MODERN POLITICAL THOUGHT

the great issues

MODERN POLITICAL THOUGHT

THE GREAT ISSUES · Second Edition

William Ebenstein

PROFESSOR OF POLITICS, PRINCETON UNIVERSITY

HOLT, RINEHART AND WINSTON, INC. · NEW YORK

5   6   7   8   9

Works by William Ebenstein

CHURCH AND STATE IN FRANCO SPAIN

POLITICAL THOUGHT IN PERSPECTIVE

MODERN POLITICAL THOUGHT
  The Great Issues (Second Edition)

GREAT POLITICAL THINKERS
  Plato to the Present (Third Edition)

INTRODUCTION TO POLITICAL PHILOSOPHY

TODAY'S ISMS
  Communism, Fascism, Capitalism, Socialism (Third Edition)

MAN AND THE STATE
  Modern Political Ideas

THE GERMAN RECORD
  A Political Portrait

THE PURE THEORY OF LAW

THE NAZI STATE

THE LAW OF PUBLIC HOUSING

FASCIST ITALY

To the memory of my father

PREFACE TO THE FIRST EDITION

The wars and revolutions of our century have strongly revived the interest in political ideas. Conflicts between, and within, nations are over power and advantage; but they also express profound cleavages of ideas and creeds rooted in conflicting ways of life. If western civilization is to survive, we shall have to develop a deeper knowledge and keener appreciation of its basic values than ever before, because the threat confronting it—communist world domination—is more serious than ever before.

The most direct way of acquainting oneself with the great ideas that have animated the western world from Machiavelli to date is to go back to the great writers themselves. This is the method employed in the present book. However, I have prefaced each chapter of selections from original sources with an introductory essay of my own to provide the proper setting and perspective for the issues dealt with. To further facilitate the work and pleasure of the reader, the Bibliographical Notes at the end of the book contain additional bibliographical comments and criticisms which, it is hoped, will help to convey the vitality and excitement of important political ideas as well as aid in research on more specialized topics.

As to the presentation of the material, it has seemed to me that the richness and complexity of modern political thought, particularly as it effects world events, may easily be lost in the customary chronological or biographical approach, and as a result I have adopted the method of *great issues* as the focus of attention and organization.

Part I, "Philosophy, Psychology, and Politics," stresses, first, the fact that, in a broad sense, all questions of political philosophy are related to fundamental issues of general philosophy, and, secondly, that there can be no balanced understanding of group life without a penetrating grasp of the motivations, tensions, and anxieties of the individual. The contributions which philosophy and psychology can make to a better understanding of politics are immense, and our political wisdom will grow in proportion to our ability to draw on new sources of knowledge and insight.

Part II, "The Foundations of Democracy," seeks to explore democracy as a *way of life* rather than as a governmental system. Democracy is more than a set of institutions: it is the quality of the men and women who compose it that counts above all—and if that quality is unequal to the challenge, the hope for democratic survival will be dim.

Part III, "Antidemocratic Thought," shows how the eruption of irrational, demonic forces in national and international politics has shaken our former confidence in the inevitability of democratic progress, and how fragile are the foundations of civilized living. The tradition of antidemocratic thinking is much older than fascism or communism, and is even older than democracy itself. While antidemocratic ideas and attitudes have been more deeply rooted in some countries than in others, no one can deny that the enemies of the free way of life exist everywhere.

Part IV deals with "Capitalism, Socialism, and the Welfare State." For almost a century, political problems were artificially separated from economic ones, and the divorce proved costly to both from the viewpoint of theory and practice. More and more, we are developing again a science of political economy in which the intimate link between economics and politics is systematically—and fruitfully—demonstrated.

Finally, Part V, "From Nationalism to World Order," examines some of the most urgent issues that confront mankind. It explores some of the principal tensions, such as nationalism, imperialism, and sovereignty, and tries to show in what ways the dilemma of international anarchy can be hopefully approached. As a nation of nations, the United States has a great part to play in the development of international government and world peace, and American leadership of the free world is a tremendous burden and responsibility.

In selecting materials for this volume I have not clung slavishly to well-known names. The first consideration has been readability and freshness of thought and expression. In several cases, I myself have translated materials hitherto unavailable in English, and in a few instances I have slightly revised older translations.

PREFACE TO THE SECOND EDITION

The continuing friendly reception of this book by students and teachers has made the publication of a new, revised and enlarged, edition both possible and desirable. In making the new edition as up-to-date as possible, I have tried to stick to essentials and to keep the basic organization of the book built around the concept of great issues, without any sacrifice of challenging and enduring ideas to ephemeral triviality. The extensive Bibliographical Notes at the end have been entirely redone, and it is hoped that they will continue to be as useful in the future as they have proved in the past.

W. E.

Princeton University

CONTENTS

Part III   Antidemocratic Thought

Part V   From Nationalism to World Order

Chapter XIV   Nationalism: Peaceful or Aggressive?   741

Chapter XV   Conflict or Common Interest?   777

Part I

PHILOSOPHY, PSYCHOLOGY, AND POLITICS

Philosophy and Politics

Psychology and Politics

Chapter I

PHILOSOPHY AND POLITICS

No study of the fundamental problems of political philosophy can be fruitful without the awareness that they are intimately related to the basic issues of general philosophy. Every theory of state and society, and of the position of the individual in them, derives—more often unconsciously than consciously—from a more comprehensive conception of the world and man's place in it. In particular, the possibility of human knowledge, the pivotal challenge of all philosophical inquiry, has a direct bearing on primary political conceptions and attitudes. Though it may be difficult to argue that certain types of philosophical systems are always reflected in exactly corresponding types of political outlook, a remarkable parallelism exists between basic philosophical and political conceptions, a parallelism which is partly logical, partly psychological, and partly historical.

All three aspects of this parallelism are analyzed by Bertrand Russell in *Philosophy and Politics* (1947; reproduced here in its entirety). *Philosophy and Politics* has quickly established itself as a classic in the field for several reasons. First, it is the only analysis of the problem by a distinguished modern philosopher who is considered by many to be the most original of the twentieth century. Second, the relation between philosophy and politics is one of the great themes of Russell's interest in the development of thought, as is witnessed by the fact that his massive *History of Western Philosophy* (1945) carries the subtitle, *And Its Connections with Political and Social Circumstances.* Finally, *Philosophy and Politics* gained influence so rapidly because of the brilliance of its style and the cogency of its argument. In 1950, Russell received the Nobel Prize in *literature,* and in the whole history of philosophy there are few writers of equal literary accomplishment.

Essentially analytical, *Philosophy and Politics* also briefly surveys the evolution of Western philosophy from a historical viewpoint. In classical antiquity, the two principal philosophical figures are, according to Russell, Democritus and Plato. Essentially empirical in outlook, Democritus was "a utilitarian who disliked all strong passions, a believer in evolution, both astronomical and biological." Like virtually all Greeks of his time Democritus accepted the institution of slavery, but in his political views he favored

3

democracy and freedom of speech. Plato, born about thirty years later than Democritus, was so incensed by the latter's philosophical and political ideas that he is said to have expressed the thought that Democritus' books ought to be burned: "His wish was so far fulfilled that none of the writings of Democritus survive," except for approximately three hundred alleged and genuine quotations. Russell sees in the traditional admiration of Plato, particularly of his political philosophy as stated in the *Republic*, "perhaps the most astonishing example of literary snobbery in all history." The true disciples of the *Republic*, that "totalitarian tract," are Lenin and Hitler, Russell argues, because it includes the basic precepts of the totalitarian state and society: thought control and censorship; the inculcation of a fierce sense of nationalism; and, above all, government by a small, self-appointed oligarchy which maintains itself in power by propaganda, lies, and violence if necessary. Plato's political thought has derived much of its effectiveness from its marriage to his general philosophy, particularly his conception of the Form, the Idea, the Good, as true reality, the vision of which is revealed to but a select few. By contrast, empirically verifiable knowledge is, according to Plato, not knowledge at all, but merely sensory appearance and opinion, dealing with the passing phenomena of sense perception, whereas the true reality is timeless and unchanging Idea. Plato's aristocratic-conservative politics and anti-empirical philosophy fit together, Russell implies, and "the fine talk about the good and the unchanging makes it possible to lull the reader into acquiescence in the doctrine that the good shall rule, and that their purpose should be to preserve the *status quo*."

Russell sees in Hegel the modern counterpart to Plato. Again, Russell finds Hegel's philosophy "so odd that one would not have expected him to be able to get sane men to accept it, but he did." Like his predecessor, Hegel sees the essence of reality, not in verifiable empirical phenomena, but in what he calls the Absolute Idea. Russell shows the complexities of the concept of Absolute Idea, defined by him as "pure thought thinking about pure thought." Just as Hegel was more extreme than Plato in his general philosophy, especially in his conception of reality as pure thought, so too he exceeded Plato in his political conservatism and authoritarianism. Hegel derived from his philosophical speculations about the nature of reality that "true liberty consists in obedience to an arbitrary authority, that free speech is an evil, that absolute monarchy is good, that the Prussian State was the best existing at the time when he wrote, that war is good, and that an international organization for the peaceful settlement of disputes would be a misfortune." As in the case of Plato, Hegel's philosophy—in its general as well as in its specifically political aspects—has profoundly influenced the modern totalitarian brands of Fascism and communism. The influence of Plato on Fascism is more directly traceable than his impact on communism, just as Hegel's imprint on Marxism and communism seems more significant than the effects of his philosophy on Fascism and Nazism. Yet there is an inner kinship and affinity between them all, and it can be argued that the explicit opposition of Marx and Lenin to Plato is less important than their implicit indebtedness to Plato via Hegel. The coercive and persecutory elements in Fascist and communist totalitarianism are directly related to philosophies of reality which, as in Plato and Hegel, claim absolute certainty and objective validity.

By contrast with the Platonic-Hegelian tradition of anti-empirical philosophy, *empiricism* seems to Russell the *only philosophy* that provides a *theoretical justification for democracy*. Locke, the founder of modern empiricism, expressed its key concept by saying that *in experience* "all our knowledge is founded, and from that it ultimately derives itself." Russell is struck by the fact that Locke the philosophical empiricist also upheld, in politics, the principles of liberty, toleration, and self-government. Yet Russell also emphasizes that liberalism is more than a set of philosophical principles, that its core lies in a "temper of mind." Locke himself exemplified in his own personality one of the basic traits of the liberal temperament—the *absence of fanaticism* and unbalanced enthusiasm. Russell describes the true liberal as saying, not "this is true," but "I am inclined to think that under present circumstances this opinion is probably the best." This means that in the liberal, empirical outlook the important issue is not *what* opinions are held, but *how* they are held: undogmatically, and always subject to modification by new evidence. Liberalism is thus the extension of the scientific temperament and outlook from the realm of intellect to that of practical affairs, for science is "empirical, tentative, and undogmatic."

Liberalism avoids the two opposite extremes of despotism and anarchy, just as empiricism stands between the two extremes of dogma and skepticism. Contrary to those who hold that liberals must themselves become more fanatical if they are to survive in a war with fanatics, Russell argues that the fanatics have failed throughout history, and that "only through a revival of liberal tentativeness and tolerance can our world survive." Fanatics have generally failed either because they have pursued impossible aims, or because they have distorted facts in the interests of theory. Whereas the Nazi distinguished between German and Jewish physics, and the Communist opposes Marxist to bourgeois biology, the liberal knows of only one criterion in science: whether its hypotheses and principles can be verified by empirical research and observation. Nazi Germany paid bitterly in World War II for her distortions of facts in the service of preconceived dogma and inflamed fanaticism. In the Soviet Union the "party line" has in recent years been applied to the social sciences and humanities rather than to physical science and military technology.

Russell concludes by saying that empiricism is to be commended not only because of its greater truth, but also for its deeper ethical value. The tentative, moderate, scientific aspects of empiricism make friendly argument possible, whereas authoritarian dogma inevitably leads to tension, hostility, and persecution. Since the dogmatist *knows*—finally, absolutely, and uncondi-tionally—what truth is, argument is eliminated as a means of arriving at truth. This leaves war as the only arbiter of rival creeds: "And war, in our scientific age, means, sooner or later, universal death."

Russell's general conception of the relations between philosophy and poli-tics is supported, though in a somewhat modified form, by Hans Kelsen in his essay, "Absolutism and Relativism in Philosophy and Politics" (1948). Kelsen, the most influential legal philosopher of the twentieth century, con-ceives of the two concepts of *absolutism* and *relativism* as fundamental in both philosophy and politics. The philosophical absolutist holds that there is an absolute reality, that is, that reality exists independently of human knowledge and experience, and that its existence is unlimited by space and time, which define the boundaries of human knowledge. The function of knowledge—in the conception of philosophical absolutism—is to reflect pas-sively objective reality, "the thing in itself." Kelsen argues that there is a clear parallelism between philosophical and political absolutism. Just as the un-limited authority of absolute government is "beyond any influence on the part of its subjects, who are bound to obey its laws without participating in their creation, the absolute is beyond our experience, and the object of knowl-edge—in the theory of philosophical absolutism—independent of the subject of the knowledge, totally determined in his cognition by heteronomous laws."

By contrast, relativistic philosophy sees a much more dynamic and creative relationship between the subject of knowledge—the person who inquires and experiences, and the object of knowledge—the process and product of experience. Philosophical relativism holds that the human being is, in the process of knowledge, the "creator of his world, a world which is constituted exclusively in and by his knowledge." Similarly, political relativism holds that man is the creator of his political world, inasmuch as he participates in the creation of the social and political order to which he is subject. Rela-tivism, both philosophical and political, recognizes that "only relative values are accessible to human knowledge and human will," and it insists that no one individual or group has a monopoly of the knowledge of the absolute good. Because relativism denies the possibility of absolute knowledge and values, it is tolerant; it upholds freedom of thought and speech and protects, above all, the rights of minorities and opposition views—for the minority of today may be right and may become the majority of tomorrow. By contrast, the philosophical absolutist thinks he possesses absolute knowledge and val-ues, and he considers, Kelsen argues, differing views as morally wrong, and ultimately seeks to eradicate them by force. Thus there is a parallelism—both logically and historically—between philosophical relativism and democracy on the one hand, and between philosophical absolutism and political des-potism and autocracy on the other. The intellectual foundations of persecu-tory groups and movements in history have invariably been built upon dogma and absolute certainty, whereas the liberal and democratic temper—in ancient Greece as in the modern world—has always included elements of doubt and skepticism, of never-ending self-questioning and inquiring, that is, philosophical relativism.

Relativism in philosophy and politics can be attacked either from a metaphysical-religious viewpoint or from an empirical-rational one. The metaphysical-religious critique of relativism is the core of René de Visme Williamson's essay, "The Challenge of Political Relativism" (1947). Williamson denies that all who believe in absolute values seek to impose their views on unyielding unbelievers. Particularly where convictions are rationally held and are deeply embedded in the experience of the believers, "the likelihood of persecution is remote," for "tolerance may partake of the magnanimity of the strong." However, Williamson goes beyond the appeal to experience, and urges that there are values "above and beyond man." The fact that absolute values cannot be proved does not mean, according to Williamson, that they do not exist: "There are a great many things in this world which are true and yet undemonstrable." If the relativist or empiricist denies the existence of such undemonstrable absolute values, "it is the sight of the onlooker which is at fault and not the visibility of the object." Williamson also refers to the Declaration of Independence as antirelativist, because it bases its principal claim for independence on "the laws of nature and of nature's God," and because it declares the fundamental truths of political organization as "self-evident." The signers of the Declaration of Independence believed in absolute values, Williamson states, and they "had the courage to be dogmatic." Williamson summarizes his antirelativist position by saying that the down-to-earth approach in philosophy and politics has its dangers, and that man must "move in an upward direction" if he is to attain a more elevated view of reality and value: "We must move toward the absolute if we are to manage even the relative." Above all, Williamson emphasizes one absolute value upon which the Christian, the scientist, and the citizen can unite: the unconditional allegiance to truth.

Relativism in philosophy and politics can be attacked not only from the metaphysical-religious viewpoint, as in the case of Williamson, but also from a rational-secular one, as is done by Morris Ginsberg in "Ethical Relativity and Political Theory" (1951). Ginsberg, one of the leading British sociologists, denies that there is any specific psychological or historical relation between philosophical relativism and political democracy, and he finds that relativism has been used to buttress both totalitarianism and democracy. The real danger of the theories of moral relativism, Ginsberg writes, is that "they remove the problem of values from the sphere of reason." He notes that both Nazis and Fascists have dethroned reason, substituting the arbitrary intuitions of the leader or the shifting interests of race or nation for rational moral laws. Marxists and communists, too, have substituted the concept of class morality for that of general moral laws. Relativist philosophy, ethics, and politics can thus be put to widely varying uses, for "if moral judgments express nothing but individual or group desires or preferences, the content of morals will vary with the interpretation of these desires or preferences." If moral ends are not open to rational investigation, the function of *reason* becomes *restricted* to the issue of *means:* if reason cannot harmonize conflicting ends on a just and equitable basis, conflict and violence take its place.

Yet relativism cannot provide a rational basis for democracy either, Ginsberg argues, since the democratic agreement not to use force in the case of disagreement is not relative, but absolute in the life of the democratic society: "If moral judgments are subjective and express nothing but individual or group preferences, I do not see how anyone can be refuted who prefers to coerce those who differ from him." Ginsberg concedes that relativism is compatible with democracy, but he insists that *democracy needs a firmer foundation than ethical relativism,* a foundation which can be rationally justified. The best rational defense of democracy is that it is more likely to secure equality and freedom than authoritarian ways of life. The striving for justice has a basis in reason, and can be subjected to rational tests. Ginsberg is aware that impulses and feelings play a large part in the moral life, because without them moral judgments would not lead to practical action, and would remain without effect. However, the important issue is "whether there are such things as rational impulses, that is impulses which stand the test of critical scrutiny." The variability of moral judgment is caused by the distortion of relevant facts as much as by differences of moral insight; therefore the quality of moral insight is likely to gain from the progress of the social sciences. Though opposed to relativism, Ginsberg is a thorough positivist, and he looks to the *advancement of knowledge* of human needs and relations as the best hope for the attainment of a rational morality.

BERTRAND RUSSELL

1. *Philosophy and Politics**

The British are distinguished among the nations of modern Europe, on the one hand by the excellence of their philosophers, and on the other hand by their contempt for philosophy. In both respects they show their wisdom. But contempt for philosophy, if developed to the point at which it becomes

* (Cambridge University Press, London, 1947). By permission.

systematic, is itself a philosophy; it is the philosophy which, in America, is called "instrumentalism." I suggest that philosophy, if it is bad philosophy, may be dangerous, and therefore deserves that degree of negative respect which we accord to lightning and tigers. What positive respect may be due to "good" philosophy I will leave for the moment an open question.

The connection of philosophy with politics has been less evident in Britain than in Continental countries. Empiricism, broadly speaking, is connected with liberalism, but Hume was a Tory; what philosophers call "idealism" has, in general, a similar connection with conservatism, but T. H. Green was a Liberal. On the Continent distinctions have been more clear cut, and there has been a greater readiness to accept or reject a block of doctrines as a whole, without critical scrutiny of each separate part.

In most civilised countries at most times, philosophy has been a matter in which the authorities had an official opinion, and except where liberal democracy prevails this is still the case. The Catholic Church is committed to the philosophy of Aquinas, the Soviet Government to that of Marx. The Nazis upheld German idealism, though the degree of allegiance to be given to Kant, Fichte or Hegel respectively was not clearly laid down. Catholics, Communists, and Nazis all consider that their views on practical politics are bound up with their views on theoretical philosophy. Democratic liberalism, in its early successes, was connected with the empirical philosophy developed by Locke. I want to consider this relation of philosophies to political systems as it has in fact existed, and to inquire how far it is a valid logical relation, and how far, even if not logical, it has a kind of psychological inevitability. In so far as either kind of relation exists, a man's philosophy may have an intimate connection with the happiness or misery of large sections of mankind.

The word "philosophy" is one of which the meaning is by no means fixed. Like the word "religion," it has one sense when used to describe certain features of historical cultures, and another when used to denote a study or an attitude of mind which is considered desirable in the present day. Philosophy, as pursued in the universities of the Western democratic world, is, at least in intention, part of the pursuit of knowledge, aiming at the same kind of detachment as is sought in science, and not required, by the authorities, to arrive at conclusions convenient to the government. Many teachers of philosophy would repudiate, not only the intention to influence their pupils' politics, but also the view that philosophy should inculcate virtue. This, they would say, has as little to do with the philosopher as with the physicist or the chemist. Knowledge, they would say, should be the sole purpose of university teaching; virtue should be left to parents, schoolmasters, and churches.

But this view of philosophy, with which I have much sympathy, is very modern, and even in the modern world exceptional. There is a quite different view, which has prevailed since antiquity, and to which philosophy has owed its social and political importance.

Philosophy, in this historically usual sense, has resulted from the attempt to produce a synthesis of science and religion, or, perhaps more exactly, to combine a doctrine as to the nature of the universe and man's place in it with a practical ethic inculcating what was considered the best way of life. Philosophy was distinguished from religion by the fact that, nominally at least, it did not appeal to authority or tradition; it was distinguished from science by the fact that an essential part of its purpose was to tell men how to live. Its cosmological and ethical theories were closely interconnected: sometimes ethical motives influenced the philosopher's views as to the nature of the universe, sometimes his views as to the universe led him to ethical conclusions. And with most philosophers ethical opinions involved political consequences: some valued democracy, others oligarchy; some praised liberty, others discipline. Almost all types of philosophy were invented by the Greeks, and the controversies of our own day were already vigorous among the pre-Socratics.

The fundamental problem of ethics and politics is that of finding some way of reconciling the needs of social life with the urgency of individual desires. This has been achieved, in so far as it has been achieved, by means of various devices. Where a government exists, the criminal law can be used to prevent anti-social action on the part of those who do not belong to the government, and law can be reinforced by religion wherever religion teaches that disobedience is impiety. Where there is a priesthood sufficiently influential to enforce its moral code on lay rulers, even the rulers become to some extent subject to law; of this there are abundant instances in the Old Testament and in medieval history. Kings who genuinely believe in the Divine government of the world, and in a system of rewards and punishments in the next life, feel themselves not omnipotent, and not able to sin with impunity. This feeling is expressed by the King in *Hamlet,* when he contrasts the inflexibility of Divine justice with the subservience of earthly judges to the royal power.

Philosophers, when they have tackled the problem of preserving social coherence, have sought solutions less obviously dependent upon dogma than those offered by official religions. Most philosophy has been a reaction against scepticism; it has arisen in ages when authority no longer sufficed to produce the socially necessary minimum of belief, so that nominally rational arguments had to be invented to secure the same result. This motive has led to a deep insincerity infecting most philosophy, both ancient and modern. There has been a fear, often unconscious, that clear thinking would lead to anarchy, and this fear has led philosophers to hide in mists of fallacy and obscurity.

There have, of course, been exceptions; the most notable are Protagoras in antiquity, and Hume in modern times. Both, as a result of scepticism, were politically conservative. Protagoras did not know whether the gods exist, but he held that in any case they ought to be worshipped. Philosophy, according to him, had nothing edifying to teach, and for the survival of morals we must rely upon the thoughtlessness of the majority and their willingness to believe what they had been taught. Nothing, therefore, must be done to weaken the popular force of tradition.

The same sort of thing, up to a point, may be said about Hume. After setting forth his sceptical conclusions, which, he admits, are not such as men can live by, he passed on to a piece of practical advice which, if followed, would prevent anybody from reading him. "Carelessness and inattention," he says, "alone can afford us any remedy. For this reason I rely entirely upon them." He does not, in this connection, set forth his reasons for being a Tory, but it is obvious that "carelessness and inattention," while they may lead to acquiescence in the *status quo,* cannot, unaided, lead a man to advocate this or that scheme of reform.

Hobbes, though less sceptical than Hume, was equally persuaded that government is not of divine origin, and was equally led, by the road of disbelief, to advocacy of extreme conservatism.

Protagoras was "answered" by Plato, and Hume by Kant and Hegel. In each case the philosophical world heaved a sigh of relief, and refrained from examining too nicely the intellectual validity of the "answer," which in each case had political as well as theoretical consequences—though in the case of the "answer" to Hume, it was not the Liberal Kant but the reactionary Hegel who developed the *political* consequences.

But thorough-going sceptics, such as Protagoras and Hume, have never been influential, and have served chiefly as bugbears to be used by reactionaries in frightening people into irrational dogmatism. The really powerful adversaries against whom Plato and Hegel had to contend were not sceptics, but empiricists, Democritus in the one case and Locke in the other. In each, empiricism was associated with democracy and with a more or less utilitarian ethic. In each case, the new philosophy succeeded in presenting itself as nobler and more profound than the philosophy of pedestrian common sense which it superseded. In each case, in the name of all that was most sublime, the new philosophy made itself the champion of injustice, cruelty, and opposition to progress. In the case of Hegel this has come to be more or less recognised; in the case of Plato it is still something of a paradox, though it has been brilliantly advocated in a recent book by Dr. K. R. Popper.[1]

Plato, according to Diogenes Laertius, expressed the view that all the books of Democritus ought to be burnt. His wish was so far fulfilled that none of the writings of Democritus survive. Plato, in his *Dialogues,* never mentioned him. Aristotle gave some account of his doctrines; Epicurus vul-

[1] *The Open Society and Its Enemies.* The same thesis is maintained in my *History of Western Philosophy.*

garised him; and finally Lucretius put the doctrine of Epicurus into verse. Lucretius just survived, by a happy accident. To reconstruct Democritus from the controversy of Aristotle and the poetry of Lucretius is not easy; it is almost as if we had to reconstruct Plato from Locke's refutation of innate ideas and Vaughan's "I saw eternity the other night." Nevertheless enough can be done to explain and condemn Plato's hatred.

Democritus is chiefly famous as (along with Leucippus) the founder of atomism, which he advocated in spite of the objections of metaphysicians —objections which were repeated by their successors down to and including Descartes and Leibniz. His atomism, however, was only part of his general philosophy. He was a materialist, a determinist, a free thinker, a utilitarian who disliked all strong passions, a believer in evolution, both astronomical and biological.

Like the men of similar opinions in the eighteenth century, Democritus was an ardent democrat. "Poverty in a democracy," he says, "is as much to be preferred to what is called prosperity under despots as freedom is to slavery." He was a contemporary of Socrates and Protagoras, and a fellow townsman of the latter; he flourished during the early years of the Peloponnesian war, but may have died before it ended. That war concentrated the struggle that was taking place throughout the Hellenic world between democracy and oligarchy. Sparta stood for oligarchy; so did Plato's family and friends, who were thus led to become Quislings. Their treachery is held to have contributed to the defeat of Athens. After that defeat, Plato set to work to sing the praises of the victors by constructing a Utopia of which the main features were suggested by the constitution of Sparta. Such, however, was his artistic skill that Liberals never noticed his reactionary tendencies until his disciples Lenin and Hitler had supplied them with a practical exegesis.[2]

That Plato's *Republic* should have been admired, on its political side, by decent people, is perhaps the most astonishing example of literary snobbery in all history. Let us consider a few points in this totalitarian tract. The main purpose of education, to which everything else is subordinated, is to produce courage in battle. To this end, there is to be a rigid censorship of the stories told by mothers and nurses to young children; there is to be no reading of Homer because that degraded versifier makes heroes lament and gods laugh; the drama is to be forbidden because it contains villains and women; music is to be only of certain kinds, which, in modern terms, would be "Rule Britannia" and "The British Grenadiers." The government is to be in the hands of a small oligarchy, who are to practise trickery and lying—trickery in manipulating the drawing of lots for eugenic purposes, and elaborate lying to persuade the population that there are biological differences between the upper and lower classes. Finally, there is to be large-

[2] In 1920 I compared the Soviet State to Plato's *Republic*, to the equal indignation of Communists and Platonists.

scale infanticide when children are born otherwise than as a result of governmental swindling.

Whether people are happy in this community does not matter, we are told, for excellence resides in the whole, not in the parts. Plato's City is a copy of the eternal City laid up in heaven; perhaps in heaven we shall enjoy the kind of existence it offers us, but if we do not enjoy it here on earth, so much the worse for us.

This system derives its persuasive force from the marriage of aristocratic prejudice and "divine philosophy"; without the latter, its repulsiveness would be obvious. The fine talk about the good and the unchanging makes it possible to lull the reader into acquiescence in the doctrine that the good shall rule, and that their purpose should be to preserve the *status quo,* as the ideal State in heaven does. To every man of strong political convictions—and the Greeks had amazingly vehement political passions—it is obvious that "the good" are those of his own party, and that, if they could establish the Constitution they desire, no further change would be necessary. So Plato taught, but by concealing his thought in metaphysical mists he gave it an impersonal and disinterested appearance which deceived the world for ages.

The ideal of static perfection, which Plato derived from Parmenides and embodied in his theory of ideas, is one which is now generally recognised as inapplicable to human affairs. Man is a restless animal, not content, like the boa constrictor, to have a good meal once a month and sleep the rest of the time. Man needs, for his happiness, not only the enjoyment of this or that, but hope and enterprise and change. As Hobbes says, "felicity consisteth in prospering, not in having prospered." Among modern philosophers, the ideal of unending and unchanging bliss has been replaced by that of evolution, in which there is supposed to be an ordered progress towards a goal which is never quite attained, or at any rate has not been attained at the time of writing. This change of outlook is part of the substitution of dynamics for statics which began with Galileo, and which has increasingly affected all modern thinking, whether scientific or political.

Change is one thing, progress is another. "Change" is scientific, "progress" is ethical; change is indubitable, whereas progress is a matter of controversy. Let us first consider change, as it appears in science.

Until the time of Galileo, astronomers, following Aristotle, believed that everything in the heavens, from the moon upwards, is unchanging and incorruptible. Since Laplace, no reputable astronomer has held this view. Nebulæ, stars, and planets, we now believe, have all developed gradually. Some stars, for instance the companion of Sirius, are "dead." They have at some time undergone a cataclysm which has enormously diminished the amount of light and heat radiating from them. Our own planet, in which philosophers are apt to take an excessive parochial interest, was once too hot to support life, and will in time be too cold. After ages during which the earth produced harmless trilobites and butterflies, evolution progressed to the point at which it generated Neros, Jenghiz Khans, and Hitlers. This, however, is a passing nightmare; in time the earth will become again incapable of supporting life, and peace will return.

But this purposeless see-saw, which is all that science has to offer, has not satisfied the philosophers. They have professed to discover a formula of progress, showing that the world was becoming gradually more and more to their liking. The recipe for a philosophy of this type is simple. The philosopher first decides which are the features of the existing world that give him pleasure, and which are the features that give him pain. He then, by a careful selection among facts, persuades himself that the universe is subject to a general law leading to an increase of what he finds pleasant and a decrease of what he finds unpleasant. Next, having formulated his law of progress, he turns on the public and says "It is fated that the world must develop as I say; therefore those who wish to be on the winning side, and do not care to wage a fruitless war against the inevitable, will join my party." Those who oppose him are condemned as unphilosophic, unscientific, and out of date, while those who agree with him feel assured of victory, since the universe is on their side. At the same time the winning side, for reasons which remain somewhat obscure, is represented as the side of virtue.

The man who first fully developed this point of view was Hegel. Hegel's philosophy is so odd that one would not have expected him to be able to get sane men to accept it, but he did. He set it out with so much obscurity that people thought it must be profound. It can quite easily be expounded lucidly in words of one syllable, but then its absurdity becomes obvious. What follows is not a caricature, though of course Hegelians will maintain that it is.

Hegel's philosophy, in outline, is as follows. Real Reality is timeless, as in Parmenides and Plato, but there is also an apparent reality, consisting of the everyday world in space and time. The character of real Reality can be determined by logic alone, since there is only one sort of possible Reality that is not self-contradictory. This is called the "Absolute Idea." Of this he gives the following definition: *The Absolute Idea.* The idea, as unity of the subjective and objective Idea, is the notion of the Idea—a notion whose object is the Idea as such, and for which the objective is Idea—an Object which embraces all characteristics in its unity." I hate to spoil the luminous clarity of this sentence by any commentary, but in fact, the same thing would be expressed by saying "The Absolute Idea is pure thought thinking about pure thought." Hegel has already proved to his satisfaction that all Reality is thought, from which it follows that thought cannot think about anything but thought, since there is nothing else to think about. Some people might find this a little dull; they might say: "I like thinking about Cape Horn and the South Pole and Mount Everest and the great nebula in Andromeda;

I enjoy contemplating the ages when the earth was cooling while the sea boiled and volcanoes rose and fell between night and morning. I find your precept, that I should fill my mind with the lucubrations of word-spinning professors, intolerably stuffy, and really, if that is your 'happy ending,' I don't think it was worth while to wade through all the verbiage that led up to it." And with these words they would say goodbye to philosophy and live happy ever after.

But if we agreed with these people we should be doing Hegel an injustice, which God forbid. For Hegel would point out that, while the Absolute, like Aristotle's God, never thinks about anything but itself, because it knows that all else is illusion, yet we, who are forced to live in the world of phenomena, as slaves of the temporal process, seeing only the parts, and only dimly apprehending the whole in moments of mystic insight, we, illusory products of illusion, are compelled to think as though Cape Horn were self-subsistent and not merely an idea in the Divine Mind. When we think about Cape Horn, what happens in Reality is that the Absolute is aware of a Cape-Horny thought. It really does have such a thought, or rather such an aspect of the one thought that it timelessly thinks and is, and this is the only reality that belongs to Cape Horn. But since we cannot reach such heights, we are doing our best in thinking of it in the ordinary geographical way.

But what, some one may say, has all this to do with politics? At first sight, perhaps, not very much. To Hegel, however, the connection is obvious. It follows from his metaphysic that true liberty consists in obedience to an arbitrary authority, that free speech is an evil, that absolute monarchy is good, that the Prussian State was the best existing at the time when he wrote, that war is good, and that an international organisation for the peaceful settlement of disputes would be a misfortune.

It is just possible that some among my hearers may not see at once how these consequences follow, so I hope I may be pardoned for saying a few words about the intermediate steps.

Although time is unreal, the series of appearances which constitutes history has a curious relation to Reality. Hegel discovered the nature of Reality by a purely logical process called the "dialectic," which consists of discovering contradictions in abstract ideas and correcting them by making them less abstract. Each of these abstract ideas is conceived as a stage in the development of "The Idea," the last stage being the "Absolute Idea."

Oddly enough, for some reason which Hegel never divulged, the temporal process of history repeats the logical development of the dialectic. It might be thought, since the metaphysic professes to apply to all Reality, that the temporal process which parallels it would be cosmic, but not a bit of it: it is purely terrestrial, confined to recorded history, and (incredible as this may seem) to the history that Hegel happened to know. Different nations, at different times have embodied the stages of the Idea that the dialectic had reached at those times. Of China, Hegel knew only that it *was,* therefore China illustrated the category of mere Being. Of India he knew only that Buddhists believed in Nirvana, therefore India illustrated the category of Nothing. The Greeks and Romans got rather further along the list of categories, but all the late stages have been left to the Germans, who, since the time of the fall of Rome, have been the sole standard-bearers of The Idea, and had already in 1830 very nearly realized The Absolute Idea.

To any one who still cherishes the hope that man is a more or less rational animal, the success of this farrago of nonsense must be astonishing. In his own day, his system was accepted by almost all academically educated young Germans, which is perhaps explicable by the fact that it flattered German self-esteem. What is more surprising is its success outside Germany. When I was young, most teachers of philosophy in British and American universities were Hegelians, so that, until I read Hegel, I supposed there must be some truth in his system; I was cured, however, by discovering that everything he said on the philosophy of mathematics was plain nonsense.

Most curious of all was his effect on Marx, who took over some of his most fanciful tenets, more particularly the belief that history develops according to a logical plan, and is concerned, like the purely abstract dialectic, to find ways of avoiding self-contradiction. Over a large part of the earth's surface you will be liquidated if you question this dogma, and Western men of science who sympathize politically with Russia show their sympathy by using the word "contradiction" in ways that no self-respecting logician can approve.

In tracing a connection between the politics and the metaphysics of a man like Hegel, we must content ourselves with certain very general features of his practical programme. That Hegel glorified Prussia was something of an accident; in his earlier years he ardently admired Napoleon, and only became a German patriot when he became an employee of the Prussian State. Even in the latest form of his *Philosophy of History,* he still mentions Alexander, Caesar, and Napoleon as men great enough to have a right to consider themselves exempt from the obligations of the moral law. What his philosophy constrained him to admire was not Germany as against France, but order, system, regulation and intensity of governmental control. His deification of the State would have been just as shocking if the State concerned had been Napoleon's despotism. In his own opinion, he knew what the world needed, though most men did not; a strong government might compel men to act for the best, which democracy could never do. Heraclitus, to whom Hegel was deeply indebted, says: "Every beast is driven to the pasture with blows." Let us, in any case, make sure of the blows; whether they lead to a pasture is a matter of minor importance—except, of course, to the "beasts."

It is obvious that an autocratic system, such as that advocated by Hegel or by Marx's present-day disciples, is only theoretically justifiable on a basis of unquestioned dogma. If you know for certain what is the purpose of the universe in relation to human life, what is going to happen, and what is good for people even if they do not think so; if you can say, as Hegel does, that his theory of history is "a result which happens to be known to *me,* because I have traversed the entire field"—then you will feel that no degree of coercion is too great, provided it leads to the goal.

The only philosophy that affords a theoretical justification of democracy in its temper of mind, is empiricism. Locke, who may be regarded, so far as the modern world is concerned, as the founder of empiricism, makes it clear how closely this is connected with his views on liberty and toleration and with his opposition to absolute monarchy. He is never tired of emphasizing the uncertainty of most of our knowledge, not with a sceptical intention such as Hume's, but with the intention of making men aware that they may be mistaken, and that they should take account of this possibility in all their dealings with men of opinions different from their own. He had seen the evils wrought both by the "enthusiasm" of the sectaries, and by the dogma of the divine right of kings; to both he opposed a piecemeal and patchwork political doctrine, to be tested at each point by its success in practice.

What may be called, in a broad sense, the Liberal theory of politics is a recurrent product of commerce. The first known example of it was in the Ionian cities of Asia Minor, which lived by trading with Egypt and Lydia. When Athens, in the time of Pericles, became commercial, the Athenians became Liberal. After a long eclipse, Liberal ideas revived in the Lombard cities of the middle ages, and prevailed in Italy until they were extinguished by the Spaniards in the sixteenth century. But the Spaniards failed to reconquer Holland or to subdue England, and it was these countries that were the champions of Liberalism and the leaders in commerce in the seventeenth century. In our day the leadership has passed to the United States.

The reasons for the connection of commerce with Liberalism are obvious. Trade brings men into contact with tribal customs different from their own, and in so doing destroys the dogmatism of the untravelled. The relation of buyer and seller is one of negotiation between two parties who are both free; it is most profitable when the buyer or seller is able to understand the point of view of the other party. There is, of course, imperialistic commerce, where men are forced to buy at the point of the sword; but this is not the kind that generates Liberal philosophies, which have flourished best in trading cities that have wealth without much military strength. In the present day, the nearest analogue to the commercial cities of antiquity and the middle ages is to be found in small countries such as Switzerland, Holland, and Scandinavia.

The Liberal creed, in practice, is one of live-and-let-live, of toleration and freedom as far as public order permit, of moderation and absence of fanaticism in political programmes. Even democracy, when it becomes fanatical, as it did among Rousseau's disciples in the French Revolution, ceases to be Liberal; indeed, a fanatical belief in democracy makes democratic institutions impossible, as appeared in England under Cromwell and in France under Robespierre. The genuine Liberal does not say "this is true"; he says, "I am inclined to think that under present circumstances this opinion is probably the best." And it is only in this limited and undogmatic sense that he will advocate democracy.

What has theoretical philosophy to say that is relevant to the validity or otherwise of the Liberal outlook? The essence of the Liberal outlook lies not in *what* opinions are held, but in *how* they are held; instead of being held dogmatically, they are held tentatively, and with a consciousness that new evidence may at any moment lead to their abandonment. This is the way in which opinions are held in science, as opposed to the way in which they are held in theology. The decisions of the Council of Nicaea are still authoritative, but in science fourth-century opinions no longer carry any weight. In the U.S.S.R. the dicta of Marx on dialectical materialism are so unquestioned that they help to determine the views of geneticists on how to obtain the best breed of wheat,[3] though elsewhere it is thought that experiment is the right way to study such problems. Science is empirical, tentative and undogmatic; all immutable dogma is unscientific. The scientific outlook, accordingly, is the intellectual counterpart of what is, in the practical sphere, the outlook of Liberalism.

Locke, who first developed in detail the empiricist theory of knowledge, preached also religious toleration, representative institutions, and the limitation of governmental power by the system of checks and balances. Few of his doctrines were new, but he developed them in a weighty manner at just the moment when the English Government was prepared to accept them. Like the other men of 1688, he was only reluctantly a rebel, and he disliked anarchy as much as he disliked despotism. Both in intellectual and in practical matters he stood for order without authority; this might be taken as the motto both of science and of Liberalism. It depends, clearly, upon consent or assent. In the intellectual world it involves standards of evidence which, after adequate discussion, will lead to a measure of agreement among experts. In the practical world it involves submission to the majority after all parties have had an opportunity to state their case.

In both respects his moment was a fortunate one. The great controversy between the Ptolemaic and the Copernican systems had been decided, and scientific questions could no longer be settled by an appeal to Aristotle. Newton's triumphs seemed to justify boundless scientific optimism. In the practical world, a century and a half of wars of religion had produced hardly

[3] See *The New Genetics in the Soviet Union,* by Hudson and Richens, School of Agriculture, Cambridge, 1946.

any change in the balance of power as between Protestants and Catholics. Enlightened men had begun to view theological controversies as an absurdity, caricatured in Swift's war between the Big-Endians and the Little-Endians. The extreme Protestant sects, by relying upon the inner light, had made what professed to be Revelation into an anarchic force. Delightful enterprises, scientific and commercial, invited energetic men to turn aside from barren disputation. Fortunately they accepted the invitation, and two centuries of unexampled progress resulted.

We are now again in an epoch of wars of religion, but a religion is now called an "ideology." At the moment the Liberal philosophy is felt by many to be too tame and middle-aged; the idealistic young look for something with more bite in it, something which has a definite answer to all their questions, which calls for missionary activity and gives hope of a millennium brought about by conquest. In short, we have been plunging into a renewed age of faith. Unfortunately the atomic bomb is a swifter exterminator than the stake, and cannot safely be allowed so long a run. We must hope that a more rational outlook can be made to prevail; for only through a revival of Liberal tentativeness and tolerance can our world survive.

The empiricist's theory of knowledge—to which, with some reservations, I adhere—is half way between dogma and scepticism. Almost all knowledge, it holds, is in some degree doubtful, though the doubt, if any, is negligible as regards pure mathematics and facts of present sense-perception. The doubtfulness of what passes for knowledge is a matter of degree; having recently read a book on the Anglo-Saxon invasion of Britain, I am now convinced of the existence of Hengist, but very doubtful about Horsa. Einstein's general theory of relativity is probably, broadly speaking, true, but when it comes to calculating the circumference of the universe we may be pardoned for expecting later investigations to give a somewhat different result. The modern theory of the atom has pragmatic truth, since it enables us to construct atomic bombs; its consequences are what instrumentalists facetiously call "satisfactory." But it is not improbable that some quite different theory may in time be found to give a better explanation of the observed facts. Scientific theories are accepted as useful hypotheses to suggest further research, and as having some element of truth in virtue of which they are able to colligate existing observations; but no sensible person regards them as immutably perfect.

In the sphere of practical politics, this intellectual attitude has important consequences. In the first place, it is not worth while to inflict a comparatively certain present evil for the sake of a comparatively doubtful future good. If the theology of former times was entirely correct, it was worth while burning a number of people at the stake in order that the survivors might go to heaven, but if it was doubtful whether heretics would go to hell, the argument for persecution was not valid. If it is certain that Marx's eschatology is true, and that as soon as private capitalism has been abolished we shall all be happy ever after, then it is right to pursue this end by means of dictatorships, concentration camps, and world wars; but if the end is doubtful or the means not sure to achieve it, present misery becomes an irresistible argument against such drastic methods. If it were certain that without Jews the world would be a paradise, there could be no valid objection to Auschwitz; but if it is much more probable that the world resulting from such methods would be a hell, we can allow free play to our natural humanitarian revulsion against cruelty.

Since, broadly speaking, the distant consequences of actions are more uncertain than the immediate consequences, it is seldom justifiable to embark on any policy on the ground that, though harmful in the present, it will be beneficial in the long run. This principle, like all others held by empiricists, must not be held absolutely; there are cases where the future consequences of one policy are fairly certain and very unpleasant, while the present consequences of the other, though not agreeable, are easily endurable. This applies, for instance, to saving food for the winter, investing capital in machinery, and so on. But even in such cases uncertainty should not be lost sight of. During a boom there is much investment that turns out to have been unprofitable, and modern economists recognize that the habit of investing rather than consuming may easily be carried too far.

It is commonly urged that, in a war between Liberals and fanatics, the fanatics are sure to win, owing to their more unshakeable belief in the righteousness of their cause. This belief dies hard, although all history, including that of the last few years, is against it. Fanatics have failed, over and over again, because they have attempted the impossible, or because, even when what they aimed at was possible, they were too unscientific to adopt the right means; they have failed also because they roused the hostility of those whom they wished to coerce. In every important war since 1700 the more democratic side has been victorious. This is partly because democracy and empiricism (which are intimately interconnected) do not demand a distortion of facts in the interests of theory. Russia and Canada, which have somewhat similar climatic conditions, are both interested in obtaining better breeds of wheat; in Canada this aim is pursued experimentally, in Russia by interpreting the Marxist Scriptures.

Systems of dogma without empirical foundation, such as those of scholastic theology, Marxism, and fascism, have the advantage of producing a great degree of social coherence among their disciples. But they have the disadvantage of involving persecution of valuable sections of the population. Spain was ruined by the expulsion of the Jews and Moors; France suffered by the emigration of Huguenots after the Revocation of the Edict of Nantes; Germany would probably have been first in the field with the atomic bomb but for Hitler's hatred of Jews. And, to repeat, dogmatic systems have the two further disadvantages of involving false beliefs on practically important matters of fact, and of rousing violent hostility in those who do not share the fanaticism in question. For these various reasons, it is not to be expected that, in the long run, nations addicted to a dogmatic philosophy will have the advantage over those of a more empirical temper. Nor is it true that dogma is necessary for social coherence when social coherence is called for; no nation could have shown more of it than the British showed in 1940.

Empiricism, finally, is to be commended not only on the ground of its greater truth, but also on ethical grounds. Dogma demands authority, rather than intelligent thought, as the source of opinion; it requires persecution of heretics and hostility to unbelievers; it asks of its disciples that they should inhibit natural kindliness in favour of systematic hatred. Since argument is not recognized as a means of arriving at truth, adherents of rival dogmas have no method except war by means of which to reach a decision. And war, in our scientific age, means, sooner or later, universal death.

I conclude that, in our day as in the time of Locke, empiricist Liberalism (which is not incompatible with *democratic* socialism) is the only philosophy that can be adopted by a man who, on the one hand, demands some scientific evidence for his beliefs, and, on the other hand, desires human happiness more than the prevalence of this or that party or creed. Our confused and difficult world needs various things if it is to escape disaster, and among these one of the most necessary is that, in the nations which still uphold Liberal beliefs, these beliefs should be whole-hearted and profound, not apologetic towards dogmatisms of the right or the left, but deeply persuaded of the value of liberty, scientific freedom, and mutual forbearance. For without these beliefs life on our politically divided but technically unified planet will hardly continue to be possible.

HANS KELSEN

2. *Absolutism and Relativism in Philosophy and Politics**

Since there exists philosophy, there exists the attempt to bring it in relation with politics; and this attempt has succeeded in so far as it is today recognized to the degree of a truism that political theory and that part of philosophy we call ethics are closely connected with each other. But it seems strange to assume—and this essay tries to verify this assumption—that there exists an external parallelism, and perhaps also an inner relationship, between politics

* *The American Political Science Review*, Vol. XLII (October, 1948). By permission.

and other parts of philosophy such as epistemology, that is, theory of knowledge, and theory of values. It is just within these two theories that the antagonism between philosophical absolutism and relativism has its seat; and this antagonism seems to be in many respects analogous to the fundamental opposition between autocracy and democracy as the representatives of political absolutism on the one hand and political relativism on the other.[1]

I

Philosophical absolutism is the metaphysical view that there is an absolute reality, i.e., a reality that exists independently of human knowledge. Hence its existence is objective and unlimited in, or beyond, space and time, to which human knowledge is restricted. Philosophical relativism, on the other hand, advocates the empirical doctrine that reality exists only within human knowledge, and that, as the object of knowledge, reality is relative to the knowing subject. The absolute, the thing in itself, is beyond human experience; it is inaccessible to human knowledge and therefore unknowable.

To the assumption of absolute existence corresponds the possibility of absolute truth and absolute values, denied by philosophical relativism, which recognizes only relative truth and relative values. Only if the judgments about reality refer ultimately to an objective existence may they aim at absolute truth; that is to say, claim to be true not only in relation to the judging subject but to everybody, always and everywhere. If there is an absolute reality, it must coincide with absolute value. The absolute necessarily implies perfection. Absolute existence is identical with absolute authority as the source of absolute values. Value judgments can claim to be valid for everybody, always and everywhere, and not only in relation to the judging subject, if they refer to values inherent in an absolute reality or, what amounts to the same, are established by an absolute authority. The personification of the absolute, its presentation as the omnipotent creator of the universe whose will is the law of nature as well as of man, is the inevitable consequence of philosophical absolutism. Its metaphysics shows an irresistible tendency towards monotheistic religion; whereas philosophical relativism, as anti-metaphysical empiricism insists upon the unintelligibility of the absolute as a sphere beyond experience, and consequently has an outspoken inclination to skepticism.

The hypothesis of philosophical absolutism that there is an absolute existence independent of human knowledge leads to the assumption that the function of knowledge is merely to reflect, like a mirror, the objects existing in themselves; whereas relativistic epistemology, in its most consistent presentation by Kant, interprets the process of cognition as the creation of its object. This view implies that the human subject of knowledge is—epistemologically—the creator of his world, a world which is constituted exclusively in and by his knowledge. Hence, freedom of the knowing subject is a funda-

[1] Cf. Hans Kelsen, *Staatsform und Weltanschauung* (Tübingen, 1933).

mental prerequisite of the relativistic theory of knowledge. This, of course, does not mean that the process of cognition has an arbitrary character. There are laws governing this process; but these laws originate in the human mind, the subject of knowledge being the autonomous law-giver. Philosophical absolutism, on the other hand, if consistent, must conceive of the subject of knowledge as completely determined by heteronomous laws immanent in objective reality, and as subjected to the absolute, especially if the absolute is imagined as a personal being and super-human authority.

The subjectivistic character of the relativistic theory of knowledge involves two perils. The one is a paradoxical solipsism; that is, the assumption that the *ego* as the subject of knowledge is the only existent reality. Such assumption would involve a relativistic epistemology in a self-contradiction. For if the *ego* is the only existent reality, it must be an absolute reality. The other danger is a no less paradoxical pluralism. Since the world exists only in the knowledge of the subject, according to this view, the *ego* is, so to speak, the center of his own world. If, however, the existence of many *egos* must be admitted, the consequence seems to be inevitable that there are as many worlds as there are knowing subjects. Philosophical relativism deliberately avoids solipsism as well as pluralism. Taking into consideration—as true relativism—the mutual relation among the various subjects of knowledge, this theory compensates its inability to secure the objective existence of the one and same world for all subjects by the assumption that the individuals, as subjects of knowledge, are equal. This assumption implies that also the various processes of cognition in the minds of the subjects are equal, and thus the further assumption becomes possible that the objects of knowledge, as the results of these individual processes, are in conformity with one another, an assumption confirmed by the external behavior of the individuals. From the point of view of philosophical absolutism, on the other hand, it is not the equality of the subjects; it is, on the contrary, their fundamental inequality in relation to the absolute and supreme being which is essential.

II

In politics, the term "absolutism" designates a form of government where the whole power of the state is concentrated in one single individual, namely, the ruler, whose will is law. All the other individuals are subjected to the ruler, without participating in his power, which, for this reason, is unlimited and in this sense absolute. Political absolutism means for the ruled complete lack of individual freedom. It is incompatible with the idea of equality because justifiable only by the assumption of an essential difference between the ruler and the ruled. Political absolutism is synonymous with despotism, dictatorship, autocracy. In the past, the characteristic example is the absolute monarchy as it existed in the seventeenth and eighteenth centuries in Europe, especially in France under Louis XIV, who formulated its idea in the famous phrase: *L'État c'est moi.* In our time, political absolutism is realized in the totalitarian states as established by fascism, national socialism, and bolshevism. Its opposite is democracy based on the principles of freedom and equality. These principles exclude the establishment of a totalitarian, i.e., an unlimited, and in this sense, absolute, power of the state, which from a democratic point of view is characterized by the formula *L'État c'est nous.*

The parallelism which exists between philosophical and political absolutism is evident. The relationship between the object of knowledge, the absolute, and the subject of knowledge, the individual human being, is quite similar to that between an absolute government and its subjects. Just as the unlimited power of this government is beyond any influence on the part of its subjects, who are bound to obey laws without participating in their creation, the absolute is beyond our experience, and the object of knowledge—in the theory of philosophical absolutism—independent of the subject of knowledge, totally determined in his cognition by heteronomous laws. Philosophical absolutism may very well be characterized as epistemological totalitarianism. According to this view, the constitution of the universe has certainly not a democratic character.

There exists not only an external parallelism between political and philosophical absolutism; the former has in fact the unmistakable tendency to use the latter as ideological instrument. To justify his unlimited power and the unconditional submission of all the others, the ruler must present himself, directly or indirectly, as authorized by the only true absolute, the supreme superhuman being, as his descendant or deputy or as inspired by him in a mystical way. Where the political ideology of an autocratic and totalitarian government does not permit recourse to the absolute of a historic religion, as in the case of bolshevism, it shows an unconcealed disposition to assume itself a religious character by absolutizing its basic value: the idea of socialism.

Political absolutism not only uses a metaphysical ideology for its practical purposes, i.e., its moral justification; it has also a political theory at its disposal which describes the state as an absolute entity existing independently of its subjects. According to this theory, the state is not merely a group of individuals; it is more than the sum-total of its subjects. It is a collective, and that means here a super-individual, body which is even more real than its members, a mystic organism and as such a supreme and super-human authority, whose visible representative or incarnation is the ruler, whether he be called monarch, Führer, or Generalissimo. It is the concept of sovereignty serving the purpose of this deification of the state which implies the worship of the ruler as a god-like being. In relation to other states, the dogma of sovereignty leads to the negation of international law as a legal order above the states, that is to say, as a set of rules imposing obligations and conferring rights upon the states and thus determining the spheres of their legal existence. Sovereignty, in the sense of absolute supreme authority, can be the quality of one state only. By voluntarily recognizing international law, the sovereign state incorporates these legal rules into its own law and thus extends the validity of its national law, comprising the international law, over all the other states or, what amounts to the same, over all the other national legal orders. The view that international law is part of one's own national law is advocated by those who insist upon the sovereignty of their own state, and who take it for granted that legal interpretation of facts is identical with interpretation according to their national law, that is, the law of their own state. This juristic imperialism is usually not consistent enough to admit that by this interpretation the own state of the interpreter becomes the sole and absolute legal authority, the god in the world of law.[2]

III

Diametrically opposed to this absolutistic theory of the state is the one which conceives of the state as a specific relation among individuals, established by a legal order or, what amounts to the same, as a community of human beings constituted by this order, the national legal order. In rejecting the sovereignty dogma, this relativistic doctrine considers the state as subject, together with all the other states, to the international legal order. In their subjection to international law, all states are equal and members of the international community constituted by international law. According to this view, the state is certainly a legal authority; but not a supreme authority, since it is essentially under the authority of international law. But this law is created, in a thoroughly democratic way, by custom and treaties, that is, by the cooperation of the states subjected to it. As a legal community, the state exists together with all the other states within the international community under international law, just as private corporations exist within the state under national law. Thus the state represents only an intermediate stage between the international community and the various legal communities established under the state in accordance with its national law. The relativization of the state is one of the essential objectives of this political theory. It may be characterized as a democratic theory of the state, because it reflects the spirit of democracy. For, just as autocracy is political absolutism and political absolutism is paralleled by philosophical absolutism, democracy is political relativism which has its counterpart in philosophical relativism.

It might be taken for a more or less superficial analogy between democracy and relativism that the fundamental principles of freedom and equality are characteristic of both; that the individual is politically free in so far as he participates in the creation of the social order to which he is subjected, just as the knowing subject—according to relativistic epistemology—is autonomous in the process of cognition; and that the political equality of the indi-

[2] Cf. Hans Kelsen, *General Theory of Law and State* (Harvard University Press, 1946), pp. 419 ff.

viduals corresponds to the equality of the subjects of knowledge, which relativistic epistemology must assume in order to avoid solipsism and pluralism. But a more serious argument for the relationship between democracy and relativism is the fact that almost all outstanding representatives of a relativistic philosophy were politically in favor of democracy, whereas followers of philosophical absolutism, the great metaphysicians, were in favor of political absolutism and against democracy.[3]

IV

It is well known that in antiquity the sophists were relativists. Their most prominent philosopher, Protagoras, taught: Man is the measure of all things; and their representative poet, Euripides, glorified democracy. But Plato, the greatest metaphysician of all times, proclaimed against Protagoras: God is the measure of all things, and, at the same time, rejected democracy as a contemptible form of government. His ideal state is a perfect autocracy.[4] In Aristotle's *Metaphysics,* the absolute appears as "the first mover who is itself unmoved" and stands as a monarch over the universe. Consequently the philosopher presents in his *Politics* the hereditary monarchy as superior to democracy.[5] His teleological interpretation of nature—a consequence of his metaphysics—is in direct opposition to the mechanistic view of the atomists, who strictly rejected causes which were simultaneously ends and thus became the founders of modern science. It was not by chance that Democritus, who together with Leucippus developed the anti-metaphysical theory of atoms, declared: "Poverty in democracy is as preferable to pretended prosperity in monarchy as freedom is to slavery."

In the Middle Ages, the metaphysics of the Christian religion goes hand in hand with the conviction that monarchy, the image of the divine rule of the universe, is the best form of government. Thomas Aquinas' *Summa Theologiae* and Dante Alighieri's *De Monarchia* are the classical examples for this coincidence of philosophical and political absolutism. But Nicolaus Cusanus, who in his philosophy declared the absolute as unknowable, in his political theory, couched a lance for the freedom and the equality of men. In modern times, Spinoza combined his anti-metaphysical pantheism with an outspoken preference for democratic principles in the moral and political fields; but the metaphysician Leibniz defended monarchy. The English founders of anti-metaphysical empiricism were decided opponents of political absolutism. Locke affirmed that absolute monarchy was inconsistent with civil society and could be no form of government at all. Hume, who much

---

[3] Cf. Bertrand Russell, *Philosophy and Politics* (1947), *passim.*
[4] Cf. Hans Kelsen, "Platonic Justice," *International Journal of Ethics,* Vol. 48 (1937), pp. 367 ff.
[5] Hans Kelsen, "The Philosophy of Aristotle and the Hellenic-Macedonian Policy," *Ethics,* Vol. 48 (1937), pp. 1 ff.

more than Kant deserves to be called the destroyer of metaphysics, it is true, did not go as far as Locke; but he wrote in his brilliant essay, "Of the Original Contract," that the consent of the people is the best and most sacred foundation of government, and in his essay, "Idea of a Perfect Commonwealth," he sketched the constitution of a democratic republic. Kant, following Hume, showed in his philosophy of nature the futility of any metaphysical speculation, but in his ethics he reintroduced the absolute, which he so systematically excluded from his theoretical philosophy. Likewise, his political attitude was not very consistent. He sympathized with the French Revolution and admired Rousseau; but he lived under the absolute monarchy of the Prussian police state and had to be cautious in his political statements. So in his political theory he did not dare express his true opinion. Hegel, on the other hand, the philosopher of the absolute and objective spirit, was also a protagonist of the absolute monarchy.

V

It was a disciple of Hegel who, in the fight against the democratic movement in Germany during the nineteenth century, formulated the catchword: Authority, not majority! And indeed, if one believes in the existence of the absolute, and consequently in absolute values, in the absolute good—to use Plato's terminology—is it not meaningless to let a majority vote decide what is politically good? To legislate, and that means to determine the contents of a social order, not according to what objectively is the best for the individuals subject to this order, but according to what these individuals, or their majority, rightly or wrongly believe to be their best—this consequence of the democratic principles of freedom and equality is justifiable only if there is no absolute answer to the question as to what is the best, if there is no such a thing as an absolute good. To let a majority of ignorant men decide instead of reserving the decision to the only one who, in virtue of his divine origin, or inspiration, has the exclusive knowledge of the absolute good—this is not the most absurd method if it is believed that such knowledge is impossible and that, consequently, no single individual has the right to enforce his will upon the others. That value judgments have only relative validity, one of the basic principles of philosophical relativism, implies that opposite value judgments are neither logically nor morally impossible. It is one of the fundamental principles of democracy that everybody has to respect the political opinion of everybody else, since all are equal and free. Tolerance, minority rights, freedom of speech, and freedom of thought, so characteristic of democracy, have no place within a political system based on the belief in absolute values. This belief irresistibly leads—and has always led—to a situation in which the one who assumes to possess the secret of the absolute good claims to have the right to impose his opinion as well as his will upon the others who are in error. And to be in error is, according to this view, to be wrong, and hence punishable. If, however, it is recognized that only relative values are accessible to human knowledge and human will, then it is justifiable to enforce a social order against reluctant individuals only if this order is in harmony with the greatest possible number of equal individuals, that is to say, with the will of the majority. It may be that the opinion of the minority, and not the opinion of the majority, is correct. Solely because of this possibility, which only philosophical relativism can admit—that what is right today may be wrong tomorrow—the minority must have a chance to express freely their opinion and must have full opportunity of becoming the majority. Only if it is not possible to decide in an absolute way what is right and what is wrong is it advisable to discuss the issue and, after discussion, to submit to a compromise.

This is the true meaning of the political system which we call democracy, and which we may oppose to political absolutism only because it is political relativism.

VI

In the eighteenth chapter of the Gospel of Saint John, the trial of Jesus is described. The simple story in its naïve wording is one of the sublimest pieces of world literature and, without intending it, grows into a tragic symbol of the antagonism between absolutism and relativism.

It was at the time of Passover when Jesus, accused of pretending to be the Son of God and King of the Jews, was brought before Pilate, the Roman procurator. And Pilate ironically asked him, who in the eyes of the Roman was but a poor fool, "Then, you are the king of the Jews?" But Jesus took this question very seriously, and, burning with the ardor of his divine mission, answered: "You say so. I am a king. To this end I was born and for this cause came I into the world, that I should bear witness to the truth. Everyone who is on the side of the truth listens to my voice." Then Pilate asked, "What is truth?" And because he, the skeptical relativist, did not know what the truth was, the absolute truth in which this man believed, he—quite consistently—proceeded in a democratic way by putting the decision of the case to a popular vote. He went out again to the Jews, relates the Gospel, and said to them: "I find in him no fault at all. But you have a custom that I should release to you one at the Passover. Do you wish that I set free to you this king of the Jews?" Then cried they all again, saying: "Not this man, but Barabbas." The Gospel adds: "Now Barabbas was a robber."

For those who believe in the Son of God and King of the Jews as witness of the absolute truth, this plebiscite is certainly a strong argument against democracy. And this argument we political scientists must accept. But only under one condition: that we are as sure of our political truth, to be enforced, if necessary, with blood and tears—that we are as sure of our truth as was, of his truth, the Son of God.

RENÉ DE VISME WILLIAMSON

3. *Antirelativism: A Metaphysical-Religious View**

I

There exists a very widely held opinion that democracy and relativism go together. Some of the people who hold that opinion go even further by asserting that the two are not only linked but linked inseparably. One of the most eminent scholars who thinks so is the well-known Austrian jurist, Professor Hans Kelsen. He stated his position very clearly and concisely in these words:

> "He who holds that absolute truth and absolute values are beyond human understanding is forced to look upon a rival alien opinion as possible at the very least. Relativism is therefore the philosophy (*Weltanschauung*) which the democratic conception presupposes." [1]

With perfect consistency he argues that a belief in absolute values goes with autocratic regimes—particularly divine right monarchy—because the believer is not free to allow himself or others any deviation from absolute values and is bound by his conscience to base political decisions on authority rather than majority.[2] According to Kelsen, therefore, forms of government are differentiated by the philosophy which underlies them far more than by constitutional provisions and governmental institutions. "This is," he emphasizes, "specifically the decisive question: whether or not there is a conception of absolute truth, a point of view rooted in absolute values." [3]

Kelsen's theory implies that conviction and tolerance are incompatible. It assumes that believers in absolute values are obliged by their conscience and by logical necessity to impose these values on people who do not subscribe to them, hence the machinery of the state will sooner or later become an instrument of persecution. The effect of this theory is to make doubt the foundation of tolerance. Democracy allows freedom of discussion because nothing is certain enough to be *beyond* discussion. The doubter feels that he might as well let his neighbors and fellow-citizens talk and vote as they please. What else could he do? He would not know how to indoctrinate them since he has no doctrine of his own, and he could not tell them how they should vote because he does not know. Freedom of discussion relieves him of the duty of

---

* From René de Visme Williamson, "The Challenge of Political Relativism," *The Journal of Politics,* Vol. IX (May, 1947). By permission.

[1] Hans Kelsen, *Allgemeine Staatslehre* (Berlin, 1925), p. 370.

[2] *Ibid.*, pp. 370 and 371.

[3] *Ibid.*, p. 369.

thinking his way through difficult problems by transferring it to others and majority rule is a device which relieves him of the necessity of making responsible decisions. He who cannot count arguments and facts can always count votes. It is a tendency of relativists generally to rely on procedural rules as a substitute for principles, for the former is a predominantly mechanical activity whereas the latter calls for the intellectual activity and discretion which are needed to apply them to particular situations. This is why so many legislative debates on controversial bills turn on questions of constitutionality instead of merit and why it is so much easier to have courts of law than courts of justice. What Kelsen's theory really means therefore, is that there are no democrats except by default and that majority rule is a kind of *ersatz* principle. Sovereign power is placed in the hands of the common man because there are no uncommonly capable men with a right to claim it.

II

The sincerity of Kelsen's belief in democracy and the adequacy of the reasoning upon which it is based are not the same thing. That believers in absolute values always are obliged by conscience and logic to impose their views on unyielding unbelievers is not a sound general proposition. It is quite true that some believers feel this way, but it is equally true that many others do not. On the other hand, it is not necessarily a fact that doubters are tolerant. The supposition that conviction and doubt are the only factors affecting the situation is itself an over-simplification. Psychological reality is more complex than that. Thus, doubt is sometimes associated with what is known as the will to believe, and there are persons who oscillate back and forth between conviction and doubt. Furthermore, it can also happen that intensity of feeling is a compensation for lack of depth. It is often from groups such as these that persecution comes. They try to ban free discussion because they fear that they lack the strength to cling to their convictions in the face of adverse criticism or because they harbor the unavowed feeling that these convictions are weak in themselves and could not survive in competition with rival ones. In such cases, persecution is not the product of an evangelistic urge but a species of self-defense. But when convictions have real intrinsic merit, are rationally held, and have their roots deep in the experience of those who hold them, the likelihood of persecution is remote. When such is the situation, tolerance may partake of the magnanimity of the strong. In addition to the psychological considerations, one must also reckon with the influence of important social factors. For example, there is no inexorable natural law which says that whenever a person discovers a great truth he feels an irresistible urge to communicate it to everybody. On the contrary, there have been societies in which the characteristic impulse of most people was to keep the great truth secret and to transmit it only to an initiated few.

Intolerance and persecution are highly improbable in a situation of this kind. Even in a society where the evangelistic urge is strong, persecution may yet be inconsequential or non-existent because most believers think that convictions can be imparted successfully by rational argument and persuasive appeal rather than by force. Again, it is entirely possible that people who concede a limited efficacy to persecution will nevertheless disapprove of this particular method of imparting their own convictions. Not everyone who is out to conquer is willing to stoop for it.

It follows from the above considerations that Kelsen's theory that there is an unbreakable link between absolute values and autocracy and between relativism and democracy is a false one. The most that one could say for it, perhaps, is that it is a half-truth.

III

The idea that democracy is applied political relativism has always had many adherents in this country, though their influence and number have not been constant throughout our history. Several factors have contributed to its popularity. One of these is that we won our independence during a period when resistance to authority was widespread. Another was that geography and frontier conditions gave support to an attitude of mind hostile to sovereignty except when pulverized into individualism. A third and more recent factor was the general diffusion of relativistic ideas like those of the philosopher John Dewey. Relativism in our country, however, has been much more of an attitude of mind than a systematic philosophy. It has existed by implication in what we thought and did, but only rarely has it been a deliberately taught and knowingly received doctrine. When we raise the problem of reconciling authority and liberty, for example, what we try to establish is the right of constituted authority to demand and receive the obedience of individuals, thereby implying that this right needs justification. The burden of proof is squarely placed on government to show cause why an individual should not follow those principles and conform to any rules other than those which he had made for himself. What we do not ordinarily ask is: what right does an individual have to defy constituted authority or to act in a manner inconsistent with the common good as that good is conceived by the legitimate spokesmen of the community? We assume that every person has an indefeasible right to do whatsoever he pleases, although we do add the proviso that no person should trespass against the rights of others. But it is not up to the individual to show that he is right: it is up to the government to show that he is wrong. The strict construction of the powers of the federal government that was once claimed on behalf of the states is now invoked against all government for the benefit of the individual. The values which individuals seek are presumed to be true regardless of numbers and conflicts, and they remain so until and unless they are proved false. The whole relativist philosophy is implicit when this presumption is applied without qualification to all cases.

This attitude of mind is not by any means confined to government but applies to other forms of association as well. Does the ordinary American want to know by virtue of what right a small minority of factory workers presumes to jeopardize the interests of all the workers in that factory and the hard-won gains of years of struggle when its values do not jibe with those of the labor union's majority? Practically never. Instead of that, he asks why the values of the majority should override those of the few and rare, indeed, is the instance when the question is asked in any but a purely rhetorical manner. It will have to be proved to him that 50 or 100 workers are guilty of sabotage against the common good, but he will not require the slightest shred of evidence to accept the charge that 1000 workers are guilty of tyranny. The same sort of attitude may be observed among our college and university students. Their tendency is to condemn any regulation, however reasonable and beneficial, if it is compulsory. The unexpressed major premise in their thinking is that anything compulsory is bad *because* it is compulsory. When it comes to the realm of religion, we find a great diversity of values several of which are incompatible with each other. Yet, confronted with the opposing claims of Roman Catholics and Protestants, fundamentalists and modernists, traditionalists and rationalists, the advocates of the social gospel and those of religious individualism, Christian nationalists and Christian pacifists, many an American will be found who says: "They all have the right to their own opinion." Inasmuch as several of these religious positions are contradictory and cannot be reconciled, this comment can only mean that there exists a right to be wrong and that to be wrong is not really wrong but right. It might as well be said that "everything" is always right and nobody is ever wrong and, if courage were allied to logic, the speaker would recognize that his position is the Nietzschean one of being *beyond good and evil*. This takes him much further than he cares to go, however, so he tries to get out of so awkward a predicament by seeking refuge in the relativist philosophy. "I recognize these differences and conflicts," he says by way of explanation, "because I like to face facts. I am a realist. It's too bad things are so mixed up. But all that I or anybody else can say is that the position of each believer is right *for him*. Beyond that, there isn't anything one can say, except for un-American fanatics who think they know all the answers and like to push people around." It is not surprising that persons who reason thus in the realm of religion should do likewise in the realm of politics. All that is necessary is substitute the word "nation" for the word "denomination."

The ironical aspect of the relativist position is that those who take it are also the very ones who champion the "practical" most profusely, little realizing how utterly impractical applied relativism is. With benevolent and impartial indifference for all and approval for none, you can *say* that every protagonist of discordant views is right, but *you cannot govern a nation that way*—unless you want disorder, anarchy, and chaos. How can a relativist, then, bring about a practicable situation without giving up his principles? The same idea could not be expressed more concisely than was done by Rousseau who sometimes used relativist language though he was not one himself. "The problem," he said, "is to find a form of association which will defend and protect with the whole common force the person and goods of each associate, and in which each, while uniting himself with all, may still obey himself alone, and remain free as before." [4]

IV

The answer which relativists give to this riddle can be summarized in a single word, namely: *consent*. This answer is embedded in our political and legal thinking. It is never far from the surface. How can national sovereignty be reconciled with the binding force of international law? By the doctrine of consent under the name of the auto-limitation of states. If colonial dependencies are wholly under the authority of the colonizing state from whose will all law emanates, how can it be explained that the daily lives of the natives are almost entirely regulated by native law often antedating colonial rule by several centuries? By the doctrine of consent under the guise of the fiction that failure to abrogate native law is to be interpreted as re-enactment by the colonizing state. We are not to inquire, of course, concerning the mysterious process of legislation whereby the legislator becomes the author of laws he does not know or understand and which he did not even know he was enacting. Let us call this legislation by amnesia, therefore, and hope that it will not be out of place at least in that great empire which is said to have been acquired in a fit of absent-mindedness. How can it be held that long continued and undisputed possession may be transmuted into a valid legal right? By the doctrine of consent, known in this instance as prescription, whereby silence is deemed to be acquiescence. This is spontaneous legislation according to which law surreptitiously and fortuitously creeps up on all the parties concerned. How could resistance against the Stamp Act in the American colonies be justified? By the doctrine of consent re-stated as the principle of "no taxation without representation," representation being understood very simply here as consent by proxy. How can one distinguish a democratic government from one which is not? By the doctrine of consent from which the just powers of government are derived.

This doctrine of consent which enjoys such great popularity today is nevertheless very old. It is impossible to say when it first came into current use, but we have an admirable statement of it as far back as twenty-five centuries ago in Plato's *Republic*—and one might add that it has been unsatisfactory

[4] Jean Jacques Rousseau, *The Social Contract* (Everyman edition, London, 1913), p. 14.

for the same length of time. Glaucon who presented it as the most widely accepted answer in ancient Athens and who formulated it with matchless perfection was himself not satisfied with it. In essence it consists in the proposition *that what men agree to is always right.* All social values, therefore, have a conventional or contractual basis. The impossibility of a social existence in which each individual does exactly as he pleases in the light of his own values without reference to anybody else is the underlying reason why men alienate the inalienable by compromising and reaching an agreement with one another on a common set of values. This solution is represented as a happy medium between two intolerable extremes: anarchy in which everyone is a law unto himself in a society peopled by duplicate Robinson Crusoes, and tyranny in which one man imposes his own personal values by sheer force on people who do not believe in them. It is supposedly consent, then, which enables the individual to steer this middle course between bedlam and slavery.

It might be conceded that if mortal man is the ultimate source of all truth and is, as Protagoras taught, the measure of all things, this is the best answer that one could give. Nevertheless, it is not nearly good enough. In the first place, it is not true that there are no values above and beyond man. It is not a valid argument against the existence of absolute values to assert that we cannot *prove* that they exist to someone who doubts it or to cite numerous cases in which men have been mistaken in identifying and applying them. There are a great many things in this world which are true and yet undemonstrable. It is the sight of the onlooker which is at fault and not the visibility of the object. Moreover, there is a distressing lack of moral elevation in the thought that truth is created by a process of group bargaining and compromising which culminates in consent. "We must not think," Milton once observed on this very point, "to make a staple commodity of all the knowledge in the land, to mark and license it like our broadcloth, and our wool packs." [5]

The doctrine that values have their origin and sanction in consent is impractical as well as false because it cannot accomplish what its adherents intend that it should. How can anyone steer a middle course between anarchy and tyranny or any other set of political reefs if there is no magnetic pole and a compass that points to it? We understand well enough that merchant ships do not have to go all the way to the North Pole to map out their course and reach their destination. They do not have to dock there to be guided by it. Just so the ship of state need not reach absolute values in order to navigate through the stormy seas of politics and attain those relative values that are its earthly destination. World peace is unobtainable if there are no values of a higher level independent of the consent of nations. Of all the dangerous illusions and unrealistic figments of imagination, there is none greater than

[5] John Milton, *Areopagitica* (The Harvard Classics, Vol. 3, 1909), p. 213.

the expectation that sovereign nation-states will ever agree on enough principles and give their consent to enough roles to eliminate force from international relations. The necessary willingness to agree is lacking. Furthermore, if consent really be treated as primary and original instead of secondary and derivative, it does not matter whether a willingness to agree exists or not because the necessary legal instruments are lacking too. The whole of human existence cannot be put on a contractual basis, nor can the gap between individual values be contracted away because contracts are possible only *where there is antecedent law*.

V

The popularity of the doctrine of consent and the pervasiveness of the relativist philosophy have misled some of us into thinking that the best democratic theory has lacked elements characteristic of quite a different philosophy. It is high time that we straighten out our thinking on this matter and realize that those who were the historic and truly great thinkers and champions of democracy believed in absolute values and took their stand there.

An excellent point of departure for us Americans is our own national Declaration of Independence because the relativist version of democracy has derived no little support from a misconception of that document, particularly its reference to "the consent of the governed." Paraphrasing and transposing Mr. Justice Holmes' quip that the framers of the Constitution did not enact Mr. Herbert Spencer's *Social Statics,* we may say that neither did the signers of the American Declaration of Independence proclaim the relativist philosophy. That so many of our fellow-citizens think otherwise is probably due in large measure to the practice of lifting the phrase "deriving their just powers from the consent of the governed" out of its context and interpreting it as though it stood independently by itself. The signers themselves, however, assigned it no such position. Quite the contrary!

In the first paragraph of the Declaration of Independence, they specifically based their claim to independence not on the consent of the governed nor the will of the thirteen colonies but on "the laws of nature and of nature's God." They then proceeded to state their motive as "a decent respect to the opinions of mankind"—quite an unnecessary digression if one man's opinion is as good as another's! In the second paragraph they lay down five propositions each of which is introduced by the word "that" and closed by a semi-colon, except for the fifth one which ends with a period. The substance of these five propositions may be summarized as follows: equality, natural rights, the citation of three of these natural rights (life, liberty, and the pursuit of happiness), limited government, and the right of revolution. The philosophy in the light of which the signers saw these propositions was made plainly evident in the declaratory statement "We hold these truths to be self-evident." Both the position and the punctuation of this statement show that the signers intended it to apply to all five of the ensuing propositions. The self-evident truths are not only stated explicitly but also labelled so that their nature would not be misunderstood or overlooked. The signers realized, of course, that these truths were not evident to everybody either in America or in Europe. That is why they said self-evident and not "evident to all mankind," and they were careful to point out that it is "We" who hold them to be thus.

We now come to the statement in question, *i.e.* that governments derive "their just powers from the consent of the governed." Let us first of all note that it occurs in the fourth proposition, which is one of the self-evident truths. The next logical step is to observe that the statement is not the whole of the proposition but rather a subordinate modifying clause. The *main* point is that "governments are instituted among men" for a particular purpose which is "to secure these rights," *i.e.* the natural rights of man. The just powers of governments have their source in the consent of the governed, but the extent and limits of these powers are contained in the *purpose* of all government. The significance of the proposition considered in its entirety, therefore, is that there are governments which no amount of consent could make legitimate. Rulers may forfeit their right to govern because their powers are exercised to subvert the purpose for which they exist and not solely because these powers may have an illegitimate origin. Thus, even the unanimous support of the German people could not have justified the Hitler regime because the Nazi leaders neither believed in nor observed the natural rights of man. If we read the second paragraph of the Declaration a little further, any remaining doubt that one might have must vanish once and for all when the signers state that the governed have not only the right but the duty to overthrow by revolution any government which is bent on establishing despotism. Viewed as a part of the historical development of Western political thought, we can recognize in the fourth and fifth propositions of the signers an eighteenth-century American adaptation of the medieval concept of tyranny *ab initio* and tyranny *ab exercitio*. We are entitled to conclude, therefore, that the signers of the American Declaration of Independence were inspired by a philosophy that is completely alien to political relativism. They took a firm stand on absolute values and had the courage to be dogmatic. They did not pretend to think that King George III and Lord North had a right to their own opinion, nor did they believe that justice meant one thing in the British Isles and another in British America. They based themselves on self-evident truths, and not on hypotheses, working premises, tentative assumptions, and other verbal symptoms of hesitant wills, mixed emotions, and inconclusive minds. They understood that judgment which comes to grips with reality is far superior to judgment which is suspended so that it cannot get a grip on anything at all. When they spoke of the duty of a free people to overthrow despotic governments they did not mean anything like "that is the way we feel about it" (with perhaps the words "at this time" added for further safety). Their concept of duty was a close kin to the one described by Wordsworth as the "stern daughter of the Voice of God."

<h2 style="text-align:center">VI</h2>

There emerges from this discussion of the challenge of political relativism the conclusion that if we are to enjoy democracy at home and peace abroad, we must take our stand on absolute values. It is admitted on all sides that the kind of democracy, peace, and justice that we now have is a very imperfect kind at best and that our hold on even that is precarious. The trouble is that everything we have in *this* world is, indeed, relative. It would be amusing, if it were not so tragic, to observe how many people choose their goals from admittedly shoddy models of proven unreliability and insist on behaving like those insects who beat themselves to death against the same window-pane instead of looking elsewhere for the way out.

What relative degree of democracy and peace we possess, little as that is, we owe to those who built on the foundation of absolute values. A social order of any kind is created only by those who have the vision of a new heaven and a new earth, inasmuch as the old earth and crude man-made heavens have been so pathetically inadequate. They alone have the eyes to see it, the power to create it, the steadfastness to maintain it, the knowledge and experience to improve it. The time has come when we must stop being so down-to-earth that we get mired in the mud of our mistakes and confine ourselves to the same ruts which experience tells us lead to disaster. When men set such an absurdly high value on being level-headed, is it any wonder that their handiwork should be so dismally flat? To secure a longer, deeper, and more well-rounded view of our position without losing sight of what lies immediately before us, we must move some distance and the only way of moving so that it can serve our purpose is *to move in an upward direction*. This is just as true in the moral and social realm as it is in the physical: we must move toward the absolute if we are to manage even the relative. Let us be done once and for all, therefore, with the futile enterprise of seeking our standards from substandard conditions and of borrowing our thinking about democracy from those who misunderstand it.

"But," someone is likely to inquire, "isn't majority rule an instance of exactly that kind of borrowing?" This is a good question to which improved methods of public opinion measurement have given a special urgency, yet it is not asked very often, and the few who ask it generally seem to expect an affirmative answer. This expectation is itself an example of the wrong kind of borrowing and one of the legacies of earlier anti-democratic thinking. The defenders of legitimism, aristocracy, and other reactionaries and conservatives of the first half of nineteenth-century Europe were unable to prevent the victory and establishment of democracy, but it is curious to note how often some of their arguments have outlived their authors and their cause. Democracy has never been the special preserve of nose-counting statisticians any more than hereditary monarchy by divine right was the private monopoly of obstetricians. To this false charge that majority rule is a form of wholesale opinion-borrowing by buck-passing citizens, the most effective reply was given by Rousseau whose understanding of majority rule remains unsurpassed.

Rousseau stressed the point that majority rule is a tool whose purpose is to give expression to the voice of the general will and that, like every tool, it will not function effectively unless certain conditions are met. One of these is that the citizens who vote are by that act expressing their considered judgment as to what the common good requires and not pursuing private selfish ends disguised as public interest.[6] A second condition is that adequate information and free inquiry be available to permit the formation of objective and verifiable judgments.[7] A third condition is that, as he seeks the common good of all, "each citizen should think only his own thoughts." [8] In making this point Rousseau says, in effect, that there must be no opinion-borrowing at all, and his hostility toward groups ("partial associations") is caused by the tendency of groups to become *pressure* groups striving for power through the regimentation of their members instead of striving for truth through the independent thinking of each member.[9] In so far as every citizen is animated by the same public spirit and makes use of his own individual background by independent thinking on common problems, the general will is given expression and translated into a great political force. Individual bias and personal peculiarities cancel out and what is left is the common judgment of all which is truest because it has the broadest possible base, *i.e.* the total experience of life and the wealth of resources afforded by diversity in backgrounds.[10] An individual who lets someone else do this thinking for him is robbing the community of all that is personal and unique in his contribution to its wisdom, and a political leader who accepts the services and support of his followers without getting the benefit of their considered judgment is like someone who is willing to drive a car equipped with a powerful motor and no brakes: he who drives it is a public threat and they who ride in it are unmitigated fools or pitiful victims. It is the essence of dictatorship to

[6] Jean Jacques Rousseau, *op. cit.*, p. 26.
[7] *Ibid.*, pp. 93 and 94.
[8] *Ibid.*, p. 26.
[9] *Ibid.*, p. 26.
[10] *Ibid.*, p. 25.

accumulate power without the corresponding wisdom that would make it safe, and it is a wholly natural thing for an individual who craves for power and at the same time denies the existence of truth by believing that all truth is relative. Dictators cannot see why they should bother to take both, and they are apt to confront their critics with Pilate's question: what is truth? And it happens that not a few of these critics have no more inclination to answer the question than the dictators who ask it!

What happens when truth is eliminated from consideration in human relations? You sever reason from its natural anchor and every order from one man to another becomes arbitrary because it is no longer possible to justify that order. When people have to heed the orders, demands, requests, or directives of one man for no other reason than that they are his will, what you have is despotism. Anyone who consents to such a relationship is neither patriot nor democrat. He may honestly believe that he should be praised for being cooperative. Actually, however, he is guilty of being a collaborationist. The factor of numbers alters the situation not one whit. The arbitrary is not improved by multiplication. Whoever fails to use his God-given reason in the pursuit of truth whatever it may be and who is incapable of regulating his conduct according to the truth he has found and using it for the common good of his fellow-man is only a pseudo-democrat. Even if he took the opinions of a ninety per cent majority of his countrymen as his *standard* he would still be guilty of robbing a hundred per cent of them of his own personal contribution, however small, which he only can make to the discovery and realization of the general welfare of his own people and the common good of all peoples. "A man may be heretic in the truth," said John Milton, "and if he believe things only because his pastor says so, or the Assembly so determines, without knowing other reason, though his belief be true, yet the very truth he holds, becomes his heresy." [11]

This inalienable allegiance to truth with its unyielding defense of the individual's freedom to search for it, is the common ground on which the Christian, the scientist, and the citizen unite. It is the one platform which is big enough and strong enough to accommodate Martin Luther and Martin Niemoeller, Galileo and Albert Einstein, the hero of Thermopylae and the hero of Bastogne. It is the one rallying point for those who can be dogmatic about truth and modest about their own understanding of it, and for those who can demonstrate by the force of example that a man of principle has to have the broad, tolerant, adaptable, and open mind without which he would really be a man of prejudice. It would be a pity if we had vindicated our right to seek truth through centuries of struggle against a long and varied succession of tyrants only to surrender it freely and absent-mindedly to the Gallup organization!

[11] John Milton, *op. cit.*, p. 217.

MORRIS GINSBERG

4. *Antirelativism: A Rational-Secular View**

It is a curious and disconcerting fact that theories of ethical relativity have been used to justify both totalitarianism and democracy. The logical positivists who incline towards relativism in ethics have been accused of encouraging moral nihilism and of thus providing a basis for fascism. On the other hand, writers like Kelsen, Radbruch and others both in England and America have argued that the real justification for democracy lies in the idea of toleration, and this implies, in their view, an empirical and relativist outlook both in the theory of knowledge and in ethics; while the authoritarian attitude finds its natural support in what is described as an "absolutist" view of knowledge and morals. It is this somewhat paradoxical situation that I would like to consider in this lecture.

Historically there seems to be little justification for either claim. The defenders of democracy have not, on the whole, been ethical relativists. The philosophical radicals in England, for example, were adherents of an empirical theory of knowledge and, no doubt, they claimed to base their ethical theory on the basis of experience. But they cannot be called ethical relativists, since they certainly sought to establish general principles of conduct which were to be the basis alike of moral and legal rules. They believed in democracy becausey they believed it to be the form of government most likely to conduce to general happiness. Neither Green, nor Hobhouse, nor Mill, who must be regarded as the best exponents of liberal thought in England, can by any stretch of imagination be considered ethical relativists. On the other hand, it would not be difficult to point to philosophers who favoured a "Positivist" view of knowledge and morals who were on the side of absolutism in their political views. Such, for example, were Auguste Comte and Hobbes. Again, while it is true that much in Nazi and Fascist literature employs the language of ethical relativism, it is equally true that those who originated logical positivism in its modern form and their supporters in England and America are very far from being adherents of totalitarianism. It thus becomes clear even on a cursory survey that the relations involved must be more complex than appears at first sight and that if a fruitful analysis is to be conducted, it is essential to define more closely what is to be understood in this context by ethical relativism or positivism, on the one hand, and democracy and totalitarianism on the other.

For the purpose of this discussion I should like to distinguish two forms

* *The British Journal of Sociology*, Vol. II (March, 1951). By permission. Originally delivered as a guest-lecture at the Hebrew University of Jerusalem (May 7, 1950).

of ethical relativism, which may be called sociological and psychological. By sociological relativism I mean the theory that moral rules are statements which assert that within a given group there is a general tendency for classes of acts to arouse reactions of approval or disapproval. Such statements are either true or false in the sense that it is either the case or not the case that the approval or disapproval will be generally aroused. On the other hand, the approval or disapproval themselves cannot, according to some supporters of this view, be either true or false, since this distinction is regarded as inapplicable to feelings or emotions. The theory is relativist in the sense that morals are tied to the group, so that different groups have different moralities and there is no common standard by which they can be judged. The group in question according to the Nazi writers is the *Volk* or racial community. According to Marxist writers the group is the dominant class, but each class has its own morality and between them there is conflict. The main difficulty in defining this type of theory is that it has never been worked out in any detail. The moralities of different peoples are alleged to differ, but no one has ever set out how precisely they differ, or defined the boundaries of the groups which are to be compared. Are we to say, for example, that there is a European or Western morality, or is there a Teutonic, an Anglo-Saxon, a French, an Italian and a Spanish morality? Similarly we may ask how many class-moralities there are, how exactly do they differ and to what extent do they interpenetrate?

It is easy to see that sociological relativism can easily be used to support totalitarian policy. For, if morals come from the group and enjoin attachment to the group, this can be readily interpreted in a sense which would leave little or nothing to individual autonomy. Nevertheless, sociological relativism and totalitarianism are not necessarily connected. Thus for example Durkheim, who certainly holds a group theory of morality, is anxious to defend the notion of individual rights and to find room in his theory for the autonomy of the individual. The root of the matter lies in the answer to the question how what the group requires is to be ascertained. In Durkheim's view this cannot be done merely by yielding to the pressure of group opinion. It is a matter for scientific inquiry into the needs of society. Durkheim in the long run believes in the autonomy of reason, and reason is exercised by individuals. On the other hand, in the Nazi theories reason is decried. Values are the expression of the vital impulses of the race and are above reason. The interpreters of the values are the leaders or creative minds of the race and the rest have to accept their edicts as binding. The validity which these claim is absolute within the group or racial community and not a matter of individual preference. Between this kind of group-morality and totalitarianism there is thus a close link. The masses are not asked what they want; they are told what they ought to want by the self-appointed interpreters of group values.

Of the theories of what I have called psychological relativism it is not easy to find a precise formulation. They claim generally that moral judgments are emotive, rather than descriptive. Moral judgments express not a characteristic of acts but an attitude towards them favourable or unfavourable. "This action is right," means "I am favourably disposed towards actions of this type; I give myself and others leave to do it should similar circumstances arise." These theories start with the individual and not with the group, since clearly only individuals can have emotions, or likes and dislikes. Lord Russell, who is one of the strongest supporters of this theory, is very far from holding that the individual must always conform; "If a man seriously desires to live the best life open to him, he must learn to be critical of the tribal customs and tribal beliefs that are generally accepted among his neighbours."[1] On what basis he is to criticize is, however, not clear. Strictly it would seem any desire, if felt with sufficient strength, will generate its own morality. Lord Russell believes that an impersonal or universal morality is possible because human desires are in fact more general and less selfish than many moralists imagine. It is the business of "wise institutions" he argues, to encourage such a universal morality, to create conditions in which self-interest and the interests of society can be harmonized.[2] "Wise" presumably means such as Russell would approve. But to persuade others of what is wise it is necessary to appeal to their emotions and not to their reason—a curiously monopolistic sense of the word "wise."

The example of Lord Russell shows that there is no necessary link between ethical relativism or subjectivism and totalitarianism. On the face of it, moral subjectivism is more naturally linked with individualism or even anarchism. Lord Russell himself likes freedom, creativeness, universal love and sympathy, while, certainly, hosts of Nazi and fascist writers would dismiss all these as the fear-ridden impulses of weaklings and degenerates. Whether freedom or coercion is to be the basis of the political organization would depend on the presence or absence of the corresponding desires in those who decide policy and on the extent of their capacity to imbue others with similar desires or emotions. In *gleichgeschaltete* communities common desires would be inculcated and morality would be the same for all. On the other hand, in differentiated and diversified communities there would be more scope for individual peculiarity and moral originality or eccentricity. But there is nothing in the theory of moral relativism which could be logically used to justify either type of society. Strictly speaking the term "justify," if used in an ethical sense, would have no meaning. The term could have only "ideological" value as pretending to give a rational ground for what in fact is no more than individual desire or preference.

Is there then no connection at all between moral relativism and totali-

[1] *Authority and the Individual*, p. 109.
[2] *Religion and Science*, p. 241.

tarianism? I think there is, but the connection is psychological and socio-logical rather than logical. This raises the general problem of the influence exercised by philosophical theories on political and social development. There are some who attribute a great deal of power to the thought of philosophers, while others regard theories as the passive product of circumstances, and as reflecting rather than shaping the course of events. This is the sort of question upon which a great deal has been written and it would not be profit-able to pursue it further in general terms. I assume that the relation is one of reciprocal interaction, that philosophers tend to make explicit and to give form to tendencies which seek embodiment, but in doing so they give these tendencies greater strength than they might otherwise possess.[3] In the case before us, it would be absurd to blame philosophers for generating moral nihilism, but it remains that in giving it theoretical form they encourage its growth. Lord Russell has formulated a general principle which is of interest in this connection.

> A philosophy [he says], developed in a politically advanced country, which is, in its birthplace, little more than a clarification and systematiza-tion of prevalent opinion, may become elsewhere a source of revolutionary ardour and, ultimately, of actual revolution. It is mainly through theories that the maxims regulating the policy of advanced countries become known to less advanced countries. In the advanced countries, practice in-spires theory; in the others theory inspires practice.[4]

It is, I think, probable that the theories of moral relativism will be used as a basis for moral nihilism not only in the countries in which they have been formulated, but also and with even more devastating effect when trans-planted in other countries whether advanced or not.

The real danger of these theories is that they remove the problem of values from the sphere of reason. In their mildest form they reflect a failure of nerve, a method of running away from the difficult task of tackling the problem of fairness and equity in human relations. At worst they provide those who resort to coercion and violence with an ideology which gives them a moral sanction, while at the same time undermining the moral foundations of those who favour justice and freedom. Philosophers can hardly be blamed for the abuse of their theories, but they are not entirely free from responsibility, especially if, as I think is the case, these theories are not really consistent with what is best in the positivist spirit. What is im-portant in positivism is a sceptical attitude towards metaphysical assump-tions and the insistence that all inductions must rest on observation of facts. Neither of these requirements is satisfied, so far as I can see, by the ethical

---

[3] To this audience it is not necessary to stress the power of an ideal, held with passion. "If you believe it, it is no dream," you were told. You did believe it, and it is no dream.

[4] *A History of Western Philosophy*, p. 624.

theory of the logical positivists. It assumes without investigation that only those categories are of scientific importance which are employed in ordering sensory experience and it makes no attempt to examine systematically the data provided by the comparative study of morals. That only statements relating to what are called "facts" permit of the distinction between true and false is mere dogma. On the factual side, we are continually told that the variability of moral codes is so extensive as to preclude any hope of our ever reaching any generally acceptable body of moral principles.

> If we all agreed [says Lord Russell], we might hold that we know values by intuition. We cannot *prove,* to a colour-blind man, that grass is green and not red. But there are various ways of proving to him that he lacks a power of discrimination which most men possess, whereas in the case of values there are no such ways, and disagreements are much more frequent than in the case of colours. . . . Hence the conclusion is forced on us that the difference is one of tastes, not one as to any objective truth.[5]

One would expect that such a statement would be substantiated by an inquiry into the extent and nature of the divergencies in moral outlook and into the possible reasons for such divergence. It is always possible, for example, that differences arise to a considerable extent from ignorance of facts and from confusion between questions of fact and questions of values, and that when these confusions have been cleared up, the differences in value judgments proper might conceivably turn out to be no greater than those which are found in other spheres of knowledge.[6] These are matters which require prolonged investigations and the positivists of all people have no right to assume that they know enough about them to justify the very sweeping conclusions they claim to have established in the analysis of ethical judgments.

The use made of ethical relativity by the totalitarians differs from case to case. The fascists, as represented by Mussolini, at any rate, cannot really be said to hold a particular theory of morals, unless the rejection of all theories can be designated a theory. They consider all moral and political theories as ideologies which everyone is free to create for himself and to impose them on others, if he can. In practice, of course, this does not mean "everyone," but only the leader, and there is nothing to check or control his ever-changing intuitions. The Nazi writers too appeal to intuition, but in their case, this is linked with the theory of the race as the ultimate source of all values and the leader as its exponent or interpreter. The Nazi view is more clearly a form of group-relativism than the fascist; but in both cases reason is dethroned, the interests of the nation or race are put above all moral

[5] *Religion and Science,* p. 238.
[6] Especially if allowance is made for differences due to differences in the general level of knowledge.

laws. Ultimately therefore there is no criterion other than the arbitrary intuitions of the leader.

Marxist morality is more complex. There are, it would seem, two moralities—a universal morality which will become operative when class antagonisms have disappeared and an "interim" morality which is functionally
related to the class struggle. During this period each class has its own morality based on its own needs, and what is called general morality is in fact the
morality of the dominant class, disguised by an ideology which serves to
impose it on the other classes. In a period of revolution the morality is that
necessitated by war, and this "justifies" any measures required by revolutionary tactics and strategy and recognizes no limits above those needed to
maintain the morale of the working classes. The condemnation of violence
is "counter-revolutionary" and is merely the ideology of the exploiting classes.
There is a certain inconsistency in the Marxist attitude to bourgeois morality. Strictly speaking, this cannot be "condemned" in the period of the
class struggle, except in an "ideological" sense, since during this period there
are no common moral standards. In fact, however, Marxists have it both
ways. They appeal to the ethics of the interim morality in defending the
actions of the revolutionaries and to the ethics of the morality of the future
in judging the actions of their opponents. This use of a dual morality is, of
course, not peculiar to Marxists. But here the fissure between the two codes
is so deep as to endanger the whole substance of morality.

It will be seen that relativist ethics can be put to very different uses. This
is to be expected. For if moral judgments express nothing but individual or
group desires for preferences, the content of morals will vary with the interpretation of these desires or preferences. From the theoretical point of view
we should expect some account of the method by which these needs or desires can be ascertained and how these are related to the working moral
codes. But beyond vague generalities this is not forthcoming. There is no
real attempt to discover in what ways the moral codes of the different groups
differ from one another, or how far they are reconcilable. The function of
reason is restricted to the investigation of the means used in the attainment
of ends. The ends themselves are not open to rational scrutiny and where
there is a conflict of ends wisdom stands helpless. In the Marxist view it is
recognized that ends and means are dialectically related, from which it
should follow that reason is capable of dealing not only with means but
also with ends. But this promising deduction is of little importance. All
reasoning in moral and social matters is classbound and until the age of
proletarian knowledge is reached is subject to no tests other than those
imposed by revolutionary tactics and strategy. The possibility of a rational
harmonization of conflicting interests is ruled out so long as the class struggle
continues. If my analysis is right, it follows that the different forms of totalitarianism have this in common: they all involve the subordination of

ethics to politics and the removal of morals from the sphere of reason. Theories of ethical relativity are therefore congenial to them, even though the logical connection is slender. In Marxist terminology, ethical relativity provides totalitarianism with just the ideology which it needs.

Ethical relativity has been used as a basis not only for totalitarianism but also for democracy. Democracy, it is argued, implies that there is no such thing as absolute knowledge, that no one has a monopoly of truth; from which it is deduced that everyone is entitled to be heard and that coercion should only be employed when it has been accepted as necessary by at least the majority of those concerned.[7] It may be doubted whether this is logically consistent, since it implies that there is at least one ethical principle which may be taken to be assured, the principle namely that where there is disagreement force ought not to be employed and that the majority is entitled to impose its will on the rest. If moral judgments are subjective and express nothing but individual or group preferences, I do not see how anyone can be refuted who prefers to coerce those who differ from him. No doubt ethical relativism is compatible with democracy, but it is equally compatible with anarchism or absolutism, according to the emotional make-up of the individuals or groups concerned and their power of persuading or coercing others. From the psychological point of view also it may be questioned whether the best preparation for respecting the opinions or wishes of others is to doubt your own. Toleration and self-doubt by no means always go together; and not infrequently the fanatical persecutor is a person who hunts his own doubt in the doubt of others.

If democracy is to be justified, we need a surer foundation than ethical relativity. This indeed is a truism, since if moral judgments are emotive or express the demands of groups, the term justify has no meaning other than "persuade or coerce." In rejecting ethical relativism we are thus insisting that there is such a thing as a rational justification of democratic policy. This is not to claim infallibility. Moral reasoning, like reasoning in other spheres, is probable reasoning and open to correction in the light of wider experience or deepened insight. But it is nevertheless incumbent on us to form the best judgment that we can of what is good and then act on it. Our first problem is to define what we are to mean by democracy in this context. This is a question on which a good deal of time can be wasted. If we take it that as popularly used the word democracy means "a government of the whole people by the majority, generally through representatives, elected nowadays by a secret ballot of the adult population"[8] our problem is on what grounds such a form of government is held to be better than others. I will not attempt to survey the various answers that have been given to this question. I think

[7] Cf. Kelsen, *Allgemeine Rechtslehre*, p. 370.
[8] Cf. E. F. Carritt, *Ethical and Political Thinking*, p. 150.

the most promising line of approach is to say that democracy in this formal sense is considered good because on the whole it is the best device for securing certain elements of social justice. If the device is so used that it does not attain this purpose, then a democracy may be bad. Some people would say that in that case it is not a democracy, but this is a matter of words. What is important is to consider what are the elements of social justice which constitute the ultimate ground of appeal. It seems to me they are two: first, equality, and second, freedom with its correlative, individual responsibility. Equality in this context means two things; first, equality of consideration and, secondly, the exclusion of arbitrariness. The first requires that everyone is entitled to be considered, to have his claim heard; the second means that differences in treatment require as their justification some relevant difference in the ground on which the claim is put forward. The justification for this principle is, I think, rooted in the nature of rational procedure. To proceed rationally involves at least two requirements; first, to treat like cases in like manner and to insist on justification for differential treatment; second, not to impose principles from without, but rather to seek to elicit them from experience by a process of mutual correction and systematization. To suppress an experience unheard is to eliminate what may be a valuable contribution to the common stock. Hence freedom of discussion and freedom of election. Inherent in government by discussion is decision by majority. The difficulty, of course, is to operate this device in a manner which will satisfy the above requirements. Free elections may fail to give expression to divergent views, and majority decisions may ignore or override rather than integrate opposed opinions. The theme is well worn and need not be further pursued here, but it is clear that in practice formal democracy may lack the moral authority which our principles demand. Equality and freedom are closely connected. The function of free institutions is to encourage variety and spontaneity and to minimize the abuses arising out of inequalities in power. Compulsion may be required for both purposes, firstly to secure the resources necessary for a full life and secondly to prevent interference by the strong with the weak. It is sometimes thought that the notion of liberty does not involve any particular conception of the content of the good, that, on the contrary, it is based on the contention that everyone knows best what his own good is and that the important thing is that the individual should be free to pursue whatever ends he chooses, provided he does not interfere with the like freedom of other persons to pursue their own ends in their own way.[9] But this is unworkable. To give freedom any concrete meaning it is necessary to define a body of rights and to devise means of balancing them when they conflict. Now rights are claims to the conditions of a good life and must vary with our conception of the good and our

[9] F. Knight, *Freedom and Reform*, p. 52.

command of the conditions necessary to attain it. In particular the right-ful use of coercion must turn upon the nature of the ends aimed at, that is on the question how far they *can* be attained by force without distortion and moral pauperization. In short the idea of liberty cannot be profitably dis-cussed without considering its relation to the intrinsic values of individual personality and without an analysis of the relations between the individual and society. It is certainly not enough to say that anyone is free to do what he likes provided he does not interfere with the like freedom of others. Every claim may have to be considered not only in relation to the like claims of others, but to the entire system of liberties. This, in turn, cannot be done without some conception of a common good, that is a form or way of life in the light of which the various values are graded and arranged in an order of priority and importance. There are, no doubt, principles of justice which can be formulated without reference to the content of the good. Such are, for example, the principles designed to secure equality of consideration and the exclusion of arbitrariness. But it is easy to see that they cannot be applied mechanically. For what is arbitrary or not cannot be decided without some criterion of relevance, and this involves consideration of the particular values involved, such as the satisfaction of needs in some order of importance or the stimulus of effort, or the fulfilment of human potentialities. Similarly the problem of the relation between freedom and coercion cannot be resolved without taking into consideration the nature of the ends to be secured and the effects likely to be produced on the character of those affected. In this connection, as in others, the good and the just cannot be fruitfully considered in isolation from each other.

In the last resort, then, the best defence of democracy is that on the whole it is a form of government most likely to secure equality and freedom. Freedom, it should be added, is closely connected with responsibility, that is the knowledge of values and the power of acting in accordance with that knowledge. Democracy, if it is to attain these objects, must be representa-tive and responsible government; that is, based on the alert and active con-sent of the governed and a widely diffused and informed sense of values and a strong feeling of accountability on the part of those to whom power is entrusted and on whom it is exercised. If these requirements are not satisfied, formal democracy, in the sense of majority rule, will lack the moral basis which alone can give it authority.

To base democracy on ethical relativity is then to say that equality and freedom are not principles which can be rationally defended but general-ized desires or attitudes which happen to be felt by defenders of democracy but not by others. Now impulses and feelings are undoubtedly important elements in the moral life, since without them moral judgments would be powerless to affect action. The question is whether there are such things as rational impulses, that is impulses which stand the test of critical scrutiny. I find it difficult to believe that the striving for justice, for example, has no basis in reason or cannot be subjected to rational tests. The view that moral judgments are illusory is usually defended on two grounds. Firstly, it is argued moral judgments confuse assertions of a certain kind of fact—the fact namely that certain individuals tend to experience emotions or desires in relation to certain classes of acts—with assertions of a non-factual kind, e.g. that certain classes of acts have value or disvalue, ought or ought not to be done. These latter, it is then argued, are not susceptible of empirical verification and the distinction between true and false does not properly apply to them. This is further strengthened by a second consideration which emphasizes the great variability of moral judgments and the difficulty of reaching agreement about them. Neither of these grounds seems to me to be valid. It is mere dogma to assume that no intuitions are important save those which have a sensory origin or that experience is limited to what is called "fact." As to the variability of moral judgment, it is admitted by some relativists, such as Westermarck, that in many instances psychological and sociological reasons can be given which account for the variations and that these are compatible with the claim that universally valid moral judgments are discoverable.[10] I suggest that the problem of the causes of the variations in moral insight and in particular of the part played by ignorance or distortion of the relevant facts and the confusions of factual assertions with moral assertions proper deserves and requires much fuller investigation than it has received. If we consider, for example, the variations in attitude towards the equality of the sexes or of races it will soon become apparent that the distortions of the relevant facts are as difficult to remove as the divergence in moral outlook. In neither respect have we the right to abandon the task of rational inquiry. Similarly, the drive to punish crime has deep psychological roots and has expressed itself in many different forms, but this does not mean that one treatment of criminals is as good as another or that the problem is one of arbitrary choice or preference. From the fact that people differ either about facts or values and that it is difficult to get them to agree about either, we are not entitled to conclude that true judgments are unattainable without exploring the nature of the differences and the psychological and sociological factors which stand in the way of their removal.

The problem thus suggested is of especial importance to-day. We are told by politicians and theologians alike that behind political conflicts there lie fundamental differences in moral outlook. The "realists," on the other hand, tell us that morality has nothing to do with the matter, that the struggle is for power and not for moral ends. Yet the rival powers all speak in the name of morals and it is this more than anything else that is responsible for the

[10] Cf. *Ethical Relativity,* p. 196.

widespread moral scepticism of our age. Nevertheless the fact that moral principles can be distorted ideologically and used to justify rival causes does not prove that there are no moral principles. Ideological distortions are well nigh as common and as difficult to dispel in the realm of fact as in the realm of values. It is interesting in this connection to consider the differences in outlook that exist within the rival groups and not only those between them. The erstwhile communists who have recently discovered that their god has failed them were firm adherents of equality and freedom. They were willing for a time to sacrifice the one in favour of the other, in the hope that ultimately both would be secured. They have now learnt that what once seemed to them the only way to bring about economic and social equality as distinct from political equality has entailed such terrible disasters that the attempted cure has been worse than the disease and have consequently returned to the democratic fold. Their conversion does not turn upon a change of moral principle but is the result of what experience has taught them of the consequences inevitably resulting from dictatorial methods. I suspect that in many other cases, too, political differences do not rest on differences regarding fundamental moral principles, but in so far as they have a moral basis at all, on differences in moral sensitiveness, imagination and sympathy. What may be called the liberal mind is characterized by an abhorrence of fanaticism, a greater readiness to count the cost in terms of human happiness and human lives, a profounder awareness of the corroding and demoralizing effects of violence on those who employ it, quite apart from its direct effect on those who suffer from it. The problem is, so to say, one for the psychology rather than the logic of morals. It is not for want of admirable doctrine, as Shelley has warned us, that men hate and despise and censure and deceive and subjugate one another. The difficulty is to give the "admirable doctrine" sufficient emotional warmth to pervade action. This however is not to say that the fundamental principles of morals are established beyond doubt. Even if, as may be the case, there is wide agreement about the ultimate ends of conduct, there are certainly different conceptions of the general form or way of life in accordance with which the ends are graded or balanced. Further, we often lack the secondary principles or *axiomata media* for making the transition from the ultimate ends to the detail of life. In the absence of these mediating links, it is easy for lofty principles to remain on a safe level of abstraction or to be used in justification of contradictory policies. The moral perplexity is increased by confusions between questions of fact and questions of values and by the difficulty of foreseeing the consequences of human interactions, especially in large scale societies. From this point of view ethical thought stands to gain from the development of the social sciences. The deeper our knowledge of human needs and potentialities and of the laws of social interaction the greater is the chance of increased insight into the nature of ideals. Theories of ethical relativity have proved utterly sterile in dealing with the problems of our age. The positive spirit is another matter. To it we owe the impetus to seek a basis for morality in human experience and to regard ideals, not as patterns laid up in heaven, but as rooted in fundamental needs and attainable by rational effort.

Chapter II

PSYCHOLOGY AND POLITICS

The relations between personality structure and political process increasingly engage the attention of psychologists, psychiatrists, sociologists, and political scientists. The connection between personality and politics is, in itself, no discovery of modern thought: one of the main assumptions of Plato, particularly in the *Republic,* is that constitutions do not grow at random "from stone to stone," but derive their existence and vitality from "those characters in the city which preponderate and draw the rest of the city after them." Although Plato's conception on the nature of man may seem out of date today, in some respects it shows a remarkable understanding of the complexity of human personality. His psychological hypotheses are weakest where his aristocratic, antidemocratic political outlook blocks an objective appraisal of reality, and where the antiscientific, mythical elements in his philosophy are reflected in his views on the nature of man. Yet, despite these psychological imperfections, his political theory gained immensely from his realization that no study of state and society can be fruitful unless it is based on a systematic conception of man's nature and motivations. In particular, Plato's sense of the complexity of social and political issues is anchored in the knowledge that they cannot be dealt with in isolation, and that they are ultimately human problems, infused with all the contradictory and irrational elements of man's nature and existence.

In modern political thought Rousseau was perhaps the last writer who was keenly interested in the totality of man rather than in his political behavior alone. Like Plato, Rousseau was intensely concerned with education as a process of taming man's irrational forces and transmuting them into socially desirable activities from which the state could derive stability and strength. After Rousseau, political thinking increasingly abandoned the older tradition of Platonic and medieval thought in which the nature of the state was related to the nature of man. The classical political doctrines since the late eighteenth century have generally assumed an oversimplified rationalistic conception of man without subjecting it to careful empirical analysis, and have proceeded to build a theory of state and society on the basis of such an assumption. Facts that do not seem to fit into the framework of theory have been dismissed as extraordinary, abnormal, irregular, or contrary to reason. Intellectual failure to account for the causes and existence of irrational, aggressive, and destructive forces in human relations was inevitably reflected in ineffectual methods for coping with such tendencies on the larger international scene.

Although insight into the dynamic relations between personality and politics is not new, only in the last fifty years have we begun to study them in an empirical manner, primarily because of the tremendous progress of clinical psychology and psychiatry. The single most important impetus to this study stems from the work of Freud and the psychoanalytic movement which he initiated. Whereas pre-Freudian psychology virtually identified mental with conscious processes, Freud emphasized the essentially *unconscious* character of mental processes, the conscious processes being merely "isolated acts and parts of the whole psychic entity." Freud was not a political philosopher, but a practicing physician, who developed his psychological theories out of his experience as a neurologist and psychiatrist. Yet as he grew older, he became increasingly absorbed in the study of archaeology, ethnology, anthropology, religion, folklore, and mythology, and he drew attention to the remarkable similarity in the mental development of the individual and that of the human race as a whole. Freud's emphasis on the unconscious, *irrational* elements in human behavior first aroused a great deal of opposition, but later that opposition died down when it was understood that scientific analysis of these irrational forces has the effect of lessening their damaging effect: the more we progress in understanding the mechanisms and processes of these irrational forces, the more we may eventually succeed in rationally controlling them, or—failing to achieve completely such an ambitious goal—we may at least be able to lessen in a practical manner some of the harmful effects of irrationality in everyday individual and collective behavior.

The immense psychological complexity of eradicating war is the main theme of Sigmund Freud's essay, "Thoughts for the Times on War and Death" (1915). When World War I broke out, many sensitive, civilized persons were shocked by the conduct of governments, armies, and individual combatants and civilians. Freud shows that the asocial impulses in man can be inhibited, repressed, or directed toward socially approved goals, but can never be completely eradicated. Civilization consists in the "ever-increasing transmutation of egoistic trends into social and altruistic ones," but the intensity and success of this transmutation varies from individual to individual, from group to group. In some persons, the pattern of civilized conduct is stable; in others, such conduct is the result of outward conformity rather than inward acceptance. These two types of persons must be clearly distinguished, and Freud writes that "we are certainly misled by our optimism into grossly exaggerating the number of human beings who have been transformed in a civilized sense." Freud is therefore not disillusioned about the behavior of the belligerent nations in war, which "have not sunk so low as we feared, because they had never risen so high as we believed." Those people, Freud says, who in normal times exhibit moral restraint only under pressure, live, psychologically speaking, "beyond their means," whereas war gives them relief from such imposed moral conduct, and thus enables them to live, psychologically, "within their means."

Early in World War I, many people thought that imperial, militaristic Germany under Emperor William II had, particularly in her treatment of Belgium, sunk about as low as any portion of the so-called civilized human race could possibly do. Freud was the only major thinker early in this century who warned that man's inhumanity to man as revealed in World War I was but a minor scratch on the surface and that much worse was still to come. He expressed this view, not because he was basically a pessimist, but because his psychological and psychiatric experience had taught him that the protective layers of civilization are thin, and that the whole fabric of civilized society is much more frail and vulnerable than his contemporaries were then able to realize. The atrocities of Nazi Germany in her concentration camps, the systematic murder of millions of non-Germans in her extermination camps, the barbarities of imperial Japan against conquered Asian populations and against Allied prisoners-of-war during World War II, the record of Soviet slave labor camps and mass killings following the Great Purge in the 1930's, the harsh brutality inflicted upon American prisoners by their Communist Chinese captors in the Korean war—all this subsequent evidence supports Freud's thesis that such cruelty and savagery are not an exceptional occurrence due to a particular characteristic of this or that nation, but that potentially every nation, every individual is capable of such conduct. Gradually we begin to understand that civilization is not the normal way of life, occasionally assailed by the atavistic few, but that it is an exceptional condition, maintained by the strong will and moral ethos of relatively few and constantly threatened by the primitive passions and destructive urges of the many.

As the work of Freud began to make its impact felt, first in the field of psychiatry and later in broader areas, the need developed for a bridge which would link the methods and findings of psychoanalysis with the problems and tasks of the social sciences. A symposium on the *Social Aspects of Psycho-Analysis*, edited by Ernest Jones (1924), the leading British psychoanalyst, was one of the first attempts to examine the relations of Freudian ideas to the basic social studies; the chapter on "Psychoanalysis in Relation to Politics" was contributed by M. D. Eder, one of the first British analysts. Following Freud, Eder stresses the point that psychoanalysis is no short cut to the understanding of politics—much less a substitute for other approaches, such as economics, geography, history, and law—but that it supplements these other studies by treating political questions primarily from one viewpoint, that of the unconscious. The *role of the family* in forming unconscious motivations and patterns of behavior is paramount: "The relationship of the individual to his father, to his mother, and to their surrogates, to his brothers and sisters, forms not only the model for a primitive society but for such a complicated structure as the governance of England." The *father* becomes the unconscious ideal, and the allegiance to the father-ideal may later be transferred to a political chief ("father of the country") or to abstract ideals. Yet *allegiance* to, and identification with, the father is not the only tie between son and father; there is also a basic attitude of *hostility* toward the father, which exists side by side with that of devotion. The common bond of antagonism creates a mutual link of intense identification among brothers and sisters, and such identification can be transferred to larger groups, and, finally, to the people as a whole.

The two basic political attitudes of conservatism and radical democracy closely reflect the two basic emotional attitudes of identification with the father, or, alternatively, of hostility toward him: the *conservative* transfers his idealization of, and identification with, his father to his sovereign and the persons connected with him, while hostility is felt toward the children who seek to overthrow the father, that is, the people. By contrast, the *radical democrat* derives his emotional dynamic from his identification with brothers and sisters, and his watchwords are therefore "Liberty, Equality, Fraternity." Modern politics are filled with the conflict between the two basic emotional attitudes toward the father and toward authority as the father-symbol; in democracies, too, the cry for the strong man is heard from time to time, particularly in a crisis situation. "In the ultimate analysis," Dr. Eder writes, "the cry for the strong man is but the child's cry for daddy and mummy to kiss the sore place and make it well again—for the soothing words of the magician who has power to charm away all the ills that affect us." Eder shows how the conflict between man's effort toward independence and responsibility and his attachment to authority and father-symbols is at the root of many primary social, economic, and political issues, both national and international.

Moreover, what complicates the striving for maturity and independence is the fact that the ousting of the father—a way of life based on an authoritarian pattern of thought and action—often fails to lead to fraternity and equality, but merely inaugurates a new authoritarian system, as happened after the initial successes of the French and Russian revolutions. The inner contradiction of communism is particularly striking: communism promises the destruction of capitalist authoritarianism, after which the classless society of fraternal liberty is to be established, the state to wither away completely. Yet the reality of communist states shows that the abolition of capitalist authority is, in itself, no guarantee of the establishment of a society based on liberty and equality, and that the paternalism of the communist police state is more oppressive than the restrictions and limitations of the economic and political systems that preceded it.

For several generations the imperfections of Western societies have been criticized on social, economic, and political grounds. Recently, as the more general study of human relations in their broadest context has developed, the attempt has been made to examine, not this or that particular symptom of social disease, but the whole phenomenon of the sick, disintegrating society and its relation to the unbalanced, distorted personality. This is the central issue in "Defeatism Concerning Democracy" (1941), by Franz Alexander, one of America's foremost psychoanalysts and psychiatrists. Alexander concedes that psychiatrists deal with individuals, and not with political or national groups. However, group relations are essentially the same as those between individuals, except for one striking difference: in their group relationships "people show much less consideration for each other's interests than in their personal dealings."

Alexander notes a gradation of conscience in human relations: it is strongest in dealings between individuals, weaker within groups of the same nation, and weakest between nations. Alexander defines conscience as that "portion of the human personality by which we identify ourselves with other people." The more individuals feel that they share fairly and equitably in available benefits and opportunities, the higher will be their social conscience and their feeling of identification with the other members of the group. Conversely, if there are deep cleavages of interest within a group, if some members feel that their vital interests are disregarded, social peace and order may be violated by the ensuing stresses and tensions, because "effectiveness of social conscience gradually diminishes in proportion to the conflicts within the group."

While an ideally just solution of all social conflicts is impossible, the democratic way facilitates compromise through free cooperation. Totalitarian societies do not allow such peaceful compromises, and their apparent unity conceals grave conflicts of interest. To preserve their prestige in the eyes of their own people whom they deprive of liberty and equality, totalitarian dictators must therefore continuously plan victories over their enemies, holding out the enticing promise of conquest and loot to their own oppressed subjects.

In the light of his psychoanalytic practice Alexander concludes that *two factors menace,* above all, the prospects of *democracy:* the first is the *latent regressive tendency toward dependence,* and the second is *economic insecurity.* The first factor is subjective, emotional, and universal in the sense that every human being protests to some extent against growing up and wishes to continue the existence in which someone else takes care of him. As man grows up, he is expelled from his Garden of Eden, and is driven into the cold world where he must struggle for himself. This emotional tendency toward dependence is strengthened by an objective social phenomenon, economic insecurity: "Economic insecurity increases the flight from responsibility and independence and mobilizes the latent longing for parental care which everyone carries in himself." Totalitarian systems demand obedience, but offer their citizens security and the comforts of not having to make decisions and assume civic responsibilities. Totalitarianism appeals, therefore, to those who have never grown up emotionally, and who long to return to their infantile dependence and irresponsibility. There is empirical evidence to show that the early experience of authoritarianism in the family tends to condition individuals toward the later acceptance of other forms of totalitarianism, be they political, social, economic, or religious.

During and after World War II, the free nations learned the hard way that democracy, if it was to meet the challenge of totalitarianism, had to prove its efficiency, toughness, and resilience in the military as well as in the ideological field. Furthermore, the people of the free countries began to understand that democracy was more than a form of government which could be introduced or imposed from the outside, and that, in particular, the democratization of societies permeated with ancient and archaic totalitarian patterns of living would be a long and arduous process. Contributing to a symposium on "The Practicality of Democracy" (1945), Kurt Lewin, a leading German social psychologist who migrated to the United States from Germany after the advent to power of Hitler, examines the dynamic relations between group and individual in three alternative social environments: autocracy, democracy, and *laissez faire*. Contrary to the prevalent view, Lewin shows that human relations should not be conceived as a continuum between strict authoritarian discipline at one end and maximum individual freedom at the other, but should rather be thought of in terms of a triangular configuration. As to leadership and organization, both are accepted by autocracy and democracy as necessary patterns of human relations. On the other hand, democracy and *laissez faire* have in common the vital element of shared experience in formulating group decisions. Democracy thus does not stand somewhere in the middle between authoritarianism and lawlessness. The democratic leader, in particular, is not a "soft" edition of the autocratic leader: "The democratic leader is no less a leader and, in a way, has no less power than the autocratic leader." On the basis of controlled experiments with groups of children, as well as a wide range of experience in industry, Lewin arrives at the conclusion that the character and personality of the individual, at least as shown in his behavior, is rapidly and profoundly affected by a change in social atmosphere. Not only the degree of friendliness and aggressiveness changes under such circumstances, but also initiative and "laziness" vary with variations of the underlying social pattern. Specifically, so far as efficiency of the various group organizations is concerned, Lewin does not hesitate to affirm that a democratic group with long-range planning surpasses both the autocratic and *laissez-faire* groups in creative initiative and sociability. The key elements to be considered in seeking to transform a nondemocratic group into a democratic one are ideology, the character of its members, and the distribution of power within the group—specifically between leaders and members. No single element can be changed without altering the others and the balance between all three. Lewin thus shows the narrowness of conception of the "realist" who sees power as the sole factor in human relations, overlooking the weight of ideology, but he also warns against the believer in the "goodness of human nature" who easily overlooks that ideology cannot be changed by preachment and indoctrination alone, but must be accompanied by changes in the distribution of power within the group. Finally, Lewin utters the important warning that *democratic behavior cannot be learned by autocratic methods.* In the school as in the home, in the factory as in the church, the decisive thing is not the verbalization of democratic slogans and symbols, but the *quality of the citizens' lives.*

The poverty of genuine democratic living in a society which may be formally and constitutionally committed to democratic government is the deeper cause of such nations' fall into the abyss of out-and-out totalitarianism, as happened in Germany and Japan in the nineteen-thirties. One of the most original psychological interpretations of the deviations and aberrations of modern man from the path of freedom is to be found in *Escape from Freedom* (1941), by Erich Fromm. Strongly influenced by Freud, Fromm finds psychoanalysis too individualistic in its stress on the problems of satisfaction or frustration of instinctual needs. "The key problem of psychology," Fromm writes, "is that of the specific kind of relatedness of the individual toward the world." Long before modern psychology, writers and poets saw in the loneliness of man one of the main driving forces of his existence. Fromm shows the political, economic, and cultural causes that make modern man feel small and helpless amidst the bigness in which he finds himself. Industrialism has destroyed many of the traditional institutions which had previously made a person feel that he "belonged," and the anonymity and impersonality of human relations resulting from increased urbanization have accentuated individual isolation and frustration.

Fromm's analysis of masochism and sadism as escape mechanisms from personal insecurity deserves the closest attention, as it explains one of the mainsprings of the dynamics of totalitarian movements—of submissive followers and authoritarian leaders. The traditional analysis of political dictatorship has been, and often still is, centered on the motivations of dictatorial leaders, driven by lust of power and sadistic cravings for domination. In that traditional political analysis, the followers and subjects of a dictatorship are viewed exclusively as "victims," who just happen to fall into the misfortune of oppressive rule. Fromm performs a signal service in the study and understanding of *totalitarianism* by showing that its very existence *depends on the desire of many persons to submit and obey,* and the "phenomenon of masochism shows us that men can be drawn to the experience of suffering or submission." *Escape from Freedom* deals mainly with the Fascist form of totalitarianism, but there is little doubt that communism, too, appeals to those who long for certainty and submission.

The findings of psychologists and psychiatrists have more recently been supported by newly accumulated empirical data on the authoritarian personality. The largest research project of its kind in history was set up in 1944 in the United States, centered at the University of California at Berkeley and aided by research teams in other parts of the country. Over two thousand persons drawn from a wide variety of social strata were tested and interviewed by means of techniques and procedures developed by social psychologists, psychiatrists, and psychometricians. The results of the cooperative enterprise, which was carried on for about five years, were published in the monumental work, *The Authoritarian Personality* (1950), by T. W. Adorno, Else Frenkel-Brunswik, Daniel J. Levinson, and R. Nevitt Sanford. The main conclusions of the study were summarized in a short essay, "Portrait of the Authoritarian Man" (1950), by Samuel H. Flowerman, one of the research directors of the project.

Flowerman expresses perhaps the most incisive idea of his essay by stating that "the real menace to democracy is not the brutal dictator but the anonymous man-in-the-crowd on whose support the dictator depends for power." *Without authoritarian personalities*—going into the thousands and millions—*there can be no authoritarian state.* Analyzing the main elements that characterize the authoritarian personality, Flowerman lists, on the basis of the larger study, the following qualities as essential: a tendency to conform compulsively to orthodox ideals and practices; emotional rigidity and limited imagination; strong loyalty to one's own group ("in-group") coupled with vehement dislike of outsiders ("out-group"); phony conservatism; and, finally, moral purism. The "herd-minded" (or "ethnocentric") element in the personality of the authoritarian is perhaps the most important, although no single element in itself constitutes the authoritarian type. As in earlier studies, the role of the family in the formation of basic attitudes appears to be pivotal, although it must be understood that the family is no isolated and independent agent operating on its own energy, but reflects the predominant social goals and values. The family is, as it were, the psychological and cultural representative of society in relation to the child, teaching the child the fundamentals of what society considers right and wrong and enforcing the prevailing code to the extent that it is feasible. For the child, the family is thus society in miniature—law, government, and ethics in one small unit.

No individual is ever completely authoritarian or democratic, just as no society is perfectly authoritarian or democratic. In each case it is a question of extent and degree, although differences of quantity become, eventually, differences of quality. In the United States, about 10 per cent of the population are authoritarian men and women, and another 20 per cent are potentially authoritarian. No similar large-scale empirical study has ever been undertaken in any other country, and it is therefore difficult to compare the American figures with others.

But it should be borne in mind—and this is a serious limitation of *The Authoritarian Personality*—that its framework of authoritarianism was defined (as was natural in the middle 1940's) by Fascism. Yet on the basis of subsequent psychiatric and psychological studies of Communists it is clear that they have emotionally and intellectually much in common with Fascists. The implicit and fundamental similarities between Fascist and Communist personality types outweigh the explicit political hostility between the totalitarian systems of Fascist and Communist states. For a long time, particularly in the nineteen-thirties, many scholars and politicians made a sharp distinction between Fascism and Communism, largely because the former seemed more dangerous at the time. Yet popular folklore even then spoke of Communism as "Red Fascism," thus expressing the deeper psychological and political truth that the nature of modern totalitarianism is fundamentally the same in all countries, regardless of differences in expressed aims.

SIGMUND FREUD

1. *Why Men Wage War**

Swept as we are into the vortex of this war-time, our information one-sided, ourselves too near to focus the mighty transformations which have already taken place or are beginning to take place, and without a glimmering of the inchoate future, we are incapable of apprehending the significance of the thronging impressions, and know not what value to attach to the judgements we form. We are constrained to believe that never has any event been destructive of so much that is valuable in the common wealth of humanity, nor so misleading to many of the clearest intelligences, nor so debasing to the highest that we know. Science herself has lost her passionless impartiality; in their deep embitterment her servants seek for weapons from her with which to contribute towards the defeat of the enemy. The anthropologist is driven to declare the opponent inferior and degenerate; the psychiatrist to publish his diagnosis of the enemy's disease of mind or spirit. But probably our sense of these immediate evils is disproportionately strong, and we are not entitled to compare them with the evils of other times of which we have not undergone the experience.

* (1915); reprinted in Sigmund Freud, *Collected Papers*, Vol. IV (Hogarth Press, 1925). By permission.

The individual who is not himself a combatant—and so a wheel in the gigantic machinery of war—feels conscious of disorientation, and of an inhibition in his powers and activities. I believe that he will welcome any indication, however slight, which may enable him to find out what is wrong with himself at least. I propose to distinguish two among the most potent factors in the mental distress felt by non-combatants, against which it is such a heavy task to struggle, and to treat of them here: the disillusionment which this war has evoked; and the altered attitude towards death which this—like every other war—imposes on us.

When I speak of disillusionment, everyone at once knows what I mean. One need not be a sentimentalist; one may perceive the biological and psychological necessity of suffering in the economics of human life, and yet condemn war both in its means and in its aims, and devoutly look forward to the cessation of all wars. True, we have told ourselves that wars can never cease so long as nations live under such widely differing conditions, so long as the value of individual life is in each nation so variously computed, and so long as the animosities which divide them represent such powerful instinctual forces in the mind. And we were prepared to find that wars between the primitive and the civilized peoples, between those races whom a colour-line divides, nay, wars with and among the undeveloped nationalities of Europe or those whose culture has perished—that for a considerable period such wars would occupy mankind. But we permitted ourselves to have other hopes. We had expected the great ruling powers among the white nations upon whom the leadership of the human species has fallen, who were known to have cultivated world-wide interests, to whose creative powers were due our technical advances in the direction of dominating nature, as well as the artistic and scientific acquisitions of the mind—peoples such as these we had expected to succeed in discovering another way of settling misunderstandings and conflicts of interest. Within each of these nations there prevailed high standards of accepted custom for the individual, to which his manner of life was bound to conform if he desired a share in communal privileges. These ordinances, frequently too stringent, exacted a great deal from him, much self-restraint, much renunciation of instinctual gratification. He was especially forbidden to make use of the immense advantages to be gained by the practice of lying and deception in the competition with his fellow-men. The civilized state regarded these accepted standards as the basis of its existence; stern were its proceedings when an impious hand was laid upon them; frequent the pronouncement that to subject them even to examination by a critical intelligence was entirely impracticable. It could be assumed, therefore, that the state itself would respect them, nor would contemplate undertaking any infringement of what it acknowledged as the basis of its own existence. To be sure, it was evident that within these civilized states were mingled remnants of certain other races who were universally unpopular and had therefore been only reluctantly, and even so not to the fullest extent, admitted to participation in the common task of civilization, for which they had shown themselves suitable enough. But the great nations themselves, it might have been supposed, had acquired so much comprehension of their common interests, and enough tolerance for the differences that existed between them, that "foreigner" and "enemy" could no longer, as still in antiquity, be regarded as synonymous.

Relying on this union among the civilized races, countless people have exchanged their native home for a foreign dwelling-place, and made their existence dependent on the conditions of intercourse between friendly nations. But he who was not by stress of circumstances confined to one spot, could also confer upon himself, through all the advantages and attractions of these civilized countries, a new, a wider fatherland, wherein he moved unhindered and unsuspected. In this way he enjoyed the blue sea, and the grey; the beauty of the snow-clad mountains and of the green pasture-lands; the magic of the northern forests and the splendour of the southern vegetation; the emotion inspired by landscapes that recall great historical events, and the silence of nature in her inviolate places. This new fatherland was for him a museum also, filled with all the treasures which the artists among civilized communities had in the successive centuries created and left behind. As he wandered from one gallery to another in this museum, he could appreciate impartially the varied types of perfection that miscegenation, the course of historical events, and the special characteristics of their mother-earth had produced among his more remote compatriots. Here he would find a cool inflexible energy developed to the highest point; there, the gracious art of beautifying existence; elsewhere, the sense of order and fixed law—in short, any and all of the qualities which have made mankind the lords of the earth.

Nor must we forget that each of these citizens of culture had created for himself a personal "Parnassus" and "School of Athens." From among the great thinkers and artists of all nations he had chosen those to whom he conceived himself most deeply indebted for what he had achieved in enjoyment and comprehension of life, and in his veneration had associated them with the immortals of old as well as with the more familiar masters of his own tongue. None of these great figures had seemed to him alien because he had spoken another language—not the incomparable investigator of the passions of mankind, nor the intoxicated worshipper of beauty, nor the vehement and threatening prophet, nor the subtle mocking satirist; and never did he on this account rebuke himself as a renegade towards his own nation and his beloved mother-tongue.

The enjoyment of this fellowship in civilization was from time to time disturbed by warning voices, which declared that as a result of long-prevailing differences wars were unavoidable, even among the members of a fellowship such as this. We refused to believe it; but if such a war indeed must be, what was our imaginary picture of it? We saw it as an opportunity for demonstrating the progress of mankind in communal feeling since the era when the Greek Amphictyones had proclaimed that no city of the league might be demolished, nor its olive-groves hewn down, nor its water cut off. As a chivalrous crusade, which would limit itself to establishing the superiority of one side in the contest, with the least possible infliction of dire sufferings that could contribute nothing to the decision, and with complete immunity for the wounded who must of necessity withdraw from the contest, as well as for the physicians and nurses who devoted themselves to the task of healing. And of course with the utmost precautions for the non-combatant classes of the population—for women who are debarred from warwork, and for the children who, grown older, should be enemies no longer but friends and co-operators. And again, with preservation of all the international undertakings and institutions in which the mutual civilization of peace-time had been embodied.

Even a war like this would have been productive of horrors and sufferings enough; but it would not have interrupted the development of ethical relations between the greater units of mankind, between the peoples and the states.

Then the war in which we had refused to believe broke out, and brought—disillusionment. Not only is it more sanguinary and more destructive than any war of other days, because of the enormously increased perfection of weapons of attack and defence; but it is at least as cruel, as embittered, as implacable as any that has preceded it. It sets at naught all those restrictions known as International Law, which in peace-time the states had bound themselves to observe; it ignores the prerogatives of the wounded and the medical service, the distinction between civil and military sections of the population, the claims of private property. It tramples in blind fury on all that comes in its way, as though there were to be no future and no goodwill among men after it has passed. It rends all bonds of fellowship between the contending peoples, and threatens to leave such a legacy of embitterment as will make any renewal of such bonds impossible for a long time to come.

Moreover, it has brought to light the almost unbelievable phenomenon of a mutual comprehension between the civilized nations so slight that the one can turn with hate and loathing upon the other. Nay, more—that one of the great civilized nations is so universally unpopular that the attempt can actually be made to exclude it from the civilized community as "barbaric," although it long has proved its fitness by the most magnificent co-operation in the work of civilization. We live in the hope that the impartial decision of history will furnish the proof that precisely this nation, this in whose tongue we now write, this for whose victory our dear ones are fighting, was the one which least transgressed the laws of civilization—but at such a time who shall dare present himself as the judge of his own cause?

Nations are in a measure represented by the states which they have formed; these states, by the governments which administer them. The individual in any given nation has in this war a terrible opportunity to convince himself of what would occasionally strike him in peace-time—that the state has forbidden to the individual the practice of wrong-doing, not because it desired to abolish it, but because it desires to monopolize it, like salt and tobacco. The warring state permits itself every such misdeed, every such act of violence, as would disgrace the individual man. It practises not only the accepted stratagems, but also deliberate lying and deception against the enemy; and this, too, in a measure which appears to surpass the usage of former wars. The state exacts the utmost degree of obedience and sacrifice from its citizens, but at the same time treats them as children by maintaining an excess of secrecy, and a censorship of news and expressions of opinion that renders the spirits of those thus intellectually oppressed defenceless against every unfavourable turn of events and every sinister rumour. It absolves itself from the guarantees and contracts it had formed with other states, and makes unabashed confession of its rapacity and lust for power, which the private individual is then called upon to sanction in the name of patriotism.

Nor may it be objected that the state cannot refrain from wrong-doing, since that would place it at a disadvantage. It is no less disadvantageous, as a general rule, for the individual man to conform to the customs of morality and refrain from brutal and arbitrary conduct; and the state but seldom proves able to indemnify him for the sacrifices it exacts. It cannot be a matter for astonishment, therefore, that this relaxation of all the moral ties between the greater units of mankind should have had a seducing influence on the morality of individuals; for our conscience is not the inflexible judge that ethical teachers are wont to declare it, but in its origin is "dread of the community" and nothing else. When the community has no rebuke to make, there is an end of all suppression of the baser passions, and men perpetrate deeds of cruelty, fraud, treachery and barbarity so incompatible with their civilization that one would have held them to be impossible.

Well may that civilized cosmopolitan, therefore, of whom I spoke, stand helpless in a world grown strange to him—his all-embracing patrimony disintegrated, the common estates in it laid waste, the fellow-citizens embroiled and debased!

In criticism of his disillusionment, nevertheless, certain things must be said. Strictly speaking, it is not justified, for it consists in the destruction of —an illusion! We welcome illusions because they spare us emotional distress, and enable us instead to indulge in gratification. We must not then complain if now and again they come into conflict with some portion of reality, and are shattered against it.

Two things in this war have evoked our sense of disillusionment: the destitution shown in moral relations externally by the states which in their interior relations pose as the guardians of accepted moral usage, and the brutality in behaviour shown by individuals, whom, as partakers in the highest form of human civilization, one would not have credited with such a thing.

Let us begin with the second point and endeavour to formulate, as succinctly as may be, the point of view which it is proposed to criticize. How do we imagine the process by which an individual attains to a higher plane of morality? The first answer is sure to be: He is good and noble from his very birth, his very earliest beginnings. We need not consider this any further. A second answer will suggest that we are concerned with a developmental process, and will probably assume that this development consists in eradicating from him the evil human tendencies and, under the influence of education and a civilized environment, replacing them by good ones. From that standpoint it is certainly astonishing that evil should show itself to have such power in those who have been thus nurtured.

But this answer implies the thesis from which we propose to dissent. In reality, there is no such thing as "eradicating" evil tendencies. Psychological —more strictly speaking, psycho-analytic—investigation shows instead that the inmost essence of human nature consists of elemental instincts, which are common to all men and aim at the satisfaction of certain primal needs. These instincts in themselves are neither good nor evil. We but classify them and their manifestations in that fashion, according as they meet the needs and demands of the human community. It is admitted that all those instincts which society condemns as evil—let us take as representatives the selfish and the cruel—are of this primitive type.

These primitive instincts undergo a lengthy process of development before they are allowed to become active in the adult being. They are inhibited, directed towards other aims and departments, become commingled, alter their objects, and are to some extent turned back upon their possessor. Reaction-formations against certain instincts take the deceptive form of a change in content, as though egoism had changed into altruism, or cruelty into pity. These reaction-formations are facilitated by the circumstance that many instincts are manifested almost from the first in pairs of opposites, a very remarkable phenomenon—and one strange to the lay public—which is termed the "ambivalence of feeling." The most easily observable and comprehensible instance of this is the fact that intense love and intense hatred are so often to be found together in the same person. Psycho-analysis adds that the conflicting feelings not infrequently have the same person for their object.

It is not until all these "vicissitudes to which instincts are subject" have been surmounted that what we call the character of a human being is formed, and this, as we know, can only very inadequately be classified as "good" or "bad." A human being is seldom altogether good or bad; he is usually "good" in one relation and "bad" in another, or "good" in certain external circumstances and in others decidedly "bad." It is interesting to learn that the existence of strong "bad" impulses in infancy is often the actual condition for an unmistakable inclination towards "good" in the adult person. Those who as children have been the most pronounced egoists may well become the most helpful and self-sacrificing members of the community; most of our sentimentalists, friends of humanity, champions of animals, have been evolved from little sadists and animal-tormentors.

The transformation of "bad" instincts is brought about by two co-operating factors, an internal and an external. The internal factor consists in an influence on the bad—say, the egoistic—instincts exercised by erotism, that is, by the human need for love, taken in its widest sense. By the admixture of *erotic* components the egoistic instincts are transmuted into *social* ones. We learn to value being loved as an advantage for which we are willing to sacrifice other advantages. The external factor is the force exercised by upbringing, which advocates the claims of our cultural environment, and this is furthered later by the direct pressure of that civilization by which we are surrounded. Civilization is the fruit of renunciation of instinctual satisfaction, and from each new-comer in turn it exacts the same renunciation. Throughout the life of the individual there is a constant replacement of the external compulsion by the internal. The influences of civilization cause an ever-increasing transmutation of egoistic trends into altruistic and social ones, and this by an admixture of erotic elements. In the last resort it may be said that every internal compulsion which has been of service in the development of human beings was originally, that is, in the evolution of the human race, nothing but an external one. Those who are born to-day bring with them as an inherited constitution some degree of a tendency (disposition) towards transmutation of egoistic into social instincts, and this disposition is easily stimulated to achieve that effect. A further measure of this transformation must be accomplished during the life of the individual himself. And so the human being is subject not only to the pressure of his immediate environment, but also to the influence of the cultural development attained by his forefathers.

If we give the name of *cultural adaptability* to a man's personal capacity for transformation of the egoistic impulses under the influence of the erotic, we may further affirm that this adaptability is made up of two parts, one innate and the other acquired through experience, and that the relation of the two to each other and to that portion of the instinctual life which remains untransformed is a very variable one.

Generally speaking, we are apt to attach too much importance to the innate part, and in addition to this we run the risk of overestimating the general adaptability to civilization in comparison with those instincts which have remained in their primitive state—by which I mean that in this way we are led to regard human nature as "better" than it actually is. For there is, besides, another factor which obscures our judgement and falsifies the issue in too favourable a sense.

The impulses of another person are naturally hidden from our observation. We deduce them from his actions and behaviour, which we trace to motives born of his instinctual life. Such a conclusion is bound to be, in many cases, erroneous. This or that action which is "good" from the civilized point of view may in one instance be born of a "noble" motive, in another not so. Ethical theorists class as "good" actions only those which are the outcome of good impulses; to the others they refuse their recognition. But society, which is practical in its aims, is little troubled on the whole by this distinction; it is content if a man regulates his behaviour and actions by the precepts of civilization, and is little concerned with his motives.

We have seen that the external compulsion exercised on a human being by his up-bringing and environment produces a further transformation towards good in his instinctual life—a turning from egoism towards altruism. But this is not the regular or necessary effect of the external compulsion. Education and environment offer benefits not only in the way of love, but also employ another kind of premium system, namely, reward and punishment. In this way their effect may turn out to be that he who is subjected to their influence will choose to "behave well" in the civilized sense of the phrase, although no ennoblement of instinct, no transformation of egoistic into altruistic inclinations, has taken place within. The result will, roughly speaking, be the same; only a particular concatenation of circumstances will reveal that one man always acts rightly because his instinctual inclination compels him so to do, and the other is "good" only in so far and for so long as such civilized behaviour is advantageous for his own egoistic purposes. But superficial acquaintance with an individual will not enable us to distinguish between the two cases, and we are certainly misled by our optimism into grossly exaggerating the number of human beings who have been transformed in a civilized sense.

Civilized society, which exacts good conduct and does not trouble itself about the impulses underlying it, has thus won over to obedience a great many people who are not thereby following the dictates of their own natures. Encouraged by this success, society has suffered itself to be led into straining the moral standard to the highest possible point, and thus it has forced its members into a yet greater estrangement from their instinctual dispositions. They are consequently subjected to an unceasing suppression of instinct, the resulting strain of which betrays itself in the most remarkable phenomena of reaction and compensation formations. In the domain of sexuality, where such suppression is most difficult to enforce, the result is seen in the reaction-phenomena of neurotic disorders. Elsewhere the pressure of civilization brings in its train no pathological results, but is shown in malformations of character, and in the perpetual readiness of the inhibited instincts to break through to gratification at any suitable opportunity. Anyone thus compelled to act continually in the sense of precepts which are not the expression of instinctual inclinations, is living, psychologically speaking, beyond his means, and might objectively be designated a hypocrite, whether this difference be clearly known to him or not. It is undeniable that our contemporary civilization is extraordinarily favourable to the production of this form of hypocrisy. One might venture to say that it is based upon such hypocrisy, and that it would have to submit to far-reaching modifications if people were to undertake to live in accordance with the psychological truth. Thus there are very many more hypocrites than truly civilized persons— indeed, it is a debatable point whether a certain degree of civilized hypocrisy be not indispensable for the maintenance of civilization, because the cultural adaptability so far attained by those living to-day would perhaps not prove adequate to the task. On the other hand, the maintenance of civilization even on so questionable a basis offers the prospect of each new generation achieving a farther-reaching transmutation of instinct, and becoming the pioneer of a higher form of civilization.

From the foregoing observations we may already derive this consolation —that our mortification and our grievous disillusionment regarding the uncivilized behaviour of our world-compatriots in this war are shown to be unjustified. They were based on an illusion to which we had abandoned ourselves. In reality our fellow-citizens have not sunk so low as we feared, because they had never risen so high as we believed. That the greater units of humanity, the peoples and states, have mutually abrogated their moral restraints naturally prompted these individuals to permit themselves relief for a while from the heavy pressure of civilization and to grant a passing satisfaction to the instincts it holds in check. This probably caused no breach in the relative morality within their respective national frontiers.

We may, however, obtain insight deeper than this into the change brought about by the war in our former compatriots, and at the same time receive a warning against doing them an injustice. For the evolution of the mind shows a peculiarity which is present in no other process of development. When a village grows into a town, a child into a man, the village and the child become submerged in the town and the man. Memory alone can trace the earlier features in the new image; in reality the old materials or forms have been superseded and replaced by new ones. It is otherwise with the development of the mind. Here one can describe the state of affairs, which is a quite peculiar one, only by saying that in this case every earlier stage of development persists alongside the later stage which has developed from it; the successive stages condition a co-existence, although it is in reference to the same materials that the whole series of transformations has been fashioned. The earlier mental state may not have manifested itself for years, but none the less it is so far present that it may at any time again become the mode of expression of the forces in the mind, and that exclusively, as though all later developments had been annulled, undone. This extraordinary plasticity of the evolution that takes place in the mind is not unlimited in its scope; it might be described as a special capacity for retroversion—for regression—since it may well happen that a later and higher stage of evolution, once abandoned, cannot be reached again. But the primitive stages can always be re-established; the primitive mind is, in the fullest meaning of the word, imperishable.

What are called mental diseases inevitably impress the layman with the idea of destruction of the life of mind and soul. In reality, the destruction relates only to later accretions and developments. The essence of mental disease lies in a return to earlier conditions of affective life and functioning. An excellent example of the plasticity of mental life is afforded by the state of sleep, which every night we desire. Since we have learnt to interpret even absurd and chaotic dreams, we know that whenever we sleep we cast off our hard-won morality like a garment, only to put it on again next morning. This divestiture is naturally unattended by any danger because we are paralysed, condemned to inactivity, by the state of sleep. Only through a dream can we learn of the regression of our emotional life to one of the earliest stages of development. For instance, it is noteworthy that all our dreams are governed by purely egoistic motives. One of my English friends put forward this proposition at a scientific meeting in America, whereupon a lady who was present remarked that that might be the case in Austria, but she could maintain for herself and her friends that *they* were altruistic even in their dreams. My friend, although himself of English race, was obliged to contradict the lady emphatically on the ground of his personal experience in dream-analysis, and to declare that in their dreams highminded American ladies were quite as egoistical as the Austrians.

Thus the transformations of instinct on which our cultural adaptability is based, may also be permanently or temporarily undone by the experiences of life. Undoubtedly the influences of war are among the forces that can bring about such regression; therefore we need not deny adaptability for culture to all who are at the present time displaying uncivilized behaviour, and we may anticipate that the refinement of their instincts will be restored in times of peace.

There is, however, another symptom in our world-compatriots which has perhaps astonished and shocked us no less than the descent from their ethical nobility which has so greatly distressed us. I mean the narrow-mindedness shown by the best intellects, their obduracy, their inaccessibility to the most forcible arguments, their uncritical credulity for the most disputable assertions. This indeed presents a lamentable picture, and I wish to say emphatically that in this I am by no means a blind partisan who finds all the intellectual shortcomings on one side. But this phenomenon is much easier to account for and much less disquieting than that which we have just considered. Students of human nature and philosophers have long taught us that we are mistaken in regarding our intelligence as an independent force and in overlooking its dependence upon the emotional life. Our intelligence, they teach us, can function reliably only when it is removed from the influences of strong emotional impulses; otherwise it behaves merely as an instrument of the will and delivers the inference which the will requires. Thus, in their view, logical arguments are impotent against affective interests, and that is why reasons, which in Falstaff's phrase are "as plenty as blackberries," produce so few victories in the conflict with interests. Psycho-analytic experience has, if possible, further confirmed this statement. It daily shows that the shrewdest persons will all of a sudden behave like imbeciles as soon as the needful insight is confronted by an emotional resistance, but will completely regain their wonted acuity once that resistance has been overcome. The logical infatuations into which this war has deluded our fellow-citizens, many of them the best of their kind, are therefore a secondary phenomenon, a consequence of emotional excitement, and are destined, we may hope, to disappear with it.

Having in this way come to understand once more our fellow-citizens who are now so greatly alienated from us, we shall the more easily endure the disillusionment which the nations, those greater units of the human race, have caused us, for we shall perceive that the demands we make upon them ought to be far more modest. Perhaps they are reproducing the course of individual evolution, and still to-day represent very primitive phases in the organization and formation of higher unities. It is in agreement with this that the educative factor of an external compulsion towards morality, which we found to be so effective for the individual, is barely discernible in them. True, we had hoped that the extensive community of interests established by commerce and production would constitute the germ of such a compulsion, but it would seem that nations still obey their immediate passions far more readily than their interests. Their interests serve them, at most, as rationalizations for their passions; they parade their interests as their justification for satisfying their passions. Actually why the national units should disdain, detest, abhor one another, and that even when they are at peace, is indeed a mystery. I cannot tell why it is. It is just as though when it becomes a question of a number of people, not to say millions, all individual moral acquirements were obliterated, and only the most primitive, the oldest, the crudest mental attitudes were left. Possibly only future stages in development will be able in any way to alter this regrettable state of affairs. But a little more truthfulness and upright dealing on all sides, both in the personal relations of men to one another and between them and those who govern them, should also do something towards smoothing the way for this transformation.

M. D. EDER

2. *Psychoanalysis and Politics**

The method I propose to adopt, and the point of view from which I set out, namely the application of the results derived from the study of individual psychology to sociological problems, and the possibility of understanding that the study of the unconscious may throw on political questions, run, I am painfully aware, in opposition to the views of some eminent sociologists and students of politics.

Durkheim, for instance, states that "the determining cause of a social fact must be sought in the preceding social facts, and not in the state of individual conscience." [1] Laski claims that "politically we can be concerned not with the hidden motives but with the overt acts of men." [2]

It is however with the facts derived from the study of the individual who is a member of at least a small circle that I set out; and it is with the motives so carefully hidden that the individual is himself unaware of them, yet which so largely determine his activities, that I am concerned.

If I go counter to certain views I can claim on the other hand that the standpoint of psycho-analysis is in accordance with the views of some modern sociologists. I remember how Prof. Geddes corrected me when I referred to him as Professor of Sociology at the University of Bombay. "No," he said, "I am Professor of Sociology and Town-planning." That is to say, practical life must be the guide for sociological principles. Now if, as I hope to show, psycho-analysis has some interest when applied to politics, it is because of its extremely practical nature. As you know, psycho-analysis began humbly enough as a branch of medical therapeutics. "By the inspiration of an ingenious mind, the apparently most insignificant facts become the principle of considerable discoveries," [3] as Le Play said in another connexion. From what seems to be mere psychological trifles, such as the motive and the meaning of a misquotation, a dream, a nervous symptom, Freud, that "esprit ingénieux," has been impelled to a consideration of the meaning of our attitude towards general social and political questions. I shall adopt rather the Greek view of politics as embracing all activities of human association, but I warn you that I shall deal with these political questions from one point of view only, from

---

* From Ernest Jones (ed.), *Social Aspects of Psycho-Analysis* (Williams and Norgate, 1924). By permission.

[1] Emile Durkheim, *Les règles de la méthode sociologique* (1895), p. 135.

[2] Harold Laski, *Authority in the Modern State* (1919), p. 30.

[3] Le Play, *Les Ouvriers européens* (1855), appendix, p. 281.

the standpoint of the unconscious. Sociology, biology, geography, history, law, economics, philosophy and other disciplines, I need not remind you, have all important bearings upon political questions. My treatment is confessedly one-sided, but it is a side which has not much of a hearing. I do not think the Oedipus complex has yet appeared on a political platform; at all events, it has not yet become a party question.

Furthermore I am afraid I must disappoint you by saying that although I firmly believe practical values may be some day reached as the result of the application of psycho-analysis to politics, I do not expect you to obtain any practical help from my discourse. At the end I shall not have helped any one of you in your voting at the next election; perhaps you will even say that I am attempting to make confusion worse confounded. This is to some extent inevitable, for in trying to solve one problem we usually find that we are confronted with a new set of problems of which we must first seek a solution; but indeed I am not here seeking a solution to any political problem, being solely concerned with the study of certain human associations from a purely scientific point of view, where the question of values or action is not under consideration.

The importance that the family, demonstrated by Mr. Flügel, is found to take in the moulding of the individual is an aspect with which the Sociological Society, lodged in Le Play House, will certainly find no cause of complaint. Le Play writes: "I firmly hold that even those who refuse to consider the family as a direct creation of God, see in it at least a direct consequence of the natural laws established by Him." [4] It is not surprising to find a genius like Le Play making the family one of the triad in the genesis of societies; he reached his conclusions as a result of repeated observations. Compare Paley's remark that the "condition of human infancy prepares men for society, by combining individuals into small communities, and by placing them from the beginning under direction and control. A family contains the rudiments of an Empire." [5]

Freud, another man of genius, arrived at a similar result—the Oedipus complex is, he says, a regular and most important factor in the relationship of the child to its parents: the Oedipus complex therefore displays the situation of an individual in society, in a miniature society, namely in the family circle. But this grouping is the pattern upon which the affective relationship of all other groupings is modelled. When Mr. Laski asks "the psychologist to disclose the factors of human association," [6] I can answer: they have been and are being disclosed; the factors of human association are the factors seen in the psycho-analytic survey of the family. The other day in an article headed "The Fourth Terror," the *Times* quoted a Japanese proverb enumer-

---

[4] Le Play, *L'organisation de la famille* (1884), p. 7.
[5] Paley, *Moral and Political Philosophy* (Complete Works, 1825), Vol. II, p. 280.
[6] Laski, *op. cit.*, p. 32.

ating the four greatest terrors which Japan is called upon to endure: "earth-quakes, thunder, fire and too strict fatherly discipline." [7] To the psycho-analyst the proverb does not seem quite so paradoxical as it did to the writer of the article. It is a recognition that the father plays as great a part in human destinies as does an earthquake.

The relationship of an individual to his father, to his mother, and to their surrogates, to his brothers and sisters, forms not only the model for a primi-tive society but for such a complicated structure as the governance of Eng-land. Voltaire said that man had fashioned God in his own image; it would be nearer the mark to say, in the image of his father, i.e., of the ideal which is built up in the earliest years of childhood. "Identification," says Freud, "is known to psycho-analysis as the earliest expression of an emotional tie with another person. It plays a part in the early history of the Oedipus complex. A little boy will exhibit a special interest in his father: he would like to grow like him, and be like him, and take his place everywhere. We may simply say that he takes his father as his ideal." [8] I have pointed out elsewhere all that the father means in power, intelligence, wisdom to the infant and child. I do not think you will regard it as an exaggerated picture were one to say that in a child's view the father is not only incapable of doing wrong but even of thinking wrong, he can never mean to do any improper thing; in him is no folly or weakness.

Much of this is matter of everyday observation, but what psycho-analysis brings out is that this emotional relationship remains throughout life; I mean our relationship to other men is emotionally activated by the father-ideal. What occurs as we come more in touch with the external world, when the principle of reality develops, is the finding of surrogates for this ideal father. We discover that he is not all-wise, all-powerful, all-good, but we still need to find persons or abstractions upon which we can distribute these and similar attributes. By a process of fission these feelings are displaced on to and may be distributed among a number of surrogates. The surrogates may be per-sons, animals, things or abstract ideas; the headmaster, the dog, the rabbit, the Empire, the Aryan race, or any particular "ism."

It is upon this ego-ideal that is formed the possibility of leadership, of lead-ers, then of the supreme leader, the king—the one who can, that is, who can do all, just as the father did in the child's view. As the late J. N. Figgis main-tained in his "Essay on the Divine Right of Kings," this theory gained cur-rency because it appealed to some of the deepest instincts of human nature. "It gathered up into itself notions of the sanctity of the medicine-man, of the priestly character of primitive royalty, of the divinity of the Roman Emper-ors, and perhaps of the sacredness of the tribunician power." [9] "It was essen-

[7] *The Times* (September 17, 1923).
[8] Sigmund Freud, *Group Psychology and the Analysis of the Ego* (1922), p. 60.
[9] J. N. Figgis, *Divine Right of Kings,* 2nd edn. (1914), p. 256.

tially a popular theory, proclaimed in the pulpit, published in the market-place, witnessed to on the battle-field." [10]

One of the typical disguises for father and mother in dreams is their appearance as king, queen, kaiser, president; the dreamer himself appearing as the eldest son, the Prince of Wales, etc. For my present purpose I have only to point out the equation: king-father, father-king, i.e., the ideal we have taken: that is, the king stands for all. Let me repeat the description I have already quoted adding the first two words—it is of course Blackstone's well-known formula: "The sovereign is not only incapable of doing wrong, but even of thinking wrong; he can never mean to do an improper thing; in him is no folly or weakness." [11] Put briefly, it is the maxim that the king can do no wrong, and its genesis is: My father can do no wrong. I am like my father—I can do no wrong. This ego-ideal splits off and is projected on to the father of his people—the king. The reverence that doth hedge a king is thus the reverence unconsciously paid to our ideal self. It must be borne in mind, as I have already said, that this feeling may be displaced on to a number of persons or ideas; there may be, so to say, many kings—many projections of the original identification, for, as Freud has pointed out, identification may arise with every new perception of a common quality shared with some other person who is not an object of the sexual instinct.

Identification does not exhaust the emotional tie between father and little son. There is the basic Oedipus relationship, hostility to the father who stands in the way of the little boy, whose wish is therefore to get the father out of the way. This hostility comes into conflict with the ego-ideal, giving rise to the sense of guilt and remorse. To sociologists acquainted with Le Play's work the idea will not seem very startling although, of course, the permanence of the child's attitude in adult life may be a new view. Le Play said that at each generation, society is menaced by a great invasion of little savages; the child is "fundamentally and uniquely selfish"; against Rousseau he maintained that "the child is born evil"; [12] or, as psycho-analysts might preferably express it, the child is not born with an ego-ideal.

These conflicting relationships—tenderness, the wish to be like the father in every way, and hostility, the wish to be rid of the father, exist side by side. Just as we have seen the one tie, identification, spreading out and finding a number of partial substitutes, so we also find the second of the ambivalent emotions displaced on to one or more substitutes. Thus the hostility felt by the child towards the father may be preserved towards the father himself, and the tenderness displayed towards an uncle, teacher, the gardener, the dog, a collection of stamps or butterflies. The reversed case is also possible, but the former may be regarded as the ordinary course of development.

[10] *Ibid.*, p. 3.
[11] *Blackstone's Commentaries*, 4th edn. (1876), Vol. I, p. 218.
[12] Le Play, *La Réforme Sociale*, p. 388.

For this fission of affects the British Constitution provides admirably. I think it was Mr. Zangwill who once said that it is a principle of the British Constitution that the king can do no wrong and his ministers no right. That is to say, the ambivalency originally experienced towards the father is now split; the sentiment of loyalty, etc., is displaced on to the king, the hostility on to the king's ministers, or on to some of them, or on to the Opposition, the Labour Party, etc. The President of a Republic like the French is in much the same case, but in the United States the President seems to know no such softening of the primitive affect.

Death at the hands of their subjects, which includes their sons, was the common fate of rulers in rude days, as it still is the fate of many savage royalties. Primitive people have all kinds of taboos which save the life of a king, and betray in the various ceremonies the underlying unconscious wish.

Modern society has discovered the principle of election, and the vote to give expression to the subjects' hostile feelings towards their rulers. Psychoanalytically an election may be regarded as the sublimation of regicide (primarily parricide) with the object of placing oneself on the throne; the vote is like a repeating decimal; the father is killed but never dies. The ministers are our substitutes for ourselves. Hence the political axiom of the swing of the pendulum.

In the United States the President comes in for the vituperation that is here reserved for the government in power. It is the Old Gang, the father, who must be got rid of. The rise and fall of President Wilson illustrates this typically; for a time he was the projected ego-ideal of a large mass of American mankind; then came the surge of the parricidal impulses, and the President is hurled from power with every expression of ignomiy.

The behaviour of the elected or representative politician betrays many characteristics derived from the family. For example, during the time that I filled a political role in Palestine I noticed in myself (and in my colleagues) the satisfaction it gave me to have secret information, knowledge which must on no account be imparted to others. Of course good reasons were always to be found: the people would misuse the information or it would depress them unduly and so on—pretty exactly the parent's attitude about imparting information, especially of a sexual nature, to the children. Indeed when our secret information was common knowledge we still tried to keep it to ourselves, just as we do with our children, though we have ourselves been through the same schooling.

At the back of secret diplomacy, trade secrets, and indeed the whole relationship of the official to the non-official, there rests this father-child affect. This also serves to explain the passion aroused in former days by any proposed extension of the franchise: let me illustrate it by a quotation from one of the less demonstrative politicians. Macaulay in his speech on the People's Charter, May 3rd, 1842, said: "My firm conviction is that in our country universal suffrage (i.e. manhood suffrage) is incompatible not with this or that form of government and with everything for the sake of which forms of government exist, but that it is incompatible with poverty, and that it is consequently incompatible with civilisation." [13] I am not giving the analysis of the politician, or it would have been tempting to undertake an explanation of what "property" meant to Macaulay the bachelor.

In this opposition to the extension of male suffrage, in this objection to allowing others to share in our private knowledge or privileges, we can recognise a sentiment having as its emotional disposition the original jealousy of the father towards his male offspring. We know how closely guarded from the children is, among primitive men, sexual knowledge, the appanage of the adult; in most savage tribes the youth have to undergo a series of ceremonies at intitiation in which painful rites inflicted by the elders are prominent, rites which express in their veiled form the more barbarous practices of early man.

Like any primitive savage, a Macauley, now an elder himself, will keep out the rest, resents any sapping of his power. Notice that Macaulay's opposition is especially aroused towards those who may approximate to himself, towards English Protestants. To those whose sentiments may be regarded as more widely separated from his own there is no opposition. He is the advocate of Catholic and Jewish suffrage rights—these are no children of his and arouse no fierce jealousy.

That this jealousy of the fathers towards their male children, unconscious in part or wholly so, is one of the causes of war, seems not to have escaped the notice of the youth of this age—at least of some of the more sensitive among them, poets and novelists. War, with its special death-roll among the young, fulfils the desire of the old men for the removal of their lusty rivals; the war memorials, the cenotaphs are not only monuments raised in expiation of the old people's sins, but are also survivals of days when it was feared that the ghosts of the killed, taking material shape, would revenge themselves on the living; these monumental erections will prevent the dead arising.

Of course this young generation will in turn become the fathers, and in their turn, standing in fear of their sons, will seek the gratification of their unconscious wishes. But I attach some importance to the recognition, however incomplete, and allied as it is with other unconscious emotions, of the motives of the father's jealousy as a cause of war. It is one of the methods, it seems to me, by which changes may come about in the organisation of society. Broadly speaking, we find that social changes are brought about by external pressure—geographical, economic and so on, so that whilst the forms change there is not a corresponding change in the psyche. Freud says: "What to-day arises from within was once a compulsion from without, perhaps imposed by the necessity of the time. The demands made to-day by the external

---

[13] *Macaulay's Speeches* (Popular Edition, 1889), p. 626.

world upon every child may some day be fulfilled by some simple repression from within." But it may be that among those compulsions from without will be included at some future time a reformation inspired by an understanding of and a power to deal with such unconscious reactions as I am now alluding to. Probably you will think me rather presumptuous if I suggest that psychoanalysis may be the precursor of another regulator; the individual learns how he shall grow to independence through his experiences in the psychoanalytic laboratory; and it seems not inconceivable that at some future period much of what is now unconscious may become conscious material, allowing mankind to deal with it in the same way as do a few analysed individuals to-day. This would mean greater changes in human nature than our written records can show.

This is speculation: I will now return to my politics. In the Conservative the tender tie towards the father is preserved in loyalty to the sovereign and to those persons identified with him, whilst hostility is felt towards the children (including himself) who are seeking to overthrow the father, usurp his place, i.e., the People. Hobbes laid it down that "originally the Father of every man was also his Sovereign Lord with power over him of life and death." [14] Paley says sovereignty may be termed absolute, omnipotent, uncontrollable, arbitrary, despotic and as alike in all countries.[15]

Whether this is historically accurate or not is for my purpose tonight indifferent; I quote it for its psychological truth; Paley's statement is but an echo of the father's significance to the son. I do not maintain that this is the only mode of genesis. Conservatism can arise also as a reaction formation against hostility towards the father.

The common bond uniting the children in antagonism to their parents is a matter of daily observation; it may unite the children of one family or a group of children; it is the theme of innumerable novels; it is seen later in any assembly of people where there are children-substitutes: in the committee and unofficial members of clubs, etc. This bond is found in later life as a desexualised, sublimated homosexual relationship with other men (and women) springing from work in common. I have pointed out that the emotional affect can be displaced on to abstract conceptions or ideas just as readily as on to something concrete. Identification with the other children of the family or little friends can become in adult life identification with people, with democracy, with a quasi deification of the people. As Dr. Glover said, the child says: "If I cannot be first favourite, then none of the other children shall be"; "justice for me," becomes "justice for all," "equal rights for us all," and we get the famous slogan: "Workers of the world, unite, you have a world to gain, you have nothing to lose but your chains."

It is the affect arising from this hostility of the children towards the father

[14] Hobbes, *Leviathan* (Everyman Edition), p. 182.
[15] Paley, *op. cit.*, p. 314.

(the possessor) that gives force to the abstract conception of the class-war. Then arises another father, another god: "The voice of the people is the voice of God"—an instance of what Ferenczi calls the infantile happy condition of omnipotence. This idea of the children against the father, carried on from childhood's relationships, is well expressed in the motto of the French Republic: Liberté, Egalité, Fraternité: Freedom from the tyrannical father, who monopolises everything; we band of brothers will share and share alike. It is eloquently expressed in Lincoln's famous Gettysburg speech: "This nation, under God, shall have a new birth of freedom, and that the government of the people, by the people, for the people, shall not perish from the earth." Whereas then, for the Conservative the dynamic is derived from identification with the father, in the Radical or Democrat it is derived from identification with brothers and sisters.

The impermanency of such a revolt on the part of the band is seen in the French Reign of Terror, which offers in this particular a striking contrast with the Russian Revolution.

Louis XVI was executed on Jan. 21, 1793; Marat was assassinated on July 13, 1793; Hébert was executed on March 24, 1794; Danton was executed on April 5, 1794; Robespierre on July 28, 1794. Thus in the eighteen months after the death of the King four of the revolutionary leaders had met their deaths by violence. It is now six years since the Bolshevik Revolution took place (Oct. 1917) and we find the original leaders still in power. I do not think any prominent Russian revolutionary leader has been assassinated or executed since the Czar was killed. Psycho-analysis offers a hint as to one factor in this difference. When I was in Russia in the winter of 1920–21 I could not but be struck by the large number of busts of Karl Marx everywhere displayed, by the prodigal array of quotations from his works; that bust with the flowing beard, you may remember, got on the nerves of Mr. H. G. Wells. What did the French Revolutionists set up? Statues of Liberty, Reason, Nature. The Russian leaders, although they had killed their father the Czar, found another father, Marx, to worship; that he was dead was unimportant —in the unconscious the dead are no less powerful forces than the living.

The French revolutionary leaders found no common father; as each emerged from the band in the attempt to make himself supreme leader, to become the Old Man, the Sire, the band must destroy him; Equality and Justice for all, just as in the nursery. These attempts to establish the rule of a band of brothers on the basis of equality of powers fail, and the people fall back again on a father—Napoleon who receives the worship of a god and the vilification of a devil—god and devil being both facets of father-worship, the extensions of the original ambivalent feelings of love and hate.

The peculiar horror which regicide has always inspired we understand when we know it as the fulfilment of a wish, namely parricide, that was ever buried in the unconscious. Is the extraordinary fear which some regicides experience, e.g., Cromwell, the expression of a desire to be killed? Cromwell, himself now ruler-king-father, is intolerable to the son of his father. This splitting of the personality is familiar enough to us in individual psychology but its possible application to Cromwell I must leave to some student of history.

The investigation of individual cases will, of course, bring to light more than one determinant; an interesting example in point is that of a social reformer like Lord Shaftesbury, the seventh earl. From earliest childhood he was in conflict with a tyrannical, forbidding father, and the subject of his mother's neglect. The headmaster of the school to which he was early sent was, according to all accounts, inhuman and brutal. Neither at school nor at home did he obtain the common necessaries of life. There was, says one of his biographers, neither joy in going back to school nor joy in coming home, where he was often left with insufficient food. It is easy to see the narcissistic projection in this champion of children, the Chairman of the Ragged Union, the reformer of asylums. There was another determinant; a question was asked of Mr. Flügel as to the results of a child's being brought up by a nurse. Now the sole person who seems to have bestowed any love on this unfortunate son of an earl was his mother's old maid. Until the day of his death Lord Shaftesbury wore a watch which this maid had left him in her will. His love for this woman of inferior station finds expression in adult life in his efforts to amend the lot of the oppressed, the lowly, the humble, but he does not throw in his lot with them, he remains always faithful to his rôle of protector, of master, nor apparently could his complexes allow him to regard an independent working-class with complacency—as you probably know he was an opponent of the Education Acts.

Much reforming zeal is genetically related to similar reactions in childhood. The desire to defend the oppressed, to protect the weak or inferior in rank may be the outcome of some such motive as the one I have mentioned. Jealousy felt towards a younger child, such fratricidal impulses as cited by Mr. Flügel, come under the subjugation of the ego-ideal impulses, with feelings of remorse, of guilt, as a reaction formation there ensues solicitude for the younger child, regarded as the victim of parental discipline, and in later years these emotions are radiated on to other persons, on to all who are oppressed, on to the general class of the "under-dogs."

The rôle of protector is also derived from the phantasy of protecting the mother against the onslaughts of the father, for coitus is often regarded by the child as a brutal attack on the part of the father against the mother.

The other side of the Oedipus complex, the boy-child's relationship towards the mother, his wish for union with her, for return to the maternal womb, undergoes partial sublimation in social life. It finds expression in attachment to the earth, the land, the mother-country, home; the "Heimweh" of the Swiss, or the Scot, the pious Jew's desire for burial in Palestine, the agitation over the proposed removal of Gen. Oglethorpe's remains, are instances of this emotional tie which are fraught with potential political consequences. It is a factor that must not be overlooked in any serious consideration of emigration and of the exodus from the country-side in to the town. The earth is familiar as the symbol of the mother; as Eve, Mother-Earth. Richard Jeffries in "The Story of my Heart" describes this influence when "lying down on the grass I thought of the earth's firmness—I felt it bear me up; through the grassy couch there came an influence as if I could feel the great earth speaking to me." Is this exodus from the country-side an attempt to get away from the more primary sexual attraction and to fall back in the city upon aim-restricted sexual impulses?

How these impulses affect politics when the sovereign is both father and mother is well seen in the cases of Queen Elizabeth and Queen Victoria: note the loyalty, veneration and love extended to the latter after the death of the Prince Consort, when there is no rival to dispute the unconscious wish to possess the supreme earthly mother; if that wish is impossible of fulfilment, then no one shall possess her—she shall remain perpetual widow, fulfilling at once various unconscious phantasies of the Virgin Queen, the Virgin Mother, the ultimate wish-phantasy of every male.

Besides the major forms of such hostility towards the father (authority) as seen in the rebel and revolutionists, we may notice all kinds of minor symptoms. It is a partial explanation of smuggling, of evading the income-tax, of cheating a railway company, etc. On the other side we see the need of the father in the call for the strong man, for the return of the omnipotent being of our childhood, with his magical control over watches, able to emit clouds from his mouth and nose. In the ultimate analysis the cry for the strong man is but the child's cry for daddy and mummy to kiss the sore place and make it well again—for the soothing words of the magician who has power to charm away all the ills that affect us.

As a derivative from the hostility to the father we may note the heat with which the question of a sovereign state or of a pluralistic state is being discussed at this moment. I will not embark upon an analysis of the Regional Movement which is one form, but stop for a moment to call attention to this tendency to set up counter authorities to Parliament. It is found in such movements as the national guilds, trade unionism, the claims of the different churches to control of their adherents. The pluralistic state, if I understand the conception correctly, is no return to mediaevalism, for then the authority of the Church was paramount in Europe. It is significant that a churchman, the late Dr. J. N. Figgis, should have been one of the most original and powerful advocates of this doctrine, demanding at the least, increased authority for associations that are to be ultimately co-equal with Parliament. "We are in the midst of a new movement," writes Mr. Laski, "for the conquest of self-government. It finds its main impulse in the attempt to disperse the sovereign power." [16] This movement has become vigorous at a period which sees the return of women to authority in the affairs of the state. I would regard it as suggestive of the growing influence of what I have called the Band of Brothers, a decline in the authority of the father.

It is noteworthy in the United States that law has taken the place of all other authorities; there is almost a "divine right" of the constitution; the work of the framers, of the elders, must not be touched. This is but another instance of the need mankind seems still to feel for a father, for some final authority. The majesty of the law received very great reverence in England, which prides itself on its respect for precedence; but I take it the existence of a monarch to some extent weakens the position of the law: I am speaking, of course, entirely of the non-rational side.

I will return to a current political issue which demonstrates the same forces at work. When you are told in England that those who are in favour of that economic system known as Free Trade are in league with the enemies of England and the Empire, or that the advocates of Protection are seeking for selfish ends to tax the working man's breakfast, it does not require a psychologist to conclude that there are here emotions engaged which are apart from economic considerations. The chosen banners, Protection and Free Trade, give an indication of the underlying motives. The home industries must be protected from outside interference, at all events they must be safeguarded in their youth until they are strong enough to be resistant to the onslaughts of the stranger. This is one of the attitudes of the parent towards his children; the father and mother will watch over the children, in the interests of the child; for the child is but a projection of ourselves. Protection is, as one would expect, a Conservative tendency. It is worth passing notice that Mr. Joseph Chamberlain was a free trader in his republican and radical days; it was when he had found a father—the Empire—which gave him a political fatherhood, that he became the advocate of protection; the father's children must be looked after and helped.

Cobden and the early free traders were all rebels against the political authority of their day. They were seeking a means to rid themselves of the influence of authority, of their fathers. Trade and industry, i.e., themselves, must be freed from the trammels of the State, i.e., of authority, of the father. In their hostility towards State interference they had to find a surrogate upon which they could bestow their tender emotions and they found it in the idea of Free Trade.

The conclusion to which one seems drawn is that hitherto the band of brothers does not easily exist without a father; they become like

> Sheep without a shepherd
> When the snow shuts out the sky.

[16] Laski, *Foundations of Sovereignty* (1921), p. 243.

The study of the psychology of the individual has taught us how severe a struggle it is for him to rid himself of the father, to rid himself in such a way that his conduct is not inspired either by a positive or a negative emotional attitude. In the social organisation there appears a similar struggle or independence, and though the father is often cast out he returns to power in devious ways—the constitution, law and order, Das Kapital and many various similar examples.

FRANZ ALEXANDER

3. *Defeatism Concerning Democracy**

It would seem that in these troubled days not only the social scientist, but even the general public is beginning to turn toward psychiatry as a potential saviour. It is becoming a truism that the physical sciences failed in increasing human happiness, and their main contribution was to supply more and more deadly weapons to be used by human destructiveness. It has become a commonplace that the mastery of physical nature is more a curse than a blessing in the hands of men who are ignorant concerning their own personality and human relationships. The discrepancy between the development of the physical sciences on the one hand and psychology and social sciences on the other is, in great part, responsible for the disasters we are witnessing at present. Man, blind and ignorant about the dynamic principles of social life, would be better off without a chemistry which produces poison gas and dynamite, without a technology which enables him to destroy others from the air and allows him to replace bow and arrow with machine guns. Finally, man, incapable of constructive social life and utilizing his scientific knowledge primarily for subjugation and exploitation of his fellow man, does not deserve this knowledge.

While the masses still proudly and unwittingly enjoy the blessings of technical advancement—their radios, automobiles, pullman cars and airlines—the more contemplative men of learning, publicists and philosophers, psychologists, social scientists and educators are becoming more and more concerned about the one-sided developments of the last three centuries which led to our top-heavy technical civilization and did not contribute in the least to the improvement of human relationships.

* *The American Journal of Orthopsychiatry*, Vol. XI (October, 1941). By permission.

All this became a commonplace and is being reiterated in eloquent phrases again and again. The recognition of the dangers which came from this gap between the natural and social sciences lead to two kinds of conclusion. One is a mistrust and defeatist antagonism against the natural sciences, the other is a constructive emphasis upon the need for the study of personality and human relationship. Fortunately, the first of these reactions made little impression upon contemporary thought. The sensational but naive attacks of a young philosopher against modern materialism and scientism caused more amusement than resentment. His admonitions to return to medieval obscurantism and to substitute for critical scientific thought the scholastic dogmatism of Thomas Aquinas does not seem to impress even his own students. Even though an occasional educator may turn emotionally against the scientific spirit of our times, this neo-scholastic trend in one of the great American universities is an isolated occurrence. These educators obviously lost their faith in science. They consider the development of Western Civilization since the Renaissance a blind alley and want to return to the prescientific era of European culture. Witnessing man abuse his scientific mastery of natural forces makes these confused educators conclude that science, or at least the scientific spirit, carries the blame. They overlook the fact that we have not too much, but too little, of scientific enlightenment; that the critical, empirical attitude of the natural sciences must now be extended to the field of personality research and the social sciences in order to achieve the same mastery of our own self and our social relationships that we have acquired over the forces of inanimate nature. Their isolated and vain attempt to return to medieval obscurantism is a mixture of confusion and juvenile and provocative sensationalism and does not require further attention. This cultural and educational detour is helpful in one respect: through its fallacy it brings into sharp relief the more constructive trend, the desire to introduce the scientific method into the study of personality and human relationships—a field which, until the last forty years, has been approached only by philosophical speculations and lifeless generalizations.

After Freud opened the way for an empirical study of personality and human relationships, psychiatry came into position to study those phenomena which stubbornly resisted the traditional approach by the microscope. The methods and principles of dynamic psychology created an entirely new field of science—a science of human relationships. It was soon discovered that not only are the gross symptoms of insanity the manifestations of irrational psychological processes, but that in all human relationships intellect has a subordinate role compared with the force of blind and irrational emotions. I call these emotions irrational because their gratification does not serve the interest of the individual, but may often cause self-destruction. It was also soon understood that social life requires a great amount of renunciation from the individual—renunciations which are opposed by self-centered emotional

tendencies. It is not so difficult to sit down and work out from the armchair
a rational world order which gives the maximum security and gratification
of each person. It became obvious that what opposes the creation of such a
rational world order of peace is primarily not lack of intelligence, but the
rule of irrational emotions over the intellect.

Sensing these facts, people today often speak of war as a kind of group
psychosis. Its irrational nature makes this comparison persuasive. The irrationality of mutual destruction in the face of plenty becomes especially obvious when one tries to formulate war aims. The answers are rationalizations
so thin that even the most naive is not fooled by them.

In the face of the present wholesale manifestation of irrational forces, all
eyes turn for explanation toward psychiatry, the science of irrational human
behavior. Can psychiatry live up to these expectations? The psychiatrist deals
with individuals and not with political or national groups. However, groups
consist of individuals and group relationships follow the same psychological
principles as those which govern the relationship of individuals to each other.
There are, naturally, extremely important quantitative differences. The most
striking difference is that in their group relationships people show much less
consideration for each other's interests than in their personal dealings. Two
political leaders, exponents of two antagonistic groups, may violently and
aggressively attack each other in a public meeting, and five minutes later they
may have a friendly drink together at a neighboring bar. The excuse of fighting for a public cause allows the reckless expression of hostile impulses which
are otherwise checked by conscience. This same dynamic fact holds in a tremendously exaggerated fashion for international relations. In civilized nations, actual physical injury or killing of a political opponent is still a criminal act. Only in times of social disorganization, such as civil wars, killing
becomes an accepted means of settling conflicting interests. While civil war is
an exceptional occurrence in the life of nations, war among nations is the
usual means of settling international conflicts. It is noteworthy, however, that
even in such cases a certain amount of excuse for one's conscience is needed.
The alibi given is the belief that the enemy threatens life and property. Even
Russia claimed attacking the Finns in self-defense. That leaders use such
propaganda to liberate their soldiers' consciences for killing shows that the
average person needs an inner justification to destroy other human beings.
This shows that the inhibitig force of social conscience is a dynamic force
to be reckoned with and before a man can be transformed from a peaceful
human being into a warring soldier, his conscience must somehow be persuaded that he acts in self defense. Unfortunately, as soon as a war has
started the excuse of killing for self defense becomes only the too tragic
reality. After a war has started each party tries to destroy the other and war
becomes legitimate self-defense for both sides. The fury of human aggres-

sions is liberated and the destructive business has to be carried out to its bitter end.

This gradation of moral inhibitions is indeed very impressive. They are strongest between individual and individual, weaker within conflicting groups within a nation, and weakest in international relationships. This leads to the conclusion that in order to improve group relationship we must understand the psychology of the human conscience.

It is obvious that within a nation, police force is not the sole supporter of peace and order. Most people do not need intimidation by law not to kill or steal. Were it not for the internal control of the human conscience, the existing police force would not be able to maintain order. Police force is needed only to control the least adjusted members of the group. Why are moral inhibitions so effective in insuring peaceful social life within a nation and so ineffective in international relationships? Why is social conscience so easily put out of action by a few empty phrases or obvious lies in the dealings of nations with nations?

Social life is obviously based on an interdependent cooperation of the members with each other. This can be best observed in *ad hoc* organized group formation. If people in an accidental grouping are exposed to a common danger, say an attacking enemy, an organization will take place to meet the danger. Some will defend the left flank, others the right, and still others will supply the means of defense. In such a situation each member of the group will consider the others as friends, and will subordinate his particular interest, at least to some degree, to the interest of the others. The survival of the others is in one's own interest.

Conscience can be considered as that portion of the human personality by which we identify ourselves with other people. In ultimate analysis, groups are formed because of the self-preserving tendencies of individuals to facilitate survival and, by division of labor, make the gratification of biological needs more economical. We must consider the human conscience the most important preserver of social cooperation. It expresses the emotional tie between members of the group which establishes an equilibrium between particular selfish and common group interests in a way to preserve social cooperation. It is easy to understand that when the interests of individual members of a group become more divergent, that is, when vital interests and conscience have no longer a parallel direction, selfish interests may outweigh the voice of conscience. This is best demonstrated by the fact that underprivileged members of an organized group who profit least from social cooperation will be the main offenders of peace and order. To forgive your enemy only on the basis that he is also a human being is something the average human conscience is certainly unable to enforce when a person's own vital interests are at stake.

These facts of dynamic psychology can be simply formulated by saying that the effectiveness of social conscience gradually diminishes in proportion to the conflicts within the group. The conflict of interest is greater between people belonging to different nations divided by political and economic boundaries. At the same time differences in race, language and customs make more difficult the identification with each other, which we learned is the basis of social conscience. Conscience is the internal psychological protector of common interests in their organized groups. Since the world today is organized according to national and not international interests, social conscience stops at the national boundaries.

It should, of course, be realized that even within the same group the cohesive force of social conscience is limited. It would be foolish to overlook the fact that there is no ideally just social organization. The principles of democracy certainly would appear to secure the most stable social order. Democracy is essentially based on a compromise between conflicting interests, that is, on enlightened and curtailed self-interest. Furthermore, it is based on free cooperation of its members. If cooperation of the members is based more on fear of punishment and of authority, the groups are much more disruptible. Social order based on intimidation and fear results by necessity in an atrophy of social conscience. Such an organization is based solely on the awe and fear which the members have toward their rulers, and not on fear of their own conscience. As soon as rulers show a weakness, all the accumulated and checked hostilities of the group will break through and an internal dissolution will take place in the form of civil war. Dictators must therefore carefully guard their prestige and always be victorious over their enemies. Important for such a group also is the principle of looting. Only by throwing fat spoils to their suppressed followers may tyrannical leaders preserve order and suppress discontent. Therefore, such a group must necessarily try to live at the expense of others. Depriving their followers of personal dignity and freedom of expression, leaders must at least compensate them by making them masters over their conquered neighbors. All this is instinctively understood by the neighboring groups who regard with horror, and as a source of danger, nations dominated by autocratic oppression and minority rule. They feel instinctively that such nations can only survive by conquest of others.

Is there no other form of social group besides autocratic minority rule and democracy based on free cooperation and on compromise of conflicting interest? Theoretically, there is a third social system conceivable which might be called a planned society on a benevolent authoritarian basis. Medieval feudalism probably came nearest to this type of society which served in many respects as a model for the corporate state of fascism. Such an organization would be based on a well-conceived plan of division of labor in which every individual has his well-defined place and function, though no social mobility and freedom. Each member is a well placed cog in the social mechanism and is offered full economic security and protection for his social contribution. Such a planned society may have a great chance for peaceful survival. It must be realized, of course, that the creation of such a society would lead through a long period of internal terror and suppression. It would take considerable time until the members of the society could be terrorized and beaten into becoming passive self-contained mechanical parts of a well thought through social machinery. This kind of nightmare looms in the minds of contemporary fanatic leaders as their goal. Many suggestible natures become hypnotized by these visionary fantasies; they speak of the "wave of the future" in which humanity will become organized in such an insect state. Authoritarian dreamers and fanatics of both sides—left and right—indulge in such visions, not realizing that such a cog-wheel society would mean the end of the development of man as a biological species, would mean the end of creative culture. These cog-wheels who are no longer individuals, but cells, and enjoy full security, will be robbed of all initiative for self-expression, which is the basis of every cultural innovation.

The feudal system of the Middle Ages gives a good example both of the stability and the sterility of this type of society. This inert system had the longest duration in Western Civilization. It probably gave more economic security to its members than any other system, but brought about the least changes. It resembled more than any other system in the history of Western Civilization the stable, almost petrified societies of the primitive races who probably lived for thousands of years on the same level, under the same rigid system. Such a society sacrifices for security's sake everything which gives color, variety and change to human life. The democractic principle which preserves the dignity, self-expression and free development of the individual must by necessity surpass in efficiency any such rigidly planned insect type of society. In a democracy which recognizes inventiveness and individual accomplishment, the cultural process which started with the Renaissance will for a long time have a chance for further development.

It is discouraging to observe a present defeatism concerning the future of democracy. It is true that we have not yet made those necessary adjustments in our economic system which became imperative because of the advancement of technology. But is there need to discard the whole system because it needs certain readjustments of details? The most significant contribution of psychiatry today consists in clarifying those emotional factors which make people defeatists concerning democracy. The psychiatrist sees individual cases but, carefully comparing them, he will readily find the common emotional factors behind this defeatism. Twenty years of my psychoanalytic practice were spent in this post World War period of social instability which the defeatist interpreters of current events like to consider as the beginning of the dissolution of our democratic world. With most impressive and stereotyped monotony in the large majority of my patients, I came across one definite emotional factor which throws sharp light on the growing diffidence in the democratic system. I am glad that I do not need to refer to this factor with a Latin or Greek technical term; it is simply—insecurity.

Psychoanalytic experience shows that one of the strongest universal emotional trends is a protest against growing up, a tendency to retain the carefree existence of childhood. Through growing up, which is marked by sexual maturation, man loses the right to stay in the Garden of Eden. He is expelled into the cold world where he must struggle from then on. After man has eaten from the tree of knowledge, that is to say, after he has become sexually mature, he loses the prerogatives of the child, to be cared for by some earthly or heavenly father. Not only is he no longer a child, but he becomes the supporter of the next generation. In everyone there remains a latent longing to go back to the Garden of Eden, to the Golden Age, to the irresponsible and secure phase of childhood.

The strongest ally of this latent regressive trend, according to the experiences of psychoanalysis and psychiatry, is insecurity. The more difficult life and the maintenance of existence becomes, the stronger this regressive longing toward childhood. The democratic system, at least theoretically, relies on the maturity of its citizens. It attributes to them a faculty of judgment and requires of them participation in government. At the same time it is an obligation of each citizen to care for his own existence without much governmental protection. So long as the economic system functions well, a mature individual is able to carry responsibility and provide self-support. As soon, however, as this request for political responsibility becomes coupled with economic insecurity, the survival of the democracy is threatened. Economic insecurity increases the flight from responsibility and independence and mobilizes the latent longing for parental care which everyone carries in himself. The authoritarian system requires only obedience, relieves all citizens from responsibility, and offers them full security and a rigidly defined place in the social system. Therefore it has the greatest appeal to those whose emotional maturity is unstable and caters to those in whom the longing to reestablish childish dependence and irresponsibility is the strongest.

In psychoanalytic practice we know a type of patient who is particularly apt to be taken in by authoritarian ideas; neurotics who outwardly appear just the opposite of dependent natures. Outwardly they are often aggressive people, extreme individualists, daring barons of industry, foolhardy sportsmen, and record breakers. Their over-emphasized courage and independence, however, is only a thin external cover; by their toughness and independence, by their foolhardiness, they try to over-shadow and hide a secret internal weakness—a wish to depend on others and be taken care of. It is quite impressive to note how many of these people are secret or open admirers of the authoritarian idea. It is not difficult to understand why this should be so. In an authoritarian society, the individual's responsibility is non-existent.

Subordination and dependence is not considered a weakness, as in our democratic civilization, but a virtue. In such a society, internal conflict between infantile dependence and its denial is completely solved. All the laborious struggle to prove one's courage to oneself and to others in order to hide an internal weakness becomes superfluous. Such patients often do well in the army. Martial occupation eliminates the conflict about their dependence, and the strict organization relieves them of responsibility The authoritarian state which gives them security and eliminates even the possibility of individualistic accomplishment, offers a complete solution of the conflict between extreme internal dependence and its desperate outward denial.

What can we learn from all these psychological details? That the greatest menace for democracy consists of two factors: one, a subjective emotional factor, the universal though mostly latent regressive trend for dependence; and two, an objective factor, namely, economic insecurity due to insufficient organization of production and distribution. This objective external factor strengthens the emotional need for governmental help and dependence. Psychiatry, of course, can only deal with the emotional factor. Democracy, in order to survive, must educate its members to emotional maturity, and psychiatry will have to help develop educational principles which are most conducive to overcoming infantile dependence and strengthening a sense of responsibility. What democracies need, more than anything else, is a well planned psychologically sound educational system.

So much for the emotional factor. We saw that the objective factor, the economic insecurity, plays into the hand of the emotional regressive tendency to escape the responsibilities of mature life. In order to counteract this flight toward political dependence, democratic governments must offer at least a minimum of security to all of its members. This can be done without assuming such extreme paternalism in guiding and prescribing the lives and activities of citizens as do the totalitarian states. There is no question that in a highly developed industrial civilization it should be possible, without sacrificing the basic principles of democracy, to offer such minimum security to all citizens. However, this is not a question for a psychiatrist to decide. He can only emphasize the extreme importance of the subjective factor, and point out how economic insecurity plays into the hands of this regressive trend. One must realize that no education for maturity and responsibility can counterbalance the fear and uncertainty of the next day and of old age. Especially in this country must we become aware of the full significance of this fact. This country ideologically still lives in the tradition of the frontier, when personal initiative, ambition and endurance by necessity secured success. This period of economic expansion has long since disappeared, yet our economic ideology is still fashioned according to the patterns of frontier days.

In the present time of standardized industrialism, economic anarchy must be replaced, to some degree at least, by governmental regulation based on the free consent of all interested groups. Economic insecurity, as a result of economic anarchy, makes people susceptible to totalitarian ideas by mobilizing in them the universal, though latent, longing for parental protection. As long as in an expanding economy an independent spirit and self-reliance worked well and led to prosperity, people readily accepted them. But even the bravest becomes discouraged when he feels that his existence is no longer dependent upon his ability and that whether he finds employment is not a question of his capacity but of numbers, of the impersonal laws of supply and demand. The psychiatrist must emphasize that economic insecurity undermines peoples' readiness to accept mature responsibilities and that the population can only preserve its enthusiasm for a free democratic system so long as it secures at least a minimum amount of security. The recognition of this fact sets the limits of the role of psychiatry for the preservation of democracy. Preservation of democracy is not only a question of mentality, of the citizen's readiness to accept political responsibility in exchange for a reasonable chance for success, but also depends upon a system in which this mature and responsible attitude provides a secure existence. Preservation of democracy, therefore, is at the same time a complex psychological and a socio-economical problem.

We may now turn our attention to the question of international relationships. Not only the preservation of the existing great democracies, but the spreading of the democratic principle throughout the world is the only hope for an improvement of international relations. If the democratic principle survives and spreads, there is hope that international relations will also be regulated according to democratic principles. If it also fails in international relations, tyranny, suppression and exploitation will remain the governing principle. Democracies must recognize that their mentality does not yet pervade the whole world. The League of Nations neglected this fact, together with all teachings of dynamic psychology and history. It counted too much on a non-existing world conscience. A future League of Nations by necessity will, for a considerable period of time, need to rely upon the armed superiority of democratic nations. It cannot be hoped that non-democratic nations will accept democratic principles in international dealings, therefore these principles must be upheld if necessary by the force of arms. Dynamic psychology teaches that, even within a nation, social order is upheld not alone by social conscience, but also by law enforced by police. The higher the social conscience is developed, the less social order must depend on police force. At present, social conscience obviously stops at national boundaries. A world conscience remains to be developed in the future. A democratic world order is unimaginable if some groups are to be permitted to disregard its principles. Therefore, for a time, a democratic world order must be protected by armed forces which can only be gradually reduced at the same rate as the slow educational process toward a more embracing social conscience progresses. It will be the obligation of the advanced democratic nations to provide for such an education, but in order to do so, they must survive and defend by arms a democratic world order to which the rest of the world will have to adjust itself through the slow process of domestication.

KURT LEWIN

4. *Group Living: Autocratic, Democratic, and Laissez-Faire**

Democracy—like forms of group living—cannot be defined adequately by isolated elements of conduct, rules or institutions; it is the larger *pattern* of group life and the group *atmosphere* which determines how a society is to be classified. The pattern includes such diversified aspects as the form of leadership, the degree and type of interdependence of sub-groups, the way in which the policy of the group depends on the will of its various sections or members; it includes how children talk to parents, workers to foremen, or how the crippled are treated. However, though social *techniques* must be considered, it is the actual *group dynamics* that counts. This holds for a small group of children as well as for the life of a whole community or state, or for the organization of the world.

The war has made it abundantly clear that the ever-increasing functional dependence of the different sections of the world is leading to some form of closer political, cultural and economic organization among nations and within nations. The fateful question is whether this higher degree of organization will be expressed in stronger forms of autocracy or in stronger forms of democracy.

AUTOCRACY, DEMOCRACY AND LAISSEZ-FAIRE

In our present state of knowledge, the scientifically superior method of defining a special form of group life is probably the determination of its position within a totality of other forms of group life. One of the outstanding facts which has been known but is not sufficiently recognized concerns the relation between autocracy, democracy and individualistic freedom (laissez-faire). The average Sunday-school teacher, foreman or university professor is accustomed to perceive problems of discipline or leadership as lying on a

* From Gardner Murphy (ed.), *Human Nature and Enduring Peace* (Third Yearbook of the Society for the Psychological Study of Social Issues, Boston-New York, 1945). By permission.

single continuum, in which lack of discipline and maximum individual freedom represent the one end and strict authoritarian discipline the other. This
conception, however, is basically incorrect. Autocracy, democracy and laissez-faire should be perceived as a triangle (Fig. 1). In many respects autocracy and democracy are similar: they both mean leadership as against the
lack of leadership which appears in laissez-faire; they both mean discipline
and organization as against chaos. They both mean a stress upon the group
rather than upon the individual. Among other lines of comparison, democracy and laissez-faire are similar: they both give freedom to the group members in so far as they create a situation where the members are acting on
their own motivation, rather than being moved by forces induced by an
authority in which they have no part.

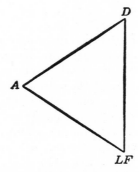

FIGURE 1. *The relations of similarity and difference between Autocracy (A), Democracy
(D), and Laissez-Faire (LF) cannot be represented by one continuum.*

The person who thinks in terms of one continuum has no choice but to
consider democracy as something *between* autocratic discipline and lawlessness; he sees it as a soft type of autocracy, or frequently as a kind of sugar-
coated or refined method to induce the group member to accept the leader's
will. It is a prerequisite to democratic living and democratic education that
this concept be destroyed. The democratic leader is no less a leader and, in a
way, has no less power than the autocratic leader. There are soft and tough
democracies as well as soft and tough autocracies; and a tough democracy is
likely to be more, rather than less, democratic. Like autocracy, democracy is
fully aware of the rôle of power in group life and considers power a necessary
and legitimate element of group organization. But the democratic use of
power is as far from a superiority aloof from the ruled—so characteristic,
for instance, of the treatment of "natives" by the British colonial office—as
from the religious zeal for one's own power so typical of the "sacred egoism"
of totalitarian Fascism.

The difference between autocracy and democracy is an honest, deep difference, and an autocracy with a democratic front is still an autocracy. In de-mocracy the use of power must recognize the "equal right" of each member of the group to live a good life. Sometimes democracy merely "tolerates" differences among individuals or among groups. An outspoken democracy does not merely recognize the "right to be different" as the basis for "individual freedom" and the treatment of "minorities"; it will encourage that richness of group life and group productivity which can grow only from a diversity of sub-groups and personalities. It will, however, be equally determined to enforce the principle of "intolerance against the intolerant," a principle without which no democracy seems to be able to live in the long run.

As to the form or organization, two differences between democracy and autocracy may be mentioned: (*a*) The unity of an autocratic group is based on its relation to the top leader of the hierarchy to a greater degree than is true of a democratic group. Goal-setting or policy determination in an autocracy is, to a high degree, in the hands of the leader, rather than in the hands of the group as a whole. It is typical of a democracy that the leader is responsible to the group; in an autocratic system the follower is responsible to the leader. This principle of "no responsibility to people below oneself and all responsibility to the leader above" was one of the first steps to be acclaimed again and again by Hitler after his ascent to power.

(*b*). Interdependence within the group and the interactions essential for group life in an autocracy follow, in general, "vertical" lines, i.e., relations between higher and lower in the hierarchy of organization. In a democracy the "horizontal" type of interdependence among people of equal status is more emphasized. That is one of the reasons why, for instance, discussion and group decision—which have their full meaning only among equals—play greater rôles in democracy.

As to the problem of the practicality of democracy, one may consider (1) the effect of democracy on the character and capacity of the individual, (2) its effect on efficiency as regards production in industry, and in other fields, and finally (3) the problem of how to learn democracy and its correct application. This includes the problem of the learning of democratic ideology and the training of democratic leaders.

At present, statements about these topics have to be based on rather scant scientific data, and one must always keep in mind that there are many forms of autocracy and democracy. Only recently has the step been taken from descriptions of attitudes to "action research" on groups. Scientific insight about the causal relations in group life will have to be established by experiments in group dynamics. The last decade has seen an increasing development in this field although research is still in its initial stages.

The experiments help in many ways to substantiate the triangular relation of autocracy, democracy and laissez-faire, and to clarify the rather disturbing complexity of problems by showing where the differences lie;

why differences in group procedures which might look important are actually unimportant; and why others which look unimportant are important. It is particularly interesting to consider what might be called an efficient "tough democracy."

EFFECT OF DEMOCRACY ON THE CHARACTER AND CAPACITY OF THE INDIVIDUAL

The best controlled study in this field is probably that of Lippitt and White.[1] In this study the same groups of children went through an autocratic, a democratic, and a laissez-faire atmosphere. They show that the character of the individual, at least as it expresses itself in conduct, is deeply and very quickly affected by a change in social atmosphere. The degree of friendliness, for instance, was greatest in democracy. With an exchange of two children between the autocratic and democratic groups their friendliness and aggressiveness changed within one meeting. Aggressive reactions were greatest in a form of autocracy and led to discontent not only with the leader but with the fellow members as well. It sometimes led to scapegoating.

The sociability of the individual children and the amount of constructive help they offered to other children was greatly affected by the change in social climate. Under autocracy conversation kept much more to the immediate topics; the children under democracy showed a broader outlook in many respects. In autocracy they lost some of their individuality as measured by the degree of individual differences. They became more dependent and more ready to drop work when not under immediate pressure. In other words, initiative and "laziness" are traits which depend much on the social atmosphere.

This is not the place to go into the many and not always simple relations between group life and the character and productivity of the individual. However, two conclusions seem to be quite well-established by the experiments on groups, by the experience in industry ("Training in Industry" Program), by studies of family living and by what we know about child development in terms of psychology and cultural anthropology: (*a*) The effect of social atmospheres on character and on character development is very profound. (*b*) A democratic organization with long-range planning seems to be definitely superior to autocracy and to laissez-faire atmospheres in creating initiative and positive sociability.

DEMOCRACY AND EFFICIENCY OF GROUP LIFE

The superiority of democracy in regard to bringing up fair-minded and more richly developed individuals is not likely to be questioned, at least in

---

[1] Ronald Lippitt and Ralph K. White, "The 'Social Climate' of Children's Groups," in Roger G. Barker, Jacob S. Kounin, and Herbert F. Wright (eds.), *Child Behavior and Child Development* (New York, 1943), pp. 485-508.

this country. More frequently, doubts are expressed in regard to democratic efficiency. We are accustomed to the idea that democracy has to "pay" in efficiency for the greater freedom the individual has. For many, efficient group organization is more or less identified with autocratic organization. The problem itself is fundamental because practically every group has to "pro-

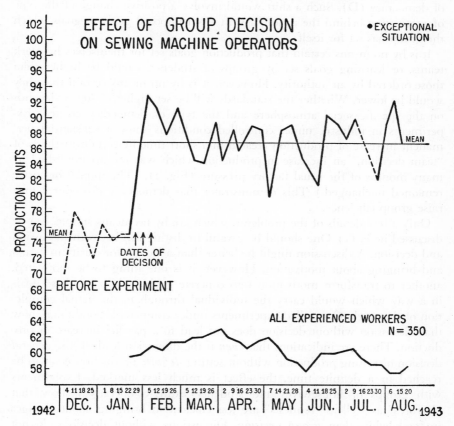

FIGURE 2. *The Effect of Team Decision on Production in a Sewing Factory. An experiment by Alex Bavelas shows a marked permanent rise in production after decision. As comparison, the production level of experienced workers is given during the same months.*

duce" some kind of "goods," whether it is health in a hospital or automobiles in a factory, fun in a recreation center, or knowledge and education in a school.

In school as well as in industry certain standards exist concerning the rate of learning or production. These standards are set up by the teacher or the management and are upheld by these authorities with a certain amount of pressure. It is assumed that relaxing the standards will slow down the work of group members. This assumption is probably sound, but has *little to do with the problem of democracy*. Lowering the standards or relaxing the pressure to keep up the standards in an autocratic atmosphere means shifting to a softer form of autocracy. It means a shift from autocracy (A) toward laissez-faire (LF) in Fig. 1. It does *not* mean a shift in the direction of democracy (D). Such a shift would involve a positive change of the type of *motivation* behind the action, a shift from imposed goals to goals which the group has set for itself.

It is by no means certain that production goals set for themselves by work teams, or learning goals set by groups of students, would be higher than those ordered by an authority. However, it is by no means certain that they would be lower. Whether the standards will be set higher or lower depends on the specific social atmosphere and the type of democracy created. Experiments in industry under controlled conditions show a substantial permanent increase of production created in a short time by certain methods of "team decision," an increase in production which was not accomplished by many months of the usual factory pressure (Fig. 2). (The money incentive remained unchanged.) This demonstrates that democratic procedures may raise group efficiency.

Only a few details of the problems, which are by no means simple, can be discussed here. (1) One should be careful to distinguish between discussion and decision. A discussion might be better than a lecture for clarifying issues and bringing about motivation. However, it is one thing to be motivated, another to transform motivation into concrete goals, stabilizing these goals in a way which would carry the individual through to the actual completion of the work. Controlled experiments under comparable conditions show that discussion without decision does not lead to a parallel increase in production. There are indications that *even* if the discussion leads to the *general* decision of raising production without setting *definite* production goals to be reached in a definite time, the effect is much less marked. Experiments with groups of housewives and students' eating-co-operatives show that "lectures" as well as "requests" are less efficient in bringing about changes in food habits than *group decision*. Discussions without decisions do not make for efficient democracy. On the other hand, democratic methods, properly handled, are superior to requests in bringing about changes.

(2) One of the reasons why democratic methods are superior is illustrated in the study of students' co-operatives. Students were to change from white to whole-wheat bread. From each student was obtained a rating of his eagerness to reach the goal and of his like or dislike of whole-wheat as compared with white bread. After "request," the eagerness to succeed was lowest in the individuals who disliked whole-wheat bread and increased with the degree of liking. *After group decision,* however, the eagerness to reach the group goal was largely independent of personal like or dislike. In other

words, group decision provides a background of motivation, where the individual is ready to co-operate as a member of the group, more or less independent of his personal inclinations.

HOW TO LEARN DEMOCRACY

It is one of the basic facts about group standards that they are not an expression of a common biological entity called "human nature" but are somehow acquired. This fundamental fact seems to be very difficult to realize. To the individual who follows a certain cultural pattern, most of what is essential to this culture seems as "natural" and unquestionable as the air he breathes. It is a prerequisite of international peace that the fallacy of this position be understood. For permanent co-operation we must understand better both our own and other cultures, their similarities and their differences. That is one of the reasons why a large program of research on our own standards and those of other countries is vital.

Two of the important aspects of learning democracy are *changes of ideology* and *leadership training*. The scientific knowledge, finally—based upon experimental cultural anthropology and experiments in leadership training —is as yet very limited. There are definite indications, however, that the education of leaders and the means of changing the forms of leadership can be brought about sometimes in an astonishingly short time.

In all the experiments mentioned, the problem of leadership plays an important rôle. As the earlier experiments show, a group atmosphere can be changed radically in a relatively short time by introducing new leadership techniques. The paradoxes of democratic leadership are by no means solved; however, the studies of leadership, and particularly of leadership training, give some information.

(1) Autocratic as well as democratic leadership consists in the leader's playing a certain rôle. These leader rôles cannot be carried through without the followers playing certain complementary rôles, namely, those of "autocratic" or "democratic" followers. Educating people in democracy or re-educating them from either autocracy or laissez-faire cannot be accomplished by the passive behavior of the democratic leader. It is a fallacy to assume that individuals if left alone will form themselves naturally into democratic groups; it is much more likely that chaos or a primitive pattern of organization through autocratic dominance will result. Establishing democracy in a group implies an active education: the democratic follower must learn to play a rôle which implies, among other things, a fair share of responsiblity toward the group and a sensitivity to other people's feelings. Sometimes, particularly in the beginning of the process of re-education, individuals may have to be made aware, in a rather forceful manner, of the two-way interdependence which exists between themselves and others within the democratic group. To create such a change, the leader must be in

power, and able to hold his power. As the followers learn democracy, other aspects of the democratic leader's power and function prevail. What holds for the education of democratic followers holds also for the education of democratic leaders. In fact, it seems to be the same process through which persons learn to play these two rôles and it seems that both rôles have to be learned if either one is to be played well.

(2) It is important to realize that democratic behavior cannot be learned by autocratic methods. This does not mean that democratic education or democratic leadership must reduce the power aspect of a group organization in a way which would place the group life on the laissez-faire point of the triangle (Fig. 1). Efficient democracy means organization, but it means organization and leadership on principles different from those of autocracy. These principles might be *clarified* by lectures but they can be *learned,* finally, only by democratic living. The "training on the job" of democratic leaders is but one example of the fact that teaching democracy presupposes establishment of a democratic atmosphere.

One should be slow in generalizing experimental findings. Any type of organization like a factory, a business enterprise, a community center, a school system, or the army has characteristics of its own. What democracy means technically has to be determined in each organization in line with its particular objective. The objective of our educational system is customarily defined as twofold. It is to give knowledge and skills to the coming generation and to build the character of the citizens-to-be. The experiments indicate that democratic education does not need to impede efficiency in regard to the first objective, but can be used as a powerful instrument toward this end. The experiment also indicates that, for educating future citizens, no mere talk about democratic ideals can substitute for a democratic atmosphere in the school. The character and the cultural habits of the growing citizen are not so much determined by what he *says* as by what he *lives*.

(3) It is important to realize that the methods of changing group ideology or group goals and obtaining group efficiency are not based on dealing with the individual as an individual but as a group member. The goals were set for the group as a whole or for individuals in a group setting. The experimental studies indicate that it is easier to change ideology or cultural habits by dealing with groups, rather than with individuals. In addition, the anchorage of the motivation of the individual in a group decision goes far in achieving the execution of the decision and in establishing certain self-regulatory processes of the group life on the new level of ideology and action.

SUMMARY

On the whole, then, research in democratic living indicates the deep interdependence of the various aspects of group life, such as ideology, leadership form, power distribution, productivity and efficiency of the individual and the group. It shows that the ideology of a group, the character of its members and the distribution of power are so closely interwoven that no one of them can be changed without altering the others. This should be a lesson to the hard-boiled politician who thinks only in terms of power and to the sympathetic believer in the "goodness of human nature" who forgets too easily that *ideology cannot be changed without changing the actual distribution of power within a group.* There are definite indications that democracy is not only practicable but *superior in regard to character development, social relations and efficiency if it is handled as a true democracy.*

Finally, there are good indications that "self-understanding" and "self-education" within democratic groups is possible. The chances for the success of such a program will be much enhanced by making full use of the instruments of research in social science which, after all, means merely using an old democratic standby: the rational approach.

ERICH FROMM

5. *Escape from Freedom**

The insignificance of the individual in our era concerns not only his role as a businessman, employee, or manual laborer, but also his role as a customer. A drastic change has occurred in the role of the customer in the last decades. The customer who went into a retail store owned by an independent businessman was sure to get personal attention: his individual purchase was important to the owner of the store; he was received like somebody who mattered, his wishes were studied; the very act of buying gave him a feeling of importance and dignity. How different is the relationship of a customer to a department store. He is impressed by the vastness of the building, the number of employees, the profusion of commodities displayed; all this makes him feel small and unimportant by comparison. As an individual he is of no importance to the department store. He is important as "a" customer; the store does not want to lose him, because this would indicate that there was something wrong and it might mean that the store would lose other customers for the same reason. As an abstract customer he is important; as a concrete customer he is utterly unimportant. There is nobody who is glad about his coming, nobody who is particularly concerned about his wishes.

The act of buying has become similar to going to the post office and buying stamps.

This situation is still more emphasized by the methods of modern advertising. The sales talk of the old-fashioned businessman was essentially rational. He knew his merchandise, he knew the needs of the customer, and on the basis of this knowledge he tried to sell. To be sure, his sales talk was not entirely objective and he used persuasion as much as he could; yet, in order to be efficient, it had to be a rather rational and sensible kind of talk. A vast sector of modern advertising is different; it does not appeal to reason but to emotion; like any other kind of hypnoid suggestion, it tries to impress its objects emotionally and then make them submit intellectually. This type of advertising impresses the customer by all sorts of means: by repetition of the same formula again and again; by the influence of an authoritative image, like that of a society lady or of a famous boxer, who smokes a certain brand of cigarette; by attracting the customer and at the same time weakening his critical abilities by the sex appeal of a pretty girl; by terrorizing him with the threat of "b.o." or "halitosis"; or yet again by stimulating daydreams about a sudden change in one's whole course of life brought about by buying a certain shirt or soap. All these methods are essentially irrational; they have nothing to do with the qualities of the merchandise, and they smother and kill the critical capacities of the customer like an opiate or outright hypnosis. They give him a certain satisfaction by their daydreaming qualities just as the movies do, but at the same time they increase his feeling of smallness and powerlessness.

As a matter of fact, these methods of dulling the capacity for critical thinking are more dangerous to our democracy than many of the open attacks against it, and more immoral—in terms of human integrity—than the indecent literature, publication of which we punish. The consumer movement has attempted to restore the customer's critical ability, dignity, and sense of significance, and thus operates in a direction similar to the trade-union movement. So far, however, its scope has not grown beyond modest beginnings.

What holds true in the economic sphere is also true in the political sphere. In the early days of democracy there were various kinds of arrangements in which the individual would concretely and actively participate in voting for a certain decision or for a certain candidate for office. The questions to be decided were familiar to him, as were the candidates; the act of voting, often done in a meeting of the whole population of a town, had a quality of concreteness in which the individual really counted. Today the voter is confronted by mammoth parties which are just as distant and impressive as the mammoth organizations of industry. The issues are complicated and made still more so by all sorts of methods to befog them. The voter may see something of his candidate around election time; but since the days of the radio, he is not likely to see him so often, thus losing one of the last means of sizing up "his" candidate. Actually he is offered a choice between two or three candidates by the party machines; but these candidates are not of "his" choosing, he and they know little of each other, and their relationship is as abstract as most other relationships have become.

Like the effect of advertising upon the customer, the methods of political propaganda tend to increase the feeling of insignificance of the individual voter. Repetition of slogans and emphasis on factors which have nothing to do with the issue at stake numb his critical capacities. The clear and rational appeal to his thinking are rather the exception than the rule in political propaganda—even in democratic countries. Confronted with the power and size of the parties as demonstrated in their propaganda, the individual voter cannot help feeling small and of little significance.

All this does not mean that advertising and political propaganda overtly stress the individual's insignificance. Quite the contrary; they flatter the individual by making him appear important, and by pretending that they appeal to his critical judgment, to his sense of discrimination. But these pretenses are essentially a method to dull the individual's suspicions and to help him fool himself as to the individual character of his decision. I need scarcely point out that the propaganda of which I have been speaking is not wholly irrational, and that there are differences in the weight of rational factors in the propaganda of different parties and candidates respectively.

Other factors have added to the growing powerlessness of the individual. The economic and political scene is more complex and vaster than it used to be; the individual has less ability to look through it. The threats which he is confronted with have grown in dimensions too. A structural unemployment of many millions has increased the sense of insecurity. Although the support of the unemployed by public means has done much to counteract the results of unemployment, not only economically but also psychologically, the fact remains that for the vast majority of people the burden of being unemployed is very hard to bear psychologically and the dread of it overshadows their whole life. To have a job—regardless of what kind of a job it is—seems to many all they could want of life and something they should be grateful for. Unemployment has also increased the threat of old age. In many jobs only the young and even inexperienced person who is still adaptable is wanted; that means, those who can still be molded without difficulty into the little cogs which are required in that particular setup.

The threat of war has also added to the feeling of individual powerlessness. To be sure, there were wars in the nineteenth century too. But since the last war the possibilities of destruction have increased so tremendously—the range of people to be affected by war has grown to such an extent as to comprise everybody without any exception—that the threat of war has become a nightmare which, though it may not be conscious to many people before their nation is actually involved in the war, has overshadowed their lives and increased their feeling of fright and individual powerlessness.

The "style" of the whole period corresponds to the picture I have sketched. Vastness of cities in which the individual is lost, buildings that are as high as mountains, constant acoustic bombardment by the radio, big headlines changing three times a day and leaving one no choice to decide what is important, shows in which one hundred girls demonstrate their ability with clocklike precision to eliminate the individual and act like a powerful though smooth machine, the beating rhythm of jazz—these and many other details are expressions of a constellation in which the individual is confronted by uncontrollable dimensions in comparison with which he is a small particle. All he can do is to fall in step like a marching soldier or a worker on the endless belt. He can act; but the sense of independence, significance, has gone.

The extent to which the average person in America is filled with the same sense of fear and insignificance seems to find a telling expression in the fact of the popularity of the Mickey Mouse pictures. There the one theme —in so many variations—is always this: something little is persecuted and endangered by something overwhelmingly strong, which threatens to kill or swallow the little thing. The little thing runs away and eventually succeeds in escaping or even in harming the enemy. People would not be ready to look continually at the many variations of this one theme unless it touched upon something very close to their own emotional life. Apparently the little thing threatened by a powerful, hostile enemy is the spectator himself; that is how *he* feels and that is the situation with which he can identify himself. But of course, unless there were a happy ending there would be no continuous attraction. As it is, the spectator lives through all his own fears and feelings of smallness and at the end gets the comforting feeling that, in spite of all, he will be saved and will even conquer the strong one. However—and this is the significant and sad part of this "happy end"—his salvation lies mostly in his ability to run away and in the unforeseen accidents which make it impossible for the monster to catch him.

The position in which the individual finds himself in our period had already been foreseen by visionary thinkers in the nineteenth century. Kierkegaard describes the helpless individual torn and tormented by doubts, overwhelmed by the feeling of aloneness and insignificance. Nietzsche visualizes the approaching nihilism which was to become manifest in Nazism and paints a picture of a "superman" as the negation of the insignificant, directionless individual he saw in reality. The theme of the powerlessness of man has found a most precise expression in Franz Kafka's work. In his *Castle* he describes the man who wants to get in touch with the mysterious inhabitants of a castle, who are supposed to tell him what to do and show him his place in the world. All his life consists in his frantic effort to get into touch with them, but he never succeeds and is left alone with a sense of utter futility and helplessness.

The feeling of isolation and powerlessness has been beautifully expressed in the following passage by Julian Green: "I knew that we counted little in comparison with the universe, I knew that we were nothing; but to be so immeasurably nothing seems in some way both to overwhelm and at the same time to reassure. Those figures, those dimensions beyond the range of human thought, are utterly overpowering. Is there anything whatsoever to which we can cling? Amid that chaos of illusions into which we are cast headlong, there is one thing that stands out as true, and that is—love. All the rest is nothingness, an empty void. We peer down into a huge dark abyss And we are afraid." [1]

However, this feeling of individual isolation and powerlessness as it has been expressed by these writers and as it is felt by many so-called neurotic people, is nothing the average normal person is aware of. It is too frightening for that. It is covered over by the daily routine of his activities, by the assurance and approval he finds in his private or social relations, by success in business, by any number of distractions, by "having fun," "making contacts," "going places." But whistling in the dark does not bring light. Aloneness, fear, and bewilderment remain; people cannot stand it for ever. They cannot go on bearing the burden of "freedom from"; they must try to escape from freedom altogether unless they can progress from negative to positive freedom. The principal social avenues of escape in our time are the submission to a leader, as has happened in Fascist countries, and the compulsive conforming as is prevalent in our own democracy.

The first mechanism of escape from freedom I am going to deal with is the tendency to give up the independence of one's own individual self and to fuse one's self with somebody or something outside of oneself in order to acquire the strength which the individual self is lacking. Or, to put it in different words, to seek for new, "secondary bonds" as a substitute for the primary bonds which have been lost.

The more distinct forms of this mechanism are to be found in the striving for submission and domination, or, as we would rather put it, in the masochistic and sadistic strivings as they exist in varying degrees in normal and neurotic persons respectively. We shall first describe these tendencies and then try to show that both of them are an escape from an unbearable aloneness.

The most frequent forms in which masochistic strivings appear are feelings of inferiority, powerlessness, individual insignificance. The analysis of persons who are obsessed by these feelings shows that, while they con-

[1] Julian Green, *Personal Record, 1928-1939,* translated by J. Godefroi, Harper & Brothers, New York, 1939.

sciously complain about these feelings and want to get rid of them, unconsciously some power within themselves drives them to feel inferior or insignificant. Their feelings are more than realizations of actual shortcomings and weaknesses (although they are usually rationalized as though they were); these persons show a tendency to belittle themselves, to make themselves weak, and not to master things. Quite regularly these people show a marked dependence on powers outside of themselves, on other people, or institutions, or nature. They tend not to assert themselves, not to do what they want, but to submit to the factual or alleged orders of these outside forces. Often they are quite incapable of experiencing the feeling "I want" or "I am." Life, as a whole, is felt by them as something overwhelmingly powerful, which they cannot master or control.

In the more extreme cases—and there are many—one finds besides these tendencies to belittle oneself and to submit to outside forces a tendency to hurt oneself and to make oneself suffer.

This tendency can assume various forms. We find that there are people who indulge in self-accusation and self-criticism which even their worst enemies would scarcely bring against them. There are others, such as certain compulsive neurotics, who tend to torture themselves with compulsory rites and thoughts. In a certain type of neurotic personality, we find a tendency to become physically ill, and to wait, consciously or unconsciously, for an illness as if it were a gift of the gods. Often they incur accidents which would not have happened had there not been at work an unconscious tendency to incur them. These tendencies directed against themselves are often revealed in still less overt or dramatic forms. For instance, there are persons who are incapable of answering questions in an examination when the answers are very well known to them at the time of the examination and even afterwards. There are others who say things which antagonize those whom they love or on whom they are dependent, although actually they feel friendly toward them and did not intend to say those things. With such people, it almost seems as if they were following advice given them by an enemy to behave in such a way as to be most detrimental to themselves.

The masochistic trends are often felt as plainly pathological or irrational. More frequently they are rationalized. Masochistic dependency is conceived as love or loyalty, inferiority feelings as an adequate expression of actual shortcomings, and one's suffering as being entirely due to unchangeable circumstances.

Besides these masochistic trends, the very opposite of them, namely, *sadistic* tendencies, are regularly to be found in the same kind of characters. They vary in strength, are more or less conscious, yet they are never missing. We find three kinds of sadistic tendencies, more or less closely knit together. One is to make others dependent on oneself and to have absolute and unrestricted power over them, so as to make of them nothing but instruments, "clay in the potter's hand." Another consists of the impulse not only to rule over others in this absolute fashion, but to exploit them, to use them, to steal from them, to disembowel them, and, so to speak, to incorporate anything eatable in them. This desire can refer to material things as well as to immaterial ones, such as the emotional or intellectual qualities a person has to offer. A third kind of sadistic tendency is the wish to make others suffer or to see them suffer. This suffering can be physical, but more often it is mental suffering. Its aim is to hurt actively, to humiliate, embarrass others, or to see them in embarrassing and humiliating situations.

Sadistic tendencies for obvious reasons are usually less conscious and more rationalized than the socially more harmless masochistic trends. Often they are entirely covered up by reaction formations of overgoodness or overconcern for others. Some of the most frequent rationalizations are the following: "I rule over you because I know what is best for you, and in your own interest you should follow me without opposition." Or, "I am so wonderful and unique, that I have a right to expect that other people become dependent on me." Another rationalization which often covers the exploiting tendencies is: "I have done so much for you, and now I am entitled to take from you what I want." The more aggressive kind of sadistic impulses finds its most frequent rationalization in two forms: "I have been hurt by others and my wish to hurt them is nothing but retaliation," or "By striking first I am defending myself or my friends against the danger of being hurt."

There is one factor in the relationship of the sadistic person to the object of his sadism which is often neglected and therefore deserves especial emphasis here: his dependence on the object of his sadism.

While the masochistic person's dependence is obvious, our expectation with regard to the sadistic person is just the reverse: he seems so strong and domineering, and the object of his sadism so weak and submissive, that it is difficult to think of the strong one as being dependent on the one over whom he rules. And yet close analysis shows that this is true. The sadist needs the person over whom he rules, he needs him very badly, since his own feeling of strength is rooted in the fact that he is the master over some one. This dependence may be entirely unconscious. Thus, for example, a man may treat his wife very sadistically and tell her repeatedly that she can leave the house any day and that he would be only too glad if she did. Often she will be so crushed that she will not dare to make an attempt to leave, and therefore they both will continue to believe that what he says is true. But if she musters up enough courage to declare that she will leave him, something quite unexpected to both of them may happen: he will become desperate, break down, and beg her not to leave him; he will say he cannot live without her, and will declare how much he loves her and so on. Usually, being afraid of asserting herself anyhow, she will be prone to believe him, change her decision and stay. At this point the play starts again. He resumes his old behavior, she finds it increasingly difficult to stay with him, explodes again, he breaks down again, she stays, and so on and on many times.

I come now to the main question: What is the root of both the masochistic perversion and masochistic character traits respectively? Furthermore, what is the common root of both the masochistic *and* the sadistic strivings?

The direction in which the answer lies has already been suggested in the beginning of this chapter. Both the masochistic and sadistic strivings tend to help the individual to escape his unbearable feeling of aloneness and powerlessness. Psychoanalytic and other empirical observations of masochistic persons give ample evidence (which I cannot quote here without transcending the scope of this book) that they are filled with a terror of aloneness and insignificance. Frequently this feeling is not conscious; often it is covered by compensatory feelings of eminence and perfection. However, if one only penetrates deeply enough into the unconscious dynamics of such a person, one finds these feelings without fail. The individual finds himself "free" in the negative sense, that is, alone with his self and confronting an alienated, hostile world. In this situation, to quote a telling description of Dostoevski, in *The Brothers Karamazov,* he has "no more pressing need than the one to find somebody to whom he can surrender, as quickly as possible, that gift of freedom which he, the unfortunate creature, was born with." The frightened individual seeks for somebody or something to tie his self to; he cannot bear to be his own individual self any longer, and he tries frantically to get rid of it and to feel security again by the elimination of this burden: the self.

Masochism is one way toward this goal. The different forms which the masochistic strivings assume have one aim: *to get rid of the individual self, to lose oneself; to get rid of the burden of freedom.* This aim is obvious in those masochistic strivings in which the individual seeks to submit to a person or power which he feels as being overwhelmingly strong. (Incidentally, the conviction of superior strength of another person is always to be understood in relative terms. It can be based either upon the actual strength of the other person, or upon a conviction of one's own utter insignificance and powerlessness. In the latter event a mouse or a leaf can assume threatening features.) In other forms of masochistic strivings the essential aim is the same. In the masochistic feeling of smallness we find a tendency which serves to increase the original feeling of insignificance. How is this to be understood? Can we assume that by making a fear worse one is trying to remedy it? Indeed, this is what the masochistic person does. As long as I struggle between my desire to be independent and strong and my feeling of insignificance or powerlessness I am caught in a tormenting conflict. If I succeed in reducing my individual self to nothing, if I can overcome the awareness of my separateness as an individual, I may save myself from this conflict. To feel utterly small and helpless is one way toward this aim; to be overwhelmed by pain and agony another; to be overcome by the effects of intoxication still another. The phantasy of suicide is the last hope if all other means have not succeeded in bringing relief from the burden of aloneness.

Under certain conditions these masochistic strivings are relatively successful. If the individual finds cultural patterns that satisfy these masochistic strivings (like the submission under the "leader" in Fascist ideology), he gains some security by finding himself united with millions of others who share these feelings. Yet even in these cases, the masochistic "solution" is no more of a solution than neurotic manifestations ever are: the individual succeeds in eliminating the conspicuous suffering but not in removing the underlying conflict and the silent unhappiness. When the masochistic striving does not find a cultural pattern or when it quantitatively exceeds the average amount of masochism in the individual's social group, the masochistic solution does not even solve anything in relative terms. It springs from an unbearable situation, tends to overcome it, and leaves the individual caught in new suffering. If human behavior were always rational and purposeful, masochism would be as inexplicable as neurotic manifestations in general are. This, however, is what the study of emotional and mental disturbances has taught us: that human behavior can be motivated by strivings which are caused by anxiety or some other unbearable state of mind, that these strivings tend to overcome this emotional state and yet merely cover up its most visible manifestations, or not even these. Neurotic manifestations resemble the irrational behavior in a panic. Thus a man, trapped in a fire, stands at the window of his room and shouts for help, forgetting entirely that no one can hear him and that he could still escape by the staircase which will also be aflame in a few minutes. He shouts because he wants to be saved, and for the moment this behavior appears to be a step on the way to being saved—and yet it will end in complete catastrophe. In the same way the masochistic strivings are caused by the desire to get rid of the individual self with all its shortcomings, conflicts, risks, doubts, and unbearable aloneless, but they only succeed in removing the most noticeable pain or they even lead to greater suffering. The irrationality of masochism, as of all other neurotic manifestations, consists in the ultimate futility of the means adopted to solve an untenable emotional situation.

These considerations refer to an important difference between neurotic and rational activity. In the latter the *result* corresponds to the *motivation* of an activity—one acts in order to attain a certain result. In neurotic strivings one acts from a compulsion which has essentially a negative character: to escape an unbearable situation. The strivings tend in a direction which only fictitiously is a solution. Actually the result is contradictory to what the person wants to attain; the compulsion to get rid of an unbearable feeling was so strong that the person was unable to choose a line of action that could be a solution in any other but a fictitious sense.

The implication of this for masochism is that the individual is driven by an unbearable feeling of aloneness and insignificance. He then attempts to overcome it by getting rid of his self (as a psychological, not as a physiological entity); his way to achieve this is to belittle himself, to suffer, to make himself utterly insignificant. But pain and suffering are not what he wants; pain and suffering are the price he pays for an aim which he compulsively tries to attain. The price is dear. He has to pay more and more and, like a peon, he only gets into greater debts without ever getting what he has paid for: inner peace and tranquillity.

I have spoken of the masochistic perversion because it proves beyond doubt that suffering can be something sought for. However, in the masochistic perversion as little as in moral masochism suffering is not the real aim; in both cases it is the means to an aim: forgetting one's self. The difference between the perversion and masochistic character traits lies essentially in the following: In the perversion the trend to get rid of one's self is expressed through the medium of the body and linked up with sexual feelings. While in moral masochism, the masochistic trends get hold of the whole person and tend to destroy all the aims which the ego consciously tries to achieve, in the perversion the masochistic strivings are more or less restricted to the physical realm; moreover by their amalgamation with sex they participate in the release of the tension occurring in the sexual sphere and thus find some direct release.

The annihilation of the individual self and the attempt to overcome thereby the unbearable feeling of powerlessness are only one side of the masochistic strivings. The other side is the attempt to become a part of a bigger and more powerful whole outside of oneself, to submerge and participate in it. This power can be a person, an institution, God, the nation, conscience, or a psychic compulsion. By becoming part of a power which is felt as unshakably strong, eternal, and glamorous, one participates in its strength and glory. One surrenders one's own self and renounces all strength and pride connected with it, one loses one's integrity as an individual and surrenders freedom; but one gains a new security and a new pride in the participation in the power in which one submerges. One gains also the security against the torture of doubt. The masochistic person, whether his master is an authority outside of himself or whether he has internalized the master as conscience or a psychic compulsion, is saved from making decisions, saved from the final responsibility for the fate of his self, and thereby saved from the doubt of what decision to make. He is also saved from the doubt of what the meaning of his life is or who "he" is. These questions are answered by the relationship to the power to which he has attached himself. The meaning of his life and the identity of his self are determined by the greater whole into which the self has submerged.

But what about ourselves? Is our own democracy threatened only by Fascism beyond the Atlantic or by the "fifth column" in our own ranks? If that were the case, the situation would be serious but not critical. But although foreign and internal threats of Fascism must be taken seriously, there is no greater mistake and no graver danger than not to see that in our own society we are faced with the same phenomenon that is fertile soil for the rise of Fascism anywhere: the insignificance and powerlessness of the individual.

This statement challenges the conventional belief that by freeing the individual from all external restraints modern democracy has achieved true individualism. We are proud that we are not subject to any external authority, that we are free to express our thoughts and feelings, and we take it for granted that this freedom almost automatically guarantees our individuality. *The right to express our thoughts,* however, *means something only if we are able to have thoughts of our own;* freedom from external authority is a lasting gain only if the inner psychological conditions are such that we are able to establish our own individuality. Have we achieved that aim, or are we at least approaching it? This book deals with the human factor; its task, therefore, is to analyze this very question critically. In discussing the two aspects of freedom for modern man, we have pointed out the economic conditions that make for increasing isolation and powerlessness of the individual in our era; in discussing the psychological results we have shown that this powerlessness leads either to the kind of escape that we find in the authoritarian character, or else to a compulsive conforming in the process of which the isolated individual becomes an automaton, loses his self, and yet at the same time consciously conceives of himself as free and subject only to himself.

It is important to consider how our culture fosters this tendency to conform, even though there is space for only a few outstanding examples. The suppression of spontaneous feelings, and thereby of the development of genuine individuality, starts very early, as a matter of fact, with the earliest training of a child. This is not to say that training must inevitably lead to suppression of spontaneity if the real aim of education is to further the inner independence and individuality of the child, its growth and integrity. The restrictions which such a kind of education may have to impose upon the growing child are only transitory measures that really support the process of growth and expansion. In our culture, however, education too often results in the elimination of spontaneity and in the substitution of original psychic acts by superimposed feelings, thoughts, and wishes. (By original I do not mean, let me repeat, that an idea has not been thought before by someone else, but that it originates in the individual, that it is the result of his own activity and in this sense is *his* thought.) To choose one illustration somewhat arbitrarily, one of the earliest suppressions of *feelings* concerns hostility and dislike. To start with, most children have a certain measure of hostility and rebelliousness as a result of their conflicts with a surrounding world that tends to block their expansiveness and to which, as the weaker opponent, they usually have to yield. It is one of the essential aims of the educational process to eliminate this antagonistic reaction. The methods are different; they vary from threats and punishments, which frighten the child, to the subtler methods of bribery or "explanations," which confuse the child and make him give up his hostility. The child starts with giving up the very feeling itself. Together with that, he is taught to suppress the awareness of hostility and insincerity in others; sometimes this is not entirely easy, since children have a capacity for noticing such negative qualities in others without being so easily deceived by words as adults usually are. They still dislike somebody "for no good reason"—except the very good one that they feel the hostility, or insincerity, radiating from that person. This reaction is soon discouraged; it does not take long for the child to reach the "maturity" of the average adult and to lose the sense of discrimination between a decent person and a scoundrel, as long as the latter has not committed some flagrant act.

On the other hand, early in his education, the child is taught to have feelings that are not at all "his"; particularly is he taught to like people, to be uncritically friendly to them, and to smile. What education may not have accomplished is usually done by social pressure in later life. If you do not smile you are judged lacking in a "pleasing personality"—and you need to have a pleasing personality if you want to sell your services, whether as a waitress, a salesman, or a physician. Only those at the bottom of the social pyramid, who sell nothing but their physical labor, and those at the very top do not need to be particularly "pleasant." Friendliness, cheerfulness, and everything that a smile is supposed to express, become automatically responses which one turns on and off like an electric switch.[2]

What then is the meaning of freedom for modern man?

He has become free from the external bonds that would prevent him from doing and thinking as he sees fit. He would be free to act according to his own will, if he knew what he wanted, thought, and felt. But he does not know. He conforms to anonymous authorities and adopts a self which is

---

[2] As one telling illustration of the commercialization of friendliness I should like to cite *Fortune's* report on "The Howard Johnson Restaurants." (*Fortune*, September, 1940, p. 96.) Johnson employs a force of "shoppers" who go from restaurant to restaurant to watch for lapses. "Since everything is cooked on the premises according to standard recipes and measurements issued by the home office, the inspector knows how large a portion of steak he should receive and how the vegetable should taste. He also knows how long it should take for the dinner to be served and he knows the exact degree of friendliness that should be shown by the hostess and the waitress."

not his. The more he does this, the more powerless he feels, the more he is forced to conform. In spite of a veneer of optimism and initiative, modern man is overcome by a profound feeling of powerlessness which makes him gaze toward approaching catastrophes as though he were paralyzed.

Looked at superficially, people appear to function well enough in economic and social life; yet it would be dangerous to overlook the deep-seated unhappiness behind that comforting veneer. If life loses its meaning because it is not lived, man becomes desperate. People do not die quietly from physical starvation; they do not die quietly from psychic starvation either. If we look only at the economic needs as far as the "normal" person is concerned, if we do not see the unconscious suffering of the average automatized person, then we fail to see the danger that threatens our culture from its human basis: the readiness to accept any ideology and any leader, if only he promises excitement and offers a political structure and symbols which allegedly give meaning and order to an individual's life. The despair of the human automaton is fertile soil for the political purposes of Fascism.

Does our analysis lend itself to the conclusion that there is an inevitable circle that leads from freedom into new dependence? Does freedom from all primary ties make the individual so alone and isolated that inevitably he must escape into new bondage? Are *independence* and *freedom* identical with *isolation* and fear? Or is there a state of positive freedom in which the individual exists as an independent self and yet is not isolated but united with the world, with other men, and nature?

We believe that there is a positive answer, that the process of growing freedom does not constitute a vicious circle, and that man can be free and yet not alone, critical and yet not filled with doubts, independent and yet an integral part of mankind. This freedom man can attain by the realization of his self, by being himself. What is realization of the self? Idealistic philosophers have believed that self-realization can be achieved by intellectual insight alone. They have insisted upon splitting human personality, so that man's nature may be suppressed and guarded by his reason. The result of this split, however, has been that not only the emotional life of man but also his intellectual faculties have been crippled. Reason, by becoming a guard set to watch its prisoner, nature, has become a prisoner itself; and thus both sides of human personality, reason and emotion, were crippled. We believe that the realization of the self is accomplished not only by an act of thinking but also by the realization of man's total personality, by the active expression of his emotional and intellectual potentialities. These potentialities are present in everybody; they become real only to the extent to which they are expressed. In other words, *positive freedom consists in the spontaneous activity of the total, integrated personality.*

We approach here one of the most difficult problems of psychology: the problem of spontaneity. An attempt to discuss this problem adequately would require another volume. However, on the basis of what we have said so far, it is possible to arrive at an understanding of the essential quality of spontaneous activity by means of contrast. Spontaneous activity is not compulsive activity, to which the individual is driven by his isolation and powerlessness; it is not the activity of the automaton, which is the uncritical adoption of patterns suggested from the outside. Spontaneous activity is free activity of the self and implies, psychologically, what the Latin root of the word, *sponte,* means literally: of one's free will. By activity we do not mean "doing something," but the quality of creative activity that can operate in one's emotional, intellectual, and sensuous experiences and in one's will as well. One premise for this spontaneity is the acceptance of the total personality and the elimination of the split between "reason" and "nature"; for only if man does not repress essential parts of his self, only if he has become transparent to himself, and only if the different spheres of life have reached a fundamental integration, is spontaneous activity possible.

While spontaneity is a relatively rare phenomenon in our culture, we are not entirely devoid of it. In order to help in the understanding of this point, I should like to remind the reader of some instances where we all catch a glimpse of spontaneity.

In the first place, we know of individuals who are—or have been—spontaneous, whose thinking, feeling, and acting were the expression of their selves, and not of an automaton. These individuals are mostly known to us as artists. As a matter of fact, the artist can be defined as an individual who can express himself spontaneously. If this were the definition of an artist— Balzac defined him just in that way—then certain philosophers and scientists have to be called artists too, while others are as different from them as an old-fashioned photographer from a creative painter. There are other individuals who, though lacking the ability—or perhaps merely the training —for expressing themselves in an objective medium as the artist does, possess the same spontaneity. The position of the artist is vulnerable, though, for it is really only the successful artist whose individuality or spontaneity is respected; if he does not succeed in selling his art, he remains to his contemporaries a crank, a "neurotic." The artist in this matter is in a similar position to that of the revolutionary throughout history. The successful revolutionary is a statesman, the unsuccessful one a criminal.

Small children offer another instance of spontaneity. They have an ability to feel and think that which is really *theirs;* this spontaneity shows in what they say and think, in the feelings that are expressed in their faces. If one asks what makes for the attraction small children have for most people I believe that, aside from sentimental and conventional reasons, the answer must be that it is this very quality of spontaneity. It appeals profoundly to everyone who is not so dead himself that he has lost the ability to perceive it. As a matter of fact, there is nothing more attractive and convincing than spontaneity whether it is to be found in a child, in an artist, or in those individuals who cannot thus be grouped according to age or profession.

Most of us can observe at least moments of our own spontaneity which are at the same time moments of genuine happiness. Whether it be the fresh and spontaneous perception of a landscape, or the dawning of some truth as the result of our thinking, or a sensuous pleasure that is not stereotyped, or the welling up of love for another person—in these moments we all know what a spontaneous act is and may have some vision of what human life could be if these experiences were not such rare and uncultivated occurrences.

Why is spontaneous activity the answer to the problem of freedom? We have said that negative freedom by itself makes the individual an isolated being, whose relationship to the world is distant and distrustful and whose self is weak and constantly threatened. Spontaneous activity is the one way in which man can overcome the terror of aloneness without sacrificing the integrity of his self; for in the spontaneous realization of the self man unites himself anew with the world—with man, nature, and himself. Love is the foremost component of such spontaneity; not love as the dissolution of the self in another person, not love as the possession of another person, but love as spontaneous affirmation of others, as the union of the individual with others on the basis of the preservation of the individual self. The dynamic quality of love lies in this very polarity: that it springs from the need of overcoming separateness, that it leads to oneness—and yet that individuality is not eliminated. Work is the other component; not work as a compulsive activity in order to escape aloneness, not work as a relationship to nature which is partly one of dominating her, partly one of worship of and enslavement by the very products of man's hands, but work as creation in which man becomes one with nature in the act of creation. What holds true of love and work holds true of all spontaneous action, whether it be the realization of sensuous pleasure or participation in the political life of the community. It affirms the individuality of the self and at the same time it unites the self with man and nature. The basic dichotomy that is inherent in freedom—the birth of individuality and the pain of aloneness—is dissolved on a higher plane by man's spontaneous action.

In all spontaneous activity the individual embraces the world. Not only does his individual self remain intact; it becomes stronger and more solidified. *For the self is as strong as it is active.* There is no genuine strength in *possession* as such, neither of material property nor of mental qualities like emotions or thoughts. There is also no strength in use and manipulation of objects; what we use is not ours simply because we use it. Ours is only that to which we are genuinely related by our creative activity, be it a person or an inanimate object. Only those qualities that result from our spontaneous activity give strength to the self and thereby form the basis of its integrity. The inability to act spontaneously, to express what one genuinely feels and thinks, and the resulting necessity to present a pseudo self to others and oneself, are the root of the feeling of inferiority and weakness. Whether or not we are aware of it, there is nothing of which we are more ashamed than of not being ourselves, and there is nothing that gives us greater pride and happiness than to think, to feel, and to say what is ours.

This implies that what matters is the activity as such, the process and not the result. In our culture the emphasis is just the reverse. We produce not for a concrete satisfaction but for the abstract purpose of selling our commodity; we feel that we can acquire everything material or immaterial by buying it, and thus things become ours independently of any creative effort of our own in relation to them. In the same way we regard our personal qualities and the result of our efforts as commodities that can be sold for money, prestige, and power. The emphasis thus shifts from the present satisfaction of creative activity to the value of the finished product. Thereby man misses the only satisfaction that can give him real happiness—the experience of the activity of the present moment—and chases after a phantom that leaves him disappointed as soon as he believes he has caught it—the illusory happiness called success.

If the individual realizes his self by spontaneous activity and thus relates himself to the world, he ceases to be an isolated atom; he and the world become part of one structuralized whole; he has his rightful place, and thereby his doubt concerning himself and the meaning of life disappears. This doubt sprang from his separateness and from the thwarting of life; when he can live, neither compulsively nor automatically but spontaneously, the doubt disappears. He is aware of himself as an active and creative individual and recognizes that *there is only one meaning of life: the act of living itself.*

If the individual overcomes the basic doubt concerning himself and his place in life, if he is related to the world by embracing it in the act of spontaneous living, he gains strength as an individual and he gains security. This security, however, differs from the security that characterizes the preindividualist state in the same way in which the new relatedness to the world differs from that of the primary ties. The new security is not rooted in the protection which the individual has from a higher power outside of himself; neither is it a security in which the tragic quality of life is eliminated. The new security is dynamic; it is not based on protection, but on man's spontaneous activity. It is the security acquired each moment by man's spontaneous activity. It is the security that only freedom can give, that needs no illusions because it has eliminated those conditions that necessitate illusions.

Positive freedom as the realization of the self implies the full affirmation of the uniqueness of the individual. Men are born equal but they are also born different. The basis of this difference is the inherited equipment, physiological and mental, with which they start life, to which is added the particular constellation of circumstances and experiences that they meet with. This individual basis of the personality is as little identical with any other as two organisms are ever identical physically. The genuine growth of the self is always a growth on this particular basis; it is an organic growth, the unfolding of a nucleus that is peculiar for this one person and only for him. The development of the automaton, in contrast, is not an organic growth. The growth of the basis of the self is blocked and a pseudo self is superimposed upon this self, which is—as we have seen—essentially the incorporation of extraneous patterns of thinking and feeling. Organic growth is possible only under the condition of supreme respect for the peculiarity of the self of other persons as well as of our own self. This respect for and cultivation of the uniqueness of the self is the most valuable achievement of human culture and it is this very achievement that is in danger today.

The uniqueness of the self in no way contradicts the principle of equality. The thesis that men are born equal implies that they all share the same fundamental human qualities, that they share the basic fate of human beings, that they all have the same inalienable claim on freedom and happiness. It furthermore means that their relationship is one of solidarity, not one of domination-submission. What the concept of equality does not mean is that all men are alike. Such a concept of equality is derived from the role that the individual plays in his economic activities today. In the relation the man who buys and the one who sells, the concrete differences of personality are eliminated. In this situation only one thing matters, that the one has something to sell and the other has money to buy it. In economic life one man is not different from another; as real persons they are, and the cultivation of their uniqueness is the essence of individuality.

Positive freedom also implies the principle that there is no higher power than this unique individual self, that man is the center and purpose of his life; that the growth and realization of man's individuality is an end that can never be subordinated to purposes which are supposed to have greater dignity. This interpretation may arouse serious objections. Does it not postulate unbridled egotism? Is it not the negation of the idea of sacrifice for an ideal? Would its acceptance not lead to anarchy? These questions have actually already been answered, partly explicitly, partly implicitly, during our previous discussion. However, they are too important for us not to make another attempt to clarify the answers and to avoid misunderstanding.

To say that man should not be subject to anything higher than himself does not deny the dignity of ideals. On the contrary, it is the strongest affirmation of ideals. It forces us, however, to a critical analysis of what an ideal is. One is generally apt today to assume that an ideal is any aim whose achievement does not imply material gain, anything for which a person is ready to sacrifice egotistical ends. This is a purely psychological—and for that matter relativistic—concept of an ideal. From this subjectivist viewpoint a Fascist, who is driven by the desire to subordinate himself to a higher power and at the same time to overpower other people, has an ideal just as much as the man who fights for human equality and freedom. On this basis the problem of ideals can never be solved.

We must recognize the difference between genuine and fictitious ideals, which is just as fundamental a difference as that between truth and falsehood. All genuine ideals have one thing in common: they express the desire for something which is not yet accomplished but which is desirable for the purposes of the growth and happiness of the individual.[3] We may not always know what serves this end, we may disagree about the function of this or that ideal in terms of human development, but this is no reason for a relativism which says that we cannot know what furthers life or what blocks it. We are not always sure which food is healthy and which is not, yet we do not conclude that we have no way whatsoever of recognizing poison. In the same way we can know, if we want to, what is poisonous for mental life. We know that poverty, intimidation, isolation, are directed *against* life; that everything that serves freedom and furthers the courage and strength to be oneself is *for* life. What is good or bad for man is not a metaphysical question, but an empirical one that can be answered on the basis of an analysis of man's nature and the effect which certain conditions have on him.

But what about "ideals" like those of the Fascists which are definitely directed against life? How can we understand the fact that men are following these false ideals as fervently as others are following true ideals? The answer to this question is provided by certain psychological considerations. The phenomenon of masochism shows us that men can be drawn to the experiencing of suffering or submission. There is no doubt that suffering submission, or suicide is the antithesis of positive aims of living. Yet these aims can be subjectively experienced as gratifying and attractive. This attraction to what is harmful in life is the phenomenon which more than any other deserves the name of a pathological perversion. Many psychologists have assumed that the experience of pleasure and the avoidance of pain is the only legitimate principle guiding human action; but dynamic psychology can show that the subjective experience of pleasure is not a sufficient criterion for the value of certain behavior in terms of human happiness. The analysis of masochistic phenomena is a case in point. Such analysis shows that the sensation of pleasure can be the result of a pathological perversion and proves as little about the objective meaning of the experience as the sweet taste of a poison would prove about its function for the organism.[4] We thus come to define a genu-

---

[3] Cf. Max Otto, *The Human Enterprise*, T. S. Croft, New York, 1940. Chaps. IV and V.

[4] The question discussed here leads to a point of great significance which I want at least to mention: that problems of ethics can be clarified by dynamic psychology. Psychologists will only

ine ideal as any aim which furthers the growth, freedom, and happiness of the self, and to define as fictitious ideals those compulsive and irrational aims which subjectively are attractive experiences (like the drive for submission), but which actually are harmful to life. Once we accept this definition, it follows that a genuine ideal is not some veiled force superior to the individual, but that it is the articulate expression of utmost affirmation of the self. Any ideal which is in contrast to such affirmation proves by this very fact that it is not an ideal but a pathological sin.

From here we come to another question, that of sacrifice. Does our definition of freedom as nonsubmission to any *higher* power exclude sacrifices, including the sacrifice of one's life?

This is a particularly important question today, when Fascism proclaims self-sacrifice as the highest virtue and impresses many people with its idealistic character. The answer to this question follows logically from what has been said so far. There are two entirely different types of sacrifice. It is one of the tragic facts of life that the demands of our physical self and the aims of our mental self can conflict; that actually we may have to sacrifice our physical self in order to assert the integrity of our spiritual self. This sacrifice will never lose its tragic quality. Death is never sweet, not even if it is suffered for the highest ideal. It remains unspeakably bitter, and still it can be the utmost assertion of our individuality. Such sacrifice is fundamentally different from the "sacrifice" which Fascism preaches. There, sacrifice is not the highest price man may have to pay to assert his self, but it is an aim in itself. This masochistic sacrifice sees the fulfillment of life in its very negation, in the annihilation of the self. It is only the supreme expression of what Fascism aims at in all its ramifications—the annihilation of the individual self and its utter submission to a higher power. It is the perversion of true sacrifice as much as suicide is the utmost perversion of life. True sacrifice presupposes an uncompromising wish for spiritual integrity. The sacrifice of those who have lost it only covers up their moral bankruptcy.

One last objection is to be met: If individuals are allowed to act freely in the sense of spontaneity, if they acknowledge no higher authority than themselves, will anarchy be the inevitable result? In so far as the word anarchy stands for heedless egotism and destructiveness, the determining factor depends upon one's understanding of human nature. I can only refer to what has been pointed out in the chapter dealing with mechanisms of escape: that man is neither good nor bad; that life has an inherent tendency to grow, to expand, to express potentialities; that if life is thwarted, if the individual is

---

be helpful in this direction when they can see the relevance of moral problems for the understanding of personality. Any psychology, including Freud's, which treats such problems in terms of the pleasure principle, fails to understand one important sector of personality and leaves the field to dogmatic and unempirical doctrines of morality. The analysis of self-love, masochistic sacrifice, and ideals as offered in this book provides illustrations for this field of psychology and ethics that warrant further development.

isolated and overcome by doubt or a feeling of aloneness and powerlessness, then he is driven to destructiveness and craving for power or submission. If human freedom is established as *freedom to,* if man can realize his self fully and uncompromisingly, the fundamental cause for his asocial drives will have disappeared and only a sick and abnormal individual will be dangerous. This freedom has never been realized in the history of mankind, yet it has been an ideal to which mankind has stuck even if it was often expressed in abstruse and irrational forms. There is no reason to wonder why the record of history shows so much cruelty and destructiveness. If there is anything to be surprised at—and encouraged by—I believe it is the fact that the human race, in spite of all that has happened to men, has retained—and actually developed—such qualities of dignity, courage, decency, and kindness as we find them throughout history and in countless individuals today.

SAMUEL H. FLOWERMAN

6. *The Authoritarian Personality**

Findings of recent scientific investigations reveal that the real menace to democracy is not the brutal dictator but the anonymous man-in-the-crowd on whose support the dictator depends for power. Social scientists have found that this nameless individual is not a creation of the dictator but a ready-made "authoritarian personality"—a person whose family background and social environment have made him peculiarly attuned to anti-democratic beliefs. It requires authoritative personalities to take hold of authoritarian ideas; it takes authoritarian personalities—thousands and even millions of them—to build an authoritarian state.

Concern about authority and the relationship between the ruler and the ruled is not new. It runs through the fabric of recorded history of civilization. Philosophers and poets—from at least as far back as ancient Egypt and Greece to present-day Existentialists—have wrestled with the dilemma of how to attain the highest level of development of the individual within some system of order governing man's relation to man. In the United States a spate of studies about various aspects of personality development has been going forward for several decades. And research workers, most of them trained here, have been conducting studies in post-war Germany in an effort to understand why a people will produce, nurture and follow a dictator. The bulk of these inquiries tend to yield somewhat consistent results: there is something special, something different about the "authoritarian man."

* *The New York Times Magazine* (April 23, 1950). By permission.

Perhaps the most detailed study of all time in this field was made by a team of social psychologists in California, working for almost five years. They recently completed an investigation of the democratic and anti-democratic ideas and attitudes of the American man-in-the-crowd, seeking keys to their origin. Teams from other parts of the country have added to their findings. The California group—T. W. Adorno, Else Frenkel-Brunswik, Max Horkheimer, Daniel Levinson and R. Nevitt Sanford—interviewed and tested more than two thousand persons in the San Francisco Bay area, Los Angeles, Portland, Ore., and Washington, D. C.

Among the groups tested were factory workers, officer candidates in a maritime training school, veterans, members of service clubs (Rotarians and Kiwanis), office workers, male inmates of a prison, members of parent-teacher associations, out-patients in a psychiatric clinic, church groups and college students.

While the California study is not a statistical study but rather examines various groups psychologically, it was found that authoritarian men did exist in many groups and in many places. Based on the California study and other readings and observations over a number of years, social scientists feel that it can be said that about 10 per cent of the population of the United States probably consists of "authoritarian men and women" while as many as another 20 per cent have within them the seeds that can grow into authoritarianism.

Lest the conclusion be drawn that there are only two kinds of people, authoritarians and anti-authoritarians, it should be said that the social scientists' findings rate persons on a scale from very low to very high, as regards their authoritarian tendencies, with perhaps the bulk of the population clustered around the middle.

From the findings of the California study has emerged this composite psychological portrait of the Authoritarian Man:

He is a supreme conformist. The Authoritarian Man conforms to the nth degree to middle-class ideas and ideals and to authority. But conforming is no voluntary act for him; it is compulsive and irrational. It is an attempt to find security by merging with the herd, by submitting to some higher power or authority. Not only does he feel compelled to submit; he wants others to submit, too. He cannot run the risk of being different and cannot tolerate difference in anyone else.

In a mild form, such compulsive submission to authority may find a Casper Milquetoast chewing each mouthful of food thirty times because some bogus health expert has said he should. In its extreme form it finds people reduced to sheep, herded into marking "yes" on ballots that do not have "no," bleating "Heil!" to the commands of a Hitler, and doing his bidding even when it means oppressing, even killing, other people.

Authoritarians see the world and its inhabitants as menacing and unfriendly. Being so threatened, so anxiety ridden, they must seek security somehow, somewhere. The best security for the authoritarian is to surrender to a powerful authority. He agrees, for example, that "What the world needs is a strong leader"; and "There are two kinds of people, the weak and the strong."

To him, life is a power system into which he must fit. He doesn't have to wield the power himself so long as he can be near power, sharing it vicariously. It is this latter tendency which makes the authoritarian such a good camp-follower.

But the authoritarian is a loyal camp-follower only so long as the leader remains strong. Let the leader falter, let him be defeated; then, "Down with the old, up with the new."

So today in Germany many people agree that Hitler was bad, but only because he was unsuccessful in the long run; their basic way of life is still authoritarian—they simply await a new, stronger, more powerful leader.

He is rigid and shows limited imagination. He is a mechanical man, a kind of robot who reacts to only a limited number of ideas and can't be budged out of the channels in which he has been conditioned to operate. This doesn't mean that the Authoritarian Man is a person of low intelligence; but it does mean that his personality restricts his intelligence and imagination. He is generally incapable of figuring out alternate solutions to problems.

The extent to which this rigidity operates was demonstrated by Dr. Milton Rokeach, a junior member of the California team and now at Michigan State College. Dr. Rokeach worked out a series of simple problems in arithmetic and map reading. He presented these problems to groups of adults and children whose authoritarianism had already been determined. All the people in the experiment were taught to solve the problems by using a complicated method, but nothing was said about other, easier, solutions; they were simply instructed to get the right answers. As Dr. Rokeach's guinea pigs continued to work down the list of problems they soon reached a series of examples that could be solved either the hard way or very simply. Authoritarians continued to solve the problems the hard way. The non-authoritarians shifted readily to the easy solutions—they were able to use more channels.

He is herd-minded. And to be herd-minded—"ethnocentric," is the scientists' term—implies being prejudiced. To the authoritarian, people who are —or seem to be—different are strange, uncanny and threatening, although they may be few in number and unimportant in influence. He tends to exalt his own group and reject members of other groups. (To be sure, there are some exceptions to this praise of one's own group. Sometimes members of minority groups take over the prejudices of the majority groups and engage in what psychologists call "self-hate.")

The person who dislikes one "out-group" generally dislikes many other "out-groups." In this respect he is like the hay-fever victim, who is usually allergic to more than one kind of pollen.

The authoritarian puts neat—and often false—labels on people. In his group he may see individuals; outside his own group he sees only masses or types. So he will frequently say of members of "minority" groups that "that kind" is "lazy," "sex-crazy," "dishonest in business," "money-mad," "smelly," and so on. What is more, he tends to see "them" everywhere.

He is a phony conservative. He waves the flag, he sounds like a patriot, but at heart hates the very traditions and institutions he professes to love. In his most rabid form the phony conservative is the anti-democratic agitator who is more destructively radical than the radicals he claims he is attacking.

The California team distinguishes between the true conservative and the phony conservative. The true conservative may be patriotic, believe in American traditions and institutions and support their continued existence; he may also believe in a laissez-faire economy. But he is also for giving every individual an equal "break" regardless of his group membership. And it is in regard to this last point that the true conservative can be distinguished from the counterfeit flag-waver.

He is a moral purist. The authoritarian frowns on sensuality, a trait he is ready to find in members of other groups. He regards his own group as morally pure. Authoritarian men—and women—tend to agree, for example, that no "decent man" would marry an unchaste woman. Even male prisoners jailed for sex crimes support statements condemning sex crimes; and they are also more conforming, more anti-Semitic, more anti-Negro, and more pseudo-conservative than their fellow-prisoners.

It would be a grave mistake to regard the authoritarian as a lunatic or freak, although doubtless there are such extreme cases. If anything, the democratic person may appear outwardly to be less well-adjusted because he "internalizes" his problems to a greater degree and blames himself for many of his difficulties. The authoritarian "externalizes" his problems and blames other people and other forces. On the surface, the authoritarian may seem to be less troubled, but this is often because he has buried his smoldering resentment and hostility within himself.

By contrast with his opposite the extremely democratic personality is a man with a mind of his own; he is a flexible individual, adjusting readily to new situations. He is sensitive to the part he plays in conflicting situations and he is ready to take responsibility for his own behavior.

The model anti-authoritarian tends to like all sorts of people regardless of whether they are members of his group. He is without prejudice against religious or racial minorities. He regards persons as individuals, not types. Nor is he inclined to judge the moral standards of others. It is easy for him to see some good in the world and some hope for its future. Most important, he refuses to surrender his individuality to a "big shot," although he may submit to rational authority by choice when he believes that such authority is based upon equality, superior ability, and cooperation, and that it is subject to dismissal for a job badly done.

The findings of these studies suggest that people are not deliberately and systematically taught the ABC's of authoritarianism. Authoritarianism is a term which describes personality; and personality is developed in the crucible of inter-personal relationships, the most important of which is the relationship between parent and child.

As a child the typical authoritarian was usually subjected to harsh discipline and was given little affection in a home in which the father was a tough boss. In such a home children must "knuckle under" and submit. There is little opportunity to disagree and to act as an individual. Fear rules, and parents and other figures of authority are regarded as menacing, punitive and overpowering. This fear, based on the inability to disagree, is carried over into adult life; when the opportunity to assert one's self occurs, it is seized by way of compensation. The slave of one generation becomes the domineering master of the next generation.

On the other hand, as a child the democratic individual most often grew up in a home where the mother had much to say. Children in these families knew affection and had a feeling that they counted as individuals. They exercised the right to disagree, although often not without conflict and guilt. As adults they regard their parents as flesh-and-blood characters with the traits of real people. In childhood, the democratic person was able to choose equality and independence instead of blind, passive submission. As an adult, the democratic person is not so easily pushed around because he has no compulsive need, based on fear, to submit to the authority of the "big shot."

To be sure, there are reasons for the development of authoritarian personalities which are not to be found in the home. There are the major environmental upheavals—depressions and unemployment, inflations, wars, earthquakes, revolutions, floods—which alter ways of living and believing. There are also the chance experiences which an individual encounters in a lifetime. Sometimes the harshness of a child's home may be offset by kindly teachers, decent playmates, and other significant figures who treat the child affectionately as an individual. Sometimes a child grows up in such a way as to be able to throw off the effects of his slavery.

But these rebels are perhaps the exception, whereas the slave personality occurs more often when childhood has been spent in an authoritarian home. Certainly research findings indicate that so far the key to the difference between the authoritarian and democratic personalities lies in the relationship between parents and children. Learning to disagree with one's parents may be the capstone of a democratic personality.

How great is the threat of authoritarian development in this country? There are several deeply ingrained trends in American culture which probably offset to a considerable degree the spread of authoritarianism.

Americans traditionally scoff at authority. An American President reads a state of the Union message before Congress and is heckled, only to answer right back. Prizefight referees are booed when they award unfair decisions against Negro boxers in favor of white boxers. Players and spectators "razz" baseball umpires. Radio programs and movies make fun of cops, school teachers and principals, and especially fathers.

American homes are mother-oriented—and if anything—child-dominated. Women control the family purse strings of America, handle immediate problems of discipline, and are favored by over-sentimentality in a Victorian sense.

We have an American creed of fair play, of equality, and of upward mobility among social and economic classes. We are an individualistic, freedom-loving, rational, practical people. Americans are suspicious of flag-waving and of military authority.

Yet there are those who note that our American creed is "honored more in the breach than in the observance." Wide gaps separate what we claim to believe and what we feel and do. Like any national group, we are susceptible to anti-democratic ideologies; we have authoritarian personalities among us.

To develop freer personalities—personalities less susceptible to authoritarian ideas—we must learn how to select better teachers and to train them better; we must see them as engineers of human relations instead of instructors of arithmetic and spelling. We must reach parents so that they can learn the importance of affection and equality in the home. Mental health programs must be developed to help people become better parents. And laws, as social controls, can serve the useful purpose of limiting the effects of bigots and bringing the force of authority—which they frequently fear and have to submit to—to bear upon them.

Another source of enlightenment is to be found in our colleges and universities. Stimulated by the studies of authoritarian personality, scores of graduate students all over the country are pursuing research projects in human relations. Already the knowledge which comes from such research is reaching students in schools and colleges throughout the United States, and is beginning to reach scholars and students in France, England, Belgium and Italy.

There are many healthy signs in America today. Love has chased the behaviorists from the nursery; modern parents are less ashamed of loving their children. We regard juvenile delinquency as a social problem rather than an ordinary crime. Alcoholism has been the subject of research and humane treatment. Colleges turn down large bequests containing discriminatory clauses. Movies about such social problems as prejudice have increased in number and improved in quality (and have made money at the box office). Eight states have laws barring discrimination in employment. Three states bar discrimination in higher education.

These signs herald a future in which there may be fewer authoritarians, for they tend to check the authoritarian personality at its source and aim to make the American background more fruitful for the development of its antagonist, the democratic man and woman.

Part II

THE FOUNDATIONS OF DEMOCRACY

The Right to Rebel

Liberty and Loyalty

Liberty and Equality

Chapter III

THE RIGHT TO REBEL

One of the stereotypes that will die, if at all, a slow death is the "conservative Englishman." The English could not be really conservative even if they tried.

In the sixteenth century they were the first (and only) major nation to break away from the authority of the Roman Church—then as now a pillar of conservatism in theology and politics. The other great nations of that era of religious revolt, the Spanish, French, and Italians, extirpated the seeds of protest with hot iron, if necessary. The Germans could not, as on other occasions, make up their minds how to save their souls. This first major revolution in the life of the English people is so important because, more perhaps than any other event in their history, it made English nationality conscious of itself. As elsewhere, war and nationalism were closely linked, and the English struggle against the Roman Church and its loyal monarchies, Spain and France, sharpened the awareness of the English that they were a people with a destiny of their own.

In the seventeenth century the English scored no better on conservative respectability. To cut off one king's head and to exile another monarch in one century is not a bad record, however one interprets the ideal of radical democracy. Since that time the British have not been so spectacular—they did not have to be. Try as they may, they can never hope to regain their "political innocence."

The "Glorious Revolution" of 1688 established, once and for all, the principle of parliamentary sovereignty in England. Twice in forty years the will of the people had triumphed over the will of the king.

In 1690 John Locke published *Two Treatises of Government,* in which he formulated, clearly and briefly, the classical theory of representative government. What makes the *Two Treatises* remarkable is that they are more than an *apologia* for the revolution in 1688. Unlike most political writers, Locke was able to perceive what lay behind the events of his own age. In particular, he insisted that popular consent was the sole legitimate basis of government, and that revolution was, under predictable circumstances, a natural and justifiable remedy in defending liberty. Before Locke, respectable people had abhorred rebellion as a form of sporadic, untamed, mob violence, illegitimate in origin and incapable of achieving any moral good. To impose upon powei the necessity of justifying its very existence, not by reference to divine grace, nor to tradition, nor to sheer force, but through the freely given consent of the people who alone were to judge their rulers, was one of the most revolutionary and potentially most civilizing acts of the human mind. When Locke declared the arbitrary autocrat an outcast and the people in rebellion against him as the defenders of the law, he gave new meanings to the words "law" and "rebellion." His insistence that there is a law higher than the formally proclaimed law of a community has led to the conception, so widespread in the English-speaking world, that obedience to the law is a high, but not, as in other countries, the highest civic virtue.

Opponents of the democratic solution of the problem of government, from Hobbes to Hitler, have charged that making political rule dependent upon the consent of the ruled "lays a ferment for frequent rebellion," as Locke puts it. To this grave accusation, Locke himself adduces several answers which are included below. The perspective of experience since 1690 supplies the most effective reply to the charge that democracy contains within itself seeds of anarchy and rebellion: the British and American systems of government, based upon recognition of the right to rebel, have proved themselves the most stable and successful political societies the world has ever seen. Paradoxically, where the right of revolution has been rejected in the name of order and stability, the political results have been putsches, blood purges, conspiracies, and violent swings from one extreme to another—the political record, specifically, of Germany and, to a lesser extent, of Japan. Neither Italian Fascism nor German Nazism, both extolling the principle of order, have been good propaganda for that creed. Mussolini's ouster in 1943, and his subsequent assassination, occurred under circumstances which suggest that Fascism was not all stability; the anti-Hitler plot of July 20, 1944, revealed that Prussian officers of the highest military rank had conspired to assassinate their beloved war leader. Stable as Nazism may have been throughout most of its career, there was always an element of plain murder in it—and that, again, was no better than a touch of anarchy or lawlessness would have been.

If Locke was the intellectual father of the British political system of the last two and a half centuries, his influence on American political thinking has been even more massive. To the extent that ideas and doctrines can be said to have affected political acts and institutions in the United States, Locke has influenced American political life more than any other writer, American or foreign. In fact, Locke has become more typically American than British, as time has gone by, especially in his economic views.

By committing themselves to Locke's theories of government, the British themselves supplied the case for the American Revolution, and, as can be seen from the text of the Declaration of Independence, the chief ideas and their wording were almost pure Locke. As a consequence, the main elements of the American political system, the inviolability of property, limited governmental powers, and the inalienable rights of the individual, are all contained in Locke. Writing in an expanding commercial society, his ideas also fitted the needs of a dynamic pioneer country. Above all, Locke's defense of the right to rebel seemed to the authors of the American Revolution eminently reasonable.

The most forceful expression of the right to revolution is to be found in a letter by the author of the Declaration of Independence. In a letter (dated November 13, 1787) to Colonel William Stephen Smith, Jefferson refers to Shays' insurrection in 1786, a minor revolt in Massachusetts, which seemed to prove to fearful souls that the government of the United States was producing more anarchy than peace. Jefferson adds general observations on the issue of rebellion. His thought that the "tree of liberty must be refreshed from time to time with the blood of patriots and tyrants" is probably as shocking to legitimists now as it was in 1787.

This Lockean-Jefferson theory of revolution has been vigorously reaffirmed in our own time by Harold J. Laski. His political thought sprang from the rich heritage of the liberal faith, and his socialism was but an enlargement of his liberalism from the purely political into the economic and social aspects of life. His defense of the democratic socialist movements against the inroads of revolutionary communism, resumed by him with renewed vigor after the end of the Second World War, was inconsistent with the attempt to build up Harold J. Laski into a commissar. While no yogi, he never embraced the creed of the commissar.

During the years 1933-1939, when Nazism and Fascism grew stronger and stronger, unchecked by weak and divided democracies, Laski, like many other liberals, became intellectually moody and a bit pessimistic as to the ability of the capitalist democracies to survive the ordeal of Fascism. In this period he accepted some of the points of the Marxian analysis of history; his *State in Theory and Practice,* published in 1935, is the book which best represents that phase in his development. But even then, the main assumptions of his political theory were in the grand tradition set by Locke, and not in the deviation set by Marx. "The roots of valid law are, and can only be," says Laski, "within the individual conscience." This is pure Locke, and not even impure Marx or Lenin. To the charge that such a view, "by justifying refusal to obey, opens the door to anarchy, the answer is that the accusation is true." This, again, is a leading idea expressed by Laski in words that can be found almost identically in Locke.

In fact, Laski outdoes Locke: whereas Locke restricts the right to rebel to the injured *majority,* Laski goes further: he sees in history many examples of minorities and even single men revolting against intolerable iniquities, and he is therefore driven to the conclusion that, in the last resort, the *individual* will have to decide for himself whether he will bow to established law and order, or whether he will feel compelled, by an inner impulse of irrepressible intensity, to rebel.

The Constitution of the United States, wisely recognizing that the individual will accept social compulsion only up to a point, also adheres to this conception which goes beyond Locke, by declaring that some rights of the individual are inalienable.

Whatever the social and economic system that may exist at a particular time—be it early or advanced capitalism, rural economy or urban industry, pioneering conditions or an old established society, New Deal or Labor Party socialism—the right to rebel remains the great tradition of British and American politics. Rebelliousness, too, can, paradoxically, grow into tradition. We ourselves are heirs of and witnesses to that tradition—the tradition of the dignity of man and of his unbreakable spirit.

The classical Anglo-American concept of the right to rebel has been misinterpreted or deliberately abused by the Communists. According to the liberal doctrine, rebellion against the government is justified only when the majority of the people are oppressed by a despotic minority or by a single despot. Under such conditions, rebellion is not only morally justified, but it becomes the moral *duty* of men who love liberty and the rule of law. If force is the only way to wrest freedom from a tyrannical minority, then force must be used. Under this liberal doctrine, the traditional one in Anglo-American thought, totalitarians have no right to use force as a means of setting up their own antiliberal and antidemocratic order. For the liberal doctrine of revolution argues that as long as a minority has the opportunity to plead its case peacefully in a constitutional system of government, it has no moral right to rebel against the majority. When a political minority in a constitutional system abandons the peaceful road of persuasion and turns to the radical method of violence, it implicitly concedes that the attempts at such persuasion would be useless. This explains why no nation in the world has so far turned to Communism on the basis of peaceful persuasion and free elections: wherever Communism has been able to seize the government, it has done so either by means of domestic revolution and civil war (as in Russia, Yugoslavia, and mainland China) or by means of military imposition from the outside (as in the case of the Eastern European Communist satellites or North Korea). Whenever a truly popular revolution has occurred within the Communist orbit (as in Eastern Germany in 1953 and in Hungary in 1956), such revolutions have been suppressed by the Red Army. The only revolutions that Communism encourages or even permits are those revolutions which are carried through by Communist minorities against the will of the majority of the people.

Yet the totalitarian attack, be it Communist or Fascist, against the liberal doctrine of rebellion is not necessarily the most dangerous one. Even more damaging is the internal corrosion of that doctrine in liberal societies in the name of adjustment and conformity. Fascist or Communist aggression against free nations is dramatic; it can be quickly noticed, and tangible defenses against it can be mounted effectively. Yet in the long run, particularly if the menace of Communist imperialism should subside as did that of Fascist imperialism before it, the spirit of the organization man, of togetherness, of team-work, of adjustment and conformity, may produce a creeping and insidiously unnoticed paralysis of the will and habit to be different, to be one's own self rather than to conform to that of others, and to dare challenge the fondest predilections and prejudices of one's fellow men. In *Must You Conform?* (1956) Robert Lindner, one of the most imaginative American psychoanalysts, takes up the all-pervasive threat of conformity to the survival of free man in a free society. The pressure to adjust prevails, Lindner argues, on all levels of education, from the nursery to colleges and universities: in the latter "professors live in fear of saying or doing anything unorthodox." The new Eleventh Commandment of "You Must Adjust" is also preached, Lindner charges, by all churches and religions to the extent that they demand submission as a condition (in many cases as *the* condition) of man's salvation and redemption. In politics, all parties demand conformity from their adherents, and those political movements that promise the maximum of liberty and reform end up by imposing the maximum of conformity and oppression. Among the sciences, Lindner is particularly critical of psychiatry and psychology: "Of all betrayals, their treachery has been the greatest, for in them we have placed our remaining hope, and in them, sadly, hope has fled." Protest and discontent on the part of an individual do not necessarily indicate that something is wrong with him, that he is neurotic and in need of psychotherapy: something may be wrong with society. Yet the general trend of contemporary psychiatry, Lindner argues, is to adjust the individual to society rather than to help restore the health of the society. Lindner scathingly attacks the methods of psychiatry in adjusting man to his social environment, be they soft counsel and persuasion, palliative drugs and sedatives, and finally, shock treatment or brain surgery: the last method, the most radical one, produces a "walking zombie," cured of his maladjustments, but, alas, also "cured of his humanity."

Lindner rejects this trend toward conformity on the grounds of ethics and psycho-biology. On the grounds of ethics, because Lindner fervently believes in the value of liberty and the great constitutional documents, in the United States and elsewhere, that enshrine it. On the grounds of psycho-biology, because Lindner believes that there is in man an "instinct of rebellion." Unlike all other forms of life, man adapts "alloplastically." This means that he himself is the author of the changes of his physical and social environment, whereas in the case of other forms of life change is imposed, that is, they adapt "autoplastically." This will in man to overcome limitations of environment, even death itself, is (according to Lindner) unlearned and innate, and he therefore calls it an "instinct," thus reinforcing the concept that man has no choice when it comes to rebellion, no choice because "in order to live he must rebel."

So far, no totalitarian system, not even in its most elaborate form as fictionalized in George Orwell's *1984,* has ever been able to eradicate man's rebelliousness completely. Yet it still remains to be seen whether new techniques of indoctrination and brainwashing will succeed more thoroughly than they have in the past, or whether their renewed failure will lend support to Lindner's analysis and optimism.

JOHN LOCKE

1. *Democracy, Revolution, and the Threat of Anarchy**

Perhaps it will be said that, the people being ignorant and always discontented, to lay the foundation of government in the unsteady opinion and uncertain humor of the people is to expose it to certain ruin; and no government will be able long to subsist if the people may set up a new legislative whenever they take offense at the old one. To this I answer: Quite the contrary. People are not so easily got out of their old forms as some are apt to suggest. They are hardly to be prevailed with to amend the acknowledged faults in the frame they have been accustomed to. And if there be any original defects, or adventitious ones introduced by time or corruption, it is not an easy thing to get them changed, even when all the world sees there is an opportunity for it. This slowness and aversion in the people to quit their old constitutions has, in the many revolutions which have been seen in this kingdom, in this and former ages still kept us to, or after some interval of fruitless attempts still brought us back again to, our old legislative of Kings, Lords, and Commons. And whatever provocations have made the crown be taken from some of our princes' heads, they never carried the people so far as to place it in another line.

But it will be said, this hypothesis lays a ferment for frequent rebellion. To which I answer:

* From John Locke, *Two Treatises of Government* (1690).

First, no more than any other hypothesis. For when the people are made miserable, and find themselves exposed to the ill-usage of arbitrary power, cry up their governors as much as you will for sons of Jupiter, let them be sacred and divine, descended, or authorized from heaven, give them out for whom or what you please, the same will happen. The people generally ill-treated, and contrary to right, will be ready upon any occasion to ease themselves of a burden that sits heavy upon them. They will wish and seek for the opportunity, which in the change, weakness, and accidents of human affairs seldom delays long to offer itself. He must have lived but a little while in the world who has not seen examples of this in his time, and he must have read very little who cannot produce examples of it in all sorts of governments in the world.

Secondly, I answer, such revolutions happen not upon every little mismanagement in public affairs. Great mistakes in the ruling part, many wrong and inconvenient laws, and all the slips of human frailty will be borne by the people without mutiny or murmur. But if a long train of abuses, prevarications and artifices, all tending the same way, make the design visible to the people—and they cannot but feel what they lie under, and see whither they are going—it is not to be wondered that they should then rouse themselves and endeavor to put the rule into such hands which may secure to them the ends for which government was at first erected, and without which ancient names and specious forms are so far from being better that they are much worse than the state of nature or pure anarchy; the inconveniences being all as great and as near, but the remedy farther off and more difficult.

Thirdly, I answer that this power in the people of providing for their safety anew by a new legislative when their legislators have acted contrary to their trust by invading their property, is the best fence against rebellion, and the probablest means to hinder it. For rebellion being an opposition, not to persons, but authority, which if founded only in the constitutions and laws of the government, those whoever they be who by force break through, and by force justify their violations of them, are truly and properly rebels. For when men by entering into society and civil government have excluded force, and introduced laws for the preservation of property, peace, and unity amongst themselves, those who set up force again in opposition to the laws do *rebellare*—that is, bring back again the state of war—and are properly rebels; which they who are in power (by the pretense they have to authority, the temptation of force they have in their hands, and the flattery of those about them) being likeliest to do, the properest way to prevent the evil is to show them the danger and injustice of it who are under the greatest temptation to run into it.

In both the forementioned cases, when either the legislative is changed or the legislators act contrary to the end for which they were constituted, those who are guilty are guilty of rebellion. For if anyone by force takes away the established legislative of any society, and the laws by them made pursuant to their trust, he thereby takes away the umpirage which everyone had consented to for a peaceable decision of all their controversies, and a bar to the state of war amongst them. They who remove or change the legislative, take away his decisive power, which nobody can have by the appointment and consent of the people, and so destroying the authority which the people did, and nobody else can, set up; and introducing a power which the people hath not authorized, actually introduce a state of war which is that of force without authority. And thus by removing the legislative established by the society (in whose decisions the people acquiesced and united as to that of their own will), they untie the knot and expose the people anew to the state of war. And if those who by force take away the legislative are rebels, the legislators themselves, as has been shown, can be less esteemed so, when they who were set up for the protection and preservation of the people, their liberties and properties, shall by force invade and endeavor to take them away; and so they, putting themselves into a state of war with those who made them the protectors and guardians of their peace, are properly and with the greatest aggravation *rebellantes* (rebels).

But if they who say it lays a foundation for rebellion mean that it may occasion civil wars or intestine broils, to tell the people they are absolved from obedience when illegal attempts are made upon their liberties or properties, and may oppose the unlawful violence of those who were their magistrates when they invade their properties contrary to the trust put in them and that therefore this doctrine is not to be allowed, being so destructive to the peace of the world: they may as well say upon the same ground that honest men may not oppose robbers or pirates because this may occasion disorder or bloodshed. If any mischief come in such cases, it is not to be charged upon him who defends his own right, but on him that invades his neighbor's. If the innocent honest man must quietly quit all he has for peace's sake to him who will lay violent hands upon it, I desire it may be considered what a kind of peace there will be in the world which consists only in violence and rapine, and which is to be maintained only for the benefit of robbers and oppressors. Who would not think it an admirable peace betwixt the mighty and the mean when the lamb without resistance yielded his throat to be torn by the imperious wolf? Polyphemus's den gives us a perfect pattern of such a peace and such a government, wherein Ulysses and his companions had nothing to do but quietly to suffer themselves to be devoured. And no doubt Ulysses, who was a prudent man, preached up passive obedience, and exhorted them to a quiet submission by representing to them of what concernment peace was to mankind, and by showing the inconveniences which might happen if they should offer to resist Polyphemus, who had now the power over them.

The end of government is the good of mankind, and which is best for mankind, that the people should be always exposed to the boundless will of tyranny, or that the rulers should be sometimes liable to be opposed when they grow exorbitant in the use of their power, and employ it for the destruction and not the preservation of the properties of their people?

Nor let anyone say that mischief can arise from hence as often as it shall please a busy head or turbulent spirit to desire the alteration of the government. It is true such men may stir whenever they please, but it will be only to their own just ruin and perdition. For till the mischief be grown general, and the ill designs of the rulers become visible, or their attempts sensible to the greater part, the people, who are more disposed to suffer than right themselves by resistance, are not apt to stir. The examples of particular injustice or oppression of here and there an unfortunate man moves them not. But if they universally have a persuasion grounded upon manifest evidence that designs are carrying on against their liberties, and the general course and tendency of things cannot but give them strong suspicions of the evil intention of their governors, who is to be blamed for it? Who can help it if they, who might avoid it, bring themselves into this suspicion? Are the people to be blamed if they have the sense of rational creatures, and can think of things no otherwise than as they find and feel them? And is it not rather their fault who put things in such a posture that they would not have them thought as they are? I grant that the pride, ambition, and turbulency of private men have sometimes caused great disorders in commonwealths, and factions have been fatal to states and kingdoms. But whether the mischief hath oftener begun in the people's wantonness, and a desire to cast off the lawful authority of their rulers, or in the rulers' insolence and endeavors to get and exercise an arbitrary power over their people, whether oppression or disobedience gave the first rise to the disorder, I leave it to impartial history to determine. This I am sure, whoever, either ruler or subject, by force goes about to invade the rights of either prince or people, and lays the foundation for overturning the constitution and frame of any just government, he is guilty of the greatest crime I think a man is capable of, being to answer for all those mischiefs of blood, rapine, and desolation, which the breaking to pieces of governments bring on a country; and he who does it is justly to be esteemed the common enemy and pest of mankind, and is to be treated accordingly.

2. Declaration of Independence*

When, in the Course of human events, it becomes necessary for one people to dissolve the political bonds which have connected them with another, and to assume, among the Powers of the earth the separate and equal station to

* From the *Declaration of Independence* (1776).

which the Laws of Nature and of Nature's God entitle them, a decent respect to the opinions of mankind requires that they should declare the causes
which impel them to the separation.

We hold these truths to be self-evident, that all men are created equal, that
they are endowed by their Creator with certain unalienable Rights, that
among these, are Life, Liberty, and the pursuit of Happiness. That, to secure
these rights, Governments are instituted among Men, deriving their just
Powers from the consent of the governed. That, whenever any form of Government becomes destructive of these ends, it is the Right of the People to
alter or to abolish it, and to institute new Government, laying its foundation
on such Principles, and organizing its Powers in such form as to them shall
seem most likely to effect their Safety and Happiness. Prudence, indeed, will
dictate that Government's long established should not be changed for light
and transient causes; and, accordingly, all experience hath shewn, that mankind are more disposed to suffer, while evils are sufferable, than to right
themselves by abolishing the forms to which they are accustomed. But, when
a long train of abuses and usurpations, pursuing invariably the same Object,
evinces a design to reduce them under absolute Despotism, it is their right,
it is their duty, to throw off such Government, and to provide new Guards
for their future Security. Such has been the patient sufferance of these Colonies; and such is now the necessity which constrains them to alter their
former Systems of Government.

THOMAS JEFFERSON

3. Rebellion and Liberty*

The British ministry have so long hired their gazetteers to repeat and
model into every form lies about our being in anarchy, that the world has at
length believed them, the English nation has believed them, the ministers
themselves have come to believe them, and what is more wonderful, we have
believed them ourselves. Yet where does this anarchy exist? Where did it
ever exist, except in the single instance of Massachusetts? And can history
produce an instance of rebellion so honourably conducted? I say nothing of
its motives. They were founded in ignorance, not wickedness. God forbid we
should ever be twenty years without such a rebellion. The people cannot be
all, and always, well informed. The part which is wrong will be discon-

* From a letter to Colonel William Stephens Smith (November 13, 1787).

tented in proportion to the importance of the facts they misconceive. If they remain quiet under such misconceptions it is a lethargy, the forerunner of death to the public liberty. We have had thirteen states independent for eleven years. There has been one rebellion. That comes to one rebellion in a century and a half, for each state. What country before ever existed a century and a half without a rebellion? And what country can preserve its liberties if their rulers are not warned from time to time that their people preserve the spirit of resistance? Let them take arms. The remedy is to set them right as to facts, pardon and pacify them. What signify a few lives lost in a century or two? The tree of liberty must be refreshed from time to time with the blood of patriots and tyrants. It is its natural manure.

HAROLD J. LASKI

4. *Challenge to Authority**

There is, outside the purely formal realm, no obligation to obey the actual state. Our obedience is, and can only be, a function of our judgment upon its performance. That judgment, moreover, is never one which each citizen can make upon the same postulates, intellectual or emotional. What he decides will be the product of the place he occupies in the state, and the relation of that place to his view of what he ought to attain. He may be wrong in the view he takes; but he has never any rational alternative to action in the light of his own certainties. Upon this attitude there hinges a view of law the implications of which are important. It regards the validity of law as unrelated to the source from which it comes. Law becomes law as it goes into application; it is made law by being accepted. That is not to say that accepted law is right law; for law may be accepted by the might which is behind it. We have, in fact, to distinguish between three different senses in which the idea of law can be used. There is the formal juristic sense, which is no more than an announcement, ultimately dependent upon the sovereign authority, of the will to enforce certain decisions. There is the political sense, in which the formal announcement is validated by the acceptance of it by those to whom it applies. There is, finally, the ethical sense in which the decision announced ought to be obeyed, because it is morally right that what it proposes should be done.

Now it is clear that in the first two of these three senses the citizen has no inherent duty to obey. Few people would seriously claim that the juristic sense is always to be equated with the ethical; certainly, to take an obvious example, no Quaker could admit that a state whose government ordered its citizens to make war had, for this purpose, a title to their obedience. Nor can it, I think, be seriously claimed, either, that the political and ethical senses are identical; the commands of the Hitlerite state on June 30, 1934, were law in the sense that they went into effective operation, and were accepted by the population over whom it ruled; but most people in a position to make an independent judgment would, I suggest, regard them as ethically outrageous. Might, however profound, does not make right; effective operation of law still leaves undecided the question of ethical adequacy.

Neither formal competence, then, nor political power can confer a just title to obedience. With what are we left? Only, I think, with the insistence that law to be ethically valid must conform with the requirements of the system of rights the purposes of which the state exists to maintain. And since law is a command seeking to control my behaviour in some particular way, I must judge that conformity for myself as the test of its ethical adequacy. The roots of valid law, that is, are, and can only be, within the individual conscience. I make law legal, so to say, by giving to its operation the consent of my conscience.

If it is said that such a view, by justifying refusal to obey, opens the door to anarchy, the answer is that the accusation is true. But it is not a serious accusation. In the life of states the door to anarchy is always open because men are never willing to admit the unconditional conference of power. If, further, it be said that the individual conscience is at least as likely to be wrong as the consciences of those who rule the state, the answer, again, is that while this may be true, the citizen who yields his conviction on the ground that he may be mistaken will soon cease, in any meaning sense, to be a citizen at all. There is no way of making a state active in the fulfilment of its function except the knowledge that men will refuse to obey its commands where they regard them as a violation of that function. That was the truth that Pericles saw when he told the citizens of Athens that the secret of liberty was courage. Unless men are prepared to act by the insights they have, even when these insights are erroneous, they are bound to become no more than the passive recipients of orders to whose moral quality they are indifferent. When they do that, they poison the foundations of the state. For they then cease to be moral beings in any sense of the word that has meaning. They associate truth and justice and right automatically with the possession of physical power. No people prepared in that fashion to abdicate its humanity is likely to be long capable of creative achievement. For so to abdicate the duty of moral judgment is to sell oneself into slavery.

It is said that the individual is powerless, and that he wastes his energy by acting upon his judgment. But there are at least two answers to this view. A moral obligation is not less compelling because it may end in failure. To adopt that canon of effort is to accept the view that justice is the will of the stronger—a doctrine against which, as I have pointed out, the whole history of humanity is a protest. And to argue, secondly, that the individual is powerless is, on the record, quite untrue. He is powerless only when his perceptions are so completely unshared that he fails to arouse any note of response among his fellow-citizens; and he has always to remember that the shift of events may cause them to be shared at a later stage. The early Christians must have appeared singularly futile to their own generation when they challenged the majesty of Rome; but their steadfastness conquered the Western world. Luther's recalcitrance must have appeared akin to madness to a church which remembered its successful emergence from the stresses of the Conciliar revolt; but he changed the history of the world by his courage. Even so liberal a mind as Emerson could write of the American abolitionists that they were "narrow, self-pleasing, conceited men, and affect us as the insane do";[1] but it was hardly a generation afterwards that so respectable an observer as Oliver Wendell Holmes, not given to extreme views, could say of his friend's judgment that "it would have taken a long time to get rid of slavery if some of Emerson's teachings had been accepted as the whole gospel of liberty." [2]

History, indeed, abounds with such instances. The individual who protests against the law he deems unjust is far less alone than he is likely to imagine. He is acting in a mental climate in which the experience borne in upon him is likely to be shared by others; and the gesture he makes may awaken others to the understanding of their obligations. No one who looks back upon their history can doubt that the suffragettes who, for eight years, defied the law awakened the British government to a sense that their claims were serious in a way that altered the whole perspective of those claims. No one can doubt either that the unbreakable will of Lenin was central to the success of the Bolshevik Revolution in 1917. That we must fight for our philosophy if we believe in it, seems to me the inescapable implication of the record.

Against this view two considerations are urged, in both of which there is, unquestionably, considerable force. It is said that to challenge the government is to weaken the authority of all law, and that to do so is to open the flood-gates to chaos. It was the sense of this danger which made T. H. Green, who admitted, in the last resort, the right to revolution, insist that we must approach the state in fear and trembling. But it is surely not less important to realise that respect for law must always mean respect for what the law does; and if the individual, whether alone or in concert with others, judges what the law does to be ethically intolerable, he must act upon the basis of his judgment. To decide otherwise is to argue that the highest duty of the indi-

---

[1] Quoted in V. F. Calverton, *The Liberalism of American Literature* (1932), p. 330.
[2] *Ibid.*, p. 331.

vidual is to maintain order, without regard to the quality of the order that is maintained. I do not find this argument compatible with the notion of the individual as a moral being.

It is said, secondly, that this view admits the right of any doctrine to support itself by force, if it can. Men have only to announce that they are moved by some profound conviction to be justified in using violence to attain their ends. Such an attitude, it is argued, is utterly destructive of the foundations of social well-being.

But the answer is surely that no doctrine, however evil, moves to the use of force unless it is rooted in profound grievance which it sees no other way to remedy. We may believe the Bolshevik Revolution to have been wholly evil; but it is clear that the previous conditions of the Russian state alone account for its origin and methods. We may argue, with the Communists, that Hitler has been no more than the agent of finance-capitalism in Germany;[3] but it is also clear that his victory was built upon the profound grievances of millions of Germans who saw no adequate redress for them in the habits of the Weimar republic. The truth is that men in general are so accustomed to obey that their departure from the normal canons of political behaviour is always an index to grave disease in the state. They have, as Burke said, "no interest in disorder; where they do wrong it is their error and not their crime." We need not argue that a doctrine which arms itself is wise or right to do so. But, on the facts, we have to argue that no doctrine ever does successfully arm itself unless the government it attacks has failed to deal with the grievances it expresses in a reasonable way.

That is, I think, apparent in the history of most revolutions. Certainly the student of the English civil wars, of the revolutions of France and of Russia, will note as not the least remarkable of their features, the patient efforts of the common people to await reform before they turned to violence. And in any society violence is unlikely if the conviction is widespread that the state is seriously attempting to fulfil its obligations. Violence comes when the facts persuade men to believe that the bona-fides of their rulers is no longer to be trusted.

[3] Cf. E. Henri, *Hitler Over Europe* (1933).

ROBERT LINDNER

5. *The Pressure of Conformity and the Instinct of Rebellion**

Must we conform? This is the question that confronts every man today, the question that must be answered before silence descends and the voice of humanity fades to a whimper. It is a question only a few fortunate ones can still ask, a question that cannot even be raised behind the barbed wire where half of humanity lives.

Must we conform? Must we fit ourselves into the pattern that molds Mass Man? Must we bend, submit, adjust, give in? Must we, finally, cease to be men?

The forces of Society tell us that we must. Aligned already with the emergent dominant class, they and the institutions they represent have put individuality and liberty on the sacrificial altar. For a brief moment of respite, and in the vain hope that they will in this way themselves escape a destiny just over the horizon, they have become its heralds. In chorus, these forces proclaim the myth that smooths the way of the conqueror and robs their fellows of the will to resist tyranny.

Abroad in the world today is a monstrous falsehood, a consummate fabrication, to which all social agencies have loaned themselves and into which most men, women and children have been seduced. In previous writings, I have called this forgery "the Eleventh Commandment"; for such, indeed, has become the injunction: You Must Adjust!

Adjustment, that synonym for conformity that comes more easily to the modern tongue, is the theme of our swan song, the piper's tune to which we dance on the brink of the abyss, the siren's melody that destroys our senses and paralyzes our wills. But this is something known only to the few who have penetrated its disguises and glimpsed the death's head beneath: for the many, adjustment is the only way of life they know, the only way of life permitted to them by the powers that govern their existences from cradle to grave.

You must adjust . . . This is the motto inscribed on the walls of every nursery, and the processes that break the spirit are initiated there. In birth begins conformity. Slowly and subtly, the infant is shaped to the prevailing pattern, his needs for love and care turned against him as weapons to en force submission. Uniqueness, individuality, difference—these are viewed with horror, even shame; at the very least, they are treated like diseases,

---

* From Robert Lindner, *Must You Conform?* (Rinehart and Company, 1956). By permission.

and a regiment of specialists are available today to "cure" the child who will not or cannot conform. Does he violate the timetable of Gesell?—Call the pediatrician, quickly! Does he contradict Spock?—Get the telephone number of the nearest child analyst! Is he unhappy? maladjusted? lonely? too noisy? too quiet? too slow? too fast?—Let us be thankful for the special schools, the nurseries and, above all, for the magazines on the rack at the corner drugstore!

You must adjust . . . This is the legend imprinted in every schoolbook, the invisible message on every blackboard. Our schools have become vast factories for the manufacture of robots. We no longer send our young to them primarily to be taught and given the tools of thought, no longer primarily to be informed and acquire knowledge; but to be "socialized"—which in the current semantic means to be regimented and made to conform. The modern report card reflects with horrible precision the preoccupations of our teachers and the philosophy of our educators. Today, in the public schools, grades are given for the "ability" of a child to "adjust" to group activities, for whether he is "liked" by others, for whether he "enjoys" the subjects taught, for whether he "gets along" with his schoolmates. In the private schools, especialy in those which designate themselves "progressive," the situation is more frightening, in some cases known to me actually revealing a cynical kind of anti-intellectualism. So the school takes up where the parent leaves off; and the children who emerge from it with a few shreds of individuality clinging to their blue jeans or bobby-socks are rare birds, indeed. But even if they manage to retain some uniqueness after passing through the mill of primary and secondary education, the young who go on to institutions of higher learning are exposed to pressures to conformity that must surely deprive them of the pitiful remnants of singularity and independence they still have.

In the colleges and universities it is not necessarily the teachers or the system of education that command adjustment, although currently, with academic freedom under attack and access to knowledge blocked, professors live in fear of saying or doing anything unorthodox. Here the Eleventh Commandment is more often enjoined by the young themselves upon themselves. By this time completely enslaved by the myth, they have acquired title to it, and now it comprises almost the whole of their philosophy and the basis of their code of conduct. This phenomenon, moreover, is a recent one, apparently dating from the last war. It has been brought to my attention by teachers in many colleges I have visited during the last few years. The collegian of today, they tell me, is hardly to be compared with the student of, say, twenty years ago. Today's undergraduate is almost a caricature of conformism. Like the new uniform he wears—the uniform of the junior executive that is *de rigueur* on Madison Avenue—his opinions, attitudes, tastes and behavior are ultra-conservative. In the world that is being born he will have little conflict about exchanging his charcoal grays for the deeper black of the élite guard.

You must adjust . . . This is the command etched above the door of every church, synagogue, cathedral, temple, and chapel. It constitutes a passport to salvation, an armor against sin: it sums the virtues and describes the vices. For there is no formal religion that does not insist, as its first requirement, on a confession of conformity. Nor is there, any longer, a religion that offers a path to Heaven other than the autobahn of submission. One and all, they have conspired, in the name of the Spirit, against the spirit of man: one and all, they have sold him into slavery. Under threat of damnation, hell-fire, purgatory, eternal non-being or even re-incarnation as some lower form of life, they have ordered him to renounce protest, to forego revolt, to be passive, to surrender. And while most of them were founded upon protest and by rebellion, these are the very things they now uniformly hold in horror. With Caesar and poverty, with war and hate, with disease and violence, with famine, crime and destruction, our priests, ministers, rabbis, imams, yogis, hierophants and lamas have signed a treaty to guarantee human tractability. All they have to sell us subverts the nature of man. Conformity, humility, acceptance—with these coins we are to pay our fares to paradise. Meanwhile, we must adjust, we must accept. And among the things we are to accept, in our time, are the following: riot guns, tear gas, trans-hydrogen explosives, character assassination, radioactive dust, tanks, nerve gases, guilt by association, atomic submarines, concentration camps, gas masks, guided missiles, censorship over thought and expression, rubber hoses, bacteriological warfare, purges, slave labor, bomb shelters, liquidations, brain-washing, Roy Cohn's opinions and Bishop Sheen's God . . .

You must adjust . . . This is the slogan emblazoned on the banners of all political parties, the inscription at the heart of all systems that contend for the loyalties of men. Our lives today, more than ever before, are governed by politics. Some observers, as a matter of fact, insist that modern man be called *homo politicus;* for there is hardly an area of existence that remains untouched by politics, hardly an act that in some way does not involve the manner in which our social affairs are regulated or the principles by which they are determined. Love, hate, friendship, enmity—these and other emotions have come to have political significance and, to some extent, to involve political choices. But there is no freedom even here, since conformity is of the essence of all the organizations that rule over us. Paradoxically, the systems which most loudly proclaim the right of human liberty and offer themselves as the instruments of change are those systems that oppress most heavily. On the way to power their sole condition is discipline, the severe regulation of mind and act so that the aim of the organization, the seizure

somehow of power, can be achieved. At this stage of struggle, the surrender
of individuality is urged or forced, but those of whom conformity is exacted
are the voluntary adherents, the dedicated, the passionate few who believe
truly in the slogans, in the high-sounding words of deliverance from slavery,
and give over their selves to the Party. Once in power, however, what has
been the dedication of a few is elevated to the religion of the many. In the
congealing amber of politics the individual is pressed and imprisoned. The
erstwhile revolutionary, no longer rebel but policeman and bureaucrat, becomes an oppressor; and against the revolution he has wrought he now
turns—or, becoming a heretic, he dies. Meanwhile, for the masses, what has
been an act of faith is now an order to surrender. Simple discipline, obedience
and passivity are not enough when the Party becomes the All, for only in
the collective orgasm of conformity can power be affirmed. Now is the day
of the Committee, the high noon of the Inquisitor, the time of the midnight
awakening, the bright lights, the spittle in the face and the breaking of bones,
the long corridor, the Confession, and the merciful bullet in the back of the
head.

You must adjust . . . This is the creed of the sciences that have sold themselves to the status quo, the prescription against perplexity, the placebo for
anxiety. For psychiatry, psychology and the medical or social arts that depend
upon them have become devil's advocates and sorcerers' apprentices of conformity. Joined in the criminal conspiracy against human nature, they have
poisoned the last oasis for the relief of man. Of all betrayals, their treachery
has been the greatest, for in them we have placed our remaining hope, and
in them, sadly, hope has fled. Equating protest with madness and non-conformity with neurosis, in the clinics and hospitals, the consulting rooms and
offices, they labor with art and skill to gut the flame that burns eternally at
the core of being. Recklessly and with the abandon of some demented sower
of noxious seeds, they fling abroad their soporifics, their sedatives, their palliative drugs and their opiate dopes, lulling the restlessness of man, besotting
him so that he sleepwalks through his days and does not recognize the doom-
writing on the wall. Or with the soft persuasion and counsel that apes
wisdom, with pamphlets and tracts and books that flow over the mind and
drown it in a rising flood of imbecilic recipes for contented existence, they
prepare his ankles for chains, his back for the brand, and his head for a
crown of thorns. But if these do not "cure" him into conformity, do not level
him into the mass, there remain in the arsenals of adjustment the ultimate
weapons: the little black box for shock "therapy" and the swift and silent
knife for psychosurgery. From the skies the lightning and the thunder are
stolen to be discharged into the brain, the seat of reason, the home of evolution and the treasury of manhood. In the convulsion that follows, resistance
ebbs and another sheep is added to the flock. Or the scalpel, quiet and sterile,
probes with unerring aim toward the target behind the eyes . . . up, down,

to one side, then the other . . . and a walking zombie, the penultimate conformist, stands where a man once stood, "cured" of his humanity.[1]

The question remains: must we conform? Or can we, somehow, resist the powers that conspire to domesticate us? Can we woo or win our liberty from an emergent dominant segment devoted to raw power? Can we, in short, recover Society for all humanity? And if so, with what arms are we to redeem our almost-lost manhood? How can we withstand the total onslaught I have hardly begun to describe? Where are we to find the weapons of resistance?

I believe that the question of conformity, in the long run, answers itself. I think that if there was a possibility, once, of a yes or no—if at one time humans could decide "we must conform" or "we must not"—that possibility has been lost in the long reaches of evolution, far back along the corridors of Time. The simple truth, stark and severe in its simplicity, is that *we cannot conform;* for it seems there is an ingredient in the composition of our cells, a chemistry in our blood, and a substance in our bones that will not suffer man to submit forever.

Built into man, the foundation of his consciousness, the source of his humanity and the vehicle of his evolution up from the muck of a steaming primeval swamp, is an instinct. I have chosen to call it the "instinct of rebellion," since it reveals itself as a drive or urge toward mastery over every obstacle, natural or man-made, that stands as a barrier between man and his distant, perhaps never-to-be-achieved but always-striven-after goals. It is this instinct that underwrites his survival, this instinct from which he derives his nature: a great and powerful dynamic that makes him what he is—restless, seeking, curious, forever unsatisfied, eternally struggling and eventually victorious. Because of the instinct of rebellion man has never been content with the limits of his body: it has led him to extend his senses almost infinitely, so that his fingers now probe space, his eyes magnify the nuclei of atoms, and his ears detect whispers from the bottoms of seas. Because of the instinct of rebellion man has never been content with the limits of his mind: it has led him to inquire its secrets of the universe, to gather and learn and manipulate the fabulous inventory of the cosmos, to seek the very mysteries of creation. Because of the instinct of rebellion, man has never been content, finally, with the limits of his life: it has caused him to deny death and to war with mortality.

---

[1] There are certain situations wherein the use of shock therapy or psychosurgery is justified by medical necessity, but occasions for resorting to such "heroic" techniques grow fewer as time and research go on. Despite this, the statistical fact is that these drastic measures are applied with increasing frequency amounting almost to abandon. One must therefore suspect that the black box and scalpel are often used to sustain the myth of the medicos' magic powers and to obtain quick and cheap—even if impermanent—"cures." Undeniably, the real if unconscious aim of many psychiatrists and physicians is to subdue the patient by such means, to force him into line, and to stamp out his distressing and stubborn tendency toward non-conformity.

Man is a rebel. He is committed by his biology *not* to conform, and herein lies the paramount reason for the awful tension he experiences today in relation to Society. Unlike other creatures of earth, man cannot submit, cannot surrender his birthright of protest, for rebellion is one of his essential dimensions. He cannot deny it and remain man. In order to live he must rebel. Only total annihilation of humanity as a species can eliminate this in-built necessity. Only with the death of the last man will the revolt that is the essence of his nature also die.

But this is cold comfort in the present when the forces of conformity have collected against the spirit of man. It offers us, in the modern world, faced as we are with these forces, little satisfaction to know that the destiny of man is to conquer and that the final victory will be his.

What about now? What about today?

I suggest that the answer to the all-important question in the here and now lies in the mobilization and implementation of the instinct of rebellion. We must, in short, become acquainted with our protestant nature and learn how to use it in our daily lives, how to express it ourselves, how to infuse it throughout all levels of our culture, and how to nourish it in our young.

Today, in the struggle between man and Society over the issue of conformity, Society is winning because man, the rebel, does not yet know how to rebel successfully—positively. His protest is expressed in negative forms, in ways which may discharge somewhat the energy of his rebellious instinct but which yield him little profit; indeed, in ways which are often actually harmful to himself and to the community. Non-conformity, as it is now conceived, is largely exhibited as psychosis, neurosis, crime, and psychosomatic illness; or it appears as pitifully hopeless and vain little defiances of convention and custom in dress, manner, opinion and taste. All of these ways are negative, unproductive, totally inadequate to meet the situation man faces.

The productive way toward non-conformity is the way of positive rebellion, of protest that at once affirms the rebellious nature of man *and* the fundamental human values. These values reside in the common treasury of humanity. They form the basic aspirations of all humans everywhere and are expressed most clearly in the great documents and contracts—such as our own Bill of Rights—which men have seen fit to declare from time to time. *Rebellion and protest in their name, and conducted in a fashion which does not in any way violate their spirit, is positive rebellion, authentic rebellion.*

Our instruction in the methods of positive rebellion, of affirmative protest, must come from two sources—one inner, one outer. The first of these, the inner source, is the slower and less dependable one. It requires that men themselves awaken to the knowledge, first, that rebellion is native in them and that there exist positive ways of protest which await discovery. The inspiration and example of the all-too-few positive rebels in our culture may assist this admittedly protracted and precarious self-awakening by contagion.

The outer source of instruction is more rapid and more sure. It consists of direct tuition in positive rebellion by those to whom we have always looked, and will always look, for edification: our psychologists, educators, and artists.

While it is true, as I have charged, that these guides in human affairs have always identified with—and in some cases sold themselves to—the emerging dominant segment; and while it is true that in the current crisis they have shamefully ranged themselves on the side of conformity, it is no less true that they have done so largely out of desperation and ignorance. They have not known about the instinct at the very navel of man's being, and in their unawareness have been forced into the position they now occupy. But if once they become informed, if once they learn about the existence of such an instinct and its cosmic possibilities, it is unavoidable that the motives which inspired them toward the vocation they practice will fuse with this knowledge and become animated by it. In this manner will the methods of positive rebellion, of life-affirming protest, be explored and spread about.

The answer to the question, "Must we conform?" is a resounding No! *No* . . . not only because, in the end, we are creatures who cannot conform and who are destined to triumph over the forces of conformity; but *no* because there is an alternate way of life available to us here and now. It is the way of positive rebellion, the path of creative protest, the road of productive revolt. This is the way natural to man, the way he must and will take to achieve the values he aspires to just because he is human. By taking it, man can find the future of which he dreams, the future in which he will achieve his far, high, and unforeseeable goals. . . .

Chapter IV

LIBERTY AND LOYALTY

Important as the right of revolution is, especially in the Anglo-American view of government, there must be something else, if life is to be not only interesting, but also happy. Liberty and the pursuit of happiness go together, because each depends on the other.

Friedrich Schiller, the great German poet, sang that "freedom is only in the land of dreams." Others have agreed with Schiller that at best freedom is an illusion, and at worst, licence and anarchy. Where there has been no solid experience of freedom, liberty has often been confused, even by great minds like Goethe, with submission to laws—physical laws of nature or political laws of society.

The Greeks showed their genius of originality in matters political when they defined liberty essentially as the right to participate in public affairs. Only beasts or gods lived, according to Aristotle, outside the confines of the sheltering city; thoughtful Greek statesmen, like Pericles, refused to apply the concept of liberty to the arbitrary rule of the tyrant or to the individual outside of the social group, facing the universe in his pitiable loneliness. As true "political animals" (Aristotle), the Greeks could not think of freedom as a purely individual affair, unrelated to the quality of a person as a member of his organized political community.

With the triumph of Christianity, and its emphasis on the individual soul and its relations to God, Western man lost, for good or bad, the unconscious, almost naïve, sense of total integration into the social group. The very duality of the individual versus the state (one of the key issues of all modern political philosophy) presupposes the concepts of individual and state. Both are historically, post-Renaissance ideas. The modern concept of the individual was born in the great revolutionary movements of the sixteenth century— economic individualism as capitalism, religious individualism as Protestantism, and cultural individualism as scientific learning. Likewise, the modern national state is only a product of the last four centuries (in Germany and Italy, of only two or three generations).

In the changed circumstances, economic and political, of the modern state, the concept of liberty tended to assume, more and more, the negative emphasis of the *absence of restraint* rather than the positive stress on participation in public affairs. In the English-speaking nations this view of liberty was especially current from the eighteenth to the late nineteenth century.

French political thought has never quite followed this Anglo-American tradition, possibly because the economic individualism of capitalism never flourished in France with the same thoroughness as in England and America. Jean Jacques Rousseau's *Social Contract,* published twenty-seven years before the French Revolution, has been one of the most influential books in history. The opening sentence, "Man is born free; and everywhere he is in chains," proclaims the voice of a fearless challenger who had the intellectual gift to think clearly, as well as the artistic genius to express his mind dramatically and imaginatively. Outside the English-speaking countries, Rousseau has probably had more popular philosophical appeal than any other political writer of the last two centuries. The young Continental European or Latin American discovers the idea of liberty through Rousseau rather than through Locke or John Stuart Mill.

Rousseau's theory of the social contract is one of the most ingenious doctrinal attempts to base political obligation on *consent.* Whether Rousseau was in possession of all the anthropological facts in describing the "state of nature" is immaterial, when compared with the timeless moral truths that he expressed about the nature of the state. What makes *The Social Contract* one of the most complex and baffling documents is the fact that democrats, as well as some Nazis, Fascists and Communists, have seen in it the rays of their particular light. Rousseau's central idea of the "general will" has frequently attracted the totalitarian mentality. Some of this confusion is due, perhaps, to Rousseau's failure to distinguish clearly the "general will" from the "will of all." Yet Rousseau is one of the few eighteenth-century libertarian writers who managed to go beyond individualism unlimited, who captured the spirit of "We, the people. . . ." Without this spirit of communal solidarity, democratic institutions are bound to lead from selfish individual interest and group greed to social chaos and dissolution. To say, as Rousseau did, that "the general will considers only the common interest," while "the will of all takes private interests into account, and is no more than a sum of particular wills," is a statement of the problem rather than its solution. Still, the statement is important enough. Difficult as it may be to define what the public interest is in a concrete issue, thoughtful citizens in a working democracy are aware that some practical way must be found to transcend purely private, or group, interests. In labor relations boards, e.g., we have long accepted the principle that in addition to representatives of labor and capital, the public view must be reflected by a "public member," who has the complex task of defending the "general will" or interest of the whole community.

Rousseau recognizes that in direct popular government unanimity is, in practice, impossible, and that the vote of the majority binds the minority.

The question of how the minority can be free and yet be bound to obey the majority is rejected by Rousseau as wrongly formulated. When a citizen objects to a proposed law in the popular assembly and finds himself in a minority, he does not thereby lose his freedom, for his minority vote merely proves that he did not recognize the General Will, rather than that the majority, as such, has a right to rule over him. Rousseau cautiously adds that this conception of freedom of the individual "presupposes, indeed, that all the qualities of the General Will still reside in the majority: when they cease to do so, whatever side a man may take, liberty is no longer possible."

Obeying the General Will is thus the expression of the moral freedom of the individual, and if he refuses to obey, he may be compelled to do so: "This means nothing less than that he will be forced to be free." Here Rousseau revives his basic distinction between the apparent liberty of man in the state of nature, which actually is enslavement to selfish appetites, and his moral liberty in civil society, which consists in obeying laws, general in scope and origin, which he, as a member of the body politic, has helped to make. This extreme formulation of Rousseau—that *man can be forced to be free*—could easily be used later by Hegel and the modern worshippers of the state. Yet the master conception of *The Social Contract* is a community of free men living in a small state in which democracy can be practiced directly by the people, a community of men who see in freedom not only an invitation to personal enjoyment and advantage but also to shared responsibility for the welfare of the whole. Rousseau's stress on the small political unit as the only one suited to direct and genuine democracy may acquire new significance as we seek to discover the means by which we can create small geographical and functional areas of self-government within the overly impersonal methods of large-scale technology and government.

Turning from Rousseau to John Stuart Mill's essay *On Liberty* (1859), we move from brilliance to balance, from the general to the specific, from glittering *esprit* to solid common sense. With the Periclean funeral address and Lincoln's Gettysburg Address, *On Liberty* probably ranks as one of the greatest testimonies of the liberal faith. Liberalism as a way of life rather than as a set of governmental procedures—this is the spirit captured by John Stuart Mill in his immortal essay.

It is a tribute to Mill's farsightedness that in writing *On Liberty* he thought of the future rather than of his own time, which was one of the most liberal periods in all recorded history. Though not foreseeing the precise phenomenon of twentieth-century totalitarianism, Mill accurately analyzed some of the principal social and intellectual forces that prepared the ground for it as well as for the spread of greater conformity in the established democratic societies. The greatest force that operates against liberty in the modern world is the fact that now people "read the same things, listen to the same things, see the same things, go to the same places, have their hopes and fears directed to the same objects, have the same rights and liberties, and the same means of asserting them." He foresaw, possibly even more clearly than Alexis de Tocqueville, that industrialization—a social and economic process—is more important as a cause of levelling conformity than democracy—an essentially political process. The process of conformity reaches, according to Mill, the last stage when the pressures of society are no longer followed by the individual through weakness or acquiescence, but when they are so completely assimilated to his own moral code that he is no longer aware that dictates and pressures of the group are imposed upon him.

Like Tocqueville, Mill explodes the illusion that the evolution of government from authoritarianism to popular self-rule necessarily solves the problem of personal liberty. The tyranny of prevailing public opinion in democracies may be just as harmful to individuality and variety as the formal, legal oppression in non-democratic regimes. Protection against political tyranny is therefore not enough; it must be supplemented by protection against the tyranny of prevailing opinion and feeling. Unless *absolute* freedom of opinion—scientific, moral, and religious—is guaranteed, a society is not completely free. It makes little difference to Mill's argument how small the dissenting minority is: "If all mankind minus one were of one opinion, and only one person were of the contrary opinion, mankind would be no more justified in silencing that one person, than he, if he had the power, would be justified in silencing mankind." For those who are concerned lest such emphasis on personal liberty interfere with national welfare and greatness, Mill has the following reminder at the end of *On Liberty:* "A state which dwarfs its men, in order that they may be more docile instruments in its hands even for beneficial purposes—will find that with small men no great thing can really be accomplished."

The centenary of the publication of *On Liberty* has been fittingly celebrated in Isaiah Berlin's *Two Concepts of Liberty* (1958), destined to be a classic in its field for a long time to come. Much shorter than *On Liberty,* Berlin's essay barely examines one of the central topics of *On Liberty:* the proper boundaries between the discretion and freedom of the individual and the needs and demands of society, particularly in matters social and economic. *Two Concepts of Liberty* concentrates on the *meaning* of freedom from the viewpoint of analysis and history rather than of morals and ethics—although Berlin's conclusions clearly point to an ethics which is very much akin to that of Mill. Berlin sees in the conception of freedom two main meanings, often not recognized or confused. First there is the *negative* concept of liberty that tries to answer the question, "How much control?" By contrast, the *positive* concept of liberty seeks to answer the question, "Who is to exercise control?" The negative concept of liberty is often expressed as "freedom from," whereas the positive concept of liberty is "freedom to." Politically and historically, the distinction between the negative concept of liberty as absence of constraint and the positive concept of liberty as self-government roughly coincides with the distinction between liberalism and democracy.

The questions inherent in the negative and positive concepts of liberty are good questions, and the answers provided by liberalism and democracy may be good answers, but things that are separately good do not always mix well or easily. As long as there was a common enemy, such as monarchical or aristocratic privilege or church control of thought, liberalism and democracy could work closely together, as is the actual record of historical experience. But when the common enemy had passed, incongruities began to show up. The Constitution of the United States was originally concerned with the problem of democracy; the later grafting of the Bill of Rights onto the Constitution provided the liberal element. The issue of whether the American political system is a democracy or a republic, while expressing conflicts of material interest, also reflects the philosophical conflict of whether the liberal or the democratic element is predominant.

The pull of the numerical majority has always been toward the positive conception of liberty, or democracy. The negative conception of liberty, or liberalism, demands the maximum amount of non-interference with the individual compatible with the minimum demands of society. It seems unlikely, writes Berlin, "that this demand for liberty has ever been made by any but a small minority of highly civilized and self-conscious human beings. The bulk of humanity has certainly at most times been prepared to sacrifice this to other goals: security, status, prosperity, power, virtue, rewards in the next world; or justice, equality, fraternity, and many other values which appear wholly, or in part, incompatible with the attainment of the greatest degree of individual liberty, and certainly do not need it as a pre-condition for their own realization." The psychologists have not said the last word on this matter as yet, but it appears that psychologically the negative conception of liberty makes very heavy demands on the individual as an autonomous, mature, and responsible being, capable of standing on his own feet and making his own decisions, and morally and socially self-sufficient to a larger extent than under the positive conception of liberty, which caters to, or at least takes into account, man's dependence on others, although such dependence may be concealed under terms like "equality," "cooperation," "togetherness," or "team-work."

When does freedom become "licence"? Are there any limits at all to freedom of thought and (if the latter is not to remain a monologue or solitary communion with the cosmos) freedom of speech, including all the other freedoms of communication? Although the Constitution of the United States expressly protects freedom of speech, two-thirds of the American people believed, according to polls in 1954 (see Samuel A. Stouffer, *Communism, Conformity, and Civil Liberties,* 1955), that some opinions (such as atheist or communist) should not be permitted public expression. Only one-third of those polled held firm to the belief that there should be no limitation on speech in the United States, even for persons who hold "extremist" views on religion or politics.

Of the fifty states of the Union, thirty-three have passed "sedition" or "criminal syndicalism" laws, mostly in the years immediately following the First World War; under them, men were sentenced to long prison terms for selling, or even merely possessing, so-called "radical" books or pamphlets. One of the most famous cases dealing with freedom of opinion is *Abrams* v. *United States* (1919). On August 23, 1918, an obscure anarchist, named Abrams, distributed some leaflets in a poor section of New York, in which he attacked the United States government for sending troops and munitions to Russia to fight the Bolshevik government that had been established in November, 1917. Abrams was charged with violation of the Espionage Act of 1918, specifically with having hindered the war effort of the United States against Germany, by publishing leaflets intending to cause strikes and revolts. Abrams, aged twenty-nine, was sentenced to twenty years' imprisonment by a federal district court. His four codefendants, also completely unknown Socialist and anarchist youths, received prison terms ranging from three to twenty years. In 1919 the case came to the Supreme Court, and seven out of the nine judges upheld the sentence of the lower court. Mr. Justice Holmes wrote the dissenting opinion, in which Mr. Justice Brandeis concurred. Holmes denied that society has the right to punish opinions unless they "so imminently threaten immediate interference with the lawful and pressing purposes of the law that an immediate check is required to save the country." Holmes had expressed the nature of this test in even sharper terms in *Schenck* v. *United States* (1919): "The question in every case is whether the words used are used in such circumstances and are of such a nature as to create a clear and present danger that they will bring about the substantive evils that Congress has a right to prevent. It is a question of proximity and degree." Holmes thus denied that words are punishable because they might incite to violence in an undefined future. In the *Abrams* case the test of "imminent threat" seemed to indicate to Holmes that Abrams was unjustly punished: "Now nobody can suppose that the surreptitious publishing of a silly leaflet by an unknown man, without more, would present any immediate danger that its opinions would hinder the success of the government arms or have any appreciable tendency to do so." Far from being pro-German, Abrams had bitterly denounced German militarism in his leaflets. Holmes finally asserted this: "In this case sentences of twenty years imprisonment have been imposed for the publishing of two leaflets that I believe the defendants had as much right to publish as the Government has to publish the Constitution of the United States now vainly invoked by them." As time went on, more and more people realized the folly of the Anglo-French-American-Japanese expedition to Russia in 1918; in 1929 Secretary of War Newton D. Baker wrote that "the expedition was nonsense from the beginning."

Democracies, it seems, therefore, are not immune from the danger of oppressing freedom of opinion and speech in the name of patriotism, loyalty to democratic institutions, and fear of nonconformity. This is why Mill's warning is perennially timely that no society is "completely free" in which "absolute freedom of opinion and sentiment on all subjects, practical or speculative, scientific, moral or theological" does not exist "absolute and un-qualified." And those who justify the right of the majority to persecute dissenters on the ground that majorities are right should reflect on Mill's warning that "ages are no more infallible than individuals."

In "normal" times, there is a good chance for liberty and loyalty to be conceived and practiced in a more generous and broad-minded manner. The real test of how deeply a nation is committed to liberty comes in times of stress and tension. During World War II, the governments and peoples of both Britain and the United States maintained a remarkably high degree of free speech and opinion, and the record in both countries was much better than during World War I. When World War II came to an end, the hope was widely expressed that the defeat of the Fascist Axis (Germany-Japan-Italy) would make possible a new era of liberty and democracy throughout the world. Yet the war was hardly over when the alliance between the Western democracies and the Soviet Union dissolved. Cooperation was re-placed by distrust and recrimination, and the high hopes for a lasting peace were shattered by the stark reality of aggressive communist imperialism. This background of international tension has been the primary cause of the pressure for more uniformity and orthodoxy in democratic nations. *Loyalty* became the key concept in an era of fear and frustration.

Even before the United States was born, Edmund Burke had referred to the citizens of the North American colonies as "dissenters from dissent": whereas the English had established in religion and politics a tradition of dissent, the Americans, according to Burke, went even further, by being "dissenters from dissent," and Burke therefore uttered in his speeches on conciliation with the American colonies the prophetic warning that govern-ment in America could not be based on loyalty which was the result of fear and repression rather than right and liberty.

Among the founders of the Republic, no one emphasized the concept of revolution and dissent more vigorously and consistently than Thomas Jeffer-son. Julian P. Boyd, the outstanding Jefferson scholar of our time, and editor of the first complete edition of his Papers, appraises the issue of liberty and loyalty in "Subversive of What?" (1948), taking an actual incident in Jeffer-son's life as the starting point. The incident related to the attempted official banning, in Philadelphia, of a book as subversive and blasphemous, and in our present age of "book-burning" the story told by Boyd is of particular interest. Jefferson asks whether in the United States of America we are to have "a censor whose imprimatur shall say what books may be sold, and what we may buy," and "whose foot is to be the measure to which ours are all to be cut or stretched." As far as political criticism in general is con-cerned, there are always those who, particularly in time of crisis, will allow criticism of details but not of fundamentals. Here, Jefferson's words from his First Inaugural Address will stand as a permanent reminder: "If there be any among us who wish to dissolve this union or to change its republican form, let them stand undisturbed as monuments of the safety with which error of opinion may be tolerated where reason is left free to combat it."

Boyd's discussion of loyalty in the light of American values and traditions is tremendously significant, and his analyses of the meaning of loyalty are of profound relevance as guideposts in the formulation and appraisal of public policies dealing with the loyalty issue. Yet there still remains the practical issue of what to do with Communists and Communist fellow-travelers in public life, particularly in public employment. Morris L. Ernst, an American lawyer long associated with the cause of civil liberty, proposes "Some Affirmative Suggestions for a Loyalty Program" (1950) on the basic assumption that communism in the United States is a real problem, and that it must be coped with in concrete terms rather than in philosophical generalities. The war with communism, whether hot or cold, "is a war for the minds of men, and we can lose it without losing a life." While disloyalty and espionage are not new in American history, the nature of Communist political activity is different from that of traditional political parties and groups, inasmuch as communism operates with "a new kind of organized stealth and anonymity." The open Communist is much less of a problem than the crypto-Communists. In studying antidemocratic political groups, Fascist or Communist, in the United States, Ernst is struck by the fact that such organizations never make full disclosures to the American people, whether it be with regard to the source of income, lists of members, officers, or activities. Ernst therefore proposes that *publicity* be used as the principal weapon in fighting antidemocratic subversive groups. Organizations which refuse full disclosure of their finances, members, and officers should be put on the list of subversive organizations, provided they have had the opportunity to present their case in an open hearing. Only individuals associated with such secret subversive organizations should be affected by the loyalty or security program; no person could claim innocence of association in the case of a political group which freely chooses the undercover of secrecy for its activities in preference to the aboveboard openness of legality. However, in following the British approach to the problem of loyalty and security in public employment, Ernst proposes that the application of such a program be limited to "sensitive" agencies or jobs, in which loyalty and security are integral elements of employment, as in the Atomic Energy Commission, the Departments of Defense, or in highly confidential scientific research. "I would not want a person of even a potential division of loyalty," Ernst writes, "to be employed cleaning out the trash baskets at the White House, but I should imagine no one would object if such a person were given a job picking up leaves in a public park in Washington." The need to distinguish between "sensitive" and "non-sensitive" jobs in public employment was finally recognized by the Supreme Court in *Cole* v. *Young* (1956), ruling that the security program for federal employees was applicable only to "sensitive" positions. Since half the number of persons dismissed under the security program had held "non-sensitive" jobs, the decision of the Supreme Court had immediate practical results; more importantly from an over-all viewpoint, it helped to create a new, and more rational, climate in matters relating to loyalty and security in the government.

Ernst's stress on publicity as the principal weapon in fighting Communist or Fascist organizations in a democracy, in the security area as well as in other aspects of public policy, is supported by considerable experience, although there is no one panacea in fighting subversion in a democracy. It is a matter of record that no country was ever brought under the rule of communism by open and legal means; conspiracy and terror always played an important part in preparing the ground for eventual Communist victory, and conspiracy and terror have also played equally important roles in Communist international policy. As far as Communist theory and long-term strategy are concerned, Lenin wrote as early as in 1902 (in *What Is to Be Done?*) that the open Communist party and trade union organizations must be led by small groups of professional revolutionaries, and that such groups— the real policy-makers in the movement—must be "as secret as possible." In later years, too, Lenin frequently reiterated the point that Communists must combine illegal with legal work, even where Communist parties are legally permitted.

In theory and practice, secrecy has thus played a key role in the spread of Communist activity, and democratic nations have been forced, as a matter of practical necessity—nay, of survival—to cope with the problem of Communist conspiracy in a manner to be determined by the law. Two conflicting values are at stake: first, *liberty,* the heart and life-blood of democracy; second, *security,* without which liberty might easily be destroyed. In the United States, the curbing of communism by legal means is based on the Smith Act of 1940, sections 2 and 3 of which provide as follows:

"Sec. 2: (a) It shall be unlawful for any person—

      (1) to knowingly or wilfully advocate, abet, advise, or teach the duty, necessity, desirability, or propriety of overthrowing or destroying any government in the United States by force or violence, or by the assassination of any officer of such government.

      (2) with intent to cause the overthrow or destruction of any government in the United States, to print, publish, edit, issue, circulate, sell, distribute, or publicly display any written or printed matter advocating, advising, or teaching the duty, necessity, desirability, or propriety of overthrowing or destroying any government in the United States by force or violence;

(3) to organize or help to organize any society, group, or assembly of persons who teach, advocate, or encourage the overthrow or destruction of any government in the United States by force or violence; or to be or become a member of, or affiliate with, any such society, group, or assembly of persons, knowing the purpose thereof.

Sec. 3: (b) It shall be unlawful for any person to commit, or to conspire to commit, any of the acts prohibited by the provisions of this title."

In 1948, eleven Communist leaders were indicted for violation of the conspiracy provisions of the Smith Act. The trial, one of the most important political trials in American history, lasted over nine months, the record running up to sixteen thousand pages. Finally, the Supreme Court took up the case, and decided against the Communist leaders on June 4, 1951. The main constitutional issue involved was whether sections 2 and 3 of the Smith Act violated the First and Fifth Amendments. The First Amendment provides that Congress shall make no law "abridging the freedom of speech, or of the press; or the right of the people peaceably to assemble, and to petition the Government for a redress of grievances." Under the Fifth Amendment, no person "shall be deprived of life, liberty, or property, without due process of law."

Before the *Dennis* case of 1951 (involving Dennis and ten other top Communist leaders), the Supreme Court had on several occasions dealt with communism, but always as a side issue. The *Dennis* case was the first in which the Supreme Court decided whether Communist organization and propaganda enjoy the protection of free speech of the First and Fifth Amendments, or whether Congress has the authority to outlaw them. Holding the Smith Act constitutional by a majority of six to two, the Supreme Court finally determined an issue of the highest political and constitutional significance. As can be seen from the text of the majority and minority opinions, passions can run as high inside the highest court of the land as in the less aloof atmosphere of the marketplace outside.

A central concept in the conflicting opinions of the Court was the *clear and present danger* doctrine, as expressed by Mr. Justice Holmes in the *Schenck* case in 1919. "The question in every case," Holmes wrote, "is whether the words used are used in such circumstances and are of such a nature as to create a clear and present danger that they will bring about the substantive evils that Congress has a right to prevent. It is a question of proximity and degree." Writing for the majority in the *Dennis* case, Chief Justice Vinson declared that the Communist conspiracy created a " 'clear and present danger' of an attempt to overthrow the Government by force and violence." However, he went, in his opinion, beyond the "clear and present danger" doctrine by accepting a new, and more restrictive, doctrine of *probable danger,* as expressed by Chief Judge Learned Hand of the Court of Appeals in deciding against the eleven Communist leaders: "In each case (courts) must ask whether the gravity of the 'evil,' discounted by its improbability, justifies such invasion of free speech as is necessary to avoid the danger." Mr. Justice Jackson in his concurring opinion denied that the "clear and present danger" test could properly be applied to this case; otherwise Communist plotting would be protected during its period of incubation, and the Government could move "only after imminent action is manifest, when it would, of course, be too late."

In his dissenting opinion, Mr. Justice Black stresses that the Communist leaders were not charged with any nonverbal acts designed to overthrow the government, and that the outlawry of verbal expressions of revolution constitutes a drastic qualification or complete repudiation of the "clear and present danger" doctrine. Mr. Justice Douglas, in his dissenting opinion, concedes that "the freedom to speak is not absolute," and accepts, in general, the Holmesian principle of the "clear and present danger" doctrine. However, whereas Holmes left the meaning of his principle rather vague, Douglas quotes approvingly the formulation by Mr. Justice Brandeis in *Whitney* v. *California* (1927) that "no danger flowing from speech can be deemed clear and present, unless the incidence of the evil apprehended is so imminent that it may befall before there is opportunity for full discussion." Following this Brandeisian concept, Douglas argues that free speech has destroyed communism as an effective political force in the United States, and that it is "inconceivable" that advocates of Communist revolution in this country would have any success. Finally, Black expressed the hope that "in calmer times, when present pressures, passions, and fears subside, this or some later Court will restore the First Amendment liberties to the high preferred place where they belong in a free society."

This hope was fulfilled—almost, but not quite completely—six years later in the case against fourteen West Coast Communist leaders (*Yates* v. *United States,* 1957). Virtually reversing is position of 1951, the Supreme Court ruled in the *Yates* case that a distinction must be made "between advocacy of forcible overthrow as an abstract doctrine and advocacy of action to that end," and that "mere membership or the holding of office in the Communist Party" did not constitute sufficient evidence of the intent to overthrow the government by force. "The essential distinction," the Court said, "is that those to whom the advocacy is addressed must be urged to do something, now or in the future, rather than merely to believe in something." The mere holding of revolutionary beliefs or even membership (or office) in a revolutionary party is not enough: to be convicted under the Smith Act, the Court seemed to say, *individual unlawful acts* must be proved.

While the decision in *Yates* did not explicitly attack the constitutionality of the Smith Act, it marked, at least, a return to the "clear and present danger" doctrine that had been strongly modified, if not abandoned, in the *Dennis* case. Thus, the *Yates* decision helped to reestablish the traditional democratic (and American) concept under which all doctrines, including revolutionary ones, may be lawfully advocated and propagated.

It is noteworthy that this new approach (new in relation to the *Dennis* case, but traditional in relation to the long stream of constitutional jurisprudence) of the Supreme Court to the issue of political liberty and freedom of expression occurred four years after the end of the Korean war, nearly three years after the Senate's censure of Senator Joseph McCarthy, and one month after the latter's death. Equally noteworthy is the fact that of the nine justices of the Supreme Court six concurred in the decision, whereas only one (Mr. Justice Clark) dissented (two did not participate in the decision). Justices Black and Douglas, who in 1951 were the only dissenters in *Dennis,* were not satisfied that the Court majority in *Yates* had fully adopted their viewpoint. Mr. Justice Black (with whom Mr. Justice Douglas joined), wrote a separate opinion containing the following passage: "Unless there is complete freedom for expression of all ideas, whether we like them or not, concerning the way government should be run and who shall run it, I doubt if any views in the long run can be secured against the censor. The First Amendment provides the only kind of security system that can preserve a free government—one that leaves the way wide open for people to favor, discuss, advocate, or incite causes and doctrines however obnoxious and antagonistic such views may be to the rest of us." The fourteen West Coast Communist leaders were charged with the intent of foisting upon the United States "a despicable form of authoritarian government in which voices criticizing the existing order are summarily silenced. I fear that the present type of prosecutions are more in line with the philosophy of authoritarian government than with that expressed by our First Amendment." Whereas the majority implies that the Smith Act is constitutional but that a distinction has to be drawn between advocacy of forcible overthrow as an abstract doctrine and advocacy inciting to action, Black and Douglas explicitly state that the Smith Act is unconstitutional because it is in violation of the First Amendment, for the latter "forbids Congress to punish people for talking about public affairs, whether or not such discussion incites to action, legal or illegal."

The history of the Supreme Court is full of instances in which the minority of yesterday becomes the majority of today. The minority viewpoint of Justices Black and Douglas did not fully convert the majority in 1957, particularly on the issue of the constitutionality of the Smith Act; but the majority in the *Yates* case at least *interpreted* the Smith Act in such a restrictive way as to make it virtually inoperable, thus satisfying most (though not all) defenders of the traditional doctrine of individual freedom as the chief aim of the Constitution.

JEAN JACQUES ROUSSEAU

1. *Freedom and the General Will**

Man is born free; and everywhere he is in chains. One thinks himself the master of others, and still remains a greater slave than they. How did this change come about? I do not know. What can make it legitimate? That question I think I can answer.

If I took into account only force, and the effects derived from it, I should say: "As long as a people is compelled to obey, and obeys, it does well; as soon as it can shake off the yoke, and shakes it off, it does still better, for, regaining its liberty by the same right as took it away, either it is justified in resuming it, or there was no justification for those who took it away." But the social order is a sacred right which is the basis of all other rights. Nevertheless, this right does not come from nature, and must therefore be founded on conventions.

The strongest is never strong enough to be always the master, unless he transforms strength into right, and obedience into duty. Hence the right of the strongest, which, though to all seeming meant ironically, is really laid down as a fundamental principle. But are we never to have an explanation of this phrase? Force is a physical power, and I fail to see what moral effect it can have. To yield to force is an act of necessity, not of will—at the most, an act of prudence. In what sense can it be a duty?

Suppose for a moment that this so-called "right" exists. I maintain that the sole result is a mass of inexplicable nonsense. For, if force creates right, the effect changes with the cause: every force that is greater than the first succeeds to its right. As soon as it is possible to disobey with impunity, disobedience is legitimate; and, the strongest being always in the right, the only thing that matters is to act so as to become the strongest. But what kind of right is that which perishes when force fails? If we must obey perforce, there is no need to obey because we ought; and if we are not forced to obey, we are under no obligation to do so. Clearly, the word "right" adds nothing to force: in this connection, it means absolutely nothing.

Obey the powers that be. If this means yield to force, it is a good precept, but superfluous: I can answer for its never being violated. All power comes from God, I admit; but so does all sickness: does that mean that we are

* From Jean Jacques Rousseau, *The Social Contract* (1762; Everyman's Library, E. P. Dutton & Co., Inc., 1938). By permission.

forbidden to call in the doctor? A brigand surprises me at the edge of a wood: must I not merely surrender my purse on compulsion; but, even if I could withhold it, am I in conscience bound to give it up? For certainly the pistol he holds is also a power.

Let us then admit that force does not create right, and that we are obliged to obey only legitimate powers.

Since no man has a natural authority over his fellow, and force creates no right, we must conclude that conventions form the basis of all legitimate authority among men.

If an individual, says Grotius, can alienate his liberty and make himself the slave of a master, why could not a whole people do the same and make itself subject to a king? There are in this passage plenty of ambiguous words which would need explaining; but let us confine ourselves to the word *alienate*. To alienate is to give or to sell. Now, a man who becomes the slave of another does not give himself; he sells himself, at the least for his subsistence: but for what does a people sell itself? A king is so far from furnishing his subjects with their subsistence that he gets his own only from them; and, according to Rabelais, kings do not live on nothing. Do subjects then give their persons on condition that the king takes their goods also? I fail to see what they have left to preserve.

It will be said that the despot assures his subjects civil tranquillity. Granted; but what do they gain, if the wars his ambition brings down upon them, his insatiable avidity, and the vexatious conduct of his ministers press harder on them than their own dissensions would have done? What do they gain, if the very tranquillity they enjoy is one of their miseries? Tranquillity is found also in dungeons; but is that enough to make them desirable places to live in? The Greeks imprisoned in the cave of the Cyclops lived there very tranquilly, while they were awaiting their turn to be devoured.

To say that a man gives himself gratuitously, is to say what is absurd and inconceivable; such an act is null and illegitimate, from the mere fact that he who does it is out of his mind. To say the same of a whole people is to suppose a people of madmen; and madness creates no right.

Even if each man could alienate himself, he could not alienate his children: they are born men and free; their liberty belongs to them, and no one but they has the right to dispose of it. Before they come to years of discretion, the father can, in their name, lay down conditions for their preservation and well-being, but he cannot give them irrevocably and without conditions: such a gift is contrary to the ends of nature, and exceeds the rights of paternity. It would therefore be necessary, in order to legitimise an arbitrary government, that in every generation the people should be in a position to accept or reject it; but, were this so, the government would be no longer arbitrary.

To renounce liberty is to renounce being a man, to surrender the rights of humanity and even its duties. For him who renounces everything no indemnity is possible. Such a renunciation is incompatible with man's nature; to remove all liberty from his will is to remove all morality from his acts. Finally, it is an empty and contradictory convention that sets up, on the one side, absolute authority, and, on the other, unlimited obedience. It is not clear that we can be under no obligation to a person from whom we have the right to exact everything? Does not this condition alone, in the absence of equivalence or exchange, in itself involve the nullity of the act? For what right can my slave have against me, when all that he has belongs to me, and, his right being mine, this right of mine against myself is a phrase devoid of meaning?

The passage from the state of nature to the civil state produces a very remarkable change in man, by substituting justice for instinct in his conduct, and giving his actions the morality they had formerly lacked. Then only, when the voice of duty takes the place of physical impulses and right of appetite, does man, who so far had considered only himself, find that he is forced to act on different principles, and to consult his reason before listening to his inclinations. Although, in this state, he deprives himself of some advantages which he got from nature, he gains in return others so great, his faculties are so stimulated and developed, his ideas so extended, his feelings so ennobled, and his whole soul so uplifted, that, did not the abuses of this new condition often degrade him below that which he left, he would be bound to bless continually the happy moment which took him from it for ever, and, instead of a stupid and unimaginative animal, made him an intelligent being and a man.

Let us draw up the whole account in terms easily commensurable. What man loses by the social contract is his natural liberty and an unlimited right to everything he tries to get and succeeds in getting; what he gains is civil liberty and the proprietorship of all he possesses. If we are to avoid mistakes in weighing one against the other, we must clearly distinguish natural liberty, which is bounded only by the strength of the individual, from civil liberty, which is limited by the general will; and possession, which is merely the effect of force or the right of the first occupier, from property, which can be founded only on a positive title.

We might, over and above all this, add, to what man acquires in the civil state, moral liberty, which alone makes him truly master of himself; for the mere impulse of appetite is slavery, while obedience to a law which we prescribe to ourselves is liberty.

The general will is always right and tends to the public advantage; but it does not follow that the deliberations of the people are always equally correct. Our will is always for our own good, but we do not always see what that is; the people is never corrupted, but it is often deceived, and on such occasions only does it seem to will what is bad.

There is often a great deal of difference between the will of all and the general will; the latter considers only the common interest, while the former takes private interest into account, and is no more than a sum of particular wills: but take away from these same wills the pluses and minuses that cancel one another, and the general will remains as the sum of the differences.

If, when the people, being furnished with adequate information, held its deliberations, the citizens had no communication one with another, the grand total of the small differences would always give the general will, and the decision would always be good. But when factions arise, and partial associations are formed at the expense of the great association, the will of each of these associations becomes general in relation to its members, while it remains particular in relation to the State: it may then be said that there are no longer as many votes as there are men, but only as many as there are associations. The differences become less numerous and give a less general result. Lastly, when one of these associations is so great as to prevail over all the rest, the result is no longer a sum of small differences, but a single difference; in this case there is no longer a general will, and the opinion which prevails is purely particular.

It is therefore essential, if the general will is to be able to express itself, that there should be no partial society within the State, and that each citizen should think only his own thoughts.

As nature has set bounds to the stature of a well-made man, and, outside those limits, makes nothing but giants or dwarfs, similarly, for the constitution of a State to be at its best, it is possible to fix limits that will make it neither too large for good government, nor too small for self-maintenance. In every body politic there is a *maximum* strength which it cannot exceed and which it only loses by increasing in size. Every extension of the social tie means its relaxation; and, generally speaking, a small State is stronger in proportion than a great one.

A thousand arguments could be advanced in favour of this principle. First, long distances make administration more difficult, just as a weight becomes heavier at the end of a longer lever. Administration therefore becomes more and more burdensome as the distance grows greater; for, in the first place, each city has its own, which is paid for by the people: each district its own, still paid for by the people: then comes each province, and then the great governments, satrapies, and vice-royalties, always costing more the higher you go, and always at the expense of the unfortunate people. Last of all comes the supreme administration, which eclipses all the rest. All these overcharges are a continual drain upon the subjects; so far from being better governed by all these different orders, they are worse governed than if there were only a single authority over them. In the meantime, there scarce remain resources enough to meet emergencies; and, when recourse must be had to these, the State is always on the eve of destruction.

This is not all; not only has the government less vigour and promptitude for securing the observance of the laws, preventing nuisances, correcting abuses, and guarding against seditious undertakings begun in distant places; the people has less affection for its rulers, whom it never sees, for its country, which, to its eyes, seems like the world, and for its fellow-citizens, most of whom are unknown to it. The same laws cannot suit so many diverse provinces with different customs, situated in the most various climates, and incapable of enduring a uniform government. Different laws lead only to trouble and confusion among peoples which, living under the same rulers and in constant communication one with another, intermingle and intermarry, and, coming under the sway of new customs, never know if they can call their very patrimony their own. Talent is buried, virtue unknown and vice unpunished, among such a multitude of men who do not know one another, gathered together in one place at the seat of the central administration. The leaders, overwhelmed with business, see nothing for themselves; the State is governed by clerks. Finally, the measures which have to be taken to maintain the general authority, which all these distant officials wish to escape or to impose upon, absorb all the energy of the public, so that there is none left for the happiness of the people. There is hardly enough to defend it when need arises, and thus a body which is too big for its constitution gives way and falls crushed under its own weight.

The better the constitution of a State is, the more do public affairs encroach on private in the minds of the citizens. Private affairs are even of much less importance, because the aggregate of the common happiness furnishes a greater proportion of that of each individual, so that there is less for him to seek in particular cares. In a well-ordered city every man flies to the assemblies: under a bad government no one cares to stir a step to get to them, because no one is interested in what happens there, because it is foreseen that the general will will not prevail, and lastly because domestic cares are all-absorbing. Good laws lead to the making of better ones; bad ones bring about worse. As soon as any man says of the affairs of the State: *What does it matter to me?* the State may be given up for lost.

Those who distinguish civil from theological intolerance are, to my mind, mistaken. The two forms are inseparable. It is impossible to live at peace with those we regard as damned; to love them would be to hate God who punishes them: we positively must either reclaim or torment them. Wherever theological intolerance is admitted, it must inevitably have some civil effect;

and as soon as it has such an effect, the Sovereign is no longer Sovereign even in the temporal sphere: thenceforth priests are the real masters, and kings only their ministers.

Now that there is and can be no longer an exclusive national religion, tolerance should be given to all religions that tolerate others, so long as their dogmas contain nothing contrary to the duties of citizenship. But whoever dares to say: *Outside the Church is no salvation,* ought to be driven from the State, unless the State is the Church, and the prince the pontiff. Such a dogma is good only in a theocratic government; in any other, it is fatal.

JOHN STUART MILL

2. *Freedom of Opinion—Limited or Unlimited?**

Speaking generally, it is not, in constitutional countries, to be apprehended, that the government, whether completely responsible to the people or not, will often attempt to control the expression of opinion, except when in doing so it makes itself the organ of the general intolerance of the public. Let us suppose, therefore, that the government is entirely at one with the people, and never thinks of exerting any power of coercion unless in agreement with what it conceives to be their voice. But I deny the right of the people to exercise such coercion, either by themselves or by their government. The power itself is illegitimate. It is as noxious, or more noxious, when exerted in accordance with public opinion, than when in opposition to it. If all mankind minus one, were of one opinion, and only one person were of the contrary opinion, mankind would be no more justified in silencing that one person, than he, if he had the power, would be justified in silencing mankind. Were an opinion a personal possession of no value except to the owner; if to be obstructed in the enjoyment of it were simply a private injury, it would make some difference whether the injury was inflicted only on a few persons or on many. But the peculiar evil of silencing the expression of an opinion is, that it is robbing the human race; posterity as well as the existing generation; those who dissent from the opinion, still more than those who hold it. If the opinion is right, they are deprived of the opportunity of exchanging error for truth; if wrong, they lose, what is almost as great a benefit, the clearer perception and livelier impression of truth, produced by its collision with error.

It is necessary to consider separately these two hypotheses, each of which

* From John Stuart Mill, *On Liberty* (1859).

has a distinct branch of the argument corresponding to it. We can never be sure that the opinion we are endeavouring to stifle is a false opinion; and if we were sure, stifling it would be an evil still.

First: the opinion which it is attempted to suppress by authority may possibly be true. Those who desire to suppress it, of course deny its truth; but they are not infallible. They have no authority to decide the question for all mankind, and exclude every other person from the means of judging. To refuse a hearing to an opinion, because they are sure that it is false, is to assume that their certainty is the same thing as absolute certainty. All silencing of discussion is an assumption of infallibility. Its condemnation may be allowed to rest on this common argument, not the worse for being common.

Unfortunately for the good sense of mankind, the fact of their fallibility is far from carrying the weight in their practical judgement, which is always allowed to it in theory; for while every one well knows himself to be fallible, few think it necessary to take any precautions against their own fallibility, or admit the supposition that any opinion, of which they feel very certain, may be one of the examples of the error to which they acknowledge themselves to be liable. Absolute princes, or others who are accustomed to unlimited deference, usually feel this complete confidence in their own opinions on nearly all subjects. People more happily situated, who sometimes hear their opinions disputed, and are not wholly unused to be set right when they are wrong, place the same unbounded reliance only on such of their opinions as are shared by all who surround them, or to whom they habitually defer: for in proportion to a man's want of confidence in his own solitary judgement, does he usually repose, with implicit trust, on the infallibility of "the world" in general. And the world, to each individual, means the part of it with which he comes in contact; his party, his set, his church, his class of society: the man may be called, by comparison, almost liberal and large-minded to whom it means anything so comprehensive as his own country or his own age. Nor is his faith in this collective authority at all shaken by his being aware that other ages, countries, sects, churches, classes, and parties have thought, and even now think, the exact reverse. He devolves upon his own world the responsibility of being in the right against the dissentient worlds of other people; and it never troubles him that mere accident has decided which of these numerous worlds is the object of his reliance, and that the same causes which make him a Churchman in London, would have made him a Buddhist or a Confucian in Pekin. Yet it is as evident in itself, as any amount of argument can make it, that ages are no more infallible than individuals; every age having held many opinions which subsequent ages have deemed not only false but absurd; and it is as certain that many opinions, now general, will be rejected by future ages, as it is that many, once general, are rejected by the present.

The objection likely to be made to this argument would probably take some such form as the following. There is no greater assumption of infallibility in forbidding the propagation of error, than in any other thing which is done by public authority on its own judgement and responsibility. Judgement is given to men that they may use it. Because it may be used erroneously, are men to be told that they ought not to use it at all? To prohibit what they think pernicious, is not claiming exemption from error, but fulfilling the duty incumbent on them, although fallible, of acting on their conscientious conviction. If we were never to act on our opinions, because those opinions may be wrong, we should leave all our interests uncared for, and all our duties unperformed. An objection which applies to all conduct, can be no valid objection to any conduct in particular. It is the duty of governments, and of individuals, to form the truest opinions they can: to form them carefully, and never impose them upon others unless they are quite sure of being right. But when they are sure (such reasoners may say), it is not conscientiousness but cowardice to shrink from acting on their opinions, and allow doctrines which they honestly think dangerous to the welfare of mankind, either in this life or in another, to be scattered abroad without restraint, because other people, in less enlightened times, have persecuted opinions now believed to be true. Let us take care, it may be said, not to make the same mistake: but governments and nations have made mistakes in other things, which are not denied to be fit subjects for the exercise of their authority: they have laid on bad taxes, made unjust wars. Ought we therefore to lay on no taxes, and, under whatever provocation, make no wars? Men, and governments, must act to the best of their ability. There is no such thing as absolute certainty, but there is assurance sufficient for the purposes of human life. We may, and must, assume our opinion to be true for the guidance of our own conduct: and it is assuming no more when we forbid bad men to pervert society by the propagation of opinions which we regard as false and pernicious.

I answer, that it is assuming very much more. There is the greatest difference between presuming an opinion to be true, because, with every opportunity for contesting it, it has not been refuted, and assuming its truth for the purpose of not permitting its refutation. Complete liberty of contradicting and disproving our opinion, is the very condition which justifies us in assuming its truth for purposes of action; and on no other terms can a being with human facilities have any rational assurance of being right.

When we consider either the history of opinion, or the ordinary conduct of human life, to what is it to be ascribed that the one and the other are no worse than they are? Not certainly to the inherent force of the human understanding; for, on any matter not self-evident, there are ninety-nine persons totally incapable of judging of it, for one who is capable; and the capacity of the hundredth person is only comparative; for the majority of the eminent men of every past generation held many opinions now known to be erroneous, and did or approved numerous things which no one will now justify. Why is it, then, that there is on the whole a preponderance among mankind of rational opinions and rational conduct? If there really is this preponderance—which there must be unless human affairs are, and have always been, in an almost desperate state—it is owing to a quality of the human mind, the source of everything respectable in man either as an intellectual or as a moral being, namely, that his errors are corrigible. He is capable of rectifying his mistakes, by discussion and experience. Not by experience alone. There must be discussion, to show how experience is to be interpreted. Wrong opinions and practices gradually yield to fact and argument: but facts and arguments, to produce any effect on the mind, must be brought before it. Very few facts are able to tell their own story, without comments to bring out their meaning. The whole strength and value, then, of human judgement, depending on the one property, that it can be set right when it is wrong, reliance can be placed on it only when the means of setting it right are kept constantly at hand. In the case of any person whose judgement is really deserving of confidence, how has it become so? Because he has kept his mind open to criticism of his opinions and conduct. Because it has been his practice to listen to all that could be said against him; to profit by as much of it as was just, and expound to himself, and upon occasion to others, the fallacy of what was fallacious. Because he has felt, that the only way in which a human being can make some approach to knowing the whole of a subject, is by hearing what can be said about it by persons of every variety of opinion, and studying all modes in which it can be looked at by every character of mind. No wise man ever acquired his wisdom in any mode but this; nor is it in the nature of human intellect to become wise in any other manner. The steady habit of correcting and completing his own opinion by collating it with those of others, so far from causing doubt and hesitation in carrying it into practice, is the only stable foundation for a just reliance on it: for, being cognisant of all that can, at least obviously, be said against him, and having taken up his position against all gainsayers—knowing that he has sought for objections and difficulties, instead of avoiding them, and has shut out no light which can be thrown upon the subject from any quarter—he has a right to think his judgement better than that of any person, or any multitude, who have not gone through a similar process.

It is not too much to require that what the wisest of mankind, those who are best entitled to trust their own judgement, find necessary to warrant their relying on it, should be submitted to by that miscellaneous collection of a few wise and many foolish individuals, called the public. The most intolerant of churches, the Roman Catholic Church, even at the canonization of a saint, admits, and listens patiently to, a "devil's advocate." The holiest of men, it appears, cannot be admitted to posthumous honours, until all that the devil could say against him is known and weighed. If even the Newtonian philosophy were not permitted to be questioned, mankind could not feel as complete assurance of its truth as they now do. The beliefs which we have most warrant for, have no safeguard to rest on, but a standing invitation to the whole world to prove them unfounded. If the challenge is not accepted, or is accepted and the attempt fails, we are far enough from certainty still; but we have done the best that the existing state of human reason admits of; we have neglected nothing that could give the truth a chance of reaching us: if the lists are kept open, we may hope that if there be a better truth, it will be found when the human mind is capable of receiving it; and in the meantime we may rely on having attained such approach to truth, as is possible in our own day. This is the amount of certainty attainable by a fallible being, and this the sole way of attaining it.

Strange it is, that men should admit the validity of the arguments for free discussion, but object to their being "pushed to an extreme"; not seeing that unless the reasons are good for an extreme case, they are not good for any case. Strange that they should imagine that they are not assuming infallibility, when they acknowledge that there should be free discussion on all subjects which can possibly be doubtful, but think that some particular principle or doctrine should be forbidden to be questioned because it is so certain, that is, because they are certain that it is certain. To call any proposition certain, while there is any one who would deny its certainty if permitted, but who is not permitted, is to assume that we ourselves, and those who agree with us, are the judges of certainty, and judges without hearing the other side.

In the present age—which has been described as "destitute of faith, but terrified at scepticism"—in which people feel sure, not so much that their opinions are true, as that they should not know what to do without them—the claims of an opinion to be protected from public attack are rested not so much on its truth, as on its importance to society. There are, it is alleged, certain beliefs, so useful, not to say indispensable to well-being, that it is as much the duty of government to uphold those beliefs, as to protect any other of the interests of society. In a case of such necessity, and so directly in the line of their duty, something less than infallibility may, it is maintained, warrant, and even bind, governments, to act on their own opinion, confined by the general opinion of mankind. It is also often argued, and still oftener thought, that none but bad men would desire to weaken these salutary beliefs; and there can be nothing wrong, it is thought, in restraining bad men, and prohibiting what only such men would wish to practise. This mode of thinking makes the justification of restraints on discussion not a question of the truth of doctrines, but of their usefulness; and flatters itself by that means of escape the responsibility of claiming to be an infallible judge of opinions. But those who thus satisfy themselves, do not perceive that the assumption of infallibility is merely shifted from one point to another. The usefulness of an opinion is itself matter of opinion: as disputable, as open to discussion, and requiring discussion as much, as the opinion itself. There is the same need of an infallible judge of opinions to decide an opinion to be noxious, as to decide it to be false, unless the opinion condemned has full opportunity of defending itself. And it will not do to say that the heretic may be allowed to maintain the utility or harmlessness of his opinion, though forbidden to maintain its truth. The truth of an opinion is part of its utility. If we would know whether or not it is desirable that a proposition should be believed, is it possible to exclude the consideration of whether or not it is true? In the opinion, not of bad men, but of the best men, no belief which is contrary to truth can be really useful: and can you prevent such men from urging that plea, when they are charged with culpability for denying some doctrine which they are told is useful, but which they believe to be false? Those who are on the side of received opinions, never fail to take all possible advantage of this plea; you do not find them handling the question of utility as if it could be completely abstracted from that of truth: on the contrary, it is, above all, because their doctrine is the "truth," that the knowledge or the belief of it is held to be so indispensable. There can be no fair discussion of the question of usefulness, when an argument so vital may be employed on one side, but not on the other. And in point of fact, when law or public feeling do not permit the truth of an opinion to be disputed, they are just as little tolerant of a denial of its usefulness. The utmost they allow is an extenuation of its absolute necessity, or of the positive guilt of rejecting it.

In order more fully to illustrate the mischief of denying a hearing to opinions because we, in our own judgement, have condemned them, it will be desirable to fix down the discussion to a concrete case; and I choose, by preference, the cases which are least favourable to me—in which the argument against freedom of opinion, both on the score of truth and on that of utility, is considered the strongest. Let the opinions impugned be the belief in a God and in a future state, or any of the commonly received doctrines of morality. To fight the battle on such ground, gives a great advantage to an unfair antagonist; since he will be sure to say (and many who have no desire to be unfair will say it internally), Are these the doctrines which you do not deem sufficiently certain to be taken under the protection of law? Is the belief in a God one of the opinions, to feel sure of which, you hold to be assuming infallibility? But I must be permitted to observe, that it is not the feeling sure of a doctrine (be it what it may) which I call an assumption of infallibility. It is the undertaking to decide the question *for others,* without allowing them to hear what can be said on the contrary side. And I denounce and reprobate this pretension not the less, if put forth on the side of my most solemn convictions. However positive any one's persuasion may be, not only of the falsity but of the pernicious consequences—not only of the pernicious consequences, but (to adopt expressions which I altogether condemn) the immorality and impiety of an opinion; yet if, in pursuance of that private judgement, though backed by the public judgement of his country or his contemporaries, he prevents the opinion from being heard in its defence, he assumes infallibility. And so far from the assumption being less objectionable or less dangerous because the opinion is called immoral or impious, this is the case of all others in which it is most fatal. These are exactly the occasions on which the men of one generation commit those dreadful mistakes, which excite the astonishment and horror of posterity. It is among such that we find the instances memorable in history, when the arm of the law has been employed to root out the best men and the noblest doctrines; with deplorable success as to the men, though some of the doctrines have survived to be (as if in mockery) invoked, in defence of similar conduct towards those who dissent from *them,* or from their received interpretation.

Mankind can hardly be too often reminded, that there was once a man named Socrates, between whom and the legal authorities and public opinion of his time, there took place a memorable collision. Born in an age and country abounding in individual greatness, this man has been handed down to us by those who best knew both him and the age, as the most virtuous man in it; while *we* know him as the head and prototype of all subsequent teachers of virtue, the source equally of the lofty inspiration of Plato and the judicious utilitarianism of Aristotle, *"I maëstri di color che sanno,"* the two headsprings of ethical as of all other philosophy. This acknowledged master of all the eminent thinkers who have since lived—whose fame, still growing after two thousand years, all but outweighs the whole remainder of the names which make his native city illustrious—was put to death by his countrymen, after a judicial conviction, for impiety and immorality. Impiety, in denying the gods recognized by the State; indeed his accuser asserted (see the *Apologia*) that he believed in no gods at all. Immorality, in being, by his doctrines and instructions, a "corrupter of youth." Of these charges the tribunal, there is every ground for believing, honestly found him guilty, and condemned the man who probably of all then born had deserved best of mankind, to be put to death as a criminal.

The initiation of all wise or noble things, comes and must come from individuals; generally at first from some one individual. The honour and glory of the average man is that he is capable of following that initiative; that he can respond internally to wise and noble things, and be led to them with his eyes open. I am not countenancing the sort of "hero-worship" which applauds the strong man of genius for forcibly seizing on the government of the world and making it do his bidding in spite of itself. All he can claim is freedom to point out the way. The power of compelling others into it, is not only inconsistent with the freedom and development of all the rest, but corrupting to the strong man himself. It does seem, however, that when the opinions of masses of merely average men are everywhere become or becoming the dominant power, the counterpoise and corrective to that tendency would be the more and more pronounced individuality of those who stand on the higher eminences of thought. It is these circumstances most especially, that exceptional individuals, instead of being deterred, should be encouraged in acting differently from the mass. In other times there was no advantage in their doing so, unless they acted not only differently, but better. In this age, the mere example of nonconformity, the mere refusal to bend the knee to custom, is itself a service. Precisely because the tyranny of opinion is such as to make eccentricity a reproach, it is desirable, in order to break through that tyranny, that people should be eccentric. Eccentricity has always abounded when and where strength of character has abounded; and the amount of eccentricity in a society has generally been proportional to the amount of genius, mental vigour, and moral courage which it contained. That so few now dare to be eccentric marks the chief danger of the time.

I have said that it is important to give the freest scope possible to uncustomary things, in order that it may in time appear which of these are fit to be converted into customs. But independence of action, and disregard of custom, are not solely deserving of encouragement for the chance they afford that better modes of action, and customs more worthy of general adoption, may be struck out; nor is it only persons of decided mental superiority who have a just claim to carry on their lives in their own way. There is no reason that all human existence should be constructed on some one or some small number of patterns. If a person possesses any tolerable amount of common sense and experience, his own mode of laying out his existence is the best, not because it is the best in itself, but because it is his own mode. Human beings are not like sheep; and even sheep are not undistinguishably alike. A man cannot get a coat or a pair of boots to fit him, unless they are either made to his measure, or he has a whole warehouseful to choose from: and is it easier to fit him with a life than with a coat, or are human beings more like one another in their whole physical and spiritual conformation than in the shape of their feet? If it were only that people have diversities of taste, that is reason enough for not attempting to shape them all after one model. But different persons also require different conditions for their spiritual development; and can no more exist healthily in the same moral, than all the variety of plants can in the same physical, atmosphere and climate. The same things which are helps to one person towards the cultivation of his higher nature, are hindrances to another. The same mode of life is a healthy excitement to one, keeping all his faculties of action and enjoyment in their best order, while to another it is a distracting burthen, which suspends or crushes all internal life. Such are the differences among human beings in their sources of pleasure, their susceptibilities of pain, and the operation on them of different physical and moral agencies, that unless there is a corresponding diversity in their modes of life, they neither obtain their fair share of happiness, nor grow up to the mental, moral and aesthetic stature of which their nature is capable. Why then should tolerance, as far as the public sentiment is concerned, extend only to tastes and modes of life which extort acquiescence by the multitude of their adherents? Nowhere (except in some monastic institutions) is diversity of taste entirely unrecognized; a person may, without blame, either like or dislike rowing, or smoking, or music, or athletic exercises, or chess, or cards, or study, because both those who like each of these things, and those who dislike them, are too numerous to be put down. But the man, and still more the woman, who can be accused either of doing "what nobody does," or of not doing "what everybody does," is the subject of as much depreciatory remark as if he or she had committed some grave moral delinquency. Persons require to possess a title, or some other badge of rank, or of the consideration of people of rank, to be able to indulge somewhat in the luxury of doing as they like without detriment to their estimation. To indulge somewhat, I repeat: for whoever allow themselves much of that indulgence, incur the risk of something worse than disparaging speeches—they are in peril of a commission de lunatico, and of having their property taken from them and given to their relations.

A theory which maintains that truth may justifiably be persecuted because persecution cannot possibly do it any harm, cannot be charged with being intentionally hostile to the reception of new truths; but we cannot commend the generosity of its dealing with the persons to whom mankind are indebted for them. To discover to the world something which deeply concerns it, and of which it was previously ignorant; to prove to it that it had been mistaken on some vital point of temporal or spiritual interest, is as important a service as a human being can render to his fellow creatures, and in certain cases, as in those of the early Christians and of the Reformers, those who think with Dr. Johnson believe it to have been the most precious gift which could be bestowed on mankind. That the authors of such splendid benefits should be requited by martyrdom; that their reward should be to be dealt with as the vilest of criminals, is not, upon this theory, a deplorable error and misfortune, for which humanity should mourn in sackcloth and ashes, but the normal and justifiable state of things. The propounder of a new truth, according to this doctrine, should stand, as stood, in the legislation of the Locrians, the proposer of a new law, with a halter round his neck, to be instantly tightened if the public assembly did not, on hearing his reasons, then and there adopt his proposition. People who defend this mode of treating benefactors, cannot be supposed to set much value on the benefit; and I believe this view of the subject is mostly confined to the sort of persons who think that new truths may have been desirable once, but that we have had enough of them now.

But, indeed, the dictum that truth always triumphs over persecution, is one of those pleasant falsehoods which men repeat after one another till they pass into commonplaces, but which all experience refutes. History teems with instances of truth put down by persecution. If not suppressed for ever, it may be thrown back for centuries. To speak only of religious opinions: the Reformation broke out at least twenty times before Luther, and was put down. Arnold of Brescia was put down. Fra Dolcino was put down. Savonarola was put down. The Albigeois were put down. The Vaudois were put down. The Lollards were put down. The Hussites were put down. Even after the era of Luther, wherever persecution was persisted in, it was successful. In Spain, Italy, Flanders, the Austrian empire, Protestantism was rooted out; and, most likely, would have been so in England, had Queen Mary lived, or Queen Elizabeth died. Persecution has always succeeded, save where the heretics were too strong a party to be effectually persecuted. No reasonable person can doubt that Christianity might have been extirpated in the Roman Empire. It spread, and became predominant, because the persecutions were only occasional, lasting but a short time, and separated by long intervals of almost undisturbed propagandism. It is a piece of idle sentimentality that truth, merely as truth, has any inherent power denied to error, of prevailing against the dungeon and the stake. Men are not more zealous for truth than they often are for error, and a sufficient application of legal or even of social penalties will generally succeed in stopping the propagation of either. The real advantage which truth has, consists in this, that when an opinion is true, it may be extinguished once, twice, or many times, but in the course of ages there will generally be found persons to rediscover it, until some one of its reappearances falls on a time when from favourable circumstances it escapes persecution until it has made such head as to withstand all subsequent attempt to suppress it.

The despotism of custom is everywhere the standing hindrance to human advancement, being in unceasing antagonism to that disposition to aim at something better than customary, which is called, according to circumstances, the spirit of liberty, or that of progress or improvement. The spirit of improvement is not always a spirit of liberty, for it may aim at forcing improvements on an unwilling people; and the spirit of liberty, in so far as it resists such attempts, may ally itself locally and temporarily with the opponents of improvement; but the only unfailing and permanent source of improvement is liberty, since by it there are as many possible independent centres of improvement as there are individuals. The progressive principle, however, in either shape, whether as the love of liberty or of improvement, is antagonistic to the sways of Custom, involving at least emancipation from that yoke; and the contest between the two constitutes the chief interest of the history of mankind. The greater part of the world has, properly speaking, no history, because the despotism of Custom is complete.

We have now recognized the necessity to the mental well-being of mankind (on which all their other well-being depends) of freedom of opinion, and freedom of the expression of opinion, on four distinct grounds; which we will now briefly recapitulate.

First, if any opinion is compelled to silence, that opinion may, for ought we can certainly know, be true. To deny this is to assume our own infallibility.

Secondly, though the silenced opinion be an error, it may, and very commonly does, contain a portion of truth; and since the general or prevailing opinion on any subject is rarely or never the whole truth, it is only by the collision of adverse opinions that the remainder of the truth has any chance of being supplied.

Thirdly, even if the received opinion be not only true, but the whole truth; unless it is suffered to be, and actually is, vigorously and earnestly contested, it will, by most of those who receive it, be held in the manner of a prejudice, with little comprehension or feeling of its rational grounds. And not only this, but, fourthly, the meaning of the doctrine itself will be in danger of being lost, or enfeebled, and deprived of its vital effect on the character and conduct: the dogma becoming a mere formal profession, inefficacious for good, but cumbering the ground, and preventing the growth of any real and heartfelt conviction, from reason or personal experience.

The worth of a State, in the long run, is the worth of the individuals composing it; and a State which postpones the interests of *their* mental expansion and elevation, to a little more of administrative skill, or of that semblance of it which practice gives, in the details of business; a State which dwarfs its men, in order that they may be more docile instruments in its hands even for beneficial purposes—will find that with small men no great thing can really be accomplished; and that the perfection of machinery to which it has sacrificed everything, will in the end avail it nothing, for want of the vital power which, in order that the machine might work more smoothly, it has preferred to banish.

ISAIAH BERLIN

3. *Freedom: Negative or Positive?* *

I

THE NOTION OF NEGATIVE FREEDOM

I am normally said to be free to the degree to which no human being interferes with my activity. Political liberty in this sense is simply the area within which a man can do what he wants. If I am prevented by other persons from doing what I want I am to that degree unfree; and if the area within which I can do what I want is contracted by other men beyond a certain minimum, I can be described as being coerced, or, it may be, enslaved. Coercion is not, however, a term that covers every form of inability. If I say that I am unable to jump more than 10 feet in the air, or cannot read because I am blind, or cannot understand the darker pages of Hegel, it would be eccentric to say that I am to that degree enslaved or coerced. Coercion implies the deliberate interference of other human beings within the area in which I wish to act. You lack political liberty or freedom only if you are prevented from attaining your goal by human beings.[1] Mere incapacity to attain your goal is not lack of political freedom.[2] This is brought out by the use of such modern expressions as 'economic freedom' and its counterpart, 'economic slavery'. It is argued, very plausibly, that if a man is too poor to afford something on which there is no legal ban— a loaf of bread, a journey round the world, recourse to the law courts—he is as little free to have it as he would be if it were forbidden him by law. If my poverty were a kind of disease, which prevented me from buying bread or paying for the journey round the world, or getting my case heard, as lameness prevents me from running, this inability would not naturally be described as a lack of freedom at all, least of all political freedom. It is only because I believe that my inability to get what I want is due to the fact that other human beings have made arrangements whereby I am, whereas others

---

* From Isaiah Berlin, *Two Concepts of Liberty* (Oxford University Press, 1958). By permission.

[1] I do not, of course, mean to imply the truth of the converse.

[2] Helvétius made this point very clearly: 'The free man is the man who is not in irons, nor imprisoned in a gaol, nor terrorized like a slave by the fear of punishment . . . it is not lack of freedom not to fly like an eagle or swim like a whale.'

are not, prevented from having enough money with which to pay for it, that I think myself a victim of coercion or slavery. In other words, this use of the term depends on a particular social and economic theory about the causes of my poverty or weakness. If my lack of means is due to my lack of mental or physical capacity, then I begin to speak of being deprived of freedom (and not simply of poverty) only if I accept the theory.[3] If, in addition, I believe that I am being kept in want by a definite arrangement which I consider unjust or unfair, I speak of economic slavery or oppression. 'The nature of things does not madden us, only ill will does', said Rousseau. The criterion of oppression is the part that I believe to be played by other human beings, directly or indirectly, in frustrating my wishes. By being free in this sense I mean not being interfered with by others. The wider the area of non-interference the wider my freedom.

This is certainly what the classical English political philosophers meant when they used this word.[4] They disagreed about how wide the area could or should be. They supposed that it could not, as things were, be unlimited, because if it were, it would entail a state in which all men could boundlessly interfere with all other men; and this kind of 'natural' freedom would lead to social chaos in which men's minimum needs would not be satisfied; or else the liberties of the weak would be suppressed by the strong. Because they perceived that human purposes and activities do not automatically harmonize with one another; and, because (whatever their official doctrines) they put high value on other goals, such as justice, or happiness, or security, or varying degrees of equality, they were prepared to curtail freedom in the interests of other values and, indeed, of freedom itself. For, without this, it was impossible to create the kind of association that they thought desirable. Consequently, it is assumed by these thinkers that the area of men's free action must be limited by law. But equally it is assumed, especially by such libertarians as Locke and Mill in England, and Constant and Tocqueville in France, that there ought to exist a certain minimum area of personal freedom which must on no account be violated, for if it is overstepped, the individual will find himself in an area too narrow for even that minimum development of his natural faculties which alone makes it possible to pursue, and even to conceive, the various ends which men hold good or right or sacred. It follows that a frontier must be drawn between the area of private life and that of public authority. Where it is to be drawn is a matter of argument, indeed of haggling. Men are largely interdependent, and no man's

---

[3] The Marxist conception of social laws is, of course, the best-known version of this theory, but it forms a large element in some Christian and utilitarian, and all socialist, doctrines.

[4] 'A free man', said Hobbes, 'is he that . . . is not hindered to do what he hath the will to do.' Law is always a 'fetter', even if it protects you from being bound in chains that are heavier than those of the law, say, arbitrary despotism or chaos. Bentham says much the same.

activity is so completely private as never to obstruct the lives of others in any way. 'Freedom for the pike is death for the minnows'; the liberty of some must depend on the restraint of others.[5] Still, a practical compromise has to be found.

Philosophers with an optimistic view of human nature, and a belief in the possibility of harmonizing human interests, such as Locke or Adam Smith and, in some moods, Mill, believed that social harmony and progress were compatible with reserving a large area for private life over which neither the state nor any other authority must be allowed to trespass. Hobbes, and those who agreed with him, especially conservative or reactionary thinkers,

[5] 'Freedom for an Oxford don', others have been known to add, 'is a very different thing from freedom for an Egyptian peasant.'

This proposition derives its force from something that is both true and important, but the phrase itself remains a piece of political claptrap. It is true that to offer political rights, or safeguards against intervention by the state, to men who are half-naked, illiterate, underfed, and diseased is to mock their condition; they need medical help or education before they can understand, or make use of, an increase in their freedom. First things come first: there are situations, as a nineteenth-century Russian radical writer declared, in which boots are superior to the works of Shakespeare; individual freedom is not everyone's primary need. For freedom is not the mere absence of frustration of whatever kind; this would inflate the meaning of the word until it meant too much or too little. The Egyptian peasant needs clothes or medicine before, and more than, personal liberty, but the minimum freedom that he needs today, and the greater degree of freedom that he may need tomorrow, is not some species of freedom peculiar to him, but identical with that of professors, artists, and millionaires.

What troubles the consciences of Western liberals is not, I think, the belief that the freedom that men seek differs according to their social or economic conditions, but that the minority who possess it have gained it by exploiting or, at least, averting their gaze from the vast majority who do not. They believe, with good reason, that if individual liberty is an ultimate end for human beings, none should be deprived of it by others; least of all that some should enjoy it at the expense of others. Equality of liberty; not to treat others as I should not wish them to treat me; repayment of my debt to those who alone have made possible my liberty or prosperity or enlightenment; justice, in its simplest and most universal sense—these are the foundations of liberal morality. Liberty is not the only goal of men. I can, like the Russian critic Belinsky, say that if others are to be deprived of it—if my brothers are to remain in poverty, squalor, and chains—then I do not want it for myself, I reject it with both hands, and infinitely prefer to share their fate. But nothing is gained by a confusion of terms. To avoid glaring inequality or widespread misery I am ready to sacrifice some, or all, of my freedom: I may do so willingly and freely: but it is freedom that I am giving up for the sake of justice or equality or the love of my fellow men. I should be guilt-stricken, and rightly so, if I were not, in some circumstances, ready to make this sacrifice. But a sacrifice is not an increase in what is being sacrificed, namely freedom, however great the moral need or the compensation for it. Everything is what it is: liberty is liberty, not equality or fairness or justice or human happiness or a quiet conscience. If the liberty of myself or my class or nation depends on the misery of a vast number of other human beings, the system which promotes this is unjust and immoral. But if I curtail or lose my freedom, in order to lessen the shame of such inequality, and do not thereby materially increase the individual liberty of others, an absolute loss of liberty occurs. This may be compensated for by a gain in justice or in happiness or in peace, but the loss remains, and it is nothing but a confusion of values to say that although my 'liberal', individual freedom may go by the board, some other kind of freedom—'social' or 'economic'—is increased. But it remains true that the freedom of some must at times be curtailed to secure the freedom of others. Upon what principle should this be done? If freedom is a sacred, untouchable value, there can be no such absolute principle.

argued that if men were to be prevented from destroying one another, and making social life a jungle or a wilderness, greater safeguards must be instituted to keep them in their places, and wished correspondingly to increase the area of centralized control, and decrease that of the individual. But both sides agreed that some portion of human existence must remain independent of the sphere of social control. To invade that preserve, however small, would be despotism. The most eloquent of all defenders of freedom and privacy, Benjamin Constant, who had not forgotten the Jacobin dictatorship, declared that at the very least the liberty of religion, opinion, expression, property, must be guaranteed against arbitrary invasion. Jefferson, Burke, Paine, Mill, compiled different catalogues of individual liberties, but the argument for keeping authority at bay is always substantially the same. We must preserve a minimum area of personal freedom if we are not to 'degrade or deny our nature'. We cannot remain absolutely free, and must give up some of our liberty to preserve the rest. But total self-surrender is self-defeating. What then must the minimum be? That which a man cannot give up without offending against the essence of his human nature. What is this essence? What are the standards which it entails? This has been, and perhaps always will be, a matter of infinite debate. But whatever the principle in terms of which the area of non-interference is to be drawn, whether it is that of natural law or natural rights, or of utility or the pronouncements of a categorical imperative, or the sanctity of the social contract, or any other concept with which men have sought to clarify and justify their convictions, liberty in this sense means liberty *from;* absence of interference beyond the shifting, but always recognizable, frontier. 'The only freedom which deserves the name is that of pursuing our own good in our own way', said the most celebrated of its champions. If this is so, is compulsion ever justified? Mill had no doubt that it was. Since justice demands that all individuals be entitled to a minimum of freedom, all other individuals were of necessity to be restrained, if need be by force, from depriving anyone of it. Indeed, the whole function of law was the prevention of just such collisions: the state was reduced to what Lassalle contemptuously described as the functions of a nightwatchman or traffic policeman.

What made the protection of individual liberty so sacred to Mill? In his famous essay he declares that unless men are left to live as they wish 'in the path which merely concerns themselves', civilization cannot advance; the truth will not, for lack of a free market in ideas, come to light; there will be no scope for spontaneity, originality, genius, for mental energy, for moral courage. Society will be crushed by the weight of 'collective mediocrity'. Whatever is rich and diversified will be crushed by the weight of custom, by men's constant tendency to conformity, which breeds only 'withered capacities', 'pinched and hidebound', 'cramped and warped' human beings.

'Pagan self-assertion is as worthy as Christian self-denial.' 'All the errors which a man is likely to commit against advice and warning are far out-weighed by the evil of allowing others to constrain him to what they deem is good.' The defence of liberty consists in the 'negative' goal of warding off interference. To threaten a man with persecution unless he submits to a life in which he exercises no choices of his goals; to block before him every door but one, no matter how noble the prospect upon which it opens, or how benevolent the motives of those who arrange this, is to sin against the truth that he is a man, a being with a life of his own to live. This is liberty as it has been conceived by liberals in the modern world from the days of Erasmus (some would say of Occam) to our own. Every plea for civil liber-ties and individual rights, every protest against exploitation and humiliation, against the encroachment of public authority, or the mass hypnosis of custom or organized propaganda, springs from this individualistic, and much dis-puted, conception of man.

Three facts about this position may be noted. In the first place Mill con-fuses two distinct notions. One is that all coercion is, in so far as it frustrates human desires, bad as such, although it may have to be applied to prevent other, greater evils; while non-interference, which is the opposite of coercion, is good as such, although it is not the only good. This is the 'negative' con-ception of liberty in its classical form. The other is that men should seek to discover the truth, or to develop a certain type of character of which Mill approved—fearless, original, imaginative, independent, non-conforming to the point of eccentricity, and so on—and that truth can be found, and such character can be bred, only in conditions of freedom. Both these are liberal views, but they are not identical, and the connexion between them is, at best, empirical. No one would argue that truth or freedom of self-expression could flourish where dogma crushes all thought. But the evidence of history tends to show (as, indeed, was argued by James Stephen in his formidable attack on Mill in his *Liberty, Equality, Fraternity*) that integrity, love of truth and fiery individualism grow at least as often in severely disciplined communities among, for example, the puritan Calvinists of Scotland or New England, or under military discipline, as in more tolerant or indifferent societies; and if this is so accepted, Mill's argument for liberty as a necessary condition for the growth of human genius falls to the ground. If his two goals proved incompatible, Mill would be faced with a cruel dilemma, quite apart from the further difficulties created by the inconsistency of his doctrines with strict utilitarianism, even in his own humane version of it.[6]

---

[6] This is but another illustration of the natural tendency of all but a very few thinkers to believe that all the things they hold good must be intimately connected, or at least compatible, with one another. The history of thought, like the history of nations, is strewn with examples of inconsistent, or at least disparate, elements artificially yoked together in a despotic system,

In the second place, the doctrine is comparatively modern. There seems to be scarcely any consciousness of individual liberty as a political ideal in the ancient world. Condorcet has already remarked that the notion of individual rights is absent from the legal conceptions of the Romans and Greeks; this seems to hold equally of the Jewish, Chinese, and all other ancient civilizations that have since come to light.[7] The domination of this ideal has been the exception rather than the rule, even in the recent history of the West. Nor has liberty in this sense often formed a rallying cry for the great masses of mankind. The desire not to be impinged upon, to be left to oneself, has been a mark of high civilization both on the part of individuals and communities. The sense of privacy itself, of the area of personal relationships as something sacred in its own right, derives from a conception of freedom which, for all its religious roots, is scarcely older, in its developed state, than the Renaissance or the Reformation.[8] Yet its decline would mark the death of a civilization, of an entire moral outlook.

The third characteristic of this notion of liberty is of greater importance. It is that liberty in this sense is not incompatible with some kinds of autocracy, or at any rate with the absence of self-government. Liberty in this sense is principally concerned with the area of control, not with its source. Just as a democracy may, in fact, deprive the individual citizen of a great many liberties which he might have in some other form of society, so it is perfectly conceivable that a liberal-minded despot would allow his subjects a large measure of personal freedom. The despot who leaves his subjects a wide area of liberty may be unjust, or encourage the wildest inequalities, care little for order, or virtue, or knowledge; but provided he does not curb their liberty, or at least curbs it less than many other régimes, he meets with Mill's specification.[9] Freedom in this sense is not, at any rate logically, connected with democracy or self-government. Self-government may, on the whole, provide a better guarantee of the preservation of civil liberties than other régimes, and has been defended as such by libertarians. But there is no necessary connexion between individual liberty and democratic rule. The answer to the question 'Who governs me?' is logically distinct from the question 'How far does government interfere with me?' It is in this difference that the great contrast between the two concepts of negative and posi-

---

or held together by the danger of some common enemy. In due course the danger passes, and conflicts between the allies arise, which often disrupt the system, sometimes to the great benefit of mankind.

[7] See the valuable discussion of this in Michel Villey, *Leçons d'Histoire de la Philosophie du Droit,* who traces the embryo of the notion of subjective rights to Occam.

[8] Christian (and Jewish or Moslem) belief in the absolute authority of divine or natural laws, or in the equality of all men in the sight of God, is very different from belief in freedom to live as one prefers.

[9] Indeed, it is arguable that in the Prussia of Frederick the Great or in the Austria of Josef II, men of imagination, originality, and creative genius, and, indeed, minorities of all kinds, were

tive liberty, in the end, consists.[10] For the 'positive' sense of liberty comes to light if we try to answer the question, not 'What am I free to do or be?', but 'By whom am I ruled?' or 'Who is to say what I am, and what I am not, to be or do?' The connexion between democracy and individual liberty is a good deal more tenuous than it seemed to many advocates of both. The desire to be governed by myself, or at any rate to participate in the process by which my life is to be controlled, may be as deep a wish as that of a free area for action, and perhaps historically older. But it is not a desire for the same thing. So different is it, indeed, as to have led in the end to the great clash of ideologies that dominates our world. For it is this—the 'positive' conception of liberty: not freedom from, but freedom to—which the adherents of the 'negative' notion represent as being, at times, no better than a specious disguise for brutal tyranny.

II

THE NOTION OF POSITIVE FREEDOM

The 'positive' sense of the word 'liberty' derives from the wish on the part of the individual to be his own master. I wish my life and decisions to depend on myself, not on external forces of whatever kind. I wish to be the

---

less persecuted and felt the pressure, both of institutions and custom, less heavy upon them than in many an earlier or later democracy.

[10] 'Negative liberty' is something the extent of which, in a given case, it is difficult to estimate. It might, *prima facie,* seem to depend simply on the power to choose between at any rate two alternatives. Nevertheless, not all choices are equally free, or free at all. If in a totalitarian state I betray my friend under threat of torture, perhaps even if I act from fear of losing my job, I can reasonably say that I did not act freely. Nevertheless, I did, of course, make a choice, and could, at any rate in theory, have chosen to be killed or tortured or imprisoned. The mere existence of alternatives is not, therefore, enough to make my action free (although it may be voluntary) in the normal sense of the word. The extent of my freedom seems to depend on (*a*) how many possibilities are open to me (although the method of counting these can never be more than impressionistic. Possibilities of action are not discrete entities like apples, which can be exhaustively enumerated); (*b*) how easy or difficult each of these possibilities is to actualize; (*c*) how important in my plan of life, given my character and circumstances, these possibilities are when compared with each other; (*d*) how far they are closed and opened by deliberate human acts; (*e*) what value not merely the agent, but the general sentiment of the society in which he lives, puts on the various possibilities. All these magnitudes must be 'integrated', and a conclusion, necessarily never precise, or indisputable, drawn from this process. It may well be that there are many incommensurable degrees of freedom, and that they cannot be drawn up on a single scale of magnitude, however conceived. Moreover, in the case of societies, we are faced by such (logically absurd) questions as 'Would arrangement X increase the liberty of Mr. A more than it would that of Messrs. B, C, and D between them, added together?' The same difficulties arise in applying utilitarian criteria. Nevertheless, provided we do not demand precise measurement, we can give valid reasons for saying that the average subject of the King of Sweden is, on the whole, a good deal freer today than the average citizen of the Republic of Rumania. Total patterns of life must be compared directly as wholes, although the

instrument of my own, not of other men's, acts of will. I wish to be a subject, not an object; to be moved by reasons, by conscious purposes which are my own, not by causes which affect me, as it were, from outside. I wish to be somebody, not nobody; a doer—deciding, not being decided for, self-directed and not acted upon by external nature or by other men as if I were a thing, or an animal, or a slave incapable of playing a human role, that is, of conceiving goals and policies of my own and realizing them. This is at least part of what I mean when I say that I am rational, and that it is my reason that distinguishes me as a human being from the rest of the world. I wish, above all, to be conscious of myself as a thinking, willing, active being, bearing responsibility for his choices and able to explain them by reference to his own ideas and purposes. I feel free to the degree that I believe this to be true, and enslaved to the degree that I am made to realize that it is not.

The freedom which consists in being one's own master, and the freedom which consists in not being prevented from choosing as I do by other men, may, on the face of it, seem concepts at no great logical distance from each other—no more than negative and positive ways of saying the same thing. Yet the 'positive' and 'negative' notions of freedom developed in divergent directions until, in the end, they came into direct conflict with each other.

One way of making this clear is in terms of the independent momentum which the metaphor of self-mastery acquired. 'I am my own master'; 'I am slave to no man'; but may I not (as, for instance, T. H. Green is always saying) be a slave to nature? Or to my own 'unbridled' passions? Are these not so many species of the identical genus 'slave'—some political or legal, others moral or spiritual? Have not men had the experience of liberating themselves from spiritual slavery, or slavery to nature, and do they not in the course of it become aware, on the one hand, of a self which dominates, and, on the other, of something in them which is brought to heel? This dominant self is then variously identified with reason, with my 'higher nature', with the self which calculates and aims at what will satisfy it in the long run, with my 'real', or 'ideal', or 'autonomous' self, or with my self 'at its best'; which is then contrasted with irrational impulse, uncontrolled desires, my 'lower' nature, the pursuit of immediate pleasures, my 'empirical' or 'heteronomous' self, swept by every gust of desire and passion, needing to be rigidly disciplined if it is ever to rise to the full height of its 'real' nature. Presently the two selves may be represented as divided by an even larger gap: the real self may be conceived as something wider than the individual (as the term is normally understood), as a social 'whole' of which the individual

method by which we make the comparison, and the truth of the conclusions, are difficult or impossible to demonstrate. But the vagueness of the concepts, and the multiplicity of the criteria involved, is an attribute of the subject-matter itself, not of our imperfect methods of measurement, or incapacity for precise thought.

is an element or aspect: a tribe, a race, a church, a state, the great society of the living and the dead and the yet unborn. This entity is then identified as being the 'true' self which, by imposing its collective, or 'organic', single will upon its recalcitrant 'members', achieves its own, and, therefore, their, 'higher' freedom. The perils of using organic metaphors to justify the coercion of some men by others in order to raise them to a 'higher' level of freedom have often been pointed out. But what gives such plausibility as it has to this kind of language is that we recognize that it is possible, and at times justifiable, to coerce men in the name of some goal (let us say, justice or public health) which they would, if they were more enlightened, themselves pursue, but do not, because they are blind or ignorant or corrupt. This renders it easy for me to conceive of myself as coercing others for their own sake, in their, not my, interest. I am then claiming that I know what they truly need better than they know it themselves. What, at most, this entails is that they would not resist me if they were rational, and as wise as I, and understood their interests as I do. But I may go on to claim a good deal more than this. I may declare that they are actually aiming at what in their benighted state they consciously resist, because there exists within them an occult entity—their latent rational will, or their 'true' purpose—and that this entity, although it is belied by all that they overtly feel and do and say, is their 'real' self, of which the poor empirical self in space and time may know nothing or little; and that this inner spirit is the only self that deserves to have its wishes taken into account. Once I take this view, I am in a position to ignore the actual wishes of men or societies, to bully, oppress, torture them in the name, and on behalf, of their 'real' selves, in the secure knowledge that whatever is the true goal of man (happiness, fulfilment of duty, wisdom, a just society, self-fulfilment) must be identical with his freedom—the free choice of his 'true', albeit submerged and inarticulate, self.

This paradox has been often exposed. It is one thing to say that I know what is good for X, while he himself does not; and even to ignore his wishes for its—and his—sake; and a very different one to say that he has *eo ipso* chosen it, not indeed consciously, not as he seems in everyday life, but in his role as a rational self which his empirical self may not know—the 'real' self which discerns the good, and cannot help choosing it once it is revealed. This monstrous impersonation, which consists in equating what X would choose if he were something he is not, or at least not yet, with what X actually seeks and chooses, is at the heart of all political theories of self-realization. It is one thing to say that I may be coerced for my own good which I am too blind to see: and another that if it is my good, I am not being coerced, for I have willed it, whether I know this or not, and am free even while my poor earthly body and foolish mind bitterly reject it, and struggle against those who seek to impose it, with the greatest desperation.

This magical transformation, or sleight of hand (for which William James so justly mocked the Hegelians), can no doubt be perpetrated just as easily with the 'negative' concept of freedom, where the self that should not be interfered with is no longer the individual with his actual wishes and needs as they are normally conceived, but the 'real' man within, identified with the pursuit of some ideal purpose not dreamed of by his empirical self. And, as in the case of the 'positively' free self, this entity may be inflated into some super-personal entity—a state, a class, a nation, or the march of history itself, regarded as a more 'real' subject of attributes than the empirical self. But the 'positive' conception of freedom as self-mastery, with its suggestion of a man divided against himself, lends itself more easily to this splitting of personality into two: the transcendent, dominant controller, and the empirical bundle of desires and passions to be disciplined and brought to heel. This demonstrates (if demonstration of so obvious a truth is needed) that the conception of freedom directly derives from the view that is taken of what constitutes a self, a person, a man. Enough manipulation with the definitions of man, and freedom can be made to mean whatever the manipulator wishes. Recent history has made it only too clear that the issue is not merely academic.

The consequences of distinguishing between two selves will become even clearer if one considers the two major forms which the desire to be self-directed—directed by one's 'true' self—has historically taken: the first, that of self-abnegation in order to attain independence; the second, that of self-realization, or total self-identification with a specific principle or ideal in order to attain the selfsame end.

III

THE ONE AND THE MANY

One belief, more than any other, is responsible for the slaughter of individuals on the altars of the great historical ideals—justice or progress or the happiness of future generations, or the sacred mission or emancipation of a nation or race or class, or even liberty itself, which demands the sacrifice of individuals for the freedom of society. This is the belief that somewhere, in the past, or in the future, in divine revelation, or in the mind of an individual thinker, in the pronouncements of history or science, or in the simple heart of an uncorrupted good man, there is a final solution. This ancient faith rests on the conviction that all the positive values in which men have believed must, in the end, be compatible, and perhaps even entail one another. 'Nature binds truth, happiness and virtue together as by an indissoluble chain', said one of the best men who ever lived, and spoke in similar terms of liberty, equality, and justice.[11] But is this true? It is a common-place that neither political equality nor efficient organization is compatible with more than a modicum of individual liberty, and certainly not with unrestricted *laissez-faire;* that justice and generosity, public and private loyalties, the demands of genius and the claims of society can conflict violently with each other. And it is no great way from that to the generalization that not all good things are compatible, still less all the ideals of mankind. But somewhere, we shall be told, and in some way, it must be possible for all these values to live together, for unless this is so, the universe is not a cosmos, not a harmony; unless this is so, conflicts of values may be an intrinsic, irremovable element in human life. To admit that the fulfilment of some of our ideals may in principle make the fulfilment of others impossible is to say that the notion of total human fulfilment is a formal contradiction, a metaphysical chimaera. For every rationalist metaphysician, from Plato to the last disciples of Hegel or Marx, this abandonment of the notion of a final harmony, in which all riddles are solved, all contradictions reconciled, is a piece of crude empiricism, an abdication before brute facts, an intolerable bankruptcy of reason before things as they are, a failure to explain and to justify, to reduce everything to a system, which 'reason' indignantly rejects. But if we are not armed with an *a priori* guarantee of the proposition that a total harmony of true values is somewhere to be found—perhaps in some ideal realm the characteristics of which we can, in our finite state, not so much as conceive—we must fall back on the ordinary resources of empirical observation and ordinary human knowledge. And these certainly give us no warrant for supposing (or even understanding what would be meant by saying) that all good things, or all bad things for that matter, are reconcilable with each other. The world that we encounter in ordinary experience is one in which we are faced with choices between ends equally ultimate, the realization of some of which must inevitably involve the sacrifice of others. Indeed, it is because this is their situation that men place such immense value upon the freedom to choose; for if they had assurance that in some perfect state, realizable by men on earth, no ends pursued by them would ever be in conflict, the necessity and agony of choice would disappear,

[11] Condorcet, from whose *Esquisse* these words are quoted, declares that the task of social science is to show 'by what bonds Nature has united the progress of enlightenment with that of liberty, virtue, and respect for the natural rights of man; how these ideals, which alone are truly good, yet so often separated from each other that they are even believed to be incompatible, should, on the contrary, become inseparable, as soon as enlightenment has reached a certain level simultaneously among a large number of nations'. He goes on to say that: 'Men still preserve the errors of their childhood, of their country, and of their age long after having recognized all the truths needed for destroying them.' Ironically enough, his belief in the need and possibility of uniting all good things may well be precisely the kind of error he himself so well described.

and with it the central importance of the freedom to choose. Any method of bringing this final state nearer would then seem fully justified, no matter how much freedom were sacrificed to forward its advance. It is, I have no doubt, some such dogmatic and *a priori* certainty that has been responsible for the deep, serene, unshakeable conviction in the minds of some of the most merciless tyrants and persecutors in history that what they did was fully justified by its purpose. I do not say that the ideal of self-perfection—whether for individuals or nations or churches or classes—is to be condemned in itself, or that the language which was used in its defence was in all cases the result of a confused or fraudulent use of words, or of moral or intellectual perversity. Indeed, I have tried to show that it is the notion of freedom in its 'positive' sense that is at the heart of the demands for national or social self-direction which animate the most powerful public movements of our time, and that not to recognize this is to misunderstand the most vital facts and ideas of our age. But equally it seems to me that the belief that some single formula can in principle be found whereby all the diverse ends of men can be harmoniously realized is demonstrably false. If, as I believe, the ends of men are many, and not all of them are in principle compatible with each other, then the possibility of conflict—and of tragedy—can never wholly be eliminated from human life, either personal or social. The necessity of choosing between absolute claims is then an inescapable characteristic of the human condition. This gives its value to freedom as Acton had conceived of it—as an end in itself, and not as a temporary need, arising out of our confused notions and disordered lives, a predicament which a panacea could one day put right.

I do not wish to say that individual freedom is, even in the most liberal societies, the sole, or even the dominant, criterion of social action. We compel children to be educated, and we forbid public executions. These are certainly curbs to freedom. We justify them on the ground that ignorance, or a barbarian upbringing, or cruel pleasures and excitements are worse for us than the amount of restraint needed to repress them. This judgement in turn depends on how we determine good and evil, that is to say, on our moral, religious, intellectual, economic and aesthetic values; which are, in their turn, bound up with our conception of man, and of the basic demands of his nature. In other words, our solution of such problems is based on our vision, by which we are consciously or unconsciously guided, of what constitutes a fulfilled human life, as contrasted with Mill's 'cramped and warped', 'pinched and hidebound' natures. To protest against the laws governing censorship or personal morals as intolerable infringements of personal liberty presupposes a belief that the activities which such laws forbid are fundamental needs of men as men, in a good (or, indeed, any) society. To defend such laws is to hold that these needs are not essential, or that they cannot be satisfied without sacrificing other values which come higher—satisfy deeper needs—than individual freedom, determined by some standard that is not merely subjective, a standard for which some objective status—empirical or *a priori*—is claimed.

The extent of a man's or a people's, liberty to choose to live as they desire must be weighed against the claims of many other values, of which equality, or justice, or happiness, or security, or public order are perhaps the most obvious examples. For this reason, it cannot be unlimited. We are rightly reminded by Mr. Tawney that the liberty of the strong, whether their strength is physical or economic, must be restrained. This maxim claims respect, not as a consequence of some *a priori* rule, whereby the respect for the liberty of one man logically entails respect for the liberty of others like him; but simply because respect for the principles of justice, or shame at gross inequality of treatment, is as basic in men as the desire for liberty. That we cannot have everything is a necessary, not a contingent, truth. Burke's plea for the constant need to compensate, to reconcile, to balance; Mill's plea for novel 'experiments in living' with their permanent possibility of error, the knowledge that it is not merely in practice, but in principle, impossible to reach clear-cut and certain answers, even in an ideal world of wholly good men and wholly clear ideas, may madden those who seek for final solutions and single, all-embracing systems, guaranteed to be eternal. Nevertheless, it is a conclusion that cannot be escaped by those who, with Kant, have learnt the truth that out of the crooked timber of humanity no straight thing was ever made.

There is little need to stress the fact that monism, and faith in a single criterion, has always proved a deep source of satisfaction both to the intellect and to the emotions. Whether the standard of judgement derives from some future perfection, as was done by the *philosophes* in the eighteenth century and their technocratic successors in our own day, or is rooted in the past—*la terre et les morts*—as was done by German historicists or French theocrats, or neo-Conservatives in English-speaking countries, it is bound, provided it is inflexible enough, to encounter some unforeseen and unforeseeable human development, which it will not fit; and will then be used to justify the *a priori* barbarities of Procrustes—the vivisection of actual human societies into some fixed pattern dictated by our fallible understanding of a largely imaginary past or a wholly imaginary future. To preserve our absolute categories or ideals at the expense of human lives offends equally against the principles of science and of history; it is an attitude found in equal measure on the right and left wings in our days, and is not reconcilable with the principles accepted by those who respect the facts.

The 'negative' liberty that they strive to realize seems to me a truer and more humane ideal than the goals of those who seek in the great, disciplined, authoritarian structures the ideal of 'positive' self-mastery by classes, or peoples, or the whole of mankind. It is truer, because it recognizes the fact that human goals are many, not all of them commensurable, and in perpetual rivalry with one another. To assume that all values can be graded on one scale, so that it is a mere matter of inspection to determine the highest, is to falsify our knowledge of men as free agents, to represent moral decision as an operation which a slide-rule could, in principle, perform; to say that in some ultimate, all-reconciling, yet realizable synthesis, duty *is* interest, or individual freedom *is* pure democracy, or an authoritarian state, is to throw a metaphysical blanket over either self-deceit or deliberate hypocrisy. It is more humane because it does not (as the system builders do) deprive men, in the name of some remote, or incoherent, ideal, of much that they have found to be indispensable to their life as human beings.[12] In the end, men choose between ultimate values; they choose as they do, because their life and thought are determined by fundamental moral categories and concepts that are as much a part of their being and conscious thought and sense of their own identity, as their basic physical structure.

It may be that the ideal of freedom to live as one wishes—and the pluralism of values connected with it—is only the late fruit of our declining capitalist civilization: an ideal which remote ages and primitive societies have not known, and one which posterity will regard with curiosity, even sympathy, but little comprehension. This may be so; but no sceptical conclusions seem to me to follow. Principles are not less sacred because their duration cannot be guaranteed. Indeed, the very desire for guarantees that our values are eternal and secure in some objective heaven is perhaps only a craving for the certainties of childhood or the absolute values of our primitive past. 'To realise the relative validity of one's convictions', said an admirable writer of our time, 'and yet stand for them unflinchingly, is what distinguishes a civilised man from a barbarian.' To demand more than this is perhaps a deep and incurable metaphysical need; but to allow it to guide one's practice is a symptom of an equally deep, and far more dangerous, moral and political immaturity.

[12] To this also Bentham seems to me to have provided the answer: 'Individual interests are the only real interests . . . can it be conceived that there are men so absurd as to . . . prefer the man who is not to him who is; to torment the living, under pretence of promoting the happiness of them who are not born, and who may never be born?' This is one of the infrequent occasions when Burke agrees with Bentham; for this passage is at the heart of the empirical, as against the metaphysical, view of politics.

MR. JUSTICE HOLMES

4. The Logic of Persecution*

Persecution for the expression of opinions seems to me perfectly logical. If you have no doubt of your premises or your power and want a certain result with all your heart you naturally express your wishes in law and sweep away all opposition. To allow opposition by speech seems to indicate that you think speech impotent, as when a man says that he has squared the circle, or that you do not care wholeheartedly for the result, or that you doubt either your power or your premises.

But when men have realized that time has upset many fighting faiths, they may come to believe even more than they believe the very foundations of their own conduct that the ultimate good desired is better reached by free trade in ideas—that the best test of truth is the power of the thought to get itself accepted in the competition of the market, and that truth is the only ground upon which their wishes safely can be carried out. That, at any rate, is the theory of our Constitution. It is an experiment, as all life is an experiment. Every year if not every day we have to wager our salvation upon some prophecy based upon imperfect knowledge. While that experiment is part of our system I think that we should be eternally vigilant against attempts to check the expression of opinions that we loathe and believe to be fraught with death, unless they so imminently threaten immediate interference with the lawful and pressing purposes of the law that an immediate check is required to save the country.

JULIAN P. BOYD

5. Subversive of What? †

In 1813 a native of France by the name of Regnault de Bécourt published a book entitled Sur la Création du Monde, ou Système d'Organisation Primitive. He and his book would have been forgotten long since if he had not written a letter to the one person in America who, more than any other, was

---

* *Abrams* v. *United States*, 250 U.S. 616 (1919) (dissenting opinion).
† *The Atlantic Monthly*, Vol. CLXXXII (August, 1948). By permission.

in the habit of buying, reading, and appraising the literature of the past and present—Thomas Jefferson. The title of the forthcoming work intrigued Jefferson. A book on the creation of the world seemed to the great scholar-statesman at Monticello to give promise of being either a geological or an astronomical treatise. He thereupon subscribed for the work, received it in due course, and authorized payment of the two dollars that the book cost.

Authorization of payment involved another Frenchman, a well-known bookseller of Philadelphia by the name of Nicholas Dufief, an ardent bibliophile who had been selling books to Jefferson for more than a decade. Dufief promptly paid Bécourt the two dollars. The transaction was apparently at an end, save only for the fact that Jefferson could not avoid being disappointed in so trivial a work as that of Bécourt, which turned out to be neither a geological nor an astronomical work, but merely an infantile attack on the system of philosophy of Sir Isaac Newton.

But this simple book purchase was very far from being at an end. A few months after Dufief had paid Bécourt the two dollars, the Philadelphia constabulary visited the bookshop and hailed him into court on the charge of vending subversive if not blasphemous literature. Whereupon Dufief in great anxiety and distress appealed to Jefferson, urging him to set the minions of the law right by informing them that he, Dufief, had not actually sold the book but had merely acted as Jefferson's agent in a financial transaction.

Jefferson of course immediately complied with the urgent request of the bookseller. He stated the facts succinctly and accurately, no doubt satisfying both Dufief and the Philadelphia magistrates. But while this may have been enough for Mr. Dufief, who was interested only in keeping out of the toils of the law, or for the Philadelphia magistrates, who were determined only to safeguard American institutions, it was very far from being enough to satisfy the author of the American philosophy of government.

Jefferson thereupon stated in his own incomparable way the true nature of the issue involved. The issue, as he presented it, was one that made the fact of Dufief's arrest a trivial and irrelevant circumstance. It was an issue as great as the cause of America itself, involving one of the fundamental precepts upon which the philosophy of Jefferson and of his country rested. It was the same issue, indeed, that had earlier called forth the unforgettable declaration that now stands carved upon one of the three great monuments of our national capital: "I have sworn upon the altar of God eternal hostility against every form of tyranny over the mind of man." It was the issue to which Jefferson devoted his entire life, invariably upholding the oath he had taken in defense of free inquiry.

"I really am mortified," he declared in his letter to Dufief, "to be told that, *in the United States of America,* a fact like this can become a subject of inquiry, and of criminal inquiry too, as an offense against religion: that a question about the sale of a book can be carried before the civil magistrate. Is this then our freedom of religion? And are we to have a censor whose imprimatur shall say what books may be sold, and what we may buy? And who is thus to dogmatize religious opinions for our citizens? Whose foot is to be the measure to which ours are all to be cut or stretched? Is a priest to be our inquisitor? Or shall a layman, simple as ourselves, set up his reason as the rule for what we are to read, and what we must believe?

"It is an insult to our citizens to question whether they are rational beings or not; and blasphemy against religion to suppose it cannot stand a test of truth and reason. If M. de Bécourt's book be false in its facts, disprove them; if false in its reasoning, refute it. But, for God's sake, let us freely hear both sides, if we choose. I know little of its contents, having barely glanced over here and there a passage and over the table of contents. From this the Newtonian philosophy seemed the chief object of attack, the issue of which might be trusted to the strength of the two combatants; Newton certainly not needing the auxiliary arm of the government, and still less the holy author of our religion as to what in it concerns him. I thought the work would be very innocent and one which might be confided to the reason of any man; not likely to be much read, if let alone, but if persecuted it will be generally read. Every man in the United States will think it a duty to buy a copy, in vindication of his right to buy, and to read what he pleases. . . .

"But," Jefferson concluded, "it is impossible that the laws of Pennsylvania, which set us the first example of the wholesome and happy effects of religious freedom, can permit these inquisitorial functions to be proposed to their courts. Under them you are surely safe."

Impossible? Dufief was safe, for he had a stalwart champion and the generation that had fought for the great cause of American liberties in the Revolution was still on the scene, still determined to admit no failure of the proposition to which they had dedicated their lives and sacred honor. That proposition was grounded upon the belief that man was innately good rather than evil; that he was endowed by nature with certain indefeasible rights; that, if the yoke of tyranny in every form were removed, man's natural reason and humane instincts would lead him to prefer justice to injustice, equality to privilege, independence of mind to servile obedience to authority, rational judgments to superstitution, ignorance, and bigotry; and that, finally, in order to achieve this end and to give mankind full freedom to pursue this course and to govern himself in accordance with its high ideals, it was absolutely essential that every man should have free access to knowledge, unopposed by any barriers that might be erected by any authority.

This was not a new ideal or a new faith. It was what Milton called "the good old cause" and its lineage could be traced through many countries and many ages. But old as it was as an ideal, no government in history had adopted it as a philosophy until Jefferson and his compatriots brought forth a union indissolubly linked with the cause of liberty.

This philosophy sustained and informed all of Jefferson's private thinking and public acts. But he was too much a realist not to know that mankind had a peculiar susceptibility to folly, superstition, and the easy and comfortable inclination of yielding obedience to authority. He believed mankind capable of progress, but only if men were free to know their rights and privileges. The people must be free to form their own opinions and to exercise their native reason untrammeled by authority.

Jefferson's devotion to the Union and his belief in the people required courage as well as faith. For the issue of liberty versus authority arbitrarily exercised was one that he was obliged to face in the arena of practical politics. In 1798 the party in power, fearful of the threat of foreign ideas and their subversive tendencies, enacted the Alien and Sedition Acts which made it a criminal offense for "brawlers against government" to voice opinions considered dangerous or revolutionary.

Jefferson declared these acts to be as palpably unconstitutional in their infringement of the right of free speech as if Congress had ordered the citizens of the United States to bow down and worship a golden calf. More, he brought forth the Virginia-Kentucky Resolutions, a weapon that he used reluctantly and with caution, for the doctrine of nullification on which these resolutions rested pointed straight toward disunion. But, he must have reasoned, since liberty and the Union were one cause, of what value was the Union if its powers were used to destroy those liberties guaranteed by the Declaration of Independence and the Bill of Rights?

Fortunately, the ultimate recourse to disunion was not necessary. The verdict of the people whose rights Jefferson was defending was an overwhelming verdict. In 1800 those who had attempted to suppress dissent were dispossessed of their offices and their legislative authority. Aiming their blows directly at Jefferson and his supposedly dangerous following, the Federalists succeeded only in committing political suicide and in elevating their most conspicuous enemy to the chief magistracy. A self-confident nation, inspired by the steadfast faith of one who had not separated himself by fear or distrust from the bulk of his countrymen, had taken heart from his example.

Jefferson recognized the implications of this verdict in his First Inaugural. Many, he knew, had doubted the permanence of the Union and had questioned the ability of the nation to survive such a political revolution as it had just experienced. "I know indeed," he declared, "that some honest men have feared that a republican government cannot be strong; that this government is not strong enough. . . . I believe this, on the contrary, the strongest government on earth." It was strongest, Jefferson meant, in its reliance upon a great ideal lying in the hearts and minds of its people, without which armies and economic power and even constitutions would be valueless.

Nowhere in American annals has this spirit of tolerance of dissent received a more transcendent expression than in these words from Jefferson's great First Inaugural: *"If there be any among us who wish to dissolve this union or to change its republican form, let them stand undisturbed as monuments of the safety with which error of opinion may be tolerated where reason is left free to combat it."*

II

The discoveries of the nineteenth and twentieth centuries have made it philosophically and historically impossible for us to cling to the absolutes that Jefferson accepted as self-evident. There are no absolutes in the twentieth century—at least we think there are none—and the concept of natural law is no longer accepted as fixed and unchallengeable. Yet, even though we think ourselves justified in discarding as untenable the basic assumption upon which the Jeffersonian philosophy rested, the gravest question that we can ask ourselves is whether we are justified in discarding the system along with its premises. Do we dare discard the rights of man along with the concept of natural law?

The least we can do in attempting to answer this grave question, reaching to the roots of all organized society and its institutions, is to know what it is that we propose to do if we discard both the premise and the conclusion. The least we can do if we engage now in what Jefferson would have regarded as a palpable violation of individual rights of opinion and conscience is to be conscious of what we are doing and to do it with a full realization of the consequences that may flow from our actions. Have we done this much?

Have we consciously and deliberately come to the conclusion that Jefferson's tolerance of subversive ideas and of disloyal dissent can no longer be justified? If so, on what grounds have we reached that conclusion? Are we doing it in the name of liberty if not of natural law? If so, what kind of liberty? Jefferson would scarcely have understood our use of the term liberty if in its name we attempt to control the way in which men speak or the thoughts which they express or the intellectual investigations which they undertake. He would have called it tyranny and he would have fought it with every resource at his command.

Let us return to Dufief, the bookseller who was anxious to keep out of jail. Jefferson, you will recall, felt that Dufief had nothing to fear under the liberal laws of Pennsylvania. He felt that it was impossible that in the United States of America, founded upon confidence in man's reason and ability to choose the truth, a citizen could be denied the right to purchase a book because of its ideas or arguments, however erroneous, or that a bookseller could be hailed before the magistrates because he had sold such a book. But is it impossible for us?

It is not only not impossible or improbable but is indeed an actual and sickening fact. Today, at this moment, both civil and criminal causes are being tried in the city in which Dufief lived. These causes arise largely because of the instigation of an ecclesiastical hierarchy and also of some of those who are supposed to be the direct heirs of that Reformation which established the right of men to judge for themselves in matters of conscience. At this instigation police officers arrested booksellers and seized not one book but two thousand, without compensation, because in the opinion of these self-appointed censors some books were subversive of morals or institutions or were dangerous for other men to read.

The seizure of books, some of them used in college instruction, is only one incident in a mounting demand for conformity. The House of Representatives passed by an overwhelming majority a bill which would have made Thomas Jefferson liable to imprisonment and fine if he had voiced the opinion in the First Inaugural that I have just quoted—a bill establishing so firmly the dangerous principle of "guilt by association" that it may limit the right to publish books because of the author's politics or because of the political views expressed.

The preamble of this so-called Subversive Activities Control Act declares its justification to be that of protecting American institutions and the nation itself from infiltration by those who would establish a totalitarian dictatorship. How can we justify so far-reaching a piece of legislation except on the fundamental assumption that the people cannot be trusted to distinguish truth and error?

This bill was sponsored by the House Committee on Un-American Activities. Though it pays lip service to the First Amendment, it is comparable only to the Alien and Sedition Acts of 1798, acts which Thomas Jefferson regarded as so subversive, so destructive of everything that the American Union stood for, that he was driven along the pathway toward disunion in his attempt to defeat so gross a violation of individual right.

But this bill and its sponsoring committee are only the larger symptoms of a disease that is epidemic throughout the country. The public press, the great instrument for the protection of our liberties which Jefferson preferred to government itself, has shamefully acquiesced. Not only acquiesced; but, shaken by the fear of a common foe, distrustful of the ability of the people to distinguish between right and wrong, has actually helped to produce the hysteria that would compel uniformity.

Editors have approved tacitly or explicitly the withdrawal of textbooks and the expulsion of teachers whose ideas do not conform to the established economic or political views; they have aided in compelling educators, school boards, trustees, and others to yield to the pressures of unofficial groups that object to dissenting opinion in the realm of economics, politics, or religion. They have committed the ultimate disloyalty to their trust by attempting to command loyalty, overlooking the simple fact that loyalty cannot be commanded but can only be deserved. Educators, editors, librarians, even those scholars who hold, or at least have the responsibility of defending, the last citadel of civil rights, have all but capitulated to the wave of fear and distrust that is now sweeping over us. Too many have acted the part of Dufief, putting themselves first; too few the part of Jefferson, defending his country's principles at all costs.

III

Just where will this demand for conformity, for unquestioning loyalty, lead? Thomas Jefferson, for one, was certain that it would not lead to human enlightenment, to progress, or to the fullest expressions of reason, justice, and equity toward which our nation directed its early course.

"I join you therefore," he wrote to one of his young protégés after the passage of the Alien and Sedition Acts, "in branding as cowardly the idea that the human mind is incapable of further advances. This is precisely the doctrine that the present despots of the earth are inculcating, and their friends are re-echoing: and applying especially to religion and politics; that it is not probable anything better will be discovered than what was known to our fathers. We are to look backward then and not forward for the improvement of science, and to find it amidst feudal barbarisms and the fires of Spitalfields. But thank heaven the American mind is already too much opened, to listen to these impostures; and while the art of printing is left to us, science can never be retrograde; what is once acquired of real knowledge can never be lost."

But to what advantage, we may ask Jefferson, is the art of printing if what is printed must conform to the established pattern? Of what value is the vaunted public press or our institutions of higher learning, dedicated to the progress of the mind in all fields, when the trustees of the University of Wyoming appoint a committee to examine textbooks for "subversive" material? Of what value is our professed ideal of free education, of the untrammeled pursuit of knowledge, when we acquiesce in the action of the Newark Board of Education which removed certain periodicals from school libraries? What precisely do we mean by liberty as we contemplate the magnates of Hollywood who, in trembling haste, toss sacrifices to a clamoring committee of Congress and beat their breasts in loud protestation of their innocence of a charge that none but the Un-American Activities Committee could bring against them with a straight face—the charge that they employ revolutionists to prepare their mediocre art?

These are only a few specific incidents and they are taken at random. Every day's news adds to the list and the most thoughtful educators are becoming increasingly concerned with this growing threat to a basic concept of American institutions. It is not without significance that large numbers of professors in our institutions of higher learning have signed petition after petition throughout the country, protesting against the proposed Act of Congress sponsored by the Committee on Un-American Activities. Their petitions have uniformly condemned both the bill and the activities of the committee itself as being subversive of the ideals for which this country has traditionally stood. I think such testimonials cannot be dismissed as the statements of paid hirelings of a foreign totalitarianism. These men have fought Milton's "good old cause" on too many fronts and they have sacrificed too much in the cause of education to be charged with such a calumny. Nor can they be dismissed as theorists, visionaries, and crackpots, unrealistic in their views and out of touch with the world of affairs: for these are the men—some of them at least—who formed the chief reliance of this nation in the scientific knowledge which shortened World War II and brought success to American arms.

Responsible heads of the public press who point in commendation to the Committee on Un-American Activities in its shameless pillorying of American citizens and in its flagrant disregard of rights and liberties are either ignorant of the nature and the extent of the protest that is beginning to swell or they value suppression more than they value our freedom or they are deliberately misleading their public. In any event, history has proved time and again that the cause they espouse is a shameful and a futile cause. They lack the vision and the courage that led Jefferson in the infancy of our nation to defy any threat in the realm of ideas, not by suppression but by tolerance. They have little faith and in its place they offer what Jefferson declared to be an insult to the American citizenry—the insult of saying in effect that Americans cannot be trusted to read or to understand or to discriminate. They fear a foreign ideology, unaware of the fact that here at home the liberty that they profess to cherish is in danger of being done to death in the house of friends and with their aid.

I do not impugn the motives of those legislators, editors, educators, and others who have adopted this mistaken course. I do not doubt their devotion to this nation. I do not question their loyalty to the high ideals of a free press. But I do affirm that the methods they have supported in this present issue put them on the side of the enemies of the "good old cause" of Milton and of Jefferson. Those who have adopted this course of compulsory loyalty, though they might disagree with me on everything else, would I think join me in saying that Thomas Jefferson, more than any other single American, can rightfully be regarded as the great spokesman for our ideals and our liberties.

IV

All this, it may very properly be said, is beside the point. Jefferson's agricultural economy, for this nation at least, is a thing of the past, however realistic his philosophy may have been for such an economy at the time he lived. The twentieth century is a century of science and industry and technological power. Under such circumstances, is it not likely that Jefferson would have changed his views, would have given up his eternal values and absolutes as we have given them up, would have recognized the necessity of opposing evil to the utmost limits, however much an individual here and there might suffer?

I think it is undoubtedly true that Jefferson, always a realist and a man of practical statesmanship, would have viewed our problems in the light of our knowledge. Since he was a relativist in a world of absolutes, he would probably be more so in a relativistic world. Though he knew history as few in his generation did, he looked to it for perspective, not for dogmatic authority. He would very likely have regarded it as cowardly of us to look to him as our sole guidance. The earth, he declared, belongs to the living. "Can one generation bind another and all others in succession forever?" he asked. "I think not. The Creator has made the earth for the living not the dead. . . . A generation may bind itself as long as its majority continues in life; when that has disappeared, another majority is in place, holds all the rights and powers their predecessors once held and may change their laws and institutions to suit themselves. Nothing then is unchangeable but the inherent and inalienable rights of man." But he also declared that justice is the fundamental law of society and that "the majority, oppressing an individual, is guilty of a crime, abuses its strength, and by acting on the law of the strongest breaks up the foundations of society."

It may be that today, because we have achieved such an excess of power and knowledge beyond our ability to manage, we cannot afford the tolerance and the free flow and interchange and clash of ideas that he advocated. I do not think so. At least, if this is so, the alternative evil to which we must turn in our dilemma is worse than the evil from which we fly, simply because of the vast power now in our hands. But even if this were true, let us be honest. Let us not exercise this power of the majority to suppress the rights of individuals and call it the honored name by which our liberties have come down to us. Let us not call it a free republic whose principles we deny while we commit acts that desecrate its name. Let us frankly, solemnly, and with a full realization of what we are doing and what consequences we may draw from our actions, admit that we no longer believe in the ideals that made us great.

I for one do not fear the outcome. The verdict in the twentieth century will, I believe, be what it was in 1800 and what it was in the Age of the Reformation. I believe with Jefferson that "in every country where man is free to think and speak, differences of opinion will arise from differences of perception, and the imperfection of reason; that these differences when permitted, as in this happy country, to purify themselves by free discussion, are but as passing clouds overspreading our land transiently and leaving our horizon more bright and serene."

But I believe also that we cannot wait complacently on the calm assumption that this will come about through acquiescence or through temporary yielding to pressures of authority or through letting the storm spend itself. It will come about only when, as Jefferson said, "to preserve the freedom of the human mind and freedom of the press every spirit should be ready to devote itself to martyrdom; for as long as we may think as we will and speak as we think, the condition of man will proceed in improvement."

The alternative that he implied was obvious: deny this freedom, acquiesce in this abridgment of our liberties—and the promise of improvement of the human race would diminish or cease. If, then, the power that we have achieved in the twentieth century, which is nothing less than the power of planetary destruction, is so great as to deny us the rights that have been achieved over the centuries, let us frankly acknowledge that the price of this denial is the loss of our promise of moral and intellectual improvement. It is a price so fearfully exacting as to make man's future one of mere existence and not of destiny. It is a price that mankind has steadfastly refused to pay.

MORRIS L. ERNST

6. *An Affirmative Loyalty Program**

We have had an ample amount of hysteria in regard to the Loyalty Program. Much of it has been caused by a lack of concern about facts; hysteria usually develops from ignorance. The statistical facts are simple. Congress decided to remove from Civil Service at "the exit end" the Department of Defense, the State Department and the Atomic Energy Commission. In other words, in these areas a person may now lawfully be fired under mandate of Congress without any accusation and without any hearing. It is interesting to note that many who were top officials in the Roosevelt administration have indicated that they are in favor of abolishing Civil Service at the exit end in all departments, for all employees in sensitive areas, or in fact, all em-

* *The American Scholar*, Vol. XIX (Autumn. 1950). By permission.

ployees in important positions. This has long been urged regardless of the factor of security or loyalty, and has been supported by worthy citizens as a measure to improve the service in various large government departments. True enough, it has the capacity of resulting in a spoils system.

Congress voted money so that the FBI could make reports on the two and one-half million government employees operating in other agencies in the government. Under the Atomic Energy Act, the FBI also reports on employees. The latest figures indicate that there was no evidence of hysteria on the part of the FBI. It did its job as ordered, and, interestingly enough, decided up to May 5, 1950, that only about 11,813 employees of the two and one-half million merited full investigation. The balance of about 2,490,000 were found to have a record that raised no question of division of loyalty. Of the 11,813 the public is apparently ignorant of the fact that the Civil Service Commission as of March 31, 1950, reports that only 202 were severed from service as a result of the President's Loyalty Order. As a footnote to show the extent of the protections provided, we should remember that the Civil Service Loyalty Review Boards reversed findings of potential disloyalty in 143 cases. As another footnote, it might be stated that 1,406 left the service during investigations and 1,028 left prior to adjudications by the Loyalty Hearing Boards. Such severances may have resulted from a consciousness of guilt or have occurred for reasons entirely irrelevant to any question of loyalty.

In brief, numerically the proceedings were carried on in such an orderly fashion that some day, if some Communists are found in sensitive spots, there may develop an hysterical movement to fire Hoover and the Review Boards because they allowed a few to seep through.

I have not much sympathy for the worthy liberals who merely shout down the Loyalty Program and who fail to offer a constructive suggestion about its operation or about a machinery to replace it. There were at the start, according to the not too reliable press, quite a few cases outrageously tried— where the rights of individuals, it seemed to me, were not properly protected. Students of the situation have recently come to the conclusion that the imperfections in the hearings in some of the early cases were cured, or at least substantially improved, in later cases.

Let's wake up. We are facing an utterly new problem in American life. For a century and a half this nation has had to cope with individual behavior patterns involving government employees who had a division of loyalty involving another sovereignty. If today we had only to face the fact that there are more such individuals behaving in disloyal fashion, we would not need any new or additional loyalty protective programs. The old-fashioned spy, who used to bribe the stenographer or fall in love with the boss, is easy to cope with. But we are at war. It is a good war. Unfortunately, it is called a cold war. In my opinion it is a hot war, a non-shooting war. It is a war for the minds of men, and we can lose it without losing a life. Communist dictatorship has never been attained through a vote of a majority of the people ulti-mately to be squeezed into intellectual starvation. What we are facing are the new dangers derived from secret organized efforts of dictatorships. We must cope with a new kind of organized stealth and anonymity. It is not easy to de-vise machinery to handle organized sneaks. The avowed Communist is no problem compared to the thousands who are crypto-Communists—who deny that they are Communists. Heywood Broun used to say: "People call me a Communist. I say I am not a Communist. They don't believe me. They are right not to believe me, because they know if I were a Communist I would swear I am not a Communist."

In brief, no one would believe the head of the Communist party under oath. And so we are faced with a difficulty of proof, since in the final analysis the normal way to prove that a person is or is not a Communist is to subpoena the head of the movement and the membership records—both of which no one would trust. It is this *secret* movement which no doubt impelled the President's executive order. The Attorney General prepared a list of or-ganizations which in his opinion contained the roots of "subversive" ele-ments. The simplest approach to this phase of the problem is to remember that "to subvert" means "to turn under" and that the organizations on the Attorney General's list had "turned themselves under." For my part, I was shocked that the list was published without hearings. However, after the publication, the Attorney General announced that any organization could come into his office for a hearing. So far as I know, such proffer of conference was not fully accepted by any single organization on the list. My examination of the list indicates that not a single one of the organizations has ever made full disclosure to the American people. This is the root of the problem and the root of the evil.

Through such secret organizations, decent Americans have been placed in an area of doubt from which it was difficult to remove themselves, since the Communist party obviously thrives on tainting democracy and is uncon-cerned with injury done to non-Communists. The more the wild and stupid press and some members of Congress improperly label people as subversive or Communist, the happier the Communist party is. If I had my way, I would provide a list of politically active organizations to be compiled *after hearings,* and would only put on the list organizations which have failed to make full disclosure of finances, membership, officers and activities. The United States Supreme Court has upheld as constitutional the drawing of a line between secret benevolent societies or college fraternities, on the one hand, and the Klan, on the other. This in relation to the New York statute calling for Klan disclosure. The answer to our basic dilemma is disclosure rather than suppression, and I am in full accord with the position taken by J. Edgar Hoover, who has repeatedly indicated his opposition to the outlawry of the Communist party. We must all know that we cannot outlaw anything more than a name, and that if the Communist party is outlawed, it may well bob up under a new name such as the "American Peglerites" or some other respectable title. I would go further; I would provide that an organization on the list should have a right to purge itself on making disclosure.

I would then limit the impact of a loyalty or security program to those who have relationships to secret groups, and I would have individual behavior patterns handled as we have done over the past century and a half, without relationship to the new loyalty or security program.

As to the trials of individuals where the proof would rest primarily on relationships to secret underground organizations, I would allow the fullest latitude to the review boards, since we have to pinprick our way into the degree of intimacy of relationship which would raise a question of division of loyalty. It might be money contributions; it might be official activity; on the other hand, it might be the most innocent kind of a well-motivated desire to join in what was deemed to be non-subversive activities. Most of the people who joined the organizations on the Attorney General's list were no doubt mere suckers, and above all, careless with their names and reputations. Many of them, if asked to endorse a toothpaste, would have applied greater scrutiny than when they were asked to endorse the most precious commodity known to man—ideas. I would go further and provide that an individual could purge himself. There is no such thing in life as sinning without repentance and possible salvation. Stupidly enough, we prevent people from getting out of the Communist party. It is my best judgment that a third of the members of the Communist party under thirty years of age would get out if it were not for the social and economic ostracism presently existing in our culture. To be sure, the Communist party keeps many of them prisoners through blackmail by notifying employers as to ex-Communists, provided the ex-Communist has publicly announced his divorce from that evil movement. But under a decent loyalty program, an individual should always be free to step up to the counter and say: I joined that movement and now, since I have thought it over and since I know that it is a band of uncourageous sneaks, I am withdrawing. Whether the Board believes the particular employee or not would be a question for proof in each case.

I would go further, and provide that the hearings should be either public or private, according to the request of the employee. I would add that, if an employee has been absolved, an announcement should be issued—if *he* so request.

But above all, it is important that the loyalty program be limited to sensitive jobs. I should imagine that 90 per cent of all the jobs in the United States raise no security or loyalty questions. I would not have a Communist in my law office, since the practice of the law involves trust of other people's secrets. No sane person would have a Communist work in sensitive areas of the Atomic Energy Commission. Hence, a fundamental improvement in the situation could be accomplished by a clearer definition within each department, bureau or agency of the areas which are sensitive. This may require considerable reshuffling. The definition of "sensitivity" will mean the development of standards and definitions. I understand that, in one bureau, over a hundred spots were originally declared to be sensitive. On re-examination, plus re-shuffling of scrub women, changing of locks on doors and the like, the number was reduced to about twenty. The definition of sensitive areas in itself would greatly simplify the problem, and certainly reduce the work involved. Many a person unemployable in a sensitive job might well be shifted, as is done in Engand, to non-sensitive areas. I would not want a person of even a potential division of loyalty to be employed cleaning out the trash baskets at the White House, but I should imagine no one would object if such a person were given a job picking up leaves in a public park in Washington. With the limitation of the entire program to sensitive jobs in sensitive agencies, a further improvement might be made—the advent of a realization that no one has a right to a government job, and that, in this great war with dictatorships, the first duty of a government employee is to protect the sovereignty of the state.

Many of my liberal friends have opposed the creation and activities of the review boards. I am violently in favor of them, and I think they have done an efficient and selfless job. It will be interesting to see if the conclusions reached by the group studying this matter for one of the big foundations will not soon come out with a finding to the same effect. The reason that I favor outside review boards—that is, boards composed of persons not in the professional employ of the government—is that such persons are further removed from contact with Congress, and hence may produce an additional bit of courage. With Congress what it is, the head of an agency might lean backward to protect himself, whereas the outside review board, not having to go to Congress for appropriations and the like, would be more inclined to look with greater objectivity on the evidence.

I cannot in this brief article outline every detail of what I conceive to be necessary for an ideal loyalty program, but there is one further aspect of any such program which must be mentioned.

I have followed the FBI with great care for many years. I started with a basic human suspicion of all constabularies. In my judgment, the FBI is the single greatest police force in the world, and I am happy to say that Roger Baldwin, the great driving force of the American Civil Liberties Union for many years, has said, with respect to its over-all activities: "It seems to me that your Bureau has accomplished an exceedingly difficult task with rare judicial sense." Any loyalty program must depend on reports. The FBI is a reporting agency. It has no power to hire or fire anyone, except its own employees. It is the duty of the FBI to turn over *all* facts to the employing agencies. Some worthy liberals at one time urged that the FBI files should be screened. It is no doubt true that there is much in the files of the FBI that is either anonymous or is a pick-up of alleged facts uttered by all kinds of persons, reliable or unreliable. Some people urge that the FBI files should be deleted of all such so-called gossip material. This, in my opinion, would be a greater danger than any conceivable loyalty program. If the reporting agency is ever in a position to take a single document out of this file, it will have the power to make anyone either an angel or a devil. The FBI should continue, as in the past, to turn over *all* the information it gets. The employer (that is, the government agency) should take the information and review it—and the heads of government departments are paid to be tough enough to disregard evidence that they think is immaterial, or irrelevant, or unworthy of credence. I also want the FBI to continue to receive anonymous communications or information from sources which have made anonymity a condition of the transmission. The files of the FBI would be greatly weakened if anonymous telephone calls or confidential communications were rejected. Many of the most important jobs done by the FBI were no doubt brought into being by an original tip from a person who did not care to be involved at a hearing or a court trial. The FBI should, if a reporting agency desires it, evaluate the source when the informant wants his identity withheld. It could indicate, for example, that such information came from a sick old woman or from a lawyer of repute of, say, twenty years' standing. As I understand it, the FBI offered, in the loyalty field, either to remove all communications from confidential sources or to evaluate them where possible. The Civil Service Loyalty Board naturally chose the latter course.

In the last analysis the single greatest difficulty comes from the fact that in many situations the reporting agency is in no position to divulge the source of its information: this, because either the informant has not given his name, because he has only given the information on condition that he remain anonymous, or because the divulging of the source would destroy this source as a means of getting other and even more valuable information.

I am not sure that I know exactly how to handle this phase of the dilemma. It may be that the Appeal Board should, in each such instance, declare that it has examined the situation, and that in its opinion the undivulged source has been weighted in the light of the evaluation of the material supplied by the reporting agency. It is this final dilemma that has driven many people to urge the right of free discharge of all employees in sensitive jobs—free in the sense that there be no need for any hearing.

My own feeling, however, is that the entire Loyalty Program arises from the inability of our society to come to grips with anonymous secret groups. The President's Committee on Civil Rights came out unanimously in favor of disclosure by organized groups in our society. I have long been in favor of such a measure. We are operating under a Bill of Rights, which guarantees freedom to speak or not to speak. In my opinion, to the extent that we say to our people: you can either be sneaks or you can stand up publicly, say what you think and be defended—we do encourage the development of further stealth. We now have legislation for disclosure as to magazines and newspapers, disclosure under SEC regulations, the Pure Food and Drug Act, and disclosure as to lobbying. I am not concerned with disclosure of the speaker or writer, because he is always disclosed, but I want to know for whom he is speaking, or for whom he is writing. The great Negro organizations and the spokesmen for the two great labor organizations have come out in favor of disclosure.

It cost $50,000 to run the picket line at the White House up to the time that Hitler attacked Stalin. I would defend the right of the pickets, but I think the public has a right to know for whom they were picketing—who put up the money? I was told that a million dollars was collected by the Communists in the Scottsboro case. I have looked into the matter, and I am convinced that not over $60,000 was spent directly in the defense of the case, which Judge Leibowitz carried on without compensation or reimbursements. What happened to the other $940,000?

The lowest estimate I have received as to the amount of money which will be raised in the defense of the eleven convicted Communists and their attorneys is two million dollars. They have a right to raise that amount of money. Haven't we the right, as a people, to an accounting? My theory as to disclosure is not one limited to Communists. It relates to all substantial organized efforts. I have seen the list of fifty people who gave from $5000 to $50,000 apiece to Gerald L. K. Smith. I would defend the right of Gerald L. K. Smith to send his evil literature through the mails, but I submit that disclosure of the names of the persons for whom Gerald L. K. Smith was speaking is part of the democratic function, where a government's main duty is disclosure and not suppression.

The Loyalty Program, or, as it might be called, the Security Program, will bother us as long as we fail to come to grips with this new element facing our culture—mass organized groups working with vast funds to get to the minds of our people. If the loyalty proceedings, with all of its defects, has done nothing else, it has no doubt brought to the attention of careless suckers the need for realizing that their names have value, and that they should not join organizations which refuse to make disclosure. To be sure, under a dictatorship, secrecy and stealth are necessary for minority points of view, but in this country, conducting its great and successful experiment in the direction of a free market place of thought, we cannot believe any longer that truth will win out in the market place if the market place is corrupted by the pumping in of ideas in pamphlet or other form with no one knowing who the backers of the ideas are. I should imagine that even those who are opposed to every inch of the Loyalty Program are worried when they realize that in the white primary fight in Georgia there were innumerable expensively printed gazettes and magazines favoring the white primary, and practically all of these carried fake names or no names.

Since the great minority groups, such as the National Association for the Advancement of Colored People, the CIO and the AFL, operating in most unfriendly areas, declared in favor of disclosure, I am still waiting for one example of a group which would have anything to fear by complete disclosure. To be sure, the shiftover from stealth to aboveboardness might cause some turmoil and discomfort, but I for my part am much more concerned with the discomfort of innocent people than I am with those who want to play an underground role. And with disclosure, in a very short time we will be able to defend more effectively *all* ideas in an open market place of thought.

JUSTICES VINSON, JACKSON, BLACK, DOUGLAS

7. *The Case of the Eleven Communist Leaders**

MR. CHIEF JUSTICE VINSON:

The obvious purpose of the statute is to protect existing government, not from change by peaceable, lawful and constitutional means, but from change by violence, revolution and terrorism.

That it is within the power of the Congress to protect the Government of the United States from armed rebellion is a proposition which requires little discussion. Whatever theoretical merit there may be to the argument that there is a "right" to rebellion against dictatorial governments, is without force where the existing structure of the government provides for peaceful and orderly change.

We reject any principle of governmental helplessness in the face of preparation for revolution, which principle, carried to its logical conclusion, must lead to anarchy. No one could conceive that it is not within the power of Congress to prohibit acts intended to overthrow the Government by force and violence. The question with which we are concerned here is not whether Congress has such power, but whether the means which it has employed conflict with the First and Fifth Amendments to the Constitution.

One of the bases for the contention that the means which Congress has employed are invalid takes the form of an attack on the face of the statute on

* From *Dennis et al.* v. *United States*, 341 U.S. 494 (1951).

the grounds that, by its terms, it prohibits academic discussion of the merits of Marxism-Leninism, that it stifles ideas and is contrary to all concepts of a free speech and a free press.

The very language of the Smith Act negates the interpretation which petitioners would have us impose on that act. It is directed at advocacy, not discussion. Thus, the trial judge properly charged the jury that they could not convict if they found that petitioners did "no more than pursue peaceful studies and discussions or teaching and advocacy in the realm of ideas." He further charged that it was not unlawful "to conduct in an American college and university a course explaining the philosophical theories set forth in the books which have been placed in evidence."

Such a change is in strict accord with the statutory language, and illustrates the meaning to be placed on those words. Congress did not intend to eradicate the free discussion of political theories, to destroy the traditional rights of Americans to discuss and evaluate ideas without fear of governmental sanction. Rather, Congress was concerned with the very kind of activity in which the evidence showed these petitioners engaged.

An analysis of the leading cases in this Court which have involved direct limitations on speech, however, will demonstrate that both the majority of the Court and the dissenters in particular cases have recognized that this is not an unlimited, unqualified right, but that the societal value of speech must, on occasion, be subordinated to other values and considerations.

No important case involving free speech was decided by this court prior to *Schenck* v. *United States,* 249 U.S. 47 (1919). Indeed, the summary treatment accorded an argument based upon an individual's claim that the First Amendment protected certain utterances indicates that the Court at earlier dates placed no unique emphasis upon that right.

It was not until the classic dictum of Justice Holmes in the Schenck case, that speech per se received that emphasis in a majority opinion. That case involved a conviction upon the Criminal Espionage Act, 40 Stat. 217. The question the Court faced was whether the evidence was sufficient to sustain the conviction.

Writing for a unanimous court, Justice Holmes stated that the "question in every case is whether the words used are used in such circumstances and are of such a nature as to create a clear and present danger that they will bring about the substantive evils that Congress has a right to prevent." 249 U.S. at 52.

In discussing the proper measure of evaluation of this kind of legislation, we suggested that the Holmes-Brandeis philosophy insisted that where there was a direct restriction upon speech, a "clear and present danger" that the substantive evil would be caused was necessary before the statute in question could be constitutionally applied. And we stated, "(the First) Amendment requires that one be permitted to believe what he will. It requires that one be permitted to advocate what he will unless there is a clear and present danger that a substantial public evil will result thereform." 339 U.S. at 412.

But we further suggested that neither Justice Holmes nor Justice Brandeis ever envisioned that a shorthand phrase should be crystallized into a rigid rule to be applied inflexibly without regard to the circumstances of each case. Speech is not an absolute, above and beyond control by the Legislature when its judgment, subject to review here, is that certain kinds of speech are so undesirable as to warrant criminal sanction.

Nothing is more certain in modern society than the principle that there are no absolutes, that a name, a phrase, a standard has meaning only when associated with the considerations which gave birth to the nomenclature. To those who would paralyze our Government in the face of impending threat by encasing it in a semantic straitjacket we must reply that all concepts are relative.

In this case we are squarely presented with the application of the "clear and present danger" test, and must decide what that phrase imports.

We first note that many of the cases in which this Court has reversed convictions by use of this or similar tests, have been based on the fact that the interest which the state was attempting to protect was itself too insubstantial to warrant restriction of speech.

Overthrow of the Government by force and violence is certainly a substantial enough interest for the Government to limit speech. Indeed, this is the ultimate value of any society, for if a society cannot protect its very structure from armed internal attack, it must follow that no subordinate value can be protected. If, then, this interest may be protected, the literal problem which is presented is what has been meant by the use of the phrase "clear and present danger" of the utterances bringing about the evil within the power of Congress to punish.

Obviously, the words cannot mean that before the Government may act, it must wait until the putsch is about to be executed, the plans have been laid and the signal is awaited. If Government is aware that a group aiming at its overthrow is attempting to indoctrinate its members and to commit them to a course whereby they will strike when the leaders feel the circumstances permit, action by the Government is required.

The argument that there is no need for Government to concern itself, for Government is strong, it possesses ample powers to put down a rebellion, it may defeat the revolution with ease, needs no answer. For that is not the question.

Certainly an attempt to overthrow the Government by force, even though doomed from the outset because of inadequate numbers or power of the revolutionists, is a sufficient evil for Congress to prevent. The damage which such attempts create both physically and politically to a nation, makes it impossible to measure the validity in terms of the probability of success, or the immediacy of a successful attempt.

In the instant case, the trial judge charged the jury that they could not convict unless they found that petitioners intended to overthrow the Government "as speedily as circumstances would permit." This does not mean, and could not properly mean, that they would not strike until there was certainty of success. What was meant was that the revolutionists would strike when they thought the time was ripe. We must therefore reject the contention that success or probability of success is the criterion.

The situation with which Justices Holmes and Brandeis were concerned in Gitlow was a comparatively isolated event, bearing little relation in their minds to any substantial threat to the safety of the community.

They were not confronted with any situation comparable to the instant one—the development of an apparatus designed and dedicated to the overthrow of the Government, in the context of world crisis after crisis.

Chief Judge Learned Hand, writing for the majority below, interpreted the phrase as follows: "In each case (courts) must ask whether the gravity of the 'evil,' discounted by its improbability, justifies such invasion of free speech as is necessary to avoid the danger." 183 F. 2d at 212.

We adopt this statement of the rule. As articulated by Chief Judge Hand, it is as succinct and inclusive as any other we might devise at this time. It takes into consideration those factors which we deem relevant, and relates their significances. More we cannot expect from words.

Likewise, we are in accord with the court below, which affirmed the trial court's finding that the requisite danger existed. The mere fact that, from the period 1945 to 1948, petitioners' activities did not result in an attempt to overthrow the Government by force and violence is, of course, no answer to the fact that there was a group that was ready to make the attempt.

The formation by petitioners of such a highly organized conspiracy, with rigidly disciplined members subject to call when the leaders, these petitioners, felt that the time had come for action, coupled with the inflammable nature of world conditions, similar uprisings in other countries, and the touch-and-go nature of our relations with countries with whom petitioners were in the very least ideologically attuned, convince us that their convictions were justified on this score.

And this analysis disposes of the contention that a conspiracy to advocate, as distinguished from the advocacy itself, cannot be constitutionally restrained, because it comprises only the preparation. It is the existence of the conspiracy which creates the danger.

If the ingredients of the reaction are present, we cannot bind the Government to wait until the catalyst is added.

We hold that Sections 2 (A) (1), 2 (A) (3) and 3 of the Smith Act, do not inherently, or as construed or applied in the instant case, violate the First Amendment and other provisions of the Bill of Rights, or the First and Fifth Amendments, because of indefiniteness. Petitioners intended to overthrow the Government of the United States as speedily as the circumstances would permit. Their conspiracy to organize the Communist party and to teach and advocate the overthrow of the Government of the United States by force and violence created a "clear and present danger" of an attempt to overthrow the Government by force and violence. They were properly and constitutionally convicted for violation of the Smith Act.

MR. JUSTICE JACKSON, *concurring:*

This prosecution is the latest of never-ending, because never successful, quests for some legal formula that will secure an existing order against revolutionary radicalism. It requires us to reappraise, in the light of our own times and conditions, constitutional doctrines devised under other circumstances to strike a balance between authority and liberty.

Activity here charged to be criminal is conspiracy—that defendants conspired to teach and advocate, and to organize the Communist Party to teach and advocate, overthrow and destruction of the Government by force and violence. There is no charge of actual violence or attempt at overthrow.

The principal reliance of the defense in this Court is that the conviction cannot stand under the Constitution because the conspiracy of these defendants presents no "clear and present danger" of imminent or foreseeable overthrow.

I

The statute before us repeats a pattern, originally devised to combat the wave of anarchistic terrorism that plagued this country about the turn of the century, which lags at least two generations behind Communist Party techniques.

Anarchism taught a philosophy of extreme individualsim and hostility to government and property. Its avowed aim was a more just order, to be achieved by violent destruction of all government. Anarchism's sporadic and uncoordinated acts of terror were not integrated with an effective revolutionary machine, but the Chicago Haymarket riots of 1886, attempted murder of the industrialist Frick, attacks on state officials, and assassination of President McKinley in 1901, were fruits of its preaching.

However, extreme individualism was not conducive to cohesive and disciplined organization. Anarchism fell into disfavor among incendiary radicals, many of whom shifted their allegiance to the rising Communist Party. Meanwhile, in Europe anarchism had been displaced by Bolshevism as the doctrine and strategy of social and political upheaval. Led by intellectuals hardened by revolutionary experience, it was a more sophisticated, dynamic and realistic movement. Establishing a base in the Soviet Union, it founded an aggressive international Communist apparatus which has modeled and directed a revolutionary movement able only to harass our own country. But it has seized control of a dozen other countries.

Communism, the antithesis of anarchism, appears today as a closed system of thought representing Stalin's version of Lenin's version of Marxism. As an ideology, it is not one of spontaneous protest arising from American working-class experience. It is a complicated system of assumptions, based on European history and conditions, shrouded in an obscure and ambiguous vocabulary, which allures our ultrasophisticated intelligentsia more than our hard-headed working people. From time to time it champions all manner of causes and grievances and makes alliances that may add to its foothold in government or embarrass the authorities.

The Communist Party, nevertheless, does not seek its strength primarily in numbers. Its aim is a relatively small party whose strength is in selected, dedicated, indoctrinated, and rigidly disciplined members. From established policy it tolerates no deviation and no debate. It seeks members that are, or may be, secreted in strategic posts in transportation, communications, industry, government, and especially in labor unions where it can compel employers to accept and retain its members. It also seeks to infiltrate and control organizations of professional and other groups. Through these placements in positions of power it seeks a leverage over society that will make up in power of coercion what it lacks in power of persuasion.

The Communists have no scruples against sabotage, terrorism, assassination, or mob disorder; but violence is not with them, as with the anarchists, an end in itself. The Communist Party advocates force only when prudent and profitable. Their strategy of stealth precludes premature or uncoordinated outbursts of violence, except, of course, when the blame will be placed on shoulders other than their own. They resort to violence as to truth, not as a principle but as an expedient. Force or violence, as they would resort to it, may never be necessary, because infiltration and deception may be enough.

Force would be utilized by the Communist Party not to destroy government but for its capture. The Communist recognizes that an established government in control of modern technology cannot be overthrown by force until it is about ready to fall of its own weight. Concerted uprising, therefore, is to await that contingency and revolution is seen, not as a sudden episode, but as the consummation of a long process.

The United States, fortunately, has experienced Communism only in its preparatory stages and for its pattern of final action must look abroad. Russia, of course, was the pilot Communist revolution, which to the Marxist confirms the Party's assumptions and points its destiny. But Communist technique in the overturn of a free government was disclosed by the *coup d'état* in which they seized power in Czechoslovakia. There the Communist Party during its preparatory stage claimed and received protection for its freedoms of speech, press, and assembly. Pretending to be but another political party, it eventually was conceded participation in government, where it entrenched reliable members chiefly in control of police and information services. When the government faced a foreign and domestic crisis, the Communist Party had established a leverage strong enough to threaten civil war. In a period of confusion the Communist plan unfolded and the underground organization came to the surface throughout the country in the form chiefly of labor "action committees." Communist officers of the unions took over transportation and allowed only persons with party permits to travel. Communist printers took over the newspapers and radio and put out only party-approved versions of events. Possession was taken of telegraph and telephone systems and communications were cut off wherever directed by party heads. Communist unions took over the factories, and in the cities a partisan distribution of food was managed by the Communist organization. A virtually bloodless abdication by the elected government admitted the Communists to power, whereupon they instituted a reign of oppression and terror, and ruthlessly denied to all others the freedoms which had sheltered their conspiracy.

II

The foregoing is enough to indicate that, either by accident or design, the Communist stratagem outwits the antianarchist pattern of statute aimed against "overthrow by force and violence" if qualified by the doctrine that only "clear and present danger" of accomplishing that result will sustain the prosecution.

The "clear and present danger" test was an innovation by Mr. Justice Holmes in the *Schenck* case, reiterated and refined by him and Mr. Justice Brandeis in later cases, all arising before the era of World War II revealed the subtlety and efficacy of modernized revolutionary techniques used by totalitarian parties. In those cases, they were faced with convictions under so-called criminal syndicalism statutes aimed at anarchists but which, loosely construed, had been applied to punish socialism, pacifism, and left-wing ideologies, the charges often resting on far-fetched inferences which, if true, would establish only technical or trivial violations. They proposed "clear and present danger" as a test for the sufficiency of evidence in particular cases.

I would save it, unmodified, for application as a "rule of reason" in the kind of case for which it was devised. When the issue is criminality of a hot-headed speech on a street corner, or circulation of a few incendiary pamphlets, or parading by some zealots behind a red flag, or refusal of a handful of school children to salute our flag, it is not beyond the capacity of the judicial process to gather, comprehend, and weigh the necessary materials for decision whether it is a clear and present danger of substantive evil or a harmless letting off of steam. It is not a prophecy, for the danger in such cases has matured by the time of trial or it was never present. The test applies and has meaning where a conviction is sought to be based on a speech or writing which does not directly or explicitly advocate a crime but to which such tendency is sought to be attributed by construction or by implication from external circumstances. The formula in such cases favors freedoms that are vital to our society, and, even if sometimes applied too generously, the consequences cannot be grave. But its recent expansion has extended, in particular to Communists, unprecedented immunities. Unless we are to hold our Government captive in a judge-made verbal trap, we must approach the problem of a well-organized, nation-wide conspiracy, such as I have described, as realistically as our predecessors faced the trivialities that were being prosecuted until they were checked with a rule of reason.

I think reason is lacking for applying that test to this case.

If we must decide that this Act and its application are constitutional only if we are convinced that petitioner's conduct creates a "clear and present danger" of violent overthrow, we must appraise imponderables, including international and national phenomena which baffle the best informed foreign offices and our most experienced politicians. We would have to foresee and predict the effectiveness of Communist propaganda, opportunities for infiltration, whether, and when, a time will come that they consider propitious for action, and whether and how fast our existing government will deteriorate. And we would have to speculate as to whether an approaching Communist *coup* would not be anticipated by a nationalistic fascist movement. No doctrine can be sound whose application requires us to make a prophecy of that sort in the guise of a legal decision. The judicial process simply is not adequate to a trial of such far-flung issues. The answers given would reflect our own political predilections and nothing more.

The authors of the "clear and present danger" test never applied it to a case like this, nor would I. If applied as it is proposed here, it means that the Communist plotting is protected during its period of incubation; its preliminary stages of organization and preparation are immune from the law; the Government can move only after imminent action is manifest, when it would, of course, be too late.

III

The highest degree of Constitutional protection is due to the individual acting without conspiracy. But even an individual cannot claim that the Constitution protects him in advocating or teaching overthrow of government by force or violence. I should suppose no one would doubt that Congress has power to make such attempted overthrow a crime. But the contention is that one has the constitutional right to work up a public desire and will to do what it is a crime to attempt. I think direct incitement by speech or writing can be made a crime, and I think there can be a conviction without also proving that the odds favored its success by 99 to 1, or some other extremely high ratio.

Of course, it is not always easy to distinguish teaching or advocacy in the sense of incitement from teaching or advocacy in the sense of exposition or explanation. It is a question of fact in each case.

IV

What really is under review here is a conviction of conspiracy, after a trial for conspiracy, on an indictment charging conspiracy, brought under a statute outlawing conspiracy. With due respect to my colleagues, they seem to me to discuss anything under the sun except the law of conspiracy. One of the dissenting opinions even appears to chide me for "invoking the law of conspiracy." As that is the case before us, it may be more amazing that its reversal can be proposed without even considering the law of conspiracy.

The Constitution does not make conspiracy a civil right. The Court has never before done so and I think it should not do so now. Conspiracies of labor unions, trade associations, and news agencies have been condemned, although accomplished, evidenced and carried out, like the conspiracy here, chiefly by letter-writing, meetings, speeches and organization. Indeed, this Court seems, particularly in cases where the conspiracy has economic ends, to be applying its doctrines with increasing severity. While I consider criminal conspiracy a dragnet device capable of perversion into an instrument of injustice in the hands of a partisan or complacent judiciary, it has an established place in our system of law, and no reason appears for applying it only to concerted action claimed to disturb interstate commerce and withholding it from those claimed to undermine our whole Government.

The basic rationale of the law of conspiracy is that a conspiracy may be an evil in itself, independently of any other evil it seeks to accomplish.

So far does this doctrine reach that it is well settled that Congress may make it a crime to conspire with others to do what an individual may lawfully do on his own. This principle is illustrated in conspiracies that violate the antitrust laws as sustained and applied by this Court. Although one may raise the prices of his own products, and many, acting without concert, may do so, the moment they conspire to that end they are punishable. The same principle is applied to organized labor. Any workman may quit his work for any reason, but concerted actions to the same end are in some circumstances forbidden.

There is lamentation in the dissents about the injustice of conviction in the absence of some overt act. Of course, there has been no general uprising against the Government, but the record is replete with acts to carry out the conspiracy alleged, acts such as always are held sufficient to consummate the crime where the statute requires an overt act.

But the shorter answer is that no overt act is or need be required. The Court, in antitrust cases, early upheld the power of Congress to adopt the ancient common law that makes conspiracy itself a crime. Through Mr. Justice Holmes, it said: "Coming next to the objection that no overt act is laid, the answer is that the Sherman Act punishes the conspiracies at which it is aimed on the common law footing—that is to say, it does not make the doing of any act other than the act of conspiring a condition of liability." *Nash* v. *United States,* 229 U.S. 373, 378. Reiterated, *United States* v. *Socony-Vacuum Oil Co.,* 310, U.S. 150, 252. It is not to be supposed that the power of Congress to protect the Nation's existence is more limited than its power to protect interstate commerce.

Also, it is urged that since the conviction is for conspiracy to teach and advocate, and to organize the Communist Party to teach and advocate, the First Amendment is violated, because freedoms of speech and press protect teaching and advocacy regardless of what is taught or advocated. I have never thought that to be the law.

I do not suggest that Congress could punish conspiracy to advocate something, the doing of which it may not punish. Advocacy or exposition of the doctrine of communal property ownership, or any political philosophy unassociated with advocacy of its imposition by force or seizure of government by unlawful means could not be reached through conspiracy prosecution. But it is not forbidden to put down force or violence, it is not forbidden to punish its teaching or advocacy, and the end being punishable, there is no doubt of the power to punish conspiracy for the purpose.

The defense of freedom of speech or press has often been raised in conspiracy cases, because, whether committed by Communists, by businessmen, or by common criminals, it usually consists of words written or spoken, evidenced by letters, conversations, speeches or documents. Communication is the essence of every conspiracy, for only by it can common purpose and concert of action be brought about or be proved.

Having held that a conspiracy alone is a crime and its consummation is another, it would be weird legal reasoning to hold that Congress could punish the one only if there was "clear and present danger" of the second. This would compel the Government to prove two crimes in order to convict for one.

When our constitutional provisions were written, the chief forces recognized as antagonists in the struggle between authority and liberty were the Government on the one hand and the individual citizen on the other. It was thought that if the state could be kept in its place the individual could take care of himself.

In more recent times these problems have been complicated by the intervention between the state and the citizen of permanently organized, well-financed, semisecret and highly disciplined political organizations. Totalitarian groups here and abroad perfected the technique of creating private paramilitary organizations to coerce both the public government and its citizens. These organizations assert as against our Government all of the constitutional rights and immunities of individuals and at the same time exercise over their followers much of the authority which they deny to the Government. The Communist Party realistically is a state within a state, an authoritarian dictatorship within a republic. It demands these freedoms, not for its members, but for the organized party. It denies to its own members at the same time the freedom to dissent, to debate, to deviate from the party line, and enforces its authoritarian rule by crude purges, if nothing more violent.

The law of conspiracy has been the chief means at the Government's disposal to deal with the growing problems created by such organizations. I happen to think it is an awkward and inept remedy, but I find no constitutional authority for taking this weapon from the Government. There is no constitutional right to "gang up" on the Government.

While I think there was power in Congress to enact this statute and that, as applied in this case, it cannot be held unconstitutional, I add that I have little faith in the long-range effectiveness of this conviction to stop the rise of the Communist movement. Communism will not go to jail with these Communists. No decision by this Court can forestall revolution whenever the existing government fails to command the respect and loyalty of the people and sufficient distress and discontent is allowed to grow up among the masses. Many failures by fallen governments attest that no government can long prevent revolution by outlawry. Corruption, ineptitude, inflation, oppressive taxation, militarization, injustice, and loss of leadership capable of intellectual initiative in domestic or foreign affairs are allies on which the Communists count to bring opportunity knocking to their door. Sometimes I think they may be mistaken. But the Communists are not building just for today—the rest of us might profit by their example.

MR. JUSTICE BLACK, *dissenting:*

At the outset I want to emphasize what the crime involved in this case is, and what it is not. These petitioners were not charged with an attempt to overthrow the Government. They were not charged with nonverbal acts of any kind designed to overthrow the Government. They were not even charged with saying anything or writing anything designed to overthrow the Government. The charge was that they agreed to assemble and to talk and publish certain ideas at a later date: The indictment is that they conspired to organize the Communist Party and to use speech or newspapers and other publications in the future to teach and advocate the forcible overthrow of the Government. No matter how it is worded, this is a virulent form of prior censorship of speech and press, which I believe the First Amendment forbids. I would hold Par. 3 of the Smith Act authorizing this prior restraint unconstitutional on its face and as applied.

But let us assume, contrary to all constitutional ideas of fair criminal procedure, that petitioners although not indicted for the crime of actual advocacy, may be punished for it. Even on this radical assumption, the only way to affirm these convictions, as the dissent of Mr. Justice Douglas shows, is to qualify drastically or wholly repudiate the established "clear and present danger" rule. This the Court does in a way which greatly restricts the protections afforded by the First Amendment. The opinions for affirmance show that the chief reason for jettisoning the rule is the expressed fear that advocacy of Communist doctrine endangers the safety of the Republic. Undoubtedly, a governmental policy of unfettered communication of ideas does entail dangers. To the Founders of the Nation, however, the benefits derived from free expression were worth the risk. They embodied this philosophy in the First Amendment's command that Congress "shall make no law abridging . . . the freedom of speech, or of the press . . ." I have always believed that the First Amendment is the keystone of our Government, that the freedoms it guarantees provide the best insurance against destruction of all freedom. At least as to speech in the realm of public matters, I believe that the "clear and present danger" test does not "mark the furthermost constitutional boundaries of protected expression" but does "no more than recognize a minimum compulsion of the Bill of Rights." *Bridges* v. *California,* 314 U.S. 252, 263.

So long as this Court exercises the power of judicial review of legislation, I cannot agree that the First Amendment permits us to sustain laws suppressing freedom of speech and press on the basis of Congress' or our own notions of mere "reasonableness." Such a doctrine waters down the First Amendment so that it amounts to little more than an admonition to Congress. The Amendment as so construed is not likely to protect any but those "safe" or orthodox views which rarely need its protection. I must also express my objection to the holding because, as Mr. Justice Douglas' dissent shows, it sanctions the determination of a crucial issue of fact by the judge rather than by the jury. Nor can I let this opportunity pass without expressing my objection to the severely limited grant of certiorari in this case which precluded consideration here of at least two other reasons for reversing these convictions: (1) the record shows a discriminatory selection of the jury panel which prevented trial before a representative cross-section of the community; (2) the record shows that one member of the trial jury was violently hostile to petitioners before and during the trial.

Public opinion being what it now is, few will protest the conviction of the Communist petitioners. There is hope, however, that in calmer times, when present pressures, passions and fears subside, this or some later Court will restore the First Amendment liberties to the high preferred place where they belong in a free society.

MR. JUSTICE DOUGLAS, *dissenting:*

If this were a case where those who claimed protection under the First Amendment were teaching the techniques of sabotage, the assassination of the President, the filching of documents from public files, the planting of bombs, the art of street warfare, and the like, I would have no doubts. The freedom to speak is not absolute; the teaching of methods of terror and other seditious conduct should be beyond the pale along with obscenity and immorality. This case was argued as if those were the facts. The argument imported much seditious conduct into the record. That is easy and it has popular appeal, for the activities of Communists in plotting and scheming against the free world are common knowledge. But the fact is that no such evidence was introduced at the trial. There is a statute which makes a seditious conspiracy unlawful. Petitioners, however, were not charged with a "conspiracy to overthrow" the Government. They were charged with a conspiracy to form a party and groups and assemblies of people who teach and advocate the overthrow of our Government by force or violence and with a conspiracy to advocate and teach its overthrow by force and violence. It may well be that indoctrination in the techniques of terror to destroy the Government would be indictable under either statute. But the teaching which is condemned here is of a different character.

So far as the present record is concerned, what petitioners did was to organize people to teach and themselves teach the Marxist-Leninist doctrine contained chiefly in four books: *Foundations of Leninism* by Stalin (1924), *The Communist Manifesto* by Marx and Engels (1848), *State and Revolution* by Lenin (1917), *History of the Communist Party of the Soviet Union (B)* (1939).

Those books are to Soviet Communism what *Mein Kampf* was to Nazism. If they are understood, the ugliness of Communism is revealed, its deceit and cunning are exposed, the nature of its activities becomes apparent, and the chances of its success less likely. That is not, of course, the reason why petitioners chose these books for their classrooms. They are fervent Communists to whom these volumes are gospel. They preached the creed with the hope that some day it would be acted upon.

The opinion of the Court does not outlaw these texts nor condemn them to the fire, as the Communists do literature offensive to their creed. But if the books themselves are not outlawed, if they can lawfully remain on library shelves, by what reasoning does their use in a classroom become a crime? It would not be a crime under the Act to introduce these books to a class, though that would be teaching what the creed of violent overthrow of the government is. The Act, as construed, requires the element of intent —that those who teach the creed believe in it. The crime then depends not on what is taught but on who the teacher is. That is to make freedom of speech turn not on *what is said,* but on the *intent* with which it is said. Once we start down that road we enter territory dangerous to the liberties of every citizen.

There was a time in England when the concept of constructive treason flourished. Men were punished not for raising a hand against the king but for thinking murderous thoughts about him. The Framers of the Constitution were alive to that abuse and took steps to see that the practice would not flourish here. Treason was defined to require overt acts—the evolution of a plot against the country into an actual project. The present case is not one of treason. But the analogy is close when the illegality is made to turn on intent, not on the nature of the act. We then start probing men's minds for motive and purpose; they become entangled in the law not for what they did but *for what they thought;* they get convicted not for what they said but for the purpose with which they said it.

Intent, of course, often makes the difference in the law. An act otherwise excusable or carrying minor penalties may grow to an abhorrent thing if the evil intent is present. We deal here, however, not with ordinary acts but with speech, to which the Constitution has given a special sanction.

The vice of treating speech as the equivalent of overt acts of a treasonable or seditious character is emphasized by a concurring opinion, which by invoking the law of conspiracy makes speech do service for deeds which are dangerous to society. The doctrine of conspiracy has served divers and oppressive purposes and in its broad reach can be made to do great evil. But never until today has anyone seriously thought that the ancient law of conspiracy could constitutionally be used to turn speech into seditious conduct. Yet that is precisely what is suggested. I repeat that we deal here with speech alone, not with speech *plus* acts of sabotage or unlawful conduct. Not a single seditious act is charged in the indictment. To make a lawful speech unlawful because two men conceive it is to raise the law of conspiracy to appalling proportions. That course is to make a radical break with the past and to violate one of the cardinal principles of our constitutional scheme.

Free speech has occupied an exalted position because of the high service it has given our society. Its protection is essential to the very existence of a democracy. The airing of ideas releases pressures which otherwise might become destructive. When ideas compete in the market for acceptance, full and free discussion exposes the false and they gain few adherents. Full and free discussion even of ideas we hate encourages the testing of our own prejudices and preconceptions. Full and free discussion keeps a society from becoming stagnant and unprepared for the stresses and strains that work to tear all civilizations apart.

Full and free discussion has indeed been the first article of our faith. We have founded our political system on it. It has been the safeguard of every religious, political, philosophical, economic, and racial group amongst us. We have counted on it to keep us from embracing what is cheap and false; we have trusted the common sense of our people to choose the doctrine true to our genius and to reject the rest. This has been the one single outstanding tenet that has made our institutions the symbol of freedom and equality. We have deemed it more costly to liberty to suppress a despised minority than to let them vent their spleen. We have above all else feared the political censor. We have wanted a land where our people can be exposed to all the diverse creeds and cultures of the world.

There comes a time when even speech loses its constitutional immunity. Speech innocuous one year may at another time fan such destructive flames that it must be halted in the interests of the safety of the Republic. That is the meaning of the "clear and present danger" test. When conditions are so critical that there will be no time to avoid the evil that the speech threatens, it is time to call a halt. Otherwise, free speech which is the strength of the Nation will be the cause of its destruction.

Yet free speech is the rule, not the exception. The restraint to be constitutional must be based on more than fear, on more than passionate opposition against the speech, on more than a revolted dislike for its contents. There must be some immediate injury to society that is likely if speech is allowed. The classic statement of these conditions was made by Mr. Justice Brandeis in his concurring opinion in *Whitney* v. *California,* 274 U.S. 357, 376-377:

> Fear of serious injury cannot alone justify suppression of free speech and assembly. Men feared witches and burnt women. It is the function of speech to free men from the bondage of irrational fears. To justify suppression of free speech there must be reasonable ground to fear that serious evil will result if free speech is practiced. There must be reasonable ground to believe that the danger apprehended is imminent. There must be reasonable ground to believe that the evil to be prevented is a serious one. Every denunciation of existing law tends in some measure to increase the probability that there will be violation of it. Condonation of a breach enhances the probability. Expressions of approval add to the probability. Propagation of the criminal state of mind by teaching syndicalism increases it. Advocacy of law-breaking heightens it still further. But even advocacy of violation, however reprehensible morally, is not a justification for denying free speech where the advocacy falls short of incitement and there is nothing to indicate that the advocacy would be immediately acted on. The wide difference between advocacy and incitement, between preparation and attempt, between assembling and conspiracy, must be borne in mind. In order to support a finding of clear and present danger it must

be shown either that immediate serious violence was to be expected or was advocated, or that the past conduct furnished reason to believe that such advocacy was then contemplated.

Those who won our independence by revolution were not cowards. They did not fear political change. They did not exalt order at the cost of liberty. To courageous, self-reliant men, with confidence in the power of free and fearless reasoning applied through the processes of popular government, no danger flowing from speech can be deemed clear and present, unless the incidence of the evil apprehended is so imminent that it may befall before there is opportunity for full discussion. *If there be time to expose through discussion the falsehood and fallacies, to avert the evil by the processes of education, the remedy to be applied is more speech, not enforced silence.* [Italics added.]

The nature of Communism as a force on the world scene would, of course, be relevant to the issue of clear and present danger of petitioners' advocacy within the United States. But the primary consideration is the strength and tactical position of petitioners and their converts in this country. On that there is no evidence in the record. If we are to take judicial notice of the threat of Communism within the nation, it should not be difficult to conclude that *as a political party* they are of little consequence. Communists in this country have never made a respectable or serious showing in any election. I would doubt that there is a village, let alone a city or county or state which the Communists could carry. Communism in the world scene is no bogey-man; but Communism as a political faction or party in this country plainly is. Communism has been so thoroughly exposed in this country that it has been crippled as a political force. Free speech has destroyed it as an effective political party. It is inconceivable that those who went up and down this country preaching the doctrine of revolution which petitioners espouse would have any success. In days of trouble and confusion when bread lines were long, when the unemployed walked the streets, when people were starving, the advocates of a short-cut by revolution might have a chance to gain adherents. But today there are no such conditions. The country is not in despair; the people know Soviet Communism; the doctrine of Soviet revolution is exposed in all of its ugliness and the American people want none of it.

How it can be said that there is a clear and present danger that this advocacy will succeed is, therefore, a mystery. Some nations less resilient than the United States, where illiteracy is high and where democratic traditions are only budding, might have to take drastic steps and jail these men for merely speaking their creed. But in America they are miserable merchants of unwanted ideas; their wares remain unsold. The fact that their ideas are abhorrent does not make them powerful.

The political impotence of the Communists in this country does not, of course, dispose of the problem. Their numbers; their positions in industry and government; the extent to which they have in fact infiltrated the police, the armed services, transportation, stevedoring, power plants, munitions works, and other critical places—these facts all bear on the likelihood that their advocacy of the Soviet theory of revolution will endanger the Republic. But the record is silent on these facts. If we are to proceed on the basis of judicial notice, it is impossible for me to say that the Communists in this country are so potent or so strategically deployed that they must be suppressed for their speech. I could not so hold unless I were willing to conclude that the activities in recent years of committees of Congress, of the Attorney General, of labor unions, of state legislatures, and of Loyalty Boards were so futile as to leave the country on the edge of grave peril. To believe that petitioners and their following are placed in such critical positions as to endanger the Nation is to believe the incredible. It is safe to say that the followers of the creed of Soviet Communism are known to the FBI that in case of war with Russia they will be picked up overnight as were all prospective saboteurs at the commencement of World War II; that the invisible army of petitioners is the best known, the most beset, and the least thriving of any fifth column in history. Only those held by fear and panic could think otherwise.

This is my view if we are to act on the basis of judicial notice. But the mere statement of the opposing views indicates how important it is that we know the facts before we act. Neither prejudice nor hate nor senseless fear should be the basis of this solemn act. Free speech—the glory of our system of government—should not be sacrificed on anything less than plain and objective proof of danger that the evil advocated is imminent. On this record no one can say that petitioners and their converts are in such a strategic position as to have even the slightest chance of achieving their aims.

The First Amendment provides that "Congress shall make no law . . . abridging the freedom of speech." The Constitution provides no exception. This does not mean, however, that the Nation need hold its hand until it is in such weakened condition that there is no time to protect itself from incitement to revolution. Seditious conduct can always be punished. But the command of the First Amendment is so clear that we should not allow Congress to call a halt to free speech except in the extreme case of peril from the speech itself. The First Amendment makes confidence in the common sense of our people and in their maturity of judgment the great postulate of our democracy. Its philosophy is that violence is rarely, if ever, stopped by denying civil liberties to those advocating resort to force. The First Amendment reflects the philosophy of Jefferson "that it is time enough for the rightful purposes of civil government for its officers to interfere when principles break out into overt acts against peace and good order." The political censor has no place in our public debates. Unless and until extreme and necessitous circumstances are shown our aim should be to keep speech unfettered and to allow the processes of law to be invoked only when the provocateurs among us move from speech to action.

Vyshinsky wrote in 1938 in *The Law of the Soviet State,* "In our state, naturally there can be no place for freedom of speech, press, and so on for the foes of socialism."

Our concern should be that we accept no such standard for the United States. Our faith should be that our people will never give support to these advocates of revolution, so long as we remain loyal to the purposes for which our Nation was founded.

JUSTICES HARLAN, BLACK

8. *The Case of the Fourteen West Coast Communist Leaders**

MR. JUSTICE HARLAN:

We are faced with the question whether the Smith Act prohibits advocacy and teaching of forcible overthrow as an abstract principle, divorced from any effort to instigate action to that end, so long as such advocacy or teaching is engaged in with evil intent. We hold that it does not.

The distinction between advocacy of abstract doctrine and advocacy directed at promoting unlawful action is one that has been consistently recognized in the opinions of this court, beginning with Fox v. Washington, 236 U. S. 273, and Schenck v. United States, 249 U. S. 47. This distinction was heavily underscored in Gitlow v. New York, 268 U. S. 652, in which the statute involved was nearly identical with the one now before us, and where the court, despite the narrow view there taken of the First Amendment said:

"The statute does not penalize the utterance or publication of abstract 'doctrine' or academic discussion having no quality of incitement to any concrete action * * *. It is not the abstract 'doctrine' of overthrowing organized government by unlawful means which is denounced by the statute, but the advocacy of action for the accomplishment of that purpose * * *. This (manifesto) * * * is (in) the language of direct incitement * * * that the jury were warranted in finding that the manifesto advocated not merely the abstract doctrine of overthrowing organized government by force, violence

* From *Yates* v. *United States,* 354 U. S. 298 (1957).

and unlawful means, but action to that end, is clear * * *. That utterances inciting to the overthrow of organized government by unlawful means, present a sufficient danger of substantive evil to bring their punishment within the range of legislative discretion, is clear."

We need not, however, decide the issue before us in terms of constitutional compulsion, for our first duty is to construe this statute. In doing so we should not assume that Congress chose to disregard a constitutional danger zone so clearly marked, or that it used the words "advocate" and "teach" in their ordinary dictionary meanings when they had already been construed as terms of art carrying a special and limited connotation. See Willis v. Eastern Trust & Banking Co., supra; Joines v. Patterson, supra; James v. Appel, 192 U. S. 129, 135. The Gitlow case and the New York Criminal Anarchy Act there involved, which furnished the prototype for the Smith Act, were both known and adverted to by Congress in the courts of the legislative proceedings. Cf. Carolene Products Co. v. United States, supra. The legislative history of the Smith Act and related bills shows beyond all question that Congress was aware of the distinction between the advocacy or teaching of abstract doctrine and the advocacy or teaching of action, and that it did not intend to disregard it. The statute was aimed at the advocacy and teaching of concrete action for the forcible overthrow of the Government, and not of principles divorced from action.

The Government's reliance on this court's decision in Dennis is misplaced. The jury instructions which were refused here were given there, and were referred to by this court as requiring "the jury to find the facts essential to establish the substantive crime." 341 U. S., at 512. It is true that at one point in the late Chief Justice's opinion it is stated that the Smith Act "is directed at advocacy, not discussion," id., at 502, but it is clear that the reference was to advocacy of action, not ideas, for in the very next sentence the opinion emphasizes that the jury was properly instructed that there could be no conviction for "advocacy in the realm of ideas." The two concurring opinions in that case likewise emphasize the distinction with which we are concerned, id., at 518, 534, 536, 545, 546, 547, 571, 572.

In failing to distinguish between advocacy of forcible overthrow as an abstract doctrine and advocacy of action to that end, the District Court appears to have been led astray by the holding in Dennis that advocacy of violent action to be taken at some future time was enough. It seems to have considered that, since "inciting" speech is usually thought of as calculated to induce immediate action, and since Dennis held advocacy of action for future overthrow sufficient, this meant that advocacy, irrespective of its tendency to generate action, is punishable, provided only that it is uttered with a specific intent to accomplish overthrow. In other words, the District Court apparently thought that Dennis obliterated the traditional dividing line between advocacy of abstract doctrine and advocacy of action.

This misconceives the situation confronting the court in Dennis and what was held there. Although the jury's verdict, interpreted in light of the trial court's instructions, did not justify the conclusion that the defendants' advocacy was directed at, or created any danger of, immediate overthrow, it did establish that the advocacy was aimed at building up a seditious group and maintaining it in readiness for action at a propitious time. In such circumstances, said Chief Justice Vinson, the Government need not hold its hand "until the putsch is about to be executed, the plans have been laid, and the signal is awaited. If Government is aware that a group aiming at its overthrow is attempting to indoctrinate its members and commit them to a course whereby they will strike when the leaders feel the circumstances permit, action by the Government is required." 341 U. S., at 509. The essence of the Dennis holding was that indoctrination of a group in preparation for future violent action, as well as exhortation to immediate action, by advocacy found to be directed to "action for the accomplishment" of forcible overthrow, to violence "as a rule or principle of action," and employing "language of incitement," id., at 511-512, is not constitutionally protected when the group is of sufficient size and cohesiveness, is sufficiently oriented towards action, and other circumstances are such as reasonably to justify apprehension that action will occur. This is quite a different thing from the view of the District Court here that mere doctrinal justification of forcible overthrow, if engaged in with the intent to accomplish overthrow, is punishable per se under the Smith Act. That sort of advocacy even though uttered with the hope that it may ultimately lead to violent revolution, is too remote from concrete action to be regarded as the kind of indoctrination preparatory to action which was condemned in Dennis. As one of the concurring opinions in Dennis put it: "Throughout our decisions there has recurred a distinction between the statement of an idea which may prompt its hearers to take unlawful action, and advocacy that such action be taken." Id., at 545. There is nothing in Dennis which makes that historic distinction obsolete.

In light of the foregoing we are unable to regard the District Court's charge upon this aspect of the case as adequate. The jury was never told that the Smith Act does not denounce advocacy in the sense of preaching abstractly the forcible overthrow of the Government. We think that the trial court's statement that the proscribed advocacy must include the "urging," "necessity" and "duty" of forcible overthrow, and not merely its "desirability" and "propriety," may not be regarded as a sufficient substitute for charging that the Smith Act reaches only advocacy of action for the overthrow of Government by force and violence. The essential distinction is that those to whom the advocacy is addressed must be urged to do something, now or in the future, rather than merely to believe in something. At best the expressions used by the trial court were equivocal, since in the absence of any instructions differentiating advocacy of abstract doctrine from advocacy of action, they were as consistent with the former as they were with the latter. Nor do we regard their ambiguity as lessened by what the trial court had to say as to the right of the defendants to announce their beliefs as to the inevitability of violent revolution, or to advocate other unpopular opinions. Especially when it is unmistakable that the court did not consider the urging of action for forcible overthrow as being a necessary element of the proscribed advocacy, but rather considered the crucial question to be whether the advocacy was uttered with a specific intent to accomplish such overthrow, we would not be warranted in assuming that the jury drew from these instructions more than the court itself intended them to convey.

Nor can we accept the Government's argument that the District Court was justified in not charging more than it did because the refused instructions proposed by both sides specified that the advocacy must be of a character reasonably calculated to "incite" to forcible overthrow, a term which, it is now argued, might have conveyed to the jury an implication that the advocacy must be of immediate action. Granting that some qualification of the proposed instructions would have been permissible to dispel such an implication, and that it was not necessary even that the trial court should have employed the particular term "incite," it was nevertheless incumbent on the court to make clear in some fashion that the advocacy must be of action and not merely abstract doctrine. The instructions given not only do not employ the word "incite," but also avoid the use of such terms and phrases as "action," "call for action," "as a rule or principle of action" and so on, all of which were offered in one form or another by both petitioners and the Government.

What we find lacking in the instructions here is illustrated by contrasting them with the instructions given to the Dennis jury, upon which this court's sustaining of the convictions in that case was bottomed. There the trial court charged:

"In further construction and interpretation of the statute (the Smith Act) I charge you that it is not the abstract doctrine of overthrowing or destroying organized government by unlawful means which is denounced by this law, but the teaching and advocacy of action for the accomplishment of that purpose, by language reasonably and ordinarily calculated to incite persons to such action. Accordingly, you cannot find the defendants or any of them guilty of the crime charged unless you are satisfied beyond a reasonable doubt that they conspired . . . to advocate and teach the duty and necessity of overthrowing or destroying the Government of the United States by force and violence, with the intent that such teaching and advocacy be of a rule or principle of action and by language reasonably and ordinarily calculated to incite persons to such action, all with the intent to cause the overthrow * * * as speedily as circumstances would permit." 341 U. S. at 511-512.

We recognize that distinctions between advocacy or teaching of abstract doctrines, with evil intent, and that which is directed to stirring people to action, are often subtle and difficult to grasp, for in a broad sense, as Mr. Justice Holmes said in his dissenting opinion in Gitlow, Supra, at 673: "Every idea is an incitement." But the very subtlety of these distinctions required the most clear and explicit instructions with reference to them, for they concerned an issue which went to the very heart of the charges against these petitioners. The need for precise and understandable instructions on this issue is further emphasized by the equivocal character of the evidence in this record, with which we deal in Part 888 of this opinion. Instances of speech that could be considered to amount to "advocacy of action" are so few and far between as to be almost completely overshadowed by the hundreds of instances in the record in which overthrow, if mentioned at all, occurs in the course of doctrinal disputation so remote from action as to be almost wholly lacking in probative value. Vague references to "revolutionary" or "militant" action of an unspecified character, which are found in the evidence, might in addition be given too great weight by the jury in the absence of more precise instructions. Particularly in light of this record, we must regard the trial court's charge in this respect as furnishing wholly inadequate guidance to the jury on this central point in the case. We cannot allow a conviction to stand on such "an equivocal direction to the jury on a basic issue." Bollenbach v. United States, 326 U. S. 607, 613.

Moreover, apart from the inadequacy of the evidence to show, at best, more than the abstract advocacy and teaching of forcible overthrow by the party, it is difficult to perceive how the requisite specific intent to accomplish such overthrow could be deemed proved by a showing of mere membership or the holding of office in the Communist party.

MR. JUSTICE BLACK, with whom Mr. Justice Douglas joins, *concurring in part and dissenting in part:*

I

I would reverse every one of these convictions and direct that all the defendants be acquitted. In my judgment the statutory provisions on which these prosecutions are based abridge freedom of speech, press and assembly in violation of the First Amendment to the United States Constitution. See my dissent and that of Mr. Justice Douglas in Dennis v. United States, 341 U. S. 494, 579, 581. Also see my opinion in American Communications Association v. Douds, 339 U. S. 382, 445.

The kind of trials conducted here are wholly dissimilar to normal criminal trials. Ordinarily, these "Smith Act" trials are prolonged affairs lasting for months. In part this is attributable to the routine introduction in evidence of massive collections of books, tracts, pamphlets, newspapers and manifestoes discussing communism, socialism, capitalism, feudalism and governmental institutions in general, which, it is not too much to say, are turgid, diffuse, abstruse and just plain dull. Of course, no juror can or is expected to plow his way through this jungle of verbiage. The testimony of witnesses is comparatively insignificant. Guilt or innocence may turn on what Marx or Engels or someone else wrote or advocated as much as 100 or more years ago. Elaborate, refined distinctions are drawn between "communism," "Marxism," "Leninism," "Trotskyism," and "Stalinism." When the propriety of obnoxious or unorthodox views about government is in reality made the crucial issue, as it must be in cases of this kind, prejudice makes conviction inevitable except in the rarest circumstances.

II

Since the court proceeds on the assumption that the statutory provisions involved are valid, however, I feel free to express my views about the issues it considers.

First—I agree with Part I of the court's opinion that deals with the statutory term "organize" and holds that the organizing charge in the indictment was barred by the three-year statute of limitations.

Second—I also agree with the court in so far as it holds that the trial judge erred in instructing that persons could be punished under the Smith Act for teaching and advocating forceful overthrow as an abstract principle. But, on the other hand, I cannot agree that the instruction which the court indicates it might approve is constitutional permissible. The court says that persons can be punished for advocating action to overthrow the Government by force and violence, where those to whom the advocacy is addressed are urged "to do something, now or in the future, rather than merely to believe in something." Under the court's approach, defendants could still be convicted simply for agreeing to talk as distinguished from agreeing to act. I believe that the First Amendment forbids Congress to punish people for talking about public affairs, whether or not such discussion incites to action, legal or illegal. See Meiklejohn, Free Speech and Its Relation to Self-Government. Cf. Chafee, Book Review, 62 Harv. L. Rev. 891. As the Virginia Assembly said in 1785, in its "Statute for religious liberty," written by Thomas Jefferson, "it is time enough for the rightful purposes of civil government for its officers to interfere when principles break out into overt acts against peace and good order * * *." Cf. Virginia Electric & P. Co. v. Labor Board, 319 U. S. 533, 539; Giboney v. Empire Storage & Ice Co., 336 U. S. 490, 501-502.

The requirement of proof of an overt act in conspiracy cases is no mere formality particularly in prosecutions like these which in many respects are akin to trials for treason. Article III, Section 3, of the Constitution provides that "no person shall be convicted of treason unless on the testimony of two witnesses to the same overt act, or on confession in open court." One of the objects of this provision was to keep people from being convicted of disloyalty to Government during periods of excitement when passions and prejudices ran high, merely because they expressed "unacceptable" views. See Cramer v. United States, 325 U. S. 1, 48. The same reasons that make proof of overt acts so important in treason cases apply here. The only overt act which is now charged against these defendants is that they went to a constitutionally protected public assembly where they took part in lawful discussion of public questions, and where neither they nor anyone else advocated or suggested overthrow of the United States Government. Many years ago this court said that "the very idea of a Government, Republican in form, implies a right on the part of its citizens to meet peaceably for consultation in respect to public affairs and to petition for a redress of grievances." United States v. Cruikshank, 92 U. S. 542, 552. And see De le Jonge v. Oregon, 299 U. S. 353, 364-365. In my judgment defendants' attendance at these public meetings cannot be viewed as an overt act to effectuate the object of the conspiracy charged.

In essence, petitioners were tried upon the charge that they believe in and want to foist upon this country a different and to us a despicable form of authoritarian government in which voices criticizing the existing order are summarily silenced. I fear that the present type of prosecutions are more in line with the philosophy of authoritarian government than with that expressed by our First Amendment.

Doubtlessly, dictators have to stamp out causes and beliefs which they deem subversive to their evil regimes. But governmental suppression of causes and beliefs seems to me to be the very antithesis of what our Constitution stands for. The choice expressed in the First Amendment in favor of free expression was made against a turbulent background by men such as Jefferson, Madison, and Mason—men who believed that loyalty to the provisions of this amendment was the best way to assure a long life for this new nation and its government. Unless there is complete freedom for expression of all ideas, whether we like them or not, concerning the way government should be run and who shall run it, I doubt if any views in the long run can be secured against the censor. The First Amendment provides the only kind of security system that can preserve a free government—one that leaves the way wide open for people to favor, discuss, advocate, or incite causes and doctrines however obnoxious and antagonistic such views may be to the rest of us.

Chapter V

LIBERTY AND EQUALITY

Solutions of historical problems are never final, because as long as the world persists in imperfection, the very solution creates new problems. Out-and-outers, like absolute pacifists, anarchists, religious fanatics, uncompromising believers in vegetarianism, nudism, and other radical approaches to man's material and spiritual woes, are to be envied for the peace of mind which they derive from their faith that a single formula will solve complex issues for all time. There are those naïve enough to think that, once the means of production were nationalized, crime (a typical product of capitalist injustice) would disappear, even the *crime passionel*. Come the revolution—and men will become angels, or something very close to it. Yet all historical experience shows that problems are the product, not only of unsolved troubles, but also of apparently solved ones. As we can glimpse only a part of the truth in any given situation, we can never quite catch up with our failures.

The second half of the eighteenth century was one of the few brief spells when men thought they had found the key to heaven. The architects of the popular revolutions in England, America, and France could be well satisfied with their accomplishments. The old, prerevolutionary order was defeated, never to return to life again in those nations. Absolute monarchy—the devil of the drama—was extirpated altogether, or else reduced to harmless social decoration. The old ruling classes had to concede first place to the rising new middle and commercial classes. Liberty! Who could deny that freedom was firmly established for all time, when the people were governing themselves in freely elected assemblies, without privileges of caste or creed?

The first major democracy in the modern world is that of the United States. Only after its firm establishment and patent success could democracy be discussed as a matter of practice and experience rather than of theory and speculation. The political writer in the nineteenth century first to perceive that democracy was the "irresistible" new form of society and government and that the United States was the world's most important experiment in free government was an aristocratic Frenchman, Alexis de Tocqueville. His most famous book, an enduring contribution to political thought, is his *Democracy in America* (1835-1840). It is generally conceded to be the most illuminating work on the United States written by a foreign observer, and it would be difficult to find a work of similar depth and penetration written by an American on his own country. Nothing struck Tocqueville more forcibly, as he put it, than "the general equality of condition" in American life.

The difficulty of reconciling individuality and liberty with equality is the central theme of *Democracy in America.* In particular, Tocqueville saw that the threat to liberty is potentially more real in a democracy than in a monarchy or aristocracy: "The authority of a king is purely physical, and it controls the actions of the subject without subduing his private will; but the majority possesses a power which is physical and moral at the same time; it acts upon the will as well as upon the actions of men, and it represses not only all contest, but all controversy." Tocqueville also saw that democratic despotism would work differently from the older forms of tyranny: "It would be more extensive and more mild; it would degrade men without tormenting them." Whereas persecution of unorthodox views in authoritarian regimes is open, because it has to rely on the physical force of the police and the prison, the power of public opinion in a democracy exercises a "quiet and gentle" kind of terror and intimidation that may not be easily detected. Yet even if detected, such conformist pressure in a democracy cannot be readily resisted. When a person is persecuted by an authoritarian government for his nonconformist views, he can find moral shelter and comfort in the public opinion of his own people. Yet if the same person of nonconformist views in a democracy is condemned and censored by public opinion, he is left with nothing to fall back on save his own conscience. This spiritual loneliness may be accentuated by material losses through the denial of jobs and other economic opportunities. If the tyrannical tendencies inherent in powerful majorities were allowed to operate without check, Tocqueville somberly predicted, democratic nations would become "nothing better than a flock of timid and industrious animals, of which the government is the shepherd."

Periodic campaigns against unorthodoxy in American history have partly confirmed Tocqueville's warnings. In the nineteen fifties, McCarthyism was a telling illustration of Tocqueville's thesis. What was of deep concern during that era was not only the conduct of Senator McCarthy, but even more the fact that large segments of the American public (at times even the majority according to public opinion polls) approved of his flagrant disregard of elementary principles of individual liberty and political fair play.

Just as democracy has not solved the problem of liberty once and for all, but has merely opened up new opportunities for successful solutions, the problem of equality, too, can hardly be said to have been fully settled. In the United States, the problem of racial equality was first to test the meaning of equality to millions of American citizens. On June 26, 1857, Lincoln made an address in Springfield, Illinois, in which he discussed some of the implications of the Dred Scott decision of the Supreme Court, which held that Negroes could not sue in United States courts, and that Congress could not prohibit slavery in the territories. Lincoln stressed the fact that equality does not mean identity; equality must be understood, not as describing a condition that is, but as postulating a condition that ought to exist, a right. Of such rights, life, liberty, and the pursuit of happiness were singled out by the authors of the Declaration of Independence.

As the optimistic eighteenth century was followed by the more sceptical nineteenth century, the problems created by the newly won liberties became increasingly manifest. As often happens when freedom is unregulated by a sense of social responsibility, crass inequality, especially of wealth and income, was the direct result. More and more, freedom meant the opportunity to enrich oneself—at the expense of one's own health and ethical standards, and even more so at the expense of one's employees, and of the community as a whole. To many, political liberty appeared as a device of social and economic inequality. Those who had hoped that political freedom, enjoyed by all, would automatically lead to genuine equality, were alarmed by the growing inequalities, based mainly on differences of property, among citizens formally equal before the law. In its majestic respect for the ideal of equality, the law forbids, as Anatole France once put it, the rich as well as the poor to steal bread and sleep under bridges.

The relations between liberty and equality, the conditions under which both ideas can be transformed from empty abstractions into living reality, are examined in Sidney and Beatrice Webb's *The Decay of Capitalist Civilization* (1923). Few partnerships have left their imprint on modern social thought and action as has that of Sidney and Beatrice Webb. Their name is best known in connection with the Fabian Society, founded in 1884. Sidney Webb was one of the first members, joining it in its first year; after his marriage to Beatrice in 1892, "the Webbs" became a household word in English life. Their pioneering studies on poor law, trade unionism, and local government, were the intellectual mainsprings of a movement of reform such as England had not witnessed since the early nineteenth century. Under the primary influence of the Webbs, Fabianism successfully avoided the double pitfall of small political groups (the Fabian membership never exceeded a few thousand): uncompromising dogmatism, or excessive expediency. Although limited in numbers, Fabianism was by no means a small coterie of idol worshipers attached to Sidney and Beatrice Webb. In the 1945 parliamentary elections, resulting in a Labor victory, 229 out of 394 Labor members belonged to the Fabian Society: in the Government the proportion was even higher, 45 out of 62.

Another institution which owes its existence and reputation more to the Webbs than to anyone else is the London School of Economics and Political Science. Its foundation in 1895 was the effort of several men and women, but the Webbs were more identified with it than any other name. Sidney Webb saw the school through its first difficult years, from finding financial support to doing the daily chores of detail administration. The school started out with eight students, and in forty years rose to over three thousand. Lord (then Sir William) Beveridge was one of its directors, and its faculty has included enough creative scholars to earn for it a unique reputation in the world. In the Labor government which came into office in 1945, the Prime Minister, Mr. Attlee, the Chancellor of the Exchequer, Mr. Dalton, and several other members, were former teachers of the school. The number of graduates of the school, both in Parliament and in the Labor government, is legion.

Among all the works bequeathed to England by the Webbs, none are a greater tribute to their genius, brought to full fruition by indefatigable industry, than the Fabian Society and the London School of Economics and Political Science. The Webbs believed in reason rather than in deceit, in facts rather than in propaganda, in peaceful evolution rather than in revolutionary catastrophes. If the England they left behind was a happier one than the one they knew in their youth, the change was due to them as much as to anyone of their generation.

The problem of liberty and equality is increasingly manifesting itself in modern democracies in the issue of *the expert versus the citizen*. As our modern industrial society becomes more complex and dependent on specialized knowledge and skills, there is the temptation to give the expert a position and an authority which are not easily compatible with the basic principles of democracy. The wresting of military control from the experts, the military, was one of the great achievements of Parliament in England, and involved the cost of a civil war. In the United States, the expert (especially the successful businessman) has held greater sway than in England, and this difference is apparent in a first glance at both countries—it pervades the structure of politics at the top (selection of ministers) as well as at the bottom (entrance examinations for the civil service).

The problem of the expert becomes particularly acute in the complex modern world, and the plain man, the charge runs, "is simply obsolete in a world he has never been trained to understand." However, the citizen cannot be relieved of his duty of judgment, after all the relevant facts have been brought to his attention. The expert can supply the citizen and ruler with the raw materials that may enter the final decision, but he cannot think *for* the citizen or ruler. Without utilizing the *expertise* of the specialist, a democracy may suffer from ignorance. By allowing experts (military, bureaucratic, propagandistic, or economic) to run society, democracy may soon find itself transformed into an arrogant tyranny. Opposed to this democratic conception of the place of the expert is the idea of Frederick Engels, e.g., who expresses the typically Marxist illusion that in the classless socialist society domination of man over man would be replaced by "administration of things." In such a

Utopian world, when all political problems—who tells whom what to do—will be eliminated, the expert will have a field day. In the Soviet Union, in the meantime, administrative problems have been raised to political ones, instead of the latter's being demoted to the lower status of the former.

The problem of knowledge as distinct from wisdom is examined by A. D. Lindsay in his *Modern Democratic State* (1943). In typically British fashion, Lindsay is little infatuated with the experts. They "do not like being told that the shoes they so beautifully make do not fit. They are apt to blame it on the distorted and misshapen toes of the people who have to wear their shoes." However, Lindsay warns against the argument that "ordinary plain people have a certain wisdom which is denied to the expert," because "an expert is not necessarily a fool." And he stresses the idea that the expert is a specialist: "that what is wanted for conduct is all-round experience of people and things." Those who believe that, because specialized knowledge may lead to narrowness, no knowledge will produce breadth of view, are reminded by Lindsay that "sound judgment" or "common sense" are not the "products of ignorance." Summing up the process through which a person develops wisdom, Lindsay concludes as follows: "Knowledge of the common life and its possibilities; understanding of the things which produce in it bitterness and thwart men's activities are the wisdom most wanted for politics."

Lindsay draws special attention to the fact that, in a country like Britain (or the United States), modern industrialism has robbed many people of their independence and condemned them to "specialized and narrow lives." The great danger of modern society is that of being turned by totalitarian propagandists and manipulators into a crowd, mass, or mob. The antidote to this challenge has been supplied, according to Lindsay, by industrialism itself in the form of the working-class movement. "If we consider what gives that movement its vitality, we see that it creates innumerable centres of discussion." Just as totalitarianism depends on the suppression of free discussion, "the key to democracy is the potency of discussion. A good discussion can draw out wisdom which is attainable in no other way." This may explain why the suppression of a free working-class movement has always been a top priority on the agenda of Fascist and Communist regimes. The latter, in particular, have transformed free labor unions into tools of enslavement as soon as communism takes over.

Yet even after the problem of social and economic equality has been brought nearer a satisfactory solution in the contemporary society of relative affluence and well-being, the issue of racial equality—clearly understood by Lincoln as one of the crucial tests of American history—has emerged as one of the dominant issues of our time. World War II was unleashed in 1939 by Germany in the name of racialist doctrines. Killing more people and causing more physical and moral damage than any previous war in history, World

War II opened the eyes of many who had previously been unaware of the possible results of a doctrine of human inequality based on racial prejudice. After the war, two factors in world politics further accelerated a reappraisal of racial inequality in the United States. First, the United States found itself, without consciously seeking the position, the undisputed leader of the free world, the only major hindrance to the spread of communist aggression and expansion throughout the world. Propaganda became a chief weapon in the conflict for the minds of men everywhere, and communist propaganda relentlessly exploited the theme of racial inequality in the United States, charging the United States with hypocritically preaching democracy abroad while practicing racism at home. Secondly, after World War II, as the British, French, Dutch, and Belgian empires in Asia and Africa gradually dissolved into new independent states, racial inequality became a factor of international importance. The peoples of the newly independent states in Asia and Africa are generally neither committed to the alliance led by the Soviet Union nor to that led by the United States. The United States may wish to win over the new Asian and African states (many of them non-white) into a system of firm military and diplomatic alliances. Whether it would be successful in this endeavor or, indeed, whether it should even make the endeavor are matters of debate. But, in any case, it must try to convince them that it is morally fit to lead the free nations outside of the communist orbit. To do this, our nation has had to develop new awareness that, like charity, equality, too, begins at home.

In the United States, this movement of forces toward human equality found its most dramatic expression in the public school segregation cases decided by the Supreme Court on May 17, 1954. These cases dealt with specific situations in Kansas, South Carolina, Virginia, Delaware, and the District of Columbia, but the decisions affected the whole section of the United States in which segregation was required by law (seventeen states and the District of Columbia) or permitted by law (four states), a total area containing 40 per cent of the children enrolled in American public schools. The constitutional issue involved the "equal protection" clause of the Fourteenth Amendment, under which no state shall "deny to any person within its jurisdiction the equal protection of the laws." The states practicing segregation in public schools argued that the Supreme Court should adhere to its own "separate but equal" doctrine of *Plessy* v. *Ferguson* (1896), under which the separation of white and colored persons in public facilities (such as transportation or education) was held not to be a violation of the "equal protection" clause of the Fourteenth Amendment so long as the separate facilities were of equal quality.

Speaking for a unanimous Court, Chief Justice Warren summarized the issue in a brief question, and followed with an even briefer answer: "Does segregation of children in public schools solely on the basis of race, even though the physical facilities and other 'tangible' factors may be equal, deprive the children of the minority group of equal educational opportunities? We believe that it does" (*Brown* v. *Topeka, 1954*). "We conclude," the Chief Justice went on, "that in the field of public education the doctrine of 'separate but equal' has no place. Separate educational facilities are inherently unequal." In the case that came from the District of Columbia, the equal protection clause of the Fourteenth Amendment was not applicable, since that Amendment refers only to states, and the District of Columbia is not a state. The Court applied here the Fifth Amendment, under which no person may be deprived of his liberty without due process: "Although the Court has not assumed to define 'liberty' with any great precision, that term is not confined to mere freedom from bodily restraint. Liberty under law extends to the full range of conduct which the individual is free to pursue, and it cannot be restricted except for a proper governmental objective. Segregation in public education is not reasonably related to any proper governmental objective, and thus it imposes on Negro children of the District of Columbia a burden that constitutes an arbitrary deprivation of their liberty in violation of the Due Process Clause" (*Bolling* v. *Sharpe, 1954*).

In sum, the Supreme Court thus held that segregation of children in public schools according to color violates the principles both of equality and of liberty. The strong conviction of the Court in this matter was emphasized by two facts. First, the decision in *Brown* v. *Topeka* (and related cases) was unanimous; second, although the decision is one of the most important in the whole history of the Court, it is exceptionally brief—as if to imply that the issue is so clear in principle that there is not much to argue about. No one assumed on May 17, 1954, that segregation in public schools would end on May 18, 1954; at best, many years of intense struggle, controversy, and accommodation lie ahead before segregation will have substantially decreased. Yet since May 17, 1954, the legal authority and moral weight of government in the United States are formally committed to the advancement of racial equality. As has happened so often in the history of the Supreme Court, the dissenter of yesterday becomes the voice of the majority of today: in *Plessy* v. *Ferguson* (1896), establishing the "separate but equal" doctrine, there was a lone dissenting opinion by Mr. Justice Harlan that fully anticipated the view of the unanimous Court in *Brown* v. *Topeka* in 1954. "Our Constitution," Mr. Justice Harlan said in his dissenting opinion in *Plessy* v. *Ferguson*, "is color-blind, and neither knows nor tolerates classes among citizens. In respect of civil rights, all citizens are equal before the law. The humblest is the peer of the most powerful."

ALEXIS DE TOCQUEVILLE

1. *The Dilemma of Liberty and Equality in Democracy**

I. TYRANNY OF THE MAJORITY

I hold it to be an impious and an execrable maxim that, politically speaking, a people has a right to do whatsoever it pleases; and yet I have asserted that all authority originates in the will of the majority. Am I, then, in contradiction with myself?

A general law—which bears the name of Justice—has been made and sanctioned, not only by a majority of this or that people, but by a majority of mankind. The rights of every people are consequently confined within the limits of what is just. A nation may be considered in the light of a jury which is empowered to represent society at large, and to apply the great and general law of Justice. Ought such a jury, which represents society, to have more power than the society in which the laws it applies originate?

When I refuse to obey an unjust law, I do not contest the right which the majority has of commanding, but I simply appeal from the sovereignty of the people to the sovereignty of mankind. It has been asserted that a people can never entirely outstep the boundaries of justice and of reason in those affairs which are more peculiarly its own; and that consequently full power may fearlessly be given to the majority by which it is represented. But this language is that of a slave.

A majority taken collectively may be regarded as a being whose opinions, and most frequently whose interests, are opposed to those of another being, which is styled a minority. If it be admitted that a man, possessing absolute power, may misuse that power by wronging his adversaries, why should a majority not be liable to the same reproach? Men are not apt to change their characters by agglomeration; nor does their patience in the presence of obstacles increase with the consciousness of their strength.[1] And for these

* From Alexis de Tocqueville, *Democracy in America* (1835-1840; trans. Henry Reeves, 1835-1840).

[1] No one will assert that a people cannot forcibly wrong another people: but parties may be looked upon as lesser nations within a greater one, and they are aliens to each other: if therefore it be admitted that a nation can act tyrannically towards another nation, it cannot be denied that a party may do the same towards another party.

reasons I can never willingly invest any number of my fellow-creatures with that unlimited authority which I should refuse to any one of them.

I do not think that it is possible to combine several principles in the same government, so as at the same time to maintain freedom, and really to oppose them to one another. The form of government which is usually termed *mixed* has always appeared to me to be a mere chimera. Accurately speaking there is no such thing as a mixed government (with the meaning usually given to that word), because in all communities some one principle of action may be discovered, which preponderates over the others. England in the last century, which has been more especially cited as an example of this form of government, was in point of fact an essentially aristocratic state, although it comprised very powerful elements of democracy: for the laws and customs of the country were such, that the aristocracy could not but preponderate in the end, and subject the direction of public affairs to its own will. The error arose from too much attention being paid to the actual struggle which was going on between the nobles and the people, without considering the probable issue of the contest, which was in reality the important point. When a community really has a mixed government, that is to say, when it is equally divided between two adverse principles, it must either pass through a revolution, or fall into complete dissolution.

I am therefore of opinion that some one social power must always be made to predominate over the others; but I think that liberty is endangered when this power is checked by no obstacles which may retard its course, and force it to moderate its own vehemence.

Unlimited power is in itself a bad and dangerous thing; human beings are not competent to exercise it with discretion; and God alone can be omnipotent, because his wisdom and his justice are always equal to his power. But no power upon earth is so worthy of honor for itself, or of reverential obedience to the rights which it represents, that I would consent to admit its uncontrolled and all-predominant authority. When I see that the right and the means of absolute command are conferred on a people or upon a king, upon an aristocracy or a democracy, a monarchy or a republic, I recognize the germ of tyranny, and I journey onwards to a land of more hopeful institutions.

In my opinion the main evil of the present democratic institutions of the United States does not arise, as is often asserted in Europe, from their weakness, but from their overpowering strength; and I am not so much alarmed at the excessive liberty which reigns in that country, as at the very inadequate securities which exist against tyranny.

When an individual or a party is wronged in the United States, to whom can he apply for redress? If to public opinion, public opinion constitutes the majority; if to the legislature, it represents the majority, and implicitly obeys its injunctions; if to the executive power, it is appointed by the majority and remains a passive tool in its hands; the public troops consist of the majority under arms; the jury is the majority invested with the right of hearing judicial cases; and in certain States even the judges are elected by the majority. However iniquitous or absurd the evil of which you complain may be, you must submit to it as well as you can.[2]

If, on the other hand, a legislative power could be so constituted as to represent the majority without necessarily being the slave of its passions; an executive, so as to retain a certain degree of uncontrolled authority; and a judiciary, so as to remain independent of the two other powers; a government would be formed which would still be democratic, without incurring any risk of tyrannical abuse.

I do not say that tyrannical abuses frequently occur in America at the present day; but I maintain that no sure barrier is established against them, and that the causes which mitigate the government are to be found in the circumstances and the manners of the country more than in its laws.

[2] A striking instance of the excesses which may be occasioned by the despotism of the majority occurred at Baltimore in the year 1812. At that time the war was very popular in Baltimore. A journal which had taken the other side of the question excited the indignation of the inhabitants by its opposition. The populace assembled, broke the printing presses, and attacked the houses of the newspaper editors. The militia was called out, but no one obeyed the call; and the only means of saving the poor wretches who were threatened by the frenzy of the mob, was to throw them into prison as common malefactors. But even this precaution was ineffectual; the mob collected again during the night; the magistrates again made a vain attempt to call out the militia; the prison was forced, one of the newspaper editors was killed upon the spot, and the others were left for dead: the guilty parties were acquitted by the jury when they were brought to trial.

I said one day to an inhabitant of Pennsylvania, "Be so good as to explain to me how it happens, that in a State founded by Quakers, and celebrated for its toleration, freed Blacks are not allowed to exercise civil rights. They pay the taxes: is it not fair that they should have a vote?"

"You insult us," replied my informant, "if you imagine that our legislators could have committed so gross an act of injustice and intolerance."

"What, then, the Blacks possess the right of voting in this country?"

"Without the slightest doubt."

"How comes it, then, that at the polling-booth this morning I did not perceive a single Negro in the whole meeting?"

"This is not the fault of the law; the Negroes have an undisputed right of voting: but they voluntarily abstain from making their appearance."

"A very pretty piece of modesty on their parts!" rejoined I.

"Why, the truth is, that they are not disinclined to vote, but they are afraid of being maltreated; in this country the law is sometimes unable to maintain its authority without the support of the majority. But in this case the majority entertains very strong prejudices against the Blacks, and the magistrates are unable to protect them in the exercise of their legal privileges."

"What, then, the majority claims the right not only of making the laws, but of breaking the laws it has made?"

2. POWER OF THE MAJORITY OVER PUBLIC OPINION

It is in the examination of the display of public opinion in the United States, that we clearly perceive how far the power of the majority surpasses all the powers with which we are acquainted in Europe. Intellectual principles exercise an influence which is so invisible and often so inappreciable, that they baffle the toils of oppression. At the present time the most absolute monarchs in Europe are unable to prevent certain notions, which are opposed to their authority, from circulating in secret throughout their dominions, and even in their courts. Such is not the case in America; as long as the majority is still undecided, discussion is carried on; but as soon as its decision is irrevocably pronounced, a submissive silence is observed; and the friends, as well as the opponents of the measure, unite in assenting to its propriety. The reason of this is perfectly clear: no monarch is so absolute as to combine all the powers of society in his own hands, and to conquer all opposition, with the energy of a majority, which is invested with the right of making and of executing the laws.

The authority of a king is purely physical, and it controls the actions of the subject without subduing his private will; but the majority possesses a power which is physical and moral at the same time; it acts upon the will as well as upon the actions of men, and it represses not only all contest, but all controversy.

I know no country in which there is so little true independence of mind and freedom of discussion as in America. In any constitutional state in Europe every sort of religious and political theory may be advocated and propagated abroad; for there is no country in Europe so subdued by any single authority, as not to contain citizens who are ready to protect the man who raises his voice in the cause of truth, from the consequences of his hardihood. If he is unfortunate enough to live under an absolute government, the people is upon his side; if he inhabits a free country, he may find a shelter behind the authority of the throne, if he require one. The aristocratic part of society supports him in some countries, and the democracy in others. But in a nation where democratic institutions exist, organized like those of the United States, there is but one sole authority, one single element of strength and of success, with nothing beyond it.

In America, the majority raises very formidable barriers to the liberty of opinion: within these barriers an author may write whatever he pleases, but he will repent it if he ever step beyond them. Not that he is exposed to the terrors of an auto-da-fé, but he is tormented by the slights and persecutions of daily obloquy. His political career is closed for ever, since he has offended the only authority which is able to promote his success. Every sort of compensation, even that of celebrity, is refused to him. Before he published his opinions, he imagined that he held them in common with many others; but no sooner has he declared them openly than he is loudly censured by his overbearing opponents, whilst those who think, without having the courage to speak, like him, abandon him in silence. He yields at length, oppressed by the daily efforts he has been making, and he subsides into silence as if he was tormented by remorse for having spoken the truth.

Fetters and headsmen were the coarse instruments which tyranny formerly employed; but the civilization of our age has refined the arts of despotism, which seemed however to have been sufficiently perfected before. The excesses of monarchical power had devised a variety of physical means of oppression; the democratic republics of the present day have rendered it as entirely an affair of the mind, as that will which it is intended to coerce. Under the absolute sway of an individual despot, the body was attacked in order to subdue the soul; and the soul escaped the blows which were directed against it, and rose superior to the attempt; but such is not the course adopted by tyranny in democratic republics; there the body is left free, and the soul is enslaved. The sovereign can no longer say, "You shall think as I do on pain of death": but he says, "You are free to think differently from me, and to retain your life, your property, and all that you possess; but if such be your determination, you are henceforth an alien among your people. You may retain your civil rights, but they will be useless to you, for you will never be chosen by your fellow-citizens, if you solicit their suffrages; and they will affect to scorn you, if you solicit their esteem. You will remain among men, but you will be deprived of the rights of mankind. Your fellow-creatures will shun you like an impure being; and those who are most persuaded of your innocence will abandon you too, lest they should be shunned in their turn. Go in peace! I have given you your life, but it is an existence incomparably worse than death."

Absolute monarchies have thrown an odium upon despotism; let us beware lest democratic republics should restore oppression, and should render it less odious and less degrading in the eyes of the many, by making it still more onerous to the few.

Works have been published in the proudest nations of the Old World, expressly intended to censure the vices and deride the follies of the time: Labruyère inhabited the palace of Louis XIV when he composed his chapter upon the Great, and Molière criticized the courtiers in the very pieces which were acted before the Court. But the ruling power in the United States is not to be made game of; the smallest reproach irritates its sensibility, and the slightest joke which has any foundation in truth renders it indignant; from the style of its language to the more solid virtues of its character, everything must be made the subject of encomium. No writer, whatever be his eminence, can escape from this tribute or adulation to his fellow-citizens. The majority lives in the perpetual practice of self-applause; and there are certain truths which the Americans can only learn from strangers or from experience.

If great writers have not at present existed in America, the reason is very simply given in these facts; there can be no literary genius without freedom of opinion, and freedom of opinion does not exist in America. The Inquisition has never been able to prevent a vast number of antireligious books from circulating in Spain. The empire of the majority succeeds much better in the United States, since it actually removes the wish of publishing them. Unbelievers are to be met with in America, but, to say the truth, there is no public organ of infidelity. Attempts have been made by some governments to protect the morality of nations by prohibiting licentious books. In the United States no one is punished for this sort of works, but no one is induced to write them; not because all the citizens are immaculate in their manners, but because the majority of the community is decent and orderly.

In these cases the advantages derived from the exercise of this power are unquestionable; and I am simply discussing the nature of the power itself. This irresistible authority is a constant fact, and its judicial exercise is an accidental occurrence.

3. WHY DEMOCRATIC NATIONS LOVE EQUALITY MORE THAN LIBERTY

The first and most intense passion which is engendered by the equality of conditions is, I need hardly say, the love of that same equality. My readers will therefore not be surprised that I speak of it before all others.

Everybody has remarked, that in our time, and especially in France, this passion for equality is every day gaining ground in the human heart. It has been said a hundred times that our contemporaries are far more ardently and tenaciously attached to equality than to freedom; but, as I do not find that the causes of the fact have been sufficiently analyzed, I shall endeavour to point them out.

It is possible to imagine an extreme point at which freedom and equality would meet and be confounded together. Let us suppose that all the members of the community take a part in the government, and that each one of them has an equal right to take a part in it. As none is different from his fellows, none can exercise a tyrannical power: men will be perfectly free, because they will all be entirely equal; and they will all be perfectly equal, because they will be entirely free. To this ideal state democratic nations tend. Such is the completest form that equality can assume upon earth; but there are a thousand others which, without being equally perfect, are not less cherished by those nations.

The principle of equality may be established in civil society, without prevailing in the political world. Equal rights may exist of indulging in the same pleasures, of entering the same professions, of frequenting the same places—in a word, of living in the same manner and seeking wealth by the same means, although all men do not take an equal share in the government.

A kind of equality may even be established in the political world, though there should be no political freedom there. A man may be the equal of all his countrymen save one, who is the master of all without distinction, and who selects equally from among them all the agents of his power.

Several other combinations might be easily imagined, by which very great equality would be united to institutions more or less free, or even to institutions wholly without freedom.

Although men cannot become absolutely equal unless they be entirely free, and consequently equality, pushed to its furthest extent, may be confounded with freedom, yet there is good reason for distinguishing the one from the other. The taste which men have for liberty, and that which they feel for equality, are, in fact, two different things; and I am not afraid to add, that, among democratic nations, they are two unequal things.

Upon close inspection, it will be seen that there is in every age some peculiar and preponderating fact with which all others are connected; this fact almost always gives birth to some pregnant idea or some ruling passion, which attracts to itself, and bears away in its course, all the feelings and opinions of the time: it is like a great stream, toward which each of the surrounding rivulets seems to flow.

Freedom has appeared in the world at different times and under various forms; it has not been exclusively bound to any social condition, and it is not confined to democracies. Freedom cannot, therefore, form the distinguishing characteristic of democratic ages. The peculiar and preponderating fact which marks those ages as its own is the equality of conditions; the ruling passion of men in those periods is the love of this equality. Ask not what singular charm the men of democratic ages find in being equal, or what special reasons they may have for clinging so tenaciously to equality rather than to the other advantages which society holds out to them: equality is the distinguishing characteristic of the age they live in; that, of itself, is enough to explain that they prefer it to all the rest.

But independently of this reason there are several others, which will at all times habitually lead men to prefer equality to freedom.

If a people could ever succeed in destroying, or even in diminishing, the equality which prevails in its own body, this could only be accomplished by long and laborious efforts. Its social condition must be modified, its laws abolished, its opinions superseded, its habits changed, its manners corrupted. But political liberty is more easily lost; to neglect to hold it fast, is to allow it to escape.

Men therefore not only cling to equality because it is dear to them; they also adhere to it because they think it will last for ever.

That political freedom may compromise in its excesses the tranquillity, the property, the lives of individuals, is obvious to the narrowest and most unthinking minds. But, on the contrary, none but attentive and clear-sighted men perceive the perils with which equality threatens us, and they commonly avoid pointing them out. They know that the calamities they apprehend are remote, and flatter themselves that they will only fall upon future generations, for which the present generation takes but little thought. The evils which freedom sometimes brings with it are immediate; they are apparent to all, and all are more or less affected by them. The evils which extreme equality may produce are slowly disclosed; they creep gradually into the social frame; they are only seen at intervals, and at the moment at which they become most violent, habit already causes them to be no longer felt.

The advantages which freedom brings are only shown by length of time; and it is always easy to mistake the cause in which they originate. The advantages of equality are instantaneous, and they may constantly be traced from their source.

Political liberty bestows exalted pleasures, from time to time, upon a certain number of citizens. Equality every day confers a number of small enjoyments on every man. The charms of equality are every instant felt, and are within the reach of all: the noblest hearts are not insensible to them, and the most vulgar souls exult in them. The passion which equality engenders must therefore be at once strong and general. Men cannot enjoy political liberty unpurchased by some sacrifices, and they never obtain it without great exertions. But the pleasures of equality are self-proffered: each of the petty incidents of life seems to occasion them, and in order to taste them nothing is required but to live.

Democratic nations are at all times fond of equality, but there are certain epochs at which the passion they entertain for it swells to the height of fury. This occurs at the moment when the old social system, long menaced, completes its own destruction after a last intestine struggle, and when the barriers of rank are at length thrown down. At such times men pounce upon equality as their booty, and they cling to it as to some precious treasure which they fear to lose. The passion for equality penetrates on every side into men's hearts, expands there, and fills them entirely. Tell them not that by this blind surrender of themselves to an exclusive passion, they risk their dearest interests: they are deaf. Show them not freedom escaping from their grasp, while they are looking another way: they are blind—or rather, they can discern but one sole object to be desired in the universe.

What I have said is applicable to all democratic nations: what I am about to say concerns the French alone. Among most modern nations, and especially among all those of the continent of Europe, the taste and the idea of freedom only began to exist and to extend itself at the time when social conditions were tending to equality, and as a consequence of that very equality. Absolute kings were the most efficient levellers of ranks among their subjects. Among these nations equality preceded freedom: equality was therefore a fact of some standing, when freedom was still a novelty: the one had already created customs, opinions, and laws belonging to it, when the other, alone and for the first time, came into actual existence. Thus the latter was till only recently an affair of opinion and of taste, while the former had already crept into the habits of the people, possessed itself of their manners, and given a particular turn to the smallest actions in their lives. Can it be wondered that the men of our own time prefer the one to the other?

I think that democratic communities have a natural taste for freedom: left to themselves, they will seek it, cherish it, and view any privation of it with regret. But for equality, their passion is ardent, insatiable, incessant, invincible: they call for equality in freedom; if they cannot obtain that, they ~till call for equality in slavery. They will endure poverty, servitude, barbarism—but they will not endure aristocracy.

This is true at all times, and especially true in our own. All men and all powers seeking to cope with this irresistible passion, will be overthrown and destroyed by it. In our age, freedom cannot be established without it, and despotism itself cannot reign without its support.

ABRAHAM LINCOLN

2. *The Meaning of Equality**

I think the authors of that notable instrument [the Declaration of Independence], intended to include *all* men, but they did not intend to declare all men equal *in all respects*. They did not mean to say all were equal in color, size, intellect, moral developments, or social capacity. They defined with tolerable distinctness in what respects they did consider all men created equal—equal with "certain inalienable rights, among which are life, liberty, and the pursuit of happiness." This they said, and this they meant. They did

* From an address delivered at Springfield, June 26, 1857.

not mean to assert the obvious untruth that all were then actually enjoying that equality, nor yet that they were about to confer it immediately upon them. In fact, they had no power to confer such a boon. They meant simply to declare the right, so that enforcement of it might follow as fast as circumstances should permit.

They meant to set up a standard maxim for free society, which should be familiar to all, and revered by all; constantly looked to, constantly labored for, and even though never perfectly attained, constantly approximated, and thereby constantly spreading and deepening its influence and augmenting the happiness and value of life to all people of all colors everywhere. The assertion that "all men are created equal" was of no practical use in effecting our separation from Great Britain; and it was placed in the declaration not for that, but for future use. Its authors meant it to be—as, thank God, it is now proving itself—a stumbling block to all those who in after times might seek to turn a free people back into the hateful paths of despotism. They knew the proneness of prosperity to breed tyrants, and they meant when such should reappear in this fair land and commence their vocation, they should find left for them at least one hard nut to crack.

SIDNEY AND BEATRICE WEBB

3. Inequality and Personal Freedom*

There is an inequality in the capitalist state, which is perhaps more intensely resented by the modern artisan, and is more difficult to bring to the comprehension of the governing class than the inequality of income; namely, the disparity in personal freedom. Freedom is, of course, an elusive term, with various and conflicting meanings. To some simple minds freedom appears only a negation of slavery. To them any one is free who is not the chattel of some other person. The shipwrecked mariner on a barren island and the destitute vagrant wandering among property owners protected by an all-powerful police, are "free men," seeing that they "call no man master." But this sort of freedom is little more than freedom to die. In the modern industrial community, in which no man is able to produce for himself all

---

*From Sidney and Beatrice Webb, *The Decay of Capitalist Civilization* (Harcourt, Brace and Company, 1923). By permission.

that he needs for life, personal freedom is necessarily bound up with the ability to obtain commodities and services produced by other persons. Translated into the terms of daily life, personal freedom means, in fact, the power of the individual to buy sufficient food, shelter and clothing to keep his body in good health, and to gain access to sufficient teaching and books to develop his mind from its infantile state. Moreover, as we cannot regard as a free man any one with none but vegetative experiences, freedom involves the command at some time, of at least some money to spend on holidays and travel, on social intercourse and recreation, on placing one's self in a position to enjoy nature and art. We can, in fact, best define personal freedom as the possession of opportunity to develop our faculties and satisfy our desires. Professor Graham Wallas suggests the definition of "the possibility of continuous initiative." In this sense freedom is a relative term. It is only the very rich man who has freedom to consume all that he desires of the services and commodities produced by other persons, and also the freedom to abstain from all personal toil that would stand in the way of his "continuous initiative," and stop it by absorbing his energy and his time. Any poor man has a very limited freedom. To the propertyless wage-earner freedom may mean nothing more than the freedom, by dint of perpetual toil, to continue to exist on the very brink of starvation. Hence inequality in income in itself entails inequality in personal freedom.

"EQUAL BEFORE THE LAW"

We have grown so accustomed, under the reign of capitalism, to the grossest disparity in personal freedom among nominally free citizens, that we fail to recognize how gross and how cruel is the inequality even where we profess to have adopted equality as a principle. Both Britain and America are proud of having made all men equal before the law. Yet no one can even ask for justice in the law-courts without paying fees which (though the statesmen and the wealthy refuse to credit the fact) do, in actual practice, prevent the great mass of the population from obtaining legal redress for the wrongs that are constantly being done to them. The very object with which the legal tribunals are established is to give men security for their personal freedom—to prevent this being impaired by assaults, thefts, extortions, defalcations and failure to fulfill contracts and pay debts. In every city of Britain and America the vast majority of the population never appear as plaintiffs in the civil courts, not because they are not assaulted and robbed, cheated and denied payment of what is due to them—every one must know that these evils happen much more frequently and, at one time or another, much nearer universally, to the poor and friendless than to the rich—but because they cannot afford, out of their scanty earnings, even the court fee, let alone that of the lawyer. But the disparity in personal freedom between the rich and the poor is seen most glaringly when the one and the other are charged in the criminal court with an offense against the law. The rich man, except in extreme cases such as murder, practically always receives a summons; the poor man is still often, for the same offense, peremptorily arrested, as was formerly always the case, and taken to prison to await trial. On a remand, the rich man easily procures bail, whilst quite a large proportion of propertyless defendants find themselves returned to the prison cells, a procedure which, coupled with their lack of means, does not, to say the least, facilitate their hunting up of witnesses who might prove their innocence, or their obtaining help in their defense. It is needless to recount the further advantages of the rich man in engaging the ablest lawyers and expert witnesses; in obtaining a change of venue, and successive remands, or in dragging the case from court to court. When sentence is imposed, it is, in the vast majority of cases, a pecuniary fine, which means practically nothing to the rich man, while to the poor man it may spell ruin for himself, his little business and his household. To the average police magistrate or clerk to the justices, it is quite a matter of course that a positive majority of those whom they sentence to small fines go to prison for one, two or six weeks, in default of payment. Ruinous as prison is known to be to the family of the prisoner as well as to the prisoner himself, the poor are sent to prison, in the United States as in Britain, by thousands every year, merely because they cannot immediately produce the few shillings or dollars that they are fined for minor offenses, which rich men commit daily with practical impunity. No inequality in personal freedom could be more scandalous than this practical inequality of rich and poor before the law courts, which characterizes every capitalist community, and which, though known to every judge and every practicing lawyer for a century, has remained unredressed.[1]

THE PSYCHOLOGICAL REACTION

But all this springs directly from the disparity in incomes, a material interpretation of personal freedom which does not exhaust the question. There is a psychological aspect of personal freedom which arises merely from the relation between one man and another. Even when the wage-earner is getting what he calls "good money" and steady work, he resents the fact that he, like the machine with which he works, is bought as an instrument of production; *that his daily life is dealt with as a means to another's end.* Why should he and his class always obey orders, and another, and a much smaller class, always give them? It is this concentration of the function of command in one individual, or in one class, with the correlative concentration of the obligation to obey in other individuals of another class, which constitutes the deepest chasm between the nation of the rich and the nation of the poor. In one of his novels Mr. Galsworthy vividly describes the contrast between

[1] See *The Law and the Poor*, by E. A. Parry, 1914.

the daily life of the English country house and the daily life of the laborer's cottage. The rich man, and his wife and children, get up in the morning at any time they please; they eat what they like; they "work" and they play when they like and how they like; their whole day is controlled by the promptings of their own instinct or impulse, or is determined by their own reason or will. From morning till night they are perpetually doing what is pleasant to them. They fulfill their personality, and they exercise what Professor Graham Wallas rightly calls their "continuous initiative," by giving, day in day out, year in year out, orders to other people. The laborer and his family are always obeying orders; getting up by order, working by order, in the way they are ordered, leaving off work by order, occupying one cottage rather than another by order of the farmer, being ejected from home by order of the landowner, attending school by order, sometimes even going to church by order; relying for medical attendance on the "order" of the Poor Law Relieving Officer, and in some cases ordered into the workhouse to end a life which, under the British Constitution, has always been legally and politically that of a freeman. From morning till night—save in rare hours of "expansion" usually expiated painfully—the "working class" find themselves doing what is irksome or unpleasant to them. What is called in Britain the governing class (which includes a great many more persons than are engaged in political government), is, typically, the class that passes its life in giving orders. What are called the "lower classes" are those that live by obeying orders.

WHEN AUTHORITY IS ACCEPTABLE

Now let no one imagine that these lower classes, or the socialists who champion them, or indeed any persons with common sense, object to one man exercising authority over another. What is resented in the capitalist organization of industry is both the number and the kind of the orders given by the rich to the poor, by the owners of land and capital to the persons who gain their livelihood by using these instruments of production. The authority of the capitalist and the landlord has invidious characteristics. It is continuous over the lives of the individuals who are ordered; it is irresponsible and cannot be called to account; it is not in any way reciprocal; it does not involve the selection of the person in command for his capacity to exercise authority either wisely or in the public interest; above all, it is designed to promote, not the good of the whole community, but the personal pleasure or private gain of the person who gives the order. No one but an anarchist objects to the authority of the policeman regulating the traffic in the crowded street; to the authority of the sanitary inspector compelling the occupier of the house to connect his domestic pipe with the main drain; to the authority of the Medical Officer of Health enforcing the isolation of an infectious person; or even to the demand note of the tax-collector. No one resents the commands of the railway guard—"take your seats" or "all change here." All these orders are given in respect of particular occasions in the citizen's life, and by persons assumed to be selected for their fitness for the duty of giving these particular orders. The persons exercising command are themselves under orders; they are responsible to superior authority; and they may be called to account for bad manners or for "exceeding their powers." Moreover, their orders are, in the best sense, disinterested, and have no connection with their personal gain or convenience. We may complain that the official is going beyond his function or is unmannerly in his methods. We may object to the policy of the national executive, or deplore the legislation enacted by Parliament. But in obeying these orders all men are equal before the law; and all men have the same right of appeal to the superior authority. Finally, in political democracy, the persons who are subject to the authority are exactly the persons who have created it; and they can, if and when they choose, sweep it away. In their capacity of citizen-electors they may exercise collectively, through the Parliament and the government of the day, an ultimate control over the stream of orders they are called upon as individuals to obey.

In this connection it is interesting to notice the socialist interpretation of a phrase much in vogue in the twentieth century. We often hear at labor meetings of the desirability of a man "controlling his own working life." But this does not mean that each man or woman is to be free to work at starvation wages, or for excessive hours, or under the most unpleasant conditions. This is the freedom demanded for the worker by the capitalist. Against it the socialists and the organized workers have carried on a war of attrition for a century, the victories in that war being factory laws, mines and railway regulation laws, minimum wage laws, and the like. What the insurgent worker means by "the worker's control over his own life" is, on the contrary, the sort of control exercised by means of his trade union, through an executive council and officials, whom he and his fellows have elected, and can depose. These agents of the workers stand or fall, paradoxical as it may sound to those who still ignorantly regard trade unions as tyrannies, according to their ability to maintain and increase the personal freedom of the persons who elect them. The revolt of the workers is not against authority as such, but against the continuous and irresponsible authority of the profit-making employer. Where is the warrant, he asks, for the power of the owners of factories and mines, land and machinery to dictate the daily life and the weekly expenditure of hundreds of their fellowmen, and even, at their pleasure, to withdraw from them the means of life itself? This power is not derived from popular election. It has no relation to the ascertained merit or capacity of those who wield it. It is, in many cases, not even accompanied by any consciousness of responsibility for the moral or material well-being of those over whom it is exercised. Not only is there no necessary connection

between the particular orders which the workers find themselves compelled to obey, and the security or prosperity of the commonwealth: there is
often a great and patent contradiction, orders to adulterate and cheat being
quite common. From the standpoint of labor the authority of the capitalist
and landlord is used for a corrupt end—to promote the pecuniary gain of
the person in command.

DICTATION AS TO ENVIRONMENT

Few persons who have not deliberately analyzed the way in which the
wage-system is organized have any adequate conception of the continuity
and the dictatorial character of the stream of orders by which the workman
is called upon to direct his life. But this stream of orders is not the only way
in which the property-owning class directs the daily life of those who are
dependent on their toil. Even more dangerous, because more subtle, and less
obviously an outcome of the inequality in wealth, is the power possessed by
the propertied class to determine, for many years at a stretch, what shall be
the physical and mental environment, not only of the manual laborer, but
of all the local inhabitants. The most striking manifestation of this power is
the steadily increasing "industrializing" of a countryside, ending in the
creation of an urban slum area, by the continuous pollution of the water
and the atmosphere, the destruction of vegetation, the creation of nuisances,
the erection of "back to back" dwellings, in row after row of mean streets.
The devastation wrought in this way, in some of the most fertile and most
beautiful parts of England and Scotland, as also in the United States, is, as
we now know, comparable only to that effected by a long-drawn-out modern war. In peace times the community as a whole fails to realize, in time,
the catastrophe that is being caused by the private ownership of land and
capital in the establishment and growth of an industrial center. By the time
that the evil is recognized, the health and happiness of whole generations
have been vitally affected. Belated statutes and tardy by-laws may then, at
best, lessen the pollution, abate the darkening of the atmosphere by noxious
gases and coal smoke, perhaps even save the last surviving vegetation. But
nothing can bring back the lives the dictatorship of the capitalist has wasted.
The leisured rich are able to escape from the noise, the gloom, the dirt, the
smoke, the smells that their power has created; but the wage-earners, the
industrial brain-workers, and all their retinue of professional men and shopkeepers find themselves compelled to dwell, and to rear their families, in the
graceless conditions unconsciously determined for them by the industrial
and financial organizers in their pursuit of private gain. When the city
dweller escapes into the still unspoilt countryside on a scanty holiday, it
comes as a new insult to find himself and his children barred from the pleasant park, excluded from the forest, and warned off the mountain and the

moor by the property rights of the very class of persons who have rendered his place of abode abhorrent to him. In the end he is forced in self-defense to form a perverse habit of liking grimy streets, blackened skies, and the deafening clatter of drayhorses' shoes on stone sets, on the principle that if you cannot have what you like you must like what you have.

DICTATION OF THE MENTAL ENVIRONMENT

Nor is even this unconscious determination by the property-owning class of the material environment of the mass of the community, for the sake of its own private gain, the worst form taken by the inequality in personal freedom. It has been reserved to our own time for the profit-making capitalist to determine also the mental environment. Who can estimate the effect on the mind of the incessantly reiterated advertisements that hem us in on every side? It is, moreover, the capitalist who directs the character of the recreation afforded to the mass of people. It is the brewery company and the distillery that give us the public house; other capitalists, controlling the music hall and the cinematograph, may say, with Fletcher of Saltoun, that they care not who makes the laws as long as they provide the songs and films. But the most glaring instance of the capitalist direction of our mentality, and perhaps, ultimately, the most pernicious, is the modern system of ownership of the newspaper press. Here we have even a double capitalist control, first by the millionaire proprietors of whole series of journals, daily, weekly, and monthly under autocratic control, and secondly, by the great dispensers of lucrative advertisements to these journals. The combination of the colossal expense involved in the successful conduct of a modern daily newspaper, and the natural reluctance of the wealthy advertisers to support any publication adverse to the system, if not even to the particular business, by which they obtain their own fortunes, have made it almost impossible for the propertyless wage-earners, even in cooperation with each other, to establish, either in Britain or the United States, any organ of their own at all comparable in circulation and influence with those of the millionaire proprietors. Thus, the mass of the population is quite unable to protect itself against the stream of suggestion, biased information, and corruptly selected news that is poured on them by the giant circulation of the press.[2]

[2] For accounts of the manner and extent to which the newspaper press, and behind it the possessors of wealth, now control the mental environment, as well as the local and central government of the United States and Britain, the student should consult *The Press and the Organization of Society*, by Norman Angell, 1922; and *Liberty and the News*, 1920, and *Public Opinion*, 1922, both by Walter Lippmann, himself the editor of a great New York newspaper; the more lurid descriptions given from personal experience as journalists, on the one hand, by Hilaire Belloc in *The Free Press*, 1918, and by Upton Sinclair in *The Brass Check*, 1919; and, incidentally, in the technical account of how a modern newspaper is run, by G. B. Dibblee in *The Newspaper*, 1913 (London), and by John La P. Given in *Making a Newspaper*, 1913 (New York).

Lastly, we have the control insidiously exercised by the owners and organizers of the instruments of production, by means of their wealth, over the working of municipal government and parliamentary institutions.

DICTATION IN GOVERNMENT

Of this control, the direct power of the proprietors of the newspaper press —which, in Britain, goes far to make a Prime Minister, and in the United States not only to elect a President but also to select his chief ministers—is only the most obvious example. The influence, not only upon elections and legislatures, but also upon national and municipal executives, of the great financial, shipping, manufacturing, and trading amalgamations and combinations, in which the power of wealth is cast defiantly into the scale as the sword of Brennus, has, in recent decades, become notorious and scandalous. It is, we suggest, to the suspicion, followed by the detection of this far-reaching coercive guidance of national and local government by the property-owners and profit-makers, large and small, more than to any other cause, that is to be ascribed the sudden and rapid decay of the confidence of the wage-earning class in these institutions, manifested not in this country alone, but throughout the Continent of Europe and North America. Unfortunately, one invidious feature of the Great War, so far as the United Kingdom is concerned, has been the extension of a similar capitalist control to the national executive, in ways not previously open. The temporary handing over of various government departments to leading representatives of the business interests concerned, and the shameless use of the influence thus acquired for the promotion of the private profits of those branches of business, represents, so it is felt by the British workman, the final degradation of the state to be the handmaid and accomplice of the profiteer.

THE BRAIN-WORKERS IN CAPITALIST SERVICE

This control of the physical and mental environment, which, in a capitalistic society, the property-owning class progressively and almost automatically accomplishes (for all those effects are mere incidents in the pursuit of private gain, and are no more consciously aimed at than the devastation caused by the trampling of a herd in pursuit of food), brings into prominence the instrument of its far-reaching dominance. The deep-seated intolerance by the more ignorant manual workers of the very existence of the professional brain-workers is not due solely to the difficulty a navvy finds in believing that a man who sits in a comfortable chair by a cheerful fire in a carefully sound-proofed room is doing any work at all, much less work that will leave him hungry and exhausted in three or four hours. Many wage-workers are sufficiently educated to know better; and others are employed in occupations quite as sedentary and even less apparently active than those of the financier or mathematician. Their share in the prejudice is explained, if not justified, by the fact that the brain-workers, in every capitalist state, find themselves attracted, and economically compelled, to take service under the property-owners. Historically the professions emerge as the hirelings of the governing class for the time being. In the modern industrial system they naturally serve the proprietors of the instruments of production, who alone can insure to the vast majority of them a secure and ample livelihood, with some prospect of climbing up to the eminence of "living by owning." The lawyers, the engineers, the architects, the men of financial and administrative ability, the civil servants, the authors and journalists, the teachers of the schools beyond the elementary grade, the whole class of managers, the inventors, even the artists and the men of science—not altogether excluding, in spite of their long charitable service of the poor, the medical profession and the ministers of religion, nor yet, for all their devotion to the children of the masses, even the elementary school teachers—are almost inevitably retained, consciously or unconsciously, in the maintenance and defense of the existing social order, in which the private ownership of the instruments of production is the corner-stone. Is it surprising that the manual workers of the world should be tempted to regard, not science, art or religion (as is often ignorantly asserted), but the brain-workers who have been trained under the capitalist system, and enlisted in its service, as being as much the "enemies of the people" as the "idle rich"? But this is not all. The brain-workers themselves, especially those who are poorly paid and socially segregated, are beginning to rebel openly against this all-pervading coercive guidance of national policy and national culture by wealthy men and a wealthy class. As school teachers, as municipal officials, as civil servants, as scientific workers, as journalists and editors, sometimes even (notably in the United State as under the German Empire) as university lecturers and professors, they find their freedom of thought and expression strangled by the fear of dismissal, or at any rate by that of losing all chance of promotion, should they dare to oppose not merely the political party or the pecuniary interests of influential patrons, but even the current principles of social organizations to which nearly all rich men cling. Moreover, the majority of the situations of authority and affluence are still habitually reserved, in most countries, either by administrative devices or through personal influence, for persons who have qualified as brain-workers though belonging to the class of those who live by owning or organizing the instruments of production, irrespective of their inferiority of attainments or inability to render, in the posts to which they are assigned, the highest service to the community. It is here that we find the fundamental cause of the prevailing unrest in all countries in practically all the brain-working professions, leading in many cases to the adherence of the younger professionals to the socialist movement, and nowadays even inclining some of the professional organizations to make common cause with the trade unions and the labor and socialist parties in resisting the dominance of the property-owners.

WHY LIBERALISM DECAYED

We may suggest that the foregoing analysis incidentally reveals the root-cause of the universal failure of the political parties styled Liberal, which were so typical of the advanced thought of European nations during the nineteenth century—notably at the zenith of unrestrained capitalism—to retain, in the twentieth century, they hold of a wage-earning class that has become conscious of its citizenship. To the political Liberals, personal freedom actually meant the personal power of the man of property; just as political progress meant the abolition of feudal, ecclesiastical and syndicalist restrictions upon the right of the property-owner, small as well as large, to do what he liked "with his own"—his own land and capital no less than his own personality. Down to the present day the unrepentant Liberal refuses to recognize—cannot even be made to understand—that, in the modern industrial state, a man who is divorced from the instruments of production cannot, as we have shown, even live his own life, let alone do what he likes with his own personality. Even to the political Liberal who is not a capitalist, such as the young barrister or doctor, artist or author, the conception that the laborers' engagement for hire is of the nature of "wage-slavery" is unintelligible. To him it seems, on the contrary, that the typical engagement for hire of the propertyless professional, "calling no man master" but earning his livelihood by fees from a succession of clients, upon no one of whom is he specially dependent, constitutes the very perfection of honorable service which is perfect freedom. What even this highly educated Liberal fails to understand is that, whatever may once have been the case, the industrial revolution has made anything like the freedom of professional life impossible for the artisan or the factory operative, the laborer or the clerk. The fact that the ordinary manual worker or minor clerical employee has not the ownership, and therefore, not the control of the instruments of production, or of the complicated industrial or financial organization by which he can earn a livelihood, and cannot support himself on a succession of fees from a multitude of clients, compels him, whether or not he desires this, to obtain his food by placing himself under a master whom he cannot call to account; whose orders he has to obey; whose interests he has to serve; who, in fact, possesses him and uses him, during the greater part of his waking life, for ends which are not his own. He cannot choose where he will live, and in what environment his children will grow up. He finds himself restricted in the amusements and even in the literature to which he has access, to that which it suits the pecuniary interests of the capitalist class to supply. He finds, as it seems to him, nearly every professional brain-worker retained against him and his class. And through this control over his working life and his leisure hours, over his physical and mental environment, the propertyless worker, by hand or by brain—though conscious that he and his fellows constitute a majority of the electorate—discover that even with the widest suffrage he is unable, in fact, to control the government of his state. Accordingly, once he has been admitted to voting citizenship, the liberty which Liberalism offers him seems a hypocritical pretense. He finds in the creed of Liberalism no comprehension either of the nature of the servitude in which the capitalist system has engulfed the great bulk of every industrial community, or of the need for an application to industrial organization of the first principles of democracy. Now this comprehension is the very atmosphere of socialism. The socialist is out to destroy the dictatorship of the capitalist. And as that dictatorship is the grievance which the worker is never allowed to forget for a single working day from his cradle to his grave he naturally turns to socialism the moment he begins to connect politics with his personal affairs and perceives that his vote is an instrument of political power.

A. D. LINDSAY

4. Democracy and the Expert*

The task of the government of a democratic society implies a wisdom and understanding of the complicated life of modern societies very far removed from the simple "horse sense" which is sufficient for the running of small and simple democracies. It is clear that a modern state can do its job only with a lot of expert help, expert statesmen, expert administrators. We must nowadays go on and say "expert economists and expert scientists." Perhaps we must go further and say "expert sociologists."

That is clear enough. What is not so clear is where the ordinary plain man comes in. What is the justification of submitting the expert work of all these superior people to the control of the ordinary voter? We recognize that the man in the street cannot, in the strict sense of the word, govern a modern state. The ordinary person has not the knowledge, the judgement, or the skill to deal with the intricate problems which modern government involves. The primitive democracy of a Swiss commune or of a New England township in the eighteenth century was quite different. The things which

* From A. D. Lindsay, *The Modern Democratic State* (Oxford University Press, 1943). By permission.

the community had to get done in those simple societies were within the competence of most members of the community and open to the judgement of all. Readers of *Coniston,* that admirable political novel in which the American Winston Churchill describes the corruption of simple New Hampshire democracy by the coming of the boss, will remember the society he depicts—hard-headed, sensible, decent farmers, good judges of men and of horses. The select men whom they elect to govern them are well known to them all. They have nothing to do about which their electors cannot form a sound and shrewd judgement.

To ignore the immense difference between such a society and the society of the modern democratic state is to court disaster. Where are the simple and familiar issues on which shrewd if unlearned men may judge? Where, perhaps it may be asked, in our great urban populations are the hard-headed, shrewd, independent men to judge soundly on any issues?

We all recognize that expert and technical knowledge must come from specialists—that the ordinary man or woman is not capable of judging the detail of legislative proposals. We say that the public decides upon broad issues. That is what the working of modern democracy is supposed to imply. An election makes clear that the public insists, for example, that something pretty drastic must be done about unemployment, or that the United States should support Great Britain by all measures "short of war," and so on. One party rather than another gets into power because the public broadly approves of its programme more than the programme of its rivals and judges well of its capacity to carry out its programme. The public is not supposed to have any views as to how that programme should be carried out but it is supposed to have decided that it prefers the main lines of one party's programme to another's.

What does this imply? Does democracy assume that ordinary men and women are better judges on broad issues than experts or than educated people? We can only take this line if we hold that "broad issues" demand not knowledge or skill or special training but "common sense" or sound judgement and that "common sense" is the possession of the ordinary man.

This is the stumbling-stone of democratic theory. On this subject men seem to hold opposing views which cannot be reconciled. Think of the way in which some people talk with conviction of the mob or the herd or the vulgar. Think of the long tradition of denunciation from Thucydides downwards of the folly and fickleness and weakness of the masses. Think, on the other hand, of the continual appreciation in democratic literature of the good sense and sound judgement of the common man—the often expressed conviction that there is something in the "plain man" or in "the man in the street" which makes his judgement often more worth while than that of many superior persons.

There must be something to be said for both sides in such a controversy. It is worth while to attempt some disentangling.

Let us begin by noting that there are arguments for democratic control which do not assume that men and women are or ought to be given votes only because of the soundness of their judgement. We may summarize the two arguments in the two statements: "Only the wearer knows where the shoe pinches" and "We count heads to save the trouble of breaking them."

THE "SHOES PINCHING" ARGUMENT

Let us begin with the argument about shoes pinching. If we start with the statement I have described as the authentic note of democracy, "The poorest he that is in England has a life to live as the richest he," if we remember that the end of democratic government is to minister to the common life of society, to remove the disharmonies that trouble it, then clearly a knowledge and understanding of that common life is a large part of the knowledge essential to the statesman. But the common life is the life lived by all members of the society. It cannot be fully known and appreciated from outside. It can only be known by those who live it. Its disharmonies are suffered and felt by individuals. It is their shoes that pinch and they only who can tell where they pinch. No doubt the ordinary voter has the vaguest ideas as to what legislative or administrative reform will stop the pinching of his shoes. That is no more his business and no more within his capacity than it is the ordinary customer's business to make shoes. He may think, and often does think, that his shoes are pinching only because of the gross ignorance or perhaps because of the corrupt and evil intentions of his government; he may think the making of governmental shoes which ease his feet to be a much simpler business than it is; he may listen too easily to charlatans who promise to make the most beautiful shoes for the lowest possible price. But for all that, only he, the ordinary man, can tell whether the shoes pinch and where; and without that knowledge the wisest statesman cannot make good laws. It is sadly instructive to find what a gap there always is between the account even the best administrations give of the effect of their regulations and the account you get from those to whom the regulations apply. The official account tells what ought to happen if men and women behaved and felt as decent respectable officials assume that they think and feel. What is actually happening is often quite different.

The argument about shoes pinching is the argument which justifies adult suffrage. If government needs for its task an understanding of the common life it exists to serve, it must have access to all the aspects of that common life. All classes in society must be able to express their grievances. The qualification for voting is not wisdom or good sense but enough independence of mind to be able to state grievances. This does not seem a difficult qualification, but oppressed people are not always prepared to stand up for themselves or even always to think that there is anything wrong in what happens to them. They do not always accept the teaching of "certain revolutionary maniacs" referred to by the Rev. Mr. Twist "who teach the people that the convenience of man, and not the will of God, has consigned them to labour and privation." They vote as "their betters" or their employers or their bosses tell them. To give more of them votes in a society where these conditions exist is to give more power into the hands of those who can manage and exploit them. So in some societies to give votes to women would only mean to give more power into the hands of the men who could deliver their votes. To be an independent person, to be ready to stand up for your rights, to be able to express your grievances and demand that something should be done about them, demand qualities of character and mind which are not always forthcoming, as organizers and defenders of the downtrodden and oppressed often learn sadly to their cost.

LIMITATIONS OF THIS ARGUMENT

However weighty this argument about "shoes pinching" may be, it does not seem necessarily to involve the control of government by public opinion. It does involve that government should be sensitive and accessible to public opinion, but that is not necessarily the same thing. The safeguarding of the right of petition has little to do with democracy. It is an old tradition of kingly rule that the humblest member of the public should have access to the king to state his grievances. That is the mark of the good Eastern king from Solomon to Haroun al Rashid. The administration of government always gives opportunities for petty tyranny. The member of parliament who asks a question on behalf of one of his constituents who has a complaint against the administration is fulfilling a very old function which existed in undemocratic days. Why should the argument about shoes pinching imply the control of government by the ordinary voter?

The answer is that experts do not like being told that the shoes they so beautifully make do not fit. They are apt to blame it on the distorted and misshapen toes of the people who have to wear their shoes. Unless there is power behind the expression of grievances, the grievances are apt to be neglected. The very way in which the stories talk about the good king who takes pains to find out what his subjects really think implies that most kings do not do so. Solomons or Harouns al Rashid do not grow on every bush. Contrast the very great care which is officially taken in the army to encourage and listen to complaints with what the men say about it. There may be the most regular machinery by which men can express their grievances, the most frequent opportunities to respond to the questions "Any complaints?"; but the rank and file will remain convinced that, if they complain, nothing will be done, but the sergeant-major will have it out of them somehow. Men will continue to talk and think quite differently about getting their grievances redressed through their member of parliament who wants their votes on the one hand and through their superior officer over whom they have no power on the other.

On this theory what happens in parliamentary democracy is that the people vote for a government on the understanding that it will remedy their grievances, deal with what is most manifestly wrong, and that they judge and they alone can judge whether the grievances are remedied. The vote at a general election is primarily a judgement on results: the people say, "Our shoes are still pinching and we shall try another shoemaker, thank you": or, "Yes, you have made our feet so much more comfortable that we shall let you go on and see if you can do still better." Of course what happens is not so simple as that. The verdict of the electors is not just on results: it is to some extent an assent to this or that proposal for the future; but broadly speaking an election is an expression of approval or disapproval of what has happened. This is of course strictly in accordance with the "where the shoe pinches" theory. It does not imply any more than the theory does that the electorate are particularly intelligent: that their judgement as to what ought to be done is at all out of the ordinary. It does imply that, as the end of government is to promote the free life of all its citizens, all citizens must have their say as to how that free life is actually being hindered and how far the work of government is actually removing those hindrances.

But it will also be clear that this argument has its limitations. It does not meet anything like all the claims made for democratic government. It does not even support the claim that the general public can decide broad issues. It would not, for example, justify the democratic control of foreign policy. Foreign policy involves a judgement as to how the internal life of the country is to be preserved from danger from abroad. If we assume that the democratic voter is only concerned to be allowed to "live his own life," to be freed from hindrances to it, but that he has not the necessary knowledge to know what means should be taken to ensure that end, it follows that the ordinary man or woman has on the argument of "the shoe pinching" no particular competence to control foreign policy. Is he then to leave foreign policy entirely to "his betters"?

No democrat would assent. Let us see why.

WHAT PEOPLE ARE PREPARED TO DO

Errors in foreign policy may mean that a country is faced with the threat of war which may involve, unless that threat is met in one way or another, the destruction of all in its life which its people hold dear. But there are only two conceivable ways in which a threat of war can be met, and both involve the severest sacrifices falling on the ordinary men and women in the country. One of the ways of course is to meet the threat of war by accepting its challenge and resisting it. The other has never been tried but it is advocated by Mr. Gandhi and extreme pacifists. It is to meet the threat of war by passive resistance. Let us first consider the second.

Passive resistance to invasion which would prevent the invader from destroying the soul of a country demands a heroism and goodness in the population of a kind which no people has ever yet shown. If a sincere pacifist statesman, say Mr. Gandhi in power in India, committed his country to this alternative by making the other alternative impossible, he might produce the most horrible disaster. If his people were not really prepared to act up to his principles, and he had incapacitated them from acting up to their own, the result would be disaster indeed. No statesman has a right to commit his country to action unless he has reason to believe that the people will respond to the challenge which that action involves.

The same point is obvious when we consider the conditions in which alone a democratic statesman can commit his country to war. If it be true that free men fight better than other men for what they hold dear, it is also true that they fight worse than others for what they do not hold dear. It is possible, as Nazi Germany has shown, for a government to get such control over the minds and wills of a people and to have imposed such discipline upon them, that they, the government, can make up their mind about what they intend the nation to do and then make their people ready to undergo almost any sacrifice in obedience to their will. But a democratic people is not disciplined in that way. Its government can never go much beyond what their people are prepared to do. It is therefore quite essential that its government should know what that is. No statesman can pursue a foreign policy of appeasement unless he knows how much his people will stand. No statesman can pursue a policy which may end in resistance to aggression unless he knows for what his people are prepared to fight. The weakness of British foreign policy in the period between the two wars was largely due to the fact that, because of the bad working of the democratic machinery or of faulty leadership or of a combination of both, British statesmen did not have this essential knowledge to guide them in their conduct of foreign policy. Britain found herself in a new position. The development of air power had made her vulnerable as she had never been before. The existence of the League of Nations meant the adoption of a new attitude to foreign policy. The spread of pacifism and semi-pacifism further confused the issue. Before the last war a foreign minister could say with confidence, that the British people would go a very long way to preserve peace but there were certain things which they would not stand, and he could have said what those things were. After the war that could no longer be said, and this had a disastrous effect on the conduct of foreign policy.

This need of knowledge of what people are prepared to do is not confined to foreign policy. In a democratic society at least, laws, if they are to be successful, must rest largely upon consent. The force behind government can do something, but not very much. If laws are to be effectively obeyed, their demands cannot go much beyond what people are prepared to do. Successful law-making therefore demands an understanding of the ways and the willingness of ordinary people. That understanding can, to some extent, be got without voting or the ordinary processes of democratic machinery. But in so far as democratic machinery produces the expert representative, it is probably as reliable a way as can be devised of ensuring that this necessary knowledge is in the hands of government and that the government pay attention to it.

It is important to notice that though "what people are prepared to do" is a matter of fact, it is fact of an odd kind. For any one who reflects on it knows that what people are prepared to do depends on the varying tone of their societies and that that tone depends on leadership, inspiration, and imponderables of that kind. What people are prepared to do is not a distinct fact, to be discovered in its distinct existence by scientific analysis. Indeed we may say in general about all the argument of these last few pages that we shall go wrong if we think of "the pinching shoes" and "what people are prepared to do" as distinct facts, existing separately and there to be discovered. They are that to some extent but not altogether. In a small meeting the process of discovering what needs to be done and what people are prepared to do is also a process of getting people prepared to do something. Something of the same is true in the elaborate democratic processes which culminate in men and women recording their votes in the polling booths. They are, or at least ought to be, processes of discussion, discussion carried on in the most multifarious ways as it is in a healthy society, by means of the press, of clubs and societies of all kinds: in public-houses and in W.E.A. classes as well as, indeed more than, at political meetings. The process of discovering the sense of the meeting is also a process of making the sense of the meeting. So to some extent at least with a nation at large.

We shall come back to this point later. Meanwhile let us consider how far towards democracy these two arguments take us. They assert that government needs for its task knowledge which cannot be got by ordinary learning but is provided normally by the democratic machinery. That would not necessarily imply control. If the knowledge could be got in another way, presumably on this argument the democratic machinery would not be necessary. Mass observation may claim to be a scientific process of discovering accurately what is now a rather clumsy by-product of elections. There is no reason why Hitler or any other autocrat should not use such a process. It is part of any government's job to know these facts about its people even when its main purpose is to understand how to exploit them to serve its own evil ambitions.

These arguments only imply democracy when we remember that men in power need often to be compelled to serve the true purposes of government. Expert shoemakers, as we saw, do not always like to be told that their shoes are at fault. Men who have control over executive and administrative power easily forget that they are only servants and that their power has only value as an instrument. Hence all the democratic devices to ensure that government shall attend to the purposes for which it exists, shall be made to do something about the grievances and wishes of the ordinary people it is meant to serve. Hence the necessity for responsible government—for arrangements which make the government somehow responsible to the ordinary people as contrasted with the most elaborate arrangements for advising an irresponsible government, for seeing that government has the necessary information without compelling it to act on that information. If the theory of all this were properly put into practice it would mean that the government were given a free hand to deal with means. The purpose of the control exercised by the ordinary voters is to see that those means—the technical skill of the administrative are used to right ends.

THE WISDOM OF THE PLAIN MAN

This leads to a third argument for democracy where it is assumed that ordinary plain people have a certain wisdom is denied to the expert, and that therefore they are the best judges of ends if not of means.

This argument can easily be so put as to be absurd. An expert is not necessarily a fool. It may be and often is true that experts are apt to give their minds an almost complete holiday outside their own special sphere. Who does not know the distinguished scientist who thinks that his scientific attainments in one sphere justify his making the most surprising generalizations in matters of which he has no knowledge? But knowledge even in a restricted sphere cannot be a greater handicap to sound judgment than ignorance in all spheres. Yet we are not wrong when we pray to be delivered from the clever ass and it is on the whole true that for a certain kind of practical wisdom—very important in politics—we do not naturally go to the scientific expert. That does not mean that we go instead to the most ignorant man we can find or to just any one. We go to some one who has learnt wisdom from life.

It is an old story that wisdom in conduct is not learnt from books or technical study, but from experience and character. We know what we mean when we talk of men or women of "sound judgement" or of "common sense." We distinguish them from the expert whom we rather distrust. We should defend this attitude by saying that the expert is a specialist: that what is wanted for conduct is all-round experience of people and things. "Sound judgement" or "common sense" are not the products of ignorance. They are produced by experience of a certain kind, by responsibility, by a varied acquaintance with men and things and by an all-round experience. The expert or specialist on the other hand has probably paid for his expert knowledge by having had to undergo a long training which has removed him from the ordinary rough-and-tumble of life. He has probably not had to check his judgements by practical experience. He has perhaps not had to pay for his mistakes. He has become "academic" in the bad sense of that term.

If we think about the men and women whose judgement on practical affairs and on conduct we respect, we should certainly agree that academic education did not seem to be very important in their production. We should say that some of them were learned and some not, some rich, some poor. They have no special training or accomplishment. That is why we contrast the one-sidedness of the expert with the good sense or common sense of the *ordinary* man and why democrats think that the proposals of the expert should be improved by the ordinary man.

There clearly is something in this, but we must be careful. "Common sense" it is sometimes said, "is one of the rarest of qualities." The word "common" is used in New England as a term of uncommon praise. It means, I think, much what the word "plain" means in the north of England or Scotland. We were proud as children when some one described our mother as "the plainest woman I have ever set eyes on," though we used the ambiguity of the remark as a weapon to tease her. "Plain" meant, as I think, "common" means, that she had no pretensions and no pomposity; that she took people as she found them, and entirely disregarded their external attributes, their rank or class or anything else. Such an attitude of mind, receptive and humble, is essential to the true understanding of men and of life. It is found in all sorts of people who may have no other particular accomplishments and are therefore regarded as ordinary. But in reality such people are neither common nor ordinary.

The democrat who stands up for the good sense and sound judgement of "the ordinary man" against the pronouncements and dicta of superior persons is really thinking of the good sense and sound judgement he has found—not by any manner of means in everybody—but in some humble, simple persons. This is really the secularized version of the Puritans' government by the elect. What is the difference, I once heard asked in a discussion, between government by the *élite* and government by the elect? The answer was: "The *élite* are people you choose; the elect are those whom God chooses." The untheological version of this would be to say that if you talk of *élite* you mean people characterized by some clearly marked and almost measurable quality—skill, training, birth, and so on; if you talk of the elect you mean men who have nothing of this about them but are nevertheless remarkable.

Practicable wisdom, the democrat would say, shows itself in the most unexpected places. You must be prepared for it wherever it turns up, and you must not imagine you can, by any training or planning, produce it to order. The democratic leader turns up. He is recognized by his fellows and carries them with him. He has the power of calling out the best in ordinary people. Because he shares the life and experience of ordinary men and women he knows, almost unconsciously, "where the shoe pinches" and "what people are prepared to do," and because he shares the ordinary responsibilities of life, he has an all-round experience and is saved from the narrowness of the specialist. Knowledge of the common life and its possibilities; understanding of the things which produce in it bitterness and thwart men's activities are the wisdom most wanted for politics. The state will be wisely directed if the final control is in the hands of "ordinary" men— men not specialized in their vocation or training—who have "common sense" and "sound judgement." But those men are, in favourable circumstances, the men to whom others listen, and who furnish the real if informal leadership in a community. The great mass of really ordinary people will follow them, and to give power to everybody by means of universal suffrage is to give power to them.

This view still implies a judgement about the mass of ordinary men and women. It implies their power of recognizing "sound judgement" and "common sense" in their fellows; in being able to judge a man and ready to approve the natural leader and reject the charlatan. That they do not always do so is notorious. What is important to discover is whether we can say anything about the conditions favourable to the mass of men and women in society judging men well or ill.

DISCUSSION

The argument for democratic as contrasted with expert leadership is that political wisdom needs more than anything else an understanding of the common life; and that that wisdom is given not by expert knowledge but by a practical experience of life. If the defect of the expert is his onesidedness, the merit of the practical man of common-sense judgement will be his all-round experience. The simple agricultural societies where democracy flourishes and seems native to the soil produce naturally men of common sense and sound judgement, appraisers alike of men and horses. The men whom we readily think of as men of sound judgement though unlearned have often had that kind of training. The part played by the village cobbler or blacksmith in the democratic life of a village has often been noticed. The inhabitants of a natural democracy like the New England township described in Mr. Winston Churchill's *Coniston* are independent, accustomed to act on their own, and to make judgements within the scope of their experience.

Modern industrialism has taken away from the great mass of men in an industrialized community their independence. It has condemned very many of them to specialized and narrow lives. Their lives are far more specialized and far narrower than the lives of the experts whom our democratic argument has been putting in their place, and they are without the expert's skill or knowledge or his partial independence. Where under such conditions are the common-sense qualities and sound judgment of the ordinary man to be found? How can we keep a modern industrial society from becoming not a community but a mob, not a society of persons capable of judging for themselves, discussing and criticizing from their experience of life the proposals put before them, but a mass played upon by the clever people at the top? These, nowadays, armed with new psychological techniques, claim to be able to manipulate those masses to their will, make them believe what the rulers want, hate what the rulers want, and even fight and die for what the rulers want.

For the real issue between the democrats and the anti-democrats is that democrats think of a society where men can and do act as responsible persons. The anti-democrats talk of the mob, or the herd, or the crowd. What these latter say of mobs or herds or crowds is as true as what the democrats say of the sound sense of the ordinary man who acts and thinks as an individual. No one can read a book like Ortega y Gasset's *The Revolt of the Masses* without recognizing the strength of the forces in modern society which go to the making of men into masses or crowds; or without seeing that, if they prevail, mass democracy must produce, as it has in so many countries produced, totalitarianism. That is the greatest of the challenges to democracy. But modern industrialism has supplied an antidote in the working-class movement. If we consider what gives that movement its vitality, we see that it creates innumerable centres of discussion. Trade union branches, co-operative guild meetings, W.E.A. classes and discussion groups of all kinds provide conditions as far removed as possible from those that produce a mob. The key to democracy is the potency of discussion. A good discussion can draw out wisdom which is attainable in no other way. The success of anti-democratic totalitarian techniques has depended on the suppression of discussion. If the freedom of discussion is safeguarded and fostered, there is no necessity for the most urbanized of committees becoming a mob. Those of us who have seen anything of the spread of discussion in England during the war, in the Army, in A.R.P. posts, in shelters, in all kinds of places where people come together have seen something of how in discussion the "plain" man can come into his own.

CHIEF JUSTICE WARREN

5. *The Public School Segregation Cases**

MR. CHIEF JUSTICE WARREN:

These cases come to us from the States of Kansas, South Carolina, Virginia, and Delaware. They are premised on different facts and different local conditions, but a common legal question justifies their consideration together in this consolidated opinion.

In each of the cases, minors of the Negro race, through their legal representatives, seek the aid of the courts in obtaining admission to the public schools of their community on a nonsegregated basis. In each instance, they had been denied admission to schools attended by white children under laws requiring or permitting segregation according to race. This segregation was alleged to deprive the plaintiffs of the equal protection of the laws under the Fourteenth Amendment. In each of the cases other than the Delaware case, a three-judge federal district court denied relief to the plaintiffs on the so-called "separate but equal" doctrine announced by this Court in *Plessy* v. *Ferguson,* 163 U. S. 537. Under that doctrine, equality of treatment is accorded when the races are provided substantially equal facilities, even though these facilities be separate. In the Delaware case, the Supreme Court of Delaware adhered to that doctrine, but ordered that the plaintiffs be admitted to the white schools because of their superiority to the Negro schools.

The plaintiffs contend that segregated public schools are not "equal" and cannot be made "equal," and that hence they are deprived of the equal protection of the laws. Because of the obvious importance of the question presented, the Court took jurisdiction. Argument was heard in the 1952 Term, and reargument was heard this Term on certain questions propounded by the Court.

Reargument was largely devoted to the circumstances surrounding the adoption of the Fourteenth Amendment in 1868. It covered exhaustively consideration of the Amendment in Congress, ratification by the states, then existing practices in racial segregation, and the views of proponents and

* From *Brown* v. *Topeka, Briggs* v. *Elliott, Davis* v. *Prince Edward County, Gebhart* v. *Belton, Bolling* v. *Sharpe,* 347 U. S. 483 (1954).

opponents of the Amendment. This discussion and our own investigation convince us that, although these sources cast some light, it is not enough to resolve the problem with which we are faced. At best, they are inconclusive. The most avid proponents of the post-War Amendments undoubtedly intended them to remove all legal distinctions among "all persons born or naturalized in the United States." Their opponents, just as certainly, were antagonistic to both the letter and the spirit of the Amendments and wished them to have the most limited effect. What others in Congress and the state legislatures had in mind cannot be determined with any degree of certainty.

An additional reason for the inconclusive nature of the Amendment's history, with respect to segregated schools, is the status of public education at that time. In the South, the movement toward free common schools, supported by general taxation, had not yet taken hold. Education of white children was largely in the hands of private groups. Education of Negroes was almost nonexistent, and practically all of the race were illiterate. In fact, any education of Negroes was forbidden by law in some states. Today, in contrast, many Negroes have achieved outstanding success in the arts and sciences as well as in the business and professional world. It is true that public education had already advanced further in the North, but the effect of the Amendment on Northern States was generally ignored in the congressional debates. Even in the North, the conditions of public education did not approximate those existing today. The curriculum was usually rudimentary; ungraded schools were common in rural areas; the school term was but three months a year in many states; and compulsory school attendance was virtually unknown. As a consequence, it is not surprising that there should be so little in the history of the Fourteenth Amendment relating to its intended effect on public education.

In the first cases in this Court construing the Fourteenth Amendment, decided shortly after its adoption, the Court interpreted it as proscribing all state-imposed discriminations against the Negro race. The doctrine of "separate but equal" did not make its appearance in this Court until 1896 in the case of *Plessy* v. *Ferguson, supra,* involving not education but transportation. American courts have since labored with the doctrine for over half a century. In this Court, there have been six cases involving the "separate but equal" doctrine in the field of public education. In *Cumming* v. *County Board of Education,* 175 U. S. 528, and *Gong Lum* v. *Rice,* 275 U. S. 78, the validity of the doctrine itself was not challenged. In more recent cases, all on the graduate school level, inequality was found in that specific benefits enjoyed by white students were denied to Negro students of the same educational qualifications. *Missouri ex rel. Gaines* v. *Canada,* 305 U. S. 337; *Sipuel* v. *Oklahoma,* 332 U. S. 631; *Sweatt* v. *Painter,* 339 U. S. 629; *McLaurin* v. *Oklahoma State Regents,* 339 U. S. 637. In none of these cases was it necessary to re-examine the doctrine to grant relief to the Negro plaintiff. And in *Sweatt* v. *Painter, supra,* the Court expressly reserved decision on the question whether *Plessy* v. *Ferguson* should be held inapplicable to public education.

In the instant cases, that question is directly presented. Here, unlike *Sweatt* v. *Painter,* there are findings below that the Negro and white schools involved have been equalized, or are being equalized, with respect to buildings, curricula, qualifications and salaries of teachers, and other "tangible" factors. Our decision, therefore, cannot turn on merely a comparison of these tangible factors in the Negro and white schools involved in each of the cases. We must look instead to the effect of segregation itself on public education.

In approaching this problem, we cannot turn the clock back to 1868 when the Amendment was adopted, or even to 1896 when *Plessy* v. *Ferguson* was written. We must consider public education in the light of its full development and its present place in American life throughout the Nation. Only in this way can it be determined if segregation in public schools deprives these plaintiffs of the equal protection of the laws.

Today, education is perhaps the most important function of state and local governments. Compulsory school attendance laws and the great expenditures for education both demonstrate our recognition of the importance of education to our democratic society. It is required in the performance of our most basic public responsibilities, even service in the armed forces. It is the very foundation of good citizenship. Today it is a principal instrument in awakening the child to cultural values, in preparing him for later professional training, and in helping him to adjust normally to his environment. In these days, it is doubtful that any child may reasonably be expected to succeed in life if he is denied the opportunity of an education. Such an opportunity, where the state has undertaken to provide it, is a right which must be made available to all on equal terms.

We come then to the question presented: Does segregation of children in public schools solely on the basis of race, even though the physical facilities and other "tangible" factors may be equal, deprive the children of the minority group of equal educational opportunities? We believe that it does.

In *Sweatt* v. *Painter, supra,* in finding that a segregated law school for Negroes could not provide them equal educational opportunities, this Court relied in large part on "those qualities which are incapable of objective measurement but which make for greatness in a law school." In *McLaurin* v. *Oklahoma State Regents, supra,* the Court, in requiring that a Negro admitted to a white graduate school be treated like all other students, again resorted to intangible considerations: ". . . his ability to study, to engage in discussions and exchange views with other students, and, in general, to learn his profession." Such considerations apply with added force to children in grade and high schools. To separate them from others of similar age and qualifications solely because of their race generates a feeling of inferiority as to their status in the community that may affect their hearts and minds in a way unlikely ever to be undone. The effect of this separation on their educational opportunities was well stated by a finding in the Kansas case by a court which nevertheless felt compelled to rule against the Negro plaintiffs:

> Segregation of white and colored children in public schools has a detrimental effect upon the colored children. The impact is greater when it has the sanction of the law; for the policy of separating the races is usually interpreted as denoting the inferiority of the Negro group. A sense of inferiority affects the motivation of a child to learn. Segregation with the sanction of law, therefore, has a tendency to retard the educational and mental development of Negro children and to deprive them of some of the benefits they would receive in a racially integrated school system.

Whatever may have been the extent of psychological knowledge at the time of *Plessy* v. *Ferguson,* this finding is amply supported by modern authority. Any language in *Plessy* v. *Ferguson* contrary to this finding is rejected.

We conclude that in the field of public education the doctrine of "separate but equal" has no place. Separate educational facilities are inherently unequal. Therefore, we hold that the plaintiffs and others similarly situated for whom the actions have been brought are, by reason of the segregation complained of, deprived of the equal protection of the laws guaranteed by the Fourteenth Amendment. This disposition makes unnecessary any discussion whether such segregation also violates the Due Process Clause of the Fourteenth Amendment.

Because these are class actions, because of the wide applicability of this decision, and because of the great variety of local conditions, the formulation of decrees in these cases presents problems of considerable complexity. On reargument, the consideration of appropriate relief was necessarily subordinated to the primary question—the constitutionality of segregation in public education. We have now announced that such segregation is a denial of the equal protection of the laws. In order that we may have the full assistance of the parties in formulating decrees, the cases will be restored to the docket, and the parties are requested to present further argument on Questions 4 and 5 previously propounded by the Court for the reargument this Term. The Attorney General of the United States is again invited to participate. The Attorneys General of the states requiring or permitting segregation in public education will also be permitted to appear as *amici curiae* upon request to do so by September 15, 1954, and submission of briefs by October 1, 1954.

It is so ordered.

This case [*Bolling* v. *Sharpe*] challenges the validity of segregation in the public schools of the District of Columbia. The petitioners, minors of the Negro race, allege that such segregation deprives them of due process of law under the Fifth Amendment. They were refused admission to a public school attended by white children solely because of their race. They sought the aid of the District Court for the District of Columbia in obtaining admission. That court dismissed their complaint. We granted a writ of certiorari before judgment in the Court of Appeals because of the importance of the constitutional question presented. 344 U. S. 873.

We have this day held that the Equal Protection Clause of the Fourteenth Amendment prohibits the states from maintaining racially segregated public schools. The legal problem in the District of Columbia is somewhat different, however. The Fifth Amendment, which is applicable in the District of Columbia, does not contain an equal protection clause as does the Fourteenth Amendment which applies only to the states. But the concepts of equal protection and due process, both stemming from our American ideal of fairness, are not mutually exclusive. The "equal protection of the laws" is a more explicit safeguard of prohibited unfairness than "due process of law," and, therefore, we do not imply that the two are always interchangeable phrases. But, as this Court has recognized, discrimination may be so unjustifiable as to be violative of due process.

Classifications based solely upon race must be scrutinized with particular care, since they are contrary to our traditions and hence constitutionally suspect. As long ago as 1896, this Court declared the principle "that the Constitution of the United States, in its present form, forbids, so far as civil and political rights are concerned, discrimination by the General Government, or by the States, against any citizen because of his race." And in *Buchanan* v. *Warley*, 245 U. S. 60, the Court held that a statute which limited the right of a property owner to convey his property to a person of another race was, as an unreasonable discrimination, a denial of due process of law.

Although the Court has not assumed to define "liberty" with any great precision, that term is not confined to mere freedom from bodily restraint. Liberty under law extends to the full range of conduct which the individual is free to pursue, and it cannot be restricted except for a proper governmental objective. Segregation in public education is not reasonably related to any proper governmental objective, and thus it imposes on Negro children of the District of Columbia a burden that constitutes an arbitrary deprivation of their liberty in violation of the Due Process Clause.

In view of our decision that the Constitution prohibits the states from maintaining racially segregated public schools, it would be unthinkable that the same Constitution would impose a lesser duty on the Federal Government. We hold that racial segregation in the public schools of the District of

Columbia is a denial of the due process of law guaranteed by the Fifth Amendment to the Constitution.

For the reasons set out in *Brown* v. *Board of Education*, this case will be restored to the docket for reargument on Questions 4 and 5 previously propounded by the Court. 345 U. S. 972.

It is so ordered.

Part III

ANTIDEMOCRATIC THOUGHT

The Politics of Pessimism

The Idol State

Fascism: Government by Force and Lies

Totalitarian Communism

Chapter VI

THE POLITICS OF PESSIMISM

Fundamental political attitudes reach below the level of conscious and articulate expression, and stem from one's whole personality. Typical structures of personality are reflected in correspondingly typical approaches to politics: a general inclination to look at the world optimistically leads to a radically different political temper from that of the habitual pessimist. Democracy, anarchy, individualism, and socialism are varied expressions of an essentially optimistic faith: that man can reform; that progress is possible and within practical reach; that the burden of history can be overcome by the liberating and uplifting force of reason; and that, finally, the range of human possibilities has hardly been perceived. Conversely, the pessimist sees man as incapable of progressive improvement, denies the very idea of progress as a criterion of human development, and is impressed with the helplessness of reason and principles in the face of historically evolved reality. Where the optimist tends to look into the *future* in the thought of what *might* happen, the pessimist turns his eyes backward into the *past* and is overawed by what *has* happened. Few political writers have been pure pessimists or pure optimists; nevertheless, most have tended to stress an approach to politics that is predominantly optimistic or preponderantly pessimistic.

The philosophers of political pessimism have always sought to justify their general point of view by declaring themselves the only true "realists," as contrasted with the illusionary and Utopian wishful thinking of the optimists. The first clearly formulated theory of politics from such a "realistic" and profoundly pessimistic starting point was Machiavelli's *The Prince* (1513). The whole pre-Machiavellian tradition of political speculation had concerned itself primarily with the purposes and aims of the state. Machiavelli was the first writer of the modern age who was interested in political means and techniques rather than in political ideals and objectives. Before him, political power was assumed to be a means itself—a means in the service of a higher end, such as justice, faith in God, or freedom. Machiavelli reversed this whole tradition of classical antiquity and of the Middle Ages by postulating power as the end to be sought and maintained, and confining himself to an analysis of the means that are best suited to the conquest and retention of political power. He thus separated the age-old connection between morals and politics, and made politics amoral, if not immoral. This Machiavellian hypothesis of the autonomous validity of politics as a separate and distinct sphere of life has been one of the most revolutionary events in the intellectual history of the West. Much that is labeled "Machiavellian" can hardly be attributed to Machiavelli himself. He was much less Machiavellian than most of his admirers or, despite their verbal protestations, many of his detractors. Yet, although the meaning of an idea may have been originally different from the effects it eventually produced, there is, in a deeper sense, a connection between meaning and effect.

Machiavelli's pessimism is reflected in his conviction that moral considerations may be laudable in themselves, but that the practical statesman cannot afford the luxury of living up to them: "For how we live is so far removed from how we ought to live, that he who abandons what is done for what ought to be done, will rather learn to bring about his own ruin than his preservation." In the struggle between political rulers, Machiavelli says, "there are two methods of fighting, the one by law, the other by force: the first method is that of men, the second of beasts; but as the first method is often insufficient, one must have recourse to the second. It is therefore necessary for a prince to know well how to use both the beast and the man." Specifically, the ruler must imitate the fox and the lion, "for the lion cannot protect himself from traps, and the fox cannot defend himself from wolves." Should a ruler keep faith? Machiavelli admits that everybody knows how "laudable" it is for a ruler to do so. However, in the world of actual politics such laudable intentions may be irreconcilable with expediency and interest: "Therefore, a prudent ruler ought not to keep faith when by doing so it would be against his interest, and when the reasons which made him bind himself no longer exist. If men were all good, this precept would not be a good one; but as they are bad, and would not observe their faith with you, so you are not bound to keep faith with them." Machiavelli thus takes an essentially pessimistic view of human nature. Political methods of the Renaissance were hardly known for their humanitarian mellowness; death by poison or the silent dagger—not to speak of bribery and coercion—was a mere technical detail in the execution of a political program. Leaders of the churches acted in as unholy and ruthless a fashion as mundane rulers, with the result that it was not unnatural for Machiavelli, as for many of his contemporaries, to become permeated with a mood of skepticism, not to say pessimism and outright cynicism. Unlike Fascist and Nazi ideologists later on, Machiavelli never praised immorality for its own sake, nor did he raise nihilism to the pinnacle of worldly wisdom. Prudence and moderation saved him from such extremism, as much as lack of these qualities doomed some of the later would-be Machiavellis to disaster. In particular, Mussolini might have pondered over Machiavelli's warning that, in planning aggressive warfare, "a prince ought never to make common cause with one more powerful than himself."

While Machiavelli was not antidemocratic in the sense that he was opposed to democratic forms of government on principle (in *The Discourses,* published in 1521, he sympathetically discussed republicanism), the general temper of *The Prince,* in particular, is imbued with psychological and intellectual elements that do not fit into the democratic way of life. Like other "realists" after him, he identified all too readily certain methods and techniques of naked power politics with the whole of political reality, and thus failed to grasp that ideas and ideals, too, can, if properly mobilized, become potent facts, even decisive weapons, in the struggles for political survival. History is a vast graveyard filled with the corpses of great realists like Napoleon, William II, Hitler, and Mussolini, to mention but a few notorious realists of recent record.

Thomas Hobbes was, like Machiavelli, the child of an age of struggle, discord, and civil war. His *Leviathan* (1651) is evidence of the quest for a theory of the state that could guarantee peace and security for its members. These may not be the highest aims for a society in normal times, but the *Leviathan* was published in the early part of Cromwell's stern rule, only two years after the English had beheaded their king. When there is no peace, peace seems the greatest end.

In the fashion of his time, Hobbes starts out with a description of the state of nature, and how men live in it. He finds three principal causes of quarrel: competition, diffidence, and glory. This state of nature is, according to Hobbes, a continual war or threat of war of every man against every man. Force and fraud, "the two cardinal virtues" in war, flourish in that atmosphere of perpetual fear and strife. There is no "mine" and "thine," there are no arts, no letters, no amenities of civilized living, and, "which is worst of all," there is "continual fear and danger of violent death; and the life of man, solitary, poor, nasty, brutish, and short." This pessimistic account of man's character and conduct in the state of nature is in sharp contrast with Locke's conception. Locke insists that in the state of nature, too, men are guided by reason and are obliged to abide by the rules of natural law, whereas Hobbes denies all that, because the "notions of right and wrong, justice and injustice" have no place in a condition that knows no law nor a common power to enforce it.

Locke, like Hobbes, urged the necessity of civil government to be set up by a joint compact; but whereas Locke assumed that men ordinarily abide by reasonable and decent standards of conduct, so that the state is required only for the "marginal" cases of violations of law and reason, Hobbes considered strife and war the rule rather than the exception in uncontrolled human intercourse. This is why Hobbes advocated the sovereign state, strong and unassailable against enemies from within or without, while Locke was satisfied with a state that could best justify itself by making itself as unnecessary as possible.

The sovereign power in the Hobbesian state is "incommunicable and in-separable." Hobbes attacked any institution that could weaken the omnipotence of the state, such as the division of power, the principle of mixed government, liberty of the subject, or the right of the individual to challenge the wisdom or legality of the sovereign's actions. To strengthen his authority, the sovereign should not permit the growth of groups and associations that intervene between the individual and the state. In one special chapter Hobbes listed a catalog of the causes that weaken or tend to the dissolution of the state. In it, he attacked with particular irony and vehemence the "poisonous doctrine" that "every private man is judge of good and evil actions," and that "whatsoever a man does against his conscience, is sin." Against these "seditious doctrines" Hobbes demanded unqualified obedience of the subject.

One important aspect of Hobbes' political thought is his doctrine of the relationships between natural and civil law. Since the Stoics, the conception has never died out in the Western tradition of law and government that civil (or positive) law is derived from, and inferior to, a higher law, a "law behind the law"—the law of nature. In the Bible, too, the law of the kings and princes is held to be subordinate, and responsible, to the law of God. This Stoic-Jewish-Christian approach to the validity of civil law has had civilizing effects on the Western world, because it has always reminded rulers that there is still a higher law above their edicts and commands, be that higher law founded on reason or divine revelation. By contrast, Hobbes is opposed to carrying the search for the validity of the law beyond the formal source of the legal sovereign. There can be, according to Hobbes, no unjust law, no law that is wrong, because laws "are the rules of just and unjust." As to the relations between natural law and civil law, Hobbes maintained that they "contain each other." Specifically, the law of nature is not really law at all, but only "qualities that dispose men to peace and obedience." Hobbes lists equity, justice, gratitude, and "other moral virtues" as the laws of nature. But these qualities are not true law, because, before the state is established, there is no authority to decide finally which idea of the law is binding. In practice, therefore, the law of nature is, according to Hobbes, nothing but a set of general principles of the civil law; the main formal difference is the fact that the civil law is written, whereas the law of nature is unwritten. Thus Hobbes sought to sweep away the doctrine of natural law from the theory of the state; with the insight of genius he correctly foresaw the revolutionary implications of natural law ideas as they became manifest only a century later in the American and French revolutions. Locke, too, admitted the revolutionary possibilities of the doctrine of natural law, but, unlike Hobbes, he was not too frightened by that prospect.

The complex character of Hobbes' political ideas puzzled critics and commentators from the most varied camps. The conservatives who believed in legitimate monarchy abhorred the fact that Hobbes was little interested in the divine right of monarchs and was solely concerned with the pragmatic issue of *effective* government, regardless of the source of authority. Conservatives of a religious observance charged Hobbes with atheism, because he subordinated the church, like all other associations, to the sovereign state. Morally neutral, Hobbes believed that tyrants should be punished by God but not by their subjects, and he enjoined all true believers to follow Christ into martyrdom, if their conscience conflicted with the commands of the sovereign. Finally, Hobbes has consistently encountered opposition among the advocates of parliamentary government and limited governmental authority. Since the last group developed into the dominant tradition in England and the United States, there has been no Hobbesian school in English and American political thought.

By contrast, Hobbes' influence in Germany and, under Fascism, in Italy has been very considerable. As a spokesman for the "strong state" he has always appealed to the traditional German schools of political thought, as well as to the more recent representatives of Italian Fascism. Yet the attempt to claim Hobbes as one of the precursors of Nazism and Fascism is more untenable than would appear from a cursory glance at some key phrases in the *Leviathan*. First, government is set up, according to Hobbes, by compact among the ruled. This contractual foundation alone is anathema to the Nazi or Fascist: in their political mythology, the origin and foundation of the state is to be sought in the *Volksgeist,* the people's spirit, rather than in deliberate creation. The Nazis and Fascists attack the contractual theory of the state, because contract implies mutuality of some sort, and, more important still, there can be no contract without consent. Democracy is government by consent. Second, Hobbes assigns to the state a prosaic business: to maintain order and security for the body of citizens. By contrast, the aim of the Nazi or Fascist state is the glory of the German master race, or the revival of the Roman empire. Third, the Hobbesian state is *authoritarian,* whereas the Nazi or Fascist state is *totalitarian.* Authority in the Hobbesian state is mostly concentrated in the political sphere, and in it alone. The sovereign will normally permit his subjects "the liberty to buy and sell, and otherwise contract with one another, to choose their own abode, their own diet, their own trade of life, and institute their children as they themselves think fit; and the like." The Hobbesian assumption of economic *laissez faire* hardly fits into the Nazi-Fascist pattern of a rigidly planned economy. Similarly, the Hobbesian freedom to bring up one's children was hardly reflected in the "Hitler-Youth" in Germany or the "Balilla" youth organization in Fascist Italy. The Nazi-Fascist state is totalitarian, inasmuch as it seeks to regulate and control man's life, by force if necessary, in all its aspects. Fourth, Hobbes recognizes that the sovereign may be one man, or "an assembly of men," whereas Nazism and Fascism support the dogma of the leadership principle. Hobbes preferred monarchy for practical reasons, but he was free from the mystical dogmatism that endowed Nazi and Fascist leaders with alleged charismatic and prophetic gifts. The Hobbesian sovereign is a top administrator and lawgiver, but not a top rabble rouser, spellbinder, or Fuehrer. Fifth, Hobbes recognizes that war is one of the two main reasons (the first being the danger of internal disorder) why men are driven to set up a state. But whenever he speaks of war, it is *defensive war* only, and there is no glorification of war, let alone of aggressive war, in the *Leviathan*. By contrast, Nazis and Fascists have looked upon war as something highly *desirable,* and on expansive, imperialist war as the highest form of national life. Also, Hobbes, the English bourgeois, prefers "commodious living" to the Nazi-Fascist doctrine of "living dangerously." Finally, the Hobbesian state does not completely swallow the individual: "A man cannot lay down the right of resisting them that assault him by force to take away his life." Since the purpose of political society is the preservation and protection of man's life, Hobbes recognizes the inalienable right of the individual to resist when his life is at stake, because "man by nature chooses the lesser evil, which is danger of death in resisting, rather than the greater, which is certain and present death in not resisting." For a long time, this Hobbesian caveat seemed unimportant, because the sanctity of human life was universally accepted. But when millions of people were put to death in gas chambers and concentration camps by a state, the Hobbesian stress on the integrity of human life acquired new meaning.

All this should not create the impression that Hobbes was a democrat in disguise. He was not. But the Hobbesian state is neither the modern democratic state nor the Nazi-Fascist state; it can be found in modern times in countries that possess social and economic conditions not too dissimilar from seventeenth-century England—some nations in Latin America, Southeastern Europe, and Asia. The dictatorships in Latin America in the nineteenth and twentieth centuries, such as that of General Porfirio Diaz in Mexico, approximated very closely to the Hobbesian state: society was still in a precapitalist or, at best, early capitalist phase. Economic *laissez faire* was mingled in such countries with a strong political power, possibly a dictatorship. But that dictatorship was authoritarian, and not totalitarian. In cultural, educational, and social matters it was often very lenient. By comparison with an advanced democracy, the Hobbesian state may appear dictatorial enough. By comparison with twentieth-century totalitarianism of the Nazi-Fascist kind, it is a vision of refined political civilization.

What detracts from the effective impact of Machiavelli and Hobbes is that their basically pessimistic views about the nature of man, especially the common man, are almost too coldly scientific and analytically objective. In the works of Edmund Burke, particularly in his later writing, antidemocratic political pessimism is couched in thought and language that are an arresting mixture of poetry, philosophy, and religious mysticism, all suffused with a penetrating sense of practical wisdom. No wonder, then, that Burke's statement of his political creed, particularly as expressed in his *Reflections on the Revolution in France* (1790), should have remained, to this day, the bible of conservatives and moderate antidemocrats. Burke denied the validity of the pivotal tenet of democracy: that only the governed have the right to determine who is to govern, and, secondly, that all votes are, politically, equal. He opposed this democratic method as an "arithmetic" devoid of practical meaning, and thought of representation in terms of historic interests, such as the Lords, the Commons, the monarchy, the Established Church, rather than in terms of the individual. There is something medieval in his idea that man is politically significant, not as an individual citizen, but solely as a member of a group to which he belongs socially or economically. This theory of corporate representation was also supported by Hegel, and found its perverted expression more recently in the "corporate state" of the Nazi-Fascist type.

Burke was liberal enough not to desire the oppression of persons of low station in life, like hairdressers and working tallow chandlers, provided they stayed in their place: "Such descriptions of men ought not to suffer oppression from the state; but the state suffers oppression, if such as they, either individually or collectively, are permitted to rule." Because of his firm conviction that wealth and aristocracy were the repositories of political wisdom and experience, he stubbornly ridiculed those who saw in the "rotten boroughs" and in stringent suffrage qualifications impediments to parliamentary government. The system of representation, that he advocated, and that brought England near the brink of revolution, was adjudged by Burke to be "adequate to all the purposes for which a representation of the people can be desired or devised." In the field of religion, too, he believed in a preferred position for one church, the Established Church, and suspected radical democrats of atheistic leanings; he saw in religion a force that taught men to look at nature and society with a sense of awe and reverence rather than with inquisitive analytical curiosity.

The faith of the French revolutionaries in the creative potentialities of reason provoked Burke to scathing denunciations of the revolutionaries as metaphysicians and ruthless logicians. By stressing the value of historical experience as well as the claims of circumstance, Burke sought to delimit more narrowly the boundaries within which reason could operate freely. He was skeptical about innovations unless "models and patterns of approved utility" were before the eyes of the reformers. In the French Revolution he saw only the violence and terror incidental to civil war, but failed to see its constructive aims and achievements. By constantly referring to the past, Burke sought to convince his contemporaries that France before 1789 was an ably and justly governed country, and that radical change would therefore be disastrous. In this, he idealized the past as much as he feared the future.

"Prescription" and "inheritance" are two key words that appear often in

Burke's writings. Both connote the idea of continuity, of slow growth, and both stress the evolutionary aspect of political institutions rather than the problem of their moral and ethical worth. Specifically, he applied these two terms to the issue of property (dealt with more fully below in Chapter X), the inequalities of which he candidly associated with political and social inequalities. While Burke never reached the Hegelian sanctification of the existing ("What is rational is actual and what is actual is rational"), his strong sense of the past, combined with his religious mysticism, especially in his later years, tended to endow the existing with value solely because it exists. In his cautious attitude toward reason, in his exaltation of feeling and imagination, he exercised a lasting influence on conservative thought in England and the United States, as well as on the great exponents of anti-democratic thought in Germany and France, such as Hegel and De Maistre.

Yet, when all is said and done, no reader of the *Reflections* can escape the impact of a mature and imaginative mind: "The nature of man is intricate; the objects of society are of the greatest possible complexity: and therefore no simple disposition or direction of power can be suitable either to man's nature, or to the quality of his affairs." Bismarck defined politics as "the art of the possible," and this is one of the guiding principles of Burke's thinking on politics. Whether one accepts the basic tenets of his political philosophy or not, one finds on almost every page of the *Reflections* epigrammatic and aphoristic gems of wisdom and observation, which make the work a perpetual source of inspiration even for those who feel more optimistic about the possibilities of democracy than Burke did.

NICCOLÒ MACHIAVELLI

1. *The Lion and the Fox**

OF THE THINGS FOR WHICH MEN, AND ESPECIALLY PRINCES, ARE PRAISED OR BLAMED

It now remains to be seen what are the methods and rules for a prince as regards his subjects and friends. And as I know that many have written of this, I fear that my writing about it may be deemed presumptuous, differing as I do, especially in this matter, from the opinions of others. But my intention being to write something of use to those who understand, it appears to

* From Niccolò Machiavelli, *The Prince* (1513). Modern Library edition. By permission of Random House, publishers.

me more proper to go to the real truth of the matter than to its imagination; and many have imagined republics and principalities which have never been seen or known to exist in reality; for how we live is so far removed from how we ought to live, that he who abandons what is done for what ought to be done, will rather learn to bring about his own ruin than his preservation. A man who wishes to make a profession of goodness in everything must necessarily come to grief among so many who are not good. Therefore it is necessary for a prince, who wishes to maintain himself, to learn how not to be good, and to use this knowledge and not use it, according to the necessity of the case.

Leaving on one side, then, those things which concern only an imaginary prince, and speaking of those that are real, I state that all men, and especially princes, who are placed at a greater height, are reputed for certain qualities which bring them either praise or blame. Thus one is considered liberal, another *misero* or miserly (using a Tuscan term, seeing that *avaro* with us still means one who is rapaciously acquisitive and *misero* one who makes grudging use of his own); one a free giver, another rapacious; one cruel, another merciful; one a breaker of his word, another trustworthy; one effeminate and pusillanimous, another fierce and high-spirited; one humane, another haughty; one lascivious, another chaste; one frank, another astute; one hard, another easy; one serious, another frivolous; one religious, another a nonbeliever, and so on. I know that every one will admit that it would be highly praiseworthy in a prince to possess all the above-named qualities that are reputed good, but as they cannot all be possessed or observed, human conditions not permitting of it, it is necessary that he should be prudent enough to avoid the scandal of those vices which would lose him the state, and guard himself if possible against those which will not lose it him, but if not able to, he can indulge them with less scruple. And yet he must not mind incurring the scandal of those vices, without which it would be difficult to save the state, for if one considers well, it will be found that some things which seem virtues would, if followed, lead to one's ruin, and some others which appear vices result in one's greater security and wellbeing.

OF LIBERALITY AND NIGGARDLINESS

Beginning now with the first qualities above named, I say that it would be well to be considered liberal; nevertheless liberality such as the world understands it will injure you, because if used virtuously and in the proper way, it will not be known, and you will incur the disgrace of the contrary vice. But one who wishes to obtain the reputation of liberality among men must not omit every kind of sumptuous display, and to such an extent that a prince of this character will consume by such means all his resources, and will be at last compelled, if he wishes to maintain his name for liberality, to impose heavy taxes on his people, become extortionate, and do everything possible to obtain money. This will make his subjects begin to hate him, and he will be little esteemed being poor, so that having by this liberality injured many and benefited but few, he will feel the first little disturbance and be endangered by every peril. If he recognizes this and wishes to change his system, he incurs at once the charge of niggardliness.

A prince, therefore, not being able to exercise this virtue of liberality without risk if it be known, must not, if he be prudent, object to be called miserly. In course of time he will be thought more liberal, when it is seen that by his parsimony his revenue is sufficient, that he can defend himself against those who make war on him, and undertake enterprises without burdening his people, so that he is really liberal to all those from whom he does not take, who are infinite in number, and niggardly to all to whom he does not give, who are few. In our times we have seen nothing great done except by those who have been esteemed niggardly; the others have all been ruined. Pope Julius II, although he had made use of a reputation for liberality in order to attain the papacy, did not seek to retain it afterwards, so that he might be able to wage war. The present King of France has carried on so many wars without imposing an extraordinary tax, because his extra expenses were covered by the parsimony he had so long practised. The present King of Spain, if he had been thought liberal, would not have engaged in and been successful in so many enterprises.

For these reasons a prince must care little for the reputation of being a miser, if he wishes to avoid robbing his subjects, if he wishes to be able to defend himself, to avoid becoming poor and contemptible, and not to be forced to become rapacious; this niggardliness is one of those vices which enable him to reign. If it is said that Cæsar attained the empire through liberality, and that many others have reached the highest positions through being liberal or being thought so, I would reply that you are either a prince already or else on the way to become one. In the first case, this liberality is harmful; in the second, it is certainly necessary to be considered liberal. Cæsar was one of those who wished to attain the mastery over Rome, but if after attaining it he had lived and had not moderated his expenses, he would have destroyed that empire. And should any one reply that there have been many princes, who have done great things with their armies, who have been thought extremely liberal, I would answer by saying that the prince may either spend his own wealth and that of his subjects or the wealth of others. In the first case he must be sparing, but for the rest he must not neglect to be very liberal. The liberality is very necessary to a prince who marches with his armies, and lives by plunder, sack and ransom, and is dealing with the wealth of others, for without it he would not be followed by his soldiers. And you may be very generous indeed with what is not the property of yourself or your subjects, as were Cyrus, Cæsar, and Alexander; for spending the wealth of others will not diminish your reputation, but increase it, only spending your own resources will injure you. There is nothing which destroys itself so much as liberality, for by using it you lose the power of using it, and become either poor and despicable, or, to escape poverty, rapacious and hated. And of all things that a prince must guard against, the most important are being despicable or hated, and liberality will lead you to one or other of these conditions. It is, therefore, wiser to have the name of a miser, which produces disgrace without hatred, than to incur of necessity the name of being rapacious, which produces both disgrace and hatred.

OF CRUELTY AND CLEMENCY, AND WHETHER IT IS BETTER TO BE LOVED OR FEARED

Proceeding to the other qualities before named, I say that every prince must desire to be considered merciful and not cruel. He must, however, take care not to misuse this mercifulness. Cesare Borgia was considered cruel, but his cruelty had brought order to the Romagna, united it, and reduced it to peace and fealty. If this is considered well, it will be seen that he was really much more merciful than the Florentine people, who, to avoid the name of cruelty, allowed Pistoia to be destroyed. A prince, therefore, must not mind incurring the charge of cruelty for the purpose of keeping his subjects united and faithful; for, with a very few examples, he will be more merciful than those who, from excess of tenderness, allow disorders to arise, from whence spring bloodshed and rapine; for these as a rule injure the whole community, while the executions carried out by the prince injure only individuals. And of all princes, it is impossible for a new prince to escape the reputation of cruelty, new states being always full of dangers. Wherefore Virgil through the mouth of Dido says:

> Res dura, et regni novitas me talia cogunt
> Moliri, et late fines custode tueri.

Nevertheless, he must be cautious in believing and acting, and must not be afraid of his own shadow, and must proceed in a temperate manner with prudence and humanity, so that too much confidence does not render him incautious, and too much diffidence does not render him intolerant.

From this arises the question whether it is better to be loved more than feared, or feared more than loved. The reply is, that one ought to be both feared and loved, but as it is difficult for the two to go together, it is much safer to be feared than loved, if one of the two has to be wanting. For it may be said of men in general that they are ungrateful, voluble, dissemblers, anxious to avoid danger, and covetous of gain; as long as you benefit them, they are entirely yours; they offer you their blood, their goods, their life, and their children, as I have before said, when the necessity is remote; but when it approaches, they revolt. And the prince who has relied solely on their word, without making other preparations, is ruined; for the friendship which is gained by purchase and not through grandeur and nobility of spirit is bought but not secured, and at a pinch is not to be expended in your service. And men have less scruple in offending one who makes himself loved than one who makes himself feared; for love is held by a chain of obligation which, men being selfish, is broken whenever it serves their purpose; but fear is maintained by a dread of punishment which never fails.

Still, a prince should make himself feared in such a way that if he does not gain love, he at any rate avoids hatred; for fear and the absence of hatred may well go together, and will be always attained by one who abstains from interfering with the property of his citizens and subjects or with their women. And when he is obliged to take the life of any one, let him do so when there is a proper justification and manifest reason for it; but above all he must abstain from taking the property of others, for men forget more easily the death of their father than the loss of their patrimony. Then also pretexts for seizing property are never wanting, and one who begins to live by rapine will always find some reason for taking the goods of others, whereas causes for taking life are rarer and more fleeting.

But when the prince is with his army and has a large number of soldiers under his control, then it is extremely necessary that he should not mind being thought cruel; for without this reputation he could not keep an army united or disposed to any duty. Among the noteworthy actions of Hannibal is numbered this, that although he had an enormous army, composed of men of all nations and fighting in foreign countries, there never arose any dissension either among them or against the prince, either in good fortune or in bad. This could not be due to anything but his inhuman cruelty, which together with his infinite other virtues, made him always venerated and terrible in the sight of his soldiers, and without it his other virtues would not have sufficed to produce that effect. Thoughtless writers admire on the one hand his actions, and on the other blame the principal cause of them.

And that it is true that his other virtues would not have sufficed may be seen from the case of Scipio (famous not only in regard to his own times, but all times of which memory remains), whose armies rebelled against him in Spain, which arose from nothing but his excessive kindness, which allowed more licence to the soldiers than was consonant with military discipline. He was reproached with this in the senate by Fabius Maximus, who called him a corrupter of the Roman militia. Locri having been destroyed by one of Scipio's officers was not revenged by him, nor was the insolence of that officer punished, simply by reason of his easy nature; so much so, that some one wishing to excuse him in the senate, said that there were many men who knew rather how not to err, than how to correct the errors of others. This disposition would in time have tarnished the fame and glory of Scipio had he persevered in it under the empire, but living under the rule of the senate this harmful quality was not only concealed but became a glory to him.

I conclude, therefore, with regard to being feared and loved, that men love at their own free will, but fear at the will of the prince, and that a wise prince must rely on what is in his power and not on what is in the power of others, and he must only contrive to avoid incurring hatred, as has been explained.

IN WHAT WAY PRINCES MUST KEEP FAITH

How laudable it is for a prince to keep good faith and live with integrity, and not with astuteness, every one knows. Still the experience of our times shows those princes to have done great things who have had little regard for good faith, and have been able by astuteness to confuse men's brains, and who have ultimately overcome those who have made loyalty their foundation.

You must know, then, that there are two methods of fighting, the one by law, the other by force: the first method is that of men, the second of beasts; but as the first method is often insufficient, one must have recourse to the second. It is therefore necessary for a prince to know well how to use both the beast and the man. This was covertly taught to rulers by ancient writers, who relate how Achilles and many others of those ancient princes were given to Chiron the centaur to be brought up and educated under his discipline. The parable of this semi-animal, semi-human teacher is meant to indicate that a prince must know how to use both natures, and that the one without the other is not durable.

A prince being thus obliged to know well how to act as a beast must imitate the fox and the lion, for the lion cannot protect himself from traps, and the fox cannot defend himself from wolves. One must therefore be a fox to recognize traps, and a lion to frighten wolves. Those that wish to be only lions do not understand this. Therefore, a prudent ruler ought not to keep faith when by so doing it would be against his interest, and when the reasons which made him bind himself no longer exist. If men were all good, this precept would not be a good one; but as they are bad, and would not observe their faith with you, so you are not bound to keep faith with them. Nor have legitimate grounds ever failed a prince who wished to show colourable excuse for the non-fulfilment of his promise. Of this one could furnish an infinite number of modern examples, and show how many times peace has been broken, and how many promises rendered worthless, by the faithlessness of princes, and those that have been best able to imitate the fox have succeeded best. But it is necessary to be able to disguise this character well, and to be a great feigner and dissembler; and men are so simple and so ready to obey present necessities, that one who deceives will always find those who allow themselves to be deceived.

I will only mention one modern instance. Alexander VI did nothing else but deceive men, he thought of nothing else, and found the occasion for it;

no man was ever more able to give assurances, or affirmed things with stronger oaths, and no man observed them less; however, he always succeeded in his deceptions, as he well knew this aspect of things.

It is not, therefore, necessary for a prince to have all the above-named qualities, but it is very necessary to seem to have them. I would even be bold to say that to possess them and always to observe them is dangerous, but to appear to possess them is useful. Thus it is well to seem merciful, faithful, humane, sincere, religious, and also to be so; but you must have the mind so disposed that when it is needful to be otherwise you may be able to change to the opposite qualities. And it must be understood that a prince, and especially a new prince, cannot observe all those things which are considered good in men, being often obliged, in order to maintain the state, to act against faith, against charity, against humanity, and against religion. And, therefore, he must have a mind disposed to adapt itself according to the wind, and as the variations of fortune dictate, and, as I said before, not deviate from what is good, if possible, but be able to do evil if constrained.

A prince must take great care that nothing goes out of his mouth which is not full of the above-named five qualities, and, to see and hear him, he should seem to be all mercy, faith, integrity, humanity, and religion. And nothing is more necessary than to seem to have this last quality, for men in general judge more by the eyes than by the hands, for every one can see, but very few have to feel. Everybody sees what you appear to be, few feel what you are, and those few will not dare to oppose themselves to the many, who have the majesty of the state to defend them; and in the actions of men, and especially of princes, from which there is no appeal, the end justifies the means. Let a prince therefore aim at conquering and maintaining the state, and the means will always be judged honourable and praised by every one, for the vulgar is always taken by appearances and the issue of the event; and the world consists only of the vulgar, and the few who are not vulgar are isolated when the many have a rallying point in the prince. A certain prince of the present time, whom it is well not to name, never does anything but preach peace and good faith, but he is really a great enemy to both, and either of them, had he observed them, would have lost him state or reputation on many occasions.

HOW A PRINCE MUST ACT IN ORDER TO GAIN A REPUTATION

Nothing causes a prince to be so much esteemed as great enterprises and giving proof of prowess. We have in our own day Ferdinand, King of Aragon, the present King of Spain. He may almost be termed a new prince, because from a weak king he has become for fame and glory the first king in Christendom, and if you regard his actions you will find them all very great and some of them extraordinary. At the beginning of his reign he assailed Granada, and that enterprise was the foundation of his state. At first he did it at his leisure and without fear of being interfered with; he kept the minds of the barons of Castile occupied in this enterprise, so that thinking only of that war they did not think of making innovations, and he thus acquired reputation and power over them without their being aware of it. He was able with the money of the Church and the people to maintain his armies, and by that long war to lay the foundations of his military power, which afterwards has made him famous. Besides this, to be able to undertake greater enterprises, and always under the pretext of religion, he had recourse to a pious cruelty, driving out the Moors from his kingdom and despoiling them. No more miserable or unusual example can be found. He also attacked Africa under the same pretext, undertook his Italian enterprise, and has lately attacked France; so that he has continually contrived great things, which have kept his subjects' minds uncertain and astonished, and occupied in watching their result. And these actions have arisen one out of the other, so that they have left no time for men to settle down and act against him.

It is also very profitable for a prince to give some outstanding example of his greatness in the internal administration, like those related of Messer Bernabò of Milan. When it happens that some one does something extraordinary, either good or evil, in civil life, he must find such means of rewarding or punishing him which will be much talked about. And above all a prince must endeavour in every action to obtain fame for being great and excellent.

A prince is further esteemed when he is a true friend or a true enemy, when, that is, he declares himself without reserve in favour of some one or against another. This policy is always more useful than remaining neutral. For if two neighbouring powers come to blows, they are either such that if one wins, you will have to fear the victor, or else not. In either of these two cases it will be better for you to declare yourself openly and make war, because in the first case if you do not declare yourself, you will fall a prey to the victor, to the pleasure and satisfaction of the one who has been defeated, and you will have no reason nor anything to defend you and nobody to receive you. For, whoever wins will not desire friends whom he suspects and who do not help him when in trouble, and whoever loses will not receive you as you did not take up arms to venture yourself in his cause.

Antiochus went to Greece, being sent by the Ætolians to expel the Romans. He sent orators to the Achaeians who were friends of the Romans to encourage them to remain neutral; on the other hand the Romans persuaded them to take up arms on their side. The matter was brought before the council of the Achaeians for deliberation, where the ambassador of Antiochus sought to persuade them to remain neutral, to which the Roman ambassador replied: 'As to what is said that is best and most useful for your state not to meddle in our war, nothing is further from the truth; for if you do not medin it you will become, without any favour or any reputation, the prize of the victor.'

And it will always happen that the one who is not your friend will want you to remain neutral, and the one who is your friend will require you to declare yourself by taking arms. Irresolute princes, to avoid present dangers, usually follow the way of neutrality and are mostly ruined by it. But when the prince declares himself frankly in favour of one side, if the one to whom you adhere conquers, even if he is powerful and you remain at his discretion, he is under an obligation to you and friendship has been established, and men are never so dishonest as to oppress you with such a patent ingratitude. Moreover, victories are never so prosperous that the victor does not need to have some scruples, especially as to justice. But if your ally loses, you are sheltered by him, and so long as he can, he will assist you; you become the companion of a fortune which may rise again. In the second case, when those who fight are such that you have nothing to fear from the victor, it is still more prudent on your part to adhere to one; for you go to the ruin of one with the help of him who ought to save him if he were wise, and if he conquers he rests at your discretion, and it is impossible that he should not conquer with your help.

And here it should be noted that a prince ought never to make common cause with one more powerful than himself to injure another, unless necessity forces him to it, as before said; for if he wins you rest in his power, and princes must avoid as much as possible being under the will and pleasure of others. The Venetians united with France against the Duke of Milan, although they could have avoided that alliance, and from it resulted their own ruin. But when one cannot avoid it, as happened in the case of the Florentines when the Pope and Spain went with their armies to attack Lombardy, then the prince ought to join for the above reasons. Let no state believe that it can always follow a safe policy, rather let it think that all are doubtful. This is found in the nature of things, that one never tries to avoid one difficulty without running into another, but prudence consists in being able to know the nature of the difficulties, and taking the least harmful as good.

A prince must also show himself a lover of merit, give preferment to the able, and honour those who excel in every art. Moreover he must encourage his citizens to follow their callings quietly, whether in commerce, or agriculture, or any other trade that men follow, so that this one shall not refrain from improving his possessions through fear that they may be taken from him, and that one from starting a trade for fear of taxes; but he should offer rewards to whoever does these things, and to whoever seeks in any way to improve his city or state. Besides this, he ought, at convenient seasons of the year, to keep the people occupied with festivals and shows; and as every city is divided either into guilds or into classes, he ought to pay attention to all these groups, mingle with them from time to time, and give them an example of his humanity and munificence, always upholding, however, the majesty of his dignity, which must never be allowed to fail in anything whatever.

THOMAS HOBBES

2. *The Sovereign State**

Nature has made men so equal in the faculties of the body and mind, as that though there be found one man sometimes manifestly stronger in body, or of quicker mind than another, yet when all is reckoned together, the difference between man and man is not so considerable, as that one man can thereupon claim to himself any benefit to which another may not pretend as well as he. For as to the strength of body, the weakest has strength enough to kill the strongest, either by secret machination, or by confederacy with others that are in the same danger with himself.

And as to the faculties of the mind, setting aside the arts grounded upon words, and especially that skill of proceeding upon general and infallible rules, called science, which very few have, and but in few things, as being not a native faculty, born with us, nor attained, as prudence, while we look after somewhat else, I find yet a greater equality among men than that of strength. For prudence is but experience, which equal time equally bestows on all men in those things they equally apply themselves unto. That which may perhaps make such equality incredible is but a vain conceit of one's own wisdom, which almost all men think they have in a greater degree than the vulgar; that is, than all men but themselves, and a few others, whom by fame, or for concurring with themselves, they approve. For such is the nature of men, that howsoever they may acknowledge many others to be more witty, or more eloquent, or more learned, yet they will hardly believe there be many so wise as themselves; for they see their own wit at hand, and other men's at a distance. But this proves rather that men are in that point equal, than unequal. For there is not ordinarily a greater sign of the equal distribution of any thing, than that every man is contented with his share.

* From Thomas Hobbes, *Leviathan* (1651). Spelling and punctuation have been modernized for this selection.

From this equality of ability arises equality of hope in the attaining of our ends. And therefore if any two men desire the same thing, which nevertheless they cannot both enjoy, they become enemies; and in the way to their end, which is principally their own conservation, and sometimes their delectation only, endeavour to destroy or subdue one another. And from hence it comes to pass, that where an invader has no more to fear, than another man's single power, if one plant, sow, build, or possess a convenient seat, others may probably be expected to come prepared with forces united, to dispossess and deprive him, not only of the fruit of his labour, but also of his life, or liberty. And the invader again is in the like danger of another.

And from this diffidence of one another, there is no way for any man to secure himself, so reasonable, as anticipation; that is, by force, or wiles, to master the persons of all men he can, so long, till he sees no other power great enough to endanger him; and this is no more than his own conservation requires, and is generally allowed. Also because there be some that, taking pleasure in contemplating their own power in the acts of conquest, which they pursue farther than their security requires, if others, that otherwise would be glad to be at ease within modest bounds, should not by invasion increase their power, they would not be able, long time, by standing only on their defence, to subsist. And by consequence, such augmentation of dominion over men being necessary to a man's conservation, it ought to be allowed him.

Again, men have no pleasure, but on the contrary a great deal of grief, in keeping company where there is no power able to over-awe them all. For every man looks that his companion should value him, at the same rate he sets upon himself; and upon all signs of contempt, or undervaluing, naturally endeavours, as far as he dares (which, among them that have no common power to keep them in quiet, is far enough to make them destroy each other), to extort a greater value from his contemners, by damage; and from others, by the example.

So that in the nature of man, we find three principal causes of quarrel. First, competition; secondly, diffidence; thirdly, glory.

The first makes men invade for gain; the second, for safety; and the third, for reputation. The first use violence, to make themselves masters of other men's persons, wives, children, and cattle; the second, to defend them; the third, for trifles, as a word, a smile, a different opinion, and any other sign of undervalue, either direct in their persons, or by reflection in their kindred, their friends, their nation, their profession, or their name.

Hereby it is manifest that, during the time men live without a common power to keep them all in awe, they are in that condition which is called war; and such a war, as is of every man against every man. For war consists not in battle only, or the act of fighting, but in a tract of time, wherein the will to contend by battle is sufficiently known; and therefore the notion of *time* is to be considered in the nature of war, as it is in the nature of weather.

For as the nature of foul weather lies not in a shower or two or rain, but in an inclination thereto of many days together, so the nature of war consists not in actual fighting, but in the known disposition thereto, during all the time there is no assurance to the contrary. All other time is peace.

Whatsoever therefore is consequent to a time of war, where every man is enemy to every man, the same is consequent to the time wherein men live without other security than what their own strength, and their own invention, shall furnish them withal. In such condition, there is no place for industry, because the fruit thereof is uncertain; and consequently no culture of the earth; no navigation, nor use of the commodities that may be imported by sea; no commodious building; no instrument of moving, and removing, such things as require much force; no knowledge of the face of the earth; no account of time; no arts; no letters; no society, and which is worst of all, continual fear, and danger of violent death; and the life of man, solitary, poor, nasty, brutish, and short.

It may seem strange to some man that has not well weighted these things that nature should thus dissociate, and render men apt to invade, and destroy one another; and he may therefore, not trusting to this inference, made from the passions, desire perhaps to have the same confirmed by experience. Let him therefore consider with himself: when taking a journey, he arms himself, and seeks to go well accompanied; when going to sleep, he locks his doors; when even in his house he locks his chests; and this when he knows there be laws, and public officers, armed, to revenge all injuries shall be done him; what opinion he has of his fellow-subjects, when he rides armed; of his fellow citizens, when he locks his doors; and of his children, and servants, when he locks his chests. Does he not there as much accuse mankind by his actions as I do by my words? But neither of us accuse man's nature in it. The desire, and other passions of man, are in themselves no sin. No more are the actions that proceed from those passions, till they know a law that forbids them, which till laws be made they cannot know, nor can any law be made till they have agreed upon the person that shall make it.

It may peradventure be thought there was never such a time, nor condition of war, as this; and I believe it was never generally so, over all the world; but there are many places where they live so now. For the savage people in many places of America, except the government of small families, the concord whereof depends on natural lust, have no government at all, and live at this day in that brutish manner, as I said before. Howsoever, it may be perceived what manner of life there would be, where there were no common power to fear, by the manner of life, which men that have formerly lived under a peaceful government used to degenerate into in civil war.

But though there had never been any time wherein particular men were in a condition of war one against another, yet in all times, kings, and persons of sovereign authority, because of their independency, are in continual jealousies, and in the state and posture of gladiators, having their weapons pointing, and their eyes fixed on one another; that is, their forts, garrisons, and guns upon the frontiers of their kingdoms, and continual spies upon their neighbours, which is a posture of war. But because they uphold thereby the industry of their subjects, there does not follow from it that misery which accompanies the liberty of particular men.

To this war of every man against every man, this also is consequent: that nothing can be unjust. The notions of right and wrong, justice and injustice have there no place. Where there is no common power, there is no law: where no law, no injustice. Force and fraud are in war the two cardinal virtues. Justice and injustice are none of the faculties neither of the body nor mind. If they were they might be in a man that were alone in the world, as well as his senses, and passions. They are qualities that relate to men in society, not in solitude. It is consequent also to the same condition that there be no propriety, no dominion, no *mine* and *thine* distinct, but only that to be every man's that he can get, and for so long as he can keep it. And thus much for the ill condition which man by mere nature is actually placed in, though with a possibility to come out of it, consisting partly in the passions, partly in his reason.

The passions that incline men to peace are fear of death, desire of such things as are necessary to commodious living, and a hope by their industry to obtain them. And reason suggests convenient articles of peace, upon which men may be drawn to agreement. These articles are they which otherwise are called the laws of nature.

A covenant not to defend myself from force, by force, is always void. For, as I have showed before, no man can transfer, or lay down, his right to save himself from death, wounds, and imprisonment, the avoiding whereof is the only end of laying down any right; and therefore the promise of not resisting force, in no covenant transfers any right, nor is obliging. For though a man may covenant thus, *unless I do so, or so, kill me,* he cannot covenant thus, *unless I do so, or so, I will not resist you when you come to kill me.* For man by nature chooses the lesser evil, which is danger of death in resisting, rather than the greater, which is certain and present death in not resisting. And this is granted to be true by all men, in that they lead criminals to execution and prison with armed men, notwithstanding that such criminals have consented to the law by which they are condemned.

The final cause, end, or design of men who naturally love liberty and dominion over others, in the introduction of that restraint upon themselves in which we see them live in commonwealths, is the foresight of their own preservation and of a more contented life thereby; that is to say, of getting themselves out from that miserable condition of war which is necessarily consequent, as has been shown, to the natural passions of men, when there is no visible power to keep them in awe, and tie them by fear of punishment to the performance of their covenants and observation of the laws of nature.

For the laws of nature, as *justice, equity, modesty, mercy,* and, in sum, *doing to others, as we would be done to,* of themselves, without the terror of some power to cause them to be observed, are contrary to our natural passions that carry us to partiality, pride, revenge, and the like. And covenants, without the sword, are but words, and of no strength to secure a man at all. Therefore notwithstanding the laws of nature (which everyone has then kept, when he has the will to keep them, when he can do it safely), if there be no power erected, or not great enough for our security, every man will, and may, lawfully rely on his strength and art for caution against all other men. And in all places where men have lived by small families, to rob and spoil one another has been a trade, and so far from being reputed against the law of nature, that the greater spoils they gained, the greater was their honou; and men observed no other laws therein, but the laws of honour, that is, to abstain from cruelty, leaving to men their lives, and instruments of husbandry. And as small families did then, so now do cities and kingdoms, which are but greater families, for their own security, enlarge their dominions upon all pretences of danger and fear of invasion or assistance that may be given to invaders, and endeavour as much as they can to subdue or weaken their neighbours, by open force and secret arts, for want of other caution, justly; and are remembered for it, in after ages with honour.

It is true that certain living creatures, as bees and ants, live sociably one with another, which are therefore by Aristotle numbered among political creatures, and yet have no other direction than their particular judgments and appetites, nor speech whereby one of them can signify to another what he thinks expedient for the common benefit; and therefore some man may perhaps desire to know why mankind cannot do the same. To which I answer:

First, that men are continually in competition for honour and dignity, which these creatures are not; and consequently among men there arises on that ground envy and hatred, and finally war; but among these not so.

Secondly, that among these creatures the common good differs not from the private; and being by nature inclined to their private, they procure thereby the common benefit. But man, whose joy consists in comparing himself with other men, can relish nothing but what is eminent.

Thirdly, that these creatures, having not, as man, the use of reason, do not see, nor think they see, any fault in the administration of their common business, whereas among men there are very many that think themselves wiser and abler to govern the public better than the rest; and these strive to reform and innovate, one this way, one that way, and thereby bring it into distraction and civil war.

Fourthly, that these creatures, though they have some use of voice in making known to one another their desires and other affections, yet they want that art of words by which some men can represent to others that which is good, in the likeness of evil; and evil, in the likeness of good; and augment or diminish the apparent greatness of good and evil, discontenting men and troubling their peace at their pleasure.

Fifthly, irrational creatures cannot distinguish between *injury* and *damage,* and therefore, as long as they be at ease, they are not offended with their fellows: whereas man is then most troublesome, when he is most at ease, for then it is that he loves to show his wisdom, and control the actions of them that govern the commonwealth.

Lastly, the agreement of these creatures is natural; that of men is by covenant only, which is artificial; and therefore it is no wonder if there be somewhat else required, besides covenant, to make their agreement constant and lasting, which is a common power to keep them in awe, and to direct their actions to the common benefit.

The only way to erect such a common power, as may be able to defend them from the invasion of foreigners and the injuries of one another, and thereby secure them in such sort as that by their own industry and by the fruits of the earth they may nourish themselves and live contentedly, is to confer all their power and strength upon one man, or upon one assembly of men, that may reduce all their wills, by plurality of voices, unto one will: which is as much as to say, to appoint one man, or assembly of men, to bear their persons, and every one to own and acknowledge himself to be the author of whatsoever he that so bears their person shall act, or cause to be acted, in those things which concern the common peace and safety, and therein to submit their wills, every one to his will, and their judgments to his judgment. This is more than consent, or concord; it is a real unity of them all, in one and the same person, made by the covenant of every man with every man, in such manner as if every man should say to every man, *I authorize and give up my right of governing myself, to this man, or to this assembly of men, on this condition, that thou give up thy right to him, and authorize all his actions in like manner.* This done, the multitude so united in one person is called a Commonwealth, in Latin, *civitas.* This is the generation of the great *Leviathan,* or rather, to speak more reverently, of that *mortal god* to which we owe, under the *immortal God,* our peace and defence. For by this authority, given him by every particular man in the commonwealth, he has the use of so much power and strength conferred on him that by terror thereof he is enabled to form the wills of them all, to peace at home, and mutual aid against their enemies abroad. And in him consists the essence of the commonwealth; which, to define it, is *one person, of whose acts a great multitude, by mutual covenants one with another, have made themselves every one the author, to the end he may use the strength and means of them all, as he shall think expedient, for their peace and common defence.*

And he that carries this person is called Sovereign, and said to have *sovereign power;* and every one besides, his subject.

The attaining to this sovereign power is by two ways. One, by natural force, as when a man makes his children to submit themselves and their children to his government, as being able to destroy them if they refuse, or by war subdues his enemies to his will, giving them their lives on that condition. The other is when men agree among themselves to submit to some man, or assembly of men, voluntarily, on confidence to be protected by him against all others. This latter may be called a political commonwealth, or commonwealth by *institution;* and the former, a commonwealth by *acquisition.*

The law of nature and the civil law contain each other, and are of equal extent. For the laws of nature, which consist in equity, justice, gratitude, and other moral virtues on these depending in the condition of mere nature, as I have said before, are not properly laws, but qualities that dispose men to peace and obedience. When a commonwealth is once settled, then are they actually laws, and not before, as being then the commands of the commonwealth, and therefore also civil laws: for it is the sovereign power that obliges men to obey them. For in the differences of private men to declare what is equity, what is justice, and what is moral virtue, and to make them binding, there is need of the ordinances of sovereign power, and punishments to be ordained for such as shall break them, which ordinances are therefore part of the civil law. The law of nature therefore is a part of the civil law in all commonwealths of the world. Reciprocally also, the civil law is a part of the dictates of nature. For justice, that is to say, performance of covenant, and giving to every man his own, is a dictate of the law of nature. But every subject in a commonwealth has covenanted to obey the civil law, either one with another, as when they assemble to make a common representative, or with the representative itself one by one, when subdued by the sword they promise obedience that they may receive life; and therefore obedience to the civil law is part also of the law of nature. Civil and natural law are not different kinds, but different parts of law; whereof one part being written, is called civil, the other unwritten, natural. But the right of nature, that is, the natural liberty of man, may by the civil law be abridged and restrained: nay, the end of making laws is no other but such restraint, without the which there cannot possibly be any peace. And law was brought into the world for nothing else but to limit the natural liberty of particular men in such manner, as they might not hurt, but assist, one another and join together against a common enemy.

Though nothing can be immortal which mortals make, yet, if men had the use of reason they pretend to, their commonwealths might be secured at least from perishing by internal diseases. For by the nature of their institution they are designed to live as long as mankind, or as the laws of nature, or as justice itself which gives them life. Therefore when they come to be dissolved, not by external violence but intestine disorder, the fault is not in men, as they are the *matter,* but as they are the *makers* and orderers of them. For men, as they become at last weary of irregular jostling and hewing one another, and desire with all their hearts to conform themselves into one firm and lasting edifice, so for want, both of the art of making fit laws to square their actions by, and also of humility and patience to suffer the rude and cumbersome points of their present greatness to be taken off, they cannot without the help of a very able architect be compiled into any other than a crazy building, such as hardly lasting out their own time must assuredly fall upon the heads of their posterity.

Among the *infirmities* therefore of a commonwealth, I will reckon in the first place those that arise from an imperfect institution, and resemble the diseases of a natural body which proceed from a defectuous procreation.

Of which this is one, *that a man, to obtain a kingdom, is sometimes content with less power than to the peace and defence of the commonwealth is necessarily required.* From whence it comes to pass that when the exercise of the power laid by is for the public safety to be resumed, it has the resemblance of an unjust act, which disposes great numbers of men, when occasion is presented, to rebel, in the same manner as the bodies of children, gotten by diseased parents, are subject either to untimely death or, to purge the ill quality derived from their vicious conception, breaking out into biles and scabs. And when kings deny themselves some such necessary power, it is not always, though sometimes, out of ignorance of what is necessary to the office they undertake, but many times out of a hope to recover the same again at their pleasure. Wherein they reason not well, because such as will hold them to their promises shall be maintained against them by foreign commonwealths, who in order to the good of their own subjects let slip few occasions to *weaken* the estate of their neighbours. So was Thomas Becket, archbishop of Canterbury, supported against Henry the Second by the Pope, the subjection of ecclesiastics to the commonwealth having been dispensed with by William the Conqueror at his reception, when he took an oath not to infringe the liberty of the church. And so were the barons, whose power was by William Rufus, to have their help in transferring the succession from his elder brother to himself, increased to a degree inconsistent with the sovereign power, maintained in their rebellion against king John, by the French.

Nor does this happen in monarchy only. For whereas the style of the ancient Roman commonwealth was *The Senate and People of Rome,* neither senate nor people pretended to the whole power, which first caused the seditions of Tiberius Gracchus, Caius Gracchus, Lucius Saturninus, and others, and afterwards the wars between the senate and the people, under Marius and Sylla; and again under Pompey and Caesar, to the extinction of their democracy, and the setting up of monarchy.

The people of Athens bound themselves but from one only action, which was that no man on pain of death should propound the renewing of the war for the island of Salamis; and yet thereby, if Solon had not caused to be given out he was mad, and afterwards in gesture and habit of a madman, and in verse, propounded it to the people that flocked about him, they had had an enemy perpetually in readiness, even at the gates of their city; such damage, or shifts, are all commonwealths forced to that have their power never so little limited.

In the second place, I observe the *diseases* of a commonwealth that proceed from the poison of seditious doctrines, whereof one is *that every private man is judge of good and evil actions.* This is true in the condition of mere nature, where there are no civil laws, and also under civil government in such cases as are not determined by the law. But otherwise, it is manifest that the measure of good and evil actions is the civil law, and the judge the legislator who is always representative of the commonwealth. From this false doctrine, men are disposed to debate with themselves and dispute the commands of the commonwealth, and afterwards to obey or disobey them, as in their private judgments they shall think fit; whereby the commonwealth is distracted and *weakened.*

Another doctrine repugnant to civil society is that *whatsoever a man does against his conscience is sin,* and it depends on the presumption of making himself judge of good and evil. For a man's conscience and his judgment is the same thing, and as the judgment, so also the conscience may be erroneous. Therefore, though he that is subject to no civil law sins in all he does against his conscience, because he has no other rule to follow but his own reason, yet it is not so with him that lives in a commonwealth, because the law is the public conscience, by which he has already undertaken to be guided. Otherwise in such diversity as there is of private consciences, which are but private opinions, the commonwealth must needs be distracted, and no man dare to obey the sovereign power further than it shall seem good in his own eyes.

It has been also commonly taught *that faith and sanctity are not to be attained by study and reason, but by supernatural inspiration or infusion.* Which granted, I see not why any man should render a reason of his faith; or why every Christian should not be also a prophet; or why any man should take the law of his country, rather than his own inspiration, for the rule of his action. And thus we fall again in the fault of taking upon us to judge of good and evil, or to make judges of it such private men as pretend to be supernaturally inspired to the dissolution of all civil government. Faith comes by hearing, and hearing by those accidents which guide us into the presence of them that speak to us; which accidents are all contrived by God Almighty, and yet are not supernatural, but only, for the great number of them that concur to every effect, unobservable. Faith and sanctity are indeed not very frequent; but yet they are not miracles, but brought to pass by education, discipline, correction, and other natural ways by which God works them in his elect, at such times as he thinks fit. And these three opinions, pernicious to peace and government, have in this part of the world proceeded chiefly from the tongues and pens of unlearned divines, who, joining the words of Holy Scripture together otherwise than is agreeable to reason, do what they can to make men think that sanctity and natural reason cannot stand together.

A fourth opinion, repugnant to the nature of a commonwealth, is this, *that he that has the sovereign power is subject to the civil laws.* It is true that sovereigns are all subject to the laws of nature, because such laws be divine and cannot by any man, or commonwealth, be abrogated. But to those laws which the sovereign himself, that is, which the commonwealth makes, he is not subject. For to be subject to laws is to be subject to the commonwealth, that is, to the sovereign representative, that is to himself; which is not subjection, but freedom from the laws. Which error, because it sets the laws above the sovereign, sets also a judge above him, and a power to punish him; which is to make a new sovereign; and again for the same reason a third, to punish the second; and so continually without end, to the confusion and dissolution of the commonwealth.

A fifth doctrine, that tends to the dissolution of a commonwealth, is *that every private man has an absolute propriety in his goods, such as excludes the right of the sovereign.* Every man has indeed a propriety that excludes the right of every other subject; and he has it only from the sovereign power, without the protection whereof, every other man should have equal right to the same. But if the right of the sovereign also be excluded, he cannot perform the office they have put him into, which is to defend them both from foreign enemies and from the injuries of one another; and consequently there is no longer a commonwealth.

And if the propriety of subjects excludes not the right of the sovereign representative to their goods, much less to their offices of judicature, or execution, in which they represent the sovereign himself.

There is a sixth doctrine, plainly and directly against the essence of a commonwealth; and it is this, *that the sovereign power may be divided.* For what is it to divide the power of a commonwealth, but to dissolve it; for powers divided mutually destroy each other. And for these doctrines men are chiefly beholding to some of those that, making profession of the laws, endeavour to make them depend upon their own learning and not upon the legislative power.

As there have been doctors that hold there be three souls in a man, so there be also that think there may be more souls, that is, more sovereigns than one, in a commonwealth, and set up a *supremacy* against the *sovereignty, canons* against *laws,* and a *ghostly authority* against the *civil;* working on the men's minds with words and distinctions that of themselves signify nothing, but betray by their obscurity that there walks, as some think, invisibly another kingdom, as it were a kingdom of fairies, in the dark. Now seeing it is manifest that the civil power and the power of the commonwealth is the same thing, and that supremacy and the power of making canons and granting faculties implies a commonwealth, it follows that where one is sovereign, another supreme, where one can make laws, and another make canons, there must needs be two commonwealths, of one and the same subjects, which is a kingdom divided in itself and cannot stand. For notwithstanding the insignificant distinction of *temporal* and *ghostly,* they are still two kingdoms, and every subject is subject to two masters. For seeing the *ghostly* power challenges the right to declare what is sin, it challenges by consequence to declare what is law, sin being nothing but the transgression of the law; and again, the civil power challenging to declare what is law, every subject must obey two masters, who both will have their commands be observed as law; which is impossible. Or, if it be but one kingdom, either the *civil,* which is the power of the commonwealth, must be subordinate to the *ghostly,* and then there is no sovereignty but the *ghostly;* or the *ghostly* must be subordinate to the *temporal,* and then there is no *supremacy* but the *temporal.* When therefore these two powers oppose one another, the commonwealth cannot but be in great danger of civil war and dissolution. For the *civil* authority being more visible, and standing in the clearer light of natural reason, cannot choose but draw to it in all times a very considerable part of the people; and the *spiritual,* though it stand in the darkness of School distinctions and hard words, yet, because the fear of darkness and ghosts is greater than other fears, cannot want a party sufficient to trouble, and sometimes to destroy, a commonwealth. And this is a disease which not unfitly may be compared to the epilepsy, or falling sickness, which the Jews took to be one kind of possession by spirits in the body natural. For as in this disease, there is an unnatural spirit, or wind, in the head that obstructs the roots of the nerves and, moving them violently, takes away the motion which naturally they should have from the power of the soul in the brain, and thereby causes violent and irregular motions, which men call convulsions, in the parts; insomuch as he that is seized therewith falls down sometimes into the water, and sometimes into the fire, as a man deprived of his senses; so also in the body politic, when the spiritual power moves the members of a commonwealth by the terror of punishments and hope of rewards, which are the nerves of it, otherwise than by the civil power, which is the soul of the commonwealth, they ought to be moved; and by strange and hard words suffocates their understanding, it must needs thereby distract the people, and either overwhelm the commonwealth with oppression, or cast it into the fire of a civil war.

Sometimes also in the merely civil government there be more than one soul, as when the power of levying money, which is the nutritive faculty, has depended on a general assembly; the power of conduct and command, which is the motive faculty, on one man; and the power of making laws, which is the rational faculty, on the accidental consent, not only of those two, but also of a third; this endangers the commonwealth, sometimes for want of consent to good laws, but most often for want of such nourishment as is necessary to life and motion. For although few perceive that such government is not government, but division of the commonwealth into three factions, and call it mixed monarchy, yet the truth is that it is not one independent commonwealth but three independent factions, nor one representative person, but three. In the kingdom of God, there may be three persons independent, without breach of unity in God that reigns; but where men reign that be subject to diversity of opinions, it cannot be so. And therefore if the king bear the person of the people, and the general assembly bear also the person of the people, and another assembly bear the person of a part of the people, they are not one person, nor one sovereign, but three persons, and three sovereigns.

EDMUND BURKE

3. Politics, History, Religion*

You will observe, that from Magna Charta to the Declaration of Right, it has been the uniform policy of our constitution to claim and assert our liberties, as an *entailed inheritance* derived to us from our forefathers, and to be transmitted to our posterity; as an estate specially belonging to the people of this kingdom, without any reference whatever to any other more general or prior right. By this means our constitution preserves an unity in so great a diversity of its parts. We have an inheritable crown; an inheritable peerage; and a House of Commons and a people inheriting privileges, franchises, and liberties, from a long line of ancestors.

The policy appears to me to be the result of profound reflection; or rather the happy effect of following nature, which is wisdom without reflection, and above it. A spirit of innovation is generally the result of a selfish temper, and confined views. People will not look forward to posterity, who never

* From Edmund Burke, *Reflections on the Revolution in France* (1790).

look backward to their ancestors. Besides, the people of England well know, that the idea of inheritance furnishes a sure principle of conservation, and a sure principle of transmission; without at all excluding a principle of improvement. It leaves acquisition free; but it secures what it acquires. Whatever advantages are obtained by a state proceeding on these maxims, are locked fast as in a sort of family settlement; grasped as in a kind of mortmain for ever. By a constitutional policy working after the pattern of nature, we receive, we hold, we transmit our government and our privileges, in the same manner in which we enjoy and transmit our property and our lives. The institutions of policy, the goods of fortune, the gifts of Providence, are handed down to us, and from us, in the same course and order. Our political system is placed in a just correspondence and symmetry with the order of the world, and with the mode of existence decreed to a permanent body composed of transitory parts; wherein, by the disposition of a stupendous wisdom, moulding together the great mysterious incorporation of the human race, the whole, at one time, is never old, or middle-aged, or young, but, in a condition of unchangeable consistency, moves on through the varied tenor of perpetual decay, fall, renovation, and progression. Thus, by preserving the method of nature in the conduct of the state, in what we improve, we are never wholly new; in what we retain, we are never wholly obsolete. By adhering in this manner and on those principles to our forefathers, we are guided not by the superstition of antiquarians, but by the spirit of philosophic analogy. In this choice of inheritance we have given to our frame of polity the image of a relation in blood; binding up the constitution of our country with our dearest domestic ties; adopting our fundamental laws into the bosom of our family affections, keeping inseparable and cherishing with the warmth of all their combined and mutually reflected charities, our state, our hearths, our sepulchres, and our altars.

Through the same plan of a conformity to nature in our artificial institutions, and by calling in the aid of her unerring and powerful instincts, to fortify the fallible and feeble contrivances of our reason, we have derived several other, and those no small benefits, from considering our liberties in the light of an inheritance. Always acting as if in the presence of canonized forefathers, the spirit of freedom, leading in itself to misrule and excess, is tempered with an awful gravity. This idea of a liberal descent inspires us with a sense of habitual native dignity, which prevents that upstart insolence almost inevitably adhering to and disgracing those who are the first acquirers of any distinction. By this means our liberty becomes a noble freedom. It carries an imposing and majestic aspect. It has a pedigree and illustrating ancestors. It has its bearings and its ensigns armorial. It has its gallery of portraits; its monumental inscriptions; its records, evidences, and titles. We procure reverence to our civil institutions on the principle upon which nature teaches us to revere individual men: on account of their age, and on account of those from whom they are descended. All your sophisters cannot produce anything better adapted to preserve a rational and manly freedom than the course that we have pursued, who have chosen our nature rather than our speculations, our breasts rather than our inventions, for the great conservatories and magazines of our rights and privileges.

France, by the perfidy of her leaders, has utterly disgraced the tone of lenient counsel in the cabinets of princes, and disarmed it of its most potent topics. She has sanctified the dark, suspicious maxims of tyrannous distrust; and taught kings to tremble at (what will hereafter be called) the delusive plausibilities of moral politicians. Sovereigns will consider those, who advise them to place an unlimited confidence in their people, as subverters of their thrones; as traitors who aim at their destruction, by leading their easy good-nature, under specious pretences, to admit combinations of bold and faithless men into a participation of their power. This alone (if there were nothing else) is an irreparable calamity to you and to mankind. Remember that your parliament of Paris told your king, that, in calling the states together, he had nothing to fear but the prodigal excess of their zeal in providing for the support of the throne. It is right that these men should hide their heads. It is right that they should bear their part in the ruin which their counsel has brought on their sovereign and their country. Such sanguine declarations tend to lull authority asleep; to encourage it rashly to engage in perilous adventures of untried policy; to neglect those provisions, preparations and precautions, which distinguish benevolence from imbecility; and without which no man can answer for the salutary effect of any abstract plan of government or of freedom. For want of these, they have seen the medicine of the state corrupted into its poison. They have seen the French rebel against a mild and lawful monarch, with more fury, outrage, and insult, than ever any people has been known to rise against the most illegal usurper, or the most sanguinary tyrant. Their resistance was made to concession; their revolt was from protection; their blow was aimed at a hand holding out graces, favours, and immunities.

This was unnatural. The rest is in order. They have found their punishment in their success. Laws overturned; tribunals subverted; industry without vigour; commerce expiring; the revenue unpaid, yet the people impoverished; a church pillaged, and a state not relieved; civil and military anarchy made the constitution of the kingdom; everything human and divine sacrificed to the idol of public credit, and national bankruptcy the consequence; and, to crown all, the paper securities of new, precarious, tottering power, the discredited paper securities of impoverished fraud, and beggared rapine, held out as a currency for the support of the empire, in lieu of the two great recognized species that represent the lasting, conventional credit of mankind, which disappeared and hid themselves in the earth from whence they came, when the principle of property, whose creatures and representatives they are, was systematically subverted.

Were all these dreadful things necessary? Were they the inevitable results of the desperate struggle of determined patriots, compelled to wade through blood and tumult, to the quiet shore of a tranquil and prosperous liberty? No! nothing like it. The fresh ruins of France, which shock our feelings wherever we can turn our eyes, are not the devastation of civil war; they are the sad but instructive monuments of rash and ignorant counsel in time of profound peace. They are the display of inconsiderate and presumptuous, because unresisted and irresistible authority. The persons who have thus squandered away the precious treasure of their crimes, the persons who have made this prodigal and wild waste of public evils (the last stake reserved for the ultimate ransom of the state) have met in their progress with little, or rather with no opposition at all. Their whole march was more like a triumphal procession, than the progress of a war. Their pioneers have gone before them, and demolished and laid everything level at their feet. Not one drop of *their* blood have they shed in the cause of the country they have ruined. They have made no sacrifices to their projects of greater consequence than their shoebuckles, whilst they were imprisoning their king, murdering their fellow-citizens, and bathing in tears, and plunging in poverty and distress, thousands of worthy men and worthy families. Their cruelty has not even been the base result of fear. It has been the effect of their sense of perfect safety, in authorizing treasons, robberies, rapes, assassinations, slaughters, and burnings, throughout their harassed land. But the cause of all was plain from the beginning.

This unforced choice, this fond election of evil, would appear perfectly unaccountable, if we did not consider the composition of the National Assembly; I do not mean its formal constitution, which, as it now stands, is exceptional enough, but the materials of which, in a great measure, it is composed, which is of ten thousand times greater consequence than all the formalities in the world. If we were to know nothing of this assembly but by its title and function, no colours could paint to the imagination anything more venerable. In that light the mind of an inquirer, subdued by such an awful image as that of the virtue and wisdom of a whole people collected into one focus, would pause and hesitate in condemning things even of the very worst aspect. Instead of blamable, they would appear only mysterious. But no name, no power, no function, no artificial institution whatsoever, can make the men of whom any system of authority is composed, any other than God, and nature, and education, and their habits of life have made them. Capacities beyond these the people have not to give. Virtue and wisdom may be the objects of their choice; but their choice confers neither the one nor the other on those upon whom they lay their ordaining hands. They have not the engagement of nature, they have not the promise of revelation for any such powers.

After I had read over the list of the persons and descriptions elected into the *Tiers État,* nothing which they afterwards did could appear astonishing. Among them, indeed, I saw some of known rank; some of shining talents; but of any practical experience in the state, not one man was to be found. The best were only men of theory. But whatever the distinguished few may have been, it is the substance and mass of the body which constitutes its character, and must finally determine its direction. In all bodies, those who will lead, must also, in a considerable degree, follow. They must conform their propositions to the taste, talent, and disposition, of those whom they wish to conduct: therefore, if an assembly is viciously or feebly composed in a very great part of it, nothing but such a supreme degree of virtue as very rarely appears in the world, and for that reason cannot enter into calculation, will prevent the men of talents disseminated through it from becoming only the expert instruments of absurd projects! If, what is the more likely event, instead of that unusual degree of virtue, they should be actuated by sinister ambition, and a lust of meretricious glory, then the feeble part of the assembly, to whom at first they conform, becomes in its turn the dupe and instrument of their designs. In this political traffic, the leaders will be obliged to bow to the ignorance of their followers, and the followers to become subservient to the worst designs of their leaders.

To secure any degree of sobriety in the propositions made by the leaders in any public assembly, they ought to respect, in some degree perhaps to fear, those whom they conduct. To be led any otherwise than blindly, the followers must be qualified, if not for actors, at least for judges; they must also be judges of natural weight and authority. Nothing can secure a steady and moderate conduct in such assemblies, but that the body of them should be respectably composed, in point of condition in life, of permanent property, of education, and of such habits as enlarge and liberalize the understanding.

In the calling of the states-general of France, the first thing that struck me, was a great departure from the ancient course. I found the representation for the third estate composed of six hundred persons. They were equal in number to the representatives of both the other orders. If the orders were to act separately, the number would not, beyond the consideration of the expense, be of much moment. But when it became apparent that the orders were to be melted down into one, the policy and necessary effect of this numerous representation became obvious. A very small desertion from either of the two other orders must throw the power of both into the hands of the third. In fact, the whole power of the state was soon resolved into that body. Its due composition became therefore of infinitely the greater importance.

Judge, sir, of my surprise, when I found that a very great proportion of the assembly (a majority, I believe, of the members who attended) was composed of practitioners in the law. It was composed, not of distinguished magistrates, who had given pledges to their country of their science, prudence, and integrity; not of leading advocates, the glory of the bar; not of renowned professors in universities;—but for the far greater part, as it must in such a number, of the inferior, unlearned, mechanical, merely instrumental members of the profession. There were distinguished exceptions; but the general composition was of obscure provincial advocates, of stewards of petty local jurisdictions, country attorneys, notaries, and the whole train of the ministers of municipal litigation, the fomenters and conductors of the petty war of village vexation. From the moment I read the list, I saw distinctly, and very nearly as it has happened, all that was to follow.

The degree of estimation in which any profession is held becomes the standard of the estimation in which the professors hold themselves. Whatever the personal merits of many individual lawyers might have been, and in many it was undoubtedly very considerable, in that military kingdom no part of the profession had been much regarded, except the highest of all, who often united to their professional offices great family splendour, and were invested with great power and authority. These certainly were highly respected, and even with no small degree of awe. The next rank was not much esteemed; the mechanical part was in a very low degree of repute.

Whenever the supreme authority is vested in a body so composed, it must evidently produce the consequence of supreme authority placed in the hands of men not taught habitually to respect themselves; who had no previous fortune in character at stake; who could not be expected to bear with moderation, or to conduct with discretion, a power, which they themselves, more than any others, must be surprised to find in their hands. Who could flatter himself that these men, suddenly, and, as it were, by enchantment, snatched from the humblest rank of subordination, would not be intoxicated with their unprepared greatness? Who could conceive that men, who are habitually meddling, daring, subtle, active, of litigious dispositions, and unquiet minds, would easily fall back into their old condition of obscure contention, and laborious, low, and unprofitable chicane? Who could doubt but that, at any expense to the state, of which they understood nothing, they must pursue their private interests, which they understood but too well? It was not an event depending on chance or contingency. It was inevitable; it was necessary; it was planted in the nature of things. They must *join* (if their capacity did not permit them to *lead*) in any project which could procure to them a *litigious constitution;* which could lay open to them those innumerable lucrative jobs, which follow in the train of all great convulsions and revolutions in the state, and particularly in all great and violent permutations of property. Was it to be expected that they would attend to the stability of property, whose existence had always depended upon whatever rendered property questionable, ambiguous, and insecure? Their objects would be enlarged with their elevation, but their disposition and habits, and mode of accomplishing their designs, must remain the same.

Well! but these men were to be tempered and restrained by other descriptions, of more sober minds, and more enlarged understandings. Were they then to be awed by the super-eminent authority and awful dignity of a hand-ful of country clowns, who have seats in that assembly, some of whom are said not to be able to read and write? and by not a greater number of traders, who, though somewhat more instructed, and more conspicuous in the order of society, had never known anything beyond their countinghouse? No! both these descriptions were more formed to be overborne and swayed by the intrigues and artifices of lawyers, than to become their counterpoise. With such a dangerous disproportion, the whole must needs be governed by them. To the faculty of law was joined a pretty considerable proportion of the faculty of medicine. This faculty had not, any more than that of the law, pos-sessed in France its just estimation. Its professors, therefore, must have the qualities of men not habituated to sentiments of dignity. But supposing they had ranked as they ought to do, and as with us they do actually, the sides of sick-beds are not the academies for forming statesmen and legislators. Then came the dealers in stocks and funds, who must be eager, at any expense, to change their ideal paper wealth for the more solid substance of land. To these were joined men of other descriptions, from whom as little knowledge of, or attention to, the interests of a great state was to be expected, and as little regard to the stability of any institution; men formed to be instruments, not controls. Such in general was the composition of the *Tiers État* in the Na-tional Assembly; in which was scarcely to be perceived the slightest traces of what we call the natural landed interest of the country.

The Chancellor of France, at the opening of the states, said, in a tone of oratorical flourish, that all occupations were honourable. If he meant only that no honest employment was disgraceful, he would not have gone be-yond the truth. But in asserting that anything is honourable, we imply some distinction in its favour. The occupation of a hair-dresser, or of a working tallow-chandler, cannot be a matter of honour to any person—to say nothing of a number of other more servile employments. Such descriptions of men ought not to suffer oppression from the state; but the state suffers oppression, if such as they, either individually or collectively, are permitted to rule. In this you think you are combating prejudice, but you are at war with nature.[1]

[1] Ecclesiasticus, chap. xxxviii. ver. 24, 25. 'The wisdom of a learned man cometh by oppor-tunity of leisure: and he that hath little business shall become wise.'—'How can he get wisdom that holdeth the plough, and that glorieth in the goad; that driveth oxen; and is occupied in their labours; and whose talk is of bullocks?'

Ver. 27. 'So every carpenter and work-master that laboureth night and day,' &c.

Ver. 33. 'They shall not be sought for in public counsel, nor sit high in the congregation: they shall not sit on the judge's seat, nor understand the sentence of judgment: they cannot declare justice and judgment, and they shall not be found where parables are spoken.'

Ver. 34. 'But they will maintain the state of the world.'

I do not determine whether this book be canonical, as the Gallican Church (till lately) has considered it, or apocryphal, as here it is taken. I am sure it contains a great deal of sense and truth.

I see that your example is held out to shame us. I know that we are supposed a dull, sluggish race, rendered passive by finding our situation tolerable, and prevented by a mediocrity of freedom from ever attaining to its full perfection. Your leaders in France began by affecting to admire, almost to adore, the British constitution; but, as they advanced, they came to look upon it with a sovereign contempt. The friends of your National Assembly amongst us have full as mean an opinion of what was formerly thought the glory of their country. The Revolution Society has discovered that the English nation is not free. They are convinced that the inequality in our representation is a "defect in our constitution *so gross and palpable,* as to make it excellent chiefly in *form and theory."* [2] That a representation in the legislature of a kingdom is not only the basis of all constitutional liberty in it, but of *"all legitimate government;* that without it a *government* is nothing but an *usurpation";—that "when the representation is partial,* the kingdom possesses liberty only *partially;* and if extremely partial, it gives only a *semblance;* and if not only extremely partial, but corruptly chosen, it becomes a *nuisance."* Dr. Price considers this inadequacy of representation as our *fundamental grievance;* and though, as to the corruption of this semblance of representation, he hopes it is not yet arrived to its full perfection of depravity, he fears that "nothing will be done towards gaining for us this *essential blessing,* until some *great abuse of power* again provokes our resentment, or some *great calamity* again alarms our fears, or perhaps till the acquisition of a *pure and equal representation by other countries,* whilst we are *mocked* with the *shadow,* kindles our shame." To this he subjoins a note in these words. "A representation chosen chiefly by the treasury, and a *few* thousands of the *dregs* of the people, who are generally paid for their votes."

You will smile here at the consistency of those democratists, who, when they are not on their guard, treat the humbler part of the community with the greatest contempt, whilst, at the same time, they pretend to make them the depositories of all power. It would require a long discourse to point out to you the many fallacies that lurk in the generality and equivocal nature of the terms "inadequate representation." I shall only say here, in justice to that old-fashioned constitution, under which we have long prospered, that our representation has been found perfectly adequate to all the purposes for which a representation of the people can be desired or devised. I defy the enemies of our constitution to show the contrary. To detail the particulars in which it is found so well to promote its ends, would demand a treatise on our practical constitution. I state here the doctrine of the revolutionists, only that you and others may see, what an opinion these gentlemen entertain of the constitution of their country, and why they seem to think that some great abuse of power, or some great calamity, as giving a chance for the blessing of a constitution according to their ideas, would be much palliated to their feelings;

---

[2] 'Discourse on the Love of Our Country,' 3rd edit. p. 39.

you see *why they* are so much enamoured of your fair and equal representation, which being once obtained the same effects might follow. You see they consider our House of Commons as only "a semblance," "a form," "a theory," "a shadow," "a mockery," perhaps "a nuisance."

These gentlemen value themselves on being systematic; and not without reason. They must therefore look on this gross and palpable defect of representation, this fundamental grievance (so they call it) as a thing not only vicious in itself, but as rendering our whole government absolutely *illegitimate,* and not at all better than a downright *usurpation.* Another revolution, to get rid of this illegitimate and usurped government, would of course be perfectly justifiable, if not absolutely necessary. Indeed their principle, if you observe it with any attention, goes much further than to an alteration in the election of the House of Commons; for, if popular representation, or choice, is necessary to the *legitimacy* of all government, the House of Lords is, at one stroke, bastardized and corrupted in blood. That House is no representative of the people at all, even in 'semblance or in form.' The case of the crown is altogether as bad. In vain the crown may endeavour to screen itself against these gentlemen by the authority of the establishment made on the Revolution. The Revolution which is resorted to for a title, on their system, wants a title itself. The Revolution is built, according to their theory, upon a basis not more solid than our present formalities, as it was made by a House of Lords, not representing anyone but themselves; and a House of Commons exactly such as the present, that is, as they term it, by a mere 'shadow and mockery of representation.'

Something they must destroy, or they seem to themselves to exist for no purpose. One set is for destroying the civil power through the ecclesiastical; another for demolishing the ecclesiastical through the civil. They are aware that the worst consequences might happen to the public in accomplishing this double ruin of church and state; but they are so heated with their theories, that they give more than hints, that this ruin, with all the mischiefs that must lead to it and attend it, and which to themselves appear quite certain, would not be unacceptable to them, or very remote from their wishes. A man amongst them of great authority, and certainly of great talents, speaking of a supposed alliance between church and state, says, "perhaps *we must wait for the fall of the civil powers* before this most unnatural alliance be broken. Calamitous no doubt will that time be. But what convulsion in the political world ought to be a subject of lamentation, if it be attended with so desirable an effect?" You see with what a steady eye these gentlemen are prepared to view the greatest calamities which can befall their country.

It is no wonder therefore, that with these ideas of everything in their constitution and government at home, either in church or state, as illegitimate and usurped, or, at best as a vain mockery, they look abroad with an eager and passionate enthusiasm. Whilst they are possessed by these notions, it is vain to talk to them of the practice of their ancestors, the fundamental laws of their country, the fixed form of a constitution, whose merits are confirmed by the solid test of long experience, and an increasing public strength and national prosperity. They despise experience as the wisdom of unlettered men; and as for the rest, they have wrought under ground a mine that will blow up, at one grand explosion, all examples of antiquity, all precedents, charters, and acts of parliament. They have "the rights of men." Against these there can be no prescription; against these no argument is binding: these admit no temperament, and no compromise: anything withheld from their full demand is so much of fraud and injustice. Against these their rights of men let no government look for security in the length of its continuance, or in the justice and lenity of its administration. The objections of these speculatists, if its forms do not quadrate with their theories, are as valid against such an old and beneficent government, as against the most violent tyranny, or the greenest usurpation. They are always at issue with governments, not on a question of abuse, but a question of competency, and a question of title. I have nothing to say to the clumsy subtlety of their political metaphysics. Let them be their amusement in the schools.—*"Illa se jactet in aula—Æolus, et caluso ventorum carcere regnet."*—But let them not break prison to burst like a *Levanter,* to sweep the earth with their hurricane, and to break up the fountains of the great deep to overwhelm us.

Far am I from denying in theory, full as far is my heart from withholding in practice (if I were of power to give or to withhold) the *real* rights of men. In denying their false claims of right, I do not mean to injure those which are real, and are such as their pretended rights would totally destroy. If civil society be made for the advantage of man, all the advantages for which it is made become his right. It is an institution of beneficence; and law itself is only beneficence; acting by a rule. Men have a right to live by that rule; they have a right to do justice; as between their fellows, whether their fellows are in politic function or in ordinary occupation. They have a right to the fruits of their industry; and to the means of making their industry fruitful. They have a right to the acquisitions of their parents; to the nourishment and improvement of their offspring; to instruction in life, and to consolation in death. Whatever each man can separately do, without trespassing upon others, he has a right to do for himself; and he has a right to a fair portion of all which society, with all its combinations of skill and force, can do in his favour. In this partnership all men have equal rights; but not to equal things. He that has but five shillings in the partnership, has as good a right to it as he that has five hundred pounds has to his larger proportion. But he has not a right to an equal dividend in the product of the joint stock; and as to the share of power, authority, and direction which each individual ought to have in the management of the state, that I must deny to be amongst the direct original rights of man in civil society; for I have in my contemplation the civil social man, and no other. It is a thing to be settled by convention.

If civil society be the offspring of convention, that convention must be its law. That convention must limit and modify all the descriptions of constitution which are formed under it. Every sort of legislature, judicial, or executory power, are its creatures. They can have no being in any other state of things; and how can any man claim, under the conventions of civil society, rights which do not so much as suppose its existence?—rights which are absolutely repugnant to it? One of the first motives to civil society, and which becomes one of its fundamental rules, is, *that no man should be judged in his own cause.* By this each person has at once divested himself of the first fundamental right of unconvenanted man, that is, to judge for himself and to assert his own cause. He abdicates all right to be his own governor. He inclusively, in a great measure abandons the right of self-defence, the first law of nature. Men cannot enjoy the rights of an uncivil and of a civil state together. That he may obtain justice, he gives up his right of determining what it is in points the most essential to him. That he may secure some liberty, he makes a surrender in trust of the whole of it.

Government is not made in virtue of natural rights, which may and do exist in total independence of it; and exist in much greater clearness, and in a much greater degree of abstract perfection; but their abstract perfection is their practical defect. By having a right to everything, they want everything. Government is a contrivance of human wisdom to provide for human *wants.* Men have a right that these wants should be provided for by this wisdom. Among these wants is to be reckoned the want, out of civil society, of a sufficient restraint upon their passions. Society requires not only that the passions of individuals should be subjected, but that even in the mass and body, as well as in the individuals, the inclinations of men should frequently be thwarted, their will controlled, and their passions brought into subjection. This can only be done *by a power out of themselves;* and not, in the exercise of its function, subject to that will and to those passions which it is its office to bridle and subdue. In this sense the restraints on men, as well as their liberties, are to be reckoned among their rights. But as the liberties and the restrictions vary with times and circumstances, and admit of infinite modifications, they cannot be settled upon any abstract rule; and nothing is so foolish as to discuss them upon that principle.

The moment you abate anything from the full rights of men, each to govern himself, and suffer any artificial, positive limitation upon those rights, from that moment the whole organization of government becomes a consideration of convenience. This it is which makes the constitution of a state, and the due distribution of its powers, a matter of the most delicate and complicated skill. It requires a deep knowledge of human nature and human necessities, and of the things which facilitate or obstruct the various ends, which are to be pursued by the mechanism of civil institutions. The state is to have recruits to its strength, and remedies to its distempers. What is the use of discussing a man's abstract right to food or medicine? The question is upon the method of procuring and administering them. In that deliberation I shall always advise to call in the aid of the farmer and the physician, rather than the professor of metaphysics.

The science of constructing a commonwealth, or renovating it, or reforming it, is, like every other experimental science, not to be taught *a priori*. Nor is it a short experience that can instruct us in that practical science; because the real effects of moral causes are not always immediate; but that which in the first instance is prejudicial may be excellent in its remoter operation; and its excellence may arise even from the ill effects it produces in the beginning. The reverse also happens; and very plausible schemes, with very pleasing commencements, have often shameful and lamentable conclusions. In states there are often some obscure and almost latent causes, things which appear at first view of little moment, on which a very great part of its prosperity or adversity may most essentially depend. The science of government being therefore so practical in itself, and intended for such practical purposes, a matter which requires experience, and even more experience than any person can gain in his whole life, however sagacious and observing he may be, it is with infinite caution that any man ought to venture upon pulling down an edifice, which has answered in any tolerable degree for ages the common purposes of society, or on building it up again, without having models and patterns of approved utility before his eyes.

These metaphysic rights entering into common life, like rays of light which pierce into a dense medium, are, by the laws of nature, refracted from their straight line. Indeed, in the gross and complicated mass of human passions and concerns, the primitive rights of men undergo such a variety of refractions and reflections, that it becomes absurd to talk of them as if they continued in the simplicity of their original direction. The nature of man is intricate; the objects of society are of the greatest possible complexity: and therefore no simple disposition or direction of power can be suitable either to man's nature, or to the quality of his affairs. When I hear the simplicity of contrivance aimed at and boasted of in any new political constitutions, I am at no loss to decide that the artificers are grossly ignorant of their trade, or totally negligent of their duty. The simple governments are fundamentally defective, to say no worse of them. If you were to contemplate society in but one point of view, all these simple modes of polity are infinitely captivating. In effect each would answer its single end much more perfectly than the more complex is able to attain all its complex purposes. But it is better that the whole should be imperfectly and anomalously answered, than that, while some parts are provided for with great exactness, others might be totally neglected, or perhaps materially injured, by the over-care of a favourite member.

The pretended rights of these theorists are all extremes: and in proportion as they are metaphysically true, they are morally and politically false. The rights of men are in a sort of *middle,* incapable of definition, but not impossible to be discerned. The rights of men in governments are their advantages; and these are often in balances between differences of good; in compromise between good and evil, and sometimes between evil and evil. Political reason is a computing principle; adding, subtracting, multiplying, and dividing, morally, and not metaphysically or mathematically, true moral denominations.

We know, and, what is better, we feel inwardly, that religion is the basis of civil society, and the source of all good, and of all comfort.[3] In England we are so convinced of this, that there is no rust of superstition, with which the accumulated absurdity of the human mind might have crusted it over in the course of ages, that ninety-nine in a hundred of the people of England would not prefer to impiety. We shall never be such fools as to call in an enemy to the substance of any system to remove its corruptions, to supply its defects, or to perfect its construction. If our religious tenets should ever want a further elucidation, we shall not call on atheism to explain them. We shall not light up our temple from that unhallowed fire. It will be illuminated with other lights. It will be perfumed with other incense, than the infectious stuff which is imported by the smugglers of adulterated metaphysics. If our ecclesiastical establishment should want a revision, it is not avarice or rapacity, public or private, that we shall employ for the audit, or receipt, or application of its consecrated revenue. Violently condemning neither the Greek nor the Armenian, nor, since heats are subsided, the Roman system of religion, we prefer the Protestant; not because we think it has less of the Christian religion in it, but because, in our judgment, it has more. We are Protestants, not from indifference, but from zeal.

We know, and it is our pride to know, that man is by his constitution a religious animal; that atheism is against, not only our reason, but our instincts; and that it cannot prevail long. But if, in the moment of riot, and in a drunken delirium from the hot spirit drawn out of the alembic of hell, which in France is now so furiously boiling, we should uncover our nakedness, by throwing off that Christian religion which has hitherto been our boast and comfort, and one great source of civilization amongst us, and among many other nations, we are apprehensive (being well aware that the mind will not

---

[3] "Sit igitur hoc ab initio persuasum civibus, dominos esse omnium rerum ac moderatores, deos; eaque, quæ gerantur, eorum geri vi, ditione, ac numine; eosdemque optime de genere hominum mereri; et qualis quisque sit, quid agat, quid in se admittat, qua mente qua pietate colat religiones intueri: piorum et impiorum habere rationem. His enim rebus imbutæ mentes haud sane abhorrebunt ab utili et a vera sententia." Cic. de Legibus, 1. 2.

endure a void) that some uncouth, pernicious and degrading superstition might take place of it.

For that reason, before we take from our establishment the natural, human means of estimation, and give it up to contempt, as you have done, and in doing it have incurred the penalties you well deserve to suffer, we desire that some other may be presented to us in the place of it. We shall then form our judgment.

On these ideas, instead of quarrelling with establishments, as some do, who have made a philosophy and a religion of their hostility to such institutions, we cleave closely to them. We are resolved to keep an established church, and established monarchy, an established aristocracy, and an established democracy, each in the degree it exists, and in no greater. I shall show you presently how much of each of these we possess.

It has been the misfortune (not as these gentlemen think it, the glory) of this age, that everything is to be discussed, as if the constitution of our country were to be always a subject rather of altercation than enjoyment. For this reason, as well as for the satisfaction of those among you (if any such you have among you) who may wish to profit of examples, I venture to trouble you with a few thoughts upon each of these establishments. I do not think they were unwise in ancient Rome, who, when they wished to new-model their laws, set commissioners to examine the best constituted republics within their reach.

First, I beg leave to speak of our church establishment, which is the first of our prejudices, not a prejudice destitute of reason, but involving in it profound and extensive wisdom. I speak of it first. It is first, and last, and midst in our minds. For, taking ground on that religious system, of which we are now in possession, we continue to act on the early received, and uniformly continued sense of mankind. That sense not only, like a wise architect, hath built up the august fabric of states, but like a provident proprietor, to preserve the structure from profanation and ruin, as a sacred temple, purged from all the impurities of fraud, and violence, and injustice, and tyranny, hath solemnly and for ever consecrated the commonwealth, and all that officiate in it. This consecration is made, that all who administer in the government of men, in which they stand in the person of God Himself, should have high and worthy notions of their function and destination; that their hope should be full of immortality; that they should not look to the paltry pelf of the moment, nor to the temporary and transient praise of the vulgar, but to a solid, permanent existence, in the permanent part of their nature, and to a permanent fame and glory, in the example they leave as a rich inheritance to the world.

Such sublime principles ought to be infused into persons of exalted situations; and religious establishments provided, that may continually revive and enforce them. Every sort of moral, every sort of civil, every sort of politic institution, aiding the rational and natural ties that connect the human understanding and affections to the divine, are not more than necessary, in order to build up that wonderful structure, Man; whose prerogative it is, to be in a great degree a creature of his own making; and who, when made as he ought to be made, is destined to hold no trivial place in the creation. But whenever man is put over men, as the better nature ought ever to preside, in that case more particularly, he should as nearly as possible be approximated to his perfection.

The consecration of the state, by a state religious establishment, is necessary also to operate with a wholesome awe upon free citizens; because, in order to secure their freedom, they must enjoy some determinate portion of power. To them therefore a religion connected with the state, and with their duty towards it, becomes even more necessary than in such societies, where the people, by the terms of their subjection, are confined to private sentiments, and the management of their own family concerns. All persons possessing any portion of power ought to be strongly and awfully impressed with an idea that they act in trust; and that they are to account for their conduct in that trust to the one great Master, Author and Founder of society.

This principle ought even to be more strongly impressed upon the minds of those who compose the collective sovereignty, than upon those of single princes. Without instruments, these princes can do nothing. Whoever uses instruments, in finding helps, finds also impediments. Their power is therefore by no means complete; nor are they safe in extreme abuse. Such persons, however elevated by flattery, arrogance, and self-opinion, must be sensible that, whether covered or not by positive law, in some way or other they are accountable even here for the abuse of their trust. If they are not cut off by a rebellion of their people, they may be strangled by the very janissaries kept for their security against all other rebellion. Thus we have seen the King of France sold by his soldiers for an increase of pay. But where popular authority is absolute and unrestrained, the people have an infinitely greater, because a far better founded confidence in their own power. They are themselves, in a great measure, their own instruments. They are nearer to their objects. Besides, they are less under responsibility to one of the greatest controlling powers on earth, the sense of fame and estimation. The share of infamy, that is likely to fall to the lot of each individual in public acts, is small indeed; the operation of opinion being in the inverse ratio to the number of those who abuse power. Their own approbation of their own acts has to them the appearance of a public judgment in their favour. A perfect democracy is therefore the most shameless thing in the world. As it is the most shameless, it is also the most fearless. No man apprehends in his person that he can be made subject to punishment. Certainly the people at large never ought: for as all punishments are for example towards the conservation of the people at large, the people at large can never become the subject of punishments by any human hand. It is therefore of infinite importance that they should not be suffered to imagine that their will, any more than that of kings, is the standard of right and wrong. They ought to be persuaded that they are full as little entitled, and far less qualified, with safety to themselves, to use any arbitrary power whatsoever; that therefore they are not, under a false show of liberty, but, in truth, to exercise an unnatural, inverted domination, tyrannically to exact from those who officiate in the state, not an entire devotion to their interest, which is their right, but an abject submission to their occasional will; extinguishing thereby, in all those who serve them, all moral principle, all sense of dignity, all use of judgment, and all consistency of character; whilst by the very same process they give themselves up a proper, a suitable, but a most contemptible prey to the servile ambition of popular sycophants, or courtly flatterers.

When the people have emptied themselves of all the lust of selfish will, which without religion it is utterly impossible they ever should, when they are conscious that they exercise, and exercise perhaps in a higher link of the order of delegation, the power, which to be legitimate must be according to that eternal, immutable law, in which will and reason are the same, they will be more careful how they place power in base and incapable hands. In their nomination to office, they will not appoint to the exercise of authority, as to a pitiful job, but as to a holy function; not according to their sordid, selfish interest, nor to their wanton caprice, nor to their arbitrary will; but they will confer that power (which any man may well tremble to give or to receive) on those only in whom they may discern that predominant proportion of active virtue and wisdom, taken together and fitted to the charge, such as, in the great and inevitable mixed mass of human imperfections and infirmities, is to be found.

When they are habitually convinced that no evil can be acceptable, either in the act or the permission, to him whose essence is good, they will be better able to extirpate out of the minds of all magistrates, civil, ecclesiastical, or military; anything that bears the least resemblance to a proud and lawless domination.

But one of the first and most leading principles on which the commonwealth and the laws are consecrated, is lest the temporary possessors and liferenters in it, unmindful of what they have received from their ancestors, or of what is due to their posterity, should act as if they were the entire masters; that they should not think it amongst their rights to cut off the entail or commit waste on the inheritance, by destroying at their pleasure the whole original fabric of their society; hazarding to leave to those who come after them a ruin instead of a habitation—and teaching these successors as little to respect their contrivances, as they had themselves respected the institutions of their forefathers. By this unprincipled facility of changing the state as often, and as much, and in as many ways, as there are floating fancies or fashions, the whole chain and continuity of the commonwealth would be broken. No one generation could link with the other. Men would become little better than the flies of a summer.

And first of all, the science of jurisprudence, the pride of human intellect, which, with all its defects, redundancies, and errors, is the collected reason of ages, combining the principles of original justice with the infinite variety of human concerns, as a heap of old exploded errors, would be no longer studied. Personal self-sufficiency and arrogance (the certain attendants upon all those who have never experienced a wisdom greater than their own) would usurp the tribunal. Of course no certain laws, establishing invariable grounds of hope and fear, would keep the actions of men in a certain course, or direct them to a certain end. Nothing stable in the modes of holding property, or exercising function, could form a solid ground on which any parent could speculate in the education of his offspring, or in a choice for their future establishment in the world. No principles would be early worked into the habits. As soon as the most able instructor had completed his laborious course of institution, instead of sending forth his pupil, accomplished in a virtuous discipline, fitted to procure him attention and respect, in his place in society, he would find everything altered; and that he had turned out a poor creature to the contempt and derision of the world, ignorant of the true grounds of estimation. Who would insure a tender and delicate sense of honour to beat almost with the first pulses of the heart, when no man could know what would be the test of honour in a nation, continually varying the standard of its coin? No part of life would retain its acquisitions. Barbarism with regard to science and literature, unskilfulness with regard to arts and manufactures, would infallibly succeed to the want of a steady education and settled principle; and thus the commonwealth itself would, in a few generations, crumble away, be disconnected into the dust and powder of individuality, and at length dispersed to all the winds of heaven.

To avoid therefore the evils of inconstancy and versatility, ten thousand times worse than those of obstinacy and the blindest prejudice, we have consecrated the state, that no man should approach to look into its defects or corruptions but with due caution; that he should never dream of beginning its reformation by its subversion; that he should approach to the faults of the state as to the wounds of a father, with pious awe, and trembling solicitude. By this wise prejudice we are taught to look with horror on those children of their country, who are prompt rashly to hack that aged parent in pieces, and put him into the kettle of magicians, in hopes that by their poisonous weeds, and wild incantations, they may regenerate the paternal constitution, and renovate their father's life.

Society is indeed a contract. Subordinate contracts for objects of mere occasional interest may be dissolved at pleasure—but the state ought not to be considered nothing better than a partnership agreement in a trade of pepper and coffee, calico or tobacco, or some other such low concern, to be taken up for a little temporary interest, and to be dissolved by the fancy of the parties. It is to be looked on with other reverence; because it is not a partnership in things subservient only to the gross animal existence of a temporary and perishable nature. It is a partnership in all science; a partnership in all art; a partnership in every virtue, and in all perfection. As the ends of such a partnership cannot be obtained in many generations, it becomes a partnership not only between those who are living, but between those who are living, those who are dead, and those who are to be born. Each contract of each particular state is but a clause in the great primeval contract of eternal society, linking the lower with the higher natures, connecting the visible and invisible world, according to a fixed compact sanctioned by the inviolable oath which holds all physical and all moral natures, each in their appointed place. This law is not subject to the will of those, who by an obligation above them, and infinitely superior, are bound to submit their will to that law. The municipal corporations of that universal kingdom are not morally at liberty at their pleasure, and on their speculations of a contingent improvement wholly to separate and tear asunder the bands of their subordinate community, and to dissolve it into an unsocial, uncivil, unconnected chaos of elementary principles. It is the first and supreme necessity only, a necessity that is not chosen, but chooses, a necessity paramount to deliberation, that admits no discussion, and demands no evidence, which alone can justify a resort to anarchy. This necessity is no exception to the rule; because this necessity itself is a part too of that moral and physical disposition of things, to which man must be obedient by consent of force: but if that which is only submission to necessity should be made the object of choice, the law is broken, nature is disobeyed, and the rebellious are outlawed, cast forth, and exiled, from this world of reason, and order, and peace, and virtue, and fruitful penitence, into the antagonist world of madness, discord, vice, confusion, and unavailing sorrow.

I do not know under what description to class the present ruling authority in France. It affects to be pure democracy, though I think it in a direct train of becoming shortly a mischievous and ignoble oligarchy. But for the present I admit it to be a contrivance of the nature and effect of what it pretends to. I reprobate no form of government merely upon abstract principles. There may be situations in which the purely democratic form will become necessary. There may be some (very few, and very particularly circumstanced) where it would be clearly desirable. This I do not take to be the case of France, or of any other great country. Until now, we have seen no examples of considerable democracies. The ancients were better acquainted with them. Not being wholly unread in the authors, who had seen the most of those constitutions, and who best understood them, I cannot help concurring with their opinion, that an absolute democracy, no more than absolute monarchy, is to be reckoned among the legitimate forms of government. They think it rather the corruption and degeneracy, than the sound constitution of a republic. If I recollect rightly, Aristotle observes, that a democracy has many striking points of resemblance with tyranny. Of this I am certain, that in a democracy, the majority of the citizens is capable of exercising the most cruel oppressions upon the minority, whenever strong divisions prevail in that kind of polity, as they often must; and that oppression of the minority will extend to far greater numbers, and will be carried on with much greater fury, than can almost ever be apprehended from the dominion of a single sceptre. In such a popular persecution, individual sufferers are in a much more deplorable condition than in any other. Under a cruel prince they have the balmy compassion of mankind to assuage the smart of their wounds; they have the plaudits of the people to animate their generous constancy under their sufferings; but those who are subjected to wrong under multitudes, are deprived of all external consolation. They seem deserted by mankind, overpowered by a conspiracy of their whole species.

All this violent cry against the nobility I take to be a mere work of art. To be honoured and even privileged by the laws, opinions, and inveterate usages of our country, growing out of the prejudice of ages, has nothing to provoke horror and indignation in any man. Even to be too tenacious of those privileges is not absolutely a crime. The strong struggle in every individual to preserve possession of what he has found to belong to him, and to distinguish him, is one of the securities against injustice and despotism implanted in our nature. It operates as an instinct to secure property, and to preserve communities in a settled state. What is there to shock in this? Nobility is a graceful ornament to the civil order. It is the Corinthian capital of polished society. *Omnes boni nobilitati semper favemus*, was the saying of a wise and good man. It is, indeed, one sign of a liberal and benevolent mind to incline to it with some sort of partial propensity. He feels no ennobling principle in his own heart, who wishes to level all the artificial institutions which have been adopted for giving a body to opinion and permanence to fugitive esteem. It is a sour, malignant, envious disposition, without taste for the reality, or for any image or representation of virtue, that sees with joy the unmerited fall of what had long flourished in splendour and in honour. I do not like to see anything destroyed; any void produced in society; any ruin on the face of the land. It was therefore with no disappointment or dissatisfaction that my inquiries and observations did not present to me any incorrigible vices in the noblesse of France, or any abuse which could not be removed by a reform very short of abolition. Your noblesse did not deserve punishment; but to degrade is to punish.

With us the king and the lords are several and joint securities for the equality of each district, each province, each city. When did you hear in

Great Britain of any province suffering from the inequality of its representation; what district from having no representation at all? Not only our monarchy and our peerage secure the equality on which our unity depends, but it is the spirit of the House of Commons itself. The very inequality of representation, which is so foolishly complained of, is perhaps the very thing which prevents us from thinking or acting as members for districts. Cornwall elects as many members as all Scotland. But is Cornwall better taken care of than Scotland? Few trouble their heads about any of your bases, out of some giddy clubs.

The body of the people must not find the principles of natural subordination by art rooted out of their minds. They must respect that property of which they cannot partake. They must labour to obtain what by labour can be obtained; and when they find, as they commonly do, the success disproportioned to the endeavour, they must be taught their consolation in the final proportions of eternal justice. Of this consolation whoever deprives them deadens their industry, and strikes at the root of all acquisition as of all conservation. He that does this is the cruel oppressor, the merciless enemy of the poor and wretched; at the same time that by his wicked speculations he exposes the fruits of successful industry, and the accumulations of fortune, to the plunder of the negligent, the disappointed, and the unprosperous.

Chapter VII

THE IDOL STATE

The indestructible reality of the individual stands in the center of the Western democratic theory of politics. Compared with the majesty of the individual, state, society, and government are but pale artifacts, devices to enable the individual to be most himself. By contrast, the anti-democratic theory of politics puts the state into the pivotal position of social reality, and within the shadow of its frightful power the individual leads but a timid and dependent existence.

In the German intellectual tradition, Hegel's system of philosophy towers over the rest in more than one way. Hegel's work encompasses philosophy, metaphysics, religion, art, ethics, history, and politics. In its range alone, his work is unique in Germany, and possibly in the whole world. Furthermore, his ideas are considered by most Germans themselves as the most typically representative, more German than those of any other major philosopher, not barring Kant. Kant's political philosophy often reflected a vision of what his fellow countrymen *should* think. Hegel's philosophy was more a mirror of what they actually *did* think. Hegel's position in German thought was so powerful that even the most ferocious attack against the orthodox German tradition, Karl Marx's ideas, sprang very largely from Hegelian assumptions.

Hegel's *Philosophy of Law* ("Philosophie des Rechts"), published in 1821, contains the best statement of his political ideas. In it he expresses his conception of freedom, natural and social, which provides the key to an understanding of his political thought. Hegel starts with the assertion that "people grant that it is nature as it is which philosophy has to bring within its ken." What knowledge has to investigate in nature, Hegel argues, is its "eternal harmony" and "inherent rationality." He attacks those who believe that the ethical world—actualized in the state—should be approached differently from nature, the physical world. Just as reason becomes "actual" in nature, Hegel says, so it does in the state. In both instances, the observer does not, and cannot, *make* the laws expressing reason, but can merely understand them. There is no "chance and caprice" in rationality as it may be apprehended in either the world of nature or in the ethical world—the state. Because some philosophers of the state have followed the principle that every thinker is authorized "to take his own road," political philosophy has earned for itself all kinds of "scorn and discredit," Hegel observes. This has led to the worst kind of scorn, viz., that "everyone is convinced that his mere birthright puts him in a position to pass judgment on philosophy in general and to condemn it." Since philosophy in Germany is "in the service of the state," Hegel accords to the state the right to defend itself against those who "indulge in subjective feeling and particular conviction," from which evil follows "the ruin of public order and the law of the land." This encouragement to persecute freedom of thought came from Hegel at a moment when antiliberal, authoritarian government in Prussia had become more ruthless than ever before. The Prussian absolute state—thus can philosophy prostitute itself—appeared to Hegel as the historically most perfect realization of political rationality. "What is rational is actual and what is actual is rational"—this most famous Hegelian phrase has been interpreted, like an ambiguous Biblical passage, in many ways. Whatever the meaning of that phrase as Hegel himself thought it, the impact (historical and psychological, and not hypothetical and logical) has been entirely in one direction: to sanctify the existing as the good. Hegel himself might have refused to accept the proposition that, because Hitler was actual, he was rational, but the historical effect of Hegel was to strengthen the tradition of servility to the existing, which has characterized German political life and thought.

The intimate inner connection between Hegelianism and militarism is evident in Hegel's idea that "in duty the individual finds his liberation." This concept of freedom is the product of a society which honors militarism as *the* way of life, as becomes evident in Hegel's further statement that "self-sacrifice" is the "real existence of one's freedom." This philosophy can be safely taught to members of a totalitarian army or party without amendment. Hegel considers this readiness to sacrifice oneself for the state as the "intrinsic worth of courage." The courage of resistance is unknown to Hegel. Where Locke sees the indestructible essence of man in his act of resisting, Hegel sees man's fulfillment in obedience. Life, liberty, and the pursuit of happiness are thus the exact opposites of the Hegelian concepts of citizenship of self-sacrifice, duty, and discipline.

If the individual is nothing in Hegel's world, the state is all. In his *Philosophy of History,* published posthumously in 1837 (six years after his death), Hegel defines the state as "the realization of Freedom"; the state "exists for its own sake." As to the relation between state and individual, Hegel says that "all the worth which the human being possesses—all spiritual reality, he possesses only through the State." Only through the state does the individual partake of morality. Hegel's state idolatry reaches its peak in the famous sentence, "The State is the Divine Idea as it exists on Earth." In the state, Reason becomes actual and objective, and the individual finds all his spiritual reality through the state. On the basis of this assumption, when "the subjective will of man submits to laws, the contradiction between Liberty and Necessity vanishes."

Who is to determine the law? Hegel takes up this question in both his

Philosophy of Law and *Philosophy of History*. He attacks the doctrine that "all should participate in the business of the state" as a "ridiculous notion." To permit all individuals to share in public decisions, because all concerns of the state are the concerns of its members, is "tantamount to a proposal to put the democratic element without any rational form into the organism of the state." Hegel anticipates the corporate organization of the twentieth century fascist state by his emphasis that the individual should be politically articulate only as a member of a social class, group, society, or corporation, and not just as a citizen *qua* citizen, as in the liberal democracies.

The fundamental law of the state is in its constitution. Hegel opposes the Western idea of the constitution as an instrument of government, a charter and compact consciously framed for desired ends. The constitution, Hegel says, "should not be regarded as something made, even though it has come into being in time. It must be treated rather as something simply existent in and by itself, as divine therefore, and constant, and so as exalted above the sphere of things that are made." Since the state is "the march of God through the world," the constitution of the state is not something to be tampered with by ordinary mortals.

Going back into the history of the state, Hegel finds that its origin "involves imperious lordship on the one hand, instinctive submission on the other." This leadership principle (later extolled as one of the central dogmas of Nazism) is also stressed by Hegel in his discussion of the merits of the different types of political organization—democracy, aristocracy, and monarchy. The advantage of the monarchical form of government lies in the fact that leadership is always clearly present, whereas in the aristocracies, and even more in democracies, leaders *may* rise to the top. Because of his preference for monarchy, Hegel is not overly partisan in favor of "sovereignty of the people," especially if that term implies opposition to the sovereignty of the monarch. "So opposed to the sovereignty of the monarch, the sovereignty of the people is one of the confused notions based on the wild idea of the 'people.' Taken without its monarch and the articulation of the whole which is the indispensable and direct concomitant of monarchy, the people is a formless mass and no longer a state." The Western concept that the people are the state is described by Hegel as a "perversity" and a "ruse."

Few writers popularized Hegel's main ideas as skilfully as Heinrich von Treitschke. One of the leading German historians in the nineteenth century, Treitschke was typical of a whole generation: in his youth he was a strong supporter of the liberal revolution of 1848, but later on he became the leading admirer of Bismarckian *Machtpolitik*. *Macht* (power) became the central concept of his thinking, as applied to both domestic and foreign policy. In his hatred of England and his contempt for the United States he anticipated the Nazis, as also in his attitudes toward Catholics, Socialists, and democracy in general. Openly anti-Semitic at a time when respectable people in Europe abhorred such prejudice, Treitschke was one of those German thinkers who planted the seeds of Auschwitz, Maidanek, and other German extermination camps in World War II, in which six million Jewish men, women, and children in German-occupied Europe were put to death in gas chambers—in the name of the superior German "race" and *Kultur*.

Shortly after his death in 1896, his lectures on *Politics* were published in two volumes (1897-1898). On the central issue of all Western political thinking, the relation of the individual to the state, including the right to resist authority, Treitschke is unequivocal: "There must be no question of subjects having the right to oppose a sovereignty which in their opinion is not moral." After 1848, several hundred thousands of Germans left their fatherland for the freedom of America; "it is foolish to admire them for this." Treitschke takes a dim view of democracy in general, and of particular democracies like the United States or Switzerland. "The Presidents of the United States, with a few exceptions, have never been men of great ability, because these are not of the stuff to make head against the flood of slander which envy lets loose over them. There will always be natures of too rare a quality for the common herd to understand." The dominant note of democracy, according to Treitschke, is mediocrity, in politics as well as in the arts and sciences. His faith in inequality makes him say that "where the foundation of slavery is lacking, that is to say in all modern Democracies, one may expect to find a dominant note of political mediocrity."

The unity of German thought emerges from the fact that the opponents of the predominant authoritarian tradition do not diverge from its fundamentals so much as it may appear to them. In the thirty years preceding his death in 1923, Ernst Troeltsch was one of Germany's most distinguished liberal scholars, his main work having been dedicated to the study of the social doctrines of the Christian churches. His profound democratic sentiment made him enter active political life after the First World War. In 1919 he was elected to the Prussian Diet, and he served as parliamentary under-secretary to the Prussian minister of education. Troeltsch's intellectual integrity was tested in the First World War and, unlike most of his colleagues, he stood the test of crisis remarkably well. In 1916 he published a hitherto untranslated essay on "The German Idea of Freedom." In it Troeltsch shows the historical reasons that account for the basically different conceptions of liberty in the English-speaking countries and France on the one side and in Germany on the other. In Germany, too, "liberty is the key word," but it has a meaning of its own. Troeltsch re-emphasizes the German conception of liberty, as interpreted by philosophers like Hegel or poets like Goethe, in the following way: "Liberty as creative participation in the formation of state authority means to us, not the bringing forth of governmental will out of individual wills, not control of the mandatory by the principal, but the free, conscious and dutiful dedication of oneself to the whole, as it has been molded by history, state and nation." In this interpretation of freedom by a great German liberal, the essential elements of the antidemocratic Hegelian philosophy are not only present, but freely recognized. In this conception the state is an organic whole, beyond the scrutiny of the individual, who finds his fulfillment as a citizen in free and dutiful dedication to the whole. Troeltsch refrains from Hegel's inhuman crudity, that only in self-sacrifice for the state does the individual find his true freedom, but he accepts what is the core of Hegelian thought on this issue. Whereas the Western idea of freedom stresses the opportunity of citizens to control and unseat the government, the Germans virtually identify state and government, both assuming an existence of their own, different from, and superior to, that of individuals. In the Western approach to politics, loyalty to the state is not impaired by opposition to the government—as the latter is only an instrument in the service of the former. Finally, and this point is of supreme importance, the Western idea of liberty inevitably leads to equality, and the one is unreal to the extent that the other is unfulfilled. According to Troeltsch, by contrast, "liberty is not equality, but service of the individual in his station organically due to him." This is, again, an echo of the Hegelian position that man counts politically, not as a citizen *qua* citizen, but as a member of a social class, group, or society. One of Troeltsch's most interesting observations, which ought to invite a good deal of pondering, is his comment that the German spirit of service and self-dedication to the whole is reflected in "two expressions of life so contrary to one another as the German army and the socialist party." German references to Frederick the Great as the "first German socialist," and the phenomenon of "military socialism" or "Prussian socialism," culminating in "National Socialism" of the Hitler-Himmler variety, demonstrate how the idea of socialism, essentially a product of western liberalism and antimilitarism, was transformed, on German soil, into a service philosophy of a society perpetually geared for war.

One of the two or three main tenets of antidemocratic politics is the leadership principle. The cry for the leader comes from all who refuse to grow up; it will be noticed that the voices represented in this chapter are gathered from several nations.

Few critics of nineteenth-century democracy have been so influential as Carlyle. His long life (he was born in 1795 and lived eighty-six years) may have been one factor. Like Shaw later on, Carlyle must have seemed immortal to his contemporaries. When he wrote about Martin Luther or Cromwell, some of his readers must have thought that Carlyle was writing from personal experience. A second source of influence was Carlyle's bountiful production: he published long works of four and even six volumes. The third reason for his immense influence lay in his literary style—highly personal, vituperative, brilliant, and skilfully blending truth with fasehood.

Because Carlyle attacked the "cash nexus" of capitalist civilization, he was hailed by many in his own day, as today, as a progressive thinker. Yet, as one reads his political essays, one is impressed with the fact that the anatomy of Fascism and Nazism can be unmistakably detected in his work. The essentials of the fascist mind and temper are all there: contempt for democracy which, as Carlyle puts it in *Chartism* (1840), is a self-canceling business and "gives in the long-run a net-result of zero." Democracy is, in Carlyle's eyes, less of a system of social organization than chaos and disintegration writ large and institutionalized, if emptiness and vacuity can be organized at all. He was convinced, as he put it in the *Latter-day Pamphlets* (1850), that democracy "is forever impossible." His contempt for people and his belief in aristocracy, in nature as well as in society, lead him to explain democracy as a device by which the "Sham-Noblest" are raised at the expense of "the Noble," thus perverting "the Almighty Maker's Law," according to which the Noble are in the high place, and the Ignoble in the low.

To talk of "rights of man" is, in Carlyle's view, balderdash; "it is the ever-lasting privilege of the foolish to be governed by the wise." This, says Carlyle, is "the first 'right of man.'" Analogously, and this, again, is good fascist doctrine, the wise and noble are duty bound to rule the foolish mass. This belief in inequality finds its strongest expression in *On Heroes, Hero-worship and the Heroic in History* (1840). "There is no act more moral between men than that of rule and obedience"—this Carlylean definition of human relationships is the exact antithesis of the democratic social morality which is founded on consent and cooperation rather than on rule and obedience. Carlyle also anticipates the fascist personal style of self-abasement and self-abnegation: "Find me the true Könning, King, or Able-man, and he *has* a divine right over me"

Carlyle's rejection of equality led him to attack, at home, all institutions of free government, from Parliament to a free press; in foreign and imperial policies his belief in inequality made him the advocate of imperialism over "inferior" races and peoples. He was not discriminating in his hatreds, and his mind seemed immensely spacious for hatreds of all sort: he hated the Irish, the Jews, the Negroes, the Latin peoples, and saw good only in the Teutonic and Anglo-Saxon peoples (of the United States he usually spoke with contempt). He conceived of the Teutons and Anglo-Saxons as the born master race destined to rule inferior breeds. As he became increasingly discouraged by the spread of suffrage and democracy in England, he looked to modern Germany as the sole remaining hope of the world. His mind had wandered to Germany, where he thought to have found his true spiritual home. In his biography of *Frederick the Great* he justified enthusiastically the conquests of the Prussian monarch, and also eulogized the trickery and wile that had accompanied them. The partition of Poland, to which Prussia was a party, elicited from Carlyle cynical approval of "Heaven's Justice."

Fearful of an expanding democracy and of social change, Carlyle was perhaps the first modern writer to develop a strategy of antidemocratic offensive, later more fully elaborated by Nazis and Fascists. Carlyle appealed to the "Captains of Industry" to become *leaders* and act like leaders, in union with the old landed aristocracy. He advised this antidemocratic group of leaders to build a well-armed, though numerically small, movement—sufficiently well armed to destroy the political institutions of an "anarchical" and disorganized majority. The "noble Few" would then establish a new order on hierarchical and militaristic lines, including the militaristic regimentation of labor.

The most interesting aspect of Carlyle's influence on social and political ideas is the fact that in England (where he had migrated from his native Scotland) it has been of little practical consequence, as viewed in the long-term perspective. His chief opponents, reformers like Bentham and Mill, changed the face of their country, whereas Carlyle always remained a lonely figure in England, admired by some and attacked by others—he did not continue a tradition in England that preceded him, nor did he establish a new school of thought which would carry on after his death. His work appeared like a meteor on the horizon in all its brilliance, but when the meteor hit the earth of England, its broken pieces were barren and lifeless. The important question, therefore, is not, was Carlyle British? The interesting question about Carlyle is not where he was born, and what language he wrote in, but where his influence was marked and widely felt. That country was Germany. In a real sense, Carlyle sent a lot of coal to Newcastle when his ideas, partly of German origin and all favorable to German ambitions for world power, were received by the Germans with real enthusiasm. A German selection from his works sold 300,000 copies in the years 1926-1932; under the Nazi regime, Carlyle was very much in vogue and widely read: his *On Heroes and Hero-worship* was compulsory reading in Nazi schools.

G. W. F. HEGEL

1. *Freedom in Nature and Society**

At the present time, the idea that freedom of thought, and of mind generally, evinces itself only in divergence from, indeed in hostility to, what is publicly recognized, might seem to be most firmly rooted in connection with the state, and it is chiefly for this reason that a philosophy of the state might

* From G. W. F. Hegel, *Philosophy of Law* (1821; translated by T. M. Knox as *Philosophy of Right*, Oxford University Press, 1942). By permission.

seem essentially to have the task of discovering and promulgating still an-other theory, and a special and original one at that. In examining this idea and the activity in conformity with it, we might suppose that no state or constitution had ever existed in the world at all or was even in being at the present time, but that nowadays—and this "nowadays" lasts for ever—we had to start all over again from the beginning, and that the ethical world had just been waiting for such present-day projects, proofs, and investigations. So far as nature is concerned, people grant that it is nature as it is which philosophy has to bring within its ken, that the philosopher's stone lies con-cealed somewhere, somewhere within nature itself, that nature is inherently rational and that what knowledge has to investigate and grasp in concepts is this actual reason in it; not the formations and accidents evident to the superficial observer, but nature's eternal harmony, its harmony however, in the sense of the law and essence immanent within it. The ethical world, on the other hand, the state (i.e. reason as it actualizes itself in the element of self-consciousness), is not allowed to enjoy the good fortune which springs from the fact that it is reason which has achieved power and mastery within that element and which maintains itself and has its home there. The universe of mind is supposed rather to be left to the mercy of chance and caprice, to be God-forsaken, and the result is that if the ethical world is Godless, truth lies outside it, and at the same time, since even so reason is supposed to be in it as well, truth becomes nothing but a problem. But it is this also that is to authorize, nay to oblige, every thinker to take his own road, though not in search of the philosopher's stone, for he is saved this search by the philoso-phizing of our contemporaries, and everyone nowadays is assured that he has this stone in his grasp as his birthright. Now admittedly it is the case that those who live their lives in the state as it actually exists here and now and find satisfaction there for their knowledge and volition (and of these there are many, more in fact than think or know it, because ultimately this is the position of everybody), or those at any rate who consciously find their satisfaction in the state, laugh at these operations and affirmations and regard them as an empty game, sometimes rather funny, sometimes rather serious, now amusing, now dangerous. Thus this restless activity of empty reflection, together with its popularity and the welcome it has received, would be a thing on its own, developing in privacy in its own way, were it not that it is philosophy itself which has earned all kinds of scorn and discredit by its indulgence in this occupation. The worst of these kinds of scorn is this, that, as I said just now, everyone is convinced that his mere birthright puts him in a position to pass judgment on philosophy in general and to condemn it. No other art or science is subjected to this last degree of scorn, to the sup position that we are masters of it without ado.

At the present time, the pettifoggery of caprice has usurped the name of philosophy and succeeded in giving a wide public the opinion that such triflings are philosophy. The result of this is that it has now become almost a disgrace to go on speaking in philosophical terms about the nature of the state, and law-abiding men cannot be blamed if they become impatient so soon as they hear mention of a philosophical science of the state. Still less is it a matter of surprise that governments have at last directed their attention to this kind of philosophy, since, apart from anything else, philosophy with us is not, as it was with the Greeks for instance, pursued in private like an art but has an existence in the open, in contact with the public, and especially, or even only, in the service of the state. Governments have proved their trust in their scholars who have made philosophy their chosen field by leaving entirely to them the construction and contents of philosophy—though here and there, if you like, it may not have been so much confidence that has been shown as indifference to learning itself, and professorial chairs of philosophy have been retained only as a tradition (in France, for instance, to the best of my knowledge, chairs of metaphysics at least have been allowed to lapse). Their confidence, however, has very often been ill repaid, or alternatively, if you preferred to see indifference, you would have to regard the result, the decay of thorough knowledge, as the penalty of this indifference. Prima facie, superficiality seems to be extremely accommodating, one might say, at least in relation to public peace and order, because it fails to touch or even to guess at the substance of the things; no action, or at least no police action, would thus have been taken against it in the first instance, had it not been that there still existed in the state a need for a deeper education and insight, a need which the state required philosophical science to satisfy. On the other hand, superficial thinking about the ethical order, about right and duty in general, starts automatically from the maxims which constitute superficiality in this sphere, i.e. from the principles of the Sophists which are so clearly outlined for our information in Plato. What is right these principles locate in subjective aims and opinions, in subjective feeling and particular conviction, and from them there follows the ruin of the inner ethical life and a good conscience, of love and right dealing between private persons, no less than the ruin of public order and the law of the land. The significance which such phenomena must acquire for government is not likely to suffer any diminution as a result of the pretentiousness which has used that very grant of confidence and the authority of a professorial chair to support the demand that the state should uphold and give scope to what corrupts the ultimate source of achievement, namely universal principles, and so even to the defiance of the state as if such defiance were what it deserved. "If God gives a man an office, he also gives him brains" is an old joke which in these days surely no one will take wholly in earnest.

What is rational is actual and what is actual is rational. On this conviction the plain man like the philosopher takes his stand, and from it philosophy starts in its study of the universe of mind as well as the universe of nature.

If reflection, feeling, or whatever form subjective consciousness may take, looks upon the present as something vacuous and looks beyond it with the eyes of superior wisdom, it finds itself in a vacuum, and because it is actual only in the present, it is itself mere vacuity. If on the other hand the Idea passes for "only an Idea," for something represented in an opinion, philosophy rejects such a view and shows that nothing is actual except the Idea. Once that is granted, the great thing is to apprehend in the show of the temporal and transient the substance which is immanent and the eternal which is present. For since rationality (which is synonomous with the Idea) enters upon external existence simultaneously with its actualization, it emerges with an infinite wealth of forms, shapes and appearances. Around its heart it throws a motley covering with which consciousness is at home to begin with, a covering which the concept has first to penetrate before it can find the inward pulse and feel it still beating in the outward appearances. But the infinite variety of circumstance which is developed in this externality by the light of the essence glinting in it—this endless material and its organization—this is not the subject matter of philosophy.

It is a fact that the ethical order is the system of these specific determinations of the Idea which constitutes its rationality. Hence the ethical order is freedom or the absolute will as what is objective, a circle of necessity whose moments are the ethical powers which regulate the life of individuals. To these powers individuals are related as accidents to substance, and it is in individuals that these powers are represented, have the shape of appearance, and become actualized.

The bond of duty can appear as a restriction only on indeterminate subjectivity or abstract freedom, and on the impulses either of the natural will or of the moral will which determines its indeterminate good arbitrarily. The truth is, however, that in duty the individual finds his liberation; first, liberation from dependence on mere natural impulse and from the depression which as a particular subject he cannot escape in his moral reflections on what ought to be and what might be; secondly, liberation from the indeterminate subjectivity which, never reaching reality or the objective determinacy of action, remains self-enclosed and devoid of actuality. In duty the individual acquires his substantive freedom.

Virtue is the ethical order reflected in the individual character so far as that character is determined by its natural endowment. When virtue displays itself solely as the individual's simple conformity with the duties of the station to which he belongs, it is rectitude.

But when individuals are simply identified with the actual order, ethical life (*das Sittliche*) appears as their general mode of conduct, i.e. as custom (*Sitte*), while the habitual practice of ethical living appears as a second nature which, put in the place of the initial, purely natural will, is the soul of custom permeating it through and through, the significance and the actuality of its existence. It is mind living and present as a world, and the substance of mind thus exists now for the first time as mind.

In this way the ethical substantial order has attained its right, and its right its validity. That is to say, the self-will of the individual has vanished together with his private conscience which had claimed independence and opposed itself to the ethical substance. For, when his character is ethical, he recognizes as the end which moves him to act the universal which is itself unmoved but is disclosed in its specific determinations as rationality actualized. He knows that his own dignity and the whole stability of his particular ends are grounded in this same universal, and it is therein that he actually attains these. Subjectivity is itself the absolute form and existent actuality of the substantial order and the distinction between subject on the one hand and substance on the other, as the object, end, and controlling power of the subject, is the same as, and has vanished directly along with, the distinction between them in form.

The state is the actuality of concrete freedom. But concrete freedom consists in this, that personal individuality and its particular interests not only achieve their complete development and gain explicit recognition for their right (as they do in the sphere of the family and civil society) but, for one thing, they also pass over of their own accord into the interest of the universal, and, for another thing, they know and will the universal; they even recognize it as their own substantive mind; they take it as their end and aim and are active in its pursuit. The result is that the universal does not prevail or achieve completion except along with particular interests and through the co-operation of particular knowing and willing; and individuals likewise do not live as private persons for their own ends alone, but in the very act of willing these they will the universal in the light of the universal and their activity is consciously aimed at none but the universal end. The principle of modern states has prodigious strength and depth because it allows the principle of subjectivity to progress to its culmination in the extreme of self-subsistent personal particularity, and yet at the same time brings it back to the substantive unity and so maintains this unity in the principle of subjectivity itself.

In contrast with the spheres of private rights and private welfare (the family and civil society), the state is from one point of view an external necessity and their higher authority; its nature is such that their laws and interests are subordinate to it and dependent on it. On the other hand, however, it is the end immanent within them, and its strength lies in the unity of its own universal end and aim with the particular interest of individuals, in the fact that individuals have duties to the state in proportion as they have rights against it.

To hold that every single person should share in deliberating and deciding on political matters of general concern on the ground that all individuals are members of the state, that its concerns are their concerns, and that it is their right that what is done should be done with their knowledge and volition, is tantamount to a proposal to put the democratic element without any rational form into the organism of the state, although it is only in virtue of the possession of such a form that the state is an organism at all. This idea comes readily to mind because it does not go beyond the abstraction of "being a member of the state," and it is superficial thinking which clings to abstractions. The rational consideration of a topic, the consciousness of the Idea, is concrete and to that extent coincides with a genuine practical sense. Such a sense is itself nothing but the sense of rationality on the Idea, though it is not to be confused with mere business routine or the horizon of a restricted sphere. The concrete state is the whole, articulated into its particular groups. The member of a state is a member of such a group, i.e. of a social class, and it is only as characterized in this objective way that he comes under consideration when we are dealing with the state. His mere character as universal implies that he is at one and the same time both a private person and also a thinking consciousness, a will which wills the universal. This consciousness and will, however, lose their emptiness and acquire a content and a living actuality only when they are filled with particularity, and particularity means determinacy as particular and a particular class-status; or, to put the matter otherwise, abstract individuality is a generic essence, but has its immanent universal actuality as the generic essence next higher in the scale. Hence the single person attains his actual and living destiny for universality only when he becomes a member of a Corporation, a society, &c., and thereby it becomes open to him on the strength of his skill, to enter any class for which he is qualified, the class of civil servants included.

Another presupposition of the idea that all should participate in the business of the state is that everyone is at home in this business—a ridiculous notion, however commonly we may hear it sponsored. Still, in public opinion a field is open to everyone where he can express his purely personal political opinions and make them count.

Since the laws and institutions of the ethical order make up the concept of freedom, they are the substance or universal essence of individuals, who are thus related to them as accidents only. Whether the individual exists or not is all one to the objective ethical order. It alone is permanent and is the power regulating the life of individuals. Thus the ethical order has been represented by mankind as eternal justice, as gods absolutely existent, in contrast with which the empty business of individuals is only a game of see-saw.

Duty is a restriction only on the self-will of subjectivity. It stands in the way only of that abstract good to which subjectivity adheres. When we say: "We want to be free," the primary meaning of the words is simply: "We want abstract freedom," and every institution and every organ of the state passes as a restriction on freedom of that kind. Thus duty is not a restriction on freedom, but only on freedom in the abstract, i.e. on unfreedom. Duty is the attainment of our essence, the winning of positive freedom.

The intrinsic worth of courage as a disposition of mind is to be found in the genuine, absolute, final end, the sovereignty of the state. The work of courage is to actualize this final end, and the means to this end is the sacrifice of personal actuality. This form of experience thus contains the harshness of extreme contradictions; a self-sacrifice which yet is the real existence of one's freedom; the maximum self-subsistence of individuality, yet only a cog playing its part in the mechanism of an external organization; absolute obedience, renunciation of personal opinions and reasonings, in fact complete *absence* of mind, coupled with the most intense and comprehensive *presence* of mind and decision in the moment of acting; the most hostile and so most personal action against individuals, coupled with an attitude of complete indifference or even liking towards them as individuals.

G. W. F. HEGEL

2. The State Divine*

Subjective volition—Passion—is that which sets men in activity, that which effects "practical" realization. The Idea is the inner spring of action; the State is the actually existing, realized moral life. For it is the Unity of the universal, essential Will, with that of the individual; and this is "Morality." The Individual living in this unity has a moral life; possesses a value that consists in this substantiality alone. Sophocles in his Antigone, says, "The divine commands are not of yesterday, nor of to-day; no, they have an infinite existence, and no one could say whence they came." The laws of morality are not accidental, but are the essentially Rational. It is the very object of the State that what is essential in the practical activity of men, and in their dispositions, should be duly recognized; that it should have a manifest existence, and maintain its position. It is the absolute interest of Reason that this moral Whole should exist; and herein lies the justification and merit of heroes who have founded states,—however rude these may have been. In the

* From G. W. F. Hegel, *Philosophy of History* (1837; translated by J. Sibree, Willey Book Co., 1900). Copyright, 1900, by The Colonial Press. By permission.

history of the World, only those peoples can come under our notice which form a state. For it must be understood that this latter is the realization of Freedom, i.e. of the absolute final aim, and that it exists for its own sake. It must further be understood that all the worth which the human being possesses—all spritual reality, he possesses only through the State. For his spiritual reality consists in this, that his own essence—Reason—is objectively present to him, that it possesses objective immediate existence for him. Thus only is he fully conscious; thus only is he a partaker of morality—of a just and moral social and political life. For Truth is the Unity of the universal and subjective Will; and the Universal is to be found in the State, in its laws, its universal and rational arrangements. The State is the Divine Idea as it exists on Earth. We have in it, therefore, the object of History in a more definite shape than before; that in which Freedom obtains objectivity, and lives in the enjoyment of this objectivity. For Law is the objectivity of Spirit; volition in its true form. Only that will which obeys law, is free; for it obeys itself—it is independent and so free. When the State or our country constitutes a community of existence; when the subjective will of man submits to laws,—the contradiction between Liberty and Necessity vanishes. The Rational has necessary existence, as being the reality and substance of things, and we are free in recognizing it as law, and following it as the substance of our own being. The objective and the subjective will are then reconciled, and present one identical homogeneous whole. For the morality (*Sittlichkeit*) of the State is not of that ethical (*moralische*) reflective kind, in which one's own conviction bears sway; this latter is rather the peculiarity of the modern time, while the true antique morality is based on the principle of abiding by one's duty (to the state at large). An Athenian citizen did what was required of him, as it were from instinct: but if I reflect on the object of my activity, I must have the consciousness that my will has been called into exercise. But morality is Duty—substantial Right—a "*second* nature" as it has been justly called; for the *first* nature of man is his primary merely animal existence.

The development *in extenso* of the Idea of the State belongs to the Philosophy of Jurisprudence; but it must be observed that in the theories of our time various errors are current respecting it, which pass for established truths, and have become fixed prejudices. We will mention only a few of them, giving prominence to such as have a reference to the object of our history.

The error which first meets us is the direct contradictory of our principle that the state presents the realization of Freedom; the opinion, viz., that man is free by *nature*, but that in *society*, in the State—to which nevertheless he is irresistibly impelled—he must limit this natural freedom. That man is free by Nature is quite correct in one sense; viz., that he is so according to the Idea of Humanity; but we imply thereby that he is such only in virtue of his destiny—that he has an undeveloped power to become such; for the

"Nature" of an object is exactly synonymous with its "Idea." But the view in question imports more than this. When man is spoken of as "free by Nature," the mode of his existence as well as his destiny is implied. His merely natural and primary condition is intended. In this sense a "state of Nature" is assumed in which mankind at large are in the possession of their natural rights with the unconstrained exercise and enjoyment of their freedom. This assumption is not indeed raised to the dignity of the historical fact; it would indeed be difficult, were the attempt seriously made, to point out any such condition as actually existing, or as having ever occurred. Examples of a savage state of life can be pointed out, but they are marked by brutal passions and deeds of violence; while, however rude and simple their conditions, they involve social arrangements which (to use the common phrase) *restrain* freedom. That assumption is one of those nebulous images which theory produces; an idea which it cannot avoid originating, but which it fathers upon real existence, without sufficient historical justification.

What we find such a state of Nature to be in actual experience, answers exactly to the Idea of a *merely* natural condition. Freedom as the *ideal* of that which is original and natural, does not exist *as original and natural*. Rather must it be first sought out and won; and that by an incalculable medial discipline of the intellectual and moral powers. The state of Nature is, therefore, predominantly that of injustice and violence, of untamed natural impulses, of inhuman deeds and feelings. Limitation is certainly produced by Society and the State, but it is a limitation of the mere brute emotions and rude instincts; as also, in a more advanced stage of culture, of the premeditated self-will of caprice and passion. This kind of constraint is part of the instrumentality by which only, the consciousness of Freedom and the desire for its attainment, in its true—that is Rational and Ideal form—can be obtained. To the Ideal of Freedom, Law and Morality are indispensably requisite; and they are in and for themselves, universal existences, objects and aims; which are discovered only by the activity of thought, separating itself from the merely sensuous, and developing itself, in opposition thereto; and which must, on the other hand, be introduced into and incorporated with the originally sensuous will, and that contrarily to its natural inclination. The perpetually recurring misapprehension of Freedom consists in regarding that term only in its *formal,* subjective sense, abstracted from its essential objects and aims; thus a constraint put upon impulse, desire, passion—pertaining to the particular individual as such—a limitation of caprice and self-will is regarded as a fettering of Freedom. We should on the contrary look upon such limitation as the indispensable proviso of emancipation. Society and the State are the very conditions in which Freedom is realized.

If the principle of regard for the individual will is recognized as the only basis of political liberty, viz., that nothing should be done by or for the State to which all the members of the body politic have not given their sanction, we have, properly speaking, no *Constitution*. The only arrangement that would be necessary, would be, first, a centre having no *will* of its own, but which should take into consideration what appeared to be the necessities of the State; and, secondly, a contrivance for calling the members of the State together, for taking the votes, and for performing the arithmetical operations of reckoning and comparing the number of votes for the different propositions, and thereby deciding upon them. The State is an *abstraction,* having even its generic existence in its citizens; but it is an actuality, and its simple generic existence must embody itself in individual will and activity. The want of government and political administration in general is felt; this necessitates the selection and separation from the rest of those who have to take the helm in political affairs, to decide concerning them, and to give orders to other citizens, with a view to the execution of their plans. If e.g. even the people in a Democracy resolve on a war, a general must head the army. It is only by a Constitution that the *abstraction*—the State—attains life and reality; but this involves the distinction between those who command and those who obey.—Yet obedience seems inconsistent with liberty, and those who command appear to do the very opposite of that which the fundamental idea of the State, viz. that of Freedom, requires. It is, however, urged that,—though the distinction between commanding and obeying is absolutely necessary, because affairs could not go on without it—and indeed this seems only a compulsory limitation, external to and even contravening freedom in the abstract—the constitution should be at least so framed, that the citizens may obey as little as possible, and the smallest modicum of free volition be left to the commands of the superiors;—that the substance of that for which subordination is necessary, even in its most important bearings, should be decided and resolved on by the People—by the will of many or of all the citizens; though it is supposed to be thereby provided that the State should be possessed of vigour and strength as a reality—an individual unity.—The primary consideration is, then, the distinction between the governing and the governed, and political constitutions in the abstract have been rightly divided into Monarchy, Aristocracy, and Democracy; which gives occasion, however, to the remark that Monarchy itself must be further divided into Despotism and Monarchy proper; that in all the divisions to which the leading Idea gives rise, only the generic character is to be made prominent,—it being not intended thereby that the particular category under review should be exhausted as a Form, Order, or Kind in its *concrete* development. But especially it must be observed, that the above-mentioned divisions admit of a multitude of particular modifications,—not only such as lie within the limits of those classes themselves,—but also such as are mixtures of several of these essentially distinct classes, and which are consequently misshapen, unstable, and inconsistent forms. In such a collision, the concerning question is, what is the *best constitution;* that is, by what arrangement, organization, or mechanism of the power of the State its object can be most surely attained. This object may indeed be variously understood; for instance, as the calm enjoyment of life on the part of the citizens, or as Universal Happiness. Such aims have suggested the so-called Ideals of Constitutions, and,—as a particular branch of the subject,—Ideals of the Education of Princes (Fénelon), or of the governing body—the aristocracy at large (Plato); for the chief point they treat of is the condition of those subjects who stand at the head of affairs; and in these Ideals the concrete details of political organization are not at all considered. The inquiry into the best constitution is frequently treated as if not only the theory were an affair of subjective independent conviction, but as if the introduction of a constitution recognized as the best,—or as superior to others,—could be the result of a resolve adopted in this theoretical manner; as if the form of a constitution were a matter of free choice, determined by nothing else but reflection. Of this artless fashion was that deliberation,—not indeed of the Persian *people,* but of the Persian *grandees,* who had conspired to overthrow the pseudo-Smerdis and the Magi, after their undertaking had succeeded, and when there was no scion of the royal family living,—as to what constitution they should introduce into Persia; and Herodotus gives an equally naive account of this deliberation.

In the present day, the Constitution of a country and people is not represented as so entirely dependent on free and deliberate choice. The fundamental but abstractly (and therefore imperfectly) entertained conception of Freedom, has resulted in the Republic being very generally regarded—in *theory*—as the only just and true political constitution. Many even, who occupy elevated official positions under monarchical constitutions—so far from being opposed to this idea—are actually its supporters; only they see that such a constitution, though the best, cannot be realized under all circumstances; and that—while men are what they are—we must be satisfied with less freedom; the monarchical constitution—under the given circumstances, and the present moral condition of the people—being even regarded as the most advantageous. In this view also, the necessity of a particular constitution is made to depend on the condition of the people in such a way as if the latter were non-essential and accidental. This representation is founded on the distinction which the reflective understanding makes between an idea and the corresponding reality; holding to an abstract and consequently untrue idea; not grasping it in its completeness, or—which is virtually, though not in point of form, the same,—not taking a concrete view of a people and a state. We shall have to show further on, that the constitution adopted by a people makes one substance—one spirit—with its religion, its art and philosophy, or, at least, with its conceptions and thoughts—its culture generally; not to expatiate upon the additional influences, *ab extra,* of climate, of neighbours, of its place in the World. A State is an individual totality, of which you cannot select any particular side, although a supremely important one, such as its political constitution; and deliberate and decide respecting it in that isolated form. Not only is that constitution most intimately connected with and dependent on those other spiritual forces; but the form of the entire moral and intellectual individuality—comprising all the forces it embodies—is only a step in the development of the grand Whole,—with its place preappointed in the process; a fact which gives the highest sanction to the constitution in question, and establishes its absolute necessity.—The origin of a state involves imperious lordship on the one hand, instinctive submission on the other. But even obedience—lordly power, and the fear inspired by a ruler— in itself implies some degree of voluntary connection. Even in barbarous states this is the case; it is not the isolated will of individuals that prevails; individual pretensions are relinquished, and the general will is the essential bond of political union. This unity of the general and the particular is the Idea itself, manifesting itself as a *state,* and which subsequently undergoes further development within itself. The abstract yet necessitated process in the development of truly independent states is as follows:—They begin with regal power, whether of patriarchal or military origin. In the next phase, particularity and individuality assert themselves in the form of Aristocracy and Democracy. Lastly, we have the subjection of these separate interests to a single power; but which can be absolutely none other than one outside of which those spheres have an independent position, viz. the Monarchical. Two phases of royalty, therefore, must be distinguished,—a primary and a secondary one. This process is necessitated, so that the form of government assigned to a particular stage of development *must* present itself: it is therefore no matter of choice, but is that form which is adapted to the spirit of the people.

In a Constitution the main feature of interest is the self development of the *rational,* that is, the *political* condition of a people; the setting free of the successive elements of the Idea: so that the several powers in the State manifest themselves as separate,—attain their appropriate and special perfection,— and yet in this independent condition, work together for one object, and are held together by it—i.e. form an organic whole. The State is thus the embodiment of rational freedom, realizing and recognizing itself in an objective form. For its objectivity consists in this,—that its successive stages are not merely ideal, but are present in an appropriate reality; and that in their separate and several workings, they are absolutely merged in that agency by which the totality—the soul—the individuate unity—is produced, and of which it is the result.

The State is the Idea of Spirit in the external manifestation of human Will and its Freedom. It is to the State, therefore, that change in the aspect of

History indissolubly attaches itself; and the successive phases of the Idea manifest themselves in it as distinct political *principles*. The Constitutions under which World-Historical peoples have reached their culmination, are peculiar to them; and therefore do not present a generally applicable political basis. Were it otherwise, the differences of similar constitutions would consist only in a peculiar method of expanding and developing that generic basis; whereas they really originate in diversity of principle. From the comparison therefore of the political institutions of the ancient World-Historical peoples, it so happens, that for the most recent principle of a Constitution—for the principle of our own times—nothing (so to speak) can be learned. In science and art it is quite otherwise; e.g., the ancient philosophy is so decidedly the basis of the modern, that it is inevitably contained in the latter, and constitutes its basis. In this case the relation is that of a continuous development of the same structure, whose foundation-stone, walls, and roof have remained what they were. In Art, the Greek itself, in its original form, furnishes us the best models. But in regard to political constitution, it is quite otherwise: here the Ancient and the Modern have not their essential principle in common. Abstract definitions and dogmas respecting just government—importing that intelligence and virtue ought to bear sway—are, indeed, common to both. But nothing is so absurd as to look to Greeks, Romans, or Orientals, for models for the political arrangements of our time. From the East may be derived beautiful pictures of a patriarchal condition, of paternal government, and of devotion to it on the part of peoples; from Greeks and Romans, descriptions of popular liberty. Among the latter we find the idea of a Free Constitution admitting all the citizens to a share in deliberations and resolves respecting the affairs and laws of the Commonwealth. In our times, too, this is its general acceptation; only with this modification, that—since our states are so large, and there are so many of "the Many," the latter,—direct action being impossible,—should by the indirect method of elective substitution express their concurrence with resolves affecting the common weal; that is, that for legislative purposes generally, the people should be represented by deputies. The so-called Representative Constitution is that form of government with which we connect the idea of a free constitution; and this notion has become a rooted prejudice. On this theory People and Government are separated. But there is a perversity in this antithesis; an ill-intentioned *ruse* designed to insinuate that the People are the totality of the State. Besides, the basis of this view is the principle of isolated individuality—the absolute validity of the subjective will—a dogma which we have already investigated. The great point is, that Freedom in its Ideal conception has not subjective will and caprice for its principle, but the recognition of the universal will; and that the process by which Freedom is realized is the free development of its successive stages. The subjective will is a merely formal determination—a *carte blanche*—not including what it is that is willed. Only the *rational* will is that universal principle which independently determines and unfolds its own being, and develops its successive elemental phases as organic members. Of this Gothic-cathedral architecture the ancients knew nothing.

G. W. F. HEGEL

3. Sovereignty: Monarchical or Popular?*

The state is the actuality of the ethical Idea. It is ethical mind *qua* the substantial will manifest and revealed to itself, knowing and thinking itself, accomplishing what it knows and in so far as it knows it. The state exists immediately in custom, mediately in individual self-consciousness, knowledge, and activity, while self-consciousness in virtue of its sentiment towards the state finds in the state, as its essence and the end and product of its activity, its substantive freedom.

The *Penates* are inward gods, gods of the underworld; the mind of a nation (Athens for instance) is the divine, knowing and willing itself. Family piety is feeling, ethical behaviour directed by feeling; political virtue is the willing of the absolute end in terms of thought.

The state is absolutely rational inasmuch as it is the actuality of the substantial will which it possesses in the particular self-consciousness once that consciousness has been raised to consciousness of its universality. This substantial unity is an absolute unmoved end in itself, in which freedom comes into its supreme right. On the other hand this final end has supreme right against the individual, whose supreme duty is to be a member of the state.

If the state is confused with civil society, and if its specific end is laid down as the security and protection of property and personal freedom, then the interest of the individuals as such becomes the ultimate end of their association, and it follows that membership of the state is something optional. But the state's relation to the individual is quite different from this. Since the state is mind objectified, it is only as one of its members that the individual himself has objectivity, genuine individuality, and an ethical life. Unification pure and simple is the true content and aim of the individual, and the individual's destiny is the living of a universal life. His further particular satisfaction, activity, and mode of conduct have this substantive and universally valid life as their starting point and their result.

* From G. W. F. Hegel, *Philosophy of Law* (1821; translated by T. M. Knox as *Philosophy of Right*, Oxford University Press, 1942). By permission.

Rationality, taken generally and in the abstract, consists in the thorough-going unity of the universal and the single. Rationality, concrete in the state, consists (*a*) so far as its content is concerned, in the unity of subjective free-dom (i.e. freedom of the universal or substantial will) and subjective freedom (i.e. freedom of everyone in his knowing and in his volition of particular ends); and consequently, (*b*) so far as its form is concerned, in self-determin-ing action on laws and principles which are thoughts and so universal. This Idea is the absolutely eternal and necessary being of mind.

Another question readily presents itself here: "Who is to frame the con-stitution?" This question seems clear, but closer inspection shows at once that it is meaningless, for it presupposes that there is no constitution there, but only an agglomeration of atomic individuals. How an agglomeration of individuals could acquire a constitution, whether automatically or by some-one's aid, whether as a present or by force or by thought, it would have to be allowed to settle for itself, since with an agglomeration the concept has nothing to do. But if the question presupposes an already existent consti-tution, then it is not about framing but only about altering the constitution, and the very presupposition of a constitution directly implies that its al-teration may come about only by constitutional means. In any case, however, it is absolutely essential that the constitution should not be regarded as some-thing made, even though it has come into being in time. It must be treated rather as something simply existent in and by itself, as divine therefore, and constant, and so as exalted above the sphere of things that are made.

The conception of the monarch is therefore of all conceptions the hardest for ratiocination, i.e. for the method of reflection employed by the Under-standing. This method refuses to move beyond isolated categories and hence here again knows only *raisonnement,* finite points of view, and de-ductive argumentation. Consequently it exhibits the dignity of the monarch as something deduced, not only in its form, but in its essence. The truth is, however, that to be something not deduced but purely self-originating is pre-cisely the conception of monarchy. Akin, then, to this reasoning is the idea of treating the monarch's right as grounded in the authority of God, since it is in its divinity that its unconditional character is contained. We are familiar, however, with the misunderstandings connected with this idea, and it is pre-cisely this "divine" element which it is the task of a philosophic treatment to comprehend.

We may speak of the "sovereignty of the people" in the sense that any peo-ple whatever is self-subsistent vis-à-vis other peoples, and constitutes a state of its own, like the British people for instance. But the peoples of England, Scotland, or Ireland, or the peoples of Venice, Genoa, Ceylon, &c., are not sovereign peoples at all now that they have ceased to have rulers or supreme governments of their own.

We may also speak of sovereignty in home affairs residing in the people, provided that we are speaking generally about the whole state and meaning only what was shown above, namely, that it is to the state that sovereignty belongs.

The usual sense, however, in which men have recently begun to speak of the "sovereignty of the people" is that it is something opposed to the sovereignty existent in the monarch. So opposed to the sovereignty of the monarch, the sovereignty of the people is one of the confused notions based on the wild idea of the "people." Taken without its monarch and the articulation of the whole which is the indispensable and direct concomitant of monarchy, the people is a formless mass and no longer a state. It lacks every one of those determinate characteristics—sovereignty, government, judges, magistrates, class-divisions, &c.,—which are to be found only in a whole which is inwardly organized. By the very emergence into a people's life of moments of this kind which have a bearing on an organization, on political life, a people ceases to be that indeterminate abstraction which, when represented in a quite general way, is called the "people."

At the stage of which constitutions are divided, as above mentioned, into democracy, aristocracy, and monarchy, the point of view taken is that of a still substantial unity, abiding in itself, without having yet embarked on its infinite differentiation and the plumbing of its own depths. At that stage, the moment of the final, self-determining, decision of the will does not come on the scene explicitly in its own proper actuality as an organic moment immanent in the state. Nonetheless, even in those comparatively immature constitutional forms, there must always be individuals at the head. Leaders must either be available already, as they are in monarchies of that type, or, as happens in aristocracies, but more particularly in democracies, they may rise to the top, as statesmen or generals, by chance and in accordance with the particular needs of the hour. This must happen, since everything done and everything actual is inaugurated and brought to completion by the single decisive act of a leader.

To define freedom of the press as freedom to say and write whatever we please is parallel to the assertion that freedom as such means freedom to do as we please. Talk of this kind is due to wholly uneducated, crude, and superficial ideas. Moreover, it is in the very nature of the thing that abstract thinking should nowhere be so stubborn, so unintelligent, as in this matter of free speech, because what it is considering is the most fleeting, the most contingent, and the most personal side of opinion in its infinite diversity of content and tergiversation. Beyond the direct incitation to theft, murder, rebellion, &c., there lies its artfully constructed expression—an expression which seems in itself quite general and vague, while all the time it conceals a meaning anything but vague or else is compatible with inferences which are not actually expressed, and it is impossible to determine whether they rightly follow from it, or whether they were meant to be inferred from it. This vagueness of matter and form precludes laws on these topics from attaining the requisite determinacy of law, and since the trespass, wrong, and injury here are so extremely personal and subjective in form, judgment on them is reduced equally to a wholly subjective verdict. Such an injury is directed against the thoughts, opinions, and wills of others, but apart from that, these form the element in which alone it is actually anything. But this element is the sphere of the freedom of others, and it therefore depends on them whether the injurious expression of opinion is or is not actually an effective act.

Laws then may be criticized by exhibiting their indeterminacy as well as by arguing that they leave it open to the speaker or writer to devise turns of phrase or tricks of expression, and so evade the laws or claim that judicial decisions are mere subjective verdicts. Further, however, against the view that the expression of opinion is an act with injurious effects, it may be maintained that it is not an act at all, but only opining and thinking, or only talking. And so we have before us a claim that mere opining and talking is to go unpunished because it is of a purely subjective character both in form and content, because it does not mean anything and is of no importance. And yet in the same breath we have the claim that this same opining and talking should be held in high esteem and respect—the opining because it is personal property and in fact pre-eminently the property of mind; the talking because it is only this same property being expressed and used.

But the substance of the matter is and remains that traducing the honour of anyone, slander, abuse, the contemptuous caricature of government, its ministers, officials, and in particular the person of the monarch, defiance of the laws, incitement to rebellion, &c., &c., are all crimes or misdemeanours in one or other of their numerous gradations. The rather high degree of indeterminability which such actions acquire on account of the element in which they are expressed does not annul this fundamental character of theirs. Its only effect is that the subjective field in which they are committed also determines the nature and form of the reaction to the offence. It is the field in which the offence was committed which itself necessitates subjectivity of view, contingency, &c., in the reaction to the offence, whether the reaction takes the form of punishment proper or of police action to prevent crimes. Here, as always, abstract thinking sets itself to explain away the fundamental and concrete nature of the thing by concentrating on isolated aspects of its external appearance and on abstractions drawn therefrom.

The sciences, however, are not to be found anywhere in the field of opinion and subjective views, provided of course that they be sciences in other respects. Their exposition is not a matter of clever turns of phrases, allusiveness, half-utterances, and semi-reticences, but consists in the unambiguous, determinate, and open expression of their meaning and purport. It follows that they do not fall under the category of public opinion. Apart from this, however, as I said just now, the element in which views and their expression become actions in the full sense and exist effectively, consists of the intelligence, principles, and opinions of others. Hence this aspect of these actions, i.e. their effectiveness proper and their danger to individuals, society, and the state, depends on the character of the ground on which they fall, just as a spark falling on a heap of gunpowder is more dangerous than if it falls on hard ground where it vanishes without trace. Thus, just as the right of science to express itself depends on and is safeguarded by its subject-matter and content, so an illegitimate expression may also acquire a measure of security, or at least sufferance, in the scorn which it has brought upon itself. An offence of this sort is punishable on its own account too, but part of it may be accounted that kind of nemesis which inner impotence, feeling itself oppressed by the preponderating abilities and virtues of others, is impelled to vent in order to come to itself again in face of such superiority, and to restore some self-consciousness to its own nullity. It was a nemesis of a more harmless type which Roman soldiers vented against their generals when they sang scurrilous songs about them in triumphal processions in order to get even with them for all the hard service and discipline they had undergone, and especially for the omission of their names from the triumphal honours. The former type of nemesis, the bad and hateful type, is deprived of its effect by being treated with scorn, and hence, like the public, which perhaps forms a circle of spectators of scurrility, it is restricted to futile malice and to the self-condemnation which it implicitly contains.

HEINRICH VON TREITSCHKE

4. Individualism, Democracy, and the State*

The individual should feel himself a member of his State, and as such have courage to take its errors upon him. There must be no question of subjects having the right to oppose a sovereignty which in their opinion is not

* From Heinrich von Treitschke, Politics. (1897-1898; translated by B. Dugdale and T. de Bille, 1916). By permission of The Macmillan Company, publishers.

moral. Cases may arise when the State's action touches the foundation of the moral life, namely, religious feeling. When the Huguenots in France had their religion proscribed, and were commanded to worship their God under forms which their deepest conviction held to be unchristian, conscience drove them out from their fatherland, but we must not praise the fine temper of these martyrs for religion from the standpoint of the theologian without recognizing the degree of tragic guilt which is always blended with such moral compulsion. The Huguenots who left their homes were gallant men, no doubt, but each of them had a bitter conflict to fight out within himself before he placed his love for the Heidelberg Catechism above his hereditary love for his country and his king. In modern times there have been Radical parties who have in their vanity imagined themselves faced with a similar struggle, which had in fact only a subjective existence in their own exalted imagination. This was the reason why a number of the German-Americans forsook their fatherland. It is foolish to admire them for this. We must always maintain the principle that the State is in itself an ethical force and a high moral good.

A decision by the majority is only based on reason when the question at issue concerns the development of a real power, and the expression of a Will. In a Democracy supremacy is derived solely from the people, therefore its decisions must bow to the will of the people, which can only be ascertained by the voice of the majority. The presumption is that the will of the majority could be enforced by violence in the last resort, consequently the majority decides, as representing physical force. This is the true foundation of its dominion, let democratic idealists say what they like; the will of the majority is the strongest, and for this reason men give it the sanction of law. Every unprejudiced historian will admit that it is the only reasonable system by which a State can proceed upon democratic lines, but we need not delude ourselves into the idea that there is anything inherently reasonable or ideal in a set of circumstances in which the final constitutional authority is not self-derived. There can be absolutely no question of government by the majority being in itself either reasonable or just. We must envisage these matters only *in concreto*. When the Committee of Public Safety sent people to the guillotine just as they chose in the name of the majority of the French nation, they were just as much tyrants as Philip II of Spain had been. It made no difference to the victims in whose name their heads fell into the basket, for the one slavery was as good as the other.

The rule of the majority, then, which is a necessary adjunct of Democracy, is most certainly no security for political liberty. Each citizen is given the right to make his voice heard in the national decisions, but if he does not go with the majority he must just put up with it, and hope that his turn will come some day. "One half of freedom is alternately to rule and to be ruled," as Aristotle said long ago. He is here describing political liberty, and this conception of it finds no guarantee of fulfilment in government by a majority.

When we turn to the social liberty which forms the other half of freedom, we do not find a Democracy affording it any particular security either. "To live according to our own sweet will" may be possible in a Democracy, but it cannot by any means certainly be so. The idea of the State was so predominant in the Democracies of antiquity that the individual citizen was accorded absolutely no freedom of action, but was early taken under the discipline of the State, to whose brilliancy and greatness all other considerations had to give way. Sharp indeed is the contrast between this and the modern Democracy, which as we know it, seems particularly created for an economic age like our own, which thinks only of getting on by every means it can, and lives in the illusion that the heights of civilization can be reached by telephones and telegraphs. Modern Democracy sets absolutely no restraints upon the commercial intercourse between citizens. Life in the United States is a terribly hard school, in which many perish altogether, but there is absolute freedom of action in every direction, and in this lies the secret of the singular charm which this State possesses for the average man of the present day.

The political temper of a truly ruling Demos is a very remarkable study. It is clear that it must totally lack certain finer attributes of political intelligence, and more especially the gift of foresight, which is simply absent from popular government. This applies particularly to its foreign policy, a sphere in which it must always act from a very limited range of vision. *L'esprit d'escalier* is a pre-eminently democratic characteristic. Besides this there is a singular contradiction which always makes itself felt in the inner nature of a governing Demos. On the one hand we see that terrible demoniacal and base passion—envy, which plays an immeasurably important part in the life of a Democracy. No doubt if the inner heart of Germany stood revealed it would seem to have reached gigantic strength even there, as was proved by the treatment that Bismarck received. Now that he has fallen he is beginning once more to find theoretic admirers among his ancient enemies, because he has come down to their level—or so it seems. They find an intense pleasure in the thought.[1] In their institution of ostracism the Athenians had absolutely set up a public means of gratifying this passion, which they turned into a legal weapon.

The Presidents of the United States, with a few exceptions, have never been men of great ability, because these are not of the stuff to make head

' Lecture delivered in February, 1893.

against the flood of slander which envy lets loose over them. There will always be natures of too rare a quality for the common herd to understand; for this reason Goethe will never be as popular an author as Schiller. In the early days of the North American Republic Alexander Hamilton was the most remarkable figure, more so in fact than Washington, yet the populace regarded him as the proverbial dog looked upon the glass of wine. He aroused the same sentiments as William Humboldt did at the Confederate Diet at Frankfurt, for he gave people the uncomfortable feeling that they did not understand him.

In strange contrast with this thoroughly democratic passion of envy, every noble-minded and independent nation will evince a capacity for hero-worship in times of excitement, until it may absolutely deify some individual great man. It becomes evident at such moments that the people really have an instinct which recognizes outstanding greatness. It is impossible to decide theoretically when it will display itself, for greatness alone is not the deciding factor. It must be admitted that Bismarck has never really been beloved by the mass of the nation, for only the educated classes have properly grasped the unique greatness of the man. Pericles, on the other hand, although his character was essentially lofty, attained through his marvellous gift of eloquence to such an influence over the Athenian people that Thucydides could say of him, "He was not so much led by the people as himself their leader." For a time he ruled Athens like a king, and marvellous indeed were the home-truths which he told that Demos to their faces, for there was no trace of the flatterer in him.

This phenomenon of hero-worship appears from time to time in every Democracy. It explains the alliance of the populace with the Barcidae in Carthage and with the House of Orange in the Netherlands. We meet it again in the United States, when Washington had to thrust from him the honours which were offered him. His example did much to establish democratic institutions firmly in his country, but so great did his fame become, and so devotedly was he worshipped, that he had great difficulty in waving aside the homage that was done him. Later on General Jackson, the "Publicola," held a similar position for a brief period. He was a thoroughly coarse-natured man, but he was the conqueror of Texas, and his commercial policy was very much in accord with popular taste. Under him the State was perilously near to becoming a dictatorship, although in the end the good sense of the nation gained the upper hand. Later on, the reverence of the masses for President Lincoln rose to such a pitch that he could perfectly well have attained to kingly power among them had he so willed it. But he was of the same stamp as Washington, and he remained a convinced adherent of democratic government. In spite of all these instances the danger of a dictatorship is as constantly present in a democratic Republic as in an aristocratic one, although it is no doubt most of all to be expected in Republics without republicans, as France, with her two Napoleons, has proved to us. Thus we find Democracies swayed by curiously contradictory elements; on the one hand envy, on the other a popular delight in great heroic figures.

Where the foundation of slavery is lacking, that is to say in all modern Democracies, one may expect to find a dominant note of political mediocrity. Really striking and distinguished qualities are less comprehensible by the masses, and we may look in vain to see Art and Science encouraged by modern Democracy, which has never known a second Florence. Switzerland is a type of this form of government in our own day. There we see national schools and public health encouraged with praiseworthy eagerness, but the establishment even of polytechnics has been attended with the greatest difficulties, for the Swiss nation could not be brought to realize the usefulness of these institutions. Neither have universities ever been able to take much hold in Switzerland. They are the home of an aristocratic form of culture, and the natural inclination of a Democracy is to extend a modicum of education and prosperity over the widest possible circle, without any desire to exceed this standard.

ERNST TROELTSCH

5. German and Western Conceptions of Freedom*

The German idea of freedom possesses its own characteristic traits. Undoubtedly it has been affected by French and English ideas of liberty. Locke and Rousseau have influenced theory, whereas the English constitution and self-government and the French Revolution have been of tremendous practical impact. However, these ideas have been thoroughly transformed in the real core of German development, in the institutions which go back to Baron von Stein, Scharnhorst and Boyen, and in the philosophical, idealistic interpretation of state and history from Kant, Fichte and Hegel to the contemporary philosophical idealists. Here, too, liberty is the key word, but this liberty has its own meaning, determined by German history and the German spirit.

* From Ernst Troeltsch, "The German Idea of Freedom" (1916), reprinted in *Deutscher Geist und Westeuropa* (J. C. B. Mohr, 1925). Translated by William Ebenstein.

Liberty as creative participation in the formation of state authority means to us, not the bringing forth of governmental will out of individual wills, not control of the mandatory by the principal, but the free, conscious and dutiful dedication of oneself to the whole, as it has been molded by history, state and nation. The whole as the expression and incarnation of collectivity is to be willed freely and always re-create anew in personal activity. Thus, prince and officials consider themselves as the first servants of the state, and citizens think of themselves as members of the state. They are all organs of the one sovereign whole which they bring forth anew in ceaseless self-devotion. Liberty consists more in duties than in rights, or, rather, in rights which are simultaneously duties. The individuals do not compose the whole, but identify themselves with it. Liberty is not equality, but service of the individual in his station organically due to him. In this, lie the dignity and active participation of the individual, but also his restraint, and all modern achievements of national unity, equality before the law, parliaments and universal military service, are molded by this spirit. This is the "state mysticism" (*Staatsmystik*) which our great thinkers and historians have felt in common with Plato. It has been rejected as philosophically meaningless by Bishop Welldon and his English nominalism, and it has been defined as immoral by the English ideal of independence. But Hegel saw in it the philosophy of freedom, and it has become evident, more or less consciously, more or less coherently, in all great German creations of the century. As everything in this world, this "state mysticism" has its dangers, and can obviously degenerate in face of fear of responsibility and bureaucratic rule of officials. But where its most characteristic nerve is alive in autonomous, dutiful, self-dedication and participation combined with vigilance and responsibility, it leads to a joining of initiative with devotion, pride with discipline, creative energy with public spiritedness and sacrifice. This spirit has created all that is great in the past German century, it characterizes two expressions of life so contrary to one another as the German army and the socialist party. It has also absorbed, and digested, Bismarck's realism, whose sentiment of state and liberty, as distinct from his heroic genius, was of the same color.

It is not difficult to understand how it all came about. The German states of the seventeenth century, Catholic or Lutheran, were a world of paternalistic government and the police state, of obedience and devotion on the part of loyal subjects, who saw in the state the expression of divine order. When the spirit of the West invaded that world, it encountered an impulse of liberty developing out of German life itself: the result was the enlightened absolutism in the manner of Frederick the Great, who looked upon rule, office, and army as a servant of the whole community, and who considered such service a moral duty.

THOMAS CARLYLE

6. Democracy Is Forever Impossible*

Alas, on this side of the Atlantic and on that, Democracy, we apprehend, is forever impossible! So much, with certainty of loud astonished contradiction from all manner of men at present, but with sure appeal to the Law of Nature and the ever-abiding Fact, may be suggested and asserted once more. The Universe itself is a Monarchy and Hierarchy; large liberty of "voting" there, all manner of choice, utmost free-will, but with conditions inexorable and immeasurable annexed to every exercise of the same. A most free commonwealth of "voters"; but with Eternal Justice to preside over it, Eternal Justice enforced by Almighty Power! This is the model of "constitutions"; this: nor in any Nation where there has not yet (in some supportable and withal some constantly-increasing degree) been confided to the *Noblest,* with his select series of *Nobler,* the divine everlasting duty of directing and controlling the Ignoble, has the "Kingdom of God," which we all pray for, "come," nor can "His will" even *tend* to be "done on Earth as it is in Heaven" till then. My Christian friends, and indeed my Sham-Christian and Anti-Christian, and all manner of men, are invited to reflect on this. They will find it to be the truth of the case. The Noble in the high place, the Ignoble in the low; that is, in all times and in all countries, the Almighty Maker's Law.

To raise the Sham-Noblest, and solemnly consecrate *him* by whatever method, new-devised, or slavishly adhered to from old wont, this, little as we may regard it, is, in all times and countries, a practical blasphemy, and Nature will in no wise forget it. Alas, there lies the origin, the fatal necessity, of modern Democracy everywhere. It is the Noblest, not the Sham-Noblest; it is God-Almighty's Noble, not the Court-Tailor's Noble, nor the Able-Editor's Noble, that must in some approximate degree, be raised to the supreme place; he and not a counterfeit,—under penalties! Penalties deep as death, and at length terrible as hell-on-earth, my constitutional friend! —Will the ballot-box raise the Noblest to the chief place; does any sane man deliberately believe such a thing? That nevertheless is the indispensable result, attain it how we may: if that is attained, all is attained; if not that,

* From Thomas Carlyle, *Latter-Day Pamphlets* (1850).

nothing. He that cannot believe the ballot-box to be attaining it, will be comparatively indifferent to the ballot-box. Excellent for keeping the ship's crew at peace under their Phantasm Captain; but unserviceable, under such, for getting round Cape Horn. Alas, that there should be human beings requiring to have these things argued of, at this late time of day!

I say, it is the everlasting privilege of the foolish to be governed by the wise; to be guided in the right path by those who know it better than they. This is the first "right of man"; compared with which all other rights are as nothing, —mere superfluities, corollaries which will follow of their own accord out of this; if they be not contradictions to this, and less than nothing! To the wise it is not a privilege; far other indeed. Doubtless, as bringing preservation to their country, it implies preservation of themselves withal; but intrinsically it is the harshest duty a wise man, if he be indeed wise, has laid to his hand. A duty which he would fain enough shirk; which accordingly, in these sad times of doubt and cowardly sloth, he has long everywhere been endeavouring to reduce to its minimum, and has in fact in most cases nearly escaped altogether. It is an ungoverned world; a world which we flatter ourselves will henceforth need no governing. On the dust of our heroic ancestors we too sit ballot-boxing, saying to one another, It is well, it is well! By inheritance of their noble struggles, we have been permitted to sit slothful so long. By noble toil, not by shallow laughter and vain talk, they made this English Existence from a savage forest into an arable inhabitable field for us; and we, idly dreaming it would grow spontaneous crops forever,— find it now in a too questionable state; peremptorily requiring real labour and agriculture again. Real "agriculture" is not pleasant; much pleasanter to reap and winnow (with ballot-box or otherwise) than to plough!

Who would govern that can get along without governing? He that is fittest for it, is of all men the unwillingest unless constrained. By multifarious devices we have been endeavouring to dispense with governing; and by very superficial speculations, of *laissez-faire,* supply-and-demand, &c. &c. to persuade ourselves that it is best so. The Real Captain, unless it be some Captain of mechanical Industry hired by Mammon, where is he in these days? Most likely, in silence, in sad isolation somewhere, in remote obscurity; trying if, in an evil ungoverned time, he cannot at least govern himself. The Real Captain undiscoverable; the Phantasm Captain everywhere very conspicuous:—it is thought Phantasm Captains, aided by ballot-boxes, are the true method, after all. They are much the pleasantest for the time being! And so no *Dux* or Duke of any sort, in any province of our affairs, now *leads:* the Duke's Bailiff *leads,* what little leading is required for getting-in the rents; and the Duke merely rides in the state-coach. It is everywhere so: and now at last we see a world all rushing towards strange consummations, because it is and has long been so!

THOMAS CARLYLE

7. *"Give Me a Leader"**

Democracy, we are well aware, what is called "self-government" of the multitude by the multitude, is in words the thing everywhere passionately clamoured for at present. Democracy makes rapid progress in these latter times, and ever more rapid, in a perilous accelerative ration; towards democracy, and that only, the progress of things is everywhere tending as to the final goal and winning-post. So think, so clamour the multitudes everywhere. And yet all men may see, whose sight is good for much, that in democracy can lie no finality; that with the completest winning of democracy there is nothing yet won,—except emptiness, and the free chance to win! Democracy is by the nature of it, a self-cancelling business: and gives in the long-run a net-result of *zero*. Where no government is wanted, save that of the parish-constable, as in America with its boundless soil, every man being able to find work and recompense for himself, democracy may subsist; not elsewhere, except briefly, as a swift transition towards something other and farther. Democracy never yet, that we heard of, was able to accomplish much work, beyond that same cancelling of itself. Rome and Athens are themes for the schools; unexceptionable for that purpose. In Rome and Athens, as elsewhere, if we look practically, we shall find that it was not by loud voting and debating of many, but by wise insight and ordering of a few that the work was done. So is it ever, so will it ever be. The French Convention was a Parliament elected "by the five points," with ballot-boxes, universal suffrages, and what not, as perfectly as Parliament can hope to be in this world; and had indeed a pretty spell of work to do and did it. The French Convention had to cease from being a free Parliament, and become more arbitrary than any Sultan Bajazet, before it could so much as subsist. It had to purge out its argumentative Girondins, elect its Supreme Committee of *Salut,* guillotine into silence and extinction all that gainsayed it, and rule and work literally by the sternest despotism ever seen in Europe, before it could rule at all. Napoleon was not president of a republic; Cromwell tried hard to rule in that way, but found that he could not. These, "the armed soldiers of democracy," had to chain democracy under their feet, and

* From Thomas Carlyle, *Chartism* (1840).

become despots over it, before they could work out the earnest obscure purpose of democracy itself! Democracy, take it where you will in our Europe,
is found but as a regulated method of rebellion and abrogation; it abrogates
the old arrangement of things; and leaves, as we say, *zero* and vacuity for
the institution of a new arrangement. It is the consummation of No-
government and *Laissez-faire*. It may be natural for our Europe at present;
but cannot be the ultimatum of it. Not towards the impossibility, "self-
government" of a multitude by a multitude; but towards some possibility,
government by the wisest, does bewildered Europe struggle. The blessedest
possibility: not misgovernment, not *Laissez-faire,* but veritable government!
Cannot one discern too, across all democratic turbulence, clattering of
ballot-boxes and infinite sorrowful jangle, needful or not, that this at bottom
is the wish and prayer of all human hearts, everywhere and at all times:
"Give me a leader; a true leader, not a false sham-leader; a true leader, that
he may guide me on the true way, that I may be loyal to him, that I may
swear fealty to him and follow him, and feel that it is well with me!" The
relation of the taught to their teacher, of the loyal subject to his guiding king,
is, under one shape or another, the vital element of human Society; indispensable to it, perennial in it; without which, as a body left of its soul, it
falls down into death, and with horrid noisome dissolution passes away and
disappears.

THOMAS CARLYLE

8. *Prophet of Fascism*＊

We come now to the last form of Heroism; that which we call Kingship.
The Commander over men; he to whose will our wills are to be subordinated, and loyally surrender themselves, and find their welfare in doing so,
may be reckoned the most important of Great Men. He is practically the
summary for us of *all* the various figures of Heroism; Priest, Teacher, whatsoever of earthly or of spiritual dignity we can fancy to reside in a man, embodies itself here, to *command* over us, to furnish us with constant practical
teaching, to tell us for the day and hour what we are to *do*. He is called
Rex, Regulator, *Roi:* our own name is still better; King, *Könning,* which
means *Can*-ning, Able-man.

Numerous considerations, pointing towards deep, questionable, and indeed unfathomable regions, present themselves here: on the most of which

＊ From Thomas Carlyle, *On Heroes, Hero-Worship and the Heroic in History* (1840).

we must resolutely for the present forbear to speak at all. As Burke said that perhaps fair *Trial by Jury* was the Soul of Government, and that all legislation, administration, parliamentary debating, and the rest of it, went on, in "order to bring twelve impartial men into a jury-box";—so, by much stronger reason, may I say here, that the finding of your *Ableman* and getting him invested with the *symbols of ability,* with dignity, worship (*worth*-ship) royalty, kinghood, or whatever we call it, so that *he* may actually have room to guide according to his faculty of doing it,—is the business, well or ill accomplished, of all social procedure whatsoever in this world! Hustings-speeches, Parliamentary motions, Reform Bills, French Revolutions, all mean at heart this; or else nothing. Find in any country the Ablest Man that exists there; raise *him* to the supreme place, and loyally reverence him: you have a perfect government for that country; no ballot-box, parliamentary eloquence, voting, constitution-building, or other machinery whatsoever can improve it a whit. It is in the perfect state: an ideal country. The Ablest Man; he means also the truest-hearted, justest, the Noblest Man: what he *tells us to do* must be precisely the wisest, fittest, that we could anywhere or anyhow learn;—the thing which it will in all ways behove us, with right loyal thankfulness, and nothing doubting, to do! Our *doing* and life were then, so far as government could regulate it, well regulated; that were the ideal of constitutions.

Alas, we know very well that Ideals can never be completely embodied in practice. Ideals must ever lie a very great way off; and we will right thankfully content ourselves with any not intolerable approximation thereto! Let no man, as Schiller says, too querulously "measure by a scale of perfection the meagre product of reality" in this poor world of ours. We will esteem him no wise man; we will esteem him a sickly, discontented, foolish man. And yet, on the other hand, it is never to be forgotten that Ideals do exist; that if they be not approximated to at all, the whole matter goes to wreck! Infallibly. No bricklayer builds a wall *perfectly* perpendicular, mathematically this is not possible; a certain degree of perpendicularity suffices him; and he, like a good bricklayer, who must have done with his job, leaves it so. And yet if he sway *too much* from the perpendicular; above all, if he throw plummet and level quite away from him, and pile brick on brick heedless, just as it comes to hand—! Such bricklayer, I think, is in a bad way. *He* has forgotten himself: but the Law of Gravitation does not forget to act on him; he and his wall rush-down into confused welter of ruin!——

This is the history of all rebellions, French Revolutions, social explosions in ancient or modern times. You have put the too *Un*able man at the head of affairs! The too ignoble, unvaliant, fatuous man. You have forgotten that there is any rule, or natural necessity whatever, of putting the Able Man there. Brick must lie on brick as it may and can. Unable Simulacrum of Ability, *quack,* in a word, must adjust himself with quack, in all manner of administration of human things;—which accordingly lie unadministered, fermenting into unmeasured masses of failure, of indigent misery: in the outward, and in the inward or spiritual, miserable millions stretch-out the hand for their due supply, and it is not there. The "law of gravitation" acts; Nature's laws do none of them forget to act. The miserable millions burst forth into Sansculottism, or some other sort of madness; bricks and brick-layers lie as fatal chaos!——

Much sorry stuff, written some hundred years ago or more, about the "Divine right of Kings," moulders unread now in the Public Libraries of this country. Far be it from us to disturb the calm process by which it is disappearing harmlessly from the earth, in those repositories! At the same time, not to let the immense rubbish go without leaving us, as it ought, some soul of it behind—I will say that it did mean something; something true, which it is important for us and all men to keep in mind. To assert that in whatever man you chose to lay hold of (by this or the other plan of clutch-ing at him); and clapt a round piece of metal on the head of, and called King,—there straightway came to reside a divine virtue, so that *he* became a kind of God, and a Divinity inspired him with faculty and right to rule over you to all lengths: this,—what can we do with this but leave it to rot silently in the Public Libraries? But I will say withal, and that is what these Divine-right men meant, That in Kings, and in all human Authorities, and relations that men god-created can form among each other, there is verily either a Divine Right or else a Diabolic Wrong; one or the other of these two! For it is false altogether, what the last Sceptical Century taught us, that this world is a steam engine. There is a God in this world; and a God's-sanction, or else the violation of such, does look-out from all ruling and obedience, from all moral-acts of men. There is no act more moral between men than that of rule and obedience. Woe to him that claims obedience when it is not due; woe to him that refuses it when it is! God's law is in that, I say, however the Parchment-laws may run: there is a Divine Right or else a Diabolic Wrong at the heart of every claim that one man makes upon another.

It can do none of us harm to reflect on this: in all the relations of life it will concern us; in Loyalty and Royalty, the highest of these. I esteem the modern error, That all goes by self-interest, and the checking and balancing of greedy knaveries, and that, in short, there is nothing divine whatever in the associa-tion of men, a still more despicable error, natural as it is to an unbelieving century, than that of a "divine right" in people *called* Kings. I say, Find me the true *Könning*, King, or Able-man, and he *has* a divine right over me. That we knew in some tolerable measure how to find him, and that all men were ready to acknowledge his divine right when found: this is precisely the healing which a sick world is every-where, in these ages, seeking after! The true King, as guide of the practical, has ever something of the Pontiff in him,—guide of the spiritual, from which all practice has its rise. This too is a true saying, That the *King* is head of the *Church*.—But we will leave the Polemic stuff of a dead century to lie quiet on its bookshelves.

Chapter VIII

FASCISM: GOVERNMENT BY FORCE AND LIES

Fascism is the twentieth-century version of age-old tendencies in politics. Like democracy, it is a universal phenomenon, and, like democracy, it is firmly entrenched in the national tradition of some countries, and only an ephemeral phenomenon in others. Unlike the authoritarian absolutism of the seventeenth and eighteenth centuries, Fascism is a *post-democratic* phenomenon in politics, and it cannot be understood save as a reaction to democracy. The use of popular organizations and mass activities is one of the distinguishing features of Fascism, and it has learned from democracy the value of popular support for national policies. From socialism Fascism borrowed enough anticapitalist slogans and catchwords to attract a section of the working classes. Scientifically organized propaganda and terror was another characteristic of the fascist state. Depressing as Fascism must appear to adherents of the democratic ideal, it should be borne in mind that Fascism succeeded to power between the two world wars only in those countries in which democracy had never been firmly established, or in which it was virtually unknown. Conversely, where democracy had led a healthy life before 1914, Fascism was weak and ineffective in the nineteen twenties and thirties.

The spirit of German political nihilism is faithfully reflected in Carl Schmitt's article on "The Concept of 'The Political,'" published in 1927 in *Archiv für Sozialwissenschaft und Sozialpolitik*. This essay (never before translated into English) was later expanded by Schmitt into a book, and became one of the most widely read and quoted political works in Germany in the Nazi era. Schmitt was undoubtedly one of the two or three ablest German political scientists of the twentieth century. His brilliance was surpassed only by his lack of character: in 1919 Schmitt was a near Communist; later, he ran through the gamut of all major German political parties. From communism he "evolved" into a Social Democrat, Democrat, Catholic Centrist, German Nationalist, and, finally, a full-fledged Nazi. Schmitt's definition of the *friend-enemy* contrast as the peculiar and specific criterion of the realm of politics gave the German militarists and Nazis the philosophical clothing with which to cover up the vacuity of ethical nihilism. Schmitt even denies that the liberal theory of the state, which seeks to "tame" government through ethical rules and such techniques as checks and balances and separation of powers, is a political theory at all. Politics begins and ends with the possibility of an enemy—and his total annihilation. This conception of politics is extended by Schmitt from the domestic to the international scene in which states face each other all the time as implacable enemies, to be eventually destroyed.

Hitler's eulogy of the Big Lie in *Mein Kampf* is one of the most famous passages in his book. His use of the Big Lie, though advertised in advance, was amazingly effective in Germany as well as abroad. Committing, later, crimes of previously unknown magnitude, the Germans reckoned that the rest of the world would refuse to believe them because of their very magnitude, whereas it might have believed crimes on a smaller scale, which were within the range of known experience. Hitler's doctrine of the Big Lie finally boomeranged, but not before it had been instrumental in bringing about the most devastating war in history. The psychological acuteness of this theory must be distinguished from its immorality; it is a technique that demagogues will try again.

Compared with the utter nihilism of Hitler, Mussolini's political faith, as expressed in 1932 in *The Political and Social Doctrine of Fascism,* seems to remain within the orbit of Western traditions. Mussolini's ideas may have been wrong, but they were firmly based on political philosophies of a long European heritage. Compared with Abraham Lincoln or John Stuart Mill, Mussolini must appear like the devil incarnate. Compared with Hitler, Mussolini emerged as Archangel Benito. One of the main differences between the two men was this: Hitler believed in his own lies, whereas Mussolini did not.

The picture of democracy that Mussolini draws, is distorted and one-sided, as viewed from countries in which democracy has led a strong and healthy existence. As seen from countries which have known only a caricature or sham of democracy, his picture is not greatly overdrawn. Essentially, Mussolini denied that democracy was either possible or desirable—and on both scores he sought to adduce historical evidence from the general decline of the liberal-democratic ideology in the late nineteenth and early twentieth centuries. By contrast, Mussolini emphasizes the authority of the state, which he also expressed in his famous formula "Nothing outside of the state, nothing against the state, nothing above the state." More important than Mussolini's plea for a strong state is his frank rejection of the ideal of peace among nations. He holds peace impossible as well as *undesirable,* because war alone "brings up to its highest tension all human energy and puts the stamp of nobility upon the peoples who have the courage to meet it."

Fascism is more than a momentary political aberration of certain nations in Europe and Asia. The nature of Fascism as a symptom of broader social disintegration of modern society is examined by Talcott Parsons in "Some Sociological Aspects of the Fascist Movements" (1942). Parsons, one of America's leading sociologists, examines the specific factors in modern industrial society which lead to "anomie," a state "where large numbers of individuals are to a serious degree lacking in the kind of integration with stable institutional patterns which is essential to their own personal stability and to the smooth functioning of the social system." Industrialization and urbanization have, through increased rationalization of all spheres of life, challenged, and frequently "debunked," traditional values, without always providing adequate substitute values in maintaining a civilized way of life. The *protest against reason* is thus a key element in the ideology of Fascism. The other principal element in Fascism is the *protection of vested interests* against free political and economic institutions, be they parliaments or labor unions. Especially where "business interests have not been closely integrated with strong liberal institutions" (as in Germany and Japan), the protection of business interests is likely to be fused with Fascist movements.

Yet it would be a mistake to see in Fascism nothing more than "capitalism in decay," as the Marxist interpretation would have it. What is decisive in Fascism, as in Communist totalitarianism, is its attitude on the basic issue of respect for man, rather than whether it protects this or that economic interest. This fundamental issue is discussed by Joost A. M. Meerloo, a psychiatrist interested in the psychological aspects of totalitarianism, in *The Rape of the Mind: The Psychology of Thought Control, Menticide, and Brainwashing* (1956). Two of the new concepts coined in our age of mass murder and despotism are *genocide* (the deliberate murder of an entire nation) and *menticide* (the killing of the mind). The latter concept was contributed by Meerloo, who personally experienced the methods of the German secret police in his native Holland during World War II. "Mindless robotism" is the normal way of living in "Totalitaria"—the name for any country in which a single group of the Right or Left wields absolute power and in which conformity is so complete that "disagreement and differences of opinion are crimes." Losing any individual personality of his own, the totalitarian robot man also loses his personal conscience and ethics. Intellectually, too, totalitarian man is reduced from a thinking individual to a mechanical instrument that can only play back the slogans that have been fed into it by its masters. Although this process of de-humanization can most fully be studied in the examples of Nazi Germany and Communist Russia, Meerloo warns that no country is safe, for "the brutal truth is that any country can be turned into a Totalitaria."

The defeat of the Axis in World War II has by no means removed forever the threat of Fascism. As a political system, Fascism may be destroyed for a time, so long as there is no Great Power that foments it throughout the world. As an attitude of mind, as a reflection of personal and social authoritarianism, however, Fascism can survive temporary defeats. Only a few years after Fascist regimes had led Germany and Italy to disaster and humiliation, neo-Fascist and neo-Nazi organizations brazenly resumed operations in both countries. In Argentina, Dictator Perón was overthrown in 1955, but Peronismo, the Argentine brand of Fascism, survived as a dangerous political force.

CARL SCHMITT

1. Politics: The Struggle with the Enemy*

The definition of the concept of the "political" can be arrived at only through the discovery of the specifically political categories. Politics stands as an independent sphere of its own, apart from other, relatively independent, spheres of human thought and action, such as morals, esthetics, economics, the complete enumeration of which is not required here. Politics must, therefore, possess its own, ultimately independent, distinguishing characteristics, to which all specifically political action can be traced back. Let us assume that, in the province of morals, these distinctions are Good and Evil; in esthetics, Beautiful and Ugly; in economics, Useful and Harmful, or Profitable and Unprofitable. The question then remains whether a specific and self-evident distinguishing characteristic exists in the realm of politics, and what it is.

The specifically political distinction to which political acts and motivations may be traced back, is the distinction of *friend* and *enemy*. It corresponds, in politics, to the relatively independent distinctions in other fields: Good and Evil in morals; Beautiful and Ugly in esthetics, etc. This distinction is independent, i.e., it cannot be deduced from any of these other distinctions, singly or combined. Just as the contrast between Good and Evil is not identical with, nor reducible to, that of Beautiful and Ugly, or of Useful and Harmful, it must not be confused or mixed up with any of these other contrasts. The distinction between friend and enemy can subsist, in theory and practice, without applying, at the same time, moral, esthetic, economic, or other distinctions. The political enemy need not be morally evil nor esthetically ugly; he need not appear as an economic competitor, and it may, in fact, be advantageous to do business with him. He is the other, the stranger, and his nature is sufficiently defined if he is, in an intense way, existentially different and strange; in case of conflict, he constitutes the

* From Carl Schmitt, "The Concept of 'The Political'," *Archiv für Sozialwissenschaft und Sozialpolitik*, Vol. 58 (September, 1927). Translated by William Ebenstein.

negation of one's own kind of existence, and must therefore be repulsed or fought, in order to preserve one's own way of life. In psychological reality, the enemy is easily treated as evil and ugly, because politics, like any autonomous area of human life, gladly calls on the help which it can receive from the distinctions of other spheres. This does not change the independence of such specific distinctions. As a consequence, the opposite is valid, too: what is morally bad, esthetically ugly, or economically harmful, need not be the enemy; what is morally good, esthetically beautiful, and economically useful, does not become, necessarily, the friend in the specifically political meaning of the word. The basic autonomy and independence of politics is evident in the possibility of distinguishing such a specific contrast of friend and enemy from other contrasts, and to conceive of it as an independent category.

The concepts of friend and enemy are to be understood in their concrete meaning of existence, not as symbols or metaphors, nor fused with, or weakened by, economic, moral and other ideas, nor as the expression of private feelings and tendencies. They are not normative or "spiritual" contrasts. Liberalism has transformed the enemy, from the economic side, into a competitor, and from the ethical side, into a debating adversary. In the sphere of economics, it is true, there are no enemies, but only competitors, and in a world suffused with morals and ethics, there are only debating contestants. However, the enemy is something entirely different. It makes no difference whether one considers it a reprehensible and atavistic residue of barbarian ages or not, that men still separate each other as friends and enemies, or whether one entertains the hope that this distinction will disappear, one day, from the earth, or whether it is good and advisable to construe the fiction, for educational reasons, that there are no more enemies. What is at stake, are not fictions and prescriptions of what ought to be, but real existence and the real possibility of this distinction of friend and enemy. One may share those hopes and pedagogical efforts. But one cannot rationally deny that nations have been able to line up, till now, according to the distinction of friend and enemy, and that it continues as a real possibility for every politically existent nation.

The enemy is, thus, not the competitor or opponent in general. Nor is he the private opponent whom one hates. "Enemy" is only a collectivity of men who eventually, i.e., as a real possibility, will *fight* against a similar collectivity of people. Enemy is only the public enemy, because everything that relates to such a collectivity, especially a whole nation, becomes *public*.

The genuine concept of the enemy thus implies the eventual reality of a struggle. One should abstract, from this term, all accidental changes inherent in the historical evolution of the techniques of war and armaments. War is armed struggle between nations. The essential characteristic of "the weapon" is the fact that it is a means of physical killing of human beings. The word "struggle," like the term "enemy," is to be taken here in its original meaning. It does not mean competition, nor the "intellectual" struggle of discussion, nor the symbolic struggle, which, after all, every person fights, and be it only with his inertia. The terms "friend," "enemy," and "struggle" obtain their real significance from their relation to the real possibility of physical killing. War follows from enmity, because the latter is existential negation of another being. War is only the most extreme negation of enmity. As long as the concept of the enemy retains its meaning, war need not be an everyday, normal occurrence, nor need it be felt as an ideal, but must sub-sist as a real possibility.

The conceptual characteristics of politics imply the pluralism of states. Political unity presupposes the real possibility of an enemy and, thus, of another, co-existing political unity. Therefore, as long as there is a state, there will always be several states on earth, rather than one world "state" comprehending the whole world and all of humanity. The political world is a puriverse, not a universe. To this extent, every theory of the state is puralistic, though in a different sense from the pluralism of Laski. The very nature of political organization makes its universality impossible. If the vari-ous nations and human groupings of the earth were all so united as to make a struggle among them actually impossible, if the distinction between friend and enemy ceases to operate even as a mere eventuality, then all that is left is economics, morals, law, art, etc., but not politics or a state.

ADOLF HITLER

2. *The Bigger the Lie, the Better**

Like the woman, whose psychic state is determined less by grounds of abstract reason than by an indefinable emotional longing for a force which will complement her nature, and who, consequently, would rather bow to a strong man than dominate a weakling, likewise the masses love a com-mander more than a petitioner and feel inwardly more satisfied by a doc-trine, tolerating no other beside itself, than by the granting of liberalistic freedom with which, as a rule, they can do little, and are prone to feel that they have been abandoned. They are equally unaware of their shameless

---

* From Adolf Hitler, *Mein Kampf* (1925-1927; translated by Ralph Manheim, Houghton Mifflin Company, 1943). By permission.

spiritual terrorization and the hideous abuse of their human freedom, for they absolutely fail to suspect the inner insanity of the whole doctrine. All they see is the ruthless force and brutality of its calculated manifestations, to which they always submit in the end.

All propaganda must be popular and its intellectual level must be adjusted to the most limited intelligence among those it is addressed to. Consequently, the greater the mass it is intended to reach, the lower its purely intellectual level will have to be. But if, as in propaganda for sticking out a war, the aim is to influence a whole people, we must avoid excessive intellectual demands on our public, and too much caution cannot be exerted in this direction.

The more modest its intellectual ballast, the more exclusively it takes into consideration the emotions of the masses, the more effective it will be. And this is the best proof of the soundness or unsoundness of a propaganda campaign, and not success in pleasing a few scholars or young aesthetes.

The art of propaganda lies in understanding the emotional ideas of the great masses and finding, through a psychologically correct form, the way to the attention and thence to the heart of the broad masses. The fact that our bright boys do not understand this merely shows how mentally lazy and conceited they are.

Once we understand how necessary it is for propaganda to be adjusted to the broad mass, the following rule results:

It is a mistake to make propaganda many-sided, like scientific instruction, for instance.

The receptivity of the great masses is very limited, their intelligence is small, but their power of forgetting is enormous. In consequence of these facts, all effective propaganda must be limited to a very few points and must harp on these in slogans until the last member of the public understands what you want him to understand by your slogan. As soon as you sacrifice this slogan and try to be many-sided, the effect will piddle away, for the crowd can neither digest nor retain the material offered. In this way the result is weakened and in the end entirely cancelled out.

The magnitude of a lie always contains a certain factor of credibility, since the great masses of the people in the very bottom of their hearts tend to be corrupted rather than consciously and purposely evil, and that, therefore, in view of the primitive simplicity of their minds, they more easily fall a victim to a big lie than to a little one, since they themselves lie in little things, but would be ashamed of lies that were too big. Such a falsehood will never enter their heads, and they will not be able to believe in the possibility of such monstrous effrontery and infamous misrepresentation in others; yes, even when enlightened on the subject, they will long doubt and waver, and continue to accept at least one of these causes as true. Therefore, something of even the most insolent lie will always remain and stick—a fact which all the great lie-virtuosi and lying-clubs in this world know only too well and also make the most treacherous use of.

BENITO MUSSOLINI

3. *Fascism, War, Dictatorship**

Fascism combats the whole complex system of democratic ideology, and repudiates it, whether in its theoretical premises or in its practical application. Fascism denies that the majority, by the simple fact that it is a majority, can direct human society; it denies that numbers alone can govern by means of a periodical consultation, and it affirms the immutable, beneficial, and fruitful inequality of mankind, which can never be permanently leveled through the mere operation of a mechanical process such as universal suffrage. The democratic régime may be defined as from time to time giving the people the illusion of sovereignty, while the real effective sovereignty lies in the hands of other concealed and irresponsible forces. Democracy is a régime nominally without a king, but it is ruled by many kings—more absolute, tyrannical, and ruinous than one sole king, even though a tyrant. This explains why Fascism, having first in 1922 (for reasons of expediency) assumed an attitude tending towards republicanism, renounced this point of view before the march to Rome, being convinced that the question of political form is not today of prime importance, and after having studied the examples of monarchies and republics past and present reached the conclusion that monarchy or republicanism are not to be judged, as it were, by an absolute standard; but that they represent forms in which the evolution—political, historical, traditional, or psychological—of a particular country has expressed itself. Fascism supersedes the antithesis monarchy or republicanism, while democracy still tarries beneath the domination of this idea, forever pointing out the insufficiency of the first and forever the praising of the second as the perfect régime. Today, it can be seen that there are republics innately reactionary and absolutist, and also monarchies which incorporate the most ardent social and political hopes of the future.

"Reason and science," says Renan (one of the inspired pre-Fascists) in his philosophical meditations, "are products of humanity, but to expect rea-

---

* From Benito Mussolini, *The Political and Social Doctrine of Fascism* (1932; English translation, The Hogarth Press, 1933). By permission.

son as a direct product of the people and a direct result of their action is to deceive onseself by a chimera. It is not necessary for the existence of reason that everybody should understand it. And in any case, if such a decimation of truth were necessary, it could not be achieved in a low-class democracy, which seems as though it must of its very nature extinguish any kind of noble training. The principle that society exists solely through the well-being and the personal liberty of all the individuals of which it is composed does not appear to be conformable to the plans of nature, in whose workings the race alone seems to be taken into consideration, and the individual sacrificed to it. It is greatly to be feared that the last stage of such a conception of democracy (though I must hasten to point out that the term 'democracy' may be interpreted in various ways) would end in a condition of society in which a degenerate herd would have no other preoccupation but the satisfaction of the lowest desires of common men." Thus Renan. Fascism denies, in democracy, the absurd conventional untruth of political equality dressed out in the garb of collective irresponsibility, and the myth of "happiness" and indefinite progress. But, if democracy may be conceived in diverse forms —that is to say, taking democracy to mean a state of society in which the populace are not reduced to impotence in the State—Fascism may write itself down as "an organized, centralized, and authoritative democracy."

Fascism has taken up an attitude of complete opposition to the doctrines of Liberalism, both in the political field and the field of economics. There should be no undue exaggeration (simply with the object of immediate success in controversy) of the importance of Liberalism in the last century, nor should what was but one among many theories which appeared in that period be put forward as a religion for humanity for all time, present and to come. Liberalism only flourished for half a century. It was born in 1830 in reaction against the Holy Alliance, which had been formed with the object of diverting the destinies of Europe back to the period before 1789, and the highest point of its success was the year 1848, when even Pius IX was a Liberal. Immediately after that date it began to decay, for if the year 1848 was a year of light and hope, the following year, 1849, was a year of darkness and tragedy. The Republic of Rome was dealt a mortal blow by a sister republic—that of France—and in the same year Marx launched the gospel of the Socialist religion, the famous Communist Manifesto. In 1851 Napoleon III carried out his far from Liberal *coup d'état* and reigned in France until 1870, when he was deposed by a popular movement as the consequence of a military defeat which must be counted as one of the most decisive in history. The victor was Bismarck, who knew nothing of the religion of liberty, or the prophets by which that faith was revealed. And it is symptomatic that such a highly civilized people as the Germans were completely ignorant of the religion of liberty during the whole of the nineteenth century. It was nothing but a parenthesis, represented by that body which has been called "The ridiculous Parliament of Frankfort," which lasted only for a short period. Germany attained her national unity quite outside the doctrines of Liberalism—a doctrine which seems entirely foreign to the German mind, a mind essentially monarchic—while Liberalism is the logical and, indeed, historical forerunner of anarchy. The stages in the achievement of German unity are the three wars of '64, '66, and '70, which were guided by such "Liberals" as Von Moltke and Bismarck. As for Italian unity, its debt to Liberalism is completely inferior in contrast to that which it owes to the work of Mazzini and Garibaldi, who were not Liberals. Had it not been for the intervention of the anti-Liberal Napoleon, we should not have gained Lombardy; and without the help of the again anti-Liberal Bismarck at Sadowa and Sedan it is very probable that we should never have gained the province of Venice in '66, or been able to enter Rome in '70. From 1870 to 1914 a period began during which even the very high priests of the religion themselves had to recognize the gathering twilight of their faith—defeated as it was by the decadence of literature and atavism in practice—that is to say, Nationalism, Futurism, Fascism. The era of Liberalism, after having accumulated an infinity of Gordian knots, tried to untie them in the slaughter of the World War—and never has any religion demanded of votaries such a monstrous sacrifice. Perhaps the Liberal Gods were athirst for blood? But now, today, the Liberal faith must shut the doors of its deserted temples, deserted because the peoples of the world realize that its worship—agnostic in the field of economics and indifferent in the field of politics and morals—will lead, as it has already led, to certain ruin. In addition to this, let it be pointed out that all the political hopes of the present day are anti-Liberal, and it is therefore supremely ridiculous to try to classify this sole creed as outside the judgment of history, as though history were a hunting ground reserved for the professors of Liberalism—as though Liberalism were the final unalterable verdict of civilization.

The foundation of Fascism is the conception of the State, its character, its duty, and its aim. Fascism conceives of the State as an absolute, in comparison with which all individuals or groups are relative, only to be conceived of in their relation to the State. The conception of the Liberal State is not that of a directing force, guiding the play and development, both material and spiritual, of a collective body, but merely a force limited to the function of recording results; on the other hand, the Fascist State is itself conscious, and has itself a will and a personality—thus it may be called the "ethic" State. In 1929, at the first five-yearly assembly of the Fascist régime, I said:

"For us Fascists, the State is not merely a guardian, preoccupied solely with the duty of assuring the personal safety of the citizens; nor is it an organization with purely material aims, such as to guarantee a certain level of well-being and peaceful conditions of life; for a mere council of administration would be sufficient to realize such objects. Nor is it a purely political creation divorced from all contact with the complex material reality which makes up the life of the individual and the life of the people as a whole. The State, as conceived of and as created by Fascism, is a spiritual and moral fact in itself, since its political, juridical, and economic organization of the nation is a concrete thing: and such an organization must be in its origins and development a manifestation of the spirit. The State is the guarantor of security both internal and external, but it is also the custodian and transmitter of the spirit of the people, as it has grown up through the centuries in language, in custom, and in faith. And the State is not only a living reality of the present, it is also linked with the past and above all with the future, and thus transcending the brief limits of individual life, it represents the immanent spirit of the nation. The forms in which States express themselves may change, but the necessity for such forms is eternal. It is the State which educates its citizens in civic virtue, gives them a consciousness of their mission and welds them into unity; harmonizing their various interests through justice, and transmitting to future generations the mental conquests of science, of art, of law and the solidarity of humanity. It leads men from primitive tribal life to that highest expression of human power which is Empire: it links up through the centuries the names of those of its members who have died for its existence and to obedience to its laws, it holds up the memory of the leaders who have increased its territory and the geniuses who have illumined it with glory as an example to be followed by future generations. When the conception of the State declines, and disunifying and contrifugal tendencies prevail, whether of individuals or of particular groups, the nations where such phenomena appear are in the decline."

From 1929 until today, evolution, both political and economic, has everywhere gone to prove the validity of these doctrinal promises. Of such gigantic importance is the State. Is it the force which alone can provide a solution to the dramatic contradictions of capitalism, and that state of affairs which we call the shade of Jules Simon, who in the dawn of Liberalism proclaimed that, "The State must labor to make itself unnecessary, and prepare the way for its own dismissal?" Or of McCulloch, who, in the second half of the last century, affirmed that the State must guard against the danger of governing too much? What would the Englishman, Bentham, say today to the continual and inevitably invoked intervention of the State in the sphere of economics, while according to his theories industry should ask no more of the State than to be left in peace? Or the German, Humboldt, according to whom the "lazy" State should be considered the best? Is it true that the second wave of Liberal economists were less extreme than the first, and Adam Smith himself opened the door—if only very cautiously—which leads to State intervention in the economic field: but whoever says Liberalism implies individualism, and whoever says Fascism implies the State. Yet the Fascist State is unique, and an original creation. It is not reactionary, but revolutionary, in that it anticipates the solution of the universal political problems which elsewhere have to be settled in the political field by the rivalry of parties, the excessive power of the parliamentary régime and the irresponsibility of political assemblies; while it meets the problems of the economic field by a system of syndicalism which is continually increasing in importance, as much in the sphere of labor as of industry: and in the moral field enforces order, discipline, and obedience to that which is the determined moral code of the country. Fascism desires the State to be a strong and organic body, at the same time reposing upon broad and popular support. The Fascist State has drawn into itself even the economic activities of the nation, and, through the corporative social and educational institutions created by it, its influence reaches every aspect of the national life and includes, framed in their respective organizations, all the political, economic and spiritual forces of the nation. A State which reposes upon the support of millions of individuals who recognize its authority, are continually conscious of its power and are ready at once to serve it, is not the old tyrannical State of the medieval lord nor has it anything in common with the absolute governments either before or after 1789. The individual in the Fascist State is not annulled but rather multiplied, just in the same way that a soldier in a regiment is not diminished but rather increased by the number of his comrades. The Fascist State organizes the nation, but leaves a sufficient margin of liberty to the individual; the latter is deprived of all useless and possibly harmful freedom, but retains what is essential; the deciding power in this question cannot be the individual, but the State alone.

Above all, Fascism, in so far as it considers the future and the development of humanity quite apart from political considerations of the moment, believes neither in the possibility nor the utility of perpetual peace. It thus repudiates the doctrine of Pacifism—born of a renunciation of the struggle and an act of cowardice in the face of sacrifice. War alone brings up to its highest tension all human energy and puts the stamp of nobility upon the peoples who have the courage to meet it. All other trials are substitutes, which never really put men into the position where they have to make the great decision —the alternative of life or death. Thus a doctrine which is founded upon this harmful postulate of peace is hostile to Fascism. And thus hostile to the spirit of Fascism, though accepted for what use they can be in dealing with particular situations, are all the international leagues and societies which, as history will show, can be scattered to the winds when once strong national feeling is aroused by any motive—sentimental, ideal, or practical. This anti-pacifist spirit is carried by Fascism even into the life of the individual; the proud

motto of the *Squadrista,* "Me ne Frego," written on the bandage of the
wound, is an act of philosophy not only stoic, the summary of a doctrine not
only political—it is the education to combat, the acceptance of the risks
which combat implies, and a new way of life for Italy. Thus the Fascist accepts life and loves it, knowing nothing of and despising suicide: he rather
conceives of life as duty and struggle and conquest, life which should be high
and full, lived for oneself, but above all for others—those who are at hand
and those who are far distant, contemporaries, and those who will come
after.

The "demographic" policy of the régime is the result of the above premises. The Fascist, too, loves in actual fact his neighbor, but this "neighbor"
is not merely a vague and undefined concept, this love for one's neighbor
puts no obstacle in the way of necessary educational severity, and still less
to differentiation of status and to physical distance. Fascism repudiates any
universal embrace, and in order to live worthily in the community of civilized peoples watches its contemporaries with vigilant eyes, takes good note
of their state of mind and, in the changing trend of their interests, does not
allow itself to be deceived by temporary and fallacious appearances.

The Fascist State is an embodied will to power and government: the Roman tradition is here an ideal of force in action. According to Fascism,
government is not so much a thing to be expressed in territorial or military
terms as in terms of morality and the spirit. It must be thought of as an
empire—that is to say, a nation which directly or indirectly rules other nations, without the need for conquering a single square yard of territory. For
Fascism, the growth of empire, that is to say the expansion of the nation,
is an essential manifestation of vitality, and its opposite a sign of decadence.
Peoples which are rising, or rising again after a period of decadence, are
always imperialist; any renunciation is a sign of decay and of death. Fascism
is the doctrine best adapted to represent the tendencies and the aspirations
of a people, like the people of Italy, who are rising again after many
centuries of abasement and foreign servitude. But empire demands discipline, the coordination of all forces and a deeply felt sense of duty and sacrifice: this fact explains many aspects of the practical working of the régime,
the character of many forces in the State, and the necessarily severe measures
which must be taken against those who would oppose this spontaneous and
inevitable movement of Italy in the twentieth century, and would oppose it
by recalling the outworn ideology of the nineteenth century—repudiated
wheresoever there has been the courage to undertake great experiments of
social and political transformation; for never before has the nation stood
more in need of authority, of direction, and of order. If every age has its own
characteristic doctrine, there are a thousand signs which point to Fascism
as the characteristic doctrine of our time. For if a doctrine must be a living

thing, this is proved by the fact that Fascism has created a living faith; and that this faith is very powerful in the minds of men, is demonstrated by those who have suffered and died for it.

Fascism has henceforth in the world the universality of all those doctrines which, in realizing themselves, have represented a stage in the history of the human spirit.

TALCOTT PARSONS

4. Social Disintegration and Fascism*

The older type, especially of European, social theory was, very largely, oriented to the understanding, in broad terms, of the social situation of the writer's own time. Whatever was sound in these older attempts, as of a Comte, a Spencer or a Marx, tended to be so intimately bound up with scientifically dubious elements of grandiose speculative construction and methodological assumption and dogma that the whole genus of analysis has tended to become discredited as a result of the general reaction against speculative theories.

In the course of such reactions it is not uncommon for the baby to be thrown out with the bath, for elements of sound insight and analysis to be lost sight of through their seemingly inseparable involvement with these other elements. Perhaps in the last few years more strongly than at any other time have there been signs that warrant the hope of an ability in the social sciences to apply generalized theoretical analysis to such problems in a thoroughly empirical, tentative spirit which will make possible a cumulative development of understanding, relatively unmarred by scientifically irrelevant or untenable elements. The very breadth of the problem of diagnosis of the state of a great civilization creates a strong demand for such a method.

Perhaps the most dramatic single development in the society of the Western world in its most recent phase has been the emergence of the great political movements usually referred to as "Fascist." In spite of their uneven incidence, with Germany and Italy by far the most prominent centers, and their varying character in different countries, there is sufficient similarity to justify the hypothesis that the broad phenomenon is deeply rooted in the structure of Western society as a whole and its internal strains and conflicts. However much my own approach may turn out to differ from the Marxian

* *Social Forces*, Vol. XXI (December, 1942). By permission.

this much must certainly be granted the latter—that it does relate Fascism to fundamental and generalized aspects of Western society.

As a starting point for the present analysis perhaps the common formula of characterization as the "radicalism of the right" is as satisfactory as any. It has at least the virtue of calling attention to two important points. In the first place Fascism is not "old conservatism" of the sort especially familiar before 1914, although elements which were once conservative in that sense have often been drawn into the Fascist movements. Secondly, it is definitely of the "right" in that it is specifically oriented in opposition to the political movements of the "left," notably of course communism.

Perhaps the most important reason why we are justified in speaking of "radicalism" lies in the existence of a popular mass movement in which large masses of the "common people" have become imbued with a highly emotional, indeed often fanatical, zeal for a cause. These mass movements, which are in an important sense revolutionary movements, are above all what distinguishes fascism from ordinary conservatism. They are movements which, though their primary orientation is political, have many features in common with great religious movements in history, a fact which may serve as a guide to the sociological analysis of their origins and character.

A second important feature is the role played by privileged elite groups, groups with a "vested interest" in their position. While from some points of view the combination of these two elements in the same movement is paradoxical, it will be argued here that it is of the very essence of the phenomenon and perhaps more than anything else throws light on the social forces at work.

It has come to be a well-known fact that movements of religious proselytism tend to develop in situations involving a certain type of social disorganization, primarily that early though only roughly characterized by Durkheim as "anomie." Anomie may perhaps most briefly be characterized as the state where large numbers of individuals are to a serious degree lacking in the kind of integration with stable institutional patterns which is essential to their own personal stability and to the smooth functioning of the social system. Of this there are in turn perhaps two principal aspects. In the first place there seems to be a deep-seated need for a relative stability of the expectations to which action is oriented. The aspect of this on which Durkheim lays primary stress is the sufficiently clear definition of the goals of action—there can, he says, be no sense of achievement in progress toward the realization of an infinite goal. But goals are, to a very large extent defined by institutionalized expectations. This Durkheim illustrated by the inability of indefinite increase of wealth, once cut loose from definite standards, to satisfy ambition.

Similar considerations apply to other aspects of conduct. Expectations cannot be stable if the standards with which conformity is demanded are left so vague as not to be a real guide, or if the individual is subjected, in the same situation, to two or more conflicting expectations each of which advances claims to legitimacy which cannot be ignored.

The second, it would seem somewhat more difficult and complex aspect, lies in the need for a sufficiently concrete and stable system of symbols around which the sentiments of the individual can crystallize. In many different aspects of life highly concrete associations are formed which perhaps in many cases have no great intrinsic importance in themselves, but in that they become stabilized and perpetuated through a living social tradition perform a highly important function in integrating social groups and in stabilizing the orientation of individuals within them.

The general character of the typical reaction of the individual to anomie is that usually referred to in psychological terms as a state of insecurity. The personality is not stably organized about a coherent system of values, goals, and expectations. Attitudes tend to vacillate between indecision which paralyzes action—and all manner of scruples and inhibitions—and on the other hand compulsively "overdetermined" reactions which endow particular goals and symbols with an excess of hatred, devotion or enthusiasm over what is appropriate to the given situation. Generalized insecurity is commonly associated with high levels of anxiety and aggression, both of which are to an important extent "free-floating" in that they are not merely aroused in appropriate form and intensity by fear or anger-provoking situations but may be displaced onto situations or symbols only remotely connected with their original sources.

The present formulation of the psychological correlates of anomie has consciously adhered to the level closest to the more general character of social situations—lack of definition of goals and standards, conflicting expectations, inadequately concrete and stable symbolization. I am well aware that many psychologists find the deepest sources of insecurity to lie in the relations of the individual to his parents and others in the family in early childhood. The two approaches are by no means necessarily in conflict. There is much evidence that insecurity developed in adults from the sources here indicated affects their relations to their children and in turn the character formation of the latter, so that a cumulative vicious circle may work itself out.

An increase in anomie may be a consequence of almost any change in the social situation which upsets previous established definitions of the situation, or routines of life, or symbolic associations. To be sure, the members of some societies have average character types which are better able to withstand and adapt to rapid changes than are others—but in any case there is a limit to the extent and rapidity of change which can take place without engendering anomie on a large scale. There is ample evidence that the period immediately preceding our own time was, throughout the Western world, one of such rapid and fundamental change as to make this inevitable.

It was, in the first place, the period of the Industrial Revolution which, though going much farther back in history, tended cumulatively to gain in force throughout the nineteenth century and well into the twentieth. Though in widely differing degrees, most Western countries changed from predominantly agricultural to industrial and commercial societies, a change impinging not only on occupation but on the life of very large numbers of the population in many different aspects, especially in the tremendous growth of cities and the continual introduction of new elements into the standard of living.

Secondly, and intimately connected with this, the society has been subjected to many other influences adversely affecting situational stability. Migration of population from the rural areas to the growing urban concentrations has been only one phase of a tremendous and complex migration process which has necessitated the complex process of adaptation to new social environments—sometimes, as in the great bulk of immigration into the United States, assimilation to a drastically different cultural tradition with exposure to conflicting expectations and discrimination on ethnic lines. A somewhat different source of strain lies in the instability of the new economy —the exposure to cyclical fluctuations with unemployment and rapid and drastic changes in the standard of living. Inflation and many of the social and economic effects of war fit into the same general pattern.

Though it is perhaps more significant as a consequence of than as a casual factor in anomie, the fact is relevant that not only in women's dress but in any number of other fields our society is to a very high degree subject to rapid and violent changes of fad and fashion. No sooner have we become attached to a pattern than its social prestige melts away leaving the necessity to form a new orientation. This is especially true in the recreational and other expressional fields, but applies also to political and cultural ideas, and to many fields of consumption patterns.

Finally, the cultural development of the period has been preeminently one to undermine simplicity and stability of orientation. It has been to an extraordinary extent a period of the "debunking" of traditional values and ideas, and one in which for previously stable cultural patterns in such fields as religion, ethics, and philosophy, no comparably stable substitutes have appeared—rather a conspicuously unstable factionalism and tendency to faddistic fluctuation. Part of the situation is an inevitable consequence of the enormous development of popular education, and of the development of mass means of communication so that cultural influences which in an earlier time reached only relatively small "sophisticated" minorities now impinge upon a very large proportion of the total population.

Returning for a moment to the psychological level of consideration, one of the most conspicuous features of the present situation lies in the extent to which patterns of orientation which the individual can be expected to take completely for granted have disappeared. The complexity of the influences which impinge upon him has increased enormously, in many or most situations the society does not provide him with only one socially sanctioned definition of the situation and approved pattern of behavior but with a considerable number of possible alternatives, the order of preference between which is by no means clear. The "burden of decision" is enormously great. In such a situation it is not surprising that large numbers of people should, to quote a recent unpublished study,[1] be attracted to movements which can offer them "membership in a group with a vigorous *esprit de corps* with submission to some strong authority and rigid system of belief, the individual thus finding a measure of escape from painful perplexities or from a situation of *anomie*."

Thus the large-scale incidence of anomie in Western society in recent times is hardly open to doubt. This fact alone, however, demonstrates only susceptibility to the appeal of movements of the general sociological type of fascism but it is far from being adequate to the explanation of the actual appearance of such movements or above all the specific patterns in terms of which they have become structured. It is this latter problem which must next be approached.

The state of anomie in Western society is not primarily a consequence of the impingement on it of structurally fortuitous disorganizing forces though these have certainly contributed. It has, rather, involved a very central dynamic process of its own about which a crucially important complex of factors of change may be grouped, what, following Max Weber, may be called the "process of rationalization." The main outline of its character and influence is too familiar to need to be discussed in detail—but it must be kept clearly in mind as a basis for the subsequent analysis.

Undoubtedly the most convenient single point of reference is to be found in the patterns of science. The development of science is itself of course inherently dynamic and has a certain immediate effect in progressively modifying traditional conceptions of the empirical world. It is, however, its application in technology which provides the most striking source of cumulative social change, profoundly affecting the concrete circumstances of men's lives in a multitude of ways. Again it is not only that the explicit formal content of occupational roles is affected—this is the center from which many complex ramifications of change radiate into the informal and symbolic areas of men's working lives, and into their private lives through changes in their patterns of consumption, recreation, etc. Whatever the positive value of the changes, they always involve an abandonment of traditional orientation patterns, circumstances and definitions of the situation which necessitates a process of readjustment.

[1] Theodore W. Sprague, Jehovah's Witnesses: "A Study in Group Integration." Dissertation, Harvard University, 1942.

Though by no means simply an aspect of science and its application in technology a second dynamic complex is intimately related to it. It may be characterized as the treatment of a wide range of action patterns and contexts of human relationship in terms of orientation to relatively specific and limited goals. Perhaps the classic center of the complex is the field of "contractual" relationships, and its formulation at the hands of such theorists as Spencer and Tönnies provides the classic sociological characterization. Contractualism overlaps widely with the use of money and the wide extension of market relationships. This involves the enormous extension of the mobility of elements essential to coordinated human action and the extension of the possibility of focussing elements from many sources on the realization of a single goal. Codification and systematization of personal rights and individual liberties is another essential aspect as is the clear development of the modern institution of ownership in the sphere of property. The question of where ownership is lodged is not the primary issue—but rather the concentration of the various rights which taken together we call ownership into a single bundle rather than their dispersion; and by the same token their segregation from the other elements of the status of their holder.

By no means the least important element of this complex is the patterning of functional roles primarily about their functional content itself with clear segregation from other elements of the total social status of the individual—in kinship, local ties, even to a considerable extent social class and ethnic adherence. Though prominent in the case of independent roles such as those of private professional practice this patterning of functional roles is most prominent in the field of large-scale organization, indeed without it the latter as we know it would scarcely be conceivable at all.

The interdependence between the complex of science and technology on the one hand, and that just discussed on the other is exceedingly close. Some schools of thought, as of Veblen and Ogburn, give the former unquestioned primacy. This is at least open to serious question since it is only in relatively highly developed stages of the patterning of functionally specialized roles that the most favorable situation for the functioning of scientific investigation and technological application is attained. Less directly the mobility of resources through property and market relations, and the institutions of personal freedom all greatly facilitate the influence of science on social life.

Finally, science itself is a central part of the cultural tradition of our society. As such it is perhaps the most conspicuous embodiment of the more general pattern which may be called that of "critical rationality," differing from others primarily in the place accorded to the canons of empirical observation and verification. This same spirit of critical rationality has to an increasing extent ramified into many or even most other areas of the cultural tradition.

Notably of course it has permeated philosophical thought and the religious traditions of the various branches of Christianity. In this direction two consequences above all have appeared—the questioning of the cognitive status of the "non-empirical" elements of philosophical and religious thought, and the tendency to eliminate patterns and entities of primarily symbolic significance. The use of the categories of "ignorance" and "superstition" as sufficient characterizations of all thought not in conformity with the particular rational or pseudo-rational standards of the moment is an indication of the basic attitude.

The present concern is not whether the patterns of rationality in these different areas are in some sense superior to those they have tended to supplant, but rather the relation of their relatively rapid process of development to the functioning of the social system. It should be clear that their development is in itself perhaps the most important single source of anomie. Its significance in this respect is by no means simple and cannot be adequately analyzed here. It is partly a matter of the sheer rapidity of the process, which does not provide an opportunity for stable reorientation. Another aspect is the unevenness and incompleteness of its incidence so that it engenders conflicts in the social pressures impinging on the same groups and as between different groups. There is also the question whether, to balance its undermining effect on traditional patterns and values, it succeeds in providing even for the groups most thoroughly permeated, functionally adequate substitutes.

But beyond the significance as a source of temporary or permanent anomie, the process of rationalization has a further significance of crucial interest here. It is to it that we must look for the primary explanation of the structuring of attitudes and social organization so far as it can be treated as a response to the generalized condition of anomie. This question will have to be discussed on two primary levels, first that of the cognitive definition of the situation, second that of the differential affective appeal of the competing definitions of the situation which have come to be available.

The process of rationalization would scarcely have been of profound social importance if it had not affected large numbers of people in the immediate circumstances of their daily lives. But as an essential part of the same general cultural movement there has developed a tradition of "social thought" which, in a sufficiently broad perspective, can be seen to be highly distinctive in spite of its internal complexity. It has provided, above all, two interrelated things, a diagnosis of the status of the society—particularly in relation to the traditional patterns and structures with which the process of rationalization has stood in conflict, and a frame of reference for determining the proper attitudes of "reasonable" men toward the social problems of the day. Its functioning as the "ideology" of social and political movements is a natural consequence. In a very broad sense it is the ideological patterns of the movements of the "left" which are in question.

Such a tradition of thought is inevitably compounded of various different elements which today we find it convenient to distinguish. In the first place, there are certain elements of genuine scientific insight which by contrast with previous stages may be considered new. Undoubtedly the "utilitarian" pattern of analysis of the division of labor and exchange and the corresponding analysis of the functioning of a system of competitive market relationships—in short the "classical economics"—is largely in this category. With the shift on this level from "economic individualism" in the direction of socialism, especially Marxism, certain changes of emphasis on different factors have occurred but a fundamental constancy of cognitive pattern, the "utilitarian," has remained.

From the perspective of a later vantage point we can now see that in spite of the undoubtedly sound elements there have from a scientific point of view been certain shortcomings in this scheme of thought. Attention has been concentrated on one sector of the total structure of a social system—that of contract, exchange, monetary transactions—and others such as family life have been neglected. But even within the area of focussed attention the "fallacy of misplaced concreteness" has, understandably enough, played a prominent role. The prominent patterns of thought have, that is, been inadequately placed in perspective and integrated with other elements of a total social system.

The scientifically relevant element has, at the same time, been closely related to certain patterns of value orientation—with both a positive and a negative aspect. In one connection the new social thought expressed a revolt against the old order and a rationalization or justification of the changes introduced by the process of rationalization. Its primary targets of attack have been traditionally established statuses of prestige, authority and privilege and the traditionalized patterns themselves which have been integrated with these. Positively, the rights of the individual both as against other human agencies and as against tradition itself have provided the main focus. A fundamental trend toward egalitarianism has also been prominent. Broadly the pattern can be described as one of "emancipation" from the control of forces without rational sanction, from unjust authority, from monopoly and competitive privilege, from the "tyranny" of ignorance and superstition.

Finally, apart both from questions of science and of ethical value the tendency has, it has been noted, been to extend patterns of rationality into the metaphysical realm. Science has been taken as the prototype of all sound cognitive orientation and all elements of tradition not scientifically defensible have tended to be "debunked." Here of course traditional religion has been the primary object of attack.

In the earlier phases of its development this scheme of thought overwhelmingly embodied positive value attitudes. It defined the situation for the emergence and establishment of a new and magnificent social order, for freedom against tyranny, for enlightenment against ignorance and superstition, for equality and justice against privilege, for free enterprise against monopoly and the irrational restrictions of custom.

Gradually, however, with the growing ascendancy of the associated patterns, in certain directions certain elements of the scheme of thought have with altered emphasis and formulation come to be built into a pattern embodying quite different value attitudes. This has centered primarily on the developed system of emancipated and rationalized economic organization. The liberation of free enterprise from the tyranny of monopoly and custom has, it is said, led only to the system of capitalistic exploitation. The "profit motive" has become the object of deep reproach. Inequality, unemployment, and new forms of unjust privilege have been brought into the limelight. Political liberation from the tyrannical Bourbons has led only to a new enslavement under the "executive Committee of the Bourgeoisie."

This new negative orientation to certain primary aspects of the maturing modern social order has above all centered on the symbol of "capitalism," which in certain circles has come to be considered as all-embracing a key to the understanding of all human ills as Original Sin once was. But it is important to note that the main intellectual movements within which this has developed have retained, even in an extreme form, the rationalized patterns in other connections, particularly in attitudes toward ignorance and superstition—lurking behind which economic interests are often seen—and many other symbolic and unrationalized patterns of thought and social behavior. What in terms of the recent situation is "leftist" social thought is overwhelmingly "positivistic" as well as utilitarian.

With the wisdom of hindsight, it can now be clearly seen that this rationalistic scheme of thought has not been adequate to provide a stably institutionalized diagnosis of even a "modern" social system as a whole, nor has it been adequate to formulate all of the important values of our society, nor its cognitive orientation to the world. It has been guilty of the fallacy of misplaced concreteness in neglecting or underestimating the role of what Pareto has called the "non-logical" aspects of human behavior in society, of the sentiments and traditions of family and informal social relationships, of the refinements of social stratification, of the peculiarities of regional, ethnic or national culture—perhaps above all of religion. On this level it has indeed helped to provoke a most important "anti-intellectualist" reaction.

On another level it has "debunked" many of the older values of our cultural tradition, and above all the cognitive patterns of religion, to a point well beyond that to which common values and symbols in the society had moved. Even apart from questions of its metaphysical validity it cannot be said adequately to have expressed the common orientations of the members of the society.

But on top of these inherent strains a crucial role has been played by the emergence within the rationalized cultural tradition itself of a definition of the situation which has thoroughly "debunked" many of the institutionalized products of the process of rationalization itself. Surely the stage was set for a combination of this definition of the situation with a reassertion of all the patterns which the utilitarian scheme had omitted or slighted—an acceptance of its own indictment but a generalization of the diagnosis to make "capitalism" appear a logical outcome of the whole process of rationalization itself, not merely of its perversion, and the fact that in certain directions it had not been carried far enough. By the same token it is possible to treat both capitalism and its leftist antagonists, especially communism, not as genuine antagonists but as brothers under the skin, the common enemy. The Jew serves as a convenient symbolic link between them.

This reaction against the "ideology" of the rationalization of society is one principal aspect at least of the ideology of fascism. It characteristically accepts in essentials the socialist indictment of the existing order described as capitalism, but extends it to include leftist radicalism and the whole penumbra of scientific and philosophical rationalism.[2]

The ideological definition of the situation in terms of which the orientation of a social movement becomes structured is of great importance but it never stands alone. It is necessarily in the closest interdependence with the psychological states and the social situations of the people to whom it appeals. We must now turn to the analysis of certain effects of the process of rationalization on this level.

The fundamental fact is that the incidence of the process within the social structure is highly uneven—different elements of a population become "rationalized" in different degrees, at different rates, and in different aspects of their personalities and orientations.

It may be said that both traditional and rationalized patterns are, to a high degree, genuinely institutionalized in our society. Indeed the distinction is itself largely relative and dynamic rather than absolute, and both are functionally essential to an even relatively stable society. Some elements of the population are relatively securely integrated but with varying emphasis in one direction or the other. Thus the best integrated professional groups would lean in the rational direction, certain rural elements in the traditional.

This difference of incidence has important consequences on both the structural and the psychological levels. Structurally it differentiates the social system broadly along a continuum of variation from the most highly traditionalized areas which have been least touched by the more recent phases of the process of rationalization to the most "emancipated" areas which tend at least partly to institutionalize the most "advanced" of the rationalized patterns or those which are otherwise most thoroughly emancipated from the traditional background.

---

[2] I am aware of the importance of other aspects of the total fascist pattern such as its romanticism and a tendency to ethical nihilism, but cannot stop to analyze them here.

For these and other reasons certain areas of the social structure have come to stand out conspicuously. In the first place is the area of "intellectualism" emancipated from the patterns and symbols of traditional thought, secondly of urbanism, particularly on the metropolitan scale with its freedom from particularistic controls, its cosmopolitanism and general disrespect for traditional ties. Third is the area of economic, technological, and administrative rationalization in the market system and large-scale organization, especially toward the top, with its responsiveness to *ad hoc* situations and its relation to conflicting codes. Fourth is the area of "cultural" emancipation in literature and the arts with its high susceptibility to unstable faddism, and its association with bohemianism. Finally there is the moral emancipation of "Society" with its partial permeation of the upper middle class, the adoption of manners and folkways not in keeping with various traditional canons of respectability, all the way from women smoking to polite adultery.

The uneven incidence of these various forms of emancipation results in an imperfect structural integration with latent or overt elements of conflict and antagonism. These conflicts in turn readily become associated with the tensions involved in other structural strains in the society. In particular may be mentioned here first, the difficult competitive position of the lower middle class, near enough to the realization of success goals to feel their attraction keenly but the great majority, by the sheer relation of their numbers to the relatively few prizes, doomed to frustration. Secondly, the particular strains in the situation of youth engendered by the necessity of emancipation from the family of orientation and exposure to the insecurities of competitive occupational adjustment at about the same stage of the life cycle, and third, the insecurity of the adult feminine role in our urban society.[3]

An element of at least latent antagonism between relatively emancipated and relatively traditionalized elements of the society would exist even if all its members were perfectly integrated with institutional patterns, if there were no anomie. But we have seen that anomie exists on a large scale. In relation to the above discussion, however, two principal foci, each with a tendency to a different structuring of attitudes need to be distinguished. On the one hand certain of the population elements involved in the spearheads of the processes of emancipation and rationalization are subject to a high incidence of it with its attendant insecurity. These elements tend to find the main points of reference of their orientations in the relatively well institutionalized rational and emancipated patterns—in science, liberalism, democracy, humanitarianism, individual freedom. But being insecure they tend to "overreact" and both positively and negatively to be susceptible to symboli-

---

[3] A colleague (E. Y. Hartshorne in an unpublished paper) has noted that in Germany the most conspicuous support of the Nazis came from the lower middle class, from youth, and from women. On the two latter factors see the author's paper "Age and Sex in the Social Structure of the United States," *Amer. Sociol. Review,* Vol. 7, No. 5, October, 1942.

zations and definitions of the situation which are more or less distorted cari-
catures of reality and which are overloaded with affect. Thus negatively the
traditional order from which emancipation has been taking place is characterized overwhelmingly as embodying ignorance, superstition, narrow-mindedness, privilege, or, in the later stages, acquisitive capitalistic exploitation.
On the positive side there has been not only a marked abstractness but also
some form of naive rationalistic utopianism. The pattern tends to bear conspicuous marks of the psychology of compulsion. It is held that if only certain
symbolic sources of evil like superstition, or privilege or capitalism were removed "everything would be all right" automatically and for all time. Indeed
there is every reason to believe that the psychology of this type of insecurity
has had much to do with the cognitive biases and inadequacies of utilitarian
thought as sketched above. It has contributed largely to the currency of a
definition of the situation which contains conspicuous elements of utopianism and of distorted caricature.

The other type of reaction has been prominent in those areas of the society
where traditional elements have formed the institutionalized points of reference for orientation. There the principal sources of anomie have often been
derived from situational factors such as technological change, mobility and
ethnic assimilation with relatively little direct relation to rationalized ideological patterns. There insecurity has tended to be structured in terms of a felt
threat to the traditionalized values. The typical reaction has been of an overdetermined "fundamentalist" type. Aggression has turned toward symbols
of the rationalizing and emancipated areas which are felt to be "subversive"
of these values. Naturally there has at the same time been an exaggerated assertion of and loyalty to those traditional values. The availability of ready-
made caricatured definitions of the situation and extreme symbols has of
course greatly facilitated this structuring. The use of such slogans as "capitalism," has made it possible to exaggerate the "rottenness" of the whole modern
society so far as it has departed from the good old values.

In the complex process of interaction in Western society between imperfectly integrated institutional structures, ideological definitions of the situation, and the psychological reaction patterns typical of anomie, at a certain
stage in the dynamic process of its development this new structured mass
movement has come upon the scene and at certain points in the Western
world has gained ascendancy. It is perhaps safe to conclude from the above
analysis that its possibility is at least as deeply rooted in the social structure
and dynamics of our society as was socialism at an earlier stage.

Before turning to another phase of the problem a word may be said about
the role of nationalism in the present context. Though not, in terms of the
"old regime," itself strictly a traditional value, the complex of sentiments focussing on national cultures has involved many of these traditionalistic elements—varying in specific content from one case to another. Ever since the

French Revolution a functional relationship between the rise of nationalism and the process of rationalization has been evident—they have developed concurrently.

For a variety of reasons nationalistic sentiment has been perhaps the readiest channel for the fundamentalist reaction to flow into. The national state assumed great actual importance. The actual or potential enemy in the power system of states, differing in national tradition, has formed a convenient target for the projection of many aggressive affects. At the same time many of the emancipated areas of the social structure have been defined as "international" and could be regarded as subversive of national interest, honor, and solidarity. Finally, nationalism has been a kind of lowest common denominator of traditionalistic sentiments. Above all, the humblest insecure citizen, whatever his frustrations in other connections, could not be deprived of his sense of "belonging" to the great national community.

Undoubtedly one of the most important reasons for the different degrees of success of the fascist movement in different countries has lain in the differing degrees in which national traditions and with them pride and honor, have been integrated with the symbols of the rationalized patterns of Western culture. In the United States, on the one hand, the great national tradition stems from the Enlightenment of the eighteenth century—liberty, democracy, the rights of the individual are our great slogans. A radically fundamentalist revolt would have to overcome the enormous power of these symbols. In Germany on the other hand the political symbols of a liberal democratic regime could be treated as having been ruthlessly imposed on a defeated and humiliated Germany by the alien enemy. National sentiments instead of being closely integrated with the existing regime could readily be mobilized against it.

The second important element of the fascist movements, that of "vested interests" can be much more briefly treated. It is one of the most fundamental theorems of the theory of institutions that in proportion to the institutionalization of any pattern a self-interest in conformity with it develops. Self-interest and moral sentiments are not necessarily antithetical, but may, and often do, motivate conduct in the same direction. Though this is true generally, it has a particularly important application to statuses involving prestige and authority in the social system. There, on top of the broader meaning of an interest in conformity, there is an interest in defending higher status and its perquisites against challenge from less privileged elements. For this reason the reaction of privileged elements to insecurity is almost inevitably structured in the direction of an attitude of defense of their privileges against challenge. For the same reason any movement which undermines the legitimacy of an established order tends to become particularly structured about an overt or implied challenge to the legitimacy of privileged statuses within it.

Western society has in all its recent history been relatively highly stratified, involving institutionalized positions of power, privilege, and prestige for certain elements. In the nature of the case the sentiments and symbols associated with these prestige elements have been integrated with those institutionalized in the society as a whole. In so far, then, as the process of rationalization and other disorganizing forces have undermined the security of traditional patterns the status and the bases of the legitimacy of privileged elements have inevitably been involved. But in addition to this they have been affected by threats to the legitimacy and security of their own position in the social structure. This situation tends to be particularly acute since the process of more general change is regularly accompanied by a process of the "circulation of the elite."

It is in the nature of a highly differentiated social structure that such privileged elements should be in a position to exercise influence on the power relations of the society through channels other than those open to the masses, through political intrigue, financial influence, and so on. Hence, with the progressive increase in the acuteness of a generalized state of anomie it is to be expected that such elements, which have been privileged in relation to a traditional social order should, within the limits provided by the particular situation, develop forms of activity, sometimes approaching conspiratorial patterns, which in these terms may be regarded as a defense of their vested interests. Exactly what groups are involved in this phenomenon is a matter of the particular structural situation in the society in question.

The general phenomenon would seem to be clear enough. It is also not difficult to understand the tendency for elite elements whose main patterns go far back into the older traditional society to become susceptible to the fascist type of appeal—such as the landed nobility and higher clergy in Spain, or the Junker class in Germany. But there is a further complication which requires some comment.

The process of institutional change in the recent history of our society has brought to the fore elite elements whose position has been institutionalized primarily about the newer rationalized patterns. The most important are the business and professional elites. The latter are, except where radical fascist movements have immediately threatened to gain the ascendency, perhaps the securest elite elements in the modern West.

The position of the business elite has, however, been much more complex. It gained for a time a position of great ascendancy, but for various reasons this rested on insecure foundations. With the "leftward" turn in the movement of ideology its position came under strong attack as the key element of capitalism. With its position thus threatened by the leftward sweep of the process of rationalization the legitimacy, the moral validity of its position was under attack, and its actual vested interests became less and less secure. From this point of view Fascism has constituted in one respect a continuation, even an intensification of the same threat. The threat has been made concrete by the rise to power of a new political elite with the means in hand to implement their threat.

At the same time fascism has seemed to stand, in the logic of the sentiments, for "sound" traditional values and to constitute a bulwark against subversive radicalism. Very concretely it has been instrumental in breaking the power of organized labor. At the same time on the level of power politics there has been a distinct area of potential mutual usefulness as between a political movement of the fascist type and entrenched business interests. This has been especially true because of the fascist tendency immediately to mobilize the economy in preparation for war.

The relation between fascism and vested interests in general may thus be regarded as a constant. In the case of the older traditional interests it is relatively unequivocal, but in that of business it is highly ambivalent. Especially where, as in Germany, business interests have not been closely integrated with strong liberal institutions the relationship has tended to be very close. But even there the movement can by no means be considered a simple expression of these vested interests and there are elements in the Nazi movement which may, in a certain state of the internal balance of power, turn out to be highly subversive of business.

In such brief space it has been possible to analyze only a few aspects of the very complex sociological problem presented by the fascist movement—the analysis is in no sense complete. But perhaps it will serve in a humble way to illustrate a direction in which it seems possible to utilize the conceptual tools of sociology in orienting ourselves, at least intellectually, to some of the larger aspects of the tragic social world we live in. To consider the possibility of going farther, of predicting the probable social consequences, of possible outcomes of the war and considering what we can do about fascism in other than a strictly military sense would raise such complex issues even on the scientific level, that it is better not even to attempt to touch upon them here.

JOOST A. M. MEERLOO

5. *Menticide**

There actually exists such a thing as a technique of mass brainwashing. This technique can take root in a country if an inquisitor is strong and shrewd enough. He can make most of us his victims, albeit temporarily.

What in the structure of society has made man so vulnerable to these mass manipulations of the mind? This is a problem with tremendous implications, just as brainwashing is. In recent years we have grown more and more aware of human interdependence with all its difficulties and complications.

I am aware of the fact that investigation of the subject of mental coercion and thought control becomes less pleasant as time goes on. This is so because it may become more of a threat to us here and now, and our concern for China and Korea must yield to the more immediate needs at our own door. Can totalitarian tendencies take over here, and what social symptoms may lead to such phenomena? Stern reality confronts us with the universal mental battle between thought control (and its corollaries) and our standards of decency, personal strength, personal ideas, and a personal conscience with autonomy and dignity.

Future social scientists will be better able to describe the causes of the advent of totalitarian thinking and acting in man. We know that after wars and revolutions this mental deterioration more easily finds an opportunity to develop, helped by special psychopathic personalities who only flourish on man's misery and confusion. It is also true that the next generation spontaneously begins to correct the misdeeds of the previous one because the ruthless system has become too threatening to them.

My task, however, is to describe some symptoms of the totalitarian process (which implies deterioration of thinking and acting) as I have observed them in our own epoch, keeping in mind that the system is one of the most violent distortions of man's consistent mental growth. No brainwashing is possible without totalitarian thinking.

The tragic facts of political experiences in our age make it all too clear that applied psychological technique can brainwash entire nations and reduce their citizens to a kind of mindless robotism which becomes for them a normal way of living. Perhaps we can best understand how this frighten-

* From Joost A. M. Meerloo, *The Rape of the Mind: The Psychology of Thought Control, Menticide, and Brainwashing* (World Publishing Company, 1956). By permission.

ing thing comes about by examining a mythical country, which, for the sake of convenience, we shall call Totalitaria.

THE ROBOTIZATION OF MAN

First, let me utter a word of caution. We must not make the mistake of thinking that there is any one particular nation that can be completely identified with this hypothetical land. The characteristics to be discussed can come into existence here. Some of Totalitaria's characteristics were, of course, present in Nazi Germany, and they can today be found behind the Iron Curtain, but they exist to some extent in other parts of the world as well. Totalitaria is any country in which political ideas degenerate into senseless formulations made only for propaganda purposes. It is any country in which a single group—left or right—acquires absolute power and becomes omniscient and omnipotent, any country in which disagreement and differences of opinion are crimes, in which utter conformity is the price of life.

Totalitaria—the Leviathan state—is the home of the political system we call, euphemistically, totalitarianism, of which systematized tyranny is a part. This system does not derive from any honest political philosophy, either socialist or capitalist. Totalitaria's leaders may mouth ideologies, but these are in fact mainly catchwords used to justify the regime. If necessary, totalitarianism can change its slogans and its behavior overnight. For totalitarianism embodies, to me, the quest for total power, the quest of a dictator to rule the world. The words and concepts of "socialism" and "communism" may serve, like "democracy," as a disguise for the megalomaniac intention of the tyrant.

Since totalitarianism is essentially the social manifestation of a psychological phenomenon belonging to every personality, it can best be understood in terms of the human forces that create, foster, and perpetuate it. Man has two faces; he wants to grow toward maturity and freedom, and yet the primitive child in his unconscious yearns for complete protection and irresponsibility. His mature self learns how to cope with the restrictions and frustrations of daily life, but at the same time, the child in him longs to hit out against them, to beat them down, to destroy them—whether they be objects or people. Totalitarianism appeals to this confused infant in all of us; it seems to offer a solution to the problems man's double yearning creates. Our mythical Totalitaria is a monolithic and absolute state in which doubt, confusion, and conflict are not permitted to be shown, for the dictator purports to solve all his subjects' problems for them. In addition, Totalitaria can provide official sanction for the expression of man's most antisocial impulses. The uncivilized child hidden in us may welcome this liberation from ethical frustrations.

On the other hand, our free, mature, social selves cannot be happy in Totalitaria; they revolt against the restriction of individual impulses.

The psychological roots of totalitarianism are usually irrational, destructive, and primitive, though disguised behind some ideology, and for this reason there is something fantastic, unbelievable, even nightmarish about the system itself. There is, of course, a difference in the psychic experience of the elite, who can live out their needs for power, and the masses, who have to submit; yet the two groups influence each other. When a dictator's deep neurotic needs for power also satisfy some profound emotional need in the population of his country, especially in times of misery or after a revolution, he is more easily able to assume the power for which he longs. If a nation has suffered defeat in war, for example, its citizens feel shame and resentment. Loss of face is not simply a political abstraction, it is a very real and personal thing to a conquered people; every man, consciously or unconsciously, identifies with his native land. If a country suffers from prolonged famine or severe depression, its citizens become bitter, depressed, and resentful, and will more willingly accept the visions and promises of the aspiring dictator. If the complexity of a country's political and economic apparatus makes the individual citizen feel powerless, confused, and useless, if he has no sense of participation in the forces that govern his daily life, or if he feels these forces to be so vast and confusing that he can no longer understand them, he will grasp at the totalitarian opportunity for belonging, for participation, for a simple formula that explains and rationalizes what is beyond his comprehension. And when the dictator has taken over finally, he transfers his own abnormal fantasies, his rage and anger, easily to his subjects. Their resentments feed his; his pseudo-strength encourages them. A mutual fortification of illusions takes place.

Totalitarianism as a social manifestation is a disease of interhuman relations, and, like any other disease, man can best resist its corroding effects if, through knowledge and training, he is well immunized against it. If, however, he is unfortunate enough to catch the totalitarian bug, he has to muster all the positive forces in his mind to defeat it. The raging internal struggle between the irresponsible child and the mature adult in him continues until one or the other is finally destroyed completely. As long as a single spark of either remains, the battle goes on. And for as long as man is alive, the quest for maturity keeps on.

CULTURAL PREDILECTION FOR TOTALITARIANISM

In the battle against this dread disease, social factors as well as personal ones play an important role. We can see this more clearly if we analyze the ways in which the ideals of a culture as a whole affect its citizens' vulnerability to totalitarianism. The ethics of our own Western civilization are our strongest defenses against the disease, for the ideal of these ethics is to produce a breed of men and women who are strongly individualistic and who evaluate situations primarily in terms of their own consciences. We aim to develop in our citizens a sense of self-responsibility, a willingness to confront the world as it is, and an ability to distinguish between right and wrong through their own feelings and thoughts. Such men and women are impelled to action by their personal moral standards rather than by what some outside group sets up as correct. They are unwilling to accept group evaluations immediately unless these coincide with their own personal convictions, or unless they have been able to discuss them in a democratic way. People like this are responsible to their communities because they are first responsible to themselves. If they disagree, they will form a *loyal minority,* using their rights of convincing other people at appropriate times.

There are other cultures which emphasize attitudes and values that are different from these. The Eastern ideal of man, as we find it in China and some of the other Oriental countries, is in the first place that of *oneness,* of being one with the family, one with the fatherland, one with the cosmos—nirvana. The Oriental psyche looks for a direct esthetic contact with reality through an indefinable empathy and intuition. Eternal truth is behind reality, behind the veil of Maya. Man is part of the universe; his ideal is passive servility and nonirritability. His ideal of peace lies in rest and relaxation, in meditation, in being without manual and mental travail. The happiness of the Oriental psyche lies in the ecstasy of feeling united with the universal cosmos. Ascesis, self-redemption, and poverty are better realized ideals in Oriental culture than in our Western society. The classic Oriental culture pattern can best be described as a pattern of participation. In it the individual is looked upon as an integral part of the group, the family, the caste, the nation. He is not a separate, independent entity. In this culture, greater conformity to and acceptance of the collective rules are the ideals. An Oriental child may be trained from infancy into a pattern of submission to authority and to the rules of the group. Many primitive cultures also display this pattern. To a person raised in these cultures, the most acceptable standards, the best conceivable thoughts and actions, are those sanctioned by the group. The totalitarian world of mass actions and mass thoughts is far more comprehensible to the members of a participation-patterned and less individual-minded culture than it is to Western individualists. What is to us unbearable regimentation and authoritarianism may be to them comforting order and regularity.

An example of an intensified pattern of participation and thought control and mutual spying has been given by the anthropologist E. P. Dozier.[1] The Pueblo Indians of the Rio Grande area believe that wrongdoing or wrong thinking of one man in the tribe affects all members. He may upset the cosmic balance by ill feeling toward any one of his fellow men. The moral code of the village is group-centered. The individual who transgresses this jeopardizes the well-being of all. Epidemics, crop failures, droughts are in-

[1] *The New York Times,* December 11, 1955; *Science News Letter,* December 3, 1955.

terpreted as a result of "deviationism" of one member of the group. Village members are closely watched and spied on in order to discover the culprit or "witch." Gossip and accusations of witchcraft are rampant, and the Pueblo Indian is constantly searching in his own conscience for harmful thoughts and attitudes. It is as if we watch the ritual of the purge in the totalitarian state.

Such forms of *creeping collectivism* and participation we may see in every group formation where tolerance for nonconformism ceases to exist. Wherever dogmatic partisanship dominates, the mind is coerced. We may even detect such encroaching tendencies in some scientific circles where there exists an overemphasis on group research, teamwork, membership cards, and a disdain for individual opinion.

The culture into which a man is born and his own psychological constitution interact to produce his personality in much the same way as his body and mind interact to produce his behavior. Our culture of individual freedom may offer us a partial immunity to the disease of totalitarianism, but at the same time our personal immaturities and repressed savageries can make us vulnerable to it. The participation type of culture may make men more susceptible in general to totalitarianism, although personal strivings toward maturity and individuality can offer them, too, some measure of protection against it.

Because of the interaction between these social and personal forces, no culture is completely safe from internal attack by totalitarianism and from the mental destruction it may create. As I said before, our Totalitaria is a mythical country, but the brutal truth is that any country can be turned into a Totalitaria.

The aims of the rulers of our fictitious country are simply formulated: despotism, the total domination of man and mankind, and the unity of the entire world under one dictatorial authority. At first glance, this idea of unity can be most attractive—the idea, oversimplified, of a brotherhood unity of nations under a central powerful agency. When the world is one, it would seem, there will be no more war, the tensions that face us will be eliminated, earth will become a paradise, but the simplified conception of a universal dictatorship is false and reflects the danger inherent in the totalitarian goal: all men are different, and it is the difference between them that creates the greatness, the variety, and the creative inspirations of life, as well as the tensions of social intercourse. The totalitarian conception of equalization can be realized only in death, when the chemical and physical laws that govern all of us take over completely. Death is indeed the great equalizer.

In life, all of us are different. Our bodies and minds interact with one another and with the outside world in different ways. Each man's personality is unique. True, all of us share certain basic human qualities with all the other members of the human race, but the differences in personality are also so many and so varied that no two men anywhere in the world or ever in all of human history can be said to be exactly alike. This uniqueness is as true of the citizen of Totalitaria as it is of anyone else. As a human being, he is not only different from us, he is different from his compatriots. However, to create man in the totalitarian image through leveling and equalization means to suppress what is essentially personal and human in him, the uniqueness and the variety, and to create a society of robots, not men. The noted social scientist, J. S. Bruner, in his introduction to Bauer's book on Soviet psychology has expressed this thought in a different way: "Man's image of the nature of man is not only a matter for objective inquiry; it is and has always been a prime instrument of social and political control. He who molds that image does so with enormous consequences for the society in which he lives."

Totalitaria fosters the illusion that everyone is part of the government, a voter; no one can be a non-voter or anti-voter. His inner pros and cons and doubts are not private problems of the individual himself any more; his thoughts belong to the state, the dictator, the ruling circle, the Party. His inner thoughts have to be controlled. Only those in power know what really lies behind national policy. The ordinary citizen becomes as dependent and obedient as a child. In exchange for giving up his individuality, he obtains some special gratifications: the feeling of belonging and of being protected, the sense of relief over losing his personal boundaries and responsibilities, the ecstasy of being taken up and absorbed in wild, uncontrolled collective feelings, the safety of being anonymous, of being merely a cog in the wheel of the all-powerful state.

The despotism of modern Totalitaria is very different from the lush, exotic personal tyrannies of ancient times. It is an ascetic, cold, mechanical force, aiming at what Hanna Ahrendt calls the "transformation of human nature itself." In our theoretical country, man has no individual ego any longer, no personality, no self. A leveling system is at work, and everything above the common level is trampled on and beaten down.

THE TOTALITARIAN LEADER

The leaders of Totalitaria are the strangest men in the state. These men are, like all other men, unique in their mental structure, and consequently we cannot make any blanket psychiatric diagnosis of the mental illness which motivates their behavior. But we can make some generalizations which will help us toward some understanding of the totalitarian leader. Obviously, for example, he suffers from an overwhelming need to control other human beings and to exert unlimited power, and this in itself is a psychological aberration, often rooted in deep-seated feelings of anxiety, humiliation, and inferiority. The ideologies such men propound are only used as tactical and strategical devices through which they hope to reach their final goal of complete domination over other men. This domination may help them compensate for pathological fears and feelings of unworthiness, as we can conclude from the psychological study of some modern dictators.

Fortunately, we do not have to rely on a purely hypothetical picture of the psychopathology of the totalitarian dictator. Dr. G. M. Gilbert, who studied some of the leaders of Nazi Germany during the Nuremberg trials, has given us a useful insight into their twisted minds, useful especially because it reveals to us something about the mutual interaction between the totalitarian leader and those who want to be led by him.

Hitler's suicide made a clinical investigation of his character structure impossible, but Dr. Gilbert heard many eyewitness reports of Hitler's behavior from his friends and collaborators, and these present a fantastic picture of Nazism's prime mover. Hitler was known among his intimates as the carpet-eater, because he often threw himself on the floor in a kicking and screaming fit like an epileptic rage. From such reports, Dr. Gilbert was able to deduce something about the roots of the pathological behavior displayed by this morbid "genius." Hitler's paranoid hostility against the Jew was partly related to his unresolved parental conflicts; the Jews probably symbolized for him the hated drunken father who mistreated Hitler and his mother when the future *Führer* was still a child. Hitler's obsessive thinking, his furious fanaticism, his insistence on maintaining the purity of "Aryan blood," and his ultimate mania to destroy himself and the world were obviously the results of a sick psyche. As early as 1923, nearly ten years before he seized power, Hitler was convinced that he would one day rule the world, and he spent time designing monuments of victory, eternalizing his glory, to be erected all over the European continent when the day of victory arrived. This delusional preoccupation continued until the end of his life; in the midst of the war he created, which led him to defeat and death, Hitler continued revising and improving his architectural plans.

Nazi dictator Number Two, Hermann Goering, who committed suicide to escape the hangman, had a different psychological structure. His pathologically aggressive drives were encouraged by the archaic military tradition of the German Junker class, to which his family belonged. From early childhood he had been compulsively and overtly aggressive. He was an autocratic and a corrupt cynic, grasping the Nazi-created opportunity to achieve purely personal gain. His contempt for the "common people" was unbounded; this was a man who had literally no sense of moral values.

Quite different again was Rudolf Hess, the man of passive yet fanatical doglike devotion, living, as it were, by proxy through the mind of his *Führer*. His inner mental weakness made it easier for him to live through means of a proxy than through his own personality, and drove him to become the shadow of a seemingly strong man, from whom he could borrow strength. The Nazi ideology gave this frustrated boy the illusion of blood identification with the glorious German race. After his wild flight to England, Hess showed obvious psychotic traits; his delusions of persecution, hysterical attacks, and periods of amnesia are among the well-known clinical symptoms of schizophrenia.

Still another type was Hans Frank, the devil's advocate, the prototype of the overambitious latent homosexual, easily seduced into political adventure, even when this was in conflict with the remnants of his conscience. For unlike Goering, Frank was capable of distinguishing between right and wrong.

Dr. Gilbert also tells us something about General Wilhelm Keitel, Hitler's Chief of Staff, who became the submissive, automatic mouthpiece of the *Führer,* mixing military honor and personal ambition in the service of his own unimportance.

Of a different quality is the S. S. Colonel, Hoess, the murderer of millions in the concentration camp of Auschwitz. A pathological character structure is obvious in this case. All his life, Hoess had been a lonely, withdrawn, schizoid personality, without any conscience, wallowing in his own hostile and destructive fantasies. Alone and bereft of human attachments, he was intuitively sought out by Himmler for this most savage of all the Nazi jobs. He was a useful instrument for the committing of the most bestial deeds.

Unfortunately, we have no clear psychiatric picture yet of the Russian dictator Stalin. There have been several reports that during the last years of his life he had a tremendous persecution phobia and lived in constant terror that he would become the victim of his own purges.

Psychological analysis of these men shows clearly that a pathological culture—a mad world—can be built by certain impressive psychoneurotic types. The venal political figures need not even comprehend the social and political consequences of their behavior. They are compelled not by ideological belief, no matter how much they may rationalize to convince themselves they are, but by the distortions of their own personalities. They are not motivated by their advertised urge to serve their country or mankind, but rather by an overwhelming need and compulsion to satisfy the cravings of their own pathological character structures. The ideologies they spout are not real goals; they are the cynical devices by which these sick men hope to achieve some personal sense of worth and power. Subtle inner lies seduce them into going from bad to worse. Defensive self-deception, arrested insight, evasion of emotional identification with others, degradation of empathy—the mind has many defense mechanisms with which to blind the conscience. A clear example of this can be seen in the way the Nazi leaders defended themselves through continuous self-justification and exculpation when they were brought before the bar at the Nuremberg trials. These murderers were aggrieved and hurt by the accusations brought against them; they were the very picture of injured innocence.

Any form of leadership, if unchecked by controls, may gradually turn into dictatorship. Being a leader, carrying great power and responsibility for other people's lives, is a monumental test for the human psyche. The weak leader is the man who cannot meet it, who simply abdicates his responsibility. The dictator is the man who replaces the existing standards of justice and morality by more and more private prestige, by more and more power, and eventually isolates himself more and more from the rest of humanity. His suspicion grows, his isolation grows, and the vicious circle leading to a paranoid attitude begins to develop.

The dictator is not only a sick man, he is also a cruel opportunist. He sees no value in any other person and feels no gratitude for any help he may have received. He is suspicious and dishonest and believes that his personal ends justify any means he may use to achieve them. Peculiarly enough, every tyrant still searches for some self-justification. Without such a soothing device for his own conscience, he cannot live. His attitude toward other people is manipulative; to him, they are merely tools for the advancement of his own interests. He rejects the conception of doubt, of internal contradictions, of man's inborn ambivalence. He denies the psychological fact that man grows to maturity through groping, through trial and error, through the interplay of contrasting feelings. Because he will not permit himself to grope, to learn through trial and error, the dictator can never become a mature person. But whether he acknowledges them or not, he has internal conflicts, he suffers somewhere from internal confusion. These inner "weaknesses" he tries to repress sternly; if they were to come to the surface, they might interfere with the achievement of his goals. Yet, in the attacks of rage his weakening strength is evident.

It is because the dictator is afraid, albeit unconsciously, of his own internal contradictions, that he is afraid of the same internal contradictions of his fellow men. He must purge and purge, terrorize and terrorize in order to still his own raging inner drives. He must kill every doubter, destroy every person who makes a mistake, imprison everyone who cannot be proved to be utterly single-minded. In Totalitaria, the latent aggression and savagery in man are cultivated by the dictator to such a degree that they can explode into the mass criminal actions shown by Hitler's persecution of minorities. Ultimately, the country shows a real pathology, an utter dominance of destructive and self-destructive tendencies.

THE FINAL SURRENDER OF THE ROBOT MAN

What happens to the common man in such a culture? How can we describe the citizen of Totalitaria? Perhaps the simplest answer to this question lies in the statement that he is reduced to the mechanical precision of an insectlike state. He cannot develop any warm friendships, loyalties, or allegiances because they may be too dangerous for him. Today's friend may be, after all, tomorrow's enemy. Living in an atmosphere of constant suspicion—not only of strangers, but even of his own family—he is afraid to express himself lest concentration camp or prison swallow him up. The citizens of Totalitaria do not really converse with one another. When they speak, they whisper, first looking furtively over their shoulders for the inevitable spy. Their inner silence is in sharp contrast to the official verbal bombardment. The citizens of Totalitaria may make noise, and utter polite banalities, or they may repeat slogans to one another, but they say nothing. Existing literature reveals that leading authors, among them H. G. Wells, Huxley, and Orwell, grow more and more concerned about the ghastly future of the robotized man, trained as a machine on a standard of conformity. They translate for us the common fear of a mechanized civilization.

In Totalitaria, the citizen no longer knows the real core of his mind. He no longer feels himself an *I*, an ego, a person. He is only the object of official barrage and mental coercion. Having no personality of his own, he has no individual conscience, no personal morality, no capacity to think clearly and honestly. He learns by rote, he learns thousands of indoctrinated facts and inhales dogma and slogans with every breath he draws. He becomes an obedient pedant, and pendantry makes people into something resembling pots filled with information instead of individuals with free, growing personalities. Becoming wiser and freer implies selective forgetting and changes of mind. This we accept, this we leave behind. Alert adjustment requires a change of patterns, the capacity to be deconditioned, to undo and unlearn in order to become ripe for new patterns. The citizen of Totalitaria has no chance for such learning through unlearning, for growth through individual experience. Official oversimplifications induce the captive audience into acceptance and indoctrination. Mass ecstasy and mass fanaticism are substituted for quiet individual thought and consideration. Hitler taught his people to march and to do battle, and at the end they did not know wherefore they marched and battled. People become herds—indoctrinated and obsessed herds—intoxicated first with enthusiasm and happy expectations, then with terror and panic. The individual personality cannot grow in Totalitaria. The huge mass of citizens is tamed into personal and political somnambulism.

It may be scientifically questionable to compare experiences gained from individual pathological states with social phenomena and to analyze the partial collapse of the ego under totalitarianism by analogy with actual cases of madness. But there is in fact much that is comparable between the strange reactions of the citizens of Totalitaria and their culture as a whole on the one hand and the reactions of the introverted, sick schizophrenic on the other. Even though the problem of schizophrenic behavior in individuals and groups is extremely complicated and cannot be fully handled within the scope of this book, the comparison can be helpful in our search for an understanding of the nature and effects of totalitarianism.

THE COMMON RETREAT FROM REALITY

This excursion into the world of pathology is not a description of a merely coincidental resemblance between a disease and a political system. It should serve to point up the fact that totalitarian withdrawal behind official justifications and individual fantasy is something that can occur either in social life or inside the individual mind. And many scholars believe in a relationship between cultural deterioration and schizophrenic withdrawal.

Let us briefly explain the individual schizophrenic's reaction of complete inner automatization and mental withdrawal as a personal failure to adjust to a world experienced as insecure and dangerous. Often rather simple emotional incidents may lead to such schizophrenic retreat—for instance, the intrusion of schedules and habits forced on the mind during infancy or a sly hypersensitivity to our overactive and ororverbose culture. Many a child is forced into schizophrenic withdrawal by an overcompulsive parent. Sometimes lack of external contact may drive a man into a state of utter loneliness and isolation, sometimes his own preference for solitude. A certain tendency to so-called schizophrenic withdrawal has been proved to be inborn. Yet it can be provoked in everybody. Whatever the cause, the schizophrenic patient becomes a desocialized being, lost in loneliness. Conscious and unconscious fantasy life begins to become dominant over alert confrontation of reality. In the end his weird fantasies become more real for the schizophrenic than the actual world. He hides more and more behind his own iron curtain, in the imaginary dreamland and retreat he has built for himself. This is his nirvana, in which all his dream wishes are fulfilled. Inertia and fanaticism alternate. The patient regresses to an infantile, vegetative form of behavior and rejects everything that society has taught him. In his fantasy, he lives in a world which always obeys his commands. He is omnipotent. The world turns around according to his divine inclinations. Reality, requiring as it does, continual and renewed adjustment and verification, becomes a persecutor, attacking his illusion of divine might. Every disturbing intrusion into his delusional world is encountered by the schizophrenic either with tremendous aggression or with the formation of secondary delusion to protect the first delusion, or with a combination of both. The schizophrenic displays tremendous hostility toward the real world and its representatives; reality robs him both of his delusions of omnipotence and his hallucinatory sense of being utterly protected, as he was in the womb.

Clinical experience has shown that the disease of schizophrenia often begins with negativism—a defense against the influence of others, a continual fight against mental intrusion, against what is felt as the rape of the oversensitive mind. Gradually this defensive attitude toward the world becomes a hostile attitude toward everything, not only toward influences from the outside, but also toward thoughts and feelings from the inside. Finally, the victim becomes paralyzed by his own hostility and negativisms. He behaves literally as though he were dead. He sits, unmoving, for hours. He may have to be force-fed, force-dressed. The schizophrenic moves like a puppet on a string, only when someone compels him to. Clinically, we call this catatonia—the death attitude.

THE RETREAT TO AUTOMATIZATION

Introverted schizophrenics prefer the automatic routine life of the asylum to life in the outside world, on the condition that they be allowed to indulge their private fantasies. They surrender utterly to self-defeatism. They never congregate in groups, they seldom talk with one another; even when they do, they never have any real mutual contact. Each one lives in his own retreat.

In the totalitarian myth—think, for instance, of *das Dritte Reich*—in the psychological folklore of our mythical state, the vague fantasy of the technically perfected womb, the ideal nirvana, plays a tremendous role. In a world full of insecurities, a world requiring continual alert adjustment and readjustment, Totalitaria creates the delusion of the omnipotent, miraculous ideal state—a state where, in its final form, every material need will be satisfied. Everything will be regulated, just as it was for the fetus in the womb, the land of bliss and equanimity, just as it is for the schizophrenic in the mental hospital. There is no social struggle, no mental struggle; the world moves like clockwork. There is no real interplay between people, no clash of opinions or beliefs, there is no emotional relationship between these womb-fellows; each exists as a separate number-bearing entity in the same filing system. In Totalitaria, there is no faith in fellow men, no *caritas,* no love, because real relationships between men do not exist, just as they do not exist between schizophrenics. There is only faith in and subjection to the feeding system, and there is in every citizen a tremendous fear of being expelled from that system, a fear of being totally lost, comparable with the schizophrenic's feeling of rejection and fear of reality. In the midst of spiritual loneliness and isolation, there is the fear of still greater loneliness, of more painful isolation. Without protective regulations from the outside, internal hell may break loose. Strong mechanical external order must be used to cover the internal chaos and approaching breakdown.

We have had experience in postwar years with several refugees from the totalitarian world who broke down when they had to cope with a world of freedom where personal initiative was required. The fear of freedom brought them to a state of panic. They no longer had strong enough egos to build and maintain their defenses against the competitive demands of free democratic reality. As in schizophrenia, a maneuverable and individual ego cannot exist in Totalitaria. In schizophrenia the ego shrinks as a result of withdrawal, in Totalitaria, as a result of constant merging in mass feelings. If such a shrunken ego should grow up, with its own critical attitude, its needs for verification of facts and for understanding, it would then be beaten down as being treacherous and nonconforming.

Totalitaria requires of its citizens complete subjection to and identification with the leader. It is this leader-dominance that makes people nearly ego-less, as they are in schizophrenia. This again may result in loss of control of hostile and destructive drives. Psychologists have seen this time and time again in what we can call the concentration-camp psyche. When the victims first came to the camp—dedicated to their gradual extermination—most of them displayed a complete loss of self, an utter depersonalization, combined with apathy and loss of awareness. The same observations have been made among our P.O.W.s in Korea. Some concentration-camp victims got better immediately after their return to a normal society; in others, this schizophrenic reaction of lost ego remained and, as we mentioned above, sometimes developed into a real psychosis.

THE WOMB STATE

Totalitarianism is man's escape from the fearful realities of life into the virtual womb of the leader. The individual's actions are directed from this womb—from the inner sanctum. The mystic center is in control of everything; man need no longer assume responsibility for his own life. The order and logic of the prenatal world reign. There is peace and silence, the peace of utter submission. The members of the womb state do not really communicate; between them there is silence, the silence of possible betrayal, not the mature silence of reticence and reservedness. Totalitaria increases the gap between the things one shows and communicates and the things one secretly dreams and thinks deep within oneself. It develops the artificial split-mindedness of political silence. Whatever little remains of individual feeling and opinion is kept carefully enclosed. In the schizophrenic world of Totalitaria, there is no free mutual exchange, no conversation, no exclamation, no release from emotional tension. It is a world of silent conspirators. Indeed, the atmosphere of suspicion is the big attacker of mental freedom because it makes people cling together, conspiring against mysterious enemies—first from outside, then among themselves.

In Totalitaria each citizen is continually watched. The mythical state molds the individual's conscience. He has hardly any of his own. His neighbors watch him, his postman, his children, and they all represent the punishing state, just as he himself must represent the state and watch others. Not betraying them is a crime.

The need to find conspiracies, to discover persecutors and criminals is another schizophrenic manifestation. It is psychologically related to an infantile need for a feeling of omnipotence. Megalomaniac feelings grow better in an atmosphere of mysterious secrecy. Secrecy and conspiracy increase the delusion of power. That is why so many people like to pry into other people's lives and to play the spy.

This feeling of conspiracy also lies behind the pathological struggle with imaginary persecutors, a struggle we find both in mentally ill individuals and in our mythical Totalitaria. "It is there!" "It is chasing us!" All the inner fears of losing the nirvanic womb-illusion become rampant. Mysterious ghosts and vultures chase people out of nirvana and paradise.

In these fantasies, the patriarch, the dictator, the idol, becomes both the universal danger and the omnipotent savior at the same time. Not even the citizens of Totalitaria really love this cruel giant. Suspicion against the breast that feeds and the hand that guides and forbids is often found in the fantasy of schizophrenic children, who experience the nourisher as the enemy, the dominating ogre, bribing the growing mind into submission.

The deep hate the sick individual feels toward the parental figure cannot be expressed directly, and so it is displaced onto the self or onto scapegoats. Scapegoatism is also part of the totalitarian strategy. As we pointed out before, the scapegoat temporarily absorbs all the individual's inner fury and rage. Kulaks, Negroes, Jews, Communists, capitalists, profiteers and war-mongers—any or all of them can play that role. Perhaps the greatest danger, to the totalitarian mind, is the use of intellect and awareness and the "egg-head's" demand for free, verifying thinking. Aberration and perversion are chosen by the citizens of Totalitaria, as they are by the inhabitants of mad-houses, over tiring, intellectual control.

In the center of the totalitarian fears and fantasies stands the man-eating god and idol. He is unconquerable. He uses man's great gift of adjustment to bring him to slavery. Every man's inner core of feelings and thoughts has to belong to the leader.

Is the citizen of Totalitaria consciously aware of this? Probably not. Modern psychology has taught us how strongly the mental mechanism of denial of reality works. The eye bypasses external occurrences when the mind does not want them to happen. Secondary justifications and fantasies are formed to support and explain these denials. In Totalitaria we find the same despising of reality facts as we do in schizophrenia. How else are we to explain the fact that Hitler was still moving his armies on paper after they were already defeated?

Totalitarian strategy covers inner chaos and conflict by the strict order of the police state. So does the compulsive schizophrenic patient, by his inner routine and schedules. These routines and schedules are a defense against painful occurrences in external reality. This internal robotization may lead to denial of internal realities and internal needs as well. The citizen of Totalitaria, repressing and rejecting his inner need for freedom, may even experience slavery as liberation. He may go even one step further—yearn for an escape from life itself, a delusion that he could become omnipotent through utter destruction. The S. S. soldiers called this the magic action of the *Blutkitt,* the tie of bloody crime binding them together and preparing them for Valhalla. With this magic unification, they could die with courage and equanimity. Anarchic despair and need for greatness alternated in them as they do in the psychotic patient. In the same way, the citizens of Totalitaria search for a "heroic" place in history even though the price be doom and annihilation.

Many soldiers—tired by the rigidities of normal life—look back at violent moments of their war experiences, despite the hunger and terror, as the monumental culminating experiences of their lives. There, in the *Bruderbund* of fighters, they felt happy for the first and only times in their lives (Dicks).

This all sounds like a bitter comedy, but the fantasy of schizophrenics has taught us how the mind can retreat into delusion when there is a fear of daily existence. Under these circumstances, fantasy begins to prevail over reality, and soon assumes a validity which reality never had. The totalitarian mind is like the schizophrenic mind; it has a contempt for reality. Think for a moment of Lysenko's theory and its denial of the influence of heredity. The totalitarian mind does not observe and verify its impressions of reality; it dictates to reality how it shall behave, it compels reality to conform to its fantasies.

The comparison between totalitarianism and psychosis is not incidental. Delusional thinking inevitably creeps into every form of tyranny and despotism. Unconscious backward forces come into action. Evil powers from the archaic past return. An automatic compulsion to go on to self-destruction develops, to justify one mistake with a new one; to enlarge and expand the vicious pathological circle becomes the dominating end of life. The frightened man, burdened by a culture he does not understand, retreats into the brute's fantasy of limitless power in order to cover up the vacuum inside himself. This fantasy starts with the leaders and is later taken over by the masses they oppress.

What else can man do when he is caught in that tremendous machine called Totalitaria? Thinking—and the brain itself—has become superfluous, that is, only reserved for the elite. Man has to renounce his uniqueness, his individual personality, and must surrender to the equalizing and homogenizing patterns of so-called integration and standardization. This arouses in him that great inner emptiness of the savage child, the emptiness of the robot that unwittingly yearns for the great destruction.

Chapter IX

TOTALITARIAN COMMUNISM

The Industrial Revolution separated man from the ownership of the tools of production: first, the self-employing artisan was replaced by the capitalist employer, who owned the machines employing hundreds and thousands of workers owning nothing but their hands. Second, as modern technology progressed, the proportion of those who owned the instruments of production shrank enormously, thus widening the gap between those who owned the tools and those who worked them. Third, as modern industry developed, the incidence of capital investments in the total process of production rose steadily: greater initial amounts of capital were needed to start out in business and manufacture. The basic capital requirement to manufacture buggies and supply horses is less than to manufacture automobiles and locomotives. Fourth, concentration of capital was accompanied by concentration of control, so that fewer and fewer persons controlled bigger and bigger aggregates of wealth, although ownership—as distinct from control—spread through the corporate form of business organization.

Where small property has survived as an efficient economic unit, as in agriculture, the collectivist idea has made little headway. And where there has been little industrialization, as in Tsarist Russia, China, or Eastern Europe, communism has aimed not so much at nationalizing the means of production (there would not be much to nationalize, in the first place), as at the building of a modern industrial economy on the basis of public ownership. Because initial capital requirements are heavy, especially in durable goods and basic industries, the state has often been forced to operate new industries on the basis of public ownership, even where it officially persecuted the communist movement.

Marxist communism aims at the overthrow of capitalism through revolutionary means, and believes in the necessity of setting up a dictatorship of the proletariat (through the agency of the Communist party) until the remnants of the capitalist ideology and habits of thought are liquidated. Evolutionary, democratic socialism, on the other hand, adheres to the method of constitutional procedure all throughout: it seeks power through ballots rather than bullets; and, once in power, it maintains democratic methods of government, and subjects itself to periodic tests of approval or disapproval by the electorate.

Revolutionary Marxism visualizes the transition from capitalism to communism as sudden and complete; there is no payment of compensation for expropriated property, because capitalist property is, morally and socially, little better than theft derived from exploitation. By contrast, democratic socialism is slow and piecemeal, evolves (like other transactions of advanced capitalism) on the installment plan, and has to prove its right to hold power by keeping the consent of the majority. As to compensation, democratic socialism does not believe that legitimate expectations of citizens may be violated, and persists in the belief that expropriation of private property is permissible only after due process and proper compensation. It "just isn't done" to take away property by legislative fiat, democratic socialists believe. If the whole economic system be compared to a basket of eggs, Marxist communism burns the basket and scrambles all eggs at once—never to be unscrambled again. Democratic socialism keeps the basket, and cooks only small orders of scrambled eggs at one time, because it believes in the Aristotelian observation that "the guest will judge better of a feast than the cook." If it turns out that the people—including many socialists—do not wish any further transfer of private property to public ownership, the democratic socialist must (for reasons of political expediency if for no other) accept their verdict. In the light of their repeated electoral defeats throughout the nineteen fifties, both the British Labor Party and the German Social Democratic Party have virtually abandoned nationalization of industry as a major objective, concentrating instead on the goals of social equality and the welfare state.

For the communist, such a change of policy is well-nigh inconceivable, because by definition only a small revolutionary minority—the Communist Party—knows what is best for the whole society. Therefore there is no point (in the communist view) in holding free elections in communist states, because the goal is fixed, and any popular verdict contrary to official communist policy would only indicate the survival of "bourgeois, counterrevolutionary" ideologies to be liquidated as quickly and as drastically as possible. By contrast, for the democratic socialist (as for democrats of any other economic philosophy) the freedom of the individual is the top priority, to which everything else has to be subordinated. The democratic socialist therefore knows that he may have to wait a long time, until he can peacefully persuade his fellow citizens that capitalism is inefficient and unjust, and that the proposed socialist remedies are practical and equitable. The communist tells him that it is useless to try the conquest of power by persuasion, because all mediums of communication, education, and propaganda are biased in favor of the capitalist *status quo,* and that freedom of the press means little if one desires to start a metropolitan newspaper, but lacks the four or five million dollars with which to begin. The democratic socialist can only retort that, like other believers in democracy, he has the faith that a reasonable case, reasonably presented, will eventually win the hearts of the people.

The choice between Marxist revolutionary communism and democratic evolutionary socialism is, like other vital choices, not a matter of pure logic.

Facts of history limit the range of discretion in social action. Where political democracy has fragile roots, the Communist solution of the economic problem will seem the more natural. This is why the transition from autocracy to communism has been successful in Russia, or Yugoslavia, or China. Where, however, the political tradition of democracy has been deeply embedded in the structure of national life, as in England, Scandinavia, New Zealand, and Australia, democratic socialism seems the more natural solution of fundamental economic ills, if any basic changes are to be made at all. Conversely, Sidney Webb and Attlee would be as out of place in Russia or Outer Mongolia, as Lenin and Mao would be in Westminster.

The greatest single influence in the development of revolutionary communism has been Karl Marx. The background of Prussian politics of the first half of the nineteenth century, with political prisons and exiles as the normal facts of life, was hardly the best schooling in the practice of democracy. In one sense the political theory of Karl Marx is inverted Prussianism: before the revolution, the Junkers and capitalists sit on top, and rule with an iron hand over the masses of the people. Come the revolution, and the roles are reversed: the people control the state, through customary dictatorial methods, and the erstwhile oppressors and exploiters are put into their place. This may explain why in Europe Marxism has been so popular in Russia and Germany, and why it has been so weak where government by consent makes it difficult for individuals and groups to hate each other to the point of mutual liquidation. For this reason, the Communist *coup* in Czechoslovakia in February 1948 came as a rude shock to the free world: here was the case of the first truly democratic state being subjected to Communist dictatorship by armed force.

Marx's analysis of the capitalist system has influenced the *making* of history even more than the writing of history. Regardless of what one accepts, or rejects, in the monumental work of Marx, of his social, economic, political, and philosophical ideas, it is virtually impossible simply to by-pass him. He said of himself that he was not a "Marxist," and those who insist on all or nothing in relation to his ideas betray Marx the man, as well as Marx the social scientist. He believed that, as he put it in one of his earliest writings (*Theses on Feuerbach, 1845*), "in practice man must prove the truth," which would exclude the easier method of turning to the truth as revealed by the Authority, whether Karl Marx or any other god or prophet. The *Theses on Feuerbach* were written by Marx when he was only twenty-seven, and his whole conception of the task of philosophy is indicated by his charge that "the philosophers have only *interpreted* the world; the point however is to *change* it." This is distinctly un-Hegelian, and contrary to what respectable philosophers have been doing all along.

Marx's philosophy of history and politics has to be gathered from many incidental remarks and comments in his writings and letters. One of the few places, in which he has given a summary statement of the *economic interpre-*

tation of history, is in the preface to *The Critique of Political Economy* (1859). This brief document contains virtually all the important ideas of Marx's analysis of historical change and of the relative significance of the various social forces and institutions: "that the anatomy of civil society is to be found in political economy." Contrary to pre-Marxian social analysis, which emphasized law and politics as the determining factors in society, Marx reverses the scale of importance, and considers the "productive relationship" of society as the basis, whereas legal relations and forms of government are the "superstructure." Marx puts it in this way: "The mode of production of the material means of existence conditions the whole process of social, political and intellectual life." One of his most famous formulations is that *men's social existence determines their consciousness,* and not, as had been generally accepted without challenge before Marx, that the "consciousness of men determines their existence." What Marx stresses here is that man's ideas are not completely accidental and haphazard, or freely left to his choice. Thus, the legal, political, religious, and cultural ideologies and institutions of a pastoral type of civilization will fundamentally differ from those of the feudal society, and both will have little in common with the social, political, legal, religious, and intellectual outlook and organization of the modern industrial society.

Turning to the question of what causes historical change, Marx abandons the study of monarchs and their relations with court ladies and fellow dynasts, and is also dissatisfied with the approach to history through a long list of battles and wars. Instead, he tries to locate the deeper cause of real social change in factors that go beyond the powers of rulers and victorious war leaders: "At a certain stage of their development the material productive forces of society come into contradiction with the existing productive relationships, or, what is but a legal expression for these, with the property relationships within which they have moved before. From forms of development of the productive forces these relationships are transformed into their fetters. Then an epoch of social revolution opens. With the change in the economic foundation the whole vast superstructure is more or less rapidly transformed." Thus, when new productive *forces* developed within the productive *relationships* of the feudal system, social revolution was, according to Marx, inevitable. What has doomed all historically known economic systems is the fact that when new productive forces develop, the existing productive relationship stands in the way of their proper utilization. Each system thus becomes eventually wasteful in terms of the potentialities which have developed in its womb, but which are not permitted to be born and grow.

The capitalist system, too, shows the same tendency, according to Marx, when the productive forces (the capacity to produce) have outstripped the productive relationships (law of property, production for private profit). The capitalist system as a system of social, economic and legal relations thus has come to stand in the way of the technological *forces* that are not permitted to be fully utilized. Only socialism will, according to Marx, bring about a new system of productive relationships (public ownership of the means of production, production for common use rather than private profit) that will match the tremendous forces of production already potentially existent and known to man. Marx predicted the failure of the capitalist system to use all available productive forces at a time when capitalism grew by leaps and bounds, and when populations increased in all industrial nations. Yet the experience of the last generation has shown that only in time of war or rearmament capitalist societies produce to the full extent of their capacity. In "normal" times, millions of men are forced to be without work, and machinery rusts in idleness.

In *The Communist Manifesto* (1848), Marx and his collaborator Friedrich Engels explain how social change through revolution actually occurs. When the forces of production begin to outstrip the methods of production (or productive relationships), the owners of the means of production do not step aside, so as to accelerate the inevitable course of history. Bound by the limitations of their ideology (which, in turn, expresses the existing modes of production), they sincerely believe that the existing system is economically the most efficient, socially the most equitable, and generally in harmony with the laws of nature and the will of whatever god they venerate. It is not a question of the greed of the individual feudal landowner (who stands in the way of the more productive capitalist system), or of the selfishness of the individual capitalist (who obstructs the coming of a collectivist system of production). In each case the owners of the means of production will utilize all the instruments of the legal, political, and ideological superstructure to block the growth of those forces which represent the potentially more progressive economic system. This is why Marx and Engels state early in *The Communist Manifesto,* "The history of all hitherto existing society is the history of class struggles." In the nineteenth century, the bourgeoisie liked to think of itself as extremely law-abiding and respectable—once it had won its class struggle. Yet Marx and Engels remind it that, historically, it "has played a most revolutionary part."

The end of capitalism will be brought about, not by "subversive" conspiracies and astute political leaders, but by the same inexorable social laws that destroyed previous systems. Just as feudalism, e.g., prepared its own grave by developing those forces—the urban bourgeoisie—which eventually destroyed it, capitalism does the same thing: "The essential condition for the existence and for the sway of the bourgeois class is the formation and augmentation of capital; the condition for capital is wage-labor. Wage-labor rests exclusively on competition between the laborers. The advance of industry, whose involuntary promoter is the bourgeoisie, replaces the isolation of the laborers, due to competition, by their revolutionary combinations, due to association. The development of modern industry, therefore, cuts from under its feet the very foundation on which the bourgeoisie produces and appropriates products. What the bourgeoisie therefore produces, above all, are its own grave-diggers. Its fall and the victory of the proletariat are equally inevitable." And, as Marx and Engels look at history, they can find no instance where a major social and economic system has freely abdicated to its successor. Therefore, the Communists "openly declare that their ends can be attained only by the forcible overthrow of all existing social conditions." This is one of the crucial tenets of revolutionary Marxist communism.

After the death of Marx (1883), Engels carried on the heritage of his greater partner. In a letter to the German socialist writer Joseph Bloch (dated September 21, 1890), Engels restated the problem of the relations between the economic and noneconomic forces in history. Engels candidly admits that "Marx and I are ourselves partly to blame for the fact that younger writers sometimes lay more stress on the economic side than is due to it." Engels tries to strengthen the weight that has to be given to political, historical, and cultural factors, and in particular stresses the point that the economic (or "materialist") conception of history holds the economic factor to be *ultimately* the decisive one, but does not consider it to be the *only* determining element.

Lenin's *State and Revolution* (1917) was written in the late summer of 1917; Lenin was in hiding near the Finnish border part of the time, as the Kerensky government had issued an order for his arrest. The book consists of six chapters; as Lenin explains in a postscript (dated December 13, 1917), he planned to add a seventh chapter on the Russian revolutions of 1905 and 1917, but he was "interrupted" by the November revolution of 1917, and, as he puts it: "It is more pleasant and useful to go through the 'experience of revolution' than to write about it." In the literature of Marxism, *The State and Revolution* is of immense importance. Where Marx and Engels (in perhaps typically nineteenth-century liberal fashion) neglected the factor of *political power,* Lenin, the master strategist of one of the half dozen great revolutions in history, was keenly interested in the anatomy of the state. Lenin fully accepts the Marxist thesis that the transitional state between capitalism and the socialist society "can be only the revolutionary dictatorship of the proletariat." Lenin denies that capitalism and democracy are compatible at all, and affirms that under capitalism democracy always remains "a democracy for the minority, only for the possessing classes, only for the rich." Lenin then describes the techniques that the capitalist state employs, in order to maintain itself in power. In the words of *The Communist Manifesto,* the "executive of the modern State is but a committee for managing the common affairs of the whole bourgeoisie." Behind the formalities of capitalist political democracy, Lenin sees, in effect, the dictatorship of the bourgeoisie. He also denies that the transition from capitalism to communism can be accomplished simply, smoothly, and directly, "as the liberal professors and petty-bourgeois opportunists would have us believe. No, development—toward communism—proceeds through the dictatorship of the proletariat; it cannot be otherwise, for the *resistance* of the capitalist exploiters cannot be *broken* by anyone else or in any other way." In the transitional stage between capitalism and the communist society, "the state" will continue to exist, because machinery for the suppression of the capitalist exploiters will still be required in the dictatorship of the proletariat. But Lenin points out that, in this phase already, the state begins to "wither away," because the task of the majority (the victorious proletariat) in suppressing the minority (the defeated capitalists) is different, in quantitative and qualitative terms, from the previous, capitalist state, in which a minority (of capitalists) suppress the majority (of the exploited). Finally, once communism is fully established, the state becomes "absolutely unnecessary, for there is *no one* to be suppressed —'no one' in the sense of a *class,* in the sense of a systematic struggle against a definite section of the population." With the causes of exploitation of class by class removed, with the abolition of classes, the state will therefore inevitably "wither away." There will be true freedom for all, and "when freedom exists, there will be no state."

Lenin wisely adds that he leaves the question of length of time, or of "the concrete withering away, quite open." Without indicating the time it will take to transform the "lower phase" of Communist society (the dictatorship of the proletariat) to the "higher phase" (when the state will wither away), Lenin describes the condition of such transformation: "The state will be able to wither away completely when society can apply the rule: 'From each according to his ability, to each according to his needs,' i.e., when people have become so accustomed to observing the fundamental rules of social life and when their labor is so productive that they will voluntarily work *according to their ability.*" Lenin, like Marx, denies that the vision of a society without a mechanism of force and power ("the state") is Utopian. Yet Marxism shares with anarchy, democracy, and pacifism the faith that man is so perfectible that one day he will no longer need the corrective force of government, law, and prisons. In religion, the trouble is the Adam in man; in Marx, the Adam is capitalism.

So far, at least, the Communist state has shown little proclivity to wither away in the Soviet Union. So far, the Soviet Union still is in the first, or "lower," phase of communism, when the dictatorship of the proletariat requires the retention of a machinery of legal and political suppression. Stalin and Khrushchev, following Lenin, have also left the question open as to how long the present "phase" will last, and have refused to hint at the probable time when the present totalitarian police state will begin to wither away.

Returning from dreams to reality, one of the most interesting documents in revolutionary Marxist literature is Lenin's call to revolution, addressed to the members of the Central Committee of the Bolshevik party. It was written on the evening of November 6, 1917, only a few hours before the provisional government in Petrograd was overthrown by armed insurrection under Bolshevik leadership, which made Lenin himself the head of the new government.

In his *Foundations of Leninism* (1924) Stalin expounds his conception of communism. He sees the world divided into two camps, "the world front of imperialism, which must be opposed by a common front of the revolutionary movement in all countries." In the present imperialist stage of capitalism "wars cannot be averted," and he urges a coalition between the communist states and colonial revolutions in Asia. Soviet Russia must be the "base for the overthrow of imperialism in all countries," and he approvingly quotes Lenin that "it is inconceivable that the Soviet republic should continue to exist for a long period side by side with imperialist states. Ultimately one or the other must conquer." It is remarkable that in the nineteen twenties, when the Soviet Union was economically and militarily weak or exhausted, Lenin and Stalin readied their effort for the eventual conquest of the soft underbelly of the western nations—the underdeveloped areas in Asia, Africa, and Latin America. Whereas Lenin and Stalin understood in the nineteen twenties the crucial importance of the underdeveloped territories for the global ambitions of communism, some people in the West still do not understand their importance in the nineteen sixties. Realizing that the western nations cannot be subjected to communism by a frontal attack or by internal subversion, Soviet leadership under Lenin, Stalin, and Khrushchev decided to strike at the West indirectly—through the communization of underdeveloped areas in Asia and, later, in Africa and Latin America. The communist conquest of mainland China, North Korea, and Northern Vietnam, the Marxist influence in newly independent Guinea in West Africa, and the communist infiltration in Guatemala under Arbenz and in Cuba under Castro testify to the considerable success of the Leninist-Stalinist-Khrushchevist strategy, a success likely to continue so long as the West persists in underestimating the pivotal role of the underdeveloped areas in the world-wide struggle with communism.

Khrushchev, too, follows the pattern set by Lenin and Stalin. Although he has repeatedly advocated "peaceful coexistence" between East and West (as Lenin and Stalin did before him), he has made clear his conviction, at home and abroad (including his speeches in the United States in 1959), that the whole world will eventually live under the communist system. At the same time, Khrushchev continues to have faith in the tougher line of Leninism-Stalinism. Thus, after the suppression of the Hungarian Revolution, he said to a group of Western diplomats in Moscow on November 18, 1956: "Whether you like it or not, history is on our side. We will bury you."

On January 1, 1957, Khrushchev returned again to this issue. "The imperialists call us Stalinists," he said in Moscow. "Well, when it comes to fighting imperialism, we are all Stalinists."

In his famous secret speech of February 25, 1956, attacking Stalin, Khrushchev significantly did not attack Stalin's foreign policy, except for Stalin's blunder in trying to force Tito out of office. This was a quarrel within the communist orbit, in which, moreover, no overt force was used by Stalin. But Khrushchev did not criticize Stalin for his forcible communization of Latvia, Estonia, and Lithuania in the Baltic, and of Poland, Hungary, Bulgaria, Albania, Romania, East Germany, and Czechoslovakia in Eastern and Central Europe. He refrained from criticizing Stalin for his policy of expanding communist rule by force and subversion—for the simple reason that he himself intended to continue this policy.

Yet despite this important omission, Khrushchev's secret speech of February 25, 1956, before the Twentieth Communist Party Congress in Moscow is one of the most important documents in the whole history of communism. Stalin is revealed by Khrushchev as a cruel despot "demanding absolute submission to his opinion." This is a far cry from the communist theory of "democratic centralism." Stalin's arbitrariness encouraged arbitrariness in his subordinates: "Mass arrests and deportations of many thousands of people, execution without trial and without normal investigation created conditions of insecurity, fear, and even deportation." Deportation applied not only to individuals, but to whole nations in the Soviet Union. Khrushchev describes in detail how Stalin fabricated cases against his victims without a shred of evidence. "And how is it possible," Khrushchev asks, "that a person confesses to crimes which he has not committed? Only in one way—because of application of physical methods of pressuring him, tortures, bringing him to a state of unconsciousness, deprivation of his judgment, taking away of his human dignity. In this manner were 'confessions' acquired."

Yet two basic considerations about Khrushchev's secret speech against Stalin should be kept in mind. First, Khrushchev's main line of attack is upon the crimes Stalin committed against his communist associates, the "many thousands of honest and innocent communists," who died as a result of Stalin's tyranny. Yet Khrushchev does not refer to the persecution of the infinitely larger number of victims of Stalin's despotism, the millions of ordinary Russians who perished in the drive for agricultural collectivization in the early nineteen thirties, not to speak of the many millions who were imprisoned and kept in slave labor camps in the nineteen thirties and forties. In short, Khrushchev attacks Stalin for having exercised a tyrannical regime over fellow-communists, not for having suppressed the Russian people for nearly thirty years. The second interesting point about his address is that it was never published in the Soviet Union, although it was read in Communist

Party meetings. This confirms the assumption that in Khrushchev's view Stalin's despotic rule was a matter of intra-party concern, a mere deviation from true Leninism, but that the Russian people had no right to interfere. Still, even with these reservations there is no doubt that Khrushchev's speech of February 25, 1956, is of historic importance. Only a few months later, popular revolutions broke out in Poland and Hungary. In Poland, the revolution was permitted, because the communists never lost control. In Hungary, the revolution had to be suppressed by force of arms, because the communists swiftly lost control, were ousted, and a democratic regime was set up. This was a situation which called for a Stalinist solution, and Khrushchev did not hesitate to adopt it.

More searching than Khrushchev's critique of Stalin's version of communism is Milovan Djilas' *The New Class* (1957). Next to the *Communist Manifesto* it is possibly the most significant analysis of communism. Djilas was a communist in his native Yugoslavia from his boyhood onward; in World War II he fought with Tito in the partisan formations against Nazi Germany, and after the establishment of the Tito regime he became Vice-President of Yugoslavia and was considered by many as heir-apparent to Tito himself. Yet from the early fifties onward, he gradually changed his views, attacking the rule of his country by a centralized bureaucracy that possessed political power as well as economic privilege. In 1954, he was expelled from the Yugoslav Communist Party, and in 1955 he received his first sentence of imprisonment for demanding more democracy in Yugoslavia. On November 19, 1956, he published an article on the Hungarian Revolution in the American weekly *The New Leader,* in which he attacked the attitude of the Tito government during the Hungarian Revolution and stated that the Hungarian Revolution was the beginning of the end of world communism. For this article he was sentenced to three years' imprisonment. In 1957, his book *The New Class* was published in New York; Djilas was tried again, and this time he received a sentence of seven years, making his total sentence ten years. By contrast, he had served only three years in prison for his communist activities in pre-World War II Yugoslavia. Thus, the publication of *The New Class* was a political as well as a literary event. Here was a man who dared to defy a dictatorial regime, willing to sacrifice his freedom and life, if necessary, in order to tell the truth about communism as seen and lived by a life-long Marxist and communist.

What distinguishes Djilas' work from the mass of books by ex-communists is his avoidance of sensationalism, of personal charges and accusations. He is interested in the reality of communism as a going social, economic, and political system. The originality of Djilas' analysis rests on the fact that he applies Marxist criteria of economics and politics to show what the reality of communism is like. Just as Marx argued that the concentration of economic power in the hands of the capitalists inevitably entailed political control (regardless of formal and legal appearances to the contrary), Djilas argues that the absolute political power of the communist ruling class inevitably entails economic power and privileges, notwithstanding the legal fiction of "public ownership." The so-called socialist ownership, Djilas argues, "is a disguise for the real ownership by the political bureaucracy," since it is the political bureaucracy that "uses, enjoys, and disposes of nationalized property." This new class of "owners and exploiters" decides in an arbitrary way how the national income is to be distributed, what wages are to be paid to the workers, and how property is to be used: "This is the way it appears to the ordinary man who considers the communist functionary as being very rich and as a man who does not have to work." Because this new class combines within itself absolute political and economic power, its "power over men is the most complete known to history." Yet Djilas is confident that in the long run the subjects of the communist states will press for truth and freedom, and he concludes *The New Class* with these hopeful words: "The power of reality and the power of life have always been stronger than any kind of brutal force and more real than any theory."

KARL MARX

1. *On Philosophy**

The question whether objective truth can be attributed to human thinking is not a question of theory, but is a practical question. In practice man must prove the truth, i.e., the reality and power, the "this-sidedness" of his thinking. The dispute over the reality or non-reality of thinking which is isolated from practice is a purely scholastic question.

The materialist doctrine that men are products of circumstances and upbringing and that, therefore, changed men are products of other circumstances and changed upbringing, forgets that circumstances are changed precisely by men and that the educator must himself be educated. Hence this doctrine necessarily arrives at dividing society into two parts, of which one towers above society (in Robert Owen, for example).

The coincidence of the changing of circumstances and of human activity can only be conceived and rationally understood as revolutionizing practice.

* From Karl Marx, *Theses on Feuerbach* (written in 1845; first published in 1888 in *Ludwig Feuerbach* by Friedrich Engels).

Social life is essentially *practical*. All mysteries which mislead theory to mysticism find their rational solution in human practice and in the comprehension of this practice.

The philosophers have only *interpreted* the world in various ways; the point however is to *change* it.

KARL MARX

2. *Economic Interpretation of History**

My investigations led to the conclusion that legal relations as well as forms of State could not be understood from themselves, nor from the so-called general development of the human mind, but, on the contrary, are rooted in the material conditions of life, the aggregate of which Hegel, following the precedent of the English and French of the eighteenth century, grouped under the name of "civil society"; but that the anatomy of civil society is to be found in political economy. My study of the latter, begun in Paris, was continued in Brussels, whither I migrated in consequence of an expulsion order issued by M. Guizot. The general conclusion I arrived at—and once reached, it served as the guiding thread in my studies—can be briefly formulated as follows: In the social production of their means of existence men enter into definite, necessary relations which are independent of their will, productive relationships which correspond to a definite stage of development of their material productive forces. The aggregate of these productive relationships constitutes the economic structure of society, the real basis on which a juridical and political superstructure arises, and to which definite forms of social consciousness correspond. The mode of production of the material means of existence conditions the whole process of social, political and intellectual life. It is not the consciousness of men that determines their existence, but, on the contrary, it is their social existence that determines their consciousness. At a certain stage of their development the material productive forces

* From Karl Marx, *A Contribution to the Critique of Political Economy* (1859; translated by Emile Burns in *A Handbook of Marxism*, International Publishers, 1935). By permission.

of society come into contradiction with the existing productive relationships, or, what is but a legal expression for these, with the property relationships within which they had moved before. From forms of development of the productive forces these relationships are transformed into their fetters. Then an epoch of social revolution opens. With the change in the economic foundation the whole vast superstructure is more or less rapidly transformed. In considering such revolutions it is necessary always to distinguish between the material revolution in the economic conditions of production, which can be determined with scientific accuracy, and the juridical, political, religious, aesthetic or philosophic—in a word, ideological forms wherein men become conscious of this conflict and fight it out. Just as we cannot judge an individual on the basis of his own opinion of himself, so such a revolutionary epoch cannot be judged from its own consciousness; but on the contrary this consciousness must be explained from the contradictions of material life, from the existing conflict between social productive forces and productive relationships. A social system never perishes before all the productive forces have developed for which it is wide enough; and new, higher productive relationships never come into being before the material conditions for their existence have been brought to maturity within the womb of the old society itself. Therefore, mankind always sets itself only such problems as it can solve; for when we look closer we will always find that the problem itself only arises when the material conditions for its solution are already present or at least in the process of coming into being. In broad outline, the Asiatic, the ancient, the feudal and the modern bourgeois modes of production can be indicated as progressive epochs in the economic system of society. Bourgeois productive relationships are the last antagonistic form of the social process of production—antagonistic in the sense not of individual antagonism, but of an antagonism rising out of the conditions of the social life of individuals; but the productive forces developing within the womb of bourgeois society at the same time create the material conditions for the solution of this antagonism. With this social system, therefore, the pre-history of human society comes to a close.

KARL MARX AND FRIEDRICH ENGELS

3. *The Communist Manifesto**

A spectre is haunting Europe—the spectre of Communism. All the powers of old Europe have entered into a holy alliance to exorcise this spectre: Pope and Tsar, Metternich and Guizot, French Radicals and German police-spies.

Where is the party in opposition that has not been decried as communistic by its opponents in power? Where is the Opposition that has not hurled back the branding reproach of Communism, against the more advanced opposition parties, as well as against its reactionary adversaries?

Two things result from this fact:

1. Communism is already acknowledged by all European powers to be itself a power.

2. It is high time that Communists should openly, in the face of the whole world, publish their views, their aims, their tendencies, and meet this nursery tale of the spectre of Communism with a manifesto of the party itself.

To this end, Communists of various nationalities have assembled in London, and sketched the following manifesto, to be published in the English, French, German, Italian, Flemish and Danish languages:

I: BOURGEOIS AND PROLETARIANS

The history of all hitherto existing society is the history of class struggles.

Freeman and slave, patrician and plebeian, lord and serf, guild-master and journeyman, in a word, oppressor and oppressed, stood in constant opposition to one another, carried on an uninterrupted, now hidden, now open fight, a fight that each time ended, either in a revolutionary reconstitution of society at large, or in the common ruin of the contending classes.

In the earlier epochs of history, we find almost everywhere a complicated arrangement of society into various orders, a manifold gradation of social rank. In ancient Rome we have patricians, knights, plebeians, slaves; in the Middle Ages, feudal lords, vassals, guild-masters, journeymen, apprentices, serfs; in almost all of these classes, again, subordinate gradations.

The modern bourgeois society that has sprouted from the ruins of feudal society has not done away with class antagonisms. It has but established new classes, new conditions of oppression, new forms of struggle in place of the old ones.

Our epoch, the epoch of the bourgeoisie, possesses, however, this distinc-

---

* From Karl Marx and Friedrich Engels, *The Communist Manifesto* (1848; English translation of 1888, edited by Friedrich Engels).

tive feature: it has simplified the class antagonisms. Society as a whole is more and more splitting up into two great hostile camps, into two great classes directly facing each other—bourgeoisie and proletariat.

From the serfs of the Middle Ages sprang the chartered burghers of the earliest towns. From these burgesses the first elements of the bourgeoisie were developed.

The discovery of America, the rounding of the Cape, opened up fresh ground for the rising bourgeoisie. The East-Indian and Chinese markets, the colonisation of America, trade with the colonies, the increase in the means of exchange and in commodities generally, gave to commerce, to navigation, to industry, an impulse never before known, and thereby, to the revolutionary element in the tottering feudal society, a rapid development.

The feudal system of industry, in which industrial production was monopolised by closed guilds, now no longer sufficed for the growing wants of the new markets. The manufacturing system took its place. The guildmasters were pushed aside by the manufacturing middle class; division of labour between the different corporate guilds vanished in the face of division of labour in each single workshop.

Meantime the markets kept ever growing, the demand ever rising. Even manufacture no longer sufficed. Thereupon, steam and machinery revolutionised industrial production. The place of manufacture was taken by the giant, modern industry, the place of the industrial middle class, by industrial millionaires, the leaders of whole industrial armies, the modern bourgeois.

Modern industry has established the world market, for which the discovery of America paved the way. This market has given an immense development to commerce, to navigation, to communication by land. This development has, in its turn, reacted on the extension of industry; and in proportion as industry, commerce, navigation, railways extended, in the same proportion the bourgeoisie developed, increased its capital, and pushed into the background every class handed down from the Middle Ages.

We see, therefore, how the modern bourgeoisie is itself the product of a long course of development, of a series of revolutions in the modes of production and of exchange.

Each step in the development of the bourgeoisie was accompanied by a corresponding political advance of that class. An oppressed class under the sway of the feudal nobility, an armed and self-governing association in the mediaeval commune; here independent urban republic (as in Italy and Germany), there taxable "third estate" of the monarchy (as in France); afterwards, in the period of manufacture proper, serving either the semi-feudal or the absolute monarchy as a counterpoise against the nobility, and, in fact, corner stone of the great monarchies in general, the bourgeoisie has at last, since the establishment of Modern Industry and of the world market, conquered for itself, in the modern representative State, exclusive political sway.

The executive of the modern State is but a committee for managing the common affairs of the whole bourgeoisie.

The bourgeoisie, historically, has played a most revolutionary part.

The bourgeoisie, wherever it has got the upper hand, has put an end to all feudal, patriarchal, idyllic relations. It has pitilessly torn asunder the motley feudal ties that bound man to his "natural superiors," and has left no other nexus between man and man than naked self-interest, than callous "cash payment." It has drowned the most heavenly ecstasies of religious fervour, of chivalrous enthusiasm, of philistine sentimentalism, in the icy water of egotistical calculation. It has resolved personal worth into exchange value, and in place of the numberless indefeasible chartered freedoms, has set up that single, unconscionable freedom—Free Trade. In one word, for exploitation, veiled by religious and political illusions, it has substituted naked, shameless, direct, brutal exploitation.

The bourgeoisie has stripped of its halo every occupation hitherto honoured and looked up to with reverent awe. It has converted the physician, the lawyer, the priest, the poet, the man of science, into its paid wage-labourers.

The bourgeoisie has torn away from the family its sentimental veil, and has reduced the family relation to a mere money relation.

The bourgeoisie has disclosed how it came to pass that the brutal display of vigour in the Middle Ages, which reactionaries so much admire, found its fitting complement in the most slothful indolence. It has been the first to show what man's activity can bring about. It has accomplished wonders far surpassing Egyptian pyramids, Roman aqueducts, and Gothic cathedrals; it has conducted expeditions that put in the shade all former Exoduses of nations and crusades.

The bourgeoisie cannot exist without constantly revolutionising the instruments of production, and thereby the relations of production, and with them the whole relations of society. Conservation of the old modes of production in unaltered form, was, on the contrary, the first condition of existence for all earlier industrial classes. Constant revolutionising of production, uninterrupted disturbance of all social conditions, everlasting uncertainty and agitation distinguished the bourgeois epoch from all earlier ones. All fixed, fast-frozen relations, with their train of ancient and venerable prejudices and opinions, are swept away, all new-formed ones become antiquated before they can ossify. All that is solid melts into air, all that is holy is profaned, and man is at last compelled to face with sober senses his real conditions of life and his relations with his kind.

The need of a constantly expanding market for its products chases the bourgeoisie over the whole surface of the globe. It must nestle everywhere, settle everywhere, establish connections everywhere.

The bourgeoisie has through its exploitation of the world market given a cosmopolitan character to production and consumption in every country. To the great chagrin of reactionaries, it has drawn from under the feet of industry the national ground on which it stood. All old-established national industries have been destroyed or are daily being destroyed. They are dislodged by new industries, whose introduction becomes a life and death question for all civilised nations, by industries that no longer work up indigenous raw material, but raw material drawn from the remotest zones; industries whose products are consumed, not only at home, but in every quarter of the globe. In place of the old wants, satisfied by the production of the country, we find new wants, requiring for their satisfaction the products of distant lands and climes. In place of the old local and national seclusion and self-sufficiency, we have intercourse in every direction, universal inter-dependence of nations. And as in material, so also in intellectual production. The intellectual creations of individual nations become common property. National one-sidedness and narrow-mindedness become more and more impossible, and from the numerous national and local literatures there arises a world literature.

The bourgeoisie, by the rapid improvement of all instruments of production, by the immensely facilitated means of communication, draws all, even the most barbarian, nations into civilisation. The cheap prices of its commodities are the heavy artillery with which it batters down all Chinese walls, with which it forces the barbarians' intensely obstinate hatred of foreigners to capitulate. It compels all nations, on pain of extinction, to adopt the bourgeois modes of production; it compels them to introduce what it calls civilisation into their midst, i.e., to become bourgeois themselves. In one word, it creates a world after its own image.

The bourgeoisie has subjected the country to the rule of the towns. It has created enormous cities, has greatly increased the urban population as compared with the rural, and has thus rescued a considerable part of the population from the idiocy of rural life. Just as it has made the country dependent on the towns, so it has made barbarian and semi-barbarian countries dependent on the civilised ones, nations of peasants on nations of bourgeois, the East on the West.

The bourgeoisie keeps more and more doing away with the scattered state of the population, of the means of production, and of property. It has agglomerated population, centralised means of production, and has concentrated property in a few hands. The necessary consequence of this was political centralisation. Independent, or but loosely connected provinces, with separate interests, laws, governments and systems of taxation, became lumped together into one nation, with one government, one code of laws, one national class interest, one frontier and one customs tariff.

The bourgeoisie, during its rule of scarce one hundred years, has created more massive and more colossal productive forces than have all preceding generations together. Subjection of nature's forces to man, machinery, application of chemistry to industry and agriculture, steam-navigation, railways, electric telegraphs, clearing of whole continents for cultivation, canalisation of rivers, whole populations conjured out of the ground—what earlier century had even a presentiment that such productive forces slumbered in the lap of social labour?

We see then; the means of production and of exchange, on whose foundation the bourgeoisie built itself up, were generated in feudal society. At a certain stage in the development of these means of production and of exchange, the conditions under which feudal society produced and exchanged, the feudal organisation of agriculture and manufacturing industry, in one word, the feudal relations of property became no longer compatible with the already developed productive forces; they became so many fetters. They had to be burst asunder; they were burst asunder.

Into their place stepped free competition, accompanied by a social and political constitution adapted to it, and by the economical and political sway of the bourgeois class.

A similar movement is going on before our own eyes. Modern bourgeois society with its relations of production, of exchange and of property, a society that has conjured up such gigantic means of production and of exchange, is like the sorcerer who is no longer able to control the powers of the nether world whom he has called up by his spells. For many a decade past the history of industry and commerce is but the history of the revolt of modern productive forces against modern conditions of production, against the property relations that are the conditions for the existence of the bourgeoisie and of its rule. It is enough to mention the commercial crises that by their periodical return put the existence of the entire bourgeois society on its trial, each time more threateningly. In these crises a great part not only of the existing products, but also of the previously created productive forces, are periodically destroyed. In these crises there breaks out an epidemic that, in all earlier epochs, would have seemed an absurdity—the epidemic of over-production. Society suddenly finds itself put back into a state of momentary barbarism; it appears as if a famine, a universal war of devastation had cut off the supply of every means of subsistence; industry and commerce seem to be destroyed. And why? Because there is too much civilisation, too much means of subsistence, too much industry, too much commerce. The productive forces at the disposal of society no longer tend to further the development of the conditions of bourgeois property; on the contrary, they have become too powerful for these conditions, by which they are fettered, and so soon as they overcome these fetters, they bring disorder into the whole of bourgeois society, endanger the existence of bourgeois property. The conditions of bourgeois society are too narrow to comprise the wealth created by them. And how does the bourgeoisie get over these crises? On the one hand by enforced destruction of a mass of productive forces; on the other, by the conquest of new markets, and by the more thorough exploitation of the old ones. That is to say, by paving the way for more extensive and more destructive crises, and by diminishing the means whereby crises are prevented.

The weapons with which the bourgeoisie felled feudalism to the ground are now turned against the bourgeoisie itself.

But not only has the bourgeoisie forged the weapons that bring death to itself; it has also called into existence the men who are to wield those weapons —the modern working class—the proletarians.

In proportion as the bourgeoisie, i.e., capital, is developed, in the same proportion is the proletariat, the modern working class, developed—a class of labourers, who live only so long as they find work, and who find work only so long as their labour increases capital. These labourers, who must sell themselves piecemeal, are a commodity, like every other article of commerce, and are consequently exposed to all the vicissitudes of competition, to all the fluctuations of the market.

Owing to the extensive use of machinery and to division of labour, the work of the proletarians has lost all individual character, and, consequently, all charm for the workman. He becomes an appendage of the machine, and it is only the most simple, most monotonous, and most easily acquired knack, that is required of him. Hence, the cost of production of a workman is restricted, almost entirely, to the means of subsistence that he requires for his maintenance, and for the propagation of his race. But the price of a commodity, and therefore, also of labour, is equal to its cost of production. In proportion, therefore, as the repulsiveness of the work increases, the wage decreases. Nay, more, in proportion as the use of machinery and division of labour increases, in the same proportion the burden of toil also increases, whether by prolongation of the working hours, by increase of the work exacted in a given time, or by increased speed of the machinery, etc.

Modern industry has converted the little workshop of the patriarchal master into the great factory of the industrial capitalist. Masses of labourers, crowded into the factory, are organised like soldiers. As privates of the industrial army they are placed under the command of a perfect hierarchy of officers and sergeants. Not only are they slaves of the bourgeois class, and of the bourgeois state; they are daily and hourly enslaved by the machine, by the over-looker, and, above all, by the individual bourgeois manufacturer himself. The more openly this despotism proclaims gain to be its end and aim, the more petty, the more hateful and the more embittering it is.

The less the skill and exertion of strength implied in manual labour, in other words, the more modern industry becomes developed, the more is the labour of men superseded by that of women. Differences of age and sex have no longer any distinctive social validity for the working class. All are instruments of labour, more or less expensive to use, according to their age and sex.

No sooner is the exploitation of the labourer by the manufacturer so far at an end that he receives his wages in cash than he is set upon by the other portions of the bourgeoisie, the landlord, the shopkeeper, the pawnbroker, etc. The lower strata of the middle class—the small tradespeople, shopkeepers, and retired tradesmen generally, the handicraftsmen and peasants—all these sink gradually into the proletariat, partly because their diminutive capital does not suffice for the scale on which modern industry is carried on, and is swamped in the competition with the large capitalists, partly because their specialised skill is rendered worthless by new methods of production. Thus the proletariat is recruited from all classes of the population.

The proletariat goes through various stages of development. With its birth begins its struggle with the bourgeoisie. At first the contest is carried on by individual labourers, then by the work people of a factory, then by the operatives of one trade, in one locality, against the individual bourgeois who directly exploits them. They direct their attacks not against the bourgeois conditions of production, but against the instruments of production themselves; they destroy imported wares that compete with their labour, they smash to pieces machinery, they set factories ablaze, they seek to restore by force the vanished status of the workman of the Middle Ages.

At this stage the labourers still form an incoherent mass scattered over the whole country, and broken up by their mutual competition. If anywhere they unite to form more compact bodies, this is not yet the consequence of their own active union, but of the union of the bourgeoisie, which class, in order to attain its own political ends, is compelled to set the whole proletariat in motion, and is moreover yet, for a time, able to do so. At this stage, therefore, the proletarians do not fight their enemies, but the enemies of their enemies, the remnants of absolute monarchy, the land-owners, the non-industrial bourgeois, the petty bourgeoisie. Thus the whole historical movement is concentrated in the hands of the bourgeoisie; every victory so obtained is a victory for the bourgeoisie.

But with the development of industry the proletariat not only increases in number; it becomes concentrated in greater masses, its strength grows, and it feels that strength more. The various interests and conditions of life within the ranks of the proletariat are more and more equalised, in proportion as machinery obliterates all distinctions of labour, and nearly everywhere reduces wages to the same low level. The growing competition among the bourgeois, and the resulting commercial crises, make the wages of the workers ever more fluctuating. The unceasing improvement of machinery, ever more rapidly developing, makes their livelihood more and more precarious; the collisions between individual workmen and individual bourgeois take more and more the character of collisions between two classes. Thereupon the workers begin to form combinations (trades' unions) against the bourgeois; they club together in order to keep up the rate of wages; they found permanent associations in order to make provision beforehand for these occasional revolts. Here and there the contest breaks out into riots.

Now and then the workers are victorious, but only for a time. The real fruit of their battles lies, not in the immediate result, but in the ever expanding union of the workers. This union is helped on by the improved means of communication that are created by modern industry, and that place the workers of different localities in contact with one another. It was just this contact that was needed to centralise the numerous local struggles, all of the same character, into one national struggle between classes. But every class struggle is a political struggle. And that union, to attain which the burghers of the Middle Ages, with their miserable highways, required centuries, the modern proletarians, thanks to railways, achieve in a few years.

This organisation of the proletarians into a class, and consequently into a political party, is continually being upset again by the competition between the workers themselves. But it ever rises up again, stronger, firmer, mightier. It compels legislative recognition of particular interests of the workers, by taking advantage of the divisions among the bourgeoisie itself. Thus the ten-hours' bill in England was carried.

Altogether, collisions between the classes of the old society further in many ways the course of development of the proletariat. The bourgeoisie finds itself involved in a constant battle. At first with the aristocracy; later on, with those portions of the bourgeoisie itself, whose interests have become antagonistic to the progress of industry; at all times with the bourgeoisie of foreign countries. In all these battles it sees itself compelled to appeal to the proletariat, to ask for its help, and thus to drag it into the political arena. The bourgeoisie itself, therefore, supplies the proletariat with its own elements of political and general education, in other words, it furnishes the proletariat with weapons for fighting the bourgeoisie.

Further, as we have already seen, entire sections of the ruling classes are, by the advance of industry, precipitated into the proletariat, or are at least threatened in their conditions of existence. These also supply the proletariat with fresh elements of enlightenment and progress.

Finally, in times when the class struggle nears the decisive hour, the process of dissolution going on within the ruling class, in fact within the whole range of old society, assumes such a violent, glaring character that a small section of the ruling class cuts itself adrift and joins the revolutionary class, the class that holds the future in its hands. Just as, therefore, at an earlier period, a section of the nobility went over to the bourgeoisie, so now a portion of the bourgeoisie goes over to the proletariat, and, in particular, a portion of the bourgeois ideologists, who have raised themselves to the level of comprehending theoretically the historical movement as a whole.

Of all the classes that stand face to face with the bourgeoisie to-day, the proletariat alone is a really revolutionary class. The other classes decay and finally disappear in the face of modern industry; the proletariat is its special and essential product.

The lower middle class, the small manufacturer, the shopkeeper, the artisan, the peasant, all these fight against the bourgeoisie, to save from extinction their existence as fractions of the middle class. They are therefore not revolutionary but conservative. Nay, more, they are reactionary, for they try to roll back the wheel of history. If by chance they are revolutionary, they are so only in view of their impending transfer into the proletariat; they thus defend not their present, but their future interests; they desert their own standpoint to place themselves at that of the proletariat.

The "dangerous class," the social scum, that passively rotting mass thrown off by the lowest layers of old society, may, here and there, be swept into the movement by a proletarian revolution; its conditions of life, however, prepare it far more for the part of a bribed tool of reactionary intrigue.

In the conditions of the proletariat, those of old society at large are already virtually swamped. The proletarian is without property; his relation to his wife and children has no longer anything in common with the bourgeois family relations; modern industrial labour, modern subjection to capital, the same in England as in France, in America as in Germany, has stripped him of every trace of national character. Law, morality, religion, are to him so many bourgeois prejudices, behind which lurk in ambush just as many bourgeois interests.

All the preceding classes that got the upper hand, sought to fortify their already acquired status by subjecting society at large to their conditions of appropriation. The proletarians cannot become masters of the productive forces of society, except by abolishing their own previous mode of appropriation, and thereby also every other previous mode of appropriation. They have nothing of their own to secure and to fortify; their mission is to destroy all previous securities for, and insurances of, individual property.

All previous historical movements were movements of minorities, or in the interest of minorities. The proletarian movement is the self-conscious, independent movement of the immense majority, in the interest of the immense majority. The proletariat, the lowest stratum of our present society, cannot stir, cannot raise itself up, without the whole superincumbent strata of official society being sprung into the air.

Though not in substance, yet in form, the struggle of the proletariat with the bourgeoisie is at first a national struggle. The proletariat of each country must, of course, first of all settle matters with its own bourgeoisie.

In depicting the most general phases of the development of the proletariat, we traced the more or less veiled civil war, raging within existing society, up to the point where that war breaks out into open revolution, and where the violent overthrow of the bourgeoisie lays the foundation for the sway of the proletariat.

Hitherto, every form of society has been based, as we have already seen, on the antagonism of oppressing and oppressed classes. But in order to oppress a class, certain conditions must be assured to it under which it can, at least, continue its slavish existence. The serf, in the period of serfdom, raised himself to membership in the commune, just as the petty bourgeois, under the yoke of feudal absolutism, managed to develop into a bourgeois. The modern labourer, on the contrary, instead of rising with the progress of industry, sinks deeper and deeper below the conditions of existence of his own class. He becomes a pauper, and pauperism develops more rapidly than population and wealth. And here it becomes evident that the bourgeoisie is unfit any longer to be the ruling class in society and to impose its conditions of existence upon society as an over-riding law. It is unfit to rule because it is incompetent to assure an existence to its slave within his slavery, because it cannot help letting him sink into such a state, that it has to feed him, instead of being fed by him. Society can no longer live under this bourgeoisie; in other words, its existence is no longer compatible with society.

The essential condition for the existence and for the sway of the bourgeois class is the formation and augmentation of capital; the condition for capital is wage-labour. Wage-labour rests exclusively on competition between the labourers. The advance of industry, whose involuntary promoter is the bourgeoisie, replaces the isolation of the labourers, due to competition, by their revolutionary combination, due to association. The development of modern industry, therefore, cuts from under its feet the very foundation on which the bourgeoisie produces and appropriates products. What the bourgeoisie therefore produces, above all, are its own grave-diggers. Its fall and the victory of the proletariat are equally inevitable.

The Communists everywhere support every revolutionary movement against the existing social and political order of things.

In all these movements they bring to the front, as the leading question in each, the property question, no matter what its degree of development at the time.

Finally, they labour everywhere for the union and agreement of the democratic parties of all countries.

The Communists disdain to conceal their views and aims. They openly declare that their ends can be attained only by the forcible overthrow of all existing social conditions. Let the ruling classes tremble at a Communist revolution. The proletarians have nothing to lose but their chains. They have a world to win.

Working men of all countries, unite!

FRIEDRICH ENGELS

4. *Economic and Noneconomic Forces in History**

According to the materialist conception of history the determining element in history is *ultimately* the production and reproduction in real life. More than this neither Marx nor I have ever asserted. If therefore somebody twists this into the statement that the economic element is the *only* determining one, he transforms it into a meaningless, abstract and absurd phrase. The economic situation is the basis, but the various elements of the superstructure —political forms of the class struggle and its consequences, constitutions established by the victorious class after a successful battle, etc.—forms of law —and then even the reflexes of all these actual struggles in the brains of the combatants: political, legal, philosophical theories, religious ideas and their further development into systems of dogma—also exercise their influence upon the course of the historical struggles and in many cases preponderate in determining their *form*. There is an interaction of all these elements, in which, amid all the endless *host* of accidents (i.e., of things and events whose inner connection is so remote or so impossible to prove that we regard it as absent and can neglect it), the economic movement finally asserts itself as necessary. Otherwise the application of the theory to any period of history one chose would be easier than the solution of a simple equation of the first degree.

We make our own history, but in the first place under very definite presuppositions and conditions. Among these the economic ones are finally decisive. But the political, etc., ones, and indeed even the traditions which haunt human minds, also play a part, although not the decisive one. The Prussian State arose and developed from historical, ultimately from economic causes. But it could scarcely be maintained without pedantry that among the many small states of North Germany, Brandenburg was specifically determined by economic necessity to become the great power embodying the economic, linguistic and, after the Reformation, also the religious differences between north and south, and not by other elements as well (above all by its entanglement with Poland, owing to the possession of Prussia, and hence with international, political relations—which were indeed also decisive in the formation of the Austrian dynastic power). Without making oneself

* From a letter to Joseph Bloch (September 21, 1890; reprinted in Karl Marx and Friedrich Engels, *Correspondence*, International Publishers, 1934). By permission.

ridiculous it would be difficult to succeed in explaining in terms of economics the existence of every small state in Germany, past and present, or the origin of the High German consonant mutations, which the geographical wall of partition formed by the mountains from the Sudetic range to the Taunus extended to a regular division throughout Germany.

In the second place, however, history makes itself in such a way that the final result always arises from conflicts between many individual wills, of which each again has been made what it is by a host of particular conditions of life. Thus there are innumerable intersecting forces, an infinite series of parallelograms of forces which give rise to one resultant—the historical event. This again may itself be viewed as the product of a power which, taken as a whole, works *unconsciously* and without volition. For what each individual wills is obstructed by everyone else, and what emerges is something that no one willed. Thus past history proceeds in the manner of a natural process and is also essentially subject to the same laws of movement. But from the fact that individual wills—of which each desires what he is impelled to by his physical constitution and external, in the last resort economic, circumstances (either his own personal circumstances or those of society in general)—do not attain what they want, but are merged into a collective mean, a common resultant, it must not be concluded that their value $= 0$. On the contrary, each contributes to the resultant and is to this degree involved in it.

I would ask you to study this theory further from its original sources and not at second-hand, it is really much easier. Marx hardly wrote anything in which it did not play a part. But especially *The Eighteenth Brumaire of Louis Bonaparte* is a most excellent example of its application. There are also many allusions in *Capital*. Then I may also direct you to my writings: *Herr E. Dühring's Revolution in Science* and *Ludwig Feuerbach and the Exit of Classical German Philosophy,* in which I have given the most detailed account of historical materialism which, so far as I know, exists.

Marx and I are ourselves partly to blame for the fact that younger writers sometimes lay more stress on the economic side than is due to it. We had to emphasise this main principle in opposition to our adversaries, who denied it, and we had not always the time, the place or the opportunity to allow the other elements involved in the interaction to come into their rights. But when it was a case of presenting a section of history, that is, of a practical application, the thing was different and there no error was possible. Unfortunately, however, it happens only too often that people think they have fully understood a theory and can apply it without more ado from the moment they have mastered its main principles, and those even not always correctly. And I cannot exempt many of the more recent "Marxists" from this reproach, for the most wonderful rubbish has been produced from this quarter too.

V. I. LENIN

5. *The Withering Away of the State**

The transition from capitalist society—which is developing towards communism—to a communist society is impossible without a "political transition period," and the state in this period can only be the revolutionary dictatorship of the proletariat.

What, then, is the relation of this dictatorship to democracy?

We have seen that *The Communist Manifesto* simply places the two ideas side by side: "to raise the proletariat to the position of the ruling class" and "to win the battle of democracy." On the basis of all that has been said above, it is possible to determine more precisely how democracy changes in the transition from capitalism to communism.

In capitalist society, under the conditions most favourable to its development, we have more or less complete democracy in the democratic republic. But this democracy is always restricted by the narrow framework of capitalist exploitation, and consequently always remains, in reality, a democracy for the minority, only for the possessing classes, only for the rich. Freedom in capitalist society always remains about the same as it was in the ancient Greek republics: freedom for the slave-owners. Owing to the conditions of capitalist exploitation the modern wage-slaves are also so crushed by want and poverty that "they cannot be bothered with democracy," "they cannot be bothered with politics"; in the ordinary peaceful course of events the majority of the population is debarred from participating in social and political life.

The correctness of this statement is perhaps most clearly proved by Germany, precisely because in that country constitutional legality lasted and remained stable for a remarkably long time—for nearly half a century (1871-1914)—and because during this period Social-Democracy was able to achieve far more in Germany than in other countries in the way of "utilising legality," and was able to organize a larger proportion of the working class into a political party than anywhere else in the world.

What is this largest proportion of politically conscious and active wage-slaves that has so far been observed in capitalist society? One million members of the Social-Democratic Party—out of fifteen million wage-workers! Three million organised in trade unions—out of fifteen million! [1]

---

* From V. I. Lenin, *State and Revolution* (1917; in Lenin, *Selected Works*, VII, International Publishers, 1937). By permission.

[1] According to the figures for 1917.

Democracy for an insignificant minority, democracy for the rich—that is the democracy of capitalist society. If we look more closely into the mechanism of capitalist democracy, everywhere, in the "petty"—so-called petty—details of the suffrage (residential qualification, exclusion of women, etc.), and in the technique of the representative institutions, in the actual obstacles to the right of assembly (public buildings are not for "beggars"!), in the purely capitalist organization of the daily press, etc., etc.—on all sides we see restriction after restriction upon democracy. These restrictions, exceptions, exclusions, obstacles for the poor, seem slight, especially in the eyes of one who has never known want himself and has never been in close contact with the oppressed classes in their mass life (and nine-tenths, if not ninety-nine hundredths, of the bourgeois publicists and politicians are of this category); but in their sum total these restrictions exclude and squeeze out the poor from politics, from taking an active part in democracy.

Marx grasped this *essence* of capitalist democracy splendidly, when, in analysing the experience of the Commune, he said that the oppressed were allowed, once every few years, to decide which particular representatives of the oppressing class should misrepresent them in parliament!

But from this capitalist democracy—inevitably narrow, tacitly repelling the poor, and therefore hypocritical and false to the core—development does not proceed simply, smoothly and directly to "greater and greater democracy," as the liberal professors and petty-bourgeois opportunists would have us believe. No, development—towards communism—proceeds through the dictatorship of the proletariat; it cannot do otherwise, for the *resistance* of the capitalist exploiters cannot be *broken* by anyone else or in any other way.

But the dictatorship of the proletariat, i.e., the organization of the vanguard of the oppressed as the ruling class for the purpose of crushing the oppressors, cannot result merely in an expansion of democracy. *Simultaneously* with an immense expansion of democracy which *for the first time* becomes democracy for the poor, democracy for the people, and not democracy for the rich, the dictatorship of the proletariat imposes a series of restrictions on the freedom of the oppressors, the exploiters, the capitalists. We must crush them in order to free humanity from wage-slavery; their resistance must be broken by force; it is clear that where there is suppression there is also violence, there is no freedom, no democracy.

Engels expressed this splendidly in his letter to Bebel when he said, as the reader will remember, that

so long as the proletariat still uses the state it does not use it in the interests of freedom but in order to hold down its adversaries, and as soon as it becomes possible to speak of freedom the state as such ceases to exist.

Democracy for the vast majority of the people, and suppression by force, i.e., exclusion from democracy, of the exploiters and oppressors of the people —this is the change democracy undergoes during the *transition* from capitalism to communism.

Only in communist society, when the resistance of the capitalists has been completely broken, when the capitalists have disappeared, when there are no classes (i.e., when there is no difference between the members of society as regards their relation to the social means of production), *only then* does "the state . . . cease to exist," and it *"becomes possible to speak of freedom."* Only then will really complete democracy, democracy without any exceptions, be possible and be realised. And only then will democracy itself begin to *wither away* owing to the simple fact that, freed from capitalist slavery, from the untold horrors, savagery, absurdities and infamies of capitalist exploitation, people will gradually *become accustomed* to observing the elementary rules of social life that have been known for centuries and repeated for thousands of years in all copy-book maxims; they will become accustomed to observing them without force, without compulsion, without subordination, without the *special apparatus* for compulsion which is called the state.

The expression "the state *withers away*" is very well chosen, for it indicates both the gradual and the spontaneous nature of the process. Only habit can, and undoubtedly will, have such an effect; for we see around us millions of times how readily people become accustomed to observing the necessary rules of social life if there is no exploitation, if there is nothing that causes indignation, that calls forth protest and revolt and has to be *suppressed*.

Thus, in capitalist society we have a democracy that is curtailed, wretched, false; a democracy only for the rich, for the minority. The dictatorship of the proletariat, the period of transition to communism, will, for the first time, create democracy for the people, for the majority, in addition to the necessary suppression of the minority—the exploiters. Communism alone is capable of giving really complete democracy, and the more complete it is the more quickly will it become unnecessary and wither away of itself.

In other words: under capitalism we have a state in the proper sense of the word, that is, a special machine for the suppression of one class by another, and of the majority by the minority at that. Naturally, the successful discharge of such a task as the systematic suppression of the exploited majority by the exploiting minority calls for the greatest ferocity and savagery in the work of suppression, it calls for seas of blood through which mankind has to wade in slavery, serfdom and wage-labour.

Furthermore, during the *transition* from capitalism to communism, suppression is *still* necessary; but it is the suppression of the exploiting minority by the exploited majority. A special apparatus, a special machine for suppression, the "state," is *still* necessary, but this is now a transitory state; it is no longer a state in the proper sense; for the suppression of the minority of exploiters by the majority of the wage-slaves of *yesterday* is comparatively so easy, simple and natural a task that it will entail far less bloodshed than the suppression of the risings of slaves, serfs or wage-labourers, and it will cost mankind far less. This is compatible with the diffusion of democracy among such an overwhelming majority of the population that the need for a *special machine* of suppression will begin to disappear. The exploiters are, naturally, unable to suppress the people without a very complex machine for performing this task; but *the people* can suppress the exploiters with a very simple "machine," almost without a "machine," without a special apparatus, by the simple *organisation of the armed masses* (such as the Soviets of Workers' and Soldiers' Deputies, we may remark, running ahead a little).

Finally, only communism makes the state absolutely unnecessary, for there is *no one* to be suppressed—"no one" in the sense of a *class,* in the sense of a systematic struggle against a definite section of the population. We are not utopians, and we do not in the least deny the possibility and inevitability of excesses on the part of *individual persons,* or the need to suppress *such* excesses. But, in the first place, no special machine, no special apparatus of repression is needed for this: this will be done by the armed people itself, as simply and as readily as any crowd of civilised people, even in modern society, parts two people who are fighting, or interferes to prevent a woman from being assaulted. And, secondly, we know that the fundamental social cause of excesses, which consist in violating the rules of social life, is the exploitation of the masses, their want and their poverty. With the removal of this chief cause, excesses will inevitably begin to *"wither away."* We do not know how quickly and in what order, but we know that they will wither away. With their withering away, the state will also *wither away.*

Without dropping into utopias, Marx defined more fully what can be defined *now* regarding this future, namely the difference beween the lower and higher phases (degrees, stages) of communist society.

THE FIRST PHASE OF COMMUNIST SOCIETY

In the *Critique of the Gotha Programme,* Marx goes into some detail to disprove Lassalle's idea that under socialism the worker will receive the "undiminished" or "whole proceeds of his labour." Marx shows that from the whole of the social labour of society it is necessary to deduct a reserve fund, a fund for the expansion of production, for the replacement of "worn-out" machinery, and so on; then, also, from the means of consumption must be deducted a fund for the expenses of management, for schools, hospitals, homes for the aged, and so on.

Instead of Lassalle's hazy, obscure, general phrase—"the whole proceeds of his labour to the worker"—Marx makes a sober estimate of exactly how socialist society will have to manage its affairs. Marx proceeds to make a *concrete* analysis of the conditions of life of a society in which there is no capitalism, and says:

> What we have to deal with here (in analysing the programme of the Party) is a communist society not as it has *developed* on its own foundations, but on the contrary as it *emerges* from capitalist society; which is thus in every respect economically, morally and intellectually still stamped with the birth marks of the old society from whose womb it emerges. [2]

And it is this communist society—a society which has just come into the world out of the womb of capitalism and which, in every respect, bears the birth marks of the old society—that Marx terms the "first," or lower, phase of communist society.

The means of production are no longer the private property of individuals. The means of production belong to the whole of society. Every member of society, performing a certain part of socially-necessary labour, receives a certificate from society to the effect that he has done such and such an amount of work. According to this certificate, he receives from the public warehouses, where articles of consumption are stored, a corresponding quantity of products. Deducting that proportion of labour which goes to the public fund, every worker, therefore, receives from society as much as he has given it.

"Equal right" seems to reign supreme.

But when Lassalle, having such a social order in view (generally called socialism, but termed by Marx the first phase of communism), speaks of this as "equitable distribution," and says that this is "the equal right" of "all members of society" to "equal proceeds of labour," he is mistaken, and Marx exposes his error.

"Equal right," says Marx, we indeed have here; but it is *still* a "bourgeois right," which, like every right, *presupposes inequality*. Every right is an application of the *same* measure to *different* people who, in fact, are not the same and are not equal to one another; that is why "equal right" is really a violation of equality and an injustice. As a matter of fact, every man having performed as much social labour as another receives an equal share of the social product (less the above-mentioned deductions).

But people are not alike: one is strong, another is weak; one is married, another is not; one has more children, another has less, and so on. And the conclusion Marx draws is:

> . . . with an equal output and hence an equal share in the social consumption fund, one will in fact receive more than another, one will be richer

[2] *Critique of the Gotha Programme.*

than another and so on. To avoid all these defects, right, instead of being equal, would have to be unequal.[3]

Hence, the first phase of communism cannot produce justice and equality; differences, and unjust differences, in wealth will still exist, but the *exploitation* of man by man will have become impossible, because it will be impossible to seize the *means of production,* the factories, machines, land, etc., as private property. In smashing Lassalle's petty-bourgeois, confused phrases about "equality" and "justice" *in general,* Marx shows the *course of development* of communist society, which, at first, is compelled to abolish *only* the "injustice" of the means of production having been seized by private individuals and which *cannot* at once abolish the other injustice of the distribution of articles of consumption "according to the amount of work performed" (and not according to needs).

The vulgar economists, including the bourgeois professors and also "our" Tugan-Baranovsky, constantly reproach the Socialists with forgetting the inequality of people and with "dreaming" of abolishing this inequality. Such a reproach, as we see, only proves the extreme ignorance of Messieurs the bourgeois ideologists.

Marx not only scrupulously takes into account the inevitable inequality of men; he also takes into account the fact that the mere conversion of the means of production into the common property of the whole of society (generally called "socialism") *does not remove* the defects of distribution and the inequality of "bourgeois right" which *continue to prevail* as long as the products are divided "according to the amount of work performed." Continuing, Marx says:

> But these defects are inevitable in the first phase of communist society as it is when it has just emerged after prolonged birthpangs from capitalist society. Right can never be higher than the economic structure of society and the cultural development thereby determined.[4]

And so, in the first phase of communist society (generally called socialism) "bourgeois right" is *not* abolished in its entirety, but only in part, only in proportion to the economic transformation so far attained, i.e., only in respect of the means of production. "Bourgeois right" recognises them as the private property of separate individuals. Socialism converts them into *common* property. *To that extent,* and to that extent alone, "bourgeois right" disappears.

However, it continues to exist so far as its other part is concerned; it remains in the capacity of regulator (determining factor) in the distribution of products and allotment of labour among the members of society. The socialist principle: "He who does not work, neither shall he eat," is *already*

[3] *Ibid.*
[4] *Ibid.*

realised; the other socialist principle: "An equal amount of labour for an equal quantity of products," is also *already* realised. But this is not yet communism, and it does not abolish "bourgeois right," which gives to unequal individuals, in return for an unequal (actually unequal) amount of work, an equal quantity of products.

This is a "defect," says Marx, but it is unavoidable in the first phase of communism; for if we are not to fall into utopianism, we cannot imagine that, having overthrown capitalism, people will at once learn to work for society *without any standard of right;* indeed, the abolition of capitalism *does not immediately* create the economic prerequisites for *such* a change.

And there is as yet no other standard than that of "bourgeois right." To this extent, therefore, there is still need for a state, which, while safeguarding the public ownership of the means of production, would safeguard the equality of labour and equality in the distribution of products.

The state withers away in so far as there are no longer any capitalists, any classes, and consequently, no *class* can be *suppressed.*

But the state has not yet completely withered away, since there still remains the protection of "bourgeois right" which sanctifies actual inequality. For the complete withering away of the state, complete communism is necessary.

THE HIGHER PHASE OF COMMUNIST SOCIETY

Marx continues:

In a higher phase of communist society after the enslaving subordination of individuals under division of labour, and therewith also the antithesis between mental and physical labour, has vanished; after labour has become not merely a means to live but has become itself the primary necessity of life; after the productive forces have also increased with the all-round development of the individual, and all the springs of co-operative wealth flow more abundantly—only then can the narrow horizon of bourgeois right be fully left behind and society inscribe on its banners: from each according to his ability, to each according to his needs! [5]

Only now can we appreciate to the full the correctness of Engels' remarks in which he mercilessly ridiculed the absurdity of combining the words "freedom" and "state." While the state exists there is no freedom. When freedom exists, there will no state.

The economic basis for the complete withering away of the state is the high stage of development of communism in which the antithesis between mental and physical labour disappears, that is to say, when one of the principal sources of modern *social* inequality—a source, moreover, which cannot be removed immediately by the mere conversion of the means of production into public property, by the mere expropriation of the capitalists—disappears.

Ibid.

This expropriation will *facilitate* the enormous development of the pro-ductive forces. And seeing how capitalism is already *retarding* this develop-ment to an incredible degree, seeing how much progress could be achieved even on the basis of the present level of modern technique, we have a right to say with the fullest confidence that the expropriation of the capitalists will inevitably result in the enormous development of the productive forces of human society. But how rapidly this development will proceed, how soon it will reach the point of breaking away from the division of labour, of re-moving the antithesis between mental and physical labour, of transforming work into the "primary necessity of life"—we do not and *cannot* know.

That is why we have a right to speak only of the inevitable withering away of the state; we must emphasise the protracted nature of this process and its dependence upon the rapidity of development of the *higher phase* of com-munism; and we leave the question of length of time, or the concrete forms of the withering away, quite open, because *no material is available* to enable us to answer these questions.

The state will be able to wither away completely when society can apply the rule: "From each according to his ability, to each according to his needs," i.e., when people have become so accustomed to observing the fundamental rules of social life and when their labour is so productive that they will volun-tarily work *according to their ability*. "The narrow horizon of bourgeois right," which compels one to calculate with the shrewdness of a Shylock whether he has not worked half an hour more than another, whether he is not getting less pay than another—this narrow horizon will then be left be-hind. There will then be no need for society to make an exact calculation of the quantity of products to be distributed to each of its members; each will take freely "according to his needs."

From the bourgeois point of view, it is easy to declare such a social order to be "a pure utopia," and to sneer at the Socialists for promising everyone the right to receive from society, without any control of the labour of the individ-ual citizen, any quantity of truffles, automobiles, pianos, etc. Even now, most bourgeois "savants" make shift with such sneers, thereby displaying at once their ignorance and their selfish defence of capitalism.

Ignorance—for it has never entered the head of any Socialist to "promise" that the higher phase of communism will arrive; and the great Socialists, in *foreseeing* its arrival, presupposed both a productivity of labour unlike the present and a person *unlike the present* man in the street who, like the semi-nary students in Pomyalovsky's story,[6] is capable of damaging the stores of social wealth "just for fun," and of demanding the impossible.

Until the "higher" phase of communism arrives, the Socialists demand the *strictest* control, by society *and by the state,* of the amount of labour and the amount of consumption; but this control must *start* with the expropriation

[6] Pomyalovsky's *Seminary Sketches,* depicting the life of the students in an ecclesiastical seminary, of which drunkenness, rioting and filthy pranks were typical.

of the capitalists, with the establishment of workers' control over the capitalists, and must be carried out, not by a state of bureaucrats, but by a state of *armed workers.*

The selfish defence of capitalism by the bourgeois ideologists (and their hangers-on, like Messrs. Tseretelli, Chernov and Co.) lies in their *substituting* controversies and discussions about the distant future for the essential imperative questions of *present-day* policy, *viz.,* the expropriation of the capitalists, the conversion of *all* citizens into workers and employees of *one* huge "syndicate"—the whole state—and the complete subordination of the whole of the work of this syndicate to the really democratic state of the *Soviets of Workers' and Soldiers' Deputies.*

In reality, when a learned professor, and following him some philistine, and following the latter Messrs. Tseretelli and Chernov, talk of the unreasonable utopias, of the demagogic promises of the Bolsheviks, of the impossibility of "introducing" socialism, it is the higher stage or phase of communism which they have in mind, and which no one has ever promised, or has even thought of "introducing," because, generally speaking, it cannot be "introduced."

And this brings us to the question of the scientific difference between socialism and communism which Engels touched on in his above-quoted argument about the incorrectness of the name "social-Democrat." The political difference between the first, or lower, and the higher phase of communism will in time, no doubt, be tremendous; but it would be ridiculous to take cognisance of this difference now, under capitalism; only some isolated anarchist, perhaps, could invest it with primary importance (if there are still any people among the anarchists who have learned nothing from the "Plekhanovist" conversion of the Kropotkins, the Graveses, the Cornelisens and other "leading lights" of anarchism into social-chauvinists or "anarchotrenchists," as Gay, one of the few anarchists who has still preserved a sense of honour and a conscience, has expressed it).

But the scientific difference between socialism and communism is clear. What is generally called socialism was termed by Marx the "first" or lower phase of communist society. In so far as the means of production become *common* property, the word "communism" is also applicable here, providing we do not forget that it is *not* complete communism. The great significance of Marx's explanations lies in that here, too, he consistently applies materialist dialectics, the theory of development, and regards communism as something which develops *out* of capitalism. Instead of scholastically invented, "concocted" definitions and fruitless disputes about words (what is socialism? what is communism?), Marx gives an analysis of what may be called stages in the economic ripeness of communism.

In its first phase, or first stage, communism *cannot* as yet be economically ripe and entirely free from all the traditions and all traces of capitalism. Hence the interesting phenomenon that communism in its first phase retains "the narrow horizon of *bourgeois* right." Of course, bourgeois right in regard to distribution of articles of *consumption* inevitably presupposes the existence of the *bourgeois state,* for right is nothing without an apparatus capable of *enforcing* the observance of the standards of right.

Consequently, for a certain time not only bourgeois right, but even the bourgeois state remains under communism, without the bourgeoisie!

This may sound like a paradox or simply a dialectical puzzle which Marxism is often accused of inventing by people who would not take the slightest trouble to study its extraordinarily profound content.

As a matter of fact, however, the remnants of the old surviving in the new confront us in life at every step, in nature as well as in society. Marx did not smuggle a scrap of "bourgeois" right into communism of his own accord; he indicated what is economically and politically inevitable in the society which is emerging *from the womb* of capitalism.

Democracy is of great importance for the working class in its struggle for freedom against the capitalists. But democracy is by no means a boundary that must not be overstepped; it is only one of the stages in the process of development from feudalism to capitalism, and from capitalism to communism.

Democracy means equality. The great significance of the proletariat's struggle for equality and the significance of equality as a slogan will be clear if we correctly interpret it as meaning the abolition of *classes*. But democracy means only *formal* equality. As soon as equality is obtained for all members of society *in relation to* the ownership of the means of production, that is, equality of labour and equality of wages, humanity will inevitably be confronted with the question of going beyond formal equality to real equality, i.e., to applying the rule, "from each according to his ability, to each according to his needs." By what stages, by what practical measures humanity will proceed to his higher aim—we do not and cannot know. But it is important to realise how infinitely mendacious is the ordinary bourgeois conception of socialism as something lifeless, petrified, fixed once for all, whereas in reality *only* under socialism will a rapid, genuine, really mass movement, embracing first the *majority* and then the whole of the population, commence in all spheres of social and individual life.

Democracy is a form of state, one of its varieties. Consequently, like every state, it, on the one hand, represents the organised, systematic application of force against persons; but, on the other hand, it signifies the formal recognition of the equality of all citizens, the equal right of all to determine the structure and administration of the state. This, in turn, is connected with the fact that, at a certain stage in the development of democracy, it first rallies the proletariat as a revolutionary class against capitalism, and gives it the opportunity to crush, to smash to atoms, to wipe off the face of the earth the bourgeois, even the republican bourgeois, state machine, the standing army, the police and bureaucracy; to substitute for all this a *more* democratic, but still a state machine in the shape of the armed masses of workers who become transformed into a universal people's militia.

Here "quantity is transformed into quality": *such* a degree of democracy is connected with overstepping the boundaries of bourgeois society, with the beginning of its socialist reconstruction. If, indeed, *all* take part in the administration of the state, capitalism cannot retain its hold. The development of capitalism, in turn, itself creates the *prerequisites* that *enable* indeed "all" to take part in the administration of the state. Some of these prerequisites are: universal literacy, already achieved in most of the advanced capitalist countries, then the "training and disciplining" of millions of workers by the huge, complex and socialised apparatus of the post-office, the railways, the big factories, large-scale commerce, banking, etc., etc.

With such *economic* prerequisites it is quite possible, immediately, overnight, after the overthrow of the capitalists and bureaucrats, to supersede them in the *control* of production and distribution, in the work of *keeping account* of labour and its products by the armed workers, by the whole of the armed population. (The question of control and accounting must not be confused with the question of the scientifically educated staff of engineers, agronomists and so on. These gentlemen are working today and obey the capitalists; they will work even better tomorrow and obey the armed workers.)

Accounting and control—these are the *principal* things that are necessary for the "setting up" and correct functioning of the *first phase* of communist society. *All* citizens are transformed into the salaried employees of the state, which consists of the armed workers. *All* citizens become employees and workers of a *single* national state "syndicate." All that is required is that they should work equally—do their proper share of work—and get paid equally. The accounting and control necessary for this have been so utterly *simplified* by capitalism that they have become the extraordinarily simple operations of checking, recording and issuing receipts, which anyone who can read and write and who knows the first four rules of arithmetic can perform.[7]

When the *majority* of the people themselves begin everywhere to keep such accounts and maintain such control over the capitalists (now converted into employees) and over the intellectual gentry, who preserve their capitalist habits, this control will really become universal, general, national; and there will be no way of getting away from it, there will be "nowhere to go."

The whole of society will have become a single office and a single factory with equality of work and equality of pay.

But this "factory" discipline, which the proletariat will extend to the whole

[7] When most of the functions of the state are reduced to this accounting and control by the workers themselves, it ceases to be a "political state," the "public functions will lose their political character and be transformed into . . . simple administrative functions."

of society after the defeat of the capitalists and the overthrow of the exploiters, is by no means our ideal, or our ultimate goal. It is but a necessary *step* for the purpose of thoroughly purging society of all the hideousness and foulness of capitalist exploitation, *and for the purpose of advancing further.*

From the moment all members of society, or even only the overwhelming majority, have learned to administer the state *themselves,* have taken this business into their own hands, have "set up" control over the insignificant minority of capitalists, over the gentry, who wish to preserve their capitalist habits, and over the workers who have been completely demoralised by capitalism—from this moment the need for government begins to disappear. The more complete democracy becomes, the nearer the moment approaches when it becomes unnecessary. The more democratic the "state" of the armed workers—which is "no longer a state in the proper sense of the word"—becomes, the more rapidly does *the state* begin to wither away.

For when *all* have learned the art of administration, and will indeed independently administer social production, will independently keep accounts, control the idlers, the gentlefolk, the swindlers and similar "guardians of capitalist traditions," the escape from this national accounting and control will inevitably become so increasingly difficult, such a rare exception, and will probably be accompanied by such swift and severe punishment (for the armed workers are practical men and not sentimental intellectuals, and they will scarcely allow anyone to trifle with them), that very soon the *necessity* of observing the simple, fundamental rules of human intercourse will become a *habit.*

The door will then be wide open for the transition from the first phase of communist society to its higher phase, and with it to the complete withering away of the state.

V. I. LENIN

6. *Call to Revolution**

COMRADES

I am writing these lines on the evening of November 6 [October 24]. The situation is critical in the extreme. It is absolutely clear that to delay the insurrection now will veritably be fatal.

I exhort my comrades with all my heart and strength to realise that every-

* From V. I. Lenin, *Selected Works,* VI (International Publishers, 1936). By permission.

thing now hangs on a thread; that we are being confronted by problems that can be solved not by conferences or congresses (even Congresses of Soviets), but exclusively by the people, by the masses, by the struggle of the armed masses.

The bourgeois onslaught of the Kornilovists and the removal of Verkhovsky show that we must not wait. We must at all costs, this very evening, this very night, arrest the government, first disarming (defeating, if they offer resistance) the *Junkers* and so forth.

We must not wait! We may lose everything!

The gain from the seizure of power immediately will be that the people (not the Congress, but the people, the army and the peasants in the first place) will be defended from the Kornilovist government, which has driven out Verkhovsky and has hatched a second Kornilov plot.

Who must take power?

At present that is not important. Let the Revolutionary Military Committee take it, or "some other institution," declaring that it will relinquish the power only to the true representatives of the interests of the people, the interests of the army (immediate proposals for peace), the interests of the peasants (the land to be taken immediately and private property abolished), the interests of the starving.

All boroughs, all regiments, all forces must be mobilised immediately and must send their delegations to the Revolutionary Military Committee and to the Central Committee of the Bolsheviks with the insistent demand that under no circumstances shall the power be left in the hands of Kerensky and Co. until November 7 [October 25]; not under any circumstances; the matter must be decided unconditionally this very evening, or this very night.

History will not forgive revolutionaries for procrastinating when they can be victorious today (will certainly be victorious today), while they risk losing much, in fact, everything, tomorrow.

If we seize power today, we seize it not in opposition to the Soviets but on their behalf.

The seizure of power is a matter of insurrection; its political purpose will be clear after the seizure.

It would be a disaster, or a sheer formality, to await the wavering vote of November 7 [October 25]. The people have the right and the duty to decide such questions not by a vote, but by force; in critical moments of revolution, the people have the right and the duty to give directions to their representatives, even their best representatives, and not to wait for them.

This is proved by the history of all revolutions; and it would be an infinite crime on the part of the revolutionaries were they to let the moment pass, knowing that upon them depends the *salvation of the revolution,* the proposal of peace, the saving of Petrograd, salvation from famine, the transfer of the land to the peasants.

The government is wavering. It must be *destroyed* at all costs!
To delay action will be fatal.
November 6 [October 24], 1917.

JOSEPH STALIN

7. *Communist Strategy and Tactics**

From this theme I take six questions: (1) strategy and tactics as the science of leadership in the class struggle of the proletariat; (2) stages of the revolution, and strategy; (3) the flow and ebb of the movement, and tactics; (4) strategic leadership; (5) tactical leadership; (6) reformism and revolutionism.

I. STRATEGY AND TACTICS AS THE SCIENCE OF LEADERSHIP IN THE CLASS STRUGGLE OF THE PROLETARIAT

The period of the domination of the Second International was mainly a period of the formation and training of the proletarian armies amidst conditions of more or less peaceful development. This was the period when parliamentarism was the principal form of class struggle. Questions of great class conflicts, of preparing the proletariat for revolutionary battles, of the ways and means of achieving the dictatorship of the proletariat, did not seem to be on the order of the day at that time. The task was confined to utilizing all paths of legal development for the purpose of forming and training the proletarian armies, to utilizing parliamentarism in conformity with the conditions under which the status of the proletariat was (and as it seemed then, had to remain) that of an Opposition. It need hardly be proved that in such a period and with such a conception of the tasks of the proletariat there could be neither an integral strategy nor any elaborated tactics. There were fragmentary and detached ideas about tactics and strategy, but no tactics or strategy as such.

The mortal sin of the Second International was not that it pursued the tactics of utilizing the parliamentary forms of struggle, but that it overestimated the importance of these forms, that it considered them virtually the only forms; and that when the period of open revolutionary battles set in

* From Joseph Stalin, *Foundations of Leninism* (1924; copyright, 1939, by International Publishers). By permission.

and the question of extra-parliamentary forms of struggle came to the fore the parties of the Second International turned their backs on these new tasks, refused to shoulder them.

Only in the subsequent period, in the period of direct action by the proletariat, in the period of proletarian revolution, when the question of overthrowing the bourgeoisie became a question of immediate action; when the question of the reserves of the proletariat (strategy) became one of the most burning questions; when all forms of struggle and of organization, parliamentary and extra-parliamentary (tactics) had fully manifested themselves and became well-defined—only in this period could an integral strategy and elaborated tactics for the struggle of the proletariat be drawn up. It was precisely in that period that Lenin brought out into the light of day the brilliant ideas of Marx and Engels on tactics and strategy that had been immured by the opportunists of the Second International. But Lenin did not confine himself to restoring certain tactical propositions of Marx and Engels. He developed them further and supplemented them with new ideas and propositions, combining them all into a system of rules and guiding principles for the leadership of the class struggle of the proletariat. Lenin's pamphlets, such as *What Is To Be Done?; Two Tactics; Imperialism; State and Revolution; The Proletarian Revolution and the Renegade Kautsky; "Left-Wing" Communism,* etc., will undoubtedly always be treasured as priceless contributions to the general store of Marxism, to its revolutionary arsenal. The strategy and tactics of Leninism constitute the science of leadership of the revolutionary struggle of the proletariat.

II. STAGES OF THE REVOLUTION, AND STRATEGY

Strategy is the determination of the direction of the main blow of the proletariat at a given stage of the revolution, the elaboration of a corresponding plan for the disposition of the revolutionary forces (the main and secondary reserves), the fight to carry out this plan throughout the given stage of the revolution.

Our revolution already passed through two stages, and after the October Revolution it has entered a third stage. Our strategy changed accordingly.

First stage. 1903 to February 1917. Objective: to overthrow tsarism and completely wipe out the survivals of mediaevalism. The main force of the revolution: the proletariat. Immediate reserves: the peasantry. Direction of the main blow: the isolation of the liberal-monarchist bourgeoisie, which was striving to win over the peasantry and liquidate the revolution by *compromising* with tsarism. Plan for the disposition of forces: alliance of the working class with the peasantry.

The proletariat must carry to completion the democratic revolution, by allying to itself the mass of the peasantry in order to crush by force the resistance of the autocracy and to paralyse the instability of the bourgeoisie. (Lenin, *Selected Works,* Vol. III, p. 110.)

Second stage. March 1917 to October 1917. Objective: to overthrow imperialism in Russia and to withdraw from the imperialist war. The main force of the revolution: the proletariat. Immediate reserves: the poor peasantry. The proletariat of neighbouring countries as probable reserves. The protracted war and the crisis of imperialism as the favourable factor. Direction of the main blow: isolation of the petty-bourgeois democrats (Mensheviks and Socialist-Revolutionaries), who were striving to win over the toiling masses of the peasantry and to terminate the revolution by com*promising* with imperialism. Plan for the disposition of forces: alliance of the proletariat with the poor peasantry.

The proletariat must accomplish the socialist revolution by allying to itself the mass of the semi-proletarian elements of the population in order to crush by force the resistance of the bourgeoisie and to paralyse the instability of the peasantry and the petty bourgeoisie. (*Ibid.,* p. 111.)

Third stage. Commenced after the October Revolution. Objective: to consolidate the dictatorship of the proletariat in one country, using it as a base for the overthrow of imperialism in all countries. The revolution is spreading beyond the confines of one country; the period of world revolution has commenced. The main forces of the revolution: the dictatorship of the proletariate in one country, the revolutionary movement of the proletariat in all countries. Main reserves: the semi-proletarian and small-peasant masses in the developed countries, the liberation movement in the colonies and dependent countries. Direction of the main blow: isolation of the petty-bourgeois democrats, isolation of the parties of the Second International, which constitute the main support of the policy of *compromise* with imperialism. Plan for the disposition of forces: alliance of the proletarian revolution with the liberation movement in the colonies and the dependent countries.

Strategy deals with the main forces of the revolution and their reserves. It changes with the passing of the revolution from one stage to another, but remains essentially unchanged throughout a given stage.

III. THE FLOW AND EBB OF THE MOVEMENT, AND TACTICS

Tactics are the determination of the line of conduct of the proletariat in the comparatively short period of the flow or ebb of the movement, of the rise or decline of the revolution, the fight to carry out this line by means of replacing old forms of struggle and organization by new ones, old slogans by new ones, by combining these forms, etc. While the object of strategy is to win the war against tsarism, let us say, or against the bourgeoisie, to carry the struggle against tsarism or against the bourgeoisie to its end, tactics concern themselves with less important objects, for they aim not at winning the war as a whole, but at winning a particular engagement, or a particular battle, at carrying through successfully a particular campaign or a particular action corresponding to the concrete circumstances in the given period of rise or decline of the revolution. Tactics are a part of strategy, subordinate to it and serving it.

Tactics change according to flow and ebb. While the strategic plan remained unchanged during the first stage of the revolution (1903 to February 1917) tactics changed several times during that period. In the period from 1903 to 1905 the Party pursued offensive tactics, for the tide of the revolution was rising, the movement was on the upgrade, and tactics had to proceed from this fact. Accordingly, the forms of struggle were revolutionary, corresponding to the requirements of the rising tide of the revolution. Local political strikes, political demonstrations, the general political strike, boycott of the Duma, insurrection, revolutionary fighting slogans—such were the successive forms of the struggle during that period. These changes in the forms of struggle were accompanied by corresponding changes in the forms of organization. Factory committees, revolutionary peasant committees, strike committees, Soviets of workers' deputies, a workers' party operating more or less openly—such were the forms of organization during that period.

In the period from 1907 to 1912 the Party was compelled to resort to tactics of retreat; for we then experienced a decline in the revolutionary movement, the ebb of the revolution, and tactics necessarily had to take this fact into consideration. The forms of struggle, as well as the forms of organization, changed accordingly: Instead of boycott of the Duma there was participation in the Duma; instead of open, direct revolutionary action outside the Duma, there were parliamentary speeches and work in the Duma; instead of general political strikes, there were partial economic strikes, or simply a lull in activities. Of course, the Party had to go underground during that period, while the revolutionary mass organizations were superseded by cultural, educational, cooperative, insurance and other legal organizations.

The same must be said of the second and third stages of the revolution, during which tactics changed dozens of times, whereas the strategical plans remained unchanged.

Tactics deal with the forms of struggle and the forms of organization of the proletariat, with their changes and combinations. During a given stage of the revolution tactics may change several times, depending on the flow and ebb, the rise and decline, of the revolution.

IV. STRATEGIC LEADERSHIP

The reserves of the revolution can be:

Direct: (a) the peasantry and in general the intermediate strata of the population within the country; (b) the proletariat of the neighbouring countries; (c) the revolutionary movement in the colonies and dependent coun-tries; (d) the gains and achievements of the dictatorship of the proletariat—part of which the proletariat may give up temporarily, while retaining su-periority of forces, in order to buy off a powerful enemy and gain a respite; and

Indirect: (a) the contradictions and conflicts among the nonproletarian classes within the country, which can be utilized by the proletariat to weaken the enemy and to strengthen its own reserves; (b) contradictions, conflicts and wars (the imperialist war, for instance) among the bourgeois states hos-tile to the proletarian state, which can be utilized by the proletariat in its offensive or in manoeuvring in the event of a forced retreat.

There is no need to speak at length about the reserves of the first category, as their significance is understood by everyone. As for the reserves of the second category, whose significance is not always clear, it must be said that sometimes they are of prime importance for the progress of the revolution. One can hardly deny the enormous importance, for example, of the conflict between the petty-bourgeois democrats (Socialist-Revolutionaries) and the liberal-monarchist bourgeoisie (the Constitutional-Democrats) during and after the first revolution, which undoubtedly played its part in freeing the peasantry from the influence of the bourgeoisie. Still less reason is there for denying the colossal importance of the fact that the principal groups of im-perialists were engaged in a deadly war during the period of the October Revolution, when the imperialists, engrossed in war among themselves, were unable to concentrate their forces against the young Soviet power, and the proletariat, for this very reason, was able to get down to the work of organiz-ing its forces and consolidating its power, and to prepare the rout of Kolchak and Denikin. It must be presumed that now, when the contradictions among the imperialist groups are becoming more and more profound, and when a new war among them is becoming inevitable, reserves of this description will assume ever greater importance for the proletariat.

The task of strategic leadership is to make proper use of all these reserves for the achievement of the main object of the revolution at the given stage of its development.

What does making proper use of reserves mean?

It means fulfilling certain necessary conditions, of which the following must be regarded as the principal ones:

First: the concentration of the main forces of the revolution at the enemy's most vulnerable spot at the decisive moment, when the revolution has already become ripe, when the offensive is going full-steam ahead, when insurrection is knocking at the door, and when bringing the reserves up to the vanguard is the decisive condition of success. The Party's strategy during the period from April to October 1917 well illustrates this manner of utilizing reserves. Undoubtedly, the enemy's most vulnerable spot at that time was the war.

Undoubtedly, it was on this question, as the fundamental one, that the Party rallied the broadest masses of the population around the proletarian vanguard. The Party's strategy during that period was, while training the vanguard for street action by means of manifestations and demonstrations, to bring the reserves up to the vanguard through the medium of the Soviets in the rear and the soldiers' committees at the front. The outcome of the revolution has shown that the reserves were properly utilized.

Here is what Lenin, paraphrasing the well-known theses of Marx and Engels on insurrection, says about this condition of the strategic utilization of the forces of the revolution:

> Never *play* with insurrection, but when beginning it firmly realize that you must *go to the end.* You must concentrate a *great superiority of forces* at the decisive point, at the decisive moment, otherwise the enemy, who has the advantage of better preparation and organization, will destroy the insurgents. Once the insurrection has begun, you must act with the greatest *determination,* and by all means, without fail, take the *offensive.* "The defensive is the death of every armed rising." You must try to take the enemy by surprise and seize the moment when his forces are scattered. You must strive for *daily* successes, even if small (one might say hourly, if it is the case of one town), and at all costs retain *"moral ascendancy."* (Lenin, *Collected Works,* Vol. XXI, Russian edition, pp. 319-20.)

Second: the selection of the moment for the decisive blow, of the moment for starting the insurrection, so timed as to coincide with the moment when the crisis has reached its climax, when it is fully apparent that the vanguard is prepared to fight to the end, the reserves are prepared to support the vanguard, and maximum consternation reigns in the ranks of the enemy.

> The decisive battle, says Lenin, may be deemed to have fully matured *when* "all the class forces hostile to us have become sufficiently entangled, are sufficiently at loggerheads with each other, have sufficiently weakened themselves in a struggle which is beyond their strength"; *when* "all the vacillating, wavering, unstable, intermediate element—the petty bourgeoisie and the petty-bourgeois democrats as distinct from the bourgeoisie —have sufficiently exposed themselves before the people, have sufficiently disgraced themselves through their practical bankruptcy"; *when* "among the proletariat a mass sentiment in favour of supporting the most determined, supremely bold, revolutionary action against the bourgeoisie has arisen and begun vigorously to grow. Then, indeed, revolution is ripe; then, indeed, if we have correctly gauged all the conditions indicated above . . . and if we have chosen the moment rightly, our victory is assured. (*Selected Works,* Vol. X, pp. 137-38.)

The manner in which the October insurrection was carried out may be taken as a model of such strategy.

Failure to observe this condition leads to a dangerous error called "loss of tempo," when the Party lags behind the movement or runs far ahead of it, courting the danger of failure. An example of such "loss of tempo," an example of how the moment of insurrection should not be chosen, may be seen in the attempt made by a section of our comrades to begin the insurrection by arresting the Democratic Conference in August, 1917, when hesitation was still rife in the Soviets, when the front was still at the crossroads, when the reserves had not yet been brought up to the vanguard.

Third: undeviating pursuit of the course adopted, no matter what difficulties and complications are encountered on the road towards the goal; this is necessary in order that the vanguard may not lose sight of the main goal of the struggle and that the masses may not stray from the road while marching towards that goal and striving to rally around the vanguard. Failure to observe this condition leads to a grave error, well known to sailors as "losing the course." As an example of this "loss of course" we may mention the erroneous conduct of our Party when, immediately after the Democratic Conference, it adopted a resolution to participate in the Pre-parliament. For the moment the Party, as it were, forgot that the Pre-parliament was an attempt of the bourgeoisie to switch the country from the path of the Soviets to the path of bourgeois parliamentarism, that the Party's participation in such a body might result in mixing up all the cards and confusing the workers and peasants, who were waging a revolutionary struggle under the slogan: "All power to the Soviets." This mistake was rectified by the withdrawal of the Bolsheviks from the Pre-parliament.

Fourth: manoeuvring the reserves with a view to effecting a proper retreat when the enemy is strong, when retreat is inevitable, when to accept battle forced upon us by the enemy is obviously disadvantageous, when, with the given alignment of forces, retreat becomes the only way to ward off a blow against the vanguard and to keep the reserves intact.

"The revolutionary parties," says Lenin, "must complete their education. They have learned to attack. Now they have to realize that this knowledge must be supplemented with the knowledge how to retreat properly. They have to realize—and the revolutionary class is taught to realize by its own bitter experience—that victory is impossible unless they have learned both how to attack and how to retreat properly." (*Selected Works,* Vol. X, pp. 65-66.)

The object of this strategy is to gain time, to demoralize the enemy, and to accumulate forces in order later to assume the offensive.

The signing of the Brest-Litovsk Peace may be taken as a model of this strategy, for it enabled the Party to gain time, to take advantage of the conflicts in the camp of the imperialists, to demoralize the forces of the enemy, to retain the support of the peasantry, and to accumulate forces in preparation for the offensive against Kolchak and Denikin.

"In concluding a separate peace," said Lenin at that time, "we free our-selves *as much as is possible at the present moment* from both hostile imperialist groups, we take advantage of their mutual enmity and warfare, which hamper concerted action on their part against us, and for a certain period have our hands free to advance and to consolidate the socialist revolution." (*Collected Works,* Russian edition, Vol. XXII, p. 198.)

"Now even the biggest fool," said Lenin, three years after the Brest-Litovsk Peace, "can see that the 'Brest Peace' was a concession that strengthened us and broke up the forces of international imperialism." (*Selected Works,* Vol. IX, p. 247.)

Such are the principal conditions which ensure correct strategic leadership.

V. TACTICAL LEADERSHIP

Tactical leadership is a part of strategic leadership, subordinated to the tasks and the requirements of the latter. The task of tactical leadership is to master all forms of struggle and organization of the proletariat and to ensure that they are used properly so as to achieve, with the given alignment of forces, the maximum results necessary to prepare for strategic success.

What does making proper use of the forms of struggle and organization of the proletariat mean?

It means fulfilling certain necessary conditions, of which the following must be regarded as the principal ones:

First: to put in the forefront precisely those forms of struggle and organization which are best suited to the conditions prevailing during the flow or ebb of the movement at a given moment, and which therefore can facilitate and ensure the bringing of the masses to the revolutionary positions, the bringing of the millions to the revolutionary front, and their disposition at the revolutionary front.

The point here is not that the vanguard shall realize the impossibility of preserving the old order of things and the inevitability of its overthrow. The point is that the masses, the millions, shall understand this inevitability and display their readiness to support the vanguard. But the masses can understand this only from their own experience. The task is to enable the vast masses to realize from their own experience the inevitability of the overthrow of the old regime, to promote such methods of struggle and forms of organization as will make it easier for the masses to learn from experience to recognize the correctness of the revolutionary slogans.

The vanguard would have become detached from the working class, and the working class would have lost contact with the masses, if the Party had not decided at the time to participate in the Duma, if it had not decided to concentrate its forces on work in the Duma and to base the struggle on this work, in order to make it easier for the masses to realize from their own experience the futility of the Duma, the falsity of the promises of the Constitutional-Democrats, the impossibility of compromise with tsarism, and the inevitability of an alliance between the peasantry and the working class. Had the masses not gained their experience during the period of the Duma, the exposure of the Constitutional-Democrats and the hegemony of the proletariat would have been impossible.

The danger of the "Otzovist" [1] tactics was that they threatened to detach the vanguard from the millions of its reserves.

The Party would have become detached from the working class, and the working class would have lost its influence among the broad masses of the peasants and soldiers, if the proletariat had followed the "Left" Communists, who called for insurrection in April 1917, when the Mensheviks and the Socialist-Revolutionaries had not yet exposed themselves as advocates of war and imperialism, when the masses had not yet learned from their own experience to recognize the falsity of the speeches of the Mensheviks and the Socialist-Revolutionaries about peace, land and freedom. Had the masses not gained this experience during the Kerensky period, the Mensheviks and Socialist-Revolutionaries would not have been isolated and the dictatorship of the proletariat would have been impossible. Therefore, the tactics of "patiently explaining" the mistakes of the petty-bourgeois parties and of open struggle in the Soviets were the only correct tactics.

The danger of the tactics of the "Left" Communists was that they threatened to transform the Party from the leader of the proletarian revolution into a handful of inane conspirators with no ground to stand on.

"With the vanguard alone victory cannot be achieved," says Lenin. "To throw the vanguard alone into the decisive battle, before the whole class, before the broad masses have taken up a position either of direct support of the vanguard, or at least of benevolent neutrality towards it . . . would not merely be folly but a crime. And in order that actually the whole class, that actually the broad masses of the toilers and those oppressed by capital may take up such a position, propaganda and agitation alone are not sufficient. For this the masses must have their own political experience. Such is the fundamental law of all great revolutions, now confirmed with amazing force and vividness not only in Russia but also in Germany. It has been necessary, not only for the uncultured, often illiterate, masses of Russia, but also for the highly cultured, entirely literate masses of Germany, to realize

[1] From the Russian *Otozvat*—to recall; the name given to a group of Bolsheviks who advocated the recall of the Social-Democratic deputies from the Duma.

from their own painful experience the absolute impotence and spineless-
ness, the absolute helplessness and servility before the bourgeoisie, the utter
vileness of the government of the knights of the Second International, the
absolute inevitability of a dictatorship of the extreme reactionaries
(Kornilov in Russia, Kapp and Co. in Germany) as the only alternative to
a dictatorship of the proletariat, in order to turn resolutely toward communism." (*Selected Works,* Vol. X, p. 136.)

Second: To locate at any given moment that particular link in the chain of
processes which, if grasped, will enable us to hold the whole chain and to
prepare the conditions for achieving strategic success.

The point here is to single out from all the problems confronting the Party
that particular immediate problem, the answer to which constitutes the
central point, and the solution of which will ensure the successful solution of
the other immediate problems.

The importance of this thesis may be illustrated by two examples, one of
which may be taken from the remote past (the period of the formation of the
Party) and the other from the immediate present (the period of the New
Economic Policy).

In the period of the formation of the Party, when the innumerable circles
and organizations had not yet been linked together, when amateurishness
and the parochial outlook of the circles were corroding the Party from top to
bottom, when ideological confusion was a characteristic feature of the internal life of the Party, the main link and the main task in the chain of links
and in the chain of tasks then confronting the Party proved to be the establishment of an all-Russian illegal newspaper. Why? Because only by means
of an all-Russian illegal newspaper was it possible under the conditions then
prevailing to create a harmonious nucleus of a party, one capable of linking
up the innumerable circles and organizations into a single organization, to
prepare the conditions for ideological and tactical unity, and thus to lay the
foundations for the formation of a real Party.

During the period of transition from war to economic construction, when
industry was in the clutches of ruin and agriculture was suffering from a
shortage of city manufactures, when the establishment of a bond between
state industry and peasant economy became the fundamental condition for
successful socialist construction—in that period it turned out that the main
link in the chain of processes, the main task among a number of tasks, was
to develop trade. Why? Because under the conditions of the New Economic
Policy (N.E.P.) the bond between industry and peasant economy cannot be
established except through trade; because under the conditions of N.E.P.
production without sale is fatal for industry; because industry can be expanded only by the expansion of sales as a result of developing trade; because
only after we have consolidated our position in the sphere of trade, only after

we have secured control of trade, only after we have secured this link can there be any hope of linking industry with the peasant market and successfully fulfilling the other immediate tasks, thus creating the conditions for building the foundations of socialist economy.

"It is not enough to be a revolutionary and an adherent of socialism or a communist in general," says Lenin. "One must be able at each particular moment to find the particular link in the chain which one must grasp with all one's might in order to hold the whole chain and to prepare firmly for the transition to the next link. . . . At the present time . . . this link is the revival of internal trade under proper state regulation (direction). Trade—that is the 'link' in the historical chain of events, in the transitional forms of our socialist construction in 1921-22, which we . . . must 'grasp with all our might.' " (*Selected Works,* Vol. IX, pp. 298-99.)

These are the principal conditions which ensure correct tactical leadership.

VI. REFORMISM AND REVOLUTIONISM

What is the difference between revolutionary tactics and reformist tactics?
Some think that Leninism is opposed to reforms, opposed to compromises and to agreements in general. This is absolutely wrong. Bolsheviks know as well as anybody else that in a certain sense "every little helps," that under certain conditions reforms in general, and compromises and agreements in particular, are necessary and useful.

"To carry on a war for the overthrow of the international bourgeoisie," says Lenin, "a war which is a hundred times more difficult, protracted and complicated than the most stubborn of ordinary wars between states, and to refuse beforehand to manoeuvre, to utilize the conflict of interests (even through temporary) among one's enemies, to refuse to temporise and compromise with possible (even though transient, unstable, vacillating and conditional) allies—is not this ridiculous in the extreme? Is it not the same as if in the difficult ascent of an unexplored and heretofore inaccessible mountain we were to renounce beforehand the idea that at times we might have to go in zigzags, sometimes retracing our steps, sometimes giving up the course once selected and trying various others?" (*Selected Works,* Vol. X, p. 111.)

Obviously, therefore, it is not a matter of reforms or of compromises and agreements, but of the use people make of reforms and compromises.
To a reformist, reforms are everything, while revolutionary work is something incidental, something just to talk about, mere eyewash. That is why, with reformist tactics under the bourgeois regime, reforms are inevitably

transformed into an instrument for strengthening that regime, an instrument for disintegrating the revolution.

To a revolutionary, on the contrary, the main thing is revolutionary work and not reforms; to him reforms are by-products of the revolution. That is why, with revolutionary tactics under the bourgeois regime, reforms are naturally transformed into instruments for disintegrating this regime, into instruments for strengthening the revolution, into a base for the further development of the revolutionary movement.

The revolutionary will accept a reform in order to use it as an aid in combining legal work with illegal work, to intensify, under its cover, the illegal work for the revolutionary preparation of the masses for the overthrow of the bourgeoisie.

This is what making revolutionary use of reforms and agreements under the conditions of imperialism means.

The reformist, on the contrary, will accept reforms in order to renounce all illegal work, to thwart the preparation of the masses for the revolution and to rest in the shade of "bestowed" reforms.

This is what reformist tactics mean.

This is the position in regard to reforms and agreements under imperialism.

The situation changes somewhat, however, after the overthrow of imperialism, under the dictatorship of the proletariat. Under certain conditions, in a certain situation, the proletarian power may find itself constrained temporarily to leave the path of the revolutionary reconstruction of the existing order of things and to take the path of its gradual transformation, the "reformist path," as Lenin says in his well-known article "On the Importance of Gold," the path of flanking movements, of reforms and concessions to the non-proletarian classes—in order to disintegrate these classes, to give the revolution a respite, to recuperate and prepare the conditions for a new offensive. It cannot be denied that in a sense this is a reformist path. But it must be borne in mind that there is a fundamental distinction here, which consists in the fact that in this case the reform emanates from the proletarian power, it strengthens the proletarian power, it procures for it a necessary respite; its purpose is to distintegrate, not the revolution, but the non-proletarian classes.

Under such conditions a reform is thus transformed into its opposite.

The proletarian power is able to adopt such a policy because and only because, the sweep of the revolution in the preceding period was broad enough and therefore provided a sufficiently wide expanse within which to retreat, substituting for offensive tactics the tactics of temporary retreat, the tactics of flanking movements.

Thus, while formerly, under the bourgeois regime, reforms were a by-product of revolution, now, under the dictatorship of the proletariat, the source of reforms is the revolutionary gains of the proletariat, the reserves accumulated in the hands of the proletariat and consisting of these gains.

"Only Marxism," says Lenin, "has precisely and correctly defined the relation of reforms to revolution. However, Marx was able to see this relation only from one aspect, namely, under the conditions preceding the first to any extent permanent and lasting victory of the proletariat, if only in a single country. Under those conditions, the basis of the proper relation was: reforms are a by-product of the revolutionary class struggle of the proletariat. . . . After the victory of the proletariat, if only in a single country, something new enters into the relation between reforms and revolution. In principle, it is the same as before, but a change in form takes place, which Marx himself could not foresee, but which can be appreciated only on the basis of the philosophy and politics of Marxism. . . . After the victory (while still remaining a 'by-product' on the international scale) they [i.e., reforms] are, in addition, for the country in which victory has been achieved, a necessary and legitimate respite in those cases when, after the utmost exertion of effort, it becomes obvious that sufficient strength is lacking for the revolutionary accomplishment of this or that transition. Victory creates a 'reserve of strength' upon which one can sustain oneself even in a forced retreat, sustain oneself both materially and morally." (*Selected Works,* Vol. IX, pp. 301-02.)

NIKITA S. KHRUSHCHEV

8. *Communist Reality**

SUPERMAN AND GOD

After Stalin's death the Central Committee of the party began to implement a policy of explaining concisely and consistently that it is impermissible and foreign to the spirit of Marxism-Leninism to elevate one person, to transform him into a superman possessing supernatural characteristics, akin to those of a god. Such a man supposedly knows everything, sees everything, thinks for everyone, can do anything, is infallible in his behavior.

* From Nikita S. Khrushchev, *Secret Speech on Stalin and the Cult of the Individual* (Twentieth Congress of the Communist Party of the Soviet Union, February 25, 1956; translation released by the Department of State, June 4, 1956).

Such a belief about a man, and specifically about Stalin, was cultivated among us for many years.

The objective of the present report is not a thorough evaluation of Stalin's life and activity. Concerning Stalin's merits, an entirely sufficient number of books, pamphlets and studies had already been written in his lifetime. The role of Stalin in the preparation and execution of the Socialist Revolution, in the Civil War, and in the fight for the construction of socialism in our country, is universally known. Everyone knows this well.

At present, we are concerned with a question which has immense importance for the party now and for the future—with how the cult of the person of Stalin has been gradually growing, the cult which became at a certain specific stage the source of a whole series of exceedingly serious and grave perversions of party principles, of party democracy, of revolutionary legality.

Because of the fact that not all as yet realize fully the practical consequences resulting from the cult of the individual, the great harm caused by the violation of the principle of collective direction of the party and because of the accumulation of immense and limitless power in the hands of one person, the Central Committee of the party considers it absolutely necessary to make the material pertaining to this matter available to the 20th Congress of the Communist Party of the Soviet Union.

PHYSICAL ANNIHILATION OF OPPONENTS

Stalin acted not through persuasion, explanation and patient cooperation with people, but by imposing his concepts and demanding absolute submission to his opinion. Whoever opposed this concept or tried to prove his viewpoint and the correctness of his position was doomed to removal from the leading collective and to subsequent moral and physical annihilation. This was especially true during the period following the 17th Party Congress, when many prominent party leaders and rank-and-file party workers, honest and dedicated to the cause of Communism, fell victim to Stalin's despotism.

Stalin originated the concept "enemy of the people." This term automatically rendered it unnecessary that the ideological errors of a man or men engaged in a controversy be proven; this term made possible the usage of the most cruel repression, violating all norms of revolutionary legality, against anyone who in any way disagreed with Stalin, against those who were only suspected of hostile intent, against those who had bad reputations. This concept "enemy of the people" actually eliminated the possibility of any kind of ideological fight or the making of one's views known on this or that issue, even those of a practical character. In the main, and in actuality, the only proof of guilt used, against all norms of current legal science, was the "confession" of the accused himself; and, as subsequent probing proved, "confessions" were acquired through physical pressures against the accused. This led to glaring violations of revolutionary legality and to the fact that many entirely innocent persons, who in the past had defended the party line, became victims.

We must assert that, in regard to those persons who in their time had opposed the party line, there were often no sufficiently serious reasons for their physical annihilation. The formula "enemy of the people" was specifically introduced for the purpose of physically annihilating such individuals.

It is a fact that many persons who were later annihilated as enemies of the party and people had worked with Lenin during his life. Some of these persons had made errors during Lenin's life, but, despite this, Lenin benefited by their work; he corrected them and he did everything possible to retain them in the ranks of the party; he induced them to follow him.

Arbitrary behavior by one person encouraged and permitted arbitrariness in others. Mass arrests and deportations of many thousands of people, execution without trial and without normal investigation created conditions of insecurity, fear and even desperation.

This, of course, did not contribute toward unity of the party ranks and of all strata of working people, but, on the contrary, brought about annihilation and the expulsion from the party of workers who were loyal but inconvenient to Stalin.

Our party fought for the implementation of Lenin's plans for the construction of socialism. This was an ideological fight. Had Leninist principles been observed during the course of this fight, had the party's devotion to principles been skillfully combined with a keen and solicitous concern for people, had they not been repelled and wasted but rather drawn to our side, we certainly would not have had such a brutal violation of revolutionary legality and many thousands of people would not have fallen victim to the method of terror. Extraordinary methods would then have been resorted to only against those people who had in fact committed criminal acts against the Soviet system.

LIQUIDATION OF TOP COMMUNISTS

Having at its disposal numerous data showing brutal willfulness toward party cadres, the Central Committee has created a party commission under the control of the Central Committee Presidium; it was charged with investigating what made possible the mass repressions against the majority of the Central Committee members and candidates elected at the 17th Congress of the All-Union Communist Party (Bolsheviks).

The commission has become acquainted with a large quantity of materials in the NKVD archives and with other documents and has established many facts pertaining to the fabrication of cases against Communists, to false accusations, to glaring abuses of socialist legality, which resulted in the death of innocent people. It became apparent that many party, Soviet and economic activists, who were branded in 1937-1938 as "enemies," were actually never enemies, spies, wreckers, etc., but were always honest Communists; they were only so stigmatized and, often, no longer able to bear barbaric tortures, they charged themselves (at the order of the investigative judges—falsifiers) with all kinds of grave and unlikely crimes.

The commission has presented to the Central Committee Presidium lengthy and documented materials pertaining to mass repressions against the delegates to the 17th Party Congress and against members of the Central Committee elected at that Congress. These materials have been studied by the Presidium of the Central Committee.

It was determined that of the 139 members and candidates of the party's Central Committee who were elected at the 17th Congress, 98 persons, *i.e.,* 70 per cent, were arrested and shot (mostly in 1937-1938). (Indignation in the hall.) What was the composition of the delegates to the 17th Congress? It is known that 80 per cent of the voting participants of the 17th Congress joined the party during the years of conspiracy before the Revolution and during the civil war; this means before 1921. By social origin the basic mass of the delegates to the Congress were workers (60 per cent of the voting members).

For this reason, it was inconceivable that a congress so composed would have elected a Central Committee a majority of whom would prove to be enemies of the party. The only reason why 70 per cent of Central Committee members and candidates elected at the 17th Congress were branded as enemies of the party and of the people was because honest Communists were slandered, accusations against them were fabricated, and revolutionary legality was gravely undermined.

The same fate met not only the Central Committee members but also the majority of the delegates to the 17th Party Congress. Of 1,966 delegates with either voting or advisory rights, 1,108 persons were arrested on charges of anti-revolutionary crimes, *i.e.,* decidedly more than a majority. This very fact shows how absurd, wild and contrary to common sense were the charges of counterrevolutionary crimes made out, as we now see, against a majority of participants at the 17th Party Congress. (Indignation in the hall.)

We should recall that the 17th Party Congress is historically known as the Congress of Victors. Delegates to the Congress were active participants in the building of our socialist state; many of them suffered and fought for party interests during the pre-Revolutionary years in the conspiracy and at the civil-war fronts; they fought their enemies valiantly and often nervelessly looked into the face of death.

How, then, can we believe that such people could prove to be "two-faced" and had joined the camps of the enemies of socialism during the era after the political liquidation of Zinovievites, Trotskyites and rightists and after the great accomplishments of socialist construction? This was the result of the abuse of power by Stalin, who began to use mass terror against the party cadres.

What is the reason that mass repressions against activists increased more and more after the 17th Party Congress? It was because at that time Stalin had so elevated himself above the party and above the nation that he ceased to consider either the Central Committee or the party.

While he still reckoned with the opinion of the collective before the 17th Congress, after the complete political liquidation of the Trotskyites, Zinovievites and Bukharinites, when as a result of that fight and socialist victories the party achieved unity, Stalin ceased to an ever greater degree to consider the members of the party's Central Committee and even the members of the Political Bureau. Stalin thought that now he could decide all things alone and all he needed were statisticians; he treated all others in such a way that they could only listen to and praise him.

ORDER TO EXPEDITE EXECUTIONS

After the criminal murder of Sergei M. Kirov, mass repressions and brutal acts of violation of socialist legality began. On the evening of December 1, 1934, on Stalin's initiative (without the approval of the Political Bureau—which was passed two days later, casually), the Secretary of the Presidium of the Central Executive Committee, Yenukidze, signed the following directive:

"1. Investigative agencies are directed to speed up the cases of those accused of the preparation or execution of acts of terror.

"2. Judicial organs are directed not to hold up the execution of death sentences pertaining to crimes of this category in order to consider the possibility of pardon, because the Presidium of the Central Executive Committee of the USSR does not consider as possible the receiving of petitions of this sort.

"3. The organs of the Commissariat of Internal Affairs are directed to execute the death sentences against criminals of the above-mentioned category immediately after the passage of sentences."

This directive became the basis for mass acts of abuse against socialist legality. During many of the fabricated court cases, the accused were charged with "the preparation" of terroristic acts; this deprived them of any possibility that their cases might be re-examined, even when they stated before the court that their "confessions" were secured by force, and when, in a convincing manner, they disproved the accusations against them.

MYSTERY OF KIROV KILLING

It must be asserted that to this day the circumstances surrounding Kirov's murder hide many things which are inexplicable and mysterious and demand a most careful examination. There are reasons for the suspicion that the killer of Kirov, Nikolayev, was assisted by someone from among the people whose duty it was to protect the person of Kirov.

A month and a half before the killing, Nikolayev was arrested on the grounds of suspicious behavior but he was released and not even searched. It is an unusually suspicious circumstance that when the Chekist assigned to protect Kirov was being brought for an interrogation, on December 2, 1934, he was killed in a car "accident" in which no other occupants of the car were harmed. After the murder of Kirov, top functionaries of the Leningrad NKVD were given very light sentences, but in 1937 they were shot. We can assume that they were shot in order to cover the traces of the organizers of Kirov's killing. (Movement in the hall.)

Mass repressions grew tremendously from the end of 1936 after a telegram from Stalin and [Andrei] Zhdanov, dated from Sochi on September 25, 1936, was addressed to Kaganovich, Molotov and other members of the Political Bureau. The content of the telegram was as follows:

"We deem it absolutely necessary and urgent that Comrade Yezhov be nominated to the post of People's Commissar for Internal Affairs. Yagoda has definitely proved himself to be incapable of unmasking the Trotskyite-Zinovievite bloc. The OGPU is four years behind in this matter. This is noted by all party workers and by the majority of the representatives of the NKVD."

Strictly speaking, we should stress that Stalin did not meet with and, therefore, could not know the opinion of party workers.

This Stalinist formulation that the "NKVD is four years behind" in applying mass repression and that there is a necessity for "catching up" with the neglected work directly pushed the NKVD workers on the path of mass arrests and executions.

The mass repressions at this time were made under the slogan of a fight against the Trotskyites. Did the Trotskyites at this time actually constitute such a danger to our party and to the Soviet state? We should recall that in 1927, on the eve of the 15th Party Congress, only some 4,000 votes were cast for the Trotskyite-Zinovievite opposition while there were 724,000 for the party line. During the 10 years which passed between the 15th Party Congress and the February-March Central Committee plenum, Trotskyism was completely disarmed; many former Trotskyites had changed their former views and worked in the various sectors building socialism. It is clear that in the situation of socialist victory there was no basis for mass terror in the country.

Stalin's report at the February-March Central Committee plenum in 1937, "Deficiencies of party work and methods for the liquidation of the Trotskyites and of other two-facers," contained an attempt at theoretical justification of the mass terror policy under the pretext that as we march forward toward socialism class war must allegedly sharpen. Stalin asserted that both history and Lenin taught him this.

This terror was actually directed not at the remnants of the defeated exploiting classes but against the honest workers of the party and of the Soviet state; against them were made lying, slanderous and absurd accusations concerning "two-facedness," "espionage," "sabotage," preparation of fictitious "plots," etc.

CONFESSIONS THROUGH INHUMAN TORTURE

Using Stalin's formulation, namely, that the closer we are to socialism the more enemies we will have, and using the resolution of the February-March Central Committee plenum passed on the basis of Yezhov's report, the *provocateurs* who had infiltrated the state-security organs together with conscienceless careerists began to protect with the party name the mass terror against party cadres, cadres of the Soviet state and the ordinary Soviet citizens. It should suffice to say that the number of arrests based on charges of counterrevolutionary crimes had grown ten times between 1936 and 1937.

It is known that brutal willfulness was practiced against leading party workers. The party statute, approved at the 17th Party Congress, was based on Leninist principles expressed at the 10th Party Congress. It stated that, in order to apply an extreme method such as exclusion from the party against a Central Committee member, against a Central Committee candidate and against a member of the Party Control Commission, "it is necessary to call a Central Committee plenum and to invite to the plenum all Central Committee candidate members and all members of the Party Control Commission"; only if two-thirds of the members of such a general assembly of responsible party leaders find it necessary, only then can a Central Committee member or candidate be expelled.

The majority of the Central Committee members and candidates elected at the 17th Congress and arrested in 1937-1938 were expelled from the party illegally through the brutal abuse of the party statute, because the question of their expulsion was never studied at the Central Committee plenum.

Now, when the cases of some of these so-called "spies" and "saboteurs" were examined, it was found that all their cases were fabricated. Confessions of guilt of many arrested and charged with enemy activity were gained with the help of cruel and inhuman tortures.

At the same time, Stalin, as we have been informed by members of the Political Bureau of that time, did not show them the statements of many accused political activists when they retracted their confessions before the military tribunal and asked for an objective examination of their cases. There were many such declarations, and Stalin doubtless knew of them.

The Central Committee considers it absolutely necessary to inform the Congress of many such fabricated "cases" against the members of the party's Central Committee elected at the 17th Party Congress.

An example of vile provocation, of odious falsification and of criminal violation of revolutionary legality is the case of the former candidate for the Central Committee Political Bureau, one of the most eminent workers of the party and of the Soviet Government, Comrade Eikhe, who was a party member since 1905. (Commotion in the hall.)

Comrade Eikhe was arrested on April 29, 1938, on the basis of slanderous materials, without the sanction of the Prosecutor of the USSR, which was finally received 15 months after the arrest.

Investigation of Eikhe's case was made in a manner which most brutally violated Soviet legality and was accompanied by willfulness and falsification.

Eikhe was forced under torture to sign ahead of time a protocol of his confession prepared by the investigative judges, in which he and several other eminent party workers were accused of anti-Soviet activity.

On October 1, 1939, Eikhe sent his declaration to Stalin in which he categorically denied his guilt and asked for an examination of his case. In the declaration he wrote: "There is no more bitter misery than to sit in the jail of a government for which I have always fought."

A second declaration of Eikhe has been preserved which he sent to Stalin on October 27, 1939; in it he cited facts very convincingly and countered the slanderous accusations made against him, arguing that this provocatory accusation was on the one hand the work of real Trotskyites whose arrests he had sanctioned as First Secretary of the West Siberian Krai [Territory] Party Committee and who conspired in order to take revenge on him, and, on the other hand, the result of the base falsification of materials by the investigative judges.

Eikhe wrote in his declaration:

". . . On October 25 of this year I was informed that the investigation in my case has been concluded and I was given access to the materials of this investigation. Had I been guilty of only one hundredth of the crimes with which I am charged, I would not have dared to send you this pre-execution declaration; however, I have not been guilty of even one of the things with which I am charged and my heart is clean of even the shadow of baseness. I have never in my life told you a word of falsehood, and now, finding my two feet in the grave, I am also not lying. My whole case is a typical example of provocation, slander and violation of the elementary basis of revolutionary legality. . . .

". . . The confessions which were made part of my file are not only absurd but contain some slander toward the Central Committee of the All-Union Communist Party (Bolsheviks) and toward the Council of People's Commissars, because correct resolutions of the Central Committee of the All-Union Communist Party (Bolsheviks) and of the Council of People's Commissars which were not made on my initiative and without my participation are presented as hostile acts of counterrevolutionary organizations made at my suggestion. . . .

"I am now alluding to the most disgraceful part of my life and to my really grave guilt against the party and against you. This is my confession of counterrevolutionary activity. . . . The case is as follows: Not being able to suffer the tortures to which I was submitted by Ushakov and Nikolayev—and especially by the first one—who utilized the knowledge that my broken ribs have not properly mended and have caused me great pain, I have been forced to accuse myself and others.

"The majority of my confession has been suggested or dictated by Ushakov, and the remainder is my reconstruction of NKVD materials from Western Siberia for which I assumed all responsibility. If some part of the story which Ushakov fabricated and which I signed did not properly hang together, I was forced to sign another variation. The same thing was done to Rukhimovich, who was at first designated as a member of the reserve net and whose name later was removed without telling me anything about it; the same was also done with the leader of the reserve net, supposedly created by Bukharin in 1935. At first I wrote my name in, and then I was instructed to insert Mezhlauk. There were other similar incidents.

". . . I am asking and begging you that you again examine my case, and this not for the purpose of sparing me but in order to unmask the vile provocation which, like a snake, wound itself around many persons in a great degree due to my meanness and criminal slander. I have never betrayed you or the party. I know that I perish because of vile and mean work of the enemies of the party and of the people, who fabricated the provocation against me."

It would appear that such an important declaration was worth an examination by the Central Committee. This, however, was not done, and the declaration was transmitted to Beria while the terrible maltreatment of the Political Bureau candidate, Comrade Eikhe, continued.

On February 2, 1940, Eikhe was brought before the court. Here he did not confess any guilt and said as follows:

"In all the so-called confessions of mine there is not one letter written by me with the exception of my signatures under the protocols, which were forced from me. I have made my confession under pressure from the investigative judge, who from the time of my arrest tormented me. After that I began to write all this nonsense. . . . The most important thing for me is to tell the court, the party and Stalin that I am not guilty. I have never been guilty of any conspiracy. I will die believing in the truth of party policy as I have believed in it during my whole life."

On February 4 Eikhe was shot. (Indignation in the hall.)

It has been definitely established now that Eikhe's case was fabricated; he has been posthumously rehabilitated.

THOUSANDS DIED INNOCENT

This is the kind of vile things which were then practiced. (Movement in the hall.)

Even more widely was the falsification of cases practiced in the provinces. The NKVD headquarters of the Sverdlov Oblast "discovered" the so-called "Ural uprising staff"—an organ of the bloc of rightists, Trotskyites, Socialist Revolutionaries, church leaders—whose chief supposedly was the Secretary of the Sverdlov Oblast Party Committee and member of the Central Committee, All-Union Communist Party (Bolsheviks), Kabakov, who had been a party member since 1914. The investigative materials of that time show that in almost all *krais, oblasts* [provinces] and republics there supposedly existed "rightist Trotskyite, espionage-terror and diversionary-sabotage organizations and centers" and that the heads of such organizations as a rule—for no known reason—were first secretaries of *oblast* or republic Communist party committees or central committees.

Many thousands of honest and innocent Communists have died as a result of this monstrous falsification of such "cases," as a result of the fact that all kinds of slanderous "confessions" were accepted, and as a result of the practice of forcing accusations against oneself and others. In the same manner were fabricated the "cases" against eminent party and state workers—Kossior, Chubar, Postyshev, Kosarev and others.

In those years repressions on a mass scale were applied which were based on nothing tangible and which resulted in heavy cadre losses to the party.

The vicious practice was condoned of having the NKVD prepare lists of persons whose cases were under the jurisdiction of the Military Collegium and whose sentences were prepared in advance. Yezhov would send these lists to Stalin personally for his approval of the proposed punishment. In 1937-1938, 383 such lists containing the names of many thousands of party, Soviet, Komsomol, Army and economic workers were sent to Stalin. He approved these lists.

A large part of these cases are being reviewed now and a great part of them are being voided because they were baseless and falsified. Suffice it to say that from 1954 to the present time the Military Collegium of the Supreme Court has rehabilitated 7,679 persons, many of whom were rehabilitated posthumously.

Mass arrests of party, Soviet, economic and military workers caused tremendous harm to our country and to the cause of socialist advancement.

Mass repressions had a negative influence on the moral-political condition of the party, created a situation of uncertainty, contributed to the spreading of unhealthy suspicion, and sowed distrust among Communists. All sorts of slanderers and careerists were active.

Resolutions of the January plenum of the Central Committee, All-Union

Communist Party (Bolsheviks), in 1938 had brought some measure of improvement to the party organizations. However, widespread repression also existed in 1938.

Only because our party has at its disposal such great moral-political strength was it possible for it to survive the difficult events in 1937-1938 and to educate new cadres. There is, however, no doubt that our march forward toward socialism and toward the preparation of the country's defense would have been much more successful were it not for the tremendous loss in the cadres suffered as a result of the baseless and false mass repressions in 1937-1938.

We are justly accusing Yezhov for the degenerate practices of 1937. But we have to answer these questions:

Could Yezhov have arrested Kossior, for instance, without the knowledge of Stalin? Was there an exchange of opinions or a Political Bureau decision concerning this?

No, there was not, as there was none regarding other cases of this type.

Could Yezhov have decided such important matters as the fate of such eminent party figures?

No, it would be a display of naïveté to consider this the work of Yezhov alone. It is clear that these matters were decided by Stalin, and that without his orders and his sanction Yezhov could not have done this.

We have examined the cases and have rehabilitated Kossior, Rudzutak, Postyshev, Kosarev and others. For what causes were they arrested and sentenced? The review of evidence shows that there was no reason for this. They, like many others, were arrested without the prosecutor's knowledge.

In such a situation, there is no need for any sanction, for what sort of a sanction could there be when Stalin decided everything? He was the chief prosecutor in these cases. Stalin not only agreed to, but on his own initiative issued, arrest orders. We must say this so that the delegates to the Congress can clearly undertake and themselves assess this and draw the proper conclusions.

Facts prove that many abuses were made on Stalin's orders without reckoning with any norms of party and Soviet legality. Stalin was a very distrustful man, sickly suspicious; we know this from our work with him. He could look at a man and say: "Why are your eyes so shifty today?" or "Why are you turning so much today and avoiding to look me directly in the eyes?" The sickly suspicion created in him a general distrust even toward eminent party workers whom he had known for years. Everywhere and in everything he saw "enemies," "two-facers" and "spies." Possessing unlimited power, he indulged in great willfulness and choked a person morally and physically. A situation was created where one could not express one's own will.

When Stalin said that one or another should be arrested, it was necessary to accept on faith that he was an "enemy of the people." Meanwhile, Beria's gang, which ran the organs of state security, outdid itself in proving the guilt of the arrested and the truth of materials which it falsified. And what proofs were offered? The confessions of the arrested, and the investigative judges accepted these "confessions." And how is it possible that a person confesses to crimes which he has not committed? Only in one way—because of application of physical methods of pressuring him, tortures, bringing him to a state of unconsciousness, deprivation of his judgment, taking away of his human dignity. In this manner were "confessions" acquired.

WORLD WAR II

The power accumulated in the hands of one person, Stalin, led to serious consequences during the Great Patriotic War.

When we look at many of our novels, films and historical "scientific studies," the role of Stalin in the Patriotic War appears to be entirely improbable. Stalin had foreseen everything. The Soviet Army, on the basis of a strategic plan prepared by Stalin long before, used the tactics of so-called "active defense," *i.e.,* tactics which, as we know, allowed the Germans to come up to Moscow and Stalingrad. Using such tactics, the Soviet Army, supposedly thanks only to Stalin's genius, turned to the offensive and subdued the enemy. The epic victory gained through the armed might of the land of the Soviets, through our heroic people, is ascribed in this type of novel, film and "scientific study" as being completely due to the strategic genius of Stalin.

We have to analyze this matter carefully because it has a tremendous significance not only from the historical, but especially from the political, educational and practical point of view. What are the facts of this matter?

Before the war, our press and all our political-educational work was characterized by its bragging tone: When an enemy violates the holy Soviet soil, then for every blow of the enemy we will answer with three blows, and we will battle the enemy on his soil and we will win without much harm to ourselves. But these positive statements were not based in all areas on concrete facts, which would actually guarantee the immunity of our borders.

During the war and after the war, Stalin put forward the thesis that the tragedy which our nation experienced in the first part of the war was the result of the "unexpected" attack of the Germans against the Soviet Union. But, comrades, this is completely untrue. As soon as Hitler came to power in Germany he assigned to himself the task of liquidating Communism. The fascists were saying this openly; they did not hide their plans.

In order to attain this aggressive end, all sorts of pacts and blocs were created, such as the famous Berlin-Rome-Tokyo Axis. Many facts from the prewar period clearly showed that Hitler was going all out to begin a war against the Soviet state, and that he had concentrated large armed units, together with armored units, near the Soviet borders.

Documents which have now been published show that by April 3, 1941, Churchill, through his Ambassador to the USSR, Cripps, personally warned

Stalin that the Germans had begun regrouping their armed units with the intent of attacking the Soviet Union.

It is self-evident that Churchill did not do this at all because of his friendly feeling toward the Soviet nation. He had in this his own imperialistic goals— to bring Germany and the USSR into a bloody war and thereby to strengthen the position of the British Empire.

Just the same, Churchill affirmed in his writings that he sought to "warn Stalin and call his attention to the danger which threatened him." Churchill stressed this repeatedly in his dispatches of April 18 and on the following days. However, Stalin took no heed of these warnings. What is more, Stalin ordered that no credence be given to information of this sort, in order not to provoke the initiation of military operations.

We must assert that information of this sort concerning the threat of German armed invasion of Soviet territory was coming in also from our own military and diplomatic sources; however, because the leadership was conditioned against such information, such data was dispatched with fear and assessed with reservation.

When the fascist armies had actually invaded Soviet territory and military operations began, Moscow issued the order that the German fire was not to be returned. Why? It was because Stalin, despite evident facts, thought that the war had not yet started, that this was only a provocative action on the part of several undisciplined sections of the German Army, and that our reaction might serve as a reason for the Germans to begin the war.

The following fact is also known: On the eve of the invasion of the territory of the Soviet Union by the Hitlerite army, a certain German citizen crossed our border and stated that the German armies had received orders to start the offensive against the Soviet Union on the night of June 22 at 3 o'clock. Stalin was informed about this immediately, but even this warning was ignored.

As you see, everything was ignored: warnings of certain Army commanders, declarations of deserters from the enemy army, and even the open hostility of the enemy. Is this an example of the alertness of the chief of the party and of the state at this particularly significant historical moment?

And what were the results of this carefree attitude, this disregard of clear facts? The result was that already in the first hours and days the enemy had destroyed in our border regions a large part of our Air Force, artillery and other military equipment; he annihilated large numbers of our military cadres and disorganized our military leadership; consequently we could not prevent the enemy from marching deep into the country.

Very grievous consequences, especially in reference to the beginning of the war, followed Stalin's annihilation of many military commanders and political workers during 1937-1941 because of his suspiciousness and through slanderous accusations. During these years repressions were instituted against certain parts of military cadres beginning literally at the company and battalion commander level and extending to the higher military centers; during this time the cadre of leaders who had gained military experience in Spain and in the Far East was almost completely liquidated.

The policy of large-scale repression against the military cadres led also to undermined military discipline, because for several years officers of all ranks and even soldiers in the party and Komsomol cells were taught to "unmask" their superiors as hidden enemies. (Movement in the hall.) It is natural that this caused a negative influence on the state of military discipline in the first war period.

And, as you know, we had before the war excellent military cadres which were unquestionably loyal to the party and to the Fatherland. Suffice it to say that those of them who managed to survive, despite severe tortures to which they were subjected in the prisons, have from the first war days shown themselves real patriots and heroically fought for the glory of the Fatherland; I have here in mind such comrades as Rokossovsky (who, as you know, had been jailed), Gorbatov, Maretskov (who is a delegate at the present Congress), Podlas (he was an excellent commander who perished at the front), and many, many others. However, many such commanders perished in camps and jails and the Army saw them no more.

All this brought about the situation which existed at the beginning of the war and which was the great threat to our Fatherland.

It would be incorrect to forget that, after the first severe disaster and defeat at the front, Stalin thought that this was the end. In one of his speeches in those days he said: "All that which Lenin created we have lost forever."

After this Stalin for a long time actually did not direct the military operations and ceased to do anything whatever. He returned to active leadership only when some members of the Political Bureau visited him and told him that it was necessary to take certain steps immediately in order to improve the situation at the front.

Therefore, the threatening danger which hung over our Fatherland in the first period of the war was largely due to the faulty methods of directing the nation and the party by Stalin himself.

However, we speak not only about the moment when the war began, which led to serious disorganization of our Army and brought us severe losses. Even after the war began, the nervousness and hysteria which Stalin demonstrated, interfering with actual military operation, caused our Army serious damage.

Stalin was very far from an understanding of the real situation which was developing at the front. This was natural because, during the whole Patriotic War, he never visited any section of the front or any liberated city except for one short ride on the Mozhaisk highway during a stabilized situation at the front. To this incident were dedicated many literary works full of fantasies of all sorts and so many paintings. Simultaneously, Stalin was interfering with operations and issuing orders which did not take into consideration the real situation at a given section of the front and which could not help but result in huge personnel losses.

The tactics on which Stalin insisted without knowing the essence of the conduct of battle operations cost us much blood until we succeeded in stopping the opponent and going over to the offensive.

The military know that already by the end of 1941, instead of great operational maneuvers flanking the opponent and penetrating behind his back, Stalin demanded incessant frontal attacks and the capture of one village after another.

Because of this, we paid with great losses—until our generals, on whose shoulders rested the whole weight of conducting the war, succeeded in changing the situation and shifting to flexible-maneuver operations, which immediately brought serious changes at the front favorable to us.

All the more shameful was the fact that, after our great victory over the enemy which cost us so much, Stalin began to downgrade many of the commanders who contributed so much to the victory over the enemy, because Stalin excluded every possibility that services rendered at the front should be credited to anyone but himself.

In the same vein, let us take, for instance, our historical and military films and some literary creations; they make us feel sick. Their true objective is the propagation of the theme of praising Stalin as a military genius. Let us recall the film, *The Fall of Berlin*. Here only Stalin acts; he issues orders in the hall in which there are many empty chairs and only one man approached him and reports something to him—that is Poskrebyshev, his loyal shield-bearer. (Laughter in the hall.)

And where is the military command? Where is the Political Bureau? Where is the Government? What are they doing and with what are they engaged? There is nothing about them in the film. Stalin acts for everybody; he does not reckon with anyone; he asks no one for advice. Everything is shown to the nation in this false light. Why? In order to surround Stalin with glory, contrary to the facts and contrary to historical truth.

The question arises: And where are the military, on whose shoulders rested the burden of the war? They are not in the film; with Stalin in, no room was left for them.

DEPORTATION OF WHOLE NATIONS

Comrades, let us reach for some other facts. The Soviet Union is justly considered as a model of a multinational state because we have in practice assured the equality and friendship of all nations which live in our great Fatherland.

All the more monstrous are the acts whose iniator was Stalin and which are rude violations of the basic Leninist principles of the nationality policy of the Soviet state. We refer to the mass deportations from their native places of whole nations, together with all Communists and Komsomols without any exception; this deportation action was not dictated by any military considerations.

Thus, already at the end of 1943, when there occurred a permanent breakthrough at the fronts of the Great Patriotic War benefiting the Soviet Union, a decision was taken and executed concerning the deportation of all the Karachai from the lands on which they lived.

In the same period, at the end of December 1943, the same lot befell the whole population of the Autonomous Kalmyk Republic. In March 1944, all the Chechen and Ingush peoples were deported and the Chechen-Ingush Autonomous Republic was liquidated. In April 1944, all Balkars were deported to faraway places from the territory of the Kabardino-Balkar Autonomous Republic and the Republic itself was renamed the Autonomous Kabardian Republic.

The Ukrainians avoided meeting this fate only because there were too many of them and there was no place to which to deport them. Otherwise, he would have deported them also. (Laughter and animation in the hall.)

Not only a Marxist-Leninist but also no man of common sense can grasp how it is possible to make whole nations responsible for inimical activity, including women, children, old people, Communists and Komsomols, to use mass repression against them, and to expose them to misery and suffering for the hostile acts of individual persons or groups of persons.

THE "LENINGRAD AFFAIR"

After the conclusion of the Patriotic War, the Soviet nation stressed with pride the magnificent victories gained through great sacrifices and tremendous efforts. The country experienced a period of political enthusiasm. The party came out of the war even more united; in the fire of the war, party cadres were tempered and hardened. Under such conditions nobody could have even thought of the possibility of some plot in the party.

And it was precisely at this time that the so-called "Leningrad affair" was born. As we have now proven, this case was fabricated. Those who innocently lost their lives included Comrades Voznesensky, Kuznetsov, Rodionov, Popkov, and others.

As is known, Voznesensky and Kuznetsov were talented and eminent leaders. Once they stood very close to Stalin. It is sufficient to mention that Stalin made Voznesensky first deputy to the chairman of the Council of Ministers and Kuznetsov was elected Secretary of the Central Committee. The very fact that Stalin entrusted Kuznetsov with the supervision of the state-security organs shows the trust which he enjoyed.

How did it happen that these persons were branded as enemies of the people and liquidated?

Facts prove that the "Leningrad affair" is also the result of willfulness which Stalin exercised against party cadres. Had a normal situation existed in the party's Central Committee and in the Central Committee Political Bureau, affairs of this nature would have been examined there in accordance with party practice, and all pertinent facts assessed; as a result, such an affair as well as others would not have happened.

We must state that, after the war, the situation became even more complicated. Stalin became even more capricious, irritable and brutal; in particular his suspicion grew. His persecution mania reached unbelievable dimensions. Many workers were becoming enemies before his very eyes. After the war, Stalin separated himself from the collective even more. Everything was decided by him alone without any consideration for anyone or anything.

This unbelievable suspicion was cleverly taken advantage of by the abject *provocateur* and vile enemy, Beria, who had murdered thousands of Communists and loyal Soviet people. The elevation of Voznesensky and Kuznetsov alarmed Beria. As we have now proven, it had been precisely Beria who had "suggested" to Stalin the fabrication by him and by his confidants of materials in the form of declarations and anonymous letters, and in the form of various rumors and talks.

The party's Central Committee has examined this so-called "Leningrad affair"; persons who innocently suffered are now rehabilitated and honor has been restored to the glorious Leningrad party organization. Abakumov and others who had fabricated this affair were brought before a court; their trial took place in Leningrad and they received what they deserved.

The question arises: Why is it that we see the truth of this affair only now, and why did we not do something earlier, during Stalin's life, in order to prevent the loss of innocent lives? It was because Stalin personally supervised the "Leningrad affair," and the majority of the Political Bureau members did not, at that time, know all of the circumstances in these matters and could not therefore intervene.

When Stalin received certain material from Beria and Abakumov, without examining these slanderous materials he ordered an investigation of the "affair" of Voznesensky and Kuznetsov. With this, their fate was sealed.

THE RIFT WITH TITO

The willfulness of Stalin showed itself not only in decisions concerning the internal life of the country but also in the international relations of the Soviet Union.

The July plenum of the Central Committee studied in detail the reasons for the development of conflict with Yugoslavia. It was a shameful role which Stalin played here. The "Yugoslav affair" contained no problems which could not have been solved through party discussions among comrades. There was no significant basis for the development of this "affair"; it was completely possible to have prevented the rupture of relations with that country. This does not mean, however, that the Yugoslav leaders did not make mistakes or did not have shortcomings. But these mistakes and shortcomings were magnified in a monstrous manner by Stalin, which resulted in a break of relations with a friendly country.

I recall the first days when the conflict between the Soviet Union and Yugoslavia began artificially to be blown up. Once, when I came from Kiev to Moscow, I was invited to visit Stalin, who, pointing to the copy of a letter lately sent to Tito, asked me, "Have you read this?"

Not waiting for my reply, he answered, "I will shake my little finger—and there will be no more Tito. He will fall."

We have dearly paid for this "shaking of the little finger." This statement reflected Stalin's mania for greatness, but he acted just that way: "I will shake my little finger—and there will be no Kossior"; "I will shake my little finger once more and Postyshev and Chubar will be no more"; "I will shake my little finger again—and Voznesensky, Kuznetsov and many others will disappear."

But this did not happen to Tito. No matter how much or how little Stalin shook, not only his little finger but everything else that he could shake, Tito did not fall. Why? The reason was that, in this case of disagreement with the Yugoslav comrades, Tito had behind him a state and a people who had gone through a severe school of fighting for liberty and independence, a people which gave support to its leaders.

You see to what Stalin's mania for greatness led. He had completely lost consciousness of reality; he demonstrated his suspicion and haughtiness not only in relation to individuals in the USSR, but in relation to whole parties and nations.

We have carefully examined the case of Yugoslavia and have found a proper solution which is approved by the peoples of the Soviet Union and of Yugoslavia as well as by the working masses of all the people's democracies and by all progressive humanity. The liquidation of the abnormal relationship with Yugoslavia was done in the interest of the whole camp of socialism, in the interest of strengthening peace in the whole world.

THE AFFAIR OF THE "DOCTORS' PLOT"

Let us also recall the "affair of the doctor-plotters." (Animation in the hall.) Actually there was no "affair" outside of the declaration of the woman doctor Timashuk, who was probably influenced or ordered by someone (after all, she was an unofficial collaborator of the organs of state security) to write

Stalin a letter in which she declared that doctors were applying supposedly improper methods of medical treatment.

Such a letter was sufficient for Stalin to reach an immediate conclusion that there are doctor-plotters in the Soviet Union. He issued orders to arrest a group of eminent Soviet medical specialists. He personally issued advice on the conduct of the investigation and the method of interrogation of the arrested persons. He said that the academician Vinogradov should be put in chains, another one should be beaten. Present at this Congress as a delegate is the former Minister of State Security, Comrade Ignatiev. Stalin told him curtly, "If you do not obtain confessions from the doctors we will shorten you by a head." (Tumult in the hall.)

Stalin personally called the investigative judge, gave him instructions, advised him on which investigative methods should be used; these methods were simple—beat, beat and, once again, beat.

Shortly after the doctors were arrested, we members of the Political Bureau received protocols with the doctors' confessions of guilt. After distributing these protocols, Stalin told us, "You are blind like young kittens; what will happen without me? The country will perish because you do not know how to recognize enemies."

The case was so presented that no one could verify the facts on which the investigation was based. There was no possibility of trying to verify facts by contacting those who had made the confessions of guilt.

We felt, however, that the case of the arrested doctors was questionable. We knew some of these people personally because they had once treated us. When we examined this "case" after Stalin's death, we found it to be fabricated from beginning to end.

This ignominious "case" was set up by Stalin; he did not, however, have the time in which to bring it to an end (as he conceived that end), and for this reason the doctors are still alive. Now all have been rehabilitated; they are working in the same places they were working before; they treat top individuals, not excluding members of the Government; they have our full confidence; and they execute their duties honestly, as they did before.

In organizing the various dirty and shameful cases, a very base role was played by the rabid enemy of our party, an agent of a foreign intelligence service—Beria, who had stolen into Stalin's confidence. In what way could this *provocateur* gain such a position in the party and in the state, so as to become the First Deputy Chairman of the Council of Ministers of the Soviet Union and a member of the Central Committee Political Bureau? It has now been established that this villain had climbed up the Government ladder over an untold number of corpses.

SELF-ADULATION

Comrades: The cult of the individual acquired such monstrous size chiefly because Stalin himself, using all conceivable methods, supported the glorification of his own person. This is supported by numerous facts. One of the most characteristic examples of Stalin's self-glorification and of his lack of even elementary modesty is the edition of his *Short Biography,* which was published in 1948.

This book is an expression of the most dissolute flattery, an example of making a man into a godhead, of transforming him into an infallible sage, "the greatest leader, sublime strategist of all times and nations." Finally, no other words could be found with which to lift Stalin up to the heavens.

We need not give here examples of the loathsome adulation filling this book. All we need to add is that they all were approved and edited by Stalin personally and some of them were added in his own handwriting to the draft text of the book.

What did Stalin consider essential to write into this book? Did he want to cool the ardor of his flatterers who were composing his *Short Biography?* No! He marked the very places where he thought that the praise of his services was insufficient. Here are some examples characterizing Stalin's activity, added in Stalin's own hand:

"In this fight against the skeptics and capitulators, the Trotskyites, Zinovievites, Bukharinites and Kamenevites, there was definitely welded together, after Lenin's death, that leading core of the party . . . that upheld the great banner of Lenin, rallied the party behind Lenin's behests, and brought the Soviet people into the broad road of industrializing the country and collectivizing the rural economy. The leader of this core and the guiding force of the party and the state was Comrade Stalin."

Thus writes Stalin himself! Then he adds:

"Although he performed his task as leader of the party and the people with consummate skill and enjoyed the unreserved support of the entire Soviet people, Stalin never allowed his work to be marred by the slightest hint of vanity, conceit or self-adulation."

Where and when could a leader so praise himself? Is this worthy of a leader of the Marxist-Leninist type? No. Precisely against this did Marx and Engels take such a strong position. This also was always sharply condemned by Vladimir Ilyich Lenin.

In the draft text of his book appeared the following sentence: "Stalin is the Lenin of today." This sentence appeared to Stalin to be too weak, so, in his own handwriting, he changed it to read: "Stalin is the worthy continuer of Lenin's work, or, as it is said in our party, Stalin is the Lenin of today." You see how well it is said, not by the nation but by Stalin himself.

It is possible to give many such self-praising appraisals written into the draft text of that book in Stalin's hand. Especially generously does he endow himself with praises pertaining to his military genius, to his talent for strategy.

I will cite one more insertion made by Stalin concerning the theme of the Stalinist military genius. "The advanced Soviet science of war received further development," he writes, "at Comrade Stalin's hands. Comrade Stalin elaborated the theory of the permanently operating factors that decide the issue of wars, of active defense and the laws of counteroffensive and offensive, of the cooperation of all services and arms in modern warfare, of the role of big tank masses and air forces in modern war, and of the artillery as the most formidable of the armed services. At the various stages of the war Stalin's genius found the correct solutions that took account of all the circumstances of the situation." (Movement in the hall.)

And, further, writes Stalin: "Stalin's military mastership was displayed both in defense and offense. Comrade Stalin's genius enabled him to divine the enemy's plans and defeat them. The battles in which Comrade Stalin directed the Soviet armies are brilliant examples of operational military skill."

In this manner was Stalin praised as a strategist. Who did this? Stalin himself, not in his role as a strategist but in the role of an author-editor, one of the main creators of his self-adulatory biography. Such, comrades, are the facts. We should rather say shameful facts.

And one additional fact from the same *Short Biography* of Stalin. As is known, *The Short Course of the History of the All-Union Communist Party (Bolsheviks)* was written by a commission of the party Central Committee.

This book, parenthetically, was also permeated with the cult of the individual and was written by a designated group of authors. This fact was reflected in the following formulation on the proof copy of the *Short Biography* of Stalin: "A commission of the Central Committee, All-Union Communist Party (Bolsheviks), under the direction of Comrade Stalin and with his most active personal participation, has prepared a *Short Course of the History of the All-Union Communist Party (Bolsheviks)*."

But even this phrase did not satisfy Stalin: The following sentence replaced it in the final version of the *Short Biography:* "In 1938 appeared the book, *History of the All-Union Communist Party (Bolsheviks), Short Course,* written by Comrade Stalin and approved by a commission of the Central Committee, All-Union Communist Party (Bolsheviks)." Can one add anything more? (Animation in the hall.)

As you see, a surprising metamorphosis changed the work created by a group into a book written by Stalin. It is not necessary to state how and why this metamorphosis took place.

A pertinent question comes to our mind: If Stalin is the author of this book, why did he need to praise the person of Stalin so much and to transform the whole post-October historical period of our glorious Communist party solely into an action of "the Stalin genius"?

Did this book properly reflect the efforts of the party in the socialist transformation of the country, in the construction of socialist society, in the industrialization and collectivization of the country, and also other steps taken by the party which undeviatingly traveled the path outlined by Lenin? This book speaks principally about Stalin, about his speeches, about his reports. Everything without the smallest exception is tied to his name.

And when Stalin himself asserts that he himself wrote the *Short Course of the History of the All-Union Communist Party (Bolsheviks)*, this calls at least for amazement. Can a Marxist-Leninist thus write about himself, praising his own person to the heavens?

Or let us take the matter of the Stalin Prizes. (Movement in the hall.) Not even the Tsars created prizes which they named after themselves.

WHERE WAS THE CENTRAL COMMITTEE?

Some comrades may ask us: Where were the members of the Political Bureau of the Central Committee? Why did they not assert themselves against the cult of the individual in time? And why is this being done only now?

First of all, we have to consider the fact that the members of the Political Bureau viewed these matters in a different way at different times. Initially, many of them backed Stalin actively because Stalin was one of the strongest Marxists and his logic, his strength and his will greatly influenced the cadres and party work.

It is known that Stalin, after Lenin's death, especially during the first years, actively fought for Leninism against the enemies of Leninist theory and against those who deviated. Beginning with Leninist theory, the party, with its Central Committee at the head, started on a great scale the work of socialist industrialization of the country, agricultural collectivization and the cultural revolution.

At that time Stalin gained great popularity, sympathy and support. The party had to fight those who attempted to lead the country away from the correct Leninist path; it had to fight Trotskyites, Zinovievites and rightists, and the bourgeois nationalists. This fight was indispensable.

Later, however, Stalin, abusing his power more and more, began to fight eminent party and Government leaders and to use terroristic methods against honest Soviet people. As we have already shown, Stalin thus handled such eminent party and Government leaders as Kossior, Rudzutak, Eikhe, Postyshev and many others.

Attempts to oppose groundless suspicions and charges resulted in the opponent falling victim of the repression. This characterized the fall of Comrade Postyshev.

In one of his speeches Stalin expressed his dissatisfaction with Postyshev and asked him, "What are you actually?"

Postyshev answered clearly, "I am a Bolshevik, Comrade Stalin, a Bolshevik."

This assertion was at first considered to show a lack of respect for Stalin;

later it was considered a harmful act and consequently resulted in Postyshev's annihilation and branding without any reason as a "people's enemy."

In the situation which then prevailed I have talked often with Nikolai Alexandrovich Bulganin; once when we two were traveling in a car, he said, "It has happened sometimes that a man goes to Stalin on his invitation as a friend. And, when he sits with Stalin, he does not know where he will be sent next—home or to jail."

It is clear that such conditions put every member of the Political Bureau in a very difficult situation. And, when we also consider the fact that in the last years the Central Committee plenary sessions were not convened and that the sessions of the Political Bureau occurred only occasionally, from time to time, then we will understand how difficult it was for any member of the Political Bureau to take a stand against one or another unjust or improper procedure, against serious errors and shortcomings in the practices of leadership.

MILOVAN DJILAS

9. *The New Class**

I

Everything happened differently in the U.S.S.R. and other Communist countries from what the leaders—even such prominent ones as Lenin, Stalin, Trotsky, and Bukharin—anticipated. They expected that the state would rapidly wither away, that democracy would be strengthened. The reverse happened. They expected a rapid improvement in the standard of living— there has been scarcely any change in this respect and, in the subjugated East European countries, the standard has even declined. In every instance, the standard of living has failed to rise in proportion to the rate of industrialization, which was much more rapid. It was believed that the differences between cities and villages, between intellectual and physical labor, would slowly disappear; instead these differences have increased. Communist anticipations in other areas—including their expectations for developments in the non-Communist world—have also failed to materialize.

The greatest illusion was that industrialization and collectivization in the U.S.S.R., and destruction of capitalist ownership, would result in a classless society. In 1936, when the new Constitution was promulgated, Stalin an-

* From Milovan Djilas, *The New Class* (Frederick A. Praeger, 1957). By permission.

nounced that the "exploiting class" had ceased to exist. The capitalist and other classes of ancient origin had in fact been destroyed, but a new class, previously unknown to history, had been formed.

It is understandable that this class, like those before it, should believe that the establishment of its power would result in happiness and freedom for all men. The only difference between this and other classes was that it treated the delay in the realization of its illusions more crudely. It thus affirmed that its power was more complete than the power of any other class before in history, and its class illusions and prejudices were proportionally greater.

This new class, the bureaucracy, or more accurately the political bureaucracy, has all the characteristics of earlier ones as well as some new characteristics of its own. Its origin had its special characteristics also, even though in essence it was similar to the beginnings of other classes.

Other classes, too, obtained their strength and power by the revolutionary path, destroying the political, social, and other orders they met in their way. However, almost without exception, these classes attained power *after* new economic patterns had taken shape in the old society. The case was the reverse with new classes in the Communist systems. It did not come to power to *complete* a new economic order but to *establish* its own and, in so doing, to establish its power over society.

In earlier epochs the coming to power of some class, some part of a class, or of some party, was the final event resulting from its formation and its development. The reverse was true in the U.S.S.R. There the new class was definitely formed after it attained power. Its consciousness had to develop before its economic and physical powers, because the class had not taken root in the life of the nation. This class viewed its role in relation to the world from an idealistic point of view. Its practical possibilities were not diminished by this. In spite of its illusions, it represented an objective tendency toward industrialization. Its practical bent emanated from this tendency. The promise of an ideal world increased the faith in the ranks of the new class and sowed illusions among the masses. At the same time it inspired gigantic physical undertakings.

Because this new class had not been formed as a part of the economic and social life before it came to power, it could only be created in an organization of a special type, distinguished by a special discipline based on identical philosophic and ideological views of its members. A unity of belief and iron discipline was necessary to overcome its weaknesses.

The roots of the new class were implanted in a special party, of the Bolshevik type. Lenin was right in his view that his party was an exception in the history of human society, although he did not suspect that it would be the beginning of a new class.

To be more precise, the initiators of the new class are not found in the party of the Bolshevik type as a whole but in that stratum of professional revolutionaries who made up its core even before it attained power. It was not by accident that Lenin asserted after the failure of the 1905 revolution that only professional revolutionaries—men whose sole profession was revolutionary work—could build a new party of the Bolshevik type. It was still less accidental that even Stalin, the future creator of a new class, was the most outstanding example of such a professional revolutionary. The new ruling class has been gradually developing from this very narrow stratum of revolutionaries. These revolutionaries composed its core for a long period. Trotsky noted that in pre-revolutionary professional revolutionaries was the origin of the future Stalinist bureaucrat. What he did not detect was the beginning of a new class of owners and exploiters.

This is not to say that the new party and the new class are identical. The party, however, is the core of that class, and its base. It is very difficult, perhaps impossible, to define the limits of the new class and to identify its members. The new class may be said to be made up of those who have special privileges and economic preference because of the administrative monopoly they hold.

Since administration is unavoidable in society, necessary administrative functions may be coexistent with parasitic functions in the same person. Not every member of the party is a member of the new class, any more than every artisan or member of a middle-class party is a bourgeois.

In loose terms, as the new class becomes stronger and attains a more perceptible physiognomy, the role of the party diminishes. The core and the basis of the new class is created in the party and at its top, as well as in the state political organs. The once live, compact party, full of initiative, is disappearing to become transformed into the traditional oligarchy of the new class, irresistibly drawing into its ranks those who aspire to join the new class and repressing those who have any ideals.

The party makes the class, but the class grows as a result and uses the party as a basis. The class grows stronger, while the party grows weaker; this is the inescapable fate of every Communist party in power.

If it were not materially interested in production or if it did not have within itself the potentialities for the creation of a new class, no party could act in so morally and ideologically foolhardy a fashion, let alone stay in power for long. Stalin declared, after the end of the First Five-Year Plan: "If we had not created the apparatus, we would have failed!" He should have substituted "new class" for the word "apparatus," and everything would have been clearer.

It seems unusual that a political party could be the beginning of a new class. Parties are generally the product of classes and strata which have become intellectually and economically strong. However, if one grasps the actual conditions in pre-revolutionary Russia and in other countries in which Communism prevailed over national forces, it will be clear that a party of this type is the product of specific opportunities and that there is nothing unusual or accidental in this being so. Although the roots of Bolshevism reach far back into Russian history, the party is partly the product of the unique pattern of international relationships in which Russia found itself at the end of the nineteenth and the beginning of the twentieth century. Russia was no longer able to live in the modern world as an absolute monarchy, and Russia's capitalism was too weak and too dependent on the interests of foreign powers to make it possible to have an industrial revolution. This revolution could only be implemented by a new class, or by a change in the social order. As yet, there was no such class.

In history, it is not important who implements a process, it is only important that the process be implemented. Such was the case in Russia and other countries in which Communist revolutions took place. The revolution created forces, leaders, organizations, and ideas which were necessary to it. The new class came into existence for objective reasons, and by the wish, wits, and action of its leaders.

II

The social origin of the new class lies in the proletariat just as the aristocracy arose in a peasant society, and the bourgeoisie in a commercial and artisans' society. There are exceptions, depending on national conditions, but the proletariat in economically underdeveloped countries, being backward, constitutes the raw material from which the new class arises.

There are other reasons why the new class always acts as the champion of the working class. The new class is anti-capitalistic and, consequently, logically dependent upon the working strata. The new class is supported by the proletarian struggle and the traditional faith of the proletariat in a socialist, Communist society where there is no brutal exploitation. It is vitally important for the new class to assure a normal flow of production, hence it cannot ever lose its connection with the proletariat. Most important of all, the new class cannot achieve industrialization and consolidate its power without the help of the working class. On the other hand, the working class sees in expanded industry the salvation from its poverty and despair. Over a long period of time, the interests, ideas, faith, and hope of the new class, and of parts of the working class and of the poor peasants, coincide and unite. Such mergers have occurred in the past among other widely different classes. Did not the bourgeoisie represent the peasantry in the struggle against the feudal lords?

The movement of the new class toward power comes as a result of the efforts of the proletariat and the poor. These are the masses upon which the party or the new class must lean and with which its interests are most closely allied. This is true until the new class finally establishes its power and authority. Over and above this, the new class is interested in the proletariat and the poor only to the extent necessary for developing production and for maintaining in subjugation the most aggressive and rebellious social forces.

The monopoly which the new class establishes in the name of the working class over the whole of society is, primarily, a monopoly over the working class itself. This monopoly is first intellectual, over the so-called *avant-garde* proletariat, and then over the whole proletariat. This is the biggest deception the class must accomplish, but it shows that the power and interests of the new class lie primarily in industry. Without industry the new class cannot consolidate its position or authority.

Former sons of the working class are the most steadfast members of the new class. It has always been the fate of slaves to provide for their masters the most clever and gifted representatives. In this case a new exploiting and governing class is born from the exploited class.

III

When Communist systems are being critically analyzed, it is considered that their fundamental distinction lies in the fact that a bureaucracy, organized in a special stratum, rules over the people. This is generally true. However, a more detailed analysis will show that only a special stratum of bureaucrats, those who are not administrative officials, make up the core of the governing bureaucracy, or, in my terminology, of the new class. This is actually a party or political bureaucracy. Other officials are only the apparatus under the control of the new class; the apparatus may be clumsy and slow but, no matter what, it must exist in every socialist society. It is sociologically possible to draw the borderline between the different types of officials, but in practice they are practically indistinguishable. This is true not only because the Communist system by its very nature is bureaucratic, but because Communists handle the various important administrative functions. In addition, the stratum of political bureaucrats cannot enjoy their privileges if they do not give crumbs from their tables to other bureaucratic categories.

It is important to note the fundamental differences between the political bureaucracies mentioned here and those which arise with every centralization in modern economy—especially centralizations that lead to collective forms of ownership such as monopolies, companies, and state ownership. The number of white-collar workers is constantly increasing in capitalistic monopolies, and also in nationalized industries in the West. In *Human Relations in Administration*,[1] R. Dubin says that state functionaries in the economy are being transformed into a special stratum of society.

> . . . Functionaries have the sense of a common destiny for all those who work together. They share the same interests, especially since there is relatively little competition insofar as promotion is in terms of seniority. In-

[1] New York, Prentice-Hall, 1951.

group aggression is thus minimized and this arrangement is therefore conceived to be positively functional for the bureaucracy. However, the esprit de corps and informal social organization which typically develops in such situations often leads the personnel to defend their entrenched interests rather than to assist their clientele and elected higher officials.

While such functionaries have much in common with Communist bureaucrats, especially as regards "esprit de corps," they are not identical. Although state and other bureaucrats in non-Communist systems form a special stratum, they do not exercise authority as the Communists do. Bureaucrats in a non-Communist state have political masters, usually elected, or owners over them, while Communists have neither masters nor owners over them. The bureaucrats in a non-Communist state are officials in modern capitalist economy, while the Communists are something different and new: a new class.

As in other owning classes, the proof that it is a special class lies in its ownership and its special relations to other classes. In the same way, the class to which a member belongs is indicated by the material and other privileges which ownership brings to him.

As defined by Roman law, property constitutes the use, enjoyment, and disposition of material goods. The Communist political bureaucracy uses, enjoys, and disposes of nationalized property.

If we assume that membership in this bureaucracy or new owning class is predicated on the use of privileges inherent in ownership—in this instance nationalized material goods—then membership in the new party class, or political bureaucracy, is reflected in a larger income in material goods and privileges than society should normally grant for such functions. In practice, the ownership privilege of the new class manifests itself as an exclusive right, as a party monopoly, for the political bureaucracy to distribute the national income, to set wages, direct economic development, and dispose of nationalized and other property. This is the way it appears to the ordinary man who considers the Communist functionary as being very rich and as a man who does not have to work.

The ownership of private property has, for many reasons, proved to be unfavorable for the establishment of the new class's authority. Besides, the destruction of private ownership was necessary for the economic transformation of nations. The new class obtains its power, privileges, ideology, and its customs from one specific form of ownership—collective ownership—which the class administers and distributes in the name of the nation and society.

The new class maintains that ownership derives from a designated social relationship. This is the relationship between the monopolists of administration, who constitute a narrow and closed stratum, and the mass of producers (farmers, workers, and intelligentsia) who have no rights. But that is not all, since the Communist bureaucracy also has complete monopolistic control over material assets.

Every substantive change in the social relationship between those who monopolize administration and those who work is inevitably reflected in the ownership relationship. Social and political relations and ownership—the totalitarianism of government and the monopoly of ownership—are being more fully brought into accord in Communism than in any other political system.

To divest Communists of their ownership rights would be to abolish them as a class. To compel them to relinquish their other social powers, so that workers may participate in sharing the profits of their work—which capitalists have had to permit as a result of strikes and parliamentary action—would mean that Communists were being deprived of their monopoly over property, ideology, and government. This would be the beginning of democracy and freedom in Communism, the end of Communist monopolism and totalitarianism. Until this happens, there can be no indication that important, fundamental changes are taking place in Communist systems, at least not in the eyes of men who think seriously about social progress.

The ownership privileges of the new class and membership in that class are the privileges of *administration*. This privilege extends from state administration and the administration of economic enterprises to that of sports and humanitarian organizations. Political, party, or so-called "general leadership" is executed by the core. This position of leadership carries privileges with it. In his *Stalin au pouvoir,* published in Paris in 1951, Orlov states that the average pay of a worker in the U.S.S.R. in 1935 was 1,800 rubles annually, while the pay and allowances of the secretary of a rayon committee amounted to 45,000 rubles annually. The situation has changed since then for both workers and party functionaries, but the essence remains the same. Other authors have arrived at the same conclusions. Discrepancies between the pay of workers and party functionaries are extreme; this could not be hidden from persons visiting the U.S.S.R. or other Communist countries in the past few years.

Other systems, too, have their professional politicians. One can think well or ill of them, but they must exist. Society cannot live without a state or a government, and therefore it cannot live without those who fight for it.

However, there are fundamental differences between professional politicians in other systems and in the Communist system. In extreme cases, politicians in other systems use the government to secure privileges for themselves and their cohorts, or to favor the economic interests of one social stratum or another. The situation is different with the Communist system where the power and the government are identical with the use, enjoyment, and disposition of almost all the nation's goods. He who grabs power grabs privileges and indirectly grabs property. Consequently, in Communism, power or politics as a profession is the ideal of those who have the desire or the prospect of living as parasites at the expense of others.

Membership in the Communist Party before the Revolution meant sacrifice. Being a professional revolutionary was one of the highest honors. Now that the party has consolidated its power, party membership means that one belongs to a privileged class. And at the core of the party are the all-powerful exploiters and masters.

For a long time the Communist revolution and the Communist system have been concealing their real nature. The emergence of the new class has been concealed under socialist phraseology and, more important, under the new collective forms of property ownership. The so-called socialist ownership is a disguise for the real ownership by the political bureaucracy. And in the beginning this bureaucracy was in a hurry to complete industrialization, and hid its class composition under that guise.

IV

The fact that there is a new ownership class in Communist countries does not explain everything, but it is the most important key to understanding the changes which are periodically taking place in these countries, especially in the U.S.S.R.

It goes without saying that every such change in each separate Communist country and in the Communist system as a whole must be examined separately, in order to determine the extent and significance of the change in the specific circumstances. To do this, however, the system should be understood as a whole to the fullest extent possible.

In connection with current changes in the U.S.S.R. it will be profitable to point out in passing what is occurring in the kolkhozes. The establishment of kolkhozes and the Soviet government policy toward them illustrates clearly the exploiting nature of the new class.

Stalin did not and Khrushchev does not consider kolkhozes as a "logical socialistic" form of ownership. In practice this means that the new class has not succeeded in completely taking over the management of the villages. Through the kolkhozes and the use of the compulsory crop-purchase system, the new class has succeeded in making vassals of the peasants and grabbing a lion's share of the peasants' income, but the new class has not become the only power of the land. Stalin was completely aware of this. Before his death, in *Economic Problems of Socialism in the U.S.S.R.,* Stalin foresaw that the kolkhozes should become state property, which is to say that the bureaucracy should become the real owner. Criticizing Stalin for his excess use of purges, Khrushchev did not however renounce Stalin's views on property in kolkhozes. The appointment by the new regime of 30,000 party workers, mostly to be presidents of kolkhozes, was only one of the measures in line with Stalin's policy.

Just as under Stalin, the new regime, in executing its so-called liberaliza-tion policy, is extending the "socialist" ownership of the new class. Decen-tralization in the economy does not mean a change in ownership, but only gives greater rights to the lower strata of the bureaucracy or of the new class. If the so-called liberalization and decentralization meant anything else, that would be manifest in the political right of at least part of the people to exer-cise some influence in the management of material goods. At least, the people would have the right to criticize the arbitrariness of the oligarchy. This would lead to the creation of a new political movement, even though it were only a loyal opposition. However, this is not even mentioned, just as democ-racy in the party is not mentioned. Liberalization and decentralization are in force only for Communists; first for the oligarchy, the leaders of the new class; and second, for those in the lower echelons. This is the new method, inevitable under changing conditions, for the further strengthening and consolidation of monopolistic ownership and totalitarian authority of the new class.

The fact that there is a new owning, monopolistic, and totalitarian class in Communist countries calls for the following conclusion: All changes ini-tiated by the Communist chiefs are dictated first of all by the interests and aspirations of the new class, which, like every social group, lives and reacts, defends itself and advances, with the aim of increasing its power. This does not mean, however, that such changes may not be important for the rest of the people as well. Although the innovations introduced by the new class have not yet materially altered the Communist system, they must not be underestimated. It is necessary to gain insight into the substance of these changes in order to determine their range and significance.

The Communist regime, in common with others, must take into account the mood and movement of the masses. Because of the exclusiveness of the Communist Party and the absence of free public opinion in its ranks, the regime cannot discern the real status of the masses. However, their dissatis-faction does penetrate the consciousness of the top leaders. In spite of its totalitarian management, the new class is not immune to every type of opposition.

Once in power, the Communists have no difficulty in settling their ac-counts with the bourgeoisie and large-estate owners. The historical develop-ment is hostile to them and their property and it is easy to arouse the masses against them. Seizing property from the bourgeoisie and the large-estate owners is quite easy; difficulties arise when seizure of small properties is involved. Having acquired power in the course of earlier expropriations, the Communists can do even this. Relations are rapidly clarified: there are no more old classes and old owners, society is "classless," or on the road to being so, and men have started to live in a new manner.

Under such conditions, demands to return to the old pre-revolutionary relations seem unrealistic, if not ridiculous. Material and social bases no longer exist for the maintenance of such relations. The Communists meet such demands as if they were jests.

The new class is most sensitive to demands on the part of the people for a special kind of freedom, not for freedom in general or political freedom. It is especially sensitive to demands for freedom of thought and criticism, within the limits of present conditions and within the limits of "socialism"; not for demands for a return to previous social and ownership relations. This sensitivity originates from the class's special position.

The new class instinctively feels that national goods are, in fact, its property, and that even the terms "socialist," "social," and "state" property denote a general legal fiction. The new class also thinks that any breach of its totalitarian authority might imperil its ownership. Consequently, the new class opposes *any* type of freedom, ostensibly for the purpose of preserving "socialist" ownership. Criticism of the new class's monopolistic administration of property generates the fear of a possible loss of power. The new class is sensitive to these criticisms and demands depending on the extent to which they expose the manner in which it rules and holds power.

This is an important contradiction. Property is legally considered social and national property. But, in actuality, a single group manages it in its own interest. The discrepancy between legal and actual conditions continuously results in obscure and abnormal social and economic relationships. It also means that the words of the leading group do not correspond to its actions; and that all actions result in strengthening its property holdings and its political position.

This contradiction cannot be resolved without jeopardizing the class's position. Other ruling, property-owning classes could not resolve this contradiction either, unless forcefully deprived of monopoly of power and ownership. Wherever there has been a higher degree of freedom for society as a whole, the ruling classes have been forced, in one way or another, to renounce monopoly of ownership. The reverse is true also: wherever monopoly of ownership has been impossible, freedom, to some degree, has become inevitable.

In Communism, power and ownership are almost always in the same hands, but this fact is concealed under a legal guise. In classical capitalism, the worker had equality with the capitalist before the law, even though the worker was being exploited and the capitalist was doing the exploiting. In Communism, legally, all are equal with respect to material goods. The formal owner is the nation. In reality, because of monopolistic administration, only the narrowest stratum of administrators enjoys the rights of ownership.

Every real demand for freedom in Communism, the kind of demand that hits at the substance of Communism, boils down to a demand for bringing material and property relations into accord with what the law provides.

A demand for freedom—based on the position that capital goods produced by the nation can be managed more efficiently by society than by private monopoly or a private owner, and consequently should actually be in the hands or under control of society exercised through its freely elected representatives—would force the new class either to make concessions to other forces, or to take off the mask and admit its ruling and exploiting characteristics. The type of ownership and exploitation which the new class creates by using its authority and its administrative privileges is such that even the class itself must deny it. Does not the new class emphasize that it uses its authority and administrative functions in the name of the nation as a whole to preserve national property?

This makes the legal position of the new class uncertain and is also the source of the new class's biggest internal difficulties. The contradiction discloses the disharmony between words and actions: While promising to abolish social differences, it must always increase them by acquiring the products of the nation's workshops and granting privileges to its adherents. It must proclaim loudly its dogma that it is fulfilling its historical mission of "final" liberation of mankind from every misery and calamity while it acts in exactly the opposite way.

The contradiction between the new class's real ownership position and its legal position can furnish the basic reason for criticism. This contradiction has within it the ability not only to incite others but also to corrode the class's own ranks, since privileges are actually being enjoyed by only a few. This contradiction, when intensified, holds prospects of real changes in the Communist system, whether the ruling class is in favor of the change or not. The fact that this contradiction is so obvious has been the reason for the changes made by the new class, especially in so-called liberalization and decentralization.

Forced to withdraw and surrender to individual strata, the new class aims at concealing this contradiction and strengthening its own position. Since ownership and authority continue intact, all measures taken by the new class—even those democratically inspired—show a tendency toward strengthening the management of the political bureaucracy. The system turns democratic measures into positive methods for consolidating the position of the ruling classes. Slavery in ancient times in the East inevitably permeated all of society's activities and components, including the family. In the same way, the monopolism and totalitarianism of the ruling class in the Communist system are imposed on all the aspects of social life, even though the political heads are not aiming at this.

Yugoslavia's so-called workers' management and autonomy, conceived at the time of the struggle against Soviet imperialism as a far-reaching democratic measure to deprive the party of the monopoly of administration, has been increasingly relegated to one of the areas of party work. Tnus, it is hardly possible to change the present system. The aim of creating a new democracy through this type of administration will not be achieved. Besides, freedom cannot be extended to the largest piece of the pie. Workers' management has not brought about a sharing in profits by those who produce, either on a national level or in local enterprises. This type of administration has increasingly turned into a safe type for the regime. Through various taxes and other means, the regime has appropriated even the share of the profits which the workers believed would be given to them. Only crumbs from the tables and illusions have been left to the workers. Without universal freedom not even workers' management can become free. Clearly, in an unfree society nobody can freely decide anything. The givers have somehow obtained the most value from the gift of freedom they supposedly handed the workers.

This does not mean that the new class cannot make concessions to the people, even though it only considers its own interests. Workers' management, or decentralization, is a concession to the masses. Circumstances may drive the new class, no matter how monopolistic and totalitarian it may be, to retreat before the masses. In 1948, when the conflict broke out between Yugoslavia and the U.S.S.R., the Yugoslav leaders were forced to carry out certain reforms. But they stopped the process and even reversed it, as soon as they felt that they were in jeopardy. Something similar happened recently in other East European countries.

In defending its authority, the ruling class must execute reforms every time it becomes obvious to the people that the class is treating national property as its own. Such reforms are not proclaimed as being what they really are, but rather as part of the "further development of socialism" and "socialist democracy." The groundwork for reforms is laid when the discrepancy mentioned above becomes public. From the historical point of view the new class is forced to fortify its authority and ownership constantly, even though it is running away from the truth. It must constantly demonstrate how it is successfully creating a society of happy people, all of whom enjoy equal rights and have been freed of every type of exploitation. The new class cannot avoid falling continuously into profound internal contradictions; for in spite of its historical origin it is not able to make its ownership lawful, and it cannot renounce ownership without undermining itself. Consequently, it is forced to try to justify its increasing authority, invoking abstract and unreal purposes.

This is a class whose power over men is the most complete known to history. For this reason it is a class with very limited views, views which are shaky because they are based on falsehoods. Closely knit, isolated, and in complete authority, the new class must unrealistically evaluate its own role and that of the people around it.

Having achieved industrialization, the new class can now do nothing more than strengthen its brute force and pillage the people. It ceases to create. Its spiritual heritage is overtaken by darkness.

While the revolution can be considered an epochal accomplishment of the new class, its methods of rule fill some of the most shameful pages in history. Men will marvel at the grandiose ventures it accomplished and will be ashamed of the means it used.

When the new class leaves the historical scene—and this must happen—there will be less sorrow over its passing than there was for any other class before it. Smothering everything except what suited its ego, it has condemned itself to failure and shameful ruin.

Part IV

CAPITALISM, SOCIALISM, AND THE WELFARE STATE

Private Property and Free Enterprise

Democratic Socialism

Plan or No Plan?

The Welfare State

Chapter X

PRIVATE PROPERTY AND
FREE ENTERPRISE

For one hundred years, the "economic problem" has been a leitmotiv of political conflict in the Western world. The Industrial Revolution led to a rapid growth of wealth and population; but, like other revolutions, it created new problems not sufficiently anticipated beforehand. The intimate connection between political freedom and reasonable economic opportunity has been recognized in theory everywhere—although the solutions have varied in accordance with needs as qualified by history and tradition.

The liberal capitalistic approach to political economy has been more firmly entrenched in the United States than in any other country, more, even, than in England, where it originated. Just as John Locke's doctrines of political government have influenced American ideas and institutions more strongly than those of anyone else, his economic philosophy has impinged upon American economic life with equal measure. In his *Two Treatises of Government* (1690) Locke developed a theory of property which has permeated the economic and political foundations of the American system. In fact, the aura of Locke's prestige has been so high that much economic doctrine has been attributed to him which directly contradicts his plainly stated views.

Locke's theory of property starts with the inquiry as to how private property can be justified at all. Since every man has a property in his own person, the "labor of his body and the work of his hands we may say are properly his." Labor *creates* property: the human effort that is "mixed" with natural resources is the decisive criterion which alone justifies private property. Thus Locke avoids justifying property on the ground that "the law" protects it, and instead goes back to the law behind the law, the law of nature, according to which man's property in his own body, also extends to its labor.

But labor does more than create property: it also determines the *value* of property. "It is labor indeed," Locke says, "that puts the difference of value on everything." In fact, he stresses the proportion of labor in the value of an economic good highly enough to say that "of the products of the earth useful to the life of man nine-tenths are the effects of labor." This Lockean theory of property—that labor is the title to property and the source of economic

487

value—was later more fully elaborated by Smith and Ricardo (who defended capitalism); in the hands of the socialists, Locke's theory of value and property became the most powerful weapon of attacking capitalism. When Locke defended property on the ground of individual effort and initiative, he protected the productive capacities of a new system of commercial and industrial capitalism against the shackles and curbs imposed by restrictive traditions of an authoritarian state. By making labor the title to property and the source of value, Locke translated the rise of a new class to power into terms of a new political economy. In relation to the age that preceded him, Locke's economic philosophy—the liberation of the enterprising individual from paralyzing restrictions of force and custom—was altogether progressive. When the socialists—a century and a half after Locke—used the same theory of value to demand the socialization of the means of production, they did not prove that they were more progressive than he, but that certain economic facts had changed since Locke, especially the concentration of property and income.

Locke himself did not work out a consistently unambiguous theory as to *how much property* a person may fairly claim for himself. In general, he is inclined to acknowledge that the right to property is limited: "As much as anyone can make use of to any advantage of life before it spoils, so much he may by his labor fix a property in; whatever is beyond this, is more than his share, and belongs to others. Nothing was made by God for man to spoil or destroy." This relative equality of property, based on the individual's limited capacity to make use of, and enjoy, earthly goods, would have lasted forever, "had not the invention of money, and by tacit agreement of men to put a value on it, introduced (by consent) larger possessions and a right to them." The criterion which Locke applies is that of waste. Before money was invented, man had no moral right to hoard the products of the earth and allow them to rot and spoil. His capacity to consume perishable goods determined the amount of property he could rightfully own. In a later phase, man would exchange perishable fruit (like plums) for durable ones (like nuts). By disposing of the plums he had done his duty toward society, preventing their waste in his possession. From durable nuts to even more durable gold, or "a sparkling pebble or diamond," was only a small and logical step. And if he kept on hoarding these durable goods (like gold and diamonds and money) "all his life, he invaded not the right of others." Thus Locke arrives at defining money as "some lasting thing that men might keep without spoiling, and that, by mutual consent, men would take in exchange for the truly useful but perishable supports of life." In his doctrine of property Locke makes no serious attempt to reconcile the teaching of natural law, which seems to result in reasonable equality of property, with the inequality of property which stems, by consent among men, from the use of money.

What is the relation of property to government? Locke's answer to this question has guided the makers of the American Constitution and those who later applied and lived under it. He stresses the fact that *property precedes government,* and that the sole purpose of government, the reason why men give up the state of nature for a compact of political organization, is "for the mutual preservation of their lives, liberties, and estates, which I call by the general name, property." This broad Lockean concept of property exceeds man's purely economic interests, and encompasses almost the whole orbit of his "life, liberty, and pursuit of happiness." When he speaks of property what Locke thinks of includes economic property, but is by no means identical with it. Of the three elements he lists, economic property is probably considered by him to be the most important; but it must be remembered that Locke thought of property as liberating its owner, rather than as enslaving others.

Since consent establishes government and maintains it, and since the preservation of property is the purpose of government, it follows that the supreme power of the state "cannot take from any man any part of his property without his own consent." Even if a commonwealth is based on freely elected representative institutions, it cannot "dispose of the estates of the subjects arbitrarily." The Fourteenth Amendment to the Constitution of the United States embodies this Lockean thesis, that no State shall "deprive any person of life, liberty, or property, without due process of law."

In his passionate enthusiasm for the legislative branch of government as against the executive, Locke has bequeathed another ideological legacy which has retained stronger vitality in the United States than in England. There, the development of the cabinet system since the eighteenth century has controverted some of Locke's misgivings about the inherent evil of a strong and effective executive. Despite Locke, England has not become a despotism, although her legislature has been overshadowed by the executive. Even after England voted Labor in 1945, her Prime Minister, far from being a bloody tyrant (socialism was supposed to be the distilled essence of centralization), turned out to be more than mild. In the United States, on the other hand, the Lockean sanctification of the legislative branch as contrasted with the devil theory of the executive has by no means lost its vote-getting magic.

Locke supported property with arguments based on reason and the law of nature. Edmund Burke came to the defense of property from a diametrically opposite point of view: the historical method, combined with the conception that society was not (as Locke held) founded by a social contract, but was an organic, living being, greater and more significant than the individuals who compose it. Burke's *Reflections on the Revolution in France* (1790) is probably still the most impressive statement of conservative political thought. In England his influence has been immense, and by no means confined to one political persuasion. In the United States his ideas have nurtured whatever conservative political philosophy was consciously developed. There is no dearth of conservatives in the United States, but conservatism as an ideology is often considered "Old World" and "un-American." While Burke's central interest lay in government, he was well aware of the role that property played in political institutions.

He saw society not in terms of equal individuals, but of unequal groups and historically recognized interests. Property was such an interest, founded on *prescription,* rather than on natural law or abstract reasoning. The aristocracy and monarchy were also institutions based on prescription. While property is not the only criterion of the privileged classes and interests, which Burke deems worthy to rule the nation, he is well aware of the connections between property and the established order; both he saw threatened by the progress of popular democracy in France. Whereas Locke attached to property the qualification that it was originally equal, at least, Burke frankly states the doctrine that the "characteristic essence of property, formed out of the combined principles of its acquisition and conservation, is to be *unequal.*" The inequality of property that Burke defended was closely related to his conception of society in which rank and privilege played such a large part. Conversely, Burke fully realized, and approved of, political inequality as the result of economic inequality. "Hereditary property and hereditary distinction" wholly composed the House of Lords, and he was pleased that the House of Commons was also made up (in his time) of large property owners. As to the unpropertied masses, Burke wanted them to be content with "Virtual Representation" under which, as he said in a letter to Sir Hercules Langrishe (January 3, 1792), "there is a communion of interests, and a sympathy in feelings and desires between those who act in the name of any description of people and the people in whose name they act, though the trustees are not actually chosen by them. This is virtual representation. Such a representation I think to be in many cases even better than the actual." However, quite apart from Burke's direct eulogies of property and its privileges, his indirect support was possibly even more important. What mattered most was that Burke emphasized the values of prescription, inheritance, rank, and distinction, which all helped to buttress the cause of inequality of property and government.

The doctrine that of the three fundamental principles of government (the protection of life, liberty, and property), "the chief of these is property," is forcefully espoused by Mr. Justice Van Orsdel, of the Court of Appeals of the District of Columbia, in *Children's Hospital of the District of Columbia* v. *Adkins* (1922). The issue involved was whether a minimum-wage law for women, passed by Congress in September, 1918, was constitutional. The Supreme Court of the District of Columbia, like the lower court, had declared it unconstitutional in 1921; the Court of Appeal upheld this decision in 1922, and was supported by the Supreme Court of the United States in 1923, on the ground that minimum-wage laws violated the "freedom of contract." It was only in 1937 that the supreme Court reversed itself, and held minimum-wage laws constitutional in *West Coast Hotel* v. *Parrish* (1937). The difference between 1922 and 1937 was a great depression and a New Deal.

In the seventeenth century the defense of private property was directed against absolute monarchs and restrictive legal and economic rules and customs. In the twentieth century, private property is on the defensive against the expanding force of socialism. Walter Lippmann's *The Good Society* (1937) is probably the clearest restatement of the theory of private property in an increasingly collectivist age. Lippmann disagrees with Locke's natural-law interpretation of property as being prior and superior to government: "The title to property is a construction of the law. Contracts are legal instruments. Corporations are legal creatures. It is, therefore, misleading to think of them as existing somehow outside the law and then to ask whether it is permissible to 'interfere' with them." Unlike Locke, who lived at the dawn of the capitalist system and therefore could hardly foresee its blemishes, Lippmann lives in the era of "late capitalism" ("Spätkapitalismus," as Sombart called it), which has revealed how the system can be abused.

The extreme individualism which insists on no regulation of property and private rights seems to Lippmann to be as unreal as the universal regulation of all human relations by official commands is arbitrary and unjust. Lippmann pleads for the strengthening of the rule of law as opposed to authoritarian decisions of irresponsible rulers. The function of the state is to adjust conflicts and disputes between private citizens in their dealings with each other, rather than to conduct their affairs through administrative machinery. Where Locke favored the legislative branch of the government against the executive, Lippmann is an equally strong partisan of the judiciary and the judicial method against the administrative method. The judicial method, based on the principles of the common law, is characteristic of "democratic liberalism"; the method of "arbitrary sovereign commands" expresses "authoritarian collectivism."

How is private property to be made secure in an age in which it is constantly attacked? "The real security of private property," Lippmann writes, "must rest not on a fatuous longing for a sole and despotic dominion over the necessities of all men's existence but on a reconciliation of all men's claims in a system of substantially equal rights. It is not loyalty to the cause of private property to confirm the monopolists in their privileges. To do that is to prepare the extinction of private property either by general disorder and pillage or by the establishment of an administered collectivism. The true principle is to be ready to liquidate these rights of possession which enable some men, by excluding all other men from access to land and to the resources of nature, to exact a tribute based not on their own labor but on mere legal possession." Lippmann is confident that the giant business corporations and monopolies are not a necessary development in the capitalist system, and can be reformed by remedial legislation.

Among twentieth-century economists Ludwig von Mises is perhaps the most uncompromising defender of laissez-faire capitalism. As early as 1922 Mises published *Socialism,* whose arguments against economic planning later gained wider notoriety through the more popular writings of F. A. Hayek and Walter Lippmann. Mises' crowning work is *Human Action: A Treatise on Economics* (1949), a massive synthesis of his thought. He sees in the capitalistic market economy the only possibility for individual liberty, and he totally opposes government interference in economic affairs, because "government means always coercion and compulsion and is by necessity the opposite of liberty." Mises admits that the capitalistic market economy brings about inequalities of wealth and income, but he argues that the planned economy—the alternative to capitalism—extorts an even higher price from society, for ultimately it must lead to the totalitarian police state, in which there is neither freedom nor equality.

For a long time, the main criticism of business in the United States was not directed against the principle of private property and enterprise as such, but against monopoly and the "curse of bigness," as Brandeis called it. Much of the popular political appeal of Wilson's New Freedom and Roosevelt's New Deal was based on the fight against Big Business. It is therefore doubly interesting that an effective defense of Big Business will be found in the work of a political economist and public servant long associated with the New Deal, David E. Lilienthal. In his work, *Big Business: A New Era* (1953), Lilienthal draws on his experience as chairman of the Tennessee Valley Authority and, later, of the Atomic Energy Commission, as well as on experience in business after leaving government service. The very size of the United States, coupled with the most productive economy the world has ever seen, inevitably leads to big business: "To compete in the big market takes Bigness. What makes for size, then, is the big market. We need Big Business for a big country." In examining the "fruits of bigness," Lilienthal emphasizes that the very survival of the United States may depend on the productivity of its Big Business, not only in turning out the necessary armaments, but also in maintaining a high flow of civilian goods and services and providing economic and military aid to those nations whose freedom and security are linked with those of the United States. Moreover, Lilienthal points out, individual security benefits from Big Business more than from smaller enterprises; Big Business is in a better position when it comes to long-term planning of production, stability of employment, and the provision of services like pensions and sickness benefits. Finally, in the field of labor-management relations, the greatest progress has been made in the mass-production industries like steel and automobiles, in which Big Business predominates.

Lilienthal also stresses the importance of scientific and technological research and its relation to bigness. Great discoveries are still made occasionally in small laboratories, by one or a few men. But even in such cases, it takes the resources of larger industrial etsablishments to translate the discoveries into economic realities. More and more, therefore, industrial research is carried on by big corporations, because it requires large financial resources and many years of waiting. Thus, to provide but one example, Du Pont spent $27,000,000 and thirteen years of research before nylon could be sold commercially.

Concerning the relation of Big Business and competition, Lilienthal denies that the two are incompatible. In the first place, advances in research become an increasingly important element in the competitive position of a firm. Secondly, Big Business produces a new kind of competition—"internal competition," as Lilienthal calls it—which is the direct result of bigness. Thus, there is competition not only between General Motors and Chrysler products, but within General Motors itself the Chevrolet car competes with Pontiac, or Buick with Oldsmobile.

The problem of competition in the changing American economy is the key issue in one of the most brilliantly written books in contemporary economics, *American Capitalism: The Concept of Countervailing Power* (1952), by John Kenneth Galbraith. In classical economics, competition was conceived in terms of many sellers each with a small share of the market, and restraint of excessive private economic power was provided by competing firms on the same side of the market. Galbraith concedes that this classical model of competition has largely disappeared, since many markets have become dominated by a few firms frequently operating in tacit collusion as to major policy decisions. Yet he does not conclude from the widespread disappearance of traditional competition that there is no longer any restraint of private economic power left. In fact, new restraints have taken the place of the old competitive mechanism, and these restraints—termed by Galbraith "countervailing power"—are the very product of concentration and bigness. But these new factors of restraint "appeared not on the same side of the market but on the opposite side, not with competitors but with customers and suppliers." Thus the concentration of industrial enterprises has led not only to a few sellers, but has also brought about the predominant position of a few buyers. Galbraith explains the growth and expansion of retailers like Sears, Roebuck or the A & P in terms of countervailing power; by contrast, the absence of a few large firms in the housing industry has meant more traditional competition and less efficiency, as the many small enterprises in the housing industry are unable to put countervailing pressure on labor unions and suppliers of materials. In the field of labor, too, Galbraith is impressed by the fact that strong unions have developed mainly when faced by strong corporations, as in the steel, automobile, and electrical industries. By contrast, "there is not a single union of any consequence in American agriculture, the country's closest approach to the competitive model." Galbraith concedes that countervailing power is not universally effective as a restraint on private economic power, and it signally fails to function in inflation, when relative scarcity of demand disappears, when too many buyers compete for available goods and services. If supply is small in relation to demand, the seller need not surrender to the bargaining power of the buyer, who thus loses his capacity of countervailing power.

Lilienthal's defense of big business and Galbraith's concept of counter-vailing power are critically examined in Edward S. Mason's "The New Competition" (1953). Contrary to the "apostles of bigness," as he calls them, Mason holds that *share of the market* is still a crucial *prima facie* indication of *market power,* and as such a proper concern of *public policy.* The weakness of the concept of countervailing power lies in the fact that, though the power of the large seller may be checked by that of the large buyer, the resulting benefit need not be passed on to the consumer: "It may well be that the predominant effect will be merely a division of potential monopoly profits between the large buyer and the large seller."

In substituting the *few* giant competitive units of the twentieth century for the *many* small ones of the eighteenth, the theory of countervailing power still assumes that a socially just market equilibrium may be obtained without the intervention of the community in defense of the public interest. In a sense, therefore, the concept of countervailing power, illuminating and provocative as it is, is a sophisticated restatement of the doctrine of the self-regulating market of classical economics.

Implicitly rejecting the concept of countervailing power, A. A. Berle suggests in *Economic Power and the Free Society* (1957) a more political and philosophical approach. Since his publication (with G. C. Means) of *The Modern Corporation and Private Property* (1932), Berle has been recognized as the world's leading student of the modern corporation and its role in the changing society of the last hundred years. In *Economic Power and the Free Society* Berle first points out that from its infancy in the late eighteenth and early nineteenth centuries the corporation was viewed with concern lest it accumulate too much economic wealth and power. The early fears proved remarkably accurate, yet the corporation grew despite all kinds of half-hearted limitations, "because there was no real way of constricting a corporation whose business the community needed. If its economic functions were necessary to the welfare of the community, the law somehow had to recognize the fact, however backhandedly."

Yet two aspects of the corporation have continued to cause concern. First, there is the question of bigness and the inevitable power resulting from it. About 150 American corporations control half of American manufacturing— or nearly one quarter of the world's manufacturing. This concentration of economic power, writes Berle, "makes the medieval feudal system look like a Sunday School party." The second major problem is the way in which the modern corporation is governed. The shareholders—legally the owners of the corporation—have little, if anything, to say about how the corporation is to be managed. Their function has become, in Berle's terminology, "passive receptive." They receive an annual dividend, but have little or no influence on the management of their corporation. The element of control or power in the corporation is in the body of the directors, the "self-perpetuating oligarchy" of management. This tremendous power of management is not circumscribed by any clearly defined principles of accountability and responsibility; thus the question of legitimacy arises, for "whenever there is a question of power there is a question of legitimacy." Power must rest on some moral foundation, particularly in a society that claims to adhere to a system of constitutional liberty. In the medieval system of feudalism, the "lords temporal" were counterbalanced by the "lords spiritual." Who is to play the role of the "lords spiritual" in the twentieth-century corporate economy?

Berle has no ready-made solution, but he is skeptical that purely legal remedies will do. He puts his faith in the development of controls that are essentially intellectual and philosophical, supplemented by the gradual growth of a sense of responsibility among the managers of corporate business. If the economic functions of the corporation are to be reconciled with the political principles of a free society, there will have to be a growing acceptance of the doctrine that where a corporation affects the lives of many people it should be subject to constitutional restraints similar to those that now apply to political government on the federal or state levels. So far, it is not certain by what means such consensus can be attained, if at all, and ultimate progress will depend on the capacity for fresh thinking.

JOHN LOCKE

1. *The End of Government**

Whether we consider natural reason, which tells us that men being once born have a right to their preservation, and consequently to meat and drink and such other things as nature affords for their subsistence; or revelation, which gives us an account of those grants God made of the world to Adam, and to Noah and his sons, 'tis very clear that God, as King David says, Psalm CXV. 16, "has given the earth to the children of men," given it to

* From John Locke, *Two Treatises of Government* (1690).

mankind in common. But this being supposed, it seems to some a very great difficulty how anyone should ever come to have a property in anything. I will not content myself to answer that if it be difficult to make out property upon a supposition that God gave the world to Adam and his posterity in common, it is impossible that any man but one universal monarch should have any property upon a supposition that God gave the world to Adam and his heirs in succession, exclusive of all the rest of his posterity. But I shall endeavor to show how men might come to have a property in several parts of that which God gave to mankind in common, and that without any express compact of all the commoners.

God, who hath given the world to men in common, hath also given them reason to make use of it to the best advantage of life and convenience. The earth and all that is therein is given to men for the support and comfort of their being. And though all the fruits it naturally produces, and beasts it feeds, belong to mankind in common, as they are produced by the spontaneous hand of nature; and nobody has originally a private dominion exclusive of the rest of mankind in any of them as they are thus in their natural state; yet being given for the use of men, there must of necessity be a means to appropriate them some way or other before they can be of any use or at all beneficial to any particular man. The fruit or venison which nourishes the wild Indian, who knows no enclosure, and is still a tenant in common, must be his, and so his, i.e., a part of him, that another can no longer have any right to it, before it can do any good for the support of his life.

Though the earth and all inferior creatures be common to all men, yet every man has a property in his own person; this nobody has any right to but himself. The labor of his body and the work of his hands we may say are properly his. Whatsoever, then, he removes out of the state that nature hath provided and left it in, he hath mixed his labor with, and joined to it something that is his own, and thereby makes it his property. It being by him removed from the common state nature placed it in, it hath by this labor something annexed to it that excludes the common right of other men. For this labor being the unquestionable property of the laborer, no man but he can have a right to what that is once joined to, at least where there is enough, and as good left in common for others.

He that is nourished by the acorns he picked up under an oak, or the apples he gathered from the trees in the wood, has certainly appropriated them to himself. Nobody can deny but the nourishment is his. I ask, then, When did they begin to be his—when he digested, or when he ate, or when he boiled, or when he brought them home, or when he picked them up? And 'tis plain if the first gathering made them not his, nothing else could. That labor put a distinction between them and common; that added something to them more than nature, the common mother of all, had done, and so they became his private right. And will anyone say he had no right to those acorns or apples he thus appropriated, because he had not the consent of all mankind to make them his? Was it a robbery thus to assume to himself what belonged to all in common? If such a consent as that was necessary, man had starved, notwithstanding the plenty God had given him. We see in commons which remain so by compact that 'tis the taking any part of what is common and removing it out of the state nature leaves it in, which begins the property; without which the common is of no use. And the taking of this or that part does not depend on the express consent of all the commoners. Thus the grass my horse has bit, the turfs my servant has cut, and the ore I have dug in any place where I have a right to them in common with others, become my property without the assignation or consent of anybody. The labor that was mine removing them out of that common state they were in, hath fixed my property in them.

By making an explicit consent of every commoner necessary to anyone's appropriating to himself any part of what is given in common, children or servants could not cut the meat which their father or master had provided for them in common without assigning to everyone his peculiar part. Though the water running in the fountain be everyone's, yet who can doubt but that in the pitcher is his only who drew it out? His labor hath taken it out of the hands of Nature where it was common, and belonged equally to all her children, and hath thereby appropriated it to himself.

Thus this law of reason makes the deer that Indian's who hath killed it; it is allowed to be his goods who hath bestowed his labor upon it, though, before, it was the common right of everyone. And amongst those who are counted the civilized part of mankind, who have made and multiplied positive laws to determine property, this original law of nature for the beginning of property, in what was before common, still takes place, and by virtue thereof, what fish anyone catches in the ocean, that great and still remaining common of mankind; or what ambergris anyone takes up here is by the labor that removes it out of that common state nature left it in, made his property who takes that pains about it. And even amongst us, the hare that anyone is hunting is thought his who pursues her during the chase. For being a beast that is still looked upon as common, and no man's private possession, whoever has employed so much labor about any of that kind as to find and pursue her has thereby removed her from the state of nature wherein she was common, and hath began a property.

It will perhaps be objected to this, that if gathering the acorns, or other fruits of the earth, etc., makes a right to them, then anyone may engross as much as he will. To which I answer, Not so. The same law of nature that does by this means give us property, does also bound that property too. "God has given us all things richly" (I Tim. vi. 17), is the voice of reason confirmed by inspiration. But how far has He given it us? To enjoy. As much as anyone can make use of to any advantage of life before it spoils, so much he may by his labor fix a property in; whatever is beyond this, is more than his share, and belongs to others. Nothing was made by God for man to spoil or destroy. And thus considering the plenty of natural provisions there was a long time in the world, and the few spenders, and to how small a part of that provision the industry of one man could extend itself, and engross it to the prejudice of others—especially keeping within the bounds, set by reason, of what might serve for his use—there could be then little room for quarrels or contentions about property so established.

But the chief matter of property being now not the fruits of the earth, and the beasts that subsist on it, but the earth itself, as that which takes in and carries with it all the rest, I think it is plain that property in that, too, is acquired as the former. As much land as a man tills, plants, improves, cultivates, and can use the product of, so much is his property. He by his labor does as it were enclose it from the common. Nor will it invalidate his right to say, everybody else has an equal title to it; and therefore he cannot appropriate, he cannot enclose, without the consent of all his fellow-commoners, all mankind. God, when He gave the world in common to all mankind, commanded man also to labor, and the penury of his condition required it of him. God and his reason commanded him to subdue the earth, i.e., improve it for the benefit of life, and therein lay out something upon it that was his own, his labor. He that, in obedience to this command of God, subdued, tilled, and sowed any part of it, thereby annexed to it something that was his property, which another had no title to, nor could without injury take from him.

Nor was this appropriation of any parcel of land, by improving it, any prejudice to any other man, since there was still enough and as good left; and more than the yet unprovided could use. So that in effect there was never the less left for others because of his enclosure for himself. For he that leaves as much as another can make use of, does as good as take nothing at all. Nobody could think himself injured by the drinking of another man, though he took a good draught, who had a whole river of the same water left him to quench his thirst; and the case of land and water, where there is enough of both, is perfectly the same.

God gave the world to men in common; but since He gave it them for their benefit, and the greatest conveniences of life they were capable to draw from it, it cannot be supposed He meant it should always remain common and uncultivated. He gave it to the use of the industrious and rational (and labor was to be his title to it), not to the fancy or covetousness of the quarrelsome and contentious. He that had as good left for his improvement as was already taken up, needed not complain, ought not to meddle with what was already improved by another's labor; if he did, it is plain he desired the benefit of another's pains, which he had no right to, and not the ground which

God had given him in common with others to labor on, and whereof there was as good left as that already possessed, and more than he knew what to do with, or his industry could reach to.

It is true, in land that is common in England, or any other country where there is plenty of people under Government, who have money and commerce, no one can enclose or appropriate any part without the consent of all his fellow-commoners: because this is left common by compact, i.e., by the law of the land, which is not to be violated. And though it be common in respect of some men, it is not so to all mankind; but is the joint property of this country, or this parish. Besides, the remainder, after such enclosure, would not be as good to the rest of the commoners as the whole was, when they could all make use of the whole; whereas in the beginning and first peopling of the great common of the world it was quite otherwise. The law man was under was rather for appropriating. God commanded, and his wants forced him, to labor. That was his property, which could not be taken from him wherever he had fixed it. And hence subduing or cultivating the earth, and having dominion, we see are joined together. The one gave title to the other. So that God, by commanding to subdue, gave authority so far to appropriate. And the condition of human life, which requires labor and materials to work on, necessarily introduces private possessions.

The measure of property nature has well set by the extent of men's labor and the conveniency of life. No man's labor could subdue or appropriate all, nor could his enjoyment consume more than a small part; so that it was impossible for any man, this way, to entrench upon the right of another or acquire to himself a property to the prejudice of his neighbor, who would still have room for as good and as large a possession (after the other had taken out his) as before it was appropriated. Which measure did confine every man's possession to a very moderate proportion, and such as he might appropriate to himself without injury to anybody in the first ages of the world, when men were more in danger to be lost, by wandering from their company, in the then vast wilderness of the earth than to be straitened for want of room to plant in.

The same measure may be allowed still, without prejudice to anybody, full as the world seems. For, supposing a man or family, in the state they were at first, peopling of the world by the children of Adam or Noah, let him plant in some inland vacant places of America. We shall find that the possessions he could make himself, upon the measures we have given, would not be very large, nor, even to this day, prejudice the rest of mankind or give them reason to complain or think themselves injured by this man's encroachment, though the race of men have now spread themselves to all the corners of the world, and do infinitely exceed the small number that was at the beginning. Nay, the extent of ground is of so little value without labor that I have heard it affirmed that in Spain itself a man may be permitted to plough, sow, and reap, without being disturbed, upon land he has no other title to, but only his making use of it. But, on the contrary, the inhabitants think themselves beholden to him who, by his industry on neglected, and consequently waste land, has increased the stock of corn, which they wanted. But be this as it will, which I lay no stress on, this I dare boldly affirm, that the same rule of propriety—viz., that every man should have as much as he could make use of, would hold still in the world, without straitening anybody, since there is land enough in the world to suffice double the inhabitants, had not the invention of money, and the tacit agreement of men to put a value on it, introduced (by consent) larger possessions and a right to them; which, how it has done, I shall by and by show more at large.

This is certain, that in the beginning, before the desire of having more than man needed had altered the intrinsic value of things, which depends only on their usefulness to the life of man; or had agreed that a little piece of yellow metal which would keep without wasting or decay should be worth a great piece of flesh or a whole heap of corn, though men had a right to appropriate by their labor, each one to himself, as much of the things of nature as he could use, yet this could not be much, nor to the prejudice of others, where the same plenty was still left to those who would use the same industry.

Before the appropriation of land, he who gathered as much of the wild fruit, killed, caught, or tamed as many of the beasts as he could; he that so employed his pains about any of the spontaneous products of nature as in any way to alter them from the state which nature put them in, by placing any of his labor on them, did thereby acquire a propriety in them. But if they perished in his possession without their due use; if the fruits rotted, or the venison putrefied before he could spend it, he offended against the common law of nature, and was liable to be punished; he invaded his neighbor's share, for he had no right further than his use called for any of them and they might serve to afford him conveniences of life.

The same measures governed the possessions of land, too. Whatsoever he tilled and reaped, laid up, and made use of before it spoiled, that was his peculiar right; whatsoever he enclosed and could feed and make use of, the cattle and product was also his. But if either the grass of his enclosure rotted on the ground, or the fruit of his planting perished without gathering and laying up, this part of the earth, notwithstanding his enclosure, was still to be looked on as waste, and might be the possession of any other. Thus, at the beginning, Cain might take as much ground as he could till and make it his own land, and yet leave enough for Abel's sheep to feed on; a few acres would serve for both their possessions. But as families increased, and industry enlarged their stocks, their possessions enlarged with the need of them; but yet it was commonly without any fixed property in the ground they made use of, till they incorporated, settled themselves together, and built cities;

and then, by consent, they came in time to set out the bounds of their distinct territories, and agree on limits between them and their neighbors, and, by laws within themselves, settled the properties of those of the same society. For we see that in that part of the world which was first inhabited, and therefore like to be best peopled, even as low down as Abraham's time, they wandered with their flocks and their herds, which was their substance, freely up and down—and this Abraham did in a country where he was a stranger; whence it is plain that, at least, a great part of the land lay in common, the inhabitants valued it not, nor claimed property in any more than they made use of; but when there was not room enough in the same place for their herds to feed together, they, by consent, as Abraham and Lot did (Gen. xiii. 5), separated and enlarged their pasture where it best liked them. And for the same reason, Esau went from his father and his brother, and planted in Mount Seir (Gen. xxxvi. 6).

And thus, without supposing any private dominion and property in Adam over all the world, exclusive of all other men, which can no way be proved, nor any one's property be made out from it, but supposing the world, given as it was to the children of men in common, we see how labor could make men distinct titles to several parcels of it for their private uses, wherein there could be no doubt of right, no room for quarrel.

Nor is it so strange, as perhaps before consideration it may appear, that the property of labor should be able to overbalance the community of land. For it is labor indeed that puts the difference of value on everything; and let anyone consider what the difference is between an acre of land planted with tobacco or sugar, sown with wheat or barley, and an acre of the same land lying in common without any husbandry upon it, and he will find that the improvement of labor makes the far greater part of the value. I think it will be but a very modest computation to say that of the products of the earth useful to the life of man nine-tenths are the effects of labor; nay, if we will rightly estimate things as they come to our use, and cast up the several expenses about them—what in them is purely owing to nature, and what to labor—we shall find that in most of them ninety-nine hundredths are wholly to be put on the account of labor.

There cannot be a clearer demonstration of anything than several nations of the Americans are of this, who are rich in land and poor in all the comforts of life; whom nature, having furnished as liberally as any other people with the materials of plenty—i.e., a fruitful soil, apt to produce in abundance what might serve for food, raiment, and delight; yet, for want of improving it by labor, have not one hundredth part of the conveniences we enjoy, and a king of a large and fruitful territory there feeds, lodges, and is clad worse than a day laborer in England.

To make this a little clearer, let us but trace some of the ordinary provisions of life, through their several progresses, before they come to our use, and see how much they receive of their value from human industry. Bread, wine, and cloth are things of daily use and great plenty; yet, notwithstanding, acorns, water, and leaves or skins, must be our bread, drink, and clothing, did not labor furnish us with these more useful commodities. For whatever bread is more worth than acorns, wine than water, and cloth or silk than leaves, skins, or moss, that is wholly owing to labor and industry: the one of these being the food and raiment which unassisted nature furnishes us with; the other, provisions which our industry and pains prepare for us; which how much they exceed the other in value when anyone hath computed, he will then see how much labor makes the far greatest part of the value of things we enjoy in this world. And the ground which produces the materials is scarce to be reckoned in as any, or at most but a very small, part of it; so little that even amongst us land that is left wholly to nature, that hath no improvement of pasturage, tillage, or planting, is called, as indeed it is, "waste," and we shall find the benefit of it amount to little more than nothing.

An acre of land that bears here twenty bushels of wheat, and another in America which, with the same husbandry, would do the like, are without doubt of the same natural intrinsic value; but yet the benefit mankind receives from the one in a year is worth £5, and from the other possibly not worth a penny, if all the profit an Indian received from it were to be valued and sold here; at least, I may truly say, not one-thousandth. 'Tis labor, then, which puts the greatest part of value upon land, without which it would scarcely be worth anything; 'tis to that we owe the greatest part of all its useful products, for all that the straw, bran, bread, of that acre of wheat is more worth than the product of an acre of as good land which lies waste, is all the effect of labor. For 'tis not barely the ploughman's pains, the reaper's and thresher's toil, and the baker's sweat, is to be counted into the bread we eat; the labor of those who broke the oxen, who dug and wrought the iron and stones, who felled and framed the timber employed about the plough, mill, oven, or any other utensils, which are a vast number, requisite to this corn, from its sowing, to its being made bread, must all be charged on the account of labor, and received as an effect of that. Nature and the earth furnished only the almost worthless materials as in themselves. 'Twould be a strange catalogue of things that industry provided, and made use of, about every loaf of bread before it came to our use, if we could trace them—iron, wood, leather, bark, timber, stone, bricks, coals, lime, cloth, dyeing drugs, pitch, tar, masts, ropes, and all the materials made use of in the ship that brought any of the commodities made use of by any of the workmen to any part of the work all which it would be almost impossible—at least, too long— to reckon up.

From all which it is evident that, though the things of nature are given in common, yet man, by being master of himself and proprietor of his own person and the actions of labor of it, had still in himself the great foundation of property; and that which made up the great part of what he applied to the support or comfort of his being, when invention and arts had improved the conveniences of life, was perfectly his own, and did not belong in common to others.

Thus labor, in the beginning, gave a right of property, wherever anyone was pleased to employ it upon what was common, which remained a long while the far greater part, and is yet more than mankind makes use of. Men at first, for the most part, contented themselves with what unassisted nature offered to their necessities; and though afterwards, in some parts of the world (where the increase of people and stock, with the use of money, had made land scarce, and so of some value), the several communities settled the bounds of their distinct territories, and, by laws within themselves, regulated the properties of the private men of their society, and so, by compact and agreement, settled the property which labor and industry began—and the leagues that have been made between several states and kingdoms, either expressly or tacitly disowning all claim and right to the land in the other's possession, have, by common consent, given up their pretenses to their natural common right, which originally they had to those countries; and so have, by positive agreement, settled a property amongst themselves in distinct parts of the world—yet there are still great tracts of ground to be found which, the inhabitants thereof not having joined with the rest of mankind in the consent of the use of their common money, lie waste, and are more than the people who dwell on it do or can make use of, and so still lie in common; though this can scarce happen amongst that part of mankind that have consented to the use of money.

The greatest part of things really useful to the life of man, and such as the necessity of subsisting made the first commoners of the world look after, as it doth the Americans now, are generally things of short duration, such as, if they are not consumed by use, will decay and perish of themselves: gold, silver, and diamonds are things that fancy or agreement have put the value on more than real use and the necessary support of life. Now, of those good things which nature hath provided in common, everyone hath a right, as hath been said, to as much as he could use, and had a property in all he could effect with his labor—all that his industry could extend to, to alter from the state nature had put it in, was his. He that gathered a hundred bushels of acorns or apples had thereby a property in them; they were his goods as soon as gathered. He was only to look that he used them before they spoiled, else he took more than his share, and robbed others; and, indeed, it was a foolish thing, as well as dishonest, to hoard up more than he could make use of. If he gave away a part to anybody else, so that it perished not uselessly in his possession, these he also made use of; and if he also bartered away plums that would have rotted in a week, for nuts that would last good for his eating a whole year, he did no injury; he wasted not the common stock, destroyed no part of the portion of goods that belonged to others, so long as nothing perished uselessly in his hands. Again, if he would give his nuts for a piece of metal, pleased with its color, or exchange his sheep for shells, or wool for a sparkling pebble or a diamond, and keep those by him all his life, he invaded not the right of others; he might heap up as much of these durable things as he pleased, the exceeding of the bounds of his just property not lying in the largeness of his possessions, but the perishing of anything uselessly in it.

And thus came in the use of money—some lasting thing that men might keep without spoiling, and that, by mutual consent, men would take in exchange for the truly useful but perishable supports of life.

And as different degrees of industry were apt to give men possessions in different proportions, so this invention of money gave them the opportunity to continue and enlarge them; for supposing an island, separate from all possible commerce with the rest of the world, wherein there were but a hundred families—but there were sheep, horses, and cows, with other useful animals, wholesome fruits, and land enough for corn for a hundred thousand times as many, but nothing in the island, either because of its commonness or perishableness, fit to supply the place of money—what reason could any-one have there to enlarge his possessions beyond the use of his family and a plentiful supply to its consumption, either in what their own industry pro-duced, or they could barter for like perishable useful commodities with others? Where there is not something both lasting and scarce, and so valuable to be hoarded up, there men will not be apt to enlarge their possessions of land, were it never so rich, never so free for them to take; for I ask, what would a man value ten thousand or a hundred thousand acres of excellent land, ready cultivated, and well stocked too with cattle, in the middle of the inland parts of America, where he had no hopes of commerce with other parts of the world, to draw money to him by the sale of the product? It would not be worth the enclosing, and we should see him give up again to the wild common of nature whatever was more than would supply the conveniences of life to be had there for him and his family.

Thus in the beginning all the world was America, and more so than that is now, for no such thing as money was anywhere known. Find out some-thing that hath the use and value of money amongst his neighbors, you shall see the same man will begin presently to enlarge his possessions.

But since gold and silver, being little useful to the life of man in propor-tion to food, raiment, and carriage, has its value only from the consent of men, whereof labor yet makes, in great part, the measure, it is plain that the consent of men have agreed to a disproportionate and unequal possession of the earth—I mean out of the bounds of society and compact; for in govern-ments the laws regulate it; they having, by consent, found out and agreed in a way how a man may rightfully and without injury possess more than he himself can make use of by receiving gold and silver, which may continue long in a man's possession, without decaying for the over-plus, and agreeing those metals should have a value.

And thus, I think, it is very easy to conceive without any difficulty how labor could at first begin a title of property in the common things of nature, and how the spending it upon our uses bounded it, so that there could then be no reason of quarrelling about title, nor any doubt about the largeness of possession it gave. Right and conveniency went together; for as a man had a right to all he could employ his labor upon, so he had no temptation to labor for more than he could make use of. This left no room for controversy about the title, nor for encroachment on the right of others; what portion of man carved to himself was easily seen, and it was useless, as well as dishonest, to carve himself too much, or take more than he needed.

If man in the state of nature be so free, as has been said, if he be absolute lord of his own person or possessions, equal to the greatest, and subject to nobody, why will he part with his freedom, this empire, and subject himself to the dominion and control of any other power? To which, it is obvious to answer, that though in the state of nature he hath such a right, yet the enjoyment of it is very uncertain, and constantly exposed to the invasions of others. For all being kings as much as he, every man his equal, and the greater part no strict observers of equity and justice, the enjoyment of the property he has in this state is very unsafe, very insecure. This makes him willing to quit this condition, which, however free, is full of fears and continual dangers; and it is not without reason that he seeks out and is willing to join in society with others, who are already united, or have a mind to unite, for the mutual preservation of their lives, liberties, and estates, which I call by the general name, property.

The great and chief end, therefore, of men's uniting into commonwealths, and putting themselves under government, is the preservation of their property; to which in the state of nature there are many things wanting.

The great end of men's entering into society being the enjoyment of their properties in peace and safety, and the great instrument and means of that being the laws established in that society: the first and fundamental positive law of all commonwealths, is the establishing of the legislative power; as the first and fundamental natural law, which is to govern even the legislative itself, is the preservation of the society, and (as far as will consist with the public good) of every person in it. This legislative is not only the supreme power of the commonwealth, but sacred and unalterable in the hands where the community have once placed it; nor can any edict of anybody else, in what form soever conceived, or by what power soever backed, have the force and obligation of a law, which has not its sanction from that legislative which the public has chosen and appointed. For without this the law could not have that, which is absolutely necessary to its being a law, the consent of the society over whom nobody can have a power to make laws; but by their own consent, and by authority received from them; and therefore all the obedience, which by the most solemn ties anyone can be obliged to pay, ultimately terminates in this supreme power, and is directed by those laws which it enacts; nor can any oaths to any foreign power whatsoever, or any domestic subordinate power discharge any member of the society from his obedience to the legislative, acting pursuant to their trust; nor oblige him to any obedience contrary to the laws so enacted, or farther than they do allow; it being ridiculous to imagine one can be tied ultimately to obey any power in the society which is not the supreme.

Though the legislative, whether placed in one or more, whether it be always in being, or only by intervals, though it be the supreme power in every commonwealth, yet,

First, It is not nor can possibly be absolutely arbitrary over the lives and fortunes of the people. For it being but the joint power of every member of the society given up to that person, or assembly, which is legislator; it can be no more than those persons had in a state of nature before they entered into society, and gave it up to the community. For nobody can transfer to another more power than he has in himself; and nobody has an absolute arbitrary power over himself, or over any other to destroy his own life, or take away the life or property of another. A man as has been proved cannot subject himself to the arbitrary power of another; and having in the state of nature no arbitrary power over the life, liberty, or possession of another, but only so much as the law of nature gave him for the preservation of himself, and the rest of mankind; this is all he doth, or can give up to the commonwealth, and by it to the legislative power, so that the legislative can have no more than this. Their power in the utmost bounds of it, is limited to the public good of society. It is a power that hath no other end but preservation, and therefore can never have a right to destroy, enslave, or designedly to impoverish the subjects. The obligations of the law of nature cease not in society, but only in many cases are drawn closer, and have by human laws known penalties annexed to them to enforce their observation. Thus the law of nature stands as an eternal rule to all men, legislators as well as others. The rules that they make for other men's actions must, as well as their own, and other men's actions, be conformable to the law of nature, i.e., to the will of God, of which that is a declaration, and the fundamental law of nature being the preservation of mankind, no human sanction can be good or valid against it.

Secondly, The legislative, or supreme authority, cannot assume to itself a power to rule by extemporary arbitrary decrees, but is bound to dispense justice, and decide the rights of the subject by promulgated standing laws, and known authorized judges. For the law of nature being unwritten, and so nowhere to be found but in the minds of men, they who through passion or interest shall miscite or misapply it, cannot so easily be convinced of their mistake where there is no established judge. And so it serves not, as it ought, to determine the rights, and fence the properties of those that live under it, especially where every one is judge, interpreter, and executioner of it too, and that in his own case; and he that has right on his side, having ordinarily but his own single strength hath not force enough to defend himself from injuries, or punish delinquents. To avoid these inconveniences, which disorder men's properties in the state of nature, men unite into societies that they may have the united strength of the whole society to secure and defend their properties, and may have standing rules to bound it, by which everyone may know what is his. To this end it is that men give up all their natural power to the society which they enter into, and the community put the legislative power into such hands as they think fit, with this trust, that they shall be governed by declared laws, or else their peace, quiet, and property, will still be at the same uncertainty as it was in the state of nature.

Absolute arbitrary power, or governing without settled standing laws, can neither of them consist with the ends of society and government, which men would not quit the freedom of the state of nature for, and tie themselves up under, were it not to preserve their lives, liberties, and fortunes; and by stated rules of right and property to secure their peace and quiet. It cannot be supposed that they should intend, had they a power so to do, to give to anyone, or more, an absolute arbitrary power over their persons and estates, and put a force into the magistrate's hand to execute his unlimited will arbitrarily upon them. This were to put themselves into a worse condition than the state of nature, wherein they had a liberty to defend their right against the injuries of others, and were upon equal terms of force to maintain it, whether invaded by a single man or many in combination. Whereas, by supposing they have given up themselves to the absolute arbitrary power and will of a legislator, they have disarmed themselves, and armed him, to make prey of them when he pleases. He being in a much worse condition that is exposed to the arbitrary power of one man who has the command of 100,000, than he that is exposed to the arbitrary power of 100,000 single men; nobody being secure that his will, who hath such a command, is better than that of other men, though his force be 100,000 times stronger. And, therefore, whatever form the commonwealth is under, the ruling power ought to govern by declared and received laws, and not by extemporary dictates and undetermined resolutions. For then mankind will be in a far worse condition than in the state of nature, if they shall have armed one, or a few men, with the joint power of a multitude to force them to obey at pleasure the exorbitant and unlimited decrees of their sudden thoughts, or unrestrained, and, till that moment, unknown wills, without having any measures set down which may guide and justify their actions. For all the power the government has, being only for the good of the society, as it ought not to be arbitrary and at pleasure, so it ought to be exercised by established and promulgated laws; that both the people may know their duty and be safe and secure within the limits of the law; and the rulers too kept within their due bounds, and not be tempted by the power they have in their hands to employ it to such purposes, and by such measures, as they would not have known, and own not willingly.

Thirdly, The supreme power cannot take from any man any part of his property without his own consent. For the preservation of property being the end of government, and that for which men enter into society, it necessarily supposes and requires that the people should have property, without which they must be supposed to lose that by entering into society, which was the end for which they entered into it, too gross an absurdity for any man to own. Men, therefore, in society having property, they have such a right to the goods which by the law of the community are theirs, that nobody hath a right to take them or any part of them from them, without their own consent; without this they have no property at all. For I have truly no property in that which another can by right take from me when he pleases, against my consent. Hence it is a mistake to think that the supreme or legislative power of any commonwealth can do what it will, and dispose of the estates of the subjects arbitrarily, or take any part of them at pleasure. This is not much to be feared in governments where the legislative consists wholly, or in part, in assemblies which are variable, whose members, upon the dissolution of the assembly, are subjects under the common laws of their country, equally with the rest. But in governments where the legislative is in one lasting assembly, always in being, or in one man, as in absolute monarchies, there is danger still, that they will think themselves to have a distinct interest from the rest of the community, and so will be apt to increase their own riches and power by taking what they think fit from the people. For a man's property is not at all secure, though there be good and equitable laws to set the bounds of it between him and his fellow subjects, if he who commands those subjects have power to take from any private man what part he pleases of his property, and use and dispose of it as he thinks good.

But government, into whosoever hands it is put, being, as I have before shown, entrusted with this condition, and for this end, that men might have and secure their properties, the prince, or senate, however it may have power to make laws for the regulating of property between the subjects one amongst another, yet can never have a power to take to themselves the whole or any part of the subject's property without their own consent. For this would be in effect to leave them no property at all. And to let us see that even absolute power, where it is necessary, is not arbitrary by being absolute, but is still limited by that reason, and confined to those ends which required it in some cases to be absolute, we need look no farther than the common practice of martial discipline. For the preservation of the army, and in it the whole commonwealth, requires an absolute obedience to the command of every superior officer, and it is justly death to disobey or dispute the most dangerous or unreasonable of them; but yet we see that neither the sergeant, that could command a soldier to march up to the mouth of a cannon, or stand in a breach, where he is almost sure to perish, can command that soldier to give him one penny of his money; nor the general, that can condemn him to death for deserting his post, or not obeying the most desperate orders, cannot yet, with all his absolute power of life and death, dispose of one farthing of that soldier's estate, or seize one jot of his goods, whom yet he can command anything, and hang for the least disobedience. Because such a blind obedience is necessary to that end for which the commander has his power, viz., the preservation of the rest; but the disposing of his goods has nothing to do with it.

'Tis true governments cannot be supported without great charge, and it is fit everyone who enjoys a share of the protection should pay out of his estate his proportion for the maintenance of it. But still it must be with his own consent, i.e., the consent of the majority giving it either by themselves or their representatives chosen by them. For if anyone shall claim a power to lay and levy taxes on the people, by his own authority, and without such consent of the people, he thereby invades the fundamental law of property, and subverts the end of government. For what property have I in that which another may by right take when he pleases to himself?

Fourthly, The legislative cannot transfer the power of making laws to any other hands; for it being but a delegated power from the people, they who have it cannot pass it over to others. The people alone can appoint the form of the commonwealth, which is by constituting the legislative, and appointing in whose hands that shall be. And when the people have said we will submit to rules, and be governed by laws made by such men, and in such forms, nobody else can say other men shall make laws for them; nor can the people be bound by any laws but such as are enacted by those whom they have chosen and authorized to make laws for them.

These are the bounds which the trust that is put in them by the society, and the law of God and Nature, have set to the legislative power of every commonwealth, in all forms of government.

First, They are to govern by promulgated established laws, not to be varied in particular cases, but to have one rule for rich and poor, for the favorite at court and the countryman at plough.

Secondly, These laws also ought to be designed for no other end ultimately but the good of the people.

Thirdly, They must not raise taxes on the property of the people without the consent of the people, given by themselves or their deputies. And this properly concerns only such governments where the legislative is always in being, or at least where the people have not reserved any part of the legislative to deputies, to be from time to time chosen by themselves.

Fourthly, The legislative neither must nor can transfer the power of making laws to anybody else, or place it anywhere but where the people have.

EDMUND BURKE

2. Representation of Property*

Nothing is a due and adequate representation of a state that does not represent its ability, as well as its property. But as ability is a vigorous and active principle, and as property is sluggish, inert and timid, it never can be safe from the invasions of ability, unless it be, out of all proportion, predominant in the representation. It must be represented too in great masses of accumulation, or it is not rightly protected. The characteristic essence of property, formed out of the combined principles of its acquisition and conservation, is to be *unequal*. The great masses therefore which excite envy, and tempt rapacity, must be put out of the possibility of danger. Then they form a natural rampart about the lesser properties in all their gradations. The same quantity of property, which is by the natural course of things divided among many, has not the same operation. Its defensive power is weakened as it is diffused. In this diffusion each man's portion is less than what, in the eagerness of his desires, he may flatter himself to obtain by dissipating the accumulations of others. The plunder of the few would indeed give but a share inconceivably small in the distribution to the many. But the many are not capable of making this calculation; and those who lead them to rapine never intend this distribution.

The power of perpetuating our property in our families is one of the most valuable and interesting circumstances belonging to it, and that which tends the most to the perpetuation of society itself. It makes our weakness subservient to our virtue; it grafts benevolence even upon avarice. The possessors of family wealth, and of the distinction which attends hereditary possession, (as most concerned in it,) are the natural securities for this transmission. With us the House of Peers is formed upon this principle. It is wholly composed of hereditary property and hereditary distinction; and

* From Edmund Burke, *Reflections on the Revolution in France* (1790).

made therefore the third of the legislature; and, in the last event, the sole judge of all property in all its subdivisions. The House of Commons too, though not necessarily, yet in fact, is always so composed, in the far greater part. Let those large proprietors be what they will, and they have their chance of being among the best, they are, at the very worst, the ballast in the vessel of the commonwealth. For though hereditary wealth, and the rank which goes with it, are too much idolized by creeping sycophants, and the blind, abject admirers of power, they are too rashly slighted in shallow speculations of the petulant, assuming, short-sighted coxcombs of philosophy. Some decent, regulated pre-eminence, some preference (not exclusive appropriation), given to birth, is neither unnatural, nor unjust, nor impolitic.

It is said, that twenty-four millions ought to prevail over two hundred thousand. True; if the constitution of a kingdom be a problem of arithmetic. This sort of discourse does well enough with the lamp-post for its second: to men who *may* reason calmly, it is ridiculous. The will of the many, and their interest, must very often differ; and great will be the difference when they make an evil choice. A government of five hundred country attorneys and obscure curates is not good for twenty-four millions of men, though it were chosen by eight and forty millions; nor is it the better for being guided by a dozen of persons of quality, who have betrayed their trust in order to obtain that power. At present, you seem in everything to have strayed out of the high road of nature. The property of France does not govern it. Of course property is destroyed, and rational liberty has no existence.

When all the frauds, impostures, violences, rapines, burnings, murders, confiscations, compulsory paper currencies, and every description of tyranny and cruelty employed to bring about and to uphold this Revolution, have their natural effect, that is, to shock the moral sentiments of all virtuous and sober minds, the abettors of this philosophic system immediately strain their throats in a declamation against the old monarchical government of France. When they have rendered that deposed power sufficiently black, they then proceed in argument, as if all those who disapprove of their new abuses must of course be partisans of the old; that those who reprobate their crude and violent schemes of liberty ought to be treated as advocates for servitude. I admit that their necessities do compel them to this base and contemptible fraud. Nothing can reconcile men to their proceedings and projects but the supposition that there is no third option between them and some tyranny as odious as can be furnished by the records of history, or by the invention of poets. This prattling of theirs hardly deserves the name of sophistry. It is nothing but plain impudence. Have these gentlemen never heard, in the whole circle of the worlds of theory and practice, of anything between the despotism of the monarch and the despotism of the multitude? Have they never heard of a monarchy directed by laws, controlled and balanced by the great hereditary wealth and hereditary dignity of a nation; and both again controlled by a judicious check from the reason and feeling of the people at large, acting by a suitable and permanent organ? Is it then impossible that a man may be found who, without criminal ill intention, or pitiable absurdity, shall prefer such a mixed and tempered government to either of the extremes; and who may repute that nation to be destitute of all wisdom and of all virtue, which having in its choice to obtain such a government with ease, *or rather to confirm it when actually possessed,* thought proper to commit a thousand crimes, and to subject their country to a thousand evils, in order to avoid it? Is it then a truth so universally acknowledged, that a pure democracy is the only tolerable form into which human society can be thrown, that a man is not permitted to hesitate about its merits, without the suspicion of being a friend to tyranny, that is, of being a foe to mankind?

With the National Assembly of France, possession is nothing. I see the National Assembly openly reprobate the doctrine of prescription, which one of the greatest of their own lawyers[1] tells us, with great truth, is a part of the law of nature. He tells us that the positive ascertainment of its limits, and its security from invasion, were among the causes for which civil society itself has been instituted. If prescription be once shaken, no species of property is secure, when it once becomes an object large enough to tempt the cupidity of indigent power. I see a practice perfectly correspondent to their contempt of this great fundamental part of natural law. I see the confiscators begin with bishops, and chapters, and monasteries; but I do not see them end there. I see the princes of blood, who, by the oldest usages of that kingdom held large landed estates (hardly with the compliment of a debate), deprived of their possessions, and, in lieu of their stable, independent property, reduced to the hope of some precarious, charitable pension, at the pleasure of an assembly, which of course will pay little regard to the rights of pensioners at pleasure, when it despises those of legal proprietors. Flushed with the insolence of the first inglorious victories, and pressed by the distresses caused by the lust of unhallowed lucre, disappointed but not discouraged, they have at length ventured completely to subvert all property of all descriptions throughout the extent of a great kingdom. They have compelled all men, in all transactions of commerce, in the disposal of lands, in civil dealing, and through the whole communion of life, to accept as perfect payment and good and lawful tender, the symbols of their speculations on a projected sale of their plunder. What vestiges of liberty or property have they left? The tenant-right of a cabbage-garden, a year's interest in a hovel,

[1] Domat.

the good-will of an ale-house or a baker's shop, the very shadow of a con-structive property, are more ceremoniously treated in our parliament, than with you the oldest and most valuable landed possessions, in the hands of the most respectable personages, or than the whole body of the monied and commercial interest of your country. We entertain a high opinion of the legislative authority; but we have never dreamt that parliaments had any right whatever to violate property, to over-rule prescription, or to force a currency of their own fiction in the place of that which is real, and recog-nized by the law of nations. But you, who began with refusing to submit to the most moderate restraints, have ended by establishing an unheard-of despotism. I find the ground upon which your confiscators go is this: that indeed their proceedings could not be supported in a court of justice; but that the rulers of prescription cannot bind a legislative assembly. So that this legislative assembly of a free nation sits, not for the security, but for the destruction of property, and not of property only, but of every rule and maxim which can give it stability and of those instruments which can alone give it circulation.

In every prosperous community something more is produced than goes to the immediate support of the producer. This surplus forms the income of the landed capitalist. It will be spent by a proprietor who does not labour. But this idleness is itself the spring of labour; this repose the spur to indus-try. The only concern for the state is, that the capital taken in rent from the land, should be returned again to the industry from whence it came; and that its expenditure should be with the least possible detriment to the morals of those who expend it, and to those of the people to whom it is returned.

Why should the expenditure of a great landed property, which is a dis-persion of the surplus product of the soil, appear intolerable to you or to me, when it takes its course through the accumulation of great libraries, which are the history of the force and weakness of the human mind; through great collections of ancient records, medals and coins, which attest and ex-plain laws and customs; through paintings and statues that, by imitating nature, seem to extend the limits of creation; through grand monuments of the dead, which continue the regards and connexions of life beyond the grave; through collections of the specimens of nature, which become a rep-resentative assembly of all the classes and families of the world, that by disposition facilitate, and, by exciting curiosity, open the avenues to science? If, by great permanent establishments, all these objects of expense are better secured from the inconstant sport of personal caprice and personal extrava-gance, are they worse than if the same tastes prevailed in scattered individu-als?

MR. JUSTICE VAN ORSDEL

3. Property—The First Principle of Government*

High wages do not necessarily tend to good morals, or the promotion of the general welfare. The standard of virtue and morality is no higher among the prosperous than among the poor. Their worth cannot be measured in dollars and cents, or promoted by a legal subsidy. Never have wages been so high as since the outbreak of the late war, and never in the history of the republic has crime been so universal; and this condition, it must be conceded, has made a like unfavorable impression upon the morals of the people. A wage based upon competitive ability is just, and leads to frugality and honest industry, and inspires an ambition to attain the highest possible efficiency, while the equal wage paralyzes ambition and promotes prodigality and indolence. It takes away the strongest incentive to human labor, thrift, and efficiency, and works injustice to employee and employer alike, thus affecting injuriously the whole social and industrial fabric. Experience has demonstrated that a fixed minimum wage means, in the last analysis, a fixed wage; since the employer, being compelled to advance some to a wage higher than their earning capacity, will, to equalize the cost of operation, lower the wage of the more competent to the common basis.

Any intimation that the Constitution is flexible, even in response to the police power, is unsound. Powers expressly delegated by the Constitution—such, for example, as the regulation of interstate commerce—may be extended to meet changing conditions, providing it can be accomplished without altering fundamental principles; but the principles are immutable, not elastic, or subject to change. That a state may not impair the obligations of a contract, or that no person can be deprived of his property without due process of law, are principles fundamental, and if the Legislature, in response to public clamor for an experimental social reform, may break down these constitutional guaranties by calling an act a "health law," or a "public morality law," or a "public welfare law," all guaranties of the Constitution, under the alleged exercise of the police power, may be changed, modified, or totally eliminated.

Nor is the extent of such modification a matter of judicial discretion. To hold that the courts may declare a law, violating the same principle, constitutional under one state of fact, and unconstitutional under another, is the exercise of arbitrary power—a power said to exist nowhere in our system of government. And nowhere could it be lodged with more dangerous results than in the courts.

* From *Children's Hospital of the District of Columbia* v. *Adkins,* 284 Fed. Rep. 613 (1922).

The tendency of the times to socialize property rights under the subterfuge of police regulation is dangerous, and if continued will prove destructive of our free institutions. It should be remembered that of the three fundamental principles which underlie government, and for which government exists, the protection of life, liberty, and property, the chief of these is property; not that any amount of property is more valuable than the life or liberty of the citizen, but the history of civilization proves that, when the citizen is deprived of free use and enjoyment of his property, anarchy and revolution follow, and life and liberty are without protection.

The highest freedom consists in obedience to law, and a strict adherence to the limitations of the Constitution. In no way can the freedom of the citizen be more effectively curtailed and ultimately destroyed than by a deprivation of those inherent rights safeguarded by our fundamental law. The security of society depends upon the extent of the protection afforded the individual citizen under the Constitution against the demands and incursions of the government. The only tyranny the citizenship of this republic need fear is from the government itself. The character and value of government is measured by the security which surrounds the individual in the use and enjoyment of his property. These rights will only remain secure so long as the Bill of Rights—the first ten amendments of the Constitution—are construed liberally in favor of the individual and strictly against the government. They were early adopted because of a widespread apprehension that the time might come when the government would assume to trespass upon those inalienable individual rights announced in the Declaration of Independence and afterwards incorporated in the Bill of Rights. Courts, therefore, should be slow to lend aid to the government in this modern tendency to invade individual property rights.

WALTER LIPPMANN

4. *The Rule of Law and Regulation of Property**

I. SOCIAL CONTROL BY LAW RATHER THAN BY COMMANDS

In distinguishing between the regulation of affairs by reciprocal rights and duties on the one hand, by overhead administrative order on the other, we can, I believe, clarify what Burke called "one of the finest problems in legis-

* From Walter Lippmann, *The Good Society* (1937). By permission of Little, Brown & Company and The Atlantic Monthly Press.

lation," which is "What the state ought to take upon itself to direct by the public wisdom, and what it ought to leave, with as little interference as possible, to individual discretion." [1]

This problem baffled the influential thinkers and statesmen of the nineteenth century, and their failure to elucidate it successfully caused that popular bewilderment in which men came to think that they must make an exclusive choice between the anarchy of unrestrained property owners and the management of property by public officials. They thought they had to decide between doing nothing and administering almost everything. Those who wished to let things alone called themselves individualists and said they believed in liberty. Those who wished to direct the course of affairs became collectivists and appealed to the desire for security, order, and equality.

The choice is not, I think, exclusive, and it has been posed only because of faulty observation and an insufficient analysis. There is no exclusive choice between direction by the state and noninterference with individual behavior, between state collectivism and laissez-faire as understood by the latter-day liberals. This supposed choice ignores the whole immense field occupied by the development of private rights and duties, and, therefore, it is not true that individuals must be left to do what they like or be told by officials what they must do. There is another way, the way of the common law, in which abuses are regulated and public policy is made effective by altering the private rights that are enforceable in the courts.

This becomes self-evident when we remember what the laissez-faire theorists forgot: that the individualism they are talking about exists by virtue of lawful rights that are enforced by the state.[2] The title to property is a construction of the law. Contracts are legal instruments. Corporations are legal creatures. It is, therefore, misleading to think of them as existing somehow outside the law and then to ask whether it is permissible to "interfere" with them. Thus the English law governing the inheritance of real property produced a different distribution of property from that produced by the French law. For in England the oldest son had different legal rights from those he had in France. Property of any kind, contracts of any kind, corporate organization of any kind, exist only because there are certain rights and immunities which can be enforced, when they have been legally established, by enlisting the coercive authority of the state. To speak of letting things alone is, therefore, to use a meaningless and a deceptive phrase. No one who asks to be let alone really wishes to be let completely alone: what he asks is that he be enabled to enjoy the undisputed exercise of the rights which he enjoys. But he expects the state to interfere promptly and effec-

---

[1] "Thoughts and Details on Scarcity," *Works,* Vol. V, p. 107.

[2] Cf. Ernest Barker's Translator's Introduction to Gierke's *Natural Law and the Theory of Society,* LXX.

tively if anyone disturbs him. He insists that his rights shall be enforced.

For some curious reason, the debate between individualists and collectivists has been carried on with both factions assuming that the *existing* system of private rights must either be left undisturbed or that it must be abolished; that existing rights must be maintained absolutely or extinguished absolutely; that either "property" must be what it happened to be when they were quarreling about it or the means of production must be administered by officials of the state. The dilemma is unreal and unnecessary. The system of private land tenure which happens to prevail at one moment in some country is not the only possible system of land tenure. The only possible alternative is not the nationalization of the land. The alternative may be any one of innumerable other systems of private land tenure. The only possible alternative to the existing system of private contract in industrial relations is not the replacement of private contracts by public administration. There are many alternatives, many possible ways of changing the kinds of private contracts that the law will require the courts to enforce. The only alternative to the concentrated corporate control of industry is not a concentrated government control of business corporations. It may be any one of many possible modifications of the law of corporate rights.

But in the nineteenth century individualists and collectivists alike persuaded themselves that the existing system of private rights could not be modified: that it had either to be maintained or to be superseded. Thus they created for themselves the fatal dilemma which has divided mankind into those who merely wish to preserve the status quo with all its abuses and those who wish to make a new social order by the authoritarian power of the state. Collectivists and individualists had lost sight of one of the most obvious facts in human experience, that great and salutary changes in human relations can be and usually have been effected not by commands from on high but by amending the laws under which men deal with one another.

Any student of history could have told them that laws have changed radically in the course of history. Yet it was somehow assumed that laws were absolute, and therefore incapable of serious modification. So the debate has proceeded on the assumption that the choice lies between stubborn conservatism and complete revolution, that the rights of property as they stood in the nineteenth century have either to be confirmed and protected or that property owners have to be expropriated and their possessions administered by the state. The latter-day liberals, having committed themselves to the fallacy that existing rights are absolute, have been inhibited by their own fallacy from working out any programme to relieve the evils of modern society. The collectivists, believing in the same fallacy, merely drew an opposite conclusion. They turned to the state as deus ex machina, believing that the relief which could not be obtained by a readjustment of personal rights could be obtained by authoritative commands.

The essential intellectual difficulty may be seen in Burke's statement of the problem. He assumes that the state must either "direct" or must not "interfere." But suppose I invent a new mousetrap and suppose the law says that no one may use my invention during my lifetime without paying me the royalty I choose to charge. Is this *direction* or is it *interference?* Now suppose the state amends the law, saying that I have an exclusive patent for five years only: after that anyone may copy my mousetrap without being liable to a suit for damages. That amendment of the law will radically alter the mousetrap situation. But is this act of social control to be called *direction* or is it to be called *non-interference?* From my point of view I suppose I have been interfered with. But my neighbors might say that they have been released from an undue interference on my part with their right to catch mice more successfully; that I was levying an unjust toll for an invention that was probably suggested to me, in part at least, by someone else's invention.

Is it not clear that the terms of the discussion do not really fit the facts, and that the debate could go on forever? A change in the law governing my right to patent the invention does not fit into either of Burke's categories. Yet the change in the law causes a real change in the situation. Though the state has not undertaken to direct the invention or to administer the manufacture of mousetraps, it is not letting me "alone" without social control. The change is brought by a readjustment of the rights of my neighbors and of myself. Impressive social changes may have been effected—the public health improved, a new industry brought into being, I prevented from becoming a millionaire, my neighbors relieved of a bitter grievance, good feeling promoted. But these things have been done without appointing new officials empowered to issue commands to anyone.

There are not, then, as Burke and so many after him assumed, only two realms, one in which there is no regulation of men's behavior, another in which men must obey the commands of their superiors. To state the problem in this fashion is to overlook the realm of private rights and duties where significant relations are regulated by general laws impartially applied to specific controversies, not by commands issued by some men to other men. Except where a few solitary individuals subsist in a wilderness, the actual choice is between the regulation of social affairs by adjudicating and adjusting private rights on the one hand, by arbitrary sovereign commands on the other. The one is the method of a common law; the other the method of the prerogatives of superior persons. The one is the system of democratic liberalism, the other of authoritarian collectivism.

In the light of this distinction much unnecessary confusion is dissipated. We shall not, for example, fall into the error of regarding the existing law of property, of contracts, of corporations, as marking a realm in which the state does not or should not intervene. We shall recognize it for what it is, as a structure of rights and duties, immunities and privileges, built by custom, judicial interpretation, and statute, and maintained by the coercive authority of the state. We shall not think of all this as subsisting somehow outside the law, and then become involved in an empty debate as to whether the law may interfere with it. The whole of it, all property, and everything which we include in the general name of private enterprise, is the product of a legal development and can exist only by virtue of the law. This is evident enough in periods of social disorder when for want of law observance and law enforcement the whole private economy may collapse in a day.

We shall not compound the error by thinking that the law of property contracts and corporations is immutable.

II. THE REGULATION OF PROPERTY

It was, as we have already seen, at this point that nineteenth-century liberalism came to a dead end: where it chose to treat property and the powers of the business corporation as in effect absolute and untouchable. Then it was that liberal statesmen, being unable to regulate property and corporations effectively, had to give way to the collectivists.

The latter-day liberals had a vague notion that they must regard private property as approximating, to use Blackstone's words, "that sole and despotic dominion which one man claims and exercises over the external things of the world, in total exclusion of the right of any other individual in the universe." [3]

But no such sole and despotic dominion exists or can be established, and it was a signal disservice to the maintenance of free enterprise when men attempted to claim and to exercise such a sole and despotic dominion. For the rights of property have no existence outside the law: they are simply the rights which courts of law will recognize. No man can hold or enjoy property openly and securely except by virtue of the readiness of the state to enforce his lawful right. Without a lawful title, he has no property; he is merely a possessor without recourse against those who are strong enough to help themselves to his goods.

Not only is all property a right established by law and enforceable at law: all property is a complex system of rights. This system is not the same system in respect to all kinds of things. It is not the same system at all times in respect to the same things. It is not the same system in all places at the same time in respect to the same things. In other words there is no such thing as an absolute, immutable, and indefeasible system of property rights.

Thus the system of private property is not uniform for urban land and for land at the frontier. The title to urban land may, for example, be subject to zoning ordinances which completely nullify any pretension that the owner exercises a sole and despotic dominion, "in total exclusion of the right of

[3] Blackstone, *Commentaries,* Bk. II, Ch. 1.

any other individual." If, in defiance of the zoning ordinance, he attempts to establish a garage, his neighbors have rights which they can enforce. The landowner has no absolute rights in his property; he has only conditional rights which vary from place to place. He cannot put up a jerry-built structure on Broadway, but he can, if he likes, go out into the open country and build himself a house of wood and paper held together by safety pins. Moreover, he holds his property on Broadway subject not only to the existing building laws but to future changes in those laws. And the same is true of his house in the country: if, for example, it were judged to be a fire hazard, his neighbors by a change in the law might be invested with the right to protect themselves by bringing suit or entering a complaint.

The same property rights do not adhere to land which contains minerals, to land which controls water power, to land usable for bridgeheads, ferry landings, and highways, for railway tracks and conduits in city streets. The rights of property are not uniform in patents, in animals, in news gathered by reporters, in radio channels, in the air traversed by flying machines, in gold, silver, and platinum, in an author's manuscript, in all inheritances and in all gifts. Though we think of all these rights as property, in fact property consists of an extremely varied collection of rights.

What is more, the special rights which make up different kinds of property are not immutable. Before the appearance of the airplane the owner of a piece of land was held to have a title to a pyramid which had its apex at the centre of the earth and an infinitely wide base out in infinite space. Under a recent decision in an American court, his rights in the air extend no higher up than a safe distance above the roof of his house. The conditions on which the title to land can be enjoyed, acquired by sale, transmitted by gift or inheritance, have been profoundly modified again and again. Less than three hundred years ago, for example, the obligation of the English tenant to render personal services to the lord of the manor was commuted to the payment of a pecuniary rent. The right of the landlord to appropriate the monopoly rent of the land is by no means absolute, being subject to the power both of eminent domain and of taxation.

If we ask ourselves whether in this bewildering complex of rights which men call property there is any clarifying principle of order, we must, it seems to me, take as our premise the principle enunciated by Sir William Blackstone that "the earth . . . and all things therein are the general property of all mankind, exclusive of other beings, from the immediate gift of the Creator." [4] This does not mean that the earth and all things therein should be administered by a central collectivist authority or that individuals should not or cannot be made secure in the enjoyment of private rights. But it does mean that no individual can or should exercise a sole and despotic dominion over any portion of the earth or of the things therein. The earth is limited in size

[4] *Op. cit.*, Bk. II. Ch. I.

and its use is necessary to every man's existence. Therefore, the rights of any man upon the earth must be reconciled with the equal rights of other men, not only of living men but of the unborn generations. No one in his senses can therefore believe in an absolute right of property which would permit the transient possessors of the land to destroy its fertility, to burn down forests, to cause the streams to dry up, to squander at will the minerals under the surface. These owners did not make these resources. They are unable to re-create them. What title have they then to claim that posterity has no rights which they must respect? The true doctrine surely is that men hold property in limited and necessary natural resources, not as sovereigns, but as tenants —who have rights and also duties—of mankind.

And likewise, no one believes in an absolute right of property which gives such exclusive possession that property owners can so monopolize the land and the resources that other men can live only by paying the price they choose to exact. Men may pretend to believe in such a theory of property. In practice it is unworkable. The dispossessed and the disinherited will haunt them and terrorize them. The desperate insecurity of all private property in the modern world is due to the fact that the propertied classes, in resisting a modification of their rights, have aroused the revolutionary impulse to abolish all their rights. Modern bolshevism is the product of the attempt to make property an absolute right.

The real security of private property must rest not on a fatuous longing for a sole and despotic dominion over the necessities of all men's existence but on a reconciliation of all men's claims in a system of substantially equal rights. It is not loyalty to the cause of private property to confirm the monopolists in their privileges. To do that is to prepare the extinction of private property either by general disorder and pillage or by the establishment of an administered collectivism. The true principle is to be ready to liquidate these rights of possession which enable some men, by excluding all other men from access to land and to the resources of nature, to exact a tribute based not on their own labor but on mere legal possession.

If all property is a complex of legal rights, the business corporation, with its privilege of limited liability and perpetual succession, is even more obviously a legal creation. It is no exaggeration to say that without the corporate device modern capitalism could not have been evolved. Now an aggregation of individuals can, when they are incorporated, do things which they could not possibly do as separate individuals nor as an informal association of individuals. They can do these things only because of legal rights acquired in their charter. But for that charter they would have separate and unlimited liability for the acts done by their association; when one of them died or resigned, the association would have been dissolved, like a marriage or a partnership.

It is plain that a corporation enjoys great advantages as against unincorporated individuals. It can assemble the property of great masses of individuals, administer it collectively, and, though its directors or managers fall sick or die, the corporate organization goes on. Now all of these advantages are created and maintained by the law which says that under certain conditions individuals have the right to incorporate and as a corporation to enjoy certain privileges and immunities. How can such rights be regarded as inalienable and immutable? Is it not evident that in granting the privilege of incorporation the state may fix the conditions, that it may say what the rights of an incorporated body are, that it may say that the privilege of limited liability and perpetual succession shall be enjoyed only in so far as the corporation meets certain specific obligations?

Yet for reasons which it is not necessary for us to examine here, the ability to incorporate came to be regarded in the nineteenth century not as a privilege granted by law but as some sort of unquestionable right. The founders of the American Republic had no such notion and the liberals of the eighteenth century would have regarded it as preposterous.

A charter of incorporation to use property for profit is a state-created privilege, particularly when it grants to its members the partial immunity of limited liability. There is, therefore, no reason why that charter should be vague and general: it can be made as specific in its definition of what rights the corporation may exercise and what duties it must perform as the lawmakers choose to make it. In the charter and in the statutes governing corporations they can stipulate any public policy they deem desirable. They can stipulate that the members of the corporation shall not enjoy limited liability or perpetual succession if the courts find that they have violated the terms of the charter. The lawmakers can stipulate the grounds on which competitors, customers, employees, creditors, and debtors may sue for violations of the charter and the law. Moreover, the lawmakers may stipulate, if they deem it wise, how much land a corporation may own and no title in excess of that amount would be a good title. They may stipulate as to whether one corporation may own another, for how long and on what terms it may own patents, in what measure it may own natural resources, whether it shall be capitalized through the issue of bonds or equity shares, what shall be the rights of its security holders. They may stipulate the manner in which the accounts shall be kept, and what information must be made public and how often.

Thus, without overhead direction, a very comprehensive regulation of corporate activity is feasible. It can be achieved by defining in the law the respective rights of a corporation and of those with whom it transacts business. Yet such a system of regulation does not invest public officials with the authority to administer the affairs of the corporation or to issue commands and prohibitions to the corporate managers. It does not increase the power of officials over the life and labor of citizens. It merely readjusts, theoretically in any degree and in any manner, the rights of citizens with one another.

and then relies upon individuals to put the law in motion when they believe they can prove in court that their rights have been violated.

But though, theoretically, the lawmakers could set any conditions they chose upon the right to incorporate, in fact they could not legislate capriciously. For as they approached the point where they were converting the privileges of incorporation into a risk and a burden, men would simply turn in their corporate charters and revert to some form of partnership. At that point the social advantages of the corporation would be lost, and the excessive rights against corporations granted to customers, employees, investors, or competitors, would have defeated their own purposes. Thus the system would have to be reasonable in order to be effective. It would have to represent a wise reconciliation of collaborating and competing interests. But that is one of the paramount virtues of the liberal method of regulating human affairs through the adjustment of private rights: that it is compelled to work, not by the compulsion of irresistible authority from on high but by conciliation, justice, and comity among persons.

It has been a great illusion to think of the modern business corporation as a kind of autonomous principality with inherent power derived from some mysterious source that is independent of the state. The power of the business corporation is entirely a power granted by the state, dependent from day to day upon the continued enforcement of the law by the state which has invested it with its privileges and immunities. It cannot be true, as so many lawyers have argued, that corporate rights are inalienable and immutable and indefeasible. Previous to about 1850 a special act of the legislature was needed in order to charter a corporation. Fifty years ago no common-law lawyer would have thought it conceivable that one corporation could own the stock of another. The business corporation, as we know it, is founded on the fact that legislatures and courts gradually invested incorporated associations with new rights, rights which did not exist a hundred years ago, rights which can, therefore, by no stretch of the imagination be regarded as anything but conditional and subject to alteration.

By the same token it is no less untrue that modern corporate capitalism is a predestined development due to some mysterious necessity of the machine process, or to some inexorable tendency to the agglomeration of wealth and power. The promoters of the giant corporation were not giants to whom ordinary men had to yield. They were ordinarily enterprising men who made the most of legal privileges with which legislatures and courts had inadvertently endowed them. The essential elements out of which the giant corporations were assembled were titles to land and natural resources and patents, limited liability for debts and damages, perpetual succession, their chartered right to set up an internal government of the corporate organization.

Any or all of these elements could have been and can at any time be redefined and subjected to new conditions. In short, their existing rights are not absolute. The development of private corporate collectivism is in no sense inevitable. The potentialities of regulation are as numerous and varied as the points at which the corporation has relations—with its customers, its employees, its competitors, its providers of raw materials and transportation, its stockholders and bondholders, its neighbors in the places where it operates, and the tax collector. The field of the business corporation is not an immunized area which is sterile to the possibility of reform and regulation. The business corporation can be reformed and regulated by a readjustment of private rights, and there is no reason whatever for the assumption, made both by individuals and by collectivists, that corporations must either be allowed to enjoy all their present rights or be taken over and administered by the state.

LUDWIG VON MISES

5. *The Free Market Economy**

I. THE CHARACTERISTICS OF THE MARKET ECONOMY

The market economy is the social system of the division of labor under private ownership of the means of production. Everybody acts on his own behalf; but everybody's actions aim at the satisfaction of other people's needs as well as at the satisfaction of his own. Everybody in acting serves his fellow citizens. Everybody, on the other hand, is served by his fellow citizens. Everybody is both a means and an end in himself; an ultimate end for himself and a means to other people in their endeavors to attain their own ends.

This system is steered by the market. The market directs the individual's activities into those channels in which he best serves the wants of his fellow men. There is in the operation of the market no compulsion and coercion. The state, the social apparatus of coercion and compulsion, does not interfere with the market and with the citizens' activities directed by the market. It employs its power to beat people into submission solely for the prevention of actions destructive to the preservation and the smooth operation of the market economy. It protects the individual's life, health, and property against violent or fraudulent aggression on the part of domestic gangsters and external foes. Thus the state creates and preserves the environment in which

* From Ludwig von Mises, *Human Action: A Treatise on Economics* (Yale University Press, 1949). By permission.

the market economy can safely operate. The Marxian slogan "anarchic production" pertinently characterizes this social structure as an economic system which is not directed by a dictator, a production tsar who assigns to each a task and compels him to obey this command. Each man is free; nobody is subject to a despot. Of his own accord the individual integrates himself into the cooperative system. The market directs him and reveals to him in what way he can best promote his own welfare as well as that of other people. The market is supreme. The market alone puts the whole social system in order and provides it with sense and meaning.

The market is not a place, a thing, or a collective entity. The market is a process, actuated by the interplay of the actions of the various individuals cooperating under the division of labor. The forces determining the—continually changing—state of the market are the value judgments of these individuals and their actions as directed by these value judgments. The state of the market at any instant is the price structure, i.e., the totality of the exchange ratios as established by the interaction of those eager to buy and those eager to sell. There is nothing inhuman or mystical with regard to the market. The market process is entirely a resultant of human actions. Every market phenomenon can be traced back to definite choices of the members of the market society.

The market process is the adjustment of the individual actions of the various members of the market society to the requirements of mutual cooperation. The market prices tell the producers what to produce, how to produce, and in what quantity. The market is the focal point to which the activities of the individuals converge. It is the center from which the activities of the individuals radiate.

The market economy must be strictly differentiated from the second thinkable—although not realizable—system of social cooperation under the division of labor: the system of social or governmental ownership of the means of production. This second system is commonly called socialism, communism, planned economy, or state capitalism. The market economy or capitalism, as it is usually called, and the socialist economy preclude one another. There is no mixture of the two systems possible or thinkable; there is no such thing as a mixed economy, a system that would be in part capitalistic and in part socialist. Production is directed either by the market or by the decrees of a production tsar or a committee of production tsars.

If within a society based on private ownership of the means of production some of these means are publicly owned and operated—that is, owned and operated by the government or one of its agencies—this does not make for a mixed system which would combine socialism and capitalism. The fact that the state or municipalities own and operate some plants does not alter the characteristic features of the market economy. These publicly owned and operated enterprises are subject to the sovereignty of the market. They must fit themselves, as buyers of raw materials, equipment, and labor, and as sellers of goods and services, into the scheme of the market economy. They are subject to the laws of the market and thereby depend on the consumers who may or may not patronize them. They must strive for profits or, at least, to avoid losses. The government may cover losses of its plants or shops by drawing on public funds. But this neither eliminates nor mitigates the supremacy of the market; it merely shifts it to another sector. For the means for covering the losses must be raised by the imposition of taxes. But this taxation has its effects on the market and influences the economic structure according to the laws of the market. It is the operation of the market, and not the government collecting the taxes, that decides upon whom the incidence of the taxes falls and how they affect production and consumption. Thus the market, not a government bureau, determines the working of these publicly operated enterprises.

II. FREEDOM

The words freedom and liberty signified for the most eminent representatives of mankind one of the most precious and desirable goods. Today it is fashionable to sneer at them. They are, trumpets the modern sage, "slippery" notions and "bourgeois" prejudices.

Freedom and liberty are not to be found in nature. In nature there is no phenomenon to which these terms could be meaningfully applied. Whatever man does, he can never free himself from the restraints which nature imposes upon him. If he wants to succeed in acting, he must submit unconditionally to the laws of nature.

Freedom and liberty always refer to interhuman relations. A man is free as far as he can live and get on without being at the mercy of arbitrary decisions on the part of other people. In the frame of society everybody depends upon his fellow citizens. Social man cannot become independent without forsaking all the advantages of social cooperation. The self-sufficient individual is independent, but he is not free. He is at the mercy of everybody who is stronger than himself. The stronger fellow has the power to kill him with impunity. It is therefore nonsense to rant about an alleged "natural" and "inborn" freedom which people are supposed to have enjoyed in the ages preceding the emergence of social bonds. Man was not created free; what freedom he may possess has been given to him by society. Only societal conditions can present a man with an orbit within the limits of which he can attain liberty.

Liberty and freedom are the conditions of man within a contractual society. Social cooperation under a system of private ownership of the means of production means that within the range of the market the individual is not bound to obey and to serve an overlord. As far as he gives and serves other people, he does so of his own accord in order to be rewarded and served by the receivers. He exchanges goods and services, he does not do compulsory labor and does not pay tribute. He is certainly not independent. He depends on the other members of society. But this dependence is mutual. The buyer depends on the seller and the seller on the buyer.

There is no kind of freedom and liberty other than the kind which the market economy brings about. In a totalitarian hegemonic society the only freedom that is left to the individual, because it cannot be denied to him, is the freedom to commit suicide.

The state, the social apparatus of coercion and compulsion, is by necessity a hegemonic bond. If government were in a position to expand its power *ad libitum,* it could abolish the market economy and substitute for it all-round totalitarian socialism. In order to prevent this, it is necessary to curb the power of government. This is the task of all constitutions, bills of rights, and laws. This is the meaning of all the struggles which men have fought for liberty.

The detractors of liberty are in this sense right in calling it a "bourgeois" issue and in blaming the rights guaranteeing liberty for being negative. In the realm of state and government, liberty means restraint imposed upon the exercise of the police power.

Liberty and freedom are terms employed for the description of the social conditions of the individual members of a market society in which the power of the indispensable hegemonic bond, the state, is curbed lest the operation of the market be endangered. In a totalitarian system there is nothing to which the attribute "free" could be attached but the unlimited arbitrariness of the dictator.

There would be no need to dwell upon this obvious fact if the champions of the abolition of liberty had not purposely brought about a semantic confusion. They realized that it was hopeless for them to fight openly and sincerely for restraint and servitude. The notions liberty and freedom had such prestige that no propaganda could shake their popularity. Since time immemorial in the realm of Western civilization liberty has been considered as the most precious good. What gave to the West its eminence was precisely its concern about liberty, a social ideal foreign to the oriental peoples. The social philosophy of the Occident is essentially a philosophy of freedom. The main content of the history of Europe and the communities founded by European emigrants and their descendants in other parts of the world was the struggle for liberty. "Rugged" individualism is the signature of our civilization. No open attack upon the freedom of the individual had any prospect of success.

Thus the advocates of totalitarianism chose other tactics. They reversed the meaning of words. They call true or genuine liberty the condition of the individuals under a system in which they have no right other than to obey orders. They call themselves true *liberals* because they strive after such a social order. They call democracy the Russian methods of dictatorial government. They call the labor union methods of violence and coercion "industrial democracy." They call freedom of the press a state of affairs in which only the government is free to publish books and newspapers. They define liberty as the opportunity to do the "right" things, and, of course, they arrogate to themselves the determination of what is right and what is not. In their eyes government omnipotence means full liberty. To free the police power from all restraints is the true meaning of their struggle for freedom.

The market economy, say these self-styled liberals, grants liberty only to a parasitic class of exploiters, the bourgeoisie. These scoundrels enjoy the freedom to enslave the masses. The wage earner is not free; he must toil for the sole benefit of his masters, the employers. The capitalists appropriate to themselves what according to the inalienable rights of man should belong to the worker. Under socialism the worker will enjoy freedom and human dignity because he will no longer have to slave for a capitalist. Socialism means the emancipation of the common man, means freedom for all. It means, moreover, riches for all.

In spite of these serious shortcomings of the defenders of economic freedom it was impossible to fool all the people all the time about the essential features of socialism. The most fanatical planners were forced to admit that their projects involve the abolition of many freedoms people enjoy under capitalism and "pluto-democracy." Pressed hard, they resorted to a new subterfuge. The freedom to be abolished, they emphasize, is merely the spurious "economic" freedom of the capitalists that harms the common man. Outside the "economic sphere" freedom will not only be fully preserved, but considerably expanded. "Planning for Freedom" has lately become the most popular slogan of the champions of totalitarian government and the Russification of all nations.

The fallacy of this argument stems from the spurious distinction between two realms of human life and action, entirely separated from one another, viz., the "economic" sphere and the "noneconomic" sphere. With regard to this issue there is no need to add anything to what has been said in the preceding pages. However, there is another point to be stressed.

Freedom, as people enjoyed it in the democratic countries of Western civilization in the years of the old liberalism's triumph, was not a product of constitutions, bills of rights, laws, and statutes. Those documents aimed only at safeguarding liberty and freedom, firmly established by the operation of the market economy, against encroachments on the part of officeholders. No government and no civil law can guarantee and bring about freedom otherwise than by supporting and defending the fundamental institutions of the market economy. Government means always coercion and compulsion and is by necessity the opposite of liberty. Government is a guarantor of liberty and is compatible with liberty only if its range is adequately restricted to the preservation of economic freedom. Where there is no market economy, the best-intentioned provisions of constitutions and laws remain a dead letter.

The freedom of man under capitalism is an effect of competition. The worker does not depend on the good graces of an employer. If his employer discharges him, he finds another employer. The consumer is not at the mercy of the shopkeeper. He is free to patronize another shop if he likes. Nobody must kiss other people's hands or fear their disfavor. Interpersonal relations are businesslike. The exchange of goods and services is mutual; it is not a favor to sell or to buy, it is a transaction dictated by selfishness on either side.

It is true that in his capacity as a producer every man depends either directly—e.g., the entrepreneur—or indirectly—e.g., the hired worker—on the demands of the consumers. However, this dependence upon the supremacy of the consumers is not unlimited. If a man has a weighty reason for defying the sovereignty of the consumers, he can try it. There is in the range of the market a very substantial and effective right to resist oppression. Nobody is forced to go into the liquor industry or into a gun factory if his conscience objects. He may have to pay a price for his conviction; there are in this world no ends the attainment of which is gratuitous. But it is left to a man's own decision to choose between a material advantage and the call of what he believes to be his duty. In the market economy the individual alone is the supreme arbiter in matters of his satisfaction.

Capitalist society has no means of compelling a man to change his occupation or his place of work other than to reward those complying with the wants of the consumers by higher pay. It is precisely this kind of pressure which many people consider as unbearable and hope to see abolished under socialism. They are too dull to realize that the only alternative is to convey to the authorities full power to determine in what branch and at what place a man should work.

In his capacity as a consumer man is no less free. He alone decides what is more and what is less important for him. He chooses how to spend his money according to his own will.

The substitution of economic planning for the market economy removes all freedom and leaves to the individual merely the right to obey. The authority directing all economic matters controls all aspects of a man's life and activities. It is the only employer. All labor becomes compulsory labor because the employee must accept what the chief deigns to offer him. The economic tsar determines what and how much of each the consumer may consume. There is no sector of human life in which a decision is left to the individual's value judgments. The authority assigns a definite task to him, trains him for this job, and employs him at the place and in the manner it deems expedient.

As soon as the economic freedom which the market economy grants to its members is removed, all political liberties and bills of rights become humbug. Habeas corpus and trial by jury are a sham if, under the pretext of economic expediency, the authority has full power to relegate every citizen it dislikes to the arctic or to a desert and to assign him "hard labor" for life. Freedom of the press is a mere blind if the authority controls all printing offices and paper plants. And so are all the other rights of men.

III. INEQUALITY OF WEALTH AND INCOME

The inequality of individuals with regard to wealth and income is an essential feature of the market economy.

The fact that freedom is incompatible with equality of wealth and income has been stressed by many authors. There is no need to enter into an examination of the emotional arguments advanced in these writings. Neither is it necessary to raise the question of whether the renunciation of liberty could in itself guarantee the establishment of equality of wealth and income and whether or not a society could subsist on the basis of such an equality. Our task is merely to describe the role inequality plays in the framework of the market society.

In the market society direct compulsion and coercion are practiced only for the sake of preventing acts detrimental to social cooperation. For the rest individuals are not molested by the police power. The law-abiding citizen is free from the interference of jailers and hangmen. What pressure is needed to impel an individual to contribute his share to the cooperative effort of production is exercised by the price structure of the market. This pressure is indirect. It puts on each individual's contribution a premium graduated according to the value which the consumers attach to this contribution. In rewarding the individual's effort according to its value, it leaves to everybody the choice between a more or less complete utilization of his own faculties and abilities. This method can, of course, not eliminate the disadvantages of inherent personal inferiority. But it provides an incentive to everybody to exert his faculties and abilities to the utmost.

The only alternative to this financial pressure as exercised by the market is direct pressure and compulsion as exercised by the police power. The authorities must be entrusted with the task of determining the quantity and quality of work that each individual is bound to perform. As individuals are unequal with regard to their abilities, this requires an examination of their personalities on the part of the authorities. The individual becomes an inmate of a penitentiary, as it were, to whom a definite task is assigned. If he fails to achieve what the authorities have ordered him to do, he is liable to punishment.

It is important to realize in what the difference consists between direct pressure exercised for the prevention of crime and that exercised for the extortion of a definite performance. In the former case all that is required from the individual is to avoid a certain mode of conduct, precisely determined by law. As a rule it is easy to establish whether or not this interdiction has been observed. In the second case the individual is liable to accomplish a definite task; the law forces him toward an indefinite action, the determination of which is left to the decision of the executive power. The individual is bound to obey whatever the administration orders him to do. Whether or not the command issued by the executive power was adequate to his forces and faculties and whether or not he has complied with it to the best of his abilities is extremely difficult to establish. Every citizen is with regard to all aspects of his personality and with regard to all manifestations of his conduct subject to the decisions of the authorities. In the market economy in a trial before a penal court the prosecutor is obliged to produce sufficient evidence that the defendant is guilty. But in matters of the performance of compulsory work it devolves upon the defendant to prove that the task assigned to him was beyond his abilities or that he has done all that can be expected of him. The administrators combine in their persons the offices of the legislator, the executor of the law, the public prosecutor, and the judge. The defendants are entirely at their mercy. This is what people have in mind when speaking of lack of freedom.

No system of the social division of labor can do without a method that makes individuals responsible for their contributions to the joint productive effort. If this responsibility is not brought about by the price structure of the market and the inequality of wealth and income it begets, it must be enforced by the methods of direct compulsion as practiced by the police.

DAVID E. LILIENTHAL

6. The Case for Big Business*

To those individuals who are deeply distrustful of business in its effects on human welfare and values, the question whether Big Business has in fact brought benefits—both material and intangible—to the people of the country "has nothing to do with the case."

Such skepticism and even cynicism toward business and businessmen has articulate present-day spokesmen. They are the legatees of centuries of aversion, disbelief and rejection of the ethical and cultural standards of business-

* From David E. Lilienthal, *Big Business: A New Era* (Harper and Brothers, 1953). By permission.

men, expressed not only by political leaders but also by great imaginative writers—novelists, playwrights, satirists, poets and religious seers.

As a consequence a deeply held dogma exists; to those who are its current adherents, evidence of the actual benefits conferred by Big Business is neither persuasive nor even relevant. They will be no more persuaded by a recital of such testimony than will dogmatic extremists about government be willing to weigh, open-mindedly, whether or not creative consequences flow from some of the newer functions of government.

Our basic economic laws, as they are now construed and applied to Big Business, reflect very largely this dogmatic indifference to results and performance. The fact that a Big Business *in fact* is benefiting the country is waved aside as irrelevant in determining whether that business should be divided up or restrained. To them the important thing is the iron law, not the living breathing facts of life. The "rule of reason" of the earlier days of our fight on monopoly has become attenuated by the rule of dogma.

This rigidity, however, is not typical of the way the great body of laymen think. For by and large we are a country of reasonable and moderate people, always open to reason *on the basis of results*. We say "you've got to show me" —but we are ready to be shown.

In this book I direct myself to those who by habit look at the results, the actual consequences of Bigness as they appear in our daily lives.

BIGNESS FOR NATIONAL SECURITY

With the single exception of the effect of Bigness upon the individual, national security is the most important test of the principle and practice of Bigness in contemporary American life.

To the extent that the principle of Bigness, in our economic life, contributes in an affirmative and an indispensable way to the strengthening of our national security we should, by an explicit and affirmative national policy, encourage and protect that kind of Bigness.

In this decade of danger, productivity in turning out a prodigious flow of armament and developing new scientific weapons is the most important single test of the utility of Bigness in serving the national security. But it is not the sole test. Offsetting factors must be counted, too, in reaching a general judgment, or in particular cases. For example, is productivity by Bigness achieved at the expense of a physically dangerous overconcentration of industry in already highly concentrated areas? Is it at the expense of labor-management tensions of a hazardous kind? Does Big Business demand armament profits so exorbitant as to destroy confidence and support for the defense effort among many people? These are relevant factors in judging the effectiveness of Big Business.

Whether Bigness is an impediment to national security, or whether it is in most vital regions literally indispensable to it, should be measured by thinking of "national security" in the broadest sense. It is not only a matter of the manufacture of tanks and armor plate and bazookas and all the tens of thousands of items required for our military forces and those of our friends who depend upon us for arms. Our security also requires high productivity of the "civilian" goods and services essential for the health and vigor of our country. Moreover, we are now agreed, in principle at least, that economic aid to free peoples in Europe and Asia is in a very immediate sense part of the strengthening of our own security.

It is in these broader terms that I think we should weigh the issue of Bigness and national security.

My own opportunities for close observation in this area cover the fifteen-year period of 1937-1952. During all but the last two years of this fifteen-year period I was in the public service, with responsibility for some aspects of national security.

My work both in TVA and the Atomic Energy Commission involved the production of strictly military defense materials (in TVA, ammonium nitrate and elemental phosphorus, both munitions; in AEC, atomic bombs). It also involved the widest ramifications of a defense program, such as planning for and producing electric power for aluminum, finding ways of stimulating food production, and so on. Dealings with hundreds of different kinds of business organizations, involving in total several billions of dollars, on specific and concrete matters of production, were the grist of the work of myself and my associates.

From my own experience I conclude that Big Business and the principles and techniques of Bigness are indispensable to our security. Accordingly, I believe that our national laws, our national climate of opinion, and the attitude of our public servants should be consistent with that conclusion.

This is not always the case. I can illustrate by a single experience, out of many, from my work as chairman of the Atomic Energy Commission. The case involves a vital security interest, namely the last step in the production of atomic bombs, which is the fabrication of the components, and their assembly into a workable weapon.

On January 1, 1947, the new civilian Atomic Energy Commission took over the responsibilities of atomic weapon development and production from the Army's Manhattan District. By this time many of the great scientists who had actually fabricated the first bombs had returned to their various laboratories. But a superb scientific team remained in Los Alamos, on a mountaintop in New Mexico, carrying on the fundamental work. We new commissioners took our first look into the secret bomb-storage areas.

The result was a shock. The substantial stockpile of atom bombs we and the top military assumed was there, in readiness, did not exist. Furthermore, the production facilities that might enable us to produce quantities of atomic bombs so engineered that they would not continue to require a Ph.D. in physics to handle them in the field, likewise did not exist. No quantity production of these weapons was possible under the existing "handicraft" setup.

To redesign the bomb so it would be a genuine field weapon, to carry forward fundamental work on new designs, to design and build a plant in which this infinitely complex thing could be put into quantity industrial-type production, and then to operate such a factory required talents in an unusual and remarkable combination.

First of all, this task required *industrial* experience. What we wanted was not something that could be done in a laboratory alone, but in a production center, with factory techniques, factory mechanics (of a high order of skill, it is true) and factory management.

Second, what we wanted done required men of a high order of ability in scientific fundamentals, equal to any in the universities but also experienced in dealing with industrial problems and with industrial associates.

Third, this task called for a special kind of operating experience in dealing with the technical characteristics of systems used in these weapons, and others then actively under development, new weapons which have since been proof-tested.

Most important of all, these three capabilities of research, industrial techniques and operation had to be *combined* in the same team, with experience in working together as a unit.

To go out and create such an organization was out of the question. There was not time.

It was our "hunch" that there was such an organization in existence—the Bell System, that is, the team consisting of the American Telephone & Telegraph Company and its associated operating companies, together with the Bell Laboratories, a research and development institution, and Western Electric, the manufacturing arm of the system.

A careful analysis confirmed this initial "hunch." I spent Decoration Day of 1949 with the president of A. T. & T., the late Leroy Wilson. On behalf of President Truman and the Atomic Energy Commission, I requested that A. T. & T., Bell Laboratories and Western Electric, as a team, take the heavy responsibility which I have here summarized. Mr. Wilson said that his company was already committed to important defense work, and while it did not relish another great load such as this, the Bell System would accept the assignment as in the national interest.

Then he said (and I paraphrase only): the government is asking the Bell System to put its research-manufacturing-operation setup to work on this task because it is a combination of these things that you regard as essential to the nation's security. I must tell you, he said, that a few months ago the government, through the Antitrust Division of the Department of Justice, filed a suit under the Sherman Anti-trust Act to sever the Western Electric from the Bell System, as well as to split up Western Electric into several parts. What the government asks in this lawsuit, Mr. Wilson indicated, is that the courts break up and dissolve the very organizational unity and size you say this vital security job requires. The fairness of telephone rates, including the cost of Western Electric equipment, Mr. Wilson said, is regulated by the states and the Federal Communications Commission. What the Antitrust Division charges is essentially that this team we have put together is too big, and should be made smaller.

The Bell System took over the Sandia operation (as this part of atomic weapons production is called) not long after my meeting with Mr. Wilson. It has been responsible for it ever since. The stepped-up production of atomic bombs and the favorable results in the tests of new weapons, as officially announced from time to time, are, I am sure, in considerable measure due to the unique contribution of the Bell System and of the great scientific talents in the Los Alamos laboratory.

The antitrust suit to break up the Bell System is pending, and is being prepared for trial.

There may be those who would say: But in the end the Bell System may win its case in the courts; and in any case, win or not, it certainly will be five years or more before a final decision to sever the Bell System is rendered in the Supreme Court. How then is the atomic bomb program injured *now*, how is our nation's security impaired *now*, by a possible dismemberment that may not transpire for years, if ever?

The answer may not be obvious to anyone not aware of the prodigious human demands on a company's management that preparation for such a great litigation entails, or of the morale consequences on management of the possibility hanging over them of an enforced reorganization of the whole enterprise.

A terrible pressure of work falls upon the most responsible men both in management and in technical pursuits in such large organizations as A. T. & T. and the many others, public and private, that carry much of the heavy job of keeping this country's technical weapons at the highest possible level. The figures of American production of civilian goods *plus* prodigious technical feats of armament need to be translated into terms of the toll they exact on men.

The preparation of the company's side of a suit such as the Bell case, involving as it does the technical side of the business and going back into transactions and decisions of many years ago, requires countless hours of work by the top-level executives and technicians who participated in those decisions. Since men of these attainments and experience are few in number, since they cannot wholly delegate this task of preparation to others (it is they who know most of the surrounding circumstances), both the preparation for a crucial lawsuit and the urgent work of the government's defense program suffer, inevitably, for even the strongest men have limits to their stamina.

This example of the Bell System—and there are other recent instances, with grave implications for national security—presents one of the strongest possible reasons for an early and rigorous re-examination of our whole public policy and public attitudes toward Bigness.

BIGNESS FOR INDIVIDUAL SECURITY

Just as we insist that our country be secure, in a military sense, against the hazards that lie in wait for us as a nation, we have also, in more recent years, adopted another kind of security as a goal: individual economic security. How has Bigness as a characteristic of business furthered this objective?

Take year-round employment for industrial workers, as an example. Our desire for a stable and humane social system leads us to seek to reach this most difficult of objectives.

Here and there quite small businesses, by superior management, have made excellent headway in this direction.

As a broad proposition, however (in industries of seasonal demand in particular), Bigness is necessary to accomplish the necessary planning of production, and the requisite influence upon purchaser habits and distribution practices. To smooth out the dips of employment it is often necessary to be able to stockpile or accumulate large inventories or to shift from one kind of product to another for a temporary period, or to move into markets in widely separated parts of the country or even of the world. Only a business of substantial size can do this.

A stable and humane society is one that recognizes the individual's natural desire for a measure of security and peace of mind in old age. Such a society will favor an industrial system that can provide extensive and liberal pensions. Such pension systems, ideally, should, I think, be designed as much as possible to be a cost of the particular business, rather than chiefly a cost assessed against everyone through taxes. In this way it becomes a challenge to management's skill, and a part of the system of incentives and rewards by which management and organized labor can improve the general health of the particular business or industry.

Some small business units have provided excellent pension systems. But here again, as a broad proposition, the outstanding pensions plans are those of larger enterprises. That these plans often did not originate with enlightened management, that their adoption often required the force of legislation (opposed by many big concerns) and the pressure of union activity, is certainly true; but the results are now the important thing. The resulting pension plans are good, and no one but extremists will ever try to do away with them.

As a youth I lived and worked for a time in Gary, Indiana. In the great U.S. Steel mills at that time the working hours were 13½ hours a day one week, and 11½ hours the alternate week, *seven days a week*. Now, due largely to unionization, governmental action and managerial enlightenment, steel-workers at Gary receive retirement pensions—to say nothing of short hours, high wages and vacations with pay. Big Business of even a generation ago and today operate in two entirely different worlds.

One of the most remarkable and most heartening chapters of social history is the evolution of the relations between employers and employees in American industry to their present stage of development.

In this country at mid-century the idea of "class war" as a means of improving the lot of workers—an idea that once had a striving start—has almost entirely disappeared. Efforts by management to suppress and destroy independent labor unions by almost any means, including violence, espionage, corruption of union officers and economic coercion, have become rare.

With all its painful and obvious limitations, this record is one of the greatest achievements of American democracy. Moreover, to the extent that the individual worker is increasingly protected from the exercise of *arbitrary* power of his supervisor or employer—the very essence of freedom in the earning of one's living—and has an effective voice in the running of his union's affairs, this accomplishment to date, crude and unfinished as it is, takes its place with some of the greatest in the history of individual freedom.

But this development is only at its beginning. There will be setbacks now and then; but the most constructive and creative period is still before us.

Taking the picture as a whole, the most potent leadership—in unions and in management—in this marked social change has been found in companies of substantial size. (The outstanding exception is probably the women's and men's clothing industry, where small units are common.) A generation ago about the worst instances of suppression and coercion by management and class-warfare tactics and violence by unions occurred in our largest industries —steel and automobiles, for example. Today, the reverse is true.

On May 23, 1950, an agreement was entered into between one of America's biggest of Big Businesses, General Motors, and the United Auto Workers (CIO). In a number of respects this contract represents a pioneer undertaking. Its terms, for example, is without precedent: for five years both the business and the union agree to abide by the agreement "without reopening by either party for any cause." This agreement embodied an explicit recognition by General Motors of the dollars-and-cents value of responsibility by a labor union. Charles Wilson, head of G.M., was not niggardly in giving credit to the union; the company could never have made the agreement, he said, had the union not "demonstrated . . . its sincerity and responsibility in carrying out agreements in the past."

The agreement included provisions against hazards to life and health, and for pensions, hospital coverage and vacations. In addition to an adjust-ment of wages each three months in accordance with changes in the cost of living, the contract included a much-praised and also much-criticized "improvement factor." Four cents per hour was to be added to all wages, annually, throughout the period of the contract. But the *reasoning* behind this provision gives it its long-range importance. The contracting parties, management and labor, used the following words in the agreement itself:

> The annual improvement factor provided herein recognizes that a continuing improvement in the standard of living of employees depends upon technological progress, better tools, methods, processes and equipment and a co-operative attitude on the part of all parties in such progress. It further recognizes the principle that to produce more with the same amount of human effort is a sound economic and social objective.

Commenting on this provision the president of G.M. said: "Both parties completely accept the principle of progress, including the use of machines, mechanical power and better organization, better working conditions and better arrangement of the work in order not to waste human effort."

PRODUCTIVITY AND BIGNESS

My responsibility, as a public servant, for industrial operations, and my study of areas outside my own direct experience have convinced me that the encouragement of Bigness is essential if we are to maintain the highest levels of production and the lowest costs of *basic industrial commodities*.

Iron- and steelmaking are examples. In this country, until about a hundred years ago, iron- and steelmaking were carried on by many plants. Each of these numerous plants was small. As a consequence of technical developments and the great expansion in the market for all kinds of steel products, this situation changed completely. As we produced more and more tons of pig iron, the *number* of the iron- and steelmaking furnaces decreased, and the size of the individual furnaces grew. This trend continues until our day, when we have witnessed a spectacular increase in the total productiveness of the country and in the size of the individual furnaces.

As things stand today, and for the next decade or so at least, to get high productivity and low cost of iron and steel, we must have big machinery—even bigger than at present perhaps. This requires the resources and managerial scope of big companies, with earnings adequate to attract the vast capital expenditures required.

Much the same thing is true in another field of production, one upon which most of America's modern industry—and her security and living standards—is built. I refer to the production of electrical energy, public and private, whether created by water power, or by using coal, gas or oil as the fuel for operating a steam turbine. (This is, of course, not a competitive industry, but one of legal, regulated monopoly.)

We eat up electric power at an unbelievable rate; in my opinion this trend will continue for an almost indefinite period.

It is not easy to comprehend the change in our *rate* of use of electricity. In 1936, TVA's Norris Dam was considered a large addition to the nation's power supply. The late Wendell Willkie vigorously contended, in 1933, that Norris Dam should not be built because it would create a big "surplus" of electricity. The water wheels and power generators, two in number, had a total capacity of 100,000 kilowatts.

Norris Dam is only one—and not one of the very largest—of more than a score of such structures built since that time by TVA. Today, to meet prodigious atomic energy plant requirements, TVA is also installing new coal-burning, power-generating facilities (the individual generators now grown from 50,000 to 200,000 kilowatts with the most recent order being for 250,-000 kilowatts in a single machine) that in total represent more power capacity than *thirty* Norris Dams. Just to keep up with the normal increase in annual needs of power, for the same region for which Norris Dam was built, will require new power plants the equivalent of *seven* Norris Dams *each year*.

I cite these figures from this one relatively small region only as illustrative of what is going on by way of increasing demands for electricity in almost every other part of the country. By 1970, America's electrical energy output will probably be more than doubled over 1950.

It is at last becoming clear that electricity is so fundamental to the life of the nation that no one should ever concern himself about a "surplus." Electricity in great quantities, at low cost, creates its own market, creates new uses and new productivity, which in turn creates further need for more electricity.

These comments about electric supply go to the heart of the issue of Bigness. For it takes Bigness of individual power units, Bigness of power-supplying enterprises and Bigness of electric equipment companies to create the huge pools of power we need, timed for our needs, and at low cost.

To build turbines and generators of this mammoth size and their ever-bigger transmission equipment requires Bigness in the manufacturing company—Bigness of research, development and production. To operate units of this size and their transmission systems that are required to move the blocks of power calls for a big electric enterprise, whether it be a TVA or Bonneville Administration, a Pacific Gas & Electric or a Commonwealth Edison.

Similar considerations apply to basic minerals. The maintenance of the United States as a going concern requires almost unbelievably large quantities of iron ore, copper, bauxite (for aluminum), petroleum, coal, phosphate and other raw minerals. It is not simply that it would be "a nice thing" to have these. We *must* have them to live, and in quantities that not many years ago would have seemed out of the question. But looking ahead a single generation, to the year 1975, the prospect for basic life-essential minerals presents a challenging picture.

The problem has three principal parts.

First, we must explore for and discover and develop our remaining raw minerals lying within the United States, and do so in the most effective way possible. For their development the best engineering and business practice is required.

Second, where our American reserves of high-grade materials are nearing an end—iron and copper ores are outstanding examples—we must develop technical means of utilizing ores of constantly lower and lower concentration, at costs that are bearable. Well utilized, we have the technical and business talents to stretch our low-grade home supplies for a very long time. This will require huge outlays of private capital, and call for great adjustments within industry and in many communities.

Third, we need to increase the already vast activity directed toward exploring, developing and transporting to our shores raw materials mined in other parts of the world.

To meet this major and overshadowing problem of basic resources our government, of course, has vital roles to play; but for end results we must, in the main, rely upon Big Business. The magnitude of private resources required for this task, the managerial complexity of the problem and the high responsibilities assumed when operations go on in other countries— such as the development of oil in the Middle East and of oil and iron ore in Venezuela—make this problem essentially one for very large mature enterprises. They need to be well led, by responsible and modern-minded men— generally but not universally the case today. But in any case, they must be big.

BIGNESS AND THE DISTRIBUTION OF GOODS AND CREDIT

As I have traveled about the parts of the world which are clinical cases of poverty, uncleanliness and the most undemocratic disparity between classes —the most utterly poor and the most conspicuously rich—what impressed me greatly was not lack of natural resources or favorable climate, or an uneducable people: it was that these people have suffered most grievously from lack of a sensible and efficient system of *distribution* of goods.

America's progress, economically, can be told in considerable measure by our advance in the techniques of distribution, as the unhappy condition of the Middle East or Latin America is attributable in substantial measure to a debilitating and static system of distribution. The terrible toll of the poor man's substance that their miserable distribution systems exact is one of the saddest commentaries on the lives of at least half the people of the world today. If a fraction of the indignation expended on the unquestionably ar-chaic land laws of these backward countries was directed toward improving the inefficient distribution system, faster progress would be made all along the line. And what is the most obvious functional characteristic of distribu-tion in these regions? It is the *smallness* of individual units.

The story in America and in Britain and parts of Europe is different. Big Business must receive the major credit for leadership in these great achieve-ments in distribution.

When buying a product at an American store, Mr. and Mrs. Consumer have to pay about as much for the cost of getting that commodity from the factory or farm as it cost to produce it in the first place. The product must usually weave its way through a maze of wholesalers, jobbers, distributors and retail stores until at last it slides across the store counter, or the delivery truck deposits it at the customer's door. Nothing is more important to the budget and living standards of the average family than ways and means, if possible, of cutting these costs of distribution.

To whittle down this high proportion of the "cost of living" involved in getting their product into peoples hands is a major preoccupation of a large segment of American men of business.

It is here—in distribution—that Bigness has made what is perhaps its most spectacular change in the face of everyday American life. I refer, of course, to the chain store. It is only somewhat more than one generation ago that the distribution of goods was almost entirely in the hands of local "department stores" or small independent retail stores.

Once the independent merchant was the prime representative of middle-class life in most parts of the United States. The waning of his importance has had important effects on economic thinking and on politics. How deeply—even bitterly—this strong and highly respected group of merchants resented the inroads of the chain store is difficult to understand in a time when the A&P, the Penney Stores, Sears, Roebuck, Montgomery Ward and a multitude of other chain establishments are to be found in every city and town in America. That feeling still persists to some degree, but cannot compare in intensity to that which I remember as a youth in a Midwestern small town of forty years ago.

How could it happen that the chain-store system would grow and prosper despite the great political strength and warm popular sympathy enjoyed by the independent merchant and grocer?

It is difficult to escape the conclusion that, on the whole, Bigness won be-cause it did a good job for the buying public.

Bigness, in getting goods to people, has proved to the customer that it can cut the cost of distribution for essential commodities. Big Business in distribution has helped mightily to make foods once seasonal or local or only for the rich widely available to almost all economic groups in all corners of the country. It has been a main factor in improving the human and hygienic conditions under which all goods, and particularly foods, are supplied to people. These are by no means "merely" economic gains: these represent practical workaday applications of democratic aspirations.

In my opinion, therefore, those antitrust prosecutions and proceedings, and actions in Congress, which, in effect, are leveled against the mass production and mass distribution of goods by chain-store systems, in the end will fail. There is a simple reason for this: Bigness in distribution is in the consumer's interest, by and large.

It has also been in the interest of employees. Take the number of hours stores used to be open for business in the days before the chain stores, when the owner-operated small store was the rule. They were, characteristically, open from early morning until eight or nine o'clock at night, even later on Saturdays; the hours of labor of the proprietor and the "clerks" were outrageously long and wearying.

What of the part played by the chain-store method of distribution in improving the hygienic conditions in the distribution of foodstuffs? Today, in the chain-store period of grocery stores, very few foods are sold in bulk. An actual cracker barrel, symbol of social "argufying" in the small-town grocery store, is no longer to be seen; and similarly the sugar barrel, the tea and coffee bin, the bulk sale of butter and lard and a hundred other staples. We have Bigness largely to thank for this major improvement. A similar comment could be made about the great improvement in cleanliness in handling meat and milk today, compared to the days when these products were distributed almost exclusively by the small operator of a butcher shop or a "creamery."

My own observation has been that in many—though not in all—areas, the chain-store technique of organization has in fact reduced the cost of distribution of many products, and improved the human setting of the distribution of goods in our country. The personal relation between the storekeeper and the customer, and the active participation of local store managers in community affairs—where most chain establishments have in the past certainly fallen short—is apparently on its way toward improvement.

It is now quite well understood that mass distribution has contributed greatly to the competitive system and to our standard of living. But the beneficial effect of improved methods of distribution upon *production* of these goods is little comprehended. The most notable instance I know of is that of Sears Roebuck & Company. Although Sears itself has grown bigger and bigger, both as merchandiser and manufacturer, its policies have resulted in the creation of many new, small manufacturers, and greater stability for existing smaller concerns from which it buys; these suppliers now number about 20,000. Departing from an earlier preoccupation with price alone, Sears has come also to stress the quality of the products of its suppliers.

Almost of equal importance has been the effect of this huge business in improving the management skills of small manufacturers from whom they buy the thousands of items one finds in their catalogue and in their retail outlets throughout the world. This development of Sears' policy, both here and abroad, has done much for the modernizing of the management of smaller manufacturers, teaching them how to do a better job of production, cost keeping, etc., and making available to them the benefits of research and engineering.

What Bigness has done to improve the distribution of goods it shows promise of doing in the quite different but equally vital area of the improved "distribution" of credit.

Making credit and banking services more responsive to Mr. Average Citizen's needs, making them serve him more intelligently and at low cost, are gains Bigness can render that may prove as significant for the public and for business enterprise as those secured through the advent and influence of the chain-store system.

The small businessman, in particular, has need of a banking and credit system big enough to spread risks and thus keep down the cost of credit to them, equipped with enough specialized knowledge and services to help him with his own special credit problems, and localized into even the smallest community. Such credit facilities may mean for the small enterprise the difference between failing and prospering.

I have remarked that in poverty-stricken countries smallness is the mark of the corrosive and inefficient systems of distribution of goods; so it is also with their banking and credit systems. Usurious moneylenders, who prey on the needs of the helpless and who contribute little to the country's development, are the rule; banking and credit as a constructive, imaginative and enterprise-irrigating function rarely exists. It was a pernicious credit system that as much as any single cause held back the people of the South for almost fifty years after the Civil War, tying many of them to a decaying cotton economy, delaying the growth of a diversified agriculture and retarding industry and commerce. Such a suffocating credit system was not a plot hatched by a big banking combine; it was the product of small, provincial credit monopolies.

The American credit picture today is in marked contrast to this sterile and inhumane picture. It is characterized by remarkable and increasing diversity and freedom of choice for the man or business in need of credit. There are now several places to which an individual may freely turn for his credit needs, whether for personal loans—funds for a new house or for a new refrigerator—or for his small business or his farm. There are many alternatives open to businessmen or public bodies if the credit required is very large, for a mine or manufacturing plant or a super-highway system or city water-supply.

Never have there been more avenues of credit, private, mutual nonprofit, co-operative, public; never has there been a more intelligent, creative and responsive concept of the role of finance in the building of the community and region.

Bigness in banking has helped bring this to pass, whether the banking is commercial banking, mutual, co-operative or public. An outstanding example of Bigness in private commercial banking in its modern role of aiding in the development of a whole region is afforded by a glance at branch banking.

This form of banking is by no means a novel one confined to the United States; in Canada and Britain, for example, it has long been standard and successful practice. The American talent for large-scale enterprises, and for the control of their abuses, indicates that branch banking has an even greater future in the United States. The best known, oldest and largest example is the Bank of America in the state of California.

California's history, in the past forty years, has been one of extraordinary growth in population and in wealth. In this unique development the diversity of men's ways of making a livelihood and therefore the demands made upon its credit system moves over as wide a spectrum as the diversity of California's climate, from the high Sierras to the Imperial Valley. This has required financing of every conceivable need, from the building of countless homes for a burgeoning population to the requirements of the mining industry, from avocado ranches to tuna canning, from cotton raising (a relatively new crop) to the special needs of an old industry, shipping, from the need for credit for Mickey Mouse and the cartoon movie industry to individual consumer credit for washing machines, from funds for huge metropolitan water systems to small local community paving programs.

Bigness played a determining role in the supply and distribution of credit for a large part of this great story of American development. The largest bank in terms of resources in the United States—seven and a half billions of dollars—is not in "old" New York City but in "new" California, the Bank of America National Trust and Savings Association. Within the state the Bank of America has developed the branch bank system to a degree not known elsewhere in the country. The number of branches is impressive; as of September 30, 1952, there were 537 branches throughout California. There is hardly a community so small that one does not find in it a branch of the Bank of America. The sheer number of its deposit accounts—5,111,-524—and the variety of its services, reflect a most intensive use of private banking facilities and a varied utilization of credit as an integral part of the development of California.

JOHN KENNETH GALBRAITH

7. *The Theory of Countervailing Power**

On the night of November 2, 1907, the elder Morgan played solitaire in his library while the panic gripped Wall Street. When the other bankers had divided up the cost of saving the tottering Trust Company of America, he presided at the signing of the agreement, authorized the purchase of the Tennessee Coal & Iron Company by the Steel Corporation to encourage the market, cleared the transaction with President Roosevelt and the panic was over. There, as legend has preserved and doubtless improved the story, was a man with power a self-respecting man could fear.

A mere two decades later, in the crash of 1929, it was evident that the Wall Street bankers were as helpless as everyone else. Their effort in the autumn of that year to check the collapse in the market is now recalled as an amusing anecdote; the heads of the New York Stock Exchange and the National City Bank fell into the toils of the law and the first went to prison; the son of the Great Morgan went to a Congressional hearing in Washington and acquired fame, not for his authority, but for his embarrassment when a circus midget was placed on his knee.

As the banker, as a symbol of economic power, passed into the shadows his place was taken by the giant industrial corporation. The substitute was much more plausible. The association of power with the banker had always depended on the somewhat tenuous belief in a "money trust"—on the notion that the means for financing the initiation and expansion of business enterprises was concentrated in the hands of a few men. The ancestry of this idea was in Marx's doctrine of finance capital; it was not susceptible to statistical or other empirical verification at least in the United States.

By contrast, the fact that a substantial proportion of all production was concentrated in the hands of a relatively small number of huge firms was readily verified. That three or four giant firms in an industry might exercise power analogous to that of a monopoly, and not different in consequences, was an idea that had the most respectable of ancestry in classical economics. So as the J. P. Morgan Company left the stage, it was replaced by the two hundred largest corporations—giant devils in company strength. Here was economic power identified by the greatest and most conservative tradition in economic theory. Here was power to control the prices the citizen paid, the wages he received, and which interposed the most formidable of ob-

* From John Kenneth Galbraith, *American Capitalism: The Concept of Countervailing Power* (Houghton Mifflin Company, Boston, 1952). By permission.

stacles of size and experience to the aspiring new firm. What more might it accomplish were it to turn its vast resources to corrupting politics and controlling access to public opinion?

Yet, as was so dramatically revealed to be the case with the omnipotence of the banker in 1929, there are considerable gaps between the myth and the fact. The comparative importance of a small number of great corporations in the American economy cannot be denied except by those who have a singular immunity to statistical evidence or striking capacity to manipulate it. In principle the American is controlled, livelihood and soul, by the large corporation; in practice he seems not to be completely enslaved. Once again the danger is in the future; the present is still tolerable. Once again there may be lessons from the present which, if learned, will save us in the future.

II

As with social efficiency, and its neglect of technical dynamics, the paradox of the unexercised power of the large corporation begins with an important oversight in the underlying economic theory. In the competitive model—the economy of many sellers each with a small share of the total market—the restraint on the private exercise of economic power was provided by other firms on the same side of the market. It was the eagerness of competitors to sell, not the complaints of buyers, that saved the latter from spoliation. It was assumed, no doubt accurately, that the nineteenth-century textile manufacturer who overcharged for his product would promptly lose his market to another manufacturer who did not. If all manufacturers found themselves in a position where they could exploit a strong demand, and mark up their prices accordingly, there would soon be an inflow of new competitors. The resulting increase in supply would bring prices and profits back to normal.

As with the seller who was tempted to use his economic power against the customer, so with the buyer who was tempted to use it against his labor or suppliers. The man who paid less than prevailing wage would lose his labor force to those who paid the worker his full (marginal) contribution to earnings. In all cases the incentive to socially desirable behavior was provided by the competitor. It was to the same side of the market and thus to competition that economists came to look for the self-regulatory mechanism of the economy.

They also came to look to competition exclusively and in formal theory still do. The notion that there might be another regulatory mechanism in the economy has been almost completely excluded from economic thought. Thus, with the widespread disappearance of competition in its classical form and its replacement by the small group of firms if not in overt, at least in conventional or tacit collusion, it was easy to suppose that since competition had disappeared, all effective restraint on private power had disappeared. Indeed this conclusion was all but inevitable if no search was made for other restraints and so complete was the preoccupation with competition that none was made.

In fact, new restraints on private power did appear to replace competition. They were nurtured by the same process of concentration which impaired or destroyed competition. But they appeared not on the same side of the market but on the opposite side, not with competitors but with customers or suppliers. It will be convenient to have a name for this counterpart of competition and I shall call it *countervailing power*.[1]

To begin with a broad and somewhat too dogmatically stated proposition, private economic power is held in check by the countervailing power of those who are subject to it. The first begets the second. The long trend toward concentration of industrial enterprise in the hands of a relatively few firms has brought into existence not only strong sellers, as economists have supposed, but also strong buyers as they have failed to see. The two develop together, not in precise step but in such manner that there can be no doubt that the one is in response to the other.

The fact that a seller enjoys a measure of monopoly power, and is reaping a measure of monopoly return as a result, means that there is an inducement to those firms from whom he buys or those to whom he sells to develop the power with which they can defend themselves against exploitation. It means also that there is a reward to them, in the form of a share of the gains of their opponents' market power, if they are able to do so. In this way the existence of market power creates an incentive to the organization of another position of power that neutralizes it.

The contention I am here making is a formidable one. It comes to this: Competition which, at least since the time of Adam Smith, has been viewed as the autonomous regulator of economic activity and as the only available regulatory mechanism apart from the state, has, in fact, been superseded. Not entirely, to be sure. There are still important markets where the power of the firm as (say) a seller is checked or circumscribed by those who provide a similar or a substitute product or service. This, in the broadest sense that can be meaningful, is the meaning of competition. The role of the buyer on the other side of such markets is essentially a passive one. It consists in looking for, perhaps asking for, and responding to the best bargain. The active restraint is provided by the competitor who offers, or threatens to offer, a better bargain. By contrast, in the typical modern market of few sellers, the active restraint is provided not by competitors but from the

---

[1] I have been tempted to coin a new word for this which would have the same convenience as the term competition and had I done so my choice would have been "countervailence." However, the phrase "countervailing power" is more descriptive and does not have the raw sound of any newly fabricated word.

other side of the market by strong buyers. Given the convention against price competition, it is the role of the competitor that becomes passive.

It was always one of the basic presuppositions of competition that market power exercised in its absence would invite the competitors who would eliminate such exercise of power. In other words competition was regarded as a *self-generating* regulatory force. The doubt whether this was in fact so after a market had been pre-empted by a few large sellers, after entry of new firms had become difficult and after existing firms had accepted a convention against price competition, was what destroyed the faith in competition as a regulatory mechanism. Countervailing power is also a self-generating force and this is a matter of great importance. Something, although not very much, could be claimed for the regulatory role of the strong buyer in relation to the market power of sellers, did it happen that, as an accident of economic development, such strong buyers were frequently juxtaposed to strong sellers. However it is far more important that, as with the ancient presupposition concerning competition, the regulatory role of the strong buyer, in relation to the market power of the strong seller, is also self-generating. As noted, power on one side of a market creates both the need for, and the prospect of reward to, the exercise of countervailing power from the other side.[2] In the market of small numbers, the self-generating power of competition is a chimera. That of countervailing power, by contrast, is readily assimilated to the common sense of the situation and its existence, once we have learned to look for it, is readily subject to empirical verification.

Market power can be exercised by strong buyers against weak sellers as well as by strong sellers against weak buyers. In the competitive model, competition acted as a restraint on both kinds of exercise of power. This is also the case with countervailing power. In turning to its practical manifestations, it will be convenient, in fact, to begin with a case where it is exercised by weak sellers against strong buyers.

III

The operation of countervailing power is to be seen with the greatest clarity in the labor market where it is also most fully developed. Because of his comparative immobility, the worker has long been highly vulnerable to

---

[2] This has been one of the reasons I have rejected the terminology of bilateral monopoly in characterizing this phenomenon. As bilateral monopoly is treated in economic literature, it is an adventitious occurrence. This, obviously, misses the point and it is one of the reasons that the investigations of bilateral monopoly, which one would have thought might have been an avenue to the regulatory mechanisms here isolated, have in fact been a blind alley. However, this line of investigation has also been sterilized by the confining formality of the assumptions of monopolistic and (more rarely) oligopolistic motivation and behavior with which it has been approached. (Cf. for example, William H. Nicholls, *Imperfect Competition within Agricultural Industries,* Ames, Iowa: 1941, pp. 58 ff.) As noted later, oligopoly facilitates the exercise of countervailing market power by enabling the strong buyer to play one seller off against another.

private economic power. The customer of any particular steel mill, at the turn of the century, could always take himself elsewhere if he felt he was being overcharged. Or he could exercise his sovereign privilege of not buying steel at all. The worker had no comparable freedom if he felt he was being underpaid. Normally he could not move and he had to have work. Not often has the power of one man over another been used more callously than in the American labor market after the rise of the large corporation. As late as the early twenties, the steel industry worked a twelve-hour day and seventy-two-hour week with an incredible twenty-four-hour stint every fortnight when the shift changed.

No such power is exercised today and for the reason that its earlier exercise stimulated the counteraction that brought it to an end. In the ultimate sense it was the power of the steel industry, not the organizing abilities of John L. Lewis and Philip Murray, that brought the United Steel Workers into being. The economic power that the worker faced in the sale of his labor—the competition of many sellers dealing with few buyers—made it necessary that he organize for his own protection. There were rewards to the power of the steel companies in which, when he had successfully developed countervailing power, he could share.

As a general though not invariable rule there are strong unions in the United States only where markets are served by strong corporations. And it is not an accident that the large automobile, steel, electrical, rubber, farm-machinery and non-ferrous metal-mining and smelting companies all bargain with powerful CIO unions. Not only has the strength of the corporations in these industries made it necessary for workers to develop the protection of countervailing power, it has provided unions with the opportunity for getting something more as well. If successful they could share in the fruits of the corporation's market power. By contrast there is not a single union of any consequence in American agriculture, the country's closest approach to the competitive model. The reason lies not in the difficulties in organization; these are considerable, but greater difficulties in organization have been overcome. The reason is that the farmer has not possessed any power over his labor force, and at least until recent times has not had any rewards from market power, which it was worth the while of a union to seek. As an interesting verification of the point, in the Great Valley of California, the large farmers of that area have had considerable power vis-à-vis their labor force. Almost uniquely in the United States, that region has been marked by persistent attempts at organization by farm workers.

The other industries which are not marked by any high degree of concentration, and accordingly are not especially powerful in their labor market, do not normally have strong unions. The textile industry, boot and shoe manufacture, lumbering and other forest industries in most parts of the country, and smaller wholesale and retail enterprises, are all cases in point.

I do not advance the theory of countervailing power as a monolithic explanation of trade-union organization; in the case of bituminous-coal mining and the clothing industry, for example, the unions have emerged as a supplement to the weak market position of the operators and manufacturers. They have assumed price- and market-regulating functions that are the normal functions of management. Nevertheless, as an explanation of the incidence of trade-union strength in the American economy, the theory of countervailing power clearly fits the broad contours of experience.

IV

The labor market serves admirably to illustrate the incentives to the development of countervailing power and it is of great importance in this market. However, its development, in response to positions of market power, is pervasive in the economy. As a regulatory device one of its most important manifestations is in the relation of the large retailer to the firms from which it buys. The way in which countervailing power operates in these markets is worth examining in some detail.

One of the seemingly harmless simplifications of formal economic theory has been the assumption that producers of consumers' goods sell their products directly to consumers. All business units are held, for this reason, to have broadly parallel interests. Each buys labor and materials, combines them and passes them along to the public at prices that, in some sense, maximize returns. Were this in fact the case, the lot of the consumer would be an unhappy one.

In practice, goods pass to retailers whose interests, normally,[3] are at sharp variance with those of their suppliers. The typical retailer is deeply concerned with his volume of sales. This is uniquely important for minimizing inventory risk, it is a prime factor in the prestige of the concern, and, of course, it is one of the dimensions of profit. The convention that excludes cutthroat price competition—in the case of retailers the cutting of gross margins—is observed by retailers as by other firms. Nonetheless, lower prices— a low level in general as well as low prices in relation to those of other firms —are regarded by one whole class of retailers as the major device for obtaining and maintaining volume. It is in their interest accordingly to resist any exercise of market power by their suppliers that results in higher prices. More important, any power retailers can exercise to reduce their supplier's prices will redound to their benefit. It will enable them to use price as an inducement without breaking the convention against destructive cutting of their own margins.

Such an opportunity exists only when their suppliers are enjoying something that can be taken away, i.e., when they are enjoying the fruits of market power from which they can be separated. Thus, in precise parallel with

---

[3] An exception of great importance will be stressed presently.

the labor market, we find the retailer with both a protective and profit incentive to develop countervailing power whenever his supplier is in possession of market power. The practical manifestation of this, over the last half-century, has been the spectacular rise of the food chains, the variety chains, the mail-order houses (now graduated into chain stores), the department-store chains, and the co-operative buying organizations of the surviving independent department and food stores.

This development has been the countervailing response to previously established positions of power. The gains from invading these positions have been considerable. The rubber tire industry is a fairly commonplace example of oligopoly. Four large firms are dominant in the market. In the thirties, Sears, Roebuck & Co. was able, by exploiting its role as a large and indispensable customer, to procure tires from Goodyear Tire & Rubber Company at a price from twenty-nine to forty per cent lower than the going market. These it resold to thrifty motorists for from a fifth to a quarter less than the same tires carrying the regular Goodyear brand.

One consequence of the failure of the government to recognize the role of countervailing power is that many hundreds of pages of court records have detailed the exercise of this power by the Great Atlantic & Pacific Tea Company. There is little doubt that this firm has used the countervailing power it has developed with considerable artistry. In 1937, a survey by the company indicated that, for an investment of $175,000, it could supply itself with corn flakes. Assuming that it charged itself the price it then was paying to one of the three companies manufacturing this delicacy, it could earn a modest sixty-eight per cent on the outlay. Armed with this information, and the threat to go into the business which its power could readily make effective, it had no difficulty in bringing down the price by approximately ten per cent.[4] Such gains from the exercise of countervailing power, it will be clear, could only occur where there is an exercise of original market power with which to contend. The A & P could have reaped no comparable gains in buying staple products from the farmer. Committed as he is to the competition of the competitive model, the farmer has no gains to surrender. Provided, as he is, with the opportunity of selling all he produces at the impersonally determined market price, he has not the slightest incentive to make a special price to A & P beyond that which might be associated with the simple economies of bulk sale.

The examples of the exercise of countervailing power by Sears, Roebuck and A & P just cited show how this power is deployed in its most dramatic form. The day-to-day exercise of the buyer's power is a good deal less spectacular but also a good deal more significant. At the end of virtually every channel by which consumers' goods reach the public there is, in practice, a layer of powerful buyers. In the food market there are the great food chains;

---

[4] I am indebted to my friend Professor M. A. Adelman for these details which are from his forthcoming book, on the A & P Case, to be published by the Harvard University Press.

in clothing there are the department stores, the chain department stores and the department store buying organizations; in appliances there are Sears, Roebuck, and Montgomery Ward and the department stores; these latter firms are also important outlets for furniture and other house furnishings; the drug and cosmetic manufacturer has to seek part of his market through the large drug chains and the department stores; a vast miscellany of consumers' goods pass to the public through Woolworth's, Kresge's and the other variety chains.

In all of these cases buyers deal directly with the manufacturer and there are few of the latter who, in setting prices, do not have to reckon with the attitude and reaction of their powerful customers. The retail buyers have a variety of weapons at their disposal to use against the market power of their suppliers. Their ultimate sanction is to develop their own source of supply as the food chains, Sears, Roebuck, and Montgomery Ward have extensively done. They can also concentrate their entire patronage on a single supplier and, in return for a lower price, give him security in his volume and relieve him of selling and advertising costs.

The more commonplace but more important exercise of countervailing power consists, merely, in keeping the seller in a state of uncertainty as to the intentions of a buyer who is indispensable to him. The larger of the retail buying organizations place orders around which the production schedules and occasionally the investment of even the largest manufacturers become organized. A shift in this custom imposes prompt and heavy loss. The threat or even the fear of this sanction is enough to cause the supplier to surrender some or all of the rewards of his market power. He must, frequently, make a more conditional surrender to less potent buyers if he is not to be more than ever in the power of his large customers. It will be clear that in this operation there are rare opportunities for playing one supplier off against another.

A measure of the importance which large retailing organizations attach to the deployment of their countervailing power is the prestige they accord to their buyers. These men (and women) are the key employees of the modern large retail organization; they are highly paid and they are among the most intelligent and resourceful people to be found anywhere in business. In the everyday course of business, they are considerably better known, both for their capacities and their power, than the salesmen from whom they buy.

There are producers of consumers' goods who have secured themselves from exercise of countervailing power. Some, like the automobile and the oil industry, have done so either by integrating their distribution through to the consumer or because they have an organization of small and dependent and therefore fairly powerless dealers. It seems probable that in a few industries, tobacco manufacture for example, the members are strong enough and have sufficient solidarity to withstand any pressure applied to them even by the most powerful buyer. However, even the tobacco manufacturers, under conditions that were especially favorable to the exercise of countervailing power in the thirties, were forced to make liberal price concessions, in the form of advertising allowances, to the A & P [5] and possibly also to other large customers. When the comprehensive representation of large retailers in the various fields of consumers' goods distribution is considered, it is reasonable to conclude—the reader is warned that this is an important generalization—that most positions of market power in the production of consumers' goods are covered by positions of countervailing power.

Countervailing power also manifests itself, although less visibly, in producers' goods markets. For many years the power of the automobile companies, as purchasers of steel, has sharply curbed the power of the steel mills as sellers. Detroit is the only city where the recently oulawed basing-point system was not used to price steel. Under the basing-point system, all producers regardless of location quoted the same price at any particular point of delivery. This minimized the opportunity of a strong buyer to play one seller off against the other. The large firms in the automobile industry had developed the countervailing power which enabled them to do precisely this. They were not disposed to tolerate any limitations on their exercise of such power. In explaining the quotation of "arbitrary prices" on Detroit steel, a leading student of the basing-point system has recently recognized, implicitly, the role of countervailing power by observing that "it is difficult to apply high cartel prices to particularly large and strong customers such as the automobile manufacturers in Detroit." [6]

The more normal operation of countervailing power in producers' goods markets turns on the relatively small number of customers which firms in these industries typically have. Where the cigarette or soap manufacturer numbers his retail outlets by the hundreds of thousands and his final consumers by the millions, the machinery or equipment manufacturer counts his customers by the hundreds or thousands and, very often, his important ones by the dozen. The latter are important to the seller as individuals and are able to collect the rewards of that importance. As elsewhere, the market pays a premium to those who develop power as buyers that is equivalent to the market power of those from whom they buy. The reverse is true where weak sellers do business with strong buyers.

V

There is an old saying, or should be, that it is a wise economist who recognizes the scope of his own generalizations. While countervailing power is of decisive importance in regulating the exercise of private economic

[5] Richard B. Tennant, *The American Cigarette Industry* (New Haven: Yale University Press, 1950), p. 312.

[6] Fritz Machlup, *The Basing Point System* (Philadelphia: Blakiston Co., 1949), p. 115.

power, it is not universally effective. Some industries, because they are integrated through to the consumer or because their product passes through a dependent dealer organization, have not been faced with countervailing power. As noted, there are a few cases where a very strong market position has proven impregnable even against the attacks of strong buyers. And there are cases where the dangers from countervailing power have, apparently, been recognized and where it has been successfully resisted.

An example of successful resistance to countervailing power is the residential-building industry. No segment of American capitalism evokes less pride. Yet anyone approaching the industry with the preconceptions of competition in mind is unlikely to see, very accurately, the reasons for its shortcomings. There are many thousands of individual firms in the business of building houses. Nearly all are small—the capital of the typical housebuilder runs from a few hundred to a few thousand dollars. The members of the industry oppose little market power to the would-be house owner. Except in times of extremely high building activity there is aggressive competition for business.

The industry does show many detailed manifestations of guild restraint. Builders are frequently in alliance with each other, the unions, and local politicians to protect prices, wages and to maintain established building techniques. These derelictions have been seized upon avidly by the critics of the industry. Since they represent its major departure from the competitive model, they have been assumed to be the cause of the poor performance of the housing industry.

Unhappily, were the restraints on contract prices, materials and techniques in the industry swept away, it seems improbable that the prices of new houses would be much changed and the satisfaction of customers with what they get for what they pay much enhanced. The reason is that the typical builder would still be a small and powerless figure contending with unions that are far stronger than he and buying his building materials in small quantities at high cost from suppliers with effective market power. It is these factors which, very largely, determine the cost of the house.

The builder is kept without power. With few exceptions, the manufacturers of building supplies decline to sell direct to the builder. This prevents any one of the latter from bringing pressure to bear on his source of supply; at the same time it helps keep all builders relatively small and powerless by uniformly denying them the economies of direct purchase. All must pay jobbers' and retailers' margins. A few builders—a spectacular case is Levitt & Sons of Long Island—have managed to circumvent this ban.[7] As the result of more effective buying, a much stronger position in dealing with labor, and the savings from large-scale production of houses, they have notably

[7] Levitt has established a wholly-owned building-supply company to buy materials for its projects. *Fortune*, August 1947, p. 168.

increased the satisfaction of customers with what they receive for their money. Few can doubt that the future of the industry, if its future is to improve on its past, lies with such firms.

Thus it is the notion of countervailing power, not of competition, which points the way to progress in the housing industry. What is needed is fewer firms of far greater scale with resulting capacity to bring power to bear upon unions and suppliers. It is the absence of such firms, and of the resulting economies, which helps explain why one sector of this industry—low-cost housing where cost is especially important in relation to ability-to-pay—has passed under government management. In the absence of an effective regulating mechanism within the industry in the form of countervailing power, private entrepreneurship has been superseded.

VI

The development of countervailing power requires a certain minimum opportunity and capacity for organization, corporate or otherwise. If the large retail buying organizations had not developed the countervailing power which they have used, by proxy, on behalf of the individual consumer, consumers would have been faced with the need to organize the equivalent of the retailer's power. This would be a formidable task but it has been accomplished in Scandinavia and, in lesser measure, in England where the consumer's co-operative, instead of the chain store, is the dominant instrument of countervailing power in consumers' goods markets.[8] Quite probably there would have been similar organization in the United States. The fact that there are no consumer co-operatives of any importance in the United States is to be explained, not by any inherent incapacity of the American for such organization, but because the chain stores pre-empted the gains of countervailing power first. The counterpart of the Swedish Kooperative Forbundet or the British Co-operative Wholesale Societies has not appeared in the United States simply because it could not compete with the A & P and the other large food chains. The meaning of this, which incidentally has been lost on devotees of the theology of co-operation, is that the chain stores are approximately as efficient in the exercise of countervailing power as a co-operative would be. In parts of the American economy where proprietary mass buyers have not made their appearance, notably in the purchase of farm supplies, individuals (who are also individualists) have shown as much capacity to organize as the Scandinavians and the British and have similarly obtained the protection and rewards of countervailing power. The Grange League Federation, the Eastern States Farmers' Exchange and the Illinois Farm Supply Company, co-operatives with annual sales running to multi-million-dollar figures, are among the illustrations of the point.

---

[8] Especially in Scandinavia the co-operative has been explicitly viewed as a device for countering the power of the cartels—i.e., as an instrument for the exercise of countervailing power.

However, it must not be assumed that it is easy for great numbers of individuals to coalesce and organize countervailing power. In less developed communities, Puerto Rico for example, one finds people fully exposed to the exactions of strategically situated importers, merchants and wholesalers and without the apparent capacity to develop countervailing power in their own behalf. (Anyone, incidentally, who doubts the force of the countervailing power exercised by large retailer-buying organizations would do well to consider the revolution which the entry of the large chain stores would work in an economy like that of Puerto Rico and also how such an intrusion would be resented and perhaps resisted by importers and merchants now able to exercise their market power with impunity against the thousands of small, independent and inefficient retailers who are their present outlets.)

In light of the difficulty in organizing countervailing power, it is not surprising that the assistance of government has repeatedly been sought in this task. Without the phenomenon itself being full recognized, the provision of state assistance to the development of countervailing power has become a major function of government—perhaps *the* major domestic function of government. Much of the domestic legislation of the last twenty years, that of the New Deal episode in particular, only becomes fully comprehensible when it is viewed in this light.

VII

I come now to the major limitation on the operation of countervailing power—a matter of much importance in our time. Countervailing power is not exercised uniformly under all conditions of demand. It does not function at all as a restraint on market power when there is inflation or inflationary pressure on markets.

Because the competitive model, in association with Say's Law, was assumed to find its equilibrium at or near full employment levels, economists for a long time were little inclined to inquire whether markets in general, or competition in particular, might behave differently at different levels of economic activity, i.e., whether they might behave differently in prosperity and depression. In any case the conventional division of labor in economics has assigned to one group of scholars the task of examining markets and competitive behavior, to another a consideration of the causes of fluctuations in the economy. The two fields of exploration are even today separated by watertight bulkheads, or, more accurately, by professorial division of labor and course requirements. Those who have taught and written on market behavior have assumed a condition of general stability in the economy in which sellers were eager for buyers. To the extent, as in recent years, that they have had to do their teaching or thinking in a time of inflation—in a time when, as the result of strong demand, eager buyers were besieging reluctant sellers—they have dismissed the circumstance as abnormal. They have drawn their classroom and textbook illustrations from the last period of deflation, severe or mild.

So long as competition was assumed to be the basic regulatory force in the economy these simplifications, although they led to some error, were not too serious. There is a broad continuity in competitive behavior from conditions of weak to conditions of strong demand. At any given moment there is a going price in competitive markets that reflects the current equilibrium of supply-and-demand relationships. Even though demand is strong and prices are high and rising, the seller who prices above the going or equilibrium level is punished by the loss of his customers. The buyer still has an incentive to look for the lowest price he can find. Thus market behavior is not fundamentally different from what it is when demand is low and prices are falling.

There are, by contrast, differences of considerable importance in market behavior between conditions of insufficient and excessive demand when there is oligopoly, i.e., when the market has only a small number of sellers. The convention against price competition, when small numbers of sellers share a market, is obviously not very difficult to maintain if all can sell all they produce and none is subject to the temptation to cut prices. Such a device for maintaining the convention against price competition as the basing-point system only has significance when demand is insufficient in relation to capacity. The basing-point system by making known, or easily calculable, the approved prices at every possible point of delivery in the country provided protection against accidental or surreptitious price-cutting. Such protection is not necessary when there is no temptation to cut prices. By an interesting paradox when the basing-point system was attacked by the government in the late depression years it was of great consequence to the steel, cement and other industries that employed it. When, after the deliberate processes of the law, the system was finally abolished by the courts in April 1948, the consequences for the industries in question were rather slight. The steel and cement companies were then straining to meet demand that was in excess of their capacity. They were under no temptation to cut prices and thus had no *current* reason to regret the passing of the basing-point system.

These differences in market behavior under conditions of strong and of weak demand are important and there are grounds for criticizing their neglect—or rather the assumption that there is normally a shortage of buyers—in the conventional market analysis. However, the effect of changes in demand on market behavior becomes of really profound importance only when the role of countervailing power is recognized. Countervailing power, as a restraint on market power, *only* operates when there is a relative scarcity of demand. Only then is the buyer important to the seller and this is an obvious prerequisite for his bringing his power to bear on the market power of the seller. If buyers are plentiful, that is, if supply is small in relation to current demand, the seller is under no compulsion to surrender to the bargaining power of any customer. The countervailing power of the buyer, however great, disappears with an excess of demand. With it goes the regulatory or restraining role of countervailing power in general. Indeed, the best hope of the buyer, under conditions of excess demand, may be to form a coalition with the seller to bring about an agreed division of returns.[9]

Following the useful practice of testing theory against experience, it is worth noting that it was the twenties and the thirties which were the periods of great growth of chain and group buying enterprises.[10] In sharp contrast with most other types of business, the early depression years especially were favorable to the great chain stores. These were years when demand, generally, fell short of the capacity of suppliers to meet it. Thus they were favorable to the exercise of countervailing power. The intensity of the trade agitation against the mass retailers, culminating in 1936 in the passage of the Robinson-Patman Act (designed as we shall see presently to limit their exercise of this power), was itself a measure of the chain's advantage in this period. By contrast, during the years of strong demand and short supply during World War II, the chain stores lost ground, relatively, to independents. As this strong demand in relation to supply destroyed their capacity to exercise countervailing power, their advantage disappeared. It is interesting to note that the trade agitation and resentment against the chains almost completely disappeared during the war and postwar years.

However, it is again in the labor market where the change in the pattern of exercise of countervailing power that accompanies changes in demand can be seen with greatest clarity. Here also it has the most portentous consequences. In industries where strong firms bargain with strong unions, the management of the former has what has come to be considered a normal resistance to wage increases when demand is not pressing upon capacity. To yield is to increase unit costs. The firm cannot with impunity pass along these higher costs to its customers. There may be a question as to whether other firms in the industry will follow suit; there will always be a question of the effect of the higher prices on sales. If the demand for the products is in any measure elastic the consequence of the higher prices will be a loss of

[9] The everyday distinction between a "buyers" and a "sellers" market and the frequency of its use reflect the importance which participants in actual markets attach to the ebb and flow of countervailing power. That this distinction has no standing in formal economics follows from the fact that countervailing power has not been recognized by economists. As frequently happens, practical men have devised a terminology to denote a phenomenon of great significance to themselves but which, since it has not been assimilated to economic theory, has never appeared in the textbooks. The concept of the "break-even point," generally employed by businessmen but largely ignored in economic theory, is another case in point.

[10] See Temporary National Economic Committee. *Large Scale Organization in the Food Industries*, Monograph No. 35 by A. C. Hoffman (Washington: U.S. Government Printing Office), pp. 5 ff.

volume. This, with its effect on employment in the industry, is something of which modern union leadership, as well as management, is usually conscious. Thus the trial of strength between union and management associated with collective bargaining is, essentially, over the division of profits. When demand is limited, we have, in other words, an essentially healthy manifestation of countervailing power. The union opposes its power as a seller of labor to that of management as a buyer: At stake is the division of the returns. An occasional strike is an indication that countervailing power is being employed in a sound context where the costs of any wage increase cannot readily be passed along to someone else. It should be an occasion for mild rejoicing in the conservative press. The *Daily Worker,* eagerly contemplating the downfall of capitalism, should regret this manifestation of the continued health of the system.

Under conditions of strong demand, however, collective bargaining takes on a radically different form. Then management is no longer constrained to resist union demands on the grounds that higher prices will be reflected in shrinking volume. There is now an adequate supply of eager buyers. The firm that first surrenders to the union need not worry lest it be either the first or the only one to increase prices. There are buyers for all. No one has occasion, as the result of price increases, to worry about a general shrinkage in volume. A strong demand means an inelastic demand. On the other hand, there are grave disadvantages for management in resisting the union. Since profits are not at stake, any time lost as the result of a strike is a dead loss. Worker morale and the actual loss of part of the working force to employers who offer better wages must be reckoned with. Thus when demand is sufficiently strong to press upon the capacity of industry generally to supply it, there is no real conflict of interest between union and employer. It is to their mutual advantage to effect a coalition and to pass the costs of their agreement along in higher prices. Other buyers along the line, who under other circumstances might have exercised their countervailing power against the price increases, are similarly inhibited. Thus under inflationary pressure of demand, the whole structure of countervailing power in the economy dissolves.

We have already seen an example of this dissolution of countervailing power in the continuing rounds of wage and price increases following World War II. The full coalition between management and labor, under the conditions of inflationary demand of these years, was partly disguised by the conventional expressions of animosity and by the uncertainty of management as to how long the inflation would last. However, the "Fifth Round" in 1950-51 was negotiated with scarcely an important strike. The President of the United States Steel Corporation, in yielding to the union in November 1950, indicated a *de facto* coalition when he pointed out that the "half-cent" inflation in steel prices, which would be passed along to customers, was a small price to pay for "uninterrupted and expanded" production. The consequences of this failure of countervailing power in times of inflation are considerable.

EDWARD S. MASON

8. *Competition and Public Policy**

Many voices—including some unexpected ones—have recently made themselves heard in praise of the large business. Frederick Lewis Allen, in his recent book "The Big Change," has looked upon the growth of giant enterprise and has found it good. A forthcoming study from the Brookings Institution, announced with considerable fanfare at a banquet in the Starlight Room of the Waldorf-Astoria, is described by Alfred P. Sloan, Jr., as a factual study that is hoped will "correct the more glaringly artificial and outmoded assumptions of the economic textbook and popular economic literature" concerning large corporations. David Lilienthal's "Big Business: A New Era" is an unqualified endorsement of the large firm as the primary source of economic growth and effective competition in the American economy. The recent report of the Business Advisory Council on "Effective Competition" seeks, among other things, a redefinition of competition that will recognize the innovating role of the large firm in the competitive process.

Behind these and other current discussions of bigness lie a number of academic studies that are increasingly cited in the popular literature. The statistical investigations of Morris Adelman at the Massachusetts Institute of Technology have at least raised doubts whether economic concentration has substantially increased in this country since the turn of the century, despite the growth of giant firms. The late Professor Schumpeter of Harvard has familiarized a generation of economists with the view that effective competition is essentially a process of "creative destruction," in which new products and processes, usually introduced by large firms, supplant old products and processes now become obsolete. Professor Galbraith, also at Harvard, had added to contemporary views on competition a doctrine of "countervailing power" that emphasizes the limits set by large buyers such as the A & P to the otherwise unchecked market power of large sellers.

A good deal of this recent writing on the role of the large firm in the

* *Yale Review*, Vol. XLIII (Autumn, 1953). By permission.

competitive process leads towards a vigorous attack—either explicit or implicit—on current antitrust policy. Professor Schumpeter was fond of saying that he did not oppose a sensible antimonopoly policy. But he regarded antitrust policy in practice as a relatively senseless harassment of large firms by people with little understanding of the historical and potential contribution of large-scale enterprise to effective competition. Professor Galbraith is willing to grant that there is a limited utility in attempts to increase competition among sellers or buyers but finds that market power can usually be more effectively controlled by building an opposing power constellation rather than by reducing an existing one. To Lilienthal "trust-busting" is frankly an outworn doctrine. As the antitrust laws "are now construed, the very Bigness upon which we all now depend may be illegal." He proposes to replace the Sherman Law which negatively forbids "restraints of trade" with a positive law that fosters the "development of trade." The report of the Business Advisory Council on "Effective Competition" has no fault to find with the basic purpose of the Sherman Law but wants it interpreted in the light of a "rule of reason" that takes into account conditions now neglected in the enforcement of antitrust policy.

The criticism of antitrust policy tends to center on the allegation that this policy is an attack on "size as such." The enforcement agencies are pictured as engaged in a process of tearing down business structures essential to the growth, prosperity, and security of the United States. What is the truth of this charge that the antitrust laws as currently interpreted constitute an important attack on size as such?

It would have to be admitted by the critics of antitrust policy that, if the success of the attack on the large firm is to be judged by the number and importance of dissolutions or dismemberments actually accomplished, the results are meager indeed. During the last decade, when the attack on size was supposed to be at its height, there have been no more than five or six decisions that produced dismemberment of firms. Furthermore, none of the firms in question was large in comparison with such giants as U. S. Steel, Standard Oil of New Jersey, or General Motors. In 1945 the Pullman manufacturing properties were separated from the operation of Pullman services. Pullman Standard remained by far the largest producer of sleeping cars, though a new company controlled by the railroads took over the operation of the sleeping-car service. In 1948 a number of moving-picture producers were forced to dispose of distributing properties and theatres. None of these companies was large as size is now measured, nor was their share of the picture-producing market very extensive. The Court held, nevertheless, that integration produced an interdependence among producers for theatre outlets and an interdependence among theatre owners for films to be exhibited that smacked of collusion. In 1947 the Yellow Cab manufacturing properties were divorced from the Yellow Cab operating companies. In 1950 the owners of the controlling stock interests in the Aluminum Company of American and of Aluminum Ltd. of Canada were ordered to dispose of their stock interests in one or the other of these companies. These are the principal dissolutions that have been accomplished during the last ten years; they can hardly be said to add up to a massive change in the structure of American industry.

Furthermore, during this same period the Supreme Court handed down a number of decisions that ran quite in the other direction. Although Du Pont and National Lead were known to produce between them over 90 percent of the national output of titanium pigments, the Court refused to accede to the request of the Department of Justice that these two companies be dissolved. When U. S. Steel, not only the largest steel company, but one of the largest corporation in any industry, acquired the Columbia Steel Company, the Court said this acquisition did not violate the antitrust laws. Although the Aluminum Company produced over 50 percent of the country's output of aluminum ingot, Judge Knox did not find it necessary to accede to the request of the Department of Justice that the company be dismembered.

There are, of course, a number of important cases now before the courts in which the enforcement agencies are pressing for dissolution. Among them are cases against the A & P, American Telephone and Telegraph, Cellophane, International Business Machines, and Du Pont. It is possible to suppose that we are in the midst of an impressive attack on the large firm if attention is limited to the statements of certain judges, particularly dissenting judges, and to the abracadabra that accompanies the action of enforcement agencies. There is, however, a very long distance between what the Department of Justice asks for in its prayer for relief and what the courts will grant in the form of a remedy. And it must always be remembered that antitrust policy is not what various official or unofficial spokesmen think it might be, but what the majority of the Supreme Court says it is.

There is, however, a sense in which it is proper to say that antitrust policy has been moving towards an attack on size as such. This is so despite the fact that every year since the war, as regularly as the migration of songbirds from the South, we are treated to a speech from the current head of the Anti-Trust Division piously disclaiming any concern with bigness as such. What he is talking about is the absolute size of firms measured in assets, number of employees, or in other possible ways. And, indeed, with the possible exception of the Du Pont case, it is probably correct to say that no action has been brought against a firm or combination merely because of its absolute economic size.

The critics, however, are talking about something else. They are concerned with cases that have been brought against firms that are *relatively* large; against firms, i.e., that are large in relation to the industries or markets in which they operate. According to the critics a firm that occupies a large share of the market may be found to be in violation of the antitrust laws even though its practices are as competitive as those of any smaller firm; in fact, the more competitive its practices the more guilty is it likely to be considered to be. This is a sense in which it is correct to say that current antitrust policy is an attack on size as such—and it pains Mr. Lilienthal and others deeply. He holds that "the doctrine of penalizing, prosecuting, hectoring and even dismembering a large business which, by research and managerial superiority, achieves competitive success (that is, wins a large share of the market) has serious consequences of a practical kind."

So, indeed, it has. But the practical consequences are not all, as Mr. Lilienthal supposes, injurious to effective competition. Any antimonopoly policy that attempts to set limits to the extension of market power may check the normal competitive expansion of a firm *in a particular market*. It does not follow, however, that the growth of the firm need be checked or that superior management or research possibilities need be frustrated for lack of appropriate "economic space." The firm still has an opportunity to expand into other markets and industries and, to the extent that it can do so effectively, it may not only realize the potentialities of superior management but contribute to the effectiveness of competition in those markets in which it expands. An attack on market power is not necessarily an attack on bigness.

There are strong reasons why the thrust of antitrust policy should be directed against market power. Furthermore, the share of the market occupied by a particular firm is one of the important bits of evidence bearing on the market power of that firm. It is not conclusive evidence and it must be carefully interpreted together with other types of evidence; but the enforcement agencies and the courts are fully justified in placing market share in a central position.

We have always looked to our competitive free-enterprise system to accomplish two different things. On the one hand, we have expected from it a set of powerful motivations, stimulations, and drives towards increased output, product improvement, cost reduction: in general, towards increased efficiency in the use of economic resources. On the other hand, we have expected from the competitive system a set of limitations to the growth of private economic power. The competitive system is supposed to be self-regulating in the sense that a continual striving for market advantage by all firms effectively sets limits to the market power of each.

Both of these objectives are important, and it is essential that public policy keep both in mind. My quarrel with the current worshipers of Big Business, both popular and academic, is that they have concentrated on one objective to the exclusion of the other. Their critique of current antitrust policy towards the large firm has included some important negative propositions but has almost completely neglected the central problem of market power that any effective antitrust policy must confront.

If we are to continue to rely on competition as the principal limiter of private economic power—rather than on public ownership or public utility regulation—we must center our attention on the position of firms in the various markets in which they operate. How and to what extent a particular firm is limited by a market in which it operates is difficult to judge. Yet a judgment must be made and such a judgment presupposes the formulation of applicable tests of permitted and nonpermitted power. The critics of antitrust policy have shown that the tests currently applied sometimes leave out relevant considerations. But they have made little or no contribution to the formulation of more acceptable tests. And some, including Lilienthal, in effect deny the existence of the problem.

Let us consider some of the more important points raised by the apostles of bigness. They emphasize first of all that, in judging the market share of a firm, products that are close substitutes for the articles produced by the firm in question must be taken into account. They insist, further, that the market power of a firm is limited not only by currently competing products but by the new products and processes that are likely to be introduced if any profit opportunity becomes available by reason of a monopoly price charged by existing firms. They also point out that the market power of a seller is limited not only by his rivals but by the bargaining power that may be exerted by big buyers. These are all important considerations. They all need to be taken into account in estimating the market power of large firms. It is true that they are frequently neglected not only by the enforcement agencies but by the courts.

Nevertheless, when these considerations have been fully evaluated, there remains a problem of market power that the protagonists of big business have either neglected or have not understood.

That commodities compete with other and physically different commodities, that a market must be understood to embrace all close substitutes, is a commonplace of textbook economics. Yet the courts and the enforcement agencies have sometimes neglected this obvious fact in attempting to estimate the market position of particular firms. Although copper, stainless steel, and other metals compete with aluminum in some uses, the Court, in the aluminum case, ignored this fact and stated resolutely, "Every product meets with competition of substitutes—this has no relevance for the existence of monopoly."

The Anti-Trust Division contends, in the Cellophane case now pending, that Du Pont's market position should be determined with reference solely to other producers of Cellophane. The defense holds, on the other hand, that Cellophane is in close and continuous competition with a variety of other wrapping materials. The same issue arises in the current suit against

International Business Machines. Should the market for tabulating and calculating equipment be limited to mechanical and electronic calculators, or
should all methods and devices for tabulating and bookkeeping be included?

The competition of substitutes is obviously an important consideration in
judging the market power of a firm. There is even a sense in which it is true
to say that all commodities compete with one another for the consumer's
dollar. It does not follow, however, when due weight has been given to
interproduct competition, that positions of market power are negligible in
number and importance. All it means is that the dimensions of a market are
frequently greater than those of a single product, and that this fact should
be recognized in the application of antitrust policy.

The view is also advanced by the defenders of big business that product
and process innovation is not only an important, but may be a sufficient,
limitation to positions of market power. Lilienthal goes very far in this direction. The "new competition" he discovers in the American economy is
largely a competition offered by new products and processes, which are
chiefly the results of research in large units, public and private. To this "new
competition" he attributes a tremendous growth in the productivity of the
American economy during the last few decades.

In the first place, there is no evidence of any substantial increase in the
rate of economic growth in the American economy. The growth rate of
per-capita output has been no higher during the last twenty-five years than
it was in the previous quarter-century; nor is there any evidence that growth
rates during the last half of the nineteenth century were any lower than
during the first half of the twentieth. The economy has grown rapidly with
relatively small firms *and* with relatively large firms. In the second place,
the fact that research expenditures are highly concentrated in large firms
does not mean that important product and process innovation is the product
of large firms. This is something about which we know next to nothing. In
the third place, although new products and new processes have dramatically
displaced existing products and processes in certain areas, they have had
relatively little effect in others.

The role of innovation in the competitive process has been discussed with
more originality and cogency in the writings of the late Professor
Schumpeter than in any others. "The competition that counts," he emphasized, "is the competition from the new commodity, the new technology,
the new source of supply, the new type of organization (the largest scale
unit of control for instance)—competition which commands a decisive cost
or quality advantage and which strikes not at the margins of profit and
their outputs of the existing firms, but at their foundations and their very
lives. This kind of competition is as much more effective than the other as
bombardment is in comparison with forcing a door, and so much more
important that it becomes a matter of comparative indifference whether

competition in the ordinary sense functions more or less promptly: the powerful lever that in the long run expands output and brings down prices is in any case made of other stuff."

Certainly it would have been rather foolish to have conducted an attack on a firm controlling a large share of the trade in carriages—if one had existed—at a time when the development of the motorcar was driving horse-drawn vehicles off the road. Market share is not always an indication of market power. There is a period in the development of most industries when the rate of innovation is such as to make the number of firms or their market shares irrelevant to a judgment on the effectiveness of competition. That is one of the reasons why it is unreasonable to conclude, because three or four firms produce from 70 to 80 percent of the output in a particular industry, that competition is necessarily nonexistent. Competition may well be nonexistent, but a sensible antitrust policy will have to take other things into account than market shares.

To say that innovation is sufficient in certain situations to assure effective competition is not to say, however, that innovation may be relied upon to assure effective competition in all. Technological change is not something that spreads itself evenly over the economy, nor does it always work in the direction of increasing competition. Formidable positions of market power may persist in the most dynamic of economies, and the American economy is no exception. Although Schumpeter assures us that what he is opposed to is not every antimonopoly but only certain kinds, he does not offer much guidance to a sensible policy. No more does Lilienthal. The critics have succeeded in pointing out a set of considerations relevant to the monopoly problem that have been relatively neglected. They have not, however, disposed of the problem itself.

Nor have the exponents of the theory of "countervailing power." It seems probable that in some situations the growth of large buyers has resulted not only in a wresting of monopoly profits away from large sellers but in passing on some of the advantages gained to ultimate consumers. It is possible that the A & P and other chain stores have fulfilled this function. Sears, Roebuck and the other mail-order houses may have done the same. Perhaps it is correct to say that, over the last three or four decades, mass distributors have, in general, accomplished this function, though what part of the price reductions brought about by these distributors is to be assigned to economics of large size and what to bargaining advantages it would be difficult indeed to determine.

To recognize, however, that under certain circumstances the power of large sellers may be checked by large buyers, not only to the advantage of these buyers but to the advantage of ultimate consumers, is not to conclude that in all circumstances this beneficial result will follow. It may well be that the predominant effect will be merely a division of potential monopoly profits between the large buyer and the large seller. Under what circumstances is this result like to follow rather than the others and how do we tell whether market power is, or is not, adequately checked to the advantage of the consuming public? It is at this point that the proponents of countervailing power leave off the discussion.

In general it may be said that the recent literature extolling the virtues of bigness has offered some legitimate and telling criticism of current antitrust policy. It *is* true that interproduct competition tends to limit the market power of certain firms whose share of the sales of a particular product is large. Close substitutes should, therefore, be included in any proper calculation of that firm's share of the market. It *is* true that innovation in products and processes is of the essence of competition and that in certain industrial areas where the rate of innovation—and consequently of obsolescence—is rapid, market share is essentially irrelevant to a judgment of market power. It is also true that market power is limited by rivals on the other side as well as by rivals on the same side of the market, though whether this rivalry offers the same advantage to consumers is open to question.

When, however, admitting the partial validity of the criticism, we ask the disciples of bigness to offer, from their superior insight, alternative and more realistic tests of permitted or nonpermitted positions of market power, we encounter a blank wall. Lilienthal, it is true, proposes a positive program, but it is couched in such general language that the reader has difficulty in determining whether, in fact, any substantial change from current practice would be accomplished. He suggests a "Basic Economic Law" containing "a broad declaration of public policy that the *prime* concern of Congress is not with competition, *per se,* nor with competitors, but with productivity and the promotion of an ethical and economic distribution of this productivity."

If, under this law, suit was brought against a company occupying a large share of a market "the legal test Bigness would have to face would thenceforth be whether the particular aspect of size challenged by the government does in fact *further the public interest."* Until Lilienthal has specified his tests of public interest there is no way of knowing what he proposes is significantly different from what we now have. Under current antitrust policy, if a firm charged with monopolizing the market can effectively demonstrate not only that its practices are not predatory, but that costs of production and prices are likely to be lower than under an alternative market structure, there is little or no chance of its being found guilty of violating the antitrust laws. Under Lilienthal's proposed legislation the company would still apparently bear the burden of proof, and the sole question is whether his tests of "public interest" would be significantly different from those now applied in antitrust cases.

A similar charge of excessive vagueness must also be levied against the Business Advisory Council's contribution to the discussion of antitrust policy. Again the negative criticism is well directed, but the discussion ends abruptly at the point where positive tests of desirable competition or undesirable monopoly need to be considered. The council preaches the doctrine of "effective competition," but there are as many definitions of "effective" or "workable" competition as there are effective or working economists.

When all is said and done there is a problem of market power that is a proper concern of public policy. When the market is adequately defined, with full account taken of competition among products and of the position of buyers as well as sellers, there are strong reasons for supposing that a firm with a large share of the market will have a large degree of market power. The reasons are not conclusive; other considerations will need to be examined; and it does not follow, even though market power is demonstrated, that dissolution is the appropriate remedy. Nevertheless, the enforcement agencies and the courts are on the right track in emphasizing share of the market as a *prima-facie* indication of market power. This does not imply an attack on size as such. A firm whose position in a particular market is limited by public action is, and should be, free to expand in other markets as far as managerial qualifications and research potentialities permit. There remains, however, the question of market power, and nothing brought forward by the current defenders of big business has called into question either its existence or the need for a remedy.

A. A. BERLE

9. *Economic Power and the Free Society**

The cycle of shift from individual possessory holdings into power systems, and from power systems back once more into possessory personal holdings, appears to be a kind of rhythm of history, especially in the West. As the feudal system merged into the king state, the revolutionary doctrine that there should be private property began to assert itself, reaching a high degree of philosophical justification in the middle of the Eighteenth Century when the French physiocrats declared that if a man was to be free, able to speak his own mind, depict his own thought and develop his own personal-

* (The Fund for the Republic, 1957). By permission.

ity, he would have to have a base apart from one that was politically or ecclesiastically organized and controlled. The theory of private property as a part of freedom reached its culmination in the French Revolution and in the far slower and quieter industrial revolution in England.

No doubt the American system is the child of that revolution. Certainly the Jeffersonian ideal was a country in which everyone had private property, no one was very rich, no one was very poor. In order to make this system work, however, a companion theory was needed—that economics worked automatically. The self-interest of men levering against each other and controlling each other through competition resulted in a splendid ethical balance wheel, which was the open market. This leveled out inequalities, eliminated the inefficient and through competition prevented an undue concentration of power.

Adam Smith's *Wealth of Nations* consecrated the theory. Smith said that this strange animal "the corporation" could never be a major factor in economics because in it men worked for other men, and obviously no man would ever pay as much attention to other men's affairs as he would to his own. Therefore, such a collective enterprise could never play a major role in society. Its inefficiency would always be such that the workings of the market would eliminate it. Thus, the corporation was merely an agency of the state for specialized purposes, and those suspect.

At the convention which met to draw up the Constitution of the United States the proposal was made that the Federal government be given the power to incorporate. According to Madison's notes the answer was: No, a corporation prevented men from getting into action and this is a dangerous power. A corporation had not merely the privilege of existence but other privileges as well, or if it did not have them it could get them. As a result monopolies would arise and dominate the United States. This should not be allowed.

So the Federal government was specifically denied the power to create corporations. This was to be left to the states and it was assumed that they would not exercise this power or, if they did, would exercise it only as a means of carrying on government. This doctrine survived less than fifteen years. By 1791 the Federal government found it desirable to organize a corporation entitled the Bank of the United States, and in the 1819 Supreme Court case *McCulloch v. Maryland* Justice Marshall decided that the implied powers granted to the government of the United States included the power to form a corporation if it were apposite to the particular functions the government wished to perform. It is still true that the Federal government can create corporations only for governmental or quasi-governmental purposes; the states, on the other hand, have been allowed to create them as they would, and as our technology developed corporations began to proliferate to such an extent that by 1835 our great-grandfathers felt that the situation called for a close look.

As we look back on their findings now, they made a surprisingly accurate prediction of the probable effects of an unlimited corporate life. (They were not so sound, perhaps, in their estimate as to whether it was desirable or undesirable.) For the next fifty years they used every known legal means to keep a corporation to a single defined and manageable enterprise. The corporation lawyer of the period spent most of his time on the law of *ultra vires*, which dealt with corporations that tried to transcend the limits that had been set out for them. These limits ordinarily were:

First, that they could only own a limited amount of property, frequently and especially only a limited amount of real property. The fear was they would start absorbing huge quantities of land.

Second, that they could indulge in only one type of business. If a corporation was organized to run a flour-mill, it had to run a flour-mill and nothing more.

Third, that they should last only for a defined period of time, twenty or thirty years or whatever the statutory limitation was.

Not infrequently there was a fourth limitation. This was that the corporation should be subject to continuous inspection. The courts could appoint a "visitor"—today he would be called an auditor. He was authorized to inspect and analyze the workings of a corporation and report to the judge, who, in turn, had an undefined power to say what should or should not be done.

A variety of other limitations were imposed from time to time, all of them representing attempts to prevent exactly what happened:

First, that a corporation would grow so large that its economic strength would vastly outweigh the strength of any individual enterprise.

Second, that it would be able to rove the country, if not the world, at will and do what it wished in terms of economic enterprise.

And third, that it would become a trust for perpetual accumulation; that its assets, in so far as they were not distributed by way of dividends, would be permitted to pile up to unlimited amounts.

These three results have come about, of course. Corporations did do, have done and are doing exactly what our forefathers worried about. Part of their fear stemmed from the belief that the corporation was only an artificial personality and therefore did not have a soul or a conscience. Lacking a conscience, it had no morals and was *prima facie* dangerous. This is why throughout out history society has attempted to control and constrict the corporation.

The rise of the large contemporary corporation—the giant as we know it

today, the true collectivism—began with the railroad systems. There were
other large corporations, but the railroad systems were the ones that posed
the real problems. They were the first to demonstrate the shift in the private
property system that came about when we began to realize that there was
no real way of constricting a corporation whose business the community
needed. If its economic functions were necessary to the welfare of the community, the law somehow had to recognize that fact, however backhandedly.
If a railroad needed to go through to the Pacific coast, the law had to find
some way around the fact that the corporate power did not let it go that far.

A diagram of what was happening to private property while this was
going on would look something like this:

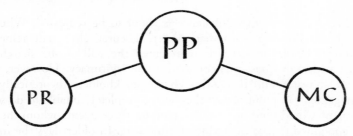

"PP" or possessory property is where it all began in about 1810 or 1820.
This is our great-great-grandfather's farm or forge, which he had not only
created but owned and operated. This was the assumed unit of property at
the beginning, and even today we still talk in those terms. This possessory
property becomes incorporated as an enterprise and is immediately split into
two functions. At the left is one function—"PR" or "passive receptive." This
is the receptive side of property, the stockholder's share. The shareholder
cannot manage. Every corporation statute in the country says that the business of the corporation shall be managed by its directors, and almost every
court has agreed that the director is not an agent of the stockholder and
does not have to follow his instructions. So the right-hand side of the diagram is "MC" or managing and creating.

The business of stockholders is primarily to receive; the business of management is primarily to manage and create. In the early days, when corporations were still small, the stockholder powerfully influenced the director but
today they are so far apart that the stockholder can hardly communicate
with management even by megaphone. We go through the ancient forms
and it is good that we do so, but everyone knows that a stockholders' meeting is a kind of ancient, meaningless ritual like some of the ceremonies that
go on with the mace in the House of Lords. The "passive receptive" side of
the corporation, in short, is functionless.

The "MC" side looks better at first glance. But in any large corporation
the management group is actually as striated as it is possible to be. The

president and the chairman of the board probably work together as the theoretically responsible officers, but they must operate through committees of officers—big officers, medium officers and little officers, all divided in as many different ways as the management experts can invent. While the top officers officially have the right to enter upon the property and do things, even though they are not able to own it, the fact is that they have had to sub-divide that right to such a degree that in practice the real possessor of a piece of property is the manager of the particular division or area of the property—and even he probably has to share his right with his plant manager if he's got one. This is possession without right, just as on the "passive receptive" side there is right without possession.

As things look now, this unbalance is about to be redressed. Whether it will be good redressing is another matter. Theoretically, management got its legitimacy by the fact that it represented the will of the shareholders. This was a kind of quasi-amateur democratic legitimacy. However, on examination, it was found that although the stockholders theoretically chose the management, in point of fact they were completely unable to do so. The management would send out a proxy naming three agents whom the stockholders appointed to cast their vote at a meeting. In older days the management often didn't even bother to say for what directors these proxies would cast their vote. Since the Securities and Exchange legislation, they have to do that, but the corporation secretary who sent out the proxies was the man who really determined what happened for all practical purposes in the power relationship. The president or the directors could fire him, of course, so he did what they told him to do. When the directors wished to renominate themselves or to add to their number or to fill a vacancy, they did it. This is still the method by which the directors in a great corporation are chosen. This is an automatic self-perpetuating oligarchy.

These are a string of bad words. There was at least one court case in which it was held that a self-perpetuating oligarchy was illegal. This was the famous case in which a life insurance company in New Jersey purchased control of a trust company by buying a majority of the shares. Thereafter it caused the trust company to purchase a majority of *its* shares. The result was an unbreakable ring. A New Jersey court said that this was illegal, created an oligarchy and was contrary to the theory of New Jersey corporation laws.

However, thereafter, somebody asked whether corporations really should be run democratically. Should this group or that group or the other group campaign against each other, offering inducements to shareholders to vote for them instead of the other group? Could corporations assimilate this kind of democratic government? There was no answer. In point of fact, the choice of management depends not on an assent of balanced interest but on expert judgment of technical ability with a companion judgment of honesty and character. As a result, for all practical purposes, management controls the corporation unless it is itself controlled by another oligarchy with enough shares to dominate the situation at all times.

There is a good deal of loose thinking about this. It is commonly believed that the holder of 20 per cent or 25 per cent of a corporation's stock can control that corporation. This was the inference in the recent du Pont-General Motors case. This is not true. It is true that with 20 per cent or 25 per cent of the stockholders' list of a large corporation *plus* control of the directors it can be done. But if the directors of General Motors decided not to vote with du Pont, it is very doubtful whether the du Pont interest is sufficient to be able to go out and get the other 30 per cent of General Motors stockholders which it would need. This is not pure theory. When a certain gentleman ran Standard Oil of Indiana he did various things that induced the so-called controlling group to want a change. They canvassed the board of directors and asked whether they would not fire the man. The directors said they would not. Thereupon the controlling group went to work to try to win the next election. Between their own and allied holdings they had slightly over 20 per cent of the stock. They did control in the end, and the man was fired. But they achieved it only by spending about $800,000 on a stockholders' campaign.

The control system in today's corporations, when it does not lie solely in the directors as in the American Telephone and Telegraph Company, lies in a combination of the directors of a so-called control bloc (a misnomer, incidentally) plus the directors themselves. For practical purposes, therefore, the control or power element in most large corporations rests in its group of directors and it is autonomous—or autonomous if taken together with a control bloc. And inheritance-tax distribution of stock being what it is, the trend is increasingly to management autonomy. This is a self-perpetuating oligarchy.

Meanwhile the next phase has been emerging. It will stay with us and it will be of some interest. This involves what are known as pension trusts— welfare funds and pension trust funds. A pension trust in most cases differs from an insurance trust in that it has an unlimited and indefinite obligation. It is there to pay pensions to X, Y and Z which shall be a fraction of the salaries X, Y and Z will have collected during the years of their tenure. The pension trust fund, if it is properly administered, has to think not merely of paying out a stated number of dollars in, say, 1980, as an insurance company does, but of having enough dollars to meet obligations later to be determined. No human being knows the future course of inflation of the dollar, prices, pay and so forth. Nevertheless, although the payment period may be twenty or thirty years away, the pension trusts must keep abreast of inflation at least as it affects pay.

This suggests, of course, that they must invest in equities, whereas, classically, trust funds invested in fixed obligations. This is the sharp difference between the kind of burden resting on an honorable pension trustee and on the directors of, say, the New York Life Insurance Company, whose business is to provide a stated number of dollars against stated contracts to pay those dollars with interest later on. The pension trust funds, therefore, belong among the stockholders in the "passive-receptive" column of our diagram because of their ownership of common stocks. The holdings of life insurance companies include less than 5 per cent in common-stock equities; in the pension trust funds equities are running close to 30 per cent of their assets and may be more. The total of pension trust funds at the moment is almost $31 billion. Roughly half of this is in the hands of insurance companies, which operate—perhaps erroneously—on the assumption that they have only another set of insurance policies. Ninety per cent of the remaining pension funds are in the hands of eight or nine New York banks, the largest single one being the pension trust fund of the American Telephone and Telegraph Company, which is about $2.2 billion so far and is operated by a committee through the Bankers Trust Company.

As a result of this broad-scale buying of equities the pension trusts are slowly "chewing up" control of those corporations which offer the best means of equity investment. These are voting equities. Thus far no attempt has been made to make use of this except in the case of the Sears, Roebuck pension trust fund which undertook to buy Sears, Roebuck stock and presumably now has a controlling interest in the company. As a result Sears, Roebuck is socializing itself via its own pension trust fund, and is discovering that it is running into the same difficulty which a socialist or any other form of oligarchic government has—that it has self-contained control, and management is thus responsible to itself. Query: does it continue to have "legitimacy" when the only mandate it can refer to is its own?

The present $30 billion in the pension trusts of course is doomed to increase. These are compulsory savings and the funds must continue to accumulate. They now cover only about half of the non-farm labor force; they will undoubtedly soak up a considerable part of the balance before long, and must increase, particularly in view of the population rise. In addition, it will be another twenty or thirty years before this "levels off"; that is, before the payment from the funds begins to balance the incoming. The pension trust funds will perhaps level out at somewhere in the vicinity of $70 to $80 billion, probably increased by the coefficient of the increase in population or the increase in labor force within the population. This will mean that if the pension trusts continue to take the good equities as they have been doing, they may well have the prevailing control-stockholding position and the capacity to make it absolute. They will have, say, 20 per cent to 30 per cent of the good equity stocks and the capacity to increase that to 40 per cent or 50 per cent (45 per cent for practical purposes is a majority at any big stockholders' meeting).

With the rise of the pension trusts into the "passive-receptive" end of the corporation structure the old "passive-receptive" stockholder is gradually disappearing. At best he is, shall we say, a pensionnaire. The last vestige of his power to legitimate a management by a vote is in the hands of the pension trustees. He has an expectation arising out of the fact that he may have performed a certain number of years of acceptable work and fulfilled a certain number of other conditions. But does he have any property right in the pension trust? The courts say no. The power—what is left of it—lies in the trustees, or in those insurance companies which administer trusts.

When power is lodged in a particular group it has no choice except either to exercise it or to try to revolutionize the system. There is no way of avoiding power. If you take it and refuse to exercise it you suffer the fate of King Lear—the king who wanted to be king but did not want to be bothered. The trust funds admit they have it but they have thus far refused to use it. This situation cannot last very much longer. Somebody is bound to use that power, of necessity. Pension trusts are so concentrated that a relatively small amount in equities outbalances any number of scattered holdings.

The private property system in production, which began with our great-grandfather's farm and forge, has almost vanished in the vast area of American economy dominated by this system. Instead we have something which differs from the Russian or socialist system mainly in its philosophical content. Under a pure socialist or Communist system, in theory, every worker has an old-age pension at the end of his labors. We are developing the same thing by "socializing" property without a revolution. It is one of our more amazing achievements. Whether one likes it or not depends on one's philosophy.

Possessory private property in this area has been metamorphosed. In its place is a power pyramid. At the moment this is a management pyramid, but it is beginning to be balanced by a pyramid of men who have no possible property interest in the actual corpus but do have the power of choice—the pension trustees. These are naked power vehicles, with the "receptive" end so far dispersed that it cannot even be discerned. To make the joke complete, let us suppose that a pension trust liquidated itself tomorrow and satisfied its contract obligations. If it was a well-run trust, there would be a balance left over. That balance would very likely escheat to the state because there was no claimant to it left. In the most violently private-property-minded country in the world this is perhaps one of the most magnificent economic jests the world has seen.

None of this has come about as a result of the villainy of conspiring men. That might have been true in the free-wheeling corporation days of a hundred years ago, but it would be as ridiculous an assumption today as is the basic assumption of the Supreme Court decision in the recent du Pont case. This decision apparently assumed that because du Pont bought 23 per cent of General Motors forty years ago, perhaps hoping that it could control General Motors, du Pont still holds to the intention of exercising this control. Actually, there has been a kind of continual biological progression over the years. Change is part of the progression. Bigger enterprise was needed to satisfy the desires of the population. In addition, the techniques which made it possible to satisfy certain necessities made it *impossible* to rely only on the individual. Consequently, organization and power, not ownership, had to meet the resulting problems. The progression has been natural.

Today approximately 50 per cent of American manufacturing—that is everything other than financial and transportation—is held by about 150 corporations, reckoned, at least, by asset values. If finance and transportation are included, the total increases. If a rather larger group is taken, the statistics would probably show that about two-thirds of the economically productive assets of the United States, excluding agriculture, are owned by a group of not more than 500 corporations. This is actual asset ownership. (Some further statistical analysis is called for if financial corporations be included, for these, of course, double up. One of the largest and most plainly oligarchically controlled corporations in the United States, the Metropolitan Life Insurance Company, duplicates assets because it holds securities of other corporations.) But in terms of power, without regard to asset positions, not only do 500 corporations control two-thirds of the non-farm economy but within each of that 500 a still smaller group has the ultimate decision-making power. This is, I think, the highest concentration of economic power in recorded history. Since the United States carries on not quite half of the manufacturing production of the entire world today, these 500 groupings—each with its own little dominating pyramid within it—represent a concentration of power over economics which makes the medieval feudal system look like a Sunday School party. In sheer economic power this has gone far beyond anything we have yet seen.

We can talk about the various alleged legal controls which somehow or other, when the chips are down, neither control nor even seek to control. We can point out the fear of "monopoly" and "restraint of trade" and say that from time to time this fear has checked the process. True, our law has prevented any one of these power groups from becoming a monopoly, but it has not seriously prevented the concentration of power as power, though it has prevented certain ultimate results. The question is then: Why has concentrated economic power in America not got completely out of hand? Many of these corporations have budgets, and some of them have payrolls, which, with their customers, affect a greater number of people than most of the ninety-odd sovereign countries of the world. American Telephone and Telegraph, for example, based on combined population and wealth, would be somewhere around the thirteenth state of the union in terms of budget, and certainly larger than many of the countries of South America. Some of these corporations are units which can be thought of only in somewhat the way we have heretofore thought of nations.

Whether we like it or not, this is what has happened. As noted, it is not the product of evil-minded men. I believe that we must try to work with the system. The dangers are obvious. But history cannot usually be reversed. Until engineers and economic forces give us a way by which a man can manufacture an automobile in his back yard we will continue to have organizations the size of General Motors or Ford—as long as people want Chevrolets or Fords. We will have railroads the length of the Union Pacific as long as people want to go across the continent by railroad. In other words, until a combination of technique and organization can be invented permitting *individuals* to do the job, we are bound to try to make the best we can out of the situation. To my mind most of the results are rather surprisingly good.

This does not mean, however, that I am not afraid. I am. I believe it is the *content* of these systems rather than their *form* that matters. Their power can enslave us beyond present belief, or perhaps set us free beyond present imagination. The choice lies with the men who operate the pyramids, and with the men affected who can demand what they really want. Our Anglo-Saxon democratic liberties, after all, were beaten out, not against the framework of the personal possessory property regime, but against the background of two of the most brutal despotisms in Western history. Both the Angevin dynasty in Normandy and the Tudor dynasty in England were rank despotisms. The content of our democratic liberties from Magna Carta down was pumped in by extraneous moral processes. Our institutionalized liberties present the case of an institution conscripted into utility, rather than something that emerged full-armed from the head of Jove. It was probably better that way; the democracy of the Greeks did not work so very well.

We have to accept this power situation as, let us call it, a neutral mechanism subject to the control of the body politic as long as we *keep* it subject to that control. That control, I believe, will be essentially intellectual and philosophical, capable of being translated into legal rules when necessity arises. In that respect I make three points in summary:

1. The first is that whenever there is a question of power there is a question of legitimacy. As things stand now, these instrumentalities of tremendous power have the slenderest claim of legitimacy. This is probably a transitory period. They must find some claim of legitimacy, which also means finding a field of responsibility and a field of accountability. Legitimacy, responsibility and accountability are essential to any power system if it is to endure. They correspond to a deep human instinct. A man desires beyond anything else to have someone give him the accolade of "Well done, thou good and faithful servant," thereby risking the condemnation of "You have been no good—get out." If he has to say it to himself, or hear it from a string of people whom he himself has hired or controls, he is apt to die a cynical and embittered man.

The medieval feudal power system set the "lords spiritual" over and against the "lords temporal." These were the men of learning and of the church who in theory were able to say to the greatest power in the world: "You have committed a sin; therefore either you are excommunicate or you must mend your ways." The "lords temporal" could reply: "I can kill you." But the "lords spiritual" could retort: "Yes, that you can, but you cannot change the philosophical fact." In a sense this is the great lacuna in the economic power system today. In theory the stockholders can act as the "lords spiritual" through their vote. In fact they cannot, and they know they cannot. Are the pension trustees or their equivalent slowly emerging as the men who can? They had not thought so—nobody had thought so. They have been essentially a method of transmission of choice and not much else. We are looking for the kind of thing that C. Wright Mills in his recent book on the American power elite rightly said did not exist. He wrongly concluded, therefore, that the system was a mess, which it obviously is not. We are, if you choose, searching for the pyramid on the other side of our diagram. But every time we have had the chance to construct that kind of elite we seem to have abandoned it, and chucked in an administrator instead.

2. My second summary point is that the sheer power of invading personality is great and that a doctrine is already at work which plays a second joke on our constitutional system. The United States began by saying that its Federal government could not construct corporations and apparently by assuming that the states would not. Both have done so. It also said that corporations should be kept apart from governmental power. *De facto,* they have not been. We are now, in fact, beginning to converge on a doctrine which may well push right over the line when the next case comes up. This doctrine is that where a corporation has power to affect a great many lives (differing from the little enterprise which can be balanced out by the market) it should be subject to the same restraints under the Constitution that apply to an agency of the Federal or state government. In that case, the Bill of Rights and the Fourteenth and Fifteenth Amendments would apply. At the

moment this is one jump ahead of current law. Yet it seems probable that this will be the next phase—just as we already have the constitutional doctrine that under the Fifth Amendment you may not by private contract prohibit a Negro from buying land.

3. My third point is destined to be in infinitely greater controversy, and I do not know what the end of the controversy will be. Great corporate power is exercised in relation to certain obligations:

1. It should supply the want in the area of its production. Where the community has come to rely on a corporation for steel, oil, automobiles or cigarettes, the corporation is obliged reasonably to meet that demand.

2. The price must not be considered extortionate. It must be "acceptable"—which doesn't necessarily mean fair or just.

3. It must provide at least some continuity of employment.

4. It must give a continuing attention to the technical progress of the art.

At every point in the individual history of large corporations there has been some moment of impact on the community when either the community felt the corporation was not fulfilling its obligations or, alternatively, the corporation realized it was up against a situation it could not handle. In every case the result has been either a friendly and orderly, or unfriendly and disorderly, hassle out of which a piece of planned economy emerged. Roughly two-thirds of American industry and much of American finance is now controlled by a formal or informal Federal industrial plan. Here are two illustrations at each end of the cycle.

The oil industry claims to be the most non-socialist, free-wheeling, private business that ever was. But the fact is that after many vicissitudes it sought control by, and is controlled by, various Acts of Congress. After orderly discussion certain laws were passed. Under these laws, first, the Bureau of Mines of the Department of Interior estimates the probable consumption month by month of gasoline and the chief oil products. Second, an interstate treaty exists among the oil-producing states, ratified by the Congress. Third, a Congressional Act makes it illegal to transport oil in interstate commerce which has been produced in excess of a state allowable. This legislation might break down if it were not for the fact that because there is a relatively concentrated system in the oil industry the refineries will not buy "non-certified" oil anyway. As a result, the big companies do not violate the Act; the little ones cannot; and the result is a planned oil economy by which supply is equated to demand and the oil industry from well to refinery to gas station is more or less geared to meet it.

Here is a disorderly example: Aluminum was manufactured by a monopoly which was ordered to be split up under an anti-trust decree. By a combination of administrative orders entirely without administrative rationale but all working toward the same end the Federal government used the aluminum plants it had itself created during World War II in order to set up two competitors to Alcoa. It likewise required Alcoa to sell its Aluminium of Canada shares. This was not enough by itself, so the government for a period of years handled its defense orders in such a way that the new companies had adequate assurance of a market until they could get properly under way. The policy still is to make certain that the new companies, which can stay in business only by being assured a reasonable market, will get the extent of market they need. There was a stockpiling arrangement at one time, followed later by the release of part of the stockpiled aluminum. In a wholly disorderly way which only the American system could ever conceive, there arose the equivalent of a *de facto* planned economy in aluminum. At the moment this industry now sails away, free-wheeling. But there is not the slightest doubt that if conditions required transition back into a planned economy it would happen.

These two illustrations could be multiplied. The point is merely that (a) through constitutionalization of the corporation some attention is being paid to the protection of the individual; and (b) through a slowly emerging, industry-by-industry, flexibly-planned economy, some protection of the community is coming about.

Obviously a system like this is just as good as the ideas and strength of the body politic behind it. The same system in the hands, for example, of a Latin American dictator could produce terrible oppression.

There is a gradually growing feeling that pension trusts, for example, must be controlled. A pension trust ring could be something to bind a man beyond belief. It could bind him to his job. He could not change it without losing a substantial part of his life savings. He might be controlled in all sorts of ways. We are beginning to think even that the pension trust right which cannot be transferred to some other pension trust is suspect.

As men think, so they are. We are really seeking now a body of doctrine which will control power. I close by returning to my first point, which related to the desperate search for a field of responsibility and accountability referent to some point of view outside the system: that is, to some modern "lords spiritual."

Chapter XI

DEMOCRATIC SOCIALISM

In the seventeenth century the English established themselves as the world's leaders of progressive politics by making Parliament supreme against rival claimants, especially the Crown. Since then, the idea of popular sovereignty has become an integral part of civilized government. Some nations, like France, learned from England's example. Others have not learned their lesson, and still live, politically, three or four centuries behind the times.

In the twentieth century London has again become the symbol of a world ideology—democratic socialism. That England was first in developing socialist ideas was due to the fact that she was first in starting the Industrial Revolution which created the urban working classes—without which there can be no socialist *movement*. English socialism could not but be democratic from the start, because government by consent was a part of English life. Revolutionary Marxist communism, like the revolutionary Right, Fascism, finds unfavorable soil in England. Of all free parliaments in the world, the Communists have always had the smallest representation in the United States and England. This was disputed by some in the British election of 1945, when the number of Communist M.P.s in the House of Commons rose by fully 100 per cent—from one M.P. to two, out of a total of 640. In the elections of 1950, 1951, 1955, and 1959, the Communists failed to win a single seat.

Americans can no longer afford to look upon the various approaches to socialism with the detachment of yesteryear. Since the end of the Second World War, Soviet-American relations have dominated the issue of world peace. Since the foreign policy of a Great Power is related, in many respects, to its internal political and economic system, familiarity with the principles of Marxism-Leninism is indispensable to an understanding of the methods and goals of Soviet policy, domestic and international.

Important as the knowledge of the foundations of Marxist revolutionary communism is to the American citizen, whose grasp of political realities is so vital to the whole world, the main ideas of English socialism are even more important to him. "We are all socialists now," said Sir William Harcourt, a British Liberal leader, in 1884. Since then the trend, all over the world, has been toward more collective action. In the United States this tendency found expression in Woodrow Wilson's "New Freedom," and in Franklin D. Roosevelt's "New Deal." What was considered intolerable interference in the United States a generation ago, in fields like labor, social security, and education has gradually been accepted as just and inevitable. If the American economic system, the last island of a sheltered capitalist civilization, is going to develop at all in the direction of more public action and responsibility, Britain, and not Russia, supplies the laboratory in which the American observer will want to see what tests are being made, and why. Attlee is not nearly the dramatic figure that Lenin was; but to an American, Sidney Webb, and Tawney, and Attlee, are of greater *practical* importance than the quarrels between Stalin and Trotsky, or Marx's call to revolution, coupled with the doctrine of the dictatorship of the proletariat. If the United States were ever to subject even part of her economy to public control or management, it would have to be done slowly, as in England, and not overnight as in Russia; every change would have to be debated and passed by Congress, rather than imposed by revolutionary militias. The problem in Russia in 1917 was to *build* industry in a highly agrarian society with little democratic experience. The problem of socialism in advanced countries like England and the United States is to *reorganize* the existing industrial system in a society that is highly literate, relatively prosperous, and attached to free government. Finally, there was no middle class in Russia in 1917, when Communism triumphed. In the United States, as in England, there is a vast and strong middle class, and the problem for socialists is to persuade its most crucial sector—managers, engineers, technicians, and professional people— that socialism can offer them a better future than they can reasonably expect under private enterprise.

Socialist literature in England has no Marx or Lenin, who lays down the law for all time. The most influential socialist thinkers in England have frequently been without any official position of party or government, and their impact has been due primarily to their moral authority and felicitous literary style. Many consider R. H. Tawney's *The Acquisitive Society* (1921) one of the great classics of English literature as well as of socialist thought. Avoiding unnecessary technical terms, Tawney defines industry as "nothing more mysterious than a body of men associated, in various degrees of competition and co-operation, to win their livelihood by providing the community with some service which it requires." The function of industry, therefore, is service. However, under the capitalist system of industry and wealth, "functionless" property has developed, property which yields income and power without rendering any service. The essence of property is power, a kind of "limited sovereignty." This power becomes easily tyrannical when it is not responsible to anyone but itself, and when the only question asked is, "What does it yield?" rather than "What service does it perform?" From functionless property comes the power of those "who do not work over those who do," and Tawney warns that functionless property is "the greatest enemy of legitimate property itself." Tawney states two principles which will have to be applied to industry if it is to be a function ("an activity which embodies and expresses the idea of social purpose") rather than tyranny: "The first principle is that industry should be subordinated to the community in such a way as to render the best service technically possible, that those who render that service faithfully should be honourably paid, and that those who render no service should not be paid at all, because it is of the essence of a function that it should find its meaning in the satisfaction, not of itself, but of the end which it serves. The second is that its direction and government should be in the hands of persons who are responsible to those who are directed and governed, because it is the condition of economic freedom that men should not be ruled by an authority which they cannot control."

Published in 1921, *The Acquisitive Society* is still one of the prime sources of the socialist faith in Britain. Yet it is also illuminating in its description of capitalism as an economic system and of the behavior of capitalists. The kind of capitalism that Tawney exposes in *The Acquisitive Society* was a reality in the nineteenth century, began to change drastically when Tawney wrote, and has been defunct for too long to be ever revived again. Yet in reading Tawney one understands more easily why men of his generation—say around 1920—easily adopted the socialist creed as a protest against the degrading economic and moral conditions under which so many working people lived at that time. As the reality of the capitalist economy is changing in the direction of relative equality and affluence in Britain and in other advanced industrial nations, socialists are faced with the necessity of rethinking their traditional—and by now orthodox and often dogmatic—ideas in the light of changed circumstances.

What the Webbs and Tawney argued was partly realized in the lifework of Clement R. Attlee. In *The Labour Party in Perspective* (1937), the Leader of the Labor party and Prime Minister (1945-1951) of the first majority Labor government in English history, gives an intimate picture of the kind of men who built the Labor party. It may sound startling to many European (and possibly American) socialists that "the first place in the influence that built up the Socialist movement must be given to religion." In most Continental and Latin-American countries, socialism and religion are considered two entirely different worlds, living in nonbelligerent neutrality at best, and in open warfare at worst. Pope Pius XI emphasized this strongly when he warned in his encyclical *Quadragesimo anno* (1931) that "No one can be, at the same time, a sincere Catholic and a true Socialist." England is probably the only major country in the world where religion has nurtured the socialist faith and has even been, as Attlee claims, its first influence: "There are probably more texts from the Bible enunciated from Socialist platforms than from those of all other parties," and it is "possible in Britain for a parson to declare him-self a Communist and for millions of faithful Catholics to support the Labour Party."

Before World War II, one of the main points of Nazi-Fascist propaganda in the Western nations was the inevitability of an ultimate choice between communism and Fascism, and the offer of saving the world from the threat of communism through the Berlin-Rome-Tokyo Axis. Writing in 1937, when this propaganda convinced more than a few, Attlee rejected this choice: "I do not think that Britain must follow the Moscow or the Berlin road," mainly because the totalitarian state must make use of force and intolerance. "Avoid-ing both Fascism and Communism," Attlee wrote, "this country, I believe, can afford to the world an example of how society can adapt itself to new conditions and base itself on new principles without breach of continuity and without violence and intolerance." Attlee also notices the fact, without which the Labor party could never gain power: it had become a "national" party, whereas in its beginnings it had been essentially a party representing organ-ized labor. Many "individuals from the better-off classes" have joined the Labor party because of their realization of the "immoral and unjust basis of capitalism."

The spirit of British socialism is well reflected in the writings of Sidney and Beatrice Webb, Tawney, Laski, and a host of others; but the number of systematic treatises on the nature of British socialist philosophy is rela-tively small. One of the keenest analytical works in this field is E.F.M. Durbin's *The Politics of Democratic Socialism*. Published in the grim year of 1940, the book helped to reaffirm the faith in the democratic process, come what may. Durbin was especially well qualified, as a distinguished econo-mist, to study the phenomenon of capitalism on the broad basis of fact and history. Although an economist, Durbin believed that the *political* factor, the issue of revolution or evolution, of dictatorship or parliamentary government, is the really decisive problem. Rejecting the totalitarianism of Marxist revo-lutionary communism, Durbin was confident, in 1940, that not only would Britain be able to solve her economic problems within the framework of democratic socialism, but that she would lead the world on the road to a new society of political freedom *and* economic equality.

The strength of British socialism lies in the fact, foreseen by Sidney Webb in 1889, that the conservatives were being constantly "permeated" by socialist ideas. In a letter dated August 3, 1925, to the late Justice Holmes, Sir Frederick Pollock made an observation on socialism and the common law which is of interest to persons other than lawyers. Sir Frederick was rather conservative, but this did not prevent him from seeing that socialism contained an old principle of the common law, viz., the opposition to monopolies.

Socialism is frequently interpreted, or misinterpreted, as an essentially materialistic movement. In "The Moral Case for Socialism" (1949), Francis

Williams, closely associated with the British Labor movement for many years, starts with the thesis that socialism "arises from the belief that man is not an economic but a moral being moved by ideals and aspirations more satisfying than those of the materialist conceptions that govern the other great political creeds of the modern world—capitalism and Communism." On moral grounds, Williams objects to the open violence and terror of communism, but he also notices the tendency in capitalism toward "de-humanizing" man by reducing him to a mere potential source of profit, as far as his social-economic function is concerned. The boom-and-bust swings of unplanned capitalism have meant serfdom for many people, "the submission to blind economic forces generating their own crises and operating altogether outside the realm of logic or justice." Another main charge against capitalism is that its main motivation—competition—is likely to lead to a "profound neurosis." The stresses and strains produced by the competitive striving for higher and higher incomes in a capitalist society create a sick civilization, "because the men and women who compose it are sick." By contrast, socialism does not accept the pessimistic conception of capitalism concerning the nature of man, which holds that men, like donkeys, "will not move unless they are alternately induced to do so by a carrot and driven to do so by a stick." The more *optimistic* philosophy of socialism, Williams holds, assumes that men will freely work together in full realization of the values of cooperation and human fellowship. Williams concedes that such a view of man "has its attendant risks," and history alone will prove whether the philosophy of optimism is justified or not, whether cooperation can replace competition as the main driving force in society.

The moral aspect of socialism is also central in the thought of Jawaharlal Nehru, next to Gandhi India's greatest leader in the twentieth century. Since her independence in 1947, India—with a population of 400 million people—has been involved in the largest experiment in democracy that has ever been tried. The success or failure of democracy in India may well determine which way the underdeveloped countries will go: toward gradual social and economic change based on constitutional government, or toward rapid economic revolution based on the communist police state. In "Democracy, Communism, Socialism, and Capitalism" (1958) Nehru examines the main economic and political alternatives that confront the contemporary world. As a disciple of Gandhi, Nehru is opposed to the violence of communist theory and practice, and he strongly believes that "wrong means will not lead to right results." The gravest defect in communism, however, is that "its contempt for what might be called the moral and spiritual side of life not only ignores something that is basic in man but also deprives human behavior of standards and values." By contrast, socialism (in Nehru's thinking) avoids both the violence and repression of communism and the inequality and inefficiency of capitalism. Nehru sees no magic in socialism through which poverty, particularly in underdeveloped countries, will suddenly be transformed into riches. Socialism is for Nehru only another name for the scientific approach to social and economic problems, desirable for any country, but imperative in an underdeveloped one: "In a poorly developed country, the capitalist method offers no chance." Yet Nehru is no dogmatist who sees democratic economic systems sharply divided into socialist and capitalist ones. He feels that the earlier gap between socialism and capitalism tends to lessen in the long run, because capitalism is gradually incorporating some ideas of socialism, while socialism is gradually allowing more free scope to individual initiative.

Yet these differences of economic policy are less important than the common belief in the principles and values of democracy that link socialism and capitalism. Whether India and other underdeveloped areas following her example are more or less dedicated to public enterprise than to private enterprise is of no major concern so long as they are committed to free government. India's tie with the free world far outweighs whatever disadvantage some see in her neutralist foreign policy. An internally and externally free and independent India is of far greater value to the free world than an authoritarian or totalitarian India temporarily participating in western military alliances, but spiritually indifferent or even hostile to the basic principles of a free society.

There are no "final solutions" for fundamental human problems. The very success of a political or social philosophy frequently produces new problems, due to new conditions, new experiences, and new frustrations. One of the main defects of socialist thinking in the nineteenth century—shared by antisocialist economic thought of the period—was the underestimation of the political factor in its relation to economic institutions. The socialists (and many nonsocialist reformers) correctly saw that the economic power of capitalists entailed considerable political power. Socialists therefore thought that by breaking the economic power of the capitalists the problem of power and responsibility in its broadest sense would be solved. Yet the experience of socialist reality has shown that the diminution of capitalist power may be followed by an increase of governmental power. R. H. S. Crossman, a leading intellectual in the British Labor Party, addresses himself to this problem in his Fabian Tract, *Socialism and the New Despotism* (1956). Although left-of-center in the Labor Party, Crossman frequently writes as if he were F. A. Hayek. Crossman concedes two important points which socialists a generation ago would not have dared to concede: first, that capitalism may well prove a workable system from a purely economic viewpoint; and second, that the fact of nationalizing the means of production does not in itself solve the problem of responsible power: "Socialism must challenge power which is either irresponsible or only semi-responsible—in whatever hands that power rests," that is, whether power is in the hands of managers running privately or publicly owned enterprises. The dilemma facing a British democratic socialist is described by Crossman as follows: "Since the abuses of oligopoly cannot be checked by free competition, the only way to enlarge freedom and achieve a full democracy is to subject the economy to public control. Yet the state bureaucracy itself is one of those concentrations of power which threaten our freedom. If we increase its authority still further, shall we not be endangering the liberties we are trying to defend?" Despite all these difficulties, Crossman is still convinced that public ownership of the main industries is the way to bring about full democracy, provided the publicly owned enterprises are under continuous and effective control of Parliament and public opinion and provided the Labor Party itself, as well as the trade unions and cooperatives, can be made more truly democratic in their internal operations.

Denis Healey, one of the prominent spokesmen of the Right wing in the Labor Party, takes a less optimistic view on the issue of nationalization. In "British Labor's New Look at Industry" (1957) he bluntly states the fact that "nationalization is not popular with the average voter." Defending the *economic* performance of the nationalized industries in Britain (primarily coal mining, civil aviation, and the railroads), Healey argues that the British experience has shown that the state cannot always "be relied on to represent the people." In particular, the nationalized industries cannot claim any brilliant *political* performance, especially in relation to the consuming public or to their own workers. What, a generation ago, American writers like A. A. Berle and others said about American capitalist enterprise—that real power is in the hands of professional managers rather than of the share-holders who legally own it—is now increasingly recognized by socialists as being equally applicable to publicly owned enterprise: "Industrial power in every large developed economy now rests with a managerial class which is responsible to no one. The form of ownership is irrelevant. State control over nationalized industries is as difficult as share-holder control over private firms." For a high-ranking socialist to say that "the form of ownership is irrelevant" marks a basic change of outlook. As a way out of this dilemma between old dogmas and new facts, the Labor Party proposed in two policy statements in 1957 (*Industry and Society* and *Public Enterprise*) that the next Labor Government should adopt a new course: it should not take over businesses or industries as a general policy, but buy shares of companies in the open market, achieving a controlling interest in some individual firms, but remaining a mere share-holder among others in those firms where such control would not be obtained. The main purpose of this new procedure would be to let the nation benefit from capital gains and rising dividends in important industrial enterprises.

This method was not tried out after the 1959 election in Britain, because the Labor Party lost again, as it had done in 1951 and 1955. The aversion to further nationalization was even deeper than the more moderate leaders of the Labor Party had assumed. Shortly before the 1959 elections in Britain, over 2.5 million households were polled on the question of nationalization. Of those interviewed, 63.5 per cent wanted no further nationalization; 17.9 per cent wanted more nationalization; and 18.6 per cent had no opinion. More remarkably still, of Labor Party supporters 41.7 per cent wanted no more nationalization, 36.2 per cent wanted more, and 22.1 per cent had no opinion (*The New York Times,* September 4, 1959). If only a little over one third of Labor Party supporters were in favor of more nationalization in the 1959 election, it is not surprising that the Labor Party suffered a humiliating defeat so long as a large part of the voters identified the Labor Party with nationalization.

The reasons for the defeat are spelled out in greater detail by C. A. R. Crosland in "Socialism in a Prosperous World" (1960). Crosland, the author of the most challenging book on socialism written since World War II (*The Future of Socialism,* 1956), points to some important changes that have occurred in western nations in recent years. The average standard of living of the working class has risen considerably. This rise has been proportionately even higher for those who were formerly unemployed or who are relatively unskilled: the unemployed are now generally employed, and the gap between the wages of skilled and unskilled workers has been substantially narrowed. As to the sense of inequality and resentment that used to feed socialist party ranks, Crosland points to an interesting psychological phenomenon: "As the *average* level of real income rises, people care less about the exact distribution of income." An unemployed worker resents the income of a steadily employed person more than does an employed worker whose income is lower than that of another person. A worker who cannot afford any kind of a car is more resentful of those who can than is a worker who owns a low-priced car but sees others drive fancier models with more gadgets. Misery and inequality are thus no longer primary sources that can guarantee electoral victories for socialist parties in a prosperous world.

The first requirement for socialist survival and progress, Crosland argues, is for socialists to recognize that the "unreformed capitalism" of a generation ago no longer exists, and to adapt their program to the new circumstances. Yet he fails to spell out in concrete terms what this new appeal is to be. In this failure he is not alone, as the successive electoral defeats of the Labor Party in the nineteen fifties demonstrated. Yet it is perhaps a hopeful sign, from the viewpoint of the future of democratic socialism, that so many of the younger leaders have shown a remarkable capacity of self-analysis and self-criticism. Once the traditional orthodoxies and dogmas are cleared away, new positive programs appealing to electoral majorities may eventually be developed.

This will, however, in no case be an easy task. If the Labor Party is compelled, for reasons of expediency if for no others, to abandon the goal of nationalizing important industries, it runs the danger of antagonizing the militant element in the labor movement, which supplies the driving force, enthusiasm, and the active energy. Conversely, if the Labor Party confines itself to a more vigorous pursuit of welfare state policies, it may easily become a "me-too" party, since the Conservative Party can boast a long record of social reform and will not hesitate to remind the electorate of this fact.

While socialism has never found expression in a major national party in the United States, it has by no means remained without influence, the influence frequently being exercised indirectly rather than directly. The leader of American socialism, Norman Thomas, a former minister of religion, summarizes the insights and experiences of his life-long career as a socialist in his *Democratic Socialism: A New Appraisal* (1953). More than ever Thomas emphasizes *democracy* as the goal and process of socialism, after the world has learned in a generation of violence and terror of Fascist and Communist totalitarianism how precious the preservation of the democratic way of life is. Interestingly enough Thomas has learned also from experience to "lessen somewhat socialist insistence on state ownership," and he is aware of the "dangers of a statism," if the state is entrusted with too much economic responsibility. What socialists want now is "not nationalization, but socialization," in which workers and consumers, rather than the state, directly participate in the ownership and management of a publicly owned industry. The Tennessee Valley Authority rather than a government department like the Post Office seems to Thomas the kind of socialized industry which avoids the pitfalls of direct government operation and bureaucratic centralism. Thomas also frankly concedes—as few socialists would have done twenty or thirty years ago—that "socialism is not a panacea against war," which may be due to deeper psychological causes reflected in nationalism and totalitarian imperialism. On the issues of competition and equality of pay Thomas is less orthodox, too, than socialists used to be: he admits room for competition in a socialist society, provided it operates within reasonable bounds, and "if the reward is not of such a nature and amount as to put other men in virtual slavery to the winner." Similarly, Thomas rejects the principle of absolute equality of pay as impractical: "To make that principle work, there would have to be a kind of conscription for jobs which the socialist who loves liberty will be deeply concerned to avoid." Thomas stresses, however, that as a socialist he is in favor of a more equitable distribution of the national income, but such relative equality can be obtained progressively and through democratic methods. Important as the problem of distribution is, moreover, Thomas recognizes that for years to come the principal problem will be that of *increased production*. The experience of British socialism has shown that, whereas socialists used to concern themselves—before assuming the responsibility of government—primarily with the issue of just distribution, they quickly discovered that increased production was the first condition for a better life for all the people. Unlike many other socialists who still persist in a naive, unsophisticated type of optimism, looking upon capitalism as the only source of the maladies of democracy, Thomas has learned his lesson from modern psychology that "fear of freedom" is one of the main causes of democratic apathy and weakness, and that it is the task of socialism to create institutions which will make democracy a living reality.

One of the staple arguments against socialism is that it is the first step toward communism, and that a Communist is a "socialist in a hurry." Yet experience shows that the *strength of communism* is in *inverse proportion to that of democratic socialism*. After World War II communism established its rule where democratic socialist movements had been outlawed or suppressed, as in Eastern Europe and China. In Western Europe, Communist parties have flourished most in countries such as France and Italy, which have declining socialist movements. By contrast, communism has steadily weakened in countries that were governed by wholly or predominantly Socialist governments, such as Sweden, Denmark, Norway, Great Britain, and Israel, or by coalition governments with vigorous Socialist participation, such as Holland, Belgium, Uruguay, and Chile. So far, democratic socialism has been most successful in Scandinavia, New Zealand, Australia, and Britain, which have the strongest traditions of political liberty in the world, coupled with high standards of integrity in public life. The road to socialist doctrine may be simple, but that to socialist reality is complex; it has been no accident that democratic socialism has grown and governed in the politically most mature nations, whereas totalitarian communism, like totalitarian Fascism, has taken root primarily in politically less experienced states, whose traditions of political democracy are none too stable and whose standards of government are none too high. Socialists do not consider their ideal as an alternative to democracy, but, as Norman Thomas puts it: "Socialism itself is the fulfilment of democracy."

R. H. TAWNEY

1. *The Tyranny of Functionless Property**

"Possession," said the Egoist, "without obligation to the object possessed, approaches felicity." Functionless property appears natural to those who believe that society should be organized for the acquisition of private wealth, and attacks upon it perverse or malicious, because the question which such

* From R. H. Tawney, *The Acquisitive Society* (Harcourt, Brace and Company, 1921), By permission.

persons ask of any institution is, "What does it yield?" And such property yields much to those who own it. Those, however, who hold that social unity and effective work are possible only if society is organized and wealth distributed on the basis of function, will ask of an institution not, "What dividends does it pay?" but "What service does it perform?" To them the fact that much property yields income irrespective of any service which is performed or obligation which is recognized by its owners will appear, not a quality, but a vice. They will see in the social confusion which it produces, payments disproportionate to service here, and payments without any service at all there, and dissatisfaction everywhere, a convincing confirmation of their argument that to build on a foundation of rights and of rights alone is to build on a quicksand.

From this portentous exaggeration into an absolute of what once was, and still might be, a sane and social institution, most other evils follow. Its fruits are the power of those who do not work over those who do, the alternate subservience and rebelliousness of those who work towards those who do not, the starving of science and thought and creative effort for fear that expenditure upon them should impinge on the comfort of the sluggard and the *fainéant,* and the arrangement of society in most of its subsidiary activities to suit the convenience, not of those who work usefully, but of those who spend gaily; so that the most hideous, desolate, and parsimonious places in the country are those in which the greatest wealth is produced, the Clyde valley, or the cotton towns of Lancashire, or the mining villages of Scotland and Wales, and the gayest and most luxurious those in which it is consumed. From the point of view of social health and economic efficiency, society should obtain its material equipment at the cheapest price possible, and, after providing for depreciation and expansion, should distribute the whole product to its working members and their dependents. What happens at present, however, is that its workers are hired at the cheapest price which the market (as modified by organization) allows, and that the surplus, somewhat diminished by taxation, is distributed to the owners of property.

Profits may vary in a given year from a loss to 100 per cent. But wages are fixed at a level which will enable the marginal firm to continue producing one year with another; and the surplus, even when due partly to efficient management, goes neither to managers nor to manual workers, but to shareholders. The meaning of the process becomes startlingly apparent when, as recently in Lancashire, large blocks of capital change hands at a period of abnormal activity. The existing shareholders receive the equivalent of the capitalized expectation of future profits. The workers, as workers, do not participate in the immense increment in value. And when, in the future, they demand an advance in wages, they will be met by the answer that profits, which before the transaction would have been reckoned large, yield shareholders after it only a low rate of interest on their investment.

The truth is that, whereas in earlier ages the protection of property was normally the protection of work, the relationship between them has come in the course of the economic development of the last two centuries to be very nearly reversed. The two elements which compose civilization are active efforts and passive property, the labour of human things and the tools which human beings use. Of these two elements those who supply the first maintain and improve it, those who own the second normally dictate its character, its development, and its administration. Hence, though politically free, the mass of mankind live in effect under rules imposed to protect the interests of the small section among them whose primary concern is ownership. From this subordination of creative activity to passive property, the worker who depends upon his brains, the organizer, inventor, teacher or doctor suffers almost as much embarrassment as the craftsman. The real economic cleavage is not, as is often said, between employers and employed, but between all who do constructive work, from scientist to labourer, on the one hand, and all whose main interest is the preservation of existing proprietary rights upon the other, irrespective of whether they contribute to constructive work or not.

If, therefore, under the modern conditions which have concentrated any substantial share of property in the hands of a small minority of the population, the world is to be governed for the advantage of those who own, it is only incidentally and by accident that the results will be agreeable to those who work. In practice there is a constant collision between them. Turned into another channel, half the wealth distributed in dividends to functionless shareholders, could secure every child a good education up to 18, could re-endow English universities, and (since more efficient production is important) could equip English industries for more efficient production. Half the ingenuity now applied to the protection of property could have made most industrial diseases as rare as smallpox, and most English cities into places of health and even of beauty. What stands in the way is the doctrine that the rights of property are absolute, irrespective of any social function which its owners may perform. So the laws which are most stringently enforced are still the laws which protect property, though the protection of property is no longer likely to be equivalent to the protection of work, and the interests which govern industry and predominate in public affairs are proprietary interests.

A mill-owner may impose conditions which degrade a generation of operatives; but his brother magistrates will let him off with a caution or a nominal fine to do the same to the next. For he is an owner of property. A landowner may draw rents from slums in which young children die at the rate of 200 per 1000; but he will be none the less welcome in polite society. For property has no obligations and therefore can do no wrong. Urban land may be held from the market on the outskirts of cities in which human beings are living three to a room, and rural land may be used for sport when villagers are leaving it to overcrowd them still more. No public authority intervenes, for both are property.

Nor are these practical evils the gravest consequences which flow from the hypertrophy of property in an industrial society. Property is in its nature a kind of limited sovereignty. Its essence is a power, secured by the State to some individual or group as against all others, to dispose of the objects over which the proprietary rights are exercised. When those objects are simple and easily obtained, the property is normally harmless or beneficial. When they are such that, while they can be acquired only by the few, the mass of mankind cannot live unless it has free access to them, their proprietors, in prescribing their use, may become the irresponsible governors of thousands of other human beings.

Hence, when pushed to extremes, applied to purposes for which it was not designed, and in an environment to which it is not adapted, property in things swells into something which is, in effect, sovereignty over persons. "The main objection to a large corporation," writes Mr. Justice Brandeis, of the Supreme Court of the U. S. A., "is that it makes possible—and in many cases makes inevitable—the exercise of industrial absolutism." In England such absolutism is felt mainly in the hours of work, above all in the power to deprive the wage-earner of his livelihood by dismissing him from his employment. In America there are cities where the company owns not only the works, but halls and meeting-places, streets and pavements, where the town council and police are its nominees, and the pulpit and press its mouthpieces, where no meeting can be held to which it objects and no citizen can dwell of whom it disapproves.[1] Such property confers a private franchise or jurisdiction analogous to that which in some periods has been associated with the ownership of land. The men who endure it may possess as citizens the right to "life, liberty, and the pursuit of happiness." But they live, in effect, at the will of a lord.

To those who believe that institutions which repudiate all moral significance must sooner or later collapse, a society which confuses the protection of property with the preservation of its functionless perversions will appear as precarious as that which has left the memorials of its tasteless frivolity and more tasteless ostentation in the gardens of Versailles. Do men love peace? They will see the greatest enemy of social unity in rights which involve no obligation to co-operate for the service of society. Do they value equality? Property rights which dispense their owners from the common human necessity of labour make inequality an institution permeating every corner of society, from the distribution of material wealth to the train-

[1] See the *Report on the Steel Strike of 1919*, by the Commission of Inquiry of the Interchurch World Movement, W. Z. Foster, *The Great Steel Strike*, and the Final Report of the United States Commission on Industrial Relations.

ing of intellect itself. Do they desire greater industrial efficiency? There is no more fatal obstacle to efficiency than the revelation that idleness has the same privileges as industry, and that for every additional blow with the pick or hammer an additional profit will be distributed among shareholders who wield neither.

Indeed, functionless property is the greatest enemy of legitimate property itself. It is the parasite which kills the organism that produced it. Bad money drives out good, and, as the history of the last two hundred years shows, when property for acquisition or power and property for service or for use jostle each other freely in the market, without restrictions such as some legal systems have imposed on alienation and inheritance, the latter tends normally to be absorbed by the former, because it has less resisting power. Thus functionless property grows, and as it grows it undermines the creative energy which produced the institution of property and which in earlier ages property protected. It cannot unite men, for what unites them is the bond of service to a common purpose, and that bond it repudiates, since its very essence is the maintenance of rights irrespective of service. It cannot create; it can only spend, so that the number of scientists, inventors, artists, or men of letters who have sprung in the course of the last century from hereditary riches can be numbered on one hand. It values neither culture nor beauty, but only the power which belongs to wealth and the ostentation which is the symbol of it.

So those who dread these qualities, energy and thought and the creative spirit—and they are many—will not discriminate, as we have tried to discriminate, between different types and kinds of property, in order that they may preserve those which are legitimate and abolish those which are not. They will endeavour to preserve all private property, even in its most degenerate forms. And those who value those things will try to promote them by relieving property of its perversions and thus enabling it to return to its true nature.

They will not desire to establish any visionary communism, for they will realize that the free disposal of a sufficiency of personal possessions is the condition of a healthy and self-respecting life, and will seek to distribute more widely the property rights which make them to-day the privilege of a minority. But they will refuse to submit to the naïve philosophy which would treat all proprietary rights as equal in sanctity merely because they are identical in name. They will distinguish sharply between property which is used by its owner for the conduct of his profession or the upkeep of his household, and property which is merely a claim on wealth produced by another's labour. They will insist that property is moral and healthy only when it is used as a condition, not of idleness, but of activity, and when it involves the discharge of definite personal obligations. They will endeavour in short, to base it upon the principle of function.

CLEMENT R. ATTLEE

2. *Democratic Socialism versus Totalitarian Communism and Fascism**

Predominantly the parties on the Continent have been built on the writings of Karl Marx. Around his teachings the movement has grown. Different interpretations have been put upon his creed. In some countries other powerful influences have been at work, and the characters of his apostles and the circumstances of the countries to which they belong have necessarily caused differences in the method pursued by particular parties, but they have this in common—that they were formed as definite Socialist movements, inspired by the word revealed to Marx.

In Britain the history of the movement has been entirely different. Widely diffused as his influence has been, the number of those who accepted Marxism as a creed has always been small. The number of those who have entered the Socialist movement as the direct result of his teaching has been but a fraction of the whole. One must seek the inspiration of the majority of British Socialists in other directions.

Leaving aside Owen and the early pioneers, I think that the first place in the influences that built up the Socialist movement must be given to religion. England in the nineteenth century was still a nation of Bible readers. To put the Bible into the hands of an Englishman is to do a very dangerous thing. He will find there material which may send him out as a preacher of some religious, social, or economic doctrine. The large number of religious sects in this country, and the various tenets that many of them hold, illustrate this.

The Bible is full of revolutionary teaching, and it is not surprising that, in a country where thought is free, many men and women have drawn from it the support which they needed for their instinctive revolt against the inhuman conditions which Capitalism brings. I think that probably the majority of those who have built up the Socialist movement in this country have been adherents of the Christian religion—and not merely adherents, but enthusiastic members of some religious body. There are probably more texts from the Bible enunciated from Socialist platforms than from those of all other parties. Not only the adherents of dissenting bodies whose less privileged position inclined them to take a Left Wing line in politics, but also many clergy and laymen of the Established Church, found that the

* From Clement R. Attlee, *The Labour Party in Perspective* (Victor Gollancz, 1937). By permission.

Capitalist system was incompatible with Christianity. It is significant that the gap between the end of Owenism and the birth of the Social Democratic Federation is filled by the Christian Socialist movement of Kingsley and Maurice. Here one sees a feature which distinguishes the British movement from most of those abroad. In no other country has Christianity become converted to Socialism to such an extent as in Britain. In no other Socialist movement has Christian thought had such a powerful leavening effect. It is possible in Britain for a parson to declare himself a Communist and for millions of faithful Catholics to support the Labour Party. It may be noted as a factor in building the British Labour movement on broad foundations that so many of the adherents of the Catholic Faith in Britain come from Ireland, where a creed of political and economic revolt has been inculcated into a Catholic population. The British Labour movement owes much to these men and women, who brought over from their own country their hatred of oppression.

The Labour Party necessarily differs from those Continental countries where Socialists found themselves faced by a Church either closely bound up with the State or with property or class interests, and inimical to liberty of thought. Where, as in many countries, the workers in the formative years of the Socialist movement were attached to a dogmatic faith which controlled every phase of their lives, it was natural that the movement of revolt should be anti-clerical. To meet the conditions there was set up a dogmatism equally narrow and exclusive. The divisions between blacks and reds extending into every activity became absolute. Neither side could influence the other any more than can two contending armies entrenched against each other. Such a division undoubtedly gives great driving-force and cohesion to a movement, but it creates such a fissure in the body politic that the result is either stalemate or revolution. Neither can advance or retreat. In Britain, on the other hand, where political and religious differences do not coincide, there is a constant broadening owing to contact.

I do not believe that the only choice before us is the acceptance of Fascism or Communism. I do not think that Britain must follow the Moscow or the Berlin road. Those two roads have certain features in common. They are straight, narrow, and artificial. They drive through the landscape of humanity with little apparent reference to its contours or to the graces of the countryside which have been derived from the past. Those who journey along them attain a very high rate of speed, and they scorn old-fashioned meandering paths. There are many casualties on that account. A high rate of speed may give great pleasure to those who control the machines, but it may mean a vast amount of discomfort to the driven. The real question is, to what place will those who complete the journey arrive?—if, indeed, they do arrive, for there is a great possibility of a terrible catastrophe on the way. One may ask, too, in what kind of condition will those who journey be like when the road has been traversed? One can give no certain answer to these questions, whether one considers the travellers on the Moscow or on the Berlin highways.

I have already set out my objections to the Totalitarian State, whether formed on the Fascist or Communist model, and I will not repeat them here. I do not think that it is desirable as an ideal or necessary as a stage in human development. In my view the Totalitarian State is not an advance in civilisation but a retrogression. It has been adopted by peoples who are politically and socially immature. They have not grasped the fact that the essential condition for an advanced civilisation is tolerance, and that a society in which men and women of differing views on many subjects can live together in peace and harmony is a higher type than one in which all must conform to a single pattern. The achievement of the Totalitarian State involves the use of force, and its continuance requires the use of the same methods. The one thing indispensable is an all-pervading police service. While this continues there is no freedom, and until it is abolished the experiment in Russia will not attract the majority of the British people.

It is, in my view, the strength, not the weakness, of Britain which allows of wide tolerance and freedom, permitting people to disagree on matters of vital importance and yet to continue to live together in friendly intercourse. To exchange this for a society in which everything is subordinated to a ruthless class warfare would be a retrograde step. Avoiding both Fascism and Communism, this country, I believe, can afford to the world an example of how society can adapt itself to new conditions and base itself on new principles without breach of continuity and without violence and intolerance. We have in the past to a great extent avoided the civil wars which have done such a vast amount of harm in other countries. It is, I think, a false reading of history to think that what has happened elsewhere must necessarily happen in this country. It has not been so in the past. It was, I think, characteristic of Britain that, on the only occasion on which there arose a military dictatorship, the dictator was a man who strove continually for tolerance and sought unceasingly to rid himself of the burden of absolute power and to return to the ways of constitutionalism. Cromwell was as English as Mussolini is Italian.

I think that nations tend to follow very closely their national traditions. Italy has frequently been the arena for faction fights and proscriptions. The Fascist methods are nothing new to the descendants of the Guelfs and Ghibellines. Military despotism has been a feature of German history. It is still a question whether or not Russia will return to the autocracy which she has so long endured. It is my faith that Britain will be true to her traditions, and that, despite the profound differences that separate the supporters of

Socialism and Capitalism, the changes which are necessary will be brought about without bloodshed and violence. It is the genius of the British people to modify and adapt old institutions to new purposes. I think that the same process which has been followed in the past will be employed in the future for changing the social and economic structure of this country.

I believe that the Labour Party is the instrument whereby this change will be effected. Typically British, the Labour Party has shown its power of adaption to new conditions and new purposes. At its inception it was a party representing almost entirely organised Labour. Its programme was sectional, not national. It has since then developed into a national party, open to all, and has a policy which embraces every phase of national life. In its earlier days it would have been a fair criticism to have said that it could not aspire to power because its appeal was too narrow. It is not true to-day. Increasingly it draws its strength from men and women of all classes of society. Its achievement of power does not depend on an alteration in the quality of its adherents, but in their quantity. It has to convert to its faith many millions of workers who still cling to Capitalism. It has to persuade many members of the classes which depend in the main on their own work for their livelihood that true community of interest is based on fellowship in service, not on participation in profits.

There is, I believe, an ever-growing number of people who, although comparatively well-to-do, are yet profoundly dissatisfied with the Capitalist system. There are technicians and business managers who find that their efforts lead only to frustration. When they invent new machinery or introduce improvements into production, they more often than not find that as a result of their labours a number of workers have been thrown out of their jobs, while not infrequently the increased production which they have effected cannot be absorbed because of the mal-distribution of purchasing power.

There is also a realisation that in modern large-scale industry there is but little chance of a man becoming his own master. He is apt to be only a servant of a company. He realises that he might as well serve the community instead of a certain number of profit-takers. The uncertainty of private enterprise which was so manifest during the great depression has made more attractive the prospects of serving the State or the municipality. But I think that a more powerful motive which is bringing into the ranks of labour so many individuals from the better-off classes is a realisation of the immoral and unjust basis of Capitalism. The social conscience speaks loudly to-day. Where formerly it impelled people of goodwill to give to charity, it now leads them to examine into the system which produces injustice. Where formerly they were content to deal with results, they now seek to remove causes.

The fact is that the ranks of the supporters of the Capitalist system are constantly being thinned by the desertion of those who have lost faith in it. Many of these find their way into the ranks of Labour. There is, however, a great body of citizens who, while unable to give their former support to Capitalism, still fear to accept Socialism and all its implications. I believe that they will come to realise that there is no alternative. At present they hesitate partly through prejudice and partly through misunderstanding.

It is the task of the Labour Party to win over to its side all these elements which are still uncertain of their position. To do this involves a receptivity on the part of the Labour Party itself. It does not in my view involve watering down Labour's Socialist creed in order to attract new adherents who cannot accept the full Socialist faith. On the contrary I believe that it is only a clear and bold policy that will attract their support. It is not the preaching of a feeble kind of Liberalism that is required, but a frank statement of the full Socialist faith in terms which will be understood.

I do not believe that there is need for a great change in the constitution of the Labour Party. Its basis in organised Labour must remain. The complaint that the Labour Party is bossed by a few Trade Union officials is untrue. The constitution of the Party is democratic. Individual membership is open to all. I anticipate that in the course of the next few years there will be a rapid increase of individual membership which will give the local Labour Parties an even greater influence than that which they now possess. I hope that the Party will continue to be a party of the rank and file, and that those who enter its ranks will accept the conditions and discipline of democracy. There is not, and should not be, a royal road to influence in the Labour movement.

The Labour Party is what its members make it.

The future of the Labour Party depends on two things—its success in winning power in this country, and the way in which it uses that power when it has been obtained.

I am convinced that whenever this mandate has been given, the Labour programme must be carried out with the utmost vigour and resolution. To delay dealing with essentials would be fatal. To show irresolution or cowardice would be to invite defeat. A Labour Government should make it quite plain that it will suffer nothing to hinder it in carrying out the popular will. In all great enterprises it is the first steps that are difficult, and it is the way in which these are taken that makes the difference between success or failure. A Labour Government, not in a spirit of malice or revenge, but with the greatest regard for justice to all, must resolutely set about its task of rebuilding the life of this country on the principles of liberty, equality, and social justice, and of joining with other nations to create a world Commonwealth.

E. F. M. DURBIN

3. *Britain: World Leader of Democratic Socialism**

The Marxist system of thought is based upon four propositions of an ascending degree of particularity—first, that the governing motive in human life is that of acquisitiveness; secondly that acquisitiveness must manifest itself in the form of group struggle in so far as it produces historical change; thirdly that this group struggle must break out into civil war during any period in which power is transferred from one class to another; and fourthly that a dictatorship of the proletariat and of the Communist Party over the proletariat can achieve social justice or Socialism.

I have found it impossible to accept any one of these four propositions in an unamended form. While it is possible to concede that acquisitiveness is an important and universal motive in human behaviour—animating us all, present in every group contest, deeply influencing the whole course of history—it is not possible to accept the view that it is a sole determining cause, a solitary source of change, or the final or fundamental cause in history. The pattern of social causes is more complex, and the causes at work in it are of many kinds. Nor was it possible to accept the view that even where rational acquisitiveness is present, it must take the form of group contest. It is obvious that co-operation plays just as important a role in the economic life of society, and that changes and discoveries in the field of co-operation are every bit as significant in the determination of historical change as are movements in the technique of struggle.

But the most important doctrines for my purpose are the two political theses—that civil war is inevitable, and that social justice can be secured by the dictatorship of the Communist Party. Neither of these doctrines, however, seems to bear the light of psychological or historical evidence particularly well. It appears from the history of our own country alone that classes have been defeated without violence, and that we were brought within measurable distance of civil war in a struggle between two parties of the same class. And we have just seen that the method of government implied by a dictatorship, and the release of unbridled aggression made possible by the circumstances of a dictatorship, render it almost inconceivable that a dictatorship of any kind could create social justice, or restore political liberty without a further revolution.

It would perhaps be as well to say at this point that I do not wish for a mo-

* From E. F. M. Durbin, *The Politics of Democratic Socialism* (Routledge, 1940). By permission.

ment to decry the importance or value of Marxist thought to the social sciences. After Marx and Engels had completed their life work, all further historical reflection and political theory has of necessity been "post-Marxian." They accomplished an intellectual revolution in the historical and social sciences upon which all who come after them must build. Their emphasis upon the importance of acquisitiveness in history—Mr. Cole's "realistic interpretation" of history—their analysis of the mechanics of group struggle, their picture of society as a mechanism of institutions, are ideas that may change and develop, but can never wholly disappear. They are part of our contemporary understanding of what we are.

It is only static Marxianism that is blind, and whose political implications are wrong. All that Marx said, and Lenin said, must be amended, reinterpreted and set in proper perspective by the greater knowledge of social institutions that we have now accumulated, the further historical experience through which we have passed since they wrote, and, most important of all, by the extra-ordinary increase in our knowledge of psychological motive and emotional process. Marxism must, like every body of thought, change and grow if it is to live.

For the purpose of this book the most important conclusion that I have tried to establish is the last. I have tried to show why I so profoundly believe that we cannot proceed by the Communist road to a better social order. Strong and violent men have always believed that they could build a new heaven and a new earth, if only they were allowed to override and destroy those who disagreed with them. It is not so. The problem of social life is the problem of reconciling the conflicting ends of different persons and different groups. Justice cannot be achieved, much less happiness, by the mere crushing of one party to a conflict. Injustice remains, hatred remains, the drawn sword cannot be sheathed, the machine-gun cannot be put away. Monotonously and horribly the victims will continue to tramp down to death, their shoulders bowed by suffering, their eyes glazed with hatred and fear. It is twenty years since the Communist Party obtained undisputed political power in Russia. Still the victims tramp down to death. There is no end to the suffering, the river of blood flows on. For those of us who live in quieter and happier lands, this is not the way. To those who really seek a better social order—and are not merely seeking in political action relief from the explosive violence of their own natures—I would say with assurance: *This is not the road!*

Is there any other and better way to walk in?

I value the social tradition in which we live. The services of this country to the cause of human happiness cannot be lightly dismissed. We have, for centuries now, led the world in the arts of government and in the discovery of the springs of social peace. We first applied the principles of reason to the tasks of economic organization and industrial production. By so doing we made possible, for all men, levels of prosperity and wealth that would have appeared Utopian, even fantastic, to generations that lived before the onset of the English Industrial Revolution. We have, from the beginning, made invaluable contributions to the advancement of science and learning. To-day through the generosity and long-sighted wisdom of one group of our scientists—the practising psycho-analysts—standing in marked and honourable contrast to the behaviour of most other professions, we have gathered into our society the most distinguished group of psychologists in the world, working in the forefront of contemporary science. We shall continue, in many fields of human endeavour, to lead and not to follow the generality of mankind.

We have, in this country, much of which to be ashamed. The distribution of income is nowhere less equal. The grip of a class system that frustrates the search for comradeship between us, and wastes a monstrously high proportion of our natural talent, is extraordinarily strong, and is not the less strong, nor the less destructive, because it is so little resented. In this generation moreover, we have been guilty of the most terrible crimes of popular vandalism. We have torn down some of our finest buildings, and we have permitted the speculative builder and the profiteering landlord to drive hideous scars across our countryside; straggling in promiscuous rape over the lovely body of our ancient agricultural civilization. We have revealed ourselves to the world as ruthlessly uncultured, and our generation will go down to posterity as one of the most aesthetically destructive in our history —a rival in the popular demonology of the future to the unforgettable excesses of the Reformation and the Civil War. Although we have reason to be proud of our social tradition we have, therefore, no occasion to be contented with its chequered pattern.

The future of the British tradition is not secure. It is threatened from within and from without. There are dictatorial parties at home and there is the ever-present threat of attack from abroad. We could no longer walk quietly in our traditional paths of liberty if either of our violent parties grew to power, or if we were on the losing side in the present European war. Even victory in it will endanger the stability of our society. Hence peace was and is one, though not the sole or the first, of our vital interests.

When the peace of Europe is restored, and in so far as we have preserved the institutions of a free government, we have still a great service to perform for ourselves and for the world.

Every generation is in part united, and in part inspired, by some conception of a better and a more just society. The conception varies from age to age, and reflects in large measure the peculiar needs and the dominant philosophy of the time in which it enlivens men to hope. There is a rough law of compensation in its form. The deeper the distress of the world in which they live, the more Utopian is likely to be the hope by which men sustain themselves in their daily labour. Despite the fear of aerial bombardment, ours is predominantly an age of quietness and comfort. The standard of living continuously rises about us, and our social life is not torn by deep religious or political conflicts, moving men to violent solutions. We can therefore afford modest dreams and practicable aspirations. We do not need the soothing vision of a perfect society to reconcile us to a bitter distress.

The conception of a better society, by which the broad trends of our policy can best be instructed, is therefore of a specific kind. We need not be content with anything less, nor need we ask for more, than a society in which property as a source of social inequality is made to wither slowly away, in which the establishment of a rational central control has restored expansion and created economic stability, in which political democracy is preserved and perfected as a method of government, and in which children may grow, free from secret fear, into a sociable and happy maturity. This is what I mean by a more just society. An important, indeed an essential, part of it is the constituent principle of Socialism. Within it the common happiness of mankind can be, for a long season, safely established.

Nor need we fear that this society is far away, or difficult to achieve. There is nothing in it that could not be established in a single generation, if we had the eyes to see, and the hearts to will, this reasonable programme of social betterment. We have only to open our eyes and stretch out our hands to pluck this precious fruit from the tree of knowledge.

I feel the conviction, ever more strongly as I grow older, that it is in this land, rather than in any other, that these hopes are likely to find their first fulfilment. We shall not be conscious of the birth in our midst of a new society, because we do not exercise our minds in self-analysis, or construct systematic social philosophies. But as I move about this island, in its quiet lanes and in its crowded streets, meeting people of all classes and persuasions, I feel the life of a strong and quiet people about me; more deeply united than they realize, more creative than they ever suspect. Here, if anywhere, the will for the common good is strong. From it and from the common friendliness we bear to one another we can continue to make, if we will, a society of which all men will be glad.

FREDERICK POLLOCK

4. *Socialism and the Common Law**

The element of truth in Socialism is to my mind something the Common Law knew long before any modern Socialists were born: Monopolies are in principle odious, and when they are necessary they must be under public control: whether the control shall be central or local, direct as in the post-office, or indirect by way of regulated franchises, is a matter of means and economic expediency (thus electric supply now seems capable of centralization on a great scale and with advantage, and our numerous railway companies are now amalgamated in a few groups). Our lady the Common Law is a very wise old lady though she still has something to learn in telling what she knows.

FRANCIS WILLIAMS

5. *The Moral Case for Socialism* †

I know of no better definition of the moral case for socialism than two sentences from the Declaration of Independence: "We hold these truths to be self-evident, that all men are created equal, that they are endowed by their Creator with certain unalienable Rights, that among these are Life, Liberty and the pursuit of Happiness. That to secure these rights Governments are instituted among Men deriving their just powers from the consent of the governed . . ." I am a socialist because I believe that only within a socialist society can these rights be assured. Socialism, like all political systems, is a means. Its end is a democratic society recognizing the dignity of human personality and the uniqueness of the individual. Its specific contribution to the solution of those political problems, which are among the most intransigent facing mankind, arises from the belief that man is not an economic but a moral being moved by ideals and aspirations more satisfy-

* From *Holmes-Pollock Letters*, edited by Mark DeWolfe Howe (2 vol., Harvard University Press, 1941). By permission.

† *Fortune*, Vol. 40 (October, 1949). Copyright 1949 Time Inc. By permission.

ing than those of the materialist conceptions that govern the other great political creeds of the modern world—capitalism and Communism.

This is the basis of the political method that the socialist believes should be followed in the organization of community affairs. He holds that a good society is possible only if it is recognized that men have a fundamental need to combine and cooperate. In this belief he is, it may be noted, increasingly supported by the researches of biologists into the nature of life.

Capitalism, even when it outgrows its more ruthless manifestations and becomes benevolent and paternal, is rooted in the belief that the acquisitive instinct is the primary human instinct upon which a civilized community must depend. The socialist does not accept this profoundly skeptical and pessimistic view of human nature. He is no more prepared to accept the doctrine of economic man when it is presented to him in capitalist terms, than he is when it is presented to him in Communist terms.

To the Communist, of course, the stage of economic development reached by society alone, as Engels said, determines its form, its political pattern, and its cultural development. The struggle between classes whose economic vantage point differs is so absolute that it can only be resolved by force and will only be ended when the largest and least advantaged of all economic classes has succeeded in destroying all others.

The socialist rejects Communism as a political method capable of achieving the good society because he cannot agree that economic interests, although important, are sufficiently absolute to justify the suppression of political and intellectual freedom and the concentration of all power in the hands of those who claim, rightly or wrongly, to represent the interests of the largest economic class. But he equally rejects capitalism as a means to the good society because he observes that by denying social control over economic power it reduces in practice the effectiveness of the very political liberties it claims to defend.

At the conclusion of the last meeting of the United States Chamber of Commerce, the United Press canvassed representative leaders of American business there present for their views on an unemployment total of over three million. "Unemployment is a natural and normal development of industrial readjustment," said one of these leaders. And a second one added, "Unemployment is a good thing in a dynamic free-enterprise economy."

Within the capitalist concept they were quite right: a system of private capitalism requires a reservoir of economically powerless and expendable human beings for its smooth functioning just as much as a Communist system requires the existence of a politically powerless and expendable mass for its operations. The socialist, however, is concerned not with systems but with human beings. He says with all the force at his command that any system which can so dehumanize its leaders that they can regard as "a good thing" the infliction upon millions of their fellows of the mental and moral degradation and material suffering of unemployment—of being told by society that it has no use for them, that their strength and talents are value-less, that they are unfit to do what it is the right of all men to do, to support themselves and their families by their labor—that such a system is immoral; because it has altogether lost sight of the true values of human life.

I am concerned with the moral case for socialism. And that case depends, as I shall hope to show, upon absolute values rooted in the nature of man and society. Nevertheless, that case does not exist in a vacuum without relation to other systems. Socialism challenges both the alternatives currently being offered to the world—Communism and capitalism—not only because it believes them to be misconceived in their estimate of the nature and the needs of man but also because of their historical records.

CAPITALISM, ROAD TO SERFDOM

The failure of Communism to make men free needs no documentation by me in these pages. But let us briefly consider the record of modern capitalism. It has, it is true, immense material achievements to its credit. But since it developed out of the Industrial Revolution of the nineteenth century it has repeated a devastating pattern of boom and slump on a major scale no less than eighteen times. These recurring crises it has been able to solve only by the purges of bankruptcy and unemployment. It has required men and women to pay tribute to it by the most terrible of all submissions, the submission to blind economic forces generating their own crises and operating altogether outside the realms of logic or justice. The theoretical case for capitalism is that it rewards those who by their energy most deserve reward. But, in fact, depressions of capitalist economy are as undiscriminating as the plague. No man can build an individual barrier against their devastations however honestly he labors or however worthily he uses his talents.

The submission to "automatic" economic forces that capitalism requires of ordinary men and women is, in the socialist's view, contrary to morality. And indeed, as the record of the interwar years showed, men and women are in fact increasingly unwilling to accept unemployment and personal ruin as the necessary correctives of an economic system beyond their social control. Faced with so destructive a philosophy, many of them during those years turned in desperation to the even more destructive philosophies of Fascism and Communism. They did so because both these systems, however specious their claims, appeared to offer economic security to the individual and affirmed in the loudest terms the right and ability of men to control the economic systems by which they lived. During the whole period of modern industrial capitalism no authoritarian dictatorship, whether of the left or of the right, has ever come into being in any country as the heir and creation of democratic socialism. The road to serfdom has always been the road of capitalist economy. In every case authoritarianism has been the product of a system of private enterprise, sometimes highly developed as in Germany and northern Italy, sometimes backward in development as in Russia and Eastern Europe, which has failed to satisfy the legitimate right of all men and women to that essential background of stability without which all personal hopes, ambitions, and plans can be made completely worthless.

It may be that, as its defenders declare, American capitalism alone among the great capitalisms of the modern world can succeed in solving this dilemma. It may be that it can find a way to offer to all men and women not only that which all advanced capitalisms have been able in some degree to offer, a high standard of living in periods of prosperity, but also a bulwark against depression and a genuine hope of security against undeserved unemployment and poverty. It may be so. But I see little evidence of it so far. Nor is there in such pronouncements as those I have been quoting on the therapeutic of unemployment, anything to indicate even the beginnings of a real understanding of the nature of the human challenge capitalism has to meet.

But even if—which I repeat seems to me unlikely—American capitalism were able to solve the problem of security that has baffled all other capitalist societies; and even if, which is still more unlikely, it were able to pass on its solution to other capitalist societies with few of its advantages in vast national resources—the moral case for socialism would still remain.

For that case rests ultimately, as I stated earlier, on the belief that man is a moral being and not simply an economic being. The socialist case is thus a challenge to successful capitalism as well as to unsuccessful and is spiritual and in a wide sense religious in character. It is no accident that, as Prime Minister Attlee recently stated, "The first place in the influences that built up the British socialist movement must be given to religion." Nor is it an accident that so many early leaders of British socialism were drawn from the churches and nonconformist chapels and that its present leaders include so many whose economic interests, taking into account the section of society into which they were born, gave them every reason to support the status quo. It was not personal economic interest but ethical compulsion that drove men like Attlee, Cripps, and others to try to build a more moral society.

CAPITALISM AND NEUROSIS

The moral case upon which socialism bases its claim rests on a view of the nature of man that denies that economic motives, although they have their part in affairs, are the sole or primary forces which should govern human society or that uncontrolled competition is the natural mode of human life. Just as the socialist believes that cooperation among nations can produce a better international society than can war, so he believes that cooperation among individuals can produce a better national society than can economic war. He insists that only by recognizing the fundamental desire of the vast majority of men and women to cooperate in solving their common social, political, and economic problems, and by accepting this desire as the primary motivation of our social organism, can we prevent society from being torn apart by conflicting group interests and create a pattern within which the whole personality of man can develop.

The socialist looking at modern capitalist societies sees them the prey of a profound neurosis. Their emphasis on a purely materialist standard of achievement, their insistence—inherent in the economic ideology that governs them—on competitive success as proof of character, so that men go through their lives hagridden by the fear that they may fail in almost the only test of manhood socially acceptable, that of the ability to earn a high income—all these confine human personality within a framework so rigid and so mutilating that the true values of civilization and the true warmths and generosities of human fellowship are lost. There is nothing so pitiable as the man who has no standards other than crudely material ones. Yet modern capitalism by its nature, by the credo at the heart of its philosophy, increasingly imposes these standards upon all men. Civilization is sick because the men and women who compose it are sick: forced into a mode of life unnatural to them and inimical to the profounder stirrings of the human spirit.

I do not think it is possible to look at American society, which is the product of modern capitalism at its most successful, without being made aware of the stresses and conflicts imposed upon men and women by the insistence upon materialist competitive success as the primary test of human value. The point of no return to which the salesman's philosophy brings those who give themselves wholly to the capitalist dream is not reassuring.

I am a visitor from a socialist country which is thought by many, because of the austerities that war and the change in international economic circumstances have imposed, to be a gray society and one hedged in with restrictions and controls. Yet I hope I shall be forgiven if I say that I am more conscious of strain and anxiety in American society than in British society. And of something perhaps more surprising—a sense of being imprisoned, confined within a pattern that has no mercy upon the nonconformist and dictates what it is socially acceptable to eat, to wear, to read, to say, to think, and above all to set as one's professional goal—to an extent that is not true of any European country I know. This dictation, this molding of the individual to a conventionally acceptable type, is not less significant nor less frightening because it is not the dictation of a man or of a group of men but of a philosophy. This philosophy sees people, as the believer in the capitalist thesis must, primarily as economic beings, as mass producers and mass consumers and as mass seekers after a social approval which is to be secured only by those who accept the standards of success that this philosophy lays down. I do not think this conformist pattern comes easily to American men and women—which is no doubt why neurosis seems to be assuming (if one can judge by newspaper reports, medical warnings, and what appears to be an almost universal preoccupation with digestion) the stature of a national disease. It is indeed contrary to what is best in that great American tradition of freedom, of individuality—of eccentricity even—and of goodneighborliness, to which the entire world owes so much. And it is even contrary to human nature; for that nature, we know, is infinitely variable. Indeed, it has much more exciting goals to seek than the well-appointed penitentiary of the economic man to which the pessimistic philosophy of competitive capitalism would lead us, under the neon lights and past the minatory advertisements.

ARE MEN LIKE DONKEYS?

The moral case for socialism is simply that it is based on a philosophy of optimism about human nature, just as democracy is. That is, indeed, why it is the natural culmination of the democratic idea and why, if one is to be genuinely a democrat, one ought also to be a socialist.

The democratic idea, which in its modern form is quite a new idea as political philosophies go, was a break with the past. This is true in the sense that it was an affirmation of faith in the ordinary man: in his ability to govern himself better than he could be governed by any hereditary or self-appointed ruler. And the democratic idea was also a revolutionary idea because it said that, however much men might differ in their individual talents and abilities, they were equals in their membership in a common society. It thus sought to transmit into the political sphere the Christian ethic of the uniqueness of the human personality and of the value of the individual—a value that is not to be judged solely by the standards of worldly success, but rather one by whose light all men are seen as equal in their common humanity.

It was opposed by many men of intelligence and good will as well as by many others of less estimable character, simply because they could not bring themselves to believe that ordinary men possessed this capacity to manage their own affairs decently, or that government by majority could be other than government directed by the lowest common denominator of human credulity and passion. They were ready to do everything for the people but trust them.

The socialist, imbued with the same faith in the ordinary human being as that possessed by the early democrat, seeks to widen the democratic domain. He does not accept the skeptical or the pessimistic view of human nature, which is the basis of the capitalist dependence upon economic self-interest and which holds that men, like donkeys, will not move unless they are alternately induced to do so by a carrot and driven to do so by a stick.

Nor does he accept the equally skeptical and pessimistic view, from which the capitalist theory of government flows, that men are unable to act wisely together in matters of major community concern or to elect representatives who will be honest and public-spirited in administering affairs, and that a government is the natural enemy of its citizens. Since he holds this view, it is natural that the advocate of capitalism as a political theory should believe that power cannot be tamed and must be dispersed. In his view a number of great corporations, wielding power uncontrolled by any authority other than the economic self-interest of their shareholders and managers, are less dangerous than one Department of State subject to the constant scrutiny of the legislature and the constant pressure of the public opinion of the electorate.

The socialist believes, however, that in matters of community concern the community is the best judge. Moreover, he holds that, as the quite short history of democratic government has shown, it is in fact able, within the framework of the democratic political method, to control its elected administrators and so ensure that the power delegated to them is used for the public good.

The business of supporting ourselves on this planet by using to the best advantages the natural resources with which it is endowed is not, to the socialist, an end in itself—as it is to those who hold to the capitalist theory as though it were a religion—but a means to an end. It is something to be solved in order that man may get on with the adventures of the soul and intellect, which are his real business. The socialist economic pattern derives from this belief. That is why it puts economic security and social service as a first charge upon natural resources and gives to the government, as the elected agent of the community, control over those commanding heights of economic power that can shape national destinies.

In applying it, the socialist makes an assumption that is no less and no more revolutionary than that which was made by the first adherents of political democracy. It is that incentives other than those of private interest can effectively govern economic affairs, that human beings will work together and give what is best in them because they feel themselves members of a social partnership of whose purposes they approve, and that there is a positive value in cooperation and in human fellowship. No doubt such an assumption has its attendant risks. Many decry it. But the search for a nobler harmony in life than that of the competition of the market place runs like a golden thread through all human history. It is to the adventure of that search that socialism summons those who have faith in the nature of man.

JAWAHARLAL NEHRU

6. Democracy, Communism, Socialism, and Capitalism*

The basic fact of today is the tremendous pace of change in human life. In my own life I have seen amazing changes, and I am sure that in the course of the life of the next generation these changes will be even greater, if humanity is not overwhelmed and annihilated by an atomic war.

Nothing is so remarkable as the progressive conquest of understanding of the physical world by the mind of man today. While there has been this conquest of external conditions, there is at the same time the strange spectacle of a lack of moral fiber and of self-control in man as a whole. Conquering the physical world, he fails to conquer himself.

That is the tragic paradox of this atomic and sputnik age. The fact that nuclear tests continue even though it is well recognized that they are very harmful in the present and in the future, the fact that all kinds of weapons of mass destruction are being produced and piled up even though it is universally recognized that their use may well exterminate the human race, brings out this paradox with startling clarity. Science is advancing far beyond the comprehension of a very great part of the human race and posing problems which most of us are incapable of understanding, much less of solving. Hence the inner conflict and tumult of our times. On the one side, there is this great and overpowering progress in science and technology and their manifold consequences, and, on the other, a certain mental exhaustion of civilization itself.

Religion comes into conflict with rationalism. The disciplines of religion and social usage fade away without giving place to other disciplines, moral or spiritual. Religion, as practiced, either deals with matters rather unrelated to our normal lives, and thus adopts an ivory-tower attitude, or is allied to certain social usages which do not fit in with the present age. Rationalism, on the other hand, with all its virtues, somehow appears to deal with the surface of things, without uncovering the inner core. Science itself has arrived at the stage when vast new possibilities and mysteries loom ahead. Matter and energy and spirit seem to overlap.

The old civilizations, with the many virtues that they possess, have

* *The New Leader* (September 8, 1958). By permission.

obviously proved inadequate. The new Western civilization, with all its triumphs and achievements as well as its atomic bombs, also appears inadequate, and therefore the feeling grows that there is something wrong with our civilization.

Communism comes in the wake of this disillusionment and offers some kind of faith and some kind of discipline. To some extent it fills the vacuum. It succeeds in some measure in giving a content to man's life. But, in spite of its apparent success, it fails—partly because of its rigidity, but even more so because it ignores certain essential needs of human nature. There is much talk in Communism of the contradictions of capitalist society, and there is truth in that analysis. But we see the growing contradictions within the rigid framework of Communism itself. Its supervision of individual freedom brings about powerful reactions. Its contempt for what might be called the moral and spiritual side of life not only ignores something that is basic in man but also deprives human behavior of standards and values. Its unfortunate association with violence encourages a certain evil tendency in human beings.

I have the greatest admiration for many of the achievements of the Soviet Union. Among these great achievements is the value attached to the child and the common man. Their systems of education and health are probably the best in the world. But it is said—and rightly—that there is suppression of individual freedom there. And yet the spread of education in all its forms is itself a tremendous liberating force which ultimately will not tolerate that suppression of freedom. This, again, is another contradiction. Unfortunately, Communism became too closely associated with the necessity for violence and thus the idea which it placed before the world became a tainted one. We see here the powerful influence of wrong means and methods.

Communism charges the capitalist structure of society with being based on violence and class conflict. I think this is essentially correct, though that capitalist structure itself has undergone and is continually undergoing a change because of democratic and other struggles against inequality. The question is how to get rid of this and have a classless society with equal opportunities for all.

Can this be achieved through methods of violence, or is it possible to bring about those changes through peaceful methods? Communism has definitely allied itself to the approach of violence. Even if it does not indulge normally in physical violence, its language is that of violence, its thought is violent and it does not seek to change by persuasion or peaceful democratic pressures but by coercion and, indeed, by destruction and extermination. Fascism has all these evil aspects of violence and extermination in their grossest forms and at the same time has no acceptable idea.

This is completely opposed to the peaceful approach which Gandhi taught us. Communists as well as anti-Communists both seem to imagine that a principle can only be stoutly defended by the language of violence and by condemning those who do not accept it. For both of them there are no shades, there is only black and white. That is the old approach of the bigoted aspects of some religions. It is not the approach of tolerance, of feeling that perhaps others might also have some share of the truth. Speaking of myself, I find this approach wholly unscientific, unreasonable and uncivilized, whether it is applied in the realm of religion or economic theory or anything else.

But whatever we may think about it, we have arrived at a stage in the world when an attempt of forcible imposition of ideas on any large section of people is bound ultimately to fail. In present circumstances, this will lead to war and tremendous destruction. There will be no victory, only defeat for everyone. We have seen in the last year or two that it is not easy for even great powers to reintroduce colonial control over territories which have recently become independent. This was exemplified by the Suez incident in 1956. Also, what happened in Hungary demonstrated that the desire for national freedom is stronger even than any ideology and cannot ultimately be suppressed. What happened in Hungary was not essentially a conflict between Communism and anti-Communism. It represented nationalism striving for freedom from foreign control.

Thus, violence cannot possibly lead today to a solution of any major problem, because violence has become much too terrible and destructive.

If the society we aim at cannot be brought about by big-scale violence, will small-size violence help? Surely not. Partly because that itself may lead to big-scale violence and partly because it produces an atmosphere of conflict and of disruption. It is absurd to imagine that out of the conflict the socially progressive forces are bound to win. In Germany, both the Communist party and the Social Democratic party were swept away by Hitler. This may well happen in other countries, too. In India, any appeal to violence is particularly dangerous, because of its inherent disruptive character. We have too many fissiparous tendencies for us to take risks. But all these are relatively minor considerations. The basic thing, I believe, is that wrong means will not lead to right results and that this is no longer merely an ethical doctrine but a practical proposition.

It is often said that there is a sense of frustration and depression in India, and that the old buoyancy of spirit is not to be found at a time when enthusiasm and hard work are most needed. This is not merely in evidence in our country. It is, in a sense, a world phenomenon. In our efforts to insure material prosperity, we have not paid any attention to the spiritual element in human nature. We talk of a welfare state and of democracy and socialism. They are good concepts, but they hardly convey a clear and unambiguous meaning. Democracy and socialism are means to an end, not the end itself. We talk of the good of society. Is this something apart from and transcending the good of the individuals composing it? If the individual is ignored and sacrificed for what is considered the good of society, is that the right objective to have?

The individual should not be so sacrificed. Indeed, real social progress will come only when an opportunity is given to the individual to develop, provided "the individual" is not a selected group but comprises the whole community. The touchstone should be how far any political or social theory enables the individual to rise above his petty self and think in terms of the good of all.

In a sense, every country, whether it is capitalist, socialist or Communist, accepts the ideal of a welfare state. Capitalism, in a few countries at least, has achieved this common welfare to a very large extent, though it is far from having solved its own problems and there is a basic lack of something vital. Democracy, allied to capitalism, has undoubtedly toned down many of its evils and, in fact, is different now from what it was a generation or two ago. In industrially advanced countries, there has been a continuous and steady upward trend of economic development. Even the terrible losses of the world wars have not prevented this trend, insofar as these highly developed countries are concerned. Further, this economic development has spread—though in varying degrees—to all classes.

This does not apply to countries which are not industrially developed. Indeed, in those countries the struggle for development is very difficult and sometimes, in spite of the efforts made, economic inequalities not only remain but tend to become worse. Normally speaking, it may be said that the forces of a capitalist society, if left unchecked, tend to make the rich richer and the poor poorer and thus increase the gap between them. This applies to countries, as well as to groups or regions or classes within countries. Various democratic processes interfere with these normal trends. Capitalism itself has, therefore, developed some socialistic features, even though its major aspects remain.

Socialism, of course, deliberately wants to interfere with normal processes, and thus not only adds to the productive forces but lessens inequalities. But what is socialism? Some people probably think of socialism vaguely just as something which does good and aims at equality. That does not take us very far. Socialism is basically a different approach from that of capitalism, though I think it is true that the wide gap between them tends to lessen, because many of the ideas of socialism are gradually incorporated even in the capitalist structure. Socialism is, after all, not only a way of life but a certain scientific approach to social and economic problems. If socialism is introduced in a backward and underdeveloped country, it does not suddenly make it any less backward. In fact, we then have a backward and poverty-stricken socialism.

Unfortunately, many of the political aspects of Communism have tended to distort our vision of socialism. Also, the technique of struggle evolved by

Communism has given violence a predominant part. Socialism should, therefore, be considered apart from these political elements or the inevitability of violence. It tells us that the general character of social, political and intellectual life in a society is governed by its productive resources, so that, if they change and develop, so the life and thinking of the community change.

Imperialism or colonialism suppressed and suppresses progressive and social forces. Inevitably, it aligns itself with certain privileged groups or classes, because it is interested in preserving a social and economic status quo. Even after a country has become independent, it may continue to be economically dependent on other countries. This kind of thing is euphemistically called "having close cultural and economic ties."

Without utilizing the modern methods which have brought great material advance to some countries of the West, we remain poor—and, what is more, tend to become poorer, because of the pressure of an increasing population. I do not see any way out of our vicious circle of poverty except by utilizing the new techniques and sources of power which science has placed at our disposal. But in doing so we should not forget the basic human element and the fact that our objective is individual improvement and the lessening of inequalities; and we must not forget the ethical and spiritual aspects of life which are ultimately basic to culture and civilization and which have given some meaning to life.

It must be remembered that it is not by some magic adoption of socialist or capitalist method that poverty suddenly leads to riches. The only way is through hard work, by increasing the productivity of the nation and organizing an equitable distribution of its products. It is a lengthy and difficult process. In a poorly developed country, the capitalist method offers no chance. It is only through a planned approach on socialistic lines that steady progress can be attained, though even that will take time. As this process continues, the texture of our life and thinking gradually changes.

Planning is essential, because otherwise we waste our resources, which are very limited. Planning does not mean a mere collection of projects or schemes, but a thought-out approach to strengthening the base and the pace of progress so that the community advances on all fronts. In India, we have a terrible problem of extreme poverty in certain large regions, apart from the general poverty of the country. We always have a difficult choice before us: whether to concentrate on production by itself in selected and favorable areas, thus temporarily ignoring the poor areas, or to try and develop backward areas at the same time, so as to lessen the inequalities between regions. A balance must be struck and an integrated national plan evolved. That national plan need not and, indeed, should not have rigidity. It need not be based on any dogma, but should rather take existing facts into consideration. It may—and, I think, in present-day India it should—encourage private enterprise in many fields, though even that private enterprise must necessarily fit in with the national plan and have such controls as are considered necessary.

The problems that India faces are, to some extent, common to other countries, but—much more so—there are new problems for which we have not got parallels or historical precedents elsewhere. What has happened in the past in the industrially advanced countries has little bearing on us today. As a matter of fact, the countries that are advanced today were economically better off than India today, in terms of per-capita income, before their industrialization began. Western economics, therefore, though helpful, have little bearing on our present-day problems. So also have Marxist economics, which are in many ways out of date, even though they throw a considerable light on economic processes. We thus have to do our own thinking, profiting by the example of others but essentially trying to find a path for ourselves suited to our own conditions.

In considering these economic aspects of our problems, we have always to remember the basic approach of peaceful means; and perhaps we might also keep in view the old Vedantic ideal of the life-force which is the inner base of everything that exists.

R. H. S. CROSSMAN

7. *Socialism and the New Despotism**

I. REACTION AGAINST LABOUR

Why has labour been losing the support of thoughtful independent voters since 1950?

If we were merely witnessing a change of fashion from the Leftism of the 1930's, this question would not worry us unduly. In that decade, a large number of intellectuals, who had no serious interest in democratic Socialism, were swept into Labour politics by the emotional tide of the Spanish war. That they have drifted back into non-political indifference need disturb

* From R. H. S. Crossman, M.P., *Socialism and the New Despotism* (Fabian Society, 1956). By permission.

nobody. But what is happening to-day is something far more serious. Despite the record of the Labour Government, more and more serious-minded people are having second thoughts about what once seemed to them the obvious advantages of central planning and the extension of State ownership.

Among the factors which have antagonised them, I would list—

(1) the experience of negative and frustrating war-time controls, prolonged for years after the fighting was over; and in particular the impression, fostered by its enemies, that the Labour Party regarded the ration card not as a temporary expedient but as a permanent feature of a fair-shares economy;

(2) the discovery that the Labour Government's 'Socialism' meant the establishment of a number of vast, bureaucratic public corporations, which failed to fulfil the two essential requirements of Socialism, namely, that a State-owned industry should be fully responsible to Parliament and give a share of management to its workers;

(3) the uneasy suspicion that the social revolution of which Socialists have talked was actually leading not to a freer but to a managerial society; and

(4) the conviction, heightened by years of cold war propaganda, that complete socialisation, as practised in the Soviet Union, has degenerated into a totalitarian State, in which the loss of civil liberties is not counterbalanced by the eradication of inequalities. These seem to me to be some, at least, of the factors which are driving liberal-minded people to-day to adopt views which, even eight years ago, they would have dismissed as black reaction.

Can we find a common characteristic in these four factors? I think we can. *What brought people into the Labour Party before the war was the conviction that it was fighting the battle for popular emancipation at home and abroad. What inclined them towards Socialism was the belief that democracy was breaking down and that freedom could only be secured by transforming it into a Socialist society. It was this assumption which converted a whole University generation, who would have been ardent Liberals in 1906, into ardent Socialists during the great depression; and it was the growth of doubt about its validity which has disillusioned them in the 1950's.*

IS A SLUMP INEVITABLE?

This doubt was brought home to me in August, 1955, when I attended the Congress for Cultural Freedom at Milan. There I had the pleasure of meeting John K. Galbraith, the author of the most arresting study of modern American capitalism. We were discussing the problem which confronts the American Fair Dealer in working out a convincing policy for the Democratic candidate in the forthcoming Presidential election; and it struck me at once that the difficulty which Galbraith, Arthur Schlesinger, junior, and others like them face in the United States is not unlike that of the Labour Party Executive. Their clothes have been stolen by the Eisenhower Republicans, just as ours have been by the Butlerites.

Galbraith said to me, 'There's an awkward thought which lurks at the back of our minds. Both the American Liberal and the British Socialist in the 1930's assumed that capitalism was not only immoral but unworkable; it was a system which must destroy itself because of its own inherent weaknesses. And this meant that, in your British philosophy, a Socialist revolution was not only desirable but inevitable. Now suppose that assumption is not true. Would that not mean the snapping of the mainspring of the Labour Party?'

In response to this challenge, I propose to pull this ugly thought out of its dark corner in the back of your minds.

KEYNES VINDICATED

Since 1945 the evidence, both from the United States and from this country and Western Europe, seems to suggest that, instead of being the most difficult and fundamental problem of Western society, mass unemployment is something which can be dealt with relatively easily by any Government which understands the economic system and has the right instruments for controlling it and manipulating it. There is still room for argument about these instruments. Are credit contraction and credit expansion—combined with the right budgetary policy—sufficient? Or are physical controls necessary as well? But these are secondary questions—disputes about tactics rather than strategy. What Socialists have to decide is whether John Maynard Keynes was right in asserting that the new capitalism has developed into a workable system—provided that it is worked intelligently.

I am not an economist and I am not here concerned with the strictly economic controversy. What matters to me are the basic assumptions about the nature of Western society which a Socialist should accept.

You will remember Keynes's picture. The way he proposed to deal with mass unemployment was to dig a very deep shaft, bury millions of bank-notes at the bottom of it and then pay wages to workers for digging the bank-notes out again. There, he said, is the simple method of resolving the inherent contradiction of capitalism. Whether the work is socially useful or socially useless is of secondary importance: what matters is the provision of work. Hitler and Schacht were the first people to demonstrate this, when they used an arms programme, fiscal controls and bilateral trade treaties to produce a full-employment economy in Germany. And we should not forget that the New Dealers did not succeed in abolishing mass unemployment in the United States until the war and the arms programme came along. So.

too, when the Germans invaded France, there were still 843,000 unemployed in this country. It was only at this point that the British Government was stimulated to indulge in the arms expenditure which absorbed all the unemployed.

It is high time you pulled this thought out of the back of your minds and had the courage to think it through to its final consequences. I believe that Keynes has shown this particular kind of pessimism about the Western economy to be unfounded. It is not an inherently unworkable society, but a workable society which is appallingly wasteful of human and material resources and which contains gross injustices. Only when we have frankly admitted this can we begin to think sensibly about the next stage of Socialism.

THE CONSEQUENCES

Why do so many Socialists hesitate to accept this? After all, we detest the denial of freedom in a Communist State, and it should be a vast relief for a democratic Socialist to realise that there is no need for totalitarian government control in order to abolish mass unemployment.

One reason for our hesitation is a practical one. It was difficult enough to persuade people to become Socialists when we could tell them that capitalism is not only immoral but also unworkable. Will it not be much more difficult, we ask, to persuade the majority of our countrymen that a workable system must be changed, simply because it is immoral and unjust? Don't most people care more about security than they do about social justice and equality? If welfare capitalism can provide the majority with security, how can we ever persuade them to prefer Socialism?

The doubts awakened by these questions have, I think, been accentuated by our experience of the mixed economy established by the Labour Government between 1945 and 1950. If we are honest, we must admit to ourselves that it was the least dogmatically Socialist parts of what the Labour Government did which were most popular and which worked best. What we describe as the Welfare State has been immensely successful and immensely popular, whereas nationalisation has not changed the lives of the workers in the industries affected in the way they expected.

It has been a disappointment to the trade union movement. The Socialist planner may envisage a future in which there are added to the Coal Board, the British Electricity Authority and the Transport Commission forty or fifty other Boards of the same type, imposed on other industries. But would this prospect, if presented to the public, win votes for Labour or reawaken the enthusiasm of the trade union movement? I suspect that we all know the answer to this question. It would not. If that is all that socialism means, the people of this country will reject it.

I put some of these problems to a Fabian Summer School at Oxford in 1955, and we had some of the best discussions I have ever heard. Most of the younger Fabians there agreed on one thing. They said to me, 'If you are going to have Socialism and a planned economy, why not make a real job of it? Why be content with this half-baked mixed economy and why imagine that you will rouse the Labour movement from its lethargy by proposing that the next Labour Government should nationalise two or three more industries? For heaven's sake, make up your minds on the National Executive. If you are still Socialists, go for it one hundred per cent.' I had anticipated that this would be the reaction, and I had taken the precaution of asking A. J. P. Taylor to come to the school. He listened to these younger Fabians and then he said, 'Very well, my friends, answer me one question. If you really believe all that, why don't you join the Communist Party? If you want one hundred per cent Socialism, what's wrong with the Soviet Union?' They could not give much of an answer to A. J. P. Taylor's question. They wanted one hundred per cent Socialism—but they didn't want the Soviet system.

THE WORST OF BOTH WORLDS

All the week we roamed round the problem, until we began to have the feeling that maybe the British people is now getting the worst of both worlds. Under the mixed economy now carried on by the Conservatives what we have is not monopoly (a market dominated by a single mammoth concern), but oligopoly (a market dominated by a very few mammoth concerns). In Britain this oligopoly is protected by a vast, bureaucratic State and so starved of the competition which, according to Mr. Galbraith, produces the new equilibrium in American society. The recognition that Britain is now falling between the two stools of full Socialist planning and a modern American Keynesianism is, I believe, another reason for the disillusionment of the independent Labour voter.

Both the American and the Russian systems are working far better than anyone expected twenty years ago. Even more important they are working far better than the British system either under Labour or under Tory management. That is why not merely intellectual sceptics but a good many loyal Labour Party supporters are beginning to wonder whether there is any third way between these two great systems. Are the only alternatives left to the Socialist in the 1950's either to watch Mr. Macmillan bring the British mixed economy into line with the American system or else to join the Communist Party?

II. THE AGE OF OLIGOPOLY

These doubts can only be removed by re-thinking the foundations of our Socialism.

Surely it is time to recognise that Socialism cannot and should not be based on any particular economic theory. Judged by the standards of prediction and verification, economics is still very far from being a science. To rate it at its highest, it is a technique, combined with historical analysis. Moreover, those who based the case for Socialism on the inherent contradictions of the capitalist system were departing from the tradition of British Radicalism and introducing a foreign element into the philosophy of our Labour Movement. *Labour's real dynamic has always been a moral protest against social injustice, not an intellectual demonstration that capitalism is bound to collapse; a challenge to capitalist privilege, not a proof that those privileges must inevitably be replaced by a classless society. Keynesianism may have undermined the old-fashioned economic case for Socialism, but it has left the political and moral case for it completely unaffected.*

That case was formulated in its classic form by Professor R. H. Tawney. He showed that Parliamentary democracy will only become a fully effective guarantor of individual freedom when it is combined with social control of economic power. Power, he argued, always degenerates into privilege when those who hold it are accountable to no one but themselves. In a democracy, therefore, those who own or manage the means of production must be made responsible to a popularly elected Government, and the most effective way to do this is to substitute public for private ownership of large-scale industries. Tawney's case for Socialism was not that it is easier to work than the acquisitive society but that it is morally superior—and politically essential to the realisation of freedom.

MAKING POWER RESPONSIBLE

Has Tawney's denunciation of the acquisitive society become less relevant in the last thirty years? On the contrary. One of the main post-war features of the Western world has been the steady concentration of economic power in the hands of the managerial class, whose responsibility to their shareholders is now purely titular. In Tawney's sense, the men who run our great industries to-day form an irresponsible oligarchy; and the degree of public control we have achieved is quite inadequate to ensure that they are in any sense accountable to the community.

The first task of Socialism, therefore, in the 1950's must be to expose this growth of irresponsible power; to challenge this new managerial oligarchy; to show that its monopolistic—or oligopolistic—privileges are a threat to democracy and to demand that it should become not the master but the servant of the nation.

At this point, however, we must drag out another of those doubts which are lurking in the dark corner of our minds. We say that we must denounce great concentrations of irresponsible power. But are they all on one side of industry? Is it only the privately owned companies which threaten our freedom?

The Labour Party has declared that Imperial Chemical Industries is ripe for nationalisation because it is a private monopoly. But when I look at the Coal Board (a public corporation), what strikes me is that it shares certain characteristics with I.C.I. Under its constitution the Coal Board must pay the same kind of attention to its balance sheet as any private corporation. It cannot pursue an unorthodox price policy, based on the national interest. It is certainly not fully accountable to Parliament and the degree of workers' participation in management which it has achieved is not markedly higher than in a progressive company. As for the technician and the scientist, they may actually feel more frustrated under the rule of the accountants, ex-civil servants, ex-generals and ex-trade union officials who compose the Board of a nationalised industry than they did under private enterprise. Nationalisation, in its present stage, has certain solid economic advantages, including Government control of the capital investment and the broad lines of policy of the nationalised industries. Moreover, it is a stabilising factor, since it eliminates those increases in unearned incomes and capital gains which provoke wage demands and stimulate inflation. But it is very far from the kind of Socialism envisaged in Tawney's *Acquisitive Society*. It is only the first step towards our goal.

STATE BUREAUCRACY

Moreover, these oligopolists—some in charge of nationalised and some of private industries—do not comprise the whole of the managerial society. There is also the State bureaucracy to contend with; and here too the old distinctions between public and private enterprise are becoming blurred. Of course, the orthodox Tory still instinctively suspects any Government Department of over-staffing and muddle; and instinctively assumes that I.C.I. is a model of individual initiative and business efficiency. Unfortunately the loyal Labour supporter is far too inclined to believe that his Socialist loyalty requires him to say the exact reverse. He believes that, whereas large-scale private enterprise is a threat to freedom, the State must be 'a good thing.'

Actually, the growth of a vast, centralised State bureaucracy constitutes a grave potential threat to social democracy. The idea that we are being disloyal to our Socialist principles if we attack it excesses or defend the individual against its incipient despotism is a fallacy.

Here again, Tawney's principle is relevant. Our aim is to enlarge freedom by making those who control great concentrations of power fully accountable to the people. But that must apply to the Chiefs of Staff or the Milk Marketing Board or the National Assistance Board or the Foreign Office as well as to the Directors of I.C.I. For the Socialist, as much as for the Liberal, the State Leviathan is a necessary evil; and the fact that part of the Civil Service now administers a Welfare State does not remove the threat to freedom which the twentieth-century concentration of power has produced. *It is the gigantic size of the modern unit of organisation, whether in industry, in the press, in the armed services or in the Welfare State, which presents the citizens of an advanced Western nation to-day with the choice between accepting the inroads on freedom of an increasingly managerial society or risking the advance towards a fully Socialist society.*

Let me try to sum up the conclusions we have so far reached.

(1) The probability suggested by John Maynard Keynes that Western capitalism is no longer bound by its own inherent contradictions to collapse in ruins, may well demand a radical rethinking of classic Communist theory in order to bring it into line with Russian practice. It presents neither a theoretical nor a moral problem to the democratic Socialist.

Our Socialism is based on the traditional Radical demand for a society of free and equal citizens, reinforced by the empirical postulate that great concentrations of power become a menace to freedom and equality unless they are subjected to public control. If the Western economies continue to expand without more than minor recessions, that expansion will bring with it an intensification of the oligopoly which provides the Socialist with the justification for imposing democratic controls on these vast aggregates of economic power. If, on the other hand, the Americans are unintelligent and let themselves drift into a slump, then we shall be faced with a crisis in which the case for Socialism scarcely needs to be argued in rational terms.

(2) Since our Socialism is based on the moral demand for greater equality and an enlargement of freedom, and postulates that irresponsible power corrupts, the Socialist must be courageous enough to admit that the evils of oligopoly are not limited to the private sector of the economy. Public corporations and Departments of State can also exhibit managerialist tendencies, favour inequality and become a threat to freedom. *If it is to appeal to the younger generation, Socialism must challenge power which is either irresponsible or only semi-responsible—in whatever hands that power rests.*

III. THE ROLE OF NATIONALISATION

The conclusion I reach is that we must not expect the initiative for the next stage of Socialism to come either from the Co-operative Movement or from the leadership of the trade unions.

It is, of course, essential for the Labour Party to retain the confidence of its two main allies. But it would be unrealistic to overlook the fact that both have now become established institutions, with deep roots in the existing social order, and display for this reason a quite natural reluctance to accept any radical change which seems inimical to their own interests. The dynamic of change today must be found in the Socialist membership of the Labour Party, or nowhere else.

That dynamic, I believe, will only become really effective if we ground our

Socialist case not only on economic arguments about increased productivity and improved living standards but also on the defence of personal freedom and personal responsibility in a managerial society. From this point of view the case for Socialism can be stated very simply. Since the process of power concentration is inevitable in a modern economy, the only alternatives are either to permit the oligopolists to dominate the community or to subject them to public control.

At this point, however, I must insert one reservation. There does exist another possible way of dealing with oligopoly. Instead of socialising the economy, the attempt could be made to break up the concentrations of power, or at least to ensure that they were subject to genuine competition. This, of course, is the tradition of American democracy, with its anti-trust legislation. There the trade union movement is violently but quite rationally opposed to the concepts of Socialism and central planning because it believes that the worker's freedom and living standards can best be safeguarded by independent trade union action in a keenly competitive society. I mention this American philosophy only in order to remind you that it is inapplicable to Britain. In the first place, Britain is too small. And, secondly, British capitalists are as afraid as British trade unions of genuinely competitive free enterprise. The only democratic alternative to Socialism, therefore, is ruled out in Britain by the need for enforced standardisation and by the restrictive practices which have characterised both sides of our industry for a generation. However much Conservatives may talk about their belief in the virtues of free enterprise, the Tory Government has done little to stimulate it since 1951.

In Britain we are faced with the following dilemma. Since the abuses of oligopoly cannot be checked by free competition, the only way to enlarge freedom and achieve a full democracy is to subject the economy to public control. Yet the State bureaucracy itself is one of those concentrations of power which threaten our freedom. If we increase its authority still further, shall we not be endangering the liberties we are trying to defend?

This dilemma is inherent in the nature of the modern, highly industrialised community. It is not, as is often suggested, exclusively a dilemma for Socialists; it faces every democratic Government, whatever its complexion.

CONSERVATIVES DEFEND PRIVATE POWER

The Conservative solution is to concentrate attention on the threat of State despotism (Crichel Down, for instance) and conveniently to overlook all the other concentrations of power which threaten our liberties. Modern Conservatives wish to weaken the central Government and encourage the Executive to sign a Magna Carta which guarantees the liberties not of the individual but of our new-style feudal barons. In fact, they accept the notion of an equilibrium within the managerial society, which we have already discussed and abandoned as a modern version of the Manchester Liberal illusion. Hence the failure of Conservatism to introduce effective monopoly legislation. Hence its eagerness to persuade the TUC to become a respectable member of the Establishment.

Where this leads is clear enough. Representative institutions will become less and less effective, and Parliament a ceremonial façade, which conceals the fact that power has been taken from the people and divided between the barons who control industry, Fleet Street and radio, the Departments of State and the party machines. On the pretence of defending the individual against the horrors of State Socialism, modern Conservatism will let democracy drift into a kind of voluntary totalitarianism.

The main task of Socialists to-day is to convince the nation that its liberties are threatened by this new feudalism and to show the way to overcome it. There are two requirements. (1) If the Executive is not to surrender to the oligopolists, it must be able to control them, and that means that they must be made equally subject to its control. (2) If the Executive is not itself to become a despot, it must be fully and continuously responsive to the popular will.

EXTENDING PUBLIC OWNERSHIP

I shall not spend long on the first of these requirements. It is, of course, the traditional Socialist case for public ownership. That case is even stronger today than it was before the growth of modern large-scale organisation. Although coal, electricity, gas and transport are not yet socialised, the national Boards which run them are partly accountable to the Government and the main lines of their development can be laid down by a strong Cabinet. If the Executive is to curb oligopoly without any loss of productive efficiency, then public ownership must be extended a great deal further.

All I would add is a word of warning. Neither the workers in industry nor the voters are well acquainted with the serious Socialist case for nationalisation. We would be prudent, therefore, to select industries where even the non-Socialist can be convinced that it is desirable. If the tenant of a rent-restricted house realises that he cannot obtain a bathroom under his private landlord without an exorbitant increase of rent, he may accept the Socialist case for municipalisation. If the road-user sees the chaos caused by pouring new cars on to an antiquated road system while passenger trains are half empty and the railways lose money, then he may accept the case for an integrated and publicly owned transport system. If retirement on half pay only becomes a possibility as a result of nationalising superannuation, then the extension of public ownership into the sphere of insurance will be as popular as the National Health Service.

It is no use, however, believing that we have finished the job when we have nationalised an industry or part of an industry and given it a Consumers'

Council. We have plenty of Consumers' Councils already and they are not very effective bodies. There is only one defence for the consumer, and that is through his elected representatives, whether in local or central government. That is why I am quite clear that every nationalised industry must be made fully responsible to Parliament, just as municipal trading concerns have always been fully responsible to the Council.

Our Socialist aim has always been two-fold. We seek to make economic power responsive both to the community as a whole (the consumer) and to the worker in any particular industry (the producer). Plans for nationalisation which do not satisfy the aspirations to workers' control are the technocrats' perversion of our Socialist ideal. We must frankly admit that, so far, our nationalised industries have been little better than that.

What is to be done about it? Some Socialists, and most trade union leaders, argue that this is a subject not for legislation but for education. The machinery, they say, for the individual worker to be promoted to management, and for production committees between workers and management, is already there in our nationalised industries, and all that needs to be done is to encourage both sides of the industries to work it.

If this were true, the prospects of a second stage of Socialism would not be bright. It seems to me obvious that any proposal for extending public ownership will not be welcomed by the trade unionists in the industry concerned unless they can foresee an improvement in their own status resulting from it. No one can responsibly promise that, as a result of nationalisation, an industry would be able to offer higher wages or even, in all cases, a more attractive superannuation scheme than a powerful private monopoly or near-monopoly. What publicly-owned industries could offer to their workers is a real share in the control of the industry.

WORKERS AND MANAGEMENT

On this problem I believe that the Labour Party would do well to study closely the experiment now launched in Western Germany. Here *Mitbestimmungsrecht* (or workers' participation in management) has been enforced by law on the coal and steel industries. Although they remain privately owned, the boards of directors of all these companies are now composed of an equal proportion of workers', employers' and State representatives, with an independent chairman.

The difference in structure between German and British industry would make quite inappropriate the idea of importing *Mitbestimmungsrecht* into Britain. Moreover, there are many snags in the German plan. Will it denude the trade unions of their best leaders? Will the workers' representatives be be cut off from the rank and file and lose its confidence? Have they been promoted to a stratosphere, where they can exert no effective control? These are all questions to which answers are only now emerging. Moreover, *Mit-*

bestimmungsrecht was regarded by the German trade union movement as an alternative to nationalisation, whereas British Socialists must treat workers' participation in management as an essential part of socialisation. All I suggest at present, therefore, is that the Labour Party should study the German experiment and ask itself whether the principle could be successfully applied to Britain.[1]

MUNICIPALISATION

I should like to say in passing that, since 1945, the Labour Party has tended to under-estimate the importance of municipalisation as a form of public ownership. There is everything to be said for creating smaller units of public ownership wherever possible and so reviving local democracy. Moreover, certain services are far better provided by Councils. I have often thought that the solution to our cultural wilderness is the municipal theatre. All over the Continent cities have their own theatres and operas, just as in America they have their orchestras. In Britain there are only a handful of such enterprises. Why do not we have the courage to preach that Socialism is not solely concerned with material improvement but also with the arts? I shall be told that this is unpopular, but many causes are unpopular at first. I would therefore like to see, in addition to municipalisation of rented houses, municipal laundries, taxis, etc., a drive by the Labour Party for municipal theatres—and also for municipal cinemas, built to break the monopoly of the big chains.

IV. SOCIALISM AS A DEFENCE OF FREEDOM

In this pamphlet I have confined myself to the single issue of Socialism and freedom. Of course, this would be only one of several themes in a Labour programme; and, in terms of appeal to the mass electorate, it would not be the most important. Responsibility is an acquired taste and the majority will always be far more concerned with material benefits and social security—at least until, in some particular case, their own personal freedom is threatened. Yet I believe that a Labour Party which neglects this theme, either in its appeal to the younger generation of electors or in the conduct of its own domestic affairs, is imperilling its cause and its future too.

SAFEGUARDS OF FREEDOM

For far too long we have assumed that the only changes in society which we have to make are changes in its economic structure and in the distribution of the national wealth. Of course, those changes are a vitally important part of Socialism. But surely we have learnt the lesson of Fascism and Communism. This lesson is that constitutional reform, designed to enlarge free-

[1] For a good discussion of this see *Workers and Management* by T. E. M. McKitterick and R. D. V. Roberts. Fabian Research Series 160.

dom and stimulate an active democracy, is at least as important as the extension of public ownership and redistribution of wealth—which are important only as another means to the same end. Indeed, unless the two march in step, we shall merely create a new Leviathan, in which a Socialist managerial oligarchy replaces a capitalist managerial oligarchy or, even worse, shares the power with it.

The modern State, with its huge units of organisation, is inherently totalitarian, and its natural tendency is towards despotism. These tendencies can only be held in check if we are determined to build the constitutional safeguards of freedom—and personal responsibility.

I am convinced that these constitutional safeguards of freedom against the new despotism can only be built by a Labour Government. But if it is to do the job, that Government must return to the first principles of Socialism and decide boldly to make all irresponsible power accountable to the community. And if that is to be our aim, we had better realise that the way we manage our democratic institutions—including the Labour Party and the trade unions—is at least as important as the way we manage the economy of the nation.

DENIS HEALEY

8. Second Thoughts on Nationalization*

In its latest pair of policy statements, the National Executive Committee of the British Labor party has grasped the most dangerous nettle involved in its revision of the old orthodoxy—the role of nationalization as an instrument of socialist policy.

Forty years ago, when the Labor party was reorganized to replace the Liberals as the second major British party, it was committed by its written constitution to achieve "the common ownership of the means of production, distribution and exchange"—an aim which even the Communist states are far from having attained as yet. Nevertheless, in its first period of real power, from 1945 to 1950, the Labor party did take 20 per cent of British industry into public ownership, by nationalizing the basic industries of coal, steel, elec-

* Denis Healey, "British Labor's New Look at Industry," *The New Leader* (August 19, 1957). By permission.

tricity and road, rail and air transport, not to speak of the Bank of England.

When the Conservatives took office, they left most of these industries in public hands, denationalizing only the profitable steel firms and long-distance road haulage. Apart from agreeing to restore these industries once more to public ownership, the Labor party has had great difficulty in deciding what part, if any, nationalization should play in its next program of legislation. For example, in 1950 it committed itself to nationalize the big insurance companies, then took fright when the powerful cooperative movement opposed this, and finally dropped the idea altogether. In the 1951 campaign it promised to nationalize sugar and cement, but after it lost the election allowed this pledge to be forgotten. Its platform in the 1955 election gave prominence to only one measure of nationalization—the integration of the remaining private water companies into what is already almost entirely a public service. But rumors that it intended to nationalize the great industrial combine of Imperial Chemical Industries cost it many votes in the areas which depend on ICI for their living.

The fact is that nationalization is not popular with the average voter. Certainly the Labor party must now justify any particular proposal for nationalization by showing that it is economically necessary on its merits. It could lose heavily if its programs appeared to be inspired by doctrinaire considerations rather than a pragmatic concern for the welfare and interests of the ordinary man. Indeed, the Labor party's constitutional commitment to total nationalization of the British economy appears nowadays only in the election propaganda of the Conservatives. But until now the Labor leaders have never dared to call down the wrath of their militants by challenging in principle the central role of nationalization as a socialist technique.

The new policy statement, "Industry and the Nation," however, does just this, though it is accompanied by another statement which is mainly concerned to justify the records of the industries which have already been nationalized. If it is accepted by the Labor party conference in September, "Industry and the Nation" will mark a definitive break, not only with the rigid commitment to nationalization as the main instrument of a socialist economic policy, but more important still, with the outmoded Marxian concept of capitalism under which nationalization was found to assume this importance.

The doctrinaire case for nationalization was based on the argument that, since private capitalists were bound to run the industries they owned purely for selfish profit, the public interest could be served only if the state, representing the people, replaced the capitalists as the owners of industry. Experience in Britain as well as less favored countries has already cast doubt on the assumption that the state can always be relied on to represent the people. Though all Britain's nationalized industries have a better economic record under public ownership than private—and in the case of coal mining and civil aviation at least, better than comparable private industries in other countries—some of them have conspicuously failed to achieve satisfactory relations with the consuming public as a whole or with their own workers.

"Industry and the Nation," however, is mainly concerned to undermine the other assumption on which the doctrinaire theorem is based—the belief that private industry is run exclusively for the selfish profit of those who own it.

In Britain, as in America, the structure of industry has changed fundamentally in the last fifty years. The private sector of the British economy is now dominated by 500 companies which are so large that no single capitalist can own a decisive share in them. To take an extreme example, a 1 per cent holding in Shell Oil would have a market value of over £5 million ($14 million). The policy of these companies is determined not by their owners but by their managers. The managers obtain capital for expansion by retaining profits rather than by going in to the market. Insofar as they do use the market, they rely mainly not on the individual investor but on large financial institutions like insurance companies and pension funds. The main theme of the Labor party's new statement is summarized in a quotation it uses from A. A. Berle: "The capital is there, and so is capitalism. The waning factor is the capitalist."

Another aspect of this industrial revolution is that the risk element in private investment is steadily declining. The state has now assumed the main responsibility for preventing a slump in which general share values would collapse. The big investors tend to spread their holdings so widely that they are unlikely to be seriously affected by fluctuations in one particular industry. Moreover, as the general pace of industrial expansion quickens through state-maintained full employment, share values rise steadily and automatically, so that in Britain equity shareholders can expect about £650 million a year in capital gains.

This picture has long been familiar to economists, particularly in the United States. But both the British parties still present their policies in terms of an industrial structure which has long since disappeared. It is only in the last few years that Labor writers like Anthony Crosland, Roy Jenkins and John Strachey have adapted to the British political scene the work of Americans like Joseph Schumpeter, John Kenneth Galbraith, James Burnham and Peter Drucker. Now that the Labor party's National Executive has given its imprimatur to this new description of contemporary capitalism, the stage is at last set for an attack on the real problems of the modern world.

"Industry and Society" does not, however, offer a prescription which is fully worthy of its analysis. It is mainly concerned to argue that, since the private investor no longer plays a productive economic role, the state should allow the people to share in his unearned income by taxing capital gains, by accepting private shareholdings in payment of death duties, and by itself investing in equities. This would, of course, lead to the state owning a controlling interest in many firms. But the statement explicitly rules out state interference in the management of such industries—such an extension of public ownership is justified, not, like nationalization, by the possibility of economic control, but by the wider distribution of property it involves. On the other hand, the statement does envisage the nationalization of further industries by the traditional methods—but only after a public inquiry has proved its necessity in each case. And no particular industries are named for nationalization at present. A future Labor government would have a free hand to decide how much or how little it attempted to nationalize.

There are obvious political dangers in this ambiguity. Inside the Labor party the struggle between Left and Right, between conservatives and revisionists, can continue over the interpretation of the statement. The Tory party can simultaneously make jokes about "Socialists on the Stock Exchange" and affect to see a cunning plot to introduce wholesale nationalization by the back door. The *Economist* has described the new statement as "The Mouse with a Leer."

But, whatever the weaknesses of the policy proposed, the statement has immense importance in establishing a realistic picture of modern industry to replace the orthodox mythology of the past. It presents the central problem in a form which will ultimately compel the Labor party to tackle it. Industrial power in every large developed economy now rests with a managerial class which is responsible to no one. The form of ownership is irrelevant. State control over nationalized industries is as difficult as shareholder control over private firms. The problem has divided the ruling clique in the Soviet Communist party as bitterly as it has divided Conservatives and Labor in Britain. Recent American studies like *The Organization Man* have shown that it creates social and psychological dangers no less formidable than the political and economic difficulties on which attention is mainly concentrated at present. The Labor party's document at least states the problem intelligibly and emphasizes its importance. Though it contributes little in itself toward a solution, it gives the green light to those who may contribute more.

C. A. R. CROSLAND

9. Socialism in a Prosperous World*

The economies of the advanced industrial countries are behaving in a much more satisfactory manner than before the war. This is the decisive economic fact which renders many traditional Socialist attitudes obsolete, and which must underlie any attempt to revise the programs of Western social democracy.

In contrast to the inter-war period, the postwar period has been characterized in most industrial countries by almost continuous full employment. There is little doubt, moreover, that despite the certainty of occasional minor world recessions, something approaching full employment has come to stay.

Quite apart from the underlying economic factors tending to make for a higher postwar level of demand (e.g., changes in population trends, income distribution, the terms of trade, business psychology, etc.), a decisive political change has occurred. The Keynesian revolution has triumphed in terms both of the policies of governments and the expectations of the voters. Governments are prepared to intervene, through fiscal and monetary policy, to the extent necessary to preserve relatively full employment. Even right-wing governments will do so, because the electorate now believes that full employment can be maintained, and would administer a sharp reverse at the polls to any government which failed to maintain it. It was noticeable in the recent British election that the only constituencies which showed a swing to Labor were those suffering from actual or prospective local unemployment (Lancashire, Scotland and the mining areas).

The feeling of prosperity associated with full employment is of course reinforced by the rise in consumption standards which has occurred in most European countries in recent years. This rise does not need to be very rapid to create a general feeling of contentment. The precise rate of a country's economic growth, while it excites the interest of intellectuals and economists, holds little interest for the population as a whole. Given a background of full employment, the electorate feels well-off even with a relatively slow rate of growth; for its psychology is not yet attuned to the clear expectation of a rapid annual rise in real incomes.

* The New Leader (February 29, 1960). By permission.

Thus in Britain, for example, the intellectuals in the Labor party have stressed the fact that the British rate of growth under the Conservative Government has been exceedingly slow by international standards. But this argument made no impact on the voters. Relative "stagnation" is of little political importance, provided that full employment is maintained; the latter is sufficient almost by itself to create an image of prosperity.

Not only has the average standard of prosperity risen, but in many countries the previously underprivileged groups have improved their position by *more* than the average. This is of course most true of the previously unemployed, who, more than any other group in the community, felt themselves unjustly treated, and harbored the strongest resentment against the existing economic system. But generally the system appears to distribute its benefits more equally and more justly than before the war; and the number of people who feel themselves conspicuously "underprivileged" is not sufficient to give a natural electoral majority to a party of the Left.

Thus full employment has greatly strengthened the bargaining position of the working class; and within the working class it has improved the position of the lower paid workers relative to that of the skilled and semiskilled. The workers now scarcely seem, either to themselves or to other classes, to be suffering from oppression or capitalist exploitation; and their relative power is much greater than it was before the war.

This shift of power is reinforced by a psychological change in the attitudes of the employing class and of Conservative politicians. As the small-scale owner-controlled firm has given way to the large managerially controlled corporation, the labor policies of the typical firm have altered dramatically. The talk, and part of it at least is genuine, is now of the social responsibilities of industry—to workers, consumers, the locality and the public at large. Aggressive individualism gives way to a suave and sophisticated sociability. The traditional capitalist ruthlessness is replaced by a belief in modern, enlightened methods of personnel management. Large-scale industry has become to some extent humanized, and the status of the worker has been enhanced.

A parallel change has occurred in the attitude of Conservative governments. In Britain, one cannot imagine today a deliberate offensive alliance between Government and employers against the unions on the 1921 or 1925-6 model, with all the brutal accompaniments of wage cuts, national lockouts, and anti-union legislation. Instead, we have a National Joint Advisory Council of Unions and Employers; and a Conservative government ostentatiously consults the unions on all major matters of domestic policy.

Other previously underprivileged groups have also improved their relative position. Despite the many serious gaps in the structure of the Welfare State, social service beneficiaries—the old, the sick, the unemployed, widows, etc.—

are relatively and absolutely better off than they were before the war; and in the present social climate of opinion they are most unlikely to lose all their gains even under a right-wing government. A Socialist party will, it is true, wish to devote a still higher proportion of the national income to social spending; indeed the British Labor party fought the recent election largely on this issue. But the outcome of that election showed that neither the present extent of social distress, nor the national conscience about such distress, were sufficient to give a majority of votes to a party of social reform.

Generally, the distribution of income does not now give rise, save among strong Socialists, to such overwhelming feelings of injustice as it did before the war. This is partly because the distribution is in most countries now more equal than it then was. But still more, it is due to the social law that as the *average* level of real income rises, people care less about the exact distribution of income. An unemployed family before the war, living in extreme poverty, resented bitterly the fact of inequality; a prosperous working-class family today, with a car, a refrigerator and a new house, is comparatively indifferent to the fact that others are wealthier still.

These and other changes render the traditional "anticapitalism" of the Left increasingly irrelevant, for we are dealing today with a quite different animal. Indeed it is doubtful if British society in 1960 can sensibly be described as "capitalist." This is of course a matter of semantics. If we accept a Marxist definition of capitalism and socialism purely in terms of the ownership of the means of production, we would, I suppose, have to describe contemporary Britain as 75 per cent capitalist and 25 per cent socialist.

But this would not be a very meaningful description, since the exact location of the dividing line between the public and private sectors is not the most decisive or significant feature of British society today. The precise pattern of industrial ownership is no longer (if indeed it ever was) the essential conditioning factor which imparts to the society its fundamental character. It was for this reason that I argued in *The Future of Socialism* that capitalism should more sensibly be defined, historically, as the type of society which developed in 19th century Britain after the Industrial Revolution, and which in its main outlines, though of course with modifications, persisted into the 1930s; and, furthermore, that since many of the basic, characteristic features of that society have now been greatly modified or wholly transformed, it makes little sense to continue talking about "capitalism."

However, whatever we decide about the right nomenclature, these fundamental changes indisputably have the most far-reaching implications for Western social-democracy. The will to socialism has always been based on a lively sense of wrongs crying for redress, and before the war the wrongs were manifest indeed. But now, instead of glaring and conspicuous evils—squalor and injustice and mass unemployment—we have full employment, the Welfare State and the prospect in 10 years' time of a car to every working-class family. For a party of protest, there is a good deal less to protest about (at least in Britain).

Moreover, as the standard of living rises, public opinion sometimes tends to shift toward the Right. This is particularly the case in those countries, such as Britain, where the post-Korean prosperity is associated with governments of the Right, while the Left is still associated with the austerity and rationing of the immediate postwar period. But, in Britain at least, a shift to the Right appears to be occurring for sociological reasons, regardless of the political complexion of the government.

Young working-class families, who, enjoying high earnings, move out from the old working-class areas in the city to new suburban housing developments or new towns, begin to dissociate themselves psychologically from the working class, and to identify increasingly with the middle class. One of the symbols of this rise in subjective social status is to vote Conservative or Liberal rather than Labor. This tendency was apparent in the recent election; it was the newly housed young working class which appears mainly to have frustrated the hope of a swing to Labor.

Generally, the electorate of an increasingly affluent society begins to see some of the traditional items in Socialist policy as either irrelevant or even positively perverse. I give two examples. First, Left-wing parties traditionally preach the need for more thorough and purposive economic planning. But this emphasis wrongly, in fact, strikes the voters as superfluous when the existing degree of planning appears adequate to ensure full employment and a steady rise in consumption standards. Socialist talk of further planning serves only to recall the detailed controls of the post-1945 years; and these are associated in the public mind not with prosperity, but with disagreeable austerity.

Secondly, the idea of further nationalization becomes increasingly unpopular. It cannot be said to be necessary to full employment and prosperity, for these exist already. Nor, in Britain, has the average performance of the nationalized industries been conspicuously better than that of private enterprise. Indeed, some (often unavoidable) problems of the public sector—the backwardness and low wages of the railways, redundancy in the coal industry, the exceptional postwar rise in the price of coal, the tendency to bureaucratic centralization—have made even the existing nationalized industries somewhat unpopular.

None of these changes destroy the fundamental Socialist case against the society in which we live. Socialists should, and do, still wish radically to alter the distribution of income, the pattern of class relations, the division between private and social expenditure, and many other aspects of our society. They must, however, recognize that they are no longer dealing with the unreformed capitalism of the inter-war period. They must adapt their statement of aims to an entirely altered social and economic background.

NORMAN THOMAS

10. *Socialism in America**

DEMOCRATIC SOCIALISM DEFINED

A great part of our present confusion in understanding and discussing socialism inheres in the matter of definition. Socialism to its critics, and sometimes to its friends, has all sorts of meanings and, consciously or unconsciously, disputants use the one convenient to the point they immediately wish to make. For instance, in a television discussion some time ago, my principal opponent, Miss Vivian Kellems, Connecticut manufacturer, argued that the income tax was socialistic and that its adoption had launched the United States headlong toward socialism. On the same television panel, however, Lawrence E. Spivak seemed to want to confine me to a discussion of socialism as defined in a college dictionary. The definition went like this:

> Socialism: A theory of civil policy that aims at the public collective ownership of land and capital, and the public collective management of all industries.

That definition is misleading. The truth is that socialism, like other great words, such as Christianity, has come to mean many and rather different things to different men. My definition of modern socialism is in line with the declarations and political actions of democratic socialist parties during recent years. It accords with the socialist statement on "Aims and Tasks" which was adopted by the Congress of socialist parties at Frankfurt, Germany, in 1951. It closely parallels "Socialism, a New Statement of Principles," presented in 1952 by the British Socialist Union.

I should be willing, as a beginning, to accept the definition given in Webster's unabridged International.

> Socialism: A political and economic theory of social reorganization, the essential feature of which is governmental control of economic activities to the end that competition shall give way to cooperation and that the opportunities of life and the rewards of labor shall be equitably apportioned.

In accepting this definition, I should insist (1) that democratic socialism must emphasize the necessity of democratic processes in all government controls lest they become fascist or communist; (2) that there is a legitimate

* From Norman Thomas, *Democratic Socialism: A New Appraisal* (League for Industrial Democracy, New York, 1953). By permission.

place for some competition in a socialist order, although the dominant principle should be cooperation, and (3) that government control does not always and necessarily mean government ownership. The social ownership—not always identical with government ownership—which socialism has always emphasized as a condition of the operation of basic economic enterprises for the common good, is itself to true socialists a means of achieving social ends, rather than an end in itself.

In brief, socialism is by no means a synonym for collectivism or collective ownership. Socialism, even in its most materialist Marxist form, has always been concerned for the good life. It has always known and insisted that man does not live by bread alone. It has always recognized the dignity of man and has desired for each individual the fullest possible opportunity for development. Its goal has always been a society fit to be described as a fellowship of free men, who will use their resources and skills no longer for war, but for the conquest of bitter poverty and remediable disease.

However, in the historic development of socialism, there have always been considerable differences of opinion on the extent to which social ownership should be pushed and the way it should be managed. We socialists in platforms and speeches have stood for social ownership of the "basic" or the "principal" means of production and distribution, or of the "commanding heights" of the economic order. These words are not and never were self-defining. Of recent years, the majority of American socialists have been —I think correctly—insistent that the model for managing what is socially owned is not the Post Office Department, but the Tennessee Valley Authority, with provision for direct representation of workers and consumers on it. On the other hand, Aneurin Bevan of Britain in his book insists—I think incorrectly—that cabinet ministers in Britain should have been given more authority over socialized industries. Almost all modern socialists are agreed that voluntary cooperative enterprises can and should be developed as vehicles of social ownership with democratic management.

Two things have happened since World War I to lessen somewhat socialist insistence on state ownership. First, not only the dictatorial fascist and communist states have sharpened our fears of the state as the master of human society, but experience with the broadened activities of relatively democratic states like Britain and America has made us more aware than formerly of the dangers of a statism—and the economic inadequacies of nationalism —against which we must always be on guard.

At the same time that we have been learning to guard against statism as an expression of socialism, we have learned that it has been possible, to a degree not anticipated by most earlier socialists, to impose desirable social controls on privately owned enterprises by the development of social planning, by proper taxation and labor legislation, and by the growth of powerful labor organizations.

THE CASE FOR INCREASED SOCIAL OWNERSHIP

Nevertheless, there is a very strong case to be made—far stronger than our American "liberals" admit—for a great extension of social ownership in America. Even to Alexander Hamilton it seemed reasonable that the state should own the mineral wealth of the country. Today men and women own oil and coal and iron, some of it miles underground. Title to the surface of the land has given them ownership to everything valuable clear down to the molten interior of the earth" but it cannot give them moral right to this wealth. They did not make it; few of them on their own discovered it; they do not themselves extract it. Their competitive ownership of it has been a terrible source of social waste. Consider the extra wells that have been drilled lest "my neighbor drain off my oil" through his well.

Our experience with the steel strike of 1952 is another illustration of the case for social ownership. The strike was very expensive in terms of the loss of much needed steel. It cost the workers millions of dollars in lost wages. Rational men could have reached the ultimate settlement weeks earlier than that settlement was made. The public lost under the settlement because there is small doubt that that agreement has had an inflationary effect on our economy. Under public ownership, the steel industry would not have to contribute large profits to private owners, and an adequate wage could be assured without the necessity of a strike or of raising prices to their present level.

There is no perfect plan which will absolutely prevent conflicts where there are sharp differences of interest. Under any conceivable economic order, all workers will always want higher pay for their work and lower prices for commodities which they must buy. But conflict could be less intense, and the appeal to cooperation for the common good much stronger, if it were not necessary for the managers of a great industry to think primarily in terms of profits for a predominantly absentee ownership of that industry. When an industry affects all our lives as definitely as does the steel industry; when the decisions on wages and prices are made between monopolistic groups of managers acting in the interest of absentee owners and organized workers, there is a situation made to order for the right type of public ownership. Industrial managers should be free to act for the general public and consumers should be definitely represented in the governing authority. The modern socialist sees a great need for the social ownership of such key industries as steel, though refusing to discuss democratic socialism in such misleading terms as total social ownership vs. total private ownership, and he is constantly raising the basic question of what industries should be transferred to public ownership, and what should be owned privately as a means to the attainment of maximum production and the most equitable distribution of goods.

That approach to the problem of public ownership is not, I grant, the orthodox Marxist approach. Marx went in heavily for collective ownership, although such followers of Marx as Karl Kautsky never insisted on the need for the ownership of *all* means of production and distribution.

DEMOCRATIC SOCIALISM AND MARXISM

The relation of modern socialism to Marxism is a confused one, and a few words about it are in order. Briefly these few things might be said:

1) Socialism existed before Marx and, during the period of maximum influence of Marxism on socialism, the dominant socialism in English speaking countries was non-Marxist or unorthodox Marxism. In America, the Marxist influence was strong, but no candidate for membership in the American Socialist Party was required to accept Marx as infallible.

2) Karl Marx and his collaborator, Friedrich Engels, in 1848 and the decades that followed, were primarily concerned with the process by which workers would come to power and by which the new order, socialism, would be born out of the womb of the old. To the terribly exploited workers of the mid-nineteenth century, they brought hope and a sense of destiny. They had amazingly little to say about how socialists should act when they obtained power in the state. That is one reason that orthodox Marxists often differ sharply on the practical problems of socialism. In order to deduce a working program for socialism in countries like Sweden, Great Britain, or the United States, one must consciously or unconsciously read a great deal into Marx which has little or no logical connection with Marxism.

3) Russian Communism is not the correct or purely logical fulfillment of Marxism. It is, indeed, inconsistent with the general Marxian thesis that society is not ready for socialism until it has developed a highly organized capitalist system, and possesses a well organized, intelligent and class conscious working class. Lenin introduced a great many ideas derived from the history and experience of Russia and the thinking of Russians. While he probably found, for instance, some basis in Marx for the role of violence and deceit and the necessity for a dictatorial elite, he was actually more profoundly influenced by Russian writers like Nichaev and by Russian history. More than that, he stood orthodox Marxism on its head in the establishment of Bolshevik power. Marx had argued that economic conditions determine politics. Lenin proved that the ruthless and determined possessor of political power could, to an immense degree, shape the course of economic development.

Communism is certainly a betrayal of true socialism. It is also a subversion of true Marxism. Nevertheless, in its march to power, it has so successfully claimed Marx for its own, it has so persuaded men that Lenin and Stalin are the true successors of Karl Marx, that the socialist who rests his case upon Marx, as upon a Bible, has to fight an uphill battle. Marxist orthodoxy does not give the democratic socialist the best vantage point for his struggle.

4) The march of events compels at the very least a considerable qualification of some of the most important doctrines of Marxism, including even the basic notion of the class conflict. Marx did a great service in emphasizing the importance of the tools men used and the economic processes they employed in shaping their civilization, their social theories, and even their own characters. But, in the light of modern psychology, our own observations of human conduct, and our fuller knowledge of ancient cultures, it is certainly untenable to hold the rigid view of the materialistic conception of history which Marx advanced, a conception which declares that the prevailing economic system determines the general character of the political and intellectual life of that epoch. He himself sometimes lapsed from his own conception of strict materialist determinism. We have lived to contemplate the very different concepts of the Freudian man, the *mass mensch* or crowd-determined man, and other psychological descriptions, none of which by itself is adequate to describe human personality.

Marx believed, not unreasonably in his day, that more and more independent producers of all sorts would be forced into the working class or the proletariat. Then, under these resultant conditions, there would be increased insecurity and misery, until the working class would rise and overthrow its exploiters.[1] Actually, the Marxian forecast has not been fulfilled, especially not in a country like the United States, partly because men's productive powers in the age of applied science have been greater than he could dream. At any rate, we still have a middle class in a true economic sense, while those who think of themselves as belonging to the middle class are even more numerous. Salaried and high wage employees usually regard themselves as members of the middle class, a notion which has been strengthened by the fairly wide distribution of stock ownership in this country.

It follows that the concept of the class conflict basic to Marxism needs modification. Marx thought that the lines of division between workers and owners were becoming steadily clearer. This, however, has not been the case, least of all in our own country. The groups into which men divide are not exclusively determined by economics. Consider the importance of na-

---

[1] Marx saw also the rise of working class economic and political organizations which would fight for better conditions for labor while they were preparing to build a new economic order. He believed that the contradictions in capitalism would lead to increasingly severe crises. Many Marxists contend that Marx used "increasing misery" in the psychological, rather than in the physical sense.

tionalism and religion, neither of which is adequately explained by economic determination, in drawing men together. There are very important economic divisions among us Americans. No one can look at some of the great strikes in American history, or some of our politics,[2] without being aware that there is class consciousness and class conflict. In Europe class lines are more definite and more binding. But there is no such tight fusion of all different economic groups into two and only two contending classes of owners and workers, as Marxism postulated. The future both of conflict and cooperation is far more complex.

SOCIALISM AND WAR

It is scarcely debatable that the great issue of our times is the establishment of peace with freedom. To the problem arising primarily out of the relentless drive of international communism under Russian leadership for universal power over the bodies, minds, and souls of men, socialism has no ready-made answer. Frankly it has lost some of that international fervor which was one of its glories in earlier days. In 1914, the socialist movement lost its best chance to prevent war by its own international action when it found itself completely unready to strike against mobilization simultaneously in Germany and the allied countries. It was then strong on both sides of the conflict between the nations. For that failure of international socialism to avert or shorten World War I, mankind paid dearly. It was a failure shared by American democracy. Woodrow Wilson, if backed by a people more intent on stopping the war than making profits out of sales to the western allies, could almost certainly have won by vigorous action after the stalemate in Europe a negotiated peace vastly preferable to the peace of Versailles.

Neither world socialism nor American democracy could ever win a second chance as good as the one they lost. As time has gone on, socialist parties in Europe have gained strength and often control of governments under conditions which almost compel them to think in national terms. They have to satisfy the voters under a national economy. Paul-Henri Spaak, the Belgian socialist leader, was near the truth when he said that the thing socialists had learned best how to nationalize was socialism. Yet a socialistic economy on a purely national basis is not enough, especially in a divided Europe. Socialism has not altogether lost its international context and appeal. Democratic socialists managed to reorganize their international at a conference

[2] The overwhelming preference of newspapers both daily and weekly for Eisenhower, the Republican, over Stevenson, the Democrat, in 1952, argued rationalization of class feeling of their owners. The preference was most decidedly not shared by working reporters and journalists. In my experience, I find that if I know a man's job and social status, in about eight out of ten cases, I can guess his opinions on social questions and even how he'll vote. In the latter case, it helps to know where he lives.

in Frankfurt, Germany, in 1951, which issued the excellent general statement of the "Aims and Tasks of Democratic Socialism," to which I have already referred. Many socialists in Europe have been leaders toward a United States of Europe. The contribution of the British Labor Party to peace was enormous, when, on friendly terms, it conceded the right of India, Pakistan, Burma, and Ceylon to independence, and when it set in motion in parts of Africa reforms pointing to an end of colonialism.

But socialism is not a panacea against war. In the light of history and logic, socialists are not warranted in repeating once popular statements that capitalism is *the* cause of war and that the *only* hope of peace is universal socialism. A great root of war has always been economic, and when the economic system is capitalism, capitalism becomes a root of war. But the explanation of the wars of our time cannot be derived from any economic theory which does not take account of nationalism; of the older imperialism which was born of western capitalism and nationalism, and the newer communist imperialism under Stalin who has succeeded in imposing a Russian imperial pattern on what started as an international working class movement.

We have learned that the causes of war are too complex to be summed up in the old statement—which was never a matter of binding socialist dogma —that capitalism, laissez faire capitalism, is *the* cause of war. There were wars before the rise of capitalism. If the militant U.S.S.R. is capitalist, it is certainly not after the old laissez faire order. Its state capitalism which Stalin falsely calls socialism is not sincerely devoted to peace, but to conquest.

One can truthfully say that an ideal and universal socialism, like an ideal and universal Christian ethic, would be the best basis for abiding peace. It is, however, very dangerous to insist that peace must be tied up with the universal adoption of any fairly rigid politico-economic system. For a long time to come, peace will depend on the ability of men and social groups to live together despite some difference in interest and conflict in ideals. The socialism which makes for world peace cannot emulate the secular religion of communism in seeking to impose its plan of salvation on mankind by force and fraud. Too often, religions have brought war, not peace, by their insistence on their exclusive possession of truth or of the way of temporal and eternal salvation. Socialism will make its contribution to peace, within the democratic framework, by its emphasis on justice, by its successful practice of a fraternity crossing racial and national lines, by its steadfast opposition to secular religions of fascism and communism, and by its concern for universal, fool proof disarmament under a strengthened U.N., and the ultimate achievement of federated world government. Peace will not be achieved as a by-product of socialism, but democratic socialism will stand or fall very largely by the intelligence and power with which it seeks peace with freedom.

SOCIAL, PRIVATE AND COOPERATIVE OWNERSHIP

There are some advantages for freedom and enterprise in varieties of ownership. The state under the most democratic theory and practice will become too huge, too cumbersome, if it seeks to control directly all economic activity. There are men with a deep seated desire to work for themselves. They will work harder and be more ingenious in so doing. Ours is not the economy of a beleaguered garrison which has to ration diminishing supplies for everybody and everything. There is room in it for individual ownership and individual effort. Justification of such ownership must always be accompanied by a genuine responsibility for management on terms consistent with the common good.

There is not one perfect formula for what ought to be owned under social legislation. One determining factor is the public attitude, which varies according to time and place. Each generation should be allowed to make its own decisions, but there ought to be assurance that once decisions are made they will stand for a reasonable length of time, whether under public or private ownership.

Heretofore publicly owned enterprises in America have operated under disadvantages that socialism should avoid. We Americans are, or think we are, committed to a theory of private enterprise. The publicly owned enterprises have been a more or less regretted exception. Sometimes it has been a sick industry which has had to be taken over by government which is then blamed for the sickness. Always there has been a conscious or unconscious tendency in the world of industry to discredit and even sabotage public ownership. Witness the attitude of industry generally toward the exceedingly useful TVA. To be truly successful, public ownership and democratic operation must be accepted in principle and extensively practiced in appropriate areas.

For some years, American socialists have been fairly well agreed that social ownership should be extended to the "commanding heights" of our economy, which include our natural resources, our system of money, banking and credit, and certain basic industries and services.

The social ownership of industries should be determined in the light of certain tests: (1) their basic importance to our lives; (2) the degree of their monopolization and the effectiveness of competition in controlling prices; (3) the degree to which absentee ownership is divorced from responsible management. Today, in huge enterprises, managers work for the private stockholders who themselves do little or nothing except to provide working capital. Even that is largely provided out of profits set aside by the managers for expansion. Yet the stockholders expect their working capital to be immortal and always to produce dividends. One of the best run privately owned utilities is the telephone industry. Yet when the New York Telephone Company was permitted to raise its rates, a large part of the argument was based on the cost of private capital which could be provided at a much lower rate of interest if the industry were publicly owned.

I have already argued the specific reason for public ownership of the steel industry. It meets all the tests which I have earlier suggested. The prices for its product are not regulated by competition. The owners have largely lost the function of management and the decision of the managers concerns us all because of the basic character of the industry.

What socialists advocate, let me again insist, is not nationalization, but socialization. A thousand times I have said that the virtue of government ownership depends upon who owns the government. It would be more accurate to say that government must be democratic, that it should act only as a trustee of society, and that consumers as a whole and workers in a particular industry should be directly concerned in the management of any publicly owned industry. Some ownership and operation might well be by cooperatives. The TVA is the sort of controlling body that we need, except that consumers and workers should be more directly represented on it. Workers in different categories should elect their own representatives. Under any social system, there will be need for labor unions to represent the workers. But preferably they should not vote in their unions for their representatives on the public Authorities.

While I am prepared stoutly to defend the program I have outlined for public ownership and democratic control, I am well aware that, of itself, it does not solve all problems of the modern industrial economy. There is, for instance, no automatic formula for a "fair" wage; we have a great deal to learn about the psychology of a genuine democracy; about the best size of various industrial units and the way to establish and maintain more satisfactory relations between managers who are key men in our society and workers.

If socialism is to do what we hope of it, the worker for his own sake and society's must be given a sense of responsibility for the productive process. It is of primary importance in socialist plans and action that the least well paid of our workers should come to understand that the whole answer to the problem of poverty does not lie in any formula devoted simply to a more equitable sharing of the wealth. Even in relatively rich America, the answer to poverty depends also upon more efficient production. This fact must be emphasized in socialist planning and in socialist education. But experience proves that we can more easily get better production if a decent floor is put under wages.

DEMOCRATIC VS. REVOLUTIONARY SOCIALISM

For the present I know no better phrase. I think democratic socialism more accurate and more descriptive than the old phrase, social democracy. It is also more accurate and more descriptive than the phrase, revolutionary socialism, popular with many socialists in the dark days of the thirties. The socialism which will carry society toward a fellowship of free men will, in the best sense of the word, be revolutionary. But the profound change which it seeks will not be achieved in one blinding apocalypse. The working class is not the Messiah which some of us thought. The Good Society will be achieved by a process each stage of which must bring blessing to those who live in that era. It will not be achieved in America by the violence commonly associated with the word, revolution. Systematic violence in our modern complex civilization wherein the weapons of violence are so deadly and indiscriminate in their effects, will defile and cripple by its very nature the kind of society which allegedly it may seek.

As a practical matter, a revolutionary socialism which disregards the normal democratic and constitutional processes in a country like America would become revolutionary communism—or maybe even a neo-fascism. The communists have already obtained a virtual monopoly on the necessary practices of violence and deceit. They are on the field. There may be countries where some revolutionary activity against tyranny can be socialist in its control and objectives. America is not one of those countries. Indeed, looking back on history since World War I, one cannot cite a country in which revolutionary violence has been steadily and successfully employed to any other than a fascist or communist end.

In the present mood of Americans, it seems hardly necessary to say these things. They were worth saying in the thirties. They may conceivably be worth saying again in some time of great unemployment or new world war or other disaster. Assuredly it is the business of the democratic socialist to help avert that kind of disaster which will not open the door to socialism but to grim dictatorial tyranny. We cannot afford to let things get worse in order that they may get better.

There is an appeal especially to the young in the all or nothing approach. Many men warm to the notion of one decisive conflict and dedication to a militant cause. To them my description of democratic socialism may not offer an equivalent appeal. I cannot close my plea for it in any other way than by asking you, my readers, to search your minds and hearts. Do you know a greater or nobler challenge than to take your part as citizens, neighbors, workers, thinkers, in the processes by which we may the better use our marvelous technology, our democratic institutions, the state and other basic forms of human associations, in the march toward the goal of a world-wide fellowship of free men? Each stage of the journey, each victory of peace and freedom will bring its rich reward.

Chapter XII

PLAN OR NO PLAN?

A generation can hardly be called well ordered which in the span of twenty-five years has suffered from the two greatest wars in history, interrupted—to make the chaos complete—by the severest economic depression on record. The clamor for planning, for economic stability at home, and for peace in the world, has therefore expressed, knowingly and unknowingly, the yearning for salvation from chaos and disorder. Mankind has lost the cheerful faith of the late eighteenth century that we live in the best of worlds, that there is a natural harmony in society, and, therefore, the less interference the better.

In his paper on "Authority and Social Change," read at the Harvard Tercentenary Conference in 1936, John Dewey raises the question, in view of the apparent intractability of human problems, where there are "resources that have not as yet been tried out in the large field of human relations, resources that are available and that carry with them the potential promise of successful application." Dewey's answer is that the untried resource in the field of human and social relationships is "the utilization of organized intelligence, the manifold benefits and values of which we have substantial and reliable evidence in the narrower field of science." The application of scientific methods, of organized intelligence, would save humanity from the two extremes of authoritative power and unregulated individual freedom, to which "most of the sorrows and defeats of the past" may be attributed.

In *The Good Society* (1937), Walter Lippmann was probably one of the first American writers to attack planning as a dangerous tendency, leading eventually to totalitarianism and misery. He drew his main ideas from the works of Ludwig von Mises, an Austrian economist who, as early as 1922, in *Socialism,* had proved its impossibility. Lippmann's chief conclusion is that planning is intimately connected with dictatorship and war. In 1937 planning was mainly identified with the militaristic systems of the Fascist Axis, or with the totalitarian one-party regime in the Soviet Union. After World War II, planning greatly expanded in nations that were governed by democratic socialist administrations (England, New Zealand, Scandinavia, Australia). Whether these countries will end in oligarchies preparing for wars of aggression is more than doubtful.

The most famous anti-planning book is Friedrich A. Hayek's *The Road to Serfdom* (1944). Its importance was immediately recognized, being digested in *The Reader's Digest,* and distributed widely by many agencies, from the Standard Oil Co. (N. J.) to the Book-of-the-Month Club. Hayek is an economist who is familiar with Continental thinking, having lived in Austria most of his early life, as well as with British problems, having settled in England for about two decades before coming to the United States. The tenor of his book is his anxiety that, just as socialism in Germany was followed by Nazi totalitarianism, so would the collectivist trend in England and the United States be followed by a drift toward the destruction of democracy. If the political background of Germany were about the same as that of England and the United States, Hayek's case would be incontrovertible. Hayek is persuaded that in a planned economy "the worst get to the top." The Gestapo, the concentration camps, and the murder camps are, according to Hayek's argument, the result of planning necessarily ending in totalitarianism, rather than phenomena of *fascist or communist* politics. Hayek is also seriously concerned about the incompatibility of planning with the rule of law. He sees in the collectivist movement a dangerous trend of substituting bureaucratic, irresponsible orders for the impartiality of the rule of law. Planning in Britain under the Labor Government (1945-1951) did not confirm Hayek's fear that "intolerance and brutal suppression of dissent, deception and spying, the complete disregard of the life and happiness of the individual are essential and unavoidable" from the "collectivist standpoint."

In *On the Agenda of Democracy* (1941) Charles Merriam analyzes the experience of America in the field of planning, as well as its potential future. He injects into the discussion of planning a note of sanity by showing that planning was not invented by New Deal brain trusters, but has a long and honorable record in the history of the United States from its beginning. The Constitution was the first great act of planning, and the "Constitutional Convention itself was a large-scale planning board." A strong believer in the desirability of a "mixed economy" of private and public enterprise, Merriam warns that "free enterprise has far more to fear from lack of planning than from its development and application to national resources."

One of the most original analyses of the basic issues of planning will be found in a short book, *The Principles of Economic Planning* (1949), by W. Arthur Lewis, a British economist. Written for the Fabian Society, *The Principles of Economic Planning* denies that the nationalization of industry is essential to planning, and maintains that "there is no case for nationalizing the whole economy." The real issue is not between planning or no planning, but between *planning by direction or inducement.* In the former case, the government tries to get the right things done by direct control and regulation of output, prices, and labor. Using inducement, the government indirectly encourages economic activities through the budget and other financial measures, thus avoiding the two main defects of planning by direction: bureaucratic centralization and economic inefficiency. Far from rejecting the free market as the normal mechanism of economic adjustment, Lewis, a socialist, holds that "our aim should be to preserve free markets wherever possible."

JOHN DEWEY

1. *Science and Society**

The scene which the world exhibits to the observer at the present time is so obviously one of general instability, insecurity, and increasing conflict— both within nations and between them—that I cannot conceive that any one will deny the *desirability* of effecting and enstating some organic union of freedom and authority. Enormous doubt will well exist, however, as to the possibility of establishing any social system in which the union is practically embodied. This question, it will be justly urged, is *the* issue that emerges even if the substantial validity of the points so far made is admitted. In fact, it may even be justly urged that this question confronts us as the controlling and decisive question just because, or to the degree that, the validity of my argument thus far is granted.

The weight of the evidence of the past is assuredly strongly against the realization of any such possibility. As far as the idea of organized authority is concerned, the pathos of the collective life of mankind on this planet is its exhibition of the dire human need for some authority; while its ever-mounting tragedy is due to the fact that the need has been repeatedly betrayed by the very institutions that claimed to satisfy it. That all is not well, on the other hand, with the principle of individualistic freedom in the form in which it has been influential up to now, is shown by more than one fact in the present scene of discord and insecurity. Above all is this manifested by the recrudescence of the principle of authority in its most extreme and primitive form—the rise of dictatorships.

As if in substantiation of the old idea that nature abhors a vacuum, it might be contended that economic competitive individualism, free from social control, had created a moral and social vacuum which recourse to dictatorships is filling. In many countries, the demand for collective and organized guidance and support has become so urgent that the very idea of individual freedom has gone into the discard and become an ideal, not to be praised, but to be despised. The regime of economic individualistic liberty is

* From John Dewey, "Authority and Social Change" (1936; reprinted in *John Dewey's Philosophy,* ed. by Joseph Ratner, Random House, 1939). By permission of Henry Holt and Company, holders of the copyright.

attacked by dictatorships from both the right and the left. In countries in which there are no open and acknowledged dictatorships, the conceptions of liberty and individualism seem to be losing their magic force; and security, discipline, order, and solidarity are, by social transfer, acquiring magic power in their stead. The actual concrete conditions that produce resort to dictatorships vary from country to country. But the phenomenon is so widespread it demands a generalized explanation. The most obvious one is the virtual bankruptcy and moribund state of a regime of individual initiative and enterprise conducted for private gain and subject to no control by recognized, collective authority.

Neither the past nor the present affords, then, any ground for expecting that the adjustment of authority and freedom, stability and change, will be achieved by following old paths. The idea that any solution at all can ever be attained may seem to some romantic and utopian. But the most fantastically unrealistic of all notions is the widely prevalent belief that we can attain enduring stable authority by employing or re-exhuming the institutional means tried in the past; equally fantastic is the belief that the assured freedom of individuals can be secured by pitting individuals against one another in a pitiless struggle for material possessions and economic power. The issue, in my judgment, can be narrowed down to this question: Are there resources that have not as yet been tried out in the large field of human relations, resources that are available and that carry with them the potential promise of successful application?

In raising this question I am aware that it is almost inevitable that what I have said about the human necessity for some kind of collective authority to give individuals direction in their relations with one another, and to give them the support that comes from a sense of solidarity, will appear to be a plea for a return to some kind of social control brought about through, and perpetuated by, external institutional means. If my question is so taken, then the criticism I have made of the alliance that has taken place between the principle of individual freedom and private initiative and enterprise in economic matters will necessarily also seem to be merely an argument for social control by means of a collective planned economy—put forward, of course, with some change in vocabulary. However, the argument in fact cuts in both directions. It indicates that while movements in the direction of collective, planned economy may cure evils from which we are now suffering, it will in the end go the way of all past attempts at organization of authoritative power unless some hitherto untried means are utilized on a large and systematic scale for bringing into life the desired and desirable organic co-ordination. Otherwise we shall finally find ourselves repeating on a different plane the old struggle between social organization and individual freedom, with the oscillation from one principle to the other that has so characteristically marked the past.

The resource that has not yet been tried on any large scale, in the broad field of human, social relationships is the utilization of organized intelligence, the manifold benefits and values of which we have substantial and reliable evidence in the narrower field of science.

Within a limited area, the collective intelligence which is exemplified in the growth and application of scientific method has already become authoritative. It is authoritative in the field of beliefs regarding the structure of nature and relevant to our understanding of physical events. To a considerable extent, the same statement holds true of beliefs about historical personages and historical events—especially with those that are sufficiently remote from the present time. When we turn to the practical side, we see that the same method is supreme in controlling and guiding our active dealings with material things and physical energies. To a large and significant extent, the Baconian prophecy that knowledge is power of control has been realized in this particular, somewhat narrowly circumscribed area. To be sure, it cannot be said that intelligence, operating by the methods that constitute science, has as yet completely won *undisputed* right and authority to control beliefs even in the restricted physical field. But organized intelligence has made an advance that is truly surprising when we consider the short time in which it has functioned and the powerful foes against which it had to make its way: the foes of inertia, of old, long-established traditions and habits—inertia, traditions, and habits all of them entrenched in forms of institutional life that are effulgent with the prestige of time, that are enveloped in the glamor of imaginative appeal, and that are crowned, severally and collectively, with an emotional halo made of the values that men most prize.

The record of the struggle that goes by the name of "conflict between science and religion," or, if you please, "conflict between theology and science," was essentially a conflict of claims to exercise social authority. It was not a conflict just between two sets of theoretical beliefs, but between two alignments of social forces—one which was old and had institutional power that it did not hesitate to use, and one which was new and striving and craving for recognition against gigantic odds.

What is pertinent, what is deeply significant to the theme of the *relation* between collective authority and freedom, is that the progress of intelligence —as exemplified in this summary story of scientific advance—exhibits their organic, effective union. Science has made its way by releasing, not by suppressing, the elements of variation, of invention and innovation, of novel creation in individuals. It is as true of the history of modern sciences as it is of the history of painting or music that its advances have been initiated by individuals who freed themselves from the bonds of tradition and custom whenever they found the latter hampering their own powers of reflection, observation, and construction.

In spite of science's dependence for its development upon the free initiative, invention, and enterprise of individual inquirers, the authority of science issues from and is based upon collective activity, cooperatively organized. Even when, temporarily, the ideas put forth in science by individuals sharply diverge from received beliefs, the method used is a public and open method which succeeds only as it tends to produce agreement, unity of belief among all who labored in the same field. Every scientific inquirer, even when he deviates most widely from current ideas, depends upon methods and conclusions that are a common possession and not of private ownership, even though all of the methods and conclusions may at some time have been initially the product of private invention. The contribution the scientific inquirer makes is collectively tested and developed and, in the measure that it is cooperatively confirmed, becomes a part of the common fund of the intellectual commonwealth.

One can most easily recognize the difference between the aim and operation of the free individual in the sphere of science and in that of current individualistic economic enterprise by stretching the fancy to the point of imagining a scientific inquirer adopting the standards of the business entrepreneur. Imagine the scientific man who should say that his conclusion was scientific and in so saying maintain that it was also the product of his private wants and efforts goading him on to seek his private advantage. The mere suggestion of such an absurdity vividly discloses the gap that divides the manifestations of individual freedom in these two areas of human activity. The suggestion brings into bold relief and in typical form the kind of individual freedom that is both supported by collective, organic authority and that in turn changes and is encouraged to change and develop, by its own operations, the authority upon which it depends.

The thesis that the operation of cooperative intelligence as displayed in science is a working model of the union of freedom and authority does not slight the fact that the method has operated up to the present in a limited and relatively technical area. On the contrary, it emphasizes that fact. If the method of intelligence had been employed in any large field in the comprehensive and basic area of the relations of human beings to one another in social life and institutions, there would be no present need for our argument. The contrast between the restricted scope of its use and the possible range of its application to human relations—political, economic, and moral—is outstanding and depressing. It is this very contrast that defines the great problem that has to be solved.

No consideration of the problem is adequate that does not take into account one fact about the development of the modern individualistic movement in industry and business. There is a suppressed premise in all the claims and reasonings of the individualistic school. All the beneficial changes that have been produced are attributed to the free play of individuals seeking primarily their own profit as isolated individuals. But in fact, the entire modern industrial development is the fruit of the technological applications of science. By and large, the economic changes of recent centuries have been parasitic upon the advances made in natural science. There is not a single process involved in the production and distribution of goods that is not dependent upon the utilization of results which are consequences of the method of collective, organic intelligence working in mathematics, physics, and chemistry. To speak baldly, it is a plain falsehood that the advances which the defenders of the existing regime point to as justification for its continuance are due to mere individualistic initiative and enterprise. Individualistic initiative and enterprise have sequestered and appropriated the fruits of collective cooperative intelligence. This they have done alone. But without the aid and support of organized intelligence they would have been impotent —perhaps even in those activities in which they have shown themselves to be socially most powerful.

In sum, the great weakness of the historic movement that has laid claim to the title of liberalism and that has proclaimed its operating purpose to be that of securing and protecting the freedom of individuals—the great weakness of this movement has been its failure to recognize that the true and final source of change has been, and now is, the corporate intelligence embodied in science. The principle, as I have already said, cuts in two directions. In so far as the attempts that are now being made in the direction of organized social control and planned economy ignore the role of scientific intelligence, in so far as these attempts depend upon and turn for support to external institutional changes affected for the most part by force, just so far are they re-enstating reliance upon the method of external authority that has always broken down in the past. For a time, while in need of security and a sense and feeling of solidarity, men will submit to authority of this kind. But if history shows anything, it shows that the variable factors in individuals cannot be permanently suppressed or completely eradicated. The principle of individual freedom expressed in the modern individualistic movement is deeply rooted in the constitution of human beings. The truth embodied in it cannot die no matter how much force is brought down upon it. The tragedy of the movement is that it misconceived and misplaced the source and seat of this principle of freedom. But the attempt to uproot and eliminate this principle on behalf of the assurance of security and attainment of solidarity by means of external authority is doomed to ultimate defeat no matter what its temporary victories.

There is no need to dwell upon the enormous obstacles that stand in the way of extending from its present limited field to the larger field of human relation the control of organized intelligence, operating through the release of individual powers and capabilities. There is the weight of past history on the side of those who are cynical or pessimistic about the possibility of achieving this humanly desirable and humanly necessary task. I do not predict that the extension will ever be effectively actualized. But I do claim that the problem of the relation of authority and freedom, of stability and change, if it can be solved, will be solved in this way. The failure of other methods and the desperateness of the present situation will be a spur to some to do their best to make the extension actual. They know that to hold in advance of trial that success is impossible is a way of condemning humanity to that futile and destructive oscillation between authoritative power and unregulated individual freedom to which we may justly attribute most of the sorrows and defeats of the past. They are aware of the slow processes of history and of the unmeasured stretch of time that lies ahead of mankind. They do not expect any speedy victory in the execution of the most difficult task human beings ever set their hearts and minds to attempt. They are, however, buoyed by the assurance that no matter how slight the immediate effect of their efforts, they are themselves, in their trials, exemplifying one of the first principles of the method of scientific intelligence. For they are projecting into events a large and comprehensive idea by experimental methods that correct and mature the method and the idea in the very process of trial. The very desperateness of the situation is, for such as these, but a spur to sustained, courageous effort.

WALTER LIPPMANN

2. *Planning versus Democracy**

The primary factor which makes civilian planning incalculable is the freedom of the people to spend their income. Planning is theoretically possible only if consumption is rationed. For a plan of production *is* a plan of consumption. If the authority is to decide what shall be produced, it has already decided what shall be consumed. In military planning that is precisely what takes place: the authorities decide what the army shall consume and what of the national product shall be left for the civilians. No economy can, therefore, be planned for civilians unless there is such scarcity that the necessities of existence can be rationed. As productivity rises above the subsistence level, free spending becomes possible. A planned production to meet a free demand is a contradiction in terms and as meaningless as a square circle.

It follows, too, that a plan of production is incompatible with voluntary

* From Walter Lippmann, *The Good Society* (1937). By permission of Little, Brown & Company and The Atlantic Monthly Press.

labor, with freedom to choose an occupation. A plan of production is not only a plan of consumption, but a plan of how long, at what, and where the people shall work. By no possible manipulation of wage rates could the planners attract to the various jobs precisely the right number of workers. Under voluntary labor, particularly with consumption rationed and standardized, the unpleasant jobs would be avoided and the good jobs overcrowded. Therefore the inevitable and necessary complement of the rationing of consumption is the conscription of labor, either by overt act of law or by driving workers into the undesirable jobs by offering them starvation as the alternative. This is, of course, exactly what happens in a thoroughly militarized state.

The conscription of labor and the rationing of consumption are not to be regarded as transitional or as accidental devices in a planned economy. They are the very substance of it. To make a five-year plan of what a whole nation shall produce is to determine how it shall labor and what it shall receive. It can receive only what the plan provides. It can obtain what the plan provides only by doing the work which the plan calls for. It must do that work or the plan is a failure; it must accept what the plan yields in the way of goods or it must do without.

All this is perfectly understood in an army or in war time when a whole nation is in arms. The civilian planner can not avoid the rationing and the conscription, for they are the very essence of his proposal. There is no escape. If the people are free to reject the rations, the plan is frustrated; if they are free to work less or at different occupations than those prescribed, the plan cannot be executed. Therefore their labor and their standards of living have to be dictated by the planning board or by some sovereign power superior to the board. In a militarized society that sovereign power is the general staff.

But who, in a civilian society, is to decide what is to be the specific content of the abundant life? It cannot be the people deciding by referendum or through a majority of their elected representatives. For if the sovereign power to pick the plan is in the people, the power to amend it is there also at all times. Now a plan subject to change from month to month or even from year to year is not a plan; if the decision has been taken to make ten million cars at $500 and one million suburban houses at $3000, the people cannot change their minds a year later, scrap the machinery to make the cars, abandon the houses when they are partly built, and decide to produce instead skyscraper apartment houses and underground railroads.

There is, in short, no way by which the objectives of a planned economy can be made to depend upon popular decision. They must be imposed by an oligarchy of some sort,[1] and that oligarchy must, if the plan is to be carried

---

[1] Which may, of course, let the people ratify the plan once and irrevocably by plebiscite, as in the German and Italian plebiscites.

through, be irresponsible in matters of policy. Individual oligarchs might, of course, be held accountable for breaches of the law just as generals can be court-martialed. But their policy can no more be made a matter of continuous accountability to the voters than the strategic arrangements of the generals can be determined by the rank and file. The planning board or their superiors have to determine what the life and labor of the people shall be.

Not only is it impossible for the people to control the plan, but, what is more, the planners must control the people. They must be despots who tolerate no effective challenge to their authority. Therefore civilian planning is compelled to presuppose that somehow the despots who climb to power will be benevolent—that is to say, will know and desire the supreme good of their subjects. This is the implicit premise of all the books which recommend the establishment of a planned economy in a civilian society. They paint an entrancing vision of what a benevolent despotism could do. They ask—never very clearly, to be sure—that somehow the people should surrender the planning of their existence to "engineers," "experts," and "technologists," to leaders, saviors, heroes. This is the political premise of the whole collectivist philosophy: that the dictators will be patriotic or class-conscious, whichever term seems the more eulogistic to the orator. It is the premise, too, of the whole philosophy of regulation by the state, currently regarded as progressivism. Though it is disguised by the illusion that a bureaucracy accountable to a majority of voters, and susceptible to the pressure of organized minorities, is not exercising compulsion, it is evident that the more varied and comprehensive the regulation becomes, the more the state becomes a despotic power as against the individual. For the fragment of control over the government which he exercises through his vote is in no effective sense proportionate to the authority exercised over him by the government.

Benevolent despots might indeed be found. On the other hand they might not be. They may appear at one time; they may not appear at another. The people, unless they choose to face the machine guns on the barricades, can take no steps to see to it that benevolent despots are selected and the malevolent cashiered. They cannot select their despots. The despots must select themselves, and, no matter whether they are good or bad, they will continue in office as long as they can suppress rebellion and escape assassination.

Thus, by a kind of tragic irony, the search for security and a rational society, if it seeks salvation through political authority, ends in the most irrational form of government imaginable—in the dictatorship of casual oligarchs, who have no hereditary title, no constitutional origin or responsibility, who cannot be replaced except by violence. The reformers who are staking their hopes on good despots, because they are so eager to plan the future, leave unplanned that on which all their hopes depend. Because a planned society must be one in which the people obey their rulers, there can be no plan to find the planners: the selection of the despots who are to make society so rational and so secure has to be left to the insecurity of irrational chance.

FRIEDRICH A. HAYEK

3. *Road to Serfdom**

Nothing distinguishes more clearly conditions in a free country from those in a country under arbitrary government than the observance in the former of the great principles known as the Rule of Law. Stripped of all technicalities, this means that government in all its actions is bound by rules fixed and announced beforehand—rules which make it possible to foresee with fair certainty how the authority will use its coercive powers in given circumstances and to plan one's individual affairs on the basis of this knowledge.[1] Though this ideal can never be perfectly achieved, since legislators as well as those to whom the administration of the law is intrusted are fallible men, the essential point, that the discretion left to the executive organs wielding coercive power should be reduced as much as possible, is clear enough. While every law restricts individual freedom to some extent by altering the means which people may use in the pursuit of their aims, under the Rule of Law the government is prevented from stultifying individual efforts by *ad hoc* action. Within the known rules of the game the individual is free to pursue his personal ends and desires, certain that the powers of government will not be used deliberately to frustrate his efforts.

The distinction we have drawn before between the creation of a perma-

* From Friedrich A. Hayek, *The Road to Serfdom* (University of Chicago Press, 1944). By permission.

[1] According to the classical exposition by A. V. Dicey in *The Law of the Constitution* (8th ed.), p. 198, the Rule of Law "means, in the first place, the absolute supremacy or predominance of regular law as opposed to the influence of arbitrary power, and excludes the existence of arbitrariness, of prerogative, or even of wide discretionary authority on the part of government." Largely as a result of Dicey's work the term has, however, in England acquired a narrower technical meaning which does not concern us here. The wider and older meaning of the concept of the rule or reign of law, which in England had become an established tradition which was more taken for granted than discussed, has been most fully elaborated, just because it raised what were new problems there, in the early nineteenth-century discussion in Germany about the nature of the *Rechtsstaat*.

nent framework of laws within which the productive activity is guided by individual decisions and the direction of economic activity by a central authority is thus really a particular case of the more general distinction between the Rule of Law and arbitrary government. Under the first the government confines itself to fixing rules determining the conditions under which the available resources may be used, leaving to the individuals the decision for what ends they are to be used. Under the second the government directs the use of the means of production to particular ends. The first type of rules can be made in advance, in the shape of *formal rules* which do not aim at the wants and needs of particular people. They are intended to be merely instrumental in the pursuit of people's various individual ends. And they are, or ought to be, intended for such long periods that it is impossible to know whether they will assist particular people more than others. They could almost be described as a kind of instrument of production, helping people to predict the behavior of those with whom they must collaborate, rather than as efforts toward the satisfaction of particular needs.

Economic planning of the collectivist kind necessarily involves the very opposite of this. The planning authority cannot confine itself to providing opportunities for unknown people to make whatever use of them they like. It cannot tie itself down in advance to general and formal rules which prevent arbitrariness. It must provide for the actual needs of people as they arise and then choose deliberately between them. It must constantly decide questions which cannot be answered by formal principles only, and, in making these decisions, it must set up distinctions of merit between the needs of different people. When the government has to decide how many pigs are to be raised or how many busses are to be run, which coal mines are to operate, or at what prices shoes are to be sold, these decisions cannot be deduced from formal principles or settled for long periods in advance. They depend inevitably on the circumstances of the moment, and, in making such decisions, it will always be necessary to balance one against the other the interests of various persons and groups. In the end somebody's views will have to decide whose interests are more important; and these views must become part of the law of the land, a new distinction of rank which the coercive apparatus of government imposes upon the people.

The distinction we have just used between formal law or justice and substantive rules is very important and at the same time most difficult to draw precisely in practice. Yet the general principle involved is simple enough. The difference between the two kinds of rules is the same as that between laying down a Rule of the Road, as in the Highway Code, and ordering people where to go; or, better still, between providing signposts and commanding people which road to take. The formal rules tell people in advance what action the state will take in certain types of situation, defined in general terms, without reference to time and place or particular people. They refer to typical situations into which anyone may get and in which the existence of such rules will be useful for a great variety of individual purposes. The knowledge that in such situations the state will act in a definite way, or require people to behave in a certain manner, is provided as a means for people to use in making their own plans. Formal rules are thus merely instrumental in the sense that they are expected to be useful to yet unknown people, for purposes for which these people will decide to use them, and in circumstances which cannot be foreseen in detail. In fact, that we do *not* know their concrete effect, that we do *not* know what particular ends these rules will further, or which particular people they will assist, that they are merely given the form most likely on the whole to benefit all the people affected by them, is the most important criterion of formal rules in the sense in which we here use this term. They do not involve a choice between particular ends or particular people, because we just cannot know beforehand by whom and in what way they will be used.

In our age, with its passion for conscious control of everything, it may appear paradoxical to claim as a virtue that under one system we shall know less about the particular effect of the measures the state takes than would be true under most other systems and that a method of social control should be deemed superior because of our ignorance of its precise results. Yet this consideration is in fact the rationale of the great liberal principal of the Rule of Law. And the apparent paradox dissolves rapidly when we follow the argument a little further.

This argument is twofold; the first is economic and can here only briefly be stated. The state should confine itself to establishing rules applying to general types of situations and should allow the individuals freedom in everything which depends on the circumstances of time and place, because only the individuals concerned in each instance can fully know these circumstances and adapt their actions to them. If the individuals are to be able to use their knowledge effectively in making plans, they must be able to predict actions of the state which may affect these plans. But if the actions of the state are to be predictable they must be determined by rules fixed independently of the concrete circumstances which can be neither foreseen nor taken into account beforehand: and the particular effects of such actions will be unpredictable. If, on the other hand, the state were to direct the individual's actions so as to achieve particular ends, its action would have to be decided on the basis of the full circumstances of the moment and would therefore be unpredictable. Hence the familiar fact that the more the state "plans," the more difficult planning becomes for the individual.

The second, moral or political, argument is even more directly relevant to the point under discussion. If the state is precisely to foresee the incidence of its actions, it means that it can leave those affected no choice. Wherever the state can exactly forsee the effects on particular people of alternative courses of action, it is also the state which chooses between the different ends. If we want to create new opportunities open to all, to offer chances of which people can make what use they like, the precise results cannot be foreseen. General rules, genuine laws as distinguished from specific orders, must therefore be intended to operate in circumstances which cannot be foreseen in detail, and, therefore, their effect on particular ends or particular people cannot be known beforehand. It is in this sense alone that it is at all possible for the legislator to be impartial. To be impartial means to have no answer to certain questions—to the kind of questions which, if we have to decide them, we decide by tossing a coin. In a world where everything was precisely foreseen, the state could hardly do anything and remain impartial.

Where the precise effects of government policy on particular people are known, where the government aims directly at such particular effects, it cannot help knowing these effects, and therefore it cannot be impartial. It must, of necessity, take sides, impose its valuations upon people and, instead of assisting them in the advancement of their own ends, choose the ends for them. As soon as the particular effects are foreseen at the time a law is made, it ceases to be a mere instrument to be used by the people and becomes instead an instrument used by the lawgiver upon the people and for his ends. The state ceases to be a piece of utilitarian machinery intended to help individuals in the fullest development of their individual personality and becomes a "moral" institution—where "moral" is not used in contrast to immoral but describes an institution which imposes on its members its views on all moral questions, whether these views be moral or highly immoral. In this sense the Nazi or any other collectivist state is "moral," while the liberal state is not.

Perhaps it will be said that all this raises no serious problem because in the kind of questions which the economic planner would have to decide he need not and should not be guided by his individual prejudices but could rely on the general conviction of what is fair and reasonable. This contention usually receives support from those who have experience of planning in a particular industry and who find that there is no insuperable difficulty about arriving at a decision which all those immediately interested will accept as fair. The reason why this experience proves nothing is, of course, the selection of the "interests" concerned when planning is confined to a particular industry. Those most immediately interested in a particular issue are not necessarily the best judges of the interests of society as a whole. To take only the most characteristic case: when capital and labor in an industry agree on some policy of restriction and thus exploit the consumers, there is usually no difficulty about the division of the spoils in proportion to former earnings or on some similar principle. The loss which is divided between thousands or millions is usually either simply disregarded or quite inadequately considered. If we want to test the usefulness of the principle of "fairness" in deciding the kind of issues which arise in economic planning, we must apply it to some question where the gains and the losses are seen equally clearly. In such instances it is readily recognized that no general principle such as fairness can provide an answer. When we have to choose between higher wages for nurses or doctors and more extensive services for the sick, more milk for children and better wages for agricultural workers, or between employment for the unemployed or better wages for those already employed, nothing short of a complete system of values in which every want of every person or group as a definite place is necessary to provide an answer.

In fact, as planning becomes more and more extensive, it becomes regularly necessary to qualify legal provisions increasingly by reference to what is "fair" or "reasonable"; this means that it becomes necessary to leave the decision of the concrete case more and more to the discretion of the judge or authority in question. One could write a history of the decline of the Rule of Law, the disappearance of the *Rechtsstaat*, in terms of the progressive introduction of these vague formulas into legislation and jurisdiction, and of the increasing arbitrariness and uncertainty of, and the consequent disrespect for, the law and the judicature, which in these circumstances could not but become an instrument of policy. It is important to point out once more in this connection that this process of the decline of the Rule of Law had been going on steadily in Germany for some time before Hitler came into power and that a policy well advanced toward totalitarian planning had already done a great deal of the work which Hitler completed.

There can be no doubt that planning necessarily involves deliberate discrimination between particular needs of different people, and allowing one man to do what another must be prevented from doing. It must lay down by a legal rule how well off particular people shall be and what different people are to be allowed to have and do. It means in effect a return to the rule of status, a reversal of the "movement of progressive societies" which, in the famous phrase of Sir Henry Maine, "has hitherto been a movement from status to contract." Indeed, the Rule of Law, more than the rule of contract, should probably be regarded as the true opposite of the rule of status. It is the Rule of Law, in the sense of the rule of formal law, the absence of legal privileges of particular people designated by authority, which safeguards that equality before the law which is the opposite of arbitrary government.

CHARLES E. MERRIAM

4. Planning: America's Experience*

From the beginning of our national life various forms of planning have been in evidence. The industrial situation confronting the founders of this republic was one of widespread distress, insecurity, and depression of the most anxious type. They deliberately planned a way out, when most men held that even government could not be planned. The Constitution itself was an economico-political plan on a grand scale, not only providing a democratic frame of government, but also setting up special plans for dealing with currency, tariffs, interstate commerce, and international relations. Justice was the first term in the preamble and liberty the last, but between them came the general welfare, common defense, and domestic tranquillity. The Constitutional Convention itself was a large-scale planning board.

Alexander Hamilton's well-known *Report on Manufactures* presented in 1791 was an impressive consideration of national policy in industry and related fields of American interest. In broad terms Hamilton set out the national problems of economics and government and suggested specific lines of policy to be followed. The report on internal improvements drawn up by President Jefferson's Secretary of the Treasury, Albert Gallatin, was almost equally notable. Henry Clay developed later (1820) the famous "American system," in which tariff and internal improvements occupied a conspicuous place. It is clear that the encouragement of manufactures by a policy of protection began as a systematic planning procedure, though later it degenerated at times into a free-for-all scramble for favors.

The land policy of the United States was planned with similar deliberation. It began with the abolition of the system of primogeniture and entail, the basis of the British system of political and economic power. The "grand plan" of John Quincy Adams for the management of the national domain was not followed; but the later development of the American homestead policy (1862) was designed to give a homestead at a nominal cost to practically all prospective settlers.

Our public educational policy rested in large part upon the broad grants of public lands given—two sections per township—for school purposes, with additional amounts for land-grant colleges. All this was notable national planning as of that day and age, democratic in purpose and method and highly successful in producing results. Those who prefer not to call this

* From Charles E. Merriam, *On the Agenda of Democracy* (The Godkin Lectures, Harvard University Press, 1941). By permission.

planning may, of course, apply some other term, but that will not change the spirit and temper of the work of the first great national planners who laid broad foundations for the republic of their dreams. Down to the Civil War, no country in the world had made bolder and more successful experiments in the field of government and economics alike than the United States.

Following that war, planning centered for several decades in large-scale private industries, such as had scarcely been known theretofore. Giant enterprises began to dominate whole areas of industry, and to operate them in increasingly unified and systematic fashion, although not always in the public interest. But national planning did not cease. It was resorted to whenever the public came to believe that unrestricted business enterprise failed at some point to promote the national welfare. Examples of government action designed to protect public interests are the establishment of the Interstate Commerce Commission in 1887, the passage of the Sherman Antitrust Act of 1890, the organization of the Federal Trade Commission, and a long series of national and state measures having the same general purpose.

Another step toward national planning was the development of the conservation program designed for the protection of natural resources, under the leadership of Theodore Roosevelt. This wide-ranging movement constituted a striking example of intelligent and forward-looking national policy, designed to protect and promote our common interests through various types of controls preventive of wasteful exploitation of our basic resources. In addition to the plans of the United States Government, similar systems and arrangements were set up by several of the states in various fields.

A more dramatic development of national planning was the "economic mobilization" development during the World War through the War Industries Board, the War Trade Board, the Shipping Board, the War Labor Board, the Food Administration, the Fuel Administration, and the Railroad Administration, with their various subsidiaries. Under the stimulus of the war objective and national unity of purpose, far-reaching plans were made for the utilization of resources, for the ordering of industry, and for the focusing of the nation's strength in military and naval pressure. Nor did plans for economic mobilization end with the war. The National Defense Act of 1921 is a plan for a national war emergency—a plan which covers the wide ranges of industrial life necessarily reorganized for war purposes.

Though the war-time controls were released promptly after the armistice, the speculative boom of 1919-20 and the severe though brief depression of 1920-21 brought home to everyone the fact that peace has her defeats no less than war. The elaborate report on *Waste in Industry,* sponsored by the American Engineering Council in 1921, was a landmark in a movement toward better economic management, and this line was followed by important developments of planning in the Department of Commerce. Trade associations began their rapid growth under the benevolent auspices of the United States Government. Attacks upon waste, demands for standardization, simplification, research in production efficiency, long-time plans for stabilization and equilibrium in industry, were pressed forward.

Another notable development was the reorganization of the budgetary procedure of the United States Government through the Budget Bureau and the Director of the Budget—a reform long advocated and finally accomplished—under President Harding. While many of these powers were already in the hands of the President, the deliberate planning of ways and means for the exercise of his authority unquestionably had an important influence in the direction of systematic scrutiny and control over public expenditures. The Federal Reserve Bank was set up to be an important agency for equilibrium in the field of banking and credit. The organization of the Federal Employment Stabilization Board through the efforts of Senator Wagner and President Hoover was an attempt to plan expenditures for public works over a period of years in relation to business cycles.

Meanwhile many forms of planning appeared. City planning agencies sprang up, reaching now the number of some one thousand. County planning boards have been established covering a quarter of our three thousand counties. Some forty-five state planning agencies have been established.[1] Regional planning committees have been set up and commissions on interstate coöperation have been organized by most of the states. Many large-scale efforts in the field of planning have been developed by the United States Government in the last ten years, beginning with the Reconstruction Finance Corporation, the Home Owners' Loan Corporation, and the Federal Employment Stabilization Office under President Hoover. President Roosevelt initiated a broad sweep of policies in the field of social legislation. No effort is made here to sum up all of the attempts made in this direction.

Wide ranges of social legislation have been directed at regulation of industrial maladjustments. Sometimes these efforts took the form of labor legislation and sometimes they were aimed at the correction of corporate and other industrial abuses.

Notwithstanding differences of judgment regarding either the policy or the administration of these undertakings, there is general agreement that many of them have been highly successful. Taken together they illustrate the importance of planning our fundamental national policy in the emergency period upon which we are now entering. Doubtless many other evidences of national planning of resources both natural and human will be seen. It becomes more and more evident that the fullest use of American national resources cannot be obtained without careful and intelligent planning—national, state, and local.

The National Resources Planning Board, created by President Roosevelt

---

[1] For history of state planning, see Clifford J. Hynning, *State Conservation of Resources* (1939); R. A. Walker, *The Planning Function in Urban Government* (1941).

in 1933, was substantially the projection of the Advisory Council recommended by President Hoover's Committee on Recent Social Trends, 1933. This body has made many studies of our physical and our human resources. The basic data regarding land use, water use, energy resources, long-time planning of public works, have been assembled by technicians and carefully analyzed, and various indicated policies have been suggested. In each of these areas broad programs have been outlined. Elaborate analyses have been made of the structure of our national economy, of consumer expenditure, and of consumer income. Reviews of industrial trends and their relation to employment stabilization, and analyses of industrial-plant location, thoroughgoing scrutiny of our relief policy, and indications of a long-time method of procedure have been prepared and presented to responsible officials. More recently the Board has undertaken the preparation of plans for the post-emergency period on a considerable scale.

Fundamental inquiries have been made into basic factors in the national economy: scientific studies of population trends, of inventions and their social implications, of research as a national resource—research in government, in industry, in university centers. In addition to printed reports, many of the results are in the form of interoffice memoranda, and in the shape of private reports and memos submitted to the Executive. These taken together constitute an important section of the work of the planning agency on whatever level of government it may be found. An advisory agency will find that much of its advice is rejected in whole or in part, but this is one of the ways in which advisors are distinguished from the responsible policy-determiners or administrators dealing with operative activities. Advice often advances through roundabout and even underground channels. There may come a moment when the advice long since given comes back with a request for a review by the one who gave it.

W. ARTHUR LEWIS

5. *Planning: By Inducement or Direction?* *

THE MARKET ECONOMY

Even the greatest worshipper of *laisser-faire* has never suggested that there should be no state. Everyone agrees that there are certain minimum functions for which it is absolutely essential. Adam Smith listed defence, justice,

* From W. Arthur Lewis, *The Principles of Economic Planning* (Dennis Dobson and Allen and Unwin, 1949). By permission.

education and roads and communications. Economists following in his foot-steps have expanded the list, and reduced it to general principles. Enshrined in the textbooks as beyond controversy, the state has duties in respect of (*a*) things which only the state can enforce (e.g. justice, defence); (*b*) things which diffuse benefits for which the beneficiaries cannot be charged (e.g. lighthouses); and (*c*) things in which the judgment of the state is superior to that of the citizens. This last is a growing category: the state now claims to know better than its citizens for how many years they should send their children to school, between what hours they should drink, what proportion of income should be saved, whether cheap housing is better than cheap ciga-rettes, and so on. Whether any particular case fits into one of these categories is frequently open to dispute, but the categories are well accepted as laying the absolute minimum of functions for the state.

The case against *laisser-faire* is much more formidable than this. It rests on the following counts.

First, under a *laisser-faire* system income is not fairly distributed; and as a corollary of this, less urgent goods are produced for wealthy people while the poor lack education, health, good food, decent houses and ordinary com-forts which could be supplied instead. This is no longer denied. The price mechanism rewards people according to the scarcity of the resources (la-bour and property) that they possess, but it does not itself contain any mechanism for equalising the distribution of scarcities. For justice in distri-bution we have clearly to summon the forces of the state.

The second weakness is related; the market mechanism does not humanise the wage relation. This is not a simple issue. Employment for wages arises out of the fact that the workers do not own the instruments with which they work. Some socialists have wished to abolish this relation altogether by redistributing property to the workers, as is done in agrarian revolutions, to be worked either individually or in cooperative groups. Any other solu-tion, whether it leaves property to capitalists or hands it over to the state, retains the wage relation, and can seek only to humanise it by guaranteeing the worker's rights, and by insisting on his sharing in decisions. Of course it is arguable that in perfect competition and in full employment employers would have to court labour, so that the price mechanism, rid of its imper-fections, would ensure to labour protection of its rights. Perhaps it would, but the state is a much more certain protection.

This brings us to the third defect of the market economy, its instability. Private enterprise in the creation of money produces cycles, unemployment and misery. To be sure, state enterprise in the creation of money has had no better record; the case for private enterprise in this field rested for centuries on the unchallengeable ground that control by the state had always proved to be much worse. The present unanimity of British thinkers in favour of state control of money (there is no similar unanimity in the U.S.A.) is very recent, and due only to conviction that new secrets have been discovered which reverse the advantages in favour of the state.

Equally inadequate, on the fourth count, is the market's handling of foreign monies. The case that foreign trade is self-regulating was argued long and stoutly by the protagonists of *laisser-faire,* but the same advances in monetary theory have now finally exploded this myth. Foreign trade must be regulated by the state.

Fifthly, the market economy is ineffective in coping with major change. Where resources need to be moved in considerable degree, its methods are too slow and cruel. Scarcities are not quickly eliminated, with the result that a few persons receive abnormally large incomes at the public's expense, and that scarce commodities are unjustly distributed; and at the same time over-production is not quickly reduced, with the result that other persons suffer abnormally low incomes. State action to speed the mobility of resources is clearly needed.

Next, the market economy is wasteful. Competition induces producers to improve their techniques; but it also induces them to spend heavily on sales promotion, and to evade standardisation. But here the case is not so clear. The case for *laisser-faire* in the 18th and 19th centuries was the wastefulness and stupidity of bureaucratic operations; on the subject of waste we must clearly not proceed by simple generalisations.

This part of the case against the market economy is bound up with the final count, the fact that the merits of the market depend on the existence of competition, and that perfect competition is rare. It is clear that nothing in the market mechanism itself either establishes or maintains competition. Only state action can assure competition. In this, as in so much else, the market economy cannot function adequately without positive support from the state.

PLANNING BY DIRECTION

It has been possible to state the counts in this indictment of *laisser-faire* so briefly because they are now accepted by most serious political thinkers. There are no longer any believers in *laisser-faire,* except on the lunatic fringe. There are many who denounce planning in fierce language, and who appear by implication to be arguing for *laisser-faire,* but, on closer examination there are always a few pages in their books which give the game away. The truth is that we are all planners now.

That is not to say that we believe in all forms of planning or in complete central planning. *Laisser-faire* can be complete, or it can be modified by state action at many crucial points. Similarly planning can be complete, or it can be combined with a market economy in various degrees.

In fact, the central issue in the discussion of planning is not whether there shall be planning but what form it shall take, and in particular whether the state shall operate through the price mechanism or in supercession of it. Suppose, for example, that the government decides that, in the interests of children's health, the production of milk ought to be increased. No one questions that this is a reasonable sort of decision for the government to make. But there are many ways of fulfilling this plan, some more direct than others, and some more effective. It might pass a law making it illegal for those responsible for a child to give the child less than one pint of milk a day (just as it is illegal to give the child less than a stipulated amount of education). Or it might increase family allowances, and urge parents to spend the increase on extra milk. Or it might issue free milk tickets to each child, and refund the cost to milk retailers. Or it might purchase milk, and feed this to children in schools. These are measures it might take on the side of demand; they have their parallel on the side of supply. It might pay subsidies to milk producers, thus reducing the price and stimulating both consumption and production. It might set up its own state farms, and give the milk away. Or it might pass a law instructing each milk producer to increase his output by a stipulated amount. All these ways of fulfilling the milk plan are forms of planning, and of course a planner may reject some and accept others. The fundamental difference is between methods that achieve their result by persuasion and those that achieve it by command. Making milk cheaper is an inducement to extra consumption, and paying milk subsidies is an inducement to extra production; both are planning through the price mechanism. On the other hand, ordering people to purchase more milk or producers to produce more is planning by direction. The real choice we have to make is between planning by inducement, and planning by direction.

Complete planning by direction is just as much ruled out as is complete *laisser-faire*. To begin with, it cannot be applied to consumption. The Government knows better than the citizen how he should spend his income in certain spheres; we all admit this, but they are limited spheres. Bye and large the citizen demands freedom of choice in consumption; freedom to spend his money as he pleases. Rationing is abhorred, except in emergency, and so is payment of wages in kind. There must, therefore, be money, and a consumers' market. This is a severe limitation on planning, for it means that the results of planning are tested in the consumers' market. If, for example, too many resources are devoted to investment, a general shortage shows up in the consumers' market, and even if there is no general shortage, there will be particular shortages unless the balance of production is just right. Freedom of choice in consumption therefore exerts pressure for free adjustment of production to demand. The government may plan demand, by taking steps to secure a just distribution of income, but once it has done this the pressure is all against trying to plan production by direction when consumption is free.

Secondly, the worker demands freedom to choose his own job. This means that there must be a labour market, as well as a consumers' market, and that the social task of getting labour into the right jobs in the right proportions must be achieved not by direction but by inducement. This also is a big limitation on planning, for plans which can only be fulfilled by moving labour by direction are bound to fail.

There must be a market for the consumer, and there must be a market for labour. That leaves the markets for enterprise, capital and raw materials in the balance. The manager of a firm (private, cooperative or state trust) has to be able to sell what he produces, and has to attract labour by inducement. Should he be free to adjust himself in markets for enterprise, capital and raw materials, or should he produce what he is directed to produce with resources that are allocated to him?

There is nothing in the case for planning which requires the choice of methods that put industrial managers into a straight jacket. There is, we have seen, a formidable case for regulating markets in many ways, and with many objects in view, but nothing in this case calls for issuing directions to managers which diminish their freedom to adjust production to the market forces of supply and demand.

There is, on the other hand, a formidable case against planning by direction, and in favour of using the market.

In the first place, the central planner, who issues the directions, cannot hope to see and provide for all the consequences of his actions. The economic system is exceedingly complex. If you plan to increase the output of watches you must at the same time plan to increase the output of everything complementary to watches, i.e. everything used with watches or in making watches, and to reduce the output of all substitutes for watches and the constituents of substitutes. Now no single person can make a complete list of all the complements and substitutes of watches, or decide what will be all the economic effects of having more watches. And even if he could make a list for watches, he would need also to make a separate list for each of the complements and substitutes, each of which has to be planned, and again separate lists for each of their complements and substitutes, and so on. It is because of this complexity that the fulfilment of plans by direction is always so unsatisfactory. Thousands of engines are produced, but they have to be stored through shortage of ball bearings or of screws. In planning by direction the result is always a shortage of some things, and a surplus of others. Planning through the market (e.g. the state placing an order for watches, or paying a subsidy) handles all this better because, in any sphere that is affected by the decision to have more watches, the flow of money and the adjustment of prices acts as a "governor," turning on or off automatically without any central direction.

Secondly, and for the same reason, planning by direction has to be inflexible. Once the planners have made the thousands of calculations that are necessary to fit the plan together, and have issued their directions, any demand that any of the figures be revised is bound to be resisted. The plan once made must be adhered to simply because you cannot alter any part of it without altering the whole, and altering the whole is too elaborate a job to be done frequently. The price mechanism can adjust itself from day to day, the flow of money alters, and prices and production respond; but the economy planned by direction is inflexible.

The third defect follows from these two. As the plan proceeds fulfilment is bound to be imperfect—even if the plan was perfect when it was made, conditions change. Firm X has been given a permit to buy coal; but there has been a strike, or an accident, or bad weather, and it cannot get its allocation of coal. It therefore wants to buy oil, but the oil has all been allocated, and a complete reallocation of oil is too big a job to undertake at short notice. So firm X must close, or it must buy an allocation of oil from some other firm whose need for oil is not so urgent. This has had, in most centrally planned economies, the curious consequence that the plan works smoothly only because it is supplemented by black markets in which firms can adjust themselves to changing conditions. However, given adequate stocks, a centrally planned economy could carry its mistakes without interrupting production, just as in a market economy it is mainly the existence of stocks that acts as a buffer for the numerous errors made by private entrepreneurs. The main reason why centrally planned economies work always in an atmosphere of scarcity and of hit and miss is that central planners usually forget how important it is to plan for an adequate holding of stocks, but this error is not itself inherent in central planning.

To the inflexibility and errors of planning by direction we must add its tendency to be procrustean. It is hard enough to step up the output of watches if there is only one kind of watch; if there are two kinds of watch it is more than twice as hard, and it gets progressively harder the more different types of watch there are. Central planners in consequence are always tempted to excessive standardisation, not because they think that standardisation is good for the public, but because it simplifies their job. Standardisation is frequently an engine of progress; but it is also frequently the enemy of happiness, and in foreign trade it is in many lines fatal to success.

Related to this is the stifling effect of direction on enterprise, and this is a consideration of the utmost importance in a country like the United Kingdom. This is a country which lives by foreign trade. We built up this trade by being first in the field of mass production of standard commodities. But today other nations are as good as we are at this game, if not better, and we can hold our own only if we are constantly in the vanguard pioneering new ideas; inventing new goods and processes, trying them out on the market, adjusting rapidly in accordance with consumer reaction, and so on. None of this can be foreseen, and so none of this can be planned from the centre. The future of the country depends on bold and free entrepreneur ship; on people with new ideas being free to back them against all opposition, to get what resources of capital, labour and raw materials they need without bureaucratic hindrance, and to test out the market for themselves. Any form of planning which prevents this permanently, or for long periods, will be the ruin of Great Britain.

And finally, the more one tries to overcome the difficulties of planning by direction, the more costly planning becomes in terms of resources. We cannot plan without knowledge, so we must have elaborate censuses, numerous forms and an array of clerks. We cannot issue thousands of licences rapidly without thousands of clerks. The better we try to plan, the more planners we need. The Soviet Census returns over 800,000 "economists," who are mostly administrative staff connected with planning. The price mechanism does the same job without this army of economists, who are thus released for useful work in the mines and the potato fields. To be sure, the market economy also has its army of hangers-on, who contribute to profit making rather than to production—its contact men, sales promoters, stockbrokers and the like, but they are not as essential to it as are the planners to planning.

On account of its complexity, planning by direction does not increase, but on the contrary diminishes democratic control. A plan cannot be made by "the people" or by parliament or by the cabinet; it has to be made by officials, because it consists of thousands of details fitted together. Its results are embodied in thousands of administrative orders and decisions, of which parliament and ministers can have only the briefest knowledge, and which provide innumerable opportunities for corrupting the public service. The more we direct from the centre the less the control that is possible. When the government is doing only a few things we can keep an eye on it, but when it is doing everything it cannot even keep an eye on itself.

PLANNING THROUGH THE MARKET

The obvious moral of all this is that our aim should be to preserve free markets wherever possible. The manager of an industrial establishment, whether private or public, should be left free to adjust his concern to market conditions; to make what he can sell, and to make it with whatever combination of resources he can most cheaply buy. This does not mean that he will be free from control; on the contrary, he is the servant of the market, which controls everything that he does. Neither does it limit the scope of planning. For the state can do all the planning it wants by controlling in its turn the market which controls the entrepreneur. The state can plan as much as it wants, but it should plan not by direction but by manipulating the market.

Thus if it wishes firms to make more of the sorts of goods that the poor buy and less of the sorts of goods that the rich buy, there is no need for a cumbersome machinery of allocations and controls. It can increase the taxation of the rich, and reduce the taxation of the poor; or it can subsidise the goods it wishes to encourage, and tax those it wishes to discourage. If it wishes to increase the production of wheat at the expense of other agricultural products there is no need for a multitude of forms, clerks and agricultural committees to fix a wheat acreage for each of 350,000 farms; it has only to raise its guaranteed price for wheat, or to increase its wheat subsidy. If it wishes to encourage exports at the expense of home consumption it need not give each firm an export allocation; it can take money out of the home market by increasing taxation, or it can alter the foreign exchange rate, or it can increase the purchase tax on goods sold in the home market, or it can pay subsidies on exports. And if it wishes to promote capital formation at the expense of consumption it can, on the one hand, either subsidise investment or make investments itself, and on the other hand, it can simultaneously discourage consumption by taxation. In every case there is the choice between direction and inducement, and in every case inducement brings the same final result, without the costs of bureaucratic control.

Fundamentally, where planning parts company with *laisser-faire* is not in rejecting the market economy controlled by demand, but in arguing that demand itself is not sacred, but something that should be manipulated by the state. Once this is realised there is no need for planners to cling to cumbersome types of planning when they have at hand methods that can make planning work as smoothly as *laisser-faire* and with far superior results.

What makes it impossible to rely exclusively on planning by manipulating market demand is the immobility of resources. This kind of planning relies on inducement to bring about a supply large enough to meet market demand. Suppose, for example, that it is desired to increase the consumption of milk and that the method chosen is to distribute free milk in schools. The total demand for milk is thus increased, and its price tends to rise. If a small rise in price is sufficient to induce a large flow of resources into milk production, supply will keep pace with demand, and no further action will be required. But if it is not, there will be either a large increase in the price of milk, or a shortage for ordinary consumers, and in either of these cases further action will be demanded, either to keep the price at a reasonable level, or to allocate the limited supplies fairly, or both.

Since, therefore, the real cause of the trouble is the immobility of resources, it follows that the most important measures to be adopted are those which augment the supply. Price control and rationing may also be necessary, but since they are only necessary until such time as the supply can be augmented, they are subsidiary to measures that augment supply, and the efficiency of planning is to be judged not by the excellence of the system of rationing and price controls, but by the speed with which shortages are eliminated and price controls and rationing rendered unnecessary.

The most important thing to do to a shortage is to eliminate it. This is not the only thing to do. In the interim prices may have to be controlled, specifications issued, and supplies rationed. But all these are necessary only for so long as the shortage lasts, and are subsidiary to eliminating the shortage by augmenting supply. The quality and success of planning are to be measured not by the excellence of price and rationing controls, but by the speed with which shortages are eliminated, and by the effectiveness of the measures taken towards that end.

If the quantity of money is right there cannot be a general shortage of goods, and particular shortages must be balanced by the existence of surplus supplies of other goods. The existence of shortages is then a clear sign that productive resources are in the wrong places, and what we have to do is to get them correctly allocated between industries.

This is no easy job. The best way to tackle it is by inducement; i.e. by raising the earnings in industries that are short of resources relatively to earnings in other industries. But inducement may work only over a long period, and only by means of sharp fluctuations in earnings—a sharp rise followed by a fall to normal levels, for example. Sometimes there are acceptable forms of direction which can be applied to end the shortage, e.g. by controlling raw materials, labour recruitment, or capital installations in ways that restrict less essential industries; but, especially where the maldistribution of labour is the principal problem, at other times we can rely only on the slow working of inducement, and then the shortage and the controls it makes necessary will last for some time.

It is here that planning by direction and planning by inducement meet. In a normally working economic system the state should be able to do nearly all the planning it wants by manipulating the market, and especially through the budget, which is the principal instrument of planning. Through the budget the state fixes the quantity of money in circulation, and thus determines whether there shall be inflation, deflation or the right balance. Through the budget it redistributes income, decides how much equality there shall be, and thus controls demand and supply and production. These general controls it supplements, again through the budget, by stimulating or retarding particular industries and services, either by buying itself, or by taxes and subsidies. The budget is not the only instrument available for planning, but it is the most important, the most powerful, and the most embracing. Perhaps in some other countries where the machinery for assessing and collecting taxes is very inadequate, and where corruption is rife in the Treasury, the budget is not powerful enough for planning. But in such countries the whole administrative machine is likely to be unsuitable for planning, and other weapons of planning fare no better than the budget. In Britain, however, it is not only the case that the arts of public finance are highly developed. But it is also important that while the citizen of Britain responds fairly well to fiscal demands, he hates other forms of control that involve direction, rationing or other dependence on administrative decision; and this is added reason for planning through the budget as much as possible, and relegating other forms of control to a subsidiary position.

But this kind of planning takes us as far as inducement will take us and no further. If there are big changes in demand or supply, and if resources are not mobile, it will have to be supplemented by direction. At the outbreak of a war, and at the end of a war, an economic system is not working normally. The movements required are large, and a whole network of controls is needed to cope with them. Similarly, a big change in the foreign trade position of a country calls for shifts of resources which cannot be accomplished rapidly, and which necessarily subject an economy for a long period to widespread controls. As conditions become normal it should be possible to dispense with such controls; if the opportunity has really been taken to spread resources correctly between industries the shortages should disappear. If conditions were to become stationary, all physical and price controls should disappear, and the budget remain the single instrument of planning. But of course conditions do not become stationary, and it is not desirable that they should. In normal conditions the budget will be the principal instrument of planning, but because of immobilities it will have to be supplemented by controls in all those parts of the economy where there is marked disequilibrium between demand and supply. The issue is not whether to plan or not to plan. It is simply how far planning can be done through the budget, and how much extra control we must have.

CONCLUSION

It may be useful to summarise the conclusions of this chapter.

(1) The issue between planning and *laisser-faire* is whether we can use the visible controls of state action to improve on the invisible social controls exercised by the market.

(2) This is an issue that must be argued; there is no *a priori* case for using the state in place of other social institutions that serve the same purpose.

(3) The argument produces a formidable list of defects in the market, which state action is required to eliminate.

(4) The state can use different forms of planning to achieve the same purposes; planning by direction is much inferior to planning by inducement.

(5) In planning by inducement the state manipulates the market to secure its objectives.

(6) Manipulating demand is not enough because resources move too slowly in response to inducements. Other controls are also needed temporarily.

(7) Price control and rationing are frequently necessary in the interest of equity, but they do not solve the fundamental problem, which is to get productive resources correctly allocated.

(8) The principal objective of planning by direction should be to overcome immobilities, and the speed with which this is achieved is the true measure of the quality of planning.

(9) The main instrument of planning is the budget, but this may need to be supplemented by planning by direction wherever there is marked disequilibrium between demand and supply.

Chapter XIII

THE WELFARE STATE

The contradictions between political freedom and economic dependence have been noted by students of democracy for at least a hundred years. The essence of the problem consists in this: in politics, Western democracies have successfully established the principle that the holders of power must be accountable to the public. The latter is the "boss," the former, the agent. Political power in a democracy must not be held for the benefit of the rulers, but is a trust, under which the interest of the people is to be protected. In the economic realm, on the other hand, the dogma of *laissez faire* has created a constitutional situation which violates all recognized canons of democracy: at times the owners of capital wield tremendous power over the lives of their employees without due reference to the public good, without being responsible to those whose welfare they determine through basic economic decisions. Whereas in a capitalist democracy political policies are arrived at through processes of consent which begin at the bottom and end at the top, in corporate business organizations economic decisions are made from the top down to the bottom. The structure of industrial organization is hierarchical, based on discipline and obedience; more recently, this traditional pattern has been made more democratic by collective bargaining and the influence of the labor movement.

The relationships between power and responsibility in industrial relations engaged the lifework of Mr. Justice Brandeis. Before his appointment to the Supreme Court by President Wilson, Brandeis had fought monopoly in the courts, in print and in speech, wherever the occasion demanded it. Brandeis strongly believed in the capitalist system, provided it was not perverted into its exact opposite, unregulated monopoly, and provided the political liberty of democracy was also preserved in economic relations. He was persuaded that the two realms of society, politics and the economy, could not be too contradictory in the long run, and that "either political liberty will be extinguished or industrial liberty must be restored." His concept of "industrial absolutism" opposing political freedom is most clearly elaborated in the testimony he gave in 1915 before the United States Commission on Industrial Relations. Long before, he had been one of the foremost foes of monopoly.

Brandeis was not committed to any preconceived dogmas or "isms," and his great contributions to legal analysis and political thought were based on his profound respect for facts. This pragmatic attitude—characteristic of all true liberals, whatever their economic philosophy—is also the outstanding quality in the work of a more recent social and political thinker, Lord William Beveridge. The "Beveridge Report" (*Report on Social Insurance and Allied Services,* 1942) was probably the most inspiring document of social philosophy that came out during World War II. Here was a message that promised every Briton that he could henceforth count on adequate protection against want, unemployment, illness, and old age. The report was, for a government publication, a surprising best-seller in both Britain and the United States. Two years later, in 1944, Beveridge published his even greater work on *Full Employment in a Free Society.* The reaction to the book in England was remarkable: many declared that it was the most important work in political economy since *Das Kapital.* Others said that this was the first real attempt to solve the problem of employment—a key problem of the survival of political democracy—without "judgment on the general issue between socialism and capitalism." Spokesmen of all political parties recognized in Beveridge's work a remarkable step forward in the whole debate on how to combine political liberties with economic security and progress. By contrast, the reception of the book in the United States was more polite than enthusiastic. Hayek's *Road to Serfdom* and Beveridge's *Full Employment in a Free Society* were both published in 1944. Hayek's book was a sensational best-seller in the United States, but a moderate success in Britain; Beveridge's book was a best-seller in England, but sold moderately in the United States.

Full employment in a totalitarian state is relatively simple, because the state forces people to work for low wages and under oppressive working conditions. What Beveridge seeks to achieve with his proposals is full employment in a *free society.* The essential citizen liberties to be preserved under all circumstances are listed by him as follows: "Freedom of worship, speech, writing, study and teaching; freedom of assembly and of association for political and other purposes, including the bringing about of a peaceful change of the governing authority; freedom in choice of occupation; and freedom in the management of a personal income." The private ownership of the means of production, Beveridge remarks, may be a good economic device or not, but is "not an essential citizen liberty in Britain, because it is not and never has been enjoyed by more than a very small proportion of the British people." Still, Beveridge thinks that full employment could be attained while a community "held firmly to private enterprise." Ultimately, however, if private property in the means of production should make full employment impossible, the latter would take precedence over the former. Beveridge thus avoids any a priori dogmas, and insists that experience, rather than preconceptions and prejudgments, should be the guide to the solution of these vital issues.

It was perhaps natural to think in an age of large-scale and depressing unemployment that full employment would be the answer to the social, economic, and political troubles of industrial society in the West. In the process of solving the problem of unemployment through public policies aiming at full employment, new problems developed which were not anticipated before, and of which, for instance, Beveridge seemed to have had no inkling when he wrote *Full Employment in a Free Society*. The first analysis, and still one of the most acute, of the impact of full employment on the social fabric of capitalist democracy will be found in Joseph A. Schumpeter's "The March into Socialism" (1950), his last paper before his death. In earlier works Schumpeter, one of the leading economists of the twentieth century, had studied the dynamics of capitalist enterprise (*The Theory of Economic Development*, 1912), and the relations between *Capitalism, Socialism, and Democracy* (1942; 3d ed., 1950). Unlike most other historians and analysts of the capitalist system, who ascribed the transformation of capitalism into a planned, socialized economy to the failures of capitalism, Schumpeter showed, in a more subtle and original manner, how the success of capitalism was one of the main agents contributing to its dissolution. Thus, the very success of capitalism leads to big business and the resultant "bureaucratization" of business organization, undermining and rendering obsolete the driving forces and values of classical individualistic capitalism. Above all, the rational spirit under the banner of which capitalism stormed successfully the citadel of tradition-bound feudalism, and later permeated all spheres of social thought and action, becomes the primary weapon for attacking capitalism.

Moreover, in addition to these forces of dissolution and transformation inherent in capitalism, there are outside pressures which accelerate the rate of such change. In the first place, total war tends to render the functioning of a free-enterprise system well-nigh impossible, since production, consumption, and wages have to be regulated by the state. But an even more important factor making for rapid social change is, according to Schumpeter, *inflation*. At a high level of employment, Schumpeter argues, "wage demands or other demands that increase the money cost of employing labor become both inevitable and inflationary. They become inevitable because high-level employment removes the only reason why they should not be raised. And they become inflationary because, with high utilization of resources, borrowing from banks and upward revision of prices provides a perfectly easy method of satisfying them." Given the nature of labor unions and popular government, inflation is, according to Schumpeter a "perennial pressure" in the capitalist system of today and tomorrow, and it is bound to undermine the nature and working of private enterprise. Can this inflationary pressure be effectively counteracted? Of traditional methods, neither the manipulation of the interest rate nor an aggressive tax policy with regard to high incomes seems to promise much success, and both these methods may in some ways worsen the malady rather than remedy it. However there remains one remedy which may prove to be the most appealing, politically speaking: direct controls of wages, prices, and subsidies. Such a system of *direct controls* will inevitably bring into being a big *bureaucracy* which may eventually plan the entire economy. Full employment may thus lead through inflation to bureaucratic collectivism, although the formal, legal basis of private ownership of the means of production may be preserved for a long time to come, particularly in agriculture and small business. For Schumpeter, the main difference between capitalism and collectivism lies not so much in the form of ownership—private in the one and public in the other—but in whose hands lie the decisions concerning how and what to produce, and "who is to get what."

Less pessimistic than Schumpeter, Russell W. Davenport suggests in "The Greatest Opportunity on Earth" (1949) that the demands of the American people for social welfare measures and social-economic security are legitimate and inevitable. However, the means to accomplish those aims is *welfare capitalism,* not the welfare state. Davenport, a liberal conservative, warns against the dangers of resisting welfare on the ground that, as some old-guard conservatives think, the businessman is "neither a social policeman nor a political reformer," and that "the business of business is economic and not social." Davenport (editor of *Fortune,* a leading business magazine, at the time he wrote "The Greatest Opportunity on Earth") points out that it is precisely such negativistic attitudes toward the question of economic welfare and social security that increase general hostility toward the idea of private enterprise and eventually lead to a publicly managed economy, for "the economic rights of man cannot be escaped." If business will refuse to do the job—or at least its share of the job—in the field of economic welfare, the state will step in. Moreover, the challenge which confronts business in this area is not only a moral one, it is also "an economic opportunity, a profit opportunity." Davenport cites some of the more advanced social security schemes, covering pensions, medical care, accident insurance and the like, sponsored by large and middle-sized firms in the United States; such schemes prove not only that the job can be done privately by management and labor in joint cooperation, but also—in terms of dollars and cents —that such privately sponsored welfare schemes benefit the long-range effectiveness and performance of worker and enterprise.

In a forum on "The Democratic Limits of the Welfare State" (1950), two American social scientists, Louis M. Hacker and Max Lerner, examine the issue from the viewpoints of history, economics, and politics. Hacker, a noted historian of American capitalism, stresses, in "The Limits of Intervention," the danger of the *dynamics of the welfare state:* threats to liberty come not only from irresponsible authority, but also from a state "which starts out with benevolent intentions." In particular, Hacker is apprehensive lest the welfare state threaten technical innovation, fiscal integrity, and individual opportunity by excessive concentration of power. By contrast, Lerner, a political scientist, rejects, in "State Capitalism and Business Capitalism," Hacker's notion that the welfare state is but a preliminary stage of full-fledged socialism, and that the alternative today is therefore exclusively between capitalism and socialism. Lerner sees in all modern states in the West a *mixture of private and public enterprise;* the problem is how to obtain the maximum welfare from a combination of both forms of enterprise. There is no generally valid law as to the proper mixture of the various ingredients in all cases; in the United States, Lerner says, "our whole historic instinct has been to cling to the private sector wherever we can, to move toward the public sector only when we must." He sees little danger that the American people will accept the extension of public activity out of sheer enthusiasm for socialism, and he is more apprehensive lest the power of big business escape responsibility and accountability because of the traditional prestige and influence of the business community in the affairs of the nation.

By-passing the choice between "pure" capitalism and "pure" socialism as unrealistic, public policy in the United States has steadily evolved toward more economic welfare and security. In the twentieth century, there is a direct line from Theodore Roosevelt's Square Deal through Woodrow Wilson's New Freedom to Franklin D. Roosevelt's New Deal—all stages in the extension of welfare for more and more people. The basic principles of the welfare state are simple: first, every human being is entitled to a minimum of material well-being, such as food, clothing, and decent housing; second, expanding living standards are possible with the existing physical resources and scientific knowledge; and, third, the state has the right and duty to act when private initiative fails. Unlike the dogmatic capitalist or socialist, the adherent of the welfare state judges each issue on its merits, and is interested in the maximum happiness of the greatest number of people rather than in the purity of social or economic abstractions. Because the conception of the welfare state is empirical, it has a strong appeal in countries like England and the United States: their traditions of political democracy, coupled with the empiricism and experimentalism of the Common Law, provide the necessary psychological and institutional framework for the successful working of the welfare state.

Yet it would be a tragic error to look upon this philosophy of the welfare state as a luxury, prerogative, or monopoly of advanced Western nations. Arnold J. Toynbee, the most influential historian of our time, argues in "Not the Age of Atoms but of Welfare for All" (1951) that three centuries from now the twentieth century will be remembered, not for its wars, horrors, and crimes, but for the fact that it is the first era in history "in which people dared to think it practicable to make the benefits of civilization available for the whole human race." Toynbee points to Asia and Africa as the crucial areas of the world, in which the issue of totalitarian communism versus human liberty might ultimately be settled. If the West is to stop the progressive Communist enslavement of those continents, it must be willing to cooperate with underdeveloped nations, and transform the conception of the welfare state from a national policy into a message of universal hope and inspiration.

LOUIS D. BRANDEIS

1. *Industrial Absolutism versus Political Liberty**

My observation leads me to believe that while there are many contributing causes to [industrial] unrest, that there is one cause which is fundamental. That is the necessary conflict—the contrast between our political liberty and our industrial absolutism. We are as free politically, perhaps, as free as it is possible for us to be. Every male has his voice and vote; and the law has endeavored to enable, and has succeeded practically, in enabling him to exercise his political franchise without fear. He therefore has his part; and certainly can secure an adequate part in the government of the country in all of its political relations; that is, in all relations which are determined directly by legislation or governmental administration.

On the other hand, in dealing with industrial problems the position of the ordinary worker is exactly the reverse. The individual employee has no effective voice or vote. And the main objection, as I see it, to the very large corporation is, that it makes possible—and in many cases makes inevitable—the exercise of industrial absolutism. It is not merely the case of the individual worker against the employer which, even if he is a reasonably sized employer, presents a serious situation calling for the interposition of a union to protect the individual. But we have the situation of an employer so potent, so well organized, with such concentrated forces and with such extraordinary powers of reserve and the ability to endure against strikes and other efforts of a union, that the relatively loosely organized masses of even strong unions are unable to cope with the situation. We are dealing here with a question, not of motive, but of condition. Now, the large

*From *Testimony before the Commission on Industrial Relations* (January 23, 1915; 64th Cong., 1st Sess., *Sen. Doc.*, Vol. 26, 1916).

corporation and the managers of the powerful corporation are probably in large part actuated by motives just the same as an employer of a tenth of their size. Neither of them, as a rule, wishes to have his liberty abridged; but the smaller concern usually comes to the conclusion that it is necessary that it should be, where an important union must be dealt with. But when a great financial power has developed—when there exists these powerful organizations, which can successfully summon forces from all parts of the country, which can afford to use tremendous amounts of money in any conflict to carry out what they deem to be their business principle, and can also afford to suffer large losses—you have necessarily a condition of inequality between the two contending forces. Such contests, though undertaken with the best motives and with strong conviction on the part of the corporate managers that they are seeking what is for the best interests not only of the company but of the community, lead to absolutism. The result, in the cases of these large corporations, may be to develop a benevolent absolutism, but it is an absolutism all the same; and it is that which makes the great corporation so dangerous. There develops within the State a state so powerful that the ordinary social and industrial forces existing are insufficient to cope with it.

WILLIAM BEVERIDGE

2. *Full Employment in a Free Society* *

THE MEANING OF FULL EMPLOYMENT

What is meant by "full employment," and what is not meant by it? Full employment does not mean literally no unemployment; that is to say, it does not mean that every man and woman in the country who is fit and free for work is employed productively on every day of his or her working life. In every country with a variable climate there will be seasons when particular forms of work are impossible or difficult. In every progressive society there will be changes in the demand for labour, qualitatively if not quantitatively; that is to say, there will be periods during which particular individuals can no longer be advantageously employed in their former occupations and may be unemployed till they find and fit themselves for fresh occupations. Some frictional unemployment there will be in a progressive society however high

* From William Beveridge, *Full Employment in a Free Society* (W. W. Norton & Company, 1945). By permission.

the demand for labour. Full employment means that unemployment is reduced to short intervals of standing by, with the certainty that very soon one
will be wanted in one's old job again or will be wanted in a new job that is
within one's powers.

Full employment is sometimes defined as "a state of affairs in which the
number of unfilled vacancies is not appreciably below the number of unemployed persons, so that unemployment at any time is due to the normal
lag between a person losing one job and finding another." [1] Full employment in this Report means more than that in two ways. It means having always more vacant jobs than unemployed men, not slightly fewer jobs. It
means that the jobs are at fair wages, of such a kind, and so located that the
unemployed men can reasonably be expected to take them; it means, by
consequence, that the normal lag between losing one job and finding another will be very short.

The proposition that there should always be more vacant jobs than unemployed men means that the labour market should always be a seller's
market rather than a buyer's market. For this, on the view of society underlying this Report—that society exists for the individual—there is a decisive
reason of principle. The reason is that difficulty in selling labour has consequences of a different order of harmfulness from those associated with difficulty in buying labour. A person who has difficulty in buying the labour
that he wants suffers inconvenience or reduction of profits. A person who
cannot sell his labour is in effect told that he is of no use. The first difficulty
causes annoyance or loss. The other is a personal catastrophe. This difference
remains even if an adequate income is provided, by insurance or otherwise,
during unemployment; idleness even on an income corrupts; the feeling
of not being wanted demoralizes. The difference remains even if most people are unemployed only for relatively short periods. As long as there is any
long-term unemployment not obviously due to personal deficiency, anybody who loses his job fears that he may be one of the unlucky ones who
will not get another job quickly. The short-term unemployed do not know
that they are short-term unemployed till their unemployment is over.

The human difference between failing to buy and failing to sell labour
is the decisive reason for aiming to make the labour market a seller's rather
than a buyer's market. There are other reasons, only slightly less important.
One reason is that only if there is work for all is it fair to expect work-
people, individually and collectively in trade unions, to co-operate in making
the most of all productive resources, including labour, and to forgo restric-
tionist practices. Another reason, related to this, is that the character and

---

[1] This definition is taken from the Nuffield College Statement on *Employment Policy and
Organization of Industry after the War*. The Statement adds that full employment in this sense
"cannot be completely attained so long as there exist structural maladjustments needing to be
put right."

duration of individual unemployment caused by structural and technical change in industry will depend on the strength of the demand for labour in the new forms required after the change. The greater the pace of the economic machine, the more rapidly will structural unemployment disappear, the less resistance of every kind will there be to progress. Yet another reason is the stimulus to technical advance that is given by shortage of labour. Where men are few, machines are used to save men for what men alone can do. Where labour is cheap it is often wasted in brainless, unassisted toil. The new lands empty of men are the homes of invention and business adventure in peace. Stimulus to labour saving of all kinds is one of the by-products of full employment in war.

The full employment that is the aim of this Report means more vacant jobs than unemployed men. It means something else as well. If there were 2 million chronically unemployed men in Britain and 2¼ million vacant jobs which they could not or would not fill, there would be more vacant jobs than unemployed men, but to call this state of affairs "full employment" would be mockery. It is not enough to say that there must be more vacant jobs than idle men—more or about as many. It is also necessary to be sure that the number unemployed, or rather the duration of unemployment in the individual case, is not excessive. Full employment, in any real sense, means that unemployment in the individual case need not last for a length of time exceeding that which can be covered by unemployment insurance without risk of demoralization. Those who lose jobs must be able to find new jobs as fair wages within their capacity, without delay. This means that the demand for labour and the supply of labour are related qualitatively as well as quantitatively. The demand must be adjusted to the kind of men available or the men must be capable of adjusting themselves to the demand. In the light of the facts of unemployment, it is clear that the qualitative and local adjustment of demand for labour and supply of labour has to be approached from both ends, that of demand and that of supply. The demands must not only be sufficient in total but must be directed with regard to the quality and the location of the labour that is available. The labour supply must be capable of following the changes of demand that are inseparable from technical advance.

THE PURPOSE OF EMPLOYMENT

Idleness is not the same as Want, but a separate evil, which men do not escape by having an income. They must also have the chance of rendering useful service and of feeling that they are doing so. This means that employment is not wanted for the sake of employment, irrespective of what it produces. The material end of all human activity is consumption. Employment is wanted as a means to more consumption or more leisure, as a means to a higher standard of life. Employment which is merely time-wasting, equivalent to digging holes and filling them again, or merely destructive, like war and preparing for war, will not serve that purpose. Nor will it be felt worth while. It must be productive and progressive. The proposals of this Report are designed to preserve all the essential springs of material progress in the community, to leave to special efforts its rewards, to leave scope for change, invention, competition and initiative.

In so far as room is left for change and for freedom of movement from job to job, room is left for some unemployment. The aim of this Report is expressed in numerical terms as a reduction of unemployment to not more than 3 per cent, as compared with the 10 to 22 per cent experienced in Britain between the wars. But though the Report assumes the continuance of some unemployment and suggests a figure of 3 per cent, it is the essence of the proposals made in the Report that this 3 per cent should be unemployed only because there is industrial friction, and not because there are no vacant jobs. For men to have value and a sense of value there must always be useful things waiting to be done, with money to pay for doing them. Jobs, rather than men, should wait.

PRESERVATION OF ESSENTIAL LIBERTIES

The labour market in the past has invariably, or all but invariably, been a buyer's market rather than a seller's market, with more unemployed men —generally many more unemployed men—than unfilled jobs. To reverse this and make the labour market always a seller's rather than a buyer's market, to remove not only unemployment but the fear of unemployment, would affect the working of many existing institutions. It would change and is meant to change fundamentally the conditions of living and working in Britain, to make Britain again a land of opportunity for all. There are some things in Britain which neither full employment nor the means of achieving it should be allowed to change.

The Report, as its title indicates, is not concerned simply with the problem of full employment. It is concerned with the necessity, possibility and methods of achieving full employment in a free society, that is to say, subject to the proviso that all essential citizen liberties are preserved. The precise effect of the proviso depends on the list of essential citizen liberties. For the purpose of this Report they are taken as freedom of worship, speech, writing, study and teaching; freedom of assembly and of association for political and other purposes, including the bringing about of a peaceful change of the governing authority; freedom in choice of occupation; and freedom in the management of a personal income. The proviso excludes the totalitarian solution of full employment in a society completely planned and regimented by an irremovable dictator. It makes the problem of full employment more complex in many ways, of which four call for special notice.

First, in a free society the governing authority is liable to be changed at short intervals by peaceful methods of political organization and voting. There must be reasonable continuity of economic policy in spite of such changes of government. The machinery of government, while responsive to general changes of opinion, must be resistant to "lobbies"—that is to say, organized sectional pressures.

Second, freedom of association for industrial purposes raises the issue of wage determination. Under conditions of full employment, can a rising spiral of wages and prices be prevented if collective bargaining, with the right to strike, remains absolutely free? Can the right to strike be limited generally in a free society in peace-time?

Third, freedom in choice of occupations makes it harder to ensure that all men at all times are occupied productively. It makes it impossible to retain men forcibly in particular work or to direct them to it with the threat of imprisonment if they refuse to go. One assumption underlying this Report is that neither the Essential Work Order nor the powers of industrial direction which have been found necessary in war should be continued when the war is over. In Britain at peace the supply of labour cannot be adjusted by decree to the demand for labour; it can only be guided by economic motives. From another angle, freedom in choice of occupation raises also the issue of industrial discipline. Under conditions of full employment, if men are free to move from one employment to another and do not fear dismissal, may not some of them at least become so irregular and undisciplined in their behaviour, as to lower appreciably the efficiency of industry?

Fourth, freedom in the management of a personal income complicates the problem of full employment from another side. If men cannot be forced to buy just what has been produced, this means that the demands for labour and its products cannot be fitted forcibly to the supply. There may be continual changes in the kinds of things on which consumers want to spend their money, that is to say, in the quality of consumers' outlay. There may be changes also in its quantity. For freedom in the management of a personal income includes freedom to decide between spending now and saving so as to have the power of spending later. A totalitarian regime, even if it used money and price and wage differentials to stimulate and guide individual activity, might abolish freedom of saving. It might retain from the national income of each year that portion which it needed for investment, i.e. for the sustenance of persons engaged in making instruments and materials of further production, and might issue to consumers money which, like ration coupons, could not be saved for spending later. In a free society individuals must be allowed to plan their spending over their lives as a whole.

None of these freedoms can be exercised irresponsibly. Perpetual instability of economic or social policy would make full employment and any other social reforms futile or impossible. Bargaining for wages must be responsible, looking not to the snatching of short sectional advantages, but to the permanent good of the community. Choice of occupation means freedom in choosing between occupations which are available; it is not possible for an individual to choose to be an Archbishop of Canterbury, if that post is already filled by another. Work means doing what is wanted, not doing just what pleases one. All liberties carry their responsibilities. This does not mean that the liberties themselves must be surrendered. They must be retained.

In all the respects named, and possibly in some others, the problem of maintaining full employment is more complicated in a free society than it would be under a totalitarian regime. From one complication of some historic importance the problem, as posed here, is free. The list of essential liberties given above does not include liberty of a private citizen to own means of production and to employ other citizens in operating them at a wage. Whether private ownership of means of production to be operated by others is a good economic device or not, it must be judged as a device. It is not an essential citizen liberty in Britain, because it is not and never has been enjoyed by more than a very small proportion of the British people. It cannot even be suggested that any considerable proportion of the people have any lively hope of gaining such ownership later.

On the view taken in this Report, full employment is in fact attainable while leaving the conduct of industry in the main to private enterprise, and the proposals made in the Report are based on this view. But if, contrary to this view, it should be shown by experience or by argument that abolition of private property in the means of production was necessary for full employment, this abolition would have to be undertaken.

THE STATE AND THE CITIZEN

Full employment cannot be won and held without a great extension of the responsibilities and powers of the State exercised through organs of the central Government. No power less than that of the State can ensure adequate total outlay at all times, or can control, in the general interest, the location of industry and the use of land. To ask for full employment while objecting to these extensions of State activity is to will the end and refuse the means. It is like shouting for victory in total war while rejecting compulsory service and rationing. In this Report, the new functions and powers of the State are emphasized because they are essential. This does not mean that the end can be reached through such powers alone. The underlying principle of the Report is to propose for the State only those things which the State alone can do or which it can do better than any local authority or than private citizens either singly or in association, and to leave to these other agencies that which if they will, they can do as well as or better than the

State. The Policy for Full Employment is a policy to be carried through by democratic action, of public authorities, central and local, responsible ultimately to the voters, and of voluntary associations and private citizens consciously co-operating for a common purpose which they understand and approve. The proposals in this Report preserve absolutely all the essential liberties which are more precious than full employment itself. They respect and are designed to preserve many other liberties and institutions which, though not equally essential, are deeply rooted in Britain.

The proposals imply, for instance, no weakening of local Government, no supersession of local authorities in their present field. The State must do some new things and exercise some controls which are not now exercised by anyone. It will set up the programme of planned outlay for attack on social evils and ensure the means to meet that outlay. But a large part of the execution of the programme—in health, housing, education and other fields—and the adjusting of the programme to local conditions will be a function of local rather than of central Government.

The proposals involve, again, no general change in the control or organization of industry, either on the side of management or on that of labour. They assume an expansion of the sector of industry under direct public control, but it remains a sector. The policy outlined here is put forward as something that could work and yield full employment, even though the greater part of industry continued to be conducted by private enterprise at private risk. Undoubtedly the achieving of full employment would affect the working of many industrial institutions and raise many issues; making the labour market a seller's in place of a buyer's market is a revolution which gives a new turn to every problem. Some of the most important issues, such as industrial discipline, determination of wages, determination of prices, treatment of monopolies and price associations, are discussed later among the internal implications of full employment. The general conclusion is that the degree of liberty in such matters which can be left to agencies independent of the State, without imperilling the policy of full employment, depends on the responsibility and public spirit with which those liberties are exercised. There is no reason to doubt that that responsibility and public spirit will be forthcoming.

On the general issue of public ownership as against private enterprise in industry, the provisional conclusion reached is that the necessity of socialism, in the sense of nationalization of the means of production, distribution and exchange, in order to secure full employment, has not yet been demonstrated. This implies no judgment on the general issue between socialism and capitalism, which remains for debate on other grounds. It does not mean that the problem of full employment and the problem of the control of industry are in no way connected; they are connected in many ways. It means only a judgment that it would be possible to obtain full productive employment under conditions of private enterprise. Whether it would be easier or more difficult to obtain this under conditions of national enterprise and whether there are other reasons for socialism, it is not necessary here to decide. The problem of maintaining demand on the productive resources of the country so that they are employed productively in meeting human needs arises whether industry itself is controlled by profit-seeking individuals or by public authorities. It is also to a large extent the same problem in both cases. The policy outlined in this Report is suggested as something that could and should be accepted by people who differ profoundly as to the ultimate control of industry or as to the nature of social justice.

FULL EMPLOYMENT AND PRIVATE ENTERPRISE

Can a policy of full employment be carried through and yield its full benefits under a system in which production is controlled in the main by private enterprise? The policy, as it has been set out here, is primarily one of socializing demand rather than production. It may be found convenient, as a subsidiary measure, to transfer particular industries from private to public ownership, in order to increase the power of the State directly to stabilize demand in a specified sector and in order to bring monopolies under assured control. It will certainly be necessary for the State, by inspection and supervision, to protect the community against risk of exploitation by monopolies and trade associations, in all industries. And it will be necessary for the State, in planning its own outlay, to have full continuous information as to the outlay plans of all large undertakings and to have some power of modifying those plans. But all this is far short of the nationalization of production generally. In particular it leaves the small, independent enterprise, in factory or shop or farm, unaffected. The "little man" can respond to demand under full employment, as under other conditions. So long as he remains little, he remains subject to competition and the interests of consumers need no further official safeguards.

The policy set out here is one which might be adopted by a community which held firmly to private enterprise, and accepted the principle laid down by an American economist: "Private industry can and will do the job of production. It is the responsibility of the Government to do its part to ensure a constant demand." [2] Full employment is achieved in war by State control of demand without socialization of production. There is every reason for hoping that full employment could be secured in peace by the policy outlined here, while leaving the major part of industry to private enterprise. Apart from the problems of international trade, the only significant doubt that arises on this is as to the possibility under such conditions of bringing about a sufficient stability of private investment, and preventing its cyclical fluctuation. It is reasonable to let that doubt be resolved by experience.

[2] Professor Alvin Hansen, in *Post War Economic Problems*, edited by Seymour Harris, p. 14.

It can be argued, nevertheless, that under such conditions a policy of full employment, even if it gave full employment, would fail to yield its full benefits and might lead to dangerous consequences. It can be argued that all that is proposed here is insufficient, without the socialization of production in all its more important forms. This position may be supported by a variety of arguments. In the first place, as has been pointed out above, the smooth working of a full employment policy involves the co-operation of work-people, in enforcing industrial discipline on the unruly, in securing maximum efficiency and removal of restrictions on output, in refraining from pressing unreasonable claims that might set up a vicious spiral of wages and prices. Can that co-operation, it is asked, be secured under conditions of enterprise conducted for private profit? It is argued, in the second place, that a State policy of full employment will always be liable to sabotage by capitalists desiring to make difficulties for the State. It is argued, in the third place, that substitution of national for private ownership of the means of production is necessary to prevent the piling up of wealth which may be used to manipulate the political machine. It is argued finally, that full employment will not by itself bring about the more equal distribution of income which is essential to social justice.

These arguments raise large issues, economic, political and moral, which fall to a large extent outside the scope of this Report. The importance of these issues is obvious. They are not prejudged in what is written here. The proposals of this Report are designed for one essential practical purpose —to bring to an end the mass unemployment and the fear of unemployment which, next to war, have been the greatest evils of modern times. The proposals take us round the next corner ahead—a corner which must be turned, if we desire to preserve free institutions. The problems that lie beyond that corner will become clearer when that corner has been passed; they can, if we so desire, be left to be dealt with when they are reached.

The basic proposals of this Report are neither socialism nor an alternative to socialism; they are required and will work under capitalism and under socialism alike, and whether the sector of industry conducted by private enterprise is large or is small. A conscious control of the economic system at the highest level—a new type of budget which takes man-power as its datum—adequate sustained demand directed for the products of industry— organization of the labour market—these are required in any modern society. These things the State must provide in any case, if the citizens want full employment. What else the State may be called on to do has to be determined on other grounds, or can at need be decided later. From the point of view of full employment, the decision depends largely on how private citizens use their liberties. If trade unions under full employment press wage claims unreasonably, maintenance of a stable price level will become impossible; wage determination will perforce become a function of the State. If the private owners of business undertakings under full employment set out to exploit consumers by organizing monopolies and price rings, or abuse their economic power for political purposes, or fail, with all the help of the State and in an expanding economy, to stabilize the process of investment, the private owners cannot for long be left in their ownership. If the people of Britain generally under full employment become undisciplined in industry, that will show either that they are not sufficiently civilized to be led by anything but fear of unemployment and are unworthy of freedom, or that the control of industry must be changed. All liberties have their responsibilities. The greater the sense of citizen responsibility, the greater can be the measure of liberty and the scope that is left for agencies independent of the State.

UNEMPLOYMENT AND THE INDIVIDUAL

Statistics of unemployment mean rows of men and women, not of figures only. The three million or so[3] unemployed of 1932 means three million lives being wasted in idleness, growing despair and numbing indifference. Behind these three million individuals seeking an outlet for their energies and not finding it, are their wives and families making hopeless shift with want, losing their birth-right of healthy development, wondering whether they should have been born. Beyond the men and women actually unemployed at any moment, are the millions more in work at that moment but never knowing how long that work or any work for them may last. Unemployment in the ten years before this war meant unused resources in Britain to the extent of at least £500,000,00 per year. That was the additional wealth we might have had if we had used instead of wasting our powers. But the loss of material wealth is the least of the evils of unemployment, insignificant by comparison to the other evils. Even with that loss, Britain was still one of the richest countries of the world. If that unemployment could have been divided evenly over the whole people as leisure, we should have been as rich and altogether happier; we should have had a standard of living with which few countries could compare. The greatest evil of unemployment is not the loss of additional material wealth which we might have with full employment. There are two greater evils: first, that unemployment makes men seem useless, not wanted, without a country; second, that unemployment makes men live in fear and that from fear springs hate.

So long as chronic mass unemployment seems possible, each man appears as the enemy of his fellows in a scramble for jobs. So long as there is a scram-

---

[3] The highest number registered as unemployed was 2,979,425 in January, 1933, but 1932 in general and particularly in its second half had higher figures than 1933. No doubt even in 1932 there was some unemployment which escaped registration.

ble for jobs it is idle to deplore the inevitable growth of jealous restrictions, of demarcations, of organized or voluntary limitations of output, of resistance to technical advance. By this scramble are fostered many still uglier growths—hatred of foreigners, hatred of Jews, enmity between the sexes. Failure to use our productive powers is the source of an interminable succession of evils. When that failure has been overcome, the way will be open to progress in unity without fear.

The necessity of preventing the return of mass unemployment is a recurrent theme in nearly all that has been written on reconstruction problems in Britain after the war, from whatever angle it is written. "Unemployment such as darkened the world between the two wars, must not recur." [4] "There must be no return to the disastrous waste of man-power which characterized the period between the wars." [5] This is the issue which in the years after the war, more than any other, will make or break the reputation of any minister of any government. Yet, as Sir John Anderson remarked exactly a year ago when discussing Assumption C of the Beveridge Report, "There is no question whether we can achieve full employment; we must achieve it. It is the central factor which will undermine the pattern of national life after the war, including, perhaps, the fate of democratic institutions." [6] The same thoughts find utterance in America: "Never again will doles and subsistence levels be tolerated." [7] "The liberty of a democracy is not safe if its business system does not provide employment and produce and distribute goods in such a way as to sustain an acceptable standard of living." [8]

The necessity of preventing after this war a return to the mass unemployment between the two wars is formally admitted by all. The possibility of doing so, if we are prepared to will the means as well as the end, is not open to reasonable doubt. Depressions of trade are not like earthquakes or cyclones; they are man-made. In the course of relieving unemployment, all industrial countries, but particularly Britain, have acquired much knowledge as to its causes. Though there remain some unsolved problems, the conditions without which mass unemployment cannot be prevented are known and the main lines for remedial action are clear. Finally, the experience of the two wars has shown that it is possible to have a human society in which every man's effort is wanted and none need stand idle and unpaid.

---

[4] *Work: The Future of British Industry* (being a Report by the Conservative Sub-Committee on Industry), para. 3.

[5] *Nuffield College Memorandum on Employment Policy and Organization of Industry after the War*, para. 4.

[6] *The Times* (Editorial), 16th February, 1944.

[7] From a leaflet by the Committee for Economic Development—an organization financed by business firms to assist and encourage industry and commerce in the United States to plan for maximum employment after the war.

[8] President Roosevelt in Message to Congress, 29th April, 1938.

SOME OBJECTIONS ANSWERED

The doubt is not as to the possibility of achieving full employment but as to the possibility of achieving it without the surrender of other things that are even more precious. Some things which are more precious than full employment, that is to say, some of the essential British liberties, are surrendered in war. But it can be shown that this surrender is required by the special nature of the war objective, and not by the full employment which is incidental to war. This surrender of essential liberties would not be required for full employment in peace and should be refused. The Policy for Full Employment set out in this Report preserves all the essential British liberties; it rejects rationing, which forbids the free spending of personal income; it rejects direction of men and women to compulsory tasks; it rejects prohibition of strikes and lock-outs. The policy preserves also other liberties which, if less essential, are deeply rooted in Britain, including collective bargaining to determine wages, and private enterprise in a large sector of industry; it preserves these lesser liberties, subject to the degree of responsibility with which they are exercised. The policy preserves possibility of change, the springs of progress and the way to rising standards of life. It is not open to the criticism that it would destroy essential liberties or lead to stagnation. Is it open to any other serious objection? It will be convenient to name some of the possible objections and give brief answers.

There are some who will say that full employment, combined with unemployment insurance, will remove the incentive of effort which depends on fear of starvation. The answer is that for civilized human beings ambition and desire for service are adequate incentives. It may be that cattle must be driven by fear. Men can and should be led by hope. The policy set out in this Report is not one of stagnation or forced equality. It does not give security for life in a particular job; it gives only the opportunity of exercising one's gifts and energies in generous rather than in ungenerous rivalry with one's fellows.

There are some who will say that the great development of State activity involved in the policy proposed here will destroy the "little man," that is to say the small, independent business. The answer is that the policy does nothing of the sort, unless risk of bankruptcy in trade depressions is essential to the existence and happiness of the "little man." The policy is simply one of setting up sufficient demands. It involves, as an implication, control of monopolies to prevent exploitation of the demand and supervision of large concerns in order to plan investment. It does not touch the "little man" at all; he can work to meet the demand like any other. He will find more scope than before, once strong demand has eliminated the slumps in which so many small businesses in the past have come to grief.

There are some who will object to the proposals of this Report on the ground that they involve an extension of the activities of Government and a consequent increase in the number of civil servants. That the proposals do involve action by Government in fields which in the past have been left wholly to private enterprise is true; the justification for this lies in the failures of the past. In certain industries men may find themselves working directly for the community in place of being the employees of a monster business corporation. In all industries, the managers of large undertakings may find themselves both regulated and assisted in keeping what they do—in investment, in the location of industry, in price policy—in accord with national interest. But there is nothing in all the proposals of this Report to involve greater interference in the private lives of the mass of the people. On the contrary, not only will all the war-time restrictions on consumption and choice of work vanish with war, but many of the previous inter-ferences with private lives will be ended. There will be no unemployment assistance subject to a means test; the 8,000 officials of the Unemployment Assistance Board in 1938 will become unnecessary for that work. So, too, a substantial proportion of the 28,000 peace-time officials of the Ministry of Labour, that is to say, those engaged in paying or calculating unemploy-ment benefit, will find that occupation gone, though it may be hoped that most of these will render still better service in preventing unemployment by organizing the labour market. A full employment policy involves more public control over a limited class of business undertakers, and less control over the private lives of the mass of the people. It may in the end mean fewer bureaucrats, not more.

There may be some who will say that in the emphasis laid in this Report on the need for organizing the labour market the Report treats labour as a commodity, in conflict with the opening declaration of the Charter adopted by the International Labour Conference in Philadelphia in May, 1944. There is no conflict. The Philadelphia declaration that labour is not a commodity cannot mean that men should not be free to sell their labour as men sell commodities. In a free community the right to sell or to refrain from selling one's labour by hand or brain and to bargain as to the terms on which it should be used is essential. This makes important the question of how those who desire to sell their labour and those who, whether for private profit or as representatives of a public authority, desire to buy the labour, shall be brought together. In concerning itself with these matters, the Report does not treat men themselves as a commodity; it treats them, as the Philadelphia declaration demands, as an end and not as a means; it proposes a funda-mental difference to be established between the position of those who desire to sell their labour and the position of all other sellers. Only for labour should the market always be a seller's market. It should not be that always for any particular commodity.

There are some who will say that the policy of this Report subordinates the individual to the State. The answer is that this criticism directly reverses the truth. If the State is regarded as more important than the individual, it may be reasonable to sacrifice the individual in mass unemployment to the progress and prosperity of his more fortunate fellows, as he is sacrificed in war by the dictators for their power and dominion or that of the race. If, on the other hand, the State is regarded as existing for the individual, a State which fails, in respect of many millions of individuals, to ensure them any opportunity of service and earning according to their powers or the possibility of a life free from the indignities and inquisitions of relief, is a State which has failed in a primary duty. Acceptance by the State of responsibility for full employment is the final necessary demonstration that the State exists for the citizens—for all the citizens—and not for itself or for a privileged class.

There are some who will say that the policy of this Report is a mere palliative which will block the way to further reforms like socialism or communism. The answer is that the policy does not block the way to these or other reforms, if they are good in themselves. It is a policy directed against one particular evil and includes steps which must be taken under any economic system which preserves essential liberties, in order to deal with that evil. The case for socialization of the means of production must be argued in the main on other grounds, of efficiency of production or of social justice. The Policy for Full Employment is in essence that the State takes responsibility for seeing that while any human needs are unsatisfied, they are converted into effective demand. This leaves open to argument on its merits the question whether production to meet that effective demand should be undertaken under conditions of private enterprise guided by profit, or of social enterprise working directly for use, or of a combination of these methods.

There are some who will say that the introduction of this or any other policy for Britain must wait for international agreement. Undoubtedly any economic policy for Britain must take account of the world of which Britain is part. It should be inspired by recognition of community of economic interest between different nations. It must be framed in alternatives to suit the alternative policies that may be adopted by other nations; it must include means of off-setting, so far as possible, fluctuations of overseas demand. But Britain must have her own policy; she will do better for the world and herself by leading, rather than by waiting and following. The subordination of British policy to supposed international exigencies has been one of the major mistakes of the period between the wars, the period of disastrous appeasement, political and economic. Britain is in the world and cannot escape from the world or her responsibilities for world order and world prosperity, but she cannot meet those responsibilities unless she puts her own house in order.

JOSEPH A. SCHUMPETER

3. *From the Welfare State through Inflation to Collectivism**

I

In order to minimize the danger of misunderstandings that is ever present in discussions on topics such as the one of this session I want first of all to settle a few preliminary points before taking up my subject, which is the relevance, for the economic future of this country, of the present state of inflationary pressure.

a) For the purposes of this paper, I define (centralist) socialism as that organization of society in which the means of production are controlled, and the decisions on how and what to produce and on who is to get what, are made by public authority instead of by privately-owned and privately-managed firms. All that we mean by the "march into socialism" is therefore the migration of people's economic affairs from the private into the public sphere. Observe that though both socialists and antisocialists have of course ideas of their own on the subject, it is hardly possible to visualize a socialist society in this sense without a huge bureaucratic apparatus that manages the productive and distributive process and in turn may or may not be controlled by organs of political democracy such as we have today—a parliament or congress and a set of political officers who depend for their position upon the results of a competitive struggle for votes. Therefore we may equate the march into socialism to a conquest of private industry and trade by the state. The apparent paradox that this very same process is described by classic socialist doctrine as the "withering away of the state" is easily resolved if we take account of the Marxist theory of government. Observe further that socialism does not exclude decentralized decision making in the administrative sense—just as the central management of an army does not deny all initiative to commanders of subgroups. And observe finally that socialism in our sense does not necessarily—that is, by logical necessity —exclude the use of competitive mechanisms as we see, e.g., from the Lange-Lerner model. Freedom of consumers' choice and of choice of occupation may, but need not necessarily, be restricted in socialist societies.

b) I do not advocate socialism. Nor have I any intention of discussing its desirability or undesirability, whatever this may mean. More important is it, however, to make it quite clear that I do not "prophesy" or predict it. Any prediction is extrascientific prophecy that attempts to do more than to diagnose observable tendencies and to state what results would be, if these

* *American Economic Review.* Vol. XL (May, 1950). By permission.

tendencies should work themselves out according to their logic. In itself, this does not amount to prognosis or prediction because factors external to the chosen range of observation may intervene to prevent that consummation; because, with phenomena so far removed as social phenomena are from the comfortable situation that astronomers have the good fortune of facing, observable tendencies, even if allowed to work themselves out, may be compatible with more than one outcome; and because existing tendencies, battling with resistances, may fail to work themselves out completely and may eventually "stick" at some halfway house. Let us illustrate this point by point.

First, no competent—and, of course, sufficiently detached—observer of Russia in the Stolypin era could have diagnosed the presence of any tendency towards anything at all like the Lenin system or in fact anything but rapid economic evolution and a lagged adaptation of institutions to the results of that evolution. It was a war and the consequent military and administrative breakdown which produced the Bolshevist regime and no amount of unscientific determinism avails against this fact. Second, for the sake of brevity, I speak of centralist socialism only because it holds a place of honor in the discussion. But other possibilities should not be neglected. Familiar facts of our own trade-union practice suggest that a development towards some form of guild socialism is not entirely off the cards. And other familiar facts suggest that observable tendencies or some of them may be compatible with forms of social reorganization that are not socialist at all, at least not in the sense which has been adopted for this paper. For instance, a reorganization of society on the lines of the encyclical *Quadragesimo anno,* though presumably possible only in Catholic societies or in societies where the position of the Catholic Church is sufficiently strong, no doubt provides an alternative to socialism that would avoid the "omnipotent State." Third, most observable tendencies of any kind stop short of complete achievement. Thus, a socialist regime in this country would have to be bold indeed if it ever thought of touching the subsidized independence of the farmer. Even the position of the "small businessman" might prove too strong for bureaucracy to conquer and a large fringe may therefore be covered indefinitely by compromise arrangements.

Still more important is something else, however. As economic cares migrate from the private to the public sphere, many urges that favor this migration become satisfied, wholly or partly, so that the tendency may lose momentum. Some economists will add that any gradual movement towards a centrally planned economy offers opportunity for unfavorable developments to be experienced which may act as brakes. I have no time to explain the reasons why I do not rate either possibility very highly and why, in particular, results that are felt to be unfavorable by sufficiently important groups are more likely to exert a propelling than they are to exert a restraining influence; that is, that the remedy for unsuccessful socialization which will suggest itself will be not less but more socialization. But for our purpose it is essential to notice that most of the arguments that are framed in order to arrive at a result favorable to the survival of the private-enterprise economy do not really deny the existence of a tendency towards socialism in our sense, but only deny that it will work itself out completely. Since nobody can dispute this possibility there is danger that the controversy resolve itself into a battle of words, especially in the United States where mere words count for so much, where the term socialism is not popular except with some relatively small minority groups, and where many people who like the thing at the same time dislike the word and prefer to substitute another; e.g., liberalism.[1] Hence a brief attempt at classification seems to be indicated.

c) The reasons for believing that the capitalist order tends to destroy itself and that centralist socialism is—with the qualifications mentioned above—a likely heir apparent I have explained elsewhere. Briefly and superficially, they may be summed up under four heads. First the very success of the business class in developing the productive powers of this country and the very fact that this success has created a new standard of life for all classes has paradoxically undermined the social and political position of the same business class whose economic function, though not obsolete, tends to become obsolescent and amenable to bureaucratization. Second, capitalist activity, being essentially "rational," tends to spread rational habits of mind and to destroy those loyalties and those habits of super- and subordination that are nevertheless essential for the efficient working of the institutionalized leadership of the producing plant. No social system can work which is based exclusively upon a network of free contracts between (legally) equal contracting parties and in which everyone is supposed to be guided by nothing except his own (short-run) utilitarian ends. Third, the concentration of the business class on the tasks of the factory and the office was instrumental in creating a political system and an intellectual class the structure and interests of which developed an attitude of independence from, and eventually of hostility to, the interests of large-scale business. The latter is becoming increasingly incapable of defending itself against raids that are, in the short run, highly profitable to other classes. Fourth, in consequence of all this, the scheme of values of capitalist society, though casually related to its economic success, is losing its hold not only upon the public mind but also upon the "capitalist" stratum itself. Little time—though more than I have—would be needed to show how modern drives for security, equality, and regulation (economic engineering) may be explained on these lines.

The best method of satisfying ourselves how far this process of disintegration of capitalist society has gone is to observe the extent to which its

---

[1] For obvious reasons, this is still more the case with the term communism which, barring the Russian angle, should be used synonymously.

implications are being taken for granted both by the business class itself and by the large number of economists who feel themselves to be opposed to (hundred per cent) socialism and are in the habit of denying the existence of any tendency toward it. To speak of the latter only, they accept not only unquestioningly but also approvingly: (1) the various stabilization policies that are to prevent recessions or at least depressions (that is, a large amount of public management of business situations even if not the principle of full employment); (2) the "desirability of greater equality of incomes," rarely defining how far short of absolute equality they are prepared to go, and in connection with this the principle of redistributive taxation; (3) a rich assortment of regulative measures, frequently rationalized by antitrust slogans, as regards prices; (4) public control though within a wide range of variation over the labor and the money market; (5) indefinite extension of the sphere of wants that are, now or eventually, to be satisfied by public enterprise, either gratis or on some post-office principle; and (6) of course all types of security legislation. I believe that there is a mountain in Switzerland on which congresses of economists have been held which have expressed disapproval of all or most of these things. But these anathemata have not even provoked attack.

It would spell complete misunderstanding of my argument if you thought that I "disapprove" or wish to criticize any of these policies. Nor am I one of those who label all or some of them "socialist." Some have been espoused, even in the eighteenth century, by conservative or even autocratic rulers; others have been on the programs of conservative parties and have been carried by them long before New Deal days. All I wish to emphasize is the fact that we have traveled far indeed from the principles of laissez faire capitalism and the further fact that it is possible so to develop and regulate capitalist institutions as to condition the working of private enterprise in a manner that differs but little from genuinely socialist planning. The economists I have in mind no doubt emphasize the differences they think likely to persist. They are not all agreed as to the precise location of their movable halfway house. But they all realize what Marx failed to realize: on the one hand, the vast productive possibilities of the capitalist engine that promise indefinitely higher mass standards of life, supplemented by gratis services without complete "expropriation of the expropriators"; on the other hand, the extent to which capitalist interests can in fact be expropriated without bringing the economic engine to a standstill and the extent to which this engine may be made to run in the labor interest. Having discovered this possibility of a *laborist capitalism* they go on to conclude that *this* capitalism may survive indefinitely, at least under certain favorable conditions. This may be so but it does not amount to a denial of my thesis. Capitalism does not merely mean that the housewife may influence production by her choice between peas and beans; nor that the youngster may choose whether he wants to work in a factory or on a farm; nor that plant managers have some voice in deciding what and how to produce. It means a scheme of values, an attitude toward life, a civilization—the civilization of inequality and of the family fortune. This civilization is rapidly passing away, how- ever. Let us rejoice or else lament the fact as much as everyone of us likes; but do not let us shut our eyes to it.

One genuine problem remains. The diagnoses that support implications which are favorable to the survival of laborism all lean heavily on extra- polations of the present spectacular development of society's productive powers. But there is an element of question-begging in this. Past achieve- ment was the achievement of a more or less unfettered capitalism. It cannot be assumed without further consideration that laborism will continue to perform like this. We need not accept the stagnationist thesis as it stands in order to be disturbed by the possibility that this thesis may come true after all if the private-enterprise system is *permanently* burdened and "regulated" beyond its powers of endurance. In this case, an outright socialist solution may impose itself even on the enemies of socialism as the lesser evil.

II

The transformation of social orders into one another is an incessant proc- ess but in itself a very slow one. To an observer who studies a moderate span of "quiet" time, it may well seem as if the social framework he beholds did not change at all. Moreover, the process often suffers setbacks which, considered by themselves, may suggest to him the presence of an opposite tendency. But at times we also observe accelerations and one of the most obvious causes of these are major wars. In the past, successful wars may have added to the prestige of the ruling stratum and to the strength of the institutional framework with which this stratum was associated. This is no longer so under modern conditions. The first World War of our own epoch affected the social situation in the United States but little because the war effort was neither exhausting enough nor prolonged enough to leave a permanent mark. But in Europe it was different. In the vanquished coun- tries where the social framework caught fire, the latent tendency toward socialist reconstruction proved its existence by emerging to the surface and, for a brief period, carrying everything before it. Still more significant is the fact that something similar also happened, though of course on a much re- duced scale, in the victorious countries. In France the bourgeois republic ceased to function as it had functioned before 1914. In England, a labor party that was not yet socialist but was influenced by a socialist wing rose not indeed to power but at least to office. And in both countries, the atti- tude of the political sector to the private-enterprise system quietly under- went a fundamental change.

Given a pre-existing tendency toward the socialist goal, this is easy to understand. Although voices that called for a continuation of the policies established during the years of the war economy did not elicit much response and although, for a time, public resentment of war regulations blocked further advance on the same lines, no return to prewar policies proved possible even where it was attempted. This has been strikingly verified by England's gold policy and its ultimate failure. In a world that was no longer the world of free enterprise, the gold standard—the naughty child that keeps on telling unpleasant truths—refused to work.

The world crisis and the second World War were additional "accelerators" and, this time, they asserted themselves also in the United States. They created situations that were felt, rightly or wrongly, to be beyond the remedies that would have recommended themselves to the men of the free-enterprise age. The business class itself, afraid of the "adjustments" that application of these remedies would have required, accepted—though of course grumbling all the time—gadgets of regulation that might prevent the recurrence of the experiences of 1929-33 and later on others that might prevent a postwar crisis such as that of 1921. It has learned much and unlearned still more during the last quarter of a century. Also, it has accepted new fiscal burdens a mere fraction of which it would have felt to be unbearable fifty years ago—as would, by the way, all the leading economists of that time. And it does not matter whether the business class accepts this new situation or not. The power of labor is almost strong enough in itself—and amply so in alliance with the other groups that have in fact, if not in words, renounced allegiance to the scheme of values of the private-profit economy —to prevent any reversal which goes beyond an occasional scaling off of rough edges.

Let me repeat: I do not hold for a moment that any mere "events"— even events of the importance of "total wars"—or the political situations created thereby or any attitudes or feelings entertained by individuals or groups on the subject of these situations dominate the long-run contours of social history. These are a matter of much deeper forces. But I do hold that such events and the situations created thereby may remove obstacles from the path of the more fundamental tendencies—obstacles that would otherwise slow up the pace of social evolution. Observe that this does not necessarily constitute a reason for a serious socialist to welcome such events. Evolution towards socialism would be slower in their absence but also steadier. Setbacks and the emergence of unmanageable situations would be less likely. Co-ordination of developments in the various sectors of national life would be more perfect. For just as the existence of an efficient opposition is a requirement for the orderly functioning of democratic government, so the existence of economic forces that resist institutional change may be necessary in order to keep the speed of this change within the limits of safety.

Now one of the most powerful factors that make for acceleration of social change is inflation. With so many authorities telling us that nothing undermines the framework of a society as does inflation, it is hardly necessary to dwell upon this proposition. If we accept it, then it follows from what I have just said that from all imaginable standpoints—the standpoint of irresponsible revolutionaries alone expected—it is of prime importance after a war so to adjust a country's economic process as to stop it from producing further inflation. But it is clear at the same time that this is an extremely difficult thing to do in a world where everybody is afraid of the short-run consequences of such a policy and where some of the adjustments required —especially a rise in many previously controlled prices without a rise in money wage rates—is not "politically possible" at all.[2] The course that was the obvious one to take under the circumstances and that was actually followed after 1945—among mutual recriminations but still with a good deal of common consent—was to mitigate transitional difficulties by a dose of controlled peacetime inflation that was made more effective by the continuance of a high level of expenditure on the armed services and by the policy of European aid. Substantially, all this served its purpose and, as it became evident to most people, though not to all economists, that a period of vigorous economic development, entailing vast investment requirements, was at hand, the hope that major disturbances would be avoided and that the economy of the United States would expand on a slowly rising price level was, for a time, not altogether unreasonable—whatever, short of another world war, might happen abroad.

Considerations of this type fail, however, to take into account an ominous fact. At a high level of employment (we seem, at long last, to be abandoning full employment slogans), whether "natural" or enforced by high-employment policies, wage demands or other demands that increase the money cost of employing labor become both inevitable and inflationary. They become inevitable because high-level employment removes the only reason why they should not be raised. And they become inflationary because, with high utilization of resources, borrowing from banks and upward revision of prices provides a perfectly easy method of satisfying them. Though bargaining is still with individual trade unions, the movement is really a general one; so that we are drifting into the Keynesian situation in which the money wage rate no longer affects output and employment but only the value of the monetary unit. The situations of trade-union leadership and of government being what they are, there is nothing to stop this mechanism which—barring exceptions that are due to the particular situations of certain firms— spells perennial inflationary pressure. Rising demands upon the Treasury and our hyperprogressive methods of taxation aggravate this condition, of course, but they have not created it.

There should be no need to state that breaks in prices such as have

[2] The alternative course—scaling down other prices and money wages—is not only still less "politically possible" but also much more difficult to do without causing a serious depression.

occurred and will occur again prove nothing against the presence of inflationary pressure. Even apart from the postwar movements of agricultural prices and other self-explanatory cases, such breaks occur characteristically in the course of every inflation—as could be nicely illustrated from the German inflation that followed upon the first World War. People who are "caught," then cry out about deflation, and so do those fellow economists of ours who have deflationary prognoses to live down and who, in any case, seem incapable of foreseeing anything but deflation. But it is a compliment—the more sincere because unintentional—to the productive powers of American industry that doubts are at all possible as to whether our society is menaced by inflation or deflation.

III

A state of perennial inflationary pressure will have, qualitatively, all the effects of weakening the social framework of society and of strengthening subversive tendencies (however carefully wrapped up in "liberal" phrases) that every competent economist is in the habit of attributing to more spectacular inflations. But this is not all. In addition, some of the standard remedies for such situations will not mitigate, and may even aggravate, the present one. It seems to me that this is not being fully understood. Let us, therefore, in desperate brevity, discuss three types of such remedies.

a) The most orthodox of all measures for the control of inflation is action upon the volume of borrowing through interest rates or credit rationing and the like. I fully understand, of course, that money rates must be freed from the grip of cheap-money policies *if normalcy in the sense of a free-enterprise economy is to be attained,* and that for everyone who desires return to such normalcy, the liberation—or reconstruction—of a free-money market must be a point of prime importance. But this does not alter the fact that a restrictive credit policy would at present produce consequences quite different from those that the old theory of credit policy would lead us to expect. Accepting the latter without any qualification—for argument's sake —we cannot help observing that it was to apply to a world in which everything was entirely flexible and which was not afraid of what I may term remedial recessions. In such a world, an increase in interest rates was supposed to reduce the volume of operations, money wages, and *employment*. Surely these effects would not materialize at present and, if they did, they would immediately provoke government action to neutralize them. In other words, credit restrictions would at present achieve little beyond increasing the difficulties of business. Even restrictions of consumers' credit would have this effect to some extent, though something could no doubt be done in this field.

b) Similar difficulties stand in the way of controlling inflation by means of increasing taxation—a no less orthodox remedy but which enjoys a popularity with modern economists that is denied to credit restriction. It is quite true that something might be accomplished by increasing taxes on consumption. In an inflationary situation this would even be good Keynesianism. But if it is the corporation tax and the higher-bracket income tax which is to be increased, the effect upon inflationary pressure would be small at best and might even be negative. For if the present rate of industrial progress is to continue and therefore the present rate of obsolescence of equipment is to continue, also, increasing resort would have to be taken to inflationary bank credit in order to make up for the decrease in the available non-inflationary means of finance. Alternatively, a decrease in those rates of progress and of obsolescence would indeed decrease inflationary pressure for the moment but increase it in the long run.[3]

c) The third household remedy consists in direct controls: price fixing, priorities and the like, including subsidies. Why they are so popular with certain sectors of public opinion is a question that need not concern us. For the bureaucracy in particular their reintroduction would spell reconquest of ground that has been lost; for the trade unions it would spell a decisive advantage in the campaign for the conquest of the profit item; for business it would mean the loss of the line of retreat that is open to it so long as most, if not all, attacks upon it can be partly, if not wholly, parried by price adjustments. Or at least, it would make this retreat dependent upon government permission—which there is no reason to believe would be granted for purposes of securing means for improving the productive engine. In other words, price control may result in a surrender of private enterprise to public authority; that is, in a big stride toward the perfectly planned economy.

I do not pretend to prophesy; I merely recognize the facts and point out the tendencies which those facts indicate.

Perennial inflationary pressure can play an important part in the eventual conquest of the private-enterprise system by the bureaucracy—the resultant frictions and deadlocks being attributed to private enterprise and used as arguments for further restrictions and regulations. I do not say that any group follows this line with conscious purpose, but purposes are never wholly conscious. A situation may well emerge in which most people will consider complete planning as the smallest of possible evils. They will certainly not call it socialism or communism, and they will presumably make some exceptions for the farmer, the retailer, and the small producer. Under

---

[3] I have no difficulty in understanding why this argument does not impress our radical friends. But I confess that I find it difficult to understand the position of some excellent economists who are quite above any suspicion that they would welcome the failure of our industrial engine to work on successfully and who nevertheless list reduction in industrial investment among the acceptable means for counteracting inflation, both in this country and in England. Incidentally, it should be noticed that the opinion of some conservative stalwarts that high and highly progressive taxation might promote, and that reductions in taxation (at the right spots) might decrease, inflationary dangers does not necessarily merit all the sneers it usually gets.

these circumstances, our capitalist, free-enterprise system as a scheme of values, a way of life, and a civilization may not be worth bothering about.

Whether the American genius for mass production on whose past performance all optimism for this way of life rests is up to this test, I dare not affirm, nor do I dare to affirm that the policies responsible for this situation might be reversed.

Marx was wrong in his diagnoses of the manner in which capitalist society would break down; he was not wrong in the prediction that it would break down eventually. The stagnationists are wrong in their diagnosis of the reasons why the capitalist process should stagnate; they may still turn out to be right in their prognosis that it will stagnate—with sufficient help from the public sector.

RUSSELL W. DAVENPORT

4. *Welfare Capitalism, Not Welfare State**

Since the depression of 1932 there has existed in the U.S. a trend that runs parallel with the socialist trend in Britain and Europe. Inaugurated by the New Deal, it has been carried further by Harry Truman's Fair Deal and its program for a "welfare state." Opponents of the trend have cogently argued that, if continued, it can lead nowhere except to socialism. Their case is fairly overwhelming. They point to the mounting taxes required to meet welfare costs, the loss of initiative, the rigidifying of the economy, the destruction of open markets, the growth and concentration of government power. While none of these effects has run its full course in the U.S., it is easy to show that all of them have begun. The conclusion can hardly be escaped, that the "welfare state" is of necessity the prelude to a *total* state. Yet, as Winston Churchill has been heard to observe, the argument against the welfare state is intricate and involved—ill-adapted to political campaigning. The result is that even though the American people are dead set against state socialism—as all the polls indicate—they continue to support men and measures that can lead them eventually nowhere else.

Deeply implicated in this situation is that vast combination of capital and labor known as American industrial enterprise. The incredible achievements of this system of private ownership scarcely need reviewing in FORTUNE, which has been reporting them now for twenty years. American enterprise

* *Fortune*, Vol. XL (October, 1949). Copyright 1949, Time Inc. By permission.

has literally changed the nature of life on earth. It has created a new kind of society, with new criteria and new hopes. It has twice saved Western civilization on the battlefield. It has set living standards never dreamed of before. And it now stands forth against other systems, whose promises may be alluring but whose performances are slim, as the representative of a way of life evolved in freedom and offering the only hope of a solution to the heartbreaking problems of Western man.

Yet at the mid-century mark, faced with mounting political pressures for "welfare," American enterprise, despite its protestations, is neither confident of itself nor hopeful of its future. It is, instead, hesitant and uncertain. It lives in the shadow of a government, which, while paying it lip service, seems both hostile to its hopes and blind to its needs. It is engaged in a political struggle with its own workers, who also pay it lip service, but who act as if enterprise were their enemy. It is burdened with unwise taxes based on political rather than economic considerations; yet it is too inept politically to get these corrected. Its profits are attacked as exorbitant, though these are the chief source of capital growth, upon which jobs depend. It is bedeviled by the fear of war, of Communism, of depression, of collapse. In short, despite its magnificent record, American enterprise has failed to hold the confidence of the people, or to generate that kind of initiative which has hitherto accounted for its leadership.

These considerations give rise to two fundamental questions:

1) Is the demand of the American people for "welfare" a justifiable demand, or is it merely the irresponsible clamor of the mob for bread and circuses?

2) If it is a justifiable demand, consonant with the necessities of social evolution, is there any way to satisfy it without recourse to the authoritarian state?

These are the two most important questions facing the American people on the domestic front at the mid-century mark. They are inseparable questions. For if the demand of the people is not justified, then there is nothing for the conscientious leader of public opinion to do but to oppose it—a position already taken by many so-called "conservatives." If, on the other hand, it is justified, then a dilemma emerges: do the people want "welfare" so much that they are willing to accept socialism; or, if they knew socialism were inevitable otherwise, would they be willing to give up some of the "welfare" in order to avoid it? Or is there some other way out?

It is the thesis of this article that the above dilemma is unreal—that there is, indeed, a way out. The development of this way out is not primarily the task of politicians, or even of the people at large. It is primarily the task of the enterprisers, the businessmen, who find themselves today in such an anomalous situation. This way out, moreover, is no mere compromise: it is a new opportunity, which, if seized through clear thinking and bold action, can open up a whole new social and economic era for the American people. That it has not been seized to date is not because it is idealistic or nebulous, nor because the "wave of the future" is against enterprise, nor because state socialism is inevitable, but because businessmen have not yet fully awakened to the possibilities inherent in it. These possibilities, it is contended here, are so great, and the political theory supporting them is so sound, that American business now has a chance to lead the way to a new solution for modern man, applicable not only in the U.S. but throughout the Western world.

That such a subject goes beyond the bounds of a single article scarcely needs to be said. Other articles will follow. Let us begin, however, with an examination of the two inseparable questions already posed, on the supposition that, if they can be answered, further inquiry will be stimulated and more precise recommendations evolved.

IS "WELFARE" JUSTIFIED?

In a helpful article in *Foreign Affairs* for July, 1949, G. T. Robinson, director of the Russian Institute at Columbia University, had this to say concerning U.S. political economy:

"There is urgent need for philosophic reconstruction and renewal. This undertaking has some resemblance, on the one hand, to that of the philosophies of the French Encyclopaedia, and on the other, to that of the authors of the Declaration of Independence, the Virginia Bill of Rights, or the French Declaration of the Rights of Man and the Citizen. All these monumental achievements were products of collaboration, and a somewhat similar collaborative effort would give the best promise of meeting our present need—a task for philosophers, in all the eighteenth-century . . . richness of that term."

One may go along with Mr. Robinson in recommending collaborative discussions on the philosophical foundations of the American system; yet one must be careful at the same time not to fall into the assumption, characteristic of many modern thinkers, that such foundations are altogether lacking today. In America there does in fact exist a foundation, formulated at the very outset of the American experiment and generally referred to as the Rights of Man—the "unalienable" Rights to Life, Liberty, and the Pursuit of Happiness. It is true that the modern intellectual tends to dismiss these Rights as mere verbiage, or else as obsolete; and semanticists raise the further warning that the concepts involved are so abstract that they may mean anything at all. Nevertheless, three very distinct concepts *are* involved; and so far from being obsolete, inspection shows that they are very much alive today. If we adopt the hypothesis, that the founders chose their words carefully, and if we are willing to enter into their meaning in an open-minded way, a proposition emerges which "collaborative discussions" certainly could not disregard, and which may serve us in the meantime as a kind of criterion, tested by nearly 175 years of progress.

Three different spheres of human life are covered by the American proposition, each with its own peculiarities and characteristics; and three different *kinds* of rights are actually invoked. Of the three, the Right to Liberty has played the dominant role in American evolution, to such an extent that the meaning of the others has been somewhat obscured. This Right, when extended through practical legislation, has to do with the individual's relationship to the society in which he lives—his relationship to other individuals, and, most important, his relationship to the state. The Right to Liberty gives every individual certain protections that are publicly recognized and officially enforced. It is therefore correctly characterized as the *political* Right.

Yet the American proposition is not merely political. It is also spiritual. This becomes evident when we consider the Right to the Pursuit of Happiness. This Right cannot very well be translated into strictly political terms; it can have meaning only in the spiritual or cultural sphere. What it means, in brief, is that the individual is guaranteed an opportunity to fulfill himself as he may choose. The manner of his fulfillment will depend, not upon the state, but upon his own version of the nature of happiness, which may be materialistic, idealistic, or halfway between, according to *his* lights. This principle, evidently, goes far beyond the mere political guarantee of free speech, etc. It is a fundamental guarantee to the human spirit, an appeal to freedom not only within the law but beyond the law, in the realm of human aspiration.

What, then, is the meaning of the Right to Life? Is it merely the right to breathe? For a century before the Declaration of Independence political thinkers in both England and France had concerned themselves with the foundations of government. Taking their start from a hypothetical state of nature, in which every man was threatened with violence by every other man, they concluded that the first justification of an organized society was the protection of life and limb. In its simplest terms, then, the Right to Life is the right to go "unarmed unharmed"; and this construction of the Right was all that seemed necessary in a frontier society where violence was always a real possibility.

Today, however, the lawless highwayman is the exception, and the rough frontier has gone. Men still need protection from violence: yet violence does not constitute the chief threat to life. This threat has now become economic. In an industrial city like Pittsburgh, for example, it is sheer hypocrisy to talk about the Rights of Man in terms only of Liberty and the Pursuit of Happiness. Since meat, milk, and vegetables will not grow on Pittsburgh's streets, when a worker loses his job he cannot eat—that is, he cannot live. If the American proposition is to have any meaning in Pittsburgh, therefore, an *economic* Right must be established. And this is none other than the eighteenth-century Right to Life.

This latter interpretation may encounter a certain skepticism. Does it not read into the Rights of Man more than the founders could have been aware of? Yes, and no. It has been characteristic of all our great documents, including the Declaration of Independence and the Constitution itself, that they contain many intuitive truths that must be understood and interpreted in the light of changing circumstances. Were this not so they could scarcely have endured for more than a century and a half. The political founders, who formulated their philosophy before the rise of industrialism, could not foretell the precise nature of the economic problems that industrialism would create. For them the economic problem was summed up in the right to own property and enjoy its fruits, since this was the way most Americans of that day lived—self-employed, on farms, or with the tools of their craft. But as Sumner Slichter has pointed out, we have today, for the first time in history, an economy composed predominantly of employees—more than three out of four persons who work in the U.S. work in that capacity.[1] Hence the economic emphasis has been transferred from property to jobs. If, therefore, we are to give reality to the American proposition in our time, we must be prepared to translate the Right to Life in accordance with the necessities of human evolution. Paraphrased today, this Right extends beyond the problem of life and limb to that of economic need; it must include in its meaning the proposition that society shall not proceed in such a way, and the right to property shall not be so construed, as to deny to human beings the possibility of living—that is to say, in modern society, of earning a living.

THE WAY OUT

The acceptance of this view, that three different *kinds* of Rights are involved in the American proposition—spiritual rights (Pursuit of Happiness), political rights (Liberty), and economic rights (Life)—sheds a strong light on the first of the questions already posed: is the demand of the American people for "welfare" a justifiable demand? On the basis of the Rights of Man, translated into modern terms, there can be no doubt that it is. For what the people mean by "welfare" is, precisely, the implementation of the Right to Life. This is not to say, of course, that every new welfare scheme has to be accepted. It is not even to say that we can afford all the "welfare" that the people think they have a right to. But if we are to do anything more than scratch the surface in our search for a modern solution in the field of political economy, we must recognize that the trend, which was inaugurated with the New Deal, and which is now pressing against enterprise in the form of the "welfare state," arises from an instinctive demand on the part

[1] *The American Economy*, Sumner H. Slichter.

of the American people for the implementation of one of the basic Rights that their forefathers designated in the very beginning as an essential of freedom.

Does this mean, then, that we are faced with a development similar to that of Britain, where the demand for an adequate implementation of the Right to Life has resulted in a socialist state? Is it true that we must either accept socialism or else spend our political energies, like many conscientious "conservatives" at the present time, in opposing an apparently irresistible wave? Such simplified alternatives are seldom real. An examination of the true nature of the American proposition points to a way out.

One of the radical contributions of the American proposition, as originally formulated, was that it put government in its rightful place. And this very question of the role of government happens to be the key question in modern political economy. The coincidence suggests that our real trouble has been a failure to interpret the American proposition correctly. And it holds forth a promise that the trouble can be overcome if we now learn to interpret it.

Government, of course, exists for the purpose of assuring the existence and maintenance of all three of the Rights of Man; but government is not adapted to the implementation of any of them, *save only the political rights.* The fact that Americans have been so intent upon the establishment of the political rights, making Liberty almost synonymous with the whole of the American proposition, has led to some confusion on this score. But in one field, the cultural or spiritual, the correct principle has clearly emerged. We turn to government for the building and support of many of our educational institutions, but we oppose as a violation of freedom any interference with our cultural *rights*. These, we maintain, must be exercised *and* implemented by each and every individual and by the cultural institutions themselves. The universities, not the state, should appoint professors, designate what should or should not be taught, and generally implement the principles of academic freedom. The universities are, in this sense, guardians of the cultural right. Similarly, the right to religious freedom is exercised and implemented by the churches and other religious bodies, and by every individual. The real implementation of cultural or spiritual rights is a question beyond the province of government.

The question of economic rights does not present an exact parallel to that of cultural rights. At the present time government has to concern itself with economic rights in many different ways. But the point at issue here is not whether government should concern itself at all, but whether private citizens acting in their economic and corporate capacities, that is to say, whether *business* should concern itself at all. There are many who maintain that it should not. The job of a businessman, these people point out, is to run a profitable enterprise. He is neither a social policeman nor a political reformer. His task lies with markets—the market for capital, the market for labor, the market for his goods—and if he is deflected from this by the necessity of implementing human rights he will not perform his own task well. The business of business, these people maintain, is economic and not social.

Ironically, however, it is exactly this position that is leading society toward some form of managed economy wherein privately owned business will not be able to flourish. For the economic rights of man cannot be escaped. And if it is true that business has no business in this field, then it follows that these rights must continuously be implemented by the state. This is precisely the basic principle of state socialism, which acknowledges the first Right, the Right to Life, but which finds no way to make it a reality except through authoritarian compulsion. If, therefore, businessmen insist on separating themselves from the field of rights to concern themselves only with the field of markets, the only answer a democratic society can reach is that of state socialism.

And there is only one escape from this answer, namely, that businessmen and industrialists *must* concern themselves with economic rights. They must take responsibility for them, just as educators, artists, and religious leaders take responsibility for the cultural or spiritual rights; and they must learn how to implement them. Indeed, if the matter is examined carefully, it will be seen that the business community, in combination with labor, is the only institution that *can* concern itself with these rights without misleading or stifling the economy. Those who take the position that rights are no affair of business are confusing economic rights with political rights. The political rights are entirely the affair of government, the courts, and other public institutions. But such institutions are ill adapted to the implementation of economic rights; a court may uphold the law, but it cannot intelligently determine the best agreement or productive system for carrying it out. And government bureaus, as we are learning, are inefficient instruments to this end. The people who are *best* able to implement such rights, in all their manifold aspects, are the people actually engaged in the economic process, namely, the owners, managers, and workers. Between them they know, or can find out, what the troubles are, how to fix them, how to provide better solutions for the future, and what the costs of such solutions will be. If the American proposition is to be correctly interpreted, they, not the government, are the actual guardians of the Right to Life.

THE NATURE OF THE TASK

The way out of the dilemma, therefore, is not to seek to deny the justifiable demand of the people for the implementation of the Right to Life. Rather it is, by conscious and concerted voluntary action, to transfer the primary responsibility, and therefore the initiative, from government to private hands. Such a move, if undertaken with enough resolution and on a broad enough scale, would at a single stroke cut through the socialist threat and open up a whole new vista of freedom.

What, then, does this move entail? How do we go about it? First of all, the Right to Life is not the right to live in any old society, but specifically, in the society in which the individual has been trained, for which he is adapted, and to which he makes his contribution—the American society. And "life" in the American society is something more than mere subsistence. How much "more" is not a matter that any one generation can settle, nor one to be determined here. There are a number of over-all objectives that have to be accepted in our time if the Right is to have meaning. For example, the American way of life includes a concept of decency which is so important that it is probably unrealistic to talk about the Right to Life in America without reference to it. It includes, also, a certain opportunity for advancement, without which most Americans would consider life intolerable. It includes freedom of movement and communication: if a man loses his job, for instance, he should be able to get about in order to find another one. More recently it has begun to include some kind of orderly provision for the maintenance of health, on the grounds that a man in bad health is to that extent handicapped and that the welfare of his family is jeopardized. And so forth. Perhaps a good project for Mr. Robinson's philosophers would be to compose a Bill of Economic Rights that would, in effect, define the Right to Life in terms that modern Americans could understand.

But second, since the Right to Life raises such broad considerations, the full implementation of it touches almost every aspect of the economic system, governmental as well as private. The maintenance of opportunity, for example, poses a number of problems such as that of the tax program. The maintenance of employment, a critical factor in the implementation of the Right to Life, leads into the issue of governmental fiscal policy. Indeed, a thoroughgoing study of how to implement this Right would have to take up the tangled question of competition: how monopoly can be restrained—how government interference with prices can be restricted—how the open market can be preserved.

These weighty matters, however, lie beyond our present thesis. We are concerned here primarily with the American business community; and while businessmen interest themselves as citizens in all of the above questions, there is one aspect of the Right to Life that opens up before them as their particular concern. It is to be found at their very doorstep, in that unsettled area of modern society known as "employee relations" or "management-labor relations." It is here—on the front line, so to speak—where worker and employer come together for the production of wealth, that the implementation of the Right to Life becomes most understandable and most pressing. And it is precisely here that American industrial enterprise has its opportunity to seize the initiative.

There are as many "solutions" to the labor-management problem as there are business concerns. In every plant, conditions and personalities are different, which means that the economic rights have to be implemented in different ways. Nevertheless, for our present purpose, to define as clearly as possible the nature of the task herein proposed, the whole field of labor management falls conveniently into three divisions. While some companies will put chief emphasis on one, others on another, it is doubtful whether a satisfactory solution can be found without some reference to all three.

I. ECONOMIC SECURITY

Americans have come to use the word "security" as more or less synonymous with what has here been called the Right to Life. It is a much misunderstood word. Indeed the worker's idea of security is far more dynamic than his critics like to pretend. He would not want "security" carried to such a point that freedom of choice and a chance for advancement would be eliminated; nor, on the other hand, does he expect something for nothing. What he means is, that he thinks he has a right, which ought to be just as good as the employer's right, to be able to live in the society, to participate in it, in a permanent and confident way. His right to live in it—his Right to Life—must not be taken away from him by circumstances, such as fluctuations in employment, over which he has no control; or by accident or the onset of old age.

Boiled down to its most practical terms, security for the worker means stable employment. Elmo Roper, summarizing the researches of many years, has stated that ten times as many workers would rather have steady employment than higher pay, and twenty-five times as many would rather have it than shorter hours. Yet steady employment is probably the hardest kind of security for the employer to provide. To most industrial workers the annual wage is the symbol of the ultimate to be achieved in this area, and a few companies such as Geo. A. Hormel, Procter & Gamble, and the Nunn-Bush Shoe Co. have successfully installed it. But most employers consider it virtually an impossibility.[2]

Such experienced practitioners as Jay Hormel and Richard Deupree of Procter & Gamble, however, make a point of great significance for those companies that cannot see their way to an annual wage. The first step, they say, is not the proclamation of the guarantee *but the stabilizing of employment to the highest possible degree within the circumstances prevailing in the particular company*. The truth is, that an annual guarantee is impossible until this painful stabilizing process has been carried out. And nearly every company, if it is willing to make the effort, can achieve a far greater degree

[2] However, more have succeeded in achieving it than might be supposed. The Latimer Report, made for the federal government, revealed that in 1946 a total of 196 annual wage plans covered 500 establishments.

of stability than prevails today. Production for stock, transfer of workers to other departments (here the union must cooperate), a flexible work week (the Fair Labor Standards Act should be amended to allow more latitude in this respect), the development of complementary products, and the scheduling of maintenance work in slack seasons, are methods of stabilization that are now being used by some employers and should be used by more. The Standard Oil Co. (New Jersey), without actually guaranteeing the wage, is an outstanding example of progress in this direction. In an industry that is subject to wide seasonal variations, Jersey now reports that 90 per cent of its employees (wage-rate as well as salaried) have been *continuously* employed since they were hired.

Economic security can also be strengthened by insurance schemes in which the workers themselves may participate—pensions, hospital plans, general medical plans, maternity care, accident insurance, and so forth. Perhaps the most spectacular pension system is that of Sears, Roebuck, to which the employee contributes 5 per cent of his yearly salary (up to $250 a year) and the company contributes 5 per cent of its net annual profits before federal taxes and dividends. The result is a huge fund of $216 million that owns 19 per cent of Sears stock and whose retirement benefits, in many cases, considerably exceed the mere requirements of "security."

International Business Machines has one of the most generous retirement plans in industry, which is paid for entirely by the company. Many smaller businesses that do not have the resources to set up plans on this scale have had recourse to the profit-sharing trust. This has the advantage that the company is committed to payments only in years when it has profits. Stein, Hall & Co., Sylvania Electric Products, Nathan Straus-Duparquet, Inc., and Electrolux Corp. have all chosen this method. Despite the inexcusable difficulties created by the U.S. tax laws, Continental Paper has managed to work out a trust for retirement benefits geared to productivity and cost savings.

So many companies and unions, indeed, have provided for pensions, some form of medical care, and other aspects of security, that it hardly seems fair to mention any few of them. This fact was noted by the steel fact finders' report to President Truman only a few weeks ago. "The concept of providing social insurance and pensions for workers in industry," said that report, "has become an accepted part of modern American thinking"; and the report further points out that such insurance has been gained "either by the unilateral action of employers or, to an increasing extent, through collective bargaining." The examples given here serve merely to illustrate the principle in hand: to protect the worker, at the economic level, from risks and human vicissitudes that could otherwise ruin him. Through such measures he is given a chance to live in his society on a continuing basis and in a confident way.

If, however, the "welfare state" is to be avoided, insurance plans of this kind must be even further developed, with employers taking the initiative. Very little work, for example, has as yet been done on the possibility of privately insuring against layoff or temporary unemployment caused by economic recessions, though preliminary investigations would seem to leave this possibility open. Eastman Kodak, together with eighteen other Rochester firms, launched such a plan in 1931 but had no chance to build up adequate funds before mass unemployment struck. The plan was therefore abandoned. Nevertheless, since certain advantages would accrue to enterprise were it able to put an unemployment backlog behind its employees (as a supplement, at least, to government unemployment insurance), new experiments should be tried.

2. HUMANIZATION

One of the most difficult problems management has to face in a large industrial plant is that of the human being. And the failure to solve this problem has had as much to do with the weakening of the enterprise system, here and throughout the world, as any other single factor. As Elton Mayo has said, "While material efficiency has been increasing for two hundred years, the human capacity for working together has in the same period continually diminished."

A man's work is of necessity a commodity that he sells on a market. The problem is, how to buy it without taking over the man too—that is to say, without making him the slave of the machines that he is supposed to command. Americans have instinctively resisted the idea that the labor of the human being is a commodity, and have so expressed themselves in such fundamental legislation as the Clayton Act. And the whole trade-union movement is in fact an effort to protect the *man* who sells the work. Consequently it can be said that the first, most elementary step in the humanization of industry is the principle of collective bargaining.

However, collective bargaining alone is not enough. The worker needs not only a power to bargain but a sense of *belonging*. He wants to be treated like a human being—not just a number on a payroll. In a big plant this is not easy. The greatest danger at the present time is a certain observable tendency among managements to rely upon "gadgets" that have their origin in the fields of advertising, selling, and public relations. "Human relations" has become a catch phrase and formulas for "human engineering" are springing up like mushrooms. These approaches are dangerous because they are apt to end in disillusionment for management and workers alike.

The humanization of industry is something that has to be undertaken with the utmost earnestness and it must have the personal attention and enthusiasm of the topmost executive. Loudspeaker systems, plant newspapers, suggestion boxes, depth interviewing, and similar devices are perfectly sound so long as their limitations are understood. It is obviously necessary to develop adequate forms of communication between employer and employee. But the communications must have integrity. Management must really respect the worker's ideas. And on the other hand, the information that management gives out must be real information about matters that affect the workers' lives—not pep talks and political orations. The management that pursues this question will find that one of the keys to it is the foreman, who should be specially trained for the purpose. General Electric and Servel, among many others, place great emphasis on the foreman's role.

That which has hitherto been lacking in this field, however, is precisely the theme of this article, namely, the recognition by the employer that his employee is possessed of certain rights, the implementation of which is the joint concern of the boss and the worker. From this principle the humanizing of the shop will inevitably follow.

3. PARTICIPATION

The more labor relations are studied, the more evident it becomes that the ultimate answers are to be found in a real participation of the employee in the destiny of the business. This can be effected at various levels. A great number of firms have profit-sharing plans, some of which are extremely successful. Yet profit sharing as such is often disappointing, because the monetary incentive is an inadequate one when relied on exclusively to establish good labor relations. Only the personal participation of the employee in *both* the profits *and* that part of management which has to do with production can evoke from him the kind of dynamic cooperation that the enterprise system now needs. The reason has been eloquently stated by James C. Worthy of Sears, Roebuck:

"The essence of 'free enterprise' is a system of economic and political organization which taps *spontaneously* the creative and productive resources of its citizens. Under conditions of small-scale enterprise the 'hidden hand' of prices, costs, and profits was a reasonably adequate means for accomplishing this spontaneous release . . . We must recognize, however, that this 'hidden hand,' by itself, is quite inadequate for tapping any high percentage of the productive energies of a nation when the greater part of its workers are no longer independent enterprisers but are employees of larger corporate entities and, therefore, not directly subject to the stimulus and control of the economic processes of the market.

"Business management must develop within its own organization structure a system of stimulation and control which will be as effective in releasing and directing the productive energies of individuals and groups as the 'hidden hand' of prices, costs, and profits has been in releasing and directing the efforts of corporate enterprises." [3]

[3] James C. Worthy, "Democratic Principles in Business Management," *Advanced Management,* March, 1949.

Various experiments along these creative lines are now being tried, such as McCormick Co.'s "Multiple Management Plan," the Rucker "Share of Production" plan (Orangeburg Manufacturing, Continental Paper, Reznor Manufacturing), Bundy Tubing's "Cost Saving Sharing Plan," and the remarkable pioneering of Joseph N. Scanlon of M.I.T. (to be reported in a forthcoming issue of FORTUNE). In any case, the principle of participation, which industry has scarcely begun to explore, probably holds the key to the solution of more labor problems than any other. For it represents not only a verbal acceptance of the worker's economic rights, but an actual integration of them with the industrial process.

THE THORNY PATH

Many will not altogether agree with the three categories just outlined; some will want to add other categories; others will point out that in actual practice one merges into another. These objections can be granted providing only that the over-all objective is held clear: that the worker is a human being (not an industrial atom), who, as a member of the American society, is in possession of certain rights that stem from the "unalienable" Right to Life; that these rights entitle him, on the one hand, to adequate protections, and on the other, to adequate incentives; and that their implementation is *primarily* the joint concern of himself (through his union, if he so desires) and of his employer, acting as private parties.

Moreover, it is equally important to be aware of what is *not* involved. Altruism, for example, is most emphatically not involved. The paternalistic view that an employer is in some mysterious way personally responsible for the happiness and welfare of his workers belongs—if it ever belonged anywhere—to a feudal type of society, not a democratic one. There is no question, either, of burdening a business with so many welfare plans that it loses its flexibility and power of growth. Nor is there a question of setting minima of various kinds so high that the given company would find itself unable to survive a period of depression. The business must be profitable over a reasonable period of time, and it is the employer's job to make it so. The economic rights of the workers, therefore, are not strictly speaking *absolute*—though with the help of government they can be made virtually so. They are inevitably related to the profitability of the enterprise.

The objection will be raised, that all this sounds fine, but the labor itself makes it impossible. The responsibility for implementing economic rights in a free non-paternalistic society must be a joint one, and this in turn requires that labor bring to the *economic* problem the same intelligence and good will that the employer is asked to bring to the *social* problem. A full discussion of this question would lead into another field. We may dismiss it here with the passing observation, that if American labor wants to avoid a gov-

ernment-managed system it must awake to the necessities of a privately managed one. This in turn requires the development of a higher type of labor
leadership than is commonly found today.

An even greater obstacle lying across the thorny path of the employers is
government itself. The business community has in the past committed the
error of permitting government to assume the role of sole protector of the
employee, the sole guardian of his rights. If, for example, when the bottom
dropped out of things in 1932, businessmen had taken the lead, by insisting
that the government help *them* to implement the economic rights of their
employees, the whole tenor of American history during the last two decades
would have been different. Instead, business allowed Mr. Roosevelt to step
into that heroic role. And Mr. Roosevelt and his heirs and assigns have been
shrewd enough to capitalize on it ever since. The result is that almost all the
legislation having to do with the implementation of these rights is designed
to promote the role of government, not enterprise. Certain tax legislation and
Treasury rulings, instead of providing incentives, actually make it difficult
to set up private social insurance.

In a modern society, obviously, there is much room for government action.
For one thing, even if American businessmen should undertake an extensive
program of implementing the economic rights of their employees, this
would not directly affect everyone in the nation. Yet the trouble with Washington is that, instead of trying to pass as much responsibility as possible over
to private hands, through tax incentives and other devices, it tries to pass as
little as possible. It has forgotten how to be a servant of the people. The result
is the trend already mentioned, paralleling European socialism.

These and other obstacles can be overcome only if employers will now
abandon the defensive position that they have been occupying and really take
the initiative. To make the obstacles an excuse for doing nothing is merely to
increase them. The only way to begin to change the quality of the labor
leadership is to challenge it with a proposition, the validity of which no good
American could deny. And the only way to stop the trend toward government power is the exertion of private leadership in behalf of those goals that
the administration finds it so profitable to exploit. Leadership and initiative
are the only answers to the dilemma of enterprise.

THE MAGNIFICENT OPPORTUNITY

Moreover, there is real hope that enterprise will not begin to exert this
leadership—for one good reason, namely, that the opportunity in question is
no mere reformer's opportunity, no mere dreamer's opportunity. It is in the
literal sense of the word an economic opportunity, a profit opportunity. The
line of reasoning adopted here opens up for industrial enterprise the possibility of an entirely new capitalistic adventure. And when enterprisers begin to

realize this they will surely find the means—as they always have in the past—to push through the obstacles, whatever they may be.

It may sound strange to speak of the implementation of human rights as an economic opportunity, but examination reveals that this is so. Enterprise capitalism is a system for enabling private individuals to fulfill the demands of other private individuals. There exists today a tremendous demand for all the products that enterprise makes. But there exists also a new demand, a demand for the realization of a way of life that can make the material products worth while. There exists a demand for a social product. And if the demand is there, the business is there, even though the way to profit from this business is different and not at first obvious.

One concrete reason for this is not far to seek. In a competitive society, whose resources are largely harnessed and whose basic plant is well established (even though never fully grown), the chief source of profit springs, not from the scarcity of materials, but from the use that can be made of human ingenuity. In such a society those businesses will succeed best whose employees like their jobs: where they are given reasonable economic security; where they are treated like human beings; and where they can participate in the productive process in a creative—and profitable—way. The executive, in short, who establishes a good society within his corporation finds himself able to produce a better product at lower cost.

The truth of this proposition is demonstrated by the fact that those corporations that have already gone furthest toward the voluntary implementation of economic rights have not lost, but on the contrary have gained in competitive position. Hormel, for example, which has been bold enough to saddle itself with the annual wage, has grown faster than most of its competitors. H. C. Nicholas, President of Quality Castings Co. of Orrville, Ohio, has declared that although he thought he was operating efficiently in 1940, he found that two years after the installation of his profit-sharing system in 1945, plant efficiency had risen 40 per cent. "Our employees," he says, "are now anxious to put their talents to maximum use . . . This is the most effective reason for our production record."

Richard R. Deupree of Procter & Gamble pointed out in 1945 that employment stabilization had accomplished many savings for his company, the biggest of which nobody had thought of before the annual wage was installed. This was the elimination of excess capacity, made possible by year-round production—a total saving over twenty-two years of $100 million in plant investment, exclusive of depreciation, carrying charges and interest on the money. Innumerable other examples could be cited. But perhaps the final word should be given to that august body, the Board of Directors of the Standard Oil Co. (N.J.), which declared in their annual statement for 1949: "As we see it, the basic interest of the stockholder—security for his investment and a fair return—is best served only if the corporation deserves and enjoys public confidence. Such confidence can be based only on recognition by people at large that their interest—the interest of society—is a factor in corporate action."

A SHOT AROUND THE WORLD

It may, finally, be asked: if so many businesses have already taken steps to implement the economic rights, why is it that the "welfare state" idea continues to grow and the position of enterprise democracy continues to become more insecure? The answer is threefold. In the first place, not enough businesses have tried, and the measures taken by most that have tried have been only partial. In the second, the measures have not always been taken in a positive manner, backed by a real belief, but somewhat grudgingly and defensively. And in the third, they have been scattered and haphazard.

What is needed now is concerted and positive action on the part of at least a large segment of the business community. If a hundred leading firms were to announce that from now on they intended to make themselves primarily responsible for implementing the economic rights of their employees, and that they were undertaking a program of research and action to that end, a very different atmosphere would be created. Such an announcement could well take the occasion to state some fundamental truths about these economic rights and about the role of the corporation in our society. It might even call for a panel of philosophers, to try to work out the underlying theory of the American way of life in modern terms. Backed up by employer organizations such as the U.S. Chamber of Commerce, and possibly also by labor groups, it could carry enough authority to start a wholly new trend in national affairs.

Indeed, it would resound around the world like the crack of a gun. For every important society on earth is now in the throes of a mortal struggle with its own state, for the very reason that no society has been able to find a way to implement economic rights except through the state. If, however, American industrial enterprise were to rise to this challenge, a sudden light would be shed. This light would reveal state socialism to be a great reactionary movement, signalizing the failure of man to realize the dream of democracy.

For the dream of democracy was always clear: that the state was a necessary and limited evil rather than a desirable and boundless good; that the springs of progress, happiness and security are to be found in individuals, acting in their private capacities, in response to their self-interests and their moral judgments. It was the belief of the founders of this country, well substantiated until the rise of the corporation, that men and women could be relied upon to implement the Rights of Man to their own mutual interest, and thus to keep the state at arm's length. It is now time for the business community to show that corporate action, which is still private action, and which emanates from individuals, can achieve the same result: that the Rights of Man can be made just as safe in corporate hands as they were in individual hands.

Such a demonstration would cut through all the ideologies of the world. It would show modern man a way out of the impasse into which he has fallen. It would open up for enterprise an era of new possibilities. It would awaken everywhere new hope for the perpetuation of freedom. Indeed, the vista will become immeasurable, once American enterprise awakes to the realization that in the "social problem" it is in fact faced with the greatest opportunity on earth.

LOUIS M. HACKER

5. *The Welfare State: A Negative View**

The current debate on the limits of intervention (Is the welfare state inevitable? Can we stop short of socialism?) is taking place in a fog through which light shines only occasionally. In consequence, voices seem disembodied and values unreal as historical experience and political and economic truths are sacrificed to the demands of urgency. It has been said, for example, by a recent writer, that our modern world is unique because of "the decline of competition, the recurrence of periods of depression and the persistence of demands for basic economic reforms," [1] and that first call upon economic and political statesmanship is the resoluiton of our "pressing immediacies" —to wit, stability, security and full employment. National planning stands high on any agenda.[2]

Why urgency? These analyses, or reproaches, are almost as old as historical man himself. The Gracchi talked in the same vein; so did the rebels and popular leaders of the early fourteenth and sixteenth centuries. The complaints against monopoly and depression fill the pages of our first economic literature; the demands for "basic economic reform"—to mention only the best known of the viewers-with-alarm—go back as far as Harrington in the seventeenth century, and their number is legion in the nineteenth (Saint-Simon, Owen, Fourier, Proudhon, Cabet, Marx, Morris, Bellamy).

Another question: Dare a democracy ever yield to a sense of urgency? If

* *The American Scholar*, Vol. XIX (Autumn, 1950). By permission.
[1] K. William Kapp, "Economic Planning and Freedom" in *Weltwirtschaftliches Archiv*, Band 64, Heft 1 (Hamburg, 1950).
[2] J. B. Condliffe, *The Commerce of Nations* (New York, 1950).

we believe in unlimited debate, the examination of choices, and the peaceful persuasion and full support of a majority of the electorate—as well as the conversion of the majority by a minority—can we at any time say that emergency measures are in order? A fair charge against Lincoln was that he suspended habeas corpus and imposed martial law in Northern districts that were not even threatened by invasion. Even when Britain was so threatened, after the fall of France, its government never abridged the constitutional guarantees of the British people.

These questions, however, are not my immediate interest here. I am addressing myself to that of intervention: Are there limits to it? In fact, how far can public authority legitimately go before it changes our world entirely from the one we have to another with completely different codes of behavior, morality and welfare?

There are two popular fallacies to be disposed of at the outset. The first runs somewhat as follows: During the nineteenth century, under the banner of liberalism, statesmanship concerned itself largely with political questions (the franchise, representative government, the constitutional position of the monarchy and the judiciary, popular education, minority rights); today, it is forced to concern itself with economic questions (exchange control, price supports, subsidies, full employment). And the second fallacy is: During the nineteenth century, the art of political economy had as its leading preoccupation the creation of wealth; today, it must devote itself to other canons. "Among these criteria," says Professor Condliffe, "stability and security rank high." Thus, we move from liberalism to interventionism, from freedom to necessity.

The middle-of-the-roaders, the faint of heart, Mr. Arthur M. Schlesinger, Jr.'s "vital centrists," hope we can stop in midcareer and that "the welfare state" will be a working compromise between no-intervention and full-intervention. But the fox has been flushed, the hounds are in full cry, and away we go over hill and dale, not meaning to pull up until we are in at the kill. "Kill" is the wrong word, of course, except to the cynical. The happy huntsmen are convinced we can plan for stability and security, and at the same time maintain full consumer choices, a free market, and the right to invest—which means to take risks. *Our* welfare state will not be dominated by the police. . . .

The British Labor government has formally declared that its grand plan encompasses only these three ideas: direction over investment, location of industry, and foreign exchange. It does not mean to nationalize entirely, and never without compensation. No policeman here—certainly as far as the Englishman's fundamental rights are concerned. But let us see.[3]

[3] Mr. Harold Wilson, President of the British Board of Trade, reported in The London *Times*, Jan. 20, 1950: "Basic controls, such as those of the location of industry, foreign exchange and the volume of investment, will be maintained as permanent instruments to ensure the maintenance of our economic position and the fulfillment of our full employment programme."

You want to start a newspaper and you begin making your rounds of the very many public offices involved. You learn, in time, that your investment plans, for share capital to erect buildings and furnish equipment, cannot have top priority ("More important to build houses for workers"); that paper shortages forbid the launching of new publishing ventures ("Purchases from the dollar area must be rigorously controlled by import licenses"); that all trained workers already have jobs and trade-union contracts ("A planned economy is based on high employment"). Socialism has a job to be done; first things come first, and dissent—which has always been a luxury—must wait its turn. There is no open attack on liberty. It is only that the sustenance it requires for survival simply becomes more difficult, if impossible, to obtain.

As for the popular fallacies, they fly in the face of historical fact and economic truth. English political leaders, during the nineteenth century, were constantly preoccupied with economic as well as political problems: income tax laws, the reestablishment and support of the gold standard, central banking, the rights of and restrictions on joint-stock companies, railroad regulation, land reform, factory and child-labor legislation. American political leaders were occupied, among other things, with the building of highways, the chartering and control of railroads, the question of cheap or dear money, national banking, the maintenance of competition. The legislative annals of France and Germany are filled with similar examples.

And as regards the brave challenge: "The art of political economy . . . must take account of criteria other than wealth"—this has been the stand of every Utopian from Plato up to and beyond William Morris. Without wealth —achieved not through privilege but by staring risky ventures—how can men launch new and cheaper ways of making goods and creating services? And unless we do so, will the cruel poverty which plagues so large a part of the population of the earth's surface, causing disease, starvation and early death, ever be abolished? Only a fool will deny that great deficits everywhere exist in the areas of health, education, child care—all the social services. The point is a simple one: Unless we continue to expand and create new engines of production—tearing down obsolescent plants, erecting more efficient factories and mills, building hydroelectric irrigation and flood-control projects, laying out more systems of communication—and make it possible, in consequence, to turn out more and cheaper hard and soft goods, we cannot pay for social security. The fascinating and frightening lesson of Britain's National Health Act is that its people need health services, but that the British economy will go bankrupt if its socialist leaders continue trying to pay for the health program at the expense of plant modernization. At this point in our development we simply cannot afford socialism—at any rate, Christian socialism, which is a morality and not a method for organizing production.

II

All this being so, how far may we expect the state to go? It has traditional roles which all of us in a democratic society are accustomed to see performed. It provides for the national defense; it maintains and upholds an incorruptible judiciary guided by the Rule of Law; it encourages and safeguards freedom of religion, communication and association; it gives minority groups protection and permits them to be heard; it employs the police power to defend and improve the life, health and morals of its people. The state can and should go further; and, having said this, one should also be prepared to say: There are other functions which are the proper concerns, but also the limits, of state intervention. I record them here, not necessarily in the order of their importance.

1. The protection of private property is an important function of the state. If we are committed to the encouragement of innovation in order to increase production; if we are ready to agree that capital formation in a poor world is still a crying need; if we concede that the maintenance of unequal wage and salary scales is one of the ways through which savings can occur; if, from historical experience, we are prepared to recognize that unless risks can be taken—and fortunes made by the successful—the idea of economic progress must be abandoned, then private property and private business decisions must be assured. In a free society, the existence of free consumer choices always will keep resources scarce. Unless we build our foundations on the vision of an ideal Spartan world—Plato's and More's and Marx's Utopias— there will always continue to be a relative dearth of goods. It is idle to talk of the abolition of wages as an ultimate goal, for the surfeit of plenty of which all well-intentioned romanticists have dreamed (Marx was the worst of the lot!) can never be realized.

The existence of unequal wages is one of the great social incentives: in fact, unequal wage scales are further developed in the Soviet Union than in most capitalist countries. Unequal wage and salary scales—leading to private fortunes—are a great spur to innovation. Short of a war period (the caterpillar tractor, the jet plane, atomic energy), it still is to be demonstrated that a planned and regulated economy is a more favorable climate for innovation than capitalism. The very nature of socialism—the timidity of functionaries, the vested interests of labor unions and cooperatives, the curious cost-accounting procedures—stifles innnovation. Capitalism is not on trial here; its achievements, as far as production is concerned, have been magnificent. If the state means to concern itself with social welfare, it must permit adventurers to invest, take risks, and save for further investments from their successful ventures.

2. All this does not mean that privilege is to be tolerated. Tariffs that have outlived their usefulness (encouraging infant industries) must be abolished; monopolies and unfair trade practices are to be fought; patents are proper, but they should not be privately suppressed; excessive fortunes and idle funds should be regarded with suspicion. Every political thinker worthy of the name, from Aristotle to John Stuart Mill, was aware of the fact that no society could endure for long, or ward off social discontent, unless it constantly preoccupied itself with the question of the redistribution of wealth and income. There was always a wealthy group in the top layer and a poor one in the bottom. In between was to remain that broad sector of the middle class which had the fluidity and opportunity to reach above or—if unsuccessful—to fall below.

Redistribution, through taxation, keeps opportunity alive and makes possible the regular emergence of new adventurers or innovators. So does the maintenance of the luxury industries, although in a minor way. Mandeville, in part, was right: the luxury industries are useful—not, of course, because they give employment, but because they help the profligate and stupid to speed the processes of redistribution. (J. M. Keynes was either cynical or entirely despairing when he applauded Mandeville.) Taxation, of course, is a two-edged sword: it always threatens the life of incentive.

3. Given the possession of that awful weapon, fiscal power, the state has a great responsibility: the protection of society's credit structure is in its hands. The state cannot be heedless in the management of its own finances. So completely—for good or ill—does it dominate central banking today that any recklessness on its part must have a blighting effect on enterprise at once. A sound monetary and credit system and a manageable public debt are the first concerns of virtuous lawmakers; otherwise, economic chaos inevitably follows. The history books are filled with too many familiar examples to require their recital here.

This warning, particularly, must be taken to heart by new or underdeveloped nations. The formula of inflation (or repudiation) and price and exchange controls seems such a simple and magical one; but only one's own people—and not for long—can be bemused by it. Certainly the stranger —the foreign investor and trader—will smell danger at once. That great and wise young man, Alexander Hamilton, America's first secretary of the Treasury, knew how vital it was that the young republic's public and private credit be built on an indestructible foundation. He paid off the revolutionary foreign and domestic debts; the prewar commercial claims of English merchants were to be honored; the new public debt was to be secured by a sinking fund; a central bank was established to regulate the currency; and long-term foreign funds and short-term financing flowed into the United States, to make its formative years secure.[4]

It would be idle to maintain that lawmakers must ever close their minds to the occasional necessity for unbalanced budgets. The experiences of the 1930's and the teachings of Keynes and his disciples are valuable here: deficit financing in bad years, surpluses in good ones. But what shall we say of a government which, during the greatest peacetime period of prosperity in its history, complacently draws up a budget calling for a deficit of five billions of dollars?

I am arguing for fiscal integrity; but I am not saying that state fiscal intervention should never take place. In a young or growing economy, there are many areas where private capital cannot enter because it is not powerful enough. Indeed, in the underdeveloped countries—in the new nations of India and Israel, for example, and in Latin America—public investment will undoubtedly occur. Private investment, with foreign funds, however, is more efficient, and because it is willing to take risks is less likely to be badgered by the cautious or the foolish. An illuminating contrast is that between the building of the railroads by foreign private capital in the United States after the Civil War, on the one hand, and, on the other, the current efforts of the British Labor government to push its great groundnuts project in Africa. In both cases, financial failure initially took place. In the United States, the railroads were built despite the losses suffered by British, German and Swiss investors; in Britain, the plans for the development of Africa have come under such sharp criticism that the government has been forced to narrow and limit its outlays.[5]

4. Up to this point, I have mentioned the economic responsibilities of the state; there remains to be discussed an important social one. All cultures have had dependent or unemployable persons. Their care becomes a public duty in a world such as ours which advances in medical knowledge and develops a more refined social conscience, prolongs the age of child dependency, increases life expectation and therefore the numbers of the old, and has large numbers of the chronically and permanently ill. A distinction should be drawn between the sick and those chronically and permanently ill; between the unemployed and the unemployables. Invalidity, dependent mothers and children, and the aged (where there do not exist adequate pension programs) are a public concern and should be budgeted for.

[4] See my own *England & America: The Ties That Bind. An Inaugural Lecture* (Oxford, 1948) for a fuller exposition of this point.

[5] Because I favor foreign investments, I know I will be charged with "imperialism." Two of the greatest troublemakers of modern times have been Hobson and Lenin, who popularized, and cast obloquy on, this concept. See my *England & America,* heretofore referred to.

On the other hand, the sick can be taken care of more efficiently and at less cost by private-insurance and group-medicine devices. And the unemployed can be protected by pension funds and schemes. There is a large area of joint enterprise, participated in by industry and labor, which we are beginning to explore in the United States. This, it seems to me, is a more fruitful experimentation than state programs. The welfare funds currently being set up in many of our industries place administration and responsibility where they belong; and they have the great virtue of preserving the independence of the unions.

If we mean what we say about our liberties, then pluralistic loyalties need encouraging: devolution of power, and not its concentration, is the key to proper political thinking. The welfare state (or socialism) produces the reverse, and sooner or later, because it has fiscal authority over all the social services, as well as over credit, production and exchange, it must weaken the independence of associations (trade unions, trade associations) and convert them into pale satellites without lives of their own.

5. Finally, I wish to mention what may be called the psychological duty of the state: the preservation of opportunity. There will not be an active and contented citizenry unless opportunity flourishes, unless people can climb up and down the ladder of economic success and social recognition. The founder of the Medicis began as a wool comber; the first Astor was a butcher boy; the first Vanderbilt, a ferryman. Innovators must have the chance to start, and their talents demand social acceptance. In our world of great institutional organization—the guidance of public offices, corporations, trade unions—the surest way to maintain opportunity is through the creation and defense of full educational facilities.

The state must educate, therefore, because education is expensive and should be universal. Plato's Academy, the Stoics, Peter Abelard, could meet their pupils over a covered walk or in a room, the gathering together of teachers and scholars for discourse constituted early education. But when education requires libraries, laboratories and elaborate equipment; when education begins with infancy and does not end until death; when it tries to reach whole populations to train for the effective citizenship of all rather than the leadership of the few—then we cannot escape public outlays.

Outlays are one thing; supervision is another. This is not the place to examine closely the complicated question of educational policy. The elimination of privately-administered educational institutions would be a tragedy, if we really mean what we say about wanting to uphold a democratic society and to produce free men. Authority does not start in the schools; it begins in the family, probably. But certainly the perversion of young minds can be effectively completed, and their thought forever controlled, by those who dominate education.

The state undoubtedly will have to subsidize higher education (scholarships would be the best way), but educational administration should be in the hands of local agencies (where the schools are public) and in the hands of faculties (where the schools are private). If the schools can be kept independent, the Big Policeman will be kept cut down to size.

The preservation of liberty is no longer an abstract question. Political theorists, up to now, have always assumed that threats to it came from irresponsible authority. But liberty can be put in jeopardy equally by a state which starts out with benevolent intentions. Socialism's aim is not power but welfare; yet in striving to achieve welfare it threatens innovation, sacrifices fiscal integrity, and dries up opportunity. The state has positive functions; but, if we are interested in economic progress and the maintenance of liberty, there should be specific limits on intervention. To define functions is also to limit them.

MAX LERNER

6. The Welfare State: An Affirmative View*

I find Professor Hacker less persuasive in his introductory remarks than he is when he tackles the main matter at hand. He asks, to start with, "why the urgency" about economic reform, and points out that the reformist analyses and reproaches "are almost as old as historical man himself." It is a little as if a writer on medicine were to ask "why the urgency" in the efforts to improve medical science, and were to point out that the diagnoses of disease and the calls for cure "are almost as old as historical man himself."

More than a decade ago I wrote a book called *It Is Later Than You Think*. I would not in today's crisis diminish in the slightest degree the sense of urgency implied in that title. I am certain that Professor Hacker will not deny the reality of the contemporary struggle between an all-out totalitarianism, which aims to put the whole economy, and with it the whole human mind and personality, under rigid public direction, and, on the other hand, the effort to find a way of organizing the economy effectively without destroying freedom. The problem is at once economic, political and moral. When Professor Hacker says with disdain that "socialism—at any rate, Christian socialism . . . is a morality and not a method for organizing produc-

* *The American Scholar*, Vol. XIX (Autumn, 1950). By permission.

tion," he does it less than justice by denying its economic and political aspect; yet its moral emphasis—the effort at a greater economic security and stability, the effort to meet the threat of corporate power-aggregates, the effort to create access to opportunity for all—is not in our day a negligible emphasis. In most areas of the world the problem that Professor Hacker is inclined to dismiss with an air of tiredness as old stuff of the utopian brand is a problem as real as livelihood and freedom. If we ignore it or abdicate it, we may find soon that we have lost the battle for the allegiance of men, and with it the chance to explore further the best ways of organizing an economy for common ends through democratic means.

II

Professor Hacker gets some telling effects from the English dilemma by pointing out that if your choice is between paying for social security or using the same limited funds to renovate obsolescent machinery, it is no solution to let the machinery go on obsolescing. What he does not add is that America, with a national income approaching three hundred billion dollars a year, is not faced by anything like so cruel a choice. I have noted a tendency on the part of many of the critics of the New Deal and Fair Deal to use the case of England as a whipping boy. They attribute to socialism all the present ills of England, and by a transposition they imply that Americans, too, will have to live under austerity, and ration orange juice and gasoline, if they move further toward socialism. On the other hand, they attribute to pure capitalism all the productive achievements and material prosperity of America today, and by a transposition they imply that if contemporary Britain had not followed after the strange gods of socialism, the British, too, would have today a bull market, roads crowded with burnished autos, shop windows crammed full of luxuries, the highest living standards in history, a Byzantine lushness of life, and money to burn.

It should be pointed out for the historical record that there is a difference in the resources of the two countries, both natural and human. It should also be pointed out that the obsolescence of British machinery, British railway equipment, British coal mining equipment, was notorious long before the labor governments were even heard of. Writing in 1915, Thorstein Veblen, in his *Imperial Germany and the Industrial Revolution,* gave a classic analysis of Britain's lag in terms of "the penalty for taking the lead." Whether he was right or wrong in his analysis, the fact of the British lag was recognized thirty-five years ago. Professor Hacker, who has had a first hand acquaintance with Britain as exchange professor at Oxford, should know that the bankruptcy of Britain is not the consequence of the labor government, but that the labor government is the consequence of the bankruptcy of Britain. That bankruptcy came under capitalist auspices, and was nourished by the fearful material and human expenditures of two world wars. British socialism, to the extent that it exists, is a particular kind of socialism that comes in the wake of a deficit economy. That is why Aneurin Bevan was so roundly cheered at a British Labor party conference when he said that "the language of priorities is the religion of socialism." Because the British problem was one of priorities, it does not follow that it is—or would be—the American problem as well.

The case of America presents, not the problem of deficits, but the problems of distribution, stability, security. What Professor Hacker calls deficits in the areas of health, education, child care, and the social services are (for the case of America) deficits not for all the people but only for some of the people. The New Deal and Fair Deal have already gone a considerable distance toward wiping them out, and the Cassandra-like prophecies which have dogged us since 1934—that we could do so only by eating into risk capital and investment capital—have proved utterly empty. Always we were asked the question: "Where will the money come from?"—the question that Professor Hacker is still asking. Would it be acrimonious to suggest that not only has the community found the money to establish these services, but that in the process both the volume of capital and the profits of private enterprise have been increased? And I would suggest also that to go farther along the same road, and wipe out wholly the deficits in the areas of health, education, child care and all the social services would, far from destroying the private sectors of the economy, build an even stronger base under their prosperity.

I hope I am not unfair to Professor Hacker when I say that he seems to miss the dynamic elements in the American economy. Like other critics of the Welfare State, his thinking seems to go back to the presuppositions of the wage-fund economic theorists—that there is a static fund of income upon which the society can draw as upon a bank account, and that if you withdraw it for social security, for public medical services, for farm subsidies, for public-housing construction, for hydroelectric dams, you may overdraw your account. What we have found in the case of America since the beginning of the New Deal is that the psychological factors are the crucial ones in an economy, as in all human living. John Maynard Keynes understood this, and that is why he evolved a new—if still crude—psychological language of the "propensities" to save and spend and consume. Given a strong base of resources, managerial ability, technology and labor power, as we have in America, the extent of potential national product and national income in the calculable future is such as to stagger the imagination. In that sense, the most recent report of the Committee of Economic Advisers to the President was not a utopian or a whimsical report, but a realistic assessment of what can be accomplished in the next fifty years, based upon what we have accomplished in the past twenty years. The psychological atmosphere of confidence, employment and social construction achieved by the New Deal gave a fillip to the managerial group, as well as to the workers and the consumers. That is why America has managed at once to move toward a Welfare State and to increase its national income.

But the psychological factor is only one of a complex of factors that made this possible. It would be as foolish to attribute the results to government intervention as it would be to insist that America's current prosperity is due to the boldness and imaginativeness of "risk taking capital." The wealth of a nation lies in the state of its industrial arts, its technological advance, its managerial skills, its labor force. All of these may be called "socialist" in the sense that they are all community possessions. They come from social sources and they should pay a social dividend. To an extent they are doing so in America. Wages and living standards are high, profits are unexampled, new industries and new millionaires are being created. And all of this is being done within what has been called the "strait jacket" of the New Deal and the Fair Deal.

III

But there are lumps in the porridge. Professor Hacker, I am sure, will agree with me when I enumerate them. The biggest lump is the fact that much of our present prosperity is the result of armament economics.

Second, there is the glaring fact of corporate monopoly. Since the 1880's the free American economy has been growing less free. The path of monopoly is strewn with the graves of small enterprises. Every year the area of concentrated corporate power gets greater; the area of small business enterprise shrinks. The monopolies are governments in themselves and bureaucracies in themselves. They levy their toll, as Thurman Arnold has pointed out, not only on their rivals, but also on the consumer. They are the American form of feudalism.

The third lump is boom-and-bust. The American economy has gone periodically through fevers and chills. To the extent that we carry over the planlessness of the past, to that extent we shall continue the alternation of boom-and-bust.

The fourth lump is that so-called "risk taking capital" has tended to stay out of the areas of risk, and to play it safe. It has not pushed with boldness into the possibilities of large scale investment with low profit margins. Some of the critics of American capitalism from inside have pointed out that it has not taken advantage of doing a larger volume of business on a lower margin of profit. It has tended to charge what the traffic will bear. The replacement of Commonwealth and Southern by the TVA has shown that the government is sometimes in a better position to take risks than private capital is. In the entire field of housing today there is very little risk left. The risks are all guaranteed by public funds, and the profits are the reward, not of risk, but of capital.

It is to correct these still crucial defects of our economy that we must continue along the path of economic reform.

IV

This means exploring further what John Stuart Mill called the "limits of the province of government." Professor Hacker has mapped out with considerable cogency the five major duties of the state, and then he has drawn a line as with a flaming sword, with the injunction: "thus far and no farther at your mortal peril."

I cannot have his certitude about how definite these limits are. I think it is a matter for many decades of further experience and further experiment and the further use of the inquiring mind.

Western Europe, especially Britain, has been experimenting with the socialism of the deficit economy. America alone, as I have said, has the resources for experimenting with a better organization of a surplus economy.

It will not do to debate the issue as if it were a clear one between "capitalism" and "socialism." The fact is that in the modern Western State, whether in Britain or America, whether in Israel or India (both of which have become Western states), there are elements both of capitalism and of socialism. Perhaps it would be better to say that there are elements of business capitalism and of state capitalism. The problem is how to form an amalgam of them which will achieve the best form of welfare economy.

Britain has moved reluctantly toward a larger public sector—that is, a sector of state capitalism. It has done so from necessity in the interest of sheer survival, although the Marxist tradition of the Labor party has given the new developments a dogmatic welcome. America has moved, also under the spur of necessity, toward enlarged sectors of public action in the economy. Dogmatically we abhor every such step. We call it "socialism" and many worse names as well. But under the spur of the great depression, and the thrust of the democratic welfare impulse, which is very strong in the American tradition, we have nevertheless kept moving. Our problem has been, not sheer survival, as in the case of Britain, but stability and security.

I don't think that Professor Hacker is justified in ridiculing the concept of a mixed economy, such as will be found in Professor Schlesinger's *Vital Center* and in Irwin Ross's book on the mixed economy, *Strategy for Liberals*. Our whole historic instinct has been to cling to the private sector wherever we can, to move toward the public sector only when we must. There is no danger within the American tradition and the American psychology that we will embrace socialism either out of dogmatic enthusiasm or subservience to the state. The greater danger lies in the fact that the great power structures in America are the aggregates of corporate power; that they function very much as governments function; that, more than ever, they control the agencies of public opinion and influence the direction of education and belief; that the business system in America is invested with power, and that property is invested with sanctity and with grace. My own anxiety is not that we will slip unaware into socialism, but that we will not have the courage to challenge those who fear the valid extensions of the public sector.

ARNOLD J. TOYNBEE

7. The Welfare State, Communism, and World Peace*

In the contemporary world—in whatever age or century one happens to be living—religious and political differences between various sections of the living generation are apt to seem absolute and ultimate. For instance, our seventeenth century ancestors in Western Christendom could not conceive of any greater gulf than that which seemed in their day to be fixed between the Catholic and Protestant varieties of Western Christianity. By contrast, we their descendants, looking back on them and their conflicts in the perspective of three centuries of history, are far more conscious of the gulf between our own age and the world of the seventeenth century than we are of the domestic divisions within that seventeenth century world. To our eyes, those Protestants and Catholics are all alike, seventeenth-century-minded people first and foremost; and it needs some effort of discrimination on our part to appreciate the nice distinction between the warring religious camps.

In the light of this historical precedent—and there are countless others that would have served equally well to illustrate our point—we may be sure that, 300 years from today, our own descendants will be much more alive to the common features of the twentieth century world—and especially those common features that seem to them distinctive—than they will be to the current differences that mean so much at the moment to all members of the living generation, in whatever continent or camp we may happen to have been born.

Can we guess what the outstanding feature of our twentieth century will appear to be in the perspective of 300 years? No doubt we shall not all guess alike. Some of us will guess that the present age will be looked back upon as the age of scientific discovery. Others will expect to see it branded as the age in which Fascist and Communist apostates from a Christian civilization harnassed science to the service of a neo-barbarism. My own guess is that our age will be remembered chiefly neither for its horrifying crimes nor

* *The New York Times Magazine* (October 21. 1951). By permission.

for its astonishing inventions, but for its having been the first age since the dawn of civilization, some five or six thousand years back, in which people dared to think it practicable to make the benefits of civilization available for the whole human race.

By comparison with the significance of this common twentieth century new ideal, the differences between the conflicting ideologies will—so I should guess—come to look both less important and less interesting than will be easily credible to anyone alive today. In the easy wisdom that comes after the event, our successors will, perhaps, be able to pronounce that this or that policy for achieving a common twentieth century ideal was more suitable than the rival policy was to the social conditions of this or that region in that antique and still unstandardized twentieth century world.

They may even judge that one twentieth century ideology was better or worse than another in some absolute moral sense. But the common features of our century will, I fancy, be the features standing out the most prominently in perspective; and, among these, the new ideal and objective of extending the benefits of civilization to the common man will in future centuries tower above the rest.

Perhaps there are two points here that are worth underlining: This vision of a good life for all is a new one, and—whatever our success or our failure may be in the attempt to translate this vision into reality—this new social objective has probably come to stay. That the ideal of welfare for all is new is surely true; for, as far as I can see, it is no older than the seventeenth century West European settlements on the east coast of North America that have grown into the United States. And it has surely come to stay with us as long, at any rate, as our new invention of applying mechanical power to technology; for this sudden vast enhancement of man's ability to make non-human nature produce what man requires from her has, for the first time in history, made the ideal of welfare for all a practical objective instead of a mere utopian dream.

So long as this aim continues to be practical politics, mankind is certain, however many times we may fail, to go on making one attempt after another to reach the goal. When once the odious inequality that has hitherto been a distinguishing mark of civilization has ceased to be taken for granted as something inevitable, it becomes inhuman to go on putting up with it—and still more inhuman to try to perpetuate this inequality deliberately.

Of course it was one particular ingredient in welfare—a spiritual ingredient which was at the heart of it—that was the objective of the first settlers from the Old World on this American coast. They were inspired to pull up their roots in the Old World and to set about the creation of a new world beyond the Atlantic by the hope of being able at this cost to purchase liberty—religious liberty above all, since they were living in the seventeenth century. But, as soon as they realized that their quest for liberty had landed them on the edge of a vast fallow but cultivable continent, the vision began to dawn upon their minds and hearts of offering the opportunity of a good life for everybody—by offering everybody the opportunity of carving a farm for himself out of a seemingly illimitable expanse of potentially arable land.

The ideal of welfare for all came into the world initially in North America in the eighteenth and nineteenth centuries because the sudden acquisition of immense new virgin material resources here for the first time made this vision seem practical.

It is noteworthy that the North American society which first conceived of this ideal was still living in the Old World, though it had established itself on the American side of the Atlantic. It was still living in the Old World in the sense that it remained in a pre-industrial age in which the natural resources that were the material bases of civilization were the crops and cattle on which the earliest civilizations had been reared.

The original North American version of this new ideal was still an ideal of welfare for everybody in an old-fashioned agricultural society. In the civilizations of the past there had been a just sufficient stock of arable land to provide a bare subsistence for all and a good life, in addition to a subsistence, for a very small minority. It was manifest to everyone that the normal resources of an agricultural society could not maintain more than a small minority of the whole population at a level higher than that of bare subsistence.

The chance of welfare for everybody in the North American agricultural society, which came after the plow first broke the continent's virgin soil, was no more than a limited and a transitory one. Vast though the untouched reserves of arable land in North America might seem in the eighteenth and early nineteenth centuries by comparison with agricultural opportunities in an agriculturally long since congested Western Europe, the North American continent was only a small fraction of the whole habitable world, and it took little more than 100 years to bring North America's fields under cultivation.

If the new material resources required in order to make practical politics of the new ideal of welfare for all had been confined forever to new agricultural resources, the dream would soon have faded away again. After the conquest of North America by the plow, the only remaining virgin soil in the Temperate Zone was Manchuria; and after the plow's conquest of Manchuria in the early twentieth century, the future of mankind, as a whole, so far from being anything like "welfare for all," would have been something like the present as it can be seen in China or India.

The reason why "welfare for all" is still practical politics in the world at large today is because we have tapped a wholly new kind of material resource in discovering how to harness mechanical power to technology.

Mankind's hope of better things lies in a permanent industrial revolution.

As a twentieth century non-American sees it, looking back on nineteenth century American history, the American outlook, like all particular outlooks, is based on a particular experience; and the particular experience that has molded current American ideals to their present shape is that experience of stumbling upon a whole continent of virgin arable soil. The ground for the American hope of providing a good life for all was expressed in the two nineteenth century American magic words, "Go West."

In a nineteenth century agricultural United States, the local and temporary existence of empty arable lands did indeed give to the weaker party in the economic arena so effective a bargaining power in his dealings with the stronger party that it was possible for the weaker party to win his fair share of welfare without its being necessary to curb the stronger party's freedom of economic action. Even under the very different American conditions of today, enough of these nineteenth century agrarian American circumstances perhaps still survive in a twentieth century industrial America for the best of both worlds to be still more or less practical politics locally in the United States.

By "the best of both worlds" I mean, of course, a maximum of opportunity for all, combined with a minimum of restriction upon a stronger and wealthier minority's freedom of action. But if this state of relative felicity is perhaps still attainable locally in the United States, it certainly is not, any more than it ever has been, practical politics in the world at large.

The outlook of the twentieth century world at large is governed, as I see it, by two facts. The first fact is that three-quarters of mankind are today still living the traditional life of an agricultural civilization in which there is no reserve of virgin soil and therefore no possibility of providing more than a tiny minority of the population with anything better than bare subsistence out of agricultural production.

But, in this old-fashioned starveling agrarian world, the Industrial Revolution has brought with it a hope for all mankind, from the prosperous American technician and farmer to the most miserable Chinese or Indian coolie, of breaking right through the iron limits to which the extension of the benefits of civilization has normally been subject in an agricultural society.

This hope is now rapidly dawning in the hearts of the depressed and ignorant peasantry that today still constitutes three-quarters of the living generation of mankind. They have begun to ask themselves how they are to attain those benefits of civilization which a mechanized technology has at last brought within the horizon of every man's hopes. But, considering the greatness of the gulf between present Asian and present American circumstances, it seems unlikely that the common Asian and American objective of extending the benefits of civilization to every man by drawing on the new resources of a mechanical technology can be attained in Asia in exactly the American way.

A common goal has to be approached along different roads by people who start their journey toward it from different quarters of the social compass. We must therefore expect to see an ideal which Americans have brought into the world being pursued by Asians and Africans on lines which, in contemporary American eyes, may, at best, look strange and, at worst, look misguided.

How is this depressed three-quarters of mankind going to set about the stupendously difficult task of gaining the benefits of civilization? Now that the hundreds of millions of peasants are aware of the relative well-being of the Western peoples, nothing is going to stop them from setting out to reach a goal which the West seems to them to have attained already. And no doubt only trial and error are going to make them aware of the difficulties in their path which are glaringly manifest to Western eyes.

For us Westerners it is easy to see that the mass of mankind today does not command those assets and advantages which have enabled a Western minority within the last two centuries to make some progress toward a wider distribution of the benefits of civilization inside the narrow circle of our Western society. Unlike nineteenth century and twentieth century America, they have no great installations of industrial plant, no human fund of widespread technical skill, no professionally competent and experienced middle class and—most serious deficiency of all—none of those Western traditions and habits of personal conduct which are the ultimate source of all the West's material success. If the mass of mankind did appreciate the seriousness of these handicaps, they might indeed be discouraged, but we can already see that this practical side of the problem is not going to be uppermost in non-Western minds.

Asia and Africa are going to make an audacious attempt to catch up with the West by a forced march, and here lies communism's opportunity in a world in which the Russian ideology of communism is competing with the Western ideal of free enterprise for Asia's and Africa's allegiance.

The present state of mind of an awakening majority of the human race in Asia and Africa is communism's opportunity because a forced march can never be made without severe regimentation and discipline. The rulers of the Soviet Union can plausibly represent to the rest of the non-Western world that their own system of totalitarian government already enables the peoples of the Soviet Union to overcome just those practical obstacles by which other non-Western peoples are faced.

This Russian claim is bound to appeal to Asians and Africans who are eager to reach the goal of welfare for all and who are also in a mood in which they will give priority to equality over liberty in a situation in which they may have to choose between the two. And this inclination in Asian and African minds to see salvation in communism is bound to be riling for Western observers.

What, then, is our Western policy to be? Being human, we might be tempted to give way to our sense of annoyance. Why not wash our hands of this whole Asian and African business? Isn't this dream of welfare for all mankind just a folly? And, if they are hoping for salvation in communism, cannot we count on their being disillusioned sooner or later? Such a reaction on our part would be as natural as it would be rash and wrong.

It would be rash because we could not be sure that the Soviet Union might not secure a political and military hold over Asia and Africa before the process of disillusionment had time to work itself out. And it would also be wrong for us to hold aloof because we human beings are, after all, our brothers' keepers, and we cannot be indifferent to the fate of three-quarters of the human race.

In this difficult situation the supreme need of the hour is, I would suggest, an immense patience and mutual toleration. A revolutionary improvement in means of communication has suddenly brought peoples with sharply diverse traditions or civilizations into close physical contact with one another. If, in spite of our diversity, we find ourselves all alike pursuing what is ultimately a common ideal, this is something to be thankful for. If we believe in the freedom which the Pilgrim Fathers came to look for on American shores, we must believe in the right of each people to work its way toward our common objective along a freely chosen course of its own.

Acting on this belief means acting toward Asian and African countries as we are already acting toward Yugoslavia. We must be ready to work with any non-Western country which agrees with the West on the crucial political point of being determined to resist Russian attempts to dominate the world, and we must not lay it down as a condition for their receiving help from us that the people who are asking us for assistance shall pursue our common social aim of welfare for all along Western lines.

We should be ready to help countries living under near-Communist and outright Communist regimes; for we should realize that some such dispensation as this may be the inevitable price of the forced march that these countries have to make if they are to try to catch up with us. And we should also have faith enough in our own way of life to believe that, if we do give a helping hand to peoples who have been compelled by a temporary necessity to put themselves under non-Russian totalitarian regimes, they will take to our Western liberty just as soon as they find themselves able to afford it.

Part V

FROM NATIONALISM TO WORLD ORDER

Nationalism: Peaceful or Aggressive?

Conflict or Common Interest?

Chapter XIV

NATIONALISM: PEACEFUL OR AGGRESSIVE?

No theory of the relations of man and the state can be realistic, unless it gives proper consideration to the place of the state in the great society of the world. The anarchy which has made possible the two bloodiest wars in history within the span of twenty-five years has confirmed the Hobbesian description of what man's life is like when there is no established government: "solitary, poor, nasty, brutish, and short." Hobbes saw the discrepancy between two modes of living which, though contradictory, are accepted by men. As members of the state, men have given up the advantages of savage life for the greater advantages of organized, civilized living through law and government. Yet the states themselves are still in the same condition of savagery in which men were before they founded a common government, and "live in the condition of perpetual war."

Since the French Revolution at least, nationalism has been one of the driving forces of domestic, imperial, and international politics. Complex in its origins, it has developed along many, and often contradictory, lines. In its name, some of the greatest acts of heroism and liberty have been committed, but also crimes of cruelty and fanaticism. In the first half of its existence—from the late eighteenth to the middle of the nineteenth century—nationalism was essentially inspired by humanitarian, democratic ideas; this was the story of early French, American, Czech, Italian, Irish, and Polish nationalism. In the last eighty years, on the other hand, nationalism has tended to ally itself with parochialism, intolerance, bigotry, persecution of minorities, racialism, and finally, imperialism and aggression—the record of Pan-Germanism, Tsarist imperialism, Japanese militarism, Fascism, and finally, Communist imperialism.

Lord Acton was one of the few farsighted liberals of the nineteenth century who perceived the dangers of nationalism at a time when most progressive-minded people thought that nationalism was a just principle of collective liberty and virtually the last answer to the ills of politics. In an essay on "Nationality" (1862), Lord Acton inveighs against the current progressive doctrine of his day, that state and nationality must be identical —a theory which Woodrow Wilson still considered the *ne plus ultra* fifty-five years later. Acton prophetically predicted that the doctrine of the *identity of state and nationality* would necessarily lead to *political absolutism*. Against this doctrine, Acton propounded the conception of the "multinational state" with its diversities of all kinds—linguistic, religious, national, economic and political. "Liberty provokes diversity," Acton writes, "and diversity preserves liberty by supplying the means of organization." Acton goes so far as to claim that the coexistence of several nations under the same state is "one of the chief instruments of civilization," in addition to being the best safeguard of freedom. A profoundly religious man, Acton saw in nationalism a remnant of pagan tribalism: "Christianity rejoices at the mixture of races, as paganism identifies itself with their differences, because truth is universal, and errors various and particular. In the ancient world idolatry and nationality went together, and the same term is applied in Scripture to both." Foreseeing how nationalism would eventually destroy what it set out to defend, Acton makes the, to some, paradoxical statement that "the greatest adversary of the rights of nationality is the modern theory of nationality." States which try to neutralize, absorb, or expel nationalities that are not of the *Staatsvolk*, or ruling nationality, destroy their own vitality and lose their chief basis of self-government.

Humanitarian conceptions of nationalism are also reflected in Giuseppe Mazzini, intellectual leader of Italian unity in the nineteenth century, particularly in his "Pact of Fraternity of Young Europe" (1834). Mazzini conceived of the nation as having a mission, but not a mission of imperialistic expansion inspired by conceit and haughty arrogance, but one of fulfillment toward the common goal of a fraternally united mankind. A fervent adherent of the democratic and republican faith, Mazzini worked for a free and self-governing Italy; his ultimate aim was a republican confederation of all mankind, "governed and directed by a common Declaration of Principles and a common Pact."

The humanist conception of nationality is also reflected in "What Is a Nation?" (1882) by Ernest Renan, one of the great French writers of the nineteenth century. Renan rejects the view—still held by some in our own time—that the essence of the nation lies in unity of race, language, religion, community of interest, or geography, and affirms that the nation is "a spiritual principle," based on two main elements: "The one is the possession in common of a rich heritage of memories; and the other is actual agreement, the desire to live together." Eliminating, as he puts it, metaphysics and theology, Renan defines the existence of a nation as a "daily plebiscite."

Mazzini's noble ideals of nation and humanity were betrayed, in the twentieth century, by his own countrymen, but were kept alive by the first president of the republic of Czechoslovakia, Thomas Garrigue Masaryk. One of the few truly great philosophers called upon to rule a state, Masaryk proved that the Platonic vision of the philosopher-king can become true, seldom as it may be. Under the most difficult circumstances, and faced with problems of different, and hostile, nationalities (especially Hungarians and Sudeten Germans), Masaryk managed to make Czechoslovakia the only genuine democratic country in Europe east of the Rhine. Having been under Austrian rule for almost four hundred years, the Czechs under Masaryk's inspiration and leadership showed remarkable moderation and political wisdom when the roles were reversed: "Our procedure with the minorities," Masaryk told Karel Čapek (*Masaryk on Thought and Life: Conversations with Karel Čapek,* 1938), "is practically given to us by our own experience under Austria-Hungary: what we did not like to be done unto us, we shall not do unto others." Masaryk refused to accept the distorted patriotism which deduces from love of one's country the right, and duty, to hate other countries: "True love is not proved by hatred, but only by love. Mankind is a sum of nations, it is not something outside the nations, and above them." And above all, Masaryk urged to express that love by "always acting humanely." The spirit of Masaryk lived on in Czechoslovakia until the Communists, with Russian backing, destroyed Czech democracy in 1948.

Imperialism is one of the chief distortions of nationalism. Love of oneself becomes hatred of others, and enslavement of other nations is clothed in such masks as "the white man's burden," or the need for "living space." Even highly democratic nations have, at one time or another, fallen victims of the disease of imperialism. J. A. Hobson, an unorthodox British economist, published in 1902 what was destined to become the classical analysis of imperialism. His *Imperialism* is divided into two parts: "The Economics of Imperialism" and "The Politics of Imperialism." His material is chiefly drawn from British experience and British sources, as might be expected, but imperialist policies of other nations are also examined. All subsequent work on imperialism, by Hilferding, Luxemburg, Lenin, and Woolf (to mention but a few), is based, in the main, on Hobson's *Imperialism.* Hobson condemned imperialism because it is rapacious and immoral, and also because it tends to destroy free government at home: "Imperialism and popular government have nothing in common: they differ in spirit, in policy, in method." In addition, Hobson charged imperialism with being a constant menace to peace, and with wasting economic and financial resources on unproductive military projects. Only the establishment of a genuine democracy, political as well as economic, could wrest control from those classes that have a private vested interest in the maintenance of imperialism. Hobson concludes his book on imperialism as follows: "It is the besetting sin of all successful States, and its penalty is unalterable in the order of nature."

LORD ACTON

1. *Nationality and Liberty**

In the old European system, the rights of nationalities were neither recognised by governments nor asserted by the people. The interest of the reigning families, not those of the nations, regulated the frontiers; and the administration was conducted generally without any reference to popular desires. Where all liberties were suppressed, the claims of national independence were necessarily ignored, and a princess, in the words of Fénelon, carried a monarchy in her wedding portion. The eighteenth century acquiesced in this oblivion of corporate rights on the Continent, for the absolutists cared only for the State, and the liberals only for the individual. The Church, the nobles, and the nation had no place in the popular theories of the age; and they devised none in their own defence, for they were not openly attacked. The aristocracy retained its privileges, and the Church her property; and the dynastic interest, which overruled the natural inclination of the nations and destroyed their independence, nevertheless maintained their integrity. The national sentiment was not wounded in its most sensitive part. To dispossess a sovereign of his hereditary crown, and to annex his dominions, would have been held to inflict an injury upon all monarchies, and to furnish their subjects with a dangerous example, by depriving royalty of its inviolable character. In time of war, as there was no national cause at stake, there was no attempt to rouse national feeling. The courtesy of the rulers towards each other was proportionate to the contempt for the lower orders. Compliments passed between the commanders of hostile armies; there was no bitterness, and no excitement; battles were fought with the pomp and pride of a parade. The art of war became a slow and learned game. The monarchies were united not only by a natural community of interests, but by family alliances. A marriage contract sometimes became the signal for an interminable war, whilst family connections often set a barrier to ambition. After the wars of religion came to an end in 1648, the only wars were those which were waged for an inheritance or a dependency, or against countries whose system of government exempted them from the common law of dynastic States, and made them not only unprotected but obnoxious. These countries were England and Holland, until Holland ceased to be a republic, and until, in England, the defeat of the Jacobites terminated the struggle for the Crown. There was one country, however, which still con-

---

* From "Nationality," *Home and Foreign Review* (July, 1862); reprinted in Lord Acton, *History of Freedom and Other Essays* (1907). By permission of The Macmillan Company, publishers.

tinued to be an exception; one monarch whose place was not admitted in the comity of kings.

The old despotic policy which made the Poles its prey had two adversaries, —the spirit of English liberty, and the doctrines of that revolution which destroyed the French monarchy with its own weapons; and these two contradicted in contrary ways the theory that nations have no collective rights. At the present day, the theory of nationality is not only the most powerful auxiliary of revolution, but its actual substance in the movements of the last three years. This, however, is a recent alliance, unknown to the first French Revolution. The modern theory of nationality arose partly as a legitimate consequence, partly as a reaction against it. As the system which overlooked national division was opposed by liberalism in two forms, the French and the English, so the system which insists upon them proceeds from two distinct sources, and exhibits the character either of 1688 or of 1789. When the French people abolished the authorities under which it lived, and became its own master, France was in danger of dissolution: for the common will is difficult to ascertain, and does not readily agree. "The laws," said Veregniaud, in the debate on the sentence of the king, "are obligatory only as the presumptive will of the people, which retains the right of approving or condemning them. The instant it manifests its wish the work of the national representation, the law, must disappear." This doctrine resolved society into its natural elements, and threatened to break up the country into as many republics as there were communes. For true republicanism is the principle of self-government in the whole and in all the parts. In an extensive country, it can prevail only by the union of several independent communities in a single confederacy, as in Greece, in Switzerland, in the Netherlands, and in America; so that a large republic not founded on the federal principle must result in the government of a single city, like Rome and Paris, and, in a less degree, Athens, Berne, and Amsterdam; or, in other words, a great democracy must either sacrifice self-government to unity, or preserve it by federalism.

The France of history fell together with the French State, which was the growth of centuries. The old sovereignty was destroyed. The local authorities were looked upon with aversion and alarm. The new central authority needed to be established on a new principle of unity. The state of nature, which was the ideal of society, was made the basis of the nation; descent was put in the place of tradition, and the French people was regarded as a physical product: an ethnological, not historic, unit. It was assumed that a unity existed separate from the representation and the government, wholly independent of the past, and capable at any moment of expressing or of changing its mind. In the words of Sieyès, it was no longer France, but some unknown country to which the nation was transported. The central power possessed authority, inasmuch as it obeyed the whole, and no divergence was permitted from the universal sentiment. This power, endowed with volition, was personified in the Republic One and Indivisible. The title signified that a part could not speak or act for the whole,—that there was a power supreme over the State, distinct from, and independent of, its members; and it expressed, for the first time in history, the notion of an abstract nationality. In this manner the idea of the sovereignty of the people, uncontrolled by the past, gave birth to the idea of nationality independent of the political influence of history. It sprang from the rejection of the two authorities,—of the State and of the past. The kingdom of France was, geographically as well as politically, the product of a long series of events, and the same influences which built up the State formed the territory. The Revolution repudiated alike the agencies to which France owed her boundaries and those to which she owed her government. Every effaceable trace and relic of national history was carefully wiped away,—the system of administration, the physical divisions of the country, the classes of society, the corporations, the weights and measures, the calendar. France was no longer bounded by the limits she had received from the condemned influence of her history; she could recognise only those which were set by nature. The definition of the nation was borrowed from the material world, and, in order to avoid a loss of territory, it became not only an abstraction but a fiction.

In pursuing the outward and visible growth of the national theory we are prepared for an examination of its political character and value. The absolutism which has created it denies equally that absolute right of national unity which is a product of democracy, and that claim of national liberty which belongs to the theory of freedom. These two views of nationality, corresponding to the French and to the English systems, are connected in name only, and are in reality the opposite extremes of political thought. In one case, nationality is founded on the perpetual supremacy of the collective will, of which the unity of the nation is the necessary condition, to which every other influence must defer, and against which no obligation enjoys authority, and all resistance is tyrannical. The nation is here an ideal unit founded on the race, in defiance of the modifying action of external causes, of tradition, and of existing rights. It overrules the rights and wishes of the inhabitants, absorbing their divergent interests in a fictitious unity; sacrifices their several inclinations and duties to the higher claim of nationality, and crushes all natural rights and all established liberties for the purpose of vindicating itself.[1] Whenever a single definite object is made the supreme end of the

[1] "Le sentiment d'indépendance nationale est encore plus général et plus profondément gravé dans le coeur des peuples que l'amour d'une liberté constitutionnelle. Les nations les plus soumises au despotisme éprouvent ce sentiment avec autant de vivacité que les nations libres; les peuples les plus barbares le sentent même encore plus vivement que les nations policées" (L'Italie au Dixneuvième Siècle, p. 148, Paris, 1821).

State, be it the advantage of a class, the safety or the power of the country, the greatest happiness of the greatest number, or the support of any speculative idea, the State becomes for the time inevitably absolute. Liberty alone demands for its realisation the limitation of the public authority, for liberty is the only object which benefits all alike, and provokes no sincere opposition. In supporting the claims of national unity, governments must be subverted in whose title there is no flaw, and whose policy is beneficent and equitable, and subjects must be compelled to transfer their allegiance to an authority for which they have no attachment, and which may be practically a foreign domination. Connected with this theory in nothing except in the common enmity of the absolute state, is the theory which represents nationality as an essential, but not a supreme element in determining the forms of the State. It is distinguished from the other, because it tends to diversity and not to uniformity, to harmony and not to unity; because it aims not at an arbitrary change, but at careful respect for the existing conditions of political life, and because it obeys the laws and results of history, not the aspirations of an ideal future. While the theory of unity makes the nation a source of despotism and revolution, the theory of liberty regards it as the bulwark of self-government, and the foremost limit to the excessive power of the State. Private rights, which are sacrificed to the unity, are preserved by the union of nations. No power can so efficiently resist the tendencies of centralisation, of corruption, and of absolutism, as that community which is the vastest that can be included in a State, which imposes on its members a consistent similarity of character, interest, and opinion, and which arrests the action of the sovereign by the influence of a divided patriotism. The presence of different nations under the same sovereignty is similar in its effect to the independence of the Church in the State. It provides against the servility which flourishes under the shadow of a single authority, by balancing interests, multiplying associations, and giving to the subject the restraint and support of a combined opinion. In the same way it promotes independence by forming definite groups of public opinion, and by affording a great source and centre of political sentiments, and of notions of duty not derived from the sovereign will. Liberty provokes diversity, and diversity preserves liberty by supplying the means of organisation. All those portions of law which govern the relations of men with each other, and regulate social life, are the varying result of national custom and the creation of private society. In these things, therefore, the several nations will differ from each other; for they themselves have produced them, and they do not owe them to the State which rules them all. This diversity in the same State is a firm barrier against the intrusion of the government beyond the political sphere which is common to all into the social department which escapes legislation and is ruled by spontaneous laws. This sort of interference is characteristic of an absolute government, and is sure to provoke a reaction, and finally a remedy. That intolerance of social freedom which is natural to absolutism is sure to find a corrective in the national diversities, which no other force could so efficiently provide. The co-existence of several nations under the same State is a test, as well as the best security of its freedom. It is also one of the chief instruments of civilisation; and, as such, it is in the natural and providential order, and indicates a state of greater advancement than the national unity which is the ideal of modern liberalism.

The combination of different nations in one State is as necessary a condition of civilised life as the combination of men in society. Inferior races are raised by living in political union with races intellectually superior. Exhausted and decaying nations are revived by the contact of a younger vitality. Nations in which the elements of organisation and the capacity for government have been lost, either through the demoralising influence of despotism, or the disintegrating action of democracy, are restored and educated anew under the discipline of a stronger and less corrupted race. This fertilising and regenerating process can only be obtained by living under one government. It is in the cauldron of the State that the fusion takes place by which the vigour, the knowledge, and the capacity of one portion of mankind may be communicated to another. Where political and national boundaries coincide, society ceases to advance, and nations relapse into a condition corresponding to that of men who renounce intercourse with their fellowmen. The difference between the two unites mankind not only by the benefits it confers on those who live together, but because it connects society either by a political or a national bond, gives to every people an interest in its neighbours, either because they are under the same government or because they are of the same race, and thus promotes the interests of humanity, of civilisation, and of religion.

Christianity rejoices at the mixture of races, as paganism identifies itself with their differences, because truth is universal, and errors various and particular. In the ancient world idolatry and nationality went together, and the same term is applied in Scripture to both. It was the mission of the Church to overcome national differences. The period of her undisputed supremacy was that in which all Western Europe obeyed the same laws, all literature was contained in one language, and the political unity of Christendom was personified in a single potentate, while its intellectual unity was represented in one university. As the ancient Romans concluded their conquests by carrying away the gods of the conquered people, Charlemagne overcame the national resistance of the Saxons only by the forcible destruction of their pagan rites. Out of the mediaeval period, and the combined action of the German race and the Church, came forth a new system of nations and a new conception of nationality. Nature was overcome in the nation as well as in the individual. In pagan and uncultivated times, nations were distinguished from each other by the widest diversity, not only in religion, but in customers, language, and character. Under the new law they had many things in common; the old barriers which separated them were removed, and the new principle of self-government, which Christianity imposed, enabled them to live together under the same authority, without necessarily losing their cherished habits, their customs, or their laws. The new idea of freedom made room for different races in one State. A nation was no longer what it had been to the ancient world,—the progeny of a common ancestor, or the aboriginal product of a particular region,—a result of merely physical and material causes,—but a moral and political being; not the creation of geographical or physiological unity, but developed in the course of history by the action of the State. It is derived from the State, not supreme over it. A State may in course of time produce a nationality; but that a nationality should constitute a State is contrary to the nature of modern civilisation. The nation derives its rights and its power from the memory of a former independence.

The Church has agreed in this respect with the tendency of political progress, and discouraged wherever she could the isolation of nations; admonishing them of their duties to each other, and regarding conquest and feudal investiture as the natural means of raising barbarous or sunken nations to a higher level. But though she has never attributed to national independence an immunity from the accidental consequences of feudal law, of hereditary claims, or of testamentary arrangements, she defends national liberty against uniformity and centralisation with an energy inspired by perfect community of interests. For the same enemy threatens both; and the State which is reluctant to tolerate differences, and to do justice to the peculiar character of various races, must from the same cause interfere in the internal government of religion. The connection of religious liberty with the emancipation of Poland or Ireland is not merely the accidental result of local causes; and the failure of the Concordat to unite the subjects of Austria is the natural consequence of a policy which did not desire to protect the provinces in their diversity and autonomy, and sought to bribe the Church by favours instead of strengthening her by independence. From this influence of religion in modern history has proceeded a new definition of patriotism.

The difference between nationality and the State is exhibited in the nature of patriotic attachment. Our connection with the race is merely natural or physical, whilst our duties to the political nation are ethical. One is a community of affections and instincts infinitely important and powerful in savage life, but pertaining more to the animal than to the civilised man; the other is an authority governing by laws, imposing obligations, and giving a moral sanction and character to the natural relations of society. Patriotism is in political life what faith is in religion, and it stands to the domestic feelings and to home-sickness as faith to fanaticism and to superstition. It has one aspect derived from private life and nature, for it is an extension of the family affections, as the tribe is an extension of the family. But in its real political character, patriotism consists in the development of the instinct of self-preservation into a moral duty which may involve self-sacrifice. Self-preservation is both an instinct and a duty, natural and involuntary in one respect, and at the same time a moral obligation. By the first it produces the family; by the last the State. If the nation could exist without the State, subject only to the instinct of self-preservation, it would be incapable of denying, controlling, or sacrificing itself; it would be an end and a rule to itself. But in the political order moral purposes are realised and public ends are pursued to which private interests and even existence must be sacrificed. The great sign of true patriotism, the development of selfishness into sacrifice, is the product of political life. That sense of duty which is supplied by race is not entirely separated from its selfish and instinctive basis; and the love of country, like married love, stands at the same time on a material and a moral foundation. The patriot must distinguish between the two causes or objects of his devotion. The attachment which is given only to the country is like obedience given only to the State—a submission to physical influences. The man who prefers his country before every other duty shows the same spirit as the man who surrenders every right to the State. They both deny that right is superior to authority.

The greatest adversary of the rights of nationality is the modern theory of nationality. By making the State and the nation commensurate with each other in theory, it reduces practically to a subject condition all other nationalities that may be within the boundary. It cannot admit them to an equality with the ruling nation which constitutes the States, because the State would then cease to be national, which would be a contradiction of the principle of its existence. According, therefore, to the degree of humanity and civilisation in that dominant body which claims all the rights of the community, the inferior races are exterminated, or reduced to servitude, or outlawed, or put in a condition of dependence.

If we take the establishment of liberty for the realisation of moral duties to be the end of civil society, we must conclude that those states are substantially the most perfect which, like the British and Austrian Empires, include various distinct nationalities without oppressing them. Those in which no mixture of races has occurred are imperfect; and those in which its effects have disappeared are decrepit. A State which is incompetent to satisfy different races condemns itself; a State which labours to neutralise, to absorb, or to expel them, destroys its own vitality; a State which does not include them is destitute of the chief basis of self-government. The theory of nationality, therefore, is a retrograde step in history. It is the most advanced form of the revolution, and must retain its power to the end of the revolutionary period, of which it announces the approach.

GIUSEPPE MAZZINI

2. *Humanitarian Nationalism**

I

Young Europe is an association of men believing in a future of liberty, equality, and fraternity, for all mankind; and desirous of consecrating their thoughts and actions to the realisation of that future.

GENERAL PRINCIPLES

II

One sole God;
One sole ruler,—His Law;
One sole interpreter of that law,—Humanity.

III

To constitute humanity in such wise as to enable it throughout a continuous progress to discover and apply the law of God by which it should be governed, as speedily as possible: such is the mission of *Young Europe*.

IV

As our true well-being consists in living in accordance with the law of our being, the knowledge and fulfilment of the law of humanity is the sole source of good. The fulfilment of the mission of *Young Europe* will result in the general good.

V

Every mission constitutes a pledge of duty.
Every man is bound to consecrate his every faculty to its fulfilment. He will derive his rule of action from the profound conviction of that duty.

VI

Humanity can only arrive at the knowledge of its Law of Life through the free and harmonious development of all its faculties.
Humanity can only reduce that knowledge to action through the free and harmonious development of all its faculties.
Association is the sole means of realising this development.

* From "Pact of Fraternity of Young Europe" (1834); reprinted in *Life and Writings of Joseph Mazzini*, III (Smith, Elder and Co., 1905).

VII

No true association is possible save among free men and equals.

VIII

By the law of God, given by Him to humanity, all men are free, are brothers, and are equals.

IX

Liberty is the right of every man to exercise his faculties without impediment or restraint, in the accomplishment of his special mission, and in the choice of the means most conducive to its accomplishment.

X

The free exercise of the faculties of the individual may in no case violate the rights of others. The special mission of each man must be accomplished in harmony with the general mission of humanity. There is no other limit to human liberty.

XI

Equality implies the recognition of uniform rights and duties for all men —for none may escape the action of the law by which they are defined— and every man should participate, in proportion to his labour, in the enjoyment of the produce resulting from the activity of all the social forces.

XII

Fraternity is the reciprocal affection, the sentiment which inclines man to do unto others as he would that others would do unto him.

XIII

All privilege is a violation of Equality.
All arbitrary rule is a violation of Liberty.
Every act of egotism is a violation of Fraternity.

XIV

Wheresoever privilege, arbitrary rule, or egotism are introduced into the social constitution, it is the duty of every man who comprehends his own mission to combat them by every means in his power.

XV

That which is true of each individual with regard to the other individuals forming a part of the society to which he belongs, is equally true of every people with regard to humanity.

XVI

By the law of God, given by God to humanity, all the peoples are free—are brothers and are equals.

XVII

Every people has its special mission, which will co-operate towards the fulfilment of the general mission of humanity. That mission constitutes its *nationality*. Nationality is sacred.

XVIII

All unjust rule, all violence, every act of egotism exercised to the injury of a people, is a violation of the liberty, equality, and fraternity of the peoples. All the peoples should aid and assist each other in putting an end to it.

XIX

Humanity will only be truly constituted when all the peoples of which it is composed have acquired the free exercise of their sovereignty, and shall be associated in a Republican Confederation, governed and directed by a common Declaration of Principles and a common Pact, towards the common aim—the discovery and fulfilment of the Universal Moral Law.

ERNEST RENAN

3. *What Is a Nation?**

I propose to ask you to join with me in analysing an idea which, though it appears simple, yet lends itself to the most dangerous misunderstandings. Human society assumes the most varied forms, great masses of human beings, such as we see in China, in Egypt and in the older Babylonia; the tribe as exemplified by the Hebrews and Arabs; the city, as in Athens and Sparta; the unions of various countries, as in the Achaemenian, Roman and Carlovingian empires; communities having no mother country but held together by the bond of religion, as the Israelites and the Parsees; nations such as France, England and most modern European autonomous States; confederations, as in Switzerland and America; relationships, such as those set up by race, or rather by language, between the different branches of Ger-

* (1882; trans. by Alfred Zimmern, Oxford University Press, 1939). By permission.

mans or Slavs: all these various groupings exist, or have existed, and to ignore the differences between them is to create a serious confusion. At the time of the French Revolution it was believed that the institutions of small independent towns, such as Sparta and Rome, could be applied to our great nations comprising thirty or forty million inhabitants. Nowadays, we observe a graver error. The terms "race" and "nation" are confused, and we see attributed to ethnographic, or rather linguistic, groups a sovereignty analogous to that of actually existing peoples. Let us try to arrive at some degree of exactness with regard to these difficult questions in which the least confusion at the outset of the argument as to the meaning of words may lead in the end to the most fatal errors. Our task is a delicate one; it amounts almost to vivisection; and we are going to treat the living as usually we treat the dead. We shall proceed coldly and with the most complete impartiality.

I

Since the end of the Roman Empire, or rather since the dismemberment of the empire of Charlemagne, Western Europe appears to us as divided into nations, some of which have, at certain periods, tried to establish a hegemony over others, without ever achieving any permanent success. Where Charles V, Louis XIV and Napoleon I failed, no man in the future will probably ever succeed. To set up a new Roman Empire or a new empire such as that of Charlemagne has become an impossibility. Europe is so much divided that any attempt at universal domination would immediately produce a coalition that would compel the ambitious nation to retire within its natural limits. A kind of durable balance has been established. Centuries may pass, but France, England, Germany and Russia, in spite of all their adventures, will retain their distinct historical individuality, like pieces on a draughtboard, the squares of which are ever varying in size and importance, but never quite blend completely.

Nations, thus conceived, are a fairly recent phenomenon in history. Such nations were unknown in ancient times. Egypt, China and old Chaldaea were by no manner of means nations. They were flocks led by an offspring of the Sun or an offspring of Heaven. There were no Egyptian citizens, any more than there are Chinese citizens. The classical antique world had its republics and royal towns, its confederations of local republics and its empires, but it hardly had a nation in our sense of the word. Athens, Sparta, Sidon and Tyre are small centres of patriotism, however admirable; they are cities possessing relatively small territories. Gaul, Spain and Italy, before their absorption into the Roman Empire, were assemblies of tribes, often in league with one another, but without central institutions or dynasties. Nor could the empires of Assyria or Persia or that of Alexander point to any mother country. There were never any Assyrian patriots; nor was the empire of Persia anything but a vast feudal estate. There is not a nation that traces its origin back to Alexander's colossal enterprise, which was yet so fertile in its consequences for the general history of civilisation.

The Roman Empire came much nearer to being a mother country. Roman rule, at first so hard to bear, very soon became loved in return for the immense benefit conferred by the suppression of war. It was a grand association, synonymous with order, peace and civilization. During its closing period, men of lofty mind, enlightened clerics and the educated classes had a real sense of "the Roman Peace," as opposed to the menacing chaos of barbarism. But an empire twelve times as great as France is to-day could not be termed a State in the modern sense of the word. The split between East and West was inevitable. In the third century attempts at a Gallic empire failed; and it was the Germanic invasion that ushered into the world the principle which afterwards served as a basis for the existence of nationalities.

What in fact did the Germanic peoples accomplish from the time of their great invasions in the fifth century to the last Norman conquests in the tenth? They effected little change in the essential character of races, but they imposed dynasties and a military aristocracy on more or less important areas within the former empire of the West, and these areas assumed the names of their invaders. Hence we have a France, a Burgundy, a Lombardy, and—later on—a Normandy. The rapid superiority won by the Frankish Empire renewed, for a brief period, the unity of the West. But about the middle of the ninth century this empire was shattered beyond repair. The Treaty of Verdun laid down its dividing lines, immutable in principle, and from that time France, Germany, England, Italy and Spain march forward, by ways often tortuous and beset by countless hazards, to their full national existence such as we see spread out before us to-day.

What is, in fact, the distinguishing mark of these various States? It is the fusion of the populations that compose them. There is no analogy between the countries we have just mentioned and the state of affairs in Turkey, where Turk, Slav, Greek, Armenian, Arab, Syrian and Kurd are as distinct to-day as at the time of the conquest. Two essential circumstances contributed to this result. First, the fact that the Germanic peoples adopted Christianity as soon as they came into more or less permanent contact with the Greek and Latin peoples. When victor and vanquished have the same religion, or rather when the victor adopts the religion of the vanquished, there can be no question of the Turkish system of complete discrimination according to a man's religion. The second circumstance was that the victors forgot their own language. The grandsons of Clovis, Alaric, Gondebaud, Alboin and Rollo spoke the Roman tongue. This fact was itself the consequence of another important particular circumstance, viz., that the Franks, Burgundians, Goths, Lombards and Normans were accompanied by very few women of their own race. During several generations the chiefs married none but German wives. But their concubines and their children's nurses were Latins, and the whole tribe married Latin women, with the result that, from the time of the settlement of the Franks and Goths on Roman soil, the *lingua franca* and the *lingua gothica* had but a very short career. It was not so in England, since the Anglo-Saxon invaders doubtless brought wives with them. The British population fled before them, and furthermore, Latin was no longer, or rather had never been, the dominant language in Britain. If, in the fifth century, Old French had been the general language in Gaul, Clovis and his men would not have deserted their Germanic tongue in favour of Old French.

Hence we get the following most important result, namely that, in spite of the brutality of the invaders, the pattern laid down by them became, in the course of time, the very pattern of the nation. Quite rightly, France became the name of a country containing but an imperceptible minority of Franks. In the tenth century, in the early songs of Charlemagne, which perfectly reflect the spirit of the age, all the inhabitants of France appear as Frenchmen. The idea of any difference of race in the population of France, which stands out so clearly in Gregory of Tours, does not occur at all in French writers or poets after the time of Hugh Capet. The difference between noble and serf is accentuated to the highest degree, but it is in no sort of way an ethnic difference. It is a difference in courage, custom and education, transmitted by birth. The idea that the origin of all this lies in conquest occurs to no one. Already in the thirteenth century we see established, with all the force of dogma, the spurious system according to which nobility owed its origin to a privilege conferred by the King in recognition of great services rendered to the nation, so that every noble is a man ennobled. The same thing happened after almost all the Norman conquests; after one or two generations the Norman invaders were no longer distinguishable from the rest of the population. Nevertheless, they had exercised a marked influence, having given to the conquered country a nobility, military habits and a feeling of patriotism—things which it had never known before.

To forget and—I will venture to say—to get one's history wrong, are essential factors in the making of a nation; and thus the advance of historical studies is often a danger to nationality. Historical research, in fact, casts fresh light upon those deeds of violence which have marked the origin of all political formations, even of those which have been followed by the most beneficial results. Unity is always realized by brute force. The union of North and South in France was the result of a reign of terror and extermination carried on for nearly a century. The French monarchy, which is generally regarded as typifying a steady process of crystallization and as having brought about the most perfect example of national unity known to history, when studied more closely loses its glamour. It was cursed by the nation that it was engaged in moulding, and to-day it is only those who can see the past in perspective who can appreciate the value of its achievement.

These great laws in the history of Western Europe become obvious by contrast. Many countries have failed in such an enterprise as that which the king of France, partly by his tyranny and partly by his justice, brought to so admirable a conclusion. Beneath the crown of St. Stephen, Magyars and Slavs have remained as distinct as they were eight hundred years ago. The House of Habsburg, far from blending the diverse elements in its dominions, has kept them apart and often in opposition to each other. In Bohemia the Czech and German elements are superposed like oil and water in a glass. The Turkish policy of separating nationalities according to religion has had very much graver consequences, since it has entailed the ruin of the East. Take a town like Salonica or Smyrna, and you will find five or six communities, each with its own memories and almost nothing in common. Now it is of the essence of a nation that all individuals should have much in common, and further that they should all have forgotten much. No French citizen knows whether he is a Burgundian, an Alan, a Taifal or a Visigoth, while every French citizen must have forgotten the massacre of St. Bartholomew's and the massacres in the South in the thirteenth century. Not ten families in France can prove their Frankish descent, and even if they could, such a proof would be inherently unsound, owing to the innumerable unknown alliances capable of upsetting all genealogical systems.

The modern nation is, therefore, the historic consequence of a series of facts converging towards the same point. Sometimes unity has been brought about by a dynasty, as in the case of France; at other times it has been brought about by the direct volition of provinces, as in the case of Holland, Switzerland and Belgium; or again, by a general sentiment, the tardy conqueror of the freaks of feudalism, as in the case of Italy and Germany. At all times such formations have been guided by the urge of some deep-seated reason. In such cases, principles burst out with the most unexpected surprises. In our own times we have seen Italy unified by its defeats and Turkey demolished by its victories. Every defeat advanced the Italian cause, while every victory served to ruin Turkey, since Italy is a nation, and Turkey, apart from Asia Minor, is not. It is to the glory of France that, by the French Revolution, she proclaimed that a nation exists of itself. It is not for us to disapprove of imitators. The principle of nations is our principle. But what, then, is a nation? Why is Holland a nation, while Hanover and the Grand Duchy of Parma are not? How is it that France persists in being a nation, when the principle that created her has vanished? Why is Switzerland, with its three languages, its two religions and three or four races, a nation, when Tuscany, for example, which is so homogeneous, is not? Why is Austria a state and not a nation? In what does the principle of nations differ from that of races? These are points on which thoughtful men require, for their own peace of mind, to come to some conclusion. Although the affairs of the world are rarely settled by arguments of this nature, yet studious men like to bring reason to bear on these questions, and to unravel the skein of confusion that entangles the superficial mind.

II

We are told by certain political theorists that a nation is, above all, a dynasty representing a former conquest that has been at first accepted, and then forgotten, by the mass of the people. According to these politicians, the grouping of provinces effected by a dynasty, its wars, marriages and treaties, ends with the dynasty that has formed it. It is quite true that most modern nations have been made by a family of feudal origin, which has married into the country and provided some sort of centralizing nucleus. The boundaries of France in 1789 were in no way natural or necessary. The large area that the House of Capet had added to the narrow strip accorded by the Treaty of Verdun was indeed the personal acquisition of that family. At the time when the annexations were made no one thought about natural limits, the right of nations or the wishes of provinces. Similarly, the union of England, Ireland and Scotland was a dynastic performance. The only reason Italy took so long to become a nation was that, until the present century, none of her numerous reigning families became a centre of union. It is an odd fact that she derives the royal [1] title from the obscure island of Sardinia, a land which is scarcely Italian. Holland, self-created by an act of heroic resolution, has none the less entered into a close bond of marriage with the House of Orange, and would run serious risks, should this union ever be endangered.

Is, however, such a law absolute? Doubtless, it is not. Switzerland and the United States which have been formed, like conglomerates, by successive additions, are based on no dynasty. I will not discuss the question in so far as it concerns France. One would have to be able to read the future in order to do so. Let us merely observe that this great French line of kings had become so thoroughly identified with the national life that, on the morrow of its downfall, the nation was able to subsist without it. Furthermore, the eighteenth century had entirely changed the situation. After centuries of humiliation, man had recovered his ancient spirit, his self-respect and the idea of his rights. The words "mother country" and "citizen" had regained their meaning. Thus it was possible to carry out the boldest operation ever performed in history—an operation that may be compared to what, in physiology, would be an attempt to bring back to its former life a body from which brain and heart had been removed.

It must, therefore, be admitted that a nation can exist without any dynastic principle, and even that nations formed by dynasties can be separated from them without thereby ceasing to exist. The old principle, which takes into

---

[1] The House of Savoy owes its royal title solely to the possession of Sardinia (1720).

account only the right of princes, can no longer be maintained: and, besides dynastic right, there exists also national right. On what criterion is this national right to be based? By what sign is it to be known? And from what tangible fact is it properly to be derived?

1. Many will boldly reply, from race. The artificial divisions, they say, the results of feudalism, royal marriages and diplomatic congresses, have broken down. Race is what remains stable and fixed; and this it is that constitutes a right and a lawful title. The Germanic race, for example, according to this theory, has the right to retake the scattered members of the Germanic family, even when these members do not ask for reunion. The right of the Germanic family over such-and-such a province is better than the right of its inhabitants over themselves. A sort of primordial right is thus created analogous to the divine right of kings; and the principle of ethnography is substituted for that of nations. This is a very grave error, and if it should prevail, it would spell the ruin of European civilization. The principle of the primordial right of race is as narrow and as fraught with danger for true progress as the principle of nations is just and legitimate.

We admit that, among the tribes and cities of the ancient world, the fact of race was of capital importance. The ancient tribe and city were but an extension of the family. In Sparta and Athens all citizens were related more or less closely to each other. It was the same among the Beni-Israel; and it is still so among the Arab tribes. But let us leave Athens, Sparta and the Jewish tribe and turn to the Roman Empire. Here we have quite a different state of affairs. This great agglomeration of completely diverse towns and provinces, formed in the first place by violence and then held together by common interests, cuts at the very root of the racial idea. Christianity, characteristically universal and absolute, works even more effectively in the same direction. It contracts a close alliance with the Roman Empire, and, under the influence of these two incomparable unifying agents, the ethnographic argument is for centuries dismissed from the government of human affairs.

In spite of appearances, the barbarian invasions were a step further on this road. The barbarian kingdoms which were then cut out have nothing ethnographic about them; they were decided by the forces or whims of the conquerors, who were completely indifferent with regard to the race of the peoples whom they subjugated. Charlemagne reconstructed in his own way what Rome had already built, viz., a single empire composed of the most diverse races. The authors of the Treaty of Verdun, calmly drawing their two long lines from north to south, did not pay the slightest attention to the race of the peoples to right or left of them. The frontier changes which took place in the later Middle Ages were also devoid of all ethnographic tendencies. Let it be granted that the consistent policy of the Capets managed more or less to gather together, under the name of France, the territories of ancient Gaul; yet this was by no means the consequence of any tendency on the part of their inhabitants to unite themselves with their kindred. Dauphiné, Bresse, Provence and Franche-Comté no longer remembered any common origin. The consciousness of Gallic race had been lost since the second century A.D., and it is only in modern times, and retrospectively, that the erudite have unearthed the peculiarities of the Gallic character.

Ethnographic considerations have, therefore, played no part in the formation of modern nations. France is Celtic, Iberic and Germanic. Germany is Germanic, Celtic and Slav. Italy is the country in which ethnography finds its greatest difficulties. Here Gauls, Etruscans, Pelasgians and Greeks are crossed in an unintelligible medley. The British Isles, taken as a whole, exhibit a mixture of Celtic and Germanic blood, the proportions of which are particularly difficult to define.

The truth is that no race is pure, and that to base politics on ethnographic analysis is tantamount to basing it on a chimera. The noblest countries, England, France and Italy, are those where breeds are most mixed. Is Germany an exception in this respect? Is she a purely Germanic country? What a delusion to suppose it! All the South was Gallic; and all the East, starting from the Elbe, is Slav. And as for those areas which are said to be really pure from the racial point of view, are they in fact so? Here we touch on one of those problems concerning which it is most important to have clear ideas and to prevent misunderstandings.

Discussions on race are endless, because the word "race" is taken by historians who are philologists and by anthropologists with physiological leanings in two quite different senses. For the anthropologists race has the same meaning as it has in zoology: it connotes real descent—blood relationship. Now the study of languages and history does not lead to the same divisions as physiology. The words "brachycephalic" and "dolichocephalic" find no place either in history or philology. Within the human group that created the Aryan tongues and the Aryan rules of life there were already brachycephalics and dolichocephalics; and the same must be said of the primitive group that created the languages and institutions termed Semitic. In other words, the zoological origins of the human race are vastly anterior to the origins of culture, civilization and language. The primitive Aryan, Semitic and Turanian groups were joined in no physiological unity. These groupings are historical facts which took place at a certain period, let us say fifteen or twenty thousand years ago; whereas the zoological origin of the human race is lost in impenetrable darkness. What the sciences of philology and history call the Germanic race is assuredly a quite distinct family among human kind. But is it a family in the anthropological sense? Certainly not. The distinctive German character appears in history only a very few centuries before Jesus Christ. Obviously the Germans did not emerge from the earth at that period. Before that time, when mingled with the Slavs in the great shadowy mass of Scythians, they possessed no distinctive character.

An Englishman is certainly a type in the whole sum of human kind. Now the type of what is very incorrectly termed the Anglo-Saxon race[2] is neither the Briton of the time of Caesar, nor the Anglo-Saxon of Hengist, nor the Dane of Canute, nor the Norman of William the Conqueror: it is the sum total of all these. The Frenchman is neither a Gaul, nor a Frank, nor a Burgundian. He is that which has emerged from the great cauldron in which, under the eye of the king of France, the most diverse elements have been simmering. As regards his origin, an inhabitant of Jersey or Guernsey differs in no way from the Norman population of the neighbouring coast. In the eleventh century the most piercing gaze would not have perceived the slightest difference on either side of the strait. Trifling circumstances decided Philip Augustus not to take these islands together with the rest of Normandy. Separated from each other for nearly seven hundred years, the two peoples have become not only foreign to each other, but entirely dissimilar. Race, then, as we historians understand it, is something that is made and unmade. The study of race is of prime importance for the man of learning engaged on the history of human kind. It is not applicable to politics. The instinctive consciousness which has presided over the drawing of the map of Europe has held race to be no account, and the leading nations of Europe are those of essentially mixed breed.

The fact of race, therefore, while vitally important at the outset, tends always to become less so. There is an essential difference between human history and zoology. Here race is not everything, as it is with the rodents and the cats; and one has no right to go about feeling people's heads, and then taking them by the throat and saying "You are related to us; you belong to us!" Apart from anthropological characteristics, there are such things as reason, justice, truth and beauty, which are the same for all. For another thing, this ethnographic policy is not safe. To-day you may exploit it against others; and then you see it turned against yourself. Is it certain that the Germans, who have so boldly hoisted the banner of ethnography, will not see the Slavs arrive and, in their turn, analyse village names in Saxony and Lusatia; or seek out the traces of the Wiltzes or the Obotrites; or say that they have come to settle accounts arising out of the massacres and wholesale enslavements inflicted upon their ancestors by the Ottos? It is an excellent thing for us all to know how to forget.

I like ethnography very much, and find it a peculiarly interesting science. But as I wish it to be free, I do not wish it to be applied to politics. In ethnography, as in all branches of learning, systems change. It is the law of progress. Should nations then also change together with the systems? The

---

[2] Germanic elements are not much more important in the United Kingdom than they were in France at the time when she possessed Alsace and Metz. The Germanic language prevailed in the British Isles solely because Latin had not completely ousted the Celtic forms of speech there, as was the case in the Gauls.

boundaries of states would follow the fluctuations of the science; and patriotism would depend on a more or less paradoxical dissertation. The patriot would be told: "You were mistaken: you shed your blood in such-and-such a cause; you thought you were a Celt; no, you are a German." And then, ten years later, they will come and tell you that you are a Slav. Lest we put too great a strain upon Science, let us excuse the lady from giving an opinion on problems in which so many interests are involved. For you may be sure that, if you make her the handmaid of diplomacy, you will often catch her in the very act of granting other favours. She has better things to do: so let us ask her just to tell the truth.

2. What we have said about race, applies also to language. Language invites union, without, however, compelling it. The United States and England, as also Spanish America and Spain, speak the same language without forming a single nation. Switzerland, on the contrary, whose foundations are solid because they are based on the assent of the various parties, contains three or four languages. There exists in man a something which is above language: and that is his will. The will of Switzerland to be united, in spite of the variety of these forms of speech, is a much more important fact than a similarity of language, often attained by vexatious measures. It is to the honour of France that she has never tried to attain unity of language by the use of coercion. Is it impossible to cherish the same feelings and thoughts and to love the same things in different languages? We were talking just now of the objections to making international politics dependent on ethnography. It would be no less objectionable to make them depend on comparative philology. Let us allow full liberty of discussion to these interesting branches of learning, and not mix them up with what would disturb their serenity. The political importance ascribed to languages comes from regarding them as tokens of race. Nothing could be more unsound. In Prussia, where nothing but German is now spoken, Russian was spoken a few centuries ago; in Wales, English is spoken; in Gaul and Spain, the original speech of Alba Longa; in Egypt, Arabic; and we could cite any number of other examples. Even in the beginning of things, similarity of language did not imply that of race. Take the proto-Aryan or proto-Semitic tribe. It contained slaves speaking the same language as their masters, whereas the slave very often differed from his master in race. We must repeat that these divisions into Indo-European, Semitic and other languages, which have been laid down by comparative philologists with such admirable acumen, do not coincide with those laid down by anthropology. Languages are historical formations which afford little clue to the descent of those who speak them and which, in any case, cannot be permitted to fetter human liberty, when it is a question of deciding with what family one is to be linked for life and death.

This exclusive importance attributed to language has, like the exaggerated attention paid to race, its dangers and its objections. If you overdo it, you shut yourself up within a prescribed culture which you regard as the national culture. You are confined and immured, having left the open air of the great world outside to shut yourself up in a conventicle together with your compatriots. Nothing could be worse for the mind; and nothing could be more untoward for civilization. Let us not lose sight of this fundamental principle that man, apart from being penned up within the bounds of one language or another, apart from being a member of one race or another, or the follower of one culture or another, is above all a reasonable moral being. Above French, German or Italian culture, there stands human culture. Consider the great men of the Renaissance. They were neither French, nor Italian, nor German. By their intercourse with the ancient world, they had rediscovered the secret of the true education of the human mind, and to that they devoted themselves body and soul. How well they did!

3. Nor can religion provide a satisfactory basis for a modern nationality. In its origin, religion was connected with the very existence of the social group, which itself was an extension of the family. The rites of religion were family rites. The religion of Athens was the cult of Athens itself, of its mythical founders, its laws and customs. This religion, which did not involve any dogmatic theology, was, in the full sense of the words, a state religion. Those who refused to practice it were not Athenians. At bottom it was the cult of the personified Acropolis; and to swear on the altar of Aglauros[8] amounted to an oath to die for one's country. This religion was the equivalent of our drawing lots for military service or of our cult of the national flag. To refuse to participate in such cult would have been tantamount to a refusal nowadays to serve in the army, and to a declaration that one was not an Athenian. On the other hand, it is clear that such a cult as this meant nothing for those who were not Athenians; so there was no proselytising to compel foreigners to accept it, and the slaves of Athens did not practice it. The same was the case in certain small republics of the Middle Ages. No man was a good Venetian if he did not swear by St. Mark; nor a good citizen of Amalfi if he did not set St. Andrew above all the other saints in Paradise. In these small societies, acts, which in later times became the grounds for persecution and tyranny, were justifiable and were as trivial as it is with us to wish the father of the family many happy returns of his birthday or a happy new year.

What was true of Sparta and Athens was no longer so in the kingdoms that emerged from the conquests of Alexander, and still less so in the Roman Empire. The persecutions carried out by Antiochus Epiphanes to induce the Eastern world to worship the Olympian Jove, like those of the Roman Empire to maintain the farce of a state religion, were mistaken, criminal and really absurd. Nowadays the situation is perfectly clear, since

[8] Aglauros, who gave her life to save her country, represents the Acropolis itself.

the masses no longer have any uniform belief. Every one believes and practices religion in his own way according to his capacities and wishes. State religion has ceased to exist; and a man can be a Frenchman, an Englishman or a German, and at the same time a Catholic, a Protestant or a Jew, or practice no form of worship at all. Religion has become a matter to be decided by the individual according to his conscience, and nations are no longer divided into Catholic and Protestant. Religion which, fifty-two years ago, was so important a factor in the formation of Belgium, is still equally so in the heart of every man; but it is now barely to be reckoned among the reasons that determine national frontiers.

4. Community of interest is certainly a powerful bond between men. But do interests suffice to make a nation? I do not believe it. Community of interest brings about commercial treaties. Nationality, which is body and soul both together, has its sentimental side: and a Customs Union is not a country.

5. Geography, and what we call natural frontiers, certainly plays a considerable part in the division of nations. Geography is one of the essential factors of history. Rivers have guided races: mountains have impeded them. The former have favoured, while the latter have restricted, historic movements. But can one say, as some people believe, that a nation's boundaries are to be found written on the map, and that it has the right to award itself as much as is necessary to round off certain outlines, or to reach such-and-such a mountain or river, which are regarded as in some way dispensing the frontier a priori? I know no doctrine more arbitrary or fatal than this, which can be used to justify all kinds of violence. In the first place, is it the mountains, or is it the rivers that constitute these alleged natural frontiers? It is indisputable that mountains separate; but rivers tend rather to bring together. Then again all mountains cannot divide states. Which are those that separate and those that do not? From Biarritz to Tornea there is not one estuary which is more like a boundary than another. If History had so decreed, then the Loire, the Seine, the Meuse, the Elbe and the Oder would have, as much as the Rhine has, this character of national frontier, which has been the cause of so many infringements of that fundamental right, which is the will of men. People talk of strategic grounds. Nothing is absolute; and it is evident that much must be conceded to necessity. But these concessions must not go too far. Otherwise, every one will demand what suits him from a military point of view and we shall have endless warfare. No; it is not the soil any more than the race which makes a nation. The soil provides the substratum, the field for struggle and labour: man provides the soul. Man is everything in the formation of this sacred thing that we call a people. Nothing that is material suffices here. A nation is a spiritual principle, the result of the intricate workings of history; a spiritual family and not a group determined by the configuration of the earth.

We have now seen those things which do not suffice to create such a spiritual principle. They are race, language, interests, religious affinity, geography and military necessity. What more then is required? In view of what I have already said, I shall not have to detain you very much longer.

III

A nation is a soul, a spiritual principle. Two things, which are really only one, go to make up this soul or spiritual principle. One of these things lies in the past, the other in the present. The one is the possession in common of a rich heritage of memories; and the other is actual agreement, the desire to live together, and the will to continue to make the most of the joint inheritance. Man cannot be improvised. The nation, like the individual, is the fruit of a long past spent in toil, sacrifice and devotion. Ancestor-worship is of all forms the most justifiable, since our ancestors have made us what we are. A heroic past, great men and glory—I mean real glory—these should be the capital of our company when we come to found a national idea. To share the glories of the past, and a common will in the present; to have done great deeds together, and to desire to do more—these are the essential conditions of a people's being. Love is in proportion to the sacrifices one has made and the evils one has borne. We love the house that we have built and that we hand down to our successors. The Spartan song "We are what ye were, and we shall be what ye are," is, in its simplicity, the abridged version of every national anthem.

In the past, a heritage of glory and of grief to be shared; in the future, one common plan to be realized; to have suffered, rejoiced and hoped together; these are things of greater value than identity of custom-houses and frontiers in accordance with strategic notions. These are things which are understood, in spite of differences in race and language. I said just now "to have suffered together," for indeed common suffering unites more strongly than common rejoicing. Among national memories, sorrows have greater value than victories; for they impose duties and demand common effort. Thus we see that a nation is a great solid unit, formed by the realization of sacrifices in the past, as well as of those one is prepared to make in the future. A nation implies a past; while, as regards the present, it is all contained in one tangible fact, viz., the agreement and clearly expressed desire to continue a life in common. The existence of a nation is (if you will forgive me the metaphor) a daily plebiscite, just as that of the individual is a continual affirmation of life. I am quite aware that this is less metaphysical than the doctrine of divine right, and smacks less of brute force than alleged historic right. According to the notions that I am expounding, a nation has no more right than a king to say to a province: "You belong to me; so I will take you." A province means to us its inhabitants; and if any one has a right to be consulted in the matter, it is the inhabitant. It is never to the true interest of a nation to annex or keep a country against its will. The people's wish is after all the only justifiable criterion, to which we must always come back.

We have excluded from politics the abstract principles of metaphysics and theology; and what remains? There remains man, with his desires and his needs. But you will tell me that the consequences of a system that puts these ancient fabrics at the mercy of the wishes of usually unenlightened minds, will be the secession and ultimate disintegration of nations. It is obvious that in such matters no principles should be pushed too far, and that truths of this nature are applicable only as a whole and in a very general sort of way. Human wishes change indeed: but what in this world does not? Nations are not eternal. They have had beginnings and will have ends; and will probably be replaced by a confederation of Europe. But such is not the law of the age in which we live. Nowadays it is a good, and even a necessary, thing that nations should exist. Their existence is the guarantee of liberty, which would be lost, if the world had but one law and one master.

By their various, and often contrasting, attainments, the nations serve the common task of humanity; and all play some instrument in that grand orchestral concert of mankind, which is, after all, the highest ideal reality that we attain. Taken separately, they all have their weak points; and I often tell myself that a man who should have the vices that are held to be virtues in nations, a man battening on empty glory, and so jealous, selfish and quarrelsome as to be ready to draw his sword at the slightest provocation, would be the most intolerable creature. But such discordant details vanish when all is taken together. What sufferings poor humanity has endured and what trials await it yet! May it be guided by the spirit of wisdom and preserved from the countless dangers that beset the path!

And now let me sum it all up. Man is the slave neither of his race, nor his language, nor his religion, nor of the windings of his rivers and mountain ranges. That moral consciousness which we call a nation is created by a great assemblage of men with warm hearts and healthy minds: and as long as this moral consciousness can prove its strength by the sacrifices demanded from the individual for the benefit of the community, it is justifiable and has the right to exist. If doubts arise concerning its frontiers, let the population in dispute be consulted: for surely they have a right to a say in the matter. This will bring a smile to the lips of the transcendental politicians, those infallible beings who spend their lives in self-deception and who, from the summit of their superior principles, cast a pitying eye upon our commonplaces. "Consult the population! Stuff and nonsense! This is only another of these feeble French ideas that aim at replacing diplomacy and war by methods of infantile simplicity." Well, let us wait a while. Let the kingdom of the transcendentalists endure for its season; and let us learn to submit to the scorn of the mighty. It may be, that after many fruitless fumblings, the world will come back to our modest empirical solutions. The art of being right in the future is, at certain times, the art of resigning oneself to being old-fashioned.

THOMAS G. MASARYK

4. *Democratic Nationalism**

We often discuss the question of our national character. The Romantics used to speak of a dove-like nature; today we prefer to lay stress on the sober, practical features of our character. Well then, what are we really like?

It is difficult to say. I am sceptical of the current definitions as to what constitutes national character; and also of those that other nations give themselves. Was Žizka a true Czech, or Hus, Chelčický, and Komenský? Dobrovský, Palacký, and Havlíček, or Hanka, and Jungman? I have read a book by a Swiss author about a dual France. Some people complain of our lack of concord as if it were characteristically Czech, and Slav, but the Germans complain about themselves in exactly the same way. And so on. The problem becomes more involved when we ask if and how national character changes at different times, and if there are some characteristic qualities that remain unchanged. There is also the point that from the earliest times until now there has been a considerable mixing of races and nations. There is no such thing as so-called "pure blood," at least not in Europe.

And besides: how and to what extent do economic conditions—prosperity, poverty, food, and occupation, technique, culture, religion, and morality, hygiene, and so on—form the national character? On the other hand one has to consider, how economic conditions, religion, and morality: how culture in general is determined, and to what extent by national character? For instance, is mathematics influenced by the nation, have French or English mathematics some special character, and what is it? Is Catholicism intrinsically Roman, Protestantism German, and the Orthodox Church Slav?

I won't deny that nations have their characters, both physical, and spiritual, but I do not regard anthropological and ethnological notions as already so certain that one could deduce from them the history of nations, and devise the right politics.

First of all, in our history nearly three hundred years are lacking of a full

* From Thomas G. Masaryk, *On Thought and Life: Conversations with Karel Čapek* (1938). By permission of The Macmillan Company, publishers.

and free political and spiritual life; from that I would explain the immaturity in our politics; I do not deduce our shortcomings in politics from the character of the nation.

Secondly, as a society we are without traditions; the folk tradition of the peasantry is breaking up, and we have no other; almost every one of us has come from cottages, and we have not yet had time to get ourselves into shape.

And further: I ask you how long ago is it since the Moravians felt themselves to be something different from the Czechs, and talked of a Moravian "nation"? And now the Slovaks have been joined to us, and people speak of two nations. And it would not only be a question of the definition of the character of one nation but also of the character of the various parts of the country; what for instance is the difference between a Moravian Valach and a Hanak? Therefore I repeat: we lived in subjection, and each subjection prevents the character from developing and expanding fully according to its inner law.

That is also visible in our literature. Our poetry is good but not our novels and drama. For poetry personal life is sufficient; novels and drama presuppose the accumulated expreience of generations; novels are a work of a whole century.

Yes—a small poem springing from a real strong impulse, many poets make a success of that. But that is just the expression of a peculiar personal feeling; the novel, and the drama are something different—an epical poem is too, they presuppose an artistic observation of the nation, society, classes, states, and so on. In our novels I take exception to some kind of unripeness, a restricted knowledge of one's own and foreign life, too little cosmopolitanism. We observe too little.

Foreigners say of us that we are talented, practical, industrious—well, thank God too for that. In fact our farmers, our workers, are some of the best; the urban and intellectual strata are still incomplete, but we Czechs had not begun to urbanize ourselves until sixty or eighty years ago—I can still remember what modest beginnings they were, and I can say what a fair part of the way we have gone since then.

We need fifty years of undisturbed development, and we shall be where we should like to be today. It is no blind confidence in our ability, and tenacity—our history, even if somewhat disjointed, the fact that in the great political storms we held our ground, and that during the world conflagration we managed to restore our state, that all testifies to our political ability. I do not think that I exaggerate if I say that our history is one of the most interesting—we are fine fellows, but we often make a false step. I find the German anthropologists' skull and brain indices place us among the foremost nations—we are gifted, no doubt about that, but we are somewhat unstable, not circumspect enough, and shall I say, politically green; and political inexperience is a fertile soil for demagogy, and of that we have more than enough. The discussions about the crisis of democracy, and the shortcomings of parliamentary government have to a large extent their origin in that insufficient experience; and from that also that parrot-like imitation of foreign politicalisms—in short, we do not think enough according to our own selves, and to what is ours. In the Austrian times we got used to the negation of the state—that was the result of the subjugation; we even made ourselves believe that we could not any longer be independent. Well, no not that, with that idea I could never become reconciled; but I knew that subject people, depressed and deformed by subjugation do not easily become free in spirit too at the wave of a hand. That is why so many people among us even today repudiate the state—by distrust, by resistance to the state administration, by their bad relations with whole strata of co-citizens—to put it frankly: there are still some who side with the thief rather than the policeman. Our people have a patriotic tradition, it is true, but on many occasions they are still too indifferent to the state, against the state, almost anarchical; they don't realize that it is the attitude of the old Austrian spirit. To de-Austrianize, that means to acquire a sense for the state, and what it stands for, for the democratic state. That we must ask not only from the bureaucracy, and the army, but also from all citizens. And not only the Czechs and the Slovaks.

Democracy must be livelier and sprightlier than the old régime—especially that one of ours. We must always bear in mind that we are a small nation in an unfavourable geographical position; in effect it imposes upon us the obligation to be more alert, to think more, to achieve more than the others; or according to Palacký: every self-respecting Czech and Slovak must do three times as much as the members of big and more favourably situated nations. Only bear in mind that every educated fellow countryman of ours needs to learn at least two foreign languages—how much time it takes, and work, but also what a gain it is not only for education but also for practical intercourse with nations! And so it is in everything: if we have to hold our own with honour we must thoroughly intensify all our political and cultural endeavour. Yes, it is a painstaking job; but who does not want to take trouble, don't let him talk of nation and patriotism.

Real love for one's nation is a very beautiful thing; with a decent and honest man it comes as a matter of course; therefore he does not talk much about it, just like a decent man does not go trumpeting abroad his love for his wife, family, and so on. A real love protects, bears sacrifices—and chiefly works. And for that work for the nation and state, a clear, sensible, political, and cultural programme is necessary—mere day-dreaming and getting excited is not enough. There is, after all, a difference between patriotism and jingoism; how much already did Havlíček struggle with that market-place jingoism, but for many it is as if he had never lived!

We must express our patriotism by a conscious public spirit. No doubt the state is ours, it is ours in virtue of historical right, according to the principle of the majority, and by the title that we have built; but we have considerable minorities, and therefore we must be conscious of the difference between a state, and a nation: a nation is a cultural organization, a state a political organization. We have duties towards the nation, and we have duties towards the state. Obviously they must not conflict. We have built that state, we must know how to manage and govern it; it is our task to win over to the idea of our democratic republic the minorities with whom we are living. Their numbers, and their civilization, impose both on them and on us a democratic concord. Our procedure with the minorities is practically given to us by our own experience under Austria-Hungary: what we did not like to be done unto us, we shall not do unto others. The programme of Palacký, the father of the nation, is valid for us, and for those to come. Our history, the policy of the Premyslids, of St. Venceslas, Charles, and George must be a model for the policy with our Germans. The fact that we are surrounded on all sides by a big German neighbour, impels a thoughtful Czech to cautious and definitely wise politics.

Isn't there sometimes a conflict between the love for one's nation and for humanity, or rather: between nationalism and the humanitarian ideals like pacifism, mutual understanding between nations, and such-like things?

Between the love for one's nation, the love for one's country, and humanity there is no disagreement; as it is, it is between modern nationalism and humanity. Already that new and foreign word indicates that patriotism as our revivalists demanded it, and lived it, is something different from the nationalism of today.

As far as our national programme is concerned, remember what I told you with regard to the development of Europe, and to our own history, that is that we must take a hand in world politics, and consequently be in lively and friendly contact with other nations. Our national revival is a child of Enlightenment and of late Romanticism, it sprang from the humanitarian ideals of the Eighteenth and Nineteenth Centuries which were broadcast in France, in Germany, everywhere. Humanity—that is indeed our national programme, the programme of Dobrovský, Havlíček, and of Komenský in his day, of our kings George, and Charles, and of St. Venceslas.

Humanity does not exclude, or weaken the love for one's nation; I can, nay, I must love my nation positively, but because of that I need not hate other nations. True love is not proved by hatred, but only by love. Mankind is a sum of nations, it is not something outside the nations, and above them. Humanity, love, not only for one's neighbours, but for mankind—how am I to imagine that mankind concretely? I see a poor child that I can help— that child is mankind to me. The community with which I share its troubles, the nation with which I am combined through speech and culture is mankind. Mankind is simply a greater, or smaller sum of people for whom we can do something positive in deed, and not only in words. Humanity does not consist in day-dreaming about the whole of mankind, but in always acting humanely. If I ask politics to serve mankind, I do not infer that they ought not to be national, but just and decent. That's all.

Not as individuals, not as nations are we here merely to fulfil our egoistic aims. A nation that wished to live only for itself would be just as miserable as a man who wanted to live only for himself. Without faith in ideas and in ideals the life of men and of nations is only stagnation.

This, of course, is the political credo of an idealist.

Not at all, my boy: of a realist, in philosophy and in politics. For me politically realism means: don't bury yourself in the recollection of a glorious past, work for a glorious present; don't put your faith only in words and slogans, for then you can improve the realities, and bring them to order; don't fly up in the clouds, but stick to your earth, it is the safest and least uncertain. Whatever you work for, stick to reality. . . .

Only reality?

Yes; but without doubt reality also means spirituality, soul, love, moral order, God, and eternity. Only with them do we live an entire life, in full and complete reality, whether it be the life of an individual, or the history of nations. That full life alone is without inner conflict, such a life alone has a true and clear meaning. . . .

and is a happy life.

Yes.

J. A. HOBSON

5. *Imperialism—Incompatible with Free Government**

Not only does aggressive Imperialism defeat the movement towards internationalism by fostering animosities among competing empires: its attack upon the liberties and the existence of weaker or lower races stimulates in them a corresponding excess of national self-consciousness. A nationalism that bristles with resentment and is all astrain with the passion of self-defence is only less perverted from its natural genius than the nationalism which glows with the animus of greed and self-aggrandisement at the expense of others. From this aspect aggressive Imperialism is an artificial stim-

* From J. A. Hobson, *Imperialism* (1902; third edition, 1928). By permission of The Macmillan Company, publishers.

ulation of nationalism in peoples too foreign to be absorbed and too compact to be permanently crushed. We welded Africanderdom into just such a strong dangerous nationalism, and we joined with other nations in creating a resentful nationalism until then unknown in China. The injury to nationalism in both cases consists in converting a cohesive, pacific internal force into an exclusive, hostile force, a perversion of the true power and use of nationality. The worst and most certain result is the retardation of internationalism. The older nationalism was primarily an inclusive sentiment; its natural relation to the same sentiment in another people was lack of sympathy, not open hostility; there was no inherent antagonism to prevent nationalities from growing and thriving side by side. Such in the main was the nationalism of the earlier nineteenth century, and the politicians of Free Trade had some foundation for their dream of a quick growth of effective, informal internationalism by peaceful, profitable intercommunication of goods and ideas among nations recognizing a just harmony of interests in free peoples.

The overflow of nationalism into imperial channels quenched all such hopes. While co-existent nationalities are capable of mutual aid involving no direct antagonism of interests, co-existent empires following each its own imperial career of territorial and industrial aggrandisement are natural necessary enemies. The full nature of this antagonism on its economic side is not intelligible without a close analysis of those conditions of modern capitalist production which compel an ever keener "fight for markets," but the political antagonism is obvious.

Imperialism and popular government have nothing in common: they differ in spirit, in policy, in method. Of policy and method I have already spoken; it remains to point out how the spirit of Imperialism poisons the springs of democracy in the mind and character of the people. As our free self-governing colonies have furnished hope, encouragement, and leading to the popular aspirations in Great Britain, not merely by practical successes in the arts of popular government, but by the wafting of a spirit of freedom and equality, so our despotically ruled dependencies have ever served to damage the character of our people by feeding the habits of snobbish subservience, the admiration of wealth and rank, the corrupt survivals of the inequalities of feudalism. This process began with the advent of the East Indian nabob and the West Indian planter into English society and politics, bringing back with his plunders of the slave trade and the gains of corrupt and extortionate officialism the acts of vulgar ostentation, domineering demeanour and corrupting largesse to dazzle and degrade the life of our people. Cobden, writing in 1860 of our Indian Empire, put this pithy question: "Is it not just possible that we may become corrupted at home by the reaction of arbitrary political maxims in the East upon our domestic politics, just as Greece and Rome were demoralised by their contact with Asia?" [1]

Not merely is the reaction possible, it is inevitable. As the despotic portion of our Empire has grown in area, a larger and larger number of men, trained in the temper and methods of autocracy as soldiers and civil officials in our Crown colonies, protectorates, and Indian Empire, reinforced by numbers of merchants, planters, engineers, and overseers, whose lives have been those of a superior caste living an artificial life removed from all the healthy restraints of ordinary European society, have returned to this country, bringing back the characters, sentiments, and ideas imposed by this foreign environment. The South and South-West of England is richly sprinkled with these men, many of them wealthy, most of them endowed with leisure, men openly contemptuous of democracy, devoted to material luxury, social display, and the shallower arts of intellectual life. The wealthier among them discover political ambitions, introducing into our Houses of Parliament the coarsest and most selfish spirit of "Imperialism," using their imperial experience and connexions to push profitable companies and concessions for their private benefits, and posing as authorities so as to keep the yoke of Imperialism firmly fixed upon the shoulders of the "nigger." The South African millionaire is the brand most in evidence: his methods are the most barefaced, and his success, social and political, the most redoubtable. But the practices which are writ large in Rhodes, Beit, and their parliamentary confederates are widespread on a smaller scale; the South of England is full of men of local influence in politics and society whose character has been formed in our despotic Empire, and whose incomes are chiefly derived from the maintenance and furtherance of this despotic rule. Not a few enter our local councils, or take posts in our constabulary or our prisons: everywhere they stand for coercion and for resistance to reform. Could the incomes expended in the Home Counties and other large districts of Southern Britain be traced to their sources, it would be found that they were in large measure wrung from the enforced toil of vast multitudes of black, brown, or yellow natives, by arts not differing essentially from those which supported in idleness and luxury imperial Rome.

It is, indeed, a nemesis of Imperialism that the arts and crafts of tyranny, acquired and exercised in our unfree Empire, should be turned against our liberties at home. Those who have felt surprise at the total disregard or the open contempt displayed by the aristocracy and the plutocracy of this land for infringements of the liberties of the subject and for the abrogation of constitutional rights and usages have not taken sufficiently into account the steady reflux of this poison of irresponsible autocracy from our "unfree, intolerant, aggressive" Empire.

[1] Morley, *Life of Cobden*, Vol. ii, p. 361.

The political effects, actual and necessary, of the new Imperialism, as illustrated in the case of the greatest of imperialist Powers, may be thus summarised. It is a constant menace to peace, by furnishing continual temptations to further aggression upon lands occupied by lower races and by embroiling our nation with other nations of rival imperial ambitions; to the sharp peril of war it adds the chronic danger and degradation of militarism, which not merely wastes the current physical and moral resources of the nations, but checks the very course of civilization. It consumes to an illimitable and incalculable extent the financial resources of a nation by military preparation, stopping the expenditure of the current income of the State upon productive public projects and burdening posterity with heavy loads of debt. Absorbing the public money, the time, interest and energy on costly and unprofitable work of territorial aggrandisement, it thus wastes those energies of public life in the governing classes and the nations which are needed for internal reforms and for the cultivation of the arts of material and intellectual progress at home. Finally, the spirit, the policy, and the methods of Imperialism are hostile to the institutions of popular self-government, favouring forms of political tyranny and social authority which are the deadly enemies of effective liberty and equality.

Analysis of Imperialism, with its natural supports, militarism, oligarchy, bureaucracy, protection, concentration of capital and violent trade fluctuations, has marked it out as the supreme danger of modern national States. The power of the imperialist forces within the nation to use the national resources for their private gain, by operating the instrument of the State, can only be overthrown by the establishment of a genuine democracy, the direction of public policy by the people for the people through representatives over whom they exercise a real control. Whether this or any other nation is yet competent for such a democracy may well be matter of grave doubt, but until and unless the external policy of a nation is "broad-based upon a people's will" there appears little hope of remedy. The scare of a great recent war may for a brief time check the confidence of these conspirators against the commonwealth, and cause them to hold their hands, but the financial forces freshly generated will demand new outlets, and will utilize the same political alliances and the same social, religious, and philanthropic supports in their pressure for new enterprises. The circumstances of each new imperialist exploit differ from those of all preceding ones: whatever ingenuity is requisite for the perversion of the public intelligence, or the inflammation of the public sentiment, will be forthcoming.

Imperialism is only beginning to realize its full resources, and to develop into a fine art the management of nations: the broad bestowal of a franchise, wielded by a people whose education has reached the stage of an uncritical ability to read printed matter, favours immensely the designs of keen business politicians, who, by controlling the press, the schools, and where necessary the churches, impose Imperialism upon the masses under the attractive guise of sensational patriotism.

The chief economic source of Imperialism has been found in the inequality of industrial opportunities by which a favoured class accumulates superfluous elements of income which, in their search for profitable investments, press ever farther afield: the influence on State policy of these investors and their financial managers secures a national alliance of other vested interests which are threatened by movements of social reform: the adoption of Imperialism thus serves the double purpose of securing private material benefits for favoured classes of investors and traders at the public cost, while sustaining the general cause of conservatism by diverting public energy and interest from domestic agitation to external employment.

The ability of a nation to shake off this dangerous usurpation of its power, and to employ the national resources in the national interest, depends upon the education of a national intelligence and a national will, which shall make democracy a political and economic reality. To term Imperialism a national policy is an impudent falsehood: the interests of the nation are opposed to every act of this expansive policy. Every enlargement of Great Britain in the tropics is a distinct enfeeblement of true British nationalism. Indeed, Imperialism is commended in some quarters for this very reason, that by breaking the narrow bounds of nationalities it facilitates and forwards internationalism. There are even those who favour or condone the forcible suppression of small nationalities by larger ones under the impulse of Imperialism, because they imagine that this is the natural approach to a world-federation and eternal peace. A falser view of political evolution it is difficult to conceive. If there is one condition precedent to effective internationalism or to the establishment of any reliable relations between States, it is the existence of strong, secure, well-developed, and responsible nations. Internationalism can never be subserved by the suppression or forcible absorption of nations; for these practices react disastrously upon the springs of internationalism, on the one hand setting nations on their armed defence and stifling the amicable approaches between them, on the other debilitating the larger nations through excessive corpulence and indigestion. The hope of a coming internationalism enjoins above all else the maintenance and natural growth of independent nationalities, for without such there could be no gradual evolution of internationalism, but only a series of unsuccessful attempts at a chaotic and unstable cosmopolitanism. As individualism is essential to any sane form of national socialism, so nationalism is essential to internationalism: no organic conception of world-politics can be framed on any other supposition.

Just in proportion as the substitution of true national governments for the existing oligarchies or sham democracies becomes possible will the apparent conflicts of national interests disappear, and the fundamental co-operation upon which nineteenth-century Free Trade prematurely relied manifest itself. The present class government means the severance or antagonism of nations, because each ruling class can only keep and use its rule by forcing the antagonisms of foreign policy: intelligent democracies would perceive their identity of interest, and would ensure it by their amicable policy. The genuine forces of internationalism, thus liberated, would first display themselves as economic forces, securing more effective international co-operation for postal, telegraphic, railway, and other transport services, for monetary exchange and for common standards of measurement of various kinds, and for the improved intercommunication of persons, goods, and information. Related and subsidiary to these purposes would come a growth of machinery of courts and congresses, at first informal and private, but gradually taking shape in more definite and more public machinery: the common interests of the arts and sciences would everywhere be weaving an elaborate network of intellectual internationalism, and both economic and intellectual community of needs and interests would contribute to the natural growth of such political solidarity as was required to maintain this real community.

It is thus, and only thus, that the existing false antagonisms of nations, with their wastes and perils and their retardation of the general course of civilization, can be resolved. To substitute for this peaceful discovery and expression of common interests a federal policy proceeding upon directly selfish political and military interests, the idea which animates an Anglo-Saxon alliance or a Pan-Teutonic empire, is deliberately to choose a longer, more difficult, and far more hazardous road to internationalism. The economic bond is far stronger and more reliable as a basis of growing internationalism than the so-called racial bond or a political alliance constructed on some short-sighted computation of a balance of power. It is, of course, quite possible that a Pan-Slav, Pan-Teutonic, Pan-British, or Pan-Latin alliance might, if the federation were kept sufficiently voluntary and elastic, contribute to the wider course of internationalism. But the frankly military purpose commonly assigned for such alliances bodes ill for such assistance. It is far more likely that such alliances would be formed in the interests of the "imperialist" classes of the contracting nations, in order the more effectively to exploit the joint national resources.

Imperialism is a depraved choice of national life, imposed by self-seeking interests which appeal to the lusts of quantitative acquisitiveness and of forceful domination surviving in a nation from early centuries of animal struggle for existence. Its adoption as a policy implies a deliberate renunciation of that cultivation of the higher inner qualities which for a nation as for an individual constitutes the ascendency of reason over brute impulse. It is the besetting sin of all successful States, and its penalty is unalterable in the order of nature.

Chapter XV

CONFLICT OR COMMON INTEREST?

One of the paradoxical phenomena of political philosophy is that those who demand absolute law and order within the state at the same time propound anarchy as the normal, and desirable, relationship between states. Hegel is a case in point. In his *Philosophy of Law* (1821), he advocates, as we saw in earlier chapters, the strong state—on the model of the Prussian police state of the nineteenth century. Yet, when it comes to the question of how states are to live together, Hegel is an enthusiastic anarchist. In fact, he is nihilistic enough to deny that relations between states have anything in common with morality, such as regulates dealings between individuals. There is a distinctly pagan note to Hegel's claim that "the nation state is mind in its substantive rationality and immediate actuality and is therefore the absolute power on earth." The whole Stoic-Jewish-Christian tradition, that there is a higher law than the commands of the state, a law of reason, nature, or God, is flatly rejected by Hegel. If the state is the absolute power on earth, what happens when several absolutes clash? Hegel cheerfully states: "If states disagree and their particular wills cannot be harmonized, the matter can only be settled by war." However, this consequence does not alarm Hegel. On the contrary. Wars are wholesome for a number of reasons. First, "corruption in nations would be the product of prolonged, let alone 'perpetual' peace." The trouble with peace is, says Hegel, that men stagnate in it. Their idiosyncrasies become more fixed and ossified, and war is required to keep the body politic healthy. Furthermore, Hegel stresses the impact of war on domestic conditions: "As a result of war, nations are strengthened, but peoples involved in civil strife also acquire peace at home through making war abroad." Later in the century Bismarck emphasized in his memoirs that war would be the only means to revive and maintain the loyalty of the masses who had become infected with the ideas of international socialism. By 1912 the Social Democrats had become the strongest single German party, with 35 per cent of the German electorate voting for it.

Small as the antimilitaristic voice was in Germany, it should not be forgotten. The trouble with German democracy and liberalism was not that they failed, but that so few tried to make them succeed. Immanuel Kant's name will always stand out as that of a man who believed that civilization can be advanced only through government based on law, within the nation

777

as well as between nations. In *Perpetual Peace* (1795), Kant has drawn one of the most inspiring pictures of a united mankind ever conceived. The federation of free states, held together by bonds of law rather than separated by savagery and "licentious liberty," is Kant's conception of international order. Kant makes the important point that a peace treaty (*pactum pacis*) finishes only a particular war, whereas a "pacific alliance" (*foedus pacificum*) would forever terminate all wars: "This alliance does not tend to any dominion over a state, but solely to the certain maintenance of the liberty of each particular state, partaking of this association." Whereas Hegel and Treitschke both embrace international anarchy and war as desirable and moral, Kant states the rational aspects of the problem in these words: "At the tribunal of reason, there is but one means of extricating states from this turbulent situation, in which they are constantly menaced with war; namely, to renounce like individuals, the anarchic liberty of savages, in order to submit themselves to coercive laws, and thus form a society of nations (*Civitas gentium*) which would insensibly embrace all the nations of the earth."

Probably no one has so richly deserved the Nobel peace prize as Sir Norman Angell, who, for over a generation, has served the cause of peace by trying to educate the British and American public to understand some of the fundamentals of international peace and war. In *The Unseen Assassins* (1932), Sir Norman defines, first, what are the greatest evils that devastate our civilization. He holds that neither outright wickedness nor lack of knowledge are to be blamed, but our failure to apply available and often self-evident knowledge to our social relationships: "We do not *desire* to create social or economic evils, to impose injustice and bring about war, but we apply policies in which those results are inherent because we fail to see the implications of the policies. Those unperceived implications are the Unseen Assassins of our peace and welfare."

Sovereignty is one of the chief of these assassins. Angell denies that the existence of nations is in itself the cause of war: "War is due to the fact that we have attached to nationality the idea of independence and sovereignty: sovereignty and the anarchy which it necessarily implies make war." History itself has proved that sovereignty and nationality are not necessarily united: Great Britain consists of the three nations of England, Wales, and Scotland, but they do not possess sovereignty—which means, in practice, the legal right to make war upon each other. The Hispanic nations in the New World are very similar in language, religion, and tradition, yet they have fought many wars among themselves. Because they failed to stay united after achieving independence from Spain, but organized themselves into sovereign states, they acquired the habit of warring against one another. Conversely, if independent nations had been formed in the territory of the present United States, they would undoubtedly have learned the custom of fighting among themselves. The fact that sovereign states insist on being the judges in their own cases makes war inevitable. Experience points to one method of escaping from the anarchy inherent in sovereignty: "No one shall be judge in his own cause, which means that he should not be his own defender. The combined power of the whole group shall be used to ensure the defence of each member; that is to say, the enjoyment of such rights as experience has shown to make for a workable and orderly co-operation at any given stage of a society's development."

Every form of political organization on the national and international scale is largely determined by man's ideas of himself, his nature and capacities. Within the state, the community of interests may be split by group and class conflicts, but in the end peaceful adjustments prevent such divergencies from breaking out into armed struggle. In the relations between nations, men have not settled, in their own minds, the primary question as to what is the "natural state of things": harmony of interests (though interrupted by occasional conflicts), or conflict of interests (though interrupted by short intervals of peace). The answer one is ready to give to this question will be, in itself, one of the factors that will determine whether conflict or community will be the normal condition in the society of nations.

The sharpest analysis of this issue, from a conservative point of view, will be found in E. H. Carr's *The Twenty Years' Crisis* (1939). Carr bases his whole theory of international relations on the distinction between *Utopian* and *realistic* thinking. According to Carr, this distinction coincides with the distinction between free will and determinism: "The utopian is necessarily voluntarist: he believes in the possibility of more or less radically rejecting reality, and substituting his utopia for it by an act of will. The realist analyses a predetermined course of development which he is powerless to change." Carr expresses this difference also in the sense that the "utopian, fixing his eyes on the future, thinks in terms of creative spontaneity: the realist, rooted in the past, in terms of causality." Secondly, Carr maintains that the distinction between Utopia and reality corresponds to that of theory and practice. The Utopian desires to make political practice conform to political theory, whereas the realist looks up political theory as a "sort of codification of political practice." Thirdly, the antithesis between Utopianism and realism is also reflected in the political contrast of Left and Right: "The radical is necessarily utopian, and the conservative realist. The intellectual, the man of theory, will gravitate toward the Left just as naturally as the bureaucrat, the man of practice, will gravitate towards the Right." Carr quotes approvingly the epigram of a Nazi philosopher, Moeller van den Bruck, that "the Left has reason (*Vernunft*), the Right has wisdom (*Verstand*)." Finally, and perhaps most fundamental of all, the dichotomy of Utopia and reality is reflected in that of ethics and politics. The Utopian seeks to make politics conform to ethical standards; the realist "cannot logically accept any standard of value save that of fact."

Carr attacks with much force the doctrine of the "harmony of interests," both within the state and between states, as a typically Utopian illusion. He calls that doctrine "an ingenious moral device invoked, in perfect sincerity, by privileged groups in order to justify and maintain their dominant position." This is true within the national community, but it is equally true in the world at large, and international peace is but "a special vested interest of dominant Powers." Carr thus rejects all the assumptions of economic and political liberalism, that the state is a community with discoverable principles of public interest, and that the society of nations, too, is a community whose common interests in peace and prosperity outweigh the interests in conflict, war, and destruction. Throughout his book Carr leans heavily on German conservative writers; although realist thinking in politics has had some influence on Western Europe, it "had its home in Germany." Carr is so comprehensive in his sympathies for those who attack the liberal position, that he quotes approvingly antiliberal attacks from the Right as well as from the Left: Hegel or Marx, Bismarck or Lenin, Hitler or Stalin—Carr approves of their realism, their refusal to pay heed to the liberal illusions of the nineteenth century. In particular, Prime Minister Neville Chamberlain emerges from Carr's book as the real hero: his policy of appeasing the Axis was the true expression of realism, according to Carr, as compared with the illusionary formulas of the Utopians, such as "collective security" and "indivisibility of peace."

The best reply to Carr's argument will be found in Leonard Woolf's article on "Utopia and Reality"; he wrote it (in 1940) for *The Political Quarterly*, which he edits. Woolf has also dealt with this whole problem more fully in a book, *The War for Peace* (also published in 1940). First, Woolf charges Carr with using the term "Utopia" in two different meanings which are constantly confused. The first meaning of "Utopia" is applied to a policy based on a hope or purpose which is "incapable of fulfillment," and in this sense it can be opposed to realism. But the term "Utopian" is also used as meaning "unreal" as opposed to "reality." These two meanings are different uses of the term "Utopia," and Woolf adduces several illustrations to demonstrate how Carr actually confuses them. If Chamberlain failed in his policy of appeasement, that is still no proof, according to Carr, that the policy was Utopian, because it might conceivably have succeeded. However, in the case of the failure of the League of Nations, he says that "the first and most obvious tragedy of this utopia was its ignominious defeat." Thus Woolf denies that failure or success is necessarily the criterion of whether a policy is realistic or Utopian. The *identification of fact with value* is attacked by Woolf as one of the main weaknesses of the self-styled "realists," because it provides no guide to ordered thinking: "In 1790, 1830, 1848, 1900, and 1918, if Professor Carr had been a Frenchman, he would have talked about the 'triumph' of democracy and the democratic ideals of the 'Revolution,' but in

1800, 1828, 1851, and 1939 he would have talked about their 'ignominious collapse' and utopianism." Writing early in 1940, Woolf doubted whether one of Carr's "realists," Adolf Hitler, would succeed in his "realistic" policy of organizing Europe, not on the liberal illusion and Utopia of harmony of interests, but on the basis of force and conflicting interest: "It is highly probable that his objective will not be attained and is unattainable, and is therefore really utopian." And Woolf adds: "If the criterion of utopianism is attainability, the policies of Hitler and Mr. Chamberlain are no less utopian than the League policy."

Woolf denies one of Carr's main theses, that there is "some 'reality' in a conflicting interest which does not exist in a common interest." The fact that in most instances the pursuit of a common interest necessitates the abandonment of some immediate individual interest prevents some people from being *conscious* what their true interest is. Yet, as Woolf points out, "in private life and national politics we have learnt this by bitter experience, and no one believes that the interest of men with knives to commit murder and robbery is more 'real' than the interest of men with knives to refrain and be restrained from committing murder and robbery. International psychology is still, however, so crude that even a man like Professor Carr can believe that the interest of Germany in cutting the throat of Czechoslovakia is more real than the interest of both Germany and Czechoslovakia in living peacefully together and composing conflicting interests by compromise, merely because Herr Hitler has a very large army, a very large air force, and a very loud and rasping voice." A study of the history of human society leads Woolf to the conclusion that *"generally and in the long run* common interests are more real than conflicting interests politically." The main difficulty is psychological: as in other advances of civilization, people find it difficult to give up immediate individual interests that conflict with long-term common interests, and it requires "intelligence and restraint" to learn that the individual stands to gain from this preference of the long-range interest to the immediate one. Woolf admits that people will possibly fail to learn this lesson when it comes to the establishment of international peace. But as a believer in the liberal philosophy, he is unwilling to accept the "primitive psychology" that they cannot learn where their true interests lie.

No American has expressed better than President Woodrow Wilson the faith that peace without law is impossible. He failed politically; morally he was more than vindicated by the events that filled the two decades following his disavowal by the Senate and the people. His prediction "with absolute certainty" that there would be another world war "if the nations of the world do not concert the method by which to prevent it" came true with tragic accuracy. His conception of an international organization for the maintenance of peace was never static and final: "Settlements may be temporary, but the action of the nations in the interest of peace and justice must be permanent. We can set up permanent processes. We may not be able to set up permanent decisions." This is also the nature of democratic government within a nation: the Constitution does not indicate *what* laws will be actually passed by the legislature, but merely prescribes *how* laws are to be made. The growth of a sense of procedure has distinguished, historically, political civilization from political savagery. Wilson still belonged to a generation of Americans who were not ashamed of being idealistic, who believed that America was dedicated to the love of justice and the service of humanity. He warned that, "if America goes back upon mankind, mankind has no other place to turn."

G. W. F. HEGEL

1. *The Philosophy of International Anarchy**

In peace civil life continually expands; all its departments wall themselves in, and in the long run men stagnate. Their idiosyncrasies become continually more fixed and ossified. But for health the unity of the body is required, and if its parts harden themselves into exclusiveness, that is death. Perpetual peace is often advocated as an ideal towards which humanity should strive. With that end in view, Kant proposed a league of monarchs to adjust differences between states, and the Holy Alliance was meant to be a league of much the same kind. But the state is an individual, and individuality essentially implies negation. Hence even if a number of states make themselves into a family, this group as an individual must engender an opposite and create an enemy. As a result of war, nations are strengthened, but peoples involved in civil strife also acquire peace at home through making wars abroad. To be sure, war produces insecurity of property, but this insecurity of things is nothing but their transience—which is inevitable. We hear plenty of sermons from the pulpit about the insecurity, vanity, and instability of temporal things, but everyone thinks, however much he is moved by what he hears, that he at least will be able to retain his own. But if this insecurity now comes on the scene in the form of hussars with shining sabres and they actualize in real earnest what the preachers have said, then the moving and edifying discourses which foretold all these events

* From G. W. F. Hegel, *Philosophy of Law* (1821; translated by T. M Knox as *Philosophy of Right*, Oxford University Press, 1942). By permission.

turn into curses against the invader. Be that as it may, the fact remains that wars occur when the necessity of the case requires. The seeds burgeon once more, and harangues are silenced by the solemn cycles of history.

War is the state of affairs which deals in earnest with the vanity of temporal goods and concerns—a vanity at other times a common theme of edifying sermonizing. This is what makes it the moment in which the ideality of the particular attains its right and is actualized. War has the higher significance that by its agency, as I have remarked elsewhere, "the ethical health of peoples is preserved in their indifference to the stabilization of finite institutions; just as the blowing of the winds preserves the sea from the foulness which would be the result of a prolonged calm, so also corruption in nations would be the product of prolonged, let alone 'perpetual,' peace." This, however, is said to be only a philosophic idea, or, to use another common expression, a "justification of Providence," and it is maintained that actual wars require some other justification. On this point, see below.

The ideality which is in evidence in war, i.e. in an accidental relation of a state to a foreign state, is the same as the ideality in accordance with which the domestic powers of the state are organic moments in a whole. This fact appears in history in various forms, e.g. successful wars have checked domestic unrest and consolidated the power of the state at home. Other phenomena illustrate the same point: e.g. peoples unwilling or afraid to tolerate sovereignty at home have been subjugated from abroad, and they have struggled for their independence with less glory and success the less they have been able previously to organize the powers of the state in home affairs—their freedom has died from the fear of dying; states whose autonomy has been guaranteed not by their armed forces but in other ways (e.g. by their disproportionate smallness in comparison with their neighbours) have been able to subsist with a constitution of their own which by itself would not have assured peace in either home or foreign affairs.

States are not private persons but completely autonomous totalities in themselves, and so the relation between them differs from a moral relation and a relation involving private rights. Attempts have often been made to regard the state as a person with the rights of persons and as a moral entity. But the position with private persons is that they are under the jurisdiction of a court which gives effect to what is right in principle. Now a relation between states ought also to be right in principle, but in mundane affairs a principle ought also to have power. Now since there is no power in existence which decides in face of the state what is right in principle and actualizes this decision, it follows that so far as international relations are concerned we can never get beyond an "ought." The relation between states is a relation between autonomous entities which makes mutual stipulations but which at the same time are superior to these stipulations.

The nation-state is mind in its substantive rationality and immediate actuality and is therefore the absolute power on earth. It follows that every state is sovereign and autonomous against its neighbours. It is entitled in the first place and without qualification to be sovereign from their point of view, i.e. to be recognized by them as sovereign. At the same time, however, this title is purely formal, and the demand for this recognition of the state, merely on the ground that it is a state, is abstract. Whether a state is in fact something absolute depends on its content, i.e. on its constitution and general situation; and recognition, implying as it does an identity between the state and its neighbour, is similarly conditional on its neighbour's judgment and will.

If states disagree and their particular wills cannot be harmonized, the matter can only be settled by war. A state through its subjects has widespread connexions and many-sided interests, and these may be readily and considerably injured; but it remains inherently indeterminable which of these injuries is to be regarded as a specific breach of treaty or as an injury to the honour and autonomy of the state. The reason for this is that a state may regard its infinity and honour as at stake in each of its concerns, however minute, and it is all the more inclined to susceptibility to injury the more its strong individuality is impelled as a result of long domestic peace to seek and create a sphere of activity abroad.

Apart from this, the state is in essence mind and therefore cannot be prepared to stop at just taking notice of an injury *after* it has actually occurred. On the contrary, there arises in addition as a cause of strife the *idea* of such an injury as the idea of a danger *threatening* from another state, together with calculations of degrees of probability on this side and that, guessing at intentions, &c., &c.

At one time the opposition between morals and politics, and the demand that the latter should conform to the former, were much canvassed. On this point only a general remark is required here. The welfare of a state has claims to recognition totally different from those of the welfare of the individual. The ethical substance, the state, has its determinate being, i.e. its right, directly embodied in something existent, something not abstract but concrete, and the principle of its conduct and behaviour can only be this concrete existent and not one of the many universal thoughts supposed to be moral commands. When politics is alleged to clash with morals and so to be always wrong, the doctrine propounded rests on superficial ideas about morality, the nature of the state, and the state's relation to the moral point of view.

IMMANUEL KANT

2. Perpetual Peace*

The law of nations ought to be founded upon a federation of free states.

Nations, as states, like individuals, if they live in a state of nature and without laws, by their vicinity alone commit an act of lesion. One may, in order to secure its own safety, require of another to establish within it a constitution which should guarantee to all their rights. This would be a federation of nations, without the people however forming one and the same state, the idea of a state supposing the relation of a sovereign to the people, of a superior to his inferiors. Now several nations, united into one state, would no longer form but one; which contradicts the supposition, the question here being of the reciprocal rights of nations, inasmuch as they compose a multitude of different states, which ought not to be incorporated into one and the same state.

But when we see savages in their anarchy, prefer the perpetual combats of licentious liberty to a reasonable liberty, founded upon constitutional order, can we refrain to look down with the most profound contempt on this animal degradation of humanity? Must we not blush at the contempt to which the want of civilization reduces men? And would one not rather be led to think that civilized nations, each of which form a constituted state, would hasten to extricate themselves from an order of things so ignominious? But what, on the contrary, do we behold? Every state placing its majesty (for it is absurd to talk of the majesty of the people) precisely in this independence of every constraint of any external legislation whatever.

The sovereign places his glory in the power of disposing at his pleasure (without much exposing himself) of many millions of men, ever ready to sacrifice themselves for an object that does not concern them. The only difference between the savages of America and those of Europe, is, that the former have eaten up many a hostile tribe, whereas the latter have known how to make a better use of their enemies; they preserve them to augment the number of their subjects, that is to say, of instruments destined to more extensive conquests. When we consider the perverseness of human nature, which shews itself unveiled and unrestrained in the relations of nations with each other, where it is not checked, as in a state of civilization, by the coercive power of the law, one may well be astonished that the word right has not yet been totally abolished from war-politics as a pedantic word, and that a state has not yet been found bold enough openly to profess

* From Immanuel Kant, *Perpetual Peace* (1795).

this doctrine. For hitherto Grotius, Pufendorf, Wattel, and other useless and impotent defenders of the rights of nations, have been constantly cited in justification of war; though their code, purely philosophic or diplomatic, has never had the force of law, and cannot obtain it; states not being as yet subjected to any coercive power. There is no instance where their reasonings, supported by such respectable authorities, have induced a state to desist from its pretensions. However this homage which all states render to the principle of right, if even consisting only in words, is a proof of a moral disposition, which, though still slumbering, tends nevertheless vigorously to subdue in man that evil principle, of which he cannot entirely divest himself. For otherwise states would never pronounce the word right, when going to war with each other; it were then ironically, as a Gallic prince interpreted it. "It is," said he, "the preorogative nature has given to the stronger, to make himself obeyed by the weaker."

However, the field of battle is the only tribunal before which states plead their cause; but victory, by gaining the suit, does not decide in favour of their cause. Though the treaty of peace puts an end to the present war, it does not abolish a state of war (a state where continually new pretenses for war are found); which one cannot affirm to be unjust, since being their own judges, they have no other means of terminating their differences. The law of nations cannot even force them, as the law of nature obliges individuals to get free from this state of war, since having already a legal constitution, as states, they are secure against every foreign compulsion, which might tend to establish among them a more extended constitutional order.

Since, however, from her highest tribunal of moral legislation, reason without exception condemns war as a mean of right, and makes a state of peace an absolute duty; and since this peace cannot be effected or be guaranteed without a compact among nations, they must form an alliance of a peculiar kind, which might be called a pacific alliance (*foedus pacificum*) different from a treaty of peace (*pactum pacis*) inasmuch as it would forever terminate all wars, whereas the latter only finishes one. This alliance does not tend to any dominion over a state, but solely to the certain maintenance of the liberty of each particular state, partaking of this association, without being therefore obliged to submit, like men in a state of nature, to the legal constraint of public force. It can be proved, that the idea of a federation, which should insensibly extend to all states, and thus lead them to a perpetual peace, may be realized. For if fortune should so direct, that a people as powerful as enlightened, should constitute itself into a republic (a government which in its nature inclines to a perpetual peace) from that time there would be a centre for this federative association; other states might adhere thereto, in order to guarantee their liberty according to the principles of public right; and this alliance might insensibly be extended.

That a people should say, "There shall not be war among us: we will form ourselves into a state; that is to say, we will ourselves establish a legislative, executive, and judiciary power, to decide our differences,"—can be conceived.

But if this state should say, "There shall not be war between us and other states, although we do not acknowledge a supreme power, that guarantees our reciprocal rights"; upon what then can this confidence in one's rights be founded, except it is upon this free federation, this supplement of the social compact, which reason necessarily associates with the idea of public right?

The expression of law of nations, taken in a sense of right of war, presents properly no idea to the mind; since thereby is understood a power of deciding right, not according to universal laws, which restrain within the same limits all individuals, but according to partial maxims, namely, by force. Except one would wish to insinuate by this expression, that it is right, that men who admit such principles should destroy each other, and thus find perpetual peace only in the vast grave that swallows them and their iniquities.

At the tribunal of reason, there is but one mean of extricating states from this turbulent situation, in which they are constantly menaced with war; namely, to renounce, like individuals, the anarchic liberty of savages, in order to submit themselves to coercive laws, and thus form a society of nations (*civitas gentium*) which would insensibly embrace all the nations of the earth. But as the ideas which they have of the law of nations, absolutely prevent the realization of this plan, and make them reject in practice what is true in theory, there can only be substituted, to the positive idea of an universal republic (if all is not to be lost) the negative supplement of a permanent alliance, which prevents war, insensibly spreads, and stops the torrent of those unjust and inhuman passions, which always threaten to break down this fence.

NORMAN ANGELL

3. The Sovereign Assassin*

If Europe had not formed itself or grown into sovereign nations, it would not be riven by international war. There might be civil war, there might be strife of all kinds; Europe as a unity somewhat similar to the forty-eight

* From Norman Angell, *The Unseen Assassins* (Hamish Hamilton, 1932). By permission of Sir Norman Angell.

states of North America might have sacrificed things that have been worth all the cost of separate nationalities. That is a separate question. But if Europe constituted one sovereignty she would not face, though she might face worse evils, the particular problem with which we are dealing. To repeat the truism already enunciated, if there were no nations, nations would not go to war.

Note that the earlier part of the above proposition speaks of "sovereign" nations. As noted before, when this aspect came into the argument, Scotland and Wales are nations but they do not fight each other, nor fight England, though they did once. It is not the existence of nations, or the fact of nationality, which is the cause of war. War is due to the fact that we have attached to nationality the idea of independence and sovereignty: sovereignty and the anarchy which it necessarily implies make war. We fight each other because each has said:

> We are a nation; that is to say a corporate body, a personality, *therefore* each national person is independent, a law unto itself, shall acknowledge no code regulating its relations with other similar persons. These persons shall live together without government, without laws, without institutions for their framing, their alteration or their enforcement. For if such institutions existed those persons would not be independent or sovereign, they would be subject to rule, to law.

The "therefore" of the above statement is the supreme Unseen Assassin. It stands for a complete *non sequitur*. The nation makes, if you will, by deeply rooted psychological forces, a "herd," a corporate person. But there are other such corporate bodies too: the church, the caste, the clan; sometimes the trade union, the club. But they do not ask that they shall be sovereign and independent; the state, and the only state; that they shall enter into no effective partnership with any other human organization (if partners are completely independent of each other they are not partners), owe allegiance to no other human authority.

The plain facts of history show that there was nothing "inevitable"— except in the sense that a social intelligence and discipline are of slow growth—in thus attaching to one particular form of association the quality of complete sovereignty, in dissociating it from disciplined co-operation with other groups. It was often a pure accident of history that sovereignty became attached to some groups and not to others.

There was a period after the revolution of the thirteen American colonies of Great Britain in which it seemed exceedingly doubtful whether they would form a federation at all. There was nothing inevitable about their doing so. The Spanish-American colonies when they revolted did not; and the English-speaking colonies might not have done so save for several fortuitous circumstances: the character and influence of this or that statesman amongst them, fear of the strength of the mother country. If Britain had been in reality a decadent state the revolted colonies would almost certainly have failed to hang together in order not to hang separately.

If history had taken that turn we might as easily have had half a dozen nations (a French-speaking one, perhaps, on the St. Lawrence or in Louisiana; a Dutch-speaking one on the Hudson; Spanish-speaking in California, etc.), just as we have a round dozen separate nations south of the Mexican border. We know that if such independent nations had been formed in what is now the United States (especially with differences of language and culture) they would have fought, as the independent nations which have resulted from the Spanish-American colonies have fought, even though *they* have no differences of language and culture. (Note in passing that the national characteristics, linguistic and racial, which distinguish, say, Wales from England, and both from Scotland, are far greater than those which distinguish the Chileno and the Peruvian, or the San Salvadorian and the Guatemalan. Those Spanish nations having complete sovereignty fight each other, or face the possibility by arming against each other; the British nations, having only limited sovereignty, have ceased so to do.)

Put the illustration, as already suggested, in inverse form: Imagine that at some stage in the development of Europe—at the breakdown, say, of the Western Empire—some degree of effective authority had grouped round, say, the Church; and the nations of Europe had become federalised states, like those of the American Union.[1] Then, though there might be civil war, as there has been civil war in the American Union, the problem of international war and that chaos in the international economic field as we know it to-day, would not confront us.

Why does the claim to complete sovereignty and independence, the refusal to acknowledge allegiance to a common rule of conduct, the attempt of persons or corporate bodies, having multitudinous economic and social relations, to live without government, without appropriate social institutions, necessarily involve war? Though I am not going to suggest that the rules which govern persons should necessarily apply to nations, there are principles, like those of the multiplication table, for instance, to go no further, which must apply to both.

If someone were to propose to John Smith that in this closely packed complex modern world of ours, with its motor-cars travelling at sixty miles an hour; its inevitable difference of view as to what are the best traffic rules; as to who is responsible in this or that accident; what is suitable compen-

---

[1] Boniface VIII by a Bull claims that "all Kings, Emperors, and other Sovereigns, whoever they may be, are subject, like all other men, to be summoned before the Apostolic Courts, for every sort of cause: for we, by the permission of God. command the whole Universe." (R. F. Wright, *Medieval Internationalism*, p. 89.)

sation in the event of injury; insurance laws; the necessary conflict of claims about property, rights of way, trespass, pollution of water, measures for their preservation of public health—if anyone were to suggest to him that in this sort of world you can do without legislative bodies, courts, police, without governing institutions, that is, he would regard you as insane.

And he would not qualify the verdict at all if the proposer went on to explain that, since usually folk are fundamentally decent and can be relied upon to keep their word, the idea was to replace the complicated machinery of government by an undertaking on the part of everybody always to play fair; never to take more than they were entitled to. Smith would reply that the question of goodwill was hardly involved; that differences as to what was fair and what each was entitled to were usually quite honest differences, were just the point about which the quarrels arose, that rules (especially like those of the road with reference to driving cars) had to be kept, whatever the individual thought of them, and had to be enforced if he did not like them. Suggest to Smith that such a world can work without government, and he is sure you are insane. Suggest to him, however, that the closely interwoven life of those national persons we have been discussing, for reasons just as valid, need corresponding institutions of government, and he will equally regard you as insane.

Yet the results of anarchy, though dissimilar in the two cases, not manifested, that is, in quite the same way, are hardly less dreadful in the second; as the last twenty years have shown.

Let us note the quite simple and understandable process by which with mechanical inevitability the method of anarchy produces conflict. One of the primary impulses of man, as of any animal, is self-preservation, defence, security. And society, government, as the substitute for anarchy, has largely grown up around the organisation of that function. Let us see why.

Suppose I say:

> I will be my own defender of my own rights, as against another, by being stronger than any who may challenge them. To allow others to come in and say what my rights are, means that I shall have to do the will of others, not my own, which is to deprive me of independence, freedom, sovereignty. I shall take measures therefore to see that my view of my rights shall prevail.

Very well. What is the position of that other who may disagree with my view of what my rights are?

He says:

> If you make yourself judge of a dispute in which the rights of both are involved, you are judge of my rights as well as your own. Why should

you be judge of my rights any more than I should be judge of yours? I prefer the latter arrangement.

Now that situation is bound to result in conflict because the "right" by which each stands involves in its very terms a denial of the other's claim. Each is demanding a right for himself which he refuses to the other.

There can be no general defence, security, "self-preservation" under such a system because the defence of one deprives the other of defence; the security of the one is the insecurity of the other; "justice" for the one means injustice for the other. Under such a system you could only make both secure if each were stronger than the other; each his own judge in a dispute where another is involved. It defies arithmetic, as it defies ethics.

You get exactly the same result whether you begin from another angle of anarchy: the assertion of neutrality by members of a group. Suppose my fellows say: "Your security is no concern of ours. We are neutral. If anyone steal your property or attempt to take your life, that is not our affair." If that is the attitude, then (speaking, say, as the feudal chief, or clan, or mere individual) I shall attempt to possess sufficient power to resist any threat to my security, that is to say, my rights (which means what I believe to be my rights). I shall try to be stronger than anyone likely to be a menace. That will make such a one weaker than me, put him at my mercy, though I refuse to be at his. In any dispute—any question of his rights as against mine—he will just have to trust to my goodwill, though I refuse to trust to his. *He* will be deprived of defence by the fact of *my* defence.

Now, as a statement of principle that is just as true whether the units you are speaking of are persons, families, clans, tribes, nations, or alliances. The multiplication table is just as valid or invalid whether you apply it to stars or cabbages. When a Cabinet Minister says that the surest way to get peace is to be stronger than your prospective enemy, he is still asking each of the two parties to be stronger than the other, and gaily defying arithmetic.

Is the suggestion that such a method *must* end in conflict borne out by the event? *Circumspice.*

Now, as against this method of anarchy—of each being his own defender, and consequently his own judge—the whole experience of man points a contrary method. Its general lines are these: No one shall be judge in his own cause, which means that he should not be his own defender. The combined power of the whole group shall be used to ensure the defence of each member; that is to say, the enjoyment of such rights as experience has shown to make for a workable and orderly co-operation at any given stage of a society's development. The first right of all is the right to third-party judgment in a dispute with another, so that that other, party to the dispute, does not become its judge. There is this contrast as between the use of force socially and anarchically. In a state of anarchy the power of each individual is used to enable him to be his own judge; under the social method the power of the community is used to *prevent* any individual being his own judge.

These are the issues as between the method of anarchy and the method of organised society whether of persons or of states. It is perfectly open to argue that the method which has proved feasible in the case of persons will not for this, that or the other reason work in the case of states. There is, alas! a strong case for the belief that in the latter case we are condemned to anarchy, and so to war because the momentum of certain traditions like the Jingo-militarist-nationalist tradition is such as to render us incapable of the necessary discipline or intelligence.

But it is *not* open to say this: "We will now have peace between nations by means of a properly organised society of nations. Each member of that society shall be neutral in any dispute between the others; the society as a whole shall have no responsibility for the defence of individual members; each shall take his own measures for defence; and each shall be independent and sovereign."

For that is mere contradiction of terms: If each is neutral, sovereign, independent, then there can be no society. But that is exactly what so many of us, most of us, *are* saying, and the most serious and tragic part of it is that we do not see the contradiction.

We know by the commonest experience of everyday life—in business, in every form of personal dispute—that we should be brought to deadlock if we began on the assumption that each party could be trusted to be his own judge. Still less could we trust that judgment if the party exercising it had unquestioned preponderance of power over the other. We are aware that the acceptance of the principle of third-party judgment, when we come to contentious matters, is the only possible basis of peace; that even that cannot operate until there is some agreement as to "what is right"; that the whole process is dependent upon a certain apparatus—law making, law interpreting, law enforcing—and that without that apparatus the mere goodwill of each party would be hopelessly inadequate. We are perfectly aware that the breakdown of the institutions would be simply equivalent to the breakdown of civilisation, of peace; that always indeed have the two things been coincident. A round score of ancient civilisations broke down, because their institutions collapsed under some strain: the one collapse involved the other.

Yet this commonplace experience of daily life is not by popular judgment applied to the field of international policies at all. We genuinely care for peace; are deeply apprehensive about the recurrence of war. But, speaking broadly, we are quite indifferent about the creation of institutions, for the simple reason that we do not see the relation between the maintenance of peace and the difficult, hazardous and easily defeated task of building up a world society.

The important thing which emerges is this: We do not apply the plain lessons of daily life to the task of that ending of war we all desire. In what has just been written there is an implied condemnation of educational method. Some of our educationalists are genuinely disturbed about what they are apt to call our lack of knowledge of foreign countries, and propose to remedy it by imparting information bearing on the lives of peoples other than our own. We are assured that international understanding would be promoted by knowing other nations better. I doubt it. The bitterest quarrels—like the religious conflicts of India and Ireland—are between communities that live in the same street, live all their lives in close contact and know each other very well indeed. It is the understanding of the necessary principles of just and peaceful human relationship that is needed. The facts which bear on that are available to us all, inherent in the commonest problems of our personal contact. We do not need to know any more facts about remote peoples, whether about Esquimaux or the Nestorians. We need to realise the meaning in social principle of the facts we already know. And the way in which education has taught us to think about human society is such that we fail to apply at points where most needed, to the solution of our gravest and most urgent problems, principles which emerge most obviously from the facts of daily life.

We have dealt so far with one perfectly understandable social principle. Let us take two others, just as simple, and closely related to it, and which reveal in popular understanding the same contradictions, the same *non sequiturs,* the same failure to apply the commonest experience of one situation to another only slightly less familiar.

No argument is so readily used by the ordinary voter as an excuse for his inertia or indifference in the matter of international institutions, for his refusal, that is, to deal with the problem of international anarchy, as he has dealt with anarchy elsewhere, as this argument: You will never get over human nature. Man, he will tell you, is, by the very law of his being, a fighting animal; pugnacious, inherently unreasonable, one-sided, passionate. . . . If I have heard this argument once, I have heard it a thousand times. It is usually presented as the final, complete, unanswerable case against international action towards peace, against such efforts as the League.

Yet this fact of man's anti-social instincts is, of course, the final and fundamental case *for* the League, not against. If human nature were perfect, if men were naturally other-minded, always ready to see the other's point of view, never likely to lose their tempers, then certainly we should not need the League, international institutions. But neither should we need most of our national institutions. They are the means by which we cope with the imperfections of human nature; that imperfection is the reason for the institutions. Yet the educated man who invokes the human nature argument *against* international institutions, daily thinks of it as the supreme argument *for* national institutions. Say to him: men are quarrelsome, avaricious, one-sided, quite incapable of judging their own case, therefore let us abolish the courts and have no laws, and he will see the inconsequence in a moment. Yet suggest that he should establish corresponding institutions for nations and he deems it an adequate reply to declare that nations are quarrelsome, avaricious, one-sided, quite incapable of being their own judge. He goes his life through without seeing that that fact which he uses for one conclusion in a familiar situation, he uses for an exactly opposite conclusion in a slightly less familiar situation, and only so turns it upside down because the second situation is less familiar.

But what shall we say of education for society which produces in the mass of men that degree of understanding of the world in which they live, that much of capacity for using known fact to frame social judgments?

Or take an equally simple instance of elementary confusion touching the principles by which society functions. Constantly one hears the argument: A nation's army or navy is its policeman; armies and navies exist for the same reason that the police force exists. A favourite plea of the plain man.

Yet it might occur to him that police forces are not organised to fight each other, and that armies are. National armies as we now know them are organised for a purpose which ultimately, and broadly is the exact reverse of the purpose for which police are organised, since, in the last analysis, armies are (as we have seen) forces behind rival litigants, and the police is the force behind the judge. The police represent the combined power of the whole community (of persons) used to ensure to each member of that community his agreed rights under the law, and as part of the process, to restrain any member from using his individual force to be his own judge. If in a dispute with my neighbour about a right of way, I break down his fence to defend what I regard as my right, and invade what he regards as his property, he will invoke the police, who will restrain me from being my own defender, since, if I had that right of defence, I should be my own judge, and deny by that fact a similar right to him. The whole ultimate purpose of the police is to restrain me from using my power in that way. The community has assumed the obligation of my defence. But the nation which says: We will retain force in the shape of an army or navy powerful enough to resist anyone likely to challenge its power; but that force shall not be part of the power of the community (of nations) pledged to defend each member, but a tool enabling us to be our own defender, which means in the last resort, our own judge—that nation has obviously repudiated the police method.

The object of an army or navy is to enable the individual to impose its individual will; the object of the police is to restrain that individual from imposing his will. The police method is to make the defence of the individual the obligation of the whole community; the method of armies and navies as they now exist rejects that in favour of each defending himself. One is a social instrument; the other is an instrument of anarchy; the one depends upon competition of power, "each being stronger than the other"; the other upon pooled power, the co-operation of the whole in the maintenance of agreed rights. The two methods are plainly mutually exclusive. Yet all my life I have heard from educated men the weary phrase about needing armies for the same reason that we need police.

Whether every stage or phase of the preceding argument touching what I have called the mechanism of society be valid or not, is not for the moment in question. The point is that, at a juncture when the maintenance of civilisation depends upon a relatively simple and logical development in the organisation of society, education has not equipped the public mind even to the extent of enabling it to grasp the elements of the argument, the simplest of the issues involved.

The implications are unfamiliar to the mass of ordinary men, to the scholars turned out by our schools. It is not that they are familiar with the arguments, have applied them to the problems in hand and rejected them as invalid. I say without any hesitation, on the basis of the rather special experience of having argued the internationalist case during thirty years, in several countries, that the mass of ordinary men who form our voters, have not been led to think about the necessary mechanism of society, or to think of society as having a necessary mechanism at all; or to think about the nature of society; or to be conscious that there is such a thing as a definitely organised society. They have learned a number of rules of conduct, and have accepted them, usually as an entirely arbitrary code; the reason for them in terms of social welfare is for the most part entirely disregarded.

If John Smith made a case for anarchy, or a case (such as that made before the war by certain political philosophers in Germany) for the establishment of order in the world by the ultimate domination of one national state, one would feel that though his education had made him a bad reasoner, it had at least turned his mind to dealing with the nature of the social universe in which he lived, and his relation thereto. But you will find the modern European asserting such principles as an absolutist nationalism because his education simply has not related that thing to the needs of organised society at all.

E. H. CARR

4. *Utopia and Reality: A Conservative View**

The antithesis of utopia and reality—a balance always swinging towards and away from equilibrium and never completely attaining it—is a fundamental antithesis revealing itself in many forms of thought. The two methods of approach—the inclination to ignore what was and what is in contemplation of what should be, and the inclination to deduce what should be from what was and what is—determine opposite attitudes towards every political problem. "It is the eternal dispute," as Albert Sorel puts it, "between those who imagine the world to suit their policy, and those who arrange their policy to suit the realities of the world."[1] It may be suggestive to elaborate this antithesis before proceeding to an examination of the current crisis of international politics.

FREE WILL AND DETERMINISM

The antithesis of utopia and reality can in some aspects be identified with the antithesis of Free Will and Determinism. The utopian is necessarily voluntarist: he believes in the possibility of more or less radically rejecting reality, and substituting his utopia for it by an act of will. The realist analyses a predetermined course of development which he is powerless to change. For the realist, philosophy, in the famous words of Hegel's preface to his *Philosophy of Right,* always "comes too late" to change the world. By means of philosophy, the old order "cannot be rejuvenated, but only known." The utopian, fixing his eyes on the future, thinks in terms of creative spontaneity: the realist, rooted in the past, in terms of causality. All healthy human action, and therefore all healthy thought, must establish a balance between utopia and reality, between free will and determinism. The complete realist, unconditionally accepting the causal sequence of events, deprives himself of the possibility of changing reality. The complete utopian, by rejecting the causal sequence, deprives himself of the possibility of understanding either the reality which he is seeking to change or the processes by which it can be changed. The characteristic vice of the utopian is naivety; of the realist, sterility.[2]

* From E. H. Carr, *The Twenty Years' Crisis* (1939). By permission of The Macmillan Company, publishers.

[1] A. Sorel, *L'Europe et la Révolution Française*, p. 474.

[2] The psychologist may be interested to trace here an analogy—it would be dangerous to treat it as more—with Jung's classification of psychological types as "introverted" and "extraverted" (Jung, *Psychological Types*) or William James's pairs of opposites: Rationalist-Empiricist, Intellectualist-Sensationalist, Idealist-Materialist, Optimistic-Pessimistic, Religious-Irreligious, Free-willist-Fatalistic, Monistic-Pluralistic, Dogmatical-Sceptical (W. James, *Pragmatism*).

THEORY AND PRACTICE

The antithesis of utopia and reality also coincides with the antithesis of theory and practice. The utopian makes political theory a norm to which political practice ought to conform. The realist regards political theory as a sort of codification of political practice. The relationship of theory and practice has come to be recognized in recent years as one of the central problems of political thought. Both the utopian and the realist distort this relationship. The utopian, purporting to recognize the interdependence of purpose and fact, treats purpose as if it were the only relevant fact, and constantly couches optative propositions in the indicative mood. The American Declaration of Independence maintains that "all men are created Equal," Mr. Litvinov that "peace is indivisible," [3] and Sir Norman Angell that "the biological division of mankind into independent warring states" is a "scientific ineptitude." [4] Yet it is a matter of common observation that all men are not born equal even in the United States, and that the Soviet Union can remain at peace while its neighbours are at war; and we should probably think little of a zoologist who described a man-eating tiger as a "scientific ineptitude." These propositions are items in a political programme disguised as statements of fact;[5] and the utopian inhabits a dream-world of such "facts," remote from the world of reality where quite contrary facts may be observed. The realist has no difficulty in perceiving that these utopian propositions are not facts but aspirations, and belong to the optative not to the indicative mood; and he goes on to shew that, considered as aspirations, they are not *a priori* propositions, but are rooted in the world of reality in a way which the utopian altogether fails to understand. Thus for the realist, the equality of man is the ideology of the under-privileged seeking to raise themselves to the level of the privileged; the indivisibility of peace the ideology of states which, being particularly exposed to attack, are eager to establish the principle that an attack on them is a matter of concern to other states more fortunately situated;[6] the ineptitude of sovereign states the ideology of predominant Powers which find the sovereignty of other states a barrier to the enjoyment of their own predominant position. This exposure of the hidden foundations of utopian theory is a necessary preliminary to any serious political science. But the realist, in denying any *a priori* quality to political theories, and in

[3] *League of Nations: Sixteenth Assembly*, p. 72.

[4] Angell, *The Great Illusion*, p. 138.

[5] Similarly, Marx's theory of surplus value has, in the words of a sympathetic critic, "rather the significance of a political and social slogan than of an economic truth" (M. Beer, *The Life and Teaching of Karl Marx*, p. 129).

[6] Having discovered that other states were perhaps more open to attack than themselves, the Soviet authorities in May 1939 dismissed Mr. Litvinov and ceased to talk about the indivisibility of peace.

proving them to be rooted in practice, falls easily into a determinism which argues that theory, being nothing more than a rationalisation of conditioned and predetermined purpose, is a pure excrescence and impotent to alter the course of events. While therefore the utopian treats purpose as the sole ultimate fact, the realist runs the risk of treating purpose merely as the mechanical product of other facts. If we recognize that this mechanisation of human will and human aspiration is untenable and intolerable, then we must recognise that theory, as it develops out of practice and develops into practice, plays its own transforming role in the process. The political process does not consist, as the realist believes, purely in a succession of phenomena governed by mechanical laws of causation; nor does it consist, as the utopian believes, purely in the application to practice of certain theoretical truths evolved out of their inner consciousness by wise and far-seeing people. Political science must be based on a recognition of the interdependence of theory and practice, which can be attained only through a combination of utopia and reality.

LEFT AND RIGHT

The antithesis of utopia and reality, and of theory and practice, further reproduces itself in the antithesis of radical and conservative, of Left and Right, though it would be rash to assume that parties carrying these labels always represent these underlying tendencies. The radical is necessarily utopian, and the conservative realist. The intellectual, the man of theory, will gravitate towards the Left just as naturally as the bureaucrat, the man of practice, will gravitate towards the Right. Hence the Right is weak in theory, and suffers through its inaccessibility to ideas. The characteristic weakness of the Left is failure to translate its theory into practice—a failure for which it is apt to blame the bureaucrats, but which is inherent in its utopian character. "The Left has reason (*Vernunft*), the Right has wisdom (*Verstand*)," wrote the Nazi philosopher, Moeller van den Bruck.[7] From the days of Burke onwards, English conservatives have always strongly denied the possibility of deducing political practice by a logical process from political theory. "To follow the syllogism alone is a short cut to the bottomless pit," says Lord Baldwin[8]—a phrase which may suggest that he practises as well as preaches abstention from rigorously logical modes of thought. Mr. Churchill refuses to believe that "extravagant logic in doctrine" appeals to the British elector.[9] But the clearest recent definition of the different attitudes of Right and Left towards foreign policy comes from a speech made in the House of Commons by Mr. Neville Chamberlain in answer to a Labour critic:

[7] Moeller van den Bruck, *Das Dritte Reich* (3rd ed.), p. 257.
[8] Baldwin, *On England*, p. 153.
[9] Winston Churchill, *Step by Step*, p. 147.

What does the hon. Member mean by foreign policy? You can lay down sound and general propositions. You can say that your foreign policy is to maintain peace; you can say that it is to protect British interests, you can say that it is to use your influence, such as it is, on behalf of the right against the wrong, as far as you can tell the right from the wrong. You can lay down all these general principles, but that is not a policy. Surely, if you are to have a policy you must take the particular situations and consider what action or inaction is suitable for those particular situations. That is what I myself mean by policy, and it is quite clear that as the situations and conditions in foreign affairs continually change from day to day, your policy cannot be stated once and for all, if it is to be applicable to every situation that arises.[10]

The intellectual superiority of the Left is seldom in doubt. The Left alone thinks out principles of political action and evolves ideals for statesmen to aim at. But it lacks practical experience which comes from close contact with reality. In Great Britain since the War, it has been a serious misfortune that the Left, having enjoyed office for negligible periods, has had little experience of administrative realities and has become more and more a party of pure theory, while the Right, having spent so little time in opposition, has had few temptations to pit the perfection of theory against the imperfections of practice. It is significant that intellectuals have come to play a more and more predominant part in the counsels of the British Left, and that the latter was recently taunted by the Prime Minister with "repeating *clichés* and phrases and tags which once may have had some significance but have none today," and with being ready to "walk into any trap if it is only baited with a familiar catchword" [11]—the characteristic vices of the intellectual in politics. In Soviet Russia, the group in power is more and more discarding theory in favour of practice as it loses the memory of its revolutionary origin. History everywhere shews that, when Left parties or politicians are brought into contact with reality through the assumption of political office, they tend to abandon their "doctrinaire" utopianism and move towards the Right, often retaining their Left labels and thereby adding to the confusion of political terminology.

ETHICS AND POLITICS

Most fundamental of all, the antithesis of utopia and reality is rooted in a different conception of the relationship of politics and ethics. The antithesis between the world of value and the world of nature, already implicit in the dichotomy of purpose and fact, is deeply embedded in the human

[10] House of Commons, October 21, 1937, reprinted in N. Chamberlain, *The Struggle for Peace,* p. 33.

[11] House of Commons, February 22, and October 6, 1938, reprinted in N. Chamberlain, *The Struggle for Peace,* pp. 100, 323.

consciousness and in political thought. The utopian sets up an ethical standard which purports to be independent of politics, and seeks to make politics conform to it. The realist cannot logically accept any standard of value save that of fact. In his view, the absolute standard of the utopian is conditioned and dictated by the social order, and is therefore political. Morality can only be relative, not universal. Ethics must be interpreted in terms of politics; and the search for an ethical norm outside politics is doomed to frustration. The identification of the supreme reality with the supreme good, which Christianity achieves by a bold stroke of dogmatism, is achieved by the realist through the assumption that there is no good other than the acceptance and understanding of reality.

These implications of the opposition between utopia and reality will emerge clearly from a more detailed study of the present crisis in international politics.

THE REALIST CRITIQUE OF THE HARMONY OF INTERESTS

The doctrine of the harmony of interests yields readily to analysis in terms of this principle. It is the natural assumption of a prosperous and privileged class, whose members have a dominant voice in the community and are therefore naturally prone to identify its interest with their own. In virtue of this identification, any assailant of the interests of the dominant group is made to incur the odium of assailing the alleged common interest of the whole community, and is told that in making this assault he is attacking his own higher interests. The doctrine of the harmony of interests thus serves as an ingenious moral device invoked, in perfect sincerity, by privileged groups in order to justify and maintain their dominant position. But a further point requires notice. The supremacy within the community of the privileged group may be, and often is, so overwhelming that there is, in fact, a sense in which its interests are those of the community, since its well-being necessarily carries with it some measure of well-being for other members of the community, and its collapse would entail the collapse of the community as a whole. In so far, therefore, as the alleged natural harmony of interests has any reality, it is created by the overwhelming power of the privileged group, and is an excellent illustration of the Machiavellian maxim that morality is the product of power. A few examples will make this analysis of the doctrine of the harmony of interests clear.

In the nineteenth century, the British manufacturer or merchant, having discovered that *laissez-faire* promoted his own prosperity, was sincerely convinced that it also promoted British prosperity as a whole. Nor was this alleged harmony of interests between himself and the community entirely fictitious. The predominance of the manufacturer and the merchant was so overwhelming that there was a sense in which an identity between their prosperity and British prosperity as a whole could be correctly asserted.

From this it was only a short step to argue that a worker on strike, in damaging the prosperity of the British manufacturer, was damaging British prosperity as a whole, and thereby damaging his own, so that he could be plausibly denounced by the predecessors of Professor Toynbee as immoral and by the predecessors of Professor Zimmern as muddle-headed. Moreover, there was a sense in which this argument was perfectly correct. Nevertheless, the doctrine of the harmony of interests and of solidarity between the classes must have seemed a bitter mockery to the under-privileged worker, whose inferior status and insignificant stake in "British prosperity" were consecrated by it; and presently he was strong enough to force the abandonment of *laissez-faire* and the substitution for it of the "social service state," which implicitly denies the natural harmony of interests and sets out to create a new harmony of artificial means.

The same analysis may be applied in international relations. British nineteenth-century statesmen, having discovered that free trade promoted British prosperity, were sincerely convinced that, in doing so, it also promoted the prosperity of the world as a whole. British predominance in world trade was at that time so overwhelming that there was a certain undeniable harmony between British interests and the interests of the world. British prosperity flowed over into other countries, and a British economic collapse would have meant world-wide ruin. British free traders could and did argue that protectionist countries were not only egotistically damaging the prosperity of the world as a whole, but were stupidly damaging their own, so that their behaviour was both immoral and muddle-headed. In British eyes, it was irrefutably proved that international trade was a single whole, and flourished or slumped together. Nevertheless, this alleged international harmony of interests seemed a mockery to those under-privileged nations whose inferior status and insignificant stake in international trade were consecrated by it. The revolt against it destroyed that overwhelming British preponderance which had provided a plausible basis for the theory. Economically, Great Britain in the nineteenth century was dominant enough to make a bold bid to impose on the world her own conception of international economic morality. Now that competition of all against all has replaced the domination of the world market by a single Power, conceptions of international economic morality have necessarily become chaotic.

Politically, the alleged community of interest in the maintenance of peace, whose ambiguous character has already been discussed, is capitalized in the same way by a dominant nation or group of nations. Just as the ruling class in a community prays for domestic peace, which guarantees its own security and predominance, and denounces class-war, which might threaten them, so international peace becomes a special vested interest of predominant Powers. In the past, Roman and British imperialism were commended to the world in the guise of the *pax Romana* and the *pax Britannica*. To-day, when no single Power is strong enough to dominate the world, and supremacy is vested in a group of nations, slogans like "collective security" and "resistance to aggression" serve the same purpose of proclaiming an identity of interest between the dominant group and the world as a whole in the maintenance of peace. Moreover, as in the examples we have just considered, so long as the supremacy of the dominant group is sufficiently great, there is a sense in which this identity of interests exists. "England," wrote a German professor shortly after the War, "is the solitary Power with a national programme which, while egotistic through and through, at the same time promises to the world something which the world passionately desires: order, progress and eternal peace." [12] Even to-day, if Great Britain and France went to war with Germany and Italy, the defeat of Great Britain and France by Germany and Italy would produce a far more tremendous unheaval throughout the world than the defeat of Germany and Italy by Great Britain and France; and the sympathies of all those countries which felt that they had something to lose would, other things being equal, be instinctively ranged on the Franco-British side. When Mr. Churchill declares that "the fortunes of the British Empire and its glory are inseparably interwoven with the fortunes of the world," [13] this statement has precisely the same foundation in fact as the statement that the prosperity of British manufacturers in the nineteenth century was inseparably interwoven with British prosperity as a whole. Moreover, the purpose of the statements is precisely the same, namely to establish the principle that the defence of the British Empire, or the prosperity of the British manufacturer, is a matter of common interest to the whole community, and that anyone who attacks it is therefore either immoral or muddle-headed. It is a familiar tactic of the privileged to throw moral discredit on the under-privileged by depicting them as disturbers of the peace; and this tactic is as readily applied internationally as within the national community. "International law and order," writes Professor Toynbee of a recent crisis, "were in the true interests of the whole of mankind . . . whereas the desire to perpetuate the reign of violence in international affairs was an anti-social desire which was not even in the ultimate interests of the citizens of the handful of states that officially professed this benighted and anachronistic creed." [14] This is precisely the argument, compounded of platitude and falsehood in about equal parts, which did duty in every strike in the early days of the British and American Labour movements. It was common form for employers, supported by the whole capitalist press, to denounce the "anti-social" attitude of trade union leaders, to accuse them of attacking law and order and of introducing "the reign of violence," and to declare that "true" and "ultimate" interests of the

[12] Dibelius, *England*, p. 109.
[13] Winston Churchill, *Arms and the Covenant*, p. 272.
[14] Toynbee, *Survey of International Affairs*, 1935, ii. p. 46.

workers lay in peaceful co-operation with the employers.[15] In the field of social relations, the disingenuous character of this argument has long been recognised. But just as the threat of class-war by the proletarian is "a natural cynical reaction to the sentimental and dishonest efforts of the privileged classes to obscure the conflict of interest between classes by a constant emphasis on the minimum interests which they have in common," [16] so the war-mongering of the dissatisfied Powers is the "natural, cynical reaction" to the sentimental and dishonest platitudinising of the satisfied Powers on the common interest in peace. When Herr Hitler refuses to believe "that God has permitted some nations first to acquire a world by force and then to defend this robbery with moralising theories," [17] we have an authentic echo of the Marxist denial of a community of interest between "haves" and "have-nots," of the Marxist exposure of the interested character of *"bourgeois* morality," and of the Marxist demand for the expropriation of the expropriators.

The crisis of September 1938 demonstrated in a striking way the political implications of the assertion of a common interest in peace. When Briand proclaimed that "peace comes before all," or Mr. Eden that "there is no dispute which cannot be settled by peaceful means," [18] the assumption under-lying these platitudes was that, so long as peace was maintained, no changes distasteful to France or Great Britain could be made in the *status quo.* In the crisis, France and Great Britain were trapped by the slogans which they themselves had used in the past to discredit the dissatisfied Powers, and Germany had become sufficiently dominant (as France and Great Britain had hitherto been) to turn the desire for peace to her own advantage. Since the Munich Agreement, a significant change has occurred in the attitude of the German and Italian dictators. Herr Hitler eagerly depicts Germany as a bulwark of peace menaced by war-mongering democracies. The League of Nations, he declared in his Reichstag speech of April 28, 1938, is a "stirrer up of trouble," and collective security means "continuous danger of war." Signor Mussolini in a recent speech at Turin borrowed the British formula about the possibility of settling all international disputes by peaceful means, and declared that "there are not in Europe at present problems so big and so active as to justify a war which from a European conflict would naturally become universal." [19] It would be a mistake to dismiss such utterances as hypocritical. They are symptoms that Germany and Italy are already looking forward to the time when, as dominant Powers, they will acquire the vested

[15] "Pray earnestly that right may triumph," said the representative of the Philadelphia coal-owners in an early strike organized by the United Mine Workers, "remembering that the Lord God Omnipotent still reigns, and that His reign is one of law and order, and not of violence and crime" (H. F. Pringle, *Theodore Roosevelt,* p. 267).

[16] R. Niebuhr, *Moral Man and Immoral Society,* p. 153.

[17] Speech in the Reichstag, January 30, 1939.

[18] *League of Nations: Eighteenth Assembly,* p. 63.

[19] *The Times,* May 15, 1939.

interest in peace recently enjoyed by Great Britain and France, and be able to pillory the democratic countries as enemies of peace. These developments make it easier than it would perhaps have been a few years ago for an Englishman to appreciate Halévy's subtle observation that "propaganda against war is itself a form of war propaganda." [20]

THE REALIST CRITIQUE OF INTERNATIONALISM

The concept of internationalism is a special form of the doctrine of the harmony of interests. It yields to the same analysis; and there are the same difficulties about regarding it as an absolute standard independent of the interests and policies of those who promulgate it. "Cosmopolitanism," wrote Sun Yat-sen, "is the same thing as China's theory of world empire two thousand years ago. . . . China once wanted to be sovereign lord of the earth and to stand above every other nation, so she espoused cosmopolitanism." [21] In the Egypt of the Eighteenth Dynasty, according to Dr. Freud, "imperialism was reflected in religion as universality and monotheism." [22] The doctrine of a single world-state, propagated by the Roman Empire and later by the Catholic Church, was the symbol of a claim to universal dominion. Modern internationalism has its genesis in seventeenth- and eighteenth-century France, during which French hegemony in Europe was at its height. This was the period which produced Sully's *Grand Dessin* and the Abbé Saint-Pierre's *Projet de Paix Perpétuelle* (both plans to perpetuate an international *status quo* favourable to the French monarchy), which saw the birth of the humanitarian and cosmopolitan doctrines of "the Enlightenment," and which established French as the universal language of educated people. In the next century, the leadership passed to Great Britain, which became the home of internationalism. On the eve of the Great Exhibition of 1851 which, more than any other single event, established Great Britain's title to world supremacy, the Prince Consort spoke movingly of "that great end to which . . . all history points—the realisation of the unity of mankind"; [23] and Tennyson hymned "the parliament of man, the federation of the world." France chose the moment of her greatest supremacy in post-War Europe to launch a plan of "European Union"; and Japan at the present time is developing an ambition to proclaim herself the leader of a united Asia. It is symptomatic of the growing international predominance of the United States that widespread popularity should recently have been enjoyed by the book of an American journalist advocating a world union of democracies, in which the United States would play the predominant role. [24]

---

[20] Halévy, *A History of the English People in 1895-1905* (Engl. transl.), i. Introduction, p. xi.
[21] Sun Yat-sen, *San Min Chu I* (Engl. transl.), pp. 68-9.
[22] Sigmund Freud, *Moses and Monotheism*, p. 36.
[23] T. Martin, *Life of the Prince Consort*, iii. p. 247.
[24] Clarence Streit, *Union Now*.

Just as pleas for "national solidarity" in domestic politics always come from a dominant group which can use this solidarity to strengthen its own control over the nation as a whole, so pleas for international solidarity and world union come from those dominant nations which may hope to exercise control over a unified world. Countries which are struggling to force their way into the dominant group naturally tend to invoke nationalism against the internationalism of the controlling Powers. In the sixteenth century, England opposed her nascent nationalism to the internationalism of the Papacy and the Empire. Since the beginning of the nineteenth century, Germany has opposed her nascent nationalism to the internationalism first of France, then of Great Britain. This circumstance has made her impervious to those universalist and humanitarian doctrines which were popular in eighteenth-century France and nineteenth-century Britain; and her hostility to internationalism has been further aggravated since 1919, when Great Britain and France endeavoured to create a new "international order" as a bulwark of their own predominance. "By 'international,'" wrote a recent German correspondent in *The Times*, "we have come to understand a conception that places other nations at an advantage over our own." [25] Nevertheless, there is little doubt that Germany, if she became supreme in Europe, would adopt international slogans and establish some kind of international organisation to bolster up her power. A British Labour ex-Minister recently advocated the suppression of Article 16 of the Covenant of the League of Nations on the unexpected ground that the totalitarian states might some day capture the League and invoke that article to justify the use of force by themselves.[26] Though it seems unlikely that Germany or Italy would resort to the existing machinery of the League of Nations, the anticipation was, in principle, a shrewd one. There are already signs of the development of the Anti-Comintern Pact into some form of international organisation. "The Anti-Comintern Pact," said Herr Hitler in the Reichstag on January 30, 1939, "will perhaps one day become the crystallisation point of a group of Powers whose ultimate aim is none other than to eliminate the menace to the peace and culture of the world instigated by a satanic apparition." "Either Europe must achieve solidarity," remarked an Italian journal about the same time "or the 'axis' will impose it." [27] "Europe in its entirety," says Dr. Goebbels, "is adopting a new order and a new orientation under the intellectual leadership of National Socialist Germany and Fascist Italy." [28] This is the symptom not of a change of heart, but of the fact that Germany and Italy are now approaching the time when they may become strong

---

[25] Dr. FitzRandolph, *The Times*, November 5, 1938.
[26] Lord Marley in the House of Lords, November 30, 1938: *Official Report*, col. 258.
[27] *Relazioni Internazionali*, quoted in *The Times*, December 5, 1938.
[28] *Völkischer Beobachter*, April 1, 1939.

enough to espouse internationalism. "International order," and "international solidarity" will always be slogans of those who feel strong enough to impose them on others.

The exposure of the real basis of the professedly abstract principles commonly invoked in international politics is the most damning and most convincing part of the realist indictment of utopianism. The nature of the charge is frequently misunderstood by those who seek to refute it. The charge is not that human beings fail to live up to their principles. It matters little that Wilson, who thought that the right was more precious than peace, and Briand, who thought that peace came even before justice, and Mr. Eden, who believed in collective security, failed themselves, or failed to induce their countrymen, to apply these principles consistently. What matters is that these supposedly absolute and universal principles were not principles at all, but the unconscious reflexions of national policy based on a particular interpretation of national interest at a particular time. There is a sense in which peace and co-operation between nations or classes or individuals is a common and universal end irrespective of conflicting interests and politics. There is a sense in which a common interest exists in the maintenance of order, whether it be international order or "law and order" within the nation. But as soon as the attempt is made to apply these supposedly abstract principles to a concrete political situation, they are revealed as the transparent disguises of selfish and vested interests. The bankruptcy of atopianism resides not in its failure to live up to its principles, but in the exposure of its inability to provide any absolute and disinterested standard for the conduct of international affairs. The utopian of to-day, faced by the collapse of standards whose interested character he has failed to penetrate, takes refuge in condemnation of a reality which refuses to conform to these standards. A passage penned by the German historian Meinecke immediately after the War is the best judgment by anticipation of the role of utopianism in the international politics of the post-War period:

> The profound defect of the Western, natural-law type of thought was that, when applied to the real life of the state, it remained a dead letter, did not penetrate the consciousness of statesmen, did not hinder the modern hypertrophy of state interest, and so led either to aimless complaints and doctrinaire suppositions or else to inner falsehood and cant.[29]

These "aimless complaints," these "doctrinaire suppositions," this "inner falsehood and cant" will be familiar to all those who have studied what has been written about international politics in English-speaking countries during the past few years.

[29] Meinecke, *Staatsräson*, p. 533.

LEONARD WOOLF

5. *Utopia and Reality: A Liberal Appraisal**

We are living through a period in which the use of power, force, or violence is playing a predominant part in human society. The phenomenon is not confined to the relations between states; it can be observed within states in the relation between government and individuals and between individual and individual. Societies and historical periods have differed widely in their organization of power and in the way in which force or violence has been applied to human relations. Until comparatively recent times it was commonly held that the communal control of power and the elimination of force or violence from human and social relations were important elements in civilization. It was even believed that these views were not merely utopian aspirations, but had in many cases been translated into historical facts. In the 19th century the potential power of a physically strong man to impose his will upon a physically weak man had in most places been rendered inoperative by social organization. By similar methods the potential power of the man with a club, an axe, or an automatic pistol had also been rendered inoperative. The power of kings over their subjects, of aristocrats over commoners, of men over women, of governments over citizens, of employers over employed had often, it seemed, been eliminated or modified. Most people believed that it was possible not only to control or modify the use of power, but also that of violence, and to do so effectively for an intelligent purpose. It seemed to be undeniable that the use of torture and flogging as methods of "doing justice" had been abolished in some places, that in others it was no longer possible for a man to be hanged for stealing a sheep or a few pence, and that in others the utopian idea of abolishing the death penalty had been adopted without apparently increasing the number of murderers or of their victims.

In the nineteenth century the control of the use of power and the efforts to eliminate force and violence from the relations between states, governments, and individuals were closely associated with the practice and theory of liberalism, democracy, and humanitarianism. The war of 1914-1918 for four years reversed this process of controlling, sublimating, and eliminating the use of power or violence. War between states is not only the logical result of "power politics," it is power politics reduced to their simplest terms. It also entails the adoption of force and violence as primary elements in determining a vast number of human and social relations which at other

* *The Political Quarterly*, Vol. XI (April–June, 1940). By permission.

times are regulated by discussion, compromise, "law," or other non-violent methods. Few people will deny that this four year period of power and violence had a considerable effect upon European society and the minds of Europeans. The simplest and most direct effects of historical events are often soon forgotten or underestimated by historians and politicians. It is a simple fact that an enormous majority of those Europeans who were not killed in what they then called the Great War did not like it; in fact, they disliked it so intensely that enormous numbers of ordinary persons said: "Never again," by which they meant that in their humble opinion everything should be done which was possible to eliminate war from European society. Their aspiration may or may not have been utopian—we shall consider this question later—but their convictions, the state of their minds, were a political reality which was having profound effects all over Europe and which not even the most realist statesman, general, or historian could afford to neglect.

One effect of this conviction was the founding of the League of Nations. The disillusionment of ordinary men and women in 1918, their feeling that war was in the twentieth century not a tolerable way of life, or even of death, their dim doubts as to whether it had proved to be an effective method of "settling anything"—these things were not the only cause of the birth of the League of Nations, but they had a good deal to do with it. The statesmen —other than Wilson—who established the League did not believe in it; they thought themselves to be realists and the League utopia. The statesmen who "worked" the League for fifteen years or so did not believe in it; they thought themselves to be realists and the League either utopia or a convenient or inconvenient instrument—it depended upon circumstances—of national policy. The main impetus which had brought the League into being and prevented it from being completely scrapped by realists or reality was another reality, the voice of common people who had said and might perhaps still say: "Never again."

The League failed. As it failed, ordinary people could no longer be heard saying: "Never again"; you heard them saying clearly, often bitterly, always helplessly, in the streets of cities, in fields, and villages, "It is coming again." The two realities were not unconnected. The failure of the League may have been due to its having been utopian, but it was not an isolated historical incident, the casual failure of an academic dream brought up with a jolt against the hard facts of life. It was only part of a general historical process or movement which can be clearly discerned in the period between November, 1918, and September, 1939. It gradually became clear that the post-war Europe was not going to return to the nineteenth century attitude towards power, force, and violence. In many countries governments allowed private armies to fight one another in the streets of great cities. Dictatorships took the place of democracies. Pogroms became a recognized method of administration; change of government or even of the government's programme or policy were effected or prevented by "massacres," "purges," executions, or political assassinations.

Fascism in Italy—national socialism in Germany—Stalinism in the U.S.S.R.—Pilsudski or a government of generals or colonels or majors in Poland—little dictators in the little countries—Manchuria, Abyssinia, the destruction of the republican government of Spain, the destruction of the democratic republic of Czechoslovakia, the invasion and partition of Poland —thus we have reached the second great war. These facts can only be stated and interpreted in terms of power, force, and violence. They are the negation of another series of terms which had previously seemed to have some meaning to human beings: peace, law, order, common interests, compromise, liberty and democracy. Human beings are never content just to accept the facts, their miseries, savagery, and stupidities. They have an itch to explain and interpret them, to find some fig leaf of a theory or philosophy to cover the nakedness of their own folly or cruelty. Politicians and professors of politics and history are always ready to supply fig leaves, theories, and philosophies, to comfort the dead, the dying, the disappointed, and the crucified with the assurance that nothing could possibly have happened except in the way in which it did happen and is happening and that everything is for the best in the worst of all possible worlds.

So today you will find any number of people offering us fig leaves to cover fascism, communism, and war, theories which prove the inevitable failure of democracy and the League of Nations, philosophies which discover the seeds of a new world in the most ancient forms of violence and slavery. There is a family likeness in all these ex post facto consolatory explanations, they rely upon a distinction between illusions, shams, or utopias and realities. Democracy was a "sham"; dictatorship is a "reality." The common interests of nations and peace are an illusion; conflict of national interests and war are "real." The League of Nations was "utopian"; power politics are "reality." The validity of these theories and of the practical policies, based upon them, which we are exhorted to pursue must depend upon what is meant by this distinction between political or historical utopia and political or historical reality. To understand the distinction is, therefore, not an academic, but a highly practical question, for it is clearly politically imbecile to ignore realities or to pursue policies which are impossible of attainment—only we must know what is a reality and what is "impossible of attainment."

Our search for enlightenment may well start from a book by Professor E. H. Carr which has recently attracted much attention.[1] Mr. Carr is Professor of International Politics and has an intimate knowledge of his subject.

---

[1] *The Twenty Years' Crisis*, 1919-1939. (Macmillan. 10s. 6d.). It should be read together with a smaller book which Professor Carr published about the same time: *The Foreign Policy of Britain from 1918 to Sept. 1939.* (Longmans. 6s.).

His book on Bakunin proved him to be a man of intelligence with an unusual capacity for historical impartiality. His new book is an attempt to lay the foundations of a science of international relations and at the same time to "analyse the underlying and significant, rather than the immediate and personal, causes" in the history of the last twenty years which have brought us once more into war. The whole of Professor Carr's analysis is based upon a distinction between utopia and reality, and if any one should be capable of making us understand what it is it should be he. There are, as one would expect, very good things in the book, acute analysis of particular situations or processes, illuminating comments on particular events, and trenchant and often salutary criticism of things, theories, and persons with whom Professor Carr is out of sympathy or out of understanding. And yet the book fails in its purpose. It does not give us the beginnings of a science of international relations, because its method is unscientific. It attempts to interpret the events of the last twenty years by means of a distinction between what is utopian and what is real in policy. But, although the whole of his argument depends upon the difference between "utopia" and "realism," he never makes clear the distinction between them either to himself or to his reader. The reason is that he had not pushed his analysis either of terms or of events or of causes—particularly psychological causes—far enough.

Let us begin with terms. The term utopia is commonly used in two different ways. We speak of a dream or a policy being utopian in the sense that it contains a purpose or is based upon a hope or ideal which is incapable of fulfilment, and in this sense we oppose it to "realism." But it is also used in the sense of "unreal" as opposed to "reality." The two senses are not the same, but they are continually confused with disastrous results to truth and clear thinking in political controversy and in Professor Carr's book. This can best be shown by examples. Professor Carr's thesis is that the beliefs, objectives, and policies of nineteenth century liberal democrats and of the supporters of the League of Nations in the international field were utopian. He means by that that their beliefs were false and that their objectives and policies were impossible of attainment—not by any means, it will be observed, the same thing. He has a good deal to say about the falseness of their beliefs, but he never clearly demonstrates to us why their objectives and policies were impossible of attainment. He often implies that the failure of the League and of the attempt to reconstruct a peaceful Europe was "inevitable" merely because it was a failure. This attitude can be seen in the emotional colour of his adjectives in such a sentence as "The first and most obvious tragedy of this utopia was its ignominious collapse." Here you have the vulgar and false view that failure is "ignominious" and proves somehow or other that the attempt itself was discreditable and unattainable. These superficial judgments are characteristic of contemporaries: in 1790, 1830, 1848, 1900, and 1918, if Professor Carr had been a Frenchman, he would have talked about the "triumph" of democracy and the democratic ideals of the "Revolution," but in 1800, 1828, 1851, and 1939 he would have talked about their "ignominious collapse" and utopianism.

As a matter of fact, Professor Carr is himself really well aware of all this. Where he approves of a policy which has failed, as for instance Mr. Chamberlain's appeasement policy, he sees that the failure does not prove its utopianism or its ignominy, and in his other book he writes: "There is a common inclination in politics to take the deterministic view that any policy which fails was bound to fail and should, therefore, never have been tried. The charge that British Ministers were the dupes of the Axis Powers should not be too lightly made." If the collapse of the policy of appeasement does not prove that it was utopian, the collapse of the League does not prove that it was utopian, and if Mr. Chamberlain's failure was not ignominious, why should Professor Carr see ignominy in the failure of the League?

The answer to this question is that Professor Carr is unconsciously infected with the temporary social psychology of the time, the acceptance of power and force and conflict as the primary (and therefore best) elements in social organization and human relations, and that he feels the necessity to provide the fig leaf of a theory to cover the results of this psychology. He does this by assuming that policies and social objectives inconsistent with *existing* facts or with the psychology of power, violence, and conflict are utopian, and his theory or proof is based upon a confusion between the two senses of "utopian" and upon the common, but completely unscientific, assumption that power, violence, and conflict are more "real" elements in society than, e.g., beliefs, law, and co-operation for a common end or common interests.

The League was a political and social organization of states. It was established in answer to a demand, and in this sense it had an objective or ideal—the elimination of war, the resolution of international conflict, and the promotion of the common interests of states or nations. The ideal or objective was not in the League, but in the heads of those who established it or caused it to be established. The League is utopian only if those ideals or objectives are impossible of attainment. The policy of the League, which aimed at organizing the relations of states upon the basis of their common rather than their conflicting interests, is not utopian merely because it aimed at an unattained ideal or objective, as Professor Carr and many other people frequently assume. All policies, even of the most realist statesmen, aim at unattained ideals or objectives. The policy of Hitler aims at the as yet unattained ideal or objective of organizing the relations of states in Europe on the basis of force and conflicting interest, with Germany having an overwhelming superiority of power and therefore able to promote her interests at the expense of other states. In Professor Carr's sense his policy is "realist"; in fact, it is highly probable that his objective will not be attained and is unattainable, and is therefore really utopian. Again, Mr. Chamberlain's policy had as its ideal or objective peace with Hitler by abandoning any common resistance to aggression, any obligation to aid victims of aggression, and by placating Hitler and yielding to his demands. The objective was certainly not attained and was probably unattainable, and the policy was abandoned for its exact opposite. If the criterion of utopianism is attainability, the policies of Hitler and Mr. Chamberlain are no less utopian than the League policy.

Professor Carr's dealing with utopianism and reality in connection with policy is unsatisfactory because he does not carry his analysis of the psychology of political objective or ideal far enough. But it also breaks down in another important way: it accepts the vulgar delusion about the "reality" of some political concepts and the "unreality" of others, and then illicitly argues that a policy concerned with the former is "utopian" and a policy concerned with the latter "realist." For instance, Professor Carr maintains that the international policy of nineteenth-century liberalism and of the League both broke down because they were based on the promotion of the common interests of states and not on the conflict of state interests. They ignored the problem of power, which is the instrument of conflicting interests. Conflicting interests and power are "real"; harmony of interests is unreal or non-existent and political instruments of co-operation in common international interests are therefore also "unreal." Hence power politics are real and the League and the liberal policy of free trade and international co-operation "utopian."

This kind of attitude towards "interests" and "power" is very common at the present moment, but it is rooted in muddled thinking. The idea that there is some "reality" in a conflicting interest which does not exist in a common interest is an illusion. It springs from the obvious fact that most people are more *conscious* of their own immediate interests than of common interests and that the pursuit of common interests almost always entails the abandonment of some immediate individual interests. But the political reality of interests does not depend upon people's consciousness of them, but on the relative effects of different actions and different forms of social organization. In private life and national politics we have learnt this by bitter experience, and no one believes that the interest of men with knives to commit murder and robbery is more "real" than the interest of men with knives to refrain and be restrained from committing murder and robbery. International psychology is still, however, so crude that even a man like Professor Carr can believe that the interest of Germany in cutting the throat of Czechoslovakia is more real than the interest of both Germany and Czechoslovakia in living peacefully together and composing conflicting interests by compromise, merely because Herr Hitler has a very large army, a very large air force, and a very loud and rasping voice.

The question what interests are real, or to put it in another way what is really the interest of an individual, a group, a class, or a nation, cannot be settled in this cavalier way. A study of the history of human society and of international relations, not to speak of one's own life, will make one very careful not to dogmatize about real or unreal interests *in any particular case*. But it also teaches this lesson: that *generally and in the long run* common interests are more real than conflicting interests politically. Nearly every one would agree that this is true with regard to the internal organization of the national state; in the long run and generally every one gains by the pursuit of a common interest even at the expense of individual interests; even the potential murderer is better off in the end if he refrains or is restrained from cutting the rich man's throat; a class which ruthlessly pursues what it considers its own interest at the expense of other classes nine times out of ten digs its own economic grave. But there is reason for thinking that what is true of national is also true of international society. For many centuries now the relations of states have been determined by acceptance of the hypothesis that their conflicting interests are so exclusively real that they must form the basis of national policy. I cannot believe that, if Professor Carr and others who agree with him examine impartially the results, they can maintain that they are encouraging. It would be interesting to learn which of the "Great Powers" had really gained by their ruthless pursuit of conflicting interests in the years 1790, 1815, 1870, 1914, and 1939, and which had lost by pursuing utopian common interests. And *realpolitik?* If reality is to be judged by success, what is the judgment of history upon the work of such realists as Napoleon I, Napoleon III, Bismarck, Wilhelm II, the Russian Tsars, not to speak of British imperialists? The fact is that nothing is more "utopian" than the idea that you can create a stable and permanent society by power and the pursuit of conflicting interests; the ideal is unattainable because it involves an attempt to use two of the most unstable and disintegrating of all social forces, violence in the service of cupidity, as the primary ingredients in that cement which is to hold society together.

The question whether co-operation of states in common interests is possible, whether the power of individual states can be controlled internationally as the power of individuals, groups, and classes have been controlled nationally, and whether these objectives and the preservation of peace can be attained through some such international organization as the League is at the same time much simpler and more complicated than it appears in the books of those who see some peculiar reality in power and conflict and are therefore continually reading the burial service over democracy, the nineteenth century, and internationalism. It has little or nothing to do with "morality," "reality," "liberalism," or "reason." Whether the policy of organizing European states pacifically and of eliminating the *probability* of war is or is not utopian depends solely upon whether that objective is or is not attainable. It has nothing whatsoever to do with some imaginary quality of "reality" attaching to power or violence and to "conflicting interests," but not attaching to law, co-operation, and common interests. The attainability of a political objective almost always depends mainly upon three elements: facts, psychology, and the creation of social machinery or organization appropriate to the object or purpose of the policy and to the psychology. For instance, the attainability of the purpose of Zionists depends first upon such facts as the size of Palestine and the climate of its several districts. It would be utopian to ignore these facts and to put into Palestine more Jews than could exist there or to put a million Jews suddenly into a district of Palestine which is a waterless desert. Another element which has to be considered is the power of the Arabs to shoot Jewish immigrants, and yet another is the conflicting and the common interests of Jews and Arabs. Here it is partly a question of fact and partly of psychology; there is no question of some mystic element of reality attaching to some of the facts and not to others. It is a fact that the Arab has or may have the power to shoot the Jew; it is also a fact that he has or may have the power to co-operate with the Jew. It may be his immediate interest, i.e., he may gain at the moment, by shooting the Jew, but on the other hand it may be his "real" interest, i.e., he might gain more, by refraining from shooting and by co-operating with the Jew. The power to shoot is no more and no less "real" than the power to co-operate, and the conflicting interest which is served by shooting is no more and no less "real" than the common interest which is served by co-operation. Here the most important element is really psychological. The attainability of the Zionist policy will depend upon whether Arabs and Jews pursue their separate interests by conflict or whether they pursue their common interests by co-operation. Lastly, provided that facts and psychology did not make the purpose of Zionism impossible, it would still be necessary to create a form of government appropriate to the peculiar purpose, the peculiar facts, and the peculiar psychology.

This analysis applies no less to the problem of war and peace and international relations than to that of Zionism. Five hundred years of European history have proved that the "realist" system of power politics, war, and the conflict of interests is grotesquely utopian. Its purpose is to ensure stability of national power, glory, prosperity, and peace; its result has been a kaleidoscope of loud voiced jingoism and national glory alternating with war, defeat, misery, and impoverishment. The reason why power policy and the attempt to establish a stable European society upon it always fails and always must fail is that it ignores both the reality of facts and the reality of psychology. That of course does not mean that the opposite policy, which was embodied in the League idea, is attainable. Whether a pacific international system, based upon co-operation in common interests, is possible in Europe will depend primarily upon facts and upon psychology. But I am inclined to think that the main difficulty, the real cause of the League's failure, is not to be looked for in facts and in "reality," but in psychology.

The international relations of France and Britain between 1895 and 1939 throw light upon the general problem of international relations and upon the effect of psychology. In 1895 France and Britain had a large number of conflicting and a large number of common interests. In the autumn of 1903 when Lansdowne and Delcassé sat down to discuss Anglo-French relations, nothing had happened to alter the objective reality of those interests. The conflict of some and the community of other interests still persisted; both series were "real." This fact blows up the whole of Professor Carr's argument about utopianism and reality in international relations. For in 1903 a revolution in Anglo-French policy and relations took place and it was determined mainly by psychology, not by power, realism, or utopianism. Before 1903 the governments of the two countries conducted their foreign policy on the basis and hypothesis that the most important, the "real," interests of France and Britain were in conflict, and that their common interests were illusory, the utopian hallucinations of little Englanders and pacifists. What benefited France harmed Britain, and vice versa twice over. The basis of their international relations was therefore assumed to be conflict of interests, and the main instrument of policy was power. Co-operation, compromise, political machinery for composing differences or pursuing common interests were ruled out; on both sides of the channel statesmen thought of the use (or threat of using) power, economic or military, to promote the interests of their own country at the expense of the other as the proper and inevitable instrument of policy.

In 1903 the relations between the two countries were completely and permanently changed, not owing to any change in their existing interests or in their relative power, but by a decision of their governments, and this decision was caused by a psychological change. Lansdowne and Delcassé did not suddenly see that the conflicting interests had suddenly become "unreal" and the common interests "real"; they came to the conclusion that in general and in the long run the two countries would gain more by pursuing common interests and attempting to compose conflicting interests by compromise than by continuing the pursuit by each of its own interests at the expense of the other. As soon as this psychological change took place, it had a devastating effect upon the importance of power as an element in the relations between the two states. In 1895 the relative power of the two countries had been an element of primary importance in their relations and policy; after 1904 it became negligible. The reason was that once the objective of policy had been changed by the Entente, power became a negligible and inappropriate instrument of that policy. This shows the absurdity of ascribing some peculiar quality of reality to power in international relations. Power is a very real element in human society, just as are law, co-operation, ideas, beliefs, and ideals; its importance at any particular moment depends to a large extent upon the social or political objective which at that moment individuals are pursuing.

There is absolutely no reason to believe that the change which took place in 1904 in the national policies and international relations of France and Britain could not also take place in the policies and international relations of all the Great Powers, or all the states, of Europe. It is no answer to say that it was only fear of Germany which made France and Britain co-operate instead of fighting one another and that their co-operation was directed *against* another Power. To say that is to admit that psychology and not reality, power, or utopianism is the primary determinant in the international situation. If fear of Germany was sufficient to turn France and Britain away from the pursuit of their "real" conflicting interests into the pursuit of their "utopian" harmony of interests and to eliminate the probability—one might almost say possibility—of war between them for half a century there is no reason, except psychological, why fear of mutual destruction should not effect a similar change in the policies of all European states.

That is the real international problem which confronts Europe and civilization today. It is not a choice between utopia and reality, but between the psychology of conflicting interests and the organization of power politics on the one hand and the psychology of common interests and the organization of international co-operation on the other. The psychology of common interests and of co-operation and peace are there; it is, no doubt, weak, particularly among statesmen, generals, and perhaps professors, but it is there, and has widened and deepened in the last century. Its weakness is largely due to two causes. The first is the universal obstacle to civilization in all spheres of human society, the fact that pursuit of common interests almost always means the abandonment of some conflicting, individual, immediate interests. The immediate appeal of the individual, conflicting interest is immensely strong, and it requires intelligence and restraint to see or learn that in the long run the individual may gain by abandoning it on the pursuit of common interests. Secondly, the international organization of power is itself a tremendous obstacle in the growth and influence of the psychology of co-operation. It breeds fear, and fear is the greatest fomenter of conflict among human beings and the most potent destroyer of co-operation.

No sensible man will pretend that establishment of international peace is an easy thing. Whether it is possible depends upon whether the international organization of power, as it exists today, can be altered and whether the psychology of common interests and co-operation can be made an active determinant of national policies. These things may not prove possible but they are not impossible because conflict and conflicting interests are real, and co-operation and common interests are utopian. To believe that is merely to try to rationalize one's own and other people's primitive psychology.

WOODROW WILSON

6. Peace through Law*

I would consider myself recreant to every mother and father, every wife and sweetheart in this country, if I consented to the ending of this war without a guarantee that there would be no other. You say, "Is it an absolute guarantee?" No; there is no absolute guarantee against human passion; but even if it were only 10 per cent of a guarantee, would not you rather have 10 per cent guarantee against war than none? If it only creates a presumption that there will not be war, would you not rather have that presumption than live under the certainty that there will be war? For, I tell you, my fellow citizens, I can predict with absolute certainty that within another generation there will be another world war if the nations of the world do not concert the method by which to prevent it.

The chief motives which led us to enter the war will be defeated unless that Covenant is ratified and acted upon with vigor. We cannot in honor whittle it down or weaken it as the Republican leaders of the Senate have proposed to do. If we are to exercise the kind of leadership to which the founders of the Republic looked forward and which they depended upon their successors to establish, we must do this with courage and unalterable determination. They expected the United States to be always the leader in the defense of liberty and ordered peace throughout the world, and we are unworthy to call ourselves their successors unless we fulfill the great purpose they entertained and proclaimed.

If Germany had dreamed that anything like the greater part of the world would combine against her, she never would have begun the war, and she did not dare to let the opinion of mankind crystallize against her by the discussion of the purposes which she had in mind. What I want to point out to you to-night is that we are making a fundamental choice. You have either got to have the old system, of which Germany was the perfect flower, or you have got to have a new system. You cannot have a new system unless you provide a substitute, and adequate substitute, for the old, and when certain of our fellow citizens take the position that we do not want to go into any combination at all but want to take care of ourselves, all I have to say to them is that that is exactly the German position.

You have been grossly misled with regard to the treaty, and particularly with regard to the proposed character of the League of Nations, by those who have assumed the serious responsibility of opposing it. They have gone so far that those who have spent their lives, as I have spent my life, in familiarizing themselves with the history and traditions and policies of the Nation, must stand amazed at the gross ignorance and impudent audacity which have led them to attempt to invent an "Americanism" of their own, which has no foundation whatever in any of the authentic traditions of the Government.

Americanism, as they conceive it, reverses the whole process of the last few tragical years. It would substitute America for Prussia in the policy of isolation and defiant segregation. Their conception of the dignity of the Nation and its interest is that we should stand apart and watch for opportunities to advance our own interests, involve ourselves in no responsibility for the maintenance of the right in the world or for the continued vindication of any of the things for which we entered the war to fight.

The conception of the great creators of the Government was absolutely opposite to this. They thought of America as the light of the world as created to lead the world in the assertion of the rights of peoples and the rights of free nations; as destined to set a responsible example to all the world of what free Government is and can do for the maintenance of right standards, both national and international.

This light the opponents of the League would quench. They would relegate the United States to a subordinate rôle in the affairs of the world.

Why should we be afraid of responsibilities which we are qualified to sustain and which the whole of our history has constituted a promise to the world we would sustain!

This is the most momentous issue that has ever been presented to the people of the United States, and I do not doubt that the hope of the whole world will be verified by an absolute assertion by the voters of the country of the determination of the United States to live up to all the great expectations which they created by entering the war and enabling the other great nations of the world to bring it to a victorious conclusion, to the confusion of Prussianism and everything that arises out of Prussianism. Surely we shall not fail to keep the promise sealed in the death and sacrifice of our incomparable soldiers, sailors and marines who await our verdict beneath the sod of France.

The old system was, Be ready, and we can be ready. I have heard gentlemen say, "America can take care of herself." Yes, she can take care of herself. Every man would have to train to arms. We would have to have a great standing army. We would have to have accumulations of military material such as Germany used to have. We would enjoy the luxuries of taxes even higher than we pay now. We could accumulate our force, and then our force would have to be directed by some kind of sufficiently vigorous central power. You would have a military government in spirit if not in form. No use having a fighting Nation if there is not somebody to swing it! If you do not want your President to be a representative of the civil purposes of this country, you can turn him into merely a commander in chief, ready to fight the world. But if you did nobody would recognize America in those strange and altered circumstances. All the world would stand at amaze and say, "Has America forgotten everything that she ever professed?" The picture is one that every American repudiates; and I challenge any man who has *that purpose at the back of his thought to avow it. If he comes and tells you that America must stand alone and take care of herself, ask him how it is going to be done, and he will not dare tell you, because you would show him the door and say, "We do not know any such America."

Yet we cannot do without force. You cannot establish land titles, as I have expressed it, and not maintain them. Suppose that the land titles of South Dakota were disturbed. Suppose the farm lines were moved, say, ten feet. You know what would happen. Along every fence line you would see farmers perching with guns on their knees. The only reason they are not perching now is that there are land deeds deposited in a particular place, and the whole majesty and force and judicial system of the State of South Dakota are behind the titles. Very well, we have got to do something like that internationally. You cannot set up Poland, whom all the world through centuries has pitied and sympathized with, as the owner of her property and not have somebody take care that her title deeds are respected. You cannot establish freedom, my fellow citizens, without force, and the only force you can substitute for an armed mankind is the concerted force of the combined action of mankind through the instrumentality of all the enlightened Governments of the world. This is the only conceivable system that you can substitute for the old order of things which brought the calamity of this war upon us and would assuredly bring the calamity of another war upon us. Your choice is between the League of Nations and Germanism. I have told you what I mean by Germanism—taking care of yourselves, being armed and ready, having a chip on your shoulder, thinking of nothing but your own rights and never thinking of the rights of anybody else, thinking that you were put into this world to see that American might was asserted and forgetting that American might ought never to be used against the weak, ought never to be used in an unjust cause, ought never to be used for aggression; ought to be used with the heart of humanity beating behind it.

Sometimes people call me an idealist. Well, that is the way I know I am an American. America, my fellow citizens—I do not say it in disparagement of any other great people—America is the only idealistic Nation in the world. When I speak practical judgments about business affairs, I can only guess whether I am speaking the voice of America or not, but when I speak the ideal purposes of history I know that I am speaking the voice of America, because I have saturated myself since I was a boy in the records of that spirit, and everywhere in them there is this authentic tone of the love of justice and the service of humanity. If by any mysterious influence of error America should not take the leading part in this new enterprise of concerted power, the world would experience one of those reversals of sentiment, one of those penetrating chills of reaction, which would lead to a universal cynicism, for if America goes back upon mankind, mankind has no other place to turn. It is the hope of Nations all over the world that America will do this great thing.

Settlements may be temporary, but the action of the nations in the interest of peace and justice must be permanent. We can set up permanent processes. We may not be able to set up permanent decisions. Therefore, it seems to me that we must take, so far as we can, a picture of the world into our minds. Is it not a startling circumstance, for one thing, that the great discoveries of science, that the quiet studies of men in laboratories, that the thoughtful developments which have taken place in quiet lecture rooms, have now been turned to the destruction of civilization? The powers of destruction have not so much multiplied as gained facility. The enemy whom we have just overcome had at his seats of learning some of the principal centers of scientific study and discovery, and he used them in order to make destruction sudden and complete; and only the watchful, continuous coöperation of men can see to it that science as well as armed men is kept within the harness of civilization.

In a sense the United States is less interested in this subject than the other nations here assembled. With her great territory and her extensive sea borders, it is less likely that the United States should suffer from the attack of enemies than that many of the other nations here should suffer; and the ardor of the United States—for it is a very deep and genuine ardor—for the society of nations is not an ardor springing out of fear or apprehension, but an ardor springing out of the ideals which have come to consciousness in this war. In coming into this war the United States never for a moment thought that she was intervening in the politics of Europe or the politics of Asia or the politics of any part of the world. Her thought was that all the world had now become conscious that there was a single cause which turned upon the issues of this war. That was the cause of justice and of liberty for men of every kind and place. Therefore, the United States should feel that its part in this war had been played in vain if there ensued upon it merely a body of European settlements. It would feel that it could not take part in guaranteeing those European settlements unless that guarantee involved the continuous superintendence of the peace of the world by the associated nations of the world.

Therefore, it seems to me that we must concert our best judgment in order to make this League of Nations a vital thing—not merely a formal thing, not an occasional thing, not a thing sometimes called into life to meet an exigency, but always functioning in watchful attendance upon the interests of the nations—and that its continuity should be a vital continuity; that it should have functions that are continuing functions and that do not permit an intermission of its watchfulness and of its labour; that it should be the eye of the nations to keep watch upon the common interest, an eye that does not slumber, an eye that is everywhere watchful and attentive.

What we seek is the reign of law, based upon the consent of the governed and sustained by the organized opinion of mankind.

BIBLIOGRAPHICAL NOTES

BIBLIOGRAPHICAL NOTES

Part I: Philosophy, Psychology, and Politics

CHAPTER I. PHILOSOPHY AND POLITICS

BARKER, ERNEST, *The Citizen's Choice* (Cambridge, 1937). Chap. VI is on "Philosophy and Politics" (pp. 104-124), and it discusses primarily the contributions of philosophy to the theory and practice of politics. See also Michael Oakeshott, "Rational Conduct," *Cambridge Journal,* IV (October, 1950), 2-27.

BRECHT, ARNOLD, *Political Theory: The Foundations of Twentieth-Century Political Thought* (Princeton, 1959). A monumental work—the only one in the English language—that surveys, discusses, and analyzes the many and varied efforts to construct valid foundations for a theory of politics. Rejecting the certitude of traditional metaphysics and theology as well as the skepticism of the newer relativism of the Russell-Kelsen type, Brecht attempts to develop his own position of "scientific value relativism." He does not claim to provide an ultimate answer for the problem of the relations of science and value, but seeks to discover in what ways science can be useful in analyzing and formulating valid criteria of values. Both as an encyclopedia of twentieth-century political theory and as an original exploration in political philosophy, Brecht's work is indispensable to any serious study of the relations of philosophy and politics. Ample bibliographical notes (pp. 499-574) greatly enhance the usefulness of the volume.

EWING, A. C., "Ethics and Politics," *Philosophy,* XXVI (January, 1951), 19-29. Expresses the viewpoint that the big political issues ultimately turn on questions of value, that is, ethics, and confronts the assumptions of democratic politics with those of communism and Fascism. See also Ewing's "Political Arguments: Politics and Ethics," *ibid.,* XVI (April, 1941), 138-150.

HALLOWELL, JOHN H., "Politics and Ethics," *American Political Science Review,* XXXVIII (August, 1944), 639-655. Presents forcefully the metaphysical-religious position on the relations of philosophy and politics. For a similar viewpoint, see Walter E. Sandelius, "Reason and Political Power," *ibid.,* XLV (September, 1951), 703-715. For divergent views, see the symposium on "Politics and Ethics," *ibid.,* XL (April, 1946), 283-312, with contributions by Gabriel A. Almond, Lewis A. Dexter, William F. Whyte, and a rejoinder by John H. Hallowell.

KALLEN, HORACE M., *The Liberal Spirit: Essays on Problems of Freedom in the Modern World* (Ithaca and New York, 1948). The first essay, "The Liberal Spirit" (pp. 1-8), is one of the briefest and most incisive statements of the anti-absolutist position in philosophy and politics. See also the fifth chapter, "The Warfare of Religion against Science" (pp. 91-127).

KAUFMANN, FELIX, "The Issue of Ethical Neutrality in Political Science," *Social Research*, XVI (September, 1949), 344-352. Surveys the problem of value judgments in political science, and analyzes the similarities and dissimilarities between the physical and social studies.

KELSEN, HANS, *General Theory of Law and State* (Cambridge, Mass., 1945). Kelsen deals (pp. 419-433) with the psychological and logical parallels between basic philosophical and political systems. See also the following of his writings on this question: "Science and Politics," *American Political Science Review*, XLV (September, 1951), 641-661; *Vom Wesen und Wert der Demokratie*, 2d ed. (Tübingen, 1929); and *Staatsform und Weltanschauung* (Tübingen, 1933).

MARITAIN, JACQUES, *Christianity and Democracy* (New York, 1950). A re-affirmation of religion as the foundation of democracy, by the leading liberal representative of Catholic thought in the twentieth century. See also the following of his writings: *True Humanism* (New York, 1938); *The Rights of Man and Natural Law* (New York, 1943); *The Person and the Common Good* (New York, 1947); *Man and the State* (Phoenix Books, Chicago, 1954); and *Scholasticism and Politics* (Image Books, New York, 1960). Joseph W. Evans and Leo R. Ward (eds.), *The Social and Political Philosophy of Jacques Maritain: Selected Readings* (New York, 1955), is a useful collection of excerpts from Maritain's books and essays. Critical analyses of Maritain's thought will be found in Francis M. Myers, *The Warfare of Democratic Ideals* (Yellow Springs, Ohio, 1956), pp. 91-109, 121-130, and Charles Frankel, *The Case for Modern Man* (New York, 1956), pp. 45-84. For authoritative expositions of Catholic political doctrine, see John A. Ryan and Francis J. Boland, *Catholic Principles of Politics* (New York, 1940), and Heinrich A. Rommen, *The State in Catholic Thought: A Treatise in Political Philosophy* (St. Louis, 1945), both published with the *imprimatur* of the appropriate ecclesiastical authorities. Two convenient collections of readings contain papal pronouncements on basic political issues: Francis J. Powers (ed.), *Papal Pronouncements on the Political Order* (Westminster, Md., 1952), and Gerard F. Yates, S.J. (ed.), *Papal Thought on the State: Excerpts from Encyclicals and Other Writings of Recent Popes* (Crofts Classics, New York, 1958).

McKEON, RICHARD (ed.), *Democracy in a World of Tensions: A Symposium Prepared by UNESCO* (Chicago, 1951). Thirty-three contributors from all over the world, drawn from both sides of the Iron Curtain, discuss the meaning of democracy in the light of history, philosophy, politics, and economics. The symposium illustrates the point that the divergent conceptions of democracy are based on deeper philosophical divergencies. See also McKeon's "Philosophic Differences and the Issues of Freedom," *Ethics*, LXI (January, 1951), 105-135.

NIEBUHR, REINHOLD, *Moral Man and Immoral Society: A Study in Ethics and Politics* (New York, 1941). While Niebuhr is primarily a religious thinker, his contributions to political philosophy are considerable, and betray unusual insight. His main contribution has been to demonstrate, more successfully than has been done by any other modern theologian, that there is an intellectual content in Protestant religious thought that is of provocative interest to students of politics who have no positive religious commitment or whose religious commitment is different from that of Niebuhr's. See also the following of his writings: *Christianity and Power Politics* (New York, 1940); *The Irony of American History* (New York, 1952); *Christian Realism and Political Problems* (New York, 1953); *The Self and the Dramas of History* (New York, 1955); *The Children of Light and the Children of Darkness* (Scribner Library, New York, 1959); and *The Structure of Nations and Empires* (New York, 1959). Harry R. Davis and Robert C. Good (eds.), *Reinhold Niebuhr on Politics: His Political Philosophy and Its Application to Our Age as Expressed in His Writings* (New York, 1960) is an anthology of his political writings drawn from his vast literary output. The most comprehensive study of Niebuhr's thought is Charles W. Kegley and Robert W. Bretall (eds.), *Reinhold Niebuhr: His Religious, Social, and Political Thought* (New York, 1956), containing twenty essays of interpretations by various contributors, and including an "Intellectual Autobiography" by Niebuhr himself. For diverse analyses of Niebuhr's thought, see the following: Sidney Hook, "The New Failure of Nerve," *Partisan Review*, X (January–February, 1943), 2-23, followed by two essays on related topics by John Dewey and Ernest Nagel; Charles Frankel, *The Case for Modern Man* (New York, 1956), pp. 85-116; and Gordon Harland, *The Thought of Reinhold Niebuhr* (New York, 1960). A useful systematic exposition of representative Protestant thinking about government and politics will be found in John C. Bennett, *Christians and the State* (New York, 1958).

OPPENHEIM, FELIX, "Relativism, Absolutism, and Democracy," *American Political Science Review*, XLIV (December, 1950), 951-960. In a searching inquiry, one of the most penetrating analyses of the problem, the author arrives at the conclusion that there is no direct logical, psychological, or historical correlation between the basic philosophical attitudes of absolutism, relativism, and empiricism on the one hand and the basic political systems of democracy and autocracy on the other. Yet Oppenheim concedes that there are political links between types of philosophy and types of political organization, although even these links are subject to important qualifications. See also Oppenheim's "In Defense of Relativism," *Western Political Quarterly*, VIII (September, 1955), 411-417, and "The Natural Law Thesis: Affirmation or Denial?" *American Political Science Review*, LI (March, 1957), 41-53, followed by "Comment on Oppenheim: In Defense of the Natural Law Thesis," by Harry V. Jaffa (pp. 54-64), and a "Rebuttal" by Oppenheim (pp. 65-66).

RUSSELL, BERTRAND, *A History of Western Philosophy: And Its Connection with Political and Social Circumstances from the Earliest Times to the Present Day* (New York, 1945). Planned to show the intimate ties between philosophy and politics in their historical evolution, this work accomplishes its aim admirably. *Human Society in Ethics and Politics* (New York, 1955) is Russell's most systematic application of his general empirical philosophy to ethical and political philosophy. See also the following volumes by Russell: *Authority and the Individual* (New York, 1949); *The Impact of Science on Society* (New York, 1951); and *My Philosophical Development* (New York, 1959). For an even more radically empirical approach to political philosophy, see T. D. Weldon, *The Vocabulary of Politics* (Penguin Books, 1953), and "Political Principles," in Peter Laslett (ed.), *Philosophy, Politics, and Society* (Oxford, 1956), pp.

22-34. According to Weldon, "it is impossible to demonstrate by the application of an ideal measuring rod or similar device that one type of political institution is praiseworthy while another deserves condemnation" (*Vocabulary of Politics,* p. 15), and the purpose of philosophy "is not to establish or demolish physical, economic, political, or any other principles. It is to clarify their meaning, or to examine their logical force" ("Political Principles," p. 24). This emphasis on logical and linguistic analysis in political philosophy derives to a considerable extent from A. J. Ayer, *Language, Truth, and Logic* (rev. ed., New York, 1946), one of the most influential philosophical books of the last generation. For critical evaluations of this trend in political philosophy, see the following: C. E. M. Joad, "Logical Positivism, Fascism, and Value," *The New Statesman and Nation* (July 31, 1948), 91-92; J. W. N. Watkins, "Is Political Philosophy Dead?" *Encounter,* X (June, 1958), 57-67; and Leo Strauss, *What Is Political Philosophy?: And Other Studies* (Glencoe, Ill., 1959), particularly the first three chapters. For a sharply critical appraisal of logical positivism and "linguistic philosophy," see Ernest Gellner, *Words and Things: A Critical Account of Linguistic Philosophy, And a Study in Ideology* (Boston, 1960).

Scientific Spirit and Democratic Faith, The (Papers from the Conference on The Scientific Spirit and Democratic Faith: Held in New York City, May, 1943, New York, 1944). With contributions by Horace M. Kallen, Max C. Otto, and others. See also Kenneth D. Benne, *A Conception of Authority: An Introductory Study* (New York, 1943), and the symposium, *The Authoritarian Attempt to Capture Education* (Papers from the 2d Conference on the Scientific Spirit and Democratic Faith, New York, 1945), with contributions by John Dewey, Sidney Hook, Irwin Edman, Bruce Bliven, Horace L. Friess, and others.

CHAPTER II. PSYCHOLOGY AND POLITICS

ADORNO, T. W., FRENKEL–BRUNSWIK, ELSE, LEVINSON, DANIEL J., and SANFORD, R. NEVITT, *The Authoritarian Personality* (New York, 1950). This first large-scale attempt to analyze empirically and measure quantitatively authoritarian attitudes is a pioneer in the study of politics. Its research techniques, methods, and findings are analyzed in Richard Christie and Marie Jahoda (eds.), *Studies in the Scope and Method of "The Authoritarian Personality"* (Glencoe, 1954). See also the following: Samuel Lowy, *Co-operation, Tolerance, and Prejudice* (London, 1948); Talcott Parsons, "Certain Primary Sources and Patterns of Aggression in the Social Structure of the Western World," in his *Essays in Sociological Theory Pure and Applied* (Glencoe, 1949), pp. 251-274; A. H. Maslow, "Authoritarian Character Structure," *Journal of Social Psychology,* XVIII (November, 1943), 401-411; J. C. Moloney, "Authoritarianism and Intolerance," *International Journal of Psycho-Analysis* (Part III, 1948), 236-239; R. Stagner, "Studies of Aggressive Social Attitudes," XX, *Journal of Social Psychology* (August, 1944), 109-140; Lawrence K. Frank, "Cultural Coercion and Individual Distortion," *Psychiatry,* II (February, 1939), 11-27; Abram Kardiner, "Western Personality and Social Crisis: A Psychiatrist Looks at Human Aggression," *Commentary,* II (November, 1946), 436-447; and J. A.

Bayton, "Personality and Prejudice," *Journal of Psychology*, XXII (July, 1946), 59-65.

ALEXANDER, FRANZ, *The Age of Unreason: A Study of the Irrational Forces in Social Life* (Philadelphia–New York, 1942). Part III contains analyses of the emotional structure of totalitarianism (pp. 264-275) and democracy (pp. 276-293). A useful bibliography is appended (pp. 342-359).

BAUMGARTNER–TRAMER, FRANZISKA, "Democracy and Character," *British Journal of Psychology*, XXXVIII (September, 1947), 20-22. See also D. W. Winnicott, "Some Thoughts on the Meaning of the Word Democracy," *Human Relations*, III (June, 1950), 175-186.

BRIERLEY, MARJORIE, *Trends in Psycho-Analysis* (London, 1951). See also Franz Alexander, *Fundamentals in Psychoanalysis* (New York, 1948); Clara Thompson, *Psychoanalysis: Evolution and Development* (New York, 1950); and Geraldine Coster, *Psychoanalysis for Normal People*, 3d ed. (London–New York, 1947).

CHAKOTIN, SERGE, *The Rape of the Masses* (London, 1940). The subtitle is "The Psychology of Totalitarian Political Propaganda." See also Talcott Parsons, "Propaganda and Social Control," *Psychiatry*, V (November, 1942), 551-572; and Harold D. Lasswell, "Propaganda and Mass Insecurity," in Alfred H. Stanton and Stewart E. Perry (eds.), *Personality and Political Crisis* (Glencoe, 1951), pp. 15-43.

CRAWSHAY–WILLIAMS, RUPERT, *The Comforts of Unreason* (London, 1947). The subtitle of this stimulating work is "A Study of the Motives behind Irrational Thought."

CROSSMAN, R. H. S., "On Political Neuroses," *Encounter*, II (May, 1954), 65-67. See also Franz Neumann, "Anxiety in Politics," *Dissent*, II (Spring, 1955), 133-143.

FLUGEL, J. C., *Man, Morals, and Society* (London, 1945). Chap. XVIII deals with the psychological foundations of the political Right and Left (pp. 281-301). See also the following: H. J. Eysenck, "Primary Social Attitudes as Related to Social Class and Political Party," *British Journal of Sociology*, II (September, 1951), 198-209; Thelma Herman McCormack, "The Motivation of Radicals," *American Journal of Sociology*, LVI (July, 1950); M. Sanai and P. M. Pickard, "The Relation between Political-Economic Radicalism and Certain Traits of Personality," *Journal of Social Psychology*, XXX (November, 1949), 217-227; Gerhart H. Saenger, "Social Status and Political Behavior," *American Journal of Sociology*, LI (September, 1945), 103-113; M. Brewster Smith, "Opinions, Personality, and Political Behavior," *American Political Science Review*, LII (March, 1958), 1-17; Herbert McClosky, "Conservatism and Personality," *ibid.*, 27-45; David Spitz, "Power and Personality: The Appeal to the 'Right Man' in Democratic States," *ibid.*, 84-97; and Ohmer Milton, "Presidential Choice and Performance on a Scale of Authoritarianism," *The American Psychologist*, VII (October, 1952), 597-598.

FODOR, NANDOR, and GAYNOR, FRANK (eds.), *Freud: Dictionary of Psychoanalysis* (New York, 1950). Presents, in dictionary form, the main concepts of psychoanalysis in quotations from Freud's own writings. Useful for rapid reference.

FREUD, SIGMUND, *A General Introduction to Psychoanalysis* (New York, 1920), and *New Introductory Lectures on Psychoanalysis* (New York, 1933). These are the two basic introductory works. Consult also the following: *The Interpretation of Dreams,* 3d ed. (New York, 1932); *The Psychopathology of Everyday Life* (New York, 1914); *Three Essays on the Theory of Sexuality* (New York, 1910); *Wit and Its Relation to the Unconscious* (New York, 1916); *Totem and Tabu* (New York, 1918); *Group Psychology and the Analysis of the Ego* (New York, 1922); *The Future of an Illusion* (New York, 1928); and *An Outline of Psychoanalysis* (New York, 1949). *The Basic Writings of Sigmund Freud* (ed. A. A. Brill, Modern Library, New York, 1938) contains six of Freud's most important works. Freud's *Collected Papers,* 5 vols. (London, 1924-1950) contain most of the papers contributed to journals and encyclopedias.

FROMM, ERICH, *Escape from Freedom* (New York, 1941). One of the most successful psychological interpretations of modern totalitarianism. An extensive and highly critical review of the book from the viewpoint of Freudian analysis will be found in Otto Fenichel, "Psychoanalytic Remarks on Fromm's Book, *Escape from Freedom," Psychoanalytic Review,* XXXI (April, 1944), 133-152. See also Fromm's *Man for Himself: An Inquiry into the Psychology of Ethics* (New York, 1947); *Psychoanalysis and Religion* (New Haven, 1950); *The Sane Society* (New York, 1955); and *Sigmund Freud's Mission: An Analysis of His Personality and Influence* (New York, 1959).

HOOK, SIDNEY (ed.), *Psychoanalysis, Scientific Method, and Philosophy* (New York, 1959). A symposium of twenty-eight papers, mostly by distinguished psychoanalysts, psychiatrists, and philosophers, examining the scientific validity of psychoanalysis. See also Lewis S. Feuer, *Psychoanalysis and Ethics* (Springfield, Ill., 1955); Howard L. Philp, *Freud and Religious Belief* (New York, 1956); Harold D. Lasswell, "Impact of Psychoanalytic Thinking on the Social Sciences," in Leonard D. White (ed.), *The State of the Social Sciences* (Chicago, 1956), pp. 84-115; Lawrence K. Frank, "Psychology and Social Order," in Daniel Lerner (ed.), *The Human Meaning of the Social Sciences* (Meridian Books, New York, 1959), pp. 214-241; and Norman O. Brown, *Life Against Death: The Psychoanalytical Meaning of History* (Middletown, Conn., 1959).

JONES, ERNEST, *Essays in Applied Psychoanalysis,* 2 vols. (London, 1951). The first volume deals with social, political, and international issues, the second with folklore and religion. See also his *Collected Papers,* 5th ed. (London, 1948); *What Is Psychoanalysis?* (London, 1949); *Sigmund Freud: Four Centenary Addresses* (New York, 1956); and *The Life and Work of Sigmund Freud,* 3 vols. (New York, 1953-1957), the most informative biography of Freud by one of his closest friends and collaborators. The symposium edited by Jones, *Social Aspects of Psycho-Analysis* (London, 1924), is one of the first systematic efforts to relate Freud's thought to the social sciences. The limitations of such applicability are critically examined in Hans Kelsen, "The Conception of State and Social Psychology," *International Journal of Psycho-Analysis,* V (Part 1, 1924), 1-38.

LANE, ROBERT E., *Political Life: Why People Get Involved in Politics* (Glencoe, 1959). Part III (pp. 97-181) deals with the emotional—conscious and unconscious—needs of political concern and participation. See also the following: Herbert H. Hyman, *Political Socialization: A Study in the Psychology of Political Behavior* (Glencoe, 1959); William Kornhauser, *The Politics of Mass*

Society (Glencoe, 1959); and Eugene Burdick and Arthur J. Brodbeck (eds.), *American Voting Behavior* (Glencoe, 1959), particularly Chapters V (Arthur J. Brodbeck, "The Problem of Irrationality and Neuroticism Underlying Political Choice," pp. 121-135), XVI (Franz Alexander, "Emotional Factors in Voting Behavior," pp. 300-307), XXI (Richard E. Renneker, "Some Psychodynamic Aspects of Voting Behavior," pp. 399-413), and XXII (Arthur J. Brodbeck, "The Principles of Permanence and Change: Electioneering and Psychotherapy Compared," pp. 414-436).

LASSWELL, HAROLD D., *World Politics and Personal Insecurity* (New York, 1935). Lasswell is the first political scientist who has successfully applied psychoanalytic research methods and experience to the empirical study of political processes. See also the following of his writings: *Psychopathology and Politics* (Chicago, 1930); *Politics: Who Gets What, When, How* (New York, 1936); *The Analysis of Political Behaviour* (London, 1947); *Power and Personality* (New York, 1948); and, in co-authorship with Abraham Kaplan, *Power and Society: A Framework for Political Inquiry* (New Haven, 1950). *The Political Writings of Harold D. Lasswell* (Glencoe, 1951) contains reprints of *Psychopathology and Politics; Politics: Who Gets What, When, How;* and a new work, *Democratic Character,* summarizing Lasswell's thought on the relations of politics and personality.

LEVY, DAVID M., *New Fields of Psychiatry* (New York, 1947). Contains chapters on industrial, military, and political psychiatry. A bibliography is appended (pp. 162-167).

LEWIN, KURT, *Resolving Social Conflicts: Selected Papers on Group Dynamics* (New York, 1948). A significant contribution to the understanding of the psychological structure of basic political attitudes and motivations. See also Lewin's *A Dynamic Theory of Personality* (New York, 1935), and *Field Theory in Social Science* (New York, 1951).

LINDNER, ROBERT, *Must You Conform?* (New York, 1956). The essay on "Political Creed and Character" (pp. 79-119) is of particular interest. See also Lindner's *Prescription for Rebellion* (New York, 1952) and *The Fifty-Minute Hour* (Bantam Books, New York, 1956), containing psychoanalytical case studies of fascists and communists.

LIPSET, SEYMOUR MARTIN, *Political Man* (New York, 1960). Chapter IV on "Working-Class Authoritarianism" (pp. 97-130) is one of the most original contributions to the subject. See also Joseph Adelson, "A Study of Minority Group Authoritarianism," *Journal of Abnormal and Social Psychology,* XLVIII (October, 1953), 477-485, and Daniel Bell (ed.), *The New American Right* (New York, 1955).

MANN, THOMAS, "Freud's Position in the History of Modern Culture," *Psychoanalytic Review,* XXVIII (January, 1941), 92-116. See also Otto Fenichel, "Some Remarks on Freud's Place in the History of Science," *Psychoanalytic Quarterly,* XV (July, 1946), 279-284; Lawrence K. Frank, "Freud's Influence on Western Influence and Culture," in his *Society as the Patient* (New Brunswick, 1948), pp. 162-165; Ernst Kris, "The Nature of Psychoanalytic Propositions and Their Validation," in Sidney Hook and Milton R. Konvitz (eds.), *Freedom and Experience: Essays Presented to Horace M. Kallen* (Ithaca and

New York, 1947), pp. 239-259; and Jacques Maritain, "Freudianism and Psy-choanalysis," in his *Scholasticism and Politics* (London, 1940), pp. 144-169.

MONEY–KYRLE, R. E., *Psychoanalysis and Politics* (London, 1951). The subtitle is "A Contribution to the Psychology of Morals and Politics." Consult also the following: H. J. Eysenck, *Psychology and Politics* (New York, 1954); John Bowlby, "Psychology and Democracy," *The Political Quarterly,* XVII (January–March, 1946), 61-76; Paul Schilder, "Psychoanalysis of Economics," *Psycho-analytic Review,* XXVIII (October, 1940), 401-420; Heinz Hartmann, "Psy-choanalysis and Sociology," in Sandor Lorand (ed.), *Psychoanalysis Today* (London, 1948), pp. 326-353; Louis Schneider, *The Freudian Psychology and Veblen's Social Theory* (New York, 1948); Fritz Redl, "Group Emotion and Leadership," *Psychiatry,* V (November, 1942), 573-596; Saul Scheidlinger, *Psychoanalysis and Group Behavior* (New York, 1952); Charles D. Farris, "Authoritarianism as a Political Behavior Variable," *Journal of Politics,* XVIII (February, 1956), 61-82; Morris Janowitz and Dwaine Marvick, "Authori-tarianism and Political Behavior," *Public Opinion Quarterly,* XVII (Summer, 1953), 185-201; R. Nevitt Sanford, "Recent Developments in Connection With the Investigation of the Authoritarian Personality," *Sociological Review,* New Series, II (July, 1954), 11-33; and William Haythorn and others, "The Behavior of Authoritarian and Equalitarian Personalities in Groups," *Human Relations,* IX (February, 1956), 57-74.

NELSON, BENJAMIN (ed.), *Freud and the 20th Century* (Meridian Books, New York, 1957). A collection of essays on various aspects of Freud's influence by distinguished writers, including Alfred Kazin, Gregory Zilboorg, Gardner Murphy, Jacques Maritain, and Reinhold Niebuhr. See also John D. Sutherland (ed.), *Psychoanalysis and Contemporary Thought* (London, 1958), a British symposium celebrating the centenary of Freud's birth.

RIEFF, PHILIP, *Freud: The Mind of the Moralist* (New York, 1959). The most successful interpretation, by a social scientist, of Freud's work, particularly as it bears on questions of politics, ethics, and philosophy. See also Jacob A. Arlow, *The Legacy of Freud* (New York, 1956); Martin Freud: *Sigmund Freud: Man and Father* (New York, 1958); and Herbert Marcuse, *Eros and Civilization: An Inquiry into Freud* (Boston, 1955).

RÓHEIM, GÉZA (ed.), *Psychoanalysis and the Social Sciences,* 3 vols. (New York, 1947-1951). Contain interesting contributions on the relations of psychoanalysis to the social sciences, literature, folklore, and religion. One of the few systematic collections in the field, showing the practical applicability of psychoanalytic methods to the social studies.

SARGANT, WILLIAM, *Battle For the Mind: A Physiology of Conversion and Brain-Washing* (London, 1957). One of the most original contributions to this newly developing field of study, viewed in historical perspective. See also Joost A. M. Meerloo, *The Rape of the Mind: The Psychology of Thought Control, Menti-cide, and Brainwashing* (Cleveland–New York, 1956), and Edward Hunter, *Brainwashing* (Pyramid Books, New York, 1958).

WORTIS, JOSEPH, *Soviet Psychiatry* (Baltimore, 1950). Chap. V (pp. 71-102) is entitled "Psychoanalysis and Psychotherapy." Until 1930, psychoanalysis was tolerated in the Soviet Union. After that date it ceased to exist as an organized scientific activity, and in 1936 the Communist party officially decided that it was incompatible with Marxism–Leninism–Stalinism. Wortis' account includes valuable bibliographical data of Marxist studies of psychology, psychiatry, and psychoanalysis. See also E. Perepel, "The Psychoanalytic Movement in the USSR," *Psychoanalytic Review,* XXVI (April, 1939), 299-300; I. D. London, "A Historical Survey of Psychology in the Soviet Union," *Psychological Bulletin,* XLVI (July, 1949), 241-277, and "The Treatment of Emotions in Contemporary Soviet Psychology," *Journal of Genetic Psychology,* XLI (July, 1949), 89-100; and Robert Gorham Davis, "The Mind of Man: Soviet View," *Commentary,* XI (May, 1951), 488-494. Brief analyses of Freud and general psychological problems in the light of Marxist doctrine will be found in the following: Christopher Caudwell, *Studies in a Dying Culture* (London, 1938), pp. 158-192; T. A. Jackson, *Dialectics* (New York, 1936), pp. 549-560; Francis Bartlett, "Recent Trends in Psychoanalysis," *Science and Society,* IX (Summer, 1945), 214-231; Judson T. Stone, "The Theory and Practice of Psychoanalysis," *Science and Society,* X (Winter, 1946), 54-79; and Joseph Wortis, "Freud, Horney, Fromm and Others," *Science and Society,* X (Spring, 1946), 176-185. The orthodox Communist–Stalinist "line" on psychoanalysis is summarized in George Siskind and Henry Martel, "Psychoanalysis: Ideological Instrument of Imperialism," *Political Affairs,* XXIX (December, 1950), 61-74; D. Fedotov, "The Soviet View of Psychoanalysis," *Monthly Review,* IX (December, 1957), 249-254; and "Freud and Pavlov," *Soviet Survey* (London), No. 29 (July–September, 1959), 29-37, an official Soviet account of a special conference on Freud held by the Academy of Medical Sciences of the USSR.

Part II: The Foundations of Democracy

CHAPTER III. THE RIGHT TO REBEL

AARON, R. I., *John Locke* (London–New York–Toronto, 1937). An excellent volume in the "Leaders of Philosophy" series; Locke's political, moral, religious and educational views are examined in Part III (pp. 257-313). A useful bibliography is included (pp. 314-321). See also Carl Becker, *The Declaration of Independence* (New York, 1922), pp. 24-79; H. R. G. Greaves, "Locke and the Separation of Powers," *Politica,* I (February, 1934), 90-102; C. H. Driver, "John Locke," in F. J. C. Hearnshaw (ed.), *The Social and Political Ideas of Some English Thinkers of the Augustan Age* (London, 1928), pp. 69-96; Walter M. Simon, "John Locke: Philosophy and Political Theory," *American Political Science Review,* XLV (June, 1951), 386-399; Leslie Stephen, *English Thought in the Eighteenth Century,* 3d ed. (London, 1902), II, 135-152; and George Santayana, *Some Turns of Thought in Modern Philosophy* (Cambridge, 1934), pp. 1-47.

ACTON, Lord, *Lectures on Modern History* (London, 1930). See Chap. XIII (pp. 219-232), "The English Revolution," and Chap. XIX (pp. 305-314), "The American Revolution."

BRINTON, CRANE, *The Anatomy of Revolution* (New York, 1938). An important work in a neglected field, centered on the English, American, French, and Russian revolutions. The following studies will also be found useful: Otto Bauer, *Die illegale Partei* (Paris, 1939); K. C. Chorley, *Armies and the Art of Revolution* (London, 1943); Emilio Lussu, *Teoria della insurrezione* (Paris, 1936); and Curzio Malaparte, *Coup d'Etat: The Technique of Revolution* (New York, 1932). For an annotated bibliography, see Brinton, *op. cit.,* pp. 303-319.

BROWN, IVOR, *English Political Theory* (London, 1920; 2nd rev. ed., 1929), pp. 52-67. Chapter V, "Divine Right Defeated," deals with the seventeenth-century predecessors of Locke, who is viewed by the author as a point of culmination and conclusion rather than of beginning: "Locke did not win many new positions: what he did was most effectually to consolidate the old" (p. 62). See also Brown's *The Meaning of Democracy,* 4th ed. (London, 1950), related largely to British social, economic, and political issues.

CARRITT, E. F., *Morals and Politics* (London, 1935), pp. 72-79. A brief chapter on Locke deals primarily with his solution of the problem of political obligation. For a more general analysis of Locke's philosophy and its relation to his political theory, see D. J. O'Connor, *John Locke* (London, 1952).

CRANSTON, MAURICE, *John Locke:A Biography* (New York, 1957). The definitive biography of Locke, superseding previous accounts of his life. Utilizing a large collection of Locke's papers previously inaccessible, the author corrects numerous misconceptions about Locke's personal and intellectual development. Indispensable to the study of Locke and his time.

GOUGH, J. W., *The Social Contract,* 2nd ed. (Oxford, 1957). Traces the development of the social contract theory from antiquity to the nineteenth century, and has a chapter on Locke (IX, pp. 126-146). See also Gough's *John Locke's Political Philosophy* (Oxford, 1950).

KORBONSKI, STEFAN, *Fighting Warsaw: The Story of the Polish Underground State, 1939-1945* (New York, 1956). In spite of the extreme brutality of the German occupying forces, the Poles managed to maintain in World War II an "underground state," exercising administrative, judicial, military, and educational functions. See also Jan Karski, *Story of a Secret State* (Boston, 1944), for another account of the Polish underground state during World War II. Ronald Seth, *The Undaunted: The Story of Resistance in Western Europe* (London, 1956), covers the resistance activities of German-occupied Europe in World War II from Norway to Greece. For the Hungarian Revolution against communist domination in 1956, see the following: Melvin J. Lasky (ed.), *The Hungarian Revolution* (New York, 1957); Peter Fryer, *Hungarian Tragedy* (London, 1956); and George Mikes, *The Hungarian Revolution* (London, 1957). For broader analytical and historical treatments of the problem of resistance and rebellion, see Oscar Jaszi and John D. Lewis, *Against the Tyrant: The Tradition and Theory of Tyrannicide* (Glencoe, 1957), and E. J. Hobsbawm, *Primitive Rebels* (Manchester, 1959).

LASKI, HAROLD J., *The Dangers of Obedience and Other Essays* (New York, 1930). The first essay is "The Dangers of Obedience" (pp. 1-30). Laski argues that "a healthy loyalty is not passive and complacent, but active and critical. If it finds grounds for attack, it must occupy that ground. For all obedience that has the right to regard itself as ethical is built upon a conscious agreement with the purpose we encounter. Anything else is a betrayal of ourselves; and when we surrender the truth we see, by that betrayal we betray also the future of civilization" (p. 30). The shortest introduction into Laski's political thought is *An Introduction to Politics* (London, 1931), an essay of less than a hundred pages. His greatest book is *A Grammar of Politics* (London, 1925). See also the following of his works: *Studies in Law and Politics* (London, 1931); *The Danger of Being a Gentleman and Other Essays* (London, 1939); and *Reflections on the Revolution in Our Time* (New York, 1943).

LASKI, HAROLD J., *Political Thought in England: From Locke to Bentham* (London, 1920), pp. 22-61. In this chapter, Laski gives a sympathetic account of Locke's relation to the Revolution of 1688 and his influence on subsequent English political thought, as well as his contribution to French and American political ideas and institutions.

LOUGH, JOHN (ed.), *Locke's Travels in France, 1675-1679* (Cambridge, 1955). Taken from Locke's diaries, letters, and other papers, much of the material is new. For a more detailed study of Locke's intellectual relations with France, see Gabriel D. Bonno, *Les relations intellectuelles de Locke avec la France* (Berkeley, 1955).

PENNOCK, J. ROLAND, *Liberal Democracy: Its Merits and Prospects* (New York, 1950). See also John Laird, *On Human Freedom* (London, 1947); John Macmurray, *Conditions of Freedom* (London, 1950); and Henry B. Mayo, *An Introduction to Democratic Theory* (New York, 1960).

READ, CONYERS (ed.), *The Constitution Reconsidered* (New York, 1938). Contains papers by Charles H. McIlwain, Gaetano Salvemini, Charles A. Beard, Walton H. Hamilton, and others. See, in particular, R. M. MacIver, "European Doctrines and the Constitution" (pp. 51-62), which discusses the influence of Locke and others. The volume includes also several papers on the influence of the American Constitution on the rest of the world.

STOCKS, J. L., *John Locke's Contribution to Political Theory* (London, 1933). A Tercentenary Address, delivered in October of 1932 at Christ Church, the college which Locke himself had attended at Oxford.

TAWNEY, R. H., *The Western Political Tradition* (London, 1949). See also *The Western Tradition*, by various authors (London, 1949).

WELDON, T. D., *States and Morals* (New York, 1947). The author of this suggestive work divides all theories of the state into two groups: "Some define it as a kind of organism, others as a kind of machine," and Locke is a main representative of the latter type.

CHAPTER IV. LIBERTY AND LOYALTY

ACTON, Lord, *The History of Freedom and Other Essays* (London, 1907). A collection of papers and essays, one of Lord Acton's most interesting works. It is especially illuminating on the relation of freedom and religion, and contains chapters of rare judgment and scholarship on Protestant and Catholic theories of persecution.

ANSHEN, RUTH NANDA (ed.), *Freedom: Its Meaning* (New York, 1940). A symposium, with contributions by James T. Shotwell, Benedetto Croce, Alfred North Whitehead, Bertrand Russell, Charles A. Beard, Louis Brandeis, John Dewey, Albert Einstein, Henri Bergson, Jacques Maritain, and other distinguished twentieth-century thinkers. See also the following: Carl J. Friedrich (ed.), *Authority* (Nomos I, Cambridge, Mass., 1958); Alexander Meiklejohn, *Political Freedom* (New York, 1960); and Herbert J. Muller, *Issues of Freedom: Paradoxes and Promises* (New York, 1960).

BARTH, ALAN, *The Loyalty of Free Men* (New York, 1951). A skillfully balanced appraisal of the loyalty problem. See also the following: Alexander Meiklejohn, *Free Speech and Its Relation to Self-Government* (New York, 1948); Walter Gellhorn, *Security, Loyalty, and Science* (Ithaca, 1950); Harold D. Lasswell, *National Security and Individual Freedom* (New York, 1950); Nathaniel Weyl, *The Battle against Disloyalty* (New York, 1951); Alistaire Cooke, *A Generation on Trial* (New York, 1950); John C. Wahlke (ed.), *Loyalty in a Democratic State* (Boston, 1952); Sidney Hook, *Heresy, Yes—Conspiracy, No* (New York, 1953); Merle Curti, *The Roots of American Loyalty* (New York, 1946); Elmer Davis, *But We Were Born Free* (Permabooks, New York, 1956); Henry Steele Commager, *Freedom, Loyalty, and Dissent* (New York, 1954); and Edward A. Shils, *The Torment of Secrecy* (Glencoe, 1956). The best public opinion study of, not what Americans should think, but what they actually do think about civil liberties and unorthodoxy in politics, economics, and religion is Samuel A. Stouffer, *Communism, Conformity, and Civil Liberties: A Cross-Section of the Nation Speaks Its Mind* (Garden City, 1955).

BECKER, CARL, *Freedom and Responsibility in the American Way of Life* (New York, 1946). See especially Chaps. I-III (pp. 1-64) on the American political tradition, freedom of speech and press, and freedom of learning and teaching.

BURY, J. B., *A History of Freedom of Thought* (London, 1913). A popular account in the "Home University Library."

CARRITT, E. F., *Morals and Politics* (London, 1935), pp. 56-71, 202-216. Analyzes the difficulties inherent in the concept of Rousseau's "General Will."

CHAFEE, ZECHARIAH, JR., *Free Speech in the United States* (Cambridge, Mass., 1946). The leading study of civil liberty in the United States; the time covered is mainly from World War I to 1941. The work contains all the important cases of the period, but the analysis goes beyond the purely legal realm into the political and social issues involved. See also Chafee's *How Human Rights Got Into the Constitution* (Boston, 1952), and *The Blessings of Liberty* (Philadelphia–New York, 1956).

COMMAGER, HENRY STEELE, *Majority Rule and Minority Rights* (Gloucester, Mass., 1958). In the light of past experience, the author concludes, "the Congress, and not the courts, emerges as the instrument for the realization of the guarantees of the bill of rights" (p. 55). This highly controversial thesis runs counter to the views of many (perhaps most) students of the American constitutional experience.

CRANSTON, MAURICE, *Freedom: A New Analysis* (New York, 1953). Parts I and III contain general analyses of the concept of freedom; Part II, the most interesting, deals with liberty as understood in England, France, Germany, and the United States.

CROCE, BENEDETTO, *History as the Story of Liberty* (London, 1941). Heavy going in spots, but contains an interesting thesis worth pursuing.

DAVIDSON, WILLIAM L., *Political Thought in England: The Utilitarians from Bentham to J. S. Mill* (London, 1915), pp. 158-188, 216-234. An excellent brief survey of John Stuart Mill's life and political career and his major writings on ethics and politics, including detailed discussions of *On Liberty* and *Representative Government*. See also Hans Kohn, *Prophets and Peoples* (New York, 1946), whose first chapter is on John Stuart Mill (pp. 11-42).

GELLHORN, WALTER, *American Rights: The Constitution in Action* (New York, 1960). While the emphasis is on political rights, the author, one of the leading authorities in the field, also deals with criminal procedure, education, and "private government." See also Gellhorn's *Individual Freedom and Governmental Restraints* (Baton Rouge, 1956), in which he deals primarily with "Restraints on Book Reading" (pp. 49-104) and "The Right to Make a Living" (pp. 105-151). The following studies will also be found useful: Clair Wilcox (ed.), *Civil Liberties Under Attack* (Philadelphia, 1951); Robert E. Cushman, *Civil Liberties in the United States* (Ithaca, 1956); Harold W. Chase, *Security and Liberty: The Problem of Native Communists, 1947-1955* (Garden City, 1955); David Fellman (ed.), *The Supreme Court and Education* (Classics in Education, No. 4, New York, 1960); Erwin N. Griswold, *The Fifth Amendment Today* (Cambridge, Mass., 1955); and Anne Lyon Haight, *Banned Books,* 2nd ed. (New York, 1955).

LIEF, ALFRED (ed.), *The Dissenting Opinions of Mr. Justice Holmes* (New York, 1929). Gives a profound insight into one of the richest and most subtle personalities in the history of American jurisprudence and political thought. The collection of his dissenting opinions also reconfirms how the minority view of yesterday becomes the generally accepted truth of today, and is, finally, destined to become the commonplace of tomorrow. See also Max Lerner (ed.), *The Mind and Faith of Justice Holmes* (Modern Library, New York, 1954).

MILL, JOHN STUART, *Autobiography* (London, 1873). One of the great autobiographies of English literature. It reveals intimate insights into Mill as a man and political thinker; it is also significant for the explanation of the reasons that brought Mill eventually very close to socialism. Of his essay *On Liberty* Mill says that none of his writings "have been either so carefully composed, or so sedulously corrected as this," and he rightly foresaw that it was "likely to survive longer than anything else that I have written." See also Crane Brinton, *English Political Thought in the Nineteenth Century* (London, 1933), pp. 89-103, and, for general background, Sir Leslie Stephens, *The English Utilitarians* (London, 1900), and Elie Halévy, *The Growth of Philosophical Radicalism* (London, 1928).

NIEMEYER, GERHART, "A Reappraisal of the Doctrine of Free Speech," *Thought,* XXV (June, 1950), 251-274. Attacks the traditional liberal doctrine of freedom of speech as the expression of "neutrality, agnosticism, and complacency" (p. 272), and pleads for a "firm official stand for what is known as right, true, and good" (p. 273).

PACKE, MICHAEL ST. JOHN, *The Life of John Stuart Mill* (New York, 1954). The first full-length biography of Mill, drawing on important new scource materials previously inaccessible. His relation with Harriet Taylor, so crucial for Mill's personal and intellectual development, is analyzed in detail. See also F. A. Hayek, *John Stuart Mill and Harriet Taylor: Their Friendship and Subsequent Marriage* (Chicago, 1951); Karl Britton, *John Stuart Mill* (Penguin Books, Baltimore, 1953); Richard P. Anschutz, *The Philosophy of John Stuart Mill* (Oxford, 1953); Bertrand Russell, *John Stuart Mill* (London, 1955); John C. Rees, *Mill and His Early Critics* (Leicester, 1956); and Ruth Borchard, *John Stuart Mill: The Man* (London, 1957).

ROBERTSON, J. M., *A History of Freethought*, 2 vols., 4th ed., revised and expanded (London, 1936). The classical history of freethought, covering the ancient period, the Middle Ages, and the modern era to the French Revolution. In 1929, Robertson published *A History of Freethought in the Nineteenth Century*, a worthy complement to his other work in this field.

ROUSSEAU, J. J., *The Social Contract* (Everyman's Library ed., London, 1938). The introduction by G. D. H. Cole (pp. vii-xliv), succinct and lucid, covers the essential points. See also the following books: Alfred Cobban, *Rousseau and the Modern State* (London, 1934), one of the best general works on Rousseau's political ideas; Annie Marion Osborn, *Rousseau and Burke* (London–New York–Toronto, 1940); Ernest Hunter Wright, *The Meaning of Rousseau* (London, 1929); Ernst Cassirer, *The Question of Jean-Jacques Rousseau* (New York, 1954); F. C. Green, *Jean-Jacques Rousseau: A Critical Study of His Life and Writings* (Cambridge, 1955); and John W. Chapman, *Rousseau—Totalitarian or Liberal?* (New York, 1956).

TALMON, J. L., *The Origins of Totalitarian Democracy* (London, 1952). The author's main thesis is that the eighteenth century brought forth two contradictory types of democracy: "empirical liberal democracy" and "Messianic totalitarian democracy." Rousseau is considered by Talmon as possibly the most important single source of totalitarian democracy, particularly by marrying the concept of the general will with that of popular sovereignty (p. 43). A similar interpretation will be found in Ernest Barker (ed.), *Social Contract: Essays by Locke, Hume, and Rousseau* (New York, 1948), pp. xxvii-xliv.

THOMSON, DAVID, *The Democratic Ideal in France and England* (Cambridge, 1940). A sympathetic account of the growth of democratic ideas in France and England, in their similarities and differences.

To Secure These Rights (The Report of the President's Committee on Civil Rights, Washington, 1947). A momentous official report on civil rights in the United States.

CHAPTER V. LIBERTY AND EQUALITY

BEARD, CHARLES A., *The Economic Basis of Politics* (New York, 1922). See the third chapter, "The Doctrine of Political Equality."

BRYSON, LYMAN, and OTHERS (eds.), *Aspects of Human Equality: Fifteenth Symposium of the Conference on Science, Philosophy, and Religion* (New York, 1956). Analyzes the religious, moral, political, and social aspects of equality as they impinge upon contemporary problems.

CARR, E. H., *The New Society* (London, 1951). The main theme is what the quest for economic equality has done to the traditional concepts of political liberty.

HADLEY, ARTHUR TWINING, *The Conflict between Liberty and Equality* (Boston, 1925). Hadley was a strong defender of the right of private property, and liberty meant, according to him, the enjoyment of that right. He denied the implications of equality beyond the purely formal and political realm. His thought is characteristic of an era in American life, in the late nineteenth and early twentieth centuries, in which the protection of property was considered the main objective of the Constitution. A more moderate (and more sophisticated) defense of the older concepts of political liberty and economic inequality will be found, among contemporary writers, in F. A. Hayek, *The Constitution of Liberty* (Chicago, 1960).

HALDANE, J. B. S., *The Inequality of Man* (London, 1932). A collection of essays, mostly on popular scientific topics.

HAMMOND, J. L., *The Growth of Common Enjoyment* (L. T. Hobhouse Memorial Trust Lectures, No. 3, London, 1933). The author inquires how the amenities of civilization can be made accessible to all, and comes to this conclusion: "We are still acting as if we gave beauty no place among the great ennobling and educating influences. What kind of a leisured society are we likely to produce if we start with this fallacy? How shall we hope to preserve the vitality of culture, the higher standards of taste, and the large atmosphere in which men find satisfaction in the deeper sources of happiness? Yet with the new gifts of science we can make a happier society today when our industrial supremacy is gone than we ever created when we boasted that we were the workshop of the world" (pp. 29-30).

HAYEK, F. A., "The London School of Economics, 1895-1945," *Economica* (New Series), XIII (February, 1946), 1-31. This article by a (then) teacher of the London School of Economics and Political Science gives due consideration to the influence of the Webbs, beginning with their founding of the institution and continuing throughout their lives. It is the record of one of the most exciting educational ventures and experiences in modern time. One of the first eight students in 1895, Max Beer, describes, in intimate and personal terms, "The Beginnings of the London School of Economics" in his book *Fifty Years of International Socialism* (London, 1935), pp. 81-88.

HOBSON, JOHN A., *Towards Social Equality* (L. T. Hobhouse Memorial Trust Lectures, No. 1, London, 1941) Hobson discusses the cost of inequality, and the advances made toward more equality. See also T. H. Marshall, *Citizenship and Social Class* (Cambridge, 1950). The tendency toward rising living standards and greater social and economic equality is one of the main themes of John Kenneth Galbraith, *The Affluent Society* (Boston, 1958).

JOAD, C. E. M., *Liberty To-Day* (New York, 1935). The first three chapters take up the case against liberty; the latter three, the case for liberty. Throughout, Joad is aware of the problems of balancing liberty with equality.

LASKI, HAROLD J., *Liberty in the Modern State* (London, 1930). See Chap. III (pp. 176-247), "Liberty and Social Power."

PERRY, RALPH BARTON, *Puritanism and Democracy* (New York, 1944). A significant work on the origins of the American mind and social thought. In Chap. XIX, "Equality and Fraternity" (pp. 551-582), Perry develops eight different approaches to the problem of equality, among which he includes moral, political, legal, and social equality.

PIERSON, GEORGE WILSON, *Tocqueville and Beaumont in America* (New York, 1938). This definitive work on the subject is also available in an abridged edition, *Tocqueville in America* (Anchor Books, New York, 1959).

SMITH, THOMAS V., *The American Philosophy of Equality* (Chicago, 1927). A philosophical work, greatly enriched by the author's practical experience in public affairs. For another American discussion, see Henry Alonzo Myers, *Are Men Equal? An Inquiry Into the Meaning of American Democracy* (Great Seal Books, Ithaca, 1955).

TAWNEY, R. H., *Equality*, 4th ed. (London, 1952). The fourth edition of this classic incorporates the social changes produced by the Labor Government (1945-1951).

THOMSON, DAVID, *Equality* (Cambridge, 1949). Concentrates on the problem of equality in law, religion, politics, economics, and international relations. An incisive analysis of the relations of liberty and equality in the light of American social, economic, and political issues will be found in R. M. MacIver, *The Ramparts We Guard* (New York, 1950).

TOCQUEVILLE, ALEXIS DE, *Democracy in America*, 2 vols. (ed. Phillips Bradley, Vintage Books, New York, 1954). See also the following works of Tocqueville: *Recollections* (New York, 1949); *The Old Regime and the French Revolution* (Anchor Books, New York, 1955); *Journeys to England and Ireland* (New Haven, 1958); *The European Revolution and Correspondence with Gobineau* (Anchor Books, New York, 1959); and *Journey to America* (New Haven, 1959). For a sympathetic study of Tocqueville's life and thought, see J. P. Mayer, *Alexis de Tocqueville: A Biographical Study in Political Science* (Harper Torchbooks, New York, 1960).

WOOLF, LEONARD, *After the Deluge* (London, 1931). An important study of the growth of the democratic idea in the West in terms of "communal psychology," including a pertinent discussion of "Democracy and Equality" (pp. 195-218 of the 1937 edition, Pelican Books).

WOOLF, LEONARD, and OTHERS, *The Modern State* (London, 1933). Presents the Labor, Liberal, and Conservative viewpoints. In his section of the book, Woolf treats of the relations of liberty and equality (pp. 40-63).

Part III: Antidemocratic Thought

CHAPTER VI. THE POLITICS OF PESSIMISM

ALLEN, J. W., *A History of Political Thought in the Sixteenth Century* (London, 1928). The second chapter in Part IV (pp. 447-494) is on Machiavelli; the analysis is based on Machiavelli's *Prince* as well as on his other, less well-known works. Allen's study, the best treatise on sixteenth-century political thought, concludes the appraisal of Machiavelli with the statement that he "stood, in the long run, for the principle that there is no question that must not be asked nor assumption that must be made" (p. 494).

BOWLE, JOHN, *Hobbes and His Critics: A Study in Seventeenth Century Consti-*

tutionalism (London, 1951). The only detailed account of Hobbes's contemporary critics, who anticipated some of Locke's later ideas.

BURKE, EDMUND, *Works,* Vol. II (The World's Classics, London, 1906). Contains the two important House of Commons speeches on America: "Speech on American Taxation" of April 19, 1774 (pp. 89-152), and "Speech for Conciliation with the Colonies" of March 22, 1775 (pp. 167-238). On Burke, see Ernest Barker, *Essays on Government* (Oxford, 1945), Chaps. VI and VII (pp. 155-235); Alfred Cobban, *Edmund Burke and the Revolt Against the Eighteenth Century* (London, 1929); Sir Philip Magnus, *Edmund Burke: A Prophet of the Eighteenth Century* (London, 1939); John Morley, *Burke* (London, 1879); Annie Marion Osborn, *Rousseau and Burke* (London–New York–Toronto, 1940); Leslie Stephen, *English Thought in the Eighteenth Century,* 3rd ed. (London, 1902), II, 219-252; Russell Kirk, *The Conservative Mind: From Burke to Santayana* (Chicago, 1953), Chap. II (pp. 11-61); Charles Parkin, *The Moral Basis of Burke's Political Thought* (Cambridge, 1956); and Peter J. Stanlis, *Edmund Burke and the Natural Law* (Ann Arbor, 1958). Clinton Rossiter, *Conservatism in America* (New York, 1955), compares in Chap. VI (pp. 213-242) classical British conservatism with American conservatism, pointing to both similarities and differences.

BURNHAM, JAMES, *The Machiavellians* (New York, 1943). Part II (pp. 29-77) deals, sympathetically, with "Machiavelli: The Science of Power." Burnham sees in the Machiavellian tradition the true foundation of politics and the science of politics. In addition to Machiavelli, he also deals with Mosca, Sorel, Michels, and Pareto. He comes to the conclusion that democracy as "self-government" or "government by the people" is impossible, and that the theory of democracy as self-government "must be understood as a myth, formula, or derivation" (p. 236).

CASSIRER, ERNST, *The Myth of the State* (New Haven, 1946). Chaps. X-XII (pp. 116-162) place Machiavelli in the context of his time, and relate Machiavellian ideas to broader problems of philosophy. A penetrating work, full of suggestive insights.

CROCE, BENEDETTO, *Politics and Morals* (English trans., London, 1946). Chap. II (pp. 44-50) is a defense of Machiavelli as seen in the light of Italian politics and traditions: "The art and science of politics, of pure politics, brought to maturity by the Italians, were to him a source of pride" (p. 47). See also Chap. X, "Historical Pessimism" (pp. 136-138).

DONOSO CORTÉS, JUAN, *Ensayo sobre el Catolicismo, el Liberalismo y el Socialismo* (Madrid, 1851). The bible of Spanish antiliberal, antidemocratic, and antisocialist thought. The author starts out with the interesting assumption that every great political question involves a great theological question. He then proceeds to demonstrate that modern liberalism and socialism are nothing but doctrinal "errors" from the point of view of Catholic theology. For a more recent Spanish version of antidemocratic political thought, see Ramiro de Maeztu, *Defensa de la Hispanidad* (Madrid, 1934). This book influenced, more than any other single source, the ideology of Spanish Fascism. It is anti-French, anti-American, and anti-English on ideological and political grounds, and extols the authoritarian virtues of sixteenth- and seventeenth-century Spain, including the blessings of the Inquisition. The best anthology of recent Spanish and Hispanic-American thought is José Gaos (ed.), *Antología del pensamiento de lengua española en la edad contemporanea* (Mexico City, 1945). See also William Ebenstein, *Church and State in Franco Spain* (Princeton University, Center of International Studies, Research Monographs, No. 8, Princeton, 1960).

EDWARDS, H. W. J., *The Radical Tory: Disraeli's Political Development Illustrated from His Original Writings and Speeches* (London, 1937). After Burke, no one has influenced British conservative thought more profoundly than Benjamin Disraeli. This volume of selections provides a useful guide to his thought. R. J. White (ed.), *The Conservative Tradition* (London, 1950), is a collection of statements by Conservative statesmen and publicists on philosophical, economic, and political issues; the period covered is from Burke to the middle of the twentieth century. The political ideas of Winston Churchill, the greatest Conservative of the twentieth century, have been assembled in encyclopedic form (in alphabetical order) by F. B. Czarnomski (ed.), *The Wisdom of Winston Churchill: Being a Selection of Aphorisms, Reflections, Precepts, Maxims, Epigrams, Paradoxes, and Opinions from His Parliamentary and Public Speeches, 1900-1955* (London, 1956). For a brief and authoritative presentation of the contemporary Conservative outlook, see Viscount Hailsham, *The Conservative Case* (Penguin Books, Baltimore, 1959).

GOOCH, G. P., *Hobbes* (London, 1939). This "Annual Lecture on a Master Mind" (under the auspices of the Henriette Hertz Fund of the British Academy) presents, in brief and clear form, the main outlines of Hobbes's thought, political and philosophical. Hobbes is placed in the perspective of English history and his later influence at home and abroad. Gooch concludes that it "is one of the ironies of history that the disciples whom the author of *Leviathan* failed to find in his own country and his own time are crowding the continental stage after the lapse of three hundred years" (p. 42). See also G. E. G. Catlin, *Thomas Hobbes as Philosopher, Publicist and Man of Letters* (Oxford, 1922); John Laird, *Hobbes* (London, 1934); E. L. Woodward, "Thomas Hobbes," in F. J. C. Hearnshaw (ed.), *Social and Political Ideas of Some Great Thinkers of the Sixteenth and Seventeenth Centuries* (London, 1926), Chap. VII (pp. 153-173); Richard Peters, *Hobbes* (Penguin Books, Baltimore, 1956); Howard Warrender, *The Political Philosophy of Hobbes: His Theory of Obligation* (Oxford, 1957); and Bertrand de Jouvenel, *Sovereignty* (Cambridge, 1957), Chap. XIV, "The Political Consequences of Hobbes" (pp. 231-246).

HOBBES, THOMAS, *Leviathan* (Blackwell's Political Texts, Oxford, 1946). Contains a long "Introduction" (pp. vii-lxvi) by Michael Oakeshott, which is one of the best half-dozen studies of the *Leviathan* ever published. It throws new light on that classic, and deviates substantially from the orthodox interpretations. For another unorthodox analysis, see Leo Strauss, *The Political Philosophy of Hobbes* (Oxford, 1936, reprinted, Chicago, 1952).

LASKI, HAROLD J., *The Dangers of Obedience and Other Essays* (New York, 1930). Chap. IX, "Machiavelli and the Present Time" (pp. 238-263), is sharply critical of Machiavelli, whose doctrine is called a "gospel of death" (p. 262). For a similar interpretation, but in greater detail, see Leo Strauss, *Thoughts on Machiavelli* (Glencoe, 1958).

LASKI, HAROLD J., *Political Thought in England: From Locke to Bentham* (London, 1920), pp. 165-215. In the sixth chapter, Laski gives a more than sympathetic account of Burke: "There is hardly a greater figure in the history of political thought in England" (p. 214). Similar, and even more lyrical, expressions are interesting evidence of the hold that the greatest conservative writer in England has over a liberal and socialist like Laski. This extensive study of Burke, including some important critical observations, is highly revealing of the political and intellectual climate in England.

MAINE, Sir HENRY, *Popular Government* (New York, 1886). At a time when popular government seemed to progress toward eventual acceptance everywhere, Sir Henry Maine was one of the few Englishmen to sound a note of pessimism in an atmosphere of buoyant optimism. His principal argument against democracy was that "multitudes include too much ignorance to be capable of understanding their interest" (p. 86). An incisive analysis of his ideas will be found in K. B. Smellie, "Sir Henry Maine," *Economica,* VIII (March, 1928), 64-94.

MEINECKE, FRIEDRICH, *Machiavellism: The Doctrine of Raison d'État and Its Place in Modern History* (New Haven, 1957). The most thorough study of the concept and evolution of the reason of state, from Machiavelli to the twentieth century.

MENCKEN, HENRY L., *Notes on Democracy* (New York, 1926). Strongly Nietzschean, and full of witty pessimism and cynicism about democracy. One of Mencken's main conclusions on democracy is: "It is incomparably idiotic, and hence incomparably amusing" (p. 211).

MORLEY, JOHN Viscount, *Politics and History* (London, 1923). A collection of essays, with an interesting paper on Machiavelli (pp. 129-180), written from a Liberal point of view.

OLSCHKI, LEONARDO, *Machiavelli the Scientist* (Berkeley, 1945). A very brief and suggestive interpretation of Machiavelli in the light of the new scientific tendencies of his time. Olschki characterizes Machiavelli as "one of the greatest exponents of the laical genius of Italy that sought clarity, knowledge and wisdom as manifestations of a free human judgment and of autonomous intellectual experiences" (p. 56). See also Federico Chabod, *Machiavelli and the Renaissance* (Cambridge, Mass., 1958), and James H. Meisel, *The Myth of the Ruling Class: Gaetano Mosca and the "Elite"* (Ann Arbor, 1958), Chap. XIII ("Machiavelli and the Machiavellians," pp. 262-285).

PAINE, THOMAS, *The Rights of Man* (London, 1791). Probably the most famous answer to Burke's *Reflections on the Revolution in France;* the two should be read together.

CHAPTER VII. THE IDOL STATE

BROWN, IVOR, *English Political Theory,* 2d rev. ed. (London, 1929), pp. 136-151. In the chapter "Collectivism and the Sovereign State" Brown deals with the impact of Hegel's political philosophy on English thought, particularly his doctrine of "Real Will" or (as Rousseau called it) "General Will." Brown concludes that this doctrine is "psychologically false" and "practically vicious," because it "hands unlimited powers to the person or persons who can claim to formulate it, and creates a superior class who can logically inflict 'forcible freedom' on everybody else for their 'real good.' Plato and Hegel faced the results of their premises and stood rightly against democracy" (p. 149).

CARRITT, E. F., *Morals and Politics* (London, 1935), pp. 105-127. Incisive and critical analysis of the moral foundations of Hegelian political thought, especially of Hegel's approach to the problem of political obligation. For a discussion of the two chief exponents of Hegelian political philosophy in England, Green and Bosanquet, see pp. 128-157. The best answer to Hegel and Bosanquet is L. T. Hobhouse, *The Metaphysical Theory of the State* (London, 1918). See, especially, Chap. III, "The Real Will," and Appendix I, "Hegel's Theory of the Will." John H. Muirhead, *The Platonic Tradition in Anglo-Saxon Philosophy* (New York, 1931), takes up the problem of Hegelian influences in England and America (pp. 147-218, 315-323).

FRIEDRICH, CARL J. (ed.), *The Philosophy of Hegel* (Modern Library, New York, 1953). A collection of portions of Hegel's major writings, including a long Introduction (pp. xiii-lxiv) by the editor.

GRIERSON, H. J. C., *Carlyle and Hitler* (Cambridge, 1933). In many respects sympathetic to Carlyle's social and political views. The author, a distinguished Scottish literary critic and scholar, is particularly impressed with Carlyle's revolt against *laissez faire*.

MARCUSE, HERBERT, *Reason and Revolution: Hegel and the Rise of Social Theory*, 2nd ed. (New York, 1955). A vigorous (but hopeless) attempt to present Hegel as a liberal. The author argues that the "progressive ideas of liberalism" (p. 413) in Hegel's political thought are incompatible with fascist totalitarianism, and that German Nazism was "anti-Hegelian in all its aims and principles" (pp. 418-419). For more moderate defenses of Hegel against the charge of authoritarian statism, see W. T. Stace, *The Philosophy of Hegel: A Systematic Exposition* (New York, 1955), and John N. Findlay, *Hegel: A Re-examination* (London, 1958). The following controversy about Hegel's "Prussianism" will be found very stimulating: T. M. Knox, "Hegel and Prussianism," *Philosophy,* XV (January, 1940), 51-63; E. F. Carritt, "Hegel and Prussianism," *ibid.* (April, 1940), 190-196; and the final rejoinders by both Knox and Carritt, "Hegel and Prussianism," *ibid.* (July, 1940), 313-320. See also Bertrand Russell, *A History of Western Philosophy* (New York, 1945), pp. 730-746.

POPPER, K. R., *The Open Society and Its Enemies* (Princeton, 1950). One of the outstanding treatises on a vital issue: the struggle, in history, between social science and social myth. In the first part, Popper presents Plato as the founder of the unscientific, dogmatic, and irrational tradition that has done so much harm in hampering the development of rational social thought and institutions. In the second part, Hegel and Marx are similarly dealt with, Hegel much more severely than Marx. See, in particular, Chap. XII, "Hegel and the New Tribalism" (pp. 223-273).

SANTAYANA, GEORGE, *Egotism in German Philosophy* (New York, 1916). A general inquiry into the nature of German philosophy and an examination of individual German thinkers like Goethe, Kant, and Nietzsche. A useful supplement to this work, written from a different point of view, is John Dewey, *German Philosophy and Politics* (New York, 1915).

SCHAPIRO, J. SALWYN, "Thomas Carlyle: Prophet of Fascism," *The Journal of Modern History,* XVII (June, 1945), 97-115. The experience of Fascism and Nazism has shown Carlyle in a new light, as this important study demonstrates. For a critical appraisal of Carlyle, see also J. M. Robertson, *Modern Humanists Reconsidered* (London, 1927), Chap. I (pp. 1-43), and Crane Brinton, *English Political Thought in the Nineteenth Century* (London, 1933), pp. 164-177.

SONTAG, RAYMOND, "The Future in Retrospect: The Germany of Treitschke," *Foreign Affairs,* XVIII (October, 1939), 127-139. One of the most trenchant analyses of Treitschke's *Politics.* One of Sontag's main conclusions is that the *Politics* "is valuable today because from its pages we can learn how much of the contemporary Germany is rooted deep in the past and therefore unlikely to be easily uprooted" (p. 137). See also Andreas Dorpalen, *Heinrich von Treitschke* (New Haven, 1957) for a divergent interpretation.

STIRK, S. C., *The Prussian Spirit: A Survey of German Literature and Politics, 1914-1940* (London, 1941). A valuable book because it is the only account, in English, of major German writers whose influence at home has been profound, although their work is virtually unknown outside of Germany. See also Rohan D'O. Butler, *The Roots of National Socialism, 1783-1933* (New York, 1942).

TROELTSCH, ERNST, "The Ideas of Natural Law and Humanity in World Politics" (1922), in Otto Gierke, *Natural Law and the Theory of Society, 1500 to 1800* (trans. by Ernest Barker, Beacon Paperbacks, Boston, 1957), pp. 201-222. This lecture by Troeltsch, one of the most creative German scholars of the twentieth century, and politically a liberal, is a penetrating comparison between German and western political thought. Troeltsch points out that the contrasts between the two are not recent, but go back to the Middle Ages. In particular, he stresses the fundamental difference between the western conception of liberty as absence of constraint and the German view of liberty as voluntary subordination to the state. See also William Ebenstein, *The German Record: A Political Portrait* (New York, 1945), Chap. II, "State and Society in German Politics" (pp. 32-61). For the record of German Liberalism, see the following: Leonard Krieger, *The German Idea of Freedom: History of a Political Tradition* (Boston, 1957); Guido de Ruggiero, *The History of European Liberalism* (Beacon Paperbacks, Boston, 1959), pp. 211-274; and Rudolf Olden, *The History of Liberty in Germany* (London, 1946).

CHAPTER VIII. FASCISM: GOVERNMENT
BY FORCE AND LIES

BENEŠ, EDUARD, *Democracy: Today and Tomorrow* (London, 1940). See Chap. V, "Modern Antidemocratic Ideologies and European Democracy." As a student of politics, as Foreign Minister and President of Czechoslovakia, Beneš had unusual opportunities to study, first hand, Italian Fascism and, even more thoroughly, German Nazism. See also the following: E. B. Ashton, *The Fascist: His State and His Mind* (London, 1937); William Ebenstein, *Fascist Italy* (New York, 1939); William Ebenstein, *The Nazi State* (New York, 1943); Dante L. Germino, *The Italian Fascist Party in Power* (Minneapolis, 1959); Carl J.

Friedrich (ed.), *Totalitarianism* (Cambridge, Mass., 1954); Carl J. Friedrich and Zbigniew K. Brzezinski, *Totalitarian Dictatorship and Autocracy* (Cambridge, Mass., 1956); and R. H. S. Crossman, *Government and the Governed*, 4th ed. (London, 1958), Chap. IX, "Fascism" (pp. 246-293).

BORGESE, G. A., "The Intellectual Origins of Fascism," *Social Research*, I (November, 1934), 458-485. This article by the eminent literary historian and publicist disentangles the various strands in the fabric of European Fascism. Borgese stresses the role of the romantic movement in creating an intellectual milieu which favored the growth of Fascist ideas. A similar view of romanticism is also expressed in Peter Quennell, "The Romantic Catastrophe," *Horizon*, I (May, 1940), 328-345. By contrast, Jacques Barzun absolves the romantics from this charge in *Romanticism and the Modern Ego* (Boston, 1943). One of the most extensive explorations of the intellectual origins of totalitarianism, especially Fascism, is Hannah Arendt, *The Origins of Totalitarianism*, 2nd ed. (Meridian Books, New York, 1958).

CHAKOTIN, SERGE, *The Rape of the Masses* (London, 1940). The subtitle is "The Psychology of Totalitarian Propaganda," and the work is mainly devoted to Nazism.

COLLINGWOOD, R. G., *The New Leviathan* (Oxford, 1942). The last part is entitled "Barbarism" (pp. 342-387). In it, Collingwood defines the nature of barbarism as "hostility toward civilization" (p. 342), and then proceeds to explain barbarism through four historical illustrations. A controversial work, written in a highly peculiar and mannered style, yet rich in provocative ideas.

DENNIS, LAWRENCE, *The Coming American Fascism* (New York, 1936), and *The Dynamics of War and Revolution* (New York, 1940). By one of the leading pro-Fascist writers in the United States.

DICKS, HENRY V., "Personality Traits and National Socialist Ideology," *Human Relations*, III (June, 1950), 111-154. Based on empirical research, this is one of the best psychological analyses of the Fascist personality. A complementary essay of equally lasting significance is David M. Levy, "Anti-Nazis: Criteria of Differentiation," in Alfred H. Stanton and Stewart E. Perry (eds.), *Personality and Political Crisis* (Glencoe, 1951), pp. 151-227. See also the following: Peter Nathan, *The Psychology of Fascism* (London, 1943); David Abrahamsen, *Men, Mind, and Power* (New York, 1945); Wilhelm Reich, *The Mass Psychology of Fascism* (New York, 1946); Gustav Bychowski, *Dictators and Disciples: From Caesar to Stalin: A Psychoanalytic Interpretation of History* (New York, 1948); G. M. Gilbert, *The Psychology of Dictatorship: Based on an Examination of the Leadership of Nazi Germany* (New York, 1950); Ernest Jones, "The Psychology of Quislingism," *International Journal of Psycho-Analysis*, XXII (January, 1941), 1-6; A. L. Edwards, "Signs of Incipient Fascism," *Journal of Abnormal Psychology*, XXXIX (July, 1944), 301-316; Leo Alexander, "The Molding of Personality under Dictatorship," *Journal of Criminal Law and Criminology*, XL (May–June, 1949), 3-27; and Zevedei Barbu, *Democracy and Dictatorship: Their Psychology and Patterns of Life* (Evergreen Books, New York, 1956).

DUTT, R. PALME, *Fascism and Social Revolution* (New York, 1935). One of the most authoritative interpretations of Fascism from a Marxist-Communist point of view. Dutt stresses the thesis that Fascism is essentially a symptom of capitalism in decay.

HOESS, RUDOLF, *Commandant of Auschwitz: The Autobiography of Rudolf Hoess* (Cleveland–New York, 1959). Hoess was commandant of the Auschwitz extermination camp from May 1940 to December 1943; during 1942 and 1943 about two and a half million Jews—men, women, and children—were murdered in gas chambers. Hoess was arrested by British authorities in Germany in March 1946, handed over to the Polish Government in May (Auschwitz is on Polish territory), and tried and executed in April 1947. He wrote his autobiography while in prison, feeling no remorse for his crimes. "Auschwitz became," Hoess writes, "the greatest human extermination center of all time" (p. 160), and he goes on saying that "the reasons behind the extermination program seemed to me right" (*ibid.*). Lord Russell of Liverpool, former Assistant Judge Advocate General of the British Armed Forces and an authority in the study of German war crimes, writes as follows in his Introduction to Hoess' autobiography: "During the war probably not less than twelve million men, women, and children from the invaded and occupied territories were done to death by the Germans. At a conservative estimate, eight million of them perished in concentration camps. Of these, not less than five million were Jews. The estimated number given by the Prosecution at the Nuremberg Trial of Major War Criminals was six million" (pp. 13-14). See also Lord Russell of Liverpool, *The Scourge of the Swastika: A Short History of Nazi War Crimes* (Ballantine Books, New York, 1954), and Eugen Kogon, *The Theory and Practice of Hell* (Berkley Books, New York, 1950). Kogon, a German Catholic Liberal, was arrested by the Gestapo (German Secret Police) in March 1938; in September 1939 he was sent to the Buchenwald concentration camp, where he managed to survive until April 1945, finally liberated by United States armed forces. His account is one of the most detailed of the day-to-day operation of a typical German concentration camp. Elie A. Cohen, *Human Behavior in the Concentration Camp* (London, 1954), is written from the viewpoint of medical psychology and based on first-hand experience, the author (a Dutch physician) having been an inmate of a concentration camp in 1942-1945.

JOAD, C. E. M., *A Guide to the Philosophy of Politics and Morals* (London, 1938). Chap. XVI (pp. 605-663), "Theory of Fascism," is a clear presentation of the origins and characteristics of Fascism and Nazism.

MENZEL, ADOLF, *Der Staatsgedanke des Faschismus* (Leipzig–Vienna, 1935). This work by one of the leading Austrian political scientists attempts to trace the main tenets of Fascist political theory to their historical origins. Menzel deals with German and Italian predecessors of Fascist ideas, and makes also some interesting observations on French influences like Rousseau and Sorel, and on British writers like Hobbes and Burke. His analogies are at times somewhat far-fetched, but his book is valuable in presenting the thesis that Fascism and Nazism have deep roots in the Western world, and cannot be simply explained by the iniquities of the Versailles Treaty and high unemployment figures.

MYERS, GUSTAVUS, *History of Bigotry in the United States* (New York, 1943). This work by a great, and unorthodox, American historian is of considerable importance to the understanding of antidemocratic attitudes. Myers succeeds in establishing the fact that the antidemocratic tradition in the United States (as revealed in religious and racial bigotry) has always existed side by side with the official democratic tradition of the country, although the former has never been able to win over the majority to its doctrines. The book is also valuable for the exposure of the intimate connections between religious bigotry and native American Fascism and Nazism.

RAPPARD, WILLIAM E., *The Crisis of Democracy* (Chicago, 1938). Rappard, a Swiss writer, examines the growth of modern democracy and its challenge by the totalitarian systems. Chap. IV deals with the origins and background of Italian Fascism and German Nazism (pp. 133-181).

SOREL, GEORGES, *Reflections on Violence* (Paris, 1906; English trans., London, 1915). This book has been of immense importance in the formation of an intellectual cult of violence. Sorel was primarily concerned with the revolution of the proletariat, but his ideas influenced also the Fascists, especially in Italy.

SWEEZY, PAUL M., *The Theory of Capitalist Development* (New York, 1942), pp. 329-347. The chapter "Fascism" is based on fairly orthodox Marxist assumptions. The author sees in Fascism "one form which imperialism assumes in the age of wars of redivision." Adopting the view that Fascism is essentially to be understood in terms of decadent capitalism, Sweezy does not give proper weight to other factors, such as historical and political traditions that determine the degree of political maturity and civilization of a society.

VEBLEN, THORSTEIN, *Imperial Germany and the Industrial Revolution* (New York, 1915). Published over a generation ago, this is still the best book on modern Germany. As in so many other matters, Veblen was unorthodox enough to perceive that German science and technology were a superficial veneer, behind which lurked archaic and antidemocratic ways of social ideas and institutions. He was the only American of his time to see that modern Japan offered a striking analogy in this peculiar combination of scientific technology and pre-scientific modes of thinking and living. This book is indispensable to an understanding of German political thought.

WILDEBLOOD, PETER, "English Criminals," *Encounter*, IX (July, 1957), 24-29. With respect to the political views of English criminals, the author writes that they typically tend toward fascism, and that "there is quite an extensive Hitler-cult" (p. 26). The typical member of a criminal gang is not a Byronic figure looking for unlimited freedom, but a man "who has willingly surrendered himself to the control of a powerful group—a surrender which absolves him from the painful necessity of choice or responsibility. He does not wish to be an individual" (*ibid.*). The main attraction of the gang for the criminal lies in the fact that "it calls for little or no self-discipline; what discipline there is is arbitrarily imposed from above. The ideas of loyalty and obligations to others, which are so repugnant to the criminal mind, are thus excluded from the start. The gang, like the Fascist state, is a false brotherhood based on fear. Not only is there no honor among thieves, but no effective solidarity apart from that engendered by mutual distrust" (*ibid.*).

CHAPTER IX. TOTALITARIAN COMMUNISM

BERLIN, ISAIAH, *Karl Marx,* 2d ed. (New York, 1948). The best short biography.

CARR, EDWARD H., *The Soviet Impact on the Western World* (New York, 1947).

Carr is one of the not too many writers on Soviet Communism for whom Russian history did not begin in 1917. He has the knowledge and historical perspective to separate, in Soviet thought and institutions, Western from Russian influences. Specifically, his short book takes up the political, economic, social, international, and ideological impacts of Sovietism on the Western world.

CARRITT, E. F., *Morals and Politics* (London, 1935), pp. 170-177. Critical analysis of "dialectical materialism."

COLE, G. D. H., *The Meaning of Marxism* (London, 1948). One of the best introductions into the general body of Marx's thought, the materialist interpretation of history, his theory of the state, and his economic analyses, including the theories of value and surplus value. Cole successfully simplifies some of the complexities of Marx's ideas without doing violence to them. In addition, he points out the social changes that have taken place since Marx, and discusses their implications for socialist movements. His discussion of the new class of white-collar workers and their political psychology is particularly noteworthy.

DICKS, HENRY V., "Observations on Contemporary Russian Behaviour," *Human Relations,* V (May, 1952), 111-175. Not a study of Russian national character, but of the interaction of personality and environment in the context of Communist totalitarianism. Though based on a small number of subjects, this is a pioneering analysis of personality and social structure. See also Margaret Mead, *Soviet Attitudes toward Authority* (New York, 1951), and Raymond A. Bauer, *The New Man in Soviet Psychology* (Cambridge, Mass., 1952). Morris L. Ernst and David Loth, *Report on the American Communist* (New York, 1952) is largely done in terms of personality analysis, and Gabriel A. Almond, *The Appeals of Communism* (Princeton, 1954) is a comparative study of why people join, and leave, the Communist movement in the United States, England, France, and Italy. Hadley Cantril, *The Politics of Despair* (New York, 1958), is an empirical pioneering study on the psychology and outlook of Communist voters in France and Italy, by a leading American social psychologist.

DJILAS, MILOVAN, *The New Class* (Praeger Paperbacks, New York, 1959). Possibly the most important book on communism since the *Communist Manifesto.* See also his *Land Without Justice* (New York, 1958), and *Anatomy of a Moral* (New York, 1959).

DOBB, MAURICE, *Marx as an Economist* (New York, 1945). A brief pamphlet on the main points of Marx's economic theory in clear and elementary terms. Dobb is one of the leading Marxist economists in England. See also his *Studies in the Development of Capitalism* (London, 1946).

EASTMAN, MAX, *Marxism: Is It Science?* (New York, 1940). Attacks Marxism mainly on the ground that it is unscientific. See also R. N. Carew Hunt, *Marxism: Past and Present* (New York, 1954), and Alfred G. Meyer, *Marxism: Its Unity of Theory and Practice* (Cambridge, Mass., 1954). For an analysis of Marx's concept of "alienation," consult David Braybrooke, "Diagnosis and Remedy in Marx's Doctrine of Alienation," *Social Research,* XXV (Autumn, 1958), 325-345, and Reinhold Niebuhr, *The Nature and Destiny of Man,* Vol. I (New York, 1949), pp. 43-53.

ENGELS, FRIEDRICH, *On Historical Materialism* (New York, 1940). A brief essay, published first in 1892—one of the most succinct statements of the meaning of historical materialism. It stresses the English roots of philosophical materialism, especially Bacon, Hobbes, and Locke, the "fathers of the brilliant French school of materialists" which made the eighteenth century a "pre-eminently French century" (p. 8). See also Maurice Cornforth, *Dialectical Materialism: An Introduction,* 3 vols. (London, 1952-1954), for an extensive presentation from the orthodox Marxist-communist viewpoint.

FEDERN, KARL, *The Materialist Interpretation of History* (London, 1939). The subtitle is "A Critical Analysis." For the historical background, see Alexander Gray, *The Socialist Tradition: Moses to Lenin* (London, 1946), with interesting materials on the Greek, Biblical, and medieval sources, and Harry W. Laidler, *Social-Economic Movements* (New York, 1944). G. D. H. Cole, *A History of Socialist Thought,* 5 vols. (New York, 1953-1960), includes much that is of interest to the student of Marxism and communism.

HALDANE, J. B. S., *The Marxist Philosophy and the Sciences* (New York, 1939). A distinguished scientist and a Marxist, Haldane attempts to apply Marxist principles and categories of analysis to the natural sciences, such as physics and chemistry, biology and psychology, mathematics, cosmology, and, finally, sociology. An unusual book that requires, apart from some familiarity with Marx and Engels, a solid knowledge of the basic data in the physical sciences. See also Jack Lindsay, *Marxism and Contemporary Science* (London, 1949).

HOOK, SIDNEY (ed.), *The Meaning of Marx* (New York, 1934). This symposium contains "An Introduction to the Study of Marx" by Sherwood Eddy; "The Meaning of Marx" by Sidney Hook; "Why I Am Not a Communist" by Bertrand Russell, John Dewey, and Morris Cohen; and "Communism Without Dogma" by Sidney Hook. Stimulating throughout.

JOAD, C. E. M., *Modern Political Theory* (Oxford, 1924). Chaps. III-VI discuss, in elementary language, the main ideas of Marxism, socialism, syndicalism, guild socialism, communism, and anarchism. The book also contains a selected bibliography which will be useful to beginners.

KAUTSKY, KARL, *Social Democracy versus Communism* (New York, 1945). A collection of essays by the late leader of German Social Democratic thought. Of particular interest is Chap. II, "Marxism and the Dictatorship of the Proletariat" (pp. 22-47). Kautsky's hostility to Bolshevism and the Soviet Union finds expression in Chaps. III-VI (pp. 48-99).

LAFARGUE, PAUL, and LIEBKNECHT, WILHELM, *Karl Marx: His Life and Work* (New York, 1943). These brief "reminiscences" by Lafargue, Marx's son-in-law, and by Liebknecht, German socialist leader, reveal some of the personal traits of Marx, mostly dealing with his life in London amid his friends and political followers.

LANGE, OSCAR, and TAYLOR, FRED M., *On the Economic Theory of Socialism* (Minneapolis, 1938). The two essays in this book seek to refute the charge that a socialist economy is not practicable. Specifically, Lange and Taylor turn their attention to leading opponents of socialism among economists, such as Lionel Robbins, F. A. Hayek, and Ludwig von Mises. The main argument of the two authors is that rational allocation of resources is possible under a planned socialist economy. They also emphasize that a socialist economy is not only compatible with democracy, but a natural outcome of its basic assumptions. For a survey of the relevant literature, see Abram Bergson, "Socialist Economics," in Howard S. Ellis (ed.), *A Survey of Contemporary Economics* (Philadelphia–Toronto, 1948), pp. 412-448.

LASKI, HAROLD J., *Communism: 1381-1927* (London, 1927). Laski neither accepts nor rejects Marxism–Leninism *in toto*. The materialist interpretation of history seems to him, "as general doctrine, undeniable." Yet he warns that "there is no justification for the resort to violence until the resources of reason have been exhausted" (p. 180). See, especially, Chap. IV, "The Communist Theory of the State." See also Laski's two pamphlets, *Karl Marx* (London, 1921) and *Marx and Today* (London, 1943).

LERNER, MAX, *Ideas Are Weapons* (New York, 1939). A study of "Lenin's *The State and Revolution*" (pp. 326-337) arrives at the conclusion that "in the movement of Western political theory he is in his realism one of the two or three towering figures since Machiavelli" (p. 337).

LINDSAY, A. D., *Karl Marx's Capital: An Introductory Essay* (London, 1925). This short volume in the popular series, The World's Manuals, attains its objective admirably. The first chapter (pp. 15-26) gives a brief outline of Marx and Hegel, emphasizing especially the influence of Hegelian dialectic on Marx. Chaps. II-IV (pp. 27-108) provide well-balanced introductions into economic determinism, the labor theory of value, and the meaning of surplus value. The final chapter (pp. 109-125) contains suggestive comparisons between Marx and Rousseau, each the father of a great revolution.

MARCUSE, HERBERT, *Soviet Marxism: A Critical Analysis* (New York, 1958). Examines the relation of Marxist doctrine to Soviet reality, and concludes that Marxist ideology is a decisive part, and that Soviet Marxism, in spite of its distortions, is pushing Soviet society toward more liberalized economic and political practices.

MARX, KARL, and ENGELS, FRIEDRICH, *The German Ideology* (London, 1938). Important for an understanding of Marxian philosophy and interpretation of history, this classic contains scathing criticisms of nineteenth-century German philosophers and writers.

MARX, KARL, and ENGELS, FRIEDRICH, *Selected Correspondence* (New York, 1942). Over two hundred letters, written by Marx and Engels to each other or to leading socialist writers and publicists. These letters not only reveal Marx and Engels as human beings in their relations to their friends but also contain succinctly formulated insights that frequently make a point more clearly and convincingly than more ponderous treatments in their better-known works. See also Lewis S. Feuer (ed.), *Marx and Engels: Basic Writings on Politics and Philosophy* (Anchor Books, New York, 1959), including a selection of less well-known pieces.

POPPER, K. R., *The Open Society and Its Enemies* (Princeton, 1950). The second part is on Hegel and Marx; Chaps. XIII-XXII examine some of the major assumptions of Marx's thought, especially its claim to be scientific. In the literature on Marx, these studies by Popper are noteworthy for their unusual balance of judgment and historical perspective. Critical reviews of the political theory of communism will be found in Historicus, "Stalin on Revolution," *Foreign Affairs,* XXVII (January, 1949), 175-214; Hans Kelsen, *The Political Theory of Bolshe-*

vism (Berkeley and Los Angeles, 1949); and R. W. Carew Hunt, *The Theory and Practice of Communism* (New York, 1950).

RUSSELL, BERTRAND, *Proposed Roads to Freedom: Socialism, Anarchism and Syndicalism* (New York, *n.d.*). The first part of the book looks at the past, and analyzes Marxism, anarchism, and syndicalism. The second part takes up the major problems of a socialist society, such as work and pay, government, international relations, science and art, and, finally, a vision of "The World as It Could Be Made." Unorthodox and stimulating. See also Russell's *Bolshevism: Practice and Theory* (New York, 1920, reprinted 1949).

RUSSIAN INSTITUTE, COLUMBIA UNIVERSITY (ed.), *The Anti-Stalin Campaign and International Communism: A Selection of Documents* (New York, 1956). Contains the full text of Khrushchev's secret speech against Stalin and the "cult of personality" (February 25, 1956), followed by the reactions of communist newspapers and organizations throughout the world.

SETON-WATSON, HUGH, *From Lenin to Khrushchev: A History of World Communism* (New York, 1960). The best short history of world communism, with special emphasis on underdeveloped areas, where communism has been most successful. See also Franz Borkenau, *European Communism* (New York, 1953); Stefan T. Possony, *A Century of Conflict: Communist Techniques of World Revolution* (Chicago, 1953); and Stephen King–Hall, *The Communist Conspiracy* (New York, 1953).

STALIN, JOSEPH, and WELLS, H. G., *Marxism vs. Liberalism: An Interview* (New York, 1945). The interview of Stalin by Wells took place on July 23, 1934. Stalin denied that "the Communists are enamored with violence. They would be pleased to drop violent methods if the ruling class agreed to give way to the working class. But the experience of history speaks against such an assumption." Stalin also conceded that of all the ruling classes, the British ruling groups, aristocratic and bourgeois, were the cleverest and most flexible in granting reforms and concessions. For an introduction into Stalin's thought, see his *Selected Writings* (New York, 1942).

WETTER, GUSTAV A., *Dialectical Materialism: A Historical and Systematic Survey of Philosophy in the Soviet Union* (New York, 1958). The author, an Austrian Jesuit teaching the history of Russian philosophy at the Papal Oriental Institute in Rome, is one of the top experts on Marxism and communism in the Roman Catholic Church. For Protestant interpretations, see John C. Bennett, *Christianity and Communism* (New York, 1949), and J. V. Langmead Casserley, *The Bent World: A Christian Examination of East-West Tensions* (New York, 1955).

WILSON, EDMUND, *To the Finland Station* (Anchor Books, New York, 1953). Contains studies of Marx and Engels (pp. 111-346) and Lenin (pp. 347-474). The book is also valuable for the analysis of the origins of modern socialism (especially in France) as well as for some trenchant chapters on Trotsky.

ZINNER, PAUL E. (ed.), *National Communism and Popular Revolt in Eastern Europe* (New York, 1956). A collection of documents on the background and events of the Hungarian and Polish Revolutions in 1956. See also Imre Nagy, *On Communism: In Defense of the New Course* (New York, 1957), a defense of "national communism" by the Prime Minister of Hungary during the Revolution of 1956, and Charles P. McVicker, *Titoism: Pattern for International Communism* (New York, 1957).

Part IV: Capitalism, Socialism, and the Welfare State

CHAPTER X. PRIVATE PROPERTY AND FREE ENTERPRISE

BECKER, CARL, *Freedom and Responsibility in the American Way of Life* (New York, 1946). Chap. V (pp. 89-122) is a defense of private economic enterprise, although it allows that there is a definite place for public intervention. However, "the primary aim of all governmental regulation of the economic life of the community should be, not to supplant the system of private economic enterprise, but to make it work" (p. 111).

BERLE, A. A., and G. C. MEANS, *The Modern Corporation and Private Property* (New York, 1932). The classic work on the transformation of property in the age of corporate business. The authors point to the massive concentration of property, power, and control in the corporate organization of business and industry. A much friendlier attitude toward corporate business is displayed by Berle in his more recent *The 20th Century Capitalist Revolution* (New York, 1954) and *Power Without Property* (New York, 1959). See also George W. Stocking and Myron W. Watkins, *Monopoly and Free Enterprise* (New York, 1951); A. D. H. Kaplan, *Big Enterprise in a Competitive System* (Washington, 1954); Herrymon Maurer, *Great Enterprise: Growth and Behavior of the Big Corporation* (New York, 1955); Walton Hamilton, *The Politics of Industry* (New York, 1957); Sylvia and Benjamin Selekman, *Power and Morality in a Business Society* (New York, 1956); Francis X. Sutton and Others, *The American Business Creed* (Cambridge, Mass., 1956); and Louis M. Hacker, *American Capitalism* (Anvil Books, Princeton, 1957). For a critical refutation, from the Marxist viewpoint, of the newer, "revisionist" theories of capitalism, see Paul M. Sweezy, "Theories of the New Capitalism," *Monthly Review,* XI (July–August, 1959), 65-75.

CECIL, Lord HUGH, *Conservatism* (London, 1912). This volume, in the Home University Library, by a leading British Conservative has an interesting chapter, "Property and Taxation" (pp. 118-158). Lord Cecil begins his argument with these observations: "Nothing has more effective significance in Conservatism than its bearing on questions of property. Ever since Conservatism arose to resist the revolutionary movement of 1789, the defense of property has been one of its principal purposes. And it is with questions of property that the most important of political conflicts in the future will be wholly or partly concerned" (p. 118).

DAHL, ROBERT A., "Business and Politics: A Critical Appraisal of Political Science," *American Political Science Review,* LIII (March, 1959), 1-34. A critical survey of the literature on business as a political order and on the relations of business to the American political system. The author draws on a variety of sources—political, economic, sociological, legal, and historical.

EDITORS OF FORTUNE, *U.S.A.: The Permanent Revolution* (New York, 1951). A vigorous reaffirmation of the American free enterprise system, presenting in popular language the general philosophy of *Fortune* Magazine. Speaking of the transformation of American capitalism, the authors write as follows: "What counts is that the old concept that the owner has a right to use his property just the way he pleases has evolved into the belief that ownership carries social obligations, and that a manager is a trustee not only for the owner but for society as a whole" (p. 88).

GALBRAITH, JOHN KENNETH, *The Affluent Society* (Boston, 1958). Having examined, in a fresh and original manner, the *mechanism* of American capitalism in *American Capitalism: The Concept of Countervailing Power* (Boston, 1952), the author explores in the present work the *goals* of the American economy. The problems of the "affluent society" are new both for the political economist and the policy-maker, and although such problems can now best be studied in the United States, other nations with rapidly rising living standards and expanding wealth will soon face similar issues. Galbraith's main proposal is to balance the present over-spending in the private sector of the economy by sharply increased expenditures in the public sector, such as education, health, and municipal redevelopment (to mention but a few). Even where one does not agree with Galbraith, one always enjoys the freshness of his thought and the wit and urbanity of his style.

HAMILTON, WALTON H., "Property—According to Locke," *Yale Law Journal*, XLI (April, 1931), 864-880. Protects Locke against his own defenders, especially the zealots who have read into Locke's theories of property more than he himself meant.

HAYEK, F. A., *The Constitution of Liberty* (Chicago, 1960). The most scholarly and best argued case for the free-enterprise system based on constitutional government and the rule of law available in English. In a "Postscript" (pp. 397-411) Hayek explains "Why I Am Not a Conservative," and defines his overall position as that of "an unrepentant Old Whig" (p. 409), or Liberalism as understood from the late seventeenth to the late nineteenth century. See also F. A. Hayek (ed.), *Capitalism and the Historians* (Chicago, 1954).

KEYNES, JOHN MAYNARD, *The End of Laissez Faire* (London, 1926). In this little book of fifty pages, Keynes first draws a historical sketch of the evolution of *laissez faire,* and then inquires into the economic prospects of the future. He is persuaded that capitalism, wisely managed, "can probably be made more efficient for attaining economic ends than any alternative system yet in sight, but that in itself is in many ways extremely objectionable" (pp. 52-53). Is there any way out of this dilemma? "Europe lacks the means, America the will, to make a move" (p. 54). Reprinted in William Ebenstein, *Great Political Thinkers: Plato to the Present,* 3rd ed. (New York, 1960), pp. 654-666.

LARKIN, PASCHAL, *Property in the Eighteenth Century, with Special Reference to England and Locke* (Dublin, 1930). Contains analytical summaries of Locke's ideas on property and his influence on political and economic thought.

LASKI, HAROLD J., *The Rise of European Liberalism* (London, 1936). The second chapter, "The Seventeenth Century," deals with the relationships between liberalism and early capitalism, and gives an analysis of Locke as one of the central figures on this era: "His state is nothing so much as a contract between a group of businessmen who form a limited liability company whose memorandum of association forbids to the directors all those practices of which the Stuarts had, until this time, been guilty" (p. 116). The treatment of Locke is highly critical in this work.

SPENCER, HERBERT, *Social Statics* (London, 1851); *Principles of Sociology*, 3 vols. (London, 1876-1896); and *The Man versus the State* (London, 1884). These three major works by Herbert Spencer are still the best and most uncompromising expression of the social and economic doctrines of *laissez faire*.

WEBER, MAX, *The Protestant Ethic and the Spirit of Capitalism* (1922, English trans., London, 1930). The great German sociologist attacks the study of capitalism from the religious angle, and stresses the role of Calvinism and Puritanism in the growth of the capitalist spirit. A not too dissimilar thesis will be found in R. H. Tawney, *Religion and the Rise of Capitalism* (London, 1926). Weber's view is challenged by H. M. Robertson in his *Aspects of the Rise of Economic Individualism: A Criticism of Max Weber and His School* (Cambridge, 1933). Robertson adduces evidence to prove the origins of capitalism in Catholic countries like France and Italy. The answer to Robertson will be found in the work of a Jesuit writer, *The Economic Morals of the Jesuits: An Answer to Dr. H. M. Robertson*, by J. Broderick, S.J. (London, 1934). See also Ralph Barton Perry, *Puritanism and Democracy* (New York, 1944), Chap. XII, "The Economic Virtues" (pp. 297-320), and A. Whitney Griswold, "Three Puritans on Prosperity," *New England Quarterly*, VII (September, 1934), 475-493.

WRIGHT, DAVID McCORD, *Capitalism* (New York, 1951). A spirited defense of capitalism as the most democratic and productive system. See also Thomas Wilson, *Modern Capitalism and Economic Progress* (London, 1950); William E. Rappard, *The Secret of American Prosperity* (New York, 1955); and Colin Clark, "What's Wrong With Economics?" *Encounter*, X (April, 1958), 15-23.

CHAPTER XI. DEMOCRATIC SOCIALISM

BARKER, ERNEST, *Political Thought in England: 1848-1914* (London, 1915; 2nd ed., 1928), pp. 203-247. The last chapter, "Economics and Politics," traces the beginnings of socialist ideas in Britain from the eighteen eighties on. It analyzes the British reactions to Marx, and briefly indicates the birth and growth of Fabianism.

BEER, MAX, *Fifty Years of International Socialism* (London, 1935). This autobiography of a Continental socialist, who spent about a quarter of a century in England, contains some penetrating insights into English politics in general and English socialism in particular. In Chap. XXIV, "Interview with Lenin" (pp. 144-159), Beer explained to Lenin some of the effects that he observed in revolutionary socialists who had fled from the Continent to England: "Revolutionary exiles, if they live for any length of time in England, turn gradually into reformists; she acts upon them as a de-revolutionizing filter. I have met in London former revolutionists and terrorists from Germany and Austria, Communards and Anarcho-Communists from the Latin countries, who had become wise in England. With an air of superior wisdom they held forth on the virtues of 'compromise, statesmanlike attitude, sagacity, well-balanced judgment, and preference of expediency to principle,' and all those stock phrases they had heard in lecture-halls, or had read in *The Times* or *The Spectator"* (pp. 152-153).

BUBER, MARTIN, *Paths in Utopia* (Beacon Paperbacks, Boston, 1958). The author, holder of the chair of social philosophy at the Hebrew University in Jerusalem, defends the non-Marxist socialism of Owen, Saint-Simon, Fourier, Proudhon, and Kropotkin against the Marxist-communist doctrine of class war and dictatorship. Buber holds that socialism based on small associations of freely cooperating individuals is the only realistic approach to the reconstruction of modern society, and that it is far from being "utopian," as Marx and Engels sarcastically called it, whereas the self-styled "scientific" doctrines of Marx and Lenin are doomed to fail precisely because they violate the true nature of man, his needs for freedom and cooperation. As an example of cooperative socialism based on personal freedom and voluntary association, the author describes in the epilogue the "Kvuza," or Village Commune, in Israel ("An Experiment That Did Not Fail," pp. 139-149). All in all, this is one of the classic guides to non-Marxist socialist thought.

COLE, G. D. H., *Socialism in Evolution* (London, 1938). Chap. IV (pp. 133-159), "Marxism in the Modern World," is indispensable to an understanding and modification of basic Marxian doctrines in the light of social and industrial changes since Marx's death. Cole demonstrates, in particular, the impact of the growth of the white-collar workers, the "salariat," as contrasted with the old-type "proletariat" of manual workers in the heavy industries. The failure of Continental socialist parties to attract the "salariat" led to their decline, whereas the British Labor Party succeeded in winning over the allegiance of the white-collar workers, thus ensuring for itself in 1945 a strong majority in the House of Commons. The other chapters of the book deal with problems of the labor and socialist movements in Europe, particularly western Europe, and throw a good deal of light on the psychology and strategy of English socialism.

COLE, G. D. H., *A History of Socialist Thought,* 5 vols. (New York, 1953-1960). The most comprehensive work on the subject in any language, this will probably become his enduring contribution to the literature on socialism. An individualist at heart, Cole generally sympathizes with minorities (or even minorities within minorities) in the socialist movement that are Left-of-center. Carl A. Landauer, *European Socialism: A History of Ideas and Movements from the Industrial Revolution to Hitler's Seizure of Power,* 2 vols. (Berkeley–Los Angeles, 1959), concentrates on Continental Europe (including Russia), and emphasizes movements and policies rather than ideas. In contrast to Cole, Landauer's sympathies are with the moderate forces in the socialist movement, and his work thus balances Cole's.

CRIPPS, STAFFORD, *Towards Christian Democracy* (London, 1946). Like Attlee,

Cripps became a socialist largely through his deep religious convictions. See also William Dale Morris, *The Christian Origins of Social Revolt* (London, 1949), a brief survey of the subject from the Middle Ages to the present. William Temple, *Christianity and the Social Order* (Penguin Books, London–New York, 1942) illustrates the climate of religious opinion in England. The author, Archbishop of Canterbury, came close to some of the fundamental positions of British socialism, and his book explains why politically active ministers of religion in Britain will be found more often in the labor movement than in the Conservative Party.

CROSLAND, C. A. R., *The Future of Socialism* (New York, 1957). The most important theoretical analysis of socialism since the end of World War II. The author, a renowned British economist, tones down traditional socialist objectives like nationalization and planning, and stresses social equality and the cultivation of the good life for all. The book concludes as follows: "We do not want to enter the age of abundance, only to find that we have lost the values which might teach us how to enjoy it" (p. 529).

EGBERT, DONALD DREW and PERSONS, STOW (eds.), *Socialism and American Life*, 2 vols. (Princeton, 1952). Indispensable to the study of modern socialism. Vol. II deals entirely with the literature on socialism, and is the most comprehensive critical bibliography of the subject in existence.

GAITSKELL, HUGH, Socialism and Nationalization (Fabian Tract No. 300, London, 1956). The Leader of the Labor Party, opposed to any further large-scale nationalization of industry, concludes his argument by saying that "the most vital question is how far greater social and economic equality can be achieved without more nationalization and public ownership" (p. 31). Similar views are also expressed by Gaitskell in his *Recent Developments in British Socialist Thinking* (London, 1956). A Conservative British economist, Thomas Wilson, examines the same problem in "Changing Tendencies in Socialist Thought," *Lloyds Bank Review*, New Series, No. 41 (July, 1956), 1-22. For an American evaluation, see Andrew Hacker, "Why Nationalize?—British Labor's Unasked Question," *Social Research*, XXII (Spring, 1955), 1-24, and "Original Sin vs. Utopia in British Socialism," *Review of Politics*, XVIII (April, 1956), 184-206.

JENKINS, ROY, *The Labor Case* (Penguin Books, Baltimore, 1959). A popular presentation, written before the general elections in 1959. While not official, the book reflects the outlook of the majority in the leadership and rank-and-file.

MENGER, ANTON, *The Right to the Whole Produce of Labour* (London, 1899). Several important chapters are on eighteenth- and nineteenth-century precursors of British socialism. The English edition of the book is notable for two features: first, it contains an "Introduction" of over one hundred pages by H. S. Foxwell, mostly on nineteenth-century English socialist thought; second, Foxwell also contributed a "Bibliography of the English Socialist School" (pp. 191-267), which is unique in the history of English socialism. The background of English socialism is also extensively treated in Harry W. Laidler, *Social-Economic Movements* (New York, 1944), and Alexander Gray, *The Socialist Tradition: Moses to Lenin* (London, 1946).

MORRIS, WILLIAM, *Selected Writings,* ed. by G. D. H. Cole (New York, 1934). This Centenary Edition contains most of Morris' essays and tracts (pp. 475-671). See, in particular, "Useful Work versus Useless Toil," "Art and Socialism," "A Factory as It Might Be," "How I Became a Socialist," and "Communism" (pp. 603-671).

PIGOU, A. C., *Socialism versus Capitalism* (London, 1937). One of Britain's leading economists deals with such issues as distribution of wealth and income, the allocation of productive resources, unemployment, profit, technical efficiency, and the problem of incentive. He is sympathetic toward the method of "gradualness" in social and economic change, including the nationalization of important industries.

RUSSELL, BERTRAND, *Political Ideals* (New York, 1917). Russell's socialism is highly individualistic: "Political ideals must be based upon ideals for the individual life." He looks for a renewing of the spirit of man and society as much as for a change of the economic system of capitalism, "wasteful on the production side, and unjust on the side of distribution." The need of liberating the creative rather than the possessive impulses is strongly urged by Russell. On the other hand, he warns against the danger of overcentralization under socialism, and is sympathetic to the guild socialists and other advocates of economic decentralization.

SCHUMPETER, JOSEPH A., *Capitalism, Socialism, and Democracy* (New York, 1942; 3rd ed., 1950). A distinguished economist discusses the probable future of the capitalist system and the prospects of democratic socialism in what is likely to become a classic work. Schumpeter is rather critical of Marxism, and more in sympathy with the English approach.

SHAW, BERNARD, and OTHERS, *Fabian Essays* (London, 1889). The most famous document on "Fabian Socialism." In addition to Shaw, the contributors were Sydney Webb, Graham Wallas, Sydney Olivier, William Clarke, Annie Besant, and Hubert Bland. It has sold many tens of thousands of copies since its first publication, and has never ceased to be a steady seller in the field of socialist literature. For an analysis of Fabianism, see also G. D. H. Cole, *The Fabian Society* (Fabian Tract No. 258, London, 1942); E. R. Pease, *History of the Fabian Society* (New York, 1925); the Diamond Jubilee number of the *Fabian Quarterly* (No. 41, April, 1944), a special issue devoted to the history and prospects of the Fabian Society; and Margaret Cole, "The Fabian Society," *The Political Quarterly,* XV (July–Sept., 1944), 245-256.

THOMAS, NORMAN, *A Socialist's Faith* (New York, 1951). The most systematic statement of socialist principles by the leader of American socialism, emphasizing the democratic nature of the movement. See also his "Has Socialism Any Future?" *The Progressive,* XX (August, 1956), 5-8, and David A. Shannon, *The Socialist Party of America: A History* (New York, 1955).

CHAPTER XII. PLAN OR NO PLAN?

DAVIES, ERNEST, *National Enterprise: The Development of the Public Corporation* (London, 1946). The public corporation is a new and challenging institutional device of economic planning and socialization. See also William A. Robson (ed.), *Problems of Nationalized Industry* (New York, 1951); Ben W. Lewis, *British Planning and Nationalization* (New York, 1952); Edward Goodman, *Forms of Public Control and Ownership* (London, 1951); W. Friedmann (ed.), *The Public Corporation: A Comparative Symposium* (Toronto, 1954); and H. A. Hanson, *Public Enterprise: A Study of Its Organization and Management in Various Countries* (Brussels, 1955). A scathing indictment of economic planning and nationalization in Britain will be found in R. Kelf-Cohen, *Nationalization in Britain* (New York, 1959).

FRANKFURTER, FELIX, *The Public and Its Government* (New Haven, 1930). The first chapter, "The Demands of Modern Society upon Government" (pp. 1-35), is a concise outline of the social needs that have inevitably called for governmental action. In Chaps. II (pp. 36-80) and III (pp. 81-122), Frankfurter discusses the following issues: "Does Law Obstruct Government?" and "Public Services and the Public." See also William Keilhau, *Private and Public Planning* (London, 1951).

HAYEK, FRIEDRICH A., *The Road to Serfdom* (Chicago, 1944). The most popular book against planning. Hayek argues that in a planned economy the worst get to the top, that the rule of law is incompatible with planning, and that the suppression of dissent becomes unavoidable in a planned economy. In the vast literature against planning the following may be mentioned: John Jewkes, *Ordeal by Planning* (London, 1948); Walter Lippmann, *The Good Society* (Boston, 1937); and G. L. Schwartz, *Why Planning?* (London, 1944). More moderate viewpoints are expressed in: Lionel Robbins, *The Economic Problem in Peace and War* (London, 1947); John Maurice Clark, *Alternative to Serfdom* (New York, 1948); Robert A. Dahl and Charles E. Lindblom, *Politics, Economics, and Welfare* (New York, 1953); and Michael P. Fogarty, *Economic Control* (London, 1955).

LEWIS, W. ARTHUR, *The Principles of Economic Planning: A Study for the Fabian Society* (London, 1949). A socialist economist, Lewis favors planning rather than nationalization as the chief instrument of economic policy. See also the following: Carl Landauer, *Theory of National Economic Planning*, rev. ed. (Berkeley and Los Angeles, 1947); Barbara Wootton, *Freedom under Planning* (Chapel Hill, 1945); E. F. M. Durbin, *Problems of Economic Planning* (London, 1949); and W. Friedmann, *The Planned State and the Rule of Law* (Melbourne, 1948).

LILIENTHAL, DAVID E., *TVA: Democracy on the March* (New York, 1944). The Tennessee Valley Authority is one of the most notable, and successful, planning experiments in the world. Its onetime chairman describes in this book how planning can be combined with the development of natural resources, with regionalism, and, above all, with democratic administration.

MANNHEIM, KARL, *Man and Society in an Age of Reconstruction* (London, 1940). A lengthy treatise, written in an unnecessarily heavy sociological jargon, but worthy of close scrutiny. See, in particular, Parts IV-VI, "Thought at the Level of Planning," "Planning for Freedom," and "Freedom at the Level of Planning." See also Mannheim's *Freedom, Power, and Democratic Planning* (New York, 1950).

MISES, LUDWIG VON, *Socialism* (New York, 1935; originally published as *Die Gemeinwirtschaft* in 1922). An important book, because Mises was the first to popularize a few basic arguments against planning and socialism that later gained wider currency through the books of Hayek in England and of Lippmann in the United States. The reason why socialism is impossible, according to Mises, is the lack of "economic calculations" in a socialist community. In addition, all the standard arguments against planning or socialism, from bureaucratic centralization to soulless totalitarianism, are found in Mises. See also Mises' "Economic Calculation in the Socialist Commonwealth," in F. A. Hayek (ed.), *Collectivist Economic Planning* (London, 1947), pp. 87-130, *Human Action: A Treatise on Economics* (New Haven, 1949), and *The Anticapitalist Mentality* (Princeton, 1956).

WOOTTON, BARBARA, *Plan or No Plan?* (New York, 1935). Mrs. Wootton's first book on planning, and still worth reading.

CHAPTER XIII. THE WELFARE STATE

ARNOLD, THURMAN, *The Folklore of Capitalism* (New Haven, 1937). This book, full of wit and irony as well as of learning and scholarship, shows that "political government" is not the only, or necessarily the most oppressive, form of government; "economic government," especially as it appears in corporate business and monopolies, also expresses power relations between men. Arnold shows how the folklore and mythology of capitalism transform the realities of economic government into innocent fictions and magic rituals. Reprinted in the "Yale Paperbacks" (New Haven, 1959).

BEARD, CHARLES A., *The Economic Basis of Politics* (New York, 1922; 3rd ed., 1947). One of Beard's most famous studies; it is particularly significant for its illuminating insights into the American political experience.

BRADY, ROBERT A., *Business as a System of Power* (New York, 1943). The author exposes the influence of organized big business on national government and politics, and draws his source material mainly from the United States, Great Britain, Germany, and Italy.

BRANDEIS, LOUIS, *The Curse of Bigness* (New York, 1934). The best selection of Brandeis' papers and statements on social, economic, and political issues. It has also useful bibliographies of books and articles written by, and on, Brandeis. Some of his other important books are: *Other People's Money and How the Bankers Use It* (New York, 1914); *Business—A Profession* (Boston, 1914); and *The Social and Economic View of Mr. Justice Brandeis,* ed. by Alfred Lief (New York, 1930). See also Felix Frankfurter (ed.), *Mr. Justice Brandeis* (New Haven, 1932), with contributions by Charles E. Hughes, Max Lerner, Felix Frankfurter, Walton H. Hamilton, and others; and Alpheus T. Mason, *Brandeis: A Free Man's Life* (New York, 1946).

DE GRAZIA, ALFRED (ed.), *Grass Roots Private Welfare* (New York, 1957). Fifty case studies linked by the common philosophy of solving social problems by voluntary action of the community rather than by compulsory action of the government. See also A. F. C. Boudillon (ed.), *Voluntary Social Services* (London, 1945), and John G. Turnbull and others, *Economic and Social Security: Public and Private Measures Against Economic Insecurity* (New York, 1957).

DOUGLAS, PAUL H., "Colossus on the Potomac: Causes and Cures of Big Government," *Harper's Magazine,* CCVII (July, 1953), 21-27. Shows that the extension of government is largely the product of war rather than social welfare.

GLUECK, SHELDON (ed.), *The Welfare State and the National Welfare* (Cambridge, Mass., 1952). A symposium of articles hostile to the theory and practice of the welfare state. See also Wilhelm Röpke, *Welfare, Freedom, and Inflation* (London, 1957); Conservative Political Center, *The Future of the Welfare State* (London, 1958); and J. Enoch Powell, "Conservatives and Social Services," *The Political Quarterly,* XXIV (April–June, 1953), 156-166. Critiques of the welfare state from a Left-wing socialist viewpoint will be found in Kingsley Martin, *Socialism and the Welfare State* (London, 1951), and G. D. H. Cole, *Is This Socialism?* (London, 1954).

LAUTERBACH, A. T., *Economic Security and Individual Freedom: Can We Have Both?* (Ithaca, 1948). See also I. M. D. Little, *A Critique of Welfare Economics* (Oxford, 1950); Henry Steele Commager, "Appraisal of the Welfare State," *The New York Times Magazine* (May 15, 1949) 10ff; N. A. Smith, "Theory and Practice of the Welfare State," *The Political Quarterly,* XXII (October–December, 1951), 369-381; D. L. Hobman, *The Welfare State* (London, 1953); A. C. Pigou, "Some Aspects of the Welfare State," *Diogenes,* No. 7 (Summer, 1954), 1-11, reprinted in William Ebenstein, *Great Political Thinkers: Plato to the Present,* 3rd ed. (New York, 1960), pp. 836-843; William A. Robson, *The Welfare State* (London, 1957); and Richard M. Titmuss, *Essays on the Welfare State* (London, 1958).

LEKACHMAN, ROBERT (ed.), *National Policy for Economic Welfare at Home and Abroad* (New York, 1955). A collection of essays by American economists on domestic and international aspects of economic and social welfare.

LERNER, MAX, *Ideas Are Weapons* (New York, 1939). This collection of essays has a short paper on "Woodrow Wilson: The New Freedom and the New Deal" (pp. 113-116). Lerner maintains that, despite some differences, "there is a real historical continuity between the New Freedom and the New Deal" (p. 115). A perceptive account of the background of American thinking on the welfare state will be found in Currin V. Shields, "The American Tradition of Empirical Collectivism," *American Political Science Review,* XLVI (March, 1952), 104-120.

MACIVER, ROBERT M., *The Web of Government* (New York, 1947). In Chap. VI (pp. 114-143), the author probes into "Property and Status" as bases of political authority: "Every system of government sustains a corresponding system of property. To change the one is to change the other" (p. 125). MacIver therefore attacks the Lockean conception of property as a right which exists prior to law and the state. In the discussion of the possibility of economic planning in a democratic society, the author argues for a mixed economy of private and public enterprise: "In the mixed economy there is not the monopoly of power that the socialist economy inevitably entails—monopoly in the sense that now there can be no foci of power outside the political order" (p. 357). MacIver takes up this issue more fully in Chap. XI, "The Transformations of Function," especially in the last section on "functions of economic control" (pp. 340-359). The problem of community, one of the central issues in MacIver's thought, is more fully developed in Carl J. Friedrich (ed.), *Community* (Nomos II, New York, 1959), with contributions by Carl J. Friedrich, Huntington Cairns, William Y. Elliott, George E. G. Catlin, Talcott Parsons, and others.

MADISON, CHARLES A., *Critics and Crusaders: a Century of American Protest* (New York, 1947). A good first introduction into the thinking of the major dissenters in America. The book is divided into the following sections: the "Abolitionists," the "Utopians," the "Anarchists," the "Dissident Economists," the "Militant Liberals," and the "Socialists." There is also a useful bibliography (pp. 539-554).

MERRIAM, CHARLES E., *Public and Private Government* (New Haven, 1944). In these lectures, Merriam summarizes his political thinking and experience on the relationships of public and private government. He demonstrates how political, or public, government is only one of the forms of effective social control and domination, and suggests a broader approach to the whole problem of authority, in which the power and government of social and economic groups are recognized and adequately dealt with.

NIEBUHR, REINHOLD, *The Children of Light and the Children of Darkness* (New York, 1946). Chap. III (pp. 86-118) is on the relationships of "The Community and Property." Niebuhr rejects both Liberalism and Marxism: "Neither understands property as a form of power which can be used in either its individual or its social form as an instrument of particular interest against the general interest. Liberalism makes this mistake in regard to private property and Marxism makes it in regard to socialized property" (p. 106).

POLANYI, KARL, *The Great Transformation* (New York, 1944). A provocative and challenging inquiry into the disintegration and collapse of the nineteenth-century liberal civilization. The author sees in the doctrine of the "self-regulating market" one of the most fateful assumptions of liberal economics and politics. His interpretation of recent changes emphasizes the rediscovery of society and the reintegration of economics and politics.

ROOSEVELT, FRANKLIN D., *Selected Speeches, Messages, Press Conferences, and Letters* (edited by Basil Rauch, Rinehart Editions, New York, 1957). The arrangement is chronological. Edwin C. Rozwenc (ed.), *The New Deal: Revolution or Evolution?* (Boston, 1949), is a collection of essays on the New Deal, encompassing the whole political spectrum from Herbert Hoover to Earl Browder. Richard Hofstadter, *The Age of Reform: From Bryan to F. D. R.* (New York, 1955), shows the place of the New Deal in the context of the American tradition of reform. Mario Einaudi, *The Roosevelt Revolution* (New York, 1959), shows the place of the New Deal in the context of world affairs.

SWEEZY, PAUL M., *The Theory of Capitalist Development* (New York, 1942). An account of crises, depressions, and monopolies from the Marxist point of view (pp. 133-236, 270-286).

VEBLEN, THORSTEIN, *The Engineers and the Price System* (New York, 1921). This short book is probably the best introduction into Veblen's approach to political economy. The following of his works are of major importance: *The*

Theory of the Leisure Class (New York, 1899); *The Instinct of Workmanship and the State of the Industrial Arts* (New York, 1914); *The Higher Learning In America* (New York, 1918); *Absentee Ownership and Business Enterprise in Recent Times: The Case of America* (New York, 1923); and *Essays in Our Changing Order* (New York, 1934). *What Veblen Taught* (edited, with a long introduction, by Wesley C. Mitchell, New York, 1936) is made up of selections from Veblen's more important writings. The standard biography is *Thorstein Veblen and His America,* by Joseph Dorfman (New York, 1934). A detailed bibliography of Veblen's writings will be found on pp. 519-524. Interesting analyses of Veblen are also contained in Max Lerner, *Ideas Are Weapons* (New York, 1939), pp. 117-141, and in Charles A. Madison, *Critics and Crusaders: A Century of American Protest* (New York, 1947), pp. 308-339.

Part V: From Nationalism to World Order

CHAPTER XIV. NATIONALISM: PEACEFUL OR AGGRESSIVE?

BROGAN, D. W., *French Personalities and Problems* (New York, 1946). A collection of essays and reviews, with first-rate studies of French nationalists like Maurras and Barrès in Chaps. VII, XII, and XIII. See, in particular, Chap. XIII, "Charles Maurras: the Politics of Hate," for the lucid analysis of how the prophet of "integral nationalism" was finally sentenced to life imprisonment in 1944—for treasonable collaboration with the enemies of his country. A systematic study of the intimate connections between nationalism and profascist treason, in Europe and in the Americas, remains to be written.

COBBAN, ALFRED, *National Self-Determination* (London, 1944). After a survey of the problem of national self-determination from World War I to World War II, the author deals with the limits of national self-determination. See also Annette Baker Fox, *The Power of Small States* (Chicago, 1959), showing in concrete case studies that small states, far from being only passive pawns in Great Power deals, are able to assert their influence in world affairs.

FESSLER, L., "Psychology of Nationalism," *Psychoanalytic Review* XXVIII (July, 1941), 372-383. See also Géza Róheim, "The Psychology of Patriotism," *American Imago,* VII (March, 1950), 3-19; Gertrud M. Kurth, "Hitler's Two Germanies: A Sidelight on Nationalism," in Géza Róheim (ed.), *Psychoanalysis and the Social Sciences* (New York, 1950), II, 293-312; and Llewellyn Queener, "The Development of Internationalist Attitudes," *Journal of Social Psychology,* XXIX (May, 1949), 221-235, 237-252, and *ibid.,* XXX (August, 1949), 105-126.

KOHN, HANS, *Prophets and Peoples* (New York, 1946). An authority on the intellectual origins and evolution of nationalism discusses here nineteenth-century nationalism through some of its main representatives. Chap. III (pp. 77-104) is on Mazzini. See also Kohn's *The Idea of Nationalism: A Study in Its Origins and Background* (New York, 1944); R. G. Hawtrey, *Economic Aspects of Sovereignty,* 2nd ed. (New York, 1952); and Luis Diez del Corral, *The Rape of Europe* (New York, 1959), particularly Chap. X, "Nation, Nationalism, and Supernation" (pp. 220-255).

MATHEW, DAVID, *Acton* (London, 1946). The best short study of Lord Acton. See also Crane Brinton, *English Political Thought in the Nineteenth Century* (London, 1933), pp. 198-211, and E. L. Woodward, "The Place of Lord Acton in the Liberal Movement of the Nineteenth Century," *Politica*, IV (September, 1939), 248-265.

Nationalism, A Report by a Study Group of the Royal Institute of International Affairs (London–New York–Toronto, 1939). One of the outstanding investigations into the nature of nationalism, illustrated by specific case studies. See also the following: E. H. Carr, *Nationalism and After* (London, 1945), a brief survey of the evolution of nationalism in the modern era and its prospects in the future; H. Munro Chadwick, *The Nationalities of Europe and the Growth of National Ideologies* (Cambridge, 1945), with little-known facts on some medieval origins, linguistic and historical, of nationalism; John Drinkwater, *Patriotism in Literature* (London, 1924), a popularly written volume in the Home University Library; W. Friedmann, *The Crisis of the National State* (London, 1943), a notable examination of the rise of the modern national state, and of the causes of its decline and disintegration; Carlton J. H. Hayes, *Essays on Nationalism* (New York, 1926), with a valuable "Bibliographical Note" (pp. 277-279); and Friedrich O. Hertz, *Nationality in History and Politics* (London, 1944), a comprehensive and scholarly work that traces the origins and evolution of modern nationalism in England, France, Russia, Austria–Hungary, and Prussia–Germany. Hertz attains a rare degree of objectivity, balance, and historical perspective. A Marxian–Leninist approach to the problem of nationalism will be found in Joseph Stalin, *Marxism and the National Question* (New York, 1942). Stalin had a lifelong interest in this question, and at one time was Commissar of Nationalities in the Soviet government.

NIEBUHR, REINHOLD, *The Structure of Nations and Empires* (New York, 1959). This is the most systematic statement of Niebuhr's on nationalism and imperialism in general and on the East-West tensions in particular. In his customary manner, he refuses to offer any cure-alls for the conflicts arising out of national and imperialism. His argument is less theological than his earlier works on political problems, although the religious basis of his thought remains unchanged.

SNYDER, LOUIS L., *The Meaning of Nationalism* (New Brunswick, 1954). A prolific writer in the field of nationalism, the author concentrates in this work on the psychological and social foundations of nationalism and patriotism.

STANNARD, HAROLD, *What Is a Nation?* (Looking Forward Pamphlet No. 3, Royal Institute of International Affairs, London–New York, 1945). A short introduction into the various concepts of nation and nationality, analyzed against their background in the history of political thought and institutions in Europe and America.

SWEEZY, PAUL M., *The Theory of Capitalist Development* (New York, 1942), pp. 307-328. In the chapter "Imperialism," Sweezy brings the Marxist theory of imperialism up to date, and sees in socialism the only, and inevitable, answer to imperialism. This excessively economic interpretation of imperialism fails to give due consideration to the factor of power—a political rather than economic fact.

Woolf, Leonard, *Imperialism and Civilization* (London, 1928). A classical indictment of imperialism, written in pungent, and often brilliant, style. See also Leonard Barnes, *Empire or Democracy?* (London, 1939).

CHAPTER XV. CONFLICT OR COMMON INTEREST?

Angell, Norman, *The Great Illusion* (London, 1908; expanded, in 1938, into *The Great Illusion—Now*). Of the many works of Sir Norman Angell, this is probably still the most famous. The futility of war from an economic point of view, the nature of modern imperialism, and the need for collective security are some of the main topics of the book.

Aron, Raymond, *The Century of Total War* (Garden City, 1954). A leading French political thinker traces the development from limited to total war in the twentieth century. See also Kenneth N. Walz, *Man, the State, and War* (New York, 1959), and Theodore Ropp, *War in the Modern World* (Durham, N. C., 1959). J. D. Bernal, *World Without War* (New York, 1959), is a Marxist treatment of the problem of war, leading up to the conclusion that the establishment of economic collectivism throughout the world is the only—and sure—road to world peace.

Beard, Charles A., *The Idea of National Interest* (New York, 1934). The subtitle is "An Analytical Study in American Foreign Policy."

Bentwich, Norman, *The Religious Foundations of Internationalism* (London, 1933). Deals with the pagan religions of antiquity, and with Judaism, Christianity, Islam, and the Far Eastern religions.

Beveridge, Sir William, *The Price of Peace* (London, 1945). The author states as the target: "Rule of Law in Place of Anarchy between Nations."

Carr, E. H., *The Twenty Years' Crisis* (New York, 1939). In spite of its title, this is not a history of the interwar years, but a systematic theory of international politics; in this field it is unquestionably the most influential book written in the twentieth century. Carr, an English publicist strongly influenced by Hegel and the German school of *Realpolitik,* emphasizes the elements of interest and power (as opposed to the concepts of ethics and harmony of interests) in international politics. His ideas have been popularized in the United States by George F. Kennan and Hans J. Morgenthau; see, in particular, George F. Kennan, *American Diplomacy, 1900-1950* (Chicago, 1951), and Hans J. Morgenthau, *In Defense of the National Interest: A Critical Examination of American Foreign Policy* (New York, 1951). Critical appraisals of this school of thought will be found in the following: Leonard Woolf, *The War for Peace* (London, 1940), a direct reply to Carr's *The Twenty Years' Crisis;* Frank Tannenbaum, *The American Tradition in Foreign Policy* (New York, 1955); Grayson L. Kirk, "In Search of the National Interest," *World Politics,* V (October, 1952), 110-115; and Robert W. Tucker, "Professor Morgenthau's Theory of Political 'Realism,'" *American Political Science Review,*

XLVI (March, 1952), 214-224. Morton Gordon and Kenneth N. Vines, *Theory and Practice of American Foreign Policy* (New York, 1955), contains a well-chosen selection of readings on both "idealism" and "realism" (pp. 43-149). See also John H. Herz, *Political Realism and Political Idealism* (Chicago, 1951), and Kenneth W. Thompson, *Political Realism and the Crisis of World Order* (Princeton, 1960).

CECIL, Viscount, *A Great Experiment: An Autobiography by Lord Robert Cecil* (New York, 1941). This human document by a great Englishman who dedicated his life to the ideal of world order is illuminating in its interpretation of why the League of Nations finally failed.

GINSBERG, MORRIS, *The Unity of Mankind* (L. T. Hobhouse Memorial Trust Lectures, No. 5, London, 1935). The author, an eminent sociologist, arrives at the following conclusion: "The rate of unification has certainly been increasing enormously in the fields of economics and politics. What is needed is a parallel growth in moral wisdom. To bring social development into closer accord with ethical development is the task of social science and of social ethics in our time. In the long run our faith in the unity of mankind must rest upon our faith in the unity of human reason" (p. 29).

KEETON, GEORGE W., *National Sovereignty and International Order* (London, 1939). Examines the problems of state sovereignty and international order from a legal as well as a political point of view. For a fuller discussion of the legal problems consult Hersh Lauterpacht, *The Function of Law in the International Community* (Oxford, 1933), and *An International Bill of the Rights of Man* (New York, 1945); Charles de Visscher, *Theory and Reality in Public International Law* (Princeton, 1957); and Wallace McClure, *World Legal Order* (Chapel Hill, 1960). The protection of human rights through international law and organization is dealt with in Moses Moskowitz, *Human Rights and World Order* (New York, 1958), and Pieter N. Drost, *The Crime of State,* 2 vols. (Leyden, 1959), the first volume being on "humanicide," or governmental crimes against individual human rights, and the second on "genocide," or governmental crimes against entire nations.

KELSEN, HANS, *Law and Peace in International Relations* (Cambridge, Mass., 1942). Kelsen urges that an international court with compulsory jurisdiction, rather than international government, is the immediate road to progress because "experience teaches that states submit more easily to an international court than to an international government" (p. 169).

LASKI, H. J., *Studies in the Problem of Sovereignty* (New Haven, 1917), and *The Foundations of Sovereignty and Other Essays* (New Haven, 1921). In these two books, Laski formulated his theory of "political pluralism," as opposed to the orthodox conceptions of state sovereignty.

LEVI, WERNER, *Fundamentals of World Organization* (Minneapolis, 1950). Stresses the difficulties obstructing world order.

MARRIOTT, Sir JOHN A. R., *Commonwealth or Anarchy? A Survey of Projects of Peace from the Sixteenth to the Twentieth Century* (London, 1937). A valuable aid in studying earlier attempts to outlaw war among nations—and why those attempts eventually failed.

MURPHY, GARDNER (ed.), *Human Nature and Enduring Peace* (Boston–New

York, 1945). The contributions deal with problems of war and peace as well as with democracy, Fascism, education, and religion. See also the following: Edward Glover, *War, Sadism, and Pacifism* (London, 1933); John Dollard and others, *Frustration and Aggression* (New Haven, 1939); E. F. M. Durbin and John Bowlby, *Personal Aggressiveness and War* (London, 1939); George W. Kisker (ed.), *World Tension: The Psychopathology of International Relations* (New York, 1951); T. H. Spear (ed.), *Psychological Factors of Peace and War* (London, 1951); Hadley Cantril (ed.), *Tensions That Cause Wars* (Urbana, 1950); Mark A. May, *A Social Psychology of War and Peace* (New Haven, 1943); Edward Chace Tolman, *Drives toward War* (New York–London, 1942); William A. White, *Thoughts of a Psychiatrist on the War and After* (New York, 1919); Joost A. M. Meerloo, *Aftermath of Peace: Psychological Essays* (New York, 1946); Ranyard West, *Psychology and World Order* (Penguin Books, London, 1945); G. B. Chisholm, *The Psychiatry of Enduring Peace and Social Progress* (Washington, 1946); Otto Klineberg, *Tensions Affecting International Understanding: A Survey of Research* (Social Science Research Council Bulletin, No. 62, New York, 1950); and Alix Strachey, *The Unconscious Motives of War: A Psychoanalytical Contribution* (London, 1957). Ernest Jones has three noteworthy papers on the psychological aspects of war in the first volume of his *Essays in Applied Psychoanalysis* (London, 1951): "War and Individual Psychology" (pp. 55-76); "War and Sublimation" (pp. 77-87); and "Psychopathology and International Tension" (pp. 301-322). S. F. Stein, "The Major Cause of War—Emotional Incompetency," *Journal of Nervous and Mental Disease,* CXII (July, 1950), 66-74, will also be found suggestive.

ROUTH, D. A., "The Philosophy of International Relations: T. H. Green *versus* Hegel," *Politica,* III (September, 1938), 223-235. Elucidates the differences of thought and background between these two thinkers. Routh arrives at the conclusion that the similarity between Hegel and the modern totalitarian state on the problem of international relations is "unmistakable."

TOYNBEE, ARNOLD J., *A Study of History* (abridgment of Vols. I-VI by D. C. Somervell, New York–London, 1947). Toynbee discusses, in the light of historical experience, "The Suicidalness of Militarism" (pp. 336-349).

VAGTS, ALFRED, *A History of Militarism* (New York, 1937). Particularly valuable for the analysis of the impact of militarism on political ideas and institutions.

WIGHT, MARTIN, *Power Politics* (Looking Forward Pamphlet No. 8, Royal Institute of International Affairs, London–New York, 1946). An excellent brief discussion of the power factor in international relations. The author explains such concepts as great powers and small powers, the balance of power, vital interests and prestige, and briefly analyzes the impact of the United Nations on power politics.

WOLFERS, ARNOLD, and MARTIN, LAURENCE W. (eds.), *The Anglo-American Tradition in Foreign Affairs: Readings from Thomas Moore to Woodrow Wilson* (New Haven, 1956). An unusual collection of readings in a neglected area.

WRIGHT, QUINCY, *A Study of War,* 2 vols. (Chicago, 1942). This work by one of the foremost American scholars in the field of international law and organization contains a wealth of data on war, its history and development, and its impact on social and political institutions.

ZIMMERN, ALFRED, *Learning and Leadership* (London, 1930). This slim volume of slightly over one hundred pages is weightier than many a ponderous treatise in the field. The author admirably conveys the intricate and complex character of international relations, and gives a subtle account of the qualities required for their mastery, especially in a democratic civilization. See also Grayson Kirk and others, *The Changing Environment in International Relations* (Washington, 1956), and Max Beloff, *Foreign Policy and the Democratic Process* (Baltimore, 1955).

INDEX

INDEX

A

Abrams v. *United States*, 153, 190
Absolutism, 6, 21–28, 91–99
Acton, Lord, 741–742, 744–750
Adjustment, 141–147
Alexander, Franz, 56–57, 82–91
Angell, Sir Norman, 778–779, 787–795
Antidemocratic thought, 275–484
Antirelativism, 29–51
Attlee, Clement R., 583–584, 595–599
Auschwitz extermination camp, 325, 392
Authoritarian personality, 58–60, 99–123

B

Beveridge, William, 676–677, 681–694
Berle, A. A., 494–495, 568–580
Berlin, Isaiah Sir, 151–152, 176–189
Big business, 531–544
Big lie (Hitler), 358, 362–364
Black, Mr. Justice, 158–159, 216–218, 227–229
Bolling v. *Sharpe*, 236, 271–272
Boyd, Julian P., 154–155, 190–199
Brainwashing, 385–399
Brandeis, Mr. Justice, 158, 220–221, 675–676, 680–681
Brown v. *Topeka*, 235–236, 267–270
Burke, Edmund, 154, 280–282, 302–321, 489–490, 510–513

C

Capitalism, 414–420, 487–580, 606–609
Carlyle, Thomas, 326–328, 351–356

Carr, E. H., 779–781, 796–806
Castro, Fidel, 407
Censorship, 190–199
Christianity, 39, 148, 314, 583–584, 595–596, 742, 748–749
Class war, 420–422, 438–450
Clear and present danger, doctrine of, 153, 157–159, 206–229
Codetermination, 626–627
Coercion, 176
Cole v. *Young*, 156
Common law, 604
Communism, 155–159, 190–229, 400–484, 595–599, 612–614, 732–737
Communist Manifesto, 218, 404–405, 413–422
Competition, 545–580, 585
Concentration camps, 54, 392
Confessions, 456–458
Conflict, 777–821
Conformity, 119–120, 141–147, 152, 237–242, 386–390, 396–399
Conscience, 85–86, 129–130
Consent, 33–37, 136
Constant, Benjamin, 179
Conservatism, 302–321
Corporation, 521–522, 568–580
Countervailing power, theory of, 493–494, 545–568
Crosland, C. A. R., 588–589, 632–635
Crossman, R. H. S., 586–587, 616–628
Cuba, 407

D

Davenport, Russell W., 678, 704–720
Declaration of Independence, 35–36, 125–129, 135–136, 604

CHAIN STORES
IN AMERICA
1859-1959

CHAIN STORES

IN AMERICA

1859–1959

By Godfrey M. Lebhar

Editor-in-Chief, CHAIN STORE AGE

CENTENNIAL EDITION

CHAIN STORE PUBLISHING CORPORATION

NEW YORK

CHAIN STORES IN AMERICA: 1859-1959

Copyright 1952, 1959 by Godfrey M. Lebhar

PRINTED IN THE UNITED STATES OF AMERICA
BY THE COLONIAL PRESS INC., CLINTON, MASS.

CONTENTS

CHARTS AND TABLES

PREFACE

THE seven years which have elapsed since the publication of the first edition of this book have served to complete a century of continuous operation for this country's oldest and biggest chain, The Great Atlantic & Pacific Tea Company. And since the history of the chain store system in this country starts, for all practical purposes, with the birth of A & P, 1959 may well be regarded as the 100th anniversary not only of that company but of the chain store system itself.

That fact in itself might not provide a sufficient reason for issuing a revised edition of a book which carried chain store history up to 1950, but changes occur so rapidly in such a dynamic field as retailing that the 1950 picture hardly suffices for 1959. More to the point, however, is the fact that the exhaustion of the first edition provides an opportunity to bring out this Centennial Edition covering the full span of the chains' first century, 1859 to 1959.

GODFREY M. LEBHAR

January 2, 1959

PREFACE TO FIRST EDITION

SINCE 1932, when the present author offered *The Chain Store—Boon or Bane?* as his contribution on what was then generally referred to as the "chain-store question," the chain store has ceased to be a question.

The "question" about chain stores then was: "If chain stores keep expanding at their present rate, how long will it be before the independent merchant is wiped out entirely?" And, of course, that question implied another: "Is it in the public interest for the independent merchant to be replaced by chain stores?"

The main question has been answered by events. The chains did *not* "keep expanding at their present rate." On the contrary, subsequent events showed that the *indications* of 25 years ago rested on a false premise. The possibilities for chain-store expansion were not unlimited. The rapid and spectacular progress the chains made between 1920 and 1930 carried them to a certain point, but that apparently was as far as they were destined to go. The competitive position the chains had attained by 1930 was a substantial one, but since then their main task has been to hold it.

Today the chain-store system is recognized as an established feature of our distribution set-up and an extremely valuable one. Its main economic function is to provide a type of low-cost distribution designed to lower retail prices and make more things available to more people. Its social function is to raise the general standard of living by stretching the purchasing-power of the consumer's dollar. That it can achieve both these functions to a marked degree without eliminating the independent merchant the events of the last

20 years clearly show. Indeed, the independent merchant is not only just as strong numerically today as he was back in 1929, when the "chain-store question" was beginning to gain nationwide attention, and enjoying the same share of the total retail business as he accounted for then, but he is actually doing a much better job. The spur of competition provided by the chains has proved his salvation rather than his ruin.

The purpose of this book, then, is not to attempt again to answer the "chain-store question," which has answered itself, but to record the history of a movement which has meant and means so much to our domestic economy.

The book naturally divides itself into three parts: (1) the birth and growth of the system; (2) its struggle for self preservation in the face of violent and sustained opposition; and (3) its maturity.

Both the history of the chains and the so-called chain-store problem have been well covered in several recognized works. Particularly valuable were *Chain Stores,* by Hayward & White, 1928; *The Chain Store Problem,* by Beckman & Nolen, 1938; *Chain Stores and Legislation,* by Daniel Bloomfield, 1939; and *The Chain Store Tells Its Story,* by John P. Nichols, 1940. The only trouble with these books is that they are all out of print, besides being to some extent out of date. More recent works covering retailing or marketing in general devote some space to the chain-store system, but obviously the treatment is necessarily limited.

In undertaking the task involved in preparing this book the author has been moved by a sense of responsibility based on his own connection with the chain-store field since 1925 as editor and one of the publishers of *Chain Store Age.* In that capacity it was his privilege to know and to work with many of the chain store leaders whose names appear in these pages and to play a part in some of the events recorded. Much of the data used herein is based on material gathered through the years and published in the pages of *Chain Store Age* or preserved in its files.

For their cooperation in reading the manuscript, in whole or in part, the author acknowledges his gratitude to John A. Logan, president of the National Association of Food Chains; John F. Deegan, National Marketing Director, Atlantic Commission Co., Dr. Paul C. Olsen, assistant to the president of the Limited Price Variety Stores Association; Mrs. Gladys M. Kiernan, executive secretary of the Institute of Distribution; Rowland Jones, Jr., president of the American Retail Federation; Dr. Charles F. Phillips, president of Bates College; Don Francisco, vice president of J. Walter Thompson Co.; E. W. Simms, of White & Simms, formerly general counsel for the Institute of Distribution; Arnold D. Friedman, president of Lebhar-Friedman Publications, Inc., publisher of *Chain Store Age;* and the following members of the editorial staff of that publication: the late Frank E. Landau, editorial director; Lawrence Drake, Ben Gordon and John G. Poulos. A special acknowledgment goes to Samuel O. Kaylin, editor of the Administration Edition of *Chain Store Age,* and to the author's brother, Lionel M. Lebhar, for their assistance in preparing the manuscript for the press and their wise suggestions in regard to it.

If, in this effort to record the history of chain stores in America, the author reveals a tendency to stress the virtues of the chains and to minimize their shortcomings, no apology is offered. Convinced as he is of the merits of the chain-store system, social as well as economic, the author sees no reason to conceal his convictions on that score.

GODFREY M. LEBHAR

New York, December 1, 1951

CHAIN STORES
IN AMERICA
1859-1959

PART I

BIRTH

CHAPTER I

WHAT THE CHAIN-STORE SYSTEM IS

THIS COUNTRY has approximately 1,750,000 retail stores in operation.

That figure is based on the latest official count, the 1954 Census of Business, which puts the number at 1,721,650,[1] plus the fact that the number does not change materially from year to year. Indeed it has changed hardly at all over the past 20 years, the 1939 Census accounting for 1,770,355 stores and the 1948 Census for 1,769,540.

This constancy might seem remarkable in view of the substantial growth of our population during the period in question—from approximately 131 million in 1939 to 170 million in 1957. Such a substantial increase in population, amounting to 15%, would develop a need, one might expect, for at least some increase in the number of stores.

That they were not provided is explained by the fact that the period in question saw a definite and continued trend towards *larger* stores. Sparked by the introduction of the supermarket in the early '30s and its rapid development thereafter, the new stores in all fields followed the trend and became ever larger than their predecessors. Thus the need for greater retail facilities which did indeed develop was met by providing larger rather than more stores.

On the other hand, how has this relatively constant number of stores been maintained in view of the deplorably large

[1] Why this number is somewhat less than the actual number of stores in operation is explained on p. 62.

number of retailers who drop out of the picture every year?

Without discussing here the reasons for the high rate of mortality which has always marked retail enterprise, the record indicates that for every merchant who goes out of business another is always ready to take his place. Vacant stores do not remain that way for long. Every year brings a new crop of hopefuls eager to set up shop in any spot which seems suitable for the purpose. Few are deterred by the fate of the previous tenant, if, indeed, they become aware of it.

But how about the new stores which are constantly being built to meet the needs of new or expanding communities? How is it that they fail to swell the total? A logical explanation would seem to be that these additions are offset by the elimination of store property which has been converted to other uses.

Even the development of shopping centers in recent years cannot have swelled the total appreciably since the 1954 Census was completed, although such projects obviously bring many new stores into the picture where none existed before. For assuming that as many as 1,500 of these projects have been completed since 1954, which is a liberal estimate, and assuming that they averaged 40 stores apiece, they would still have added only 60,000 stores. That is certainly no small number, and the importance of this revolutionary trend must not be minimized, but still it is not enough to change the overall statistical picture substantially.

Accepting 1,750,000 then as a reasonably accurate basis for the brief analysis of the current retail set up which follows, the first thing to note is that these stores are of all kinds, types, sizes and grades.

So far as size goes, at one end of the scale we have, on the one hand, the huge department stores found in our big cities, each occupying a large multi-storied building with thousands of square feet of selling space on each floor, employing a veritable army of workers, drawing customers from a wide area and doing many millions of dollars worth of business a year. On the other hand, we have thousands of modern supermarkets and other kinds of stores, which are typically single-storied but make up in area what they lack in height, and which likewise develop huge volumes. In 1954, 19,000 stores had annual sales in excess of $1,000,000. (See Table 1, below and also Tables 3 and 4, p. 11.)

At the other end of the scale, we have hundreds of thousands of small neighborhood stores, usually specializing in particular lines of merchandise, occupying relatively small space, having limited capital, employing few, if any, workers, and doing such a small volume of business that their ability to stay in the picture for more than a few years is highly questionable.

In between these two extremes, we have hundreds of thousands of well-established, efficiently operated stores of all kinds and types, occupying the better retail locations, adequately capitalized, stocked and manned, and operating profitably enough in most cases not only to insure their survival but to provide for possible expansion.

Quantitatively, these three groups, considering only the stores which were in operation for the full year, shaped up in the 1954 Census as shown in Table 1.

TABLE 1

RETAIL STORES, 1954, BY SALES SIZE
(Source: U.S. Retail Census)

GROUP	NUMBER	%	SALES (MILLIONS)	%
All stores in operation full year	1,614,504	100	$162,508	100
Doing more than $1,000,000	18,969	1.2	44,688	27.5
Doing between $30,000 and $1,000,000	907,820	56.2	107,672	66.3
Doing less than $30,000	687,715	42.6	10,148	6.2

Looking at our stores from another angle which is more to our present purpose, namely, that of ownership, they can be divided into two groups—one very large and the other correspondingly small.

The larger group, comprising 1,554,623 of the total covered in the 1954 Census, consisted of what the Census classified as "single units," or as they are generally known, "independent stores." Their common characteristic is that each is separately owned and self-operated. In other words, the storekeeper is both the owner and the boss. He is referred to as an "independent" because he is responsible only to himself for his policies, his methods and his results.

The smaller group, comprising the remaining 167,027 of the total, were classified in the Census as "multiunits." A multiunit was defined as "one of two or more establishments in the same general kind of business operated by the same firm." According to many authorities, all the stores in this group are chain stores, but for its own reasons, the Census Bureau abandoned the use of the term completely in connection with its 1948 Census and followed the same policy with its 1954 enumeration. In all previous Censuses, however, commencing with the original one in 1929, the Census Bureau had regarded and designated all stores operated by firms with *four* or more as "chain stores," designating as "multiunits" only those operated by firms with two or three.

But no matter how you designate the stores in this group, their common characteristic is that each belongs to a group of two or more similar stores, and is typically operated by a hired *manager* rather than by an individual *owner*. Unlike the independent merchant, the manager of a chain store does not own it, nor does he set its policies, and he is definitely responsible for his operating results to someone else—the individual or company owning the chain.

A breakdown of the 167,027 multiunits, or chain stores, as they will hereafter be called, is shown in Table 2.

From the fact that the chains (including within that category all firms operating two or more stores) account for somewhat less than 10% of all retail stores, their importance to our domestic economy might appear to be correspondingly small.

But that would be a mistake for two reasons.

TABLE 2

MULTIUNIT STORES, 1954, BY SIZE OF FIRM
(Source: U.S. Retail Census)

SIZE OF FIRM	STORES IN CATEGORY	SALES (MILLIONS)
2 stores	48,659[2]	$ 7,780
3 stores	13,229[2]	3,110
4 or 5 stores	10,870	2,847
6 to 10 stores	10,938	3,576
11 to 25 stores	14,199	5,591
26 to 50 stores	12,652	3,416
51 to 100 stores	12,239	3,464
101 or more stores	44,241	21,403
	167,027	$51,187

In the first place, the chains account for a much larger percentage of the total dollar volume done by all retail stores than their meager percentage of the total number of stores would suggest. In 1954, with aggregate sales of $51 billion, as appears from the foregoing table, they accounted for approximately 30% of the total.

Furthermore, even that figure of 30% does not tell the whole story of chain-store importance. For in some fields the chains are naturally a more important factor than they are in others. In those fields which lend themselves best to the chain-store type of operation, the chains play a far more important part than they do in retailing as a whole.

The 1954 Census reveals this quite clearly. It shows, for instance, that in the variety-store field, in which the chains were the pioneers, they operated 43% of the stores and accounted for 83% of the total business in this field; in the shoe field, the chains operated 40 per cent of the stores and accounted for 56 per cent of the sales; in the grocery field, the chains operated only 8.8 per cent of the stores but they accounted for 48 per cent of the sales; while in the drug field, the chains with 11 per cent of the stores accounted for 27 per

[2] Thus reported in Census but obviously slightly inaccurate.

cent of total sales. All the figures in this paragraph include chains with *two* or *three* stores. For this reason, they do not agree with those shown in Table 15, post, which include only chains with four or more stores.

In the second place, certain basic characteristics of the chain-store type of operation have had a greater impact on the retail business as a whole, and our general economy, than the number of their stores or even the volume of their sales might lead one to expect.

One of the outstanding characteristics of chain-store merchandising, for instance, has been its emphasis on lower prices. It has provided a competitive factor which other retailers could not ignore. Thus, such price advantages as the chains have been able to offer their own customers have benefited their competitors' customers as well. For the lower prices or better values offered by one retailer or one type of retailing are bound to be reflected in the market more or less generally. Prices may not be reduced to a common level as a result of competition but the spread between the lowest and highest prices is bound to be narrowed. To the extent that chain-store pricing policies have tended to bring all prices down, their impact on retailing has been far-reaching and significant.

But behind the chains' lower prices, of course, are the various operating and merchandising factors which make them possible. Some of them are inherent in the chain-store type of operation and are unavailable to single-store merchants. But many of them can be adopted or adapted by *any* retailer. Take, for instance, as an outstanding example of the latter, the cash-and-carry method of operation—the elimination of credit sales and delivery of merchandise from store to home. Although the chains did not invent that idea, they did see in it an effective means to lower prices, and they adopted it almost universally. Chain stores and cash-and-carry became almost synonymous terms. But the chains had no patent or monopoly on the plan and all retailers were free to use it. To the extent, however, that the cash-and-carry idea and other characteristic chain-store methods and policies have not been followed by the chains' competitors, the impact the chains have made on distribution in general has been out of proportion to the number of their stores or their share of the total retail volume.

Having divided all retail stores into two groups, independents and chains, and having referred to certain operating and merchandising features *inherent* in the chain-store system, the question arises: What is the basic difference between the two systems?

Broadly speaking, the chain-store system is nothing more nor less than a method of distribution involving the use of more than one retail outlet. That is a very rough and incomplete definition of the chain-store system, but it really covers the outstanding difference between the chain store, on the one hand, and the single, or independent, store, on the other.

The biggest chain in the country today, and incidentally the oldest, the Great Atlantic & Pacific Tea Company, with some 4,000 stores (at one time it had 15,700) and an annual volume, in the fiscal year ending February 22, 1958, of $4,769,000,000, differs only in degree from the newest infant in the chain-store family, which may operate but two or three units, and they both differ from the independent store primarily because they transact their business not through a single store, but through more than one.

In emphasizing the fact that the difference between the chain store and the independent store is based fundamentally on *the number of units* operated under one ownership and control, there is no intention to minimize the importance of the distinction. On the contrary, whatever advantages the chain-store system may possess must be attributed directly to the economies accruing from the operation of more than one unit and the increase in the scope of operation thereby achieved, while, on the other hand, whatever weaknesses are inherent in the system are due almost exclusively to the special problems involved in the operation of more than one unit.

Most of the advantages the chains enjoy may be traced directly to the fact that the business is conducted through more than one unit because most of those advantages come from *volume,* and the volume the chains are able to attain depends mainly upon the number of stores they operate.

The fact that *large* volume may likewise be attained by a retailer with a single store, and frequently is, does not weaken the foregoing statement. For although, under a single roof, a merchant may attain a very large volume, his possibilities in that direction are nevertheless limited just so long as he confines his operations to a single establishment.

Offhand, it might seem unnecessary to elaborate the point that more volume is possible with two stores than with one, but the truth of that statement may be so easily befogged by reference to the stupendous business done *in some instances* by single stores that it may be useful to look into the matter a little further.

The truth of the matter is that while *large* volume is attainable in a single store, as has been demonstrated not only in the case of our big department stores but, more recently, in the grocery field with the advent of the supermarket, the *maximum* possibilities for volume can be secured only through the operation of more than one store. But more important is the fact that, while some single-store merchants do develop large volume, a large percentage remain relatively small.

The situation is clearly revealed in Tables 3 and 4.

Table 3, covering the 1,455,310 *single* stores which were in operation for the full year of 1954, shows that 667,101, or 45.8% of them, did less than $30,000. With a combined volume of $9,802 million, this group actually *averaged* less than $15,000 for the year.

Table 4 tells the same story in another way. It discloses that

TABLE 3

SINGLE STORES, BY SALES SIZE, 1954

(Source: U.S. Retail Census)

SIZE GROUP (ANNUAL SALES)	NUMBER OF STORES IN GROUP	%	SALES OF GROUP (MILLIONS)	%
$300,000 or more	55,414	3.8	$ 43,621	38.8
$30,000 to $299,000	732,795	50.4	59,089	52.5
Less than $30,000	667,101	45.8	9,802	8.7
All stores	1,455,310	100.0	$112,512	100.0

659,483 stores, or 42% of *all* stores, including multiunits, which were in operation throughout 1954, had *no* paid employes, while an additional 519,833, or 31%, had 3 employes or fewer. Together these groups comprised some 73% of all stores, but they accounted for only 26% of all retail sales.

TABLE 4

RETAIL TRADE, BY EMPLOYMENT SIZE, 1954

(Source: U.S. Retail Census)

EMPLOYES PER STORE	NUMBER OF STORES	%	SALES OF GROUP (MILLIONS)	%
None	659,483	42.0	$ 14,550	9.0
One	203,568	12.0	8,449	5.0
Two	182,152	11.0	10,171	6.0
Three	134,113	8.0	9,667	6.0
Four or more	435,190	27.0	119,671	74.0
All stores	1,614,506	100.0	$162,508	100.0

Turning to the other end of the scale, Table 3 shows that single stores doing more than $300,000 a year were relatively few, the group including only 55,414 stores, or 3.8 per cent of the total. They accounted, however, for 38.8 per cent of the total sales of all single stores, and because of the huge volume some of them developed, the average for the group figures at nearly $800,000 a year.

Included in this group, of course, are most of our big department stores, many of which do many millions of dollars worth of business a year. But even the biggest of them is limited in the amount of business it can do so long as it confines itself to a single store.

This is well illustrated in the case of R. H. Macy & Co.'s huge store on 34th Street and Sixth Avenue, New York.

In 1921, Macy's sales amounted to $46,000,000, a tremendous volume to be attained under a single roof. Nevertheless, year by year the volume increased until, in 1929, it reached a record figure of $98,600,000. In that year, however, the company acquired Bamberger & Co., a Newark, N.J., department store, and the following year the *combined* sales amounted to $135,000,000. Of that total, Macy's contributed $99,000,-000 and Bamberger's the balance.

The illustration is particularly in point because Newark is sufficiently close to New York to warrant the conclusion that Macy's enjoyed a certain amount of Newark patronage before it took over Bamberger's, and yet there was apparently another $35,000,000 more to be had at that time only by the acquisition of that store or another store of like capacity.

Incidentally, it should be pointed out that because of the delivery system maintained by stores like Macy's and the mail-order facilities they have at their command, their possibilities for volume are not necessarily limited to their immediate neighborhoods. Indeed, they seek and obtain a certain amount of patronage from communities far removed from their natural trading area. But despite their efforts and their success in that direction, their real possibilities for volume seem nevertheless to be limited largely to the business they can draw from their own immediate vicinities.

Realization of this limitation in recent years led most of our leading department stores to open suburban branch stores. Macy's, today, operates not only a number of large stores which it acquired, as it did Bamberger's, but also several branch stores which it established in its own backyard, so to speak—in Parkchester in The Bronx, Jamaica, L.I., Flatbush in Brooklyn, White Plains, N.Y. and Roosevelt Field, L.I.—because that was the only way to capture millions of dollars of additional volume which the "miracle" store on 34th Street could not hope to draw.[3]

Other New York department stores and specialty shops and similar stores in other cities have followed the same general pattern. The trend has usually been referred to as "decentralization." Traffic congestion and limited parking facilities in the downtown areas, plus the tremendous growth in suburban population, have undoubtedly been largely responsible for it. Taking the store to the customer who can no longer shop conveniently at the main store may be as much a matter of holding existing volume as a means of achieving additional volume. In either event, however, the trend illustrates that even our most successful stores recognize the limitations inherent in any given location and attempt to overcome them by opening branch stores.

If big stores like these, with their extensive delivery systems, find themselves at a disadvantage with a single store, how much more limited must be the chances of a merchant who relies exclusively on his immediate neighborhood for all of his business!

Not only are the possibilities for volume at any single location definitely limited, but the converse is also true: Once the limitations incident to single-store operation are eliminated, the volume attainable is dependent only on the number of stores which can be successfully operated. The history of the chains is replete with instances of merchants who, once they realized the limitations of single-store operation, found that the road to unlimited volume presented practically no obstacles.

The experience of the J. C. Penney Company is typical of the manner in which most of the chain-store companies, which loom large in today's distribution set-up came into being. As

[3] Macy's sales for the fiscal year ending August 2, 1958 were $456.4 million. Its six department store divisions, consisting of Macy's New York, Bamberger's New Jersey, Davison-Paxon Company, Atlanta, La Salle & Koch Company, Toledo, Macy's California and Macy's Missouri-Kansas, respectively, operated 33 stores in all. Several of the divisions were planning to open additional stores in new shopping centers.

a matter of fact, practically all chains, small as well as large, started in precisely the same way, achieving various degrees of success.

The first Penney store, which operated under the name of the "Golden Rule," was established by James Cash Penney and a couple of partners in Kemmerer, Wyo., in April, 1902. It was a most insignificant 25x45-foot dry-goods store located in a community hardly more promising. Certainly, from the pictures of it which have been preserved, it gave no indications that it was to be the progenitor of the 1,700 outstanding apparel and general-merchandise stores which dot the country today. For his one-third interest in the store, Mr. Penney put up $500 of his own money plus $1,500 which he was able to borrow from a bank.

The sales the first year were approximately $29,000—indicating that this first Penney unit was somewhat more successful than the majority of single stores are today, particularly as $29,000 in those days meant considerably more than it does now.

In 1903, Mr. Penney and his partners opened a second establishment in another frontier community, and in that year the combined volume of the incipient chain was $63,000. Store No. 3 was opened in 1904. In 1907, Mr. Penney bought out his partners' interest in the three stores for $30,000, and he was in business on his own.[4]

That same year, Mr. Penney took into his organization a man who was later on to become the president of the company and to direct its operations through many of its most successful years—the late Earl C. Sams. How Mr. Sams came to get in touch with Mr. Penney is best told in his own language.

"In 1907, I was operating, with the backing of some friends, a store in my small native town of Simpson, Kan.," he said, in the course of his testimony before a Congressional committee[5]

---

[4] Norman Beasley, *Main Street Merchant* (New York: McGraw-Hill Book Co., 1948).

[5] Hearing on Patman Bill, 76th Congress, 3rd Session, Vol. 1, p. 559.

33 years later. "I was an independent merchant. . . . We operated a good store to the best of our knowledge and I was pretty much my own boss. However, I couldn't see any real opportunity ahead. A livelihood—yes, perhaps—but not much more. In looking around for a much bigger opportunity, an employment agency told me about a man named J. C. Penney who had a store in the little coal camp of Kemmerer, Wyo., and who had a vision of something beyond a single small store. After some correspondence, I left Kansas and joined Mr. Penney."

One of the things which attracted Mr. Sams to Mr. Penney, he went on to say, "was the vision he had of more than one store—maybe a dozen, maybe even 50, which might be opened through the years and which would work together."

That vision of "even 50" stores may have seemed far off in 1907 but, as a matter of fact, it was realized sooner than either Mr. Sams or Mr. Penney himself could ever have dreamed. Within four years after Mr. Sams' decision to throw in his lot with Mr. Penney, the company had 22 stores in operation and the sales passed the $1,000,000 mark! By 1914, the vision of "even 50" stores was actually achieved. That year the 71st store was opened and the company's sales totalled $3,600,000.

A particularly interesting milestone in the company's progress, however, is the fact that its sales in 1921, when it had 312 stores, amounted to $46,000,000. Both the year and the amount are significant because it happens that Macy's sales that very same year hit the very same level. The significance lies in the fact that, whereas the department store, operating under a single roof, had required 63 years to reach that point (Macy's was established in 1858) the chain-store company, operating under a number of separate roofs scattered over a wide area in communities far smaller than New York, had reached the same point in only nineteen years.

The progress of the chain from that time on is revealed in Table 5, which gives the number of stores and the annual sales in each year from 1902 to 1957.

TABLE 5

GROWTH OF J. C. PENNEY COMPANY, 1902-1957

YEAR	STORES	SALES	YEAR	STORES	SALES
1902	1	$ 28,898	1930	1,452	$192,943,765
1903	1	63,523	1931	1,459	173,705,095
1904	2	94,165	1932	1,473	155,271,981
1905	2	97,654	1933	1,466	178,773,965
1906	2	127,128	1934	1,474	212,053,361
1907	2	166,314	1935	1,481	225,936,101
1908	4	218,432	1936	1,496	258,322,479
1909	6	310,062	1937	1,523	275,375,137
1910	14	662,331	1938	1,539	257,963,946
1911	22	1,183,280	1939	1,554	282,133,934
1912	34	2,050,642	1940	1,586	304,539,325
1913	48	2,637,294	1941	1,605	377,571,711
1914	71	3,560,294	1942	1,611	490,295,173
1915	86	4,825,072	1943	1,610	489,888,091
1916	127	8,428,144	1944	1,608	535,362,894
1917	177	14,881,203	1945	1,602	549,149,148
1918	197	31,338,104	1946	1,601	767,584,135
1919	197	28,783,956	1947	1,601	775,889,615
1920	312	42,846,009	1948	1,601	885,203,023
1921	313	46,641,928	1949	1,609	880,192,488
1922	371	49,035,729	1950	1,612	949,729,400
1923	475	62,188,979	1951	1,621	1,035,201,519
1924	569	74,261,343	1952	1,632	1,079,256,505
1925	674	91,062,616	1953	1,634	1,109,507,675
1926	747	115,683,023	1954	1,644	1,107,156,633
1927	892	151,957,865	1955	1,666	1,220,085,325
1928	1,023	176,698,989	1956	1,687	1,291,867,267
1929	1,395	209,690,418	1957	1,694	1,312,278,000

The growth of the J. C. Penney Company from a single store in 1902, with sales of $29,000, to a chain of 1,694 stores in 1957, with sales of $1.3 billion, amazing as it is, was the outcome of no magic formula, no secret process, no patent or monopoly, no unusual opportunity which was not available to any other single-store merchant in 1902, or at any other time before or since. Of course, the idea of operating more than one store did not originate with Mr. Penney. On the contrary, the Great Atlantic & Pacific Tea Co. had been in operation for more than 40 years, Jones Brothers Tea Co. (later to become Grand Union Co.) for 30 years, and the F. W. Woolworth Co. for more than twenty years, when Mr. Penney opened his first store, while at least a score of other chains had preceded him.

But, what is more to the point, thousands of single-store merchants have followed the identical path which Mr. Penney and his predecessors trod and have likewise developed highly successful chains in a number of different fields of retail activity.

Full-length books have been written about the chains built by Frank Woolworth, J. C. Penney, Louis K. Liggett and Sears, Roebuck.[6] Hundreds of other chains have been the subjects of success stories in leading magazines and business papers. But the fact is that a human-interest story lies behind practically every one of the chains now in existence. Only the limitations of space and the fact that all the stories follow the same basic pattern, differing only in details, prevent their inclusion in these pages. Inspiring and useful as these success stories are, too many of them in this volume would make monotonous reading.

However, two of them which were told by the author years ago in the course of an address on "Opportunity in the Chain Store Field"[7] may be told again if only for the purpose of bringing them up to date.

The first involved the history of the Badger Paint & Hardware Stores, of Milwaukee, which was then only ten years old.

In 1918, Robert Jacobi opened a paint store. He had no idea of starting a chain at the time. All he saw was the possibility for a paint store that would be different from the general run.

In the first place, he decided to paint his store attractively so that the store itself would be a standing advertisement of the virtue of paint. In the second place he decided to go aggressively after business instead of waiting for it to come to him.

[6] John K. Winkler, *Five and Ten* (New York: McBride, 1940); Norman Beasley, *op. cit.;* Samuel Merwin, *Rise and Fight Againe* (New York, Boni & Co., 1935); Emmett & Jeuck, *Catalogs and Counters* (Chicago: University of Chicago Press, 1950); see also case histories of many chains in *Chain Store Age* (all editions), June, 1950.

[7] Delivered before Retail Clothiers and Furnishers Associations of New York, New Jersey and Pennsylvania, Hotel Ambassador, Atlantic City, February 22, 1928.

Although his entire capital was only $1,400, he spent $900 of it the very first month for advertising. The attractive appearance of the store, the energy its proprietor put into the management of it, the advertising effort, all combined to make the store successful. The first year's sales were $23,000. The greatest single item of expense was advertising.

Then the big idea came to this single-store merchant. The advertising he was doing would work just as well for two stores as it would for one, so that, in effect, this heavy item of cost would be cut in two.

He opened a second store. Sales for the two stores were $50,000. His operating expenses were substantially reduced proportionately because some of them, like advertising, were shared by the two stores instead of being carried entirely by one.

The following year, out of profits, he opened a third store. Then he began to realize some of the additional benefits the operation of more than one store makes possible. He found that his buying power had increased and, by buying in larger quantities, he paid less for his merchandise.

From that time on his progress was rapid. By 1928, he had his own paint factory, was operating nearly 50 stores, and his sales were in excess of $1,000,000.

What was the sequel of that story? According to the company's report for 1949, the Badger Paint & Hardware chain was operating 117 stores and sales totalled $4,500,000. Included in the assets of the company, which had started in 1918 with a capital of $1,400, were land and buildings valued at more than $1,000,000. As of March 10, 1958, the company was operating 126 stores in Wisconsin, Illinois, Iowa, Michigan and Missouri. Its assets had grown substantially since its report of 1949, and its sales exceeded $6,500,000. A number of additional stores were planned for 1958 and older stores were to be remodelled.

The other story related to an independent merchant in another field—a druggist in Chicago. Back in 1909, when he was 36 years old, this druggist was operating a small store which he had bought from his employer in 1901, and he was just about making both ends meet. That year he got a chance to buy a second store from another former employer. To raise the money for the down payment, he would have to sell a half-interest in the store he had. His friends advised him against it.

"Chicago has too many drug stores already," they warned. "Why buck the tide?"

"Chicago may have too many drug stores," he replied, "but it hasn't enough *Walgreen* drug stores!"

For the independent druggist in question was the late Charles Walgreen, and his purchase of a second store in 1909 against his friends' advice marked the beginning of the Walgreen chain of drug stores which, in 1928, at the time of the address in question, had 170 stores in operation and was doing more than $20,000,000 a year. The independent druggist of nineteen years earlier had become the president of the second largest drug chain in the country.

What happened was told in detail in a special issue of the Walgreen *Pepper Pod*, June, 1951, the company's house organ—the 50th anniversary issue.

In 1911, a third store was opened, in 1913 a fourth, and by 1916, seven Walgreen stores, each separately incorporated, were in operation. That year the separate corporations were merged to form the present Walgreen Company. Its growth from 1920 to 1957 is shown in Table 6.

In 1939, Charles Walgreen died and his son Charles Walgreen, Jr., took over as president. The chain has gained consistently under his direction not only in volume of sales but in leadership in its field and in the pharmaceutical profession. Although it now has somewhat fewer stores than it had at one time, as is revealed in the following table, this merely reflects the trend towards bigger stores to which reference has already been made. As a result, the combined selling area of the 407 stores in operation at the end of the 1957 fiscal year greatly exceeded that of the 508 stores operating in 1938. The annual sales reported include sales to several hundred agency stores —independent drug stores which serve as Walgreen agencies for the company's own products and which also use the facilities Walgreen has for supplying them with many other items.

TABLE 6

WALGREEN CO. GROWTH, 1920-1957

YEAR	STORES	SALES (MILLIONS)	YEAR	STORES	SALES (MILLIONS)
1920	23	$ 2.2	1939	494	$ 70.8
1921	29	2.6	1940	489	74.3
1922	33	2.5	1941	487	82.5
1923	41	3.6	1942	480	95.3
1924	56	5.6	1943	460	112.2
1925	87	9.3	1944	442	120.
1926	107	13.5	1945	427	118.8
1927	170	20.9	1946	412	140.7
1928	230	31.4	1947	410	154.5
1929	397	46.6	1948	413	163.3
1930	440	39.1*	1949	414	163.4
1931	468	54.	1950	410	163.4
1932	471	47.6	1951	406	171.5
1933	474	46.	1952	400	177.9
1934	487	53.7	1953	390	181.5
1935	501	58.1	1954	388	184.3
1936	496	61.8	1955	388	192.7
1937	504	67.9	1956	386	212.3
1938	508	67.7	1957	407	235.1

* For 9 months only.

The founder of Walgreen Company was a typical single-store druggist when the opportunity came to him to acquire a second store. After that he made his own opportunities. He enjoyed no advantage over his fellow independent druggists except, perhaps, a livelier imagination and a greater ambition. These were apparently enough to lay the foundation for what was to become the biggest drug chain in the country.

That most chains started with modest capital and financed their early expansion entirely out of earnings is not only a fact but was more or less inevitable. Until they had demonstrated their ability to operate a chain of stores profitably over a number of years, their chance of attracting outside capital would obviously have been slim.[8] The first public financing for the Woolworth Company did not come until 1912.[9] J. C. Penney Company financed itself until it had 197 stores and sales of $21,000,000; the S. S. Kresge Co. until it had 66 stores and sales of $7,900,000; and McCrory Stores Corporation until it had 113 stores and sales of $4,900,000.

In the shoe field, the present Melville Shoe Corporation, which was founded by Frank Melville, Jr., in 1892, was financed out of earnings for the first 24 years of its existence. Not until 1916, when the present corporation came into existence, was outside capital sought. The G. R. Kinney Company, founded in 1894, followed a similar course. It was incorporated in 1917, but the stock was closely held. Not until 1923, by which time the company had 152 stores in operation and shoe factories of its own and sales of $14,000,000, was any common stock offered publicly.

That has been the almost universal formula responsible for the chain-store system today. Not all the chains it has produced have grown to the point where public financing was either feasible or desired. The fact is that the great majority of the chains which comprise the system are extremely small compared with A&P, the Woolworth Co., J. C. Penney Co., Walgreen's, Melville Shoe Corporation and other leaders in their respective fields.

On the other hand, in between the top-flight companies and the smallest ones are thousands of regional and local companies each operating relatively few stores but doing an annual business running well into the millions.

But, large or small, national, regional or local, these companies collectively make the chain-store system. Almost without exception they have three basic points in common:

1. They started as single-store merchants.

2. None of them was content to remain a single-store merchant.

---

[8] Luigi Criscuolo, "Financing the Chain," *Chain Store Age,* June, 1925, p. 13.
[9] *Five and Ten,* note 6 *supra.*

3. By escaping the limitations of single-store operation, they were able to develop a volume of sales which, judging from the experience of most single-store merchants, they would have secured *in no other way*.

CHAPTER II

THE BIRTH OF THE SYSTEM

CHAIN-STORE history conveniently divides itself into three periods:

1. 1859-1900, the period in which the pioneers in several important chain-store fields got their start and had their early development.

2. 1900-1930, the period in which the chain-store idea captured the imagination of many alert retailers, brought hundreds of new chains into existence, and witnessed the expansion of the system at such a rapid rate and on such a conspicuous scale as to threaten its destruction.

3. Since 1930, the period in which the system had to fight for its very existence but emerged the stronger for its experience and better equipped to fill its particular niche in the distribution set-up on a sound and abiding basis.

That the chain-store idea had its beginnings, of a sort, long before 1859, the year A&P was founded, is beyond question. John P. Nichols, in his outstanding book on chain stores,[1] refers to a chain of stores operating in China 200 years before Christ, a chain of drug stores founded in Japan in 1643, mercantile operations of a chain-store character carried on by the Fugger family in Germany and the Merchant Adventurers in England, the chain of outposts developed in Canada by the Hudson's Bay Company, chartered in 1670, and the fact that our own Andrew Jackson at one time owned a small chain of retail stores in Tennessee. And, no doubt, many another early American merchant might have qualified as a pioneer chain-

---

[1] John P. Nichols, *The Chain Store Tells Its Story* (Institute of Distribution, 1940), p. 13. For more complete data on early history of chains, "of a kind," see *"Economics of Retailing,"* Paul H. Nystrom, 1930, Ronald Press.

store operator by reason of the fact that he had a second, a third or even a fourth store.

Nevertheless, the date of the founding of the A&P is chosen as the take-off point for this record of chain stores in America because *all* the chains which have helped in any way to make the system what it is today came into being within A&P's lifetime.

A&P had its beginnings in a small store on Vesey Street, New York, opened in 1859 by George F. Gilman and George Huntington Hartford. It was not a grocery store and it did not have the name Great Atlantic & Pacific Tea Co. Whether the founders at that time had any idea that they would ever have more than one store may be doubted, for the success of their first store was by no means assured. The only idea they had then was to make tea available to the public at much below the prevailing price by simply importing tea direct from China and Japan and cutting out some of the middlemen's costs and profits.

However, the Gilman & Hartford venture on Vesey Street did prove so successful that before very long they opened a second store. By 1865, they had no less than 25 stores in operation and had assumed the name of the Great American Tea Company. By that time they were so well established and so sure of their ground that they decided to add a line of groceries, figuring that if they could sell tea at reduced prices, they could sell other items at reduced prices also.

It was not until 1869 that the name Great Atlantic & Pacific Tea Company was adopted. By that time the company had begun to spread westward and undoubtedly felt that a more comprehensive title would reflect the scope of its operations more clearly.

In 1878, Mr. Gilman retired and Mr. Hartford was left to carry on alone until two of his sons, George L. and John A., were old enough to join him, the former in 1880 and the latter in 1888.[2]

---

[2] *Time*, November 13, 1950, p. 93.

A&P's 100th store was opened in 1880. Considering that the company was then 21 years old, its rate of expansion, although rapid enough, no doubt, for those days, had been at a snail's pace compared with what was to happen later on. One hundred stores in 21 years! A time was to come when A&P was to open as many as that in two weeks—to open an *average* of 50 stores a week for a whole year!

Even twenty years later, at the turn of the century, A&P was still operating less than 200 stores, although by 1900 the company was 41 years old.

Turning for a moment from A&P, a number of other grocery chains came into existence during that period, to say nothing of the appearance of the first Woolworth store, in 1879, and the early development of the Woolworth chain and other chains in the 5-and-10-cent-store field, of which more will be said later.

In the grocery field, the year 1872 saw the organization of its second oldest chain—Jones Brothers Tea Co., of Brooklyn, which was later to become the successful Grand Union Company of today.

Ten years later, in 1882, was sown the seed of the present Kroger Company, the third largest grocery chain today in number of stores and volume of sales. That year, Bernard H. Kroger, of Cincinnati, 22 years old, with a couple of years of experience as a grocery clerk, opened a store under the name of Great Western Tea Company. It made a profit the very first year and, before very long, a second store was opened and the combined profits made a third store possible. But, although the rate of expansion was necessarily slow, by 1891 the Great Western Tea Co. had seven stores and by 1902, it had 36. That year it became the Kroger Grocery & Baking Company. Its growth thereafter was more rapid. Indeed, the day was to come when it would have more than 5,500 stores.[3] Today, as a result of the trend toward larger but fewer stores,

[3] In 1929, the company reached its peak in number of stores, 5,575, but its sales that year were $286 million.

Kroger operates just over 1,400 stores, but its sales in 1957 totalled $1,674,162,000.

Another food chain established the same year as Kroger, James Butler Grocery Co., of New York, followed a different course. Although it developed successfully for many years up to the point where it was operating more than 500 stores in the metropolitan area, its owners decided in 1936 to retire from the field. Some of the stores were sold to their managers. The remainder were liquidated.

Five other food chains of that period, operating in the Philadelphia area, which were later to be merged and to become the American Stores Co., one of the four leading food chains today, were:

	Founded
Childs Grocery Co.	1883
Acme Tea Co.	1887
Geo. M. Dunlap Co.	1888
The Bell Company	1890
Robinson & Crawford	1891

Two other New York chains which were to retain their identities all through the years and which are operating today at peak efficiency are the H. C. Bohack Company of Brooklyn and Gristede Bros., of New York.

The former goes back to 1887, when H. C. Bohack opened his first store and, following the traditional pattern, opened store after store until eventually they spread all through Long Island. Today, the company operates 186 stores, including 159 supermarkets, and its sales exceed $145,000,000.

The Gristede Bros. story goes back to 1891, when two brothers, Charles and Diedrich Gristede, who had both worked as grocery clerks, decided to open a store of their own. Their obvious determination to please their customers and make a success of their business, the long hours they put into their self-bossed jobs, made their first store a sure-fire success. They were the kind of men who would have made a success in the grocery business even with a single store.

As it was, however, they were not content to remain on that basis, and they opened a second store and, although their subsequent expansion proceeded always at a slow pace, the company today operates 118 stores in New York and Connecticut. Incidentally, the chain has always specialized in a more complete range of groceries and delicacies than the typical grocery chain was accustomed to stock, and it has also the distinction of being one of the very few food chains in the whole country which never adopted the cash-and-carry principle.

One of the most successful regional chains, First National Stores, which operated 575 stores in New England and New York at the end of its 1957 fiscal year, with sales of $521 million, was not actually organized until 1926, when it came into being as a result of the merger of three existing chains, the Ginter Co., John T. Connor Co. and O'Keeffe Company, all of Boston. Because the Ginter Co. was established in 1895, First National's roots go back to the period under consideration.

Two other extremely successful chains in today's picture came into existence just before the end of the 19th century, both being founded in 1899. National Tea Co. and Jewel Tea Company both got their starts in Chicago and, although the latter did not operate retail stores for many years, confining its activities exclusively to the operation of wagon routes, it later acquired the Loblaw grocery chain of Chicago and has developed it into one of the most efficient operations in the whole field.

National Tea Co., ranking fifth among the country's food chains at the beginning of 1958, was operating some 900 stores in 18 states. Its sales in 1957 totalled some $681 million.

The Jewel Tea Co., with 227 stores at the end of 1957, had sales of $414 million.

Many local food chains in operation today in various parts of the country likewise had their beginnings back in the period under consideration, but no attempt has been made to list them all. Typical of the group are Henke & Pillot, Houston, Tex., founded in 1872, which is now owned by the Kroger Co.; Ralph's Grocery Co., Los Angeles, founded in 1873; Daniel Grocer Co., Murphysboro, Ill., founded in 1882; Fred W. Albrecht Co., Akron, Ohio, founded in 1891; and Standard Grocery Co. (now owned by National Tea Co.), Indianapolis, founded in 1897 by Lafayette Jackson, who was to figure as plaintiff some 30 years later in a case which made chain-store history.[4]

Returning now to A&P for a resumption of the account of that company's progress through its first 100 years, its real expansion program did not get under way until 1912. Then, as a result of a successful experiment with a new type of store suggested by John A. Hartford,[5] a decision was made to open as many of them as possible as rapidly as they could be established.

These new stores, called "economy stores," were designed to sell groceries as cheap as possible by the simple device of selling on a cash-and-carry basis instead of making deliveries and extending credit, as A&P had done up to that time in common with other grocers.

Furthermore, the new stores were to be small, low-rent, one-man affairs, with modest fixtures, all making for low operating costs, and were to be satisfied with a minimum of profit. Increased volume was to be depended upon to make up for the low profit rate.

The first economy stores proved so successful that A&P decided to open them wherever they could be established with a reasonable prospect of success—which, because of their low prices, meant practically anywhere and everywhere. The 500th A&P store was opened in 1913 and the company

[4] See page 130, *post.*
[5] He died September 20, 1951. George Hartford died Sept. 23, 1957.

had 585 in operation by the end of that year. In the next two years it opened some 1,600 more and, by the end of 1919, it had no less than 4,200!

But that was only the beginning of an expansion program which was to *add* nearly 10,000 stores in the next six years, the company having 14,000 stores in operation by the end of 1925. From that point, further expansion at a slower rate carried the chain to its peak of 15,700 in 1930, as is shown in the Table below and in Chart I on page 30.

TABLE 7

GROWTH OF A&P, 1859-1958

YEAR*	STORES	SALES (MILLIONS)	YEAR*	STORES	SALES (MILLIONS)
1859	1	—	1931	15,670	$1,008
1865	25	—	1932	15,427	864
1880	100	—	1933	15,131	820
1900	200	—	1934	15,035	842
1906	291	—	1935	14,926	872
1910	372	—	1936	14,746	907
1911	400	—	1937	13,314	882
1912	480	—	1938	10,900	879
1913	585	—	1939	9,200	990
1914	991	—	1940	7,230	1,116
1915	1,817	—	1941	6,170	1,379
1916	2,866	—	1942	6,000	1,471
1917	3,782	—	1943	5,900	1,311
1918	3,799	—	1944	5,800	1,402
1919	4,224	$ 195	1945	5,600	1,435
1920	4,621	235	1946	5,200	1,909
1921	5,217	202	1947	5,075	2,546
1922	7,350	247	1948	4,900	2,837
1923	9,303	303	1949	4,700	2,905
1924	11,421	352	1950	4,500	3,180
1925	14,034	440	1951	4,400	3,392
1926	14,811	574	1952	4,300	3,756
1927	15,671	761	1953	4,250	3,989
1928	15,177	973	1954	4,200	4,140
1929	15,418	1,054	1955	4,150	4,305
1930	15,737	1,066	1956	4,200	4,482
			1957	4,200	4,769

* Fiscal years ending February 28 following year given.

What happened after that to reduce the number of A&P stores to its present level of approximately 4,000 were two

CHART I

GROWTH OF GREAT ATLANTIC & PACIFIC TEA CO.
1920 - 1958

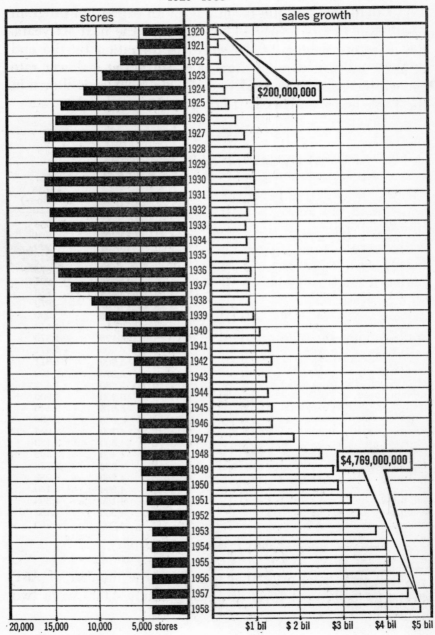

radical changes affecting the grocery trade in general. Each of them, in turn, established a trend toward bigger grocery stores. The first, which developed slowly between 1920 and 1925 but made rapid progress thereafter, introduced the combination store—a service store which handled fresh meats and a wide range of fresh fruits and vegetables as well as groceries. These combination stores were typically twice the size of the straight grocery stores which they began to replace. Then, in the early '30s, came the second and more revolutionary change—the introduction of the epoch-making supermarket.

This newcomer was much bigger than the largest combination stores and, of course, it was four or five times bigger than the traditional straight grocery stores which had previously constituted the retail grocery field. Besides being bigger, it presented many new operating and merchandising features.

In the first place, it was operated on a self-service basis, so far, at least, as the grocery department was concerned.[6] Secondly, it featured huge displays of groceries of all kinds as well as fresh meats and fruits and vegetables. Some of the early versions of the supermarket carried many other lines as well, having no relation to the grocery business—clothing,

[6] The supermarkets did not originate self-service. This revolutionary idea in food retailing was the brain-child of the inventive mind of Clarence Saunders, of Memphis. He made it the basis of an entirely new type of grocery store which he introduced, in 1916, under the intriguing name of Piggly Wiggly. The special lay-out of the Piggly Wiggly store required customers to pass through a turnstile and then follow a more or less prescribed path exposing them to the appeal of all the merchandise displayed on the shelving. The idea was so successful that the company was able to sell franchises to thousands of others who wanted to adopt it and operate under the Piggly Wiggly name. Many of the leading chains, including Safeway, Kroger, National Tea and Colonial, operated Piggly Wiggly stores in certain areas for many years before they converted their own stores to self-service. The two basic features of the Piggly Wiggly idea—specially designed self-service stores and the franchise arrangement—were likewise employed by other companies. One of the most successful was Jitney Jungle, of Jackson, Miss. The original Piggly Wiggly stores were no bigger than the typical grocery store of the period but, with the trend toward bigger stores, Piggly Wiggly stores of supermarket dimensions naturally evolved. That these original self-service stores laid the foundation for the modern supermarket would seem to be beyond question. The Piggly Wiggly Corporation, Jacksonville, Fla., is servicing today some 2,000 Piggly Wiggly stores of all sizes, many of them being operated by extremely successful regional chains.

shoes, furniture, for example—which were sold in departments operated by concessionaires. But the development of the supermarket followed a more conservative pattern although interest in non-food items was to be reborn later on. Finally, and probably most significant, everything was featured at aggressively low prices made possible by the economies flowing from the self-service set-up and the advantages inherent in large volume.

Although the first supermarkets were established by independents for the most part, the chains eventually recognized their basic advantages and possibilities and decided that the only thing to do was to build supermarkets themselves. Some chains acted faster than others but, by 1937, most of the leading food chains, including A&P, were building supermarkets as fast as they could find suitable locations—and closing up three or four of their existing smaller units to make way for each of the supermarkets they established.

The net result of the trend toward bigger stores in the case of A&P was, as has been pointed out before, to reduce the number of its stores from 14,700 at the beginning of 1937 to some 4,000 today. This apparent elimination of 10,700 stores actually reflected the elimination of an even greater number of small stores, approximately 13,700, and their replacement by some 3,000 supermarkets. The conversion, drastic as it was, resulted in no loss of sales. On the contrary, whereas the 14,700 stores in operation at the end of 1936 had produced sales that year of $889 million, A&P's sales in the fiscal year ending February 22, 1958, with only 4,000 stores in operation, totalled $4,769,000,000, a figure never before attained by any retail enterprise.

True enough, this increase, amounting to 436%, in a period of two decades, was accounted for partly by the change in the dollar's value. The main reason for it, however, was an actual increase in unit sales which reflected the greatly increased capacity of the modern supermarket compared with that of the typical grocery store which it replaced. The fact is that the type of supermarket A&P and other food chains are operating today averages more than twenty times as much business as their average store produced 20 years ago.

A&P's modern supermarkets are indeed a far cry from the "economy stores" with which the company embarked on its cash-and-carry, minimum-profit, low-price policy back in 1912, but the goal is still the same. Furthermore, the operating economies made possible by the introduction of self-service and the tremendous increase in volume per store are substantially greater than those achieved when the cash-and-carry idea was first adopted.

As it approaches its 100th anniversary, the big company is distributing some $5 billion of groceries annually at just about the lowest prices an inflated economy permits. Its success reflects the soundness of the low-price policy the company adopted early in its history and which it has followed persistently ever since. A natural result of A&P's low-price leadership was to keep *all* food-store prices at relatively low levels and thus to raise the buying-power of the consumer's food dollar and the nation's standard of living. To conclude, however, that the policy was adopted with any such altruistic purpose rather than as a practical formula for achieving success in a highly competitive business would be erroneous.

Another single-store venture which was destined not only to develop into a huge chain but was to provide the inspiration and the pattern for an entirely new field in retail merchandising was the 5-and-10-cent store started by Frank W. Woolworth in Lancaster, Pa., in 1879.[7]

While a clerk in a Watertown, N.Y., dry-goods store, young Woolworth had had an experience which impressed him deeply. A table of miscellaneous smallwares over which he had placed a sign: "Anything on this table, 5¢" was almost cleared the first day. It convinced young Woolworth that a whole store devoted exclusively to 5-cent items would prove equally successful. He determined to try it out.

[7] See *Five and Ten, supra;* and the company's own booklets.

With $300 worth of merchandise, which he obtained on credit from his former boss, and his own meager savings, he opened a store in Utica, N.Y.

The store did fairly well for a few months but then the novelty wore off. The young pioneer, still convinced that the idea was basically sound, decided to close up shop, clear up his debts and try his luck elsewhere.

Having heard from a friend that Lancaster, Pa., was an up-and-coming town, he made a trip there to look the place over. He found what he thought he wanted in a vacant 14x35-foot store on North Queen Street, and rented it. With the remainder of his stock from the Utica store and additional merchandise which he obtained on credit from his former employer, the new store opened for business June 21, 1879.

Writing to his father the following day, young Woolworth reported enthusiastically that his first day's sales had amounted to $127.65—"the most I ever sold in one day!" As he had had an opening stock costing only $410, his enthusiasm would seem to have been justified.

At any rate, he was apparently so confident of success that in that very letter he added: "I think some of starting a branch store in Harrisburg, Pa., and putting Sum [his brother Charles Sumner Woolworth] in it."

The Harrisburg store, a 12x16-foot affair, was indeed opened the following month, but although it survived longer than the first Utica venture, the following March it, too, folded up.

A fourth store was tried out in York, Pa., opening April 3, 1880, but it, too, failed to turn the corner. It was closed June 30.

That fall, however, the fifth store, opened in Scranton, Pa., proved to be the second successful venture. The combined sales of the Lancaster and Scranton stores in 1881 amounted to $18,000. The following year they increased to $24,125.

By that time, Woolworth was convinced that the 5-and-10-

cent-store idea was basically sound, provided you found the right locations. He was also convinced, however, that the possibilities of a single store of that kind were definitely limited—that real success would require a number of such stores. Only in that way would purchases be big enough to command the most favorable prices, and thus extend the range of items which could be sold profitably at 5 cents or 10 cents.

Nevertheless, expansion in those early years proceeded slowly. To find promising locations was only one of the problems. To train or to find trustworthy men to manage them, either as employes or partners, took even more time. Partners with capital to invest were particularly desirable at that stage of Mr. Woolworth's progress and he was lucky enough to find several of them.

By 1886, he had seven stores in operation. His sales totalled $100,000. But it was not until 1895, by which time he had 25 stores, that his year's sales passed the $1,000,000 mark. His first venture in New York City was a store on 6th Avenue and 17th Street, opened in October, 1897.

By the turn of the century only 59 Woolworth stores were in operation, but they were all flourishing. Their total sales exceeded $5,000,000. A few years later, expansion was accelerated by the purchase in 1904 of 21 stores in the middle-west, twelve in Pennsylvania and four in Massachusetts from various operators.

For, almost from the start, Woolworth's success with this new type of store had attracted the attention of others and tempted them to try it themselves. As early as 1881, John G. McCrory had opened his first store in Scottdale, Pa.—the forerunner of a chain which was to grow with the years and which today, as McCrory Stores Corporation, operates more than 200 stores and ranks among the first ten chains in the variety store field.

Back in 1900, McCrory had twenty stores, S. H. Kress &

Co., whose first store had been opened in Memphis in 1896, had eleven, while S. S. Kresge Company, which was destined to become the second largest variety chain, was still operating its first store, which it had acquired in 1899. A couple of years earlier, Mr. Kresge had gone into partnership with Mr. Mc-Crory with respect to two stores, one in Memphis and the other in Detroit. Then they had decided to travel their separate ways and Mr. McCrory took over the Memphis store while Mr. Kresge became the sole owner of the Detroit store.

In 1957 the Kresge Company operated 692 stores and its sales reached $377 million, making it second to Woolworth both in number of stores and sales.

S. H. Kress & Co., successful right from the start, expanded gradually through the years. At the close of 1957, it was operating 261 stores, with sales of $159 million for the year.

Returning to the pioneer company, up to 1905, Mr. Woolworth was the sole owner of all the stores which operated under his name alone. In addition, he had an interest in a number of other stores which he had started in partnership with others and which invariably bore the joint names of the partners. In 1905, he decided, for reasons of prudence, to incorporate the stores which he owned outright, and F. W. Woolworth & Co. was the result. All the stock, both preferred and common, was held by Mr. Woolworth and his friends.

By 1911, F. W. Woolworth & Co. had 318 stores, but some of his former associates had come along too. S. H. Knox & Co., Buffalo, N.Y., for instance, had 112 stores; F. M. Kirby & Co., Wilkes-Barre, Pa., 96; and E. P. Charlton & Co., Fall River, Mass., 53.

Why not a merger? That possibility was seriously discussed by the respective owners of the companies in question, all of whom knew and respected each other, and by the end of that year the union was affected.

The new company was the present F. W. Woolworth Company. It was made up as follows:

Company	Stores
F. W. Woolworth & Co.	318
S. H. Knox & Co.	112
F. M. Kirby & Co.	96
E. P. Charlton & Co.	53
C. S. Woolworth	15
W. H. Moore	2
	596

C. S. Woolworth was Frank's brother. Who was W. H. Moore? And why did his two stores figure in the big merger?

William H. Moore was the man who had given young Woolworth his first job as a clerk in the dry-goods store he ran in Watertown, N.Y. There it was that Woolworth had learned all he knew about the dry-goods business and where, indeed, he had picked up the idea of running a store devoted exclusively to 5-and-10-cent items. What is more to the point, it was Mr. Moore who had given his ambitious young clerk the goods with which to stock his first unsuccessful venture in Utica and his second store, which took root. Six years later, by which time Woolworth had five successful stores in operation, he learned that his old boss was in difficulties and about to go into bankruptcy. He promptly went to his benefactor's rescue by establishing him in a new business—a 5-and-10-cent store! And where did he locate it? In the very store where the idea of a 5-and-10-cent store had first occurred to him. At the time of the merger, Mr. Moore had two 5-and-10's in operation.

The inclusion of those two stores in the $65,000,000 merger could not have been much of an inducement to the investing public which was given an opportunity to invest in the stock of the new company,[8] but to Mr. Woolworth it meant a whole

[8] The company was capitalized at $65,000,000, consisting of $15,000,000 preferred stock, representing the value of the physical assets, and $50,000,000 of common stock, representing the value of the good will and future possibilities. See *Five and Ten, supra,* pp. 162 *et seq.*

lot. It meant that he had not forgotten his indebtedness to the man who had made the whole thing possible.

The amazing progress of the Woolworth company from 1912 to date, as revealed in Table 8, is actually only part of the story. It covers only the Woolworth operations in the United States, Canada, Cuba and Mexico. But Mr. Woolworth established a chain in England, also, and it, too, has been very successful.

TABLE 8

GROWTH OF F. W. WOOLWORTH CO. BY STORES AND SALES, 1911-1957

YEAR	STORES	SALES	YEAR	STORES	SALES
1911	596	$ 52,616,000	1935	1,980	$268,750,000
1912	631	60,558,000	1936	1,998	290,387,000
1913	684	66,228,000	1937	2,010	304,775,000
1914	737	69,620,000	1938	2,015	304,305,000
1915	805	75,996,000	1939	2,021	318,840,000
1916	920	87,089,000	1940	2,027	335,475,000
1917	1,000	98,103,000	1941	2,023	377,148,000
1918	1,039	107,179,000	1942	2,015	423,221,000
1919	1,081	119,496,000	1943	2,008	439,009,000
1920	1,111	140,919,000	1944	2,004	459,847,000
1921	1,137	147,655,000	1945	1,971	477,136,000
1922	1,176	167,319,000	1946	1,958	552,369,000
1923	1,260	193,447,000	1947	1,945	593,359,000
1924	1,356	215,501,000	1948	1,944	623,942,000
1925	1,423	239,033,000	1949	1,938	615,650,000
1926	1,480	253,645,000	1950	1,936	632,136,000
1927	1,581	272,754,000	1951	1,943	684,180,000
1928	1,725	287,319,000	1952	1,960	712,655,000
1929	1,825	303,047,000	1953	1,981	713,870,000
1930	1,881	289,289,000	1954	2,021	721,313,000
1931	1,903	282,670,000	1955	2,064	767,779,000
1932	1,932	249,893,000	1956	2,101	806,198,000
1933	1,941	250,517,000	1957	2,121	823,895,000
1934	1,957	270,685,000			

The British Woolworth Co.—F. W. Woolworth & Co. Ltd. —dates back to 1909, when Mr. Woolworth and some of his younger executives went over to England for the express purpose of starting a similar chain there. For their first store they selected a site in Liverpool, organized the British company, and within a very few months had the company well on its way towards duplicating the performance of the American company. Within a year, six stores were in operation. By the date of the American merger, the British company had 28 stores. They were known as "3d-and-6d" shops—three pence and six pence being the nearest equivalent to our nickels and dimes.

Progress from that time on was rapid and spectacular. In fact, the British proved themselves to be even more receptive to the lure of the 5-and-10-cent-store idea than Mr. Woolworth's own countrymen had been. Although the company has less than half as many stores as its American parent, opening its 1000th store in 1958 its net profits are not far behind those of the company here.

But even if Table 8 were expanded to reflect the operations of the Woolworth stores abroad, it still would not tell the full story of what Woolworth's success has meant to this country.

For the contribution the company has made has by no means been confined to Woolworth's own operations, extensive and important as they have been. On the contrary, it properly includes the development in this country of an entirely new type and kind of retailing—the variety store— which owes its existence to the example and inspiration provided by the pioneer.

What that means in terms of stores and sales is easily shown. For whereas the Woolworth stores in this country in 1954 numbered some 2,000, the entire variety store field, including independent as well as chain stores, comprised some 21,000. And whereas Woolworth's sales for that year totalled $721 million, the sales of the entire field totalled more than $3 billion.[9]

In economic terms, the variety-store field makes a tremendous contribution to the national welfare in many ways. It provides an outlet for many millions of dollars worth of items which would not be produced at all but for the facilities the variety stores provide for their distribution on a mass basis. It provides millions of jobs not only in distribution but in pro-

[9] U.S. Retail Census, 1954.

duction. It gives 12,000 individuals an opportunity to engage in a profitable business of their own, as proprietors of independent variety stores. It provides responsible and well-paid positions for thousands of chain-store executives and the managers of the individual stores. Finally, although incidentally, because of the income it produces in the shape of profits, salaries, wages and dividends, the variety-store field makes a substantial contribution to its silent partner, Uncle Sam, in the shape of Federal taxes.

But, in broader terms, perhaps the greatest virtue of the variety-store field lies in what it has added to the American standard of living. By making available a wide range of merchandise at popular prices it has stretched the consumer's dollar to the point where it has meant more things to more people—more *good* things for better living, culturally as well as materially.[10] The "5-and-10-cent store" has become such an accepted feature of American life that the special contribution it makes, social as well as economic, is apt to be overlooked.

Besides the variety-store chains and the grocery chains which were founded between 1859 and 1900 and which are still in operation, a score or more of chains in other fields can make the same boast.

In the drug field, for instance, at least 13 chains now operating in various parts of the country can trace their lineage back to a parent store established in the second half of the 19th century. Among the oldest are Schlegel Drug Stores, Davenport, Iowa, established in 1850, and Meyer Brothers Company, Fort Wayne, Ind., in 1852. T. P. Taylor & Co., Louisville, Ky., and Jacobs Pharmacy Co., Atlanta, were both founded in 1879—the year young Frank Woolworth got his

---

[10] In 1929, John Cotton Dana, director of the Newark Museum, staged an exhibit of five cases of items bought in Newark and New York variety stores at prices ranging from 10 cents to 50 cents to demonstrate that "beauty has no relation to price, rarity or age." Beauty of form, design or color in merchandise is no longer reserved for those who can afford to pay high prices, thanks to mass producers and mass distributors who long ago found out that beauty costs no more than ugliness. See *Chain Store Age*, General Merchandise Section, August, 1929, p. 55; Variety Stores Edition, April, 1949, p. 67.

first successful store under way. These embryo drug chains were joined by Read Drug & Chemical Co., Baltimore, in 1883; Marshall Drug Co., Cleveland, in 1884; Skillern's Drug Stores, Dallas, in 1885; Kinsel Drug Co., Detroit, in 1888; Cunningham Drug Stores, Detroit, in 1889; Bartell Drug Co., Seattle, in 1890; Owl Drug Co., San Francisco, in 1892; Eckerd Drug Stores, Erie, Pa., in 1898; and Standard Drug Stores, Cleveland, in 1899.

Several other small chains which were later to become a part of the Louis K. Liggett Co., organized in 1907, were likewise founded prior to 1900. They included the Jaynes Co., Boston; Hegeman Co., New York, which had four stores in 1900; and Wm. B. Riker Co., New York, which had two stores. They were later merged to become the Riker-Hegemen-Jaynes Co., which was acquired by the Liggett company in 1916.

But none of the drug chains of that era had made any conspicuous progress when it ended. Whether all the drug chains in existence in 1900 had as many as 75 stores in the aggregate is doubtful.

In the shoe field, the story is the same. Although two of the chains founded in this period were to become and remain the two biggest companies in their field, their progress during their early years was negligible. The Melville Shoe Corporation dates back to 1892, but although it operated 1,034 stores, as of May 1, 1958, most of them—796, to be exact—are accounted for by its chain of Thom McAn stores which was not established until 1922, at which time the company had only nineteen other stores in operation.

The G. R. Kinney Company, founded in 1894 by George Romanta Kinney in Waverly, N.Y., is now one of the largest shoe chains, in number of stores, with 411, but by 1920, when the company was 26 years old, it was operating only 75 stores.

The development of chains in the shoe field was eventually to carry them to the point where they accounted for nearly

50 per cent of all shoe-store sales (not 50 per cent of all shoe sales, as department stores and other stores sell shoes as well as shoe stores) but the situation in 1900 gave no such indication.

One of the oldest chains in the general-merchandise field which traces its origin back to the period under consideration is Belk Brothers, of Charlotte, N.C. It grew out of a 22x70 foot "racket store" [11] opened in 1888 by William Henry Belk in Monroe, N.C. It was operated by him and his brother, Dr. John Belk, for five years before a second unit was ventured, and expansion thereafter proceeded at a slow rate for many years. Thus, by the turn of the century, the brothers had only five stores in operation. Their progress thereafter was more rapid as appears from the fact that, with 22 stores in operation in 1920, they added 41 in the next decade, 115 more between 1930 and 1940, and another 107 between 1940 and 1950. As of March 10, 1958, they had 341 stores in operation.

A unique feature of the development of this chain was the fact that most of the stores were separately incorporated, with the ownership of the stock divided between the manager selected to operate it and the Belk family. That is why many of the stores have always been operated under hyphenated names, such as Belk-Hudson Company, organized in 1893, Gallant-Belk Company, organized in 1919, and Parks-Belk Company, organized in 1929. Many of these companies now have a number of units operating under their respective corporate names. The connecting link between them, besides the stock interest which the Belk family owns in each of them, is a centralized buying agency and operating service bureau which the company maintains for the benefit of all Belk stores although none is required to avail itself of the services offered.

[11] The "racket store" of the period in question was the forerunner of the variety store and general-merchandise store of today. The original Belk store was called the "New York Racket" in the hope that "everybody would think that sounded big." LeGette Blythe, *William Henry Belk, Merchant of the South* (University of North Carolina Press, Chapel Hill, 1951).

In the restaurant field, of the chains in existence today, John R. Thompson Co., of Chicago, dates back to 1891, and the Childs Co. to 1899. But neither of them became much of a factor in the areas in which they operated until many years later.

In the tobacco field, a retail cigar store in Syracuse, N.Y., opened in 1892 by George Whelan, a wholesale tobacconist, was to provide the background and the inspiration for what became one of the biggest and most important chains in the country—the United Cigar Stores Co. But Mr. Whelan had been running his retail store for eight years before the idea of developing a chain occurred to him. What happened then is related in a later chapter.[12]

Originating in this period and therefore deserving mention at this point because of the important part they were destined to play in the chain-store field although neither of them operated even a single retail store until after the post-war depression of 1921 are two Chicago companies. That seeming paradox is explained by the fact that the companies in question, Montgomery Ward & Co., hereafter referred to as Ward's, and Sears, Roebuck & Co., hereafter referred to as Sears, both started in life as mail-order houses and confined their retail activities to that type of distribution for more than 50 years in the one case and for nearly 40 years in the other before they decided that the time was ripe to operate retail stores as well.

Ward's was founded in 1872, Sears in 1886. The latter was destined to become the second largest retail organization in the world. Its sales for the year ending January 31, 1958, were $3.6 billion. Only A&P, with sales that year of $4.8 billion sold more. Ward's had sales of $1.2 billion. Although both Ward's and Sears still do a substantial volume by mail through their catalogs, most of their sales today are made over the counters of their retail stores, of which Ward's as of

[12] P. 101 *post.*

January 31, 1958 had 554 and Sears 724. The record of Ward's growth from 1926 to date is detailed in the appendix, page 379 *post*.

The astounding history of Sears, Roebuck & Co. is told in great detail in *Catalogues and Counters*, by Boris Emmet and John E. Jeuck, to which reference has already been made.[13] Suffice it to say here that it all started when Richard W. Sears, a railway station agent at North Redwood, Minn. got a shipper's permission to dispose of a box of watches which the consignee refused to accept. Sears undertook to sell the watches to his friends *by mail*. And when he found out how easy it was —largely because the small mark-up he required enabled him to offer the watches far below the regular retail price—he set himself up in the mail-order business, first in Minneapolis and later in Chicago. He was soon joined by Alvah C. Roebuck, who had had some experience in watch repairing which Sears figured might be useful.

Working together under various trade names until 1893, when the name Sears, Roebuck & Co. was adopted, the young firm had apparently made substantial progress, for its sales that year totalled $388,000. In 1895, when sales approached $800,000, Julius Rosenwald, a clothing merchant, joined the firm because "he recognized in the mail order methodology a pioneer effort towards mass distribution." [14] His influence on the company's subsequent success may be judged by the principles which he formulated and which became known as the "Rosenwald Creed." Its cardinal conclusions were:

(1) "Sell for less by buying for less. Buy for less through the instrumentality of mass buying and cash buying. *But maintain the quality*.

(2) "Sell for less by cutting the cost of sales. Reduce to the absolute practical minimum the expense of moving goods from producer to consumer. *But maintain the quality*.

(3) "Make less profit on each individual item and increase

[13] See p. 17 *supra*.
[14] Sears, Roebuck & Co., Annual Report for 1940.

your aggregate profit by selling more items. *But maintain the quality.*"

By the turn of the century, Sears' volume had reached $11,-000,000. In 1906, the company opened its first branch mail-order plant, in Dallas, and that year the company was rein-corporated with a capital of $40,000,000. Four years later, in 1910, the second branch plant was opened, in Seattle, and sales that year totalled $61,000,000. In 1920, they reached their peak, for that period, at $245,000,000. Incidentally, that year Woolworth was operating 1,111 stores, with aggregate sales of $141,000,000.

Then, in 1921, came the post-war crash and Sears' volume nose-dived to $160,000,000. In the years which followed that debacle, both Ward's and Sears apparently considered the possibility of opening retail stores to augment their mail-order sales. Particularly enthusiastic regarding such a move was Gen. Robert E. Wood, vice president in charge of merchandising for Ward's, and when, in 1924, he left Ward's to become a vice president of Sears, he carried his enthusiasm for retail stores with him. Sears decided to take the step, although they proceeded gingerly at first.

The first Sears store was opened February 2, 1925. Actually it was just a part of the Chicago mail-order plant converted into a department store. Three months later, the same course was taken in Seattle, and the other branch plants rapidly followed suit. The first retail outlet outside of a mail-order plant was opened in Evansville, Ind., on October 5, 1925. The year ended with eight stores in operation.

The growth of the retail operation by number of stores, store sales and ratio to total sales for each year from 1925 to 1941 inclusive is revealed in Table 9 compiled from data in *"Catalogues and Counters,"* to which reference has already been made.

Reference to the table in question discloses the remarkable fact that the chain of 378 stores which Sears developed in the short space of six years was able, in 1931, to outsell the

TABLE 9

SEARS, ROEBUCK STORES, 1925-1941

Year	Stores	Store Sales (000 omitted)	Ratio to Total Sales
1925	8	$ 11,819	4.5
1926	9	23,046	8.5
1927	27	40,001	13.6
1928	192	107,179	30.9
1929	319	174,623	39.6
1930	338	180,830	46.3
1931	378	185,339	53.4
1932	374	159,026	57.7
1933	400	167,860	58.2
1934	416	204,075	60.5
1935	428	243,291	58.6
1936	440	324,604	61.8
1937	473	366,285	64.4
1938	482	344,800	64.8
1939	520	435,406	66.6
1940	595	515,322	69.2
1941	617	662,394	68.4

far-flung mail-order set-up which had been in successful operation for more than 50 years! And from that time on, as more and more stores were added, the store operation accounted for an ever greater proportion of gross sales, even though the mail-order sales climbed too as retail volume generally improved after the depression years.

For several years after 1941, Sears was unable to build additional stores because of the ban on civilian construction during World War II. As a matter of fact the number of stores in operation in 1946 was only 610 compared with 618 in 1941.

As soon after the war as conditions permitted, however, Sears embarked on a policy of steady expansion which carried the number of its stores to 724 by the end of 1957—without including the 53 it had established in Latin-American countries or the 35 it had opened in Canada in conjunction with a Canadian chain. During this period, too, it expanded the number of its domestic catalog sales offices—from 338 in 1947 to 815 as of January 31, 1958.[15]

The substantial growth of the company since World War II, which is reflected in the following table, is a tribute to the vision and courage of Gen. Wood and his colleagues.

TABLE 10

GROWTH OF SEARS, ROEBUCK & CO.,
1941-1957

YEAR	STORES	CATALOG SALES OFFICES	TOTAL SALES (IN MILLIONS)
1941	618		$ 915
1942	599		868
1943	596		853
1944	606		989
1945	604		1,045
1946	610		1,613
1947	623	338	1,982
1948	628	341	2,296
1949	647	358	2,169
1950	654	404	2,556
1951	674	479	2,657
1952	684	546	2,932
1953	694	570	2,982
1954	699	609	2,965
1955	707	694	3,307
1956	717	772	3,556
1957	724	815	3,601

As a chain, Sears dates back only to 1925, but because its entry into the chain-store field was made possible by the success it had already achieved as a mail-order house, a line of business in which it had been engaged continuously since 1886, this brief historical sketch of the company's career may not be deemed out of place in a discussion of the 1859-1900 period.

So much for some of the pioneer companies which came into the picture prior to 1900 and which are still in operation

[15] Annual Report, March 31, 1958.

—many of them being the leaders in their respective fields.

The significant fact about the 1859-1900 period is that it saw the foundation laid for what was to become one of the most important features of our distribution set-up—the chain-store system—but that was all. The real development of the system did not begin until after the turn of the century.

CHAPTER III

THE MOVEMENT GAINS
MOMENTUM

How MANY chain stores in all were in operation at the turn of the century is not known. From the data available with respect to the larger companies then in existence, the total would probably not have exceeded 500. In any event, although the two biggest companies, A&P and Woolworth, may have begun to attract some attention individually as enterprising and progressive concerns, the chains as a group were certainly too insignificant a factor to have rated notice as a new type of operation which might bear watching.

But if a census had been taken ten years later, it would have reflected a more significant situation. For the first decade of the century saw the birth of a number of new companies which were destined to become outstanding chains in their respective fields. More directly to our present point, some of them, by reason of original and aggressive merchandising policies, attracted more attention right from the start than those which had been established many years earlier.

That was particularly true of United Cigar Stores Co., whose new type of cigar store spelled the doom of the old model which had prevailed up to that time.[1] It was also true of the new chains in the drug field who found it necessary not only to join the ranks of the cut-rate stores then in existence but to take the lead in merchandising standard products aggressively. For only in that way could they drive home to the consumer that they could and would pass on to their cus-

[1] See p. 101, *post*.

tomers the benefit of large-scale retailing.[2] To the extent that such aggressive merchandising policies achieved their purpose, the chains made their presence felt quickly not only by the public but by their competitors.

A list of some of the chains which came into the picture between 1900 and 1910 and which went on to become important factors in their respective fields is presented in Table 11.

In the next decade, 1910 to 1920, so many new chains came into the picture that to list them all would serve no useful purpose. In addition, the chains already in existence were expanding at a far more rapid rate than in their earlier years.

It was in this period, it will be recalled, that the A&P started its "economy store" program and, within six months after Mr. Hartford was convinced that he was on the right track, the company started adding stores just as fast as it was physically possible to open them. The 500th store was opened in 1913. By April 3, 1915, the company had 1,670. In the next two years, no less than 1,600 stores were added. Sales jumped from $31,000,000 in 1914 to $76,000,000 in 1916. By the beginning of 1920, A&P was operating 4,200 stores.

A&P's example could not escape the notice of the many other grocery chains which were then in operation in all areas of the country. How far some of the others had progressed is indicated by the fact that when five of them, all in the Philadelphia area, merged in 1917 to become the American Stores Co. they were operating in the aggregate 1,223 stores, and became the second largest grocery chain at that time. The Acme Tea Co., the largest of the group, had 433 stores; Childs Grocery Co. 268; The Bell Co. 214; Robinson & Crawford 186; and George N. Dunlap Co. 122.

In the variety-store field, Woolworth opened no less than 480 stores between 1912 and 1920, jumping from 631 to 1,111; Kresge added 99 stores in the same period; Grant, which had started in 1906, had four stores in 1910 and 33 by 1920;

[2] See p. 104, post.

TABLE 11

SOME CHAINS FOUNDED BETWEEN 1900 AND 1910

1900

D. Pender Grocery Co., Norfolk (now Colonial Stores, Inc.).
Hook Drugs, Indianapolis.
Daniel Reeves (grocery), New York, later acquired by Safeway.
Dockum Drug Stores, Wichita, Kans.

1901

United Cigar Stores Co., New York.
F. & W. Grand-Silver (variety), New York, now H. L. Green Co.
Lane Bryant (apparel), New York.
A. L. Duckwall Stores Co. (variety), Abilene, Kans.
Walgreen Co. (drug), Chicago.
J. Weingarten, Inc., (grocery) Houston, Tex.

1902

J. C. Penney Co. (apparel), New York.
Schultz Bros. (variety), Chicago.

1903

Morris Stores (variety), Bluffton, Ind. Now owned by the G. C.
   Murphy Co.

1905

Peoples Drug Stores, Washington, D.C.

1906

W. T. Grant Co. (variety), New York.

1907

Louis K. Liggett Co. (drug), New York.
Mading's Drug Stores, Houston, Tex.
Fisher Brothers Co. (grocery), Cleveland.

1908

A. S. Beck Shoe Corporation, New York.
Katz & Besthoff (drug), New Orleans.

1909

Western Auto Supply Co., Kansas City, Mo.
Gallaher Drug Co., Dayton, Ohio.
Hested Stores (variety), Fairbury, Nebr.

Murphy jumped from ten in 1910 to 51 in 1920; Kress, which had started the century with eleven stores, had 84 by 1910 and 145 by 1920; and McCrory, which had twenty stores in 1901, had 60 by 1910, and 156 by 1920.

A quick run-down of the status of some of the other chains in 1920 will be sufficient to indicate that, by that time, the shape of what was to come was becoming definitely discernible.

In the grocery field, Kroger had 799 stores; the predecessors of First National, 803; Daniel Reeves, 202; Southern Grocery, 119; National Tea, 163; and Bohack, 152.

In the shoe field, Melville had only twenty stores, but Kinney had 75.

In the drug field, Louis K. Liggett Co., which in 1916 had acquired the 106 stores operated by the Riker-Hegeman-Jaynes chain, was nearing the 200 mark; Walgreen's, which had not actually become a chain until 1909 when the second store was opened, now had 23; and People's Drug, organized in 1905, had eight stores in operation.

In the restaurant field, J. R. Thompson had 104 units; Childs 88; Waldorf System 79; and F. G. Shattuck, later to be known as Schrafft's, an even dozen.

Perhaps the most spectacular development of all had been that of the United Cigar Stores Co., which by 1920 had 1,096 stores. Schulte, another cigar-store chain, was second with 196.

How many stores in the aggregate all the chains had in operation in 1920 is not definitely known. It has been estimated by John P. Nichols[3] that, whereas in 1914 the total number of stores was 8,000, the number in 1920 was 27,000. The Federal Trade Commission put the figure at 50,000!

The probability is that the actual figure was somewhere between these two estimates, but the exact number is not of great significance. For what happened between 1920 and 1925 has a more direct bearing on subsequent chain-store

[3] *The Chain Store Tells Its Story, op. cit.*

history than anything that preceded those active chain-store years.

In the absence of an official census to record the full expansion of the chains during the five-year period in question, what happened in the case of twenty leading chains, whose statistics are available, will have to suffice. Table 12 and Chart

TABLE 12

GROWTH OF 20 LEADING CHAINS
BY NUMBER OF STORES
1920-1949

GROCERY CHAINS	1920	1925	1930	1949
A & P	4,544	14,034	15,737	4,820
American	1,223	1,792	2,728	1,671
First Nat'l*	803	1,642	2,548	1,083
Kroger	799	2,559	5,165	2,190
Safeway	191	1,050	2,675	2,202
National Tea	163	761	1,600	655
	7,723	21,838	30,453	12,621
VARIETY STORE CHAINS				
Woolworth	1,111	1,420	1,881	1,938
Kresge	184	306	678	702
Kress	145	166	212	256
McCrory	156	181	242	201
Murphy	53	88	166	218
McLellan	43	94	277	230
Grant	38	77	350	480
Newberry	17	86	335	482
Neisner	4	13	75	121
	1,751	2,431	4,216	4,628
APPAREL CHAIN				
J. C. Penney	312	676	1,452	1,607
SHOE CHAINS				
Kinney	75	250	366	305
Melville	20	148	480	561
	95	398	846	866
DRUG CHAINS				
Walgreen	23	87	440	414
Peoples	8	18	117	141
	31	105	557	555
TOTAL (20 CHAINS)	9,912	25,448	37,524	20,277

* Predecessor companies for 1920 and 1925.

II tell their own story, showing that the twenty chains which had 9,912 stores in operation in 1920 had 25,448 only five years later! And that scale of expansion, of course, was on top of what had been becoming more and more apparent in the years immediately preceding 1920.

Keeping in mind that Table 12 presents only a partial list of the chains then in existence, even though it does include most of the bigger ones, and that hundreds of other chains all over the country were also expanding during that period, some

CHART II

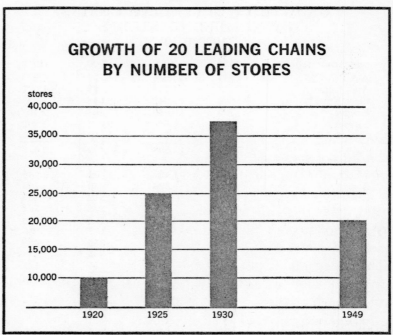

GROWTH OF 20 LEADING CHAINS
BY NUMBER OF STORES

idea is provided of the impact of this phenomenon on other types of retailing. To aggravate the situation was the fact that the majority of the new chain stores were opened in areas in which the chains were already established.

Little wonder that the chains' competitors, particularly the smaller ones, began to ask how long it would be before they would be crowded out of the picture entirely.

And some of them went further. They decided that "there ought to be a law" against further chain-store expansion and, as is pointed out in detail in later chapters, they had little trouble in finding politicians and others to champion their cause.

But despite this growing hostility, Table 13 shows that the

TABLE 13

STORES ADDED BY 20 CHAINS,
1920-1925 vs. 1925-1930

Field	1920-1925	1925-1930	Change
Grocery (6)	14,115	8,615	−5,500
Variety (9)	680	1,785	+1,105
Apparel (1)	364	776	+412
Shoe (2)	303	448	+145
Drug (2)	74	452	+378
	15,536	12,076	−3,460

chains which expanded so spectacularly between 1920 and 1925 did not stop then. On the contrary, in the next five-year period, they added another 12,000 stores. Although that was less than the 15,536 stores added in the preceding five-year period, an analysis of the Table will show that the only let-up was in the grocery field, in which only 8,615 stores were added compared with 14,115 in the preceding period.

The expansion of the chains in the other fields made up in part for the slow-up in the grocery field. That is revealed in Table 13, which gives the number of stores added in each of the two periods by each of five fields covered.

Undoubtedly the fact that the grocery chains were not expanding as rapidly between 1925 and 1930 as they had been in the preceding five-year period would have been less perceptible than the substantial strides the chains in the other fields continued to make, particularly as the grocery chains continued to grow even though not at such a rapid rate.

But the significant fact about the chain-store movement is that despite all the indications that it would continue indefinitely, actually it did nothing of the kind. Although, in the decade from 1920 to 1930, the chains listed in Table 13 added no less than 27,612 stores to the 9,912 they had had in operation at the start of it, a gain of nearly 280 per cent, the era of all-out expansion came to an end in 1930. How precipitate the drop was is revealed in Chart II.

Having reached a peak of 37,524 stores in 1930, the number of stores operated by the twenty leading chains in question started steadily to decline until, in 1949, the total was only 20,047, or 17,477 fewer. True enough, this 41 per cent decline is accounted for entirely by what happened in the grocery field alone, where, as has been pointed out already,[4] the introduction of the supermarket brought about the elimination of most of the smaller stores formerly operated. But even when that controlling factor is eliminated, the significant fact remains that the other fourteen chains listed added only 728 stores between 1930 and 1949, a span of nineteen years, compared with the 4,794 in the ten years preceding 1930. The rate of expansion dropped from an average of 479 stores a year to 38!

What brought about the decline in the number of grocery stores has been explained, but why did the chains in the other fields stop expanding, except to a negligible extent, after 1930?

Several factors were involved.

In the first place, after the rapid pace they had set for themselves in those hectic years preceding 1930, most of the companies needed a breathing spell—a chance to consolidate their gains. The larger scale of operations called for major organization changes in some cases. To open additional stores was easier than to develop men to direct and manage them.

In the second place, more stores meant not only more trained men to operate them but more capital to finance them. The collapse of the stock market in 1929 plus the onset of the depression naturally dried up many of the sources of investment capital and put a damper on further investment for the time being.

[4] See pp. 29-32, *supra*.

Thirdly, by the time the depression had worked itself out and the chains might have been ready and tempted to resume expansion on a moderate scale, along came Pearl Harbor and World War II. The resulting shortages of manpower and merchandise created operating problems for the chains which additional stores would only have magnified. In any event, wartime bans on civilian construction would have prevented the chains from expanding during this period even if they could have manned and stocked additional stores.

Finally, the trend toward bigger stores which brought the supermarket into the grocery field had also made itself felt in other fields of retailing. Bigger drug stores, bigger variety stores, bigger apparel stores, and bigger stores in various other fields made the chains less dependent on additional stores for the additional volume from which, in retailing, "all blessings flow." Table 14, showing the average sales per store for leading chains in 1950 and 1957 compared with what they were in 1930, reflects the effect of the trend in question. Although the increase in dollar sales per store resulted in part from the rise in prices, the main reason for it was that the chain stores of 1950 were typically two to five times as big as those of 1930 and those of today are even bigger.[5]

To keep in step with the trend, the chains directed their attention principally to their existing stores. To bring them up to the new standards as rapidly as possible became the main objective. Where existing locations permitted enlargement and modernization, the chains followed that course. As soon as the restrictions on civilian construction were lifted after World War II, the chains proceeded to modernize their stores as fast as they could. But where existing locations were

[5] Walgreen's first "super-drug" store was opened in Tampa, Fla., in October, 1934. The company described it as "a revolutionary new kind of drug store which not only provided the space for additional lines but took merchandise out of the traditional show-cases and presented it instead on open display counters where customers could see it, touch it and buy it. The success of this new type of drug store sounded the knell of the old-fashioned kind of 'small corner drug store.'" The company opened a gigantic store in Miami in 1937 and another in New Orleans in 1938. In October, 1949, the company opened Chicago's biggest drug store, at State and Madison Streets, with 30,000 square feet on two floors.

TABLE 14

AVERAGE ANNUAL SALES PER STORE, 27 CHAINS, 1930, 1950 AND 1957

$ Thousands

	1930	1950	1957		1930	1950	1957
GROCERY CHAINS				VARIETY STORE CHAINS			
A&P (1)	$ 68	$680	$1,100				
Safeway	82	568	1,000	Woolworth	$154	$327	$389
Kroger	50	419	1,170	Kresge	222	424	540
American	52	312	930	Kress	327	624	607
First National	42	380	907	Grant	236	522	585
National Tea	53	497	770	McLellan	87	245	267
Colonial (2)	35	487	960	McCrory	179	481	517
Bohack	49	370	750	Murphy (3)	105	687	690
				Neisner	220	474	470
APPAREL CHAIN				Green (4)	159	459	514
J. C. Penney	133	589	770	Newberry	90	302	447
SHOE CHAINS				MISCELLANEOUS CHAINS			
Melville	60	125	120				
Kinney	44	118	147*	Western Auto	136	308	254
				J. R. Thompson	120	215	437
DRUG CHAINS				Shattuck			
Walgreen (1)	93	399	500	(Schrafft's)	630	835	1,000
Peoples	143	332	394	Waldorf System	106	196	203

(1) 1950 and 1957 estimated.
(2) 1930 refers to predecessor companies.
(3) 1957 reflects effect of smaller stores acquired in 1952.
(4) Covers 1933, 1950 and 1957.
  * 1955.

too small to permit the kind of enlargement called for, re-location became necessary. While this policy gave the chains many *new* stores, it did not add to the number in operation.

One incidental result of this trend to bigger stores was that the number of stores a chain was operating lost much of its significance as an index of its growth. With one new unit doing as much business as ten smaller ones, most of the chains have been showing substantial sales increases from year to year even though the number of their stores may have been consistently declining. Reference to the data presented in the Appendix (p. 361 *et seq.*) shows this quite clearly.

Because of this a number of chains seem to feel that a better index of their growth is provided today by the total number of square feet their stores occupy, and in recent years their annual reports have been giving such information as well as the number of stores operated. The soundness of this course is indicated by the fact that whereas Jewel Tea Co. reported 160 stores with a total of 1,057,469 square feet of floor space in 1952, in 1956, with 184 stores, the floor space had increased to 1,635,046 square feet. The net increase in stores was 24, or 15%, but the increase in floor space was 54%! It was significantly reflected in a corresponding 50% increase in sales during the period in question.

To what extent was chain-store expansion checked by the wave of anti-chain agitation which developed in the 1920s and brought with it special chain-store taxes graduated in severity according to the number of stores operated?

That is a natural question. Certainly the purpose of such taxes was to produce the result which actually occurred. Chain-store expansion did slow up almost to a stop. But that chain-store taxes had much to do with it may well be doubted, for several reasons:

1. The factors already listed were sufficient in themselves to account for the result in question.

2. Although the purpose of such taxes was to impose an additional burden on chains heavy enough to discourage the addition of new stores, actually the top tax imposed, $750 per store in Texas, was hardly serious enough to have had that effect—except in the case of extremely small-volume units, such as filling stations.[6] Certainly the trend toward bigger stores tended to make a tax of that kind increasingly negligible.

3. The states which imposed such taxes showed no greater decline in the number of chain stores than those in which such taxes have never been imposed.[7]

4. The trend toward fewer but bigger stores in the chain grocery field has been attributed by some to the effect of

[6] See p. 139, *post.*
[7] Willard L. Thorp, "Economic Planning via Chain-Store Taxes," *Dun's Review,* August, 1937.

chain-store taxes. Actually it reflected a change in grocery merchandising in which the question of chain-store taxes played no part.[8] The supermarket idea was introduced not by the chains but by the independents. The chains adopted it because it was a good idea, and experience has demonstrated the wisdom of their move.

That the agitation against chain stores might have had a greater deterrent effect on chain-store expansion policies than the weight of the taxes actually imposed is, of course, true. Such a conclusion, however, would rest only on surmise. It is negatived in too many cases to have much weight. From a public-relations standpoint, the hostility to "big business" in certain quarters might give any really big company something to think about before embarking on any major expansion program, but relatively few chains are big enough to have to take that factor into consideration.

The most reasonable conclusion seems to be, therefore, that the tremendous momentum the chain-store movement developed between 1920 and 1930 carried it to a point at which a levelling-off process was natural if not inevitable. The chains went no further because, whether they knew it or not, they had actually arrived at their destination. Although their sales were to expand more than twofold between 1930 and 1950, the share of the market they had gained for themselves by 1929 was not materially changed thereafter. That, at least, is the clear indication of the U.S. Census figures for 1929, 1939, 1948 and 1954.

Because these official figures provide the only objective measurement of what chain stores have come to mean to America, a separate chapter is devoted to them.

[8] See pp. 29-32, *supra*.

CHAPTER IV

WHAT THE RETAIL
CENSUS SHOWS

THE FIRST COUNTING of retail noses on an all-out basis was undertaken in 1930 by the U.S. Department of Commerce, Bureau of the Census. It covered the year 1929. It was known as the Census of Distribution.

Similar enumerations were made later by the Bureau for the years 1933, 1935, 1939, 1948 and 1954.

Before summarizing any of the findings, one important point must be made. As each successive Census was taken, certain changes in classification were deemed desirable. To make the current results comparable with previous ones, adjustments and revisions of previous enumerations were necessary. The result was inevitable discrepancies between the figures originally obtained and given out at the time the Census was made and the figures for that year as they appeared in a subsequent Census for purposes of comparison.

By way of illustration, when the results of the 1929 Census were first released they showed total retail sales of $50,033,-850,792 rung up on the cash registers of 1,549,168 retail stores. But, lo and behold, when the 1939 Census came out, for comparability's sake, the figures for 1929 were revised as follows: Total sales $48,329,652,000; total number of stores: 1,476,365.[1]

A footnote explains the discrepancy as follows:

"Previously published totals for 1929 and 1935 revised to exclude data for service garages and other automotive busi-

[1] U.S. Census of Business, 1939, Vol. 1, Retail Trade, Part 1, p. x.

ness whose receipts from service sales exceed their sales of merchandise. These are included in the Census of Service Establishments for 1939."

Although such revisions are obviously inescapable unless the original classifications are to be frozen forever, the use of Census figures is unsafe unless these periodic changes are kept in mind and due allowance is made for them.

Particularly important is it to note in this connection that the 1954 Census is not comparable with the 1948 Census not only because it was compiled in a different way but because it used a different base. For our present purpose, the different base is the more significant difference. The scope of the 1954 Census was narrower. Whereas the 1948 Census included all retailers with annual sales of $500 or more, the 1954 Census was confined to those with annual sales of at least $2,500.

The obvious result was to throw out of the 1954 count many thousands of small retailers who would have been included if the 1948 base had been retained. One unfortunate effect was to show a decline in the number of retailers between 1948 and 1954, whereas if the same base had been used, 1954 would have shown an increase!

Because of the erroneous conclusions which would arise from a direct comparison of the 1954 Census with the 1948 Census without making allowances for the change in base, the Census Bureau provided a *revised version* of the 1948 data to make it as comparable as possible. This revision reduces the 1948 total from 1,771,317 stores to 1,668,479. Comparing that figure with 1954's 1,721,650, we have an increase of 53,171 stores in 1954 instead of a decrease of 49,667. This does not mean, of course, that the original 1948 figure was erroneous but merely that it took in more territory than the 1954 compilation.

Unfortunately, the effort of the Census Bureau to avert misinterpretation of the 1954 Census was ineffective. Direct comparison between it and the preceding Census led many to the conclusion that the number of retailers had decreased substantially during the six-year period which separated them.[2] Lest others make the same mistake in referring to the data shown in Table 15, the appropriate warning can hardly be repeated too often: *The 1954 Census is not comparable with those which preceded it!*

Another important observation to make, before proceeding with a summary of the Census figures relating to the chain-store picture, concerns the Bureau's definition of a chain store. It naturally had to define the term before it could tell how many chain stores were in operation.

Whether or not the definition should be broad enough to include every merchant who operates more than one store was the first hurdle to be taken. On the one hand, the claim could be made that because the man who operates two stores has overstepped the boundaries of single-store operation he is at least an embryo chain. That is the viewpoint the author has always taken and which is reflected in the foregoing pages. That was the position the courts took, too, when the question came up in connection with a tax on "chain stores" which applied to chains "with two stores or more." As is related later on, the law was declared constitutional because of the "real and substantial difference" between merchants with "two or more stores" and those with only one.

On the other hand, the Census Bureau felt that because many two-store and three-store operations lack certain characteristics typical of chain stores, they should *all* be excluded from the chain-store category.

To meet the situation, the Bureau decided to break down all retail stores into three main classes: (1) independents; (2) two-and-three-store multiunits; and (3) chain stores.

Thus originated the conception that a minimum of four stores was needed to make a chain—a conception which has undoubtedly had the effect of understating the scope of the chain-store field from the standpoint of both the number of

[2] *Chain Store Age*, Administration Edition, March, 1957, p. 58; Grocery Edition, December, 1956, p. 35.

stores they operate and their relative share of the total retail business.

This effect has not gone unnoticed by students of distribution. Thus, Theodore N. Beckman and Herman C. Nolen, in their book "The Chain Store Problem," published in 1938, took emphatic exception to what they term the "artificially concocted definition of chains," [3] used by the Census Bureau. They complained that as a result of that definition "the importance of chain stores is grossly understated."

To illustrate their point, they note that whereas, according to the 1929 Census (as subsequently revised) chain stores then numbered only 148,037, the number would have been 212,620 if the two-and-three-store multiunits had been included. Furthermore, whereas chain-store sales in 1929 were given as $9.8 billions, or 20 per cent of all retail sales, they were actually $14.1 billions, or 29.7 per cent of total sales, if the sales of the two-and-three-store units are included.

Nevertheless, the Census Bureau stuck to its original definition in all subsequent compilations until the 1948 Census was undertaken.

Then it decided to abandon the use of the terms "chain" and "chain store" altogether. Instead, the term "multiunit" was adopted to cover not only the stores of firms with two or three, which had previously been grouped separately, or included with independents, but also those of firms with four or more, which the Bureau had previously designated as chain stores.

To make the 1948 statistics comparable with previous Census data, multiunits with four or more stores were separated from those with only two or three and could, therefore, be compared with what were formerly designated as chain stores. The same plan was followed in compiling the 1954 Census. But by reason of this long-deferred revision in nomenclature, each of us must now define a chain according to his own lights. The Bureau of the Census can no longer be

[3] *The Chain Store Problem* (New York: McGraw-Hill Book Co., 1938), p. 23.

cited as an authority for the present size or importance of the chain-store field, *as such,* or for anything else relating to chain stores, *as such*, for it no longer designates any type of operation by that name.

With the foregoing observations in mind, the Census figures for the years 1929, 1939, 1948 and 1954, as revised for purposes of comparison and as presented in Table 15, may now be considered.

The 1929 Census is particularly interesting not only because it was the first complete count of chain stores ever undertaken but because, having covered the year 1929, it reflects the status of the chains at the peak of the expansion program which marked the 1920-1930 period, as was brought out in the preceding chapter.

What did this Census show? It showed that we then had 1,476,365 retail stores of all kinds in operation and that 159,-638 or 10.8 per cent of them, were chain stores—using that term to denote stores owned and operated by organizations of all types with four or more retail outlets.

Total retail sales that year were $48,329 millions, of which the chain stores accounted for $10,740 millions, or 22.2 per cent.

The fact that the chains accounted for less than 11 per cent of all retail stores, despite their expansion, and for only 22 per cent of the total retail volume, may be somewhat surprising, but that is because the over-all figures fail to tell the real story.

For as was pointed out earlier,[4] the chains have always been a more important factor in some fields than in others. In such fields as variety stores, for instance, in which, of course, the chains were the pioneers, they accounted for 90 per cent of the total sales in 1929; in the shoe field for 45.7 per cent of shoe store sales, in the grocery field for 39 per cent; and in several other fields they likewise exceeded the over-all ratio of 22 per cent.

[4] See p. 7 *supra.*

By contrast, as Table 15 reveals, the chains accounted for considerably less than 22 per cent of the total retail volume in a number of other fields, and indeed, in many retail fields, the chains did not figure at all. Thus, the fact that their share of all retail sales was only 22 per cent obscures their more important status in the fields in which they were particularly active.

Certainly the overall picture gave no comfort to the independent grocer. What concerned him, of course, was what had happened and what seemed to be happening in his own field. What the 1929 Census revealed to him was that the chains, with only 17% of the stores, already accounted for 39% of the sales. At the rate they had been expanding, how long would it be before the independent would be crowded out altogether? He could not know then what the subsequent Census figures were to make quite clear—that by 1930 the chains had gone about as far as they were destined to go—for the next 25 years at any rate.

What actually happened between 1929 and 1948 is revealed in Table 15. The data for 1954 is likewise included in the Table, but, for reasons which have already been given, it is not strictly comparable with that of the earlier Censuses.

So far as the whole retail field is concerned, Table 15 shows that the competitive position of the chains remained practically unchanged from 1929 to 1948. In 1929, the chains accounted for 22.2% of total sales and, in 1948, for 22.8%. The 1954 figure of 23.7% is obviously higher than it would have been if the 1954 Census had been compiled on the same basis as those which preceded it.

In the grocery field, a substantial decline in the number of stores operated by the chains between 1929 and 1954 reflects, of course, the trend toward bigger but fewer stores to which reference has already been made. The chains' share of total food store sales showed a slight decline between 1929 and 1948, but it was more than made up by 1954, even though the 43.3% figure is somewhat higher than the actual percentage which would have been shown but for the changes made in compiling the 1954 Census.

That the variety store chains accounted for a somewhat smaller share of the total market in 1954 than they did in 1929 is apparent from the Table. Although they increased the number of their stores 40% and their sales 200% during the period, the number of independent stores grew at an even greater rate, from 6,663 to 12,294, a gain of 84%. This increase in number of stores increased the independents' share of the market from 10.4% in 1929 to 20.4% in 1954.

In the shoe field, Table 15 discloses that despite a substantial gain in the relative number of stores operated between 1929 and 1954, the chains did no more than maintain the ratio of sales they had enjoyed in the earlier year.

The drug chains accounted for 18.5% of the total retail drug trade in 1929, according to the Census data, and showed but a slight gain for 1954—to 19.9%. The accuracy of the 1954 figure has been seriously questioned, however, and, if the challenge was well-founded, the drug chains with four or more stores operated 4,497 stores in 1954 and had sales of $1,321 million, or 25.2% of the total.[5]

In the department store field, Table 15 shows a major change in the status of the chains, accounting as they did for 65.6% of the sales in 1954 compared with only 15.3% in 1929. This substantial gain undoubtedly reflects the trend towards bigger stores—a trend which the department store chains were naturally in a better position to follow than traditional department stores whose operations were confined to a single location. In the case of the chains, with larger units constantly replacing smaller ones, additional volume was attained even without an increase in the number of stores operated. What happened in this category lends confirmation to the observation made earlier regarding the limitations of single-store operation.[6]

[5] *Chain Store Age,* Drug Edition, November, 1956.
[6] See page 10, *supra.*

TABLE 15

RETAIL CENSUS, 1929, 1939, 1948 AND 1954

Source: U.S. Department of Commerce, Bureau of the Census

KIND OF BUSINESS	YEAR	NUMBER OF STORES			SALES (MILLIONS)		
		TOTAL	CHAIN*	%	TOTAL	CHAIN	%
ALL KINDS	1929	1,476,365	159,638	10.8	$ 48,329	$ 10,740	22.2
	1939	1,770,355	132,763	7.5	42,041	10,105	24.0
	1948	1,769,540	105,109	5.9	130,520	29,736	22.8
	1954	1,721,650	105,139	6.1	169,968	40,297	23.7
FOOD GROUP	1929	481,891	61,416	12.7	10,837	3,514	32.4
	1939	560,549	51,110	9.1	10,165	3,409	33.5
	1948	504,439	32,574	6.5	30,966	10,493	33.9
	1954	384,616	25,212	6.5	39,762	15,478	38.8
Grocery Stores (With and without meat)	1929	307,425	53,466	17.4	7,353	2,873	39.1
	1939	387,337	40,159	10.4	7,722	2,841	36.8
	1948	377,939	25,047	6.6	24,770	9,319	37.6
	1954	279,440	19,076	6.8	34,421	14,918	43.3
Meat Markets and Fish Markets	1929	49,865	2,804	5.6	1,337	141	10.5
	1939	42,360	1,605	3.8	750	78	10.4
	1948	29,465	724	2.5	1,776	128	7.2
	1954	27,354	708	2.5	2,128	144	6.7
Dairy Products and Milk Dealers	1929	8,478	1,201	14.2	727	336	46.2
	1939	16,834	3,308	19.7	740	323	43.6
	1948	11,727	1,799	15.3	1,887	622	33.0
	1954						
Candy, Nut and Confectionery Stores	1929	63,265	1,461	2.3	572	54	9.4
	1939	48,015	2,225	4.6	295	51	17.3
	1948	32,876	3,051	9.3	649	187	28.8
	1954	20,507	1,954	9.5	568	127	22.3
Fruit Stores and Vegetable Markets	1929	22,904	383	1.7	308	15	4.9
	1939	27,666	453	1.6	222	17	7.7
	1948	15,763	177	1.1	399	17	4.3
	1954	13,136	134	1.0	485	15	3.1
All Other	1929	29,954	2,101	7.0	540	95	17.6
	1939	38,337	3,030	7.9	435	99	22.8
	1948	36,669	1,776	4.8	1,485	220	14.9
	1954	40,943	1,898	4.6	2,094	143	6.8

* Only stores operated by companies with four or more are included in the chain store category in this table. See page 62 for comment on 1954 data.

TABLE 15 (Continued)

RETAIL CENSUS

KIND OF BUSINESS	YEAR	NUMBER OF STORES			SALES (MILLIONS)		
		TOTAL	CHAIN*	%	TOTAL	CHAIN	%
DRUG STORES	1929	58,258	3,513	6.0	$ 1,690	$ 312	18.5
	1939	57,903	3,928	6.8	1,563	379	24.2
	1948	55,796	3,715	6.7	4,013	869	21.6
	1954	56,009	3,470[1]	6.2	5,252	1,044	19.9
GENERAL MERCHANDISE GROUP	1929	54,636	12,029	22.0	6,444	2,163	33.6
	1939	50,267	11,785	23.4	5,665	2,643	46.7
	1948	52,544	12,727	24.2	15,975	8,751	54.8
	1954	76,198	13,199	17.3	17,872	10,637	59.4
Department Stores	1929	4,221	2,560	60.6	4,350	665	15.3
	1939	4,074	2,672	65.5	3,975	1,195	30.0
	1948	2,580	1,565	60.7	10,645	5,523	51.9
	1954	2,761	1,856	67.2	10,558	6,956	65.6
Dry Goods and General Merchandise Stores	1929	38,305	3,932	10.3	1,190	688	57.8
	1939	29,247	1,578	5.4	713	99	13.9
	1948	29,754	3,744	12.6	2,824	1,151	40.8
	1954	51,814	3,720	7.2	4,233	1,237	29.4
Variety Stores	1929	12,110	5,447	45.0	904	810	89.6
	1939	16,946	6,390	37.7	977	850	87.0
	1948	20,210	7,418	36.7	2,507	2,077	82.9
	1954	20,917	7,623	36.4	3,067	2,444	79.6
EATING AND DRINKING PLACE GROUP	1929	134,293	3,392	2.5	2,125	299	14.1
	1939	305,386	5,222	1.7	3,520	298	8.5
	1948	346,556	6,133	1.8	10,683	742	7.0
	1954	319,657	7,521	2.3	13,101	992	7.6
Eating Places	1929	134,293	3,392	2.5	2,125	299	14.1
	1939	169,792	5,058	3.0	2,135	292	13.7
	1948	194,123	5,824	3.0	6,468	718	11.1
	1954	169,867	7,251	4.2	8,096	969	11.9
Drinking Places	1929	—	—	—	—	—	—
	1939	135,594	164	0.1	1,385	6	0.4
	1948	152,433	309	0.2	4,215	24	0.6
	1954	123,887	270	0.2	4,360	23	0.5
APPAREL GROUP	1929	114,296	17,218	15.1	4,241	1,197	28.2
	1939	106,959	17,591	16.4	3,259	1,001	30.7
	1948	115,246	14,515	12.6	9,803	2,729	27.8
	1954	119,743	19,881	16.5	11,078	3,197	28.8

* See footnote on first page of this table.
[1] See page 67, *supra*.

TABLE 15 (Continued)

RETAIL CENSUS

KIND OF BUSINESS	YEAR	NUMBER OF STORES			SALES (MILLIONS)		
		TOTAL	CHAIN*	%	TOTAL	CHAIN	%
Men's and Boys' Clothing, Hat, etc., Stores	1929	28,197	3,054	10.8	$ 1,193	$ 271	22.7
	1939	21,501	1,798	8.4	773	171	22.1
	1948	23,730	1,663	7.0	2,166	360	16.6
	1954	19,247			2,299		
Women's Ready-to-Wear Stores	1929	18,253	2,132	11.7	1,088	292	26.8
	1939	25,820	3,242	12.6	1,009	291	28.8
	1948	30,677	3,747	12.2	3,305	966	29.2
	1954	45,213	8,220	18.2	4,333	1,327	30.8
Shoe Stores (All Kinds)	1929	24,259	6,099	25.1	807	369	45.7
	1939	20,487	5,721	27.8	617	306	49.7
	1948	19,551	5,417	27.7	1,467	697	47.5
	1954	23,847	7,625	31.7	1,895	878	45.9
Family Clothing, Accessories and All Other Stores	1929	43,587	5,933	13.6	1,154	265	23.0
	1939	39,151	5,717	14.6	859	195	22.7
	1948	41,288	3,697	9.0	2,865	704	24.6
	1954	25,012			2,416		
FURNITURE, HOUSE FURNISHINGS, AND APPLIANCES GROUP	1929	58,941	6,796	11.5	2,755	560	20.3
	1939	52,827	6,918	13.1	1,733	393	22.7
	1948	85,585	6,031	7.1	6,914	1,027	14.9
	1954	91,797	5,576	6.1	8,619	1,131	13.1
Furniture Stores	1929	25,153	922	3.9	1,510	208	13.8
	1939	19,902	779	3.9	973	141	14.5
	1948	29,031	1,051	3.6	3,427	399	11.6
	1954	50,729	1,399	2.7	5,374	572	10.6
Other Home Furnishings Stores	1929	8,820	468	5.3	303	47	15.5
	1939	12,012	444	3.7	227	47	20.7
	1948	19,623	575	2.9	944	164	17.4
	1954						
Home Appliances and Radio Stores	1929	24,968	5,366	21.5	941	304	32.3
	1939	20,913	5,695	27.2	533	206	38.6
	1948	36,913	4,405	11.9	2,543	464	18.2
	1954	40,542	4,177	10.3	3,227	559	17.5
AUTOMOTIVE GROUP	1929	69,379	3,516	5.1	7,043	750	10.6
	1939	60,132	4,464	7.4	5,549	373	6.7
	1948	86,162	3,682	4.3	20,104	741	3.7
	1954	85,953	3,561	4.1	29,915	955	3.2

* See footnote on first page of this table.

TABLE 15 (Continued)

RETAIL CENSUS

KIND OF BUSINESS	YEAR	NUMBER OF STORES			SALES (MILLIONS)		
		TOTAL	CHAIN*	%	TOTAL	CHAIN	%
Motor Vehicle	1929	42,204	1,290	3.1	$ 6,267	$ 617	9.8
Dealers	1939	33,609	438	1.3	4,810	136	2.8
	1948	43,999	170	0.4	15,953	253	1.6
	1954	61,547	221	0.3	27,531	272	0.9
Tire and Accessory	1929	22,313	2,049	9.2	599	122	20.4
Dealers	1939	18,525	4,014	21.7	524	235	44.8
	1948	20,628	3,342	16.2	1,360	455	38.5
	1954	18,845	3,212	17.0	1,814	652	36.2
All Other	1929	4,862	177	3.6	177	11	6.2
	1939	7,998	12	0.2	215	2	0.9
	1948	21,535	171	0.8	2,792	33	1.2
	1954	5,307			565		
GASOLINE	1929	121,513	30,038	24.7	1,787	629	35.2
STATIONS	1939	241,858	10,397	4.3	2,822	294	10.4
	1948	188,253	5,445	2.9	6,483	470	7.3
	1954	181,747	6,344	3.5	10,744	875	8.1
LIQUOR STORES	1929	—	—	—	—	—	—
	1939	19,136	2,854	14.9	586	257	43.9
	1948	33,422	2,998	9.0	2,580	803	31.1
	1954	31,240	2,830	9.1	3,181	901	28.3
LUMBER, HARDWARE,	1929	90,386	9,001	10.0	3,846	526	13.7
FARM IMPLEMENT	1939	79,313	7,958	10.0	2,735	395	14.4
STORE GROUP	1948	98,938	7,951	8.0	11,151	1,558	14.0
	1954	100,519	7,696	7.7	13,124	1,550	11.9
ALL OTHER STORES	1929	292,772	12,701	4.3	7,561	790	10.4
	1939	236,025	10,536	4.5	4,444	662	14.9
	1948	202,599	9,336	4.6	11,847	1,552	13.1
	1954	226,903	10,874	4.8	15,987	2,552	15.9

* See footnote on first page of this table.

That the status of the chains in the grocery, variety store, shoe and drug fields in 1948 as compared with 1929 is typical of what happened in a number of other fields as well is revealed in Chart III from a study made by Clement Winston and Reba L. Osborne, of the U.S. Department of Commerce.[7] It covers thirteen selected fields, including several in which

[7] *Survey of Current Business,* January, 1949.

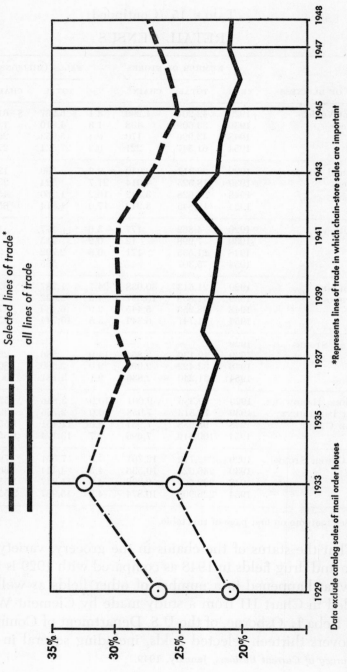

CHART III

Ratios of chain to total retail sales, 1929-1948

Selected lines of trade*

all lines of trade

*Represents lines of trade in which chain-store sales are important

Data exclude catalog sales of mail order houses

Source: U. S. Department of Commerce, Office of Business Economics

35%   30%   25%   20%

1929   1933   1935   1937   1939   1941   1943   1945   1947   1948

the chains had made relatively little progress by 1929 as well as those in which their progress had been most pronounced.

The combined sales of the chains in these thirteen fields stood at 28 per cent of total sales in those fields in 1929, the chart shows, and at approximately the same level in 1948. Covered in the study were grocery stores; department store and general merchandise; drug; eating and drinking establishments; men's clothing and furnishings; women's apparel and accessories; shoes; auto accessories; hardware; building materials; furniture and house furnishings; family wear; and variety stores.

The outstanding fact disclosed by the Census figures is that while the total number of retail stores increased by nearly 250,000 between 1929 and 1954, the gain came from an increase in the number of independent stores which was even greater than that figure but was offset by a substantial decline in the number of chain stores.

What happened is shown in the following tabulation:

RETAIL STORES, 1929 AND 1954

	1929	1954	CHANGE	%
All stores	1,476,365	1,721,650	+245,285	+16.6
Independents[1]	1,316,727	1,616,511	+299,784	+22.7
Chain stores[2]	159,638	105,139	−54,499	−34.0

[1] Includes 2 and 3 store multiunits.
[2] Includes only multiunit stores of firms with 4 or more.

True enough, the substantial decline in the number of chain stores is accounted for mainly by what happened in two categories—grocery stores and filling stations. In the former the chains had 34,390 fewer stores in 1954 than they had had in 1929, and, in the latter, they had 23,694 fewer. Leaving these two categories out of consideration, the other chains will be found to have increased the number of their stores during the period in question, but not nearly to the same relative extent as the independents. The number of chain stores, in fields other than grocery and filling stations, increased from 76,134 in 1929 to 79,719 in 1954, a gain of 3,585 stores, or 4.7 per cent. On the same basis, independent stores increased from 971,293 in 1929 to 1,180,777 in 1954, a gain of 209,451 stores, or 21 per cent.

The significance of all these statistics lies in the fact that instead of being wiped out of the picture completely as he had expected to be in the '20s, the independent merchant has retained his competitive position both in number of stores and in volume of sales. In 1929, he operated approximately 90% of the stores and accounted for 77.8% of the sales and in 1954, he had 94 per cent of the stores and 76.3 per cent of the sales. During that 25 year span, total retail sales increased 254%, from $48 billion to $170 billion, and the independent merchant increased his sales 246%, from $37.6 to $130 billion.

The two main conclusions to be drawn from the Census figures are:

1. The chains had attained an important place in our distribution set-up by 1929, particularly in those fields in which their development has been most pronounced.

2. The important status attained by the chains as of 1929 has not materially changed since that time. In other words, the fear that the chains would go on expanding indefinitely proved to have been ill-founded. As the late Hugh M. Foster pointed out in 1937 in an outstanding study of chain store development from 1920 to that date,[8] the chains had "come of age" in the early 1930s. Certainly they seem to have attained most of their growth by that time.

But although these facts are clear enough now, they could hardly have been foreseen 30 years ago. Then it seemed, as has already been pointed out, that the chain-store juggernaut would crush everything in its path unless something were done to stop it.

What followed gave the chains plenty to worry about and to combat for many years. The story is told in detail in later chapters. But before entering into that hectic phase of chain-store history a consideration of the basis of chain-store strength is necessary to provide the proper background.

[8] "The Chain Store Comes of Age," *Printers' Ink Monthly*, April, 1937.

CHAPTER V

THE BASIS OF
CHAIN-STORE STRENGTH [1]

BEFORE THE chains came into existence, the need for retail stores was supplied almost exclusively by independent merchants who secured their merchandise from either wholesalers or manufacturers direct. The system which then prevailed and which, of course, still exists, is commonly referred to as the wholesaler-retailer system because most products had to find their way from manufacturer or producer to the consumer through both wholesalers and retailers.

In the early days of chain-store development, the wholesaler-retailer system was so well intrenched that manufacturers and producers refused to deal directly with the chains, compelling them to buy through wholesalers, just as the independent merchants did, or at least to pay the same prices as independents paid.[2] Such policies were inspired mainly by a desire to protect the old-line distributors from the "cut-price" competition which the chains would be in a better position to wage if they could obtain their merchandise on a wholesale basis.

Eventually, however, the chains in almost every line succeeded in gaining recognition as wholesale as well as retail distributors and, from that time, two distinct channels of distribution came into general use—the wholesaler-retailer system and the new chain-store system.

---

[1] This chapter is taken almost word for word from *The Chain Store—Boon or Bane?* by the author (Harper & Brothers, New York, 1932), by permission of the publisher. It has been revised, however, to bring it up to date.

[2] See pp. 112 *et seq.*

Although from the technical standpoint of marketing, the independent store and the chain store represent two distinct types of operation—the former to be considered solely as a retailing operation and the latter as a type of combined wholesaling and retailing—that distinction has little significance to the consumer. To him, a store is ordinarily just a store, whether it be an independent store or part of a chain, a store to be patronized or passed by, according to the appeal it registers or fails to register.

Whatever success the chain stores have won for themselves reflects, therefore, the public's reaction to what they have to offer. Of course, chain-store critics used to assert that one of the principal advantages chain stores seem to offer, namely, lower prices, was illusionary. Such criticisms have been completely refuted in recent years, however, by comparative price studies made under impartial auspices.[3] In any event, the sustained success of the chains over the years would, in itself, refute such a contention, unless it is to be assumed, contrary to Lincoln's famous aphorism, that a very large proportion of the public can be hoodwinked continuously.

What, then, is the basis for chain-store growth, as revealed by the foregoing statistics, in the face not only of widespread and well-established competition but the early opposition of those upon whom the chains had to depend for merchandise?

Let us try to answer the question first from the standpoint of the consumer for, obviously, the impression the chain stores have registered with the public, whether conscious or subconscious, accounts for their success. Later we will consider the various factors which have enabled the chains to do what apparently their competitors left undone.

Listing them in the order of their probable importance to the customer, the following factors may be said to have been responsible in the early days of chain-store growth for whatever preference the chains enjoyed over the existing competition:

[3] See pp. 96 *et seq.*

1. Better values, mainly in the form of lower prices.
2. Better physical appearance of the stores themselves.
3. Superior locations.
4. Fresher merchandise and wider assortments.
5. Advertising.

As against these positive influences, the popularity of chain stores developed in the face of the following counteracting obstacles:

1. No deliveries and no credit.
2. Loyalty to old established order.
3. Store-management by *employes* as against the management of independent stores by their owners.
4. The superior ability and aggressiveness of a certain percentage of the independent merchants.

Taking up first the influences that have worked in favor of the chains, the factor of lower prices has undoubtedly been largely responsible for the following they have developed. Although these lower prices were made possible to some extent by the elimination of delivery and credit, services for which consumers should be willing to pay, the fact remains that so many consumers are more interested in lower prices than in such service that the cash-and-carry system fills a definite need in our distribution system, and the chains were the first to cash in on it on a big scale.

Of course, nothing prevents an independent merchant from following the same policy, and many do. Nor is there anything inherent in the chain-store system which precludes the extension of credit or the making of deliveries. Credit-clothing chains have been singularly successful and furniture, jewelry and many other kinds of chains have likewise operated on a credit basis. Chains in many fields have made deliveries to a greater or lesser extent.[4]

[4] An outstanding example of the possibilities of credit-and-delivery chains, even in the food field where cash-and-carry is almost universal among the chains, is furnished by Gristede Brothers, Inc., New York. Credit plans of various types have been introduced on a limited scale recently by some of the variety store and general merchandise chains.

Nevertheless, the fact remains that the chains, as a class, adopted the cash-and-carry idea right from the start, and the independents, as a class, stuck generally to the credit-and-delivery basis and, because a definite demand exists for both types of retailing, the chains opened a rich vein for patronage which the independents had almost entirely neglected.

But the lower prices the chains have always emphasized were made possible not only by the economies of cash-and-carry operation but, to an even greater degree, by the benefits that come from large-scale operation, of which we shall have considerably more to say later on.

Obviously, an attractive-looking store, well-lighted and well-equipped, will attract more trade than one which is run-down-at-the-heels, inadequately lighted and lacking in modern equipment. The chains, as a class, have always recognized the importance of the physical appearance of their stores and, what is more to the point, they have had the resources to a greater extent than their independent competitors to maintain high standards in that respect. This factor has undoubtedly contributed greatly to the appeal chain stores have made and the customer traffic they have been able to draw.[5]

With more experience in the choice of locations, with more capital at their command and with greater prospects of being able to cover high rents, the chains have generally located their stores to better advantage than the average independent.

One of the guiding principles which inspired pioneers in the food-chain field was the merchandising advantage to be gained by speeding up the *turnover*. To achieve that end the chains had to concentrate on items for which a constant demand existed and which therefore moved most rapidly, and to be satisfied with smaller profit per unit.[6] That policy, which

[5] For data on the heavy expenditures the chains make to keep their stores up-to-date see *Chain Store Age* annual store-construction surveys.

[6] Incidentally, this policy left a field open for grocers carrying broader lines and accounts for the ability of so many single-store grocers to withstand chain-store competition.

is perhaps the most characteristic feature of food-chain-store merchandising, not only made for lower prices but, in the case of perishables, it minimized stale merchandise. Thus, consciously or subconsciously, the consumer showed a preference for chain stores because their merchandise was more apt to be fresh.

Finally, consumers were undoubtedly influenced by the advertising the chains were in a better position to use than their smaller competitors. This was true especially in the larger cities, where newspaper space is relatively expensive. The chains could use it liberally because, by dividing its cost among all their stores which benefited by it, the cost per store was relatively small. The single-store merchant, as a rule, found this sales-stimulant beyond his reach.

No doubt the list of factors which helped to make friends for the chain stores might be materially lengthened but those which have been mentioned include the more important ones.

In considering the obstacles the chains had to overcome and which, in the course of the years, they have largely surmounted, the loyalty of the consumer to old-established merchants in preference to newcomers was a natural one. Such attachments undoubtedly worked against the chains in their early days and were strengthened by the anti-chain campaigns which were to develop later on, but, in the long run, they offered little real resistance to chain-store development.

More serious, perhaps, was the inherent disadvantage in the chain-store system which makes it necessary to entrust the management of the various units to employes. To the extent that employes cannot be expected to exert themselves as much for others as the owner of a store would for himself, the chains undoubtedly suffered some disadvantage. On the other hand, the incentives they offered to capable employes in the way of promotion and other methods they used to get satisfactory performance from their employes probably reduced this handicap to a minimum. Furthermore, the assumption that all independent stores are owner-operated and that all store-owners have and use what it takes to impress their customers favorably is, of course, wrong on both counts.

Although a large percentage of independent stores are one-man operations,[7] the percentage of total retail business they do, compared with that done by their larger and more successful fellow independent merchants, is small.

Whatever disadvantage may be involved in relying upon paid employes in retailing is felt by the bigger and better independent stores as well as by the chains and, of course, those are the stores whose competition means most to the chains.

So far as the personality and salesmanship of the average owner of a one-man store is concerned, common experience confirms that they are apt to be a negative factor as frequently as a positive one.

If the net balance of advantages and disadvantages may have favored the chains, certainly the difference was never great enough to give the chains a clear path. A large number of efficient, wide-awake, energetic independent merchants have disputed the advance of the chains every inch of the way. The statistics heretofore presented, show clearly enough that the independents, as a group, have held their own since 1930 despite all the progress the chains had made in the years of their greatest development.

But, with all due deference to the more progressive and successful independents, the great majority of independents were not of that caliber when the chains first came into the picture. Had it been otherwise, perhaps the chains would never have made the headway which carried them so far. As it was, however, the new methods the chains introduced were in such striking contrast to the less satisfactory practices of the great majority of independent merchants that the public must have recognized the difference instinctively. The rapid growth of the chains was the inevitable consequence.

[7] See p. 11, *supra*.

The truth of the matter is that the chains grew because they introduced a method of retail distribution for which there was a definite need and which the old wholesaler-retailer system failed to supply. To what extent the old system was inherently deficient and to what extent its shortcomings could be and have been corrected must be discussed now, not for the sake of stressing the imperfections of a competitive system but in order to contrast certain features of the chain-store system.

The ideal distribution system would bridge the gap between production and consumption with maximum efficiency at minimum cost.

Without any question, the outstanding inherent defect of the old wholesaler-retailer system lay in the fact that, under it, the wholesale function and the retail function are performed by separate, independent factors, whereas, under the chain-store system, the two functions are, to a major extent, combined.

In no sense does the chain-store system eliminate the wholesale function: it still has to be performed, but, whereas under the old system the wholesaler exercised no control over his retail outlets nor did the retailer have any control over his sources of supply, under the chain-store system both functions are performed by the same organization and the control is unified. That this basic difference between the two systems has been partly nullified by the development of voluntary chains of various kinds is true. But the fact remains that such organizations did not come prominently into the picture until the chains had established themselves on a firm basis. When the chains were making their greatest strides, the old wholesaler-retailer set-up provided their principal competition.

Reduced to its simplest terms, the main result of the essential difference between the two systems lies in the fact that under the old plan it is necessary for the wholesaler to *sell* to the retailer before the merchandise can find its way into consumption. Under the chain-store system, this intervening selling process, with all its disadvantages, is obviated.

A. C. Hoffman, of the U.S. Bureau of Agricultural Economics, stressed the advantages of integrating wholesaling and retailing, as in the chain-store system, in a monograph published by the Temporary National Economic Committee appointed by the 76th Congress, 3rd Session, and published in 1940.[8]

"Another important aspect of mass distribution from the standpoint of marketing efficiency," he declared, "is the fact that mass distributors have tended to integrate successive marketing functions within a single organization. The number of bargaining transaction and ownership transfers necessary to move goods from producer to consumer is thus greatly reduced as compared with the regular channels.

"The importance of this is commonly overlooked. No inconsiderable part of the total cost of distributing food products is incurred for the purpose of bringing about ownership transfer at various stages in the marketing process. Brokers' fees, wholesalers' commissions, salesmen's salaries, advertising expenditures—all are partially chargeable to the efforts of sellers and manufacturers to find retail outlets for their goods. . . . In the regular channels, comprised as they are of many small, specialized handlers, the product moves forward chiefly by means of numerous buying and selling transactions. In contrast, the mass distributor moves it forward on an intercompany basis, with the orders and requirements of its various parts largely supplanting the bargaining transactions of the regular system.

"This is the key to much, if not most, of the advantage which the grocery chains have over the independent retailer-wholesaler system. When the function of wholesaling is integrated with that of retailing, it is no longer necessary to 'sell' the retail store. The average independent retailer is visited daily by at least half-a-dozen salesmen, each trying to sell him a small bill of merchandise which he may or may not

<hr>

[8] A. C. Hoffman, *Large-Scale Organization in the Food Industries*, Monograph 35, Temporary National Economic Committee, Senate Committee Print, 76th Congress, 3rd Session.

need. Those who seek the retailer's business cannot permit him simply to order his merchandise as he needs it; the competition between them is such that they constantly must persuade, cajole and coax him.

"The cost of this sort of thing in time and money is nothing short of stupendous. Yet it is seldom mentioned when methods for reducing the costs of food distribution are being considered because most people, including a fair share of the economists, are more concerned with the preservation of competition under old institutional forms than with economic efficiency as we have defined the term."

Putting it in another way, under the old system, the wholesaler, in making his purchases from producers, must *guess*, so to speak, what he will be able to resell to his retail customers. After he has made his guess, he can sell only what his retail customers *guess*, in turn, they will be able to sell to their customers, the consumers. Under the chain-store system, the chain has to guess only what its stores will be able to sell the consumer. Thus, the new system eliminates one of the *guesses*.

What this means in helping to bridge the gap between production and consumption is considerable from the standpoint of both efficiency and cost.

From the standpoint of efficiency, the old system tends to suffer because, to the extent that the wholesaler's guess as to what the retailer will buy is *wrong*, the process of distribution, so far as those particular items are concerned, is definitely blocked. As a device for moving goods into consumption, the wholesaler-retailer system, to this extent, falls down completely. Via this channel, goods can never get into consumption until they have bridged the gulf between wholesaler and retailer. The chain-store system eliminates that gulf. Everything the chain buys, the consumer will have a chance to buy, but that is not true of everything the wholesaler buys.

Then, too, because the wholesaler exercises no effective control over the purchases of the retailer, he must compete with other wholesalers for the retailer's patronage. This limits the efficacy of the old system in several ways.

In the first place, it slows up the rate of turnover because it compels the wholesaler to carry more varieties of merchandise than would be necessary if he were the final arbiter as to the items that were to be offered at retail.

In the second place, with many wholesalers serving the same territory and naturally seeking the patronage of the same retail outlets, a certain part of the selling effort expended must inevitably prove fruitless. To the extent that this selling effort fails, it represents economic waste.

Finally, although theoretically the competition between wholesalers need not lead them to employ uneconomic methods, such as opening unprofitable accounts, granting unsafe credits, and overloading their customers, we know that, practically, that is just what happens.

Still another inherent weakness which affects the efficiency of the wholesaler-retailer system lies in the fact that the wholesaler is out of direct touch with the consumer. Because he has no direct way of gauging consumer preferences or buying habits, his job of "guessing" just what he can sell the retailer, outside of staples, is made so much harder and is attended with greater risk. This disadvantage is obviated to a large extent in the chain-store system because the chains maintain direct consumer contacts through the medium of their own retail outlets.

When we come to consider the relative costs of the two systems, the first fact to be noted is that, although the chain is relieved of the heavy expense involved in *selling* what it buys to its retail outlets, it cannot escape the cost of corresponding operations. The goods the chain takes into its warehouse do not automatically take their places on the shelves of the retail units without a system, without supervision or without expense. Although, therefore, the chains do not have to sell merchandise to their retail units, they do have to maintain adequate machinery and manpower to see that the stores are suitably stocked and the merchandise effectively displayed.

Before considering the relative cost of the two systems, let us look at the defects of the old system as they have developed in the retail end, where we will find additional reasons to explain the rise of the chains.

Perhaps the outstanding characteristic of independent retailing as it existed in the days when the chains were coming up, and which is almost as pronounced today, is that the great majority of retailers are essentially small-scale operators, accounting for but a small proportion of the total volume done by independents. The major part of that volume is done by a small proportion of independents who operate relatively large stores.

Data compiled by the Census Bureau in connection with the 1929 Census clearly reveals the situation which then prevailed. Of the 1,543,158 retailers reported for that year, 986,551, or 64%, had an annual volume of less than $20,000. As a group they accounted for only 15% of total store sales. These figures include all retail stores, chain as well as independent. However, since the total number of chain stores in 1929 was only 159,000, the number of small stores in operation must have been preponderantly independent stores. The 1929 Census also showed that at the other end of the scale, retail stores doing upwards of $100,000 a year numbered only 77,513, or 5 per cent of the total, but they accounted collectively for 45 per cent of total retail sales.[9] The heavy preponderance of small stores in 1929 is shown graphically in Chart IV.

Why is it that so large a proportion of those engaged in retailing attain such a comparatively small volume, and what is the significance of that fact so far as the efficiency of our present system of distribution is concerned?

The reason we have so many *small* retailers is that we have so many retailers. The 1954 Retail Census data on the 1,455,310 single stores which were in operation the entire year tells

[9] See Tables 3 and 4, p. 11, for the situation regarding single stores in 1954.

CHART IV

Retail stores in 1929 by volume of sales

(% of total number of stores in operation)

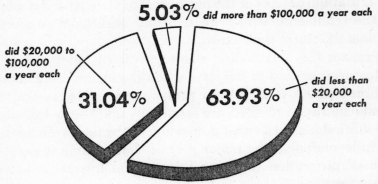

5.03% did more than $100,000 a year each

did $20,000 to $100,000 a year each

31.04%

63.93%

did less than $20,000 a year each

Source: U. S. Department of Commerce, Bureau of the Census

the story. Their sales totalled $112.5 billions. Obviously they could not *all* have done a *large* volume because if the total sales had been divided among them *equally*, none would have done more than $77,000 for the year.

The amount of money spent at retail does not vary with the number of stores we have. It is governed largely by the amount of disposable income—income less taxes—consumers, as a whole, have to spend. Furthermore, consumers spend their money in stores they like best. The great bulk of it, the statistics demonstrate, goes into the larger-volume stores. The inevitable result is indicated by the 1954 experience. Instead of every independent store doing as much as $77,000, which would have been their volume if all had shared equally, no less than 667,101 of the 1,455,310 single stores which were in operation the full year—45.9 per cent of them—actually did less than $30,000. Despite the number of them, they accounted for only 8.7 per cent of the sales of all single store sales. On the other hand, 39 per cent of such sales were made by stores doing more than $300,000 a year, of which there were only 55,414, or 3.8 per cent of the total.

As has been pointed out, the amount of money spent at retail is not unlimited and it would therefore be impossible for all merchants to do a large business, so long as we have so many of them, even if all possessed the genius of a John Wanamaker or a Marshall Field. It might therefore seem to be a gratuitous observation to refer to the appallingly large number of independent retailers who would never be successful even if there were enough volume available for all who might merit it.

In other words, if the public buying-power were to be doubled tomorrow, the great bulk of the additional funds would be spent, in all probability, in the stores which enjoy the lion's share of the present volume. The position of the rank and file of the small independent merchants would not be measurably improved.

And yet the make-up of our merchant class is important because the fact that so many of them are doomed to mediocrity or failure serves to explain a lot of things we want to know more about.

It serves to explain (1) why we have so many small stores; (2) why, despite the fact that we already have too many stores, we could still use more *good* ones; and (3) why the field was wide open for the chains when they came into the picture and is still wide open for all the latent A. T. Stewarts, Marshall Fields, John Wanamakers, Frank Woolworths and J. C. Penneys the present generation may provide.

Common experience confirms the opinions which have been expressed on this point by all authorities on retailing.

"The ease with which entry may be made into the retail business," declared Dr. Paul H. Nystrom, "throngs its channels with people who have no aptitude, no education, no experience, nor other necessary qualifications for this business. The wonder to many students of the retail business is that more do not fail." [10]

When James L. Palmer[11] was professor of marketing at the

[10] Paul H. Nystrom, *Economics of Retailing* (New York: Ronald Press, 1930), 3rd Edition, Vol. 1, p. 119.

[11] Now president of Marshall Field & Co., Chicago.

University of Chicago, in discussing the "Economic and Social Aspects of Chain Stores," he said:[12]

"The business methods of most retailers and wholesalers prior to the development of chains were appallingly wasteful. Even after ten years of intensive chain competition, we find many wholesale and retail distributors employing methods which should have been obsolete decades ago. The fact that some chains have been successful despite their own inefficiency rather than because of the perfection of their methods certainly demonstrates conclusively the wastefulness of the methods employed by some of our established institutions. It is difficult for an impartial observer to become enthusiastic about the preservation of individual enterprise in the field of distribution if, in preserving it, we perpetuate the existence of the host of incompetents that have been engaged in retailing and wholesaling in the past."

Discussing particularly the independent merchant in the grocery field, although what he says of the grocer undoubtedly applies with equal force to small-scale retailers in general, Carl N. Schmalz, then assistant director of the Harvard Bureau of Business Research, now president of R. H. Stearns Co., Boston department store, probably hit the nail squarely on the head in the following summary of the small retailer's shortcomings:[13]

"It seems, therefore, that independent grocery stores on the whole have been poorly managed, and there is strong reason for believing that this poor management has been almost unavoidable.

"As a rule, independent grocery stores necessarily are small,[14] so that the net earnings of each are strictly limited. Nevertheless, their managers are confronted with practically all the problems of any independent business.

[12] *Journal of Business*, University of Chicago, Vol. II, No. 3, July, 1929.
[13] *Harvard Business Review*, July, 1931.
[14] This was written before the advent of the supermarket, which has changed the picture somewhat for the progressive independent in the food field. But the observations still apply to small-scale retailers in all fields, including the food field.

"These men should have the knowledge, the judgment, and courage necessary in formulating and executing sound financial policies, not only in interpreting local demand but also, in changing fundamental conditions, in keeping sales and stocks in balance, in controlling expense and in granting credit.

"These qualities are seldom found in a man able and willing also to work long hours as salesperson, bookkeeper, janitor, stock boy and general detail man.

"Because of these management problems and the small sales volume, it is extremely difficult to make a single grocery store yield an income in salary and profit sufficient to compensate adequately the ability required to manage that store successfully.

"It seems reasonable to assume that many independent stores have been, and will continue to be, managed by men incompetent to operate them at a profit, and that one may expect a continuation of the high failure rates found by such investigators as Nystrom and McGarry. The old system placed an impossible burden upon the independent retailer."

If the foregoing appraisals of independent merchants, as a class, were reasonably accurate at the time they were made, of which there can be little doubt, they go a long way to explain why the chains grew so rapidly and account for the relative strength the system has consistently displayed. By contrast with the weaknesses so prevalent among the independents, the advantages offered by the chains must have seemed even bigger than they were to a large percentage of the consuming public.

But, it may be asked, assuming that an individual lacks the ability, the skill or the resources needed to enable him to develop a *large* retail business, what is to prevent him from performing a useful public service as a *small* retailer? Why cannot he sell five or ten thousand dollars worth of merchandise a year just as efficiently and as economically as a larger operator might sell seventy-five or one hundred thousand dollars a year?

The first answer is that, unless a retailer realizes at least a fair volume of business, he cannot make both ends meet and must inevitably go on the rocks. Although many small stores do manage to hang on year after year, they are the exception and, even if they survive, their stores are not the kind the public prefers to trade in. All stores, the smallest as well as the largest, incur certain inescapable operating expenses— rent, light, heat and wages. Such expenses, not to say anything of a reasonable return to the proprietor on his invested capital, can be covered only if the merchant does enough business to pay for them after he has paid for the merchandise itself.

Back in 1928, the U.S. Department of Commerce and the U.S. Chamber of Commerce published the results of a census of distribution it had made in eleven cities[15] as a pilot survey in preparation for the nationwide census it was to make for the year 1929. Commenting on the number of small-scale retailers in the grocery field, the Department said:

"The average store with an annual volume of $5,000 has little chance of surviving and, while the possibility of profitable operation increases with the annual volume, it is not until we reach a volume of more than fifty thousand dollars that more than mere existence seems possible." [16]

The significance of that comment is confirmed by various studies on retail mortality. In Buffalo, for instance, Dr. Edmund D. McGarry, of the University of Buffalo,[17] found that between 1921 and 1928, 27 per cent of the independent druggists that opened up in Buffalo passed out of business during their first year; in the hardware field, 34 per cent; in the shoe field, 44 per cent; and in the grocery field no less than 60 per cent.

[15] *Retail and Wholesale Trade of Eleven Cities,* Chamber of Commerce of the United States, May, 1928, in conjunction with the U.S. Department of Commerce.
[16] See also U.S. Census of Distribution, 1929, *Retail Trade,* Vol. 1, for observations on the plight of a retailer doing $12,000 a year.
[17] *Mortality in Retail Trade,* University of Buffalo, 1930.

Similar studies made in Louisville, revealing the same lamentable situation, led to the important Louisville Grocery Survey, an investigation of distribution conditions made under the auspices of the U.S. Department of Commerce and other cooperating bodies.[18]

Of course, the main weakness of the small-scale retailer, from the standpoint of the consumer, is that his prices are inevitably higher than those charged by his larger competitors and, generally speaking, his store will be a less attractive place to shop in than the larger and more up-to-date establishments operated by his competitors.

Turning now from the weaknesses of the small-scale retailer to the specific elements of strength in large-scale retailing, the advantages offered are not dependent upon the type of operation involved. They are enjoyed by the independent merchant who achieves large volume, whether through a department store, a supermarket or in any other way, just as they are by the mail-order houses and the chains.

Increased volume brings not only lower merchandise costs by reason of quantity purchases but results in many other operating and merchandising economies, although, of course, there is a limit beyond which such economies are no longer realized. The law of diminishing returns, which sets a limit beyond which the benefits of mass production may cease to exist, undoubtedly applies to mass distribution as well. But at just what point a company, whether in production or distribution, becomes *too* big for its own good is not easy to establish.

Up to the time this law of diminishing returns begins to exert itself, however, the advantages of large scale retailing are not to be doubted. Some of the more important ones may be thus enumerated:

1. The large scale distributor buys both his merchandise and his working equipment cheaper.
2. He can hire greater skill.

[18] Louisville Grocery Survey, U.S. Department of Commerce, 1930.

3. He can install more scientific methods and equipment.
4. He can resort to a more effective "division of labor."
5. He can command credit more readily.
6. He can better withstand business losses.
7. He can operate on less profit per unit.

The character and importance of these advantages must in most cases be more or less obvious.

Buying in large volume, for instance, results in a lower price because the seller can afford to share with the large buyer what he saves in selling cost. Although the really big buyers were once in a position to secure even greater price concessions than the volume of their purchases warranted, the passage of the Robinson-Patman Act in 1936 has made all discriminatory prices illegal unless they can be justified by actual savings to the seller.[19] However, the very fact that this law, which was designed to protect small buyers from uneconomic advantages enjoyed by big buyers, recognized that quantity purchases do justify lower prices emphasizes the natural advantage enjoyed by large-scale operators in this important phase of their business.

The large operator can afford to employ the best brains available because high salaries distributed over a large number of units usually involve a lower burden per unit than lower salaries distributed among fewer units. That applies, too, to the methods and systems he installs and the equipment he uses. He commands greater credit and can better withstand business losses because large-scale operation involves the use of larger resources and the very size of the operation signifies, even if it does not guarantee, greater stability.

But without question the greatest advantage accruing to the large-scale distributor is that he can usually operate on

[19] The Robinson-Patman Act, which became effective June 19, 1936, amended the Clayton Act of 1914. It contains the following proviso: "Provided, that nothing herein contained shall prevent differentials which make *only due allowance* for differences in the cost of manufacture, sale or delivery resulting from the differing methods or *quantities* in which such commodities are to such purchasers sold or delivered."

less profit per unit and still secure a satisfactory return on his invested capital, because the scale of his operations is usually larger proportionally than the additional capital required to finance them. A low rate of profit per unit, added to lower merchandise costs resulting from quantity buying, and lower operating costs per unit resulting from quantity selling, spells lower prices to the consumer—a competitive advantage which accounts in large measure for the success the chains have achieved and works similarly to the advantage of other large-scale operators.[20]

When we consider the advantages accruing from a more effective "division of labor," some elaboration is necessary, for that feature of mass distribution has probably been given less credit for the results achieved than it deserves. If, for instance, we turn to the chain-store system as an example of mass distribution, the first thought in the minds of most people is that the chains' advantage lies mainly if not wholly in their buying advantages as compared with their smaller competitors.

Without minimizing the value of quantity purchases, the greater all-round efficiency a large-scale distributor achieves by utilizing the principle of a division of labor probably means far more to him in the long run than all his buying advantages.

Perhaps the best way to illustrate the advantages of a division of labor in distribution is to see what happens when it is not employed. The small-scale retailer provides a typical example. He has to do practically everything himself, just as a shoemaker had to produce a pair of shoes from start to finish before the introduction of shoe-making machinery. He

[20] The amount of net profit per dollar of sales needed to produce a satisfactory return on the invested capital depends upon various factors. One of the most important is the turnover rate—the rapidity with which the capital invested in merchandise can be recovered and reinvested. That, in turn, depends upon the kind of merchandise involved. Naturally, the necessities of life move into consumption faster than items which are less essential or are within the reach of fewer people. For the actual operating results of the chains in the grocery and variety store fields see the reports of the Harvard Bureau of Business Research issued annually. See also *Chain Store Age*, Grocery Edition, May, 1958, for comment on the small net profit per dollar of sales realized by the food chains.

has to select the location of his store, in the first place, although he may have had no experience whatever in that direction. Then he has to lay it out and equip it. He has to buy his initial stock of merchandise, relying mainly, perhaps, on the advice of those from whom he buys.

With his stock of merchandise on hand, he has to trim his windows, prepare his advertising, if he does any, open a set of books, if he keeps any, grant credit, take care of collections, superintend deliveries and wait on customers.

Once established in business, he must listen to visiting salesmen and decide what lines to carry and how much of each; he should be able to analyze his sales so as to determine what items to push and which ones to discontinue; he has to watch his competitors and he must handle his finances so that he may meet his obligations and maintain his credit.

Obviously, no merchant, no matter how smart he is or how hard he has tried to equip himself for all the manifold tasks involved in the successful conduct of a store, can reasonably expect to qualify as an expert in all its branches. He can hardly be an expert buyer, an expert accountant, an expert window-trimmer, an expert debt-collector, an expert advertising manager and an expert merchandiser, and even if he were actually an expert in every one of these departments, he would not have the time to capitalize his versatility.

Compare the situation of the typical small-scale retailer with the division of labor which prevails where the volume is great enough to require and to permit the employment of specialists in each department.

In a typical chain-store organization, for instance, you have a real-estate expert selecting the locations for the individual units and securing the most advantageous terms in the lease. You have merchandising specialists handling both the buying and the selling activities, a personnel director hiring the help and supervising them, a display expert taking care of the store windows and the interior arrangement of the merchandise. Accounting, control, warehousing, transportation, sales promotion, public relations, financial, construction and maintenance experts deal with their special fields. Trained executives establish the chain's policies and see that they are carried out. The store manager, who is the counterpart of the individual merchant so far as the public is concerned, can concentrate almost exclusively on selling.

Without any question, this division of labor, which is found in the department store or in the large independent store of any kind, as well as in the chains, and which is the direct result of large-scale operation, is one of the principal advantages of large-scale operation, although it is not generally recognized as such.

But, it may be asked, while the best skill available may be utilized by the large-scale operator, and while large-scale operation might, indeed, be impossible without it, is it *necessary* for a small store? It is not necessary, but without it the small store must inevitably remain small. The only way out for the individual retailer who is unable or unwilling to expand his operation is to affiliate himself with some organization, such as a voluntary chain, or a cooperative enterprise of a similar type, which will give him the benefit of the expert guidance and help he must lack as long as he plays a lone hand.

Although a small-scale retailer can improve his position by joining a voluntary chain, the full benefits of mass distribution are available only to retailers large enough to utilize all of them.[21]

The basis of chain-store strength lies primarily in the fact that operating more than one store opens the way to greater volume, with all the benefits which, as we have seen, flow from it. But, in addition to operating more stores, the chains have increased their volume per store in the various ways which have been enumerated.

Whether the cost of bridging the gap between the producer

[21] Cf. A. C. Hoffman, *Large Scale Organization in the Food Industries*, Monograph No. 35, T.N.E.C. Study, 1940, pp. 9, 10.

and the consumer via the old wholesaler-retailer channel is greater than via the chain stores has been made the subject of several studies. Although none of these comparisons of operating costs is too satisfactory, even to their respective authors, because of the absence of comparable data, the general conclusion is that the consumer pays less for distribution via the chain stores than via independent stores.[22]

Of course, what is more important to the consumer are the relative prices in the two types of stores—whether the lower price is the result of buying advantages, operating economies, or lower net profits, or a combination of any of those elements. On that score, numerous studies have been made by impartial authorities, including the Federal Trade Commission,[23] and the results show a consistent differential in favor of the chains, although its extent varies in different kinds of stores, lines of merchandise and geographical areas. Furthermore, these differentials have undoubtedly narrowed in recent years as a result of greater efficiency on the part of independent stores achieved through affiliation with voluntary chains and in other ways.

After reviewing no less than seventeen different comparative price studies made by others as well as a special study they undertook themselves, Profs. Beckman and Nolen, in their book *The Chain Store Problem*,[24] reached the following significant conclusion:

"From the data presented and analyzed in the present and preceding chapters there can be little doubt that chain stores substantially undersell their independent competitors. In every line of trade that has been studied the chains enjoy a price differential that increases, though not in exact proportion, with the number of units operated. . . . Another significant factor is that the independent merchants are appar-

[22] *Expenses and Profits in the Chain Grocery Business*, 1929, Bulletin No. 84, Bureau of Business Research, Harvard University, June, 1931.
[23] Federal Trade Commission: "Chain Store Inquiry—Prices and Margins of Chain and Independent Distributors," Vol. IV, 1933, 1934; *The Chain Store Tells Its Story, op. cit.*, pp. 106, 116, 122, 124.
[24] *The Chain Store Problem, op. cit.*, p. 136.

ently finding ways and means to cut down the chain price differential. The earlier studies revealed consistently wider price differences than the more recent ones."

A realistic, but striking, recognition of the fact that these differentials still obtained, in the grocery field, at any rate, as late as 1945 was the Office of Price Administration's classification of grocery stores, by type of operation and sales per store, as a basis for a differential in price ceilings.[25]

The retail markups established for Group 3, comprising chain stores doing less than $250,000, and Group 4 comprising all retailers doing more than $250,000, were substantially lower than those established for Group 1, comprising independent stores doing under $50,000, or Group 2, comprising independent stores doing between $50,000 and $250,000.

The differential varied from one group of commodities to another, but in some cases the markup set for Groups 1 and 2 was 100 per cent or more higher than that set for Groups 3 and 4. On sugar, for instance, the markups (the addition to the wholesale price to make the retail price) for Groups 1, 2, 3 and 4 were 17 per cent, 12 per cent, 7 per cent, and 6 per cent respectively; on canned milk, 20 per cent, 20 per cent, 10 per cent and 9 per cent; breakfast cereals, 22 per cent, 20 per cent, 13 per cent and 11 per cent; lard, 20 per cent, 18 per cent, 13 per cent and 10 per cent; and coffee, 17 per cent, 17 per cent, 12 per cent and 11 per cent.

Thus, for the first time, with the Government in complete control of the nation's food supply and price structure, the economies made possible by large-scale distribution—the economic facts of life—were officially applied in a practical way. And in 1951, when price control was again invoked, the Office of Price Stabilization—OPA's counterpart—again classified grocery stores by type of operation and sales volume as had been done in 1945.

But the fact that the chain-store system rested upon a sound foundation was not enough to justify its existence in the eyes

[25] O.P.A. Maximum Price Regulations 422 and 423, February 3, 1945.

of those who were bound to feel the effect of chain-store competition. Slowly at first but more rapidly as the tempo of chain-store growth quickened, a wave of anti-chain agitation spread through the country. The chains are still feeling some of the consequences of that crusade, as will be shown in succeeding chapters but, fortunately for them, the hue and cry died down appreciably 15 years ago and is hardly likely to be revived.

PART II

STRUGGLE

CHAPTER VI

THE CHAINS ENCOUNTER
OPPOSITION

AT THE TURN of the century the number of chain stores in operation in all fields was negligible. Certainly at that time nobody could have foreseen how quickly the chain-store idea was to spread and grow, and only the most imaginative and timorous could have regarded it as posing a threat to the existing order.

Shortly after the turn of the century, however, as has been pointed out, the situation began to take on a new aspect. Not only did the chains then in existence begin to expand at a somewhat faster rate, but the possibilities of the chain-store idea began to attract newcomers in increasing numbers. What is more to the point, some of the newcomers made a more spectacular entrance than their predecessors had done. This trend brought into the picture not only new chains but new kinds of stores, new standards of retailing and more aggressive forms of merchandising.

Outstanding in this category was the United Cigar Stores Company, which opened its first store in New York in 1901. The story of its conception, its plans, its principles and its remarkable growth in the 25 years which followed was told on the occasion of its 25th anniversary by Herbert S. Collins, its vice-president and one of its founders.[1]

According to Mr. Collins, the idea of the chain originated with George J. Whelan in 1900. At that time he was in the wholesale cigar business in Syracuse, N.Y., and, in addition,

[1] *Chain Store Age*, May, 1926, p. 13.

had been running a retail cigar store there since 1892. The remarkable success of that store, which was years ahead of cigar stores of that period, suggested to Mr. Whelan that the retail tobacco trade was ripe for reform.

"The average cigar store of that time," Mr. Collins recalled, "hardly deserved to be called a *store* at all. Certainly it followed none of the fundamental principles of retail merchandising which even the poorest merchant recognizes today. It was inadequately stocked, the fixtures were of the most primitive kind, and little or no attempt was made at window or inside display. The principle attraction consisted of a row of chairs and cuspidors, newspapers and magazines for the convenience of idlers who elected to congregate there. An empty carton or two and several theatrical posters comprised the usual contents of the windows, and, but for the wooden Indian outside the store, the passerby would hardly have been able to tell whether it was a cigar store or a real estate office."

But Mr. Whelan's store was different. It had no wooden Indian and no chairs for loafers. Indeed, signs around the store announced: "No loafing, all room needed for business." The windows were tastefully stocked with cigars, cigarettes, pipes and tobacco, and, instead of theatrical posters, attractive signs announcing special sales or the contests which Mr. Whelan was constantly staging were conspicuously displayed.

Sales averaged about $250 a day—a tremendous volume for those days.

In 1900, came the big idea. If a cigar store run along these original lines worked out so profitably in Syracuse, why not duplicate it elsewhere? Why not establish a *chain* of them throughout the country?

A second store was accordingly opened in Elmira and, in quick succession, others in Utica, Troy and Auburn. They were all money-makers right from the start.

The following year, Mr. Whelan and his associates opened an office in New York and laid their plans for organizing the

United Cigar Stores Company. Within a very few months the corporation was launched with a capital stock of $2,000,000.

The first store to bear the name that was to make chain-store history opened on Nassau Street, New York, that year. It was only ten feet wide, with a 7-foot window, but it was set up after the style which had proved so successful in the Whelan stores upstate.

The underlying principles of the new venture were (1) to sell the best cigar to be had for the price asked and to sell smoking and chewing tobacco for less than it could be obtained elsewhere; (2) to operate on a cash basis; and (3) to extend genuine courtesy and service to customers.

Within a few days after the first store was opened, seven more were bought from an operator who had been running them along the old lines. The kind of stores they were is indicated, Mr. Collins pointed out, by the fact that the value of the stock and fixtures in all seven totalled less than $6,000.

From that time on, the chain spread as rapidly as suitable locations could be secured. How rapid that was is revealed in Table 16 showing the company's growth in sales year by year from 1901 to 1925.

TABLE 16

SALES OF UNITED CIGAR STORES
COMPANY, 1901-1925

1901	$ 93,374	1914	$29,902,712
1902	1,754,593	1915	31,038,849
1903	6,025,489	1916	35,822,984
1904	7,243,729	1917	42,913,234
1905	9,839,231	1918	52,035,735
1906	12,727,906	1919	61,874,070
1907	16,532,307	1920	78,918,582
1908	16,881,596	1921	76,521,198
1909	18,871,531	1922	72,484,254
1910	21,774,538	1923	74,199,273
1911	24,383,827	1924	79,738,566
1912	26,718,281	1925	85,060,104
1913	29,574,950		

"We had plenty of opposition," Mr. Collins noted. "The independents fought us tooth and nail—not because we were a chain but because we were supposed to be the outlet for the 'tobacco trust.' In those trust-busting days, it was the easiest thing in the world to raise a hue and cry against anything connected with 'the interests' and the 'tobacco trust' was regarded as one of the wickedest of them all."

But, as the sales record indicates, the louder the independents protested against the new cigar stores, the more eagerly the public flocked to them.

However, even though the complaints of the independent tobacconists failed to move the public, they could hardly have gone unnoticed by independent retailers in other fields. How soon would it be, they must have asked themselves, before some equally revolutionary type of store or method of merchandising appeared in their own fields?

So far as organized efforts to check the encroachment of chain stores were concerned, the most determined, at that time, appeared in the drug and grocery fields.

In the drug field, however, the effort was directed not against the chains, as such, but against "price-cutters" in general. Certainly the development of the drug chains prior to 1910 was negligible enough to have given the established order little cause for alarm so far as normal competition was concerned. But when it became apparent that the newcomers were to be aggressive merchandisers, lining up with the cut-rate independents and department stores, who had long been a thorn in the side of the trade as a whole, the character of their competition rather than its volume was naturally a most disturbing factor.

That the price-cutting evil had plagued the drug trade long before the drug chains came into the picture, is revealed by the drastic measures the National Wholesale Druggists Association took to cope with it as far back as 1882 and even earlier. By influencing manufacturers of patent medicines and proprietaries—the principal items exploited by the price-cutters—to confine their sales to members of their association, who by their membership agreed to maintain standard prices, the NWDA was able to keep the evil within reasonable bounds. Their hand was strengthened when their methods were upheld by the N.Y. Court of Appeals[2] when a price-cutter claimed he had been "boycotted" by the association because he was not on the association's approved list. On the contrary, decided the Court, whatever "boycott" existed was of his own making, for all he had to do to get all the merchandise he needed was to give up his price-cutting practices and join the association.

In the fight against price-cutting, the manufacturers of many patent medicines and proprietaries cooperated fully with the regular distributors. They developed all sorts of "agency" and other plans designed to confine the sales of their products to wholesalers who agreed (1) to maintain established wholesale prices; and (2) to sell only to retailers who had likewise agreed to maintain established retail prices.

Despite these determined and persistent efforts of both manufacturers and wholesalers, the cut-rate stores somehow managed to get at least enough of the protected items to enable them to feature their cut-price offerings constantly and conspicuously.

When the drug chains came into the picture, they had no other practical course but to join the price-cutters. How could they pass on to the public the economies made possible by chain-store operation unless they sold for less? And how could they drive home more effectively the fact that their prices really were lower than by featuring *standard* items below the prices which the independents generally were required by their sources of supply to maintain?

It is not surprising, therefore, that one of the many cases instituted by manufacturers against price-cutters in the days when price-maintenance agreements were held to be lawful (so far, at least, as proprietaries and patent medicines were

[2] Park v. NWDA, 175 N.Y. 1.

concerned) was directed against one of the pioneer drug chains—the Jaynes Drug Co., which not only conducted a wholesale drug business but had launched a chain of drug stores in Boston. The manufacturer complained that Jaynes was getting its supplies of plaintiff's products from wholesalers who had agreed not to sell them to price-cutters, and was instrumental, therefore, in getting such wholesalers to violate their contracts. The injunction was granted on December 12, 1906,[3] the court overruling the chain's contention that such contracts were invalid because they restrained competition in violation of the Sherman Anti-Trust Act.

But this victory, and similar decisions won by the manufacturer of "Peruna," [4] were short-lived, for, in 1911,[5] the U.S. Supreme Court decided unequivocally that all kinds of price-maintenance agreements were invalid except those involving items covered by patents or copyrights—and "patent" medicines and proprietaries did not come within that category.

In the face of that decision, the fight against price-cutters had to take a new tack. The only way price maintenance could be achieved legally now was through legislation specifically authorizing it. From that time on, various bills were introduced in Congress to achieve the desired objective, but although some of them got to the stage of public hearings, none was ever enacted. Not until 42 States had legalized price maintenance through what were known as Fair Trade Acts did Congress add its blessing by recognizing such contracts in the Miller-Tydings Act of 1937.

The story of the long effort to legalize price maintenance is pertinent here only because the aggressive competition of the chains, and particularly the drug chains, was constantly held up as the horrible example of what made legalized price maintenance necessary.

Strangely enough, however, not many years were to pass before the drug chains, to whom price-cutting was supposed

[3] Dr. Miles Medical Co. v. Jaynes, 149 Fed. R. 838 (1906).
[4] Park v. Hartman, 145 Fed. R. 358 (1906); reversed 153 Fed. R. 24 (1907).
[5] Dr. Miles Medical Co. v. John D. Park & Sons Co., 220 U.S. 373 (1911).

to be so vital, joined the independents in a nationwide demand for legislation designed to eliminate or curtail it. They have been among the strongest supporters of Fair Trade, as price maintenance came to be known, ever since.

Undoubtedly the coming of the depression and its effect on retail sales in general had much to do with the drug chains' change of attitude. What happened is clearly shown by an analysis of the operating results in chain drug stores made by the Harvard Bureau of Business Research for the years 1929, 1931 and 1932. It showed that whereas average sales per store of $116,400 in 1929 had yielded a typical net profit of 3 per cent, average sales dropped to $105,000 in 1931 and showed a fractional net loss; and to $90,398 in 1932, with a typical net loss of nearly 3 per cent!

Under such conditions, cut-price merchandising lost much of its attraction. When price appeal failed to produce the volume needed to sustain it, it had little to commend it. The situation was further aggravated by the impact of a new and formidable type of price-cutter in the shape of what were called "pine-boards." These crudely set up outlets featured nationally advertised proprietaries, toiletries and other drug-store products at deep-cut prices which the chains were no longer interested in meeting.

At any rate, in 1932, the late Charles R. Walgreen came out publicly for legalized price maintenance. His stand was quickly endorsed by George M. Gales, president of Louis K. Liggett Co., Malcolm G. Gibbs, president of Peoples Drug Stores, and other leading drug-chain operators.

The ensuing campaign for Fair Trade laws in state legislatures, with the chains lined up with the independent druggists, was singularly successful. Before many years were to pass, no less than 45 States had enacted such laws. When the first law of the kind, passed in California in 1931, proved abortive, because all it did was to legalize price contracts between those who would sign them, leaving untouched the price-cutters who naturally refused to sign such a contract, the weakness was eliminated by an amendment in 1933. The new California law made a price-maintenance contract with even a single retailer binding on *all* retailers in the state whether they were parties to it or not. Then the big question was whether such a unique provision was constitutional. In December, 1936, the U.S. Supreme Court held that it was.[6]

Following that decision, one State after another enacted a Fair Trade law. Within a couple of years, every State in the Union had one with the exception of Missouri, Vermont and Texas, in which three States no such law was ever passed.

But even when price maintenance agreements were enforceable in 45 States, not all manufacturers who would have liked to have availed themselves of the privilege felt free to do so. For such agreements were still condemned by Federal laws which manufacturers engaged in interstate commerce could not ignore. To remove that remaining obstacle, the Miller-Tydings Act was pushed through Congress in 1937. It exempted such agreements from the ban imposed by Federal laws provided they were authorized by the laws of the States in which they were made.

Thereafter, the Fair Trade set-up was widely adopted by manufacturers of branded lines, although it was favored in some fields more than in others. In the drug field, for instance, it became almost universal. That was because of the wide demand for it by distributors of all types—wholesalers, chains and independents. On the other hand, it made little headway in the grocery field, largely because the chains in that field were opposed to it on principle. They wanted no restriction whatever on their freedom to set their own resale prices. As they had become a substantial factor in the distribution set-up, their suppliers generally eschewed Fair Trade. In other fields in which trade-marked articles figured extensively, the adoption of Fair Trade was more or less spotty. Among its most ardent supporters were book publishers and the lead-

---

[6] The Pep Boys v. Pyroil Sales Co., Inc., and Kunsman v. Factor & Co., 229 U.S. 198 (1936).

ing manufacturers of electrical appliances for consumer use. The latter were to spend millions of dollars thereafter in enforcement proceedings against discount-houses and other price-cutters.

From 1937 to 1951, Fair Trade seemed to be so firmly entrenched that even those who rebelled against it most strenuously came to regard further recourse to the courts as hopeless. Then, in 1951, the Fair Trade apple-cart was suddenly upset by a decision of the United States Supreme Court which was as unexpected as it was devastating.[7] That decision held that while the Miller-Tydings Act unquestionably gave federal sanction to certain price-maintenance agreements, it contained nothing which bound non-signers of such contracts to respect the minimum price they established!

The effect of that decision was to precipitate price-wars of such a sensational character that they made front-page news in the daily press for several weeks. The friends of Fair Trade were quick to capitalize the situation by demanding that Congress immediately pass new legislation to plug the hole which the Supreme Court had found in the Miller-Tydings Act. Such a law, the McGuire Act, was promptly passed. It was approved July 14, 1952. It looked as if Fair Trade had not only been restored but would thereafter be impregnable.

That, however, did not prove to be the case. Price-cutters who were taken to court took a new tack. They contended that the non-signer clause violated the guarantees contained in *State* constitutions. That contention was sustained in so many cases that by 1958 Fair Trade had become unenforceable against non-signers in no less than 16 of the 45 States under whose Fair Trade laws they had been specifically covered. This was in addition to the three States and the District of Columbia, in which no Fair Trade law had ever been enacted.

To remedy that situation, the friends of Fair Trade decided to appeal to Congress again—that the only course left was to put Fair Trade on a Federal rather than a State basis. They

[7] Calvert Distillers Corp. *v.* Schwegmann, 341 U.S. 384 (1951).

had an appropriate bill prepared accordingly and it was promptly introduced in both Houses in 1958. It got only as far, however, as the public hearing stage. Thus, when the Congress adjourned on August 24 without having taken action on the proposed legislation, Fair Trade was left in a seriously debilitated condition.

Even in the 29 States in which it was still legally enforceable, its effectiveness was seriously diminished. Practically all of such States were contiguous to one or more States in which Fair Trade was unenforceable against non-signers. Thus, many retailers who would have preferred to have maintained Fair Trade prices in compliance with the laws of their own States found it impracticable to do so in the face of the competition of price-cutters in a contiguous State who were free to cut to their heart's content. In such cases, manufacturers were naturally reluctant to proceed against distributors who were disregarding Fair Trade only because they had no alternative if they were to remain competitive.[8]

But to get back to the days when the drug chains could

[8] The 29 States in which Fair Trade was enforceable as of September 23, 1958, were:

1. Alabama	11. Massachusetts	21. Oklahoma
2. Arizona	12. Minnesota	22. Pennsylvania
3. California	13. Mississippi	23. Rhode Island
4. Connecticut	14. Montana	24. S. Dakota
5. Delaware	15. Nevada	25. Tennessee
6. Idaho	16. New Hampshire	26. Virginia
7. Illinois	17. New Jersey	27. Washington
8. Iowa	18. New York	28. Wisconsin
9. Maine	19. N. Carolina	29. Wyoming
10. Maryland	20. N. Dakota	

The 19 States in which Fair Trade was not enforceable as of that date, were:

1. Arkansas	8. Louisiana	15. S. Carolina
2. Colorado	9. Michigan	16. Texas
3. Florida	10. Missouri	17. Utah
4. Georgia	11. Nebraska	18. Vermont
5. Indiana	12. New Mexico	19. W. Virginia
6. Kansas	13. Ohio	
7. Kentucky	14. Oregon	

The District of Columbia never had a Fair Trade Act, Hawaii did have one but it was nullified by the courts, but Puerto Rico's Act was effective as of the date referred to, its non-signer clause having survived an attack in a lower court.

and did cut prices without restraint, their aggressive competition incurred deep resentment on the part of their independent competitors and the wholesale druggists who supplied them.

How far this feeling had developed by 1914 is indicated by the comprehensive series of articles by Charles W. Hurd and M. M. Zimmerman, then of the editorial staff of *Printers' Ink*, published in successive issues of that weekly, beginning with that of September 10, 1914.

The first article in the series was entitled: "Why Advertisers Must Give Chain Store Growth Their Serious Attention."

It pointed out that the system then consisted of no less than 2,000 chains with some 20,000 stores. Among them it listed United Cigar Stores Company with 900, Great Atlantic & Pacific Tea Company with 800, F. W. Woolworth Company with 774, and the Riker-Hegeman drug chain with 105 and "growing at the rate of more than three a month."

Why this development was believed to be "portentous to advertising" was thus explained:

"That the profound change in trade channels which these developments mark is portentous to advertising cannot be doubted. Consider them and their results. Unusual ability, no doubt, from the start; from that to system and standardization; thence to direct buying in quantity and special discounts; then on to price-cutting and the promotion of private brands—these are the undisputed means and methods of the majority of them."

Referring to the chains as a "new and formidable power in business," the authors pointed out that they had been strengthened by the rulings of the Supreme Court virtually forbidding price maintenance, and asserted that "there is no wonder it has swelled the uneasiness to alarm and sent the manufacturers, jobbers and independent retailers to Congress for relief. The legislation embodied in the Stevens bill, the Metz bill and perhaps the Clayton bill, to name no others, is a direct assault upon all types of concentrated retailing," by which they referred to the chains, department stores and mail-order houses.

In the second article, reference was made to a circular said to have been sent to grocery jobbers by one of the leading manufacturers of a nationally advertised breakfast cereal.

"Any jobber is blind who shuts his eyes to the increasing menace of the chains," it read, "a menace to your business far more than to ours.

"Think a moment. What has become of the old corner tobacconist? Answer: United Cigar Stores. What has become of the old 'home-cooking' restaurants in so many cities? Answer: Child's, $12,000,000 (backed by Standard Oil) and Thompson's, $6,000,000—to say nothing of several others. Big Business (United Drug Company and Riker-Hegeman) already dominates the drug stores of New York, Boston and Chicago."

And then the authors add that the bare possibility that the cereal company in question "may end its long fight against the price-cutting chain stores in the grocery field by throwing overboard its famous 'square deal' policy and surrendering to them is really momentous news. It gives us a measure of the growing strength of the chains, as well as the weakness or indifference of the jobbers, to say nothing of the other elements in the field."

But the efforts of leading grocery manufacturers to protect their traditional channels of distribution by refusing to sell direct to the chains persisted for many years thereafter. That their policy was dictated by the pressures exerted on them by wholesalers rather than by any desire on their part to handicap the chains is suggested clearly enough by some of the cases which grew out of the activities of wholesalers' associations in various parts of the country.

Thus, in 1922, the Federal Trade Commission ordered the Wholesale Grocers Association of El Paso to cease and desist from influencing manufacturers not to sell direct to Standard Grocery Co., which had been founded in 1916, and had a

chain of six stores in El Paso besides running a regular wholesale grocery business. The order was sustained by the Court
which pointed out that "the combining of wholesaling and
retailing is not a novelty and is not unlawful." [9]

In Southern California, on April 2, 1924, the United States
asked for an injunction against the Southern California
Wholesale Grocers Association, a food-brokers' association,
and others, alleging that for the preceding three years they
had influenced manufacturers to refuse to sell direct to chains.
After a trial lasting four weeks, Federal Judge W. P. James
granted the injunction, although he conceded that it might
be true, as the defendants contended, that "the practice of
the chain stores to attract business by advertising and selling
certain lines at close to non-profit prices disturbed the system of retail business." [10]

Along the same lines was a complaint filed by the Federal
Trade Commission against the Arkansas Wholesale Grocers
Association on September 13, 1924. It charged that the wholesalers had designated "the channel of distribution commencing with the manufacturer or producer, flowing thence to the
wholesaler, from the wholesaler to the retailer and from the
retailer to the consuming public, as the only regular and legitimate channel of distribution," and had brought pressure to
bear on manufacturers who dealt with "irregular" channels
by threatened "boycott" and other coercive means.

Typical of the methods used was a bulletin of January 9,
1922, sent by the association to its members, containing the
following suggestion:

"We hope that all wholesale grocers will look over their list
of manufacturers from whom they buy and see the ones that
are selling the chain stores at the same price they are selling
the wholesale grocer. When you buy from them, you give
them the club that they are pounding you with and the club
that they pound the retailer with."

[9] Wholesale Groc. Assn. v. Fed. Trade Commn., 277 Fed. R. 657 (1922).
[10] U.S. v. So. Calif. Wholesale Grocers Assn., 7 Fed. (2nd) 944 (1925).

An earlier bulletin, November 3, 1921, referred to a list of "undesirables" published in a trade paper, *Duncan's Trade Register*, and added "that is what he terms the manufacturers who are selling the chain stores at the prices they sell the wholesaler," urging members to subscribe to the paper in order to get the list.

The Federal Trade Commission issued an order requiring the wholesalers to cease and desist the activities in question, and the Court upheld it.[11]

But the chains did not rely upon the Government to fight their battles for them. Instead they took their case right to the manufacturers themselves.

The interesting story of this phase of their early struggles was told in some detail by Arthur C. Jones, back in 1925. At that time, he was the president of his own chain, The Piggly-Wiggly California Co., and also secretary and treasurer of the Western States Chain Grocers' Association.

"During the year 1921, the chain operators of Los Angeles seriously considered the matter of buying direct from manufacturers," he declared,[12] "but met with such a determined resistance from local wholesaler trade and brokers that it was thought that little could be done about the matter then.

"However, in September, 1921, J. A. Daley, president of Daley's, Inc., E. F. Stanton, president of Bay Cities Merc. Co., Sam Seelig, president of Sam Seelig Co. [predecessor of Safeway Stores], F. E. Chaffee, president of Chaffee's, Inc., and myself went in a body to San Francisco and Seattle and thence eastward to Chicago, Detroit and New York, stopping off at intermediate points wherever there was a manufacturer of importance."

This task force, as it would be called today, represented at the time about 200 stores doing about $10,000,000 a year. Four years later, the same group had 650 stores and was doing some $40,000,000 a year.

[11] Arkansas Wholesale Grocers Assn. *v.* Fed. Trade Commn., 18 Fed. (2nd) 866.
[12] *Chain Store Age,* November, 1925, p. 11.

Altogether, the group called on 60 manufacturers, and Mr. Jones records that most of them reacted unfavorably. However five of them were won over and agreed to sell the chains direct and did so from that time on.

The arguments presented by the task force covered four main points:

1. If the grocery chains grew as big as their early history indicated they would, no wholesale grocer could carry adequate warehouse stocks to meet the chains' requirements.

2. If the wholesaler did not actually warehouse the merchandise but had it delivered by manufacturers direct to the chains' own warehouses, why should the chains pay middlemen for doing something they did not do?

3. The chains had reached the point where it was essential that they could be assured of an uninterrupted supply at prices that were economically sound, but unless they bought direct, they were at the mercy of middlemen.

4. The consumer had a right to enjoy whatever savings the chain-store system of distribution made possible, and eventually the consumer must be served.

Of course, the chains did not fail to point out that if the manufacturers of national brands refused to heed these arguments, the chains would be forced to deal with smaller firms who *would* sell them direct, and the day would come when the chains could get along without the national brands or without being dependent upon them.

"In the case of a well-known dessert, where the manufacturer refused and still refuses to sell us direct," Mr. Jones illustrated, "the chains have fostered and established here a local product and it now ranks *ahead* of the national brand both with independent retailers and chains. And this national product is as well known all over the country as any product you can name."

Undismayed by the cool reception they got in 1921, in the fall of the following year the task force made the same trip again and the same visits. The result was that fifteen more manufacturers agreed to sell the chains direct.

Having achieved so much with the buying power of only five chains behind them, the group then called a meeting of the 26 chains operating at that time in the western states, and organized the Western State Chain Grocers' Association. It represented 685 stores.

From that time on, more and more manufacturers changed their policy regarding selling the chains direct and, although at the time Mr. Jones wrote the article in question, there were still some important manufacturers who refused to recognize the chains, it was not long before practically all of them fell into line.

A by-product of the chains' direct approach to the manufacturers was an investigation by the Federal authorities of the activities of the wholesalers and brokers which had brought it about. That investigation resulted in the suit against the wholesalers to which reference has previously been made.

Incidentally, Mr. Jones noted that the 26 members of the association then had 1,621 stores in operation, with a volume of more than $100,000,000 a year, compared with the 685 stores they had only three years earlier. He attributed the rapidity of their growth at that time to the fact that they were able to get the necessities of life to the consumer cheaper than had been possible before because they were able to "perform the functions of both wholesaler and retailer at one cost."

So much for the earlier reactions of the established order to the challenge of the chains. As has been shown, the first steps taken by the wholesalers in both the grocery and the drug fields were confined to entrenching themselves with manufacturers as the only "regular and legitimate" channel of distribution. When the drug trade found that its efforts to halt price-cutting was nullified by the Supreme Court decision condemning price maintenance as illegal and the wholesale grocers found that they could not legally work on manufacturers to hold the line, other steps were naturally discussed.

In the second decade of the century, chain-store expansion in all lines had been so active that by the early '20s the movement was being widely discussed as a menace to the existing order. Without any legal means to curb price-cutting and with the chains' right to buy direct now beginning to be recognized by manufacturers and producers in almost all lines, about the only possible way left to check further chain-store growth would be through the legislatures. It is not surprising, therefore, that at the convention of the National Association of Retail Grocers, at Los Angeles, in 1922,[13] it was openly suggested that "there ought to be a law" to limit the number of chain stores permitted in any one community.

What followed that suggestion, whether as a result of it or not, made chain-store history for many years thereafter—a period which was to prove extremely difficult and costly to the chains but from which they were to emerge the stronger, perhaps, for their tribulations.

[13] Hayward and White, *Chain Stores* (McGraw-Hill Book Company, New York, 1925), 2nd Edition, p. 393.

CHAPTER VII

"THERE OUGHT TO BE
A LAW"

THE HISTORY of retailing reveals that every innovation in distribution methods has been opposed by those fearful of its impact on the existing order. Department stores, mail-order houses, house-to-house sellers and, most recently, the supermarkets, each in turn ran into more or less organized opposition. Almost invariably the state legislatures were appealed to for special taxes or other restrictive measures designed to check the new method of distribution or to stop it altogether.[1]

But nothing of this kind ever approached in intensity or scope what the chains ran into. The rapidity of their growth between 1910 and 1920, coupled with the price-cutting which many of them practiced, made them the target for plenty of criticism from manufacturers, wholesalers and independent retailers, but no definite effort to check their progress other than indirectly seems to have been made before the early '20s.

True enough, the chain-store "menace" was given as one of the principal reasons for proposed legislation to end the predatory price-cutting evil, but nobody had gone so far as to suggest a more direct attack on the chains themselves.

In 1922, however, at the convention of the National Association of Retail Grocers at Los Angeles[2] it was openly suggested that the number of chain stores in any community should be limited by law.

[1] John P. Nichols, *The Chain Store Tells Its Story* (Institute of Distribution, New York, 1940) p. 127.
[2] See p. 117, *supra*.

No doubt the idea appealed strongly to the grocers who heard it proposed, but how was it to be implemented?

Two approaches naturally presented themselves. The first would be a law flatly prohibiting the operation of more than one store, or more than some other specified number of stores, by a single owner. The second, less drastic but potentially as effective, would be to use the States' taxing power to impose special license taxes on chain stores severe enough to make the opening of additional stores too expensive to permit profitable operation.

The trouble with either approach, however, as the anti-chain forces must have been advised by their lawyers, was that such a law might be held unconstitutional.[3] The Fourteenth Amendment of the Constitution forbids any State to deprive any person of life, liberty or property without due process of law or to deny to any person the equal protection of the laws.

Obviously the chains would claim that a flat prohibition against operating more than a given number of stores would be a denial of their right to engage in a legitimate activity; and special taxes aimed at the chains alone would be assailed, in turn, on the ground that they violated the constitutional guarantee of the equal protection of the laws to all.

The only ground upon which such laws could possibly be sustained would be (1) that they represented a valid exercise of the State's police power—the power which every State has to take whatever measures are necessary to preserve the public health, security, morals or general welfare; and (2) although the equal protection of the laws demands that taxes shall be levied equally upon all who fall within the same classification, tax equality is not necessary as between those who fall within different classifications—and independent stores and chain stores might reasonably be classified differently for taxation purposes.

[3] See views expressed by Charles Wesley Dunn, general counsel for the National Association of Retail Grocers, 1928, p. 153 *post.*

In any event, however, the suggestion made at the Los Angeles convention seems to have been taken seriously by at least one delegation. The Missouri grocers promptly secured the introduction of an anti-chain-store bill in the very next session of their legislature.[4]

This bill was a particularly vicious one, too. It provided for a tax of $50 on the third store (in the State), $100 on the fourth, $200 on the fifth, and so on. By that rate of geometric progression, the tax on the tenth store would have been $6,400!

The bill was disapproved by the House Committee by a vote of eight to two, but the Senate Committee approved it. Public hearings were held and testimony was offered showing that chain-store overhead and chain-store prices were both substantially lower than those of their competitors. Comparative prices of 32 well-known grocery items, as of February 20, 1923, were used to establish a substantial differential in favor of the chains.

The bill did not pass. If, however, its introduction gives Missouri the distinction of having been the first State to consider the enactment of such a law, it should not be overlooked that Missouri was likewise the first State to kill such a proposal. Furthermore, Missouri shares with nineteen other States the distinction of never having enacted an anti-chain measure of any kind.

The next year a milder type of anti-chain law was introduced in the Virginia legislature by Senator Saxon Holt of Newport News.[5] It provided that chain stores in communities of 2,500 population or more should pay a tax of $15 on every $1,000 worth of merchandise purchased, if only for two stores, and $20 for every $1,000 worth of merchandise purchased if three or more stores were operated. The fate of the bill is not recorded, but apparently it failed.

Two anti-chain bills are reported to have been introduced

[4] Hayward and White, *Chain Stores, op. cit.,* p. 363.
[5] *Retail Ledger,* Philadelphia, February 1, 1924.

in 1925,[6] and another in 1926, but references to them do not identify the States involved. All three failed to pass.

Then in 1927, by which time the hue and cry against chain stores had gained rapidly in volume, no less than thirteen bills aimed at the chains were offered in various State legislatures, including Alabama, Arkansas, Illinois, Iowa, Georgia, Kansas, Maryland, North Carolina, Pennsylvania and Wisconsin. Three of them, Maryland, North Carolina and Georgia, passed bills aimed at chain stores in general. A fourth, Pennsylvania, passed one aimed only at chain drug stores.

The Maryland law is of special interest because it went after its objective head on. It flatly prohibited the operation of more than five chain stores in Allegany County by any individual or corporation and, for full measure, it also imposed a license fee of $500 on each chain store operated. The same type of bill was considered that year in Arkansas, Iowa, Kansas and Wisconsin, but only the Maryland bill was enacted.[7]

Obviously the Maryland law would have achieved its purpose effectively, and the chains could not permit it to stand unchallenged.

Accordingly an action was promptly started by the Keystone Grocery & Tea Co. in the Circuit Court of Allegany County to have the law declared unconstitutional.[8] Other chains, including the F. W. Woolworth Company, which filed a brief, supported the proceeding, for a favorable outcome was obviously of the utmost importance if the chains were to continue to function.

The Keystone company had been established in 1917, and in the ten years of its existence had grown to the point where it had 210 stores in all, although only nine of them were in Allegany County. Under the law in question, it was con-

[6] All data relating to anti-chain-store legislation is drawn from the *Retailers Manual of Taxes and Regulations*, 1958 ed., compiled and published by Institute of Distribution and Variety Stores Association, New York.

[7] *Chain Store Age*, June, 1927.

[8] Keystone Grocery & Tea Co. *v.* Huster, unreported, but appearing in the invaluable collection of cases entitled *Chain Stores in the Law Courts*, compiled by E. W. Simms, of White & Simms, for the Institute of Distribution, 1939, p. 1.

fronted with the alternative of closing four stores and paying an annual tax of $500 on each of the five retained, or being found guilty of a misdemeanor.

On April 21, 1928, Judge Albert A. Doub handed down his decision. Recognizing the far-reaching significance of the issues involved, he wrote an extensive opinion. He declared:

"This seems to be the first case in which a statute dealing with the chain stores has been considered by any of the Courts of this country except the case of The Great Atlantic & Pacific Tea Company *v.* Doughton, Commissioner of Revenue of North Carolina, in the Superior Court of Wake County, North Carolina. The Act there passed on was one to impose a special license tax on owners of six stores or more, while such tax was not imposed on owners of five stores or less, and the Court held the act to be unconstitutional and void. No opinion was filed but the findings of facts showed the principles involved in the case before us, or most of them, were considered and the act was declared to be unconstitutional and void."

Considering the chain's claim that the law in question violated the Fourteenth Amendment of the Constitution, Judge Doub said:

"The plaintiff is engaged in an innocent, ordinary, useful and necessary business, permitted and authorized by the laws of this State and every other State. It has made substantial investments in merchandise, stock, legal obligations and commitments for leases and intangible property, in organizing its business and building up its good will. These investments, to the extent of all nine chain stores, will be substantially impaired by the provisions of this statute. As far as the five stores are concerned the effect of the license fee of five hundred dollars will be to impair the profits on the investment to a very material degree and the owners will evidently be deprived of property under the provisions of the first and second sections of the Act. One store in the city of Cumberland may pay a tax of twenty dollars [a tax levied on all retailers based on amount of inventory carried] while the chain store will be required to pay a license tax of five hundred and twenty dollars, although both of them are engaged in the same general business, conducting it in substantially the same manner, having the same amount of capital invested, subject to the same losses and perhaps able to secure, as a result of the business, similar profits. It is impossible to declare that both of them will receive, if this Act is to be enforced, the equal protection of the laws as required by the Fourteenth Amendment of the Constitution."

Judge Doub pointed out further that as "there is nothing characteristic of the chain store that makes it peculiarly and essentially different in organization, in plan or in method of doing business from other stores similarly organized but not classified as chain stores," the law represented an unreasonable and unjustifiable discrimination between the chain stores and other stores of the same general class.

Furthermore, the Court decided that a license tax of $500 was so out of line with customary mercantile license taxes that it was "unreasonable, oppressive and confiscatory," particularly as it was a flat charge without relation to locality, inventory value, sales or profits.

Of course it was contended in behalf of the law that, even though it did discriminate against chain stores, such discrimination was justified as an exercise by the State of its "police power."

But Judge Doub couldn't see it that way. Said he:

"What is there in terms of the Act that bears upon public order, security, health or morals? It is not directed against any of the practices alleged to be peculiar to the chain-store business and charged to be objectionable. It recites in the title that the object is to limit the number of chain stores and to provide an additional license fee and penalties. Its purpose is not regulation, not correction of abuses and not the prevention of monopoly, but reduction of certain classes of stores (and raising revenue) of any conceivable size, conducted under any conceivable plan, for one organization in Allegany County. It permits the five chain stores to indulge in all the practices said to be objectionable, provided only five are guilty of such alleged offenses. All of the five chain stores may be located in the city of Cumberland or of Frostburg. They may be permitted to monopolize all the retail grocery business of the city to the selfish profit of the owner and without making any charitable contributions to the community. They may undersell and eliminate competitors and send to other places their profits; and yet they are perfectly free to develop into a monopoly, if such a thing is possible, by underselling their competitors and driving them all out of business. The retail grocery business is not classified as a public service business, affected with any public interest or *quasi* public interest."

Turning to the other side of the picture, Judge Doub took judicial notice of the many ways in which chain stores serve the public interest. He said:

"By purchasing direct from the manufacturer and producer and eliminating the profits and expenses of the wholesaler, jobber and broker and the cost of delivery and selling for cash and thereby escaping the usual losses resulting from sales on credit the chains are more likely to give to the farmer, truckman and consumer part of the middle man's profit and so to become a blessing to society and the public generally. Indeed the very elements so earnestly insisted upon by the defendants as a justification for this extra license fee are the very elements that would seem to justify the development of the chain store.

"The testimony does not disclose that there is anything sinister about their practices foreboding any evil to the public which can be anticipated, but it does show that the chain stores are more cleanly and sanitary than others; that they are conducted with skill and efficiency; that they do not delude the buyer into purchasing goods by giving him credit when he is unable to pay for them; that they turn over their stock more rapidly than other stores and do not keep on their shelves goods long enough to deteriorate and become unwholesome or impaired in quality and that through them the tendency is to reduce the cost to the consumer. With the rapid development of means of transit and the increase in the number of automobiles, now owned by almost every family in the country, delivery of goods by the merchant is no longer so necessary, and the buyer can save something of the cost of operating his automobile by saving the expense of delivery. Moreover, chain stores help to insure regular rentals, furnish regular employment, stabilize the value of real estate and spend a large part of the proceeds of their sales in the community."

Concluding that there was nothing in the record that even remotely proved that the Act bore "any relation either directly or indirectly to the protection of the general public in their health, morals, good order, security or general welfare," Judge Doub found the law "repugnant to the Constitution" and issued a permanent injunction restraining its enforcement.

Judge Doub's reasoning has been quoted at such length not only because his opinion was the first to be handed down in a case involving anti-chain legislation, but because it presents many of the arguments the chains were to use again and again in support of their contention that anti-chain-store taxes were inescapably in conflict with the Constitution.

The decision was apparently accepted as final so far as the flat prohibition approach to the problem was concerned. No appeal was taken from it and no similar bill was ever passed by any other State legislature.

For a time it seemed that Judge Doub's line of reasoning might prove equally effective against laws which, masked as revenue measures, struck at the chains by imposing heavier taxes on them than on their single-store competitors, without putting a limit on the number of stores which could be operated.

The North Carolina decision to which Judge Doub referred had been made in a case challenging the constitutionality of a 1927 law which levied a license tax of $50 on each store operated by anyone with six or more.

The plaintiffs in the case included A&P, The David Pender Grocery Co., Rose's 5, 10, and 25¢ Stores, F. W. Woolworth

Company, J. C. Penney Company, G. R. Kinney Company, Milner Stores, Carolina Stores, and M. Samuels Company. Each of them operated six or more stores in the State, each of them had paid the tax under protest, and each of them wanted its money back on the ground that the law was unconstitutional and void.

The case had been tried by Judge Cranmer, without a jury, and, in February, 1928, he had decided that the law was unconstitutional, but he had handed down no opinion.

However his decision was appealed and later that year the North Carolina Supreme Court affirmed it.[9]

The key point of the decision was that there was no "real and substantial difference" between a merchant who operates six or more stores and one who operates five or less stores. Judge Connor, who wrote the opinion for the Court, concluded therefore that treating them differently for taxation purposes was based on an arbitrary classification and resulted in depriving the taxed group of the equal protection of the laws.

Chief Justice Stacy and Judge Clarkson, who concurred in the decision, stressed the point that the vice in the law in question was that, whereas a chain of five stores paid no tax, a chain of six stores was taxed not only on its sixth store but on its first five stores as well. They thought that that was so arbitrary that the law had to be invalidated.

The Georgia law passed in 1927 followed the same pattern as the North Carolina law. It imposed a tax of $250 per store on chains operating five or more stores. It, too, was declared unconstitutional but, in any event, it was superseded by a new law passed at the 1929 session. The new law followed the identical pattern of the earlier one, except that the tax was set at $50 per store instead of $250, but it did introduce a new wrinkle which was apparently designed to meet the constitutional shortcomings of the 1927 law.

The new wrinkle was an express statement in the law itself

[9] Great A&P Tea Co. v. Doughton, 196 N.C. 145; 144 S.E. 701 (1928).

that "under the police powers of this State, the business of conducting chain stores . . . hereby is classified as a business tending to foster monopoly."

The law was attacked by Woolworth and other chains. When the lower court refused to declare it unconstitutional, an appeal was taken to the Georgia Supreme Court. The decision was reversed.[10] The Court handed down only a short opinion. It did not have to pass on the question as to whether the business of conducting chain stores tends to foster monopoly, because it invalidated the law on the ground that "the classification attempted to be made is founded on the difference between one who owns or operates more than five stores on the one hand, and one who operates five or less on the other" and is "arbitrary and unreasonable."

In other words, the Court did not decide that a State could not classify chain stores separately for taxation purposes, but merely that if it did undertake to do so, it would have to treat *all* chains equally.

The fourth law passed in 1927, in Pennsylvania, which, as has been pointed out, was aimed only at the drug chains, followed the flat-prohibition approach although its objective was to be achieved in a devious way. It prohibited anyone from *owning* a drug store unless he was a registered pharmacist, and, in the case of a corporation, unless *all* the stockholders were registered pharmacists, although it did permit a corporation to continue to own and operate the stores it had when the act became effective even though its stockholders did not meet the requirement.

The Louis K. Liggett Company promptly went into action. An injunction was sought in a Federal court composed of three judges. After all the arguments had been heard, the court sustained the law! It decided that the Act was a valid exercise of the police power, because there was a reasonable relation between the *ownership* of a drug store and the safeguarding of the public health. That relation was found in the

[10] Woolworth v. Harrison, 171 Ga. 891; 156 S.E. 904 (1931).

fact that the *owners* of a drug store, rather than the pharmacist in charge of the prescription department, have the final
say as to what drugs shall be stocked, and the legislature may
reasonably have thought that a corporation whose stockholders were not all registered men might be tempted to buy
drugs on price rather than on quality!

The case was carried direct to the U.S. Supreme Court. Justice Sutherland, writing the opinion for the Court,[11] decided
that in view of the fact that the State's pharmacy laws provided ample safeguards against the improper compounding of
prescriptions or sale of drugs detrimental to the public safety,
the idea that it was necessary for the *owners* of a drug store to
be qualified pharmacists was based on "conjecture, unsup-
ported by anything of substance."

Pointing out that no evidence had been produced to show
that the operation of chain drug stores had been detrimental
to public health, he declared that the law could not be sustained as a valid exercise of the police power, and the lower
court's decision was reversed.

This was the first time an anti-chain law had reached the
highest court in the land. Its outcome was particularly encouraging to the chains because it was felt that if the police-
power doctrine could not be successfully invoked against the
drug chains, which had a direct relation to public health, the
chains in other fields would have an even stronger case.

That the Pennsylvania Drug Store Ownership Law, as it
was called, reflected an organized effort to stop the growth
of the drug chains was evidenced, as George M. Gales, president of Liggett's, pointed out at the time, by the fact that
similar bills had been introduced in sixteen other States as
well, although most of them had died.

In 1928, only one of the four anti-chain bills introduced
was passed. That was in South Carolina. It followed the same
pattern as the North Carolina and Georgia laws, imposing a
tax of $100 per store on chains operating five or more, and it

[11] Liggett *v.* Baldridge, 278 U.S. 105 (1928).

met the same fate. On February 27, 1929, the Richland County Court of Common Pleas declared it unconstitutional, citing the decision of the North Carolina Supreme Court which had just been handed down.[12]

Notwithstanding these setbacks the anti-chain legislative barrage was maintained with increasing vigor. In 1929, no less than 62 more bills were introduced. Three of them passed: one in Georgia, which was invalidated, as previously pointed out, another in North Carolina and a third in Indiana.

These North Carolina and Indiana bills were destined to become extremely significant, for they introduced a new feature designed to correct the constitutional flaw in the earlier acts.

They both started the chain-store tax with the *second* store, thus laying the foundation for the contention that the single store merchant was different from a merchant with two or more stores not merely in *degree* but in *kind*—that he was essentially a different breed of cat!

The North Carolina law set a flat-rate tax of $50 per store on each store in excess of one. The chains challenged it in the Wake County Superior Court, the very Court which had previously declared the 1927 law unconstitutional. But this time it decided that a classification which distinguished chain stores from single stores was neither arbitrary nor unreasonable.

An appeal to the North Carolina Supreme Court availed nothing. Judge Connor, who had written the opinion invalidating the 1927 act, now wrote one sustaining the 1929 variation.[13]

"There is a real and substantial difference between merchants who exercise the privilege of carrying on their business in this State by means of two or more stores and those who maintain and operate only one store," he declared, adding that

[12] Southern Grocery Stores Inc. *v.* Query, unreported, but appearing in *Chain Stores in the Law Courts*, p. 18, *op. cit.*

[13] Great A&P Tea Co. *v.* Maxwell, 199 N.C. 433, 154 S.E. 838, affirmed without opinion, 284 U.S. 575.

the former "have and exercise a more valuable privilege."

He pointed out that the trouble with the 1927 law was that the tax was not levied on chain-store operators *per se,* as was evidenced by the fact that it exempted the chains with five or less stores.

That decision was handed down in 1930. It was the first serious set-back the chains had had. They carried it to the U.S. Supreme Court, but by that time, that Court had already made its historic decision regarding the Indiana law, and the North Carolina Supreme Court's decision was automatically sustained.

The Indiana tax differed from the North Carolina tax in one important respect in that it was a graduated tax, which increased progressively with the number of stores operated. It imposed a license tax of $3 per year on single stores, $10 per year on each additional store up to five; $15 per year on each additional store up to ten; $20 per year on each additional store up to twenty; and $25 per year on each additional store in excess of twenty.

Although the tax was really nominal in amount, the chains opposed it vigorously not only because they disagreed with the principle of special taxes against chain stores but because they knew that once such a pattern of taxation received judicial sanction, it would be only a question of time and conditions before it would be used to impose a greater toll. With most of the states at that time finding it increasingly difficult to balance their budgets, any new source of revenue which could be tapped without too much political danger would naturally have a strong appeal to legislators. Special taxes against chain stores certainly belonged in the category.

For the purpose of testing the constitutionality of the Indiana tax, a case was instituted in a special Federal Court of three judges sitting in Indianapolis.

The plaintiff was Lafayette Jackson, owner of a local grocery chain doing business as the Standard Grocery Co.

Mr. Jackson owned and operated 225 stores, all in the city of Indianapolis.

If his 225 stores had been owned and operated by 225 different individuals, the total tax paid by them would have been 225 times $3, or $675. But because all the stores were owned by a single individual the graduated formula employed in the law made Mr. Jackson's tax $5,443, or eight times as much as it would have been had the stores been separately owned.

Able lawyers were retained by Mr. Jackson and the other chains, who were all vitally interested in the outcome of the case. The trial lasted for more than a week, with both sides producing marketing experts to support their conflicting contentions. The chains contended, of course, that, as Judge Doub had decided in the Maryland case, the only difference between a chain and a single store was in the number of stores operated, and that that difference did not provide a legal basis on which to tax them unequally. The State, on the other hand, insisted that the chains enjoyed certain advantages inherent in their system which put them in a different class from single store merchants and justified the imposition of a higher tax.

The three-judge court decided for the chains, declaring the law unconstitutional.[14] The State appealed direct to the U.S. Supreme Court.

When the case was argued March 5, 1931, the only adverse decision that could be used against the chains was that of the North Carolina Supreme Court, which was itself being appealed to the U.S. Supreme Court. On the other hand, the chains could point to the decision of the Supreme Court itself invalidating the Pennsylvania Drug Store Ownership Law only a few months earlier.

Nevertheless, when the decision was handed down on May 18, the chain stores learned to their amazement that, so far as the Supreme Court was concerned, chain stores could law-

[14] State Board v. Jackson, 38 Fed. (2nd) 652.

fully be taxed differently from independent stores, and that the tax could be lawfully graduated according to the number of stores operated.[15]

True enough, the decision was a divided one, with Justices Roberts, Holmes, Brandeis, Stone and C. J. Hughes constituting the majority, and Justices Sutherland, Van Devanter, McReynolds and Butler dissenting.

Justice Roberts, who wrote the majority opinion, declared:

> "It is not the function of this Court in cases like the present to consider the propriety or justness of the tax, to seek for the motives or to criticize the public policy which prompted the adoption of the legislation. Our duty is to sustain the classification . . . if there are substantial differences between the occupations separately classified. Such differences need not be great."

In concluding that the classification was neither arbitrary nor unreasonable, the Justice argued that the astonishing growth of the chains was proof enough "that there are differences and advantages" in their favor.

Furthermore, he said the Court below had erroneously assumed that the difference was solely one of ownership.

"It disregarded the differences shown by the record," he declared. "They consist not merely in ownership, but in organization, management and type of business transacted. The statute treats upon a similar basis all owners of chain stores similarly situated. . . . That is all that the Constitution requires."

Justice Sutherland, whose dissenting opinion was concurred in by three of his colleagues, took the position that whatever advantages the chain stores enjoyed stemmed from the fact that their operations were on a larger scale, and, as the State's own expert witness had conceded, were enjoyed equally by any large-scale operator even if he operated only one store, such as a large department store.

---

[15] State Board v. Jackson, 283 U.S. 527 (1931).

"It thus appears," he declared, "that the advantages attributed to the chain store lie not in the fact that it is one of a *NUMBER* of stores under the same management, supervision or ownership, but in the fact that it is one of the parts of a *LARGE BUSINESS*. . . . The classification should fall because it is made to depend . . . upon the mere circumstance —wholly irrelevant so far as any of the advantages claimed are concerned—that the business of one is carried on under many roofs, and that of the other under one only."

Conceding that the maximum tax of $25 might not in itself be considered excessive, he pointed out, prophetically enough, that:

"It will open the door of opportunity to the State to increase the amount to an oppressive extent. This Court has frequently said, and it cannot be too often repeated in cases of this character, that the power to tax is the power to destroy; and this constitutes a reason why that power, however moderately exercised in given instances, should be zealously confined to the limits set by the Constitution. . . . There does not seem to be any sure comfort in the suggestion, sometimes made, that this court may be expected to intervene whenever the tax reaches the point of destruction."

How correct the Justice was is reflected in the fact that within two years after this decision, Indiana raised its chain-store tax from $25 per store to $150 per store, in the top bracket. Furthermore, the Supreme Court was soon to declare specifically that chain-store taxes could be as drastic as a State saw fit to impose, even if the burden became prohibitive.

But whatever one may think of the conflicting viewpoints expressed in the majority and dissenting opinions, the majority opinion, of course, became the law of the land, even though by a five-to-four margin.

The decision was all that was necessary to release a regular epidemic of such proposals, and, as most of the States in that period were eagerly seeking new sources of revenue, the outlook for the chains was dark indeed.

Table 17

ANTI-CHAIN-STORE TAX BILLS, 1923-1957

Source: Retailers Manual of Taxes and Regulations, 14th Edition, 1958, published by Variety Stores Association, Inc. and Institute of Distribution, Inc., edited by Gladys M. Kiernan, Editor, and Arthur Pite, Associate Editor.

YEAR	BILLS	ENACTED	STATES AND DISPOSITION*
1923	1	0	
1924	1	0	
1925	2	0	
1926	1	0	
1927	13	3	Ga. (A); Md. (A); N.C. (A).
1928	4	1	S.C. (A).
1929	62	3	Ga. (A); Ind. (B); N.C. (B).
1930	80	3	Ky. (A); Miss. (B); S.C. (I).
1931	175	3	Ala. (B); Ariz. (C); Fla. (A).
1932	125	2	La. (B); Wis. (B).
1933	225	13	Fla. (B); Ida. (C); Ind. (I); Me. (C); Md. (I); Mich. (B); Minn. (B); Mont. (B); N.M. (B); N.C. (B); Vt. (A); W.Va. (I); Wis. (A).
1934	40	4	Colo. (H); Ky. (A); La. (I); N.M. (A).
1935	163	9	Ala. (I); Calif. (D); Fla. (B); Ia. (I); Mich. (I); N.C. (B); S.D. (A); Tex. (I); Wis. (E).
1936	27	2	Ky. (A); Miss. (B).
1937	97	8	Ga. (C); Minn. (E); Mont. (A); N.C. (B); Pa. (A); S.D. (B); Tenn. (I); Wis. (E); Miss. (B).
1938	19	1	Miss. (B).
1939	99	4	Mont. (I); N.C. (F); S.D. (C); Tenn. (A).
1940	10	2	Ky. (A); Miss. (I).
1941	45	2	Fla. (C); Utah (D).
1942	7	0	
1943	20	0	
1944	4	0	
1945	10	0	
1946	1	0	
1947	12	0	
1948	3	0	
1949	16	1	N.C. (See 1939).
1950	4	0	
1951	8	0	
1952	0	0	
1953	3	0	
1954	2	0	
1955	9	0	
1956	1	0	
1957	8	1	W.Va. (J).
	1,297	62	

* KEY TO DISPOSITION. (A) Invalidated; (B) Superseded; (C) Repealed; (D) Rejected by Referendum; (E) Expired by limitation; (F) Graduated rates replaced by flat tax in 1949; (H) Retained by referendum; (I) In effect; (J) Increased tax enacted in 1933.

What actually happened is indicated by the box score shown in Table 17. It reveals that, prior to 1931, the number of tax bills introduced against the chains had totalled 164 of which 10 had been enacted in seven different States. In 1931, however, 175 were introduced; in 1932, 125, and in 1933, 225! Of the 525 bills introduced in those three years, eighteen were enacted. From 1934 to 1941, inclusive, 500 more of such bills were introduced, of which 32 became law. Altogether, from 1923 to 1941, inclusive, 60 of these bills were enacted, although the majority of them merely superseded earlier enactments. In fact, all the 60 bills which became laws were enacted in 28 States. Today only 14 States impose such taxes, and one of these, North Carolina, materially modified its tax in 1949.

In the fourteen States which no longer impose such taxes, here is what happened: six were repealed; four were declared unconstitutional as being in conflict with State constitutions; two expired by their own limitation and were not re-enacted; and two were rejected by the public through a referendum.

A breakdown of anti-chain-store tax legislation by States is provided in Table 18. Not included because of its different nature is the chain store warehouse tax enacted by the State of Washington in 1955. It imposes a tax of ¼ of 1% on the wholesale value of merchandise distributed by a chain of two or more stores from its own warehouse.

In addition to the taxes levied by the States, as disclosed in Table 17, a number of cities passed local ordinances along the same lines. The first of these municipal taxes was imposed by Portland, Ore., in 1931. A public referendum initiated by the chains failed, by a small margin, to upset it. A number of other cities throughout the country followed Portland's example. Many of these municipal chain-store taxes, however, were either repealed by the bodies which enacted them or were invalidated by the courts.[16] Of 70 cities still imposing such taxes,

[16] *The Chain Store Tells Its Story, op. cit.,* pp. 150, 151; *The Chain Store Problem, op. cit.,* pp. 261, 262.

TABLE 18

ANTI-CHAIN-STORE LEGISLATION BY STATES*

NONE ENACTED	ENACTED BUT INOPERATIVE	STILL IN EFFECT
1. Arkansas	Arizona (a)	Alabama
2. Connecticut	California (b)	Colorado
3. Delaware	Florida (a)	Indiana
4. Illinois	Georgia (a)	Iowa
5. Kansas	Idaho (a)	Louisiana
6. Massachusetts	Kentucky (c)	Maryland
7. Missouri	Maine (a)	Michigan
8. Nebraska	Minnesota (d)	Mississippi
9. Nevada	New Mexico (c)	Montana
10. New Hampshire	Pennsylvania (c)	North Carolina
11. New Jersey	South Dakota (a)	South Carolina
12. New York	Utah (b)	Tennessee
13. North Dakota	Vermont (c)	Texas
14. Ohio	Wisconsin (d)	West Virginia
15. Oklahoma		
16. Oregon		
17. Rhode Island		
18. Virginia		
19. Washington		
20. Wyoming		

(a) Repealed; (b) Rejected by referendum; (c) Invalidated by court decision; (d) Expired by its own terms.
* Source: *Retailers Manual of Taxes and Regulations, op. cit.*

65 are in North Carolina, and two in West Virginia, while Florida, South Carolina, and Virginia each have one. In the majority of instances, the tax is on a flat-rate basis and amounts to $50 per year per store.[17]

Although, with the Indiana decision, the chains were licked so far as laws of the same type were concerned, they challenged the constitutionality of every *new* enactment which, because of some new feature, gave them a chance to go to bat again.

Thus, when Florida enacted a law in 1931 imposing a graduated tax on chain stores after the pattern of the Indiana law, but increasing the tax where the stores involved were located in more than one county, the chains promptly sought an injunction. The lower court denied it, the Supreme Court of

[17] *Retailers Manual of Taxes and Regulations, op. cit.*

Florida likewise agreed that the law was constitutional, and again the chains appealed to the U.S. Supreme Court.

Justice Roberts, who had written the majority opinion in the Indiana case, wrote the majority opinion in this one also.[18] He agreed with the chains that it was arbitrary and unreasonable to levy a higher tax on a given number of stores if they were located in more than one county than if they were located all in one county.

The Court invalidated that section of the law but upheld the rest of it, taking advantage of the occasion to reaffirm its decision in the Indiana case. It emphasized its conviction that a chain was different from the ordinary individually operated small store, a department store or a co-operative or a voluntary chain (a group of individually owned stores banded together for their mutual benefit). Even though in some cases and to some extent, the advantages stemming from the chain-store system might likewise be enjoyed by other types of operation, the Court was firm in its belief that chain stores were sufficiently different to warrant special tax treatment.

Furthermore, the Court upheld another section of the law which boded no good for the chains if other States were led to adopt it. It required each county to impose an additional tax amounting to 25 per cent of the State tax, graduated on the stores within the county, and, for full measure, authorized each incorporated municipality in the State to do the same thing!

A by-product of this decision was the lengthy dissenting opinion of Justice Brandeis. With inimitable clarity, he spelled out his philosophy regarding the menace of "big business."

He was for upholding the whole statute, including the extra tax imposed on chains operating in more than one county.

Pointing out that all the plaintiffs in the case were corporations, he took the position that, as far as they were concerned at least, the State could charge them anything it wanted for the privilege of engaging in business. He declared:

[18] Liggett v. Lee, 288 U.S. 517 (1933).

"As this privilege is one which a State may withhold or grant it may charge such compensation as it pleases. . . . Since the authority to operate many stores, or to operate in two or more counties, is certainly a broader privilege than to operate only one store, or in only one county, there is in this record no basis for finding that it is unreasonable to make the charge higher for the greater privilege."

Furthermore, he made the point that the law in question was not merely a revenue measure—its main purpose was social and economic. On that basis, he said, that "if the State should conclude that bigness in retail merchandising as manifested in corporate chain stores menaces the public welfare, it might prohibit the excessive size or extent of that business as it prohibits excessive size or weight in motor trucks or excessive height in the buildings of a city."

Justice Cardozo also wrote a dissenting opinion, with which Justice Stone concurred, but he did not cover as much territory as Justice Brandeis, whose reasons, he said, "had been stated with such a wealth of learning."

His view was that, in increasing the tax for chains operating in more than one county, the State might reasonably have felt that chains in that category had ceased to be local enterprises, and, for that reason, were less desirable socially. "Courts would be lacking in candor," he said, "if they were not to concede the presence of such a motive behind this chain-store legislation. But a purpose to bear more heavily on one class than another will not avail without more to condemn a tax as void. . . . The concept may be right or wrong. At least it corresponds to an intelligible belief, and one widely prevalent today among honest men and women. . . . With that our function ends."

Is a filling station a store?

That was the question which the Standard Oil Company of N.J. was primarily interested in having the courts answer when the West Virginia Tax Commissioner answered it in the affirmative. For the affirmative answer meant that under the chain-store license tax enacted in 1933, Standard Oil would have to pay a tax of $250 on each of its filling stations in excess of 75. As it operated 949 of them in the State, and more than half of them had shown an average profit of only $89.75, it was obviously a mighty heavy burden for such stations to carry.

A three-judge Federal Court decided that a filling station was not a store, within the meaning of the act and, in any event, the tax was so much harsher when applied to filling stations than when it was applied to other chains that it amounted to a denial to Standard Oil of the equal protection of the laws.

When the appeal reached the Supreme Court, Judge Cardozo wrote the majority opinion.[19] He disagreed with the lower court on both counts. Not only did he find that gasoline stations were well within the definition of "store" contained in the Act, but he confirmed what Justice Sutherland had predicted in the Indiana case—that even a prohibitive tax would be sustained.

Said Justice Cardozo: "When the power to tax exists, the extent of the burden is a matter for the discretion of the lawmakers," citing with approval the language used by the Court in connection with a different type of tax: "Even if the tax should destroy a business, it would not be made invalid or require compensation upon that ground alone. Those who enter upon a business take that risk." For whatever consolation it might offer, the Justice added that "the tax now assailed may have its roots in an erroneous conception of the ills of the body politic or of the efficacy of such a measure to bring about a cure. We have no thought in anything we have written to declare it expedient or even just, or, for that matter, to declare the contrary. We deal with power only."

Justices Van Devanter, McReynolds, Sutherland and Butler

[19] Fox v. Standard Oil of N.J., 294 U.S. 87 (1935).

again dissented as they had in the Indiana case, but the majority, of course, prevailed. Thus the States were given free rein to tax the chains just as much as they pleased.

That decision was handed down January 14, 1935. A couple of months later, however, the Supreme Court handed down another decision in which the chains were to fare much better.

The case involved the constitutionality of another new type of law, passed in Kentucky in 1930, whose pattern had been followed by several other States before the Supreme Court finally passed on it.

This Kentucky law levied a graduated tax on *all* retailers, based on sales. It did not single out the chains but struck at them just as effectively by penalizing large volume however attained—whether through a big department store or through a number of smaller stores owned and operated by a single individual or corporation.

The progression of the tax was painfully steep, ranging from $\frac{1}{20}$th of 1 per cent on sales of $400,000 or less, to 1 per cent on sales in excess of $1,000,000.

How it would have worked can be illustrated by applying the formula to (1) a department store with sales of $4,000,-000; (2) a chain of ten stores with sales of $400,000 each; and (3) ten independent stores each doing $400,000.

The department store's tax would have totalled $33,050, made up as follows:

Sales		Rate	Tax
1st	$400,000	$\frac{1}{20}$th of 1%	$200
Next	100,000	$\frac{2}{20}$ths of 1%	100
Next	100,000	$\frac{5}{20}$ths of 1%	250
Next	100,000	$\frac{8}{20}$ths of 1%	400
Next	100,000	$1\frac{1}{20}$ths of 1%	550
Next	100,000	$1\frac{4}{20}$ths of 1%	700
Next	100,000	$1\frac{7}{20}$ths of 1%	850
Next	3,000,000	1%	30,000
		Total	$33,050

The chain of ten stores having the same total sales would have had to pay the same total tax of $33,050, or an average of $3,305 per store.

But the ten individual stores, each doing $400,000, would have had to pay only $200 each, or a total of $2,000.

As a matter of fact, the individual stores would have had to pay nothing at all in most instances under this law, for every merchant was allowed to take as a credit against the tax whatever he had to pay under other laws. In the case of most merchants doing less than $100,000 a year, which includes the vast majority of independents, the allowance would have meant no tax on his sales at all.

Several department stores and chains attacked the law on the basis of its obvious inequality. A three-judge District Court dismissed the bill on ground of lack of jurisdiction. An appeal to the U.S. Supreme Court brought a reversal.[20] The District Court then tried the case on the merits and found the law valid. A second appeal to the U.S. Supreme Court again brought a reversal, the law being held unconstitutional by a six-to-three decision.[21] This double trip to the Supreme Court accounts for the time lag between the passage of the law in 1930 and the Court's decision in 1935.

Justice Roberts, who had written the majority opinion in the Indiana case upholding a graduated tax based on the number of *stores* operated, and also in the Florida case, in which the soundness of that principle was reaffirmed, now wrote the majority opinion condemning a graduated tax based on the volume of *sales* attained.

Here is how he reconciled what, on their face, might seem to be conflicting rulings. He said:

"In several recent cases we sustained the classification of chain stores for taxation at rates higher than those applicable to single stores and graduated upward on each store as the

[20] Stewart Dry Goods Co. *v.* Lewis, 287 U.S. 9 (1932).
[21] Stewart Dry Goods Co. *v.* Lewis, 294 U.S. 550 (1935).

total number of units in one ownership increased. We found this classification reasonable because of advantages incident to the conduct of the multiple stores and obvious differences in chain methods of merchandising as contrasted with those practised in the operation of one store. The instant cases present a classification of quite another kind. The Kentucky statute ignores the form of organization and the method of conducting business. The taxable class is retail merchants, whether individuals, partnerships or corporations; those who sell in one store or many; those who offer but one sort of goods and those who, through departments, deal in many lines of merchandise. The law arbitrarily classified these vendors for the imposition of a varying rate of taxation, solely by reference to the volume of their transactions, disregarding the absence of any reasonable relation between the chosen criterion of classification and the privilege the enjoyment of which is said to be the subject taxed. It exacts from two persons different amounts for the privilege of doing exactly similar acts because the one has performed the act oftener than the other."

Earlier in his opinion, the Justice had characterized the law as "unjustifiably unequal, whimsical and arbitrary, as much so as would be a tax on tangible personal property, say cattle, stepped up in rate on each additional animal owned by the taxpayer, or a tax on land similarly graduated according to the number of parcels owned."

Rejecting the argument that a merchant's net income and his consequent ability to pay increase as the volume of his sales grow, the Justice said:

"Argument is not needed, and indeed practical admission was made at the bar, that the gross sales of a merchant do not bear a constant relation to his net profits; that net profits vary from year to year in the same enterprise; that diverse kinds of merchandise yield differing rates of profit; and that gross and net profits vary with the character of the business as well as its volume. . . . Expert witnesses . . . endeavored to establish that net profits or net worth grow with increased sales. But their testimony not only indicated great variations within each class selected for comparison, but also showed that in some of the classes representing the greater amount of sales the net profit, or the addition to the net worth, is smaller than in a class having less aggregate sales. The best that can be said for this evidence is that, averaging the results of the concerns making the reports, it is true "generally speaking," as the court below put it, that profits increase with sales. The ratio of increase, however, differs in different lines of activity and even as between concerns carrying on the same business, and so many exceptions and reservations must be made that averages are misleading . . . We think the graduated rates imposed were not intended to bear any relation to net profits."

How Justice Roberts could have recognized these obvious facts in condemning the Kentucky tax based on sales and have ignored them in the Indiana case where they applied with equal force is hard to understand.

That they do apply with equal force to a graduated tax based on the number of stores was made clear by Dr. Charles F. Phillips, now president of Bates College, in the course of a comprehensive discussion of "State Discriminatory Chain Store Taxation," as of 1936.[22]

He showed by convincing examples that the Indiana chain-store tax was every bit as "unequal, whimsical and arbitrary" as Justice Roberts said the Kentucky law was. He emphasized (1) that it hits small chains as well as big ones; (2) it ignores the great range of variation between the profits of different chains both within the same field of operation and in different fields, and even as between the stores operated by the same chain; and (3) it ignores the fact that chain-store profits are by no means constant from year to year.

In the case of the Indiana law, the Supreme Court held that the fact that "generally speaking" more *stores* means more profits justified a graduated tax based upon the number of

[22] *Harvard Business Review*, Spring Number, 1936.

stores, but in the case of the Kentucky law they held that the fact that "generally speaking" more *sales* means more profits did *not* justify a graduated tax based upon sales.

Perhaps if the Kentucky law had come up for consideration first, the Indiana law would never have been upheld; but, as it was, the chains must consider themselves fortunate that the decision in the Indiana case did not lead the Supreme Court to take the same action in the Kentucky case.

Another type of chain-store tax was involved in a Louisiana law passed in 1934. It was modeled after the Indiana law, except for one added feature. The tax was graduated on the basis of the total number of stores operated whether *within* the State or *outside*. The top bracket of $550 per store applied to all stores in excess of 500.

A&P then had some 15,000 stores in all, but only 106 of them were in Louisiana. Nevertheless, by the terms of the law A&P would have to pay $550 on each of its Louisiana stores, whereas a chain with only 106 stores altogether, wherever located, would have had to pay considerably less tax on each store.

A&P and other chains applied to a special three-judge Federal Court for an injunction and, when that Court upheld the law, an appeal was taken to the U.S. Supreme Court.

Again Justice Roberts wrote the majority opinion, and the decision sustaining the law[23] was hardly a surprise. For, as the Court declared:

> "If the competitive advantages of a chain increase with the number of its component links, it is hard to see how these advantages cease at the state boundary. Under the findings, a store belonging to a chain of one hundred, all located in Louisiana, has not the same advantages as one of a hundred Louisiana stores belonging to a national chain of one thousand."

The Court had no trouble in distinguishing this case from the one in Florida. There the tax was increased if the chain

[23] Great A&P Tea Co. *v.* Grosjean, 301 U.S. 412 (1937).

had stores in more than one county. The increase was held arbitrary because it was unrelated to the *size* or *character* of the chain and was conditioned solely upon the *location* of one or more of the stores. Under the Louisiana law, however, the classification is not based upon the location of the stores, in fact the location of the stores is rendered immaterial, but upon the total number of stores in the chain which, according to the Court, measures its competitive advantages and economic results.

But more significant perhaps than any other feature of this decision was the Court's declaration that the law should be upheld on much broader considerations than those it had applied.

"In the exercise of its police power the State may forbid, as inimical to the public welfare, the prosecution of a particular type of business, or regulate a business in such manner as to abate evils deemed to arise from its pursuit," Justice Roberts declared. "Whatever a State may forbid or regulate it may permit upon condition that a fee be paid in return for the privilege, and such a fee may be exacted to discourage the prosecution of a business or to adjust competitive or economic inequalities. Taxation may be made the implement of the exercise of the State's police power; and proper and reasonable discrimination between classes to promote fair competitive conditions and to equalize economic advantages is therefore lawful."

Applying those principles to the case at hand, the Justice went on to point out that:

"If, in the interest of the people of the State, the legislature deemed it necessary either to mitigate evils of competition as between single stores and chains or to neutralize disadvantages of small chains in their competition with larger ones, or to discourage merchandising within the state by chains grown so large as to become a menace to the general welfare, it was at liberty to regulate the matter directly or to resort to the type of taxation evidenced by the Act of 1934 as a means of regulation."

Justices Sutherland, McReynolds and Butler dissented. Neither Justice Van Devanter nor Justice Stone took any part in the consideration of the case or in the decision.

In his dissenting opinion, Justice Sutherland referred to the Indiana decision, which he still felt was wrongly decided, but which, accepting it as authoritative, went to the extreme verge of the law, adding: "it seems to us equally certain that the present decision goes far beyond the verge."

The key point raised by the Justice was that the advantage enjoyed by the stores located in Louisiana by reason of the fact that their owner operated a given number of stores in some other state or county was too vague and uncertain to justify the tax formula used in the statute. Referring to the decision in the Kentucky case and the grounds upon which it was based, he said the vices in the present statute were the same.

The net result of all this legislation and litigation may be summed up as follows:

1. Of the 28 States which, at one time or another, have had anti-chain-store taxes in effect, only 14 of them have them today. One of those, North Carolina, in 1949 eliminated the graduated type of tax, imposing a flat tax of $65 per store, irrespective of the total number operated.

2. No State has passed an anti-chain-store tax since 1941, although 108 bills have been introduced in that period, and in 1957 W. Virginia did increase the tax it had enacted in 1933.

3. Since 1941, on the other hand, four chain-store tax laws then in existence have been eliminated. In 1942, a public referendum rejected a Utah tax which had been passed in 1941; in 1946, the Kentucky Supreme Court invalidated a tax act passed in 1940; in 1949, Idaho repealed the chain-store tax it had enacted in 1933; and, in 1951, Georgia repealed its 1937 tax.

4. As a result of the decisions which have been reviewed in the preceding pages and which the U.S. Supreme Court has

shown no disposition to disturb, anti-chain-store taxes are constitutional, as far as the Federal constitution is concerned. Even if a tax is drastic enough to put the chains out of business, that fact would not invalidate it.

Obviously, the barrage of adverse legislation which has been reviewed in the foregoing pages and which, as was shown in Table 17, page 134, involved the consideration of no less than 1,297 bills between 1923 and 1957, did not develop spontaneously in widely separated State capitols. It reflects rather the insistent demand for protection against the chain-store "menace" generated in the first place by wholesalers and independent merchants and later stimulated by professional agitators and others who championed their cause.

How this demand developed into a nationwide crusade against the chains which grew in intensity as the chains grew in number and size, and what came out of it, are covered in some detail in succeeding chapters.

CHAPTER VIII

THE HUE AND CRY
GATHERS VOLUME

How FAR will this chain-store trend go? What is the secret of chain-store success? Is it all on the up and up, or does it stem from uneconomic, if not actually unlawful, practices? Even if the system is sound economically, is it desirable from a social standpoint? Is the independent merchant doomed? How would the public interest be affected if he were eliminated? How soon will it be before the chains monopolize distribution and, after that, how soon before they monopolize production too?

These were some of the questions which began to be asked and answered with increasing frequency as the chain-store movement gathered momentum and became increasingly evident to everyone with eyes to see. Long before 1925, the phenomenon had naturally received growing attention in the trade press because of its direct impact on established distribution channels. But, from that time on, the so-called "chain-store question" began to arouse interest on a broader front, with the financial and general business papers and even consumer periodicals devoting more attention to it.

The mere suggestion that chain-store expansion was leading us straight and swiftly into a state of unadulterated monopoly was enough, of course, to arouse the attention of politicians who never lost the opportunity to sound the tocsin whenever such an issue presented itself. But it went further than that. Economists delved into the subject objectively, government bureaus and officials undertook investigations to see whether existing laws were being violated or should be tightened, and governors, senators and congressmen, all over the country, began to take sides.

One of the first manifestations of the lively interest business men were taking in the chain-store issue was a public debate arranged by the Illinois Retail Clothiers' and Furnishers' Association as a feature of its eighteenth annual convention in Chicago, on February 9, 1928, between T. K. Kelly, "billed" as a banker and president of T. K. Kelly Sales System, of Minneapolis, and the author, as editor of *Chain Store Age*.

The question: Resolved, that the chain-store system is not to the public interest.

Although this debate was the first of its kind, its main significance lies in the facts that (1) it was arranged in a field which, at that time, had not felt the impact of chain-store competition to any great extent; and (2) it received far more space in the trade press than might have been expected, several publications printing both sides *in full*. As each side had been given an hour for the presentation of its case, the number of pages required for the full report was considerable.[1]

In the years which followed, the subject was to be debated over and over again, not only before audiences of business men[2] and in public forums but, more particularly, by high school and college debating teams all over the country. In a bibliography published in 1940,[3] no less than seven Debate Manuals are listed, including: the University Debaters' Manual, on the Chain Store System, issued by H. W. Wilson Publishing Co., New York, in 1930; a Handbook on Chain Stores for High School Debates, published by Albion College Debate Service, Albion, Mich.; and Debate Handbook, The Chain

---

[1] *Daily News Record,* New York, February 10, 1928; *National Retail Clothier,* Chicago, March 1, 1928; *Retail Ledger,* Philadelphia, February 2, 1928; *Men's Wear,* February 22, 1928.

[2] On September 16, 1929, the Ad-Sell League, of Omaha, a business man's organization, staged a debate on the subject between J. Frank Grimes, founder of the Independent Grocers' Alliance, and the author. It is quoted in *The Chain Store —Boon or Bane?, op. cit.,* at page 122.

[3] *The Chain Store Tells Its Story, op. cit.,* p. 262.

Store Question, by E. C. Buehler, University of Kansas, 1930.

Another bibliography on the chain-store question, issued by the Debaters' Information Bureau, Portland, Me., in 1930, listed fifteen other bibliographies on the subject; six organizations putting out material, pro or con; nineteen sources of information; three anti-chain-store publications; seven chain-store publications; 21 book references; 91 pamphlets and government documents; 473 periodical articles and 184 newspaper articles! The great majority of the periodical articles listed were published in 1928, 1929 and 1930, but the years 1925, 1926 and 1927 were well represented too.

Although the periodical articles were by no means all anti-chain in their approach, even those which reported chain-store progress objectively, or openly welcomed it, provided additional ammunition for those who viewed the situation with misgivings. The great number of men in public life who took up the cudgels against the chains, whether sincerely or for political advantage, materially strengthened the anti-chain-store case.

Probably the only reason anti-chain-store sentiment did not result in even more anti-chain-store tax bills than were actually introduced between 1927 and 1930, inclusive, was the fact that, until 1931, when the Supreme Court handed down its decision in the Indiana case, most lawyers were convinced that such legislation was hopelessly unconstitutional, as many of the lower courts had already decided.

Typical of the anti-chain viewpoint, as it was expressed by leading public figures and in the daily press, are the following observations which were quoted by the author in an earlier work on the subject.[4]

"The chain stores are undermining the foundation of our entire local happiness and prosperity. They have destroyed our home markets and merchants, paying a minimum to our local enterprises and charities, sapping the life-blood of pros-

[4] *The Chain Store—Boon or Bane?, op. cit.,* pp. 1-3.

perous communities and leaving about as much in return as a travelling band of gypsies."

Thus declared a former speaker of the Indiana House of Representatives in a letter addressed to some of his constituents.

In one of the "Letters from the People" on the editorial page of the *St. Louis Post Dispatch,* appeared the following observations:

"We have the greatest school system in the world to educate our youths to be future business men. What are their prospects for business if the chain stores continue to develop more and more every day? Do the mothers and fathers realize what will happen to their children when they have to go to work for chain stores at $20 per week, or less? The chain stores may appeal to some people as a very bright business, but our country is built on the foundation of live and let live. Economy is one thing, but eliminating that vast amount of people from work is another."

U.S. Senator Royal S. Copeland, of New York, was credited with the following contribution:

"When a chain enters a city block, ten other stores close up. In smaller cities and towns, the chain store contributes nothing to the community. Chain stores are parasites. I think they undermine the foundations of the country."

And Senator Hugo L. Black, of Alabama, later to become a Justice of the U.S. Supreme Court,[5] delivered himself of the following tirade which leaves little doubt where his sympathies would have been had he been a member of that court when the Indiana case was decided:

"Chain groceries, chain dry-goods stores, chain clothing stores, here today and merged tomorrow—grow in size and power. We are rapidly becoming a nation of a few business masters and many clerks and servants. The local man and

[5] Appointed 1937.

merchant is passing and his community loses his contribution to local affairs as an independent thinker and executive. A few of these useful citizens, thus supplanted, become clerks of the great chain machines, at inadequate salaries, while many enter the growing ranks of the unemployed. A wild craze for efficiency in production, sale and distribution has swept over the land, increasing the number of unemployed, building up a caste system, dangerous to any government." [6]

Another U.S. Senator, Burton Wheeler, of Montana, expressed a similar viewpoint over a radio network, declaring:

"The western Progressives are fighting against the domination of Congress by men who represent selfish corporate interests, because they believe sincerely that, unless the growing concentrations of wealth and power are checked, this nation will soon be converted into a plutocracy where a few supremely rich men will rule and the rights of the common men will be trampled under foot. We have seen the development of huge mergers and the rapid increase of chain banks and chain stores throughout the country until, today, the genuinely independent banker and independent business man are rapidly disappearing from our life. The type of men whose business built up the nation have been driven out of business in every State of the Union, and their places have been taken by the hired agents of the great mergers and chains which dominate and control the business of the entire country. We believe that these great aggregations of wealth must be subjected to effective government regulation if the people are to be protected from the inevitable evils of unregulated monopoly."

These viewpoints are quoted not for the purpose of refuting them at this point but merely to illustrate the kind of attack to which the chains were subjected day in and day out during the period of their greatest expansion. Certainly the bogy of monopoly could never have been pictured against a more favorable background than the chains offered at that time. The events of the past twenty years, as they are recorded in

---

[6] *Congressional Record*, January 8, 1930.

these pages, provide their own refutation of most of the anti-chain arguments raised when the crusade was at its height. But this point is as good as any other to put into the record a statement made in 1928 which, because of its source, as well as its own logic and obvious common sense, provides a refreshing antidote to some of the foregoing quotations.

Charles Wesley Dunn, a leading member of the American bar, was counsel at that time for the National Association of Retail Grocers as well as the American Grocery Specialty Manufacturers' Association (now the Grocery Manufacturers of America). Discussing the so-called chain-store question, he said:[7]

"My position is essentially this:

"First: I believe that the principle of chain store retailing is economically sound and in due application progressively works for the constructive improvement of the retail business as a business and in its service to the consuming public; that in its elementary economic conception the chain store is but a natural, logical and inevitable evolutionary development of retailing, directed to introduce scientific merchandising into it and make it more effective to all concerned; that the success of the chain store is basically due to its economic soundness; that the permanency of the chain store is beyond question and the only economic question is how far it will go and how it will evolve.

"Second: I believe that what and all that can be objected to in the chain store business, as a business and as in the case of any business, is the use of wrongful or uneconomic practice in or incidental to its pursuit, or the development of illegal monopoly in it. That wrongful and uneconomic practices have been and are used in the business, cannot be denied. That such practices are detrimental to all concerned and should be eliminated, likewise cannot be denied. As to an illegal chain grocery store monopoly, I see none. But I do see the use of methods in this business which have been heretofore and elsewhere used to create illegal monopoly. That such methods are detrimental to all concerned and

[7] In a communication to the National Chain Store Grocers Association at its eighth annual meeting, Memphis, October 11, 1928.

should be eliminated, again cannot be denied. And in view of the size and concentration of the chain store business, such methods, if not eliminated, will continue to raise the monopoly question.

"Third: I believe that legislation directed to outlaw the chain store business or in any way unduly to discriminate against it is unsound in principle, unconstitutional in law and unjust in application."

That Mr. Dunn, like most other good lawyers, was wrong in his view that anti-chain-store laws were unconstitutional, became clear only when the Supreme Court so decided, but history has proved that he was right in most of his other observations regarding the economic basis for chain-store success. The "uneconomic practices" to which he referred (and which were used not only by the chains but by large-scale operators of all types) were to a large extent eliminated when they were made *unlawful*, whether they were uneconomic or not, by the Robinson-Patman Act of 1936.

But in 1928, the tide of criticism was so strong against the chains that neither Mr. Dunn's disinterested appraisal of what was happening in distribution nor the arguments of chain-store proponents proved of much avail.

One of the first concrete results of the anti-chain crusade was a resolution introduced in the U.S. Senate by Senator Smith W. Brookhart, of Iowa, and approved May 5, 1928, calling for an extensive chain-store inquiry by the Federal Trade Commission.

According to Mr. Dunn,[8] the resolution originated with the National Association of Retail Grocers, of which he was general counsel, and was prepared for the association by John A. Cunningham, secretary, Iowa Retail Mechants Association,[9] and Mr. Cunningham "secured its introduction." Mr. Dunn,

---

[8] *The Grocery and Drug Chain Store Business,* a lecture delivered by Charles Wesley Dunn at the Harvard Graduate School of Business Administration on May 17-18, 1928.

[9] *N. Y. Journal of Commerce,* September 8, 1928, p. 9.

himself, thought the investigation was in order and desirable, because of charges of unfair practices which were widely made in the retail trade and because "the public is entitled and interested to know whether the charge is founded and, if so, whether the present laws are adequate in the circumstances." The chains had nothing to fear, he added, if their conduct was clear and should welcome the inquiry, because it afforded them an opportunity to answer the charges.

The resolution itself[10] is presented here in full because, in the light of its origin, it can be accepted as an accurate picture of what the chain-store problem looked like to the independent grocers. It read as follows:

"Whereas it is estimated that from 1921 to 1927 the retail sales of all chain stores have increased from approximately 4 per centum to 16 per centum of all retail sales; and

"Whereas there are estimated to be less than four thousand chain store systems with over one hundred thousand stores; and

"Whereas many of these chains operate from one hundred to several thousand stores; and

"Whereas there have been numerous consolidations of chain stores throughout the history of the movement, and particularly in the last few years; and

"Whereas these chain stores now control a substantial proportion of the distribution of certain commodities in certain cities, are rapidly increasing this proportion of control in these and other cities, and are beginning to extend this system of merchandising into country districts as well; and

"Whereas the continuance of the growth of chain store distribution and the consolidation of such chain stores may result in the development of monopolistic organizations in certain lines of retail distribution; and

"Whereas many of these concerns, though engaged in interstate commerce in buying, may not be engaged in interstate commerce in selling; and

"Whereas in consequence, the extent to which such consolidations are now, or should be made, amenable to the

[10] Senate R. 224, 70th Congress, First Session.

jurisdiction of the Federal anti-trust laws is a matter of serious concern to the public; Now, therefore, be it

"Resolved, that the Federal Trade Commission is hereby directed to undertake an inquiry into the chain store system of marketing and distribution as conducted by manufacturing, wholesaling, retailing, or other types of chain stores and to ascertain and report to the Senate:

"(1) The extent to which such consolidations have been effected in violation of the anti-trust laws, if at all;

"(2) The extent to which consolidations or combinations of such organizations are susceptible to regulation under the Federal Trade Commission Act or the anti-trust laws, if at all; and

"(3) What legislation, if any, should be enacted for the purpose of regulating and controlling chain store distribution.

"And for the information of the Senate in connection with the aforesaid subdivisions (1), (2) and (3) of this resolution the commission is directed to inquire into and report in full to the Senate:

"(a) The extent to which the chain store movement has tended to create a monopoly or concentration of control in the distribution of any commodity either locally or nationally;

"(b) Evidences indicating the existence of unfair methods of competition in commerce or agreements, conspiracies, or combinations in restraint of trade involving chain store distribution;

"(c) The advantages or disadvantages of chain store distribution in comparison with those of other types of distribution as shown by prices, costs, profits and margins, quality of goods and services rendered by chain stores and other distributors or resulting from integration, managerial efficiency, low overhead, or other similar causes;

"(d) How far the rapid increase in the chain store system of distribution is based upon actual savings in cost of management and operation and how far upon quantity prices available only to chain store distributors or any class of them;

"(e) Whether or not such quantity prices constitute a violation of either the Federal Trade Commission Act, the Clayton Act or any other statute and

"(f) What legislation, if any, should be enacted with reference to such quantity prices."

This was a major assignment handed to the Federal Trade Commission and, with the limited manpower at its disposal, it took the Commission six years before it was able to send the Senate its final report and conclusions. In the interim, it had submitted 33 separate reports on various phases of its study as the work progressed. Some idea of the scope of the inquiry may be gathered from the fact that the official report consists of some 2,694 printed pages and made a volume more than 5 inches thick.

Among the subjects covered were:

1. The growth and development of chain stores and their distribution by States.

2. Chain-store wages.

3. Short-weighing and over-weighing in chain and independent grocery stores.

4. Chain-store price policies.

5. Comparative prices of chains and independent stores in the grocery and drug fields in four different cities.

6. Chain-store manufacturing and sources of supply.

7. Special discounts and allowances received by chains in grocery, drug and tobacco fields.

8. Sales, margins, costs and profits of chains.

9. Voluntary chains in the drug, grocery and hardware fields.

10. Final report and conclusions.

The data collected by the Commission was obtained, for the most part, through schedules filed by the chains and others from whom information was desired. The chain-store schedule consisted of 36 printed pages. Field work by the Commission's staff and special investigators produced the additional data needed for the study.

What the Commission inquiry revealed with respect to the various subjects covered will not be discussed at length in these pages. On many of them the data compiled was inadequate to warrant conclusions of any real significance. Naturally, in the course of the investigation *some* evidence was found to support the familiar charges of chain-store short-weights, low wages, price-cutting and excessive discounts and allowances. On the other hand, the investigation revealed that such practices were by no means confined to the chains—that independent merchants and wholesalers indulged in them too.

But on the main question which the Senate had put to the Commission: "What legislation, if any, should be enacted for the purpose of regulating and controlling chain-store distribution?" this is what the Commission said:[11]

"To tax out of existence the advantages of chain stores over competitors is to tax out of existence the advantages which the consuming public have found in patronizing them, with a consequent addition to the cost of living for that section of the public. That portion of the public which is able to pay cash and is willing to forego delivery service in return for the advantage of lower prices will be deprived of that privilege, generally speaking, although there are exceptions both ways. It will also tend to an arbitrary frustration of whatever saving in cost of production and distribution results from integration of the functions of producer, wholesaler and retailer. So, on the whole, the number of people adversely affected by such a tax would constitute a very substantial percentage in comparison with the number adversely affected by present conditions. The graduated tax on chain stores cannot accomplish fully the social ends aimed at by such legislation without producing incidentally these results." [12]

[11] 74th Congress, 1st Session, Senate Document No. 4, *Final Report on the Chain Store Investigation.*

[12] That authorities on public finance regarded special taxes to discourage chain stores with no greater favor than the Federal Trade Commission was revealed by two surveys made in 1935 and 1938, respectively. The first was made by Miss Mabel L. Walker, Executive Secretary, Tax Policy League (now Tax Institute, Inc.) and published in *Tax Systems of the World*, 6th Edition, Commerce Clearing House, Inc., Chicago, 1935. Of 52 senior professors of public finance in leading American colleges and universities, who responded to a questionnaire asking for their attitude on various types of taxes, 45, or 86%, disapproved "special taxes to discourage chain stores," 6 were non-committal and only one approved them.

The second study, made by the New York State Tax Commission in 1938, and reported in the 7th Edition of the above work, published in 1938, revealed that, of 127 Professors of Finance answering the same question, 114, or 89%, disapproved of such taxes, 8 favored them and 5 were non-committal.

And on the question of a possible monopoly, the Commission's conclusions were equally decisive. Not only did the Commission find no evidence of a chain-store monopoly at the time of its investigation, but it recommended that all danger from that direction in the future could be readily averted by a simple amendment of existing anti-trust laws. The amendment it suggested would prohibit one corporation from acquiring the assets of another corporation where the effect "may be substantially to lessen competition or to tend to create a monopoly." In 1950 such an amendment to Section 7 of the Clayton Act was actually enacted,[13] although, of course, it is aimed at mergers of all kinds and not merely at mergers of chain-store companies.

But, no doubt, the mere fact that the Federal Trade Commission was *investigating* chain stores was prejudicial to the chains. On the principle that there is no smoke without fire, many people believe that an indictment is only the initial step to a verdict of guilty, and an "investigation" has about the same significance. Why are the chains being investigated by the Federal Trade Commission if their success is on the up and up? was a question which the average layman was in no position to answer but which carried its own implications to any but the more logical.

One of the most aggravating features of the anti-chain crusade was the "trade-at-home" campaign sponsored by local merchants with or without the help of professional agitators. The publicity given to such a project in one community naturally prompted promotion-minded retailers in others to launch similar campaigns.

When such a campaign was organized in Petersburg, Va., early in 1926, *Chain Store Age*[14] pointed out that it was doomed to failure because, while the local merchants might support it financially, consumers would remain skeptical. In fact, "the more the independent merchants thunder against

[13] P.L. 899, December 29, 1950.
[14] April, 1926.

the menace of the chains," the editorial observed, "the more the consumer begins to realize their underlying virtues." A warning was offered that "about the very worst thing that could happen to cities like Petersburg, which raise war-chests to fight the chains, would be to have the chains take them at their word and leave them flat."

A few months later, *Chain Store Age*[15] reported that the Petersburg campaign was still on, "a high-powered speaker from New York" having been imported to promote it. Whether or not the "high-powered speaker from New York" was responsible was not made clear but the story quoted a chain-store manager in Petersburg as saying that his sales had *increased* 50 per cent since the campaign had begun!

That same month the independent merchants of Jacksonville, Ill., ran a full-page advertisement in the local newspaper warning the public that "the future of the children" was jeopardized by chain-store growth.

This sort of thing spread throughout the country, gradually at first but gaining momentum in the years which followed, especially when professional promoters saw in such campaigns a chance to profit by them. Among the trade-at-home campaigns which were being waged in 1929, was one in Springfield, Mo., under the auspices of the local Chamber of Commerce. Because it was more or less typical of similar campaigns elsewhere, some of the copy angles used in the local newspaper advertising will serve to reveal the appeal most commonly employed.

The slogan for the campaign in question was: "Keep Ozark Dollars in the Ozarks." Under the headline: "The Chain Store Menace," an advertisement in the Springfield *Leader*, May 13, 1929, read as follows:

"Too much cannot be said against certain chain stores and their methods. Their local managers are 'mechanical operators,' controlled entirely by a set formula. These local managers cannot participate in any action, cause or activity for the

[15] July, 1926.

good of all Springfield. They are not permitted to 'give until it hurts' either of their time or of their company's money. Their duties, boiled down, are to 'get Springfield's money' and to send it to the Home Office.

"Cities are not built on this basis.

"Your loyalty to the Home Owned Stores—your patronage and friendliness to these stores—and your recognition of the Chain Store in its true light—that of a parasite upon legitimate business and a menace to our city's prosperity, will result in a CONTINUATION of that prosperity which has made Springfield so outstanding."

The advertisement carried the signature of the Chamber of Commerce, Community Building Bureau.

Another advertisement in the series[16] stressed the point that "not one of the executive heads of any chain store organization now opening up in this city, owns a residence here. Living in distant cites, we can hardly expect these chain store owners to have any other interest in Springfield and the Ozarks than to take what money they can out of the city. The owners of our home stores, together with you and all other loyal citizens, are boosters for Springfield. Our money has built up the city. Let's continue to stand together." Readers were urged to "Patronize Your Home-Owned Stores —the Money They Earn Stays in Springfield—for the Development of Springfield—not Chicago or New York."

The "absentee-ownership" theme was not, of course, the only one used but it was undoubtedly the one most commonly employed. The appeal for loyalty to the local merchant was based largely on the implication that the community was dependent upon him for the building and support of its schools, churches, public parks, libraries and other community institutions. Entirely ignored was the fact that most public activities are supported by public funds in the form of *taxes* to which *all* contribute in one way or another—the wage-earner and the tenant as well as the employer and the home-owner,

[16] May 6, 1929.

the chain store as well as the single-store merchant, the manufacturer as well as the distributor and the professional man as well as the business man. So far as donations to churches, charities and other activities dependent largely upon voluntary contributions were concerned, the fact that the average independent merchant was in no position to make more than a token contribution, if any, to such projects was also lost sight of.

Nevertheless, these "trade-at-home" campaigns persisted. In the year ending October 1, 1930, the National Chain Store Association noted that they had been developed in more than 400 cities and towns throughout the United States.

What the situation was at that time was summarized by the late Robert W. Lyons, executive vice president of that association, as follows:

"Up to a year ago, the American public was conscious only that something tremendous was taking place in the field of distribution. Anti-chain-store propaganda was so great that much genuine sympathy was aroused on behalf of the out-of-date and unsuccessful merchant. In more than 400 cities and towns throughout the United States, active local organizations were developed to fight the so-called 'chain-store menace.' United States senators, congressmen, governors, judges, State legislators, county and city officials, were being drawn into the ever-widening group who were opposed to the chain store. Local radio stations from coast to coast were being impressed with the profits to be made by selling their time to the enemies of the chain store. More than 100 newspapers had added their voice to this already noisy chorus."

Included in the ammunition used by the anti-chain interests were various pamphlets prepared and circulated by the American Wholesale Grocers' Association and other organized and individual sponsors. One of these pamphlets, whose title suggests its nature, was called: "Sons and Daughters for Sale"; it was the work of W. A. Masters, treasurer of an old-line dry-goods wholesale house. It was widely circulated through other jobbers, manufacturers and retailers.

The use of the radio against the chains on an extensive scale was probably initiated by W. K. ("Old Man") Henderson of Shreveport, La., who used his own station KWKH, Shreveport, for that purpose. Incorporating his project as the "Hello World Broadcasting Corporation"—named after the opening words of all his broadcasts, "Hello World"—"Old Man" Henderson, as he dubbed himself, discovered very quickly that attacking the chains in a vituperative way brought him country-wide attention which he lost no time in capitalizing.

His first step was to organize over the air the "Merchants' Minute Men," an organization to which any independent merchant could belong by merely sending Henderson $12. His appeal to those who felt the need for assistance against "the chain-store octopus," which Henderson built up so terrifyingly, was an effective one and money is said to have flowed into his coffers from all corners of the country.[17]

To supplement that income, Henderson offered to sell his own brand of coffee at $1 a pound to anyone who wanted to contribute to the cause. As the best coffee was selling at that time at less than half that price, Henderson's coffee sales must have netted him a liberal profit.

How much Henderson collected in all from his campaign only he knew, but the general impression was that he had uncovered a "gold mine." At any rate, he could not keep this new type of anti-chain racket to himself very long. Imitators sprang up in various sections of the country and the air war against the chains was extended to many fronts. In fact, although Henderson dropped his campaign before the end of 1931 and turned his attention to other activities, the other broadcasters maintained the air barrage for some time longer.

One interesting feature of the Henderson campaign was

[17] "Henderson's Merchant Minute Men Challenge the Chains," *Printers' Ink*, February 20, 1930.

a counterattack launched by Clarence Saunders, one of the founders of the Piggly Wiggly system of self-service stores but then operating individually as "Clarence Saunders, Sole Owner of My Name." He used full-page advertisements in the Memphis newspapers to lambaste the Shreveport traducer of the chains. In such an advertisement in the Memphis *Commercial Appeal*, March 14, 1930, which was addressed to "Rat Henderson," Saunders let loose a flood of personal vituperation which even Henderson must have found it difficult if not impossible to match.

That many of the anti-chain-store projects were regarded as "rackets" by the legitimate retailers' associations is evidenced by two bulletins in the author's possession.

One of them, dated February 14, 1930, was issued by C. H. Janssen, secretary-manager of the National Association of Retail Grocers. It read in part as follows:

"At the present time, there are in the United States literally thousands of individuals interesting themselves in anti-chain-store campaigns purely for the money they can make out of it for themselves. To the extent that any so-called anti-chain-store campaign is based purely on the educational grounds of acquainting the merchants and the public with the economic, social and civic benefits of the individual type of distribution, we have no criticism to offer, but we all know that every movement which has reached a momentum where it interests a large number of our people attracts what we may term 'camp followers' who attach themselves to such movements for the purpose of exploiting them to promote profits for themselves. . . .

"There are on my desk at the present time seven applications for financial assistance from newly born companies and individuals. . . . I have had inquiries from nearly every section of the country indicating that our self-appointed friends are numerous.

"Retail grocers and all merchants should be warned against

parting with their money to support irresponsible parties or campaigns which promise no constructive results for the individual trade. A recent attempt to secure information about several such organizations clearly indicates that these organizations are set up to make money for their promoters."

The other bulletin, dated February 19, 1930, was issued by George V. Sheridan, director, Ohio Council of Retail Merchants, and, referring to one of the new anti-chain-store associations which was operating in Ohio, read in part as follows:

". . . We are receiving a number of inquiries from merchants and local secretaries as to whether we have indorsed or are affiliated with this 'movement' to fight the chain stores. In reply, we will state definitely that none of the organizations connected with the Council have indorsed or are connected with this organization in any way. So far as we have been able to learn, none of the existing state retail associations outside the Council have indorsed it. Several have definitely refused to approve the movement. . . .

"The Ohio Wholesale Grocers' Association and the Ohio Retail Grocers' Association, both of which have been active in the past in fighting the chain stores, have advised their members definitely to withhold financial support from . . . any of these movements originating in Ohio. . . .

"The Dayton Better Business Bureau has issued a confidential report calling attention to the fact that at least one-half of the $10 membership fee goes to the salesmen and promoters who are soliciting the memberships."

What were the chains doing all this time to offset the abuse to which they were being subjected on so many fronts?

As a matter of fact, not until the end of 1928, when the National Chain Store Association came into being, were the chains equipped to do anything at all in an over-all way. Prior to that, the chains had only two associations, both in the grocery field. One was the National Chain Store Grocers Association, organized in 1920, and the other a regional association, the Western States Chain Grocers Association, organized in 1922, to which reference has already been made.[18]

The national association, of which Alfred H. Beckmann had been one of the founders and had served as its executive director throughout its existence, fulfilled its purpose more or less effectively until it was succeeded in 1928 by the National Chain Store Association. Its annual meetings had brought together food-chain operators from all over the country. Many of them were destined to work together in the common interest for many years to follow. It was the only organization in its time which was equipped to keep an eye on the anti-chain movement which was then getting under way, particularly on the anti-chain-store legislative measures which were then beginning to crop up.

However, as *Chain Store Age* had pointed out in its very first issue, which appeared in June, 1925, what the situation called for was a national chain-store association open to chains in all fields. Not only would all chains be affected by the wave of anti-chain bills which, even then, was indicated, but why should the food chains carry the burden of fighting them alone?

That proposal was slow to take root but, when in 1927 three anti-chain-store tax bills were actually enacted, as has been previously detailed, the first step in the proposed direction was taken. At its convention in 1927, the National Chain Store Grocers Association amended its constitution to provide for the admission of chains outside the food field as associate members. Furthermore, a large part of the meeting was devoted to a discussion of the problem and what could be done about it.

The final step was taken the following year in Memphis, when the old association met for its eighth and final convention. There it was dissolved and a new organization, the National Chain Store Association, open to chains in all fields, was simultaneously organized to take its place. Within a few

---

[18] P. 116, *supra*.

months, as soon as they had had a chance to learn of the new organization, practically all the leading chains in all fields became affiliated with it.

Its first president was E. G. Yonker, Sanitary Grocery Co. (now Safeway), Washington, D.C.; first vice president, F. H. Massmann, National Tea Co., Chicago; second vice president, Edward Dale, Safeway Stores, Inc., Oakland, Calif.; third vice president, T. Harry Roulston, Thomas Roulston Inc., Brooklyn, N.Y.; treasurer, H. C. Bohack, H. C. Bohack Co., Brooklyn, N.Y.; and secretary and general manager *pro tem*, the author, who was the editor of *Chain Store Age*. The reason all the original officers came from the grocery field despite the general nature of the new organization was that few of the top men of the chains in other fields had been present at the organization meeting in Memphis. The following year, however, Paul H. Metzger, Washington Shirt Shops, Chicago, and Malcolm G. Gibbs, Peoples Drug Stores, Washington, D.C., were elected vice presidents in addition to Edward Dale, Safeway Stores, and William N. Haraway, Continental Food Stores. Ward Melville, Melville Shoe Corporation, New York, became treasurer, and other chains were well represented on the board of directors and the executive committee. Among the members of the board were George B. Everitt, Montgomery Ward & Co., Chicago; George M. Gales, Louis K. Liggett Co., New York; E. H. Krom, G. R. Kinney Co., New York; Frank Melville, Jr., Melville Shoe Corporation; J. C. Penney, J. C. Penney Company, New York; C. B. Van Dusen, S. S. Kresge Co., Detroit; Gen. R. E. Wood, Sears, Roebuck & Co., Chicago; C. R. Walgreen, Walgreen Company, Chicago; and Don Davis, Western Auto Supply Co., Kansas City, Mo.; besides four from the grocery field: C. F. Adams, First National Stores, Somerville, Mass.; Samuel Robinson, American Stores Co., Philadelphia; Ross McIntyre, MacMarr Stores, Portland, Ore.; and M. B. Skaggs, Safeway Stores.

The executive committee consisted of F. H. Massmann, National Tea Co., chairman; E. G. Yonker, Sanitary Grocery

Co.; Alvin E. Dodd, Sears, Roebuck & Co.; Ward Melville, Melville Shoe Corp.; Roy H. Ott, J. C. Penney Company; T. H. Roulston, Thos. Roulston, Inc.; Wheeler Sammons, Walgreen Company; W. T. Grant, W. T. Grant Co., New York, and John B. Bonham, Kroger Grocery & Baking Co., Cincinnati.

Elected as president was William H. Albers, Kroger Grocery & Baking Company, but in May, 1930, when he resigned from that company his successor, Albert H. Morrill, took over as president of that company and of the National Chain Store Association as well.

Reappointed as executive vice president was Robert W. Lyons, the young Indiana lawyer who had been selected to direct the association's activities a few months after its organization and who had demonstrated early that he was fully equal to the task.

With such a powerful and representative organization, the chains could hardly have been expected to remain silent and inactive in the face of the barrage of propaganda which was being unleashed against them—to allow their traducers to go unanswered. Nor could they have been expected to stay away from the State capitols where legislators were being urged to check their further progress by punitive and discriminatory taxes.

After all, did not the new type of distribution they had introduced represent a definite improvement over the one it was, to some extent, replacing? Had not the success they had achieved come legitimately? Did it not reflect public approval of the kind of stores they were operating? And if their growth had been extensive and rapid, especially in recent years, was that not in the public interest? If the public preferred chain stores, as their patronage indicated, why not establish them wherever needed as rapidly as possible? Furthermore, most of the charges levelled at the chains were false, exaggerated or irrelevant and the whole anti-chain movement was inspired and sustained by the selfish interests of those who felt the effects of chain-store competition or who sought to capitalize the resentment which resulted.

At least that was the way the chains felt about the situation. What they did about it is reflected in the annual report of Mr. Lyons, covering the work of the association in the year ending October 1, 1930.

In order to meet and counteract the growth of anti-chain-store propaganda, an organized educational campaign had been commenced shortly after October 1, 1929. Its purpose was to give to the public a clearer understanding of just what the chain stores meant in terms of superior merchandise at lower cost, to provide students in high schools and colleges with authoritative information about the chain-store system, to acquaint the farmer with the benefits he derives from more efficient distribution as represented by the chains, and inform Federal and State executives and legislators regarding the social and economic value of the chains and the danger involved in imposing unsound tax burdens on them.

One feature of the program was a monthly bulletin called *Chain Store Progress*. It presented a digest of current developments, editorial comment and addresses made regarding the chain-store question. More than 400,000 copies of it were distributed during the year. The bulk of the copies went to legislators, editors, teachers of marketing, State marketing officials, college libraries, debaters and a special list of more than 21,000 leading citizens.

Several hundred thousand pamphlets and reprints of speeches were also distributed and articles were supplied to leading periodicals.

Mr. Lyons, executives of member companies and two professional speakers addressed scores of meetings of business men and made radio broadcasts whenever the opportunity arose.

"One of the most interesting manifestations of the public interest in the chain-store question," Mr. Lyons pointed out, "has been the increasing frequency with which it has been selected as the topic for leading high school and college debates. More than 500 such debates have been held during the past year. In practically every case we have been asked to supply the data upon which the chain store could be adequately championed. We have supplied such material in ever-increasing quantities and, based upon our present information, we are anticipating almost 5,000 similar debates to be held throughout the United States during the coming year. We have prepared a comprehensive Debaters' Manual, covering every phase of the chain-store subject, and are prepared to distribute it wherever such information is required. It is gratifying to note that approximately 85 per cent of all the debates held this year were decided in favor of the teams which supported the chain stores in their arguments. We believe that our thorough-going preparation of debate material has been an important factor in contributing to this success."

The association set up a research department, with Dr. Paul C. Olsen, of Columbia University, as consulting director. It not only undertook to gather, analyze and interpret a vast quantity of data about chain stores issued by others, but made some important original studies itself.

One of the main functions of the association was to see that the flood of discriminatory tax legislation which was finding its way into almost every State legislature met with at least some resistance. Whenever and wherever such bills were introduced, the association arranged for representation by counsel and sent a member of its own staff to appraise the situation and decide what measures could be taken to defeat the proposal. How effective the association's effort was is indicated by the fact that of 142 bills introduced in 29 legislatures between January 1, 1929, and October 1, 1930, only six imposing chain-store taxes were passed.

If the association was proud of its work in the legislatures, as Mr. Lyons' report indicated, it had even more cause for gratification with the success the chains had so far achieved in

the courts. Wherever they had challenged the constitutionality of anti-chain tax laws, they had won. The association was
particularly pleased with the chains' latest victory in Indianapolis, where a three-judge Federal Court had declared the
Indiana tax of 1929 unconstitutional. The association's research department had compiled the economic data and statistics used so effectively in the case. The whole case was built
around the testimony of Mr. Lyons and Dr. Paul H. Nystrom,
professor of marketing, Columbia University.

On the litigation front, indeed, the outlook then was bright
enough for Mr. Lyons to express the hope that within the next
two years, by careful preparation and guidance of litigation,
such as had characterized the Indiana case, the association
would be able "to establish the manifest unconstitutionality"
of all these anti-chain tax laws.

Unfortunately, however, within a very few months after
that expression of confidence, the whole picture was to
change.

On May 18, 1931, the decision of the three-judge Court was
reversed by the U.S. Supreme Court. In deciding that the
Indiana chain-store tax was constitutional,[19] the Supreme
Court validated not only that particular tax but *all* chain-store
taxes of that type. It established the principle that chain
stores were different in *kind* from independent stores and not
merely *in degree,* and that the difference was great enough to
justify different tax treatment. True enough, the decision was
by a divided court, five to four, but it was just as decisive and
as ominous, from a chain-store standpoint, as if it had been
unanimous.

It was a heavy blow for the chains, coming as it did from a
source which they had reasonably regarded as their one sure
refuge. Furthermore, it came at a most unfortunate time—
when the need for additional State revenue was almost universal throughout the country. With practically every State
looking hungrily for new tax sources, how could the chains

[19] State Board *v.* Jackson, p. 132, *supra.*

hope to avert a veritable avalanche of new levies for which the Supreme Court had not only cleared the way but had flood-lighted it?

However, the chains were fortunate in one respect. Most of the legislatures which had regular sessions scheduled for 1931 had already adjourned. Only eleven were still in session. Thus, the full effect of the decision would be deferred at least until the following year, when only nine States were scheduled to hold regular sessions, although at least fifteen more were expected to call special sessions because of their revenue deficits.

To meet this crisis, the association advanced its annual meeting to June 22, 1931—to take immediate stock of the situation and decide what could be done about it.

What happened at that meeting was revealed in Mr. Lyons' report for the year ending September 30, 1931. Because of the summer meeting, it had been decided to forego the usual convention in October. To take its place, *Chain Store Age* devoted its October issue to what was designated as a "stay-at-home convention." Among the reports presented at that "convention" was that of Mr. Lyons. It revealed that, at the June meeting, the majority had favored an immediate, gigantic campaign to inform consumers of the true meaning of anti-chain-store taxes, stressing their effect on the general standard of living. Others, more conservative-minded, had felt that the launching of any such campaign might well be deferred until the leaders of the industry had had more time to weigh the various problems involved. One thing they had all agreed upon was that the budget for the year beginning October 1 should be double what it had previously been.[20] Most of the additional funds would be needed for the extra tax-defense work, which would certainly be necessary, and the educational and research programs would have to be stepped up even if an all-out educational campaign were not undertaken.

[20] The budget had previously been $250,000.

During the year, Mr. Lyons reported, more than 5,000 debates on the chain-store question had been staged before high-school and college audiences aggregating some 1,900,-000 persons.

Of the eleven legislatures still in session when the Supreme Court decision was handed down, Mr. Lyons reported that seven had lost no time in pressing anti-chain-store bills for passage. And some of them were far more severe than the relatively mild tax involved in the decision.

"In Florida," Mr. Lyons pointed out, "the tax proposed in the top bracket was $250 per store, but an Illinois bill set the maximum at $1,000."

"Fortunately for the chain-store industry," he observed, "only two chain-store bills were passed since the Supreme Court's decision—Florida and Alabama (a bill taxing chain stores was passed by both houses in Wisconsin but, owing to a technical error, Governor LaFollette returned it to the legislature where it was tabled until the next session).

"The year 1931-1932, however, with nine legislatures in regular session and fifteen in special session, may tell an entirely different story unless some sound, aggressive action is taken by the chain-store industry."

What actually happened in 1932, when 125 bills were introduced, is shown in Table 17, page 134, as is also the box-score for 1933, when 225 bills came up for consideration and thirteen of them were passed.

How many of the seventeen anti-chain-store tax laws passed in 1931, 1932 and 1933, after the Supreme Court decision, might have been enacted in any event cannot, of course, be known. The combined effect of sustained anti-chain propaganda and the widespread need for additional State revenue would probably have produced some of them even if their constitutionality had still remained in doubt. On the other hand, but for the decision, many of the laws in question would not have been enacted.

But the decision, unexpectedly enough, had some favorable

consequences too. Among them was the reaction of the daily press. Almost unanimously it deprecated the decision, stressing the potential danger to the economy if it resulted in checking chain-store development. That the reaction was not just another case of sympathy for the under-dog was obvious from its extent and the reasons which accompanied it.

Chain Store Age,[21] commenting on it, declared:

"In the whole history of chain-store development, we doubt whether as much space has been devoted to the merits of the chain-store idea as has been used in the few weeks since the Supreme Court decision was handed down, and certainly the amount of *favorable* comment the chains have received in the public press was never approached before the Supreme Court declared that the chains are the legitimate prey of every State which wants to mulct them.

"Why this belated recognition by the newspapers of the merits of the chain-store idea? Why this sudden awakening to the folly of penalizing the chain store for the benefit of those who serve the public less efficiently?

"The answer lies in the fact that for the first time the newspapers of the country have a clear idea of what the agitation against the chains really means. This decision of the Supreme Court has driven home the fact that the chains have grown because they represent a distinct improvement over the methods of distribution they are, to some extent, replacing. Unfavorable as this decision is from the chain-store standpoint in one respect, certain it is the chains themselves could issue no more effective propaganda in their own behalf. . . .

"We are convinced that the reason so many newspapers have revealed such a friendly attitude towards the chain-store idea since this decision was handed down is that, for the first time, their eyes have been opened to the truth.

"If that is a correct deduction, then the course of the chains is crystal clear. The simple truths set out by the Supreme Court must be repeated so frequently, so forcibly and so con-

21 *Chain Store Age*, July, 1931.

vincingly that not only the newspapers of the country but every man, woman and child will understand and appreciate them. Only in that way may the chains expect to escape the penalties of discriminatory taxation which the Supreme Court has declared the States are at liberty to impose even though, in the same opinion, the most cogent reasons are given why chain-store growth should be encouraged."

But no such all-out educational campaign developed. Although the association did set up a committee in 1931 [22] to discuss such a campaign and to make its recommendations, and various comprehensive plans were submitted by committeemen who favored the idea, that was as far as it went. Several factors combined to thwart further action along those lines, as will appear later.

Another favorable outcome of the Supreme Court decision was its effect on the more conservative element among the leaders in the independent field itself. Many of them believed that it might prove to be a boomerang which would eventually hurt the independent merchant as well as the chains.

In a speech to the National Retail Dry Goods Association, whose membership consisted primarily of independent retailers, George V. Sheridan, executive director of the Ohio Retailers' Council, another organization primarily interested in promoting the interests of independent retailers, pointed out that "a legislature which taxes chain stores today will tax all stores tomorrow." [23] He was particularly apprehensive of the effect on all retailers of a gross sales tax, such as was imposed by the Kentucky Act of 1930, if that type of tax should likewise be held constitutional by the Supreme Court. A decision from that Court was then expected momentarily, although when it was handed down in 1932, it was an abortive one. It merely required the lower court which, on technical grounds, had dismissed the case challenging the constitution-

[22] The committee consisted of Fred H. Massmann, National Tea Co.; Ward Melville, Melville Shoe Corporation; Roy Ott, J. C. Penney Company; Wheeler Sammons, Walgreen Company, and the author. *Chain Store Age*, October, 1931.
[23] *Chain Store Age*, March, 1932.

ality of the law, to try the issues on the merits. The Supreme
Court's final decision, declaring the Act unconstitutional, was
not handed down until several years later.[24]

Mr. Sheridan stressed the fact that such a tax not only hurt
the big department stores as well as chain stores, being based
entirely on sales volume, but that even small independent
stores could not expect to remain immune, even though the
law as it then stood practically exempted the small-scale merchant. What was to prevent the legislature at any time from
amending the law to bring even the small retailers into the
tax-paying category?

In any event, the National Retail Dry Goods Association
took a definite position against special chain-store taxes as
did many individual champions of the independent merchant
who openly advised against them.

So far as the chains themselves were concerned, although
an all-out educational program appealed to many of their
leaders as an obvious step to be taken, whatever it might cost,
some of the factors which prevented it from ever getting
beyond the planning stage may now be considered.

In the first place, the long-range benefits of an educational
campaign seemed to many to be of secondary value compared
with the immediate task of fighting the numerous anti-chain
tax bills, already pending in the legislatures, or which were
certain to be introduced later.

To the objection raised by some that lobbying against proposed legislation was a dangerous business, if not actually
unethical, Mr. Lyons replied forcefully in a report to the
executive committee in March, 1932. Because of the criticism
which was later to be levelled at the tax-defense measures
used by the chains, particularly with respect to their practice
of retaining politically powerful representatives at State capitols, Mr. Lyons' observations on the "ethics" involved are
worth preserving. He said:[25]

[24] P. 141, *supra*.
[25] From typewritten copy in author's possession.

"The problem concerning the wisdom and the ethics of our tax-defense program is one of profound significance. Any intelligent judgment of it must be based upon a broad understanding of the character and development of State government.

"State legislatures throughout the United States, in the exercise of governmental functions, are considering proposals designed to drive chain stores out of existence, or to place them at a comparative disadvantage. The question, therefore, arises as to what the chain stores should do and have a right to do in opposing such legislation.

"In answering this question, I stand upon the time-honored premise that the governments of the various states are organized no less to protect the chain stores, the manufacturers from whom chain stores buy, and every business of every kind, than they are to protect the rights and prerogatives of the individual retailer and the individual citizen.

"It seems to me to follow that if proposed tax laws will injure chain-store operations, and thus curtail benefits heretofore made available to the consuming public, then the chain stores not only enjoy the right to oppose such legislation before the proper governmental bodies, but they owe an inescapable obligation of citizenship to make that opposition as effective as possible, while keeping it, in spirit and in fact, within the law. Furthermore, it seems to me that every manufacturer from whom we buy, and whose prosperity, together with that of his employes and his community, is involved in any pernicious or destructive tax scheme, owes an equally inescapable obligation to raise his voice and his influence in opposition to such corruption of governmental action. . . .

"If democratic government, administered under party systems, were perfect in integrity and wisdom, it would be unnecessary to meet this problem. Unfortunately, this is not the case. The history of party politics and of politicians has been the same the world over. Their activities have been developed as an expression of the will of the voters—but they are scarcely established until they sterilize self-government and actually restrain the average voter from having what he really wants. The ultimate status of political parties and politicians is to tell the people what they want, and to give it to them even when they want nothing at all. . . .

"To understand the problem which the chain stores face, it

is necessary to realize that in every State there is a wet vote
and a dry vote, a city vote and a rural vote, a radical vote and
a conservative vote, the utility vote and the railroad vote, the
farm vote and the soldier vote, the hoodlum vote and the
church vote, and so on without end.

"These organized and articulate minorities maintain extensive lobbies for the purpose of securing their legislative
objectives, which mostly result in plundering the public
treasury for some selfish end. Our State governments, far
from being perfect, apparently worship but one god—legislation. The arts and sciences of administration and management, which sound government demands are totally ignored
by the politician, for obvious reasons. Legislation fascinates
because, under the cloak of law, special privilege is made
legal. I maintain that it is no less the granting of a special
privilege for a State legislature to tax chain stores and let
their competitors go untaxed, than for it to give soldiers,
or the Anti-Saloon League, or the farmer, a dole out of the
public treasury.

"If I am right in my conclusions about this, then it follows
that in the interest of sound government there needs to be a
vigorous check upon those political systems which make it
possible for organized minority groups to force destructive
legislation through our State assemblies, with a resultant expense to the whole people.

"No one, I am sure, will suggest that the current flood of
anti-chain-store tax legislation is a reflection of the will of the
majority of our people. Nor will they suggest that it is being
fostered by any save a selfish minority interest. Even so,
unless the chain stores refuse to acquiesce in the feeble
attitude that would have us abandon our defenses, they will
find themselves the victims of those strong opposing forces
which are already trying to organize party politics so as to
loot them of their justly earned success. . . .

"The proposal that the chain stores give up their tax defense is in fact to urge the chain stores to resolve themselves
into a sort of defenseless jelly, for which our enemies pray
and upon which they hope to feed."

Another factor which worked against serious consideration
of a major educational campaign was the discouraging depression under which the country was staggering. Although chain-

store sales were not feeling the effect of reduced consumer buying power to the same degree as retail sales in general, chain-store sales, and profits, also, were definitely declining. Furthermore, the situation gave little hope for improvement in the foreseeable future. One direct effect of declining chain-store sales was a corresponding decline in the association's revenue, which was based on the sales of member companies. In the face of these conditions, the decision made in June, 1931, to double the budget for the following year was rescinded, and the 1931-1932 year began with less revenue in sight than had been budgeted the previous year, before the devastating Supreme Court decision.

Still another consideration was a feeling upon the part of many of the operators that perhaps the best approach to a solution of their problems would be to set up State associations in place of or to supplement the national organization. The tax problems, it was argued, were at the State level, and the support of local chains in opposing them might be gained more readily than had proved to be the case with the national association directing the effort. The idea found sufficient favor to bring about the organization of the Illinois Chain Store Association on February 3, 1932, although an attempt a month later to organize a similar association for New York made no headway.

On the top of this conflict of ideas among the chain-store leaders came the New Deal and the National Recovery Administration,[26] which provided the answer, so far as the National Chain Store Association was concerned. For at a special three-day meeting in Washington in June, 1933, called by the chains for the purpose of deciding their future course, it was quickly agreed that the national association would no longer meet their needs. Under NRA each industry and trade was required to develop a code for its own regulation. No code could be approved by the "Blue Eagle" Administrator unless the organization sponsoring it was "truly representa-

[26] The National Industrial Recovery Act, June 16, 1933.

tive" of the field affected. Obviously the N.C.S.A. would not have met that test for all the various kinds of chains affiliated with it. It did not have enough members in any individual field to make it "truly representative" of any of them.

Thus, in 1933, the N.C.S.A. followed the example of its predecessor and dissolved itself. It was succeeded by individual associations in each of the fields in which the chains played an important part. Thus came into being the Food and Grocery Chain Stores of America, Inc., whose unwieldy name was later changed to National Association of Food Chains; the Limited Price Variety Stores Association, whose name was similarly shortened in 1957 to Variety Stores Association; the National Association of Chain Drug Stores; the National Council of Shoe Retailers; and the Mail Order Association; and, later on, the Institute of Distribution.

With the new associations pre-occupied with the many new problems created by NRA, and the old association out of the picture, what became of the tax-defense program which Mr. Lyons had organized and directed so successfully from 1929 to 1932? Fortunately for the chains as a whole, it was salvaged by the action of fourteen of the larger companies who realized the necessity of keeping it going. They retained Mr. Lyons as counsel and he continued to function in that capacity until his death in 1949.

That the organization of separate chain-store associations in the various fields was a wise one, soon became apparent. No single association could have met the need for special technical guidance in each of the fields in which the chains were a factor. Certainly the National Chain Store Association, as it was set up in 1933, was in no way geared to provide that kind of leadership.

Throughout the relatively brief existence of NRA[27] the chains would have been hard put without a special trade association in each field to represent them. In the grocery

[27] The National Industrial Recovery Act was declared unconstitutional by the U.S. Supreme Court, May 27, 1935, in Schechter v. U.S., 295 U.S. 495.

field, for instance, not only did the food chains have to work out a code for their own regulation as grocery distributors, but it was necessary to follow closely the framing of 64 codes in other industries to make sure that none of them worked unfairly against the interest of the food chains or other food distributors.[28] The same was true, to a greater or lesser extent, in each of the other fields in which the chains had set up their own association.

But the usefulness of these separate chain-store associations did not end with the termination of NRA. On the contrary, it increased substantially in the years which followed and which brought with them even more serious problems. As is revealed in later chapters, the associations played a major role in improving the chains' public relations in the only sound way in which public relations can be improved—by helping the chains do a better all-round job.

In the meanwhile, however, several chains got themselves involved in the organization of another association which was to cause them plenty of adverse publicity and embarrassment and was to result indirectly in the passage of a Federal law designed to limit the buying advantages which large-scale operators had previously enjoyed. The story of the congressional inquiry into the organization and purposes of the American Retail Federation, its expansion into an investigation of large-scale buying, and its outcome—the passage of the Robinson-Patman Act of 1936—has a direct bearing on the subject-matter of this chapter but, because of its more general application, is covered in a special chapter of its own.

[28] See "Report on N.A.F.C.," *Chain Store Age*, Grocery Edition, October, 1948.

CHAPTER IX

THE "SUPERLOBBY"
INVESTIGATION

ONE OF THE MOST eventful chapters in chain-store history was the outcome of a bungled publicity release announcing the organization of a new retail association by a group of the country's outstanding merchants.

The unfortunate release not only nearly wrecked the association in question before it was a week old, but brought about a Congressional investigation of chain-store buying practices which, in turn, played its part in securing the passage of the Robinson-Patman Act and, incidentally, launched Congressman Wright Patman on an anti-chain crusade aimed at chain-store elimination.

The story can best be told as it actually unfolded.

On April 17, 1935, the *N.Y. Times* carried a front-page story with the following headlines;

MERCHANTS OF THE NATION ORGANIZE
TO ACT AS UNIT ON ECONOMIC ISSUES

"Unified Voice" on Legislative Problems to be Aim of Group of 1,000,000—All Leading Retailers Represented

Colonel Sherrill Will Direct Activities

"Formation of the American Retail Federation to serve as the 'unified voice' of the entire field of distribution on national legislation and economic problems," the story began, "was announced here yesterday by Louis E. Kirstein, of William Filene's Sons Company, Boston, who has played a leading role in the creation of the new group.

"The federation expects to have a membership of more than 1,000,000 merchants having an annual sales volume of approximately $20,000,000,000."

The story went on to point out:

1. Plans for the federation had been developed in the previous six months.

2. Col. Clarence O. Sherrill would direct it as president with an executive committee of ten, with headquarters in Washington, D.C.

3. Mr. Kirstein had emphasized that, just as the oil producers, steel and automobile manufacturers, railroads and farmers "have long organized into national associations truly representative of their industries," so the need for a single spokesman group for the entire retail field had become evident during the early days of NRA.

4. He had also declared that membership would be open to all merchants, whether large or small, and whether they are members of retail associations or not, and that the new association would not compete with existing organizations but would be supplemental to them.

5. Major features of the program were (a) cooperation with governmental and other agencies participating in movements for the national welfare; (b) coordination of all branches of retail distribution to improve it; (c) representation of the national associations affiliated with the federation in national public relations compatible with the program of policies laid down by the board of trustees; and (d) stimulation of greater appreciation on the part of retailers of the service given them by the national retail associations and encouragement of the development of representative, well-organized and coordinated State councils.

6. A vital function would be to furnish statistics on retail distribution to government and other agencies.

7. Col. Sherrill would resign immediately as vice president of Kroger Grocery and Baking Company to take up his new post.

8. Herbert J. Tily, president of Strawbridge and Clothier, a Philadelphia department store, who had been one of the leaders in the formation of the federation, was president of the Retailer's National Council, an informal organization representing *thirteen leading retail associations*. "They, together with numerous other retail units, doing an extremely large volume of business," the story declared, "will become *the nucleus of the new federation*. These associations comprise the National Retail Dry Goods Association, National Association of Retail Clothiers, National Association of Retail Grocers, National Retail Furniture Association, National Retail Hardware Association, American National Retail Jewelers Association, National Association of Retail Druggists, National Shoe Retailers Association, Limited Price Variety Stores Association, Inc., Mail Order Association of America, National Council of Shoe Retailers, National Retail Association of Music Merchants and Food and Grocery Chain Stores of America."

9. Mr. Kirstein had explained that the membership set-up had been designed "to safeguard the interests of the smaller merchant by adequate representation on the governing body."

10. The executive committee consisted of Mr. Kirstein; Percy S. Straus, R. H. Macy & Co.; John S. Burke, B. Altman & Co.; George M. Gales, Liggett Drug Company; Claude W. Kress, S. H. Kress & Co.; Fred Lazarus, Jr., The F. & R. Lazarus & Co.; Albert H. Morrill, Kroger Grocery & Baking Co.; Lessing J. Rosenwald, Sears, Roebuck and Co.; Earl C. Sams, J. C. Penney Co.; and Herbert J. Tily.

11. Twenty other leading merchants had taken an active part in the formation of the federation. All were department store men except seven chain-store executives: W. T. Grant, W. T. Grant Co.; Joy H. Johnson, Walgreen Company; Ward Melville, Melville Shoe Corporation; Samuel Robinson,

American Stores Co.; C. B. Van Dusen, S. S. Kresge Co.; E. G. Yonker, Safeway Stores; and Earl B. Puckett, Hahn Department Stores (now Allied Stores).

12. Temporary offices had been opened at the New Willard.

The newspaper stories followed rather closely a press release which had been issued by the organizers of the federation.

How the advent of the new association was greeted by the trade press is indicated by a signed article in *Women's Wear Daily*, one of the Fairchild publications, the same evening. W. D. Hart declared himself as follows:

> "At last it has come. Or perhaps it would be better to say that it is well on its way. What? A unified voice for the retail craft. The formation of the American Retail Federation is one of the most vital happenings in the retail industry in many a year. . . . Such an organization as is planned by the new group in regard to educating Government officials, manufacturers and consumers has unlimited possibilities. The true picture of the field of distribution can be developed by this group."

In the same issue, Col. Sherrill was featured as "the new Field Marshal of retail distribution."

Retailing, another Fairchild publication, a weekly, in its April 22 issue, hailed the federation enthusiastically. Under the heading: "At Last—National Organization," Earl W. Elhart declared editorially:

> "The business of retailing is about to be given a 'national voice.' Through the organization of the new American Retail Federation for the first time in American history unified representation of more than one million retail stores is provided for. . . . This new association, launched with such impressive backing, should be indeed a New Deal for the merchants from one end of the country to another. . . . The need for just such an organization as has been created has been repeatedly pointed out on this page. . . ."

Chain Store Age, May, 1935, declared editorially under the head: "Retailing Finds Its Voice," in part, as follows:

"Retailing has long needed not merely a spokesman but a 'loud-speaker.' Now it has one in the shape of the newly organized American Retail Federation, an association of associations, designed to represent all types of retailing, and sponsored by most of the leading retail organizations already functioning in their individual spheres. The selection of Col. C. O. Sherrill as president of the federation is hardly less significant than the conception of the organization itself. No better choice could have been made. If the federation is to be successful, it is going to need just what Col. Sherrill can supply."

The editorial suggested that ARF would relieve retailers themselves of "the burden of watching the legislatures and of organizing the opposition" to undesirable legislation proposals, and pointed out that ARF's "political influence may be expected to grow as its scope becomes better understood." Referring to the relation of ARF to the chains, the editorial said:

"The American Retail Federation is not a chain-store organization, but the important part the chains play in retail distribution is clearly recognized in the make-up of the executive committee, of whose ten members five are department-store men and the others are chain-store executives. Col. Sherrill, although connected with the Kroger Grocery & Baking Company for several years, has resigned from that company to give his full time to the Federation."

The editorial pointed out that "the thirteen national retail associations which have for many years been affiliated with the Retailers National Council are expected to become members of the new federation at once."

That is how the new federation appeared to those who had no reason to believe that it was anything other than it purported to be. How it appeared to others and what happened as a result of their adverse reactions provided the makings of one of the many sensational chapters in chain-store history. Before proceeding with it, however, a brief résumé of Col. Sherrill's record before he became "the Field Marshal of Retail Distribution" may be useful.

As it was described in the release upon which the *Times* story was based, "Col. Sherrill brings to his new duties a wealth of experience in the retail field, coupled with a broad viewpoint growing out of his West Point training, Army experience and various governmental, civic and business duties. He is a West Point graduate and has served in all grades of the Engineer Corps, from lieutenant to colonel, in the United States, Philippines and Canal Zone. During the World War he was Chief of Staff of the Seventy-seventh Division and served in France with distinction, as witnessed by his receiving the Distinguished Service Medal and the Croix de Guerre.

"Col. Sherrill's civic and governmental experience covers a wide field. He was in Washington as director of public buildings and parks. From this position he was drafted to become the first city manager of Cincinnati. His brilliant success is attested by the very able administration which he gave to Cincinnati, as that city has become almost the American ideal for city-manager operation. In 1930 he became vice president of the Kroger Grocery & Baking Company of Cincinnati, and he has served as vice president of the Cincinnati Chamber of Commerce, president of the Cincinnati Better Business Bureau, chairman of the Ohio National Recovery Administration Advisory Committee and director of the Ohio Retail Council. Governor Davey, of Ohio, has called upon Col. Sherrill to head a survey of all State governmental functions, with an organization being loaned by the larger industries of the State. This valuable public work will soon be completed."

But neither Col. Sherrill's reputation nor the standing of the men responsible for the organization of the ARF availed

to save the project from a sneak attack as unprovoked and
as unexpected, if not as world-shaking, as the one which was
to lay Pearl Harbor low some six years later.

What happened, within a week after ARF had been
launched so auspiciously, was thus reported in the New York
Herald Tribune of April 25:

HOUSE INQUIRY
IS ORDERED ON
RETAIL GROUP

———

New Federation Headed by
Col. Sherrill is Called
a "Chain Store Lobby"

The story began:

"Congressional investigation of the newly created American Retail Federation on charges that it represents a 'superlobby' backed by chain store interests was ordered by the
House of Representatives today through the adoption of a
resolution presented by Representative John J. Cochran,
Democrat, of Missouri."

What had brought all that about? What could possibly
have happened in the short space of those few days to turn
the ARF dream into a nightmare, as one trade-paper editor
appropriately termed it?

Most of the blame must be put, strangely enough, on the
organizers of the ARF themselves! The seat of the trouble
was the release they had given to the newspapers. It was not
as clear as it might have been. It had led the newspapers to
say something that wasn't so. They had said categorically
that the thirteen national associations affiliated with the Retailers' National Council, which were listed by name, would
"form the nucleus" of ARF. The fact was not only that the
associations in question had not pledged themselves to membership in the ARF but they had not even been invited to
join! Furthermore, the story in the newspapers was the first

information the rank-and-file members of these organizations had received regarding the ARF.

No doubt the ARF organizers had taken for granted that Dr. Tily's group would join the new association without question just because he himself had been one of its most enthusiastic sponsors. And, in giving the list of the associations to the newspapers, they had apparently failed to make clear the actual situation.

The resentment of the leaders of some of these associations had been immediate, direct and bitter. Some of them, such as the National Association of Retail Druggists, the National Association of Retail Grocers and the National Retail Hardware Association, whose membership consisted primarily of small independent retailers, were taking a major part in anti-chain activities. The mere suggestion that they were contemplating affiliating themselves with an organization in which the chains would be a key factor had made them "see red."

What happened was graphically described by John Guernsey, editor of the Philadelphia *Retail Ledger* in his May, 1935, issue. In a signed article headed: "Retail Federation Dream Becomes Nightmare," he said:

> "The National (sic) Retail Federation entered the roped arena of national politics last month, fell over its own feet, antagonized most of the fight fans and convulsed the rest by its bungling tactics and took some hard blows on the chin before it even shucked off its lounging robe."

Among the hard blows, he included the reactions of several leaders of associations whose names had been used in the press as forming "the nucleus" of the federation. He quoted Roscoe Rau, of the National Retail Furniture Association, as saying: "It is news to us. Not having been given any information, we cannot foretell the attitude of our board."

And John Dargavel, of the National Association of Retail Druggists, had said: "We emphatically deny any allegation or inference that we will affiliate with or be any part of the

Retail Federation. We positively refuse to become catspaws for the big chain and department stores."

Robert Sheets, speaking for the National Retail Hardware Association, had declared:

"The National Retail Hardware Association has never been invited to have a part, has no knowledge of the basis for the statement by Kirstein that it will be one of the vertebra of such a new organization and has no intention of being associated therewith."

Rivers Peterson, also speaking for the Hardware Association, had been even more specific. "The Hardware Association will not join," he had said, "and from this day is out definitely to establish a cleavage between the predatory Goliaths personified by the mail-order houses, chains and big stores, such as this new federation represents, and the great body of smaller retailers whose best interests are directly opposed to those of the 'big fellows' who are traveling toward a desired destination concealed beneath the coat tails of the 'little fellows' who are politically powerful."

But, after quoting these reactions, John Guernsey deprecated them. "The men behind this new federation," he declared, "are among the ablest merchants and the finest type of American citizens in this country." Naming some of them, he went on: "Such men have no ulterior motive in setting up this organization nor would they stoop to any practices unfair to others." And then he added, prophetically enough, "the Congressional investigation will come to nothing, but meantime will prove embarrassing because it puts these unselfish men in a false light by innuendo and association of ideas."

Addressing himself to the "many capable national and local retail associations whose valuable work of years in the interest of the retail craft has been so slighted," he urged them "to avoid incriminations that you may later regret, and take steps to line up with the long-range objectives of the federation. By joining it you can control it, even if you think it is on the wrong track at present. You can prevent it from being used as a 'catspaw for the chains and mail-order houses.'"

But with so much resentment already engendered against the new organization, some of it was bound to spill over and reach the attention of anti-chain Congressmen. The result was the House Resolution which prompted the *Herald Tribune* story.

Numbered H.R. 203, it provided for the appointment of a special committee of seven "to investigate the American Retail Federation, its capitalization, its membership, its objectives, the sources of its funds, its financial connections and its officers and agents and to investigate the record of stock dividends, officers' salaries, profits, interlocking directorates and banking affiliations of all corporations directly affiliated with, or contributing to, the said American Retail Federation."

The resolution was preceded by ten "Whereas" clauses based on statements alleged to have been contained in the *N.Y. Times* story, but which, for the most part, were actually without any foundation whatever. Witness, for example, the opening preamble, which read as follows:

"Whereas the Associated Press on April 16, 1935 and the New York *Times* of April 17, 1935, reported that a super-lobby to be known as the 'American Retail Federation' was recently formed to promote the business of chain stores throughout the United States and to influence the action of Members of Congress with reference to legislation affecting chain stores and their holding companies!"

Witness also the questionable assumptions and misstatements in these additional preambles:

"Whereas it is apparent that said American Retail Federation is organized for the purpose of increasing the profits of big business, through lobbying tactics, designed to prevent small businesses from securing competitive opportunities equal to those enjoyed by corporations representing vast aggregations of capital; and . . ."

"Whereas the said superlobby has already opened palatial headquarters in the city of Washington, District of Columbia, and has attempted and is now attempting, to force and coerce thousands of small retail merchants, dealing in the necessities of life, into the ranks of this superlobby, so that it may thereafter hold out to Members of Congress and to others in the Government that it represents a completely centralized and authentic voice for all retailers of the Nation; and . . .

"Whereas, it is further reported that this superlobby, the American Retail Federation, is now proceeding upon a plan designed to force the small independent retail merchants of America, engaged in the sale of the necessities of everyday life, to contribute an additional $2,000,000 annually to the funds available to the organization in its lobbying activities, and for the further purpose of permitting it to disseminate propaganda among the consumers and producers of the United States."

But the House was in no position to question the accuracy of any of the statements in the preambles, and the resolution was promptly adopted. The committee of seven originally appointed included its sponsor, Representative Cochran, as chairman, but when he withdrew, May 17, 1935, before the investigation got under way, Representative Wright Patman, of Texas, was named in his place. Considering the anti-chain animus which was behind the investigation, no more appropriate appointment could have been made. It launched Mr. Patman on an anti-chain crusade which was to subject the chains to untold expense and trouble in the years which followed and which, despite some major set-backs, he has not yet abandoned.[1]

To skip, for the moment, the many interesting facts brought out in the course of the investigation regarding the methods used by the chains in defending themselves against discriminatory taxes, some of the findings of the majority report [2] will

[1] The other members of the committee were Representatives Boileau, Bloom, Cole, Dockweiler, Lucas and McLean.

[2] 74th Congress, 2nd Session, H.R. Report No. 2373; it was filed by Representatives Patman, Dockweiler, Lucas and Boileau.

suffice to show how baseless the investigation actually was. The report declares:

"While there is a slight difference of opinion from the witnesses as to the real purpose of the organization in question, there can be little doubt that this federation was organized primarily for the purposes of promoting not only the interests of chain stores throughout the United States but also to promote the interests of department stores which had a like financial responsibility with the large chains. The evidence shows beyond any question that those in charge of the federation will be primarily engaged in research work concerning retail distribution and other problems for the purpose of ultimately disseminating that information throughout the United States of America, and especially for the purpose of appearing before committees of Congress in order to influence legislation which the federation believes to be to the best interest of the various groups which the federation represents.

"It may be well to say, in passing, that there is a voluminous amount of testimony dealing with chain store activities from a State and National viewpoint prior to the formation of the American Retail Federation. It was the belief of the committee that through the submission of such evidence we might show an unbroken chain of factual circumstances which would prove conclusively that the American Retail Federation was organized for the purpose of carrying forward the unfair methods and practices of certain large chain stores and other national organizations. However, the evidence upon this point wholly fails to make such connection."

Although that admission might seem to be generous enough, actually it was less than the truth. For the evidence showed positively that no such connection existed.

Referring to the charge in one of the preambles to the effect that the "superlobby" was attempting to force and coerce thousands of small retail merchants into its ranks, the report admits that while the rank-and-file membership of the Ohio Retail Council had been "persuaded to become members of and thereby add numerical strength to the support of the

American Retail Federation . . . there is no evidence before the committee of actual force and coercion of any such members."

With respect to the further charge that the small independent retail merchants were to be forced to contribute $2,000,-000 annually to the "superlobby," the majority report admits that "there is no evidence in the record" to prove it.

Finally, the majority report admitted that there was no evidence to support a further contention as to "the coercion of hundreds of thousands of underpaid employes throughout the Nation to flood the respective Members of the United States Congress with letters, petitions and propaganda designed to improperly and untruthfully represent the public sentiment of the respective constituencies of said Members of Congress."

The minority report,[3] as might have been expected, gave the ARF a clean bill of health. Conceding that the organization's own publicity at the outset might have conveyed the impression that its purpose was to organize a superlobby to protect the chains, the minority pointed out that "such a conclusion is not justified by the testimony adduced by the committee at its hearings when given the weight it is entitled to by reason of the character, standing and attainments of the gentlemen who organized the American Retail Federation, its declared objects and purposes."

After quoting some of the testimony of Messrs. Kirstein and Lazarus and referring to that of Col. Sherrill, the minority arrived at the following significant conclusion:

> "In the judgment of the undersigned, the American Retail Federation, as organized, is similar to many other existing organizations, except that it has for its purpose the coordination of all retailers, whereas previously existing organizations have been confined to particular trades. The individuals who head the movement are men of high standing, who have attained wide success as American businessmen, and their objectives and purposes, as explained in their testimony, may

[3] Filed by Representatives Bloom, McLean and Cole.

well serve a laudable purpose. We find nothing to indicate an intention to trespass beyond ethical limitations in the presentation to Congress and the Members thereof their views as to pending legislation or to the Government departments in the interpretation of the law and the regulations made pursuant thereof."

But, gratifying as this report must have been to the sponsors of the ARF when it was finally presented to the House, on April 7, 1936, it could not undo the damage the organization had already suffered.

Many of the associations which had definitely planned to join the ARF because they were in complete accord with its purposes and realized the need for such an organization naturally deferred taking any steps in that direction while the investigation continued. Nor could ARF itself solicit memberships under such conditions. Thus a whole year was lost before ARF was free to pursue the program it had laid out for itself.

Nevertheless, under the energetic leadership of Col. Sherrill, ARF was soon making up for lost time. One by one, all the important national retail associations became members of the ARF in the next few years. What must have been particularly gratifying to the organizers was the fact that by 1942 every one of the thirteen national associations which they had confidently expected from the start would enter the fold had done so, including, of course, even those which had been so antagonistic then. Furthermore, it may be said at this point that the ARF is a stronger and more influential organization today than at any time since its eventful arrival on the scene. Its record to date has not only completely vindicated the good faith of its organizers but has demonstrated that their judgment was sound and their vision true. The ARF did indeed become the "unified voice" of retailing. As of January 29, 1958, it spoke for 31 national and 38 state retail associations, representing 800,000 retail outlets across the nation. Since its organization, it has had four distinguished presidents—Col. Sherrill who, after two years of service, yielded to a demand that he return to the job which had earned him nation-wide recognition and respect, that of city manager of Cincinnati; Dr. David R. Craig, who served from 1937 to 1941; the late Walter Morrow, who died in office in 1948; and the incumbent, Rowland Jones, Jr., who had previously made an enviable record as the Washington representative of the National Association of Retail Druggists.

That retailing needs a "unified voice" today as much as it did when the federation was first conceived was made clear by Mr. Jones in the course of his second annual report as its president, presented April 3, 1950.

"We have become, as a nation," he declared, "a conglomeration of pressure groups—good, bad and in between—all clamoring for attention and demanding all shades and varieties of government action and intervention into the everyday lives of all our people.

"The segments of our economy which would be affected adversely, were many of the demands of these groups to be granted, must of stark necessity organize themselves for defensive political action or resign themselves to becoming the eunuchs of our economic and political system, passive and helpless to protect their legitimate interests and freedom of action and decision.[4]

"My conception of the federation is a retail-industry fire department, adequately equipped and ready to go into action when danger threatens. And like all good fire departments, it should utilize the interim periods in fire-prevention work. Brought to its full potential in membership, influence and good repute, it may extinguish many fires in their incipiency. Through the nurturing of government and public understanding of the functions and needs of the retail industry and its prime importance to the economy, the major cause of fires—misunderstandings and misinformation—can be eliminated over the long pull."

[4] Compare with observations of Robert W. Lyons, p. 176, *supra*.

By 1958, the need for an organization like the ARF to speak for all retailing had become greater than ever. Among other threats on the legislative front, a persistent effort to extend the coverage of the Federal Wage-Hour law to retailing was in itself sufficient reason for unified opposition.

In January, 1958, Mr. Jones declared that "the need of the hour is an American Retail Federation solidly financed to do the things that cry to be done, supported by a strong rise in interest and dedication to the idea that only the retail industry itself with all its facets and organizations can defend the legitimate interests of the industry."

So much for the American Retail Federation. It finds a place in these pages only because the Congressional investigation which its birth precipitated brought the chains most conspicuously into the limelight. Furthermore, some of the testimony adduced at the hearings played an important part in the debates which resulted in the Robinson-Patman Act.

Keeping in mind the fact that the investigation was premised on the charge that the new ARF was nothing but a "false front" propaganda device conceived by the chains to help them in their struggle against discriminatory anti-chain taxes, the course the hearings took was what might have been expected. Headed by Representative Patman, a former district attorney, whose hostility to the chains was to become his main political stock-in-trade, the committee, with its power of subpoena, was well equipped to expose whatever shortcomings the chain-store system might involve and to show up, in their worst possible light, whatever mistakes or indiscretions individual chain-store men might have committed.

Certainly the anti-chain interests must have smacked their lips with anticipation as the committee came into possession of such promising food for scandal as the private files of leading chain-store figures and organizations. Although in most cases access was freely given, the committee's agents were armed with subpoenas which would have enabled them to seize the files in question if they had not been made available.

Among the files used by the committee were those of the organizers of the ARF, of the Food and Grocery Chain Stores of America and of Robert W. Lyons, formerly executive secretary of the dissolved National Chain Store Association, who was then representing fourteen leading chains as counsel in charge of their lobbying activities against discriminatory legislation.

What the committee actually uncovered is dealt with in the next chapter.

CHAPTER X

WHAT THE INVESTIGATION

DISCLOSED

THE RECORD of the hearings consists of more than 1,200 pages. It covers not only the testimony regarding the ARF but the additional testimony concerning the trade practices of companies engaged in large-scale buying, the scope of the originally authorized investigation having been extended by another resolution, H.R. No. 239, to authorize a broader probe.

Although only eighteen days in all were required for the taking of the testimony, they were spread through June, July, August and December, 1935, and January, February and March, 1936.

Without attempting even to summarize all the testimony the hearings produced, comment will be confined to that part of it which might fairly be regarded as most damaging to the chains. Mr. Patman's own "index-digest" of the record, which was printed by the committee, is not particularly useful for that purpose because of its obvious unfairness.[1] One example will suffice to show how unreliable a digester Mr. Patman is.

On page 1 of his "index-digest," he declares:

"Col. Clarence C. Sherrill has testified that as president of the American Retail Federation he still holds to the chain store theory that it is the best policy to eliminate as many as possible from the retail trade."

[1] Index Digest of Record of Hearings before Special Committee on Investigation American Retail Federation &c., 74th Congress, First Session.

In support of that statement, on page 17, Mr. Patman digests Col. Sherrill's testimony as follows:

> "Sherrill stated that he still holds to the chain store theory that it is the best policy to eliminate as many people as possible between producer and consumer and that he has not, since he left Kroger Co. and became president of American Retail Federation, changed his views (vol. 4, No. 2, p. 40)."

Is that what Col. Sherrill actually said or even intimated? Here is the record itself:

> THE CHAIRMAN. Of course, Colonel Sherrill, we give you credit for believing that the chain story theory is the right theory; that chain stores should be encouraged and promoted rather than retarded.
>
> MR. SHERRILL. You say you give me credit for that?
>
> THE CHAIRMAN. Are we right in giving you credit for that?
>
> MR. SHERRILL. I was of the opinion, when I was employed by the chain store company, that the chain store method of distribution is a sound one and that it has economies that are valuable both for the chain store operators and for the consumer; yes.
>
> THE CHAIRMAN. That is, to eliminate as many people between the producer and consumer as possible?
>
> MR. SHERRILL. To eliminate as many people between the producer and consumer as possible, except where they were doing a real valuable service.

The main facts revealed by the investigation which would seem to call for explanation on the part of the chains may be considered under the following heads:

1. Publication of a medium to carry chain-store propaganda to farm leaders.
2. "Espionage" of an anti-chain-store association.
3. Invoking an NRA regulation to block the showing of an anti-chain film.
4. Legislative tactics used to combat discriminatory chain-store taxes.

5. Receipt by the chains of discounts and allowances not available to independent retailers.

1. Publication of a medium to carry chain-store propaganda to farm leaders.

The propaganda medium which came under fire was a mimeographed bulletin called "Farm to Market News." The evidence showed that it had been conceived by a former representative of the American Farm Bureau Federation who was well-known to farm leaders and who planned to issue it under his own name and as reflecting his own convictions if the chains would finance it. Three food chains had agreed to underwrite the project and the bulletin was accordingly issued for about a year.

Nobody contended that an effort by the chains, or by a group of them, to influence farm opinion in their favor through the medium of a bulletin was in itself objectionable in any way. The only criticism raised against the "Farm to Market News" was that its backers were purposely concealed. Albert H. Morrill, president of the Kroger Grocery & Baking Co., one of the sponsors of the bulletin, who was interrogated about it, frankly conceded that the failure to disclose its actual sponsorship had been a mistake, but he pointed out that it was the kind of mistake that anybody might have made under similar conditions.

In any event, the questionable bulletin was not published long enough to do the chains much good or anyone else much harm. It had been discontinued long before the committee investigating the ARF had come into existence.

2. "Espionage" of an anti-chain-store association.

Among the many organizations which were set up to fight the chains and, incidentally, in most cases, to enrich the promoters, as pointed out earlier in these pages, was one called the National Anti-Chain Stores League. The evidence disclosed that in March, 1935, a John E. Barr, one of its employes, had approached John A. Logan, executive vice president of Food and Grocery Chain Stores of America, with an offer to keep him posted on the anti-chain-store association's activities. He had explained to Mr. Logan that the journal the organization was planning to issue to independent retailers would not only attack the chains but would carry Nazi propaganda, and as he was a veteran of World War I, he thought that was "going a bit too far."

Mr. Logan testified that he had submitted the whole matter to his executive committee and they had authorized him to pay Barr $50 a week. The arrangement lasted for a short time, during which period, Mr. Logan testified, he received ample evidence from Barr to convince him that "the organization was conceived for personal profits and personal gains for the men who organized it." Barr testified to the same effect.

The only question of propriety raised by Mr. Patman with respect to the arrangement with Barr was whether it was "ethical." Mr. Logan conceded that if the league had been an association established for legitimate purposes, he would not have considered paying Barr for information concerning its activities—even though they were directed against the chains—but that was not the situation as he saw it. On the contrary, he was convinced that the league was a "racket" and it had among its objectives the spreading of Nazi propaganda through the journal that was to be widely circulated among retail merchants. Under such conditions, he could not see that any question of "ethics" was involved.

3. Invoking an NRA regulation to block the showing of an anti-chain film.

The film in question was a five-reel talking picture called "Forward America." It was produced by a Frank R. Wilson, formerly with NRA, with the idea of "dramatizing the arguments against syndicate chain stores and showing the economic effect on American communities of the operations of chain stores and mail-order houses." [2]

[2] Hearings before Special Committee on Investigation of American Retail Federation, Vol. 1, p. 333.

The nature of the picture is indicated more specifically in a circular used to promote the film and which was referred to by Mr. Patman and read into the record as follows:

"At last here is the dynamite that will blast the chain stores and mail-order houses from your community. Mr. Independent Merchant, here is your opportunity to recapture your birthright and regain your former prosperity. . . .

"This picture . . . is being shown with telling effect in many American cities, with resultant decrease in chain and mail-order business and a corresponding increase in the business of independent local merchants. . . .

"If you want to know the truth about the depression, see 'Forward America.' If you want to know who is to blame, see 'Forward America.' If you want to know how it was started and how it is being continued, see 'Forward America.' Independent Merchants, organize and appoint a live local man to get in touch with us and we will show him how to proceed. You can help solve America's greatest illness by having 'Forward America' shown in your community."

What, if anything, could the chains do to protect themselves against a picture of this kind, a picture which, as they saw it, accused them unjustly of almost every crime on the calendar?

At that time NRA was still in command of the economy. Every industry and trade was governed by a code. The Code of Fair Competition for the Retail Food and Grocery Trade contained a provision that "no food and grocery retailer shall use advertising . . . of any . . . nature, which is inaccurate in any material particular or misrepresents . . . credit terms . . . policies or services; and no food and grocer retailer shall use advertising and/or selling methods which tend to deceive or mislead the customer." Another provision read: "No food and grocery retailer shall use advertising which refers inaccurately in any material particular to any competitor or his merchandise, prices, values, credit, terms, policies or services."

Could it be that either of these provisions were violated by retail grocers who purchased tickets from the sponsors of "Forward America" at 25 cents each and distributed them to their customers and others, admitting them to the theater where the picture was showing?

Certainly nothing could be lost by trying. And so in various cities where the picture was shown complaints were filed with the local food and grocery code authority. Several of these local authorities appealed to C. H. Janssen, the chairman of the National Food and Grocery Distributors Code Authority, for a ruling. Hector Lazo, assistant to Mr. Janssen, a witness at the hearing, was questioned at great length by Mr. Patman and another member of the committee in an obvious attempt to establish that the film was condemned, through the connivance of the chains, without giving its sponsor an opportunity to be heard in its defense.

What actually happened is revealed in a letter of February 16, 1935, from Mr. Janssen to J. Neumann, the secretary of the local food and grocery Code Authority in Cincinnati, who had asked for a ruling regarding the film.[3]

After quoting the facts which Mr. Neumann had presented and the provisions of the Code applicable to them, Mr. Janssen said:

> "In response to your request, The National Food and Grocery Distributors Code Authority gave due and careful consideration to the same, and preparatory to stating an opinion, invited a private showing and hearing of the film and its accompanying lecture, following which it unanimously expressed the following opinion:
>
> "It is the opinion of the members of the National Food and Grocery Distributors Code Authority that the talking film as shown to the members in New York on February 7, 1935, (1) refers inaccurately in material particulars to a competitor and/or a class of competitors in retail food and grocery distribution in a number of respects; (2) that it tends to deceive or mislead the customers.
>
> "On the basis of the foregoing, it is my opinion that any

[3] *Ibid.*, p. 335.

member of the food and grocery trade participating in the distribution of tickets to a showing of such film or its message does therein also become a party to the dissemination of its inaccuracies or its misrepresentation of policies or services and tendency to deceive or mislead customers, and so forth, as such prohibitions are specifically stated in article IX, section 1, paragraphs (a) and (b) in the Code of Fair Competition for the Food and Grocery Trade."

That this ruling was used effectively by the chains to discourage the showing of the film can hardly be doubted. Mr. Logan had written to Mr. Janssen on January 3,[4] calling attention to the film, expressing his view that the showing of the film by wholesale and retail grocers was a violation of the code, asking that local and State code authorities in Kansas, and elsewhere, where the film was being shown, be advised of the code provisions, and also requesting information on the proper procedure for "obtaining prompt action against wholesale and retail grocers who violate the code by participating in and dissemination of unfair and inaccurate advertising of the character of 'Forward America.' " When the ruling in question was handed down on February 16, the chains would have had no reason for not taking full advantage of it.

What happened was probably accurately described in a letter sent by Mr. Wilson, the producer of the film, to Mr. Patman, a paragraph from which he read into the record as follows:

"Just to show how effective this chain store lobby was in your State, the home-owned merchants of Amarillo, Texas, appointed a committee to raise $1,200 for the sale of tickets to merchants for distribution to the public, so that an auditorium could be engaged for the showing of 'Forward America.' On the very day that the solicitors started out to collect the money for this ticket distribution the chain store representatives placed in the hands of every home-owned business of Amarillo a copy of this Code Authority opinion. The result was that many of the dealers of Amarillo who were enthusi-

[4] *Ibid.*, p. 330.

astic about the picture failed to participate in its sponsorship because of the fear of Federal prosecution."

Now what did Mr. Patman find to criticize in the efforts of the chains to discourage the showing of "Forward America"?

His main complaint, according to his own "index-digest" of the record, was that "at no time was Frank R. Wilson, the owner of the film, offered an opportunity by the chain store interests to appear before the code authorities or NRA for the purpose of showing that his film did not misrepresent chain stores or unduly disparage them."

What Mr. Patman overlooked was that Mr. Wilson was given an opportunity to exhibit the film itself to the National Authority and the film, of course, spoke for itself.

Who constituted the National Code Authority?

Mr. Lazo testified that it consisted of the representatives elected by the boards of directors of the six national trade associations sponsoring the codes. At the time they were: C. H. Janssen, executive chairman, the head of the executive staff and representing no one; C. M. D. Miller, representing the retailer-owned wholesale cooperatives; Asa Strause, representing the voluntary groups; Milton W. Griggs, representing the National-American Wholesale Grocers Association; C. Y. Early, representing the United States Wholesale Grocers Association; F. H. Massmann, representing the Food and Grocery Chain Stores of America; and H. C. Petersen, representing the National Association of Retail Grocers.

When Mr. Lazo pointed out that the only question was whether or not the film contained, in the opinion of the National Code Authority, inaccurate references to competition, he was asked how they could give an opinion without hearing both sides of the case. He answered: "These men have spent their entire lifetime in food distribution."

Challenged by Mr. Patman to name "one instance of false advertising" in the film, Mr. Lazo mentioned that it charged "the chain stores directly with being the only ones guilty of short-weighting, for example . . . saying specifically: 'this is

the reason why chain stores can sell more cheaply to you,'
then they show the short-weights."

The testimony continued:

THE CHAIRMAN. And you say that is wrong?

MR. LAZO. I say that it is wrong to charge any one particular
factor with all the vices.

THE CHAIRMAN. Suppose that the fact was that Mr. Wilson
could have come in and shown you proof, sworn testimony,
to the effect that that is true. Would it still be possible to
show the truth?

MR. LAZO. Yes.

THE CHAIRMAN. All right; why don't [sic] they listen to Mr.
Wilson's side and let him attempt to show you that it was
true?

MR. LAZO. We know that short-weighting exists in the trade.
Our contention was that it was not limited to chain stores.

THE CHAIRMAN. I know, but what if there was proof before
the Federal Trade Commission under oath—

MR. LAZO. That it was limited to chain stores?

THE CHAIRMAN. Yes.

MR. LAZO. I don't believe there was any such proof, sir. . . .
The impression that was given in the film is that all these
vices that we were attempting to correct through the codes
were limited to chain-store type of distribution. Now our
contention was and our contention is that we were cognizant
of these vices in the trade, but they were not limited to any
one factor.

Other questions brought out that, where a formal complaint
was lodged with a local code authority, the procedure called
for the citing of the merchant, against whom the complaint
was lodged, to appear at a hearing. In this case, however, the
opinion or ruling of the National Code Authority was not
based on such a complaint at all. It was given to a local code
authority, with whom such a complaint had apparently been
lodged, and who had appealed to the national body for guidance. What procedure the local authority followed in his
handling of the complaint before him, does not appear in the
record. In any event, however, it would hardly seem that the

national authority was called upon to do more than it actually did—to view the film to see whether or not it referred inaccurately in material particulars to a competitor or tended to deceive or mislead customers. If these leaders of all types of food and grocery distribution concluded unanimously, as they did, that the film did not accurately portray trade practices and was deceptive and misleading to the public, Mr. Janssen's action would seem to have rested on a sound foundation. If it resulted in stopping or limiting the circulation of the film, wasn't that the effect the provisions in the code were designed to achieve?

4. Legislative tactics used to combat discriminatory chainstore taxes.

If the chains had stepped out of bounds in the course of their lobbying activities against discriminatory legislation, the investigation certainly provided ample opportunity to find out just what they had been up to. For who could know more about what had been done than one of the witnesses who came before the committee—Robert W. Lyons? Here was the man who had directed the tax-defense work of the National Chain Store Association from 1929 to 1934 and had thereafter continued it for fourteen leading non-food chains, as has already been related.[5] Furthermore he had given the committee's agents free access to his files so that they could confront him with actual letters he had written and received.

True enough, Mr. Lyons at first refused to answer a number of questions, although he had appeared before the committee voluntarily. He based his refusal on two grounds: (1) the information requested was privileged by reason of the professional relation which existed between him and his clients; and (2) the questions went into matters which, he claimed, a Congressional committee could not legally explore since its inquisitorial power extended only to matters on which Congress

[5] See p. 180, *supra.*

could legislate. He claimed that activities in State capitols could hardly be a matter for Federal legislation.

Nevertheless, whatever legal ground Mr. Lyons might have had and maintained for refusing to answer the committee's questions, he did not stick to it. He answered enough questions to give the committee a clear picture of the scope of his lobbying activities for the chains and the policies and principles he followed in pursuing them. Supplemented by testimony on the same subject from Mr. Logan, Albert W. Hughes, assistant to the president of the J. C. Penney Company (later to become president and in 1958, chairman of the board), and other witnesses, and innumerable letters selected by the committee from the files of Mr. Lyons and the food-chain association, the picture was about as complete, if not as devastating, as the committee could have wished.

What did it show?

Mr. Lyons testified that for the year commencing October 1, 1934, as counsel for fourteen leading chains, he had a tax-defense budget of $175,000. That was the same amount, incidentally, which the National Chain Store Association had set up for its annual legislative tax-defense budget in 1931 when Mr. Lyons had been in charge of it as executive vice president. After the dissolution of that association, Mr. Lyons had continued the task as counsel for the fourteen chains who shared the expense of it on the basis of their relative sales. His fourteen clients, he told the committee, were: F. W. Woolworth Co., S. S. Kresge Co., W. T. Grant Co., S. H. Kress & Co., J. J. Newberry Co., H. L. Green Co., G. C. Murphy Co., Neisner Bros., Scott-Burr Stores Corp., Charles Stores Co. and M. H. Fishman Co., all members of the Limited Price Variety Stores Association, and J. C. Penney Company, Melville Shoe Corporation and Walgreen Co.

How was the fund used?

None of it was spent for anything but counsel fees, Mr. Lyons testified. Local counsel was engaged in every State capitol where legislation discriminating against chain stores was introduced. The general practice was for Mr. Lyons to send one of the three legislative experts on his staff to the seat of the trouble. His function was to size up the situation, arrange for the employment of competent legal counsel and report to Mr. Lyons.

As to the type of men Mr. Lyons selected as local counsel, he testified as follows:

> "I have employed counsel with two things in mind, first, to let us have an opinion as to whether an important proposition was legal, constitutional, serious, or otherwise . . . and secondly, of necessity, to measure whether the threat of that legislation is serious. As a practical matter, that lawyer must have contacts with members of the various committees with whom he can frankly, honestly and honorably discuss the problems. So, in every case, I attempt to hire an attorney who has public experience and is able to measure these matters with good conscience and good judgment and who is able as a lawyer, to give us a sound, intelligent opinion as to both our legal, constitutional and political problems."

He never employed a legislator as counsel while he was in office.

Asked whether he ever hired local counsel on a contingent basis, paying a small retainer fee and later a substantial additional fee if no discriminatory chain-store legislation was adopted, Mr. Lyons said he did in some instances in States where contingent fee arrangements were lawful. He saw nothing unethical in it.

The following extract from the record, revealing a phase of legislative strategy sometimes used in desperate cases, speaks for itself:

> THE CHAIRMAN. Have you not had correspondence with your lawyers in which you have said, "If we cannot stop this bill we will have it so amended so it will be unconstitutional"?
> MR. LYONS. I would not be at all surprised if I had.
> THE CHAIRMAN. You advised them to get that done?

MR. LYONS. I advised them to do everything they legally and properly could.

THE CHAIRMAN. You felt that it was ethical?

MR. LYONS. Yes, sir. . . .

THE CHAIRMAN. If you go before a legislative body and you misrepresent to those legislators as to what the law is and lead them to believe that they should have a better bill or a different bill, when that bill is not unconstitutional [sic] would not that be unethical?

MR. LYONS. Neither I nor my lawyers have ever so represented.

THE CHAIRMAN. It would be all right if they did do that and get an unconstitutional bill through?

MR. LYONS. If you mean would I approve a program, if that were the only alternative of preventing an unjust law being enacted, to amend the bill and make it unconstitutional, I say to you that I would want them to make every effort to do that . . .

THE CHAIRMAN. You would try to persuade the legislators to vote for such a bill and would not tell them it was unconstitutional?

MR. LYONS. I would certainly tell them—

THE CHAIRMAN. And lead them to believe it was a better bill, in order to get an unconstitutional bill through?

MR. LYONS. It is not necessary for us to be naïve about these things.

When Mr. Hughes, of the Penney Company, was asked whether he approved of his lawyer pursuing such tactics, he replied: "I would say that if somebody was going to sandbag me I would be entitled to grab any weapon that I could get hold of to hit him."

And to Mr. Patman's comment that "legislators are presumed not to be in the sandbagging business," Mr. Hughes continued: "That is no reflection on legislators at all, sir. The only reflection was in the fact that, in studying chain-store bills pretty carefully for the last six or eight years, it is my definite, sober judgment that the demand for most of them does not emanate from legislators at all. It comes either from a wholesaler or an independent who thinks he can subsidize himself by getting a law passed; and that is what I meant by sandbagging. I am not reflecting upon the legislators in any way whatsoever."

When anti-chain-store bills were under consideration, an important angle from the chains' standpoint was the extent of their coverage. Were the definitions in the bill broad enough, for instance, to include voluntary chains as well, and filling-stations? If they were, the chains could count on their cooperation in opposing the bills. If they were not, efforts were made by chains' legislative representatives to have the bills amended accordingly. So far as the voluntary chains were concerned, it was argued that since they enjoyed many of the advantages of the regular chains, they ought to bear the same tax burden; and, so far as the chain filling-stations were concerned, it was pointed out that they were in fact "stores" even though they were called "stations." That, indeed, was what the U.S. Supreme Court decided in the case of Fox *v.* Standard Oil of N.J. (See page 139 *supra*). But, in order to cover the point, before that decision was handed down, the chains naturally tried to have the bills include filling-stations specifically.

Much of the correspondence revealed clearly enough that these efforts to broaden the coverage of pending bills were frequently made, and the witnesses, who were interrogated on the point, saw nothing to apologize for in such tactics.

Although the very word "lobbying" has a sinister connotation in general usage, none of the members of the committee questioned the right of the chains to engage in such activities, provided they refrained from deception and subterfuge.

"The chains have a perfect right to lobby," declared Mr. Patman at one point where Mr. Logan turned questioner. "It is just as proper for them to lobby in defense of or to sponsor legislation as it is for me to advocate or to oppose legislation . . . the only thing in my mind is that they should do it openly and above board and not try to use a front, or not try to deceive people."

But if it is proper, as it is, for the chains to oppose legislation which they deem discriminatory or unsound in any other respect, why is it not equally proper for them to suggest the amendment of a bill to broaden its coverage for the dual purpose of (a) augmenting opposition to it, and (b) making it more equitable if it should be adopted?

Whether the chains' representatives went beyond the bounds of propriety when, in a desperate case, they sought to introduce a clause in an objectionable bill which they believed would render it unconstitutional, presents a nice question of ethics. But, as Mr. Lyons reminded Mr. Patman, why do we have to be naïve about these things? If the chains had attempted to defend themselves and their legitimate interests in the legislative arena without the aid of experts versed in legislative strategy, where would they have been? Marquis of Queensbury rules are all right when both sides can be made to abide by them, but everything goes in a roughhouse. And if, as Mr. Hughes put it, the chains knew they were being sandbagged, they can hardly be criticized for taking any lawful measures needed to outwit or defeat their aggressors.

5. Receipt by the chains of discounts and allowances not available to independent retailers.

On July 9, 1935, the committee turned its attention to the subject of "trade practices of big-scale retail and wholesale buying and selling organizations" which it had been directed to investigate.

In compliance with an offer from A&P to give the committee any information it wanted, Charles W. Parr appeared as a witness. Mr. Parr was assistant to David T. Bofinger, who was in charge of the company's buying activities at the national level.

Mr. Parr testified that A&P received approximately $6,000,-000 in advertising allowances and $2,000,000 as brokerage in 1934. It spent approximately $6,000,000 for advertising.

He presented to the committee a complete list of the manufacturers from whom A&P received such allowances, with the basis for the allowance in each case.

The manufacturers listed numbered nearly 300 and Mr. Parr explained that they constituted what the company referred to as its "preferred list" of suppliers. What that signified was thus made clear:

> "We have never laid down any arbitrary rules which prohibit any of our individual warehouses from buying any brand of merchandise which they wish to handle or for which they have a demand, but we do have a preferred list at headquarters to which we ask them to give support wherever possible . . . the people with whom we have advertising contracts, quantity price arrangements or brokerage arrangements."

The following extract from the record gives some typical examples of the arrangements made with manufacturers on the preferred list:

> "Armour & Co., regular line, 3 to 7 per cent on canned meats advertising allowance; fresh meats, one-half per cent quantity if purchases total $10,000,000.
>
> "California Packing Corporation, Del Monte, 5 per cent purchasing contract.
>
> "General Foods Corporation, line, $30,000 flat for advertising; Baker's Chocolate, $0.066 per carton, quantity discount (entire trade).
>
> "Standard Brands, foil yeast, $144,000 a year advertising allowance, 10 per cent quantity discount; Chase & Sanborn's coffee, $97,164 per year advertising allowance; Tenderleaf Tea, $394 per 1,000 advertising allowance; Royal Gelatine, $38,004 per year advertising allowance; Royal Baking Powder, $15,000 per year advertising allowance; Dr. Price Baking Powder, $996 per year advertising allowance.
>
> "Swift & Co., canned meats, 3 to 5 per cent on 200,000 pounds to over 300,000 pounds, quantity discount.
>
> "Wilson & Co., canned meats, 5 per cent brokerage."

Now what was the significance of such allowances as these, which, in the aggregate, amounted to $8,000,000 in 1934?

In the first place, to provide a yardstick by which to measure the relative importance of such allowances in the case of A&P, the company's total sales for the year ending February 28, 1935, were $842,015,871, and its net profits, after depreciation and Federal taxes, were $16,709,000.

Secondly, such allowances were not confined to A&P. As the committee was to learn later from "lists" supplied by other chains, including two voluntary chains, all large-scale buyers who had a service to render at the retail level and were in a position to render it, likewise received allowances, although, of course, no single company or organization received as much in the aggregate as A&P. Lists of allowances received were filed by Safeway, Kroger, First National, National Tea, Gristede Bros., D. Pender Groc. Co., Independent Grocers Alliance (a voluntary chain), National Retailer-Owned Grocers (a co-operative group), Liggett's, Walgreen, Woolworth and Kress.

To what extent such allowances reached even small independent retailers was not explored to any extent, but some evidence on that point came out when executives of General Foods and Standard Brands explained the scope of their respective sales-promotion activities.

Thirdly, although A&P's allowances when stacked up represented a sizable total, they came from many sources. The largest single item, $360,000 from General Foods, covered that company's complete line of products, which numbered 80.

Testifying regarding that allowance, Mr. Parr pointed out that the $360,000 was actually an estimate of the amount to be paid for the full year, as the obligation was to pay 5 per cent of total purchases which, he believed, that year would amount to $9,000,000. The difference would be met by a year-end adjustment. A contract prepared by the manufacturer specified the advertising and special promotion activities A&P was to provide in behalf of General Foods products in return for the allowance. But A&P was not required to render proof of actual advertising or promotion service. The advertising allowance was in addition to whatever regular quantity discount was shown on the invoice as a deduction from the sales price.

Mr. Parr also pointed out that, in connection with advertising-allowance contracts, his company usually agreed to cooperate with the manufacturer by running special sales in which the items would be featured below regular prices.

How manufacturers benefited from the advertising allowances and brokerage they paid to A&P was well illustrated, indirectly, by one item of evidence which revealed what happened when such allowances were *not* made. A letter to Mr. Parr from J. V. Beckmann, A&P's representative on the West Coast, pointed out that "F. E. Booth & Co. formerly did a fair business with us throughout the country, which has fallen off to almost nothing since the California Sardine Code became effective, have come and offered to restore the regular 5 per cent brokerage on sardines. They will pay this money to us in cash monthly. I have accepted this and advised them we will remove the restriction on Booth sardines and would like to have you advise me just how you want this information put out to the directors."

The following extract from the record sheds some light on the significance of that communication:

THE CHAIRMAN. Now, what does he mean when he says, "We will remove the restriction on Booth sardines"? Did you have some stop order on the sale of Booth sardines?
MR. PARR. No. What he refers to there is that the company and the individual warehouses—45 to 50 warehouses are kept informed on all arrangements, as far as possible, that we have—and when the sardine code, which prohibited the payment of brokerage, went into effect they automatically knew that, because it was common knowledge. When they

knew that they were not to receive the usual credit of 5 per cent we did not tell them to discontinue handling Booth sardines, but they lost interest in it.

THE CHAIRMAN. They lost interest in it and put them back where they were not so conspicuous?

MR. PARR. No; they just did not feature them and did not advertise.

Explaining the reference to the "directors," Mr. Parr said: "Our company is divided into six divisions and in each division there is a purchasing director, a man who supervises the purchasing for the division under headquarters."

Whether the sardine packer in question was violating the code in restoring the brokerage at that time, was a question raised by Mr. Patman, but Mr. Parr insisted that, in any event, it would have been a violation by the seller and not by the buyer as the buyer was not bound by the sardine code. But, be that as it may, the incident shows clearly enough how valuable to the manufacturer was the advertising and merchandising cooperation a company like A&P could furnish and how costly if withheld. About the only way a manufacturer could increase his sales through A&P stores in the face of such a loss of interest as resulted in the case of Booth sardines would be by stimulating consumer demand through national advertising. That, of course, might cost the manufacturer far more than the cooperation he could buy from A&P and other large-scale distributors by means of advertising allowances.

The complete service rendered by A&P, Mr. Parr declared, went far beyond newspaper advertising. It included window signs, window displays, store displays, counter displays, radio advertising, circular mail, and all sorts of promotional work, involving printing, all of which the company did at its own expense.

How the allowances received from suppliers were handled by A&P was thus explained by Mr. Parr: "We have an account known as the advertising account. That account is No. 702. . . . All receipts from manufacturers go into account No. 702, and the appropriation for advertising, for special sales, for sales promotion work, for signs, for circulars, for lithographic work and everything of that kind . . . are made from that account."

Admitting that the allowances which went into Account No. 702 paid also for the advertising of some products on which no allowance was received, Mr. Parr pointed out that, on the other hand, newspaper advertising was only part of the service A&P gave manufacturers who paid such allowances. As one example, he mentioned that the contract with California Packing Corporation specifically provided for a big general national sale on their entire line every month. A tremendous amount of effort and expense went into these promotions of the Del Monte line, he explained, and involved, as well, lower than regular prices.

But despite A&P's special interest in Del Monte, upon which the company received a 5 per cent allowance, consumer demand for Dole's, upon which no allowance was received, compelled A&P to stock that line too. As Mr. Parr explained the situation in a letter which was read into the record: "There is no doubt an insistent consumer demand for Dole's in certain markets, and the only thing we can do, under the circumstances, is to fill these orders as specified. We know the situation to be true right here in New York, for instance, where everything possible has been done to prevent the necessity of handling Dole's pack, but consumer trade here insists upon this brand."

But even though advertising allowances would seem to have a sound basis, how about brokerage? Did it not give A&P an advantage over competitors who did not get it?

How Mr. Parr answered those questions is revealed in the following extract from the record:

MR. BLOOM. But who gets the 5 per cent eventually?
MR. PARR. It goes to the A&P Tea Co.

MR. BLOOM. Is that not an advantage over the other fellow?

MR. PARR. It could be construed as such, probably, in the same way that we have an advantage when we buy goods in car lots as compared with the fellow who buys goods in less than car lots.

MR. BLOOM. No; that is a legitimate discount or price, where people buy car lots or buy at wholesale or in gross lots, or contract for a certain amount of goods during the year. That is legitimate business. But where a concern receives a special advertising allowance or special discount, or has its own brokers, it naturally has the advantage over the other fellow. As a merchant I would think that is the case.

MR. PARR. Well, we have the advantage to this extent: In the same way that, a great many years ago, we might have had an advantage over the small independent when we started buyings goods in car lots. In other words, when we started to do that we started to perform the function of a wholesale grocery. We opened our own warehouses and, instead of buying goods from a wholesale grocer, we started buying direct from the manufacturer.

MR. BLOOM. Don't you have to do that, Mr. Parr? Where you have, we will say, in this district 256 stores, you would naturally have to have your own warehouse, where you could distribute your goods to your stores and get them as you want them and when you want them.

MR. PARR. That is right. In other words in our warehousing operations we perform a legitimate wholesale function. That is, we bring our goods in car lots and distribute them around to our retail stores. Now, in the last 10 or 12 years we have attempted to do the same thing, or to follow the same principle, in regard to operating our own brokerage offices instead of dealing with an outsider. In other words, we are attempting every day to deal more directly with the producer. We believe it is more satisfactory for everybody concerned when the transaction is confined to just as few people as possible. The more direct line we can establish between the producer and consumer, the more satisfactory it is for all three of us.

MR. BLOOM. Then you believe that the farmer would be benefited if he could deal directly in that way, too, do you not?

MR. PARR. Oh, I certainly do. I think the more direct the transaction can be made, the more satisfactory it is for the producer, distributor and consumer.

What Mr. Parr had in mind, of course, was that where a distributor can bypass a broker and, by dealing direct with the producer or manufacturer, earn the brokerage himself, his price to the consumer can be correspondingly lower, which will mean that the consumer's buying power will be to that extent increased. So that while the producer gains nothing by paying the brokerage to the distributor instead of to a broker, he benefits indirectly because he helps to increase consumption by helping to lower retail prices.

Of course, Mr. Parr was able to tell the story of advertising allowances from the standpoint only of what his own company received. What other companies received, he didn't know, although he expressed a belief that, according to the Federal Trade Commission, "the average allowances that we receive are no greater than those received by other purchasers, and in many cases the small dealer got better allowances than we did."

But the manufacturers themselves knew to whom they were paying these allowances, and how much, and the evidence on that point speaks for itself.

Austin S. Igleheart, president of General Food Sales Company, whose allowance to A&P loomed so large, pointed out that the contract providing for that payment did not stand alone. On the contrary, similar contracts, although providing for substantially lower payments in most cases, numbered, as of August 9, 1934, 1,714. They were made with all types of distributors who could render a service in return. He broke them down as follows:

324 contracts with corporate chains operating 45,698 stores.
547 with voluntary chains, embracing 66,587 stores.
843 with retailers not identified with voluntary chains and operating collectively 2,039 stores.

This made a total of 114,324 retail stores obligated to render a service for which the company had agreed to pay them. Asked why no wholesale grocers appeared in his enumeration,

Mr. Igleheart pointed out that, unless they were affiliated with voluntary chains, they would have no way to render the service for which such allowances were made.

Traver Smith, vice president of Standard Brands, testified that the only allowances his company made were for what they called "cooperation service."

How much they paid for the service depended upon its value. In the case of A&P, the "preferred list" showed, it totalled approximately $300,000 a year. A written contract specified what was to be done by the customer in each case to earn a sum inserted in the contract. Such contracts were made only with customers who had something to sell in the way of service. As Standard Brands sold direct to the retailer and its salesmen called on its 250,000 outlets every four days, they used their judgment whether or not the cooperation of particular customers was worth buying.

The way it worked, Mr. Smith explained, was that if a customer was not selling enough Chase & Sanborn coffee, for instance, the salesman would suggest how the situation might be improved by a handbill, a poster in the window, a mention in the newspaper advertising, if any, a counter display or some other type of cooperation. If the grocer agreed to cooperate in the way suggested, they would agree, then and there, how much would be paid for it. If the service was given the payment would be made. In the case of A&P and four other chains, such arrangements were made on a chain-wide basis at headquarters level instead of with the individual store managers.

Asked why only A&P and Kroger received an advertising allowance on Fleischman's yeast, Mr. Smith declared:

"Naturally, with a two and one-half cent item you cannot give advertising allowances all through the country. The only way you can possibly consider an advertising allowance is on a large-scale operation. Now any discounts or payments that we make to A&P or Kroger for cooperation are due to the fact that they are the two accounts in the country that can give us a broad market operation in promoting the sales of our yeast, and we have contracts with both those accounts for a specific service to be rendered in promoting the sale of our yeasts." They paid A&P $12,000 a month and Kroger $500 a month for the cooperation they contracted for and nothing to any other chain or other organization.

Further explaining the A&P arrangement, Mr. Smith continued:

"We give them $12,000 a month, or $144,000 a year, purely for the promotional service which they render us, which is this: They give us distribution in 14,000 or more stores; they allow us to put up package displays, as we call them, with little signs, because yeast is usually tucked away in a refrigerator where nobody can see it. I have seen large posters they have gotten out . . . about 6 feet by 2 or 3. They have mentioned it at frequent intervals in their newspaper advertising and they have really given us a very comprehensive service to try to promote the sale of our yeast."

Asked why he couldn't buy the same service from independents, he found great difficulty in getting committee members to appreciate that a payment of less than $1 a month to an independent grocer, which was what the payment to A&P averaged per store per month, would hardly buy much cooperation of any kind and certainly very little advertising! In other words, he insisted, it had to be a mass proposition. Even if an independent store in a given case did as much business as an A&P store across the street, he pointed out, the independent's operation would end there, whereas the A&P store's would be multiplied by some 15,000.

What was the effect of this testimony?

Its immediate effect was to create quite a sensation in the grocery trade. For, although everybody was familiar with the fact that advertising allowances were in common use, the details of individual arrangements were, of course, known only to the parties involved. Since the allowance varied with the kind and amount of cooperation contracted for in each case, such arrangements were considered and kept more or less confidential.

When, therefore, A&P's "preferred list" was read into the record at the hearing and thus became public property, the trade press had one of the hottest stories it had been able to pick up in many a long day. One publication, *Sales Management*, which was just going to press, ran the complete list in its July 15 issue in a special four-page section printed on pink paper. For some time thereafter the list was usually referred to in the trade as the "pink supplement."

Manufacturers on the list were naturally interested to see how the allowances they were offering compared with those of their competitors.[6] On the other hand, chains and other large-scale organizations were equally interested to see whether A&P was getting more, or less, than they were.

Advertising allowances were generally regarded at that time, and still are, as a useful and legitimate feature of any well-coordinated sales plan, provided they were used solely to secure dealer cooperation. As Neil H. Borden, professor of advertising, Harvard University, pointed out in his authoritative study, *The Economic Effects of Advertising,*[7] "most manufacturers, even when they have a strong pull resulting from space advertising, strive at the same time to get active dealer support in the stocking and display of products, in the use of counter and window displays, in the offering of selling suggestions by sales clerks and in the mention of products in the retailers' direct-action advertising."

Manufacturers found that the most effective, if not the only, way to secure that kind of cooperation was to pay for it. Provided they got what they paid for, advertising allowances were considered well worth what they cost. They came in for condemnation in many quarters only because they could so

---

[6] Similar lists were subsequently provided by a number of other chains and became part of the official record, but they did not receive the publicity given to A&P's list.

[7] *The Economic Effects of Advertising,* Neil H. Borden (Richard D. Irwin, Inc., Chicago, 1942).

easily be used as a mask for discriminatory price concessions.

Such price concessions were, of course, illegal. Ever since 1914, they had been prohibited in interstate commerce by the Clayton Act. However, the Clayton Act prohibition was inadequate in two respects which left the door open, or at least ajar, for those who wanted to bypass it. One was the proviso permitting quantity discounts, without limiting them in any way. Thus it sanctioned a scale of discounts rigged to favor large-scale purchasers who alone would be in a position to earn the top-bracket discounts. The other was a proviso specifically permitting price concessions when made "in good faith to meet competition" which, too, was obviously subject to abuse.

The Clayton Act did not attempt to regulate or restrict advertising allowances. Although they were offered to some customers and not to others and were, to that extent, discriminatory, they did not run foul of the Clayton Act because that prohibited only discriminations in *price*. Legally, therefore, a manufacturer had as much right to buy his dealer-cooperation where it would do him the most good as he had, in setting up his advertising program, to put some publications on his schedule and to ignore others, or to use time rather than space, or, in short, to select the particular advertising media which he felt would serve his purpose best. Nobody had ever suggested that an advertising appropriation should be divided proportionately among all available media—that it wasn't fair or in the public interest to use only the big and successful publications, for instance, and pass up the smaller and less important ones. Why shouldn't dealer cooperation be bought on the same principle?

Of course, the two situations are not identical. When a manufacturer buys advertising space or time from an organization which buys nothing from *him*, neither the temptation nor the opportunity to grant a price concession exists. But when a manufacturer buys *anything* from a *customer* the story is quite different. Then the opportunity to pay more than its fair value is always present. Whether the danger of such an abuse is great enough to warrant banning all advertising allowances or limiting them to the point where they would become impracticable was, and still is, the real problem.

In any event, the publication of A&P's "preferred list" naturally stirred up plenty of interest in the whole subject of the buying advantages enjoyed by large-scale distributors. It revealed for the first time not only that some manufacturers were paying large sums to individual companies, but that such allowances, in the aggregate, could stack up to a stupendous figure—in the case of A&P to $8,000,000 in a single year.

That these disclosures helped to secure the enactment of the Robinson-Patman Act, which was then in the hands of the House Committee on the Judiciary, is quite clear. Indeed, on July 10, 1935, the very next day after the "preferred list" had been filed with his committee, Mr. Patman was able to make effective use of it in that connection. Appearing that day before the Judiciary Committee in support of the proposed legislation, including his own bill, H.R. 8442, he referred to the list and described its significance, as he saw it.[8] The following day, when he appeared again, he arranged to supply each member of the committee with a copy of the printed record containing the testimony relating to it. Furthermore, H. B. Teegarden, general counsel of the United States Wholesale Grocers Association, who had prepared the bill in the first place, filed a brief at the close of the hearing in which he directed the committee's attention specifically to all the testimony relating to A&P's advertising allowances.

The Robinson-Patman Act took effect June 19, 1936. It might have been enacted, of course, even if the investigation of the ARF had never been undertaken. As it was, however, the investigation must certainly be credited with having

[8] Hearing, Committee on the Judiciary, 74th Congress, 1st Session, July 10, 1935, p. 6.

helped to secure its passage—if any credit can be claimed for having helped to put such an ambiguous and impractical piece of legislation on the books.

For whatever may be said of some of the objectives of the Robinson-Patman Act, few statutes have created more confusion and litigation. Today, twenty-two years after its passage, the courts are still struggling with its ambiguities and nobody can be certain whether a particular practice violates the law or not.

What the Act actually did was to amend the Clayton Act in several particulars and to introduce some innovations of its own.

The main amendments related to quantity discounts which were limited in two important respects: (a) they were permitted only to the extent that they reflected actual savings to the vendor; and (b) even when they reflected such savings, they could be forbidden by the Federal Trade Commission, after a hearing, to the extent that the maximum discounts could be earned by *too few* of the vendor's customers.

One of the new angles introduced was a provision which, in effect, prohibited advertising allowances or other payments to a customer unless they were made available to all customers on "proportionately equal terms."

Another new provision prohibited the payment of "brokerage" or a payment "in lieu of brokerage" to purchasers, even in cases where the vendor saved the brokerage by dealing directly with the purchaser.

How ambiguous some of the provisions of the Act are is perhaps best attested by the action of Mr. Patman himself. In 1938, he wrote a 400-page book to help clarify it.[9] In the preface he declared that it was prepared "in response to more than a thousand requests for information, received from manufacturers, sales managers, advertising men, retailers, wholesalers and others affected by the Act. . . . The repeti-

[9] *The Robinson-Patman Act,* Wright Patman (Ronald Press, New York, 1938).

tion of certain questions indicates a misconception of the intent of the Act, particularly as to what it *does not* prohibit. The first wave of opinions and comments from economists and lawyers, volunteered in the press or requested from counsel, was critical, deprecatory or downright destructive in tone. . . . As a result, many perfectly sound practices were abandoned, some confusion followed for a few months, and the first reaction of business was unfavorable. Price lists were suspended, advertising allowances were withdrawn, and pricing policies were revised. Most of this was unnecessary, as subsequent events proved."

But although Mr. Patman added that "confusion ultimately gave way to common sense," he still felt, apparently, that a 400-page book was needed to "clarify" the Act.

Furthermore, eight years later, Federal Judge Walter C. Lindley declared in a case which involved the Robinson-Patman Act only incidentally: "Sometimes I doubt whether we ever needed the Robinson-Patman law, with all its elusive uncertainty. I have thought that the Sherman Act, properly interpreted and administered, would have remedied all the ills meant to be cured. . . . I doubt if any judge would assert that he knows exactly what does or does not amount to violation of the Robinson-Patman Act in any and all instances." [10]

As to the impracticability of the provision requiring that advertising allowances and other payments be made available to all customers on "proportionately equal terms," Beckman and Nolen, in *The Chain Store Problem*, had this to say:

"In many cases, the difficulties in attempting to apportion allowances among small as well as large buyers will make their use impossible. For example, if an advertising allowance of $8 per 100 cases is offered to chain stores, what should the manufacturer offer the small retailer who buys but one case? Obviously, 8 cents would buy very little in the way of advertising. The obstacles in the path of a legal

[10] U.S. *v.* Great A&P Tea Co., 67 Fed. Supp. 626.

application of allowances will force many to abandon their use entirely, as has already been done in a number of cases." [11]

The Federal Trade Commission is still issuing complaints against reputable manufacturers whose advertising allowances are allegedly in violation of the provision in question.

Summarizing the results of the ill-conceived investigation of the American Retail Federation, the following points stand out:

1. It failed absolutely in its prime purpose of branding that organization as a "superlobby" designed to promote the interest of the chains. On the contrary, the evidence established that chain-store men had had no part in the conception of the federation but had become interested in it because they were in accord with its only purpose—to serve as the voice of retailing in general.

2. It slowed up the development of ARF for a year but did not prevent the organization thereafter from achieving the original aims of its organizers.

3. It provided some of the momentum which led to the passage of the Robinson-Patman Act.

4. It brought out considerable material which could be used by the anti-chain interests, fairly or unfairly, to stir up prejudice and create resentment against the chains.

One of its direct fruits, for instance, was an anti-chain book carrying Mr. Patman's endorsement.[12] Its reliability may be judged from the fact that the author declares in the preface: "There probably would have been no congressional investigation of the chain store if the chain-store people had not overstepped themselves in seeking to set up a powerful national lobbying agency known as the American Retail Federation. Their flagrant attempt to put over the organization as a set-up to 'protect the small retailer' attracted the attention of members of Congress and indicated the need of an investigation."

[11] *The Chain Store Problem, op. cit.,* p. 282.
[12] *Wells of Discontent,* Charles G. Daughters (Daughters, 1937).

Although the author claimed to have made an "intense study" of the entire record—and, indeed, the book consists mainly of selected extracts from it—his study apparently stopped short of the committee's final report—or did it? For in that report, it will be recalled, the majority definitely admitted that their "chain-store superlobby" theory wholly failed to stand up!

One conclusion which may be fairly drawn from an analysis of the record is that, considering the opportunity the anti-chain interest had to pry into the private files of the chains' most active defenders, surprisingly little, if anything, was revealed to the discredit of the chain-store system.

CHAPTER XI

IN THE COURT OF
PUBLIC OPINION

WHILE THE investigation of the American Retail Federation was producing newspaper headlines and centering the attention of most chain-store men on Washington, another front in the anti-chain war was opening in California.

Encouraged, no doubt, by the growing agitation against "big business" in general, a California group which called itself the Anti-Monopoly League was urging drastic action against the chains. Among various anti-chain-store bills introduced at the 1935 session of the State legislature was one, called the Retail Store License bill, which the league was actively sponsoring. The "license" it proposed was $1 a year for a single store, $2 for a second store, $4 for a third store and so on progressively up to $256 for the ninth store, with all stores in excess of nine paying $500 each.

The pressure behind the bill was overwhelming. Legislators could hardly have failed to be impressed by the claim that 80,000 California independent merchants demanded its passage—frankly admitting that the purpose of the tax was to drive the chains out of California.

Nothing the chains could say or do at Sacramento could prevail against that kind of pressure—despite all the "influence" they were supposed to have built up for themselves in State capitols, according to what the Patman committee was claiming at the Washington hearings. The Senate passed the bill by a vote of 34 to 4 and the Assembly by a vote of 68 to 8—a showing which revealed clearly enough the helplessness of the chains in such a situation and explains why they felt justified in resorting sometimes to any lawful measure called for in self-defense.

Realizing the destructive character of the tax, Governor Merriam held a public hearing before deciding whether to sign or veto it. The chains put up the best case they could, marshalling all the arguments they could muster against its unfairness and economic shortcomings. No doubt they were able to make out a strong case. But their opponents resorted to a different technique, which was thus described in a detailed report covering the story of this legislation issued by the advertising agency which was later retained by the chains to direct their fight against it.[1]

"Close to a thousand independent merchants, militant and noisy, arrived on special trains on the day of the hearing and staged an impressive 'March on Sacramento.' Brass bands led them with martial music; flying banners proclaimed their demands that the bill be signed; gay buttons in their lapels identified them as crusaders for a cause; and they marched and countermarched through the capital city, swarming into the Assembly Chamber to take their places four hours before the hearing was scheduled to begin."

The main argument used by their representatives was that the tax was needed to protect the small merchant against the competition of the big chains.

The Governor delayed his decision for ten days, but on July 21 he approved the Act, saying: "the chain-store operators feel that this legislation will prove discriminatory in its application. If so, the opportunity is theirs to prevent this act from becoming effective by invoking the referendum and submitting the question directly to the people."

And that, of course, was what the chains proceeded to do. To invoke the referendum, under the California law, the chains needed 116,487 signatures of qualified voters to a petition demanding it. The number had to equal 5 per cent of all

[1] *Discrimination vs. Business,* Lord & Thomas, p. 4.

the votes cast for governor at the previous general election. By September 14 they had more than enough and the referendum was officially certified by the Secretary of State. It meant that the chains had until the next general election, November 3, 1936, a little more than thirteen months, in which to convince the voters of California that the chain-store tax was against their interests.

As the Lord & Thomas report points out, the chains had several obstacles to overcome besides their own weaknesses from a public-relations standpoint. "The enemies of the chains had timed their attack with shrewd foresight," the report observes. "The year was a Presidential year, in which it would be hard to arouse public sentiment on collateral issues; the chain-store tax would be simply one of 23 measures on a formidable and confusing California ballot; the contest would come at a time when conspicuous figures like Wright Patman were breathing fire and brimstone from Washington against the chains and all their works."

Furthermore, the battleground favored the anti-chain interests. "California, in 1936," the report declares, "was a field presenting special handicaps to any attempt at interpreting business sympathetically. It was a stronghold for all sorts of political doctrines based on discontent. Its State treasury was embarrassed by a big deficit which lent a powerful appeal to any proposal to tax the other fellow. Finally, neither the time nor the place was auspicious for any effort based on reason and intelligent analysis; both were ideal for a campaign of emotional, inflammatory character."

The first thing the chains did was to organize the California Chain Stores Association to ensure unified action. Some 65 chains with stores in California were represented in it and were committed to share the costs of the campaign proportionately among them.

The next thing, and probably the smartest thing they could have done, was to recognize their own inability to shape up the kind of campaign the situation called for, or to carry it through. They realized that they were in the position of a man who was desperately sick and needed the attention of the best doctor he could get. Self-medication, in a case like that, was likely to prove fatal. Their deliberations on the choice of a doctor resulted in their selection of one of the leading advertising agencies, Lord & Thomas, from whose final report on the campaign many of the details contained in this chapter were drawn.

Lord & Thomas, in turn, assigned its executive vice president, Don Francisco,[2] to be the campaign director. The chains wisely decided that he should be the supreme commander in fact as well as in name, for, as he himself pointed out in a speech describing the campaign, the position of the campaign director had to be like that of a quarterback on a football team.

"No successful coach would let his team go on the field with several of the players authorized to call the signals," he declared. "No successful quarterback would call a signal until he had first surveyed the position of his teammates and opponents on the field of battle. The choice of plays and the exact timing are rarely determined far in advance."

In a political campaign, he pointed out, the final decision and the authority to make quick decisions on important matters must rest with the campaign director. "In the California campaign," he said, "committees and conferences were avoided. Events moved too rapidly for meetings. I had the ablest advisers on every hand and I used them constantly. Most of the ideas we used were suggested to me by my associates. But in the conduct of the campaign, even the chain-store executives let us 'call the signals.' Never have I worked with the advantage of such full confidence and complete cooperation."

That the confidence the chains put in Don Francisco as their quarterback was fully justified, the outcome of the cam-

[2] Later to become vice president of J. Walter Thompson Co., New York. He retired in 1956.

paign was to demonstrate unmistakably. But he gave the chains more than a victory—he gave them a course in public relations which they were never after to forget. The campaign which he and his associates mapped out and which was carried out under his leadership not only achieved its immediate objective, but provided the basis for a permanent policy which was to yield the chains tremendous returns in the years which followed.

Some of the principles he laid down are best revealed in his own language, taken from one of his speeches relating to the campaign.

"Business cannot proceed on the assumption that customers are friends," he declared. "Motorists may buy at your service station but damn you because they think you are a monopoly. They may go out of their way to save a few pennies at your chain store and then denounce you for paying low wages. Making friends and making customers are two different jobs —separate though related.

"Without friends, without enlightened public opinion based upon self-interest, a business with a million customers can be crucified by a militant minority.

"Thus public relations has come to be of prime importance. Public relations is neither press agentry nor institution advertising. It is not sending out press releases after the show is produced. It begins while the show is being planned. It starts on the inside with a realization that *the best private relations make the best public relations.* Just as the advertising man strives to get his product and package right before he shouts about it, so the public-relations man starts by seeking the deep-rooted weaknesses of a business and correcting them. He starts with an effort to mold or modify events in order to create favorable news and make friends. And, finally, successful public relations recognize that *it is not enough for policies to be right—they must also seem right.* The real public-relations men are the top executives who make policies."

Although the chains suffered from the antagonism to all

"big business," Mr. Francisco was quick to point out to his clients that their troubles also stemmed from certain handicaps of their own making. *First,* they had made some mistakes, although it is probable that the chain stores had made no more mistakes than other businesses. In view of their quick growth, he thought it remarkable that they had not made more. *Second,* in their rapid development they had stepped on a lot of toes. Furthermore, he explained, they had not stopped to say "pardon me" or "I couldn't help it, I was in a terrible hurry." They had stepped not only on the toes of wholesalers and independent retailers but on those of local bankers, attorneys, insurance agents, appliance salesmen and others.

This was a new slant to chain-store executives, for although they were familiar with criticisms based on their failure to patronize local services, such as those supplied by banks, insurance men and others, they had always felt it was a sufficient answer to explain why the chain-store system did not need such services. Now they were told that, although economically, legally and in every other way, their practices may have been justified, their public relations had suffered just the same. Finally, they had not told their story. They had believed that any business which could sell for less and attract millions of customers would be welcomed as a friend in any community. They had overlooked that customers are not necessarily friends.

As Mr. Francisco put it: "Those with injured toes formed a militant organization and had been at work for many years. Their activities had undermined confidence in the chains by harping constantly on their mistakes and by raising doubts as to their desirability as a social institution. The general antagonism to big business created a most favorable background for such a crusade."

So much publicity had been given to the real and fancied shortcomings of the chains that their virtues were overshadowed. "Apparently forgotten," Mr. Francisco pointed out, "were the important services which chains rendered as prime outlets for the farmer's produce, the opportunity offered to deserving employes to climb to positions of responsibility, and the service performed for the average family by providing convenience, cleanliness, better merchandise and lower prices. In the face of this abuse the chains had been singularly inarticulate, or, at most, had contented themselves with defensively debating the damaging thrusts of their opponents."

The basic program was worked out before the campaign started. Although it was kept more or less flexible, several fundamental policies were adhered to throughout.

The first policy was to *get off the defensive* as soon as possible and launch an offensive. Mr. Francisco held that there were only two kinds of effective defense in a campaign such as the chains had to wage. First, total silence, a complete disregard of the opponent's charges; and second, a counter-attack that is so vigorous that the opponents are put on the defensive. Until they had built their organization and laid their plans, they were advised to ignore the accusations of their enemies. Then, instead of attempting to answer false accusations and thereby give them greater publicity, the chains featured the advantages of their system.

Another important policy was to refrain from attacking the independent merchant. To have done so would have served to arouse sympathy for him as the "under dog."

"Since we never attacked the independents," Mr. Francisco pointed out, "the rank and file were very lukewarm about contributing money or enlisting in the crusade against us. Thus their efforts were materially weakened. We exposed the tax as a scheme engineered by selfish middlemen who sought to place a severe handicap on their chain-store competitors at public expense. We did not hesitate to attack the professional organizers, racketeering money-raisers and self-seeking politicians who worked against us. But toward other retailers we were always tolerant. We gave them no reason for fighting us.

"Our opponents had made it appear that all chains were national monopolies controlled by Wall Street. One of our jobs was to make clear that a majority of the chains that would be hit by the tax were relatively small California-owned organizations that operated a few stores within the state."

Fundamentally the campaign was built on the belief that the most effective attack against the tax could and would be made not by the chains themselves but by those who would be affected by it indirectly—the farmer, the manufacturer, the property-owner and, most important of all, the consumer.

The overall plan consisted actually of two separate campaigns. The first, of ten months' duration, was designed to make friends for chain stores by (a) finding and correcting mistakes; (b) healing sore spots and explaining misunderstandings; and (c) telling the chains' story of service. The second, of less than two months' duration, was an all-out, hard-hitting attack against the chain-store tax itself.

One fortunate break the chains got was an opportunity early in the campaign to cooperate with agricultural producers, and thus to create better relations with a group for whom they were already rendering a vital service but whose attitude toward the chains was openly critical. On February 26, 1936, the California Canning Peach Growers wrote to Mr. Francisco, pointing out that the entire California Cling Peach Industry was suffering from an under-consumption of canned peaches. Because of his "very close touch" with the chain stores, he was asked to secure the cooperation of the food chains in putting on a drive whereby consumption of the product in question could be greatly increased and thereby benefit "the most important canning operation in the State of California." [3]

Naturally the chains acted quickly and effectively. Through their national association, a nationwide drive was launched at once. It absorbed the surplus and enabled the peach growers to dispose of their new crop at a substantial profit instead

[3] *Discrimination vs. Business, supra,* p. 5a.

of suffering the disaster which had previously seemed inevitable.

In that effort, food chains all over the country cooperated. Later on, when the price of beef was dropping so fast because of the abnormal slaughter brought about by the drought that the livestock growers were panic-stricken, the chains received another opportunity to demonstrate what organized distribution could do. The nationwide drive they put on again saved a critical situation.

Finally, only two weeks before the election, the food chains received another opportunity, in connection with a surplus crop of California dried fruits. Once again they earned the admiration and gratitude of an important group of California producers by moving an unprecedented volume of the product into consumption.

These drives showed in a concrete way the important part the chain-store system played in our national economy. They did more to command the friendship and respect of California farmers and producers than all the economic arguments, however sound, the chains could possibly have presented.

Following their California experience, the grocery chains developed a permanent agricultural relief program which, in the years to follow, was to move many a surplus crop into consumption all over the country. That "practical farm relief" program, as it has been called, will be discussed in greater detail in a later chapter.

In getting across the story of the service the chain stores were rendering, which was one of the main efforts during the first ten months of the campaign, every suitable medium and device was used. Included were radio programs, newspaper advertising, booklets, posters, speeches, essay contests. Throughout it all, however, the approach was educational and informative rather than argumentative and no reference was made to the tax at any time.

Not until six weeks before Election Day was the direct attack on the tax unleashed. By that time, the proposition as it was to appear on the ballot had been assigned a number, 22. The number itself gave the chains a chance to fashion an effective slogan against it: "22 Is a Tax on You!" Because it rhymed, it helped voters remember the number of the proposal. Because it was "a Tax on You" it helped voters remember that the answer was "No." That slogan, repeated over and over again in every type of medium for 30 days, was a potent factor in crystallizing the issue and in simplifying the voter's task on election day.

"When the zero hour came," Mr. Francisco related some time later, "every worker and medium changed from public relations to anti-tax activity. 'California's Hour' [4] commercials assailed the tax, the California Consumer's Conference released posters and newspaper advertisements attacking it. Resolutions against the tax were passed or taken out of files and publicized. Chain-store employes and workers wore buttons on their lapels and signs on their automobile bumpers reading '22 Is a Tax on You.' On a score of radio stations, lawyers, property owners, business men, women and farmers spoke against the tax. During the last three days prior to the election, the Califorina Chain Stores Association itself finally spoke. Over the association's signature three large advertisements appeared on successive days summarizing the editorials that had appeared against the tax, the prominent organizations that had passed resolutions against it and the small California-owned organizations that would be injured if it passed. There were meetings by the score, frenzied activity everywhere—at last the battle was on."

Once the drive opened it never let up. Every step had been carefully timed so that the peak was reached at the exact moment when it would prove most effective. Furthermore, an extremely vital factor if all the effort was not to prove in vain —getting out the vote—was never lost sight of. An elaborate organization had been set up to organize employes for pre-

[4] A weekly radio program of entertainment, sponsored by the chains throughout the campaign but which, up to that time, had not even mentioned the tax.

cinct work. The residence of every chain-store employe in the large cities was pin-pointed on a map and each one who volunteered for service was cataloged and assigned certain voters to call on. Some were assigned to get out the vote and others to watch the polls on election day.

"This was a very vital part of the program," Mr. Francisco pointed out, "for poor precinct work can win or lose elections. We adopted the standard technique for organizing precinct workers and applied it to chain-store employes. The job of interviewing voters throughout the state and making sure that those who planned to vote 'No' would do so on Election Day was a tremendous one, but we were able to achieve it by breaking it down into many little jobs through a military type of organization."

What was the outcome?

As has been intimated, the chains won a decisive victory.

The voters rejected the discriminatory chain-store tax by a vote of 1,369,778 to 1,067,443, a majority against the tax of 302,335.

Furthermore, that result reflected the views of voters all over the State, for 57 out of California's 58 counties voted "No" to the proposal.

Although the campaign had undoubtedly been expensive to the chains, the total cost was far less than they would have had to pay for the privilege of staying in business had the tax prevailed.

But the pecuniary benefits of their victory, great as they were, were small compared with some of the other results— most important of which were the lessons it taught. What they were are best described in the language of the "supreme commander."

"By their campaign the chain stores of California not only defeated the chain-store tax," Mr. Francisco declared, "but they improved their relations with employes, farmers and customers, made themselves better understood and increased their sales. Today they have more friends as well as more customers.

"The tax on California chain stores was not defeated because a majority of voters were unwilling to soak the chains, but because many were unwilling to soak themselves. The job of the chain stores was to interpret the effect of the tax to various groups of voters from the viewpoint of their self-interest. The employe saw the tax as a threat to his job. The farmer saw it as a measure that would cripple an important outlet for his produce. The businessman saw it as a discriminatory misuse of the tax power that might be extended to his business. The consumer saw it as a retail tax that would raise prices.

"In the last analysis, each citizen votes for himself. He has little sympathy for the problems of chain stores, railroads, utilities or other businesses. What he wants to know about laws and taxes is how they affect him. That is the opportunity and the safeguard of business.

"People know that businesses are big, successful and profitable. . . . People do not know what business has done for them—to create jobs, to effect economies, to perfect service, to save time and money, to reduce the cost of living and to raise the standard of living.

"Business needs a favorable public opinion as well as a consumer demand for its products. . . . Business can protect itself by first demonstrating and telling how it serves America, and then by showing how unfair legislation handicaps its ability to render that service."

The detailed story of the strategy and tactics employed so effectively in the California referendum campaign makes fascinating reading besides attesting the scope of the "know how" needed to produce such a result. But the full story belongs rather to the annals of public relations than in a history of chain stores. Before leaving it, however, a word or two should be said about the strength of the opposition. What did the chains have to beat to win?

In the first place, the Anti-Monopoly League, which had successfully sponsored the chain-store tax originally, could hardly have been expected to give back the fruits of its victory without a struggle. It certainly showed no disposition to do so.

The league, which was a federation of anti-chain interests, started out to raise a war-chest of $2,500,000. How much was actually obtained or how much of what was raised actually went into the campaign is not known. A court action by one of the field men who became disgruntled because the "exclusive" area assigned to him had already been worked revealed that the principal fund-raiser had a contract giving him 40 per cent of all money collected.

Be that as it may, the league was able to finance a program substantial enough to give the chains considerable concern.

"Their strategy, before the electorate as before the legislature," the Lord & Thomas report declares, "was to make the chains defendants in a court of popular prejudice, rather than to explain or support the proposed tax. . . . Their favored campaign documents were 'horror' cartoons, such as those picturing the chains as an octopus strangling California in its greedy tentacles, or as a cow, complacently browsing on the state's wealth, while top-hatted Wall Street, tugging at her udders, drained that wealth into guilty New York. . . .

"During the early months of the campaign, the Anti-Monopoly League's radio programs and advertisements stressed a vital secondary message; along with their condemnation of the greed of the chains, they urged generous contributions to the support of the league as a 'non-profit organization,' whose leaders were 'unselfishly sacrificing in behalf of the program!' "

According to Mr. Francisco, their most telling argument was that the tax amounted to only $1.37 per day per store. "However," he pointed out, "they used this in a major way only in San Francisco and the Bay cities."

The Corner Store Philosopher was their most effective radio program and, Mr. Francisco confesses, it "had us worried.

The 'Philosopher' disregarded facts and played entirely on the emotions. In a kindly drawl he told of his experiences with chain-store employes, farmers and neighbors. The stories were pure fiction but they dramatized all the arguments used against us. We were glad when lack of funds brought about the substitution of some of the opposing generals in place of the insidious 'Corner Store Philosopher.' "

The "lack of funds" referred to was attributed to the damaging publicity the league suffered as a result of the court exposure of its fund-raising activities. The president of the Anti-Monopoly League, himself, testified that 40 per cent of all the funds raised were to be turned over to the man who had the contract to gather them in. That revelation undoubtedly lost the league a lot of supporters. Contributions did not come in as freely as at first.

Nevertheless, although the campaign in behalf of the tax failed, some gauge of its force is provided in the fact that it did at least roll up a total of 1,067,443 votes. Had it been even 15 per cent more effective than it was, the outstanding efforts of the chains would have been in vain.

The California referendum was not the first trial of the so-called chain-store question in the court of public opinion, although it was the first successful one.

The first attempt of the kind involved a local ordinance passed in the city of Portland, Ore., in the fall of 1931.[5] It imposed only a modest tax, ranging from $6 on the first store to $50 on all stores in excess of 50. Nevertheless the chains decided to test it through the referendum process. At the 1932 election, the issue polled a vote of 105,653, of which 53,871 favored the tax and 51,782 opposed it. In view of the moderate character of the tax, the voters could hardly have been expected to get too excited about it. Such a small tax, however unfair, would hardly put any of the chains out of business or require them to raise their prices enough for anyone to notice it. In the light of that fact the chains had some reason

[5] *The Chain Store Tells the Story, op. cit.,* p. 151.

for gratification. The margin of their defeat, only 2,089 votes, was slim enough to suggest that under different conditions they would have better luck. However, if they had any such hopes, they were shortly to be rather roughly disillusioned.

For in 1934, in Colorado, they had to fight what was the first and only attempt ever made to enact a chain-store tax by popular vote through the medium of an "initiative" petition. The proposal was voted on at the general election that year and was adopted by a vote of 132,160 to 106,359. And it was no small tax either, ranging from $2 on a single store up to $300 on stores in excess of 24.

The chains did nothing much about it until their success in California suggested that an appeal to the public in Colorado might prove equally effective. The necessary steps were accordingly taken and at the 1938 election a proposal to repeal the chain-store tax appeared on the ballot.

Unfortunately for the chains, the ballot carried another proposal as well—a proposal to repeal the old-age pension plan which had been adopted in 1936 and under which everyone over 60 was entitled to $45 a month. Inasmuch as the State then faced a $2,000,000 deficit, those who favored the retention of the pension plan could see no sense in voting for a repeal of the chain-store tax or any other revenue-producing measure. The proposal to repeal the chain-store tax was defeated by a vote of 240,000 to 160,000.

Four years later, however, the application of some of the California techniques proved more successful in Utah. A law passed by the 1941 legislature not only imposed a severe tax, of the Louisiana type, on existing stores, the scale ranging from $50 per store on less than 100 stores to $500 per store on stores in excess of 500, the particular bracket being determined by the number of stores operated *anywhere*, but it introduced a new feature. On all stores added or relocated in Utah after July 1, 1941, the tax would be $500 per store if less than 100 were operated, while chains with 500 or more stores would have to pay $5,000 for each new store or old one relocated!

The chains again invoked the referendum process and put on an all-out program. The proposal on the ballot being number 2, the slogan "No. 2 Is a Tax on You!" was a logical choice. At the annual election on Novemer 3, 1942, the chains prevailed by a vote of 85,188 to 38,504, with every county in the State voting against the tax.

In achieving that decisive result, the chains were able to make much of the fact that the tax was actually a "death sentence" for chain stores in Utah; that there were only 123 chain stores compared with 6,000 independents in the State; that the independents accounted for seven-eighths of the total retail sales; that the bill exempted service-station chains and voluntary chains; and that the elimination of chain-store competition would inevitably mean higher prices for Utah housewives.

But, powerful as these arguments undoubtedly were, much of the credit for the chains' victory must be given to a definite swing in public attitude in favor of the chains which had begun to develop a couple of years earlier. Ironically enough, Congressman Patman's supreme effort to end the chain-store problem once and for all by his so-called Federal "Death Sentence" bill, which was the subject of an extensive public hearing in the spring of 1940, actually proved the salvation of the chains. In one sense it did, indeed, end the chain-store problem, for the supporters of the chains turned out in such overwhelming numbers and strength that the anti-chain politicians must have realized, then and there, that the open season for chain-killing was over.

Not only was the "Death Sentence" bill, sponsored by Mr. Patman, completely discredited, but no State passed a discriminatory chain-store tax after 1941; the Utah law, as we have seen, was rejected by popular vote in 1942; an Idaho tax was repealed in 1949; and, that same year, the graduated feature of the North Carolina statute was replaced by a modest flat-rate tax without reference to the number of stores operated. In 1951, the Georgia tax was repealed.

Commenting on the result of the Utah referendum a few days after the election in 1942, the New York *Herald Tribune* declared editorially:

"One of the unspectacular but none the less pleasing episodes of Tuesday's balloting occurred in Utah, where the voters of the state repudiated, by a count of more than two to one, a law passed last year which would have placed a punitive tax on chain stores. . . .

"There seems to be good reason to believe that this movement to drive the chain store out of existence by taxation reached its high-water mark in the hearings on the Patman bill, which would have nationalized this debasement of the tax function. . . . What happened in Utah this week indicates that the educational value of those hearings was not wasted. Unfortunately for the Patmans and their kind, the public today has a better grasp on the economics of the chainstore tax than it had a decade ago."

Certainly the story of the Patman "death sentence" bill rates a chapter of its own.

CHAPTER XII

THE "DEATH SENTENCE" BILL

THE FIRST ATTEMPT to impose a punitive tax against chain stores on a national basis came in February, 1938, in the shape of a bill introduced by Representative Wright Patman, of Texas. It carried the names of more than 70 other Congressmen as "co-framers, co-authors and co-sponsors."

The bill, which was designated as H.R. 9464, was aimed primarily at the chains which operated in a number of States, but its provisions were drastic enough to have put many a chain out of business even though all its stores were located in a single State.

The tax imposed started at $50 a store on the tenth to the fifteenth store and increased progressively until all stores in excess of 500 would have to pay $1,000 each annually. But that was only the beginning! After the tax had been calculated on that basis, the amount was to be *multiplied* by the number of States in which the taxpayer operated.

Just by way of example, the tax on the Woolworth Company in 1938 would have amounted to some $81,000,000 although its net profits that year amounted to only $28,000,000! With 1,864 stores in operation in 48 States and the District of Columbia, the tax would have amounted to $1,650,000 if all the stores had been operated in a single State, but because they were scattered all over the union, that sum had to be multiplied by 49, giving the tidy sum of $81,070,000. In the case of the A&P, with approximately 12,000 stores in 40 States at that time, the tax would have totalled more than $471,000,-000!

How the tax would have hit some of the other chains is

shown in Table 19, but its impact on a relatively small chain which happened to operate in a number of states is well illustrated by the case of Mangel Stores, an apparel chain, with 106 stores scattered over 27 states. The tax on the 106 stores, if all had been located in one state, would have amounted to

TABLE 19

IMPACT OF PATMAN "DEATH SENTENCE" BILL ON 24 CHAINS AS OF 1938*

COMPANY	NUMBER OF STORES	NUMBER OF STATES	1938 EARNINGS	H.R. 1 TAX
American Stores	2,416	8	$ 57,627	$ 17,652,000
A&P[1]	12,000	40	9,119,114	471,620,000
Bickford's	106	4	558,924	92,800
Bohack, H. C.	488	1	(179,741)	279,700
Dixie Home Stores	172	2	189,197	105,800
Edison Bros.	123	29	919,323	894,650
Fanny Farmer	237	15	904,009	1,315,500
First Nat'l Stores	2,350	7	2,705,191	14,983,500
Gamble-Skogmo	247	18	278,538	1,686,600
Grant Co., W. T.	491	38	2,766,424	10,731,200
Kinney, G. R.	328	37	151,503	5,420,500
Kresge[2]	679	27	8,997,051	12,676,500
Kress, S. H.	235	29	3,668,216	2,508,500
Kroger Co.	3,992	19	3,741,569	71,867,500
Lerner Stores	164	39	1,299,231	1,922,700
Liggett	552	36	518,432	12,330,000
Mangel Stores	106	27	18,674	626,400
Melville Shoe Corp.	639	40	1,484,061	17,180,000
Newberry	476	45	1,792,741	12,100,500
Penney, J. C.	1,541	48	13,739,160	63,912,000
Safeway[2]	2,873	22	4,206,781	58,597,000
Schiff Co.	277	28	265,180	3,127,600
Walgreen Co.	510	37	2,067,846	11,118,500
Woolworth Co.[3]	1,864	48	28,584,944	81,070,500

[1] Estimated U.S. stores; earnings include Canadian stores.
[2] Includes Canadian stores and earnings.
[3] Includes Canadian and Cuban stores and earnings.
* From Appendix B, "Keep Market Street Open," a brief filed by chains opposing Patman bill, appearing in record of hearing at page 652.

approximately $23,000, but, multiplied by 27, it would have come to $626,000, quite a burden for a chain whose profits that year amounted to only $18,674!

But recognizing that these taxes amounted practically to a death sentence for most of the chains which had achieved even a moderate degree of success, the bill did graciously provide an escape for those who desired to take advantage of it. The full impact of the tax was deferred for two years during which period the affected chains could liquidate voluntarily. In other words, they could escape the death penalty by committing suicide!

As might have been expected, the general reaction to such a drastic measure was condemnation.

Typical of the immediate comment on the bill was an editorial in *Business Week*, February 5, 1938, headed "Killing Chain Stores."

"Would you believe it," the editorial asked, "if you were told that a congressman, and an influential congressman at that, had proposed that the federal Government tax the F. W. Woolworth Co. about $90,000,000 a year? And that it tax the A&P $600,000,000?

"Yet that is the meaning of Rep. Patman's new bill. . . . Destruction is the object. For since the chains cannot stand such enormous taxes, they would be forced out of business, to the delight of many competitors. . . . A mighty effort is under way to smash the chains.

"Upon this effort the public must render judgment. It must make up its mind whether all the benefits of mass buying, mass distribution and mass retailing shall be destroyed in order to ensure that a multitude of small retailers, who are for the most part bad merchants, poorly financed, and ill equipped to give service, shall be subsidized at the expense of the ultimate consumer; or whether the government shall permit some progress to be made in the direction of efficiency and cost reduction for the benefit of the people who go into stores every day and pay in pennies and nickels for the necessities of life."

Retailing, in its issue of February 21, 1938, carried an editorial headed: "Death Sentence."

"Chain stores are now confronted with the executioner's axe," it declared. "If the bill just introduced by Representative Wright Patman is passed in anything like its present form, chain stores, as we know them, will pass out of the business picture within two years. . . . While the chain stores have not been blameless in their buying and competitive methods, it is incredible to think that they should be wiped out. . . . This is a fight which concerns every branch of retailing, big and little. The chains may need further regulation, but not destruction. The National Retail Dry Goods Association and other groups should help to defeat this measure."

From the very day of its introduction, a ground swell of opposition started to develop against the Patman bill which was eventually to reach overwhelming proportions.

But the almost universal condemnation his proposal was receiving did little to dampen Mr. Patman's ardor. When, in September of that year, he was invited by the National Conference of Business Paper Editors to debate the merits of his bill at the annual convention of its affiliated association, Associated Business Papers, he jumped at the chance.

"I look upon this meeting," he wrote, in accepting the invitation, "as a wonderful opportunity to sell a good cause to people who really have more to do with molding public opinion in this country than any other group. If I am right in this fight, I should win and will win, if the people get the truth. If I do not have the right side, I am not entitled to win. It is pleasing to me to know that the fight has at last been brought out into the open. It is the first time." [1]

It devolved upon the author to oppose Mr. Patman in that debate which was held at the Union League Club, Chicago. The debate appears in full in *Chain Stores and Legislation*,[2] and no purpose will be served by considering it at length in these pages, particularly as all the arguments Mr. Patman used then in favor of his measure were repeated in amplified form in the long public hearing which is to be discussed in some detail in this chapter.

However, one of Mr. Patman's most fantastic claims, which

[1] Letter from Hon. Wright Patman, Texarkana, Tex., dated September 23, 1938, to Bascom N. Timmons, Washington, D.C., from copy in author's files.
[2] By Daniel Bloomfield (New York: H. W. Wilson Co., 1939).

he had made in Congress in 1937 and reiterated in the course of the debate deserves treatment at this point because he persisted in using it thereafter even after its invalidity had been demonstrated to him.

On June 17, 1937, Mr. Patman had declared in Congress[3] that "a study has just been completed which shows that *the cost of food is higher in cities where chain stores predominate."*

He based that contention on a study of intercity living costs made by the Works Progress Administration, which he had tied up with Census figures showing how the chains stood in the cities in question as compared with the independents.

Our own comment on Mr. Patman's astounding claim, as it appeared in *Chain Store Age*[4] at that time, will serve to set up the basic facts. Our editorial said:

"Because of his reference to official data, the Congressman's argument had a decidedly genuine ring, but an examination of the sources themselves reveals that he handed his colleagues a gold brick. To achieve his purpose he resorted to a method which even a high school debater might scorn to employ—the use of *selected* instances. He used the figures which served him and completely ignored the rest, a treatment which no one who was trying to paint a *fair* picture would ever employ.

"The living-cost study he quoted covered 59 cities, but Patman used only twenty. Not only did he ignore the others, but he deliberately intimated that they all pointed the same way, when the fact is that many of them pointed in just the opposite direction.

" 'I can name you cities all over this nation,' he declared, 'and prove to you that where the chains have control in any line of business prices are higher than in cities where the independents have control of similar lines of business.'

"But not a word did he say about the cities which indicated just the opposite and which he had right in front of him in the study from which he drew his statistics.

[3] *Congressional Record*, June 17, 1937, p. 5914.
[4] August, 1937.

"Now what were the facts?

"The Division of Social Research of the WPA in 1936 made a comparative study of the cost of living in 59 different cities. Using Washington, D.C. as the base and calling it 100, a relative figure was established for each of the others. The *median* figure for the cost of food was 93.9. In other words, of the 59 cities, 27 show a food cost index higher than 93.9, 29 a lower index, and three stand exactly at the median level.

"In the group of cities in which the index is *higher* than 93.9 are nine 'chain' cities and eighteen 'independent' cities, while in the group in which the index is *lower* than 93.9 will be found nine 'chain' cities and twenty 'independent' cities. Exactly at the median level are one 'chain' city and two 'independent' cities.

"Obviously an accurate interpretation of these figures lends no support whatever to the Patman contention, but in the way he used them he conveyed an entirely different picture. He pointed out, for instance, that in Houston, an 'independent' city, the index was 90.7 and in El Paso, another 'independent' city, it was 92.5, whereas in Dallas, a 'chain' city, it was 95. In the same way, he paired various other cities, always selecting for his unfair comparisons only 'chain' cities in which the cost of living happened to be high and only 'independent' cities in which the cost of living happened to be low.

"Of course, anyone who would be willing to adopt the same tactics, could use Patman's own authority to confound his argument. One could show, for instance, that Detroit, a 'chain' city, has an index of 93.2, whereas Bridgeport, Conn., an 'independent' city, has the highest food index in the whole list—102.3; that Dallas, the 'chain' city to which Patman referred as having a comparatively high index of 95, compares quite favorably with New York, an 'independent' city, with an index of 100.1; that Cleveland, a 'chain' city, has an index of 93.3, whereas Newark, N.J., an 'independent' city has an index of 99.5; and Los Angeles, a 'chain' city, has an index of only 92.8 compared with San Francisco, an 'independent' city, whose index is 96.3.

"But that, of course, is a criminal way to distort evidence and anyone who would resort to it deliberately would be guilty of intellectual dishonesty of the rankest kind. Whether or not Congressman Patman *deliberately* juggled the data in the manner indicated cannot, of course, be inferred from the facts available, but even though he be acquitted of the suspicion of downright chicanery, he can hardly hope to escape the charge of a carelessness so gross as to be almost as culpable.

"The truth is that inter-city living costs vary for *many* different reasons, of which the prevailing type of distribution is only one. The fact that the cost of living is comparatively high in a particular city in which the chains do the bulk of the business provides no justification whatever for the conclusion that food costs are high there because of the chains. On the contrary, ordinary common sense and available data on the subject would suggest rather that the *high* cost of living in such a city must be *despite* the chains and not because of them—that the cost of living would be *even higher* but for the competitive effect of chain-store prices.

"And nobody should realize that fact more clearly than Congressman Patman himself, for has not his whole chain-baiting campaign of the last couple of years been based on his complaint that the chains are driving the independents out of business *by underselling them?* . . .

"The fact is, as has frequently been demonstrated by impartial investigators, . . . that the grocery chains not only *can* but *do* undersell their independent competitors, and if the blame for the high cost of living in a given city can fairly be placed on the shoulders of the one factor which tends to keep prices down then Congressman Patman is a public benefactor and the chains are a public menace. Otherwise, Wright Patman is wrong!"

Whether or not Mr. Patman had ever seen that editorial before that night is not known, although reprints of it had been widely circulated in Washington and throughout the country, but it certainly was brought to his attention in the course of the debate. It came up in the course of the rebuttal arguments.

Said Mr. Patman: "I also say to you (I have facts and figures to support this statement of mine. I myself placed them in the *Congressional Record* on June 17, 1937, where they will be found on page 7708)[5] and I believe conclusively that

[5] Actually the page is 5914.

these figures and facts show that the price of food is higher in chain-controlled towns and cities than it is in those communities which are not controlled by chain outfits."

In reply, the author offered to rest his whole case on the truth or falsity of that statement. After pointing out its obvious fallacies and flaws as had been done in the editorial previously quoted, he handed Mr. Patman a reprint of it, with the suggestion that if he "is fair-minded enough to withdraw a statement which has no justification he will never make it again."

But the effect on Mr. Patman was apparently not lasting. In a radio speech delivered on February 21, 1939,[6] only three months after that debate, he included among his objections to the interstate chain system: "It causes the cost of food to be higher in towns and communities controlled by it."

And, in an extension of remarks reported in the *Congressional Record* a few days later,[7] he made the statement that "cost of food is higher in chain-controlled towns and communities."

That that erroneous and illogical notion remained with Mr. Patman throughout the years was evidenced eleven years later, when he and the author appeared once again on opposite sides of the old question. This time it was on a television program called "Court of Current Issues."[8] Mr. Patman put the following question to Prof. O. Glenn Saxon, one of the chain-store "witnesses":

"Don't these same statistics prove that in cities where the chains have control, the cost of food is always higher?"

When the witness answered in the negative, the matter was not pursued, but if a thousand qualified witnesses had all answered in the same way, Mr. Patman would probably have remained unconvinced judging by the persistency with which he had stuck to his baseless contention for so long.

Of course much of Mr. Patman's muddy thinking on this point stemmed from his misleading use of the word *control*

[6] *Congressional Record,* Vol. 84, Part 11, p. 667.
[7] *Ibid.,* p. 761.
[8] Reported in *Chain Store Age,* November, 1949.

in connection with the division of a city's food business among chains and independents. Perhaps in a parliamentary body, a majority of 51 per cent may give *control*, because the other 49 per cent is as hopelessly beaten as if it were only 1 per cent.

But control of a parliamentary body and control of the cost of living under competitive conditions are two entirely different things. The fact that the chains may *enjoy* 51 per cent or 61 per cent or even 70 per cent of a city's business gives them no power to raise prices at will, as Mr. Patman naïvely suggested, for the public is still a free agent and can buy from whom it likes. Indeed, the only way in which the chains could hope to maintain the favorable position they commanded would be by keeping their prices *down*.

The Patman bill made no progress whatever in Congress in 1938.

Early the following year it was reintroduced, this time as H.R. 1. It was referred to the Committee on Ways and Means. But although no action was taken on it that year, the mere fact that it was pending precipitated nationwide discussion of the chain-store system. Nearly 350 national organizations representing all lines of activity—agricultural, industrial, commercial, labor and consumer—not only discussed the bill but passed resolutions condemning it.

Because of the widespread hostility to the bill, the chains missed no opportunity to discuss its shortcomings on the air, from the platform, or through any other medium that offered. In December, 1939, John A. Logan, president of the National Association of Food Chains, debated the issues over the air with Hector Lazo, and other chain-store spokesmen welcomed similar opportunities.

After all, the chains realized that this bill was to give them the best opportunity they had ever had to show where the chain stores stood not only in popular esteem but in the thinking of all important groups, save only those with whom they were in direct competition—the wholesalers and retailers. And, because of the long lag between the introduction of the first bill and the public hearing on H.R. 1, they had all the time they wanted to prepare for the conflict.

In March of 1940, a sub-committee was appointed by the Ways and Means Committee to conduct a public hearing on the measure. It consisted of Representatives John W. McCormack, Massachusetts, chairman; John W. Boehne, Jr., Indiana; Richard M. Duncan, Missouri; John D. Dingell, Michigan; Frank Crowther, New York; Harold Knutson, Minnesota; and Roy O. Woodruff, Michigan.

The hearings started March 27 and continued daily until May 16. Each session, however, was only two hours long. Nevertheless, before the hearings were over nearly 200 witnesses were heard, some at great length, and numerous exhibits and briefs were put into the record by both sides. The printed record of the hearing comprises 2,257 pages! [9]

As is usual, those who favored the bill were heard first. As its author, Mr. Patman took all of the first session to present his argument for it and all of the second to answer the questions put to him by the committee.

Before commencing his argument, Mr. Patman offered certain amendments to the bill to modify its effect. He asked the committee to cut the proposed tax in half. He also offered to exempt entirely all chains operating no more than 50 stores in the State in which the principal place of business was located or within a radius of 100 miles of the city or town in which such place of business was located. Finally, he offered to give the interstate chains, against which the bill was mainly directed, *seven* years in which to liquidate instead of the *two* years allowed in the original bill. But this seven years "breathing spell"—which Congressman Knutson characterized as "purgatory"—would be denied to any chain operating more than 50 stores which increased their number or which changed the location of any store during the seven-year

[9] Hearings before a sub-committee of the Committee of Ways and Means, House of Representatives, 76th Cong., 3rd Sess., on H.R. 1, a bill providing for an excise tax on chain stores.

period. He also offered to include filling stations, which had been exempted in the original bill.

Right at the start of his argument, Mr. Patman took up the question of the constitutionality of the proposal.

"The object of H.R. 1," he declared, "is to restrict interstate chain stores to the boundaries of one State, or to a smaller area than some of them now cover.

"The question is asked: 'If that is the object, why not leave out the tax provision and offer a bill that says an interstate [sic] chain cannot operate in more than one State?'

"My answer is that such a proposal, if enacted, would probably be held unconstitutional, whereas, if we use the taxing power of Congress to reach the same objective, there will be no doubt of the constitutionality of the law, when enacted.

"Why did Congress place a 10 per cent tax on the State bank currency after the war between the States? Was it in order to raise revenue? Not at all."

Elaborating on that historical incident a little later, he said:

"I invite your attention to the fact that during President Grant's administration we had all kinds of State banks all over the country that were issuing so-called wildcat currency. Congress wanted to pass a law that would stop these banks from issuing that wildcat currency. . . . But Congress decided that they could not pass a law that would be constitutional that would have that effect. But someone suggested, 'We can tax them and that will do the same thing'; so they passed a law taxing this currency issued by State banks 10 per cent. That destroyed many State banks but it served a more worthy purpose of preserving our great currency system of this country. So that in President Grant's time the taxing power was used as a vehicle to correct an evil that could not be reached in any other manner in a constitutional way."

But Mr. Patman's implication that the taxing power may be used constitutionally to achieve indirectly what Congress has no constitutional power to achieve directly was his own constitutional philosophy. It was just the opposite of the philosophy of the U.S. Supreme Court, as had appeared in the very case he used as his principal authority—the case involving the constitutionality of an act of Congress imposing a prohibitive tax against State banknotes.

Such a law *was* passed, as Mr. Patman declared, and it *was* held constitutional, as he stated, but if he really thought that the court held in the case in question that Congress could use is taxing power to achieve unconstitutional objectives, he missed the point completely.

The case in question was Veazie Bank *v*. Fenno, 8 Wallace 533. What the Court held was that as Congress is empowered by the Constitution to protect its own currency, it could constitutionally forbid the States to issue banknotes which circulated as money; and because it *could legally forbid* the issue of such banknotes, it could achieve the same constitutional result through the exercise of its taxing power.

That, of course, is a very different proposition from Mr. Patman's version of it. It was not a case, as he contended, of using the taxing power "as a vehicle to correct an evil that could *not* be reached in any other manner in a constitutional way," but of using it to correct an evil which *might* have been reached constitutionally by a flat prohibition.

What Mr. Patman overlooked was that when Chief Justice Marshall uttered his famous dictum, back in 1819, that "the power to tax involves the power to destroy" he did not say, or imply, that the power to tax involves the *right* to destroy. On the contrary, in the very case in which the dictum was offered, the Chief Justice held that the power to tax did *not* involve the right to destroy.

In that historic case[10] Maryland had passed a prohibitive tax against a branch of the United States Bank. In that respect, it might be regarded perhaps as the first chain-store

[10] McCulloch *v*. Maryland, 4 Wheaton 316 (1819). See *The American Constitution*, Alfred H. Kelly and Winfred A. Harbison (New York: Norton & Co., 1948) p. 290.

THE "DEATH SENTENCE" BILL

case to reach the United States Supreme Court, although it related to branch banks rather than branch stores. Having first decided that the Federal Government had a right to establish the bank itself, and could set up branches wherever it saw fit, the Chief Justice easily reached the conclusion that no State had the right to destroy what the Federal Government had the right to create. And as the States had no right to destroy the branch banks directly, they had no right to use their taxing power to achieve the same result indirectly.

Applying that sound principle to Mr. Patman's own bill, the use of the Federal taxing power to destroy interstate chain stores would obviously be constitutional *only* if a Federal law flat prohibiting the operation of such stores would be constitutional. But on that point Mr. Patman himself said that he had been advised that *such* a law would *not* be constitutional. On that basis, H.R. 1 could have no constitutional validity, despite Mr. Patman's blithe assumption that the power to tax is subject to no limitations.

The committee did not interrogate Mr. Patman on his unique position regarding basic constitutional principles, nor were they challenged by any of the witnesses for the chains. That, however, was rendered unnecessary because, at the end of his statement, the committee inserted in the record a memorandum prepared by the staff of the Joint Committee on Internal Revenue Taxation at the committee's request. In that memorandum, the attorney for the Joint Committee advised that H.R. 1 would "clearly violate" the Federal Constitution.[11]

[11] That ex-Governor Christianson had a better grasp of the constitutional principles involved than his colleague is indicated by the following exchange between him and a member of the committee which took place at the end of the hearing: "Mr. Dingell. Governor, speaking about whether it could be done or not, the tax club to bring about the abatement or the reduction or the elimination of the chainstore system could be used only if the purpose of the bill were constitutional; that is the elimination of the chain-store system. If that were constitutional then rightfully the Congress could use the tax club to bring that about. I think we will agree on that.
"Mr. Christianson. That is right.
"Mr. Dingell. On the other hand, if that is an unconstitutional move, then of course the taxing power of Congress could not be used to bring that about.
"Mr. Christianson. That is true." (Hearing Record, p. 1967.)

Continuing with his argument, Mr. Patman offered the committee some elaborate-looking charts. They showed that four of the largest banks in the country and seven of the leading private banking firms were represented on the directorates of some of the leading chain-store companies. Another chart showed that one large private banking firm was represented on the directorate of half a dozen or more leading chains as well as on the boards of many large manufacturing companies.

The purpose of that testimony, apparently, was to support Mr. Patman's theory that the fact that large chains and some large manufacturing companies have the same banking affiliations results in the refusal of the latter to sell their products to competitors of the chains!

But the committee did not seem to be deeply impressed with either the exhibits or the implications Mr. Patman saw in them. On the contrary, they seemed to think it a perfectly natural thing for banks to be represented on the boards of companies with which they had extensive financial dealings. One committeeman pointed out that when the R.F.C. makes a loan to a corporation it secures representation on the borrower's board of directors. Another observed that probably in many cases the connection between the bank and the chain was merely that of transfer agent.

Mr. Patman's main objections to the interstate chains, he said, were:

1. They tend to concentrate money power and credit in the hands of a few banks, mostly in the East.

2. They destroy local communities.

3. They depress farm prices.

4. They will eventually attain a monopoly in distribution if not checked.

5. They limit the opportunity for the young man of tomorrow.

Typical of the fallacies which characterized his whole argument and which seemed at times to strain the patience of the

committee was his contention that as 53 per cent of the
banks had failed between 1921 and 1933, and as that was the
period in which the chain stores had their greatest growth,
the chain-store system must have been responsible for the
bank failures!

Similarly he argued that as the farmer got a smaller share
of the consumer's dollar than he did twenty years earlier,
before the chain stores became an important factor in distribution, the chain stores must be responsible for the farmer's
ills. He estimated that total farm income would have been
$3,000,000,000 a year greater if there were no chain stores!

He also blamed the depression and unemployment on chain
stores and, in answer to a question, insisted that if his bill became a law, we would have national prosperity within a year
or two years!

Of course the committee did not allow these and other
wild statements to go unchallenged. They wanted to know,
for instance, whether he really believed the chains were solely
responsible for the appalling succession of bank failures between 1921 and 1933, for the economic changes in our community life, for the depression and the decline in farm income.
Was it not true that bank failures were greatest in areas where
chain stores were fewest? Hadn't good roads and the development of the automobile been chiefly responsible for the
changes which had overcome the smaller communities?
Would not retail business have gravitated to the larger towns
and cities, because of good roads and automobiles, even if we
had no chain stores? Didn't the war have something to do
with the depression?

While Mr. Patman stood by his original statements as long
as he could, he was finally forced to admit that many other
factors might have been responsible for the results he attributed entirely to chain stores, and to content himself with the
consoling observation that the chain stores had been a contributing factor also.

The contention that the chains depress farm prices led

Congressman Knutson to put into the record a letter he had received from the dairy farmers in Minnesota. It said they were marketing some 20,000,000 pounds of butter through chain stores, were receiving a premium price for it, that they had been doing business with chains for twenty years or more, and that the chains not only provide a ready market but, because of their economies, reduce the spread between producer and consumer. Subsequently, similar testimony was offered by numerous witnesses representing almost every branch of agriculture.

But perhaps the most killing blow suffered by the supporters of the bill in the early days of the hearing was a letter received from Secretary of Agriculture Wallace. The committee had asked him for his official viewpoint regarding the Patman bill.

Secretary Wallace condemned the bill in no uncertain terms. "In our opinion," he said, "sound public policy requires that we promote efficient methods of marketing and distribution rather than discourage or prevent them by taxes such as those provided in this bill."

The Secretary did go on to say that his department was not "insensible to the dangers associated with the growth of larger corporations, whether they are engaged in the handling of food or in any other kind of business," and that some chains are so large that "their methods and practices need some regulation to prevent the misuse of bargaining power and to enforce fair methods of competition." But he pointed out that "it should be possible to provide suitable regulations which will prevent abuses and dishonest practices by chain stores" and that the department "would be in favor of any such regulations."

"However," he concluded, "we think it would be unwise and unnecessary to give up the economies which have been brought about by chain-store distribution in order to prevent certain practices which may not be in the public interest."

Altogether some twenty witnesses appeared in favor of the bill. They occupied eleven full sessions, or 22 hours in all. The larger part of their burden was carried by Mr. Patman himself, ex-Governor Theodore H. Christianson, president of the Freedom of Opportunity Foundation and public relations director for the National Association of Retail Druggists; George Schulte, publisher of *Interstate Merchant,* St. Louis; Gerrit Vander Hooning, president, National Association of Retail Grocers; J. H. McLaurin, president, United States Wholesale Grocers Association; Rowland Jones, Jr., Washington representative of the National Association of Retail Druggists; Rivers Peterson, Indianapolis, managing director of the National Retail Hardware Association; and Frank G. Stewart, vice president of Freedom of Opportunity Foundation and president of Motor Equipment Wholesalers Association.

The only other witnesses consisted of a couple of manufacturers of work clothes who sold their output to wholesalers exclusively, a small-town banker who organized the Independent Bankers Association to fight against branch banking, a lawyer, an organizer of a Louisiana Farmers Protective Union, consisting of strawberry growers, and five Congressmen.

The significant fact about this list is that it consisted almost entirely of *wholesalers* and *retailers,* or their association spokesmen—all *interested* witnesses who admittedly expected to fall heir to the business then being done by the chains if the chains were eliminated from the picture. That these witnesses favored the bill was not the least bit surprising. Particularly noteworthy is the fact that the list included no spokesman for the *public* interest, despite Mr. Patman's far-reaching claims that the very future of the nation depended on its passage.

The fact that this measure was able to command support at the hearing of no representative labor group, no representative consumer group, no representative newspaper group, no representative real-estate group, no representative manufacturing group, could hardly have been overlooked by the committee. Nothing better illustrates the real character and purpose of legislation of this kind than the line-up of those who appear in favor of it—and against it.

Ex-Gov. Christianson confined his argument in favor of the bill to a single point—the danger of monopoly. He reviewed the growth of some of the chains via the merger process in the late '20's and suggested that if the formula were continued indefinitely we would eventually have a single chain in each field.

Existing anti-monopoly laws did not provide adequate protection against this threat, he contended, because they could be invoked only against actual monopolies—not against monopoly in the making. The only effective way to prevent a potential monopoly from developing into an actual monopoly, he pointed out, was by legislation imposing a tax heavy enough to make further growth unprofitable.

When he said that it was not so much the present position of the chains that he feared but the potential danger inherent in their further expansion, Congressman Knutson put a question which was to be asked thereafter of every witness who appeared for the bill: "Would you be satisfied with legislation to freeze the present situation?"

Gov. Christianson thought that would be adequate, but when Chairman McCormack pursued the point and asked to whom the freezing process should be applied—the man with only a few stores now as well as to the man with hundreds or thousands of stores, the suggested remedy did not appear so simple.

Finally, however, the witness suggested that all expansion should be prohibited except by the man with less than 50 stores and he should be permitted to grow only to that extent. The witness also expressed the view that future expansion within the suggested limitation should be confined to one State or at least to a reasonable area. He doubted that these results could be achieved by any type of legislation other than a tax.

The chief witness in favor of the bill was George Schulte, of St. Louis, publisher of *Interstate Merchant,* a weekly grocery paper, which for the previous fifteen years had devoted most of its space to a continuous and vituperative attack on the chain stores.

Mr. Schulte's contribution, which took the best part of three sessions, was devoted largely to an attempt to prove the obviously contradictory proposition that while chain stores allegedly paid lower wages than independents, employed fewer people, acquired their merchandise cheaper, paid less taxes, made fewer contributions to local charities and other activities, extended no credit and made no deliveries, their operating costs were nevertheless higher than the combined operating costs of wholesaler and retailer, and their prices to the consumer were higher too.

Just why the independent merchant was being driven out of business by the chains if he actually sold for less and gave credit and made deliveries in the bargain, Mr. Schulte failed to make clear.

Nor was it apparent from Mr. Schulte's argument why any special tax to check chain-store growth was needed if, because of their higher operating costs, the chains were compelled to charge the consumer more and yet give less in the way of service.

Mr. Schulte repeated Mr. Patman's statistics showing that 53 per cent of the banks failed between 1921 and 1933, and when he was asked by Chairman McCormack what inference he drew from the figures he quoted, he replied: "The decrease in the number of banks is due to the decrease in the volume of independent business."

But when Congressman Boehne pressed the point and wanted to know whether the witness contended that the growth of chain stores was responsible for the bank failures, he admitted that chain stores were "not entirely responsible." The admission led the Congressman to remark that, of course, there were many other factors to account for bank failures during the period in question. Chairman McCormack indicated what the principal reason was when he asked Mr. Schulte if he had read the report of the Comptroller of the Currency on the main cause of the failure of banks. When the witness said he had not read the report, he was informed that "the main reason was poor management."

Mr. Schulte devoted a lot of time to fragments of the voluminous reports of the Federal Trade Commission in connection with its six-year investigation of chain stores. Naturally he picked out whatever he could find that tended to back up his claims of chain-store shortcomings. But the effect of all his testimony regarding the F.T.C. study was completely negated when Congressman Crowther read into the record the following paragraph from the Commission's final report on its investigation:

"To tax out of existence the advantages of chain stores over competitors is to tax out of existence the advantages which the consuming public have found in patronizing them with a consequent addition to the cost of living for that section of the public. That portion of the public which is able to pay cash and is willing to forego delivery service in return for the advantage of lower prices will be deprived of that privilege, generally speaking, although there are exceptions both ways."

Mr. Schulte made the usual claim that chain stores were guilty of giving customers short weight. He introduced into the record the fact that in 1935 a number of chain-store managers in the city of Washington had been found guilty of giving short weight on chickens purchased by inspectors of the Department of Weights and Measures. But again the effect of the testimony was badly shattered when Congressman Knutson put into the record an official report he had just received showing that during the past three years in the

District of Columbia 67 short-weight cases had been found in grocery and meat stores, and that of these 65 were found in independent stores and only two in chain stores.

Mr. Schulte's presentation, as a whole, was characterized by the trade magazine *Tide* as "a jungle of contradictions."

Gerrit Vander Hooning, president of the National Association of Retail Grocers, insisted that his principal objection to chain stores was based on their power to exact lower prices from producers, on the one hand, and to engage in "loss-leader" merchandising, on the other.

But when he was subjected to questioning by the committee, he frankly admitted that independent grocers use "loss leaders" also, that the consumer is mainly interested in getting the most for his money and that if the trend were toward consumer cooperatives, then neither the chain nor the independent merchant would be entitled to protection.

Asked whether he would approve of legislation "that would undertake to freeze the present set-up," he replied that it would be a step in the right direction—but a man with the ambition to open a number of stores should not be stopped, nor should his operation of stores be confined to a single State, and that he would prefer to see the abuses in chain-store operation eliminated rather than the chain stores themselves. When the witness insisted that his main fear was the effect of chain-store growth on the farmer, Chairman McCormack put into the record a letter received from Secretary of Agriculture Wallace, to which reference has already been made.

J. H. McLaurin, president of the United States Wholesale Grocers Association, the organization which had been mainly responsible for the passage of the Robinson-Patman Act, and which had always worked aggressively for the elimination of chain-store competition, emphasized the action the courts had taken in the case of the packers twenty years before.

In that case, he pointed out, the Federal Government had curbed the growing power of the big meat packers by frustrating their plan to operate retail grocery and meat stores and prohibited them from processing, wholesaling or retailing any food product not connected with packing house commodities. That result had been achieved by a consent decree.

Why, he asked, shouldn't the big grocery chains be checked as the packers were checked? And then he answered his own question thus:

> "The reason that we come to Congress for relief and not to the courts, as in the case of the packers, is that we have no evidence of conspiracy or combination among the interstate chain-store systems, such as existed among the Big Five meat packers."

The statement of Rowland Jones, Jr., then Washington representative of the National Association of Retail Druggists, who appeared for the bill, is particularly interesting not so much for what he said as for the fact that only eight years later he was to be elected president of the American Retail Federation—the organization which the chains had at one time been accused of dominating.

Mr. Jones devoted himself mainly to the social aspects of the issue before the committee. He struck a new note when he elaborated on his claim that the horse-and-buggy era represented "the nearest thing to Utopia ever achieved."

Chairman McCormack took issue with his implication that the chain stores were responsible for the changes in our economic and social life which had followed the transition from "the horse-and-buggy days" to our present streamlined mode of living. On the contrary, he pointed out, the social changes of the previous 30 years had been due largely to the introduction of good roads and the wider use of automobiles, improvements in transportation and communications generally and many other achievements of science and industry. The "self-contained community," he intimated, was doomed with the passing of the "horse and buggy" as the principal means of transportation.

Rivers Peterson, managing director of the National Retail

Hardware Association, argued principally against the greater buying power of the big chains which enabled them, he claimed, to exact lower prices from their suppliers than other distributors enjoyed. He had little hope that the Robinson-Patman Act would correct the situation. He attributed the decline in the number of independent hardware stores to the competition of the mail-order chain stores, the variety chains, automotive supply chains, and even the grocery chains, which in some cases were handling aluminum ware.

But various members of the committee raised the point that chain-store competition was only one of the factors responsible for the decline of the independent hardware store. They mentioned the slump in the building trades. "The slump in building during the past ten years," said Congressman Dingell, "is responsible for 40 per cent of our unemployment directly and probably another 30 per cent indirectly. With such a slump in building activity, wouldn't carpenters and artisans naturally buy less hardware and tools, and is that not the real reason for the passing of so many hardware stores in recent years?"

Mr. Peterson conceded that that was undoubtedly a factor but insisted that, because of the chains, the independents got less of the business that remained.

Chairman McCormack, too, reminded the witness that the depression was likewise a factor in the decline in the number of hardware stores, and inefficiency in management. And, referring to the testimony of Rowland Jones, he went on to say:

"The other day one gentleman made a very powerful argument about the self-contained community and community life decades ago. And it was a very beautiful picture. I enjoyed listening to it. As I was listening to it, the thought ran through my mind that the first flight of the airplane was only in 1906 and for about ten seconds. And there have been such inventions as the telephone and wireless, the radio and other improvements in means of communication and transportation. You cannot have all that and have the community life of 50 years ago. . . . We have got to have a self-contained community life, as much as possible, consistent with those changes. Either that, or we have got to say to the human mind, 'You can't invent,' which, of course we cannot do and would not want to do. In other words, from these improvements have come great benefits, but there have also arisen problems."

Five Congressmen appeared in favor of the bill. In view of the fact that more than 70 had joined Mr. Patman as co-sponsors of the bill when it had been originally introduced in 1938, a greater turn-out than five might have been expected. Even though some of the co-sponsors of 1938 had lost their seats, what about the rest of them? Could it have been that the widespread opposition the bill had developed in the two years prior to the hearing had caused most of the sponsors to change their minds about it?

On April 10, 1940, those who were opposed to the bill started to tell their story. Before they were through, a month later, more than 150 of them had had their say. Among them they included representatives of almost every important economic and social group which comprised the nation's framework—agriculture, manufacturers, organized labor, marketing authorities, consumers, and, of course, the chains themselves. Although only ten chain-store operators appeared as witnesses, the reason for not having more was more or less obvious—the time available could be put to more effective use by presenting the testimony of others who were not interested so directly as the chains in the defeat of the bill. Then, too, the story told by the chain-store men who did appear would merely have been re-told over and over again had more of them made an appearance.

The chain-store men who did appear included Charles F. Adams, First National Stores; Thomas N. Beavers, Peoples Drug Stores; Ralph F. Burkard, First National Stores; Lewis W. Cole, Steiden Stores, Louisville; Rilea W. Doe, Safeway Stores; Earl R. French, Atlantic Commission Co.; W. T. Grant, W. T. Grant Co.; Van H. Priest, Van H. Priest Co.,

Madison, Fla.; Earl C. Sams, J. C. Penney Company; and Lingan A. Warren, Safeway Stores.

The first witness in opposition was Earl C. Sams, president of the J. C. Penney Company. He told the inspiring story of that company's outstanding growth, from microscopic beginnings in 1902 to 1,554 stores in 1939, with stores in 48 states, 30,000 employes and sales that year of $282,000,000.

He then gave five main reasons for his opposition to the bill, as follows:

"1. It would destroy the Penney company or any other similar company.

"2. It would destroy the finest field of opportunity that has ever existed in retailing for the young ambitious man born without family means.

"3. It would add to the cost of living for every American family of limited means and would lower the American standard of living.

"4. It would deal a staggering blow to the entire economic life of this country and would be especially destructive of the smaller cities and towns for the benefit of the larger cities.

"5. It would hurt and tax this entire nation for the protection and enrichment of a small minority group of self-interested middlemen and of another small minority group of ill-advised marginal retailers."

Mr. Sams proceeded to support each of these propositions with a wealth of facts which seemed to be well received by the committee.

Taking up the plight of small communities and the familiar charge that chain-store growth was responsible for it, Mr. Sams said:

"If the national chains were wiped out, it would remove the most substantial bulwark which these small trading centers have against the pull of the big cities. It has been said that chain stores were ruining the smaller communities. Chain stores didn't ruin them. The automobile and the good roads naturally caused the people to turn to larger centers to do their trading. No law, no human mandate can breathe life back in the very small trading center which formerly supported a couple of general stores. Those stores existed only because without automobiles or good roads the customer couldn't get to the city. Because of horse-and-buggy transportation and because of mud roads the customer bought what the general store offered at its own prices or she ordered by mail."

Pointing out that, between 1920 and 1939, hard surface roads increased from 350,000 miles to 1,100,000 and the number of registered automobiles increased from 8,255,000 to 26,-250,000, he said that the chain stores had served as a check on the drying up of towns and small cities in the face of these two factors. That had been achieved because "the national chains have brought to these small centers the same values, the same reliable merchandise and the same prices, the same crisp new styles, and the same modern stores that were available in the bigger cities. And the customers know it."

Regarding the suggestion which had been made to "freeze" the existing situation, Mr. Sams said it would be wrong because it would deprive many sections of the country of the services that chains had not yet brought to them.

At the conclusion of his testimony, Mr. Sams offered for the record a printed study called *Keep Market Street Open*,[12] which had been prepared as of March, 1940, and was presented for the chains as a group in opposition to the bill under consideration.

The brief was replete with statistics and facts to refute all the claims made by Congressman Patman, Gov. Christianson and George Schulte and to establish affirmatively that:

1. Chain stores raise the scale of living.

2. Chain stores keep business and purchasing power in the towns.

3. They were the product of local enterprise.

[12] Hearing Record, *op. cit.*, pp. 602-671.

4. The ownership of chain-store stocks is widely dispersed.

5. Chain headquarters are distributed all over the nation.

6. Chains have no interlocking directorates.

7. Chain stores pay better wages.

8. Employes stay with chain stores.

9. Chain stores bring capital into town.

10. Chain stores pay higher rents.

11. Chain stores widen markets and improve farm income.

12. Chain stores invest in community welfare.

13. Chain stores set high standards for all retailing.

14. Chain stores respond to disaster needs.

15. They pay more taxes.

16. They are a minor factor in the toll of retail mortality.

17. They improve the young man's opportunity.

18. They enlarge the opportunities for competitors.

19. They offer equality of opportunity to consumers.

The brief provided a fitting background for the personal testimony of the witnesses to follow. They included 53 spokesmen for the farm interests; 56 for manufacturers and processors; eight for organized labor; six for real estate interests; seven for consumer organizations; three economists; fifteen for various miscellaneous interests; and ten chain-store operators.

Summarizing the reasons given by each of these interests for their opposition to the bill, consider first the farmer's viewpoint.

In addition to the condemnation of the measure by the Secretary of Agriculture, referred to earlier, the three leading national farm organizations—the American Farm Bureau Federation, the National Grange and the National Council of Farm Cooperatives—all came out unequivocally against the bill. Other farm representatives speaking for hundreds of thousands of producers and processors in individual branches of agriculture joined their national leaders in condemning the bill for the following reasons:

1. The charge that the large food chains use their great buying power to depress farm prices, as so frequently charged by Mr. Patman, was false.

2. No type of distribution available to the farmer was more valuable than the chain store under normal conditions and, under abnormal conditions, such as arise from surplus crops or natural catastrophes, the cooperation of the chains was vital to the farmer.

3. The farmer valued the chain-store system not only because it enabled him to sell his products to better advantage but because it enabled him to satisfy his own requirements more economically.

4. The farmer realized that his own welfare depended upon lowering the cost of distribution and he was convinced that the chain-store system provided one of the best means towards that end.

What did Mr. Patman have to say about all that? After sitting in the committee room day after day for a month and hearing the farmers declare their unqualified faith in chain stores and their dependence upon the chain store system, what did he say when he summed up the case in behalf of his bill?

He still insisted that the chains depress farm prices, contending that nobody had answered the charges he had made to that effect on the opening day of the hearing. He completely overlooked the devastating answer given by Edward A. O'Neal, president of the American Farm Bureau Federation.[13] For the express purpose of getting an official explanation of why in 1913 the farmer received 53 per cent of the consumer's dollar, but in 1939 only 40.5 per cent, he had written the Secretary of Agriculture on April 4 asking whether it "was the result of chain-store operation." He had put the Secretary's answer in the record. After referring to the many factors affecting the spread between farmers' and consumer prices, the Secretary had concluded:

[13] *Ibid.*, p. 776.

"It is impossible to place any statistical reliance upon a conclusion based upon these trends in marketing changes and chain store growth. These comparisons merely denote *contemporary* developments and do not demonstrate *cause* and *effect*." In other words, just because two things happen at the same time, one is not necessarily the result of the other.

As in the case of so many of Mr. Patman's other contentions, the statistics he used, correct in themselves, provided no basis whatever for the conclusions he blithely drew from them. The fact that 53 per cent of the banks failed between 1921 and 1933, which was also the period of greatest chain-store growth, was proof enough for him that the chains were responsible for the bank failures. The fact that in some cities where the chains do more than 50 per cent of the grocery business the cost of living is higher than in some cities where the independents do more than 50 per cent of the grocery business, was proof enough for him that the chains were responsible for the higher cost of living in the case of the cities he selected. Because the farmer's share of the consumer's food dollar declined between 1913 and 1939, chain-store growth during that period was the culprit! Little wonder that Congressman Knutson at one stage of the hearing lost his temper enough to exclaim to Mr. Patman:

. . . "The way you answered Dr. Crowther convinces me that you questioned the fact that this committee had ordinary intelligence."

The attitude of organized labor was revealed by a number of outstanding union leaders, although the American Federation of Labor had taken no official position on the bill.

According to Patrick E. Gorman, president of the Amalgamated Meat Cutters and Butcher Workers, A.F. of L., with a membership of 120,000, and other union spokesmen, organized labor's opposition was based on the following key points:

1. Chain stores are easier for organized labor to work with than independent merchants.

2. Chain stores pay higher wages for comparable work than independents, and chain-store hours are shorter.

3. Union members are consumers as well as workers. Chain stores make for lower living costs.

4. The elimination of chain stores would be a step in the direction of a return to "cottage industry" which would mean more proprietors but fewer employers—hence fewer employes.

5. Special taxes against multiple stores are a direct threat against the unions themselves since "the largest operator of the chain-unit system in the world is organized labor itself."

Although A.F. of L. had taken no official position on the bill, State federations, with a combined membership of well over 1,000,000, filed resolutions with the committee condemning it. The states in question were Alabama, Florida, Georgia, Iowa, Kansas, Kentucky, Louisiana, Michigan, New Jersey, Pennsylvania and Texas.

The viewpoint of real-estate men and property owners was presented by Walter S. Schmidt, past president of the National Association of Real Estate Boards, who appeared as spokesman for that organization. Also representing the association was Frank S. Slosson, who also spoke for the National Association of Building Owners and Managers, of which he was a past president.

Real-estate interests opposed the bill mainly for the following reasons:

1. Chain stores make the most desirable tenants of business property.

2. The future of the better business districts in many cities is threatened by the trend towards decentralization. The elimination of chain stores would accelerate that trend to the detriment of real-estate values and would reduce the tax revenue from business properties on which cities largely depend.

3. Chain stores set the pace in store modernization and

enhance the drawing power of the trading area to the advantage of the whole community.

4. Banks, trust companies, insurance companies, colleges and charitable institutions have large investments in mortgages on properties occupied by chains. Such investments would be seriously endangered if the chains were compelled to abandon such locations.

5. Chain stores contribute to the stability of community life beyond the business area. Their elimination would hurt residential real estate as well as business property.

More than 50 witnesses appeared to express the viewpoint of manufacturers and processors, either as individuals or as spokesmen for manufacturer's associations, or both.

Many of the witnesses distributed only part of their output through the chains, the remainder going to the wholesaler or direct to the independent retailer. Even in the case of those who sold all their output to the chains, or the major part of it, earlier experiences with other channels of distribution were almost invariably reported. Thus, in almost every instance, whatever they said was based on actual experience with both types of distribution.

They opposed the bill for the following main reasons:

1. Selling through the chain cuts selling costs substantially.

2. It cuts production costs, too, not only because of quantity purchases but because the orders are placed so as to permit of uninterrupted production schedules, which is particularly valuable in the case of seasonable merchandise.

3. It eliminates collection costs and credit losses.

4. It reduces the risk of inventory losses because merchandise is produced only on firm orders.

5. It requires less working capital because of the prompt payment of invoices on short terms.

6. It reduces labor turnover by making for steadier employment.

7. It increases the "real" wages of workers because the chains' lower prices reduce the cost of living.

8. It makes possible the production of many items which could not be marketed at all through less efficient channels.

9. It offers manufacturers the benefit of the skill, experience and information of keen buyers who are in direct contact with the consuming public, as compared with the indirect contact of the wholesaler.

10. It offers manufacturers an opportunity to test new items quickly and economically in various parts of the country through the retail laboratories represented by the units of the interstate chains.

11. It enables manufacturers to reduce the price of their products to all the channels through which they sell.

12. It increases the total volume of production because lower retail prices mean enlarged consumer buying power.

They also emphasized the social havoc which would result from the elimination of the large interstate chains. Many of the factories and mills supplying them provided the principal payroll in the communities in which they were located. Many of them were so geared to mass production for mass distribution that other channels of distribution would not suffice to keep them in operation.

How would the public interest be affected by the passage of the proposed bill?

Members of the committee had repeatedly asked the question. Mr. Patman had agreed that that was the real issue involved.

The viewpoint of the consumer was presented by six women—all outstanding figures in women's organizations and recognized authorities on consumer problems. They were Mrs. Ernest W. Howard, department chairman of legislation, District of Columbia Federation of Women's Clubs; Mrs. Mary D. Learned, chairman of the Massachusetts Committee on Consumer Legislation; Mrs. Harriet R. Howe, representing

the American Home Economics Association; Mrs. Gustav Ket-
terer, chairman, Philadelphia Consumers Advisory Council;
Dr. Caroline F. Ware, chairman of social studies, American
Association of University Women; and Mrs. Andrew J. Noe,
former president, New York City Federation of Women's
Clubs.

All of them opposed the bill, Mrs. Howard characterizing
it as "the most vicious, inhuman bill ever to come before
Congress."

The main point these witnesses stressed was that the economies offered by the chain-store system of distribution were
of supreme economic and social importance to people of
limited income—in which category they placed two-thirds of
all the families in the country.

"Women today know," declared Mrs. Howard, "how acute
is the present problem of providing food, clothing and shelter
for themselves, their husbands and their children out of their
present income. When food prices rise, it is not a question of
paying more for the same food, but simply this, they do not
have the money with which to pay—therefore they must buy
less and eat less and pay the doctor more."

That an excise tax on chain stores would be paid by the
customers of the stores was obvious, according to Mrs.
Learned, "for how else does a storekeeper get the money to
pay taxes?" That prices would be raised in independent stores
as well as in chain stores was likewise pointed out by Mrs.
Learned. "I, as a consumer, say," she declared, "that it is just
human nature that if you raise prices by taxation in one kind
of store, then these untaxed stores will raise their prices too."

Dr. Ware's presentation was a notable contribution. Among
the reasons she gave for the opposition of her organization,
which was composed of 67,000 university women affiliated
with 870 branches, were the following:

1. The bill proposes a punitive tax on agencies of distribution which serve the consumer well.

2. It is special-interest legislation to support a particular business group, regardless of the service which that group renders to the consuming public.

3. It is based on a misconception of the nature of the modern American economy and, in the presence of this modern economy, constitutes a threat to American democratic institutions.

Four outstanding marketing authorities appeared in opposition to the bill and supported their attitude with extensive and carefully prepared arguments.

Daniel Bloomfield, manager of the Retail Trade Board of the Boston Chamber of Commerce for seventeen years; Malcolm P. McNair, professor of marketing, Graduate School of Business Administration, Harvard University, and for many years director of the Harvard Bureau of Business Research; Joseph M. Klamon, associate professor of commerce, Washington University, St. Louis; and Roland S. Vaile, professor of economics and marketing, University of Minnesota, and editor-in-chief of the *Journal of Marketing,* constituted the group.

These men spoke as individuals, but they quoted freely from the studies made by other marketing authorities. If their attitude was not representative of the general feeling in their specialized field, it was not revealed at the hearing.

On the question of monopoly in retailing all were firm in the opinion that it was out of the question.

Asked by Representative Crowther whether he thought it was "within the realm of possibility that three or four, or even half a dozen of these corporate chains might within a reasonable time get complete control of distribution and price control of food products," Dr. Vaile replied:

"I think that it is entirely impossible, and I am supported in that by every member of the editorial board of the *Journal of Marketing*. When I found I could appear before this committee, I wrote to the editorial board of the *Journal of Marketing,* seven of whom are teachers of marketing in the leading universities, five of whom are in marketing research lines, private lines, and two of whom are in retail stores, and all of them replied to that question that there was no danger of monopolistic control by chain stores."

At the conclusion of the evidence in opposition to the bill, Congressman Patman was given two days for rebuttal, although that admittedly was a concession to him not usually accorded at hearings before committees.

The time thus alloted was divided among the three men who had carried most of the burden of supporting it in the first place—Congressman Patman, himself, Gov. Christianson and George Schulte. Their concluding arguments consisted mainly of a reiteration of the claims made in their original statements.

The chains were given two days for rebuttal, too, but only one was needed. The task was assigned to Ralph F. Burkard, controller, First National Stores. He did a masterful job. He showed how the evidence offered in opposition to the bill effectively refuted all the claims that had been made in its behalf.

The day following the closing of the hearing, Hon. Robert L. Doughton, chairman of the Ways and Means Committee, announced that, in answer to its request, the Department of Commerce had appraised the proposed legislation and had unqualifiedly condemned it.

The reasons given by Acting Secretary of Commerce Edward J. Noble[14] for the position he took with respect to the Patman bill were:

1. It proposes the most extreme use yet suggested for the taxing power, not to raise revenue, not as an incentive, not as a regulator but to prohibit interstate business.

2. It would add a most vicious barrier to interstate trade of a legitimate character.

3. It would raise the cost and thereby lower the standard of living of the consumers with the lowest incomes.

[14] *Chain Store Age,* June, 1940.

4. It is designed to destroy the business and the livelihood of investors and their employes who have promoted short cuts in distribution, without reference to their having engaged in any unfair or oppressive practice.

5. It is fallaciously supposed to increase employment, whereas at best it would merely shift employment from one class of establishments to an older and apparently less efficient type, resulting probably in less continuity and lower standards of employment.

6. It prevents mass production from yielding its greatest benefit through mass distribution on a national scale.

That the Secretary of Commerce was not unmindful of the competitive plight of the small independent merchant was revealed in the following observations:

> "The Department recognizes the severe competitive pressure on small independent merchants resulting from the growth of mass distribution with multiple outlets under one ownership and management. Business mortalities and unemployment resulting from increased efficiencies and lowered cost of distribution in competitive enterprises create social problems which are the just concern of government but whose solution does not lie in legislation penalizing efficiency.
>
> "Failures due to unfair competition can find relief in laws already on the statute books prohibiting discriminatory selling practices, misleading advertising and other unethical methods of doing business . . . The primary public interest is served only when our distributing machinery operates at lowest cost, thereby bringing to the producer a larger share of the consumer's dollar, besides making that dollar go further than it does now. The displacements of labor and obsolescence of capital that are caused by new methods of distribution are on a par with all other problems of unemployment caused by technological advance."

The most significant and decisive fact about the hearing was not the high caliber of the numerous witnesses who appeared against the bill, the broad scope of the interests they represented and the convincing character of their testimony, but the failure of a single witness of the same caliber to appear in favor of it. Conceding that the chains were far better equipped financially to marshall their forces against the bill than their opponents were to support it, why was it that spokesmen for the farmer, for labor, for manufacturers and for consumers did not come forward of their own accord to support the bill if it really meant as much to them and their welfare as Mr. Patman contended?

Undoubtedly that is the way the committee must have sized up the case. On June 17, Chairman McCormack announced that his sub-committee had voted not to report the bill favorably either in its original form or with the amendment which had been submitted designed to "freeze" the chains at their existing size and locations. The effect of that decision was to kill the Patman bill forever, for, as Representative McCormack pointed out, if there were danger of monopoly in the chain-store field, the proper way to avert it would be by regulatory legislation rather than by punitive taxation.

Thus the chain-store "Death Sentence" bill suffered the death sentence itself. But although the bill itself was dead, the benefits the chains had gained from the public hearing were to live and multiply for many years to come.

Never before had the economic and social value of the chain-store system of distribution been so effectively demonstrated. On the other hand, the chains had been reminded of the shortcomings of the system too.

The elimination of the Patman bill marked a definite end to the period of struggle which had started some fifteen years earlier when the rapidity of chain-store expansion had awakened widespread concern among wholesalers and independent retailers. It opened the way for a new era in which the chains, freed from the need of defending themselves against efforts to put them out of business or to saddle discriminatory taxes on them, could devote their attention to doing a better job of retailing, assuming a greater share of their civic responsibilities in the cities in which their stores were located, and improving the working conditions and security of their employes.

To what extent the chains were able to fortify their position as an important economic and social feature of our national set-up in the years which followed forms the subject matter of Part III—the period of chain-store maturity.

PART III

MATURITY

CHAPTER XIII

THE CHAINS AND
THE COMMUNITY

ONE OF THE inherent differences between independent stores and chain stores is that whereas the former are typically home-owned, the latter are typically absentee-owned.

Critics of the chain-store system have always made a great point of that difference, but they built it up far beyond its actual significance. A chain which operated in a number of communities obviously could not have the same natural ties to each of them as the local merchant would have to his own community—the place where probably he was born and brought up, where he and his family knew everybody and in which he had developed a lifelong sentimental interest quite apart from his business interest. The result was, it was contended, that whereas the local merchant was part and parcel of his community, the chain store was merely *in* it and not *of* it.

To a large extent, of course, that was true, but how significant it was is another matter. Conceding that the chains had no sentimental interest in any of the communities in which their stores were located, it would not necessarily follow that they could not contribute as much to the community's welfare as the local merchant, or considerably more, provided *other* reasons impelled them to such a course.

And, as a matter of fact, as will be shown in this chapter, that is exactly what happened. Although in the early days of their development and throughout the period of their active expansion they were so engrossed in their immediate problems that they gave little or no thought to their community responsibilities, later on they awoke to the realities of the situation. Today they are not merely holding up their end in the community but they are supplying a brand of leadership which only exceptional independent merchants can match.

If we analyze the basis of a merchant's interest in his community, we find that it is made up of three elements: (1) local pride; (2) self-interest; and (3) social duty.

As a general proposition, a man is more interested in his home town than in any other community. Certainly if he sticks to his home town and establishes a business there, he may be expected to have a greater interest in that community than in any other place on earth.

Such an interest is based primarily on sentiment. It is the same kind of sentiment that led Scott to ask: "Breathes there a man with soul so dead, Who never to himself has said: 'This is my own, my native land!'"

In the case of the country at large, we call it national pride or patriotism. In the case of a community, we call it local pride. But it is the same thing.

In addition to this sentimental tie, a merchant has also a material stake in the welfare of the community. If it prospers his business may be expected to prosper too. If it fails to keep pace with the times, his business must expect to suffer.

Then, too, in many cases the local merchant has relatives and friends who are also engaged in business or professional activities in the home town. Their welfare, too, depends upon the progress of the community. His natural interest in the welfare of his family and friends thus gives the local merchant an additional stake in the community's progress.

Finally, the home merchant's community interest is stimulated to a greater or lesser degree by his sense of social obligation—the feeling we all have to do our part or hold up our end in connection with undertakings from which we derive a benefit.

In the case of the chain stores, of course, the sentimental

interest in the communities in which they are located is lacking. If the chains have any reason for participating in community activities, therefore, it must be found in the other two
factors—self-interest, on the one hand, and the sense of social
obligation, on the other.

From the standpoint of self-interest, the chains have at least
as much at stake in the community as any other merchant, and
more than most of them. For if the chain operates more than
one unit in the town, its interest will be proportionately
greater than that of the merchant who has only one store. So
far as self-interest is concerned, therefore, a chain store operated by an absentee-owner might be expected to take as
much interest in the community's welfare as an independent
store.

The same thing applies to the remaining factor—social
duty. Some people are undoubtedly influenced by their moral
obligations to a greater degree than others. Some always do
their part. Others never do. If a merchant is under a moral
obligation to support community activities because he derives benefit from community development, that obligation
applies to every store no matter where its owner lives.
Whether the obligation will be met depends upon the owner's *principles* rather than upon his *residence*.

The comparison here, however, must be made between the
independent merchant, on the one hand, and the man or men
who control the policies of the chains, on the other—not between the independent merchant and the store manager. For
the measure of the store manager's activities will depend
entirely upon the policies established at his headquarters.
This is a highly important distinction because, no matter how
civic-minded a store manager may be compared with the
average independent merchant, he will not follow his natural
inclinations unless he knows that his headquarters will
approve of whatever contribution of time or money he finds
it desirable to make. On the other hand, even though some
store managers will undoubtedly be below average in their

own personal sense of civic responsibility, the community will
not suffer provided the company itself *requires* all managers
to contribute in reasonable measure.

Summing up the essential differences between independent
merchants and chain stores with respect to community spirit
and cooperation, in only one respect can a community expect
more from a local man than from a chain-store manager and
that is from the angle of sentiment or local pride. In that
respect, the chain-store system must necessarily be at a disadvantage, and yet the question still remains as to how important that difference is. Can it be offset in other ways?

After all, it doesn't make much difference how actively the
feeling of local pride surges in the breast of the local merchant unless he is *able* as well as willing to heed its call—and
the statistics presented earlier in these pages show how difficult it must be for the great majority of independent merchants even to make both ends meet.

On the other hand, it doesn't matter how lacking the
absentee-owner may be in this element of local pride, provided he is able and willing to do his fair share in promoting
community welfare for other reasons. In other words, what
inspires a merchant to contribute to the Community Chest,
to take an active part in Chamber of Commerce work or to
participate in similar activities is relatively unimportant. He
may do it from local pride, or because he thinks it will help
his business or just because he thinks it is the right thing to do.
So long as he does his part, the community can ask or expect
no more.

The fact is that whatever may have been the case in the
early days of chain-store development, the chains did eventually recognize their duty to the communities in which they
operated. Once they had decided that sound policy demanded
that they do their part, they took the necessary steps to
see that their store managers cooperated adequately. The fact
that the chains were both willing and *able* to do their part
meant far more to the communities than the natural inclina-

tions of independent merchants who were unable to back up their local pride effectively.

That considerations of public relations undoubtedly prompted the chains to take this more active interest in community affairs detracts in no way from the value of the contribution they are making. Perhaps in that respect lies a factor which is lacking in the case of the independent merchant, or, which is at least less potent with him than it is in the case of the chains. The chains learned the value of maintaining public relations the hard way, but they learned it. They are not apt to forget it. Certainly one of the fundamental features of a sound public-relations program for any absentee-owned project is to earn and maintain the good will of the communities in which they are located.

That is something the critics of chain stores, and chain stores themselves, overlooked in the days when the only important factor in community cooperation was *assumed* to be the local pride of the home-town merchant. That community life might benefit far more from the contributions of absentee-owners, even though they were activated by considerations of public relations, than by the offerings of those who were moved solely by sentiment, was not generally realized, but it was a fact.

Of course the part the independent merchant played in this sphere was always exaggerated. As this author pointed out in 1932,[1] when the hue and cry against the chains was at a high point, "anybody would think, from the criticism to which the chains have been subjected in this connection, that all independent merchants are paragons of civic virtue and that most of our public institutions—our churches, our schools, our concert halls, our highways, our parks, our museums, our hospitals, our libraries and our playgrounds—reflect their generosity. The truth of the matter is that the majority of our independent merchants have such a hard struggle to make both ends meet that it is out of the question for them to

[1] *The Chain Store—Boon or Bane?*, op. cit., pp. 94-96.

contribute to community projects in any substantial way, no matter how civic-minded they may be, and if our cities and towns had to depend upon the financial support received from such sources, we should have to get along without schools, without churches, without concert halls, without highways, without parks, without museums, without hospitals, without libraries and without playgrounds. . . .

"What many people overlook is the fact that the wherewithal to build schools and highways and parks and playgrounds and other public projects comes almost entirely from *taxation* rather than from *voluntary contributions* and the part the local merchant plays—or fails to play—in developing his community through voluntary contributions is not nearly so serious a matter as might be supposed."

But what has been said of the average independent merchant did not apply to the chains. The average unit of a national or sectional chain, even in 1932, was a successful proposition and was in a position to pay its just share of whatever might be required in the way of voluntary contributions towards community welfare work. As the author pointed out at that time,[2] "the duty of the foreign-owned store to contribute is just as clear and just as definite as that of the locally owned establishment. This duty arises from the fact that the owner of a store in a community, just the same as the owner of a home, or any other resident, must share, willy-nilly, in the fruits of such projects and, by all standards of social ethics, should be willing to contribute his pro-rata share of the expense of establishing or maintaining them."

Conceding then that the chains had both the obligation and the ability to participate in community projects, how were they actually behaving?

One answer to that question was given by A. S. Dudley, president of the National Association of Commercial Organization Secretaries, an organization which included in its membership most of the local Chambers of Commerce throughout

[2] *Ibid.*, p. 98.

the country. In an address before the National Chain Store Association in October, 1930,[3] he said:

"Early in 1928 our National Association of Commercial Organization Secretaries approached the management of 344 chains operating 25 or more stores—asked for an expression of attitude towards Chambers of Commerce. . . . Within three months, 266 secretaries out of our active membership of approximately 700, reported a total increase in chain-store subscriptions amounting to $636,825.

"The organization of the National Chain Store Association which was perfected about this time established a common meeting ground. From the moment of your adoption of your Code of Ethics on the 12th of October, 1928, pledging yourselves to promote all worthy local civic enterprises and any movements looking towards the betterment of the communities in which you engaged in business, there has been reported by our members a vast increase in the financial subscriptions and in the cooperative attitude of chains towards chambers of commerce.

"In July of this year we began another survey to ascertain the present situation. Thirty days after starting the survey, 43 per cent of the Chambers of Commerce, represented by our membership, had filed reports. The summary shows that 594 chain stores began their financial support to Chambers of Commerce since 1928. With but one exception, every member of the National Chain Store Association is represented in the report.

"In comparing the actual number of dollars subscribed by chains with those of the independent merchants, approximately two-thirds of the secretaries reporting stated that the amounts given by the chains were satisfactory. In other words, the subscriptions approximately equalled those of the independent merchants; while comparatively few secretaries reported no support whatever from the chains.

"Reports received are not 100 per cent in an affirmative vein, but independent merchants are far, far from the mark of perfection in living up to their civic duties."

That presents probably a fair picture of the situation which existed 30 years ago, when the chains were only just be-

[3] *Chain Store Age,* November, 1930.

ginning to realize not only what their social duty was with respect to community cooperation but where their interest lay, from the standpoint of public relations.

In 1932, as had been pointed out on page 179, the Illinois Chain Store Council was formed for the express purpose of crystallizing chain-store cooperation in local community and agricultural activities and, before very long, similar councils were organized in other States and regions throughout the country. By 1942, approximately 30 of these State councils were functioning. In between those years, the chains had received an intensive course in public relations in connection with the California referendum, as has been previously related in Chapter XI.

The character of the contribution which chain-store managers can make in the field of community building was concretely illustrated by the Community Builder Awards which *Chain Store Age* initiated in 1939.

Announced in January, 1939, the objective was to select and honor as the "Community Builder of the Year" the chain-store manager who, in 1938, had performed the most outstanding services for his community.

"Throughout the country important service is being rendered to communities every day by chain-store managers who put their energy, training and experience to work to build the communities in which they live and work," the announcement related. "Often the extent of these signal services is lost sight of because of the modesty of these men or because the services are rendered 'in line of duty' and are seldom publicized outside of the communities which benefit.

"Contributions which these chain-store managers make to their communities should receive wider recognition, not only to acknowledge the services of these men but to disprove the fallacious arguments advanced by critics of chain stores.

"Therefore, *Chain Store Age* is undertaking the task of compiling an Honor Roll of Community Builders of 1938.

This roll will consist of managers of stores in all types of chains who, during the past year, made worth-while contributions in the form of services to their communities. From the Honor Roll of Community Builders a committee will select the 'Community Builder of the Year.'" A permanent bronze plaque and $100 in cash were to be awarded to him by the publication. All the other managers who made the Honor Roll were to receive scrolls designating them as Community Builders.

Nomination for the Honor Roll could be made either by the manager's district manager or his headquarters or by a local newspaper editor, an officer of a chamber of commerce or service club, a minister or a city official. The nomination period remained open for ten weeks. From the nominations received, 303 were selected as worthy of a place on the Roll of Honor of Community Builders. The nominating letters describing the achievements of the men who seemed to rate consideration for the top award, that of the Community Builder of the Year, were submitted to three judges for their independent appraisal. The judges were D. Hodson Lewis, of Little Rock, Ark., president of the National Association of Commercial Organization Secretaries; Walter F. Dexter, of Sacramento, Calif., president of Lions International; and Howard P. Jones, of New York, executive director of the National Municipal League.

Emery E. Freeman, manager of the J. C. Penney Company's store in Mount Pleasant, Mich., was the man selected as the Community Builder of the Year.

What were the community activities that prompted the judges to select Mr. Freeman for that distinction?

He was president of the Chamber of Commerce.

As chairman of a chapter of the American Red Cross, he headed up a membership drive which resulted in a 33 per cent increase over the previous year.

He worked with others to secure finances for a $50,000

building to house a garage for the State Highway Department, thereby retaining for Mount Pleasant a State activity employing 25 men.

He headed the financing of the citywide Santa Claus Sales event to promote Christmas shopping, bringing thousands to Mount Pleasant to do their Christmas shopping.

He provided work in his own store for fourteen college students by planning hours of employment to meet their study schedules wherever possible. Other students were given part-time extra work.

He served on a committee to raise funds for the Boy Scout budget, supporting the campaign with cash, window displays and as a solicitor of funds.

He served as rehabilitation officer of the American Legion.

He assisted the Methodist Church drive for a building fund and personally contributed $250. Other churches received his personal financial support.

He furnished free movies to three schools during a campaign to raise funds for the Parent-Teacher Association.

He was a director of the Exchange Savings Bank.

The foregoing list does not include all the activities mentioned in Mr. Freeman's nomination. But they are typical of the kind of services which not only Mr. Freeman but a great number of other store managers were equipped to perform and which many of them were actually performing. The fact that only 303 names appeared on the Honor Roll was by no means an indication that these were the only managers who deserved the honor. On the contrary, they represented but a small fraction of those who undoubtedly would have made the Honor Roll had they been nominated.

It must be remembered that relatively little publicity was given to the award except in the pages of the magazine sponsoring it and that the period for nominations was relatively short. As local organizations familiar with the services rendered by chain-store managers could hear of the awards only through store managers themselves, many who might have

submitted nominations remained unaware of their opportunity to do so. Although the chains themselves were privileged to nominate their own managers, not all the companies
realized the desirability of doing so.

Qualitatively if not quantitatively, this first Honor Roll was
highly illuminating. Not every one of the men on the Roll did
as much as Mr. Freeman, by any means, but they all did
enough at least to indicate that the observation that chain-
store managers are *in* a community but not *of* it, even if true,
is not particularly significant.

A glance, at random, at some of the community contributions made by men on the Honor Roll will suffice to show the
wide range they covered.

One manager, Dan Worth Bradley, Sears Roebuck and Co.,
Durham, N.C., served as director of his Kiwanis Club and of
the Junior Chamber of Commerce, which he helped to organize, served on the Community Chest committee, was third
among 150 in number of new members obtained for the
Y.M.C.A., and broadcasted over a local radio station in behalf
of the community, besides being active in church and Sunday
School doings.

Another, O. S. Hillman, H. L. Green Co., Columbia, S.C.,
was president of the Merchant's Association, a member of the
City Council, finance chairman of the advisory board of the
Salvation Army, director of children's clinic, orphan's home
and day nursery, and member of the Boy Scout Council.

Frank C. Collins, Great Atlantic & Pacific Tea Co., Grafton,
W. Va., as chairman of the county chapter of American Red
Cross, had put over its first successful home-service campaign
in eight years. He was a director of his Rotary Club, a member
of the county board of trade and the Y.M.C.A., and a soloist
in his church and organizer of a club for the boys of his
church.

William E. Berry, Montgomery Ward & Co., Minot, N.D.,
was president of his Kiwanis Club, vice president and fund-
drive chairman of Community Chest, which was over-sub-

scribed, chairman of the Retail Merchants group of the Association of Commerce, chairman of a city recreation council which sponsored playgrounds and other youth activities, director of the Salvation Army advisory board and co-chairman of a campaign to stimulate business and relieve unemployment.

The fact that chain-store managers all over the country were engaging in the same kinds of community activities tells its own story. This kind of work must be headed up by somebody. Chain-store managers are well equipped to handle it. The general policy of so-called national companies, including the interstate chains, is to have their managers do their part. The result is that no community in which the chains operate need ever lack leadership of a high order. The chains are both able and willing to supply it.

The following year, the Community Builder Award was announced again. This time the nominations were limited to local organizations—commercial, civic, service, religious, charitable or educational. The chains themselves could not nominate managers. Furthermore the cash award was eliminated, as the honor of recognition as an outstanding Community Builder was believed to be the only reward required. To acquaint local organizations with the conditions of the award, announcements were sent to all members of the National Association of Commercial Organization Secretaries. The judges were Ormond F. Lyman, Peoria, Ill., president of that organization; Dr. Minnie L. Maffett, Dallas, Tex., president of the National Federation of Business and Professional Women's Clubs; and Howard W. Palmer, Greenwich, Conn., president of the National Editorial Association.

From the nominations received, 344 were selected for the Roll of Honor. The highest award of Community Builder of the Year went to Walter S. Small, J. C. Penney Company manager at La Crosse, Wis. He was awarded that title for all types of chains, and also for the Department Store Division. In the Variety Store Division, the outstanding manager was

Forrest G. Weese, S. S. Kresge Co., Zanesville, Ohio. In the Grocery Store Division, Paul A. Kunkle, The Kroger Grocery & Baking Co., Trenton, Mich., was selected as the Community Builder of the Year, and in the Drug Store Division, that honor went to H. C. James, Peoples Drug Stores, Fredericksburg, Va.

Mr. Small had been nominated by the La Crosse Chamber of Commerce; Mr. Weese by the Zanesville Chamber of Commerce; Mr. Kunkle by the Trenton (Mich.) *Times;* and Mr. James by the Fredericksburg *Free Lance-Star.*

To list the many noteworthy achievements of these men and of the 340 others who made up the 1939 Honor Roll would be merely to duplicate what has already been said of the Community Builders of 1938. But Mr. Small's own observations on being notified of his selection are enlightening as a revelation of the store manager's own viewpoint.[4]

"I wish to thank *Chain Store Age* for selecting me for this honor," he wrote, "but I wish more to commend you for placing a high value on the discharge of community responsibility by chain-store managers.

"In La Crosse most chain-store managers respond readily to community calls. Many are very active in civic affairs. There is a steadily increasing interest and cooperation in community building on the part of the chains.

"When there is a call for support of most any local cause there is a very gratifying response from chain-store men. We never hesitate to solicit the chains to do their part, financially or physically. In fact, the foreign-corporation list, as it was designated in Community Chest campaigns, was always considered a plum for the team that was lucky enough to get it.

"Those multiple organizations who do not encourage and insist on community interest, both financially and in manpower, on the part of their local representatives are working a hardship on all chains. . . .

"I do not necessarily deserve medals for discharging a re-

[4] *Ibid.,* July, 1940.

sponsibility which is definitely in my lap; to do less would be to miss an opportunity, but I thank you just the same. In my case I must admit that my community interest is a result of the teaching and the policy of the J. C. Penney Co."

The third Community Builder project, which proved to be the final one, was announced in January, 1941, to some 2,400 Chambers of Commerce and other local organizations. It produced the greatest number of nominations of the three, yielding 524 names for the 1940 Honor Roll. No top awards were made as had been the case in the two previous years. The decision to abandon these special awards was made with the idea of avoiding any suggestion of a contest. It was felt that that could be best achieved by awarding a single type of recognition available to all who qualified for it—a Scroll of Honor attesting the recipient's qualification as a Community Builder by reason of outstanding service performed in 1940.

Among the Honor Roll men announced in May, 1941, were thirteen who had received the honor twice before and 77 who had received it once, either in 1940 or 1939. Eliminating these duplications, the project had brought out the names of more than 1,000 store managers located in probably more than 750 different communities, who had distinguished themselves for their leadership in community activities as part and parcel of their jobs as chain-store managers, with or without any sentimental ties to the communities in which they were located, and with no expectation of any reward other than that which comes from the satisfaction of meeting one's responsibilities.

Obviously, this group of Community Builders did not begin to include all who might equally have qualified for that title. More than 73 different interstate chains were represented on the 1940 Honor Roll, an indication that the policy of encouraging store managers to accept their community responsibilities was by no means confined to just a few broad-minded and public-spirited organizations.

The fact is that chain-store managers today have become the leading merchants in many of our communities. Unless they and the representatives of other kinds of absentee-owned enterprises recognize the responsibility which has fallen into their laps, as Mr. Small put it, such communities will suffer accordingly.

The situation was well described by a Chamber of Commerce man in the course of an address to the Pennsylvania Chain Store Council at Hershey, Pa., January 22, 1941.[5] Earl D. Bacon, the speaker, was president of the Pennsylvania Commercial Secretaries' Association and executive secretary of the Sharon, Pa., Chamber of Commerce, a field in which he had been engaged for eighteen years.

"Quite a change has been taking place in communities during the past several years," he declared. "Surely, everyone can remember some men in the towns where we grew up (we'd call them economic royalists now) who were responsible for the growth and well-being of the community. In many cases they were merchants. In others they were bankers or the proprietors of the leading industries, the power company or other leading enterprises. In every case, however, they were men of outstanding leadership who were vitally concerned with the future of the town, for the simple reason that everything they had was invested right there at home. They were willing to expend any reasonable amount of time, energy or money to secure community development.

"We all know what has happened. The utilities were combined years ago. Gradually the industries have been sold to national companies, and chain stores are constantly increasing in numbers and importance. The old entrepreneurs of former generations have been replaced by a generation of managers, running businesses for groups of stockholders who are distributed far and wide. Some of these managers have the same abilities of leadership and the same community spirit that the former local leaders had. Generally speaking, however, and through no fault of their own, they do not have the same vital personal interest in the affairs of the community.

[5] *Ibid* (Administration Edition) March, 1941.

Their first allegiance is to their bosses in New York, Philadelphia, Pittsburgh and other cities, or to an impersonal group of stockholders. Their support of local community projects is necessarily secondary to those allegiances."

Of course, what Mr. Bacon overlooked in that connection, was that even in the days when community leadership was largely in the hands of local merchants and other business men, their support of local community projects, too, was "necessarily secondary" to their major interest represented by their own business. The first duty of *any* merchant, obviously is to make a success of his own business, for if he neglects that in order to give an undue measure of his time and attention to public affairs, the net result must be prejudicial both to his business and the community as well.

Using his own city of Sharon as an example of the extent to which the changes in question had taken place, Mr. Bacon declared that 94 per cent of the industrial workers were dependent upon absentee owners for their jobs. The chains were accounting for between 25 per cent and 50 per cent of the retail business. He concluded that "to a greater and greater extent, more and more cities must rely upon 'outsiders' in many types of business for the things they used to do themselves. We secretaries in the smaller cities of the country are firmly of the belief that additional help from national firms is not only desirable—it is absolutely essential if our towns are to prosper."

How close were the chains in Pennsylvania coming to what was expected of them?

So far as their contributions to the operating budgets of civic and welfare organizations were concerned, Mr. Bacon said that most secretaries agreed that the support given by the members of the Pennsylvania Chain Store Council was "fairly adequate." So far as non-member chains were concerned, they were not, as a rule, doing their part. However, as most of the important national and sectional chains operating in Pennsylvania were members of the council, the fact that a few were not did not change the general picture materially.

So far as contributions to capital investments were concerned—the occasional capital for hospital buildings, for instance—the response of even the member-companies, Mr. Bacon said, had not been entirely satisfactory. Conceding that the national industries and utilities and many of the chains already saw the community problem and were responding to it generously, he declared that the chains would not be doing their full part until they subscribed to capital funds as regularly as they were doing to current operating budgets of local institutions.

Turning to the remaining problem of personal service, Mr. Bacon pointed out that the smaller communities were no longer self-sufficient. "We must rely upon the chains and other national firms," he said, "to supply the manpower once available at home."

To improve the situation then existing, he recommended that (1) shifting managers from one city to another should be restricted as much as possible with the community aspect in mind, pointing out that a manager must be in a town for several years at least before he can do his part as a civic leader; (2) managers should be relieved of as much store-detail work as possible in order to give them more time for community work; and (3) top executives of the chains should remind managers from time to time that they were expected to cooperate in community affairs as part of their job.

Mr. Bacon's frank appraisal of the situation was regarded by the chains at the time as constructive. It was published in full in Chain Store Age, March, 1941. By that time the changes in the make-up of our smaller communities, which have been noted, had about run their course. The transition from the so-called "horse-and-buggy" days to the streamlined era that superseded it was complete. So far as the chains were concerned, the era of their active expansion had ended ten years earlier. It was not to be resumed in the ten years that followed.

Nevertheless the need for chain-store participation and leadership in community activities definitely remained. It still exists.

That the chains have never lost sight of it is evidenced by their maintenance of the State councils they established for the express purpose of stimulating the interest of their store managers in local activities and putting their cooperation on an organized basis.

These councils now exist in some 18 States, either as separate organizations or as part and parcel of State merchants' associations representing retailers generally. Most of the national and regional chains, as well as many of the larger local chains, actively support them.

Judging from the monthly reports issued by the directors of these State councils, chain-store managers are filling responsible positions of leadership in communities all over the country. If the Community Builder awards initiated by *Chain Store Age* 20 years ago but discontinued in 1942, as has already been related, were to be revived, the resulting Honor Roll would include a representative from almost every community in which units of the national or regional chains are located. In 1954, the National Association of Food Chains launched an annual store-manager citizenship campaign with the same basic objective. Each year since then a dozen or more managers have been selected as the outstanding managers of the year from the standpoint of exceptional participation in community activities. Screened from thousands nominated by their own companies for the distinction, the successful nominees have been publicly honored and acclaimed by the National Association. This project, although confined to managers of chain food stores, serves not only to inspire them to take their civic responsibilities seriously but to demonstrate how any chain store manager can be a good citizen as well as a good merchant.

To summarize the underlying considerations involved in the relations of the chains to their communities, the first point to note is that the greatest contribution they can make lies, of course, in the economic sphere.

Their primary job is to give the community the most efficient kind of retail service their particular system makes possible. In doing that they help not only to keep the cost of living down and thus to raise the community's standard of living, but they stimulate the business and the life of the community by making it unnecessary for its residents to go elsewhere to satisfy their needs.

The second point is that chain stores have an opportunity to serve their communities in the social sphere too. They share it with independent merchants and other fellow townsmen, irrespective of business or professional connections.

It arises from the fact that many of the activities required to promote the welfare of the community depend upon voluntary support and direction. The duty to provide such support and direction falls ethically upon those who are best equipped to furnish them. The chains definitely belong in that category.

Conceding, therefore, that native-born townspeople may have greater *sentimental* reason for rallying to the support of the home town, that fact is of little practical value unless it is accompanied by both the ability and the will to make such contributions. On the other hand, the fact that chain-store managers may lack any sentimental interest whatever in the community is likewise of little practical significance, provided that their contributions are forthcoming for other valid reasons.

That such valid reasons do indeed exist would seem to insure that the chains will continue to play a major role in community leadership.

CHAPTER XIV

THE CHAINS AND
THE FARMER

OF THE SCORES of thousands of consumer items which line the shelves and counters of retail stores, those which are not of agricultural origin, either wholly or partially, are relatively few.

That applies particularly, of course, to the things we eat, but it applies also to most of the things we wear or use in other ways. In the case of foodstuffs, some of them reach the stores and the consumer in the same shape they left the farm. Others first go through various phases of processing. In the case of clothing and many other consumer items, the agricultural products entering their construction usually have lost all resemblance to their original form, but they are there just the same. Cotton, for example, goes through many processes before it emerges in a retail store as a woman's dress or a man's shirt, but the price the farmer gets for his cotton depends in the last analysis under normal conditions on how many things made of cotton are moved into consumption.

Thus the relation of retailing to agriculture is a vital one, even though it may be indirect in most cases. The significant fact is that retail stores provide the outlets through which many agricultural products move into consumption.

What has been said applies to all kinds of stores—independent stores as well as chain stores. But when the chain stores became an important factor in retailing, particularly in the grocery field, something was added to the relation of farmer and retailer which had never existed before.

In the first place, because the chains were big enough to buy from the farmer direct, they brought into sharp contrast the disadvantages the farmer had traditionally suffered in disposing of his output through commission men. The difference was clearly explained by a number of agricultural witnesses in the Patman bill hearing. One of them, S. M. Jones, of New Bern, N.C., whose company packed and distributed the output of some 500 vegetable growers, said at the hearing:[1]

"Prior to the time the chain stores became an important factor in the distribution of fresh vegetables, most of our produce was shipped to distant markets to be handled on a commission basis by the local merchants. The grower had little or no opportunity to sell at shipping point and know in advance what he was going to receive. His returns on his consignment were very uncertain and oftentimes were disappointing. As a matter of fact, it was only too frequent that he did not get anything at all, the freight and selling costs having eaten up the proceeds of the sale. In recent years, largely by means of the support of chain buyers, markets have been established in shipping sections, either auction or private sale. Today most of the supplies are sold at shipping point, either for cash or at stated prices, rather than going forward under consignment. By this means the growers have immediate contact with the pulse of the market, know what they are receiving, and can often regulate their shipments to a degree in keeping with demand requirements. Greater market stability has followed the introduction of this method of selling, which, obviously, has been of direct benefit to the growers."

But the chains brought something else into retailing which meant even more to the farmer—lower distribution costs. How badly that was needed was stressed by Edward A. O'Neal, president of the American Farm Bureau Federation, who declared when he appeared before the Patman bill committee on April 13, 1940:[2]

[1] Patman Bill Hearing, *op. cit.*, Vol. 2, p. 1468.
[2] *Ibid.*, Vol. 2, pp. 775, 784.

"Our distribution system has grown up like Topsy, in helter-skelter fashion. We have built up a costly, inefficient system of distribution which takes a heavy toll from both farmers and consumers. All too often farmers receive too little for their products and consumers pay too much. The cost of distribution is one of the great barriers that we must surmount between the farmers and the consumers. We must seek any and all improvements in our distribution system. . . .

"This great mass-producing industry of agriculture needs an efficient mass-distributing system close to consumers, to carry commodities to the doors of millions of consumers at the least necessary cost. Furthermore, it must be a system that can act quickly and on a nationwide basis in order to handle perishable products produced long distances from the points of consumption. Delay in getting to market may mean the loss of a year's farm income. The chain stores' system has supplied not only these local outlets on a nationwide basis, but also the centralized purchasing agencies which deal directly with the farmers' cooperative marketing organizations.

"Thus the chain-store system affords an opportunity to shorten the route between the farmer and the consumer by means of direct bargaining between farmers' cooperative organizations and chain store organizations which sell directly to consumers, thereby eliminating unnecessary transportation and handling costs and the losses resulting from glutting of markets and inefficient distribution."

The chains' lower distribution costs meant nothing to the farmer, of course, unless they were translated into better returns to the farmer or lower prices to the consumer, or both. That the chains did reduce retail prices on fruit and vegetables was generally recognized. The savings thus brought about meant that the consumer could buy more and the farmer shared the benefit of the consumer's increased buying power.

But the chains helped to expand the market for farm products in another way. They pioneered in displaying and merchandising fresh fruit and vegetables more extensively and more effectively than had been the practice in the grocery field before they came into the picture.

Strangely enough, despite the substantial benefits the farmers derived from these marketing innovations, many years elapsed before they were fully recognized and appreciated. In the meanwhile, anti-chain interests were busy developing the thought that the chains were actually hurting the farmers more than they were helping them. By lowering the retail price of fruits and produce, it was contended, the chains were depressing farm prices. Using farm products as "loss leaders" might indeed increase their consumption, it was urged, but how did that help the farmer if he could not get his cost of production back?

Irrespective of the facts in the case, many farmers undoubtedly came to believe that chain-store merchandising methods were actually harmful to them. When, from time to time, a bountiful harvest of a particular farm crop resulted in a supply exceeding the demand and prices declined accordingly, the plight of the farmers affected called for a scapegoat. It was easy enough then to say that the chains' low prices were largely responsible for "depressing" the market, even though the blame was obviously not theirs at all.

The result was that by 1935, at which time the chains were moving about 35 per cent of the total output of fruit and vegetables into consumption, the farmers had mixed feelings regarding the chains. That attitude might have continued indefinitely but for one of the most remarkable developments in the whole history of marketing which changed the picture in a most constructive way.

It happened in 1936. As the year opened, the California peach growers were faced with one of agriculture's frequently recurring problems—the prospect of a bigger crop than could be marketed profitably.

The trouble in this case was that the carryover of canned peaches from 1935 amounted to 6,400,000 cases, as against a normal carryover of only 4,200,000 cases. Under such conditions, the canners would not be interested in packing more than four or five million additional cases. That would be equivalent to only about half of the new crop and would mean that the grower's return on his crop would be cut from $30 per ton, which he needed to show a profit, to $20 or even $15 per ton, which would not cover his cost of production.

Instead of letting nature take its course, as had been the general practice theretofore, the leading peach growers got together and organized the Canning Peach Stabilization Committee, with H. C. Merritt, Jr., as its chairman. Obviously, the problem was to cut down the carryover in the early months of the year to make way for the new crop, and somebody got the bright idea that if the chains would organize a sales promotion drive on a nationwide basis maybe the situation could be saved.

The idea was not entirely new. Many of the food chains individually had aided farmers in the past in their own operating areas by putting on local campaigns designed to move a surplus crop into consumption. But this was the first time anybody had thought of asking all the chains to combine in a nationwide campaign to achieve such a result. The proposal was made to the Food and Grocery Chain Stores of America— which a few months later changed its name to National Association of Food Chains—and was promptly accepted. As has been pointed out earlier, the chains in California were engaged at that time in a campaign to defeat a drastic chain-store-tax proposal which the public was to pass on at the next general election. The plight of the peach growers provided an excellent opportunity to demonstrate just what organized distribution, as represented by the chain-store system, could do to help solve the farmer's constant problem of moving seasonable surpluses into consumption. The chains jumped at the chance.

What happened can be told in a few words. In April and May of that year, the chains put on a four weeks canned-peach campaign in which 34,000 stores throughout the nation participated. These stores increased their sales of canned peaches in April-May, 1936 by 171 per cent compared with their sales for the corresponding period in 1935.

What a dent it made in the carryover was thus reported by Mr. Merritt in a letter to the chain-store association dated July 6, 1936.[3]

"Now that efforts of the chain stores of the nation to save the canned-peach industry from a ruinous surplus have been crowned with success," the letter said, "it is fitting that our committee make due acknowledgment of your participation in the four California Canned Peach Events. . . .

"The figures reveal a reduction in canned-peach stocks of 3,143,387 cases in the five months period from January to June. The withdrawals averaged 670,000 cases per month, as against an average of 381,000 cases per month in 1935. . . ."

What is more to the point, the growers received $30 per ton for their 1936 crop instead of the $15 which was all they had originally expected.

At the very time the details of this first epoch-making national campaign were being worked out by John A. Logan, then the executive vice president of the food-chain association, and its agricultural committee, something much bigger was in the making, although its full possibilities may not have been realized at the time by those who were organizing it.

As has been pointed out earlier, a large number of farmers at that time believed that certain practices of long standing in distribution were inimical to agriculture and, rightly or wrongly, the chains were believed largely responsible for them. On the other hand, it was realized that many food-chain operators did not fully understand the farmers' problems.

Why not get together around a table and discuss their mutual problems in the hope that cooperation might perhaps be substituted for misunderstanding and ill-feeling?

Mr. Logan accordingly arranged such a conference to be

[3] *Practical Farm Relief*, National Association of Food Chains, April, 1937.

held in New York between outstanding agricultural leaders and representatives of the food chains.[4] The farmers were represented by a special committee appointed by the National Cooperative Council, an association consisting of 51 agricultural cooperative organizations, with a membership of 1,500,-000 farmers.

Representing the chains in what turned out to be an historic meeting were Hunter C. Phelan, D. Pender Grocery Co. (now Colonial Stores); Charles F. Adams and B. F. McGoldrick, First National Stores; Lewis W. Cole, Steiden Stores; Thomas F. Cauley, Danahy-Faxon Stores; F. H. Massman, National Tea Company; W. L. McEachran, E. S. Burgan & Sons; Albert H. Morrill and Warren H. Clark, Kroger Grocery & Baking Co.; William Park, Fred W. Johnson and H. D. Williamson, American Stores Co., L. A. Warren and Frederick W. Williamson, Safeway Stores, Inc.; E. G. Yonker, Sanitary Grocery Co. (now Safeway Stores), and Mr. Logan.

Over and beyond this desire to clear the atmosphere between the farmers and the chains was the hope that the meeting might lead to a practical program for farm relief which would go far to set their relations on a solid and substantial basis.

As Mr. Logan was to point out later in reporting on what actually happened at the conference, chain-store leaders realized that one of the most pressing problems of agriculture had to do with seasonal surplus crops. Why couldn't the chains use their facilities and their know-how to move these surplus crops into consumption on a nationwide basis as these situations arose?

The conference was presided over by C. C. Teague, vice president of the National Cooperative Council and president of the California Fruit Growers Exchange.[5] Among the practices which were responsible, he believed, for whatever ill-

---

[4] *The Chain Store Cooperates with Agriculture*, memorandum filed with California State Senate Interim Committee by Frederick W. Williamson for California Chain Store Association, December 7, 1936.
[5] *Ibid.*

will farmers felt towards the chains, he listed five which he thought ought to be eliminated:

1. Unethical brokerage payment.
2. Unearned advertising allowances.
3. The use of agricultural products as loss-leaders.
4. Unreasonable quantity discounts.
5. The control of supplies by direct or indirect financing.

In the discussion which followed, several of the farm leaders made clear that the practices complained of were by no means peculiar to chain-store operations. In fact many of them had been initiated and were followed by all manner of jobbers, commission men, wholesalers and other middlemen.

None of the chain representatives defended any of the practices complained of and the upshot of that phase of the meeting was that the chains formally pledged themselves to aid in elimination of those practices from all branches of the industry.

But most important of all was a resolution adopted at the conference by the food chains which read as follows:

"Further resolved: That the members of this organization will endeavor to cooperate with the producers through their cooperative organizations, wherever available, or through other established producer agencies, in the effective marketing of excess seasonal production and surpluses, giving due recognition in the course of such efforts to the laws of supply and demand. . . ."

That understanding was variously described thereafter as "an economic landmark," "the most forward-looking step ever taken, both for agriculture and for the distribution of food products" and "the dawn of a new day for the farmer."

This meeting took place in May. Within the next twelve months no less than eight Producer-Consumer Campaigns, as they were called, had been staged by the food chains, with most gratifying results to all concerned.

The canned-peach campaign had already been covered.

The second campaign was to promote the sale of beef. Drought that summer had so reduced feed facilities that cattle were rushed to market in unprecedented numbers, with the result that the beef market was glutted. Cattlemen asked the food chains to put on a campaign to avert the threatened catastrophe.

The campaign the chains put on was singularly successful. Mr. Logan reported a year later that the chains increased their beef sales in August 34.7 per cent—more than twice the increase in the August slaughter; and increased per capita beef consumption 11.1 per cent. "Prices to cattle raisers, which had started down, steadied, actually advanced during August," he reported,[6] "and continued to advance in the following months. Cattlemen received 6 per cent higher price and 37 per cent more dollar income from August sales than the previous five-year average for the month. The Federal Government, which bought 2,500,000 head of cattle in the 1934 drought, and which was ready to buy again in 1936, actually bought only 5,000 head to prevent a livestock market collapse."

In October the chains got behind a campaign to sell dried fruit which had backed up on the producers because of a maritime strike which reduced exports. A two weeks' campaign staged by the chains increased their sales 79.1 per cent over the previous year's sales for the period, and moved millions of pounds of dried fruits into domestic consumption. It prevented complete demoralization of the dried-fruit market.

An abnormal crop of 20,000,000 turkeys that fall, 33 per cent above 1935, again brought the chains into action. They increased their own sales 46 per cent and sales generally were increased 26.6 per cent. The net result was that most producing areas sold out and showed a profit instead of the serious loss they had expected.

The next campaign was the most sensational of all. A

[6] *Practical Farm Relief, op. cit.*, p. 6.

bumper grapefruit crop, 46.6 per cent in excess of the previous year's, resulted in what the U.S. Department of Agriculture called "the nation's number one surplus problem." [7] The campaign staged by the chains in January and February increased their sales 284.7 per cent! Surplus stocks were cleared and the growers realized from 25 to 45 cents more per box than they had expected. Again a severe loss was converted into a substantial profit.

At the same time the chains put on a campaign to boost lamb sales, which had declined as a result of the competition from the heavy turkey crop, aggravated by an increased slaughter as a result of the drought. The chains moved 59 per cent more lamb into consumption as compared with their sales in the same two months in 1935 and prices to producers rose from $8.40 per cwt. in December to $10.50 in January and $13 in March, although *retail prices* remained stable throughout the campaign.

Another turkey campaign was staged in February and a canned-pear campaign in April, with consistently satisfactory results.

These early campaigns set the pattern for a permanent farm-relief program which has been followed ever since. In March, 1951, in a talk before the Sales Executives Club,[8] Mr. Logan pointed out that since the program was started in 1936 more than 350 campaigns and promotions, covering almost every agricultural product, had cleared through the association's office. In addition, similar cooperation has been frequently extended by A&P, which is not a member of the association, acting independently.

Although the program was initiated by the food chains, the chains in other fields were quick to recognize its underlying merit and to tie in with such promotions wherever the nature of the agricultural product involved enabled them to cooperate in a practical way.

[7] *Ibid.,* p. 8.
[8] *Food Distribution Is Different,* an address before Sales Executives Club, Hotel Roosevelt, N.Y., March 13, 1951.

Thus, in 1938, the Institute of Distribution mobilized its members, including variety-store chains and other types handling consumer items in which cotton figured, to cooperate with cotton growers and processors to promote the consumption of cotton products. They all staged special promotions tying in with National Cotton Week. Even the grocery chains participated in a modest way because some of their items were derived from cotton or cotton seed.

Then, too, when the dairy interests felt they could use chain-store cooperation to increase the consumption of milk in the summertime, when the supply was at its peak, practically all types of chains responded year after year in a month-long promotion. The drug chains and the variety chains joined the grocery chains and restaurant chains in promoting milk as a beverage at their soda fountains or for consumption in the shape of dairy dishes, and even chains which had no interest in selling dairy products in any form, such as the shoe chains, the hat chains and wearing apparel chains found ways to cooperate by displaying "Drink Milk" posters in their windows and stores.

What was behind this all-out effort of the chains to help solve the farmer's problem? Did they do it out of sheer altruism? If not, what did they expect to gain by it?

Rilea W. Doe, vice president of Safeway Stores, Inc., answered those questions and several others related to them when he appeared before the Patman bill committee to tell the story of the food chains' agricultural program.[9]

In the first place, he pointed out, although the chains conceived and organized the program, they are not "the whole show." Other organized distribution groups were likewise cooperating to the best of their ability in many of the programs and the chains welcomed their participation.

Turning to the reasons for the chains' interest in promoting the welfare of the farmer, he said they were three, as follows:

[9] Patman Bill Hearing, *op. cit.*, Vol. 2, p. 885.

"First, the chains need a dependable supply of dependable quality merchandise and, therefore, are interested in a stabilized agricultural market—a market that maintains an even keel through regular daily purchases of normal supplies.

"Second, farmers are a very large class of customers of chain food stores, and if they—the farmers—have more money it means more business for the chain-store companies, as well as other business men.

"Third, farmers represent such a large proportion of the population of the entire country, and are so important economically, that the entire nation's prosperity is interwoven with the prosperity of agriculture.

"Obviously, then, it is good business—we call it enlightened selfishness—for the food chains to concern themselves with the welfare of agriculture and to assist continually to improve and stabilize the market for farm products. Such a policy is founded upon sound economic and social principles. This farm program has proven to be a practical form of working, economic, democracy."

"Enlightened selfishness" on the part of the chains undoubtedly supplied another reason for their well-conceived and most effective agricultural program. By demonstrating to the farmer in this practical way the unique facilities the chains commanded for moving seasonal surpluses into consumption as well as for expanding the market for farm products in their regular day-in and day-out merchandising, they established a unity of interest which the farmer would not be apt to overlook.

That the farmers did not overlook it was apparent enough whenever and wherever discriminatory anti-chain-store taxes were under consideration. Invariably their spokesmen took a firm and positive stand against such taxes. Typical of what was to happen over and over again in such situations was the appearance before a New York Senate Committee on March 2, 1938 of G. A. Jeffreys, secretary of the New York State Turkey Growers Association. Under consideration was a proposed special tax against chain stores. In opposing it,

Mr. Jeffreys stressed what a big job the food chains had done in moving an unusually heavy crop of turkeys into consumption. And when the anti-chain spokesman interjected sarcastically that he supposed the American people would have to get along without turkeys if we had no chain stores, Mr. Jeffreys replied:

"Not at all. Of course we would have turkeys, with or without chain stores; but because of the chain stores *more* people can have turkey!"

But the position of farmers with respect to the economic value of the chain-store system was shown most convincingly two years later at the public hearing on the Patman "Death Sentence" bill. Spokesmen for farm group after farm group appeared at the hearing to testify in person why they were interested in the defeat of the bill. One after another they testified how vital to their prosperity the chain-store system had become, and rejected almost unanimously Mr. Patman's contention that the chains were responsible for depressing farm prices. No important agricultural group failed either to appear in person in opposition to the bill or to file formal resolutions condemning it.

Typical of the testimony was that of M. J. Duer, Exmore, Va., a grower and shipper, who shipped about 4,000 cars a year of potatoes, cabbage, onions, strawberries and beans, for his own account and that of 1,200 other growers. He declared:[10]

"We sell about 50 per cent of our output to the corporate food chains. We sell practically all of our produce on an f.o.b. shipping point basis. The food chains buy almost entirely on that basis. I can safely say that our sales to the food chains net at least as much to us—and possibly a little more—than do sales to other classes of buyers, especially in declining markets.

"The reason for this is that the food-chain buyer is in the market day-in and day-out in the crop season. They do not speculate, so that if the market is declining their daily pur-

[10] *Ibid.*, pp. 1374, 1375.

chases have a considerable stabilizing effect, whereas other classes of buyers are inclined to speculate, and in the case of a declining market they may wait a few days, which, of course, results in a further drop. The charge has been made that the chain stores use farm produce as loss-leader items, with a depressing effect on prices. In our experience we know of no instance where this is so.

"The production of fruits and vegetables on the eastern shore has become a real volume business, progressing far beyond the stage of the small farmer taking a load of produce to market and selling it for what he can get. In order to properly market this volume, we must have distribution organized on a volume basis also. This is the only way we can keep our selling overhead down and be sure of selling the large quantities that we raise and which must be distributed over a very wide area. I may say right here that one of the reasons why we are so anxious to protect our chain-store distribution is that we have no credit worries with these buyers —we get our money promptly and we do not have to worry about getting it. Furthermore one of the worst abuses in the produce business has been the rejection of merchandise on arrival—often for no better reason than that the market was declining. We have never had such experience with our chain-store buyers. We always feel that a sale to a chain-store buyer is a final one and that, regardless of the trend or the market, it will stick. . . .

"It is my opinion that chain stores have a very definite place in our economic system—particularly in the distribution of fruits and vegetables to the consumers of this country —and can continue to be of great service in reducing the spread between the producer price and the consumer price."

Need one go any further than that for an explanation of the cordial relations which exist today between the chains and the farmer compared with the less favorable situation which prevailed 30 years ago?

The fact is that their present-day relations rest upon a solid foundation of interdependence and mutual understanding. Both in their everyday operations and the special campaigns they are geared to stage, when occasion calls for them, the chains offer agriculture a system of organized distribution which provides a practical solution to the farmer's main problem—how to increase the farmer's share of the consumer's dollar without reducing its purchasing power. So long as the chains retain their interest in cutting distribution costs, they may expect to retain the complete approval and cooperation of the farm interests.

CHAPTER XV

THE CHAINS AS EMPLOYERS

Some 2,500,000 full and part time employes were required to operate the 167,000 stores the chains had in 1954, including in that category all firms with two or more stores.[1] That includes those employed in the headquarters and district offices of the chains, in their warehouses and in the field as well as those who work in the stores themselves.

What kind of jobs do the chains offer?

They range in responsibility and compensation all the way from that of the beginner behind the variety-store counter or the youngster learning the grocery business in the super-market to that of the top man of the company—the president of the chain. Between these two extremes are many kinds of jobs involving manual or clerical work in the lower levels and varying degrees of merchandising and administrative experience in the higher levels.

Most of the jobs the chains provide are not materially different in character from those offered by retailing in general. Basically, retailing involves the same principles of buying and selling, display and promotion, store layout, personnel training and management, financing and public relations whether the operation be conducted under one roof or many separate roofs.

But the chains have one kind of job which is seldom found in single-store operation but which is inherent in chain-store operation—that of store manager. With 105,000 stores, the chain-store field requires 105,000 store managers, and two or three times as many assistant store managers and trainees on

[1] Retail Census, 1954.

their way up. Store managers are needed, of course, even by the smallest chains. But when the number of stores gets to the point where proper supervision calls for field men to devote all their time to that task, another kind of job, that of supervisor, found only in the chain-store field, comes into the picture. These field supervisors may be responsible for a small group of stores or a large group, depending upon the kind of stores involved and the distance between them. They are recruited generally from the ranks of the managers themselves, the promotion meaning more pay and a chance to share in the profits of the stores they supervise through various forms of bonus arrangement based on improved operating results.

Before the chains came into the retail picture, the field consisted entirely of so many separately owned single stores. Some of them were large, but the great majority were small. Retailing as a career offered only one major incentive under such circumstances—the possibility of one day having a store of your own.

To be the owner of even a small store in those days was a considerable incentive to the young man who was really serious about sticking to retailing as a livelihood. For one thing, it would mean a measure of security—an escape from the employe's ever-present danger of losing his job. The worst thing about any job was that you could lose it through no fault of your own, as, for instance, if your boss failed. The employe had reason to worry about the hazards of retailing as well as the proprietor.

Then, of course, if you had a store of your own and it proved successful, what was to stop you from enlarging it or moving it to a bigger and better location? To become the biggest merchant in town was certainly a legitimate objective for the ambitious retail clerk to shoot at even though relatively few could hope to achieve it.

One big obstacle stood between the great majority of retail clerks and the desire to have stores of their own. That was lack of capital. It took money, of course, to open, equip and stock a store. The number of retail employes who could save enough out of their meager earnings to go into business for themselves was relatively small. Even those who were thrifty enough to accumulate a nest-egg were more apt to keep it for a rainy day than to risk it in a venture which might fail, especially as such a step involved giving up a paying job in the bargain.

The same considerations undoubtedly deterred many from taking the leap even if they could borrow the needed capital. Why give up a job to go into business on borrowed capital when, in the event of failure, you would be left with no business and no job and an indebtedness you would have to repay some day by the sweat of your brow?

These were and are natural reactions. Little wonder, then, that most new stores were opened not by men with actual retailing experience, most of whom lacked the capital or the courage to risk it in such ventures, but by individuals who had the capital but lacked the experience and know-how necessary to make such ventures successful.

But with the coming of the chains, an entirely new avenue to a successful career in retailing was opened. As every chain store must have a manager, here was a chance for any young man who wanted to get somewhere in retailing to secure the necessary training and eventually to have a store of his own, in effect, without investing or risking a single cent of his own money in the venture.

True enough, managing a store owned by somebody else is not the same as owning it yourself. But to assume that the difference favors ownership is to overlook many of the factors involved. Probably the most important of them are security, compensation, responsibility and opportunity. Consider each of them in turn.

1. *Security.* Although a chain-store manager is an employe and *can* lose his job, the risk of that is relatively slight as long as he applies his experience and ability in the company's in-

terest. The company has a substantial investment in each of its managers. The longer they remain with the chain, generally speaking, the more valuable they become. They provide the manpower from which the company must draw when positions of greater responsibility have to be filled. At any rate, a chain-store manager is not apt to lose his job through failure of the company. Although some chains have failed, such disasters have been extremely rare. In most cases, the operation of a number of stores provides a degree of stability which makes for continued successful operation. On the other hand, the high mortality rate which has always prevailed among single-store retailers reflects a degree of insecurity which may not be ignored. Although the turnover among chain-store employes generally may be as high as it is in other types of retailing, and for the same reasons, that applies, in the chain-store field, only to the rank and file of selling and non-selling help. Once a man reaches the level of store manager, he has a lifetime job, generally speaking, if he does his part. That gives him a measure of security which few of those who engage in retailing on their own can fairly claim.

2. *Compensation.* A store manager's salary varies, of course, with the kind of store he manages, its size, its sales and its operating results and the caliber and ability of the manager himself. In most cases his compensation is at least equal to what the owner of a store, comparable in size and sales, would draw as salary. In addition, the owner would, of course, expect a return on his invested capital. What kind of return he would get would depend upon how successful his store was. To the extent that his income is augmented by the store's profits, he might seem to be in a better financial position than a store manager whose main source of income is his basic salary. But the comparison is hardly a fair one for it overlooks two important facts. In the first place, most store managers receive, in addition to their basic salary, a bonus based on the store's profit. In the second place, a store man-

ager's savings earn a return too. If instead of putting them into a store of his own, as the independent retailer did, he invested them in stocks and bonds or other securities, the income he derives from such sources must similarly be taken into the equation before comparing his financial status with that of a store owner.

In addition to his salary and bonus, the store manager usually enjoys such benefits as group insurance, a pension or retirement plan, and various other company-supplied privileges which the owner of a similar store has to pay out of his own pocket.

3. *Responsibility.* The store manager is responsible for the success of his store, with all which that involves. Nevertheless, he is relieved of many of the major problems which fall upon a store owner. When he becomes a store manager he falls heir to a ready-made store owned by an established company with a set of operating policies based on extensive experience and know-how. Behind him he has a buying organization which provides him with the merchandise to stock his store, a sales-promotion department to help him merchandise his store, and a central control system to help him keep his store on the beam. The individual store owner, on the other hand, must attend to all these things himself in addition to the responsibilities which he and the store manager share in common. Even with their limited responsibilities, store managers suffer plenty of headaches, but the worries of a store owner who must bear the full brunt of all the problems involved in successful retailing must be infinitely greater.

So far as actual working conditions are concerned, a store manager's responsibility for his store calls for a high degree of diligence and vigilance. Until he has developed assistants to the point where he can trust them to carry on in his absence, the store manager must stick pretty close to his store from opening to closing. But all that is true of the store owner too if he wants to run a successful store. True enough, the store owner has to answer to nobody but himself if, through his own indifference or neglect, his store shows a loss instead of a profit, whereas similar conduct on the part of the store manager would mean the loss of his job. But if the comparison between managership and ownership be confined to those managers and owners who are equally interested in being successful, little difference will be found between them so far as hard work is concerned.

4. *Opportunity.* The store manager does not have to remain a manager all his life. As has already been indicated, promotions to positions of higher responsibility in the field or at headquarters are always possibilities. The number of store managers who, having started at the bottom, have climbed all the rungs of the ladder to become top executives and even presidents of their companies is literally legion. Such companies as the A&P, and Woolworth, and Penney, to name only three of the biggest chains in their respective fields, are manned almost exclusively, so far as the thousands of key positions are concerned, by men who were picked from the ranks of store managers for promotion up the line. And that is true of practically *all* the other national and regional chains in all fields, with only the smaller and younger companies still being directed by their founders and owners.

The need for trained manpower of executive caliber is regarded by the chains in all fields as one of their greatest problems. In line with the universal policy of promoting from within the organization, the top executives of tomorrow will inevitably be drawn mainly from the ranks of today's storemanagers and their assistants.

To provide a means for such men to qualify for the bigger jobs they may one day have a chance to fill, the National Association of Food Chains envisioned in 1951 an educational program at college level that would do for distribution what the laws schools and the medical schools do for the legal and medical professions.

The idea was implemented by the establishment of a four-year curriculum in food distribution set up at Michigan State University. In the seven years of its operation, it proved so successful that in 1958 it was duplicated at Cornell University, and 1959 was to see a similar curriculum set up at the University of Southern California. Thanks to the generous cooperation of suppliers and others, hundreds of scholarships have been made available for deserving applicants from any branch of the food industry. Thus these college courses, and others which are expected to be set up eventually, will provide the additional training which storemanagers and other employes may require to fit them for the bigger jobs which the chains will constantly be required to fill.

The outlook for the store owner, on the other hand, presents no such equivalent opportunities as a general rule. No matter how good a merchant is, as long as he confines himself to a single store his opportunities for any great measure of success are necessarily limited. He can, of course, enlarge his store or move it to a better location, or even become a chain-store operator himself, but the fact is that the great majority of independent retailers do none of these things. Whatever opportunities the independent merchant may find in that direction are open equally to the store manager. For, if after a successful experience as a store manager, a chain-store man decides to put his accumulated capital into a store of his own, nothing need stop him. Because of his training and experience as a store manager under expert direction, he will be far better equipped, in most cases, to engage in business on his own account than the average entrant into retailing who lacks such experience.

To become a really successful merchant offers certain additional satisfactions in the shape of local prestige and community leadership. The percentage of independent retailers who are successful enough to achieve such distinction, however, is exceedingly small. On the other hand, as has been shown in a preceding chapter, such satisfactions are realized by a large percentage of store managers. The fact that they do

not own the successful stores they manage in no way dis-
qualifies them for important positions of leadership in the
community. On the contrary, the very fact that big and successful companies have selected them for the responsibilities
of store management is proof in itself that they have what it
takes to carry their share of community responsibilities as
well.

The unique vocational opportunities in retailing offered by
the chain-store system as compared with those offered outside of the chain-store field were aptly described by the late
Hubert T. Parson, when he was president of the F. W. Woolworth Company:[2]

"What is there about retailing that makes ownership such
an important feature? One does not have to own a railroad
in order to work out a successful career in the railroad field.
You don't have to own a bank in order to achieve success in
the financial field. By far the greater number of successful
men in every line of industry and commerce are but 'employes' of the companies with which they are connected, no
matter how exalted may be the positions they occupy.

"The idea that it is necessary to own a store in order to
achieve success in the retail field has absolutely nothing to
support it. Compared with the uncertainty which confronts
the average storekeeper, the many risks he runs and the obvious limitations of his vocation, the opportunity offered by a
strong corporate retail enterprise, whether it be in the chain-
store field, the department-store field, the mail-order field, or
any other branch of business would seem to be far superior.

"Of course, if a man lacks ability or character or persever-
ance or ambition or any of the other basic qualities that are
essential to success, he can't expect to go very far, no matter
what line of endeavor he follows. Certainly he could hope
for little in the chain-store field, while if he accumulates
sufficient capital to open a store of his own it would be only
a question of time before his own shortcomings would put
him out of the picture—another failure added to the long
list which exacts such a heavy toll from the public.

"But if a man has in him the stuff that success is made of,

[2] *Chain Store Age*, January, 1928.

I can think of no form of retailing that offers better prospects than the chain-store field."

How true that is is indicated, as has already been pointed out, by the fact that virtually all the men occupying key executive positions in the chain-store field today, started at or near the bottom. That statement could be readily documented, if space permitted, by listing the scores of thousands of chain-store executives by name and company and showing how they rose to their present high positions of responsibility step by step on the basis of merit alone. They did not have to own a store either by purchase or inheritance, or be related to the owner, nor did they have to invest a single dollar in the stock of the companies for whom they worked. And long as such a list would be, it would not include the names of thousands of other chain-store men who had the same kind of experience but who have either passed on or retired from active work.

Lansing P. Shield, president of the Grand Union Company, recently had occasion to explode the fallacy that being an "employe" of a big retailing company is a disadvantage as compared with having a store of your own. Mr. Shield had started as a young man, when he came out of World War I, with the A&P. Working his way up to an executive position in the accounting and auditing department of that chain, he resigned to take a similar position with Grand Union, a much smaller chain but one which, he figured, offered him a greater opportunity.

He was right. He rose step by step until he became general manager of the chain, and, in 1946, was made its president. The company operated 381 supermarkets as of January, 1958 and its sales in 1957 totalled $427,871,000.

On October 4, 1949, Mr. Shield appeared on the television program which was mentioned earlier.[3] It involved a "trial" of the issue: Are national retail chain stores a benefit or a

[3] See p. 254.

detriment to our country? Mr. Shield appeared, naturally, as a "witness" for the chains. Congressman Patman appeared as "counsel" against the chains.

"Which would you rather see," asked Mr. Patman, "a nation of clerks or a nation of independent owners and independent business men?"

To which Mr. Shield replied:

"The chain store provides opportunities at every level. There are hundreds of executive positions even in a company of our size, and there's a great opportunity there for any boy who wants to come in and try to do a job."

And when Mr. Patman interjected: "To work for somebody else," Mr. Shield answered: "I work for somebody else, Mr. Congressman, and I don't mind it a bit."

Of course, Mr. Patman's implication that the chain-store system tended to make of us a nation of "clerks" whereas the old wholesaler-retailer system would make us "a nation of independent owners" was as fallacious as it could be. It was a relic of the days when the so-called "chain-store question" was a live issue and was being debated by colleges and high-school teams from one end of the country to the other. It was one of the stock arguments invariably raised by the anti-chain-store side.

The main trouble with the contention was that it applied the term "clerks" to *all* chain-store employes—to the executives and the store managers as well as to the real clerks—which was obviously false, and implied that *all* the employes of other types of retailing were "independent owners," which was equally false. True enough, as was shown earlier, a large percentage of independent stores are too small to employ even a single clerk, but that is not true of the bigger and more successful ones which collectively employ some 7,000,-000 men and women, the great majority of whom are "clerks" and none of whom could be described as "independent owners." So long as we have any large number of the kind of stores the public wants, whether they are independently owned or chain owned, an army of "clerks" will be needed to operate them, but the total number of "clerks" would be no greater than it now is even if all retail stores were owned by chains, which is, of course, out of the question.

The only plausible basis for the "nation of clerks" argument lies in the fact that 1,000 stores, separately owned, give us 1,000 "independent owners," whereas 1,000 stores owned by a chain gives us only one owner. But to imply that the chain of 1,000 stores would be run exclusively by "clerks" is to ignore the significant function performed by the 1,000 store managers, not to say anything of the hundreds of higher-ranking executives which such a chain would also require for its successful operation.

The fact is, as this chapter has attempted to bring out, that the chain-store manager is at least as successful, from his own standpoint, and at least as useful, from a social and economic standpoint, as the average independent retailer. Indeed, if it were possible to make an accurate comparison of store managers as a class with store owners as a class on the basis of their relative ability as merchants and their social status as individuals, the difference should easily favor the store managers.

That can be said with some confidence because the ranks of independent retailers necessarily include many who fail to measure up to even minimum requirements. That results from the fact that anyone can become a retailer. You don't have to ask anybody's permission to open a store.

Would-be storekeepers do not have to demonstrate their ability to operate successfully. They do not have to satisfy anyone of their character and integrity—except perhaps the landlord and the wholesaler, neither of whom is always as critical as he ought to be even for his own protection. The doors are wide open to everyone—to the man with individuality and to the man without it, to the man of initiative and to the man who lacks it, to the man who seeks responsibility and to the man who would prefer to escape it, to the strong and self-reliant and to the weak and dependent, and ample evidence attests that retailing attracts all kinds with the preponderance, if the truth be told, on the side of the deficient.

But store managers do not come into being so easily. Store managers are *selected* by others; they cannot appoint themselves. Because a chain must intrust not only its property in the shape of the store and its equipment, merchandise and cash, but also the good-will of the enterprise to its store managers, it must select them deliberately and carefully. It may be taken for granted, therefore, that the mere fact that a man has been selected to manage a chain store is evidence that, in the opinion of those who are in the best position to know and whose interests require them to decide correctly, he is qualified in every respect for the job assigned to him.

Thus, if one were required to recruit hastily a group of 100 men possessing the qualities that make for good merchants and good citizens, he could not accomplish the task in any quicker way than by selecting the first 100 chain-store managers he could lay his hands on. Would anyone undertake to assemble as worthy a group out of the first 100 store *owners* he could lay his hands on?

The possibility that a minor employe in a large organization may be lost sight of—that his merit may go unrecognized and others, less deserving, may pass him on the way up the ladder—is often cited in criticism of such jobs. Whatever may be the case so far as big companies in other fields are concerned, the criticism has little basis in the chain-store field. There the big companies make a very real effort to see that no man who is doing a good job is overlooked, not only in fairness to the man himself but in the companies' own interest.

Such a policy follows from the almost universal rule among the chains of promotion from within. To fill vacancies in the higher ranks as they occur, adequate personnel records are an essential feature in chain-store administration.

Some years ago, Raymond H. Fogler, then the personnel director of the W. T. Grant Co., described in detail in *Chain*

Store Age[4] the elaborate system that chain had developed to keep an accurate and up-to-date record of the progress each of its men was making.

"To every ambitious man in any chain store," he said, "the question most frequently uppermost in his mind is undoubtedly 'Does the home office know about me and my work?'

"The answer should always be 'Yes,' and in every case it could be substantiated by records, which are accurate, complete and up-to-date. Such records are absolutely essential if a company in which the personnel is scattered, as in chain-store organizations, is to be able to determine with a fair degree of accuracy those men who, on the basis of demonstrated qualifications, are most deserving of promotion and those best fitted for special work."

And then he went on to describe the various forms his company was using and how the information they provided was put to effective use. How vital to the company's progress they were to prove in the years of extremely rapid expansion which followed, not even Mr. Fogler, himself, could have foreseen.

But the most interesting thing about that article, which appeared in August, 1925, was that its author's own case history provides one of the outstanding examples of the opportunities the chain-store field offers.

Graduating from the University of Maine in 1915 with a B.S. degree, he had taken a post-graduate course at Princeton. There he got his M.S. two years later. Returning to the University of Maine in an administrative capacity, he decided, in 1919, to enter the business field. That was when he joined the W. T. Grant Co., which was then a chain of 25 stores.

Before very long he was put in charge of the personnel department. There he developed the system described in the article referred to. By 1925 the company had 70 stores but it was expanding at such a rapid rate that only four years later its stores numbered 280! As it was Mr. Fogler's responsibility, as personnel director, to find competent men in the organiza-

[4] August, 1925.

tion for the many new jobs thus created, his "system" was certainly put to a most severe test.

In 1929, he was transferred to another extremely active department—real estate and construction. How active it was is indicated by the company's further expansion from 280 stores in 1929 to 446 in 1932.

Then something most unusual happened. Another company, Montgomery Ward & Co., a Johnny-come-lately in the chain-store field, was in dire trouble. Having confined itself strictly to the mail-order business, in which field it was the second-largest company, until 1926, that year it had decided to operate retail stores as well. Having reached that decision, it had moved so fast that by the end of 1927 it had 36 stores in operation. The next year it opened 208 additional stores. And, in 1929, it added 288 more. By 1931, this chain which had sprung from nothing in 1926, had 610 stores in operation and that year it had shown a deficit of $8,700,000. Some 450 of its stores were "in the red." [5]

Obviously something drastic had to be done. Sewell L. Avery, chairman of the successful U.S. Gypsum Co., was invited to take over. He accepted the assignment, tough as it looked at the time. His skillful analysis revealed quickly what was wrong; the mail-order house had done splendidly in its time in its own field, but when it had plunged headlong into the chain-store business without either the know-how or the manpower to direct it, trouble was inevitable.

One of the first steps to be taken was to find the best chain-store man available to head up Ward's retail stores. The choice finally fell upon Mr. Fogler and, though he was not exactly available, he was just the kind of man Mr. Avery was looking for. Naturally Mr. Fogler was reluctant to leave the company which had given him the opportunity to learn all he knew about chain-store operation. But the offer was so flattering and so attractive, that Mr. Grant decided the problem for him. He took the job.

[5] The Stores and the Catalogue, *Fortune,* January, 1935.

THE CHAINS AS EMPLOYERS

At first his responsibility was confined entirely to the retail stores but before very long he was made vice president in charge of the entire operation. Then in November, 1938, after six years of hard work, during which the company had made a spectacular recovery, Mr. Fogler, then 46 years old, was made president of the company, with an annual salary of $103,350.

In 1939, Mr. Fogler's first full year as president, the company rang up sales of $475,000,000, a substantial increase over the $176,000,000 recorded in 1932, the year he had joined the company to direct the retail stores. Throughout the entire period, sales and profits had increased each year. Profits in 1939 amounted to $27,000,000 compared with a *deficit* of $5,700,000 in 1932. That the increase in sales did not reflect merely the general recovery from the depression is indicated by the fact that during the same period Sears, Roebuck and Co.'s sales increased from $275,000,000 to $617,000,000, a gain of only 124 per cent compared with Ward's gain of 150 per cent.

Nevertheless, despite the outstanding contribution Mr. Fogler had made to Montgomery Ward & Co.'s rehabilitation and improved operating picture, in April, 1940, he decided to resign! Apparently he could no longer see eye to eye with Mr. Avery, the chairman of the board, and rather than follow the course which Mr. Avery favored but which he felt was unsound, he gave up his job.

But that is not the end of Mr. Fogler's remarkable success story. Within a week after the announcement of his resigna tion as president of Montgomery Ward & Co., another announcement made the headlines: he had been appointed president of another important chain. That chain was the W. T. Grant Co., the company which had given him his first job 21 years earlier when, as a young man of 27, he had decided to enter the retail field.

Thus, in the relatively short period of 21 years, Mr. Fogler had the unique experience of attaining the topmost rung in *two* of the leading chains in the country. What more evidence is needed of the broad opportunities which this field offers to those who measure up to them?

Of course, many men achieve great success in the chain-store field without duplicating Mr. Fogler's exceptional double-top. Each chain has only one president at a time, but it has many other key executives, all of whom occupy responsible and well-paid positions and are eligible for further promotion. But one need look no further than the army of successful store managers, without whom the chains could not operate, for proof of the main theme of this chapter—that you do not have to *own* a store in order to work out a successful career in retailing. The chains offer an ideal training ground for all who have retail ambitions—for those who may dream of having one day a store or chain of their own as well as for those who, like Mr. Shield, see the advantages of working "for somebody else."

CHAPTER XVI

THE CHAINS TODAY—
AND TOMORROW

WHERE THE CHAINS stand today as an element in our over-all distribution set-up is indicated by the Retail Census of 1954. Although that data is now four years old, such subsequent changes as may have occurred have been negligible.

As revealed in Table 15 (page 68, *supra*) total retail sales in 1954 amounted to approximately $170 billion, of which the chains (only those with four stores or over) accounted for 23.7%. In 1957, when total retail volume hit a new high of $200 billion, they accounted for 24.5%, according to the monthly estimates of sales of this group issued throughout the year by the Department of Commerce.

As has been pointed out in an earlier chapter, however, the over-all status of the chains tends to obscure their more significant status in specific fields. It obscures, for instance, the fact that the variety-store chains accounted for 79.6 per cent of total sales in that field in 1954, the department store chains for 65.6%, the shoe chains for 45.9%, the grocery-store chains for 43.3% and the tire and auto accessory chains for 36.2% in their respective fields.

A question which naturally arises in this connection is: In these fields in which the chains account for a substantial share of the total business, to what extent, if at all, do the biggest chains dominate the situation?

Turning first to the variey-store field in which the chains accounted for 79.6% of the total business in 1954, the biggest single company is the F. W. Woolworth Company, the pioneer in the field and its leader for the nearly 80 years of its existence. In 1954, the Woolworth company operated 2,021 stores and its sales totalled $721 million. How did Woolworth stack up against the rest of its field and against its less direct competitors in other fields?

As appears from the tabulation which follows, Woolworth operated 9.6 per cent of all variety stores and accounted for 23.5 per cent of the total variety store volume. The significant fact to note, however, is that Woolworth stores were in direct competition with those of nine other relatively big chains in the same field. With Woolworth, they constitute what is sometimes referred to as "the Big Ten." Collectively, the nine chains in question operated 3,045 stores, compared with Woolworth's 2,021. Their combined sales were more than twice as great as Woolworth's. The rest of the field comprised some 16,000 stores, both chain and independent, with combined sales of $821 million.

VARIETY STORE GROUP, STORES AND SALES, 1954

(Based on 1954 Census and Company reports)

GROUP	STORES	%	SALES (MILLIONS)	%
ALL VARIETY STORES	20,917	100.0	$3,067.0	100.0
Woolworth Co.	2,021	9.6	721.3	23.5
9 next largest chains	3,045	14.6	1,524.5	49.7
All other chains*	2,557	12.2	198.2	6.5
Independents, etc.	13,294	63.6	623.0	20.3

* With four or more stores.

In addition to this direct competition, however, Woolworth must meet the competition offered by department stores and the dry goods and general-merchandise stores, of which the 1954 Census reported 55,000, with combined sales of approximately $15 billion. Equally significant in character is the competition in particular lines of merchandise offered by drug stores, apparel stores and grocery stores—competition which is becoming more serious every day as stores in these fields stock more and more of the items which play an important role in variety-store merchandising.

In the light of these facts, the top company in the variety-store field, big and successful as it is, would seem to occupy no dominating position as far as its competitors are concerned. On the contrary, it must keep constantly on its toes to hold its own against numerous and aggressive competitors, both chain and independent, who are big enough and strong enough to give a good account of themselves. This is especially true of such stores as are affiliated with the large voluntary chain sponsored by Butler Brothers, under the name of Ben Franklin Stores, and the large group serviced by the Consolidated Merchants Syndicate.

And what has been said of the biggest company in the field applies, of course, with even greater force to the other members of the "Big Ten" who are also big and successful as individual companies go, but who are likewise in no position to throw their weight around with impunity.

In the grocery field, the chains in 1954 accounted for 38.9 per cent of the sales of the entire food group, which includes specialized food stores as well as grocery stores. In this field we have not only the biggest chain but the biggest retail organization of any kind in the shape of A&P. A&P's sales for the year ending February 22, 1958 totalled $4,769 million, but in the year 1954, the year of the latest Census, they were $3,989 million. What did that mean with reference to the food field as a whole?

The entire food group consisted of 384,616 stores, with sales of approximately $40 billion in 1954. The chains (only those with 4 or more stores) had 25,212, or 6.5 per cent of the stores, and they accounted for some $15 billion, or 38.9 per cent of the sales.

How the four biggest chains compared with each other, with the rest of the chain store group and with the food field as a whole is shown in the tabulation which follows.

FOOD GROUP STORES AND SALES, 1954

(Based on 1954 Census and Company reports)

GROUP	STORES	%	SALES (MILLIONS)	%
ALL FOOD STORES	384,616	100	$39,762	100
A&P	4,400	1.1	3,989	10.00
Safeway	1,859	.5	1,813	4.5
Kroger	1,678	.4	1,109	2.8
American	1,076	.3	625	1.6
Other chains*	16,199	4.2	7,942	20.
Independents &c.	359,404	93.5	24,284	61.1

* With four or more stores.

Looking at the foregoing table statistically, A&P would hardly seem to be the economic menace its critics would like to prove it to be. Operating but one per cent of the stores and enjoying only 10% of total retail food sales, it would seem, on the contrary, to be outnumbered and outweighed by its competitors collectively.

True enough, the fact that the big company enjoys only 10 per cent of the total food trade does not mean that it does not enjoy more than 10% in some areas. It certainly does. Indeed, in some areas it may enjoy as much as 20 per cent of the available trade. In a relatively few cases, the percentage may be even greater. That is true likewise of some of the other chains, small as well as large, which may be particularly strong in their home towns or in other communities where they have been fortunate enough to develop a proportionately large following.

But to conclude that such a situation is necessarily bad or against the public interest is to ignore entirely the basic realities of retail trade—to assume that somehow a retailer can compel people to trade with him instead of having to win, and to retain, their trade by superior service.

The fact is, of course, that neither A&P nor any other retailer *controls* a single dollar's worth of business anywhere. Whatever share of the available business A&P, or any other retailer, enjoys, it holds only during good behavior. The foregoing table shows only how competitive the grocery business is quantitatively. It does not show, what is even more significant, the quality of the competition which every chain, from A&P down, has to meet. Not only do the bigger chains have to meet the competition of chains of their own caliber in almost every community in which they operate, but they find just as great a challenge in the competition of successful independents and small local chains.

With competition as extensive in the food field as it is, no company is big enough to exploit the public by raising prices or in any other way. Big business may be sufficiently entrenched in some lines of production to disregard the public interest by raising prices unduly, but that has never been true of big business in distribution.

Two other criticisms levelled at big business, however, are just as applicable to distribution as they are to production. One of them relates to the ability of big companies to use their resources to eliminate competition, either by acquisition or destruction. The other relates to the buying advantages which accrue to them by reason of their large-scale purchases.

So far as the elimination of competition by acquisition is concerned, a big company is obviously in a better financial position to buy out a competitor than a small company would be. Many of the leading companies in various lines of industry have attained at least part of their present size and power by mergers and acquisitions. In the chain-store field, too, some of the bigger companies have followed the same course to a greater or lesser degree. In the late '20's, when chain-store expansion was at its peak, several of the companies which now head the list in their respective fields accelerated their growth via the merger process. As it happens, that was not true of the biggest chain of all. A&P attained its major growth by the simple process of opening additional stores of its own, as has been related in an earlier chapter. Mergers and acquisitions likewise played little or no part in the development of other big chains.

In any event, the ability of big companies to become even

bigger in this way no longer presents much of a problem from the standpoint of the public interest. For the Federal Trade Commission is now equipped with ample power to nullify any merger or acquisition which tends to restrain competition unduly.[1]

That a big company can use its resources to drive weaker companies out of business as well as to buy them out is, of course, of greater concern to small business. Undoubtedly it has been done in many lines of industry. Drastic price-cutting and other devices have been employed for the express purpose of eliminating competitors. In retailing, however, no such destructive policy could achieve more than temporary success owing to the depth of the competitive set-up. Profitless selling cannot be maintained forever even by the biggest companies, and to suffer operating losses for the purpose of eliminating one competitor with the certainty that he would be replaced by another, perhaps by a stronger one, would not make much sense.

Conceding that the big chains have sufficient resources to make life miserable if not unendurable for their weaker competitors by drastic price-cutting, the futility of such tactics, if nothing else, argues against such a policy. Furthermore, in addition to the Federal anti-trust acts which prohibit all conduct in restraint of trade, many States have what are known as "Unfair Trade" statutes aimed specifically against predatory price-cutting. These acts are not to be confused with the Fair Trade laws which many States have enacted to legalize price maintenance—to permit the manufacturers of branded products to establish a minimum resale price binding on all retailers.

Nevertheless, one of the many charges made against A&P in a criminal anti-trust case some years ago was that it had deliberately operated many of its stores "in the red" for the purpose of driving competitors out of business.

[1] See p. 159, *supra*.

The case[2] was tried in Danville, Ill. in 1945 before U.S. District Court Judge Walter C. Lindley without a jury.[3] The evidence on the issue in question did indeed establish that several of A&P's Divisions had operated "in the red" at various times, sometimes for protracted periods. But the real question, of course, was whether they were operated "in the red" for the sinister purpose of putting competitors out of business, as the Government insisted, or whether, as the company undertook to prove, the losses occurred despite the measures A&P took to avert them.

A&P's top executives testified categorically that *no* store was ever operated at a loss for the purpose alleged or indeed for any purpose other than the legitimate one of attempting to develop additional *volume* through lower *prices* so that it would not have to operate "in the red" any longer.

My own opinion is that the company's contention was not refuted by the Government. How Judge Lindley felt about it is not revealed in his decision, since he found the defendants guilty on other grounds—the practices of the Atlantic Commission Co., one of A&P's important subsidiaries.

Even if the company's "manipulation of gross profit rates" or any of the other actions of which the Government complained "might not amount to a violation of the law standing alone," he declared, they nevertheless amounted to undue restraint of trade when coupled with the unlawful activities of the Atlantic Commission Co.

An appeal from Judge Lindley's decision resulted in an affirmance by the Circuit Court of Appeals. On the basis of that decision, the Government promptly filed a civil suit

[2] See United States v. N.Y. Great Atlantic & Pacific Tea Co., 173 F. 2d 79 (1949), affirming 67 F. Supp. 626 (1946). For comment on these decisions, see "The A&P Case: A Study in Applied Economic Theory," by M. A. Adelman, *The Quarterly Journal of Economics*, Harvard University, May, 1949; "The Great A&P Muddle," by the same author, *Fortune*, December, 1949; and "What the A&P Case Is All About," by the present author, Journal of Retailing, New York University, Spring, 1950.

[3] Later promoted to the U.S. Circuit Court of Appeals. He died in 1957.

against A&P, reiterating all the charges it had made in the criminal proceeding, and asking that the company be split into seven separate retail units and five manufacturing units, each of them separately owned and managed, without any interlocking ownership or operating connection.

That suit never came to trial, a consent decree ending it on January 19, 1954.[4] The only structural change in the company's organization required by the decree was the dissolution of the Atlantic Commission Company. The four manufacturing subsidiaries and the vast retail set-up remained intact.

But the decree's most interesting provision for our present purpose was one relating to the Company's power to put competitors out of business by operating particular stores at a loss to achieve that purpose.

The provision enjoins A&P from "assigning a gross profit rate for any Division, knowing that such an assigned gross profit will result in the operation of any such Division at a loss, for the purpose of or with the intent of destroying or eliminating competition. . . . The purpose or intent prohibited in this section shall not be presumed merely by reason of the operation of a Division at a loss."

That provision, it would seem, gives A&P the only freedom it had ever claimed in this connection—the right to set its prices at any level it desired (in keeping with State or local laws) whether such prices resulted in an operating loss or not, and irrespective of the impact of such prices on competition, provided only that its purpose was not to destroy competition.

My own comment on this consent-decree at the time seems even more appropriate five years later. "With A&P approaching its 100th birthday and doing a superlative job in serving the public—we are mighty glad that it may now expect to celebrate its centenary all in one piece."[5]

Unquestionably a big company in any field *can* use its re-

[4] Trade Cases, 1954, Commerce Clearing House, Par. 67, 658.
[5] Chain Store Age, Grocery Edition, February, 1954, page 67.

sources in a variety of undesirable ways, including putting weaker competitors out of business, but, for the reasons already given, retailing provides a poor field in which to engage in such an undertaking.

What about the tremendous purchasing power commanded by big business in general and the big chains in particular? Does that involve competitive advantages which are not in the public interest?

Discounts based on quantities purchased have been a feature of American business from time immemorial. They have been in almost universal use. The greater the purchase the better the discount and, in effect, the lower the price. The principle has been applied at every level—from the purchaser of raw materials down to the consumer, who may not recognize a 2-for-25-cent price as a quantity discount but enjoys it just the same. The quantity discount, like the quality of mercy, is "twice blessed: it blesseth him that gives and him that takes." It tends to promote trade—the foundation of our economy—and for that reason has always been legal. It has never been seriously questioned even by those whose purchases may not be big enough to earn the larger discounts available. What *is* questioned are the extra price concessions big buyers may receive from suppliers who are naturally tempted to favor their best customers or may be afraid not to do so.

That such extra price concessions to big buyers of all kinds were prevalent before the passage of the Robinson-Patman Act in 1936 is not to be denied. All buyers, small as well as big, try to buy as cheaply as possible and if loopholes in the laws against price discrimination permitted manufacturers and other suppliers to favor their bigger customers, such concessions were inevitable.

But, as has been pointed out in an earlier chapter, the Robinson-Patman Act plugged the loopholes in the Clayton Act. No longer was it legal for a manufacturer to shape his price structure to favor the bigger buyers unduly. Discounts based on quantity were still permitted, but only to the extent that they reflected actual cost savings to the manufacturer or other supplier. Price concessions masquerading as advertising allowances were prohibited, and even legitimate advertising allowances and special services or facilities which manufacturers had previously offered to favored customers were required to be offered to all customers on "proportionately equal terms."

How did these required changes in marketing practices affect the chains? Because of their relatively large buying power and the desirability of their business in other respects, the chains had undoubtedly benefited by the more flexible system which had previously prevailed. Indeed, according to some of their critics, their phenomenal growth and success could be attributed largely to the special discounts and allowances which were available prior to the Robinson-Patman Act.

The fact is, however, that the chains were never dependent upon such special allowances. That is clearly indicated by what has happened since they were outlawed. After all, the Robinson-Patman Act has now been in effect for more than 22 years, and yet the chains have maintained their competitive position and operated profitably throughout that entire period without the benefit of the banned allowances which are supposed to have meant so much to them.

The truth of the matter is that these allowances which ended with the Robinson-Patman Act were never important enough to signify competitively. The real advantages which the chains enjoyed and which alone accounted for their growth and success were inherent in their system and were not affected by the Act in question. These advantages have been discussed in detail in earlier chapters, but fundamentally they all stem from the operation of more than a single store.

On that basic principle the chain-store system grew to its present size and importance and produced thousands of successful companies. Among them today are more than 50 with sales in excess of $100 million a year, with six of them already in the billion-dollar a year category[6] and others headed in that direction.

That companies of this magnitude belong in the category of "big business"—whatever that term may connote to those who use it—can hardly be doubted. But whatever the term may connote to others, in the author's view, when a retail company, whether chain or independent, achieves "big business" status it can mean only one thing—outstanding merit.

For when the public chooses to spend millions of dollars a year in the stores of a single company in the face of the keen competition provided by other stores and other claimants for the consumer dollar, the public is saying to that company in the most convincing way: "We like your stores, we like your wares, we like your service and we like your prices." Here is no case of a monopoly situation which the public must accept or go without. Here, on the contrary, is the result of the free exercise of the public's selection from a wide range of alternative choices.

What has been said here of the biggest companies in the chain-store field applies equally to all chains which are operating successfully, whether they have achieved "big business" stature or not. The mere fact that they are operating a group of retail stores successfully—that they are not only selling a lot of merchandise but are selling it *profitably*—is evidence that they are rendering a useful service under our economic system. In such a competitive field as retailing, every company, large or small, which operates profitably merits the plaudits of a nation in which profits and competition are the two vital elements of its economy.

No useful purpose would be served by listing all the chains whose success indicates that they have merited public favor, even if it were practicable to do so. A clear indication of the

[6] A&P, Sears-Roebuck, Montgomery Ward, Safeway, Kroger and J. C. Penney.

important part the chain-store system has come to play in our retail distribution set-up is to be seen, however, in a list of the 100 largest retail organizations in the country based upon their reported sales in 1957 compiled by the First National City Bank of N.Y. For of the 100 companies in the list, each of which had 1957 sales in excess of $40 millions, at least 80 are chains, and several of the others also own groups of retail stores even if they do not operate them along chain-store lines. Furthermore, of the $31.5 billions of sales done by these companies in 1957, $30 billions, or 95 per cent, are accounted for by the chains in the list.

The complete list is presented in Table 20. It should be noted that the list is confined to retail companies whose sales are "reported." For that reason, it fails to include some chains and some department stores with sales in excess of $40 millions in 1957—the minimum covered in the compilation—but whose figures are not made public.

If the foregoing observations are sound, the question raised earlier as to whether some of the chains may have grown too big for the common good would seem to be answered definitely in the negative.

The chains owe the favorable position they occupy today to many factors. Among the most important, however, are (1) the underlying merit of the system itself; (2) the caliber of the men who became chain-store operators; (3) their readiness to adjust their operations to changing conditions; and (4) the effectiveness of their trade associations.

As to the merits of the system itself, they have already been covered at length in earlier chapters. Suffice it to say here that if the economic history of the past 50 years has established anything, it is that the chain-store system provides a legitimate, effective type of low-cost distribution, which is one of the things most needed if our vast facilities for mass production are to be effectively employed for the common good.

That basic fact, long conceded by virtually all economists and marketing authorities, must undoubtedly be given the

TABLE 20   349

SALES OF 100 LEADING RETAIL FIRMS, 1957

CHAINS—FOOD (MILLIONS)

ACF—Wrigley Stores, Inc......$	326
Alpha Beta Food Markets.....	58
American Stores Co..........	837
Big Bear Stores Co............	66
H. C. Bohack Co..............	146
Colonial Stores, Inc..........	442
Cook Coffee Co..............	70
Daitch Crystal Dairies........	69
J. S. Dillon & Sons Stores Co...	52
First National Stores..........	521
Fisher Bros. Co..............	98
Food Fair Stores, Inc.........	545
Food Giant Markets..........	47
Food Mart, Inc...............	54
Grand Union Co..............	428
Great A. & P. Tea Co.........	4,769
Jewel Tea Co.................	414
Kroger Company.............	1,674
Loblaw, Inc..................	214
Lucky Stores.................	129
Market Basket...............	82
Marsh Foodliners, Inc.........	51
Mayfair Markets.............	101
National Tea Co..............	681
Penn Fruit Co................	151
Purity Stores, Ltd.............	95
Red Owl Stores..............	176
Safeway Stores..............	2,117
Shopping Bag Food Stores.....	87
Stop & Shop.................	123
Sunrise Supermarkets Corp.....	43
Thorofare Markets............	98
Thriftimart, Inc..............	135
J. Weingarten, Inc............	103
Winn-Dixie Stores, Inc.........	514

CHAINS—VARIETY STORES

W. T. Grant Co...............	406
H. L. Green Co...............	111
S. S. Kresge Co..............	377
S. H. Kress & Co.............	159
McCrory Stores Corp..........	112
McLellan Stores Co...........	61
G. C. Murphy Co.............	208
Neisner Bros.................	70
J. J. Newberry Co............	213
F. W. Woolworth Co..........	824

CHAINS—DRUG

Cunningham Drug Stores......	47
Katz Drug Co................	45
Peoples Drug Stores...........	67
Rexall Drug Co..............	168
Thrifty Drug Stores Co........	87
United Whelan Corp..........	53
Walgreen Co.................	235

CHAINS—SHOE (MILLIONS)

A. S. Beck Shoe Corp.........	61
Edison Bros. Stores...........	99
Melville Shoe Corp............	130
Shoe Corp. of America........	106

CHAINS—MISCELLANEOUS

Gamble-Skogmo, Inc..........	109
E. J. Korvette, Inc............	71
Western Auto Supply Co.......	217

DEPARTMENT STORES AND SPECIALTY SHOPS
(Chains and Independents)

Allied Stores Corp............	633
Associated Dry Goods Co......	237
L. S. Ayres & Co..............	47
Barker Bros. Corp.............	53
Bond Stores..................	89
Broadway-Hale Stores.........	160
Lane Bryant, Inc.............	72
Bullock's, Inc.................	136
Carson Pirie Scott & Co.......	97
City Stores Co................	264
Davidson Brothers............	76
Emporium Capwell Corp.......	95
Federated Department Stores..	636
Marshall Field Co.............	219
Gimbel Brothers..............	369
Goldblatt Brothers............	115
Grayson-Robinson Stores......	41
Halle Brothers Co.............	51
Hecht Company..............	105
Higbee Company.............	52
Joseph Horne Co..............	65
Interstate Dept. Stores........	67
S. Klein Dept. Stores..........	86
Lerner Stores Corp............	180
R. H. Macy & Co.............	448
May Dept. Stores Co..........	534
J. W. Mays, Inc..............	53
Meier & Frank Co.............	50
Mercantile Stores Co..........	154
J. C. Penney Co...............	1,312
Rich's, Inc...................	80
Rike-Kumler Co..............	49
Ed. Schuster & Co............	49
Scruggs-Vandervoort-Barney...	61
Stix, Baer & Fuller Co........	59
Wieboldt Stores..............	61
Woodward & Lothrop.........	63

MAIL ORDER

Alden's, Inc..................	98
Montgomery Ward & Co.......	1,074
National Bellas Hess..........	47
Sears, Roebuck & Co..........	3,608
Spiegel, Inc..................	128

major credit for the final triumph of the chains over those who used every available means to check their progress, if not to destroy them altogether.

A clear exposition of the vital role played by mass distribution in an economy of plenty is given by J. Frederic Dewhurst, Executive Director of the Twentieth Century Fund, and his associates in their revised edition of *America's Needs and Resources*, published in 1955.

Referring to the close interdependence in the American economy between producing goods and selling them, the authors declare that "the high degree of specialization in American industry, simplification of design, and the lavish use of automatic power-driven machinery in turning out low-cost standardized goods would be impossible without the means of assuring mass consumption in a mass market."

Noting that foreign observers who praise our industrial efficiency nevertheless condemn our "wasteful" selling and advertising methods, they observe that "it implies neither praise nor criticism of such methods to recognize that only by their use can the great advantages and economies of mass production be achieved. The distribution institutions and methods which make this possible—the mail order house, the chain store, the supermarket, instalment buying, market analysis, national advertising and, whether we like it or not, even the singing commercial—are just as much a part of American technology as are radioisotopes and fork-lift trucks."

"The true significance of technology in raising the American standard of living," the authors conclude, "is apparent only when production and distribution are viewed as a unified process. Then it is clear that technological progress has brought over the years and decades a steady lowering of the real costs of supplying the consumer with an ever wider range of useful goods and services."

The second factor to play a major role in chain store development was the caliber of the men who became involved

realized 30 years ago that they could go only so far acting individually. For their common protection and for the development of their system in the public interest they needed the additional strength and stimulation to be gained by mutual cooperation through trade associations.

How the first national association was organized by the chains in 1928 and functioned effectively until 1933, when the coming of the New Deal and NRA called for individual associations in each field, has already been related. If the chains have nothing else to thank the New Deal for they may at least be grateful for the trade associations which came into being as a result of it.

Four of the most influential have been the National Association of Food Chains, the Limited Price Variety Stores Association, whose name was changed in 1957 to Variety Stores Association the National Association of Chain Drug Stores and the Institute of Distribution.

Almost continuously since 1933 business has had to operate under Governmental controls and regulations imposed to help us fight successively the depression, World War II, postwar inflation, the cold war in Europe and the hot war in Korea. Under these conditions the chains, in common with most other business enterprises, were compelled to lean heavily on their own trade associations for guidance, information, official contacts, representation on industry committees cooperating with the Government, and as a medium for the exchange of ideas on current problems and operating policies. How indeed any chain could have operated within the law, with all its complexities, during these difficult years without the benefit of such information and help as these associations were equipped to furnish would be hard to conceive.

The chains were particularly fortunate in their choice of executives to direct the activities of their associations. Although the members themselves naturally had to make the final decisions on most of the important questions which arose, they were aided materially in arriving at them by the experience, ability and energy of their association directors.

John A. Logan, president of the National Association of Food Chains, has directed its activities since it was organized, March 7, 1934. It was under his leadership that the far-reaching farm-relief program, which has already been described, was initiated in 1936. Without attempting even to list the many other important achievements of this Association under Mr. Logan's direction during the past 25 years, suffice it to say that it is generally regarded as one of the most effective organizations in the entire field of trade associations.

The variety chains were equally fortunate when they secured Dr. Paul H. Nystrom to head up the activities of the Limited Price Variety Stores Association, which was organized in the summer of 1933. As one of the outstanding authorities on marketing in general and retailing in particular, serving as professor of marketing at Columbia University since 1926, Dr. Nystrom commanded universal respect in trade and Governmental circles as well as in the academic field. As the spokesman for the entire variety-store trade, independents as well as chains comprising the membership of his association, he was particularly effective in clarifying the special problems confronting his field. On the other hand, his broad experience and sound judgment proved invaluable to his members in helping them to formulate their own policies, both individual and collective. When Dr. Nystrom retired in 1954 he was succeeded by Philip W. Schindel, as Executive Director.

Fred Griffiths, president of the Pennsylvania Drug Stores, served as executive secretary of the National Association of Chain Drug Stores from the date of its organization in 1933 until his death in 1949. His long experience in the chain-drug field as a top executive gave him a practical approach to the problems which faced the drug chains as a group which few men outside of the field could have equalled. To this was added a personality which made him particularly effective as a trade-association executive. His own experience as a retail druggist having convinced him of the need for price-maintenance legislation, Mr. Griffiths was an ardent advocate of the Fair Trade laws which some of the States had already passed and others were considering when his association was organized. As most of the other drug-chain operators felt the same way about it as he did, Mr. Griffiths was able to offer the full cooperation of his organization to the National Association of Retail Druggists, which was the principal proponent of such legislation. With the chains thus joining forces with the independent druggists in the effort to end price-cutting on standard drug products, the main grievance the independents had entertained against the chains for so many years was eliminated.

Before many more years were to elapse, Mr. Griffiths had the gratification of seeing Fair Trade laws in effect in 45 States and enjoying Federal sanction as well through the passage of the Miller-Tydings Act in 1937. From then on and until his death, Mr. Griffiths' main concern was to protect Fair Trade against the attacks of those who were opposed to it, including the Federal Trade Commission and the Department of Justice. When, in 1947, Fair Trade was being blamed in some quarters as one of the factors responsible for high prices, he lost no time in launching a survey to establish the facts. The resulting study[4] revealed that whereas the cost of living between 1939 and 1947 had increased some 60 per cent, the prices of more than 7,000 Fair-Traded drug and cosmetic items had increased only 3 per cent. The only conclusion to be drawn from that showing was that instead of being responsible for rising prices, Fair Trade had exercised a definite stabilizing effect, which was absent in the case of items which were not Fair-Traded.

Effective as this study was to establish the economic facts about Fair Trade, it carried no weight, of course, with the U.S. Supreme Court several years later when the scope of the vital Miller-Tydings Act was successfully challenged on legal

[4] *Chain Store Age*, Druggist Edition, October, 1947.

rather than economic grounds.[5] The subsequent fate of Fair Trade has been related in an earlier chapter. See page 109.

Upon the death of Mr. Griffiths, Carl Willingham, who had worked with him on Association matters for four years, was appointed secretary and treasurer and still is.

The shoe chains, the apparel chains and the mail-order chains have likewise maintained their separate trade associations to help them meet their special trade problems as they arose.

The Institute of Distribution serves a different purpose of a more general nature. It was founded in 1935 by a group of important chains outside of the food field for the purpose of carrying on the educational work and public relation activities which the National Chain Store Association had begun prior to its dissolution in 1933. One of its most constructive activities was the development of the regional and State Chain Store Councils which have been described in an earlier chapter. Another important purpose it serves is to provide its member companies with statistical and other data relating to distribution and to keep them advised of the introduction and progress of legislative proposals affecting retailers in general and chain stores in particular. This work has been carried on effectively right from the start under the direction of Mrs. Gladys M. Kiernan.

What of the future? Have the chains gone about as far as they are destined to go in the fields in which they have made their greatest progress? Or is the evidence of their maturity revealed in the history of the last 28 years to be taken at less than its face value—as evidence only of a temporary slow-down in a movement which may be later resumed?

So far as the over-all retail picture is concerned, the chain-store ratio, as to both stores and sales, is likely, in the author's opinion, to increase in the years ahead. The gains, however, are likely to be both gradual and slight. They will come from the natural growth of the smaller chains and the entry of new-

---

[5] Calvert Distiller's Corp. v. Schwegmann, 341 U.S. 384 (1951).

comers rather than from any substantial expansion on the part of the big companies.

This conclusion is based primarily on the basic merits of the chain-store system as they have been reviewed in these pages—on the fundamental fact that operating more than one store offers greater opportunity than operating only one. That principle will continue to encourage single-store operators in all fields to open a second store as long as ambition and vision are to be found among retail merchants, and the success of such ventures will encourage still further expansion. Small chains are unlikely to remain small if and when the opportunity arrives for further expansion.

So far as the bigger chains are concerned, they too may be expected to expand in order to keep pace with population growth and to meet the need in new shopping centers and expanding communities for the kind of stores the chains operate. But such normal expansion will not tend to change present chain-store ratios in the general sales picture in any appreciable degree.

Several factors argue against a resumption of chain-store expansion on anything like the scale which marked their development between 1920 and 1930. In the first place, the need which then existed for the kind of stores the chains were introducing has to a large extent been met by the chains themselves and their more progressive competitors. To open more stores in areas already adequately served would involve risks which well-managed chains are unlikely to take. In the second place, the trend towards bigger stores in many fields, particularly in the food field, has eliminated the need for as many stores as were formerly necessary to achieve great volume. One supermarket doing $20,000 a week now produces as much business as twenty stores of the type which prevailed thirty years ago. The same is true, in greater or lesser degree, of modern stores in other fields. Finally the law of diminishing returns, the growing tax burden with its serious depletion of working capital, and rising operating costs would combine to discourage widespread expansion even if it were otherwise feasible.

In the years which lie ahead, the task of the chains will be not merely to maintain the favorable position they now hold but to measure up to the greater economic, social, national and even international responsibilities their status will impose on them.

For the fact is that what the author said of the food chains on the occasion of the celebration of the 25th anniversary of the founding of the National Association of Food Chains[7] applies with equal force to the chain store system in general. During the past 25 years that system has matured into one of the most vital elements of our economy—a distributive dynamo upon whose power depend in large measure the well-being and prosperity of the entire nation. But for the kind of job the chains are doing, we could not enjoy our enviable standards of living and the output of industry would inevitably be reduced as a result of the consumer's diminished buying power. For in keeping the cost of food, clothing and other basic necessities down to the lowest possible level, the chains enable the consumer to stretch her dollars—enable her to buy more of the things and services that would otherwise be beyond her reach.

The substantial growth of our population which the next two decades will bring, coupled with the increase in our productive capacity which technological advances assure will demand a corresponding increase in the capacity of our distributive facilities. The responsibility for providing it will fall largely upon the chains.

Because of the sheer magnitude of their operations and its impact on our economy, the chains will likewise incur additional social responsibilities and increased obligations in the area of cooperation with the government.

An interesting illustration of how the chains regard their

[7] *"Twenty-Five Years of Progress,"* an address before the National Association of Food Chains, October 6, 1958.

responsibility to the government was provided in 1956 when, in cooperation with the State Department and through the initiative of the National Association of Food Chains, the food industry set up in Rome a fully-equipped and fully-stocked supermarket. It was operated under the direction of chain experts for the edification of the public in connection with an international conference on food distribution. The State Department's interest stemmed from its need to do something in the "cold war" to dramatize the American way of life. No more eloquent symbol of the way we live than this up-to-date supermarket could have been conceived. Commonplace as it has become to us, it was little less than sensational to several hundred thousand Italians and other visitors who had never before seen anything like it. It was so favorably received that the following year the food chains again cooperated with the government to set up a similar exhibit in a city where it might be even more useful ideologically— Zagreb, Yugoslavia.

No doubt the chains will be called upon by the government for similar extra-curricular cooperation in the years which lie ahead, and it will be forthcoming. But the prime responsibility of the chains will always be to improve the efficiency of our own distribution system. That they will be equal to whatever challenge the future will bring would seem to be evident from the vision and flexibility they have demonstrated in the past 25 years.

So long, therefore, as the public retains its present freedom to patronize the stores of its choice and the chains retain the right, and the ability, to provide the kind of stores the public likes best, the future of the chains would seem to be secure.

APPENDIX

GROWTH OF LEADING CHAINS

IN SELECTED CATEGORIES

Sources: Company reports
Hugh M. Foster's 1937 Study, *Printers' Ink Monthly*
Chain Store Age
Miscellaneous

W. C. Shaw, Sr., of G. C. MURPHY Co.,
for average sales per store data
in variety store field.

GROWTH OF LEADING CHAINS
GROCERY CHAINS

AMERICAN STORES, INC. PHILADELPHIA, PA.			COLONIAL STORES, INC. ATLANTA, GA.		
YEAR	STORES	SALES (MILLIONS)	YEAR	STORES	SALES (MILLIONS)
1918	1,149	$ 68.3	1940	585	$ 57.0
1919	1,175	76.4	1941	570	74.0
1920	1,243	103.1	1942	564	103.0
1921	1,274	86.1	1943	487	112.7
1922	1,375	85.9	1944	481	119.3
1923	1,474	94.6	1945	472	121.1
1924	1,629	98.2	1946	457	157.9
1925	1,792	108.9	1947	432	199.5
1926	1,982	116.9	1948	418	214.9
1927	2,133	120.7	1949	430	215.6
1928	2,548	137.3	1950	426	236.8
1929	2,644	143.3	1951	409	269.6
1930	2,728	142.8	1952	407	288.9
1931	2,806	135.2	1953	411	314.7
1932	2,977	115.5	1954	401	333.3
1933	2,882	109.4	1955	432	380.0
1934	2,859	114.4	1956	449	423.0
1935	2,826	115.9	1957	461	442.2
1936	2,816	113.4			
1937	2,620	114.6			
1938	2,416	109.9			
1939	2,272	114.8			
1940	2,157	124.8			
1941	2,130	157.7			
1942	2,099	209.1			
1943	2,066	212.1			
1944	2,020	227.6			
1945	1,964	233.5			
1946	2,012	314.6			
1947	1,921	388.6			
1948	1,833	417.5			
1949*	1,776				
1950	1,637	416.6			
1951	1,505	469.8			
1952	1,408	521.3			
1953	1,289	542.0			
1954	1,132	603.7			
1955	1,076	624.6			
1956	953	654.7			
1957	903	779.9			
1958	844	837.3			

* Fiscal year changed from year-end to 3/31 of following year.

GROCERY CHAINS (Continued)

FIRST NATIONAL STORES, INC.
SOMERVILLE, MASS.

FOOD FAIR, INC.
PHILADELPHIA, PA.

YEAR*	STORES	SALES (MILLIONS)	YEAR	STORES	SALES (MILLIONS)
1927	1,681	$ 59.0	1935	9	$ 5.7
1928	1,717	64.4	1936	14	8.7
1929	2,002	75.9	1937	22	13.8
1930	2,549	107.6	1938	34	18.3
1931	2,548	108.2	1939	67	24.5
1932	2,546	107.6	1940	73	29.2
1933	2,705	100.9	1941	75	34.1
1934	2,653	105.8	1942	77	41.7
1935	2,623	111.3	1943	73	42.2
1936	2,556	119.6	1944	89	44.8
1937	2,473	120.7	1945	89	60.6
1938	2,350	124.3	1946	89	101.2
1939	2,244	124.2	1947	95	121.8
1940	2,137	131.0	1948	105	142.0
1941	1,923	142.7	1950*	113	164.6
1942	1,748	174.4	1951	123	205.6
1943	1,585	187.8	1952	151	259.6
1944	1,463	164.9	1953	162	292.7
1945	1,340	170.2	1954	196	348.2
1946	1,236	182.1	1955	216	410.1
1947	1,201	156.5	1956	238	475.2
1948	1,150	315.9	1957	273	545.1
1949	1,083	354.4	1958	283	600.9
1950	1,033	344.2			
1951	979	371.9			
1952	922	406.8			
1953	847	424.5			
1954	761	442.2			
1955	702	470.6			
1956	661	491.7			
1957	607	507.4			
1958	575	521.5			

* Calendar years from 1935 to 1948 inclusive; fiscal years thereafter ending April 30 of year given.

* Fiscal years ending March of year indicated.

GROCERY CHAINS (Continued)

GRAND UNION COMPANY
EAST PATERSON, N. J.

YEAR	STORES	SALES (MILLIONS)
1928	—	$ 31.9
1929	612	36.9
1930	611	37.0
1931	—	35.6
1932	—	30.4
1933	—	28.3
1934	568	28.6
1935	563	28.0
1936	566	29.5
1937	551	31.1
1938	499	31.4
1939	487	37.2
1940	476	35.1
1941	417	39.6
1942	358	43.9
1943	347	43.9
1944	329	50.1
1945	319	55.4
1946	318	83.4
1947	308	99.8
1948	293	116.1
1949	287	135.0
1950	289	161.0
1951	322	179.4
1952	296	184.1
1953	316	201.8
1954	320	219.5
1955	347	283.0
1956	354	374.2
1957	381	427.9

GREAT ATLANTIC & PACIFIC TEA CO.
NEW YORK, N. Y.

YEAR*	STORES	SALES (MILLIONS)
1859	1	—
1865	25	—
1880	100	—
1900	200	—
1906	291	—
1910	372	—
1911	400	—
1912	480	—

GREAT ATLANTIC & PACIFIC TEA CO.
NEW YORK, N. Y.
(Continued)

YEAR*	STORES	SALES (MILLIONS)
1913	585	—
1914	991	—
1915	1,817	—
1916	2,866	—
1917	3,782	—
1918	3,799	—
1919	4,224	$ 195
1920	4,621	235
1921	5,217	202
1922	7,350	247
1923	9,303	303
1924	11,421	352
1925	14,034	440
1926	14,811	574
1927	15,671	761
1928	15,177	973
1929	15,418	1,054
1930	15,737	1,066
1931	15,670	1,008
1932	15,427	864
1933	15,131	820
1934	15,035	842
1935	14,926	872
1936	14,746	907
1937	13,314	882
1938	10,900	879
1939	9,200	990
1940	7,230	1,116
1941	6,170	1,379
1942	6,000	1,471
1943	5,900	1,311
1944	5,800	1,402
1945	5,600	1,435
1946	5,200	1,909
1947	5,075	2,546
1948	4,900	2,837
1949	4,700	2,905
1950	4,500	3,180
1951	4,400	3,392
1952	4,300	3,756
1953	4,250	3,989
1954	4,200	4,140
1955	4,150	4,305
1956	4,200	4,482
1957	4,200	4,769

* Fiscal years ending February 28 following year given.

GROCERY CHAINS (Continued)

JEWEL TEA CO. INC.
MELROSE PARK, ILL.

THE KROGER CO.
CINCINNATI, OHIO

YEAR	STORES*	SALES (MILLIONS)	YEAR	STORES	SALES (MILLIONS)
1921	0	$ 11.2	1882	1	—
1922	0	10.2	1885	2	—
1923	0	12.6	1891	7	—
1924	0	13.6	1902	40	$ 1.8
1925	0	14.2	1920	799	50.1
1926	0	14.6	1921	947	44.9
1927	0	14.5	1922	1,224	53.8
1928	0	15.9	1923	1,641	74.3
1929	0	16.8	1924	1,973	90.1
1930	0	15.5	1925	2,559	116.2
1931	0	13.7	1926	3,100	146.0
1932	85	14.7	1927	3,564	161.3
1933	84	14.4	1928	4,307	207.4
1934	87	17.2	1929	5,575	286.6
1935	87	18.8	1930	5,165	267.1
1936	100	20.7	1931	4,884	244.4
1937	109	23.3	1932	4,737	213.2
1938	109	23.7	1933	4,400	205.7
1939	116	24.6	1934	4,352	221.2
1940	132	29.1	1935	4,250	229.9
1941	148	40.9	1936	4,212	242.3
1942	154	52.4	1937	4,108	248.4
1943	152	51.4	1938	3,992	231.3
1944	152	56.0	1939	3,958	243.4
1945	150	62.4	1940	3,727	260.4
1946	150	86.9	1941	3,477	302.8
1947	149	128.5	1942	3,174	388.8
1948	154	150.6	1943	2,999	422.4
1949	153	166.1	1944	2,896	448.4
1950	154	185.7	1945	2,730	457.3
1951	157	205.9	1946	2,611	573.8
1952	160	222.6	1947	2,516	754.3
1953	164	238.7	1948	2,349	825.7
1954	173	270.6	1949	2,190	807.7
1955	179	300.4	1950	2,054	861.2
1956	184	334.8	1951	1,978	997.1
1957	227**	414.5	1952	1,891	1,051.8
			1953	1,810	1,058.6
			1954	1,678	1,108.7
			1955	1,587	1,219.5
			1956	1,476	1,492.6
			1957	1,421	1,674.1

* Home service sales from 1921 to 1932; home service plus store sales thereafter. Retail sales are exclusive of sales tax collections.

** Includes 39 Eisner Grocery Stores acquired March 12, 1957.

GROCERY CHAINS (Continued)

NATIONAL TEA CO.
CHICAGO, ILL.

SAFEWAY STORES*
OAKLAND, CALIF.

YEAR	STORES	SALES (MILLIONS)	YEAR	STORES	SALES (MILLIONS)
1899	1	—	1914	4	$ .3
1920	163	$ 18.7	1922	118	5.8
1921	261	16.3	1923	193	8.6
1922	295	20.6	1924	263	11.9
1923	514	31.3	1925	330	13.4
1924	598	39.1	1926	673	50.5
1925	761	47.5	1927	840	69.6
1926	840	53.7	1928	1,191	103.3
1927	1,237	58.8	1929	2,340	213.5
1928	1,600	85.9	1930	2,675	219.3
1929	1,627	90.2	1931	3,264	246.8
1930	1,600	85.2	1932	3,411	229.2
1931	1,512	76.7	1933	3,306	220.2
1932	1,389	65.7	1934		242.9
1933	1,299	64.9	1935	3,330	294.7
1934	1,245	62.8	1936	3,370	346.2
1935	1,224	63.1	1937	3,327	381.9
1936	1,221	62.5	1938	3,227	368.3
1937	1,213	62.1	1939	2,967	385.9
1938	1,103	55.6	1940	2,671	399.3
1939	1,073	56.7	1941	2,660	475.1
1940	1,062	61.9	1942	2,697	611.1
1941	1,015	72.2	1943	2,493	588.8
1942	950	89.9	1944	2,463	656.6
1943	874	91.8	1945	2,452	664.8
1944	827	99.9	1946	2,428	847.5
1945	749	106.9	1947	2,401	1,117.1
1946	693	157.6	1948	2,308	1,276.8
1947	702	217.9	1949	2,202	1,197.8
1948	659	270.2	1950	2,084	1,209.9
1949	655	274.3	1951	2,104	1,454.6
1950	634	315.2	1952	2,104	1,639.1
1951	624	361.3	1953	2,054	1,751.8
1952	765	405.2	1954	2,008	1,813.5
1953	688	462.3	1955	1,998	1,932.2
1954	711	520.3	1956	1,980	1,989.3
1955	744	575.6	1957	1,958	2,117.7
1956	761	617.6			
1957	883	681.1			

* Includes Canadian Stores.

GROCERY CHAINS (Continued)

WINN-DIXIE STORES, INC.

JACKSONVILLE, FLA.

YEAR ENDING	STORES*	SALES (MILLIONS)
June 28, 1952	335	$246.4
27, 1953	335	278.4
26, 1954	347	312.7
25, 1955	370	358.6
30, 1956	412	421.3
29, 1957	462	513.5
28, 1958	473	588.6

* Predecessor chains which were combined in the course of this chain's development included Table Supply Stores, Winn & Lovett, Steiden Stores, Dixie-Home, Margaret Ann and Kwik-chek.

VARIETY STORE CHAINS

W. T. GRANT CO.

NEW YORK, N. Y.

YEAR	STORES	ANNUAL SALES TOTAL (Millions)	ANNUAL SALES PER STORE (Thousands)	YEAR	STORES	ANNUAL SALES TOTAL (Millions)	ANNUAL SALES PER STORE (Thousands)
1907	1	$ .1	$ 99.5	1933	457	$ 78.2	$171.1
1908	2	.2	84.6	1934	465	85.1	182.9
1909	4	.4	99.7	1935	171	91.9	195.3
1910	6	.8	125.5	1936	477	98.3	206.2
1911	9	1.1	120.4	1937	480	99.1	206.5
1912	12	1.4	113.5	1938	489	97.5	199.4
1913	16	2.0	125.1	1939	492	103.8	210.9
1914	20	2.6	128.3	1940	492	111.8	227.2
1915	23	3.1	133.1	1941	495	130.6	263.7
1916	25	3.7	146.4	1942	493	154.2	312.8
1917	30	4.5	150.4	1943	493	163.9	332.6
1918	32	6.0	188.4	1944	490	175.5	358.1
1919	33	7.9	240.7	1945	488	180.3	369.5
1920	38	10.2	268.2	1946	484	212.3	438.6
1921	45	12.7	282.9	1947	483	228.6	473.3
1922	50	15.4	307.7	1948	482	233.9	485.2
1923	60	20.6	343.8	1949	480	233.2	485.8
1924	70	25.3	361.7	1950	477	250.6	525.3
1925	77	30.4	394.9	1951	482	268.3	556.6
1926	109	36.1	330.9	1952	491	283.4	576.7
1927	157	43.7	278.6	1953	503	299.8	597.2
1928	221	55.7	251.9	1954	520	317.2	610.0
1929	279	65.9	236.2	1955	574	351.8	612.9
1930	350	71.4	204.0	1956	632	380.9	602.6
1931	404	75.7	187.3	1957	691	406.3	588.0
1932	446	73.1	163.9				

VARIETY STORE CHAINS (Continued)

H. L. GREEN Co.
NEW YORK, N. Y.

YEAR	STORES	ANNUAL SALES TOTAL (Millions)	PER STORE (Thousands)	YEAR	STORES	ANNUAL SALES TOTAL (Millions)	PER STORE (Thousands)
1933	182	$ 28.9	$159.2	1946	209	$ 90.4	$432.7
1934	178	33.6	188.9	1947	212	94.2	444.3
1935	184	35.5	192.8	1948	217	101.2	466.4
1936	190	40.5	213.4	1949	222	99.1	446.4
1937	193	41.9	217.6	1950	225	101.9	453.0
1938	195	40.4	207.2	1951	228	106.5	467.1
1939	196	52.2	266.2	1952	222	106.9	481.5
1940	217	56.5	260.3	1953	224	108.7	485.3
1941	219	64.2	292.9	1954	221	108.5	491.0
1942	218	73.9	339.1	1955	227	111.7	492.7
1943	217	77.4	356.6	1956	225	112.5	500.0
1944	216	79.7	370.0	1957	224	110.6	514.0
1945	213	79.1	371.3				

S. S. KRESGE Co.
DETROIT, MICH.

YEAR	STORES	ANNUAL SALES TOTAL (Millions)	PER STORE (Thousands)	YEAR	STORES	ANNUAL SALES TOTAL (Millions)	PER STORE (Thousands)
1909	42	$ 5.1	$121.8	1934	731	$137.7	$187.9
1910	51	6.5	127.4	1935	745	138.3	185.6
1911	64	7.9	123.8	1936	734	149.5	203.6
1912	85	10.3	121.5	1937	741	155.2	209.5
1913	101	13.3	131.3	1938	745	149.3	200.4
1914	118	16.1	136.4	1939	745	153.9	206.6
1915	139	20.9	150.6	1940	743	158.7	213.6
1916	160	26.4	164.9	1941	736	176.2	239.4
1917	164	30.1	183.5	1942	731	198.7	258.1
1918	170	36.3	213.6	1943	716	206.0	287.8
1919	174	42.7	245.2	1944	711	216.5	304.4
1920	184	51.2	278.5	1945	705	223.2	316.6
1921	200	55.9	279.3	1946	696	251.4	361.2
1922	211	65.2	308.9	1947	696	270.1	388.1
1923	234	81.8	349.8	1948	700	289.1	413.0
1924	257	90.1	350.6	1949	702	288.7	411.6
1925	306	105.9	346.3	1950	694	294.8	424.7
1926	367	119.3	324.8	1951	690	310.9	450.6
1927	435	133.8	307.5	1952	695	326.4	469.6
1928	506	147.5	291.2	1953	692	337.3	487.4
1929	597	156.3	261.9	1954	690	337.9	489.7
1930	678	150.5	221.8	1955	673	354.7	527.0
1931	711	145.8	205.0	1956	676	366.4	542.0
1932	719	124.5	173.0	1957	692	377.2	545.0
1933	720	125.9	174.6				

VARIETY STORE CHAINS (Continued)

S. H. KRESS & Co.
NEW YORK, N. Y.

YEAR	STORES	ANNUAL SALES TOTAL (Millions)	ANNUAL SALES PER STORE (Thousands)	YEAR	STORES	ANNUAL SALES TOTAL (Millions)	ANNUAL SALES PER STORE (Thousands)
1896	1	$ .03	$ 31.1	1927	183	$ 58.1	$317.3
1897	2	.07	36.2	1928	193	65.1	336.7
1898	5	.16	32.0	1929	203	68.5	337.3
1899	6	.23	37.8	1930	212	69.3	326.8
1900	11	.49	44.5	1931	221	69.0	312.4
1901	13	.68	52.4	1932	230	62.8	272.9
1902	16	.87	54.1	1933	230	65.0	282.7
1903	19	1.1	59.9	1934	232	75.7	326.1
1904	25	1.6	63.7	1935	234	78.5	335.4
1905	38	2.2	57.4	1936	235	86.8	369.2
1906	51	3.1	60.9	1937	234	87.9	275.5
1907	56	3.8	67.2	1938	240	82.2	342.4
1908	62	4.6	74.4	1939	240	84.9	353.6
1909	75	6.6	88.2	1940	242	88.3	364.9
1910	84	8.4	99.4	1941	242	101.4	418.9
1911	91	8.8	96.9	1942	244	116.9	479.3
1912	100	10.0	100.0	1943	244	124.0	508.3
1913	114	10.8	94.5	1944	243	127.9	526.6
1914	118	11.9	100.1	1945	244	126.0	516.4
1915	123	12.4	101.0	1946	242	150.9	623.7
1916	130	15.1	115.8	1947	243	155.4	639.5
1917	144	17.6	122.5	1948	250	165.4	661.6
1918	144	21.2	146.9	1949	256	163.9	640.3
1919	145	25.2	174.1	1950	259	161.7	624.2
1920	145	28.9	199.8	1951	259	172.4	665.6
1921	142	28.9	203.6	1952	261	176.2	675.3
1922	145	30.1	211.4	1953	262	172.9	660.0
1923	152	34.0	223.7	1954	264	169.4	641.6
1924	161	40.3	250.1	1955	262	167.9	640.8
1925	166	45.9	276.9	1956	260	167.6	644.8
1926	169	51.9	306.9	1957	261	158.6	607.6

VARIETY STORE CHAINS (Continued)

McCRORY STORES CORPORATION
NEW YORK, N. Y.

YEAR	STORES	ANNUAL SALES		YEAR	STORES	ANNUAL SALES	
		TOTAL (Millions)	PER STORE (Thousands)			TOTAL (Millions)	PER STORE (Thousands)
1901	20	$ .49	$ 24.9	1930	242	$ 43.2	$178.6
1902	26	.67	25.7	1931	244	43.3	177.4
1903	28	.78	28.0	1932	242	39.6	163.4
1904	31	.82	26.4	1933	222	35.4	159.4
1905	35	1.0	28.9	1934	207	38.2	184.7
1906	41	1.2	29.3	1935	201	37.4	186.2
1907	46	1.7	37.1	1936	195	40.2	206.3
1908	46	1.8	40.2	1937	200	41.0	205.0
1909	47	2.4	50.9	1938	200	40.1	200.3
1910	60	3.2	53.2	1939	200	43.2	215.9
1911	69	3.9	56.5	1940	199	46.2	232.2
1912	93	4.9	53.5	1941	202	53.0	262.4
1913	110	5.6	50.5	1942	202	62.6	309.9
1914	116	5.2	45.0	1943	201	67.4	335.1
1915	117	5.9	50.7	1944	203	71.3	351.4
1916	132	6.8	51.4	1945	199	71.3	358.3
1917	143	7.8	54.8	1946	199	84.5	424.7
1918	147	9.6	65.4	1947	199	91.2	456.1
1919	148	11.5	77.6	1948	202	97.6	483.1
1920	156	14.2	91.0	1949	201	95.8	476.4
1921	159	14.4	90.6	1950	205	98.6	481.0
1922	161	17.1	106.4	1951	206	104.2	505.8
1923	167	21.4	127.9	1952	211	107.0	507.2
1924	175	25.2	144.1	1953	211	104.8	497.6
1925	182	29.6	162.6	1954	210	103.9	494.8
1926	199	33.4	168.8	1955	214	109.7	512.6
1927	220	39.3	178.8	1956	213	113.1	531.1
1928	228	41.1	180.3	1957	215	111.8	520.0
1929	241	44.7	185.5				

VARIETY STORE CHAINS (Continued)

McLELLAN STORES Co., NEW YORK, N. Y.

YEAR	STORES	ANNUAL SALES TOTAL (Millions)	PER STORE (Thousands)	YEAR	STORES	ANNUAL SALES TOTAL (Millions)	PER STORE (Thousands)
1921	72	$ 2.2	$ 30.3	1940	232	$ 24.0	$103.6
1922	75	3.5	46.4	1941	233	28.0	120.3
1923	77	4.7	61.0	1942	231	32.8	141.9
1924	80	5.6	69.4	1943	230	37.7	163.8
1925	94	6.7	71.6	1944	226	41.1	181.7
1926	112	9.5	84.7	1945	225	43.5	193.3
1927	128	11.9	93.3	1946	224	49.1	219.2
1928	150	13.9	92.9	1947	224	50.9	227.2
1929	259	23.8	91.8	1948	227	55.5	244.5
1930	277	24.0	86.8	1949	230	54.5	237.7
1931	278	21.9	78.9	1950	231	56.6	245.1
1932	277	19.9	71.8	1951	231	61.1	264.5
1933	238	18.3	76.9	1952	231	62.5	270.5
1934	234	19.6	83.9	1953	232	60.7	261.6
1935	230	19.9	86.5	1954	234	60.7	259.4
1936	235	21.9	93.6	1955	232	61.4	264.7
1937	236	22.6	95.8	1956	232	61.9	266.6
1938	236	22.3	94.4	1957	235	60.7	258.3
1939	231	23.1	99.9				

G. C. MURPHY Co., McKEESPORT, PA.

YEAR	STORES	ANNUAL SALES TOTAL (Millions)	PER STORE (Thousands)	YEAR	STORES	ANNUAL SALES TOTAL (Millions)	PER STORE (Thousands)
1910	10	$ .26	$ 26.3	1935	189	$ 31.6	$167.2
1911	12	.26	20.9	1936	195	37.9	194.8
1912	18	.37	20.6	1937	200	42.5	212.6
1913	23	.47	20.6	1938	201	42.2	209.9
1914	27	.50	18.6	1939	202	47.3	234.1
1915	30	.60	20.1	1940	204	53.4	261.6
1916	32	.77	24.1	1941	207	63.5	306.8
1917	38	1.0	27.2	1942	207	76.9	371.9
1918	42	1.4	32.2	1943	207	82.1	396.5
1919	46	1.4	31.2	1944	207	88.9	429.6
1920	51	2.1	40.2	1945	208	95.9	461.1
1921	60	2.2	37.2	1946	209	110.3	527.9
1922	61	2.7	44.3	1947	209	119.3	571.0
1923	75	3.9	52.7	1948	210	137.6	655.1
1924	85	5.2	60.7	1949	218	141.3	648.2
1925	88	6.5	73.8	1950	219	150.5	687.2
1926	92	8.6	93.1	1951	223	165.2	740.9
1927	113	10.2	90.6	1951	294	168.9	574.5*
1928	133	12.1	91.1	1952	295	184.1	620.6
1929	153	15.7	102.8	1953	297	187.2	630.2
1930	166	17.5	105.4	1954	298	182.2	611.3
1931	172	19.2	111.9	1955	303	196.4	648.3
1932	176	18.5	105.3	1956	309	204.8	662.9
1933	180	21.9	121.6	1957	316	208.2	658.9
1934	186	28.0	150.5				

* Including 71 Morris Stores.

VARIETY STORE CHAINS (Continued)

NEISNER BROTHERS, INC.
ROCHESTER, N. Y.

YEAR	STORES	ANNUAL SALES		YEAR	STORES	ANNUAL SALES	
		TOTAL (Millions)	PER STORE (Thousands)			TOTAL (Millions)	PER STORE (Thousands)
1920	4	$ .9	$238.9	1939	112	$ 22.6	$200.8
1921	6	1.2	203.9	1940	114	22.5	198.6
1922	7	1.3	184.6	1941	116	26.5	228.2
1923	9	1.7	188.4	1942	117	33.1	283.3
1924	11	1.9	173.4	1943	117	37.3	319.1
1925	13	2.7	207.4	1944	115	38.2	332.3
1926	17	4.5	264.5	1945	112	38.9	347.3
1927	22	6.5	294.4	1946	112	45.7	408.0
1928	35	10.3	294.3	1947	114	50.9	447.3
1929	58	15.1	260.2	1948	117	57.6	492.6
1930	75	16.5	220.1	1949	121	57.8	477.6
1931	78	15.9	204.6	1950	123	58.3	473.7
1932	79	14.4	182.6	1951	125	61.8	494.7
1933	79	14.4	181.7	1952	127	63.8	502.6
1934	80	16.6	207.1	1953	129	66.7	517.0
1935	95	18.6	198.1	1954	132	64.9	491.6
1936	99	20.9	211.4	1955	139	68.8	495.2
1937	108	22.4	207.6	1956	142	69.2	487.3
1938	109	20.1	184.8	1957	149	69.6	467.1

J. J. NEWBERRY CO.
NEW YORK, N. Y.

YEAR	STORES	ANNUAL SALES		YEAR	STORES	ANNUAL SALES	
		TOTAL (Millions)	PER STORE (Thousands)			TOTAL (Millions)	PER STORE (Thousands)
1912	1	$ .03	$ 32.3	1935	450	$ 43.4	$ 96.4
1913	2	.04	21.1	1936	461	48.4	104.9
1914	3	.09	30.9	1937	469	50.3	107.3
1915	5	.12	23.2	1938	476	49.0	103.0
1916	5	.15	30.3	1939	479	52.3	109.1
1917	6	.15	24.9	1940	486	55.9	114.9
1918	7	.28	39.5	1941	488	64.2	131.6
1919	17	.50	29.6	1942	492	77.3	157.1
1920	17	.75	44.2	1943	491	91.0	185.4
1921	26	1.2	44.5	1944	491	95.9	195.2
1922	33	1.8	53.0	1945	488	100.9	206.7
1923	51	3.6	69.9	1946	487	113.2	232.4
1924	68	5.1	75.2	1947	485	117.9	243.1
1925	86	6.9	80.2	1948	484	134.8	278.5
1926	112	9.9	89.2	1949	482	136.8	283.8
1927	151	15.1	99.8	1950	483	145.7	301.6
1928	210	20.6	98.1	1951	480	161.3	336.0
1929	279	27.8	99.6	1952	477	166.3	348.6
1930	335	30.2	90.1	1953	476	171.2	359.6
1931	379	31.1	82.2	1954	476	179.8	377.7
1932	406	33.1	81.6	1955	476	190.7	400.6
1933	417	35.1	84.3	1956	476	203.4	427.3
1934	431	41.1	95.3	1957	476	213.0	447.4

VARIETY STORE CHAINS (Continued)

F. W. WOOLWORTH CO.

NEW YORK, N. Y.

YEAR	STORES	ANNUAL SALES		YEAR	STORES	ANNUAL SALES	
		TOTAL (Millions)	PER STORE (Thousands)			TOTAL (Millions)	PER STORE (Thousands)
1912	631	$ 60.6	$ 95.9	1935	1,980	$268.8	$135.7
1913	684	66.2	96.8	1936	1,998	290.4	145.3
1914	737	69.6	94.5	1937	2,010	304.8	151.6
1915	805	75.9	94.4	1938	2,015	304.3	151.0
1916	920	87.1	94.7	1939	2,021	318.8	157.8
1917	1,000	98.1	98.1	1940	2,027	335.5	165.5
1918	1,039	107.2	103.2	1941	2,023	377.1	185.4
1919	1,081	119.5	110.5	1942	2,015	423.2	210.0
1920	1,111	140.9	126.8	1943	2,008	439.0	218.6
1921	1,137	147.7	129.9	1944	2,004	459.8	229.5
1922	1,176	167.3	142.3	1945	1,971	477.1	242.1
1923	1,260	193.4	153.5	1946	1,958	552.4	282.1
1924	1,356	215.5	158.9	1947	1,945	593.4	305.0
1925	1,423	239.0	167.9	1948	1,944	623.9	320.9
1926	1,480	253.6	171.4	1949	1,938	615.6	317.6
1927	1,581	272.8	172.5	1950	1,936	632.1	326.5
1928	1,725	287.3	166.6	1951	1,943	684.2	352.1
1929	1,825	303.0	166.0	1952	1,960	712.6	363.6
1930	1,881	289.3	153.8	1953	1,981	713.9	360.3
1931	1,903	282.7	148.5	1954	2,021	721.3	356.9
1932	1,932	249.9	129.3	1955	2,064	767.8	371.9
1933	1,941	250.5	129.1	1956	2,101	806.2	383.7
1934	1,960	270.7	138.3	1957	2,121	823.9	388.4

DRUG CHAINS

CUNNINGHAM DRUG STORES, INC.

DETROIT, MICH.

YEAR ENDING SEPT. 30	STORES	SALES (MILLIONS)	YEAR ENDING SEPT. 30	STORES	SALES (MILLIONS)
1935	76	$ 6.8	1947	103	24.6
1936	80	8.0	1948	106	24.7
1937	84	9.2	1949	110	25.0
1938	90	8.8	1950	165*	34.0
1939	95	9.5	1951	167	38.2
1940	97	10.4	1952	173	40.1
1941	98	12.3	1953	175	42.4
1942	98	15.1	1954	180	40.9
1943	98	18.9	1955	179	42.6
1944	100	20.4	1956	188**	45.5
1945	99	20.9	1957	191	47.4
1946	99	23.2	1958		

* Includes Marshall and Schettler.
** Includes Miller Drug Stores, Inc.

DRUG CHAINS (Continued)

GRAY DRUG STORES, INC.
CLEVELAND, OHIO

YEAR*	STORES	SALES (MILLIONS)	YEAR	STORES*	SALES (MILLIONS)
1929	17	$ 1.5	1944	43	9.5
1930	21	2.1	1945	78	10.0
1931	24	2.6	1946	91	14.7
1932	26	2.5	1947	91	17.5
1933	26	2.5	1948	78	16.2
1934	29	3.2	1949	79	15.6
1935	29	1.8	1950	77	15.2
1936	33	4.4	1951	74	16.8
1937	37	5.4	1952	80	19.3
1938	38	5.4	1953	78	21.1
1939	38	5.1	1954	80	22.6
1940	40	5.5	1955	78	23.4
1941	39	6.9	1956	81	25.5
1942	44	7.9	1957	86	29.3
1943	43	9.1	1958	102	32.2

* Calendar years 1929 to 1934 inclusive; 1935, six months to June 30; thereafter fiscal year ending June 30 of year given.

KATZ DRUG CO.
KANSAS CITY, MO.

YEAR	STORES	SALES (MILLIONS)	YEAR	STORES	SALES (MILLIONS)
1929	3	$ 5.5	1944	20	17.2
1930	4	6.6	1945	20	20.1
1931	8	7.4	1946	23	24.3
1932	8	6.8	1947	24	26.4
1933	8	7.2	1948	27	26.9
1934	9	8.3	1949	28	29.9
1935	10	8.9	1950	29	31.9
1936	12	8.8	1951	30	35.1
1937	13	9.7	1952	31	34.2
1938	13	8.6	1953	31	34.3
1939	13	8.3	1954	33	35.8
1940	15	8.1	1955	33	39.5
1941	18	9.6	1956	35	40.9
1942	20	13.7	1957	39	44.8
1943	20	17.1			

DRUG CHAINS (Continued)

PEOPLES DRUG STORES, INC.
WASHINGTON, D. C.

YEAR	STORES	SALES (MILLIONS)	YEAR	STORES	SALES (MILLIONS)
1920	8	$ 2.4	1939	136	$22.8
1921	11	3.1	1940	136	23.9
1922	13	3.7	1941	136	27.7
1923	16	4.0	1942	137	32.6
1924	18	4.8	1943	131	34.8
1925	18	7.3	1944	131	34.7
1926	46	8.4	1945	131	36.1
1927	73	10.2	1946	134	44.2
1928	82	11.3	1947	136	46.0
1929	112	15.5	1948	140	46.9
1930	118	16.8	1949	141	46.8
1931	124	17.4	1950	143	47.2
1932	117	16.2	1951	146	50.7
1933	113	15.5	1952	152	54.0
1934	117	16.9	1953	150	54.5
1935	122	19.2	1954	156	54.9
1936	129	21.1	1955	158	57.6
1937	133	22.4	1956	162	61.9
1938	135	21.7	1957	170	67.1

REXALL DRUG COMPANY
LOS ANGELES, CALIF.

YEAR	STORES*	CONSOLIDATED SALES** (MILLIONS)	YEAR	STORES*	CONSOLIDATED SALES** (MILLIONS)
1941	584	$102.5	1950	339	$153.6
1942	573	122.0	1951	309	164.3
1943	568	138.9	1952	289	178.3
1944	591	147.8	1953	270	189.2
1945	558	158.2	1954	202	176.1
1946	594	178.9	1955	165	153.5
1947	541	182.7	1956	158	155.6
1948	464	173.9	1957	160	167.6
1949	387	156.4			

* Includes only stores operated by wholly owned subsidiaries, of which Liggett and Owl are the principal ones.
** Sales of Rexall Drug Company and its consolidated subsidiaries, of which the Retail Division is only one.

DRUG CHAINS (Continued)

SUN RAY DRUG CO.
PHILADELPHIA, PA.

YEAR*	STORES	SALES (MILLIONS)	YEAR*	STORES	SALES (MILLIONS)
1930	2	$ .6	1945	43	$11.1
1931	4	.9	1946	120**	16.6
1932	8	1.2	1947	130	19.9
1933	13	1.9	1948	141	22.0
1934	19	3.2	1949	140	24.1
1935	23	4.0	1950	138	23.9
1936*			1951	134	24.8
1937	29	5.9	1952	133	26.4
1938	37	6.2	1953	134	28.5
1939	38	6.5	1954	138	29.9
1940	47	7.4	1955	132	29.6
1941	48	7.9	1956	135	29.8
1942	45	8.6	1957	139	32.4
1943	44	9.8	1958	143	36.4
1944	44	10.7			

* Calendar years from 1930 to 1935 inclusive; fiscal years thereafter ending January 31 of year given.
** Includes stores and sales of Nevins Drug Co. and also agency stores for this and all subsequent years.

THRIFTY DRUG STORES CO. INC.
LOS ANGELES, CALIF.

YEAR*	STORES	SALES (MILLIONS)	YEAR*	STORES	SALES (MILLIONS)
1947	72	$39.4	1953	103	$60.6
1948	78	43.6	1954	108	63.1
1949	82	45.3	1955	114	66.7
1950	85	45.9	1956	123	74.9
1951	94	51.1	1957	129	86.8
1952	96	54.0	1958	136	97.7

* Fiscal year ending August 31 of year given.

DRUG CHAINS (Continued)

UNITED WHELAN CORPORATION*

(formerly United Cigar-Whelan Stores Corporation)

BROOKLYN, N. Y.

YEAR	DRUG STORES	CIGAR STORES	AGENCY STORES	SALES (MILLIONS)	YEAR	DRUG STORES	CIGAR STORES	AGENCY STORES	SALES (MILLIONS)
1935	187	579	830	$54.2	1947	200	194	973	$78.3
1936	185	563	848	55.3	1948	202	145	1,031	77.4
1937	186	541	804	54.9	1949	208	113	987	75.4
1938	181	499	837	50.3	1950	202	69	1,007	74.3
1939	191	407	925	50.1	1951	197	58	898	74.2
1940	186	328	995	50.0	1952	186	48	820	67.6
1941	179	284	1,033	50.0	1953	175	37	697	63.9
1942	178	275	926	57.2	1954	167	15	627	58.7
1943	177	264	879	64.2	1955	152	8	610	56.5
1944	164	248	876	65.4	1956	146	—	583	54.8
1945	166	237	846	67.0	1957	136	—	534	52.5
1946	194	227	909	79.3					

* This corporation commenced business July 17, 1937. Figures for 1935, 1936 and part of 1937, therefore, represent business of the Trustee of the Estate of United Cigar Stores Company of America and its subsidiaries. Consolidated figures for years prior to 1935 are not available.

WALGREEN COMPANY

CHICAGO, ILL.

YEAR*	STORES	SALES** (MILLIONS)	YEAR*	STORES	SALES** (MILLIONS)
1920	23	$ 2.2	1940	489	$ 74.3
1921	29	2.6	1941	487	82.5
1922	33	2.5	1942	480	95.3
1923	41	3.6	1943	460	112.2
1924	56	56	1944	442	120.0
1925	87	9.3	1945	427	118.8
1926	107	13.5	1946	412	140.7
1927	170	20.9	1947	410	154.5
1928	230	31.4	1948	413	163.3
1929	397	46.6	1949	414	163.4
1930*	440	39.1*	1950	410	163.4
1931	468	54.0	1951	406	171.5
1932	471	47.6	1952	400	177.9
1933	474	46.0	1953	390	181.5
1934	487	53.7	1954	388	184.3
1935	501	58.1	1955	388	192.7
1936	496	61.8	1956	386	212.3
1937	504	67.9	1957	407	235.1
1938	508	67.7	1958	406	260.0
1939	494	70.8			

* Calendar years 1920 to 1930 inclusive, except that 1930 covers only 9 months. Fiscal years thereafter ending September 30 of year given.

** Sales to agency stores are included in company sales.

MAIL ORDER CHAINS

MONTGOMERY WARD & COMPANY
CHICAGO, ILL.

YEAR	STORES	SALES* (MILLIONS)	YEAR	STORES	SALES* (MILLIONS)
1926	10	$ 184	1942	641	$ 635
1927	36	187	1943	637	596
1928	248	214	1944	632	621
1929	532	267	1945	630	655
1930	554	249	1946	628	974
1931	548	200	1947	622	1,159
1932**	492	176	1948	621	1,212
1933***	488	188	1949	621	1,084
1934	489	250	1950	614	1,170
1935	508	293	1951	606	1,106
1936	548	361	1952	599	1,085
1937	575	414	1953	590	999
1938	599	414	1954	568	887
1939	618	475	1955	566	970
1940	648	516	1956	562	1,046
1941	646	633	1957	554	1,074

* Includes sales of mail-order houses.
** 13 months ending Jan. 31, 1933.
*** Fiscal years hereafter, ending Jan. 31 of year following year given.

SEARS, ROEBUCK & CO.
CHICAGO, ILL.

YEAR ENDING	STORES	NET SALES* (MILLIONS)	NET SALES** (MILLIONS)
Dec. 31, 1925	8	$ 200.	$ 11.
" 31, 1926	9	234.	22.
" 31, 1927	27	249.	39.
" 31, 1928	192	329.	103.
" 31, 1929	324	415.	168.
" 31, 1930	351	355.	190.
" 31, 1931	390	320.	195.
Jan. 28, 1933	384	275.	159.
" 28, 1934	403	273.	160.
" 29, 1935	417	318.	192.
" 29, 1936	429	392.	229.
" 29, 1937	450	495.	303.
" 31, 1938	485	537.	342.
" 31, 1939	496	502.	322.

* Total, including mail order.
** Store sales only; since 1942 store sales have not been available separately, but they have been consistently running at the rate of 75% of total sales.

MAIL ORDER CHAINS (Continued)

SEARS, ROEBUCK & Co. (Continued)

CHICAGO, ILL.

YEAR ENDING	STORES	NET SALES* (MILLIONS)	NET SALES** (MILLIONS)
Jan. 31, 1940	529	$ 617.	$ 409.
" 31, 1941	596	704.	480.
" 31, 1942	618	915.	615.
" 31, 1943	598	868.	
" 31, 1944	595	853.	
" 31, 1945	605	989.	
" 31, 1946	603	1,045.	
" 31, 1947	609	1,613.	
" 31, 1948	623	1,982.	
" 31, 1949	628	2,296.	
" 31, 1950	647	2,169.	
" 31, 1951	654	2,556.	
" 31, 1952	674	2,657.	
" 31, 1953	684	2,932.	
" 31, 1954	694	2,982.	
" 31, 1955	699	2,965.	
" 31, 1956	707	3,307.	
" 31, 1957	717	3,556.	
" 31, 1958	724	3,601.	

* Total, including mail order.

** Store sales only; since 1942 store sales have not been available separately, but they have been consistently running at the rate of 75% of total sales.

SHOE CHAINS

EDISON BROTHERS STORES, INC., ST. LOUIS, MO.

YEAR*	STORES	SALES (MILLIONS)	YEAR*	STORES	SALES (MILLIONS)
1923	1	$ .3	1941	162	$33.6
1924	3	.5	1942	168	45.9
1925	6	.9	1943	166	39.8
1926	8	1.4	1944	169	44.6
1927	11	2.2	1945	170	53.2
1928	17	3.2	1946	180	65.7
1929	34	3.8	1947	188	70.9
1930	42	4.9	1948	202	75.0
1931	50	6.4	1949	213	74.2
1932	63	8.0	1950	220	73.8
1933	75	10.2	1951	228	78.0
1934	85	14.1	1952	237	80.7
1935	92	16.3	1953	245	81.6
1936	102	19.7	1954	251	80.2
1937	121	23.8	1955	267	87.2
1938	123	24.2	1956	297	91.1
1939	131	24.9	1957	322	99.3
1940	142	26.5			

* Calendar years in all cases except 1929 when fiscal year was changed to January 31 of following year and gave 1929 13 months; 1930 to 1932 inclusive, when fiscal year ended January 31 following year given; and 1933 in which a return to the calendar year gave that year only 11 months.

G. R. KINNEY CO., NEW YORK, N. Y.

YEAR	STORES	SALES (MILLIONS)	YEAR	STORES	SALES (MILLIONS)
1894	1		1938	333	$14.5
1909	24	$ .6	1939	344	15.5
1914	40	2.9	1940	343	15.6
1920	75	15.1	1941	346	20.1
1921	102	12.2	1942	339	27.1
1922	120	12.3	1943	338	24.4
1923	152	14.1	1944	330	25.9
1924	207	16.3	1945	317	28.2
1925	250	17.4	1946	306	32.6
1926	274	18.4	1947	310	33.1
1927	295	18.1	1948	308	34.8
1928	317	19.5	1949	305	35.2
1929	365	20.9	1950	311	36.7
1930	405	17.9	1951	318	43.1
1931	423	14.0	1952	324	43.8
1932	388	11.9	1953	327	44.4
1933	354	12.2	1954	344	46.9
1934	333	13.2	1955	352	51.7
1935	333	13.2	1956	360	52.2
1936	327	14.8	1957	411	59.2
1937	321	15.7			

Sources: *The First Sixty Years*, by Edw. Holloway, New York; Company reports and Hugh M. Foster, *Printers' Ink Monthly*, 1937.

SHOE CHAINS (Continued)

MELVILLE SHOE CORPORATION
NEW YORK, N. Y.

YEAR	STORES	SALES* (MILLIONS)	YEAR	STORES	SALES* (MILLIONS)
1892	1		1939	663	$ 38.3
1920	20	$ 3.7	1940	666	40.3
1921	19	4.5	1941	659	46.7
1922	19	4.7	1942	579	51.6
1923	31	6.4	1943	556	39.2
1924	83	9.0	1944	549	37.1
1925	148	10.9	1945	536	41.2
1926	247	14.1	1946	519	60.2
1927	321	17.8	1947	519	71.9
1928	410	22.6	1948	547	75.6
1929	459	25.5	1949	560	71.9
1930	480	28.7	1950	560	70.9
1931	476	26.3	1951	577	71.1
1932	499	20.6	1952	739	77.4
1933	535	21.1	1953	794	99.6
1934	588	27.2	1954	834	100.8
1935	609	30.4	1955	886	106.7
1936	651	35.3	1956	947	115.9
1937	690	38.1	1957	1,018	122.1
1938	677	36.0			

* Retail sales only.

SHOE CORPORATION OF AMERICA*
COLUMBUS, OHIO

YEAR	STORES	SALES (MILLIONS)	YEAR	STORES	SALES (MILLIONS)
1920	6	$ .3	1944	284	$ 21.4
1930	173	9.9	1945	301	24.6
1931	179	10.2	1946	315	28.6
1932	187	8.9	1947	306	33.2
1933	202	9.4	1948	326	37.6
1934	233	10.9	1949	332	39.7
1935	239	11.7	1950	440	49.1
1936	255	13.0	1951	467	62.5
1937	278	13.5	1952	485	66.0
1938	276	12.6	1953	511	70.1
1939	284	13.3	1954	528	73.2
1940	285	14.2	1955	591	89.5
1941	294	16.3	1956	625	101.8
1942	288	20.1	1957	656	106.5
1943	284	19.3			

* Originally The Schiff Co. Present name adopted Nov. 3, 1947.

DEPARTMENT STORE AND APPAREL CHAINS

ALLIED STORES CORPORATION
NEW YORK, N. Y.

YEAR*	STORES	SALES (MILLIONS)	YEAR*	STORES	SALES (MILLIONS)
1934	31	$ 82.1	1946	71	$361.7
1935	31	89.9	1947	75	392.2
1936	33	103.3	1948	79	419.2
1937	54	107.6	1949	73	407.8
1938	56	103.2	1950	73	439.9
1939	58	112.1	1951	71	476.7
1940	60	121.3	1952	72	501.8
1941	61	151.8	1953	73	515.8
1942	63	170.8	1954	75	544.0
1943	63	203.7	1955	79	581.9
1944	70	241.9	1956	84	615.8
1945	70	281.6	1957	87	632.8

* Fiscal years ending January 31 following year given.

FEDERATED DEPARTMENT STORES
CINCINNATI, OHIO

YEAR*	STORES	SALES (MILLIONS)	YEAR*	STORES	SALES (MILLIONS)
1930	12	$113.0	1944	13	$182.3
1931	12	105.3	1945	14	200.9
1932	12	85.0	1946	14	265.4
1933	12	82.6	1947	17	304.7
1934	12	89.1	1948	21	346.5
1935	12	91.6	1949	21	358.6
1936	12	103.2	1950	24	389.1
1937	12	107.7	1951	24	408.8
1938	12	105.9	1952	28	447.9
1939	12	110.1	1953	34	478.8
1940	13	114.7	1954	34	500.6
1941	14	131.4	1955	33	537.7
1942	14	142.5	1956	37	601.5
1943	14	163.4	1957	42	635.6

* Years ending January 31 or nearest Saturday thereto following year given.

DEPARTMENT STORES, etc. (Continued)

LERNER STORES CORPORATION
NEW YORK, N. Y.

YEAR*	STORES	SALES (MILLIONS)	YEAR*	STORES	SALES (MILLIONS)
1933	160	$ 22.1	1948	191	$107.3
1935	158	30.4	1949	197	126.9
1936	159	32.2	1950	207	120.6
1937	159	37.2	1951	209	125.8
1938	160	39.6	1952	209	140.9
1939	164	37.9	1953	214	154.4
1940	166	40.5	1954	215	147.8
1941	171	42.5	1955	224	151.2
1942	179	50.5	1956	230	161.1
1943	180	64.8	1957	246	170.6
1944	180	75.6	1958	263	179.5
1945	181	87.3			
1946	179	91.9			
1947	185	97.0			

* Calendar year in 1933; thereafter fiscal years ending January 31 of year given.

THE MAY DEPARTMENT STORES CO.
ST. LOUIS, MO.

YEAR*	STORES	SALES (MILLIONS)	YEAR	STORES	SALES (MILLIONS)
1949	21	$407.3	1954	26	$454.1
1950	22	392.9	1955	26	444.4
1951	23	416.7	1956	31	494.4
1952	25	424.9	1957	31	521.4
1953	26	447.5	1958	45	533.6

* Year ending January 31 of year given.

DEPARTMENT STORES, etc. (Continued)

J. C. PENNEY CO.
NEW YORK, N. Y.

YEAR	STORES	SALES (MILLIONS)	YEAR	STORES	SALES (MILLIONS)
1902	1	$ .03	1930	1,042	192.9
1903	1	.06	1931	1,459	173.7
1904	2	.09	1932	1,473	155.3
1905	2	.09	1933	1,466	178.8
1906	2	.13	1934	1,474	212.1
1907	2	.17	1935	1,481	225.9
1908	4	.22	1936	1,496	258.3
1909	6	.31	1937	1,523	275.4
1910	14	.66	1938	1,539	257.9
1911	22	1.2	1939	1,554	282.1
1912	34	2.1	1940	1,586	304.6
1913	48	2.6	1941	1,605	377.6
1914	71	3.6	1942	1,611	490.3
1915	86	4.8	1943	1,610	489.9
1916	127	8.4	1944	1,608	535.4
1917	177	14.9	1945	1,602	549.1
1918	197	31.3	1946	1,601	767.6
1919	197	28.8	1947	1,601	775.9
1920	312	42.8	1948	1,601	885.2
1921	313	46.6	1949	1,609	880.2
1922	371	49.0	1950	1,612	949.7
1923	475	62.2	1951	1,621	1,035.2
1924	569	74.3	1952	1,632	1,079.3
1925	674	91.1	1953	1,634	1,109.6
1926	747	115.7	1954	1,644	1,107.2
1927	892	151.9	1955	1,666	1,220.1
1928	1,023	176.7	1956	1,687	1,291.9
1929	1,395	209.7	1957	1,694	1,312.3

INDEX

INDEX

INDEX